# Soft Computing
## with MATLAB Programming

N.P. Padhy
*Professor*
*Department of Electrical Engineering*
*Indian Institute of Technology Roorkee*

S.P. Simon
*Assistant Professor*
*Department of Electrical and Electronics Engineering*
*National Institute of Technology, Tiruchirappalli*

# OXFORD
UNIVERSITY PRESS

Oxford University Press is a department of the University of Oxford.
It furthers the University's objective of excellence in research, scholarship,
and education by publishing worldwide. Oxford is a registered trade mark of
Oxford University Press in the UK and in certain other countries.

Published in India by
Oxford University Press
YMCA Library Building, 1 Jai Singh Road, New Delhi 110001, India

© Oxford University Press 2015

The moral rights of the author/s have been asserted.

First published in 2015

All rights reserved. No part of this publication may be reproduced, stored in
a retrieval system, or transmitted, in any form or by any means, without the
prior permission in writing of Oxford University Press, or as expressly permitted
by law, by licence, or under terms agreed with the appropriate reprographics
rights organization. Enquiries concerning reproduction outside the scope of the
above should be sent to the Rights Department, Oxford University Press, at the
address above.

You must not circulate this work in any other form
and you must impose this same condition on any acquirer.

ISBN-13: 978-0-19-945542-3
ISBN-10: 0-19-945542-2

Typeset in Times New Roman
by Mukesh Technologies Pvt. Ltd., Puducherry 605005
Printed in India by Magic International, Greater Noida

Third-party website addresses mentioned in this book are provided
by Oxford University Press in good faith and for information only.
Oxford University Press disclaims any responsibility for the material contained therein.

# Preface

*"How much better is it to get wisdom than fine gold, and the getting of intelligence to be preferred to silver?"*

*King Solomon*

Soft computing has emerged as one of the vital fields within computer science, where solutions for a complex problem can be obtained by incorporating certain processes resembling biological and nature-inspired phenomena. These processes are used intelligently in places where solutions cannot be obtained especially in polynomial time and often remain intractable to conventional mathematical and analytical methods.

Soft computing deals with imprecision, uncertainty, partial truth, and approximation to achieve practicability, robustness, and low solution cost. Soft computing techniques include expert systems, artificial neural networks, fuzzy logic systems, and evolutionary computation. Evolutionary computation techniques include evolutionary algorithms, genetic algorithms, metaheuristics, and swarm intelligent techniques such as ant colony optimisation, particle swarm optimisation, bees algorithms, and cuckoo search.

## About the Book

*Soft Computing with MATLAB Programming* is a comprehensive textbook designed for undergraduate students studying computer science, information technology, electrical and electronics, and electronics and communication engineering, as well as those pursuing an MCA degree. It aims to familiarize students with soft computing fundamentals and approaches for solving real-world problems. This text illustrates all the prominent soft computing techniques in one volume—filling in a long-time requirement of the learner community.

Beginning with an overview of soft computing, the book offers an exhaustive coverage of artificial neural networks (ANNs), discussing in detail ANN tracking in all the three generations of neural networks and their developments. This is followed by detailed chapters discussing fuzzy logic features and applications. The chapter on genetic algorithms (GAs) explains various GA operators such as crossover and mutation with suitable examples and illustrations. Finally, swarm intelligent systems are illustrated in detail, also discussing the engineering applications of particle swarm intelligent systems.

MATLAB codes have been used throughout the text to illustrate the applications of the concepts discussed.

## Key Features

- Illustrative description of the inherent principles of soft computing, eliminating heavy mathematical treatment
- Exclusive chapter on swarm intelligent systems

- Extensive coverage of neural networks and fuzzy logic concepts
- About 30 MATLAB programs with step-by-step comments and 80 general, solved problems

## Online Resources

The following resources are available to help the faculty and the students using the text:

*For Faculty*

- Chapter-wise Lecture PPTs
- Solutions Manual

*For Students*

- Additional MATLAB codes and exercises for practice
- Solutions to model question papers

## Content and Coverage

The text is divided into 8 chapters. A brief outline of each chapter is given as follows.

**Chapter 1** elaborates the *Concept of Soft Computing*. Other than the significance of important soft computing technologies, a segment on *Expert System (ES)*, which is considered as one of the earliest soft computing approaches, has been provided. The chapter discusses the chaining of rules in an *Expert Program*, *System Architecture*, and development stages of an ES, ES tools, and its applications.

**Chapter 2** discusses *Artificial Neural Networks* (ANNs). It explains how in an ANN, simple artificial nodes, also known as 'neurons', 'neurodes', 'processing elements' (PEs) or 'units', are connected together to form a network of nodes mimicking the biological neural network. The chapter presents the *First-generation Neural Networks* where the ANNs can solve simple logical functions such as AND, OR, XOR, etc. Simple neural networks such as McCulloch Pitts model, Perceptrons, and Adaline are explained with illustrations and MATLAB programs.

**Chapter 3** evaluates *Second-generation Neural Networks*. Here, the ANN can not only process logical functions but also learn by updating weights that depicts the value of strength between any two neuronal units. It explains both supervised and unsupervised neural networks with their applications such as character recognition and clustering. *Support Vector Machine* networks and an application on forecasting have been solved and explained briefly using Neural Network MATLAB Tool Box in this chapter.

**Chapter 4** explores *Third-generation Neural Networks* and focuses on the latest trend in the development of ANN, the so-called *Spiking Neural Networks* (SNNs). The information processing, which is similar to the brain by communicating via the precise timing of spikes or a sequence of spikes, has been very well introduced in this chapter. The chapter discusses the various types of neural network models, along with a forecasting application of the electrical load patterns using SNN.

**Chapters 5** and **6** study in detail the *Fuzzy Logic System*. The reason for fuzziness and the fundamentals of fuzzy theory with respect to the classical set theory have been addressed in Chapter 5. Insights on fuzzy set operation, fuzzy arithmetics, fuzzy relation, fuzzy composition, linguistic hedges, fuzzy inference system, and defuzzification method have also been dealt with in this chapter. The *fuzzy applications* related to engineering aspects are presented using MATLAB programming as well as Fuzzy Logic MATLAB Tool Box in Chapter 6. The recent developments of fuzzy logic called 'intuitionist fuzzy set' have also been introduced in this chapter.

**Chapter 7** provides a detailed discussion on *Genetic Algorithm* (GA) and *Evolutionary Programming* (EP), explaining various GA operators such as crossover and mutation with MATLAB programs with suitable representation and diagrams.

**Chapter 8** analyses the emergence of *Swarm Intelligent System* with its fundamental concepts of exploration and exploitation. Various swarm intelligent systems that have evolved and established their presence in engineering applications such as *Ant Colony Optimisation* (ACO) and *Particle Swarm Optimisation* (PSO) have been discussed in detail. Other evolving swarm-based algorithms like *Artificial Bee Colony* (ABC) algorithm and *Cuckoo Search* (CS) algorithm have been discussed with suitable applications. Most of these algorithms are implemented and explained in an easy step-by-step approach using MATLAB programming in this chapter.

## Acknowledgements

We acknowledge the Almighty for giving us the wisdom and knowledge to carry out this project. We would like to remember our family members, including Nibedita, Smitha, Apurba, Mithasha, Anjan, and Mariesha, for their constant moral support and compromises throughout the writing of this book.

We are thankful to our students K. Chandrasekaran, C. Christopher Columbus, C.H. Ramjethmalani, Rohit Rajan Eapen, M. Senthil Kumar, and Nandkishor Wasudeorao Kinhekar for extending their support.

We express our gratitude to the reviewers for their valuable suggestions and the editorial team at OUP for their support throughout the development. We also thank all those who directly or indirectly stand behind the success story of the book even though their names have not been mentioned.

Although all effort has been made to publish an error-free text, any suggestion for improvement and feedback may be sent to the publisher via their website or to us at nppeefee@iitr.ac.in or sishajpsimon@nitt.edu.

**Narayana Prasad Padhy**
**Sishaj Pulikottil Simon**

# Features of

**LEARNING OBJECTIVES**

*This chapter will enable the reader to:*
- Familiarize with the basic concept of intelligent systems and soft computing techniques
- Explain the expert system architecture and programming
- Utilize the rule-based expert system
- Analyse the expert system tools and applications
- Compare the various intelligent techniques

**Learning Objectives**

Highlight the topics and concepts to be discussed in each chapter.

## MATLAB Programs

About 30 MATLAB programs with step-by-step comments have been used to illustrate the applications of the concepts discussed. MATLAB Tool Boxes specific to fuzzy logic and neural networks have also been explained.

**MATLAB Program 1.1**

```
%%%%%%%%%%%%%%%%%%%%%%%%%%%%%%%%%%%%%%%%%%%%%%%%%%%%%%%%%%%%
% CONDITION OF THE POWER SYSTEM BASED ON THE GENERATION LEVEL
%%%%%%%%%%%%%%%%%%%%%%%%%%%%%%%%%%%%%%%%%%%%%%%%%%%%%%%%%%%%

% CLEARING ALL PREVIOUS DATA

clear workspace
clear all
clc
format long

% GET THE INPUT LOAD FOR THE GENERATORS

I=input('Give the input load between 200MW to 1000MW =');
% Enter the system load as input
if (200<=I)&(I<=1000),
% The program executes if only the data input is correct
else
disp('Input load is not correct');
% Displays the data given as input is incorrect
disp('Give load data between 200MW to 1000MW');
% Corrective action to be taken for the input data to be given
end
```

**Example 8.1** In this example, we discuss the basic features of an ant algorithm for optimizing a simple one-variable function. Let us consider that the same function and the initial procedure are similar to the one discussed in Section 7.4.

$$\text{Min } f(x) = x. \sin(10\pi . x) + 1.0 \tag{8.3}$$

**Examples**

Demonstrate the practical aspects of the concepts discussed in the chapter.

## Illustrative Problems

Support important topics like genetic algorithm operators (especially, crossover and mutation).

**7.10 ILLUSTRATIVE PROBLEMS**

**Problem 7.1**
Find the length of a binary string required to represent a variable '$X$', with a precision of 3 digits after a decimal point, where $15 \leq X \leq 50$.

**Solution:** Given that precision $p = 3$,

$$X^u = 50, X^l = 15,$$

Length of binary string required, $n = \log_2\left[\dfrac{X^u - X^l}{p}\right]$

# the Book

**SUMMARY**
- Swarm intelligence is the term used for the collective behaviour of a group (swarm) of animals as a single living creature, where via grouping and communication a *collective intelligence* emerges that actually results in more successful foraging for each individual in the group.
- Swarm intelligent searches the solution through exploration and exploitation.
- The two ways in which random numbers can be generated are: (i) through any physical phenomenon and (ii) through computational algorithms.
- The collective behaviour of the agents *natural* or *artificial* in a system should lead to the ultimate intelligence behaviour through proper convergence.
- An AACS is a population-based heuristic algorithm on agents that simulate the natural behaviour of ants developing mechanisms of cooperation and learning which enables the exploration of the positive feedback between agents as a search mechanism.

**Summary**
Provides brief conclusion on the key topics discussed in the chapter in bulleted points for easy recapitulation.

**EXERCISES**

**Part A Short-answer Questions**
1. What are 'evolutionary algorithms'?
2. Why is it said that *genetic algorithms + data structures = evolution programs*?
3. Explain the terms natural genetics and natural selection.
4. Classify the applications of GAs.
5. How do GAs differ from conventional optimisation algorithms?

**Part B Long-answer Questions**
1. Solve the following optimisation problems:
   (a) Maximize $F(X, Y) = X \sin(4\pi X) + Y \sin(20\pi X)$
   subject to
   $-3.0 \leq X \leq 12.1$
   $4.1 \leq Y \leq 5.8$
   (b) Minimize $F(X) = X \sin^2(10\pi X) + 1$
   subject to
   $-1 \leq X \leq 2$

**Part C Practical Exercises**
1. To actually see ants finding their food source, go to a garden or any place where you a piece of sweet a little far away from the nest. Make a set-up in which the ants have of the two paths of different lengths to go near the sweet. Note the timings and watch carefully and describe the events.

**Exercises**
A rich set of chapter-end exercises divided into 3 sections: (i) short-answer questions, (ii) long-answer questions, and (iii) practical exercises, which enhance learning and can be used for review and classroom discussion.

## Glossary

*Accuracy* It explains how close the instrument reading is to the true value.
*Activation function* A function that defines the output of the neuron by comparing with a threshold value.
*Artifici...*
perform
*Batch t...*

**MODEL QUESTION PAPER I**

Duration: 3 hours
Max. marks: 100

I. Answer the following questions: (10 × 2 = 20)

1. List the strengths and weaknesses of artificial neural network.
2. How do you select the number of hidden-layer neurons according to Kolomogorov's theorem?
3. Name few fuzzy logic applications with examples.
4. Why fuzzy logic is misconceived as imprecise logic?

**Glossary and Model Question Papers**
A list of key terms and a set of 5 model question papers have been provided at the end of the book for a thorough revision.

# Brief Contents

*Preface* — iii
*Features of the Book* — vi
*Detailed Contents* — ix

1. **Introduction to Soft Computing**   1

2. **Artificial Neural Networks—First Generation**   63

3. **Artificial Neural Networks—Second Generation**   118

4. **Artificial Neural Networks—Third Generation**   253

5. **Fuzzy Logic**   283

6. **Fuzzy Logic Applications**   385

7. **Genetic Algorithms and Evolutionary Programming**   445

8. **Swarm Intelligent System**   547

**Appendix A: Model Question Papers**   637
**Appendix B: MATLAB Tutorial**   646
**Glossary**   655
**Index**   659
**About the Authors**   669

# Detailed Contents

*Preface*   *iii*
*Features of the Book*   *vi*
*Brief Contents*   *viii*

**1. Introduction to Soft Computing**   **1**

   1.1 Introduction   1
   1.2 Artificial Intelligence   4
      1.2.1 Intelligent Systems   4
   1.3 Artificial Neural Networks   7
      1.3.1 Development of ANNs   9
      1.3.2 Strengths and Weaknesses of ANNs   10
      1.3.3 Neural Computing vs Conventional Computing   11
      1.3.4 Scope of ANN   12
   1.4 Fuzzy Systems   13
      1.4.1 Acceptance of Fuzzy Logic   15
      1.4.2 Fuzzy Logic Applications   16
      1.4.3 Misconceptions in Fuzzy Logic   16
      1.4.4 Scope of Fuzzy Logic   18
   1.5 Genetic Algorithm and Evolutionary Programming   19
      1.5.1 History of GAs and EPs   22
      1.5.2 Scope of GAs and EPs   22
   1.6 Swarm Intelligent Systems   23
      1.6.1 Strengths and Weaknesses of SI Techniques   25
      1.6.2 Applications of SI Techniques   26
      1.6.3 Scope of Swarm Intelligent Systems   27
   1.7 Expert Systems   27
      1.7.1 Expert System Architecture   28
      1.7.2 Rule-based Expert System   30
      1.7.3 Backward Chaining and Forward Chaining   32
      1.7.4 Expert System Knowledge Base   37
      1.7.5 Basic Activities of an Expert System   38
      1.7.6 Verification, Validation, and Design of Expert Systems   39
      1.7.7 Expert System Tools   51
      1.7.8 Expert System-building Tools   54
      1.7.9 Expert System Shells   55
      1.7.10 Application of Expert Systems   56
      1.7.11 Future Scope of Expert Systems   57
   1.8 Comparison among Intelligent Systems   57

## 2. Artificial Neural Networks—First Generation  63

2.1 Introduction to Neural Networks  63
2.2 Biological Inspiration  64
    2.2.1 Comparison between Brain and Computer  65
2.3 Biological Neural Networks to Artificial Neural Networks  67
    2.3.1 Information Processing at the Neurons and Synapses  68
2.4 Classification of ANNs  74
    2.4.1 Neural Network Architecture  74
    2.4.2 Learning/Training  77
    2.4.3 Training and Testing Modes  79
    2.4.4 Activation/Transfer Function  80
2.5 First-generation Neural Networks  83
    2.5.1 McCulloch and Pitts Neuron Model  83
    2.5.2 Learning Rules: Hebbian and Delta  85
2.6 Perceptron Network  91
    2.6.1 Perceptron Linear Separability  99
2.7 Adaline Network  101
2.8 Madaline Network  104
2.9 Illustrative Problems  110

## 3. Artificial Neural Networks—Second Generation  118

3.1 Introduction to Second-generation Neural Networks  118
3.2 Backpropagation Neural Networks  118
    3.2.1 Backpropagation Training for Multi-layer Neural Network  122
    3.2.2 Calculation of Weights for Output-layer Neurons  124
    3.2.3 Calculation of Weights for Hidden-layer Neurons  126
    3.2.4 Factors Influencing Backpropagation Training  129
    3.2.5 Character Recognition Using Backpropagation Neural Network  142
3.3 Kohonen Neural Network  153
    3.3.1 Illustration on Clustering of Bipolar Input Patterns  153
    3.3.2 Clustering of Numerical Characters  159
3.4 Learning Vector Quantization  164
    3.4.1 Clustering of Bipolar Input Patterns in LVQ  165
    3.4.2 Classification of Numerical Characters  172
3.5 Hamming Neural Network  175
    3.5.1 Illustration on Finding the Best Match with Standard Vector  178
    3.5.2 Character Recognition through Clustering of Numerical Characters  181
3.6 Hopfield Neural Network  186
    3.6.1 Illustration of Settlement of Stable Input Patterns  187
    3.6.2 Character Recognition through Stabilization of Input Test Patterns  191
3.7 Bi-directional Associative Memory  197
    3.7.1 Illustration of Settlement of Stable Input Patterns  200
    3.7.2 BAM for Character Mapping  204
3.8 Adaptive Resonance Theory Neural Networks  208
3.9 Boltzman Machine Neural Networks  211

3.10  Radial Basis Function Neural Networks   216
3.11  Support Vector Machines   222
3.12  Electrical Load Forecasting using MATLAB Neural Network Toolbox   227
3.13  Illustrative Problems   242

4. **Artificial Neural Networks—Third Generation   253**

   4.1  Introduction to Third-generation Neural Networks   253
   4.2  Introduction to Spikes   253
   4.3  Spike Neuron Models   259
       4.3.1  Threshold-fire Models   259
       4.3.2  Conductance-based Response Model   263
   4.4  Electrical Load Forecasting using Spike Response Model   267
       4.4.1  Temporal Encoding in Spiking Neural Networks   267
       4.4.2  Spike Propagation Algorithm   268
       4.4.3  Control Parameter Setting   270
       4.4.4  Implementation of SNN for STLF   271
       4.4.5  Performance Evaluation   275
       4.4.6  Results and Discussions   276

5. **Fuzzy Logic   283**

   5.1  Introduction to Fuzzy Logic   283
   5.2  Human Learning Ability, Imprecision, and Uncertainty   285
   5.3  Undecidability   286
   5.4  Probability Theory vs Possibility Theory   287
   5.5  Classical Sets and Fuzzy Sets   288
       5.5.1  Representation of a Classical Set   289
       5.5.2  Representation of a Fuzzy Set   290
       5.5.3  Basic Properties of Fuzzy Sets   293
   5.6  Fuzzy Set Operations   297
       5.6.1  Intersection of Fuzzy Sets   298
       5.6.2  Union of Fuzzy Sets   301
       5.6.3  Complement of Fuzzy Sets   303
       5.6.4  Important Terminologies in Fuzzy Set Operations   305
       5.6.5  Properties of Fuzzy Sets   306
       5.6.6  Fuzzy Arithmetics   308
   5.7  Fuzzy Relations   321
       5.7.1  Operations on Fuzzy Relations   323
   5.8  Fuzzy Composition   323
       5.8.1  Max-Min Composition   324
       5.8.2  Max-Star Composition   324
       5.8.3  Max-Product Composition   325
       5.8.4  Max-Average Composition   325
   5.9  Natural Language and Fuzzy Interpretations   328
       5.9.1  Linguistic Modifiers   329
       5.9.2  Logical Operations using Linguistic Modifiers   334

## xii Detailed Contents

    5.10  Structure of Fuzzy Inference System   335
           5.10.1  Fuzzification   335
           5.10.2  Fuzzy Propositions   337
           5.10.3  Fuzzy Connectives   338
           5.10.4  Fuzzy Implication Relations   339
           5.10.5  Fuzzy Inference Procedures   341
           5.10.6  Fuzzy Inference Algorithms   349
           5.10.7  De-fuzzification   350
           5.10.8  Assessment of de-fuzzification Methods   358
    5.11  Illustrative Problems   360

**6. Fuzzy Logic Applications   385**
    6.1  Introduction to Fuzzy Logic Applications   385
    6.2  Fuzzy Controllers   385
           6.2.1  Antecedent/Consequent Variables   388
           6.2.2  IF/THEN Rules and Inference   389
           6.2.3  Fuzzy Decision-making   396
    6.3  MATLAB Implementation of Fuzzy Logic Applications   400
           6.3.1  Automatic Fuzzy Acceleration Controller   400
           6.3.2  Selection of a Bridegroom for a Bride   403
           6.3.3  Selection of Cricket Players from a Group of Players   409
           6.3.4  Illustration of Hydel Power Plant Operation Estimation   419
    6.4  Hybrid Techniques   434
           6.4.1  Neuro-Fuzzy Systems   434
           6.4.2  Fuzzy Genetic Algorithms   435
    6.5  Intuitionistic Fuzzy Sets   435
    6.6  Illustrative Problems   438

**7. Genetic Algorithms and Evolutionary Programming   445**
    7.1  Introduction to Genetic Algorithms   445
    7.2  Genetic Algorithms   448
    7.3  Procedures of GAs   451
           7.3.1  Genetic Representations   452
           7.3.2  Selection   461
           7.3.3  Genetic Operators   470
           7.3.4  Mutation   480
           7.3.5  Natural Inheritance Operators   485
    7.4  Working of GAs   490
           7.4.1  Binary or Discrete GA (Case 1)   490
           7.4.2  Real or Continuous GA (Case 2)   498
    7.5  Genetic Algorithm Applications   505
           7.5.1  Travelling Salesman Problem   505
           7.5.2  Economic Power Dispatch Problem   512
           7.5.3  Optimisation of Weights in ANNs   527

7.6 Applicability of Genetic Algorithms    530
    7.6.1 Parallel GA    530
    7.6.2 Convergence Proof of GA    530
7.7 Evolutionary Programming    531
7.8 Working of Evolutionary Programming    532
7.9 Genetic Algorithm-based Machine Learning Classifier System    533
    7.9.1 Machine Learning Classifier System    534
    7.9.2 Working Principle of GA Machine Learning Classifier System    535
7.10 Illustrative Problems    535

## 8. Swarm Intelligent System    547

8.1 Introduction to Swarm Intelligence    547
8.2 Background of Swarm Intelligent Systems    550
8.3 Ant Colony System    552
    8.3.1 Biological Ant Colony System    552
    8.3.2 Artificial Ant Colony System    554
    8.3.3 Working of an Ant Colony System    554
    8.3.4 Probabilistic Transition Rule    554
    8.3.5 Pheromone Updating    555
    8.3.6 Solution Evaluation    556
8.4 Working of Ant Colony Optimisation    557
8.5 Ant Colony Optimisation Algorithm for TSP    563
    8.5.1 Travelling Salesman Problem Formulation    563
    8.5.2 Implementation of Ants in TSP Search Space    564
8.6 Unit Commitment Problem    573
    8.6.1 Minimize the Operational Cost    574
8.7 Particle Swarm Intelligent Systems    582
    8.7.1 Basic PSO Method    584
    8.7.2 Characteristic Features of PSO    584
    8.7.3 Procedure of the Global Version    585
    8.7.4 Parameters of PSO    586
    8.7.5 Comparison with Other EC Techniques    588
    8.7.6 Engineering Applications of PSIS and Future Research    589
    8.7.7 Working of PSO    589
8.8 Artificial Bee Colony System    599
    8.8.1 Working of ABC    601
8.9 Cuckoo Search Algorithm    613
    8.9.1 Working of CSA    616
    8.9.2 A Simple Economic Dispatch Problem    625

**Appendix A: Model Question Papers    637**
**Appendix B: MATLAB Tutorial    646**
**Glossary    655**
**Index    659**
**About the Authors    669**

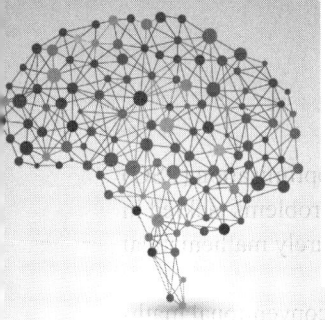

# 1 Introduction to Soft Computing

*'What you have learnt is a handful of earth, what you haven't learnt is the Earth'*

*Avvaiyar*

### LEARNING OBJECTIVES

*This chapter will enable the reader to:*
- Familiarize with the basic concept of intelligent systems and soft computing techniques
- Explain the expert system architecture and programming
- Utilize the rule-based expert system
- Analyse the expert system tools and applications
- Compare the various intelligent techniques

## 1.1 INTRODUCTION

Eric Hoffer (1902–1983), the US writer, had rightly said, 'The wise learn from the experience of others, and the creative know how to make a crumb of experience go a long way'. To some extent, based on statistics, this may be agreeable, and the wise person may be intelligent. Even though the learning from others' experience may be a wise decision, the outcome need not be same for everyone. Yet, solutions in an intelligent manner can be obtained from other people's experience.

It should be noted that most of the solutions in this scientific world need not be solved with rigid mathematics and 100 per cent perfect models. An intelligent model may do the job or provide a solution without any proof or not necessarily being perfect. Forecasting the annual profit in a business organization is possible using the previous historical data on various facts and experiences related to change in consumer preferences, local and cultural indicators, economic conditions, and technology transformation indicators.

Conventional forecasting techniques use rigorous mathematical models such as time series analysis and multiple regression analysis. These models need comprehensive and complete dataset to analyse and forecast. These mathematical models may fail when data during certain time periods are not available or due to the non-availability of data sample in a particular location. However, intelligent models such as neural network forecasting can efficiently handle non-linearity and non-availability of certain parts of the data, and still forecast with greater accuracy.

Now consider a mathematical function $f(x) = (\log(x))^{|e(x)|} + |\sin(x)^{e(x \times \log(e(x)))}|$ to be minimized, such that $x$ ranges between $-1$ and $2$. The conventional mathematical models may fail to give a solution. However, non-conventional optimisation techniques such as genetic algorithm (GA) and particle swarm optimisation (PSO) techniques will be able to give a feasible solution. Most of the problems tackled in a non-conventional style cannot be easily broken down into a purely mathematical approach.

In the past, computational approaches were carried out with conventional mathematics and precise analytical models. However, non-conventional methodologies are characterized by the use of inexact solutions to computationally hard tasks such as the solution of NP-complete problems, for which there is no known algorithm that can compute an exact solution in polynomial time. Therefore, *soft computing* can be understood as a domain of methodologies that exploits the tolerance for imprecision, uncertainty, and partial truth in solving a problem that involves information processing. From the 1990s, due to its importance and capability in various problem-solving domains, soft computing has become one of the important subjects in the field of computer science.

The Wright Brothers spent enormous amount of time for understanding the birds in flight. They noticed that birds soared into the wind and understood that the air flowing over the curved surface of their wings created lift. Birds change the shape of their wings to turn and manoeuvre. They believed that they could use this technique to obtain roll control by warping, or changing the shape, of a portion of the wing. Similarly, the concept of aerodynamic automobiles came from the boxfish, whose base, movement, and bone structure were copied in their design.

Daimler Chrysler developed the Bionic car. Using the shape of the boxfish, designers achieved 20 per cent less fuel consumption and as much as an 80 per cent reduction in nitrogen oxide emissions. Suppose a person wants to walk upon walls or across ceilings. Gecko Tape may be the way to do it. This tape is a material covered with nanoscopic hairs that mimic those found on the feet of gecko lizards. These millions of tiny, flexible hairs exert van der Waals forces, which provide a powerful adhesive effect. They are very well used in underwater and space station applications; therefore, researchers from a number of institutions are working hard. By mimicking the way light reflects from the scales on a butterfly's wings, the Qualcomm Company has developed Mirasol Displays that make use of the reflected light principle.

All the aforementioned developments come into a branch of study called 'Biomimetics—Inventions that Mimic Nature'. Similarly, most of the soft computing techniques such as expert systems, neural networks, fuzzy logic systems, GAs, and swarm intelligence systems have evolved by mimicking the concepts from nature which are detailed in the following sections. That is why Janine M. Benyus, a famous American natural science writer, innovation consultant, and author has rightly quoted, 'Life has already solved the challenges that we're trying to solve, there are literally as many ideas as there are organisms'. Therefore, it is true that in future many soft computing techniques will continuously evolve by mimicking ideas from nature and solve complex problems in a simpler fashion.

The major differences between hard computing and soft computing have been summarized in Table 1.1.

Table 1.1 Hard computing vs soft computing

| Hard computing | Soft computing |
| --- | --- |
| Precisely stated analytical model is required | Imprecision is tolerable |
| More computational time is required | Computational time required is less as it involves intelligent computational steps |
| It involves binary logic, crisp systems and numerical analysis | It involves nature-inspired systems such as neural networks, fuzzy logic systems and swarm intelligent system |
| Precision is observed within the computation | Approximation is observed in the computation |
| Imprecision and uncertainty are undesirable properties | Tolerance for imprecision and uncertainty is exploited to achieve tractability, lower cost, high Machine Intelligence Quotient (MIQ) and economy of communication |
| Programs are written which follow standard rules of programming | Programs are evolved which require new laws and theories to be created and justified while programming |
| The outcome is deterministic, i.e., on every trial run, the output is same | The outcome is stochastic or random in nature and need not be deterministic |
| It requires exact input data | It can deal with ambiguous and noisy input data |
| It strictly follows sequential computations | It allows parallel computations |
| It produces precise answers | It can produce approximate answers |

In a highly automated digital world, traditional electronic computations tend to be black and white. When working in binary code, with sequences of zeros and ones, there is no chance for anything else but simple yes or no answers. This may be a usual and satisfactory manner of computing stuff, even, though soft computing takes a diverse approach. It allows the computer to take on a certain level of inexactness in its work. Sometimes, it may be equated with artificial intelligence, in that it is similar to the way the human brain works.

As an individual's perspective, soft computing introduces compromises into a computer's processing, which are not present in hard computing. Table 1.1 gives the difference between hard and soft computing. As an illustration, while adding two numbers, the first option is simple to say that the sum of three plus four is seven. As a second option, it is also correct to say that the sum of three plus four is somewhere between 6 and 8. It is a known fact that the objective is to come up with the most accurate answer. However, the computer may be convinced to ignore the second option, whereas soft computing looks at the second one as a potential option.

Therefore, soft computing differs from conventional (hard) computing in that it is tolerant of imprecision, uncertainty, partial truth, and approximation. It should be noted that the application areas of soft computing include decision support, process and system control, signal and image processing, pattern recognition, fault diagnosis, system integration, human machine interface, data mining, virtual reality, robotics, process optimisation, forecasting applications, etc.

## 1.2 ARTIFICIAL INTELLIGENCE

Soft computing techniques solve problems in an intelligent way. This forces to elucidate the meaning of *intelligence*. The exact meaning of the term *intelligence* is debatable. It had initially started with the fact that human beings are intelligent. Therefore, the word may be interpreted as the act of thinking fast, knowing a lot, perceiving things in the right way, or giving new ideas. Some may say that it is a combination of all of the earlier characteristics along with several others. The ability to effectively propagate ones thoughts and feelings while understanding others' expressions may be considered as exhibiting intelligence. Organizing knowledge so as to stay updated, modifying existing knowledge to include latest developments, and adding new facts also constitute intelligence.

Incorporating all the points mentioned previously, we could say that an intelligent being is one who can think, applying the knowledge he/she has gained through experience, communicate his/her thoughts to others while comprehending what they are trying to share with him/her, and learn new concepts and facts so as to keep his/her knowledge relevant. How efficiently a person accomplishes these tasks defines how intelligent he is. However, solving problems in an intelligent manner requires the right strategies to be adopted in the right place for the right reasons.

Sometimes applied soft computing can be considered as applying artificial intelligence (AI) to problem-solving. Artificial intelligence is a field of study that encompasses computational techniques for performing tasks that apparently require intelligence when performed by humans. A simple example of AI application is the Panasonic microcomputer-controlled Fuzzy Logic® Rice Cooker, SR-MGS102 which uses fuzzy logic technology to adjust power and cooking time automatically for precise and consistent results every time. Artificial intelligence has enjoyed tremendous growth since its birth during and after the Second World War, the later part of the twentieth century, and in the beginning of the twenty-first century.

Artificial intelligence has been classified as an interdisciplinary branch rather than a branch of computer science because fields as different as psychology, biology, electrical engineering also have a bearing on the development of this field. Therefore, it is important to know the initial development of AI techniques mostly involved in soft computing applications. Important developments of AI techniques are given in Fig. 1.1.

A widely recognized goal of AI is the creation of artificial facts that can emulate humans in their ability to reason symbolically, as discussed in typical AI domains such as planning, natural language understanding, diagnosis, and tutoring. A good example is the expert system which uses the knowledge base and logical reasoning to solve a problem. This will be discussed in the upcoming sections in detail.

### 1.2.1 Intelligent Systems

Another area of applied soft computing techniques is to emulate the strategies and mechanisms involved in the Intelligent Systems for problem-solving. Systems such as biological neural systems and fuzzy logic systems relate the human way

Introduction to Soft Computing 5

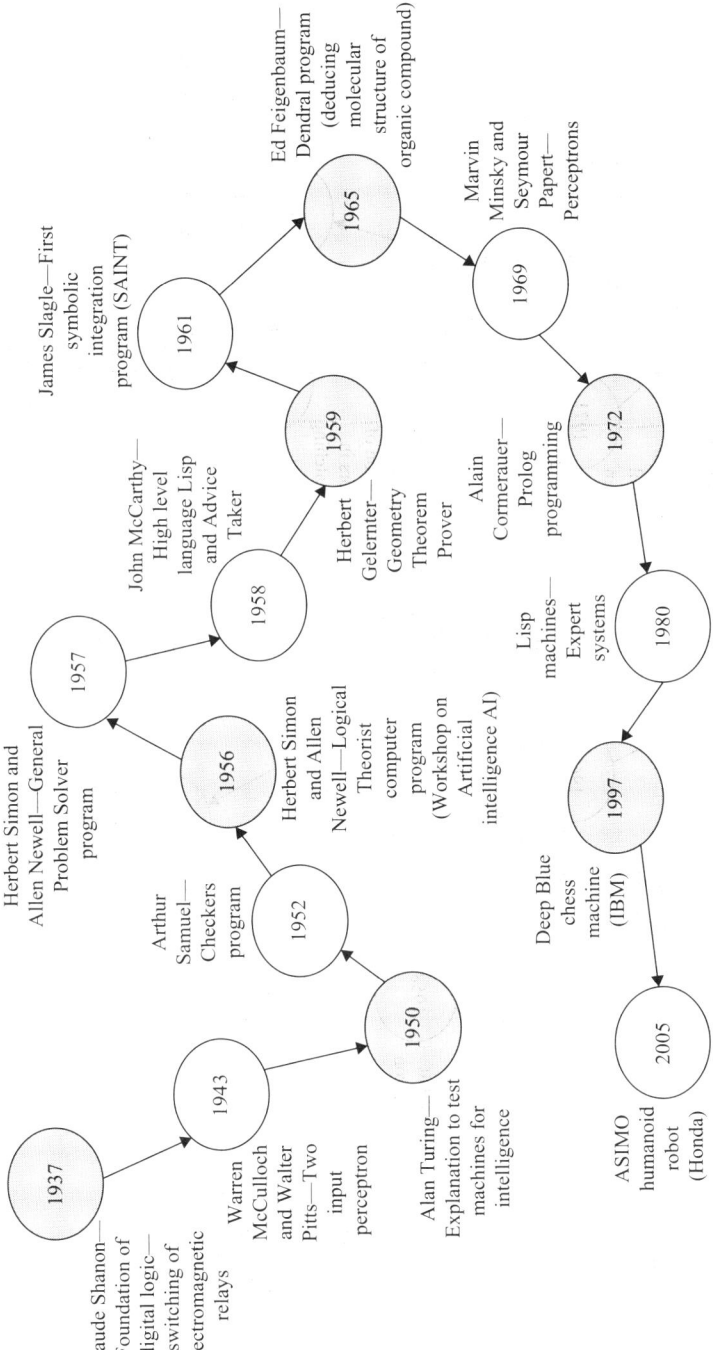

Fig. 1.1 Development of AI

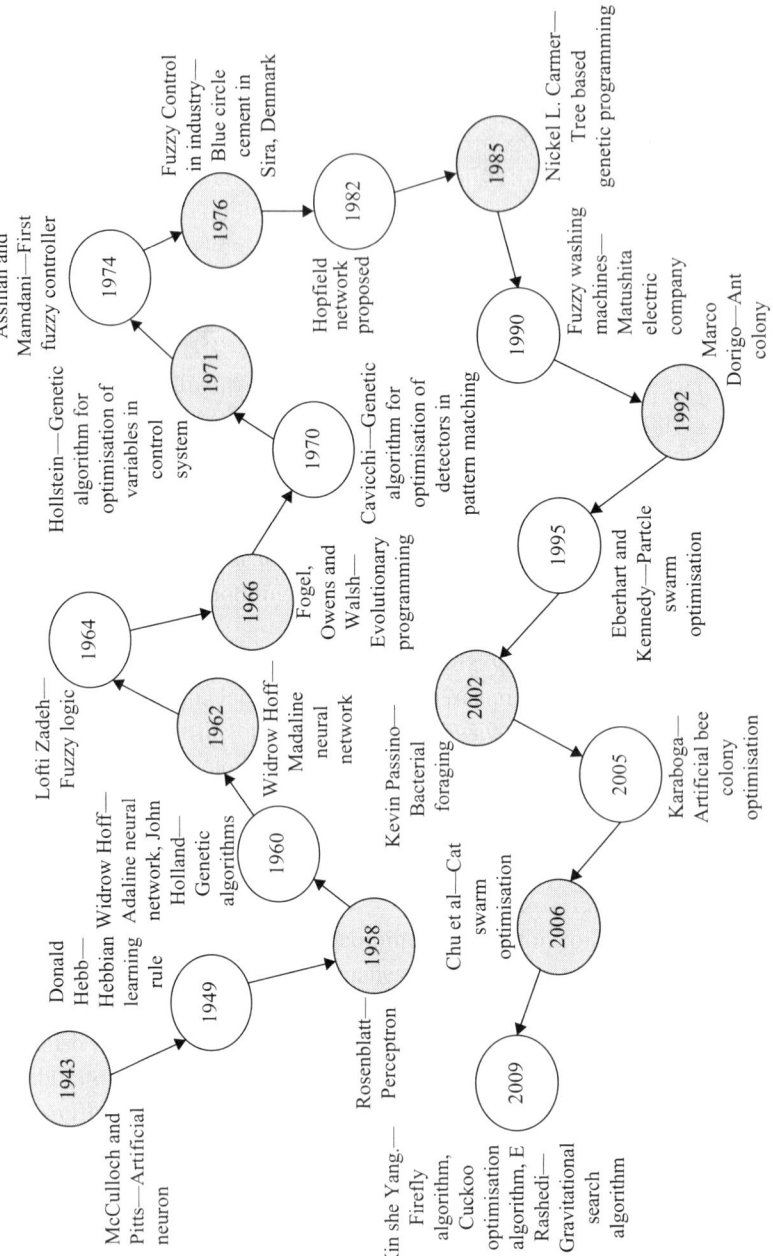

**Fig. 1.2** Development of intelligent systems

of thinking and interpretation. Systems such as genetics and evolutionary systems relates to a biological process in which the systems improves with time.

Swarm intelligence (SI) systems such as ant colony optimisation (ACO), PSO, artificial bee colony (ABC), cuckoo search algorithm (CSA), gravitational search algorithms, and so on, mimic the intelligent behaviour involved in animals, birds, insects, microorganisms or any individual living in groups to solve complex problems in a more efficient manner.

The modelling and simulation of the aforesaid intelligent strategies can be constructed from explicit, declarative knowledge bases, which in turn are operated by general, formal-reasoning mechanisms. The initial development of these intelligent systems is given in Fig. 1.2.

## 1.3 ARTIFICIAL NEURAL NETWORKS

Artificial neural networks (ANNs) are basically an *information processing system* with highly interconnected processing elements or units that simulates the behavioural aspects of a biological neural network or a brain with certain assumptions. It can be also put forth as a mathematical model inspired by biological neural network. Robert Hecht-Nielsen, an adjunct professor of electrical and computer engineering at the University of California, San Diego in 2005, and also the inventor of one of the first neuro-computer, had proposed the fundamental mechanism of thought process called *confabulation theory*. He defines neural network as a 'computing system made up of a number of simple, highly interconnected processing elements (Fig. 1.3), which process information by their dynamic state response to external inputs'.

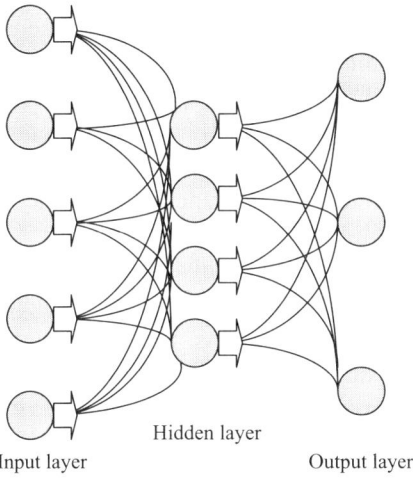

Input layer    Hidden layer    Output layer

**Fig. 1.3** Interconnected processing elements

Some of the periodically asked questions about neural networks from various sources are as follows:

What is a neural network (NN)?
When did these networks evolve?

Why is it called an 'intelligent network'?
How do NNs operate as a network?
What can you do with an NN and what not?
How many kinds of NNs exist?
Does this network system have a strong theoretical and mathematical proof?
Does it really solve real engineering problems? If so, tell something about it.
Does it have any relation to expert system, fuzzy system, or swarm intelligent systems?
What is the latest thing happening around the world using this network?
Does it have any role in the futuristic technologies?
Why should one know about NN?

The first question may be ill-posed since the focus is about ANNs. First of all, when we are talking about NN, we should say ANN because that is what we mean most of the time in applied soft computing. Biological neural networks are much more complicated than the mathematical models we use for ANNs. It should be noted that there is no universally accepted definition for NN. However, most of the people who have some understanding about NN would agree that NN is a network with many simple processors (units), each possibly having a small amount of local memory. These processors are interconnected by communication channels (connections) which carry information (data) encoded by various means. These units operate only on their local data and on the inputs they receive via the connections. The local information is modified or relaxed during the training phase or the learning phase.

The ANNs are evolved by mimicking exactly the way biological neural networks function. Some NNs are models of biological neural networks and some are not, but historically, much of the inspiration for the field of NNs came from the desire to produce artificial systems capable of sophisticated, perhaps 'intelligent', computations similar to those that the human brain routinely performs, and thereby possibly to enhance our understanding of the human brain. Since ANNs have certain analogous features of the functioning of the human brain, these networks can be called 'intelligent networks'.

In general, the operation of NNs involves learning of data through a 'training rule' where the strength of the connections, called weights, is adjusted. In other words, NNs 'learn' from examples or facts, as children learn to distinguish an apple from a mango based on examples of apples and mangoes. If trained carefully, NNs may exhibit some capability for generalization beyond the training data (i.e., to produce approximately correct results for new cases that were not used for training).

Some of the sample definitions of NNs are given as follows:

Haykin [1] writes: 'A neural network is a massively parallel distributed processor that has a natural propensity for storing experiential knowledge and making it available for use'. It resembles the brain in the following two respects:

1. Knowledge is acquired by the network through a learning process.
2. Interneuron connection strengths known as synaptic weights are used to store the knowledge.

Zurada [2] defines artificial neural systems, or neural networks, are physical cellular systems which can acquire, store, and utilize experiential knowledge.

According to the *Merriam-Webster Dictionary*, neural network is a computer architecture in which a number of processors are interconnected in a manner suggestive of the connections between neurons in a human brain and which is able to learn by a process of trial and error.

*Webopedia* describes neural network as a type of artificial intelligence that attempts to imitate the way a human brain works.

*Techtarget,* in the domain of information technology, defines neural network as a system of programs and data structures that approximates the operation of the human brain.

### 1.3.1 Development of ANNs

The development of ANNs dates back to the early twentieth century. The major classification of NN is given in Fig. 1.4. The initial works of Warren McCulloch and Walter Pitts [3] in a research paper that model a simple NN with electronic circuits paved the way for a new technological revolution of NN. Such NNs constitute the *first-generation NNs.* Afterwards, as computers emerged in the 1950s, several researchers attempted to make use of the new technology to construct enhanced NNs.

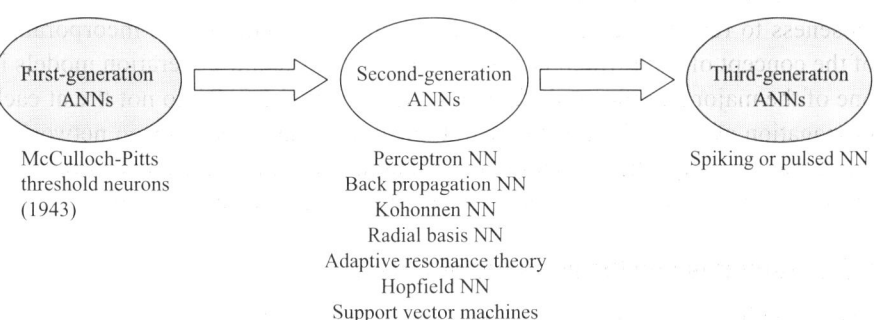

**Fig. 1.4** Classification of ANNs

Donald Hebb [4] proposed an artificial neuron that more closely mimicked the biological neuron, where each neuron would have numerous interconnections with other neurons. Each of these interconnections would have a weight' multiplier associated with it. Learning would be achieved by changing the weight multipliers of each of the interconnections.

Frank Rosenblatt [5] implemented a Hebb neuron, which he called a 'Perceptron'. Frank Rosenblatt, a neurobiologist at Cornell who was researching vision in flies, understood the neural processing that occurred within the eye itself, which particularly intrigued him and thus formed the origin of his 'Perceptron' NN. The Perceptron and other models showed great promise with many initial successes.

These networks are able to learn data with certain training rules and can be called *second-generation NNs*.

The initial successes of ANNs caused a great deal of publicity within the media. This eventually led to dissatisfaction as earlier claims were left unfulfilled. The reason was the very limited computing power available at the time. In addition, the published work of Marvin Minsky and Seymour Papert [6] discussed some of the limitations of the Perceptron model. The effect of these problems had reduced much of the funding available for research into ANNs. In 1974, Paul Werbos [7] in his PhD thesis first described the process of training ANNs through a process called the *Back propagation of Errors*. The weight multipliers are updated in such a way that the errors are decreased while training.

Just as Frank Rosenblatt developed the ideas of Donald Hebb, in 1986, David E. Rumelhart, Geoffrey E. Hinton, and Ronald J. Williams took the idea of Paul Werbos and developed a practical back propagation algorithm, which led to a re-birth in the field of ANN research. These second-generation NNs are able to learn and adapt the training data through various training schemes. Afterwards, various NN models such as Hopfield neural network, Kohonnen neural networks, Radial basis neural network, Adaptive Resonance Theory networks, and Support Vector Machines have been developed. These have been explained in detail in Chapter 3.

Recent developments in the area of NNs has evolved spiking neural networks (SNN) or pulsed neural networks, *the third-generation networks* which have the closeness to real biological neurons in a neural simulation. The incorporation of the concept of time which is not available in the second-generation models is one of the major significant differences. Neurons in the SNN do not fire at each propagation cycle (as it happens with typical multi-layer perceptron networks), but rather fire only when a membrane potential—an intrinsic quality of the neuron related to its membrane electrical charge—reaches a specific value.

### 1.3.2 Strengths and Weaknesses of ANNs

The strengths and weaknesses of ANNs can be understood from the answer for the aforecited posted question, 'What can you do with an NN and what not?' In principle, NNs can compute any computable function, that is, they can do everything a normal digital computer can do or perhaps even more, under some reasonable assumptions. Neural networks are universal approximators, and they work best if the system you are using to model them has a high tolerance to error. They can capture associations or discover regularities within a set of patterns.

Neural networks work well where the volume, number of variables, or diversity of the data are very high and the relationships between variables are vaguely understood; or, the relationships are difficult to describe adequately with conventional approaches. That is, it applies to problems where the relationships may be quite dynamic or non-linear. Artificial neural networks provide an analytical alternative to conventional techniques which are often limited by strict assumptions of normality, linearity, variable independence, etc.

The strength of the ANN depends upon its training. However, for training to be successful, one may need lots of training data and lots of computer time to do the training. In many applications, such as image and text processing, the person will have to do a lot of work to select appropriate input data and to code the data as numeric values. It should be noted that the networks are trained by an error minimization technique that aims to achieve the global minimum. Such minimization is computationally intractable except in small or simple problems. However, a conventional training algorithm updates weights through gradient-decent techniques where convergence proof is available in the literature. There are other training schemes similar to heuristic training using non-conventional methods such as GAs, PSO, simulated annealing, and so on, which do not have a strong mathematical proof of convergence. The developments in the area of ANNs are still carried out with few thousands of units and with certain symmetrical structure for the convenience of the programming and using data structures. However, it may not be a long way when information processing is carried out with the same number of processors as the number of neurons in the brain.

There are many advantages and limitations to NN analysis, and to discuss this subject properly, we would have to look at each individual type of network, which is not necessary for this general discussion. It should be noted that there are so many problems that are so difficult that an NN will be unable to learn them without memorizing the entire training set, such as predicting random or pseudo-random numbers, factoring large integers, determining whether a large integer is prime or composite, and decrypting anything encrypted by a good algorithm. And it is important to understand that there is no method for training NNs that can magically create information that is not contained in the training data.

According to David J. Chalmers' [8] published work titled *The Conscious Mind-in search of fundamental theory*, the human consciousness and emotions have some relation to information processing in the brain. Simulating this phenomenon is still considered to be science fiction. Certain characteristics in ANN such as perception and cognition may be considered as some of the pre-requisite for consciousness. However, it should be noted that ANNs are not able to provide any insight for the same. Even though ANNs are able to mimic a few of the functions in the brain, still it poses a challenge to answer questions such as, 'How does the brain respond to environmental stimulus?', 'How does it understand the information?','How do we simulate the internal states of mind, emotions, and consciousness?', and 'Why is all this information processing accompanied by an experienced inner life?'

### 1.3.3 Neural Computing vs Conventional Computing

In general, the conventional method of computing can be understood from the functioning of the traditional computers such as the 'Von Neumann machine'. Here, instructions are obtained from memory, the CPU then processes data according to these instructions, and this procedure is repeated until all instructions are completed. The operation is performed serially to solve problems using a series of well-defined steps (an algorithm) such as when searching for an item on a database.

Conventional computing does have several limitations. Primarily, all the details with perfection must be told in advance to the computers. It is very difficult to express even with advanced and rigid algorithms to convey simple tasks such as recognizing the facial expressions. In addition, even if an algorithm has identified the data used, it must be as exact as possible. Conventional computers are often unable to manage the inconsistency of data obtained in the real world. These two issues account for many of the areas in which computers have traditionally been weak, such as data prediction and classification. The differences between neural computing and conventional computing are presented in Table 1.2.

Table 1.2  Functional differences between conventional and neuro-computing

| Conventional computing | Neuro-computing |
|---|---|
| Computational process is sequential and deterministic | Computation is not sequential or necessarily deterministic |
| A single processing unit is present, which is a complex central processor | Many simple processing units are present, which generally do nothing other than taking the weighted sum of their inputs from other processors |
| Respond to any programmed instruction | Do not respond to programmed instruction; but respond in parallel such as the simulated or actual responses for the pattern of inputs presented to it |
| Separate memory addresses for storing data | No separate memory addresses for storing data; however, information is contained in the overall activation 'state' of the network |
| Knowledge is centrally located; if certain parts of data are lost, retrieval is not possible | Knowledge is distributed; data retrieval may be possible if a certain part of data is lost (i.e., similar to the memory retrieval in human brain) |
| Not suited in situations where there are no clear-cut algorithmic solutions | Well suited to situations where algorithmic solutions are not possible |
| Cannot handle noisy imprecise data | Can manage noisy imprecise data |

## 1.3.4 Scope of ANN

Neural networks are applied to various engineering and scientific applications such as control systems, forecasting, pattern recognitions, classification, data mining, and so on, to every field of application. For example, in medical diagnosis, it helps in diagnosing the patients by knowing the reported indicators such as blood pressure, heart rate, temperature, sugar level, blood test details, personal information, and physical activity. Neural network can envisage the possible health condition of the patient such as the type of fever, possible organ failures, and possible diseases. It has been very well used in decision-making problems where inconsistency of data exists. It is used as a hybrid method with other techniques such as fuzzy systems, expert system, and other intelligent systems. The strength and weakness of ANNs can be compensated with these systems to develop high-end applications. The futuristic technologies will depend more on ANNs, as these days, people want everything smart, such as smart cities, smart phone, smart grid, smart gadgets, and smart weapons.

The third-generation ANNs may give a tremendous boost to accomplish smart things in the very future. The mathematical models of the third generation may be very much closer to the way the neurons in the brain function. Neural hardwares are already in great use and will be used in most of the applications. Therefore, the scope and assurance observed in this technology justify the reason for learning this subject and will be of great use.

## 1.4 FUZZY SYSTEMS

In general, fuzzy means 'not clear, distinct, or real-world vagueness'. Sometimes, if a person is confused, we say, 'He looks fuzzy'. Suppose, when the climatic temperature of the atmosphere is 42 degrees centigrade, it may be too hot for one person to bear, whereas it may be normal for another person. Therefore, it may be perceived or felt differently by different persons at different times. The ways an individual understands, thinks, or feels is inherently not the same, and it varies with various degrees. An old saying that conveys 'One man's meat is another man's poison' may be true to quote at this juncture. Therefore, the way we perceive the world is continually changing and cannot always be defined in true or false statements.

Various definitions are available for fuzzy logic systems. The following are some of the sample definitions.

*Merriam-Webster Dictionary* describes fuzzy system as: 'A system of logic in which a statement can be true, false, or any of a continuum of values in between'.

On the website of *Wiktionary* organization, fuzzy logic is stated as: 'A form of reasoning, derived from fuzzy set theory, whereby a truth value need not be exactly zero (false) or one (true), but rather can be zero, one, or any value in between'.

*Techtarget* introduces fuzzy logic as an approach to computing based on the 'degrees of truth' rather than the usual 'true or false' (1 or 0) Boolean logic on which the modern computer is based.

*Investopedia* describes fuzzy logic as a mathematical logic that attempts to solve problems by assigning values to an imprecise spectrum of data in order to arrive at the most accurate conclusion possible.

*Collins Dictionary* [9] mentions fuzzy logic as a branch of logic designed to allow degrees of imprecision in reasoning and knowledge, typified by terms such as 'very', 'quite possibly', and 'unlikely', to be represented in such a way that the information can be processed by computer.

Some of the periodically asked questions about fuzzy logic from various sources are as follows, which will give a warm-up before getting into the details given in Chapter 5. The questions raised are as follows:

What is 'fuzzy logic'?
What is the need for fuzzy logic? Where is fuzzy logic used? Why is it studied?
What are fuzzy logic's applications?
What are fuzzy logic's salient features?

Is behaviour of fuzzy system non-deterministic?
Is fuzzy logic a better alternative as compared to linear control systems?
What is 'possibility theory'? How is it different from fuzzy logic?
What is the difference between fuzzy theory and probability theory?
Why cannot we use a lookup table instead of fuzzy logic?
Whether fuzzy theory means a theory without clear meaning?

Computers are very well known for crunching numbers applying various arithmetical operations such as addition, subtraction, multiplication, and division. We also know from literature that computers can also be used for reasoning, especially for deductive reasoning. In deductive reasoning, whenever the assumptions given are either true or false, and also their truth value is given, then whatever may be their consequence, it is deterministic. However, in day-to-day life, while doing tasks or while conversing and understanding things, it is not possible for us to have a precise functional deterministic way of operation in order to solve everyday problems. So for this purpose, one of the ways of handling these imprecisions is through fuzzy logic.

Suppose we say 'Mr X is a nice person' or 'He is a healthy person'. There may be various parameters for the person to be nice or healthy. He may be nice since he helps poor people or he may be nice in the way he behaves with his neighbours or friends. However, at times, he becomes angry if he fails in a class test. Just because he is angry at one instance, we cannot deny Mr X being a nice person. In addition, the person being healthy has various parameters such as temperature, blood pressure, sugar level, and so on. The person may be healthy even if his sugar level or blood pressure is above the normal level. These issues make the statement imprecise, and the words 'nice' or 'healthy' are not the ones that have deterministic values.

Suppose you add one sugar cube in a glass of milk. You say the milk is sweet. Again you add 3 cubes to the same glass of milk; then again you say that the milk is sweet. As you add many more sugar cubes, the milk may get sweeter and sweeter; still you say the milk is sweet. We cannot say at what point the milk has become sweet, but it depends on the variation of the degree of sweetness. However, we cannot precisely say when the milk has become sweet.

Therefore, the adjectives or the expressions that we use in our daily life cannot be mathematically evaluated in a deterministic sense. Even when not deterministic, these expressions or notions are still used in solutions for problems in our daily life. Now certain questions that arises are, 'How to capture these notions?, How is it possible to solve the power of reasoning used by human beings in solving problems involving such non-deterministic variables? How this power of reasoning can be used in a computer system for solving the problem under consideration, since computers are designed for precise work?' The answer to all these questions lies in the powerful mathematical tool called fuzzy logic.

Fuzziness pertains to uncertainty associated with the system, i.e., nothing can be predicted with exact preciseness. All real-life situations have some degree of uncertainty or fuzziness. In 1965, Lotfi A. Zadeh [10] introduced fuzzy sets, where a more flexible sense of membership is possible. However, in practical scenario, the value of variables is not always known precisely; rather an approximate value of the variables is more likely to be known. This theory provides a strict mathematical framework in which vague conceptual phenomenon can be studied rigorously. In this theory, the variables, functions, and so on are connected with the imprecise phenomenon to be studied are expressed as fuzzy variables and fuzzy functions and hence their operation becomes important.

However, based on the outline proposed by Zadeh [11], it should be noted that the fuzzy logic is found to have the following characteristics:

- Exact reasoning is viewed as a limiting case of approximate reasoning.
- Everything is a matter of degree.
- Knowledge is interpreted as a collection of elastic, fuzzy constraints on a collection of variables.
- Inference is viewed as a process of propagation of elastic constraints.
- Any logical system can be 'fuzzified'.

### 1.4.1 Acceptance of Fuzzy Logic

During the initial days of fuzzy logic evolution, a stiff opposition is seen against the fuzzy sets and fuzzy logic system. The academic circles were not accepting the fact that fuzzy is an alternative for representing the impreciseness. This may be the fact that underlying mathematics had not yet been explored. The following statements from academicians may help us understand the scenario:

> *'Fuzzy theory is wrong, wrong, and pernicious. What we need is more logical thinking, not less. The danger of fuzzy logic is that it will encourage the sort of imprecise thinking that has brought us so much trouble. Fuzzy logic is the cocaine of science.'*
>
> William Kahan, UC Berkeley

> *'Fuzzification' is a kind of scientific permissiveness. It tends to result in socially appealing slogans unaccompanied by the discipline of hard scientific work and patient observation.*
>
> Rudolf Kalman, University of Florida

> *'Fuzziness is probability in disguise. I can design a controller with probability that could do the same thing that you could do with fuzzy logic'.*
>
> Myron Tribus, University of Michigan

The large inertia seen in the acceptance of fuzzy logic is due to the controversy in certain grey areas. Even though fuzzy logic had a broad track record of successful applications, some of the engineers working in the area of control system had rejected it for validation and other reasons. In addition, some statisticians who hold the view that probability is the only rigorous mathematical description of uncertainty also have problem in accepting fuzzy logic. Some argue that it cannot be a super-set of ordinary set theory since membership functions are defined in terms of conventional sets. Whatever may be the reasons for its successful application and problem-solving capabilities in science and engineering have made fuzzy logic a versatile mathematical tool.

## 1.4.2 Fuzzy Logic Applications

Fuzzy logic has now penetrated in almost all engineering applications ranging from decision-making to control applications. Almost any control system can be replaced with a fuzzy logic-based control system. However, it simplifies the design of many more complicated cases and to provide better control. During the 1970s, C.B. Brown and his colleagues tried in applying fuzzy logic to structural analysis. Assilian and Mamdani [12] of UK have developed a controller for a steam engine which has been the first major application of fuzzy logic. Their initial efforts at creating a controller were unsatisfactory because the adaptive system was taking too long to establish equilibrium. To speed up the adaptation time, S. Assilian and E. Mamdani [13] tried creating some rules based upon linguistics. These worked so well that a whole new line of research was opened up.

In 1976, the first industrial application of fuzzy logic was developed by Blue Circle Cement and SIRA in Denmark and implemented 6 years later in 1982. Dubois applied the fuzzy set concept to traffic conditions in the year 1977. It was not until the late 1970s that Japanese research began to develop the applications of fuzzy logic. As in many matters in Japan, there was a Kanto and a Kansai version [14] of this effort. Kanto means the Tokyo area and Kansai the Osaka area. At Tokyo University, H. Shibata and T. Terano led this research. In Osaka, K. Asai and K. Tanaka were the leaders. As elsewhere in the world there was a tendency for people who knew nothing of the topic except its name to dismiss it as trivial and unimportant.

One of the most famous applications of fuzzy logic is that of the Sendai subway system in Sendai, Japan. In 1979, Seiji Yasunobu at Hitachi started trying to develop a system for the operation of the subway trains of Sendai. This control of the Nanboku line, developed by Hitachi, used a fuzzy controller to run the train all day long. This made the line one of the smoothest running subway systems in the world and increased efficiency as well as stopping time. This is also an example of the earlier acceptance of fuzzy logic in the East since the subway went into operation in 1988.

In 1985, Fuji Electrical offered commercially a control mechanism based upon fuzzy logic. The successes that Japanese companies were achieving with fuzzy logic prompted the Japanese government agency Ministry of International Trade and Industry (MITI) to set up in 1988 a major collaborative research project called the Laboratory for International Fuzzy Engineering Research (LIFE). This was a major effort program involving 50 companies in a 6-year, $5 billion program. However, fuzzy logic has been elevated to become an important subject in engineering colleges as it has been widely used in many engineering applications and decision-making.

## 1.4.3 Misconceptions in Fuzzy Logic

Fuzzy logic technology has become matured enough, based on its wide range of applications and advantages. However, there are certain grey areas where there is a need for clarity [14]. They are dealt in the following paragraphs.

### (a) Fuzzy logic is the same as 'imprecise logic'

Fuzzy logic is not an imprecise logic. It cannot be put as less precise than any other form of logic. It is true that the word fuzzy means unclear and not complete; however, fuzzy logic does not mean that the logic is unclear. It is an organized mathematical tool or techniques for handling imprecise concepts. The concept of 'hotness' cannot be expressed in an equation, because although temperature is a quantity, 'hotness' is not. However, people have an idea of what 'hot' is, and agree that there is no sharp cut-off between 'hot' and 'not hot', where something is 'hot' at $T$ degrees but 'not hot' at $T + 1$ degree.

This concept cannot be handled using the classical logic due to the principle of bivalence. The principle of bivalence states that every declarative sentence expressing a proposition (of a theory under inspection) has exactly one truth value, either true or false. Therefore, for the previous idea of what 'hot' is, has no definite answer but only can have a 'fuzzy' answer. However, when using fuzzy logic, individuals in the fuzzy set will have membership values between [0 1], (i.e., values between truth and false). Therefore, the application of fuzzy logic technique will help us in dealing with this impreciseness.

### (b) Fuzzy logic is an alternate way of expressing probability

In general, both fuzzy logic and probability are different ways of expressing uncertainty. Both theories look to be related in the sense that both are concerned with some type of uncertainty and both use the interval [0, 1] for their measures as the range of their respective functions. Fuzzy logic uses a set membership to infer 'how much a variable is in a set'. However, probability infers *'how probable do I think that a variable is in a set'*. To put in clear-cut terms, probability measures the likelihood of an event to occur while fuzzy logic measures the degree to which an outcome belongs to an event. Lotfi Zadeh, the creator of fuzzy logic, put forth that fuzzy logic is different in character from probability, and is not a replacement for it.

### (c) Behaviour of fuzzy is non-deterministic

This statement is false, since fuzzy handles the imprecise statements with the help of fuzzy mathematical sets. All fuzzy operations are evaluated as membership values as a 'degree of truth' which has deterministic values and therefore the output of fuzzy is deterministic. Even in real-time control engineering applications where fuzzy logic is applied, the output of the system is deterministic and real. It goes through a process of fuzzification, inference mechanism, and defuzzification to get the real output. This is discussed in detail in Chapter 5.

### (d) Probability theory, possibility theory, and fuzzy theory all look the same

Professor Lotfi Zadeh first introduced possibility theory in 1978 as an extension of his theory of fuzzy sets and fuzzy logic. Possibility measures the degree of ease for a variable to take a value, whereas probability measures the likelihood for a variable to take a value. So they deal with two different types of uncertainty. Possibility theory handles imprecision and probability theory handles likelihood of occurrence. This fundamental difference leads to different mathematical properties of their distributions. Being a measure of occurrence, the probability distribution of a variable must add up exactly 1. The possibility distribution is not subject to this restriction since a variable can have multiple possible values. Fuzzy theory and possibility theory is not the same. However, *fuzzy* set theory can define set membership as a *possibility distribution*. The general rule for this can be expressed as: $F: [0, 1]^n \to [0, 1]$, where $n$ is some number of possibilities.

**(e) Lookup tables are enough than using a fuzzy logic**
Lookup tables are arrays or a matrix that consist of pre-calculated information generally where the basic linear information can be directly searched for or picked up without modification. However, fuzzy logic offers a higher-level language that is easier to comprehend and modify, which a simple lookup table cannot. It takes into account the non-linear relationship, which may not be possible with the lookup table.

**(f) Fuzzy logic is no better alternative to linear control**
Most of the real-life physical systems are actually non-linear systems. Conventional design approaches use different approximation methods to handle non-linearity. Some typical choices are linear, piecewise linear, and lookup table approximations to trade-off factors of complexity, cost, and system performance. Fuzzy logic is a linear approximation technique and is relatively simple; however, it tends to limit control performance and may be costly to implement.

Piecewise linear technique works better, although it is tedious to implement, because it often requires the design of several linear controllers. A lookup table technique may help improve control performance, but it is difficult to debug and tune. Furthermore in complex systems, where multiple inputs exist, a lookup table becomes impractical due to its large memory requirements. Fuzzy logic provides an alternative solution to non-linear control because it is closer to the real world. Non-linearity is handled by rules, membership functions, and the inference process which results in improved performance, simpler implementation, and reduced design costs.

### 1.4.4 Scope of Fuzzy Logic

Today, fuzzy logic is used in many day-to-day appliances, since it allows more human-like interpretation and reasoning in machines by considering intermediate values between true/false, hot/cold, bright/dark, clean/dirty, etc. In future, more and more systems can be built using fuzzy logic which incorporate human thinking, experience and reasoning instead of limiting it to only true/false values. Hybrid technologies such as neuro-fuzzy systems, genetic-neuro-fuzzy systems, etc., are already explored to a larger extent.

Type-II fuzzy sets are becoming prominent so that more uncertainties can be handled. In 1986, Attanassov [15] proposed a new kind of fuzzy logic called intuitionist fuzzy sets. In intuitionist fuzzy logic, instead of describing a truth value as a single number $t$, we describe the truth value by a pair of numbers $(t, f)$, where $t$ is the degree to which we believe (truth) in a given statement, and $f$ is a degree to which we believe in its negation (false) with the same statement. This new branch of intuitionistic fuzzy sets may offer a great deal in the futuristic intelligent technologies.

## 1.5 GENETIC ALGORITHM AND EVOLUTIONARY PROGRAMMING

Genetic algorithms (GAs) and evolutionary programming techniques belong to a class of metaheuristic algorithms. The word 'meta' means higher level, whereas the word 'heuristics' means to find. In computer science, metaheuristic designates a computational method that optimizes a problem by iteratively trying to improve a candidate solution with regard to a given measure of quality. Metaheuristics make few or no assumptions about the problem being optimized and can search very large spaces of candidate solutions. However, metaheuristics do not guarantee an optimal solution is ever found. Many metaheuristics implement some form of stochastic optimisation. Other terms similar in meaning to metaheuristic are: derivative-free, direct search, black-box, or indeed just heuristic optimizer [16, 17].

Genetic algorithms and EPs belong to class of evolutionary algorithms. The other types of evolutionary algorithms are genetic programming and evolutionary strategies. They belong to natural inspired and population-based algorithms. They mimic and simulate the nature in a more implicit manner. There is no rigorous definition of 'genetic algorithm' or 'evolutionary programming' accepted by all in the evolutionary-computation community that differentiates GAs and EPs from other evolutionary-computation methods. However, it can be said that most methods called 'GAs' have at least the following elements in common: populations of chromosomes, selection according to fitness, crossover to produce new offspring, and random mutation of new offspring. Similarly, evolutionary programming [18], is a stochastic optimisation strategy similar to GAs, but rather places emphasis on the behavioural linkage between parents and their offspring, rather than seeking to emulate specific genetic operators as observed in nature. The evolutionary programming was originally conceived by Lawrence J. Fogel in 1960.

Some of the periodically asked questions about GAs and EPs from various sources are summarized as follows, which will give a warm-up before getting into the detail given in Chapter 7. The questions raised are as follows:

What is a 'genetic algorithm'?
How is genetic algorithm different from genetic programming?
What is 'evolutionary programming'?
How is evolutionary programming different from evolutionary strategy?
What is the significant difference of GAs and EPs, different from hill climbing, simulated annealing, and tabu search?
Are GAs and EPs deterministic algorithms?
How is GA different from EP?
What can GAs and EPs do that the other conventional algorithms cannot do?
Why should one learn GAs and EPs?

According to H. Grefenstette [19], 'A genetic algorithm is an iterative procedure maintaining a population of structures that are candidate solutions to specific domain challenges. During each temporal increment (called a generation), the structures in the current population are rated for their effectiveness as domain solutions, and on the basis of these evaluations, a new population of candidate solutions is formed using specific genetic operators such as reproduction, crossover, and mutation'.

It is a model of machine learning which derives its behaviour from a metaphor of some of the mechanisms of evolution in nature. This is done by the creation within a machine of a population of individuals represented by chromosomes, in essence a set of character strings that are analogous to the base-4 chromosomes that we see in our own DNA. The individuals in the population then go through a process of simulated 'evolution'.

Before entering into much detail in Chapter 7, we should understand the difference between GA and genetic programming (GP) which is also one of the classes of evolutionary program. Genetic programming developed by John Koza [20] can be considered as an extension of the genetic model of evolutionary programs. In GP, the bits or objects that constitute the population are not fixed-length character strings that encode possible solutions to the problem at hand.

However, they are programs, when executed, are the candidate solutions to the problem. These programs are expressed in GP as parse trees, rather than as lines of code or using a suitable data structure using Lisp (Locator/Identifier Separation Protocol) and non-Lisp programming techniques to represent exactly the problem in space. For example, '2 − B/A' 'B + C', 'B(E + AC)' can be represented as in Figs 1.5 and 1.6. The population in the program constitute of elements from a function set and terminal set, which are typically fixed sets of symbols selected to precisely represent the solution of problem in hand. It should be noted that GP implements the recombinant operation by randomly selecting sub-trees within the population and exchange them. In addition, GP does not use any mutation operator as in GAs [21, 22].

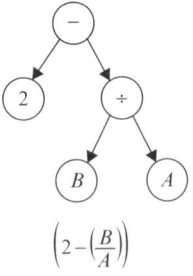

$$\left(2 - \left(\frac{B}{A}\right)\right)$$

**Fig. 1.5** Tree representation of objects

+ (+ B C) corresponds to $B + C$.
+ (* B (+ E (* A C))) corresponds to $B(E + AC)$.

**Fig. 1.6** Lisp representation of objects

Even though, GA and EP belong to the same class of evolutionary programs, EP differs in the approach they solve the problems [23]. The basic EP method involves three steps: (1) choose an initial population of trial solutions at random, (2) each solution is replicated into a new population plus mutation is carried out, and (3) each offspring solution is assessed by computing its fitness through stochastic tournament selection. However, the significant difference between GA and EP is that, EP does not use any crossover as a genetic operator. It should be understood that EPs differ from GAs in two main aspects, and they are as follows:

(a) GA has no constraint in the representation of the problem. That is, it involves the problem solutions as a string of representative tokens, the genome. However, in EP, the representation is constrained and follows from the problem.
(b) In EP, mutation is the one that changes aspects of the solution according to a statistical distribution which weighs variations in the behaviour of the offsprings.

Sometimes evolutionary strategy (ES) and evolutionary programming looks the same. While collaborating on experiments for the wind tunnel experiments and searching the optimal shapes of bodies in a flow, Rechenberg got the idea of trying random changes in the parameters defining the shape, following the example of natural mutations (Rechenberg, 1963). However, Hans-Paul Schwefel (1977) generalized the strategies by imitating the following basic principles of organic evolution: a population, leading to the possibility of recombination with random mating, mutation, and selection. However, the main difference between EP and ES are as follows:

(a) During selection, EP uses stochastic tournament selection, that is, each trial solution in the population faces competition against a pre-selected number of opponents and receives a 'win' if it is at least as good as its opponent in each encounter. Selection then eliminates those solutions with the least wins. However, in ES, the selection scheme is carried out deterministically in which the worst solutions are purged from the population based directly on their function evaluation.
(b) EP does not use crossover mechanism (recombination), whereas ES uses many from of recombination methods.

Similar to GAs and EPs, there are other heuristic search algorithms such as hill climbing simulated annealing and tabu search which are classified as single-solution-based algorithms work on a single solution. That is, during start of the search, they start from a single point solution in the domain. However, GAs and EP along with various swarm intelligent algorithms are population-based algorithms that work on a population of solutions. Though GAs and EPs tries to give a solution, they are non-deterministic or non-unique as in the case of conventional algorithms. This is due to the fact that GAs and EPs involves randomness.

While programming, pseudo-random numbers generated by the computers are used to explore the solution in the search space. The differences of GAs and EPs with respect to the conventional algorithms are explained in Chapter 7. This difference makes the advantage of GAs and EPs able to solve efficiently at places where conventional algorithms fail to provide a solution. Therefore, GAs and EPs are widely used in many engineering problems and its importance is definitely seen as one of the versatile tools of applied soft computing.

### 1.5.1 History of GAs and EPs

In the 1950s and 1960s, several computer scientists independently studied evolutionary systems with the idea that evolution could be used as an optimisation tool for engineering problems. The idea behind this was to evolve a population of candidate solutions to a given problem, using operators inspired by natural genetic variation and natural selection.

In the 1960s, Rechenberg introduced 'evolution strategies,' a method he used to optimize real-value parameters for devices such as aerofoils [17]. This idea was further developed by Schwefel. The field of evolution strategies has become an active area for the research. Lawrence J. Fogel, Alvin Owens, and Michael Walsh [24] developed evolutionary programming technique in which possible solutions to a given tasks were represented as finite state machines, which were evolved by randomly mutating their state transition diagrams and selecting the fittest. Together, evolution strategies, evolutionary programming, and GAs form the backbone of the field of evolutionary computation.

Several other people working in the 1950s and 1960s developed algorithms for optimisation and machine learning. In addition, a number of evolutionary biologists used computers to simulate evolution for the purpose of controlled experiments. Genetic algorithms were invented by John Holland in the 1960s and were developed by Holland and his students and colleagues at the University of Michigan in the 1960s and 1970s [17]. In contrast with evolution strategies and evolutionary programming, Holland's original goal was not to design algorithms to solve specific problems, but to study the phenomenon of adaptation as it occurs in nature and to develop ways in which the mechanisms of natural adaptation might be imported into computer systems.

Holland's 1975 book *Adaptation in Natural and Artificial Systems* presented the GA as an abstraction of biological evolution and gave a theoretical framework for adaptation under the GA. Holland's GA is a method for moving from one population of chromosomes to a new population by using a kind of natural selection together with the genetics inspired operators of crossover, mutation, and inversion. Holland was the first to attempt to put computational evolution on a firm theoretical footing. For decades, there has been a good interaction among the researchers studying various evolutionary-computation methods, and the boundaries between GAs, evolution strategies, evolutionary programming, and other evolutionary approaches have broken down to some extent.

### 1.5.2 Scope of GAs and EPs

GAs and EPs are generally machine learning techniques. The application of GAs ranges from bioinformatics, phylogenetics, computer science engineering, economics, chemistry, manufacturing, mathematics, physics, pharmacometrics and other fields. Though, GAs are used in a larger sense than EPs, EPs are also quite successful in the applications similar to GA. GAs are considered to be one of the robust non-conventional optimisation tool. There are various software packages such as genitor, genesis, LibGA, and hypergen available in the market.

GAs can be easily hybridized with ANN and fuzzy logic technologies to improve the efficiency of the system performance. Though it was quite successful in early days, there are some specific application and limitation where GAs cannot perform to an expected level. Sometimes they do not scale well with complexity. GAs may not be able to get the global optimum solution for certain domain of applications, and may trap in the local optimum which is one of the prominent limitation. This fact may be due to the size of the search space involved in some problems. In addition, the justification of obtaining the better solution is only in comparison to other solutions. As a result, the stop criterion is not clear in every problem.

Sometimes, other swarm intelligent algorithms such as PSO and ACO are able to give better solution than GA for some specific application. Even with all these limitations, GAs are proven technology which have theorems like 'Schema Theorem' for convergence proof and is quite successful in the past decades even before the evolution of swarm intelligent algorithms. Therefore, the importance of GA cannot be neglected and is still one of the popular soft computing techniques that are worth learning.

## 1.6 SWARM INTELLIGENT SYSTEMS

*Collins Dictionary* considers the term 'swarm intelligence (SI)' as a noun and describes as 'the collective behaviour of a group of animals', esp. social insects such as ants, bees, and termites that are each following very basic rules. It also describes SI as an AI approach to problem-solving using algorithms based on the collective behaviour of social insects.

The expression SI was first introduced by Gerardo Beni and Jing Wang in 1989, in the context of cellular robotic systems [25]. The noun word 'Intelligence' in the *Oxford Dictionary* describes the ability to acquire and apply knowledge and skills. Therefore, this collective intelligence is able to do intelligent tasks or capable of solving large complex problems. Not only in a narrow sense, a swarm of insects interacting among themselves, but in a broad sense, every matter in this universe is an intelligent design which constitutes the energy matter that interacts among them to generate an intelligent property. That is, the information exchange among individual matter exhibit intelligence. In an interview with Eric Bonabeau, the founder CEO of ICOSYTEMS and one of the world's leading experts in complex systems and distributed adaptive problem-solving has quoted as follows with respect to SI.

> 'And that swarm intelligence offers an alternative way of designing 'intelligent' systems in which autonomy, emergence, and distributedness replace control, pre-programming, and centralization.'

> *'In social insects, errors and randomness are not 'bugs'; rather, they contribute very strongly to their success by enabling them to discover and explore in addition to exploiting. Self-organization feeds itself upon errors to provide the colony with flexibility (the colony can adapt to a changing environment) and robustness (even when one or more individuals fail, the group can still perform its tasks).'*
>
> —Eric Bonabeau (2007)

During the initial developments, there are two popular swarm inspired methods in computational intelligence areas: Ant colony optimisation (ACO) and PSO. Ant colony optimisation was inspired by the behaviours of ants and has many successful applications in discrete optimisation problem which was developed by Italian scientist Marco Dorigo et al. [26]. Particle swarm optimisation is a population-based stochastic optimisation technique developed by Dr. Eberhart and Dr. Kennedy in 1995, inspired by social behaviour of bird flocking or fish schooling. However, the recent developments in this field are enormous which lead to the developments of various techniques such as ABC system, firefly systems, CSA, and gravitational search systems.

In the near future, such techniques will play an important role in most of the smart applications. From the olden days, where the term 'e' was very popular, has now declined. However, the well-known electronic applications such as e-books, e-commerce, e-mail, e-resources, and e-gadgets will soon be replaced with smart books, smart commerce, smart mails, smart resources, and smart gadgets.

Some of the periodically asked questions about swarm intelligent systems from various sources are summarized as follows, which will give an overview of the same before getting into the detail given in Chapter 8. The questions raised are as follows:

What is the difference between artificial intelligence and swarm intelligence?
How can an SI solve realistic problems?
Does an SI have any mathematical proof for its validity?
Does a swarm intelligent system give deterministic solution?
How can SI techniques differ within themselves?
Which SI technique is considered so far as the best one?
Can genetic algorithms be called swarm intelligent?
Can the SI be called 'heuristic and population-based algorithms'?
What types of SI applications are successful?
Why is SI more successful compared to conventional techniques?

Swarm intelligence can be considered as a sub-field of AI. The functioning of SI as a sub-field implies that intelligent systems can cluster and work alone as clusters, solving problems, where each sub-system within each cluster depends on peer systems to solve an ultimate problem. In addition, it can be thought of as SI intersecting AI multi-agent system as well as operation research-optimisation fields.

Most of the SI techniques can solve realistic problems. This can be explained with a real-life experience of mine. Once, my friend and I went to a village, somewhere close to our institute, to purchase some furniture. Being unfamiliar with the area, we could not re-trace our way to our destination. We decided that without asking for directions from local people, we will find our way back on our own using ant colony intelligent technique for this purpose. The idea was to follow the path where more people were seen flocking on the road. The idea worked and we were somehow able to reach our destination.

In the aforementioned example, the idea of ant's foraging behaviour in finding food in the shortest path through a phenomenon of laying a chemical substance called pheromone had been applied. The more the pheromone, the more the ants traverse the path which leads to the shortest path in reaching the food source. The analogous is more the number of people in a path, more the chance of finding the national highway. Swarm intelligence is applied in many real-time applications, which is discussed in detail in Chapter 8.

The mathematical proof of its validity is only in the infant stage. However, its successful applications confirm its validity as an intelligent tool for various scientific and engineering applications. The solution obtained is not deterministic as in conventional algorithms. The reason is the randomness involved in exploring new solutions. Statistical analysis is carried out in determining the best solutions. However, SI can give solution where conventional algorithms fail to give one.

Sometimes, it may be confusing to choose the right SI technique for a particular application. Therefore, it necessitates identifying the best among the SI techniques. From various literatures, the comparison of various SI techniques is carried out using standard benchmark objective functions and problems. However, the justification still depends on how effectively the SI technique is implemented for a particular application. Therefore, the argument in telling one technique better than another one is baseless. However, it should be judiciously judged in connection to a specific application and its implementation. The two common phenomena in any SI technique are exploration and exploitation which has to be balanced. The trade-off between the two features helps us in realizing the potential of an individual SI technique.

Most of the metaheuristic algorithms such as GA, EP, and ES have some common features with respect to SI systems. Genetic algorithm belongs to population-based algorithms. The interaction of individual genes between chromosomes through crossover mechanism is carried out as a group in which collective intelligence behaviour is seen emerging. It may be true in arguing that GA can be onsidered to be a class of swarm intelligent techniques. Both GA and SI techniques are mostly heuristic and population-based intelligent techniques. However, different types of SI techniques function differently mimicking the collective intelligence that evolves from a swarm.

### 1.6.1 Strengths and Weaknesses of SI Techniques

Swarm intelligent techniques are adaptable, evolvable, redundant, extendable, and innovative. During a course of an application, swarm can adjust or self-organize among themselves to a new stimulus or changeable according to certain dynamic constraints. The individual of the swarm which fits to the process are alive while others die bringing in new adaptable solutions.

The interaction of individuals through exchange of information pop up a new form of collective intelligence emerging which orient in getting the best possible solution. The redundant nature of the swarm is basically due to the distributed nature of information available with every individual in the swarm. Even if the information available among few individuals in a swarm is lost, the swarm still is capable enough to get a solution which may not be possible in a conventional approach where the information is centrally controlled. Hence they are error tolerant.

Swarm intelligence is extendable and can be built in or extended with another structure. They can be easily hybridized or combined with other techniques to evolve a new powerful approach. The exponential combinations of individuals hide countless possibilities in getting a novel solution. It brings more innovative solutions for a problem in hand. However, the advantages of the SI techniques need to be explored as its potential usage is very high in many fields of application.

If the success of SI systems is observed in one side of coin, then the limitations of SI should be also identified on the other side of the coin. Some of the limitations are non-optimal, non-controllable, non-predictable, and non-understandable. Swarm intelligence techniques sometimes produce non-optimal solutions. The reason is the randomness involved in the process and it is a fact that no one can control randomness. It should be noted, while implementing SI techniques in computers, pseudo-randomness is the one that is used while developing programme codes.

The emergent behaviour of swarm, though observed as a strength, should also be seen as a weakness as it evolves without any control. For example, there is no ruler or a leader in an ant colony system. However, the system itself evolves to sustain itself ensuring sufficient amount of food in the summer and worries no more in the winter through a nature-inspired successful foraging scheme. The functioning of swarm is extremely complex as it bends in unforeseeable ways to arrive at a solution. Hence, the swarm is sometimes unpredictable. As the complexity of its functioning involving stochastic phenomenon is observed, it is quite difficult to understand the way the swarm operates. Therefore, the trade-off between the strength and weakness while implementing the SI technique has to be studied before applying to different application.

### 1.6.2 Applications of SI Techniques

Swarm intelligent techniques such as ACO, PSO, ABC, Firefly, CSA, and Gravitational Search algorithms are applied successfully to various applications. Contribution of ACO to diverse fields, such as traffic congestion, swarm robots, control, structural optimisation, manufacturing, scheduling, optimisation, vehicle routing, bioinformatics, and machine, is significant. Particle swarm optimisation can be applied to solve most of the optimisation problems and the problems that can be converted to optimisation problems. The potential applications are system design, multi-objective optimisation, classification, pattern recognition, biological system modelling, signal processing, robotic applications, decision-making, simulation, and identification.

Not only the applications that are mentioned earlier, both ACO and PSO can also be used in applications such as planning, decision-making, and hybrid technologies, for example, as training of weights in NN training, designing fuzzy membership functions, and so on. Recently developed ABC, Firefly, CSA, and Gravitational Search are also finding in application where ACO and PSO have already contributed significantly.

Swarm intelligence techniques are successful in both discrete and continuous problems which are both dynamic and static in nature, respectively. Nowadays, many SI techniques are emerging and need to be analysed and implemented suitably.

### 1.6.3 Scope of Swarm Intelligent Systems

'Sweating the assets' is a phrase used in many industries and organizations which aim to get as much as possible from what is already present. Swarm intelligence systems can be effectively used to improve the already available systems which are seen as untapped potential. Most of the hurdles lie in convincing the people about its validity of successful applications. It may take some time to understand its reliable performance because mathematical proofs for SI systems are still in the infant stage.

However, if the industrialists and business men are able to get convinced about the realistic performance, then the growth of SI applications will be significant than what is observed today. Therefore, SI systems have nowadays become one of the important fields to be studied as a course work in universities and colleges. It is a known fact that, 'The right person in the wrong place and wrong person in the right place can become a disaster'. Therefore, the challenge lies in suitable application of its strength in the right place.

## 1.7 EXPERT SYSTEMS

Expert system is one of the important branches of AI. They are intelligent computer programs that use expertise knowledge and inference schemes for solving problems, thereby emulating the decision-making like a human expert. Human beings generally make decisions as *Yes* and *No*. They also reason as *True* or *False*. Digital computers are sometimes called *intelligent* as they can process their decisions similar to human beings (e.g., *yes* (1) or *no* (0) reasoning).

The initial developments of digital computers had brought much of the computing success; however, it had severe shortcomings while dealing with logical reasoning similar to human thinking process. This limitation paved way for developing an entirely new way of computer programming called the *'expert system'*.

Expert systems provide the following important features:

- Facility for non-expert personnel to solve problems that require some expertise
- Speedy solutions
- Reliable solutions
- Cost reduction
- Elimination of uncomfortable and monotonous operations (e.g., autopilot operations)
- Power to manage without human experts
- Wider access to knowledge

In addition to the advantages mentioned previously, the use of expert systems is especially recommended when the following conditions hold:

- Human experts are difficult to find
- Human experts are expensive
- Knowledge improvement is needed
- Knowledge is difficult to acquire and is based on rules that can only be learnt through experience
- The available information is poor, partial, incomplete
- Problems are incompletely defined
- There is a lack of knowledge among all those who need it
- The problem is subject to rapidly changing legal rules and codes

Sometimes a human being may have multiple areas of expertise. Consider a power system engineer who has an extraordinary proficiency for diagnosing power transformers. The engineer can apply power and hence voltage to the input terminal and measure the output voltage and current. Based on this information, the engineer with his knowledge or expertise can detect defective or faulty parts. He has possibly learnt and acquired this knowledge through experience over a prolonged period of time and education. In case this engineer is no more or left the place, will it be possible to retain the expert's knowledge to be used by a new candidate replaced in his position?

To come to a conclusion, a question can be put forth: Is it possible to implant the same knowledge in a computer program so that it can replace the human expert? The answer is 'yes', because computers are capable of replacing decision-making of human beings in most of the areas.

### 1.7.1 Expert System Architecture

Figure 1.7 shows the basic elements of an expert system. However, the architecture of the expert system is independent of the computer hardware.

The *user interface* allows the system user to enter rules and facts about a particular situation and ask questions of the system, provides responses to user requests. It supports all other communication between the system and the user. The knowledge of a human expert on a particular subject is contained in a structured format within the *knowledge base* (KB) which is easy to read and interpret.

The *knowledge base editor* helps the expert or knowledge engineer to continuously update information with ease and verify the KB. The structured format of the KB will be typically in the form of a set of IF-THEN rules relevant to the elements of the subject domain. These rules are formatted so that they can be used by the program. The expert systems that represent knowledge in a rule format are known as *rule-based expert systems*.

The *case specific data* includes both data provided by the user and the partial conclusions (along with certainty measures) based on this data. These databases could be managed by a database management system. The KB is constantly updated so that the system provides the most relevant and complete assistance to

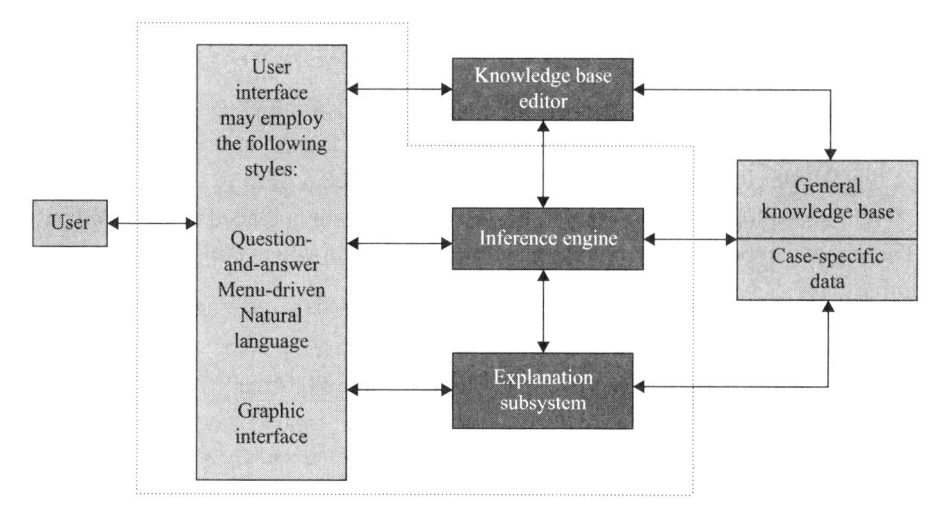

**Fig. 1.7** Expert system architecture

the user. Most of the expert systems use dedicated modules only for updating the KB. These modules are often called as *knowledge acquisition facility*.

The knowledge acquisition facility is normally used by the knowledge engineer to transfer the knowledge from the human expert to the computer-based expert system. It provides a two way communication platform between the human expertise and the computer system for acquiring human knowledge in the form of rules and facts. After obtaining the requisite knowledge, this facility stores the rules in the knowledge database and the facts in the domain database.

New facts are inferred by the *inference engine* using the information from the KB and the user. It compares the user's information with the data in KB, and gets whatever possible logical conclusions. This procedure is simulated through the deductive thought processes of an expert with the help of *explanation sub-system*. It provides a mechanism to trace the rules used and thereby justifies its conclusions.

*Self-training* is another important role of expert systems. Whenever an expert system derives a new fact through its inference scheme, this new information can be added to its KB and also pass on to the user. The self-training facility accepts the facts derived by the inference engine and compares these derived facts with the facts stored in the domain database. If a new derived fact is not already present in the domain database, it can be added to the database. Thus, the self-training facility helps in the constant updating of KB.

Expert system design and development must be carefully programmed if success is desired. Some of the main steps to be followed are given here:

- Statement of the problem to be solved
- Search for a human expert or the equivalent data or experience
- Design of the expert system
- Selection of the degree of participation of the user
- Selection of the development tool, shell, or programming language for development

- Development of a prototype
- Prototype checking
- Refinement and generalization
- Maintenance
- Updating

While developing an expert system, errors may occur and need to be sorted out. The errors can be classified in the most likely stages in which they occur, as given in Fig. 1.8.

**Expert**
- The human expert can be erroneous with incorrect and incomplete knowledge

**Knowledge engineer**
- Semantic errors can occur between the knowledge engineer and human expert
- Knowledge engineer may not completely transfer the information from the human expert

**Knowledge base**
- Syntax errors can be observed in the structured format content errors may be present due to the incorrect and incomplete knowledge and uncertainty in rules and facts

**Inference engine**
- The inference engine and programs of the expert system tool can contain bugs

**Inference chain**
- Inference errors occur due to the incorrect priority of rules, incorrect interactions of rules, errors in the knowledge base, and errors due to non-monotonic inference

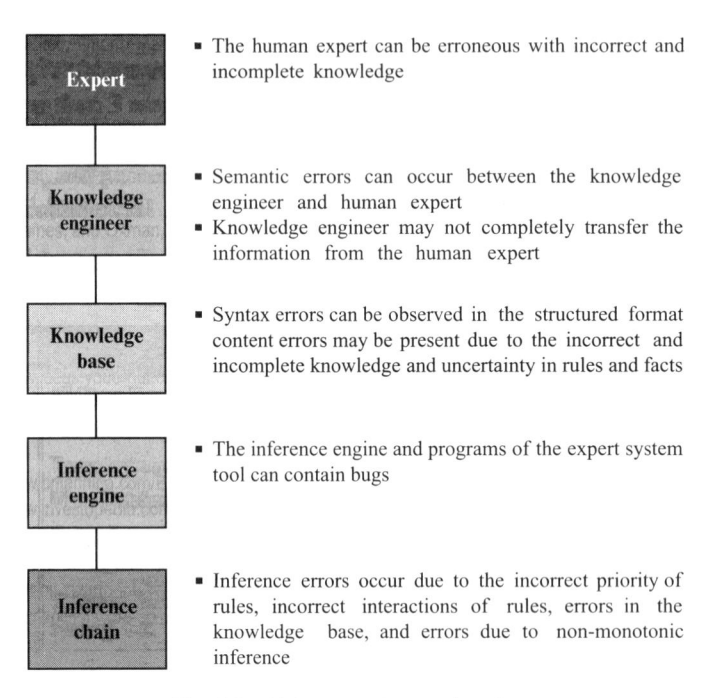

**Fig. 1.8** Major errors in expert systems

## 1.7.2 Rule-based Expert System

The knowledge base of an expert system in general is represented by using rules and objects. Let us try to understand with an illustration. In a power system, two generators each of capacity 500 MW can supply a load of up to 1,000 MW. The generators should also compensate for the transmission loses. Therefore, the power system should cater various loads from 200 MW to 950 MW. During peak load, utmost care related to load shedding and other peak load management need to be carried out. Therefore, the status of the power system can be classified into these conditions (expertise data/knowledge base) as follows:

'*If* the generation is between 200 MW and 500 MW, *then* the system operation is normal and reliable'. That is, even in case of an outage of one generator, another one can compensate the load.

'*If* the generation is between 501 MW and 950 MW, *then* the system operation is normal but unreliable'. That is, in case of an outage of one generator, load shedding needs to be carried out.

'*If* the generation is between 951 MW and 1,000 MW, *then* the system operation is abnormal and unreliable'. This condition is critical as it may cause congestion and increases losses in transmission lines. In addition, peak load management should be brought at any instant of time as the load is dynamic in nature and may cross the alarming level of 1,000 MW.

The following MATLAB code illustrates the conditions with a simple expert system program.

### MATLAB Program 1.1

```
%%%%%%%%%%%%%%%%%%%%%%%%%%%%%%%%%%%%%%%%%%%%%%%%%%%%%%%%
% CONDITION OF THE POWER SYSTEM BASED ON THE GENERATION LEVEL
%%%%%%%%%%%%%%%%%%%%%%%%%%%%%%%%%%%%%%%%%%%%%%%%%%%%%%%%

% CLEARING ALL PREVIOUS DATA

clear workspace
clear all
clc
format long

% GET THE INPUT LOAD FOR THE GENERATORS

I=input('Give the input load between 200MW to 1000MW =');
% Enter the system load as input
if (200<=I)&(I<=1000),
% The program executes if only the data input is correct

if (200<=I)&(I<=500),                                   % IF (rule condition),
disp('The system operation is normal and reliable');    % Then (Object)
end
if (501<=I)&(I<=900),                                   % IF (rule condition),
disp('The system operation is normal but unreliable'); % Then (Object)
end
if (951<=I)&(I<=1000),                                  % IF (rule condition),
disp('The system operation is abnormal and unreliable'); % Then (Object)
end

else
disp('Input load is not correct');
% Displays the data given as input is incorrect
disp('Give load data between 200MW to 1000MW');
% Corrective action to be taken for the input data to be given
end
```

If KB consists of the facts based on the system load, it will match the condition of the rule. Suppose the total generation of the load is 980 MW, the rule is thus satisfied and we can conclude that the system is abnormal and unreliable.

A rule that corresponds to a small modular collection of knowledge is called a *chunk*. Chunks of knowledge are organized in an unrestricted arrangement, with links relating one to another. An example of a rule representing a chunk of knowledge is

IF
You want to get good marks
You want to get a good job
:
THEN
Work hard
IF
You want to get poor marks
You want to get a poor job
:
THEN
Be lazy

The following MATLAB code illustrates the use of collection of knowledge in a simple expert system program.

## MATLAB Program 1.2

```
%%%%%%%%%%%%%%%%%%%%%%%%%%%%%%%%%
% DISPLAYING THE CHUNK OF KNOWLEDGE
%%%%%%%%%%%%%%%%%%%%%%%%%%%%%%%%%

% CLEARING ALL PREVIOUS DATA

clear workspace
clear all
clc
format long

% SELECTING KNOWLEDGE FROM CHUNK BASED ON FACTS

disp('Type good marks/poor marks/good jobs/poor jobs within single quote')
chunk = input('What do you want?');

switch lower(chunk)
case {'good marks','good jobs'}    % Chunk 1
disp('Then work hard')
% Based on the input knowledge rule, the condition of the rule is matched
case{'poor marks','poor jobs'}    % Chunk 2
disp('Then be lazy')
% Based on the input knowledge rule, the condition of the rule is matched
end
```

Newell and Simon popularized the use of rules to represent human knowledge and showed how reasoning could be done with the help of rules.

### 1.7.3 Backward Chaining and Forward Chaining

Backward chaining and forward chaining are strategies used to specify how rules contained in a knowledge-based rule system are to be executed [25]. To illustrate how these two reasoning mechanisms are used, consider the following:

IF
I get 1000 golden eggs
AND
A luxurious house
THEN
I will marry                                                                                          (1)
IF
I marry
THEN
I will have two children                                                                              (2)
IF
I have two children
THEN
They will take care of my business                                                                    (3)
IF
They take care of my business
THEN
I will be happy                                                                                       (4)

1. ***Backward chaining***: Suppose we want to establish the fact that 'I will be happy', assuming that we know only that 'I get 1000 golden eggs' and 'a luxurious house'. Backward chaining works backwards from the conclusion.

    | Is this fact known? | → | No |
    |---|---|---|
    | Can it be obtained from a rule? | → | Yes, from Rule (4) |
    | Which facts need to be known? | → | 'They take care of my business' |
    | Is this fact known? | → | No |
    | Can it be obtained from a rule? | → | Yes, from Rule (3) |
    | Which facts need to be known? | → | 'I have two children' |
    | Is this fact known? | → | No |
    | Can it be obtained from a rule? | → | Yes, from Rule (2) |
    | Which facts need to be known? | → | 'I marry' |
    | Is this fact known? | → | No |
    | Can it be obtained from a rule? | → | Yes, from Rule (1) |
    | Are these facts known? | → | Yes, 'I get 1000 golden eggs' and 'a luxurious house' |

    Therefore, it is true that 'I marry'.
    Therefore, it is true that 'I have two children'.
    Therefore, it is true that 'They take care of my business'
    Therefore, it is true that 'I will be happy'

    We started with the fact we wanted to prove and tried to establish all the facts needed to reach that goal. This reasoning method is called backward chaining. In general, backward chaining is applied when a goal or a hypothesis is chosen as the starting point for problem-solving. Backward chaining is also called goal-directed, top-down, or consequence-driven reasoning.

The following MATLAB code illustrates the use of backward chaining in a simple expert system program.

## MATLAB Program 1.3

```matlab
%%%%%%%%%%%%%%%%%%%%%%%%%%%%%%%%%%%%%%%%
% DEMONSTRATING BACKWARD CHAINING METHOD
%%%%%%%%%%%%%%%%%%%%%%%%%%%%%%%%%%%%%%%%

% Note: This expert program works only for the assumed fact
% It will give erroneous results for other facts

% CLEARING ALL PREVIOUS DATA

clear workspace
clear all
clc
format long

disp('Given facts');
disp('%%%%%%%%%%%%%%%%%%%%%%%%%%%%%%%%%%%%%%%%');

fact = ''I get 1000 golden eggs' and 'a luxurious house'';    % Assumed fact
fact_1 = ''I marry'';                                          % Rule No.1
fact_2 = ''I have two children'';                              % Rule No.2
fact_3 = ''They take care of my business'';                    % Rule No.3
fact_4 = ''I will be happy'';                                  % Rule No.4

% DISPLAYING THE GIVEN FACTS

disp('fact');disp(fact);
disp('fact_1');disp(fact_1);
disp('fact_2');disp(fact_2);
disp('fact_3');disp(fact_3);
disp('fact_4');disp(fact_4);
disp('%%%%%%%%%%%%%%%%%%%%%%%%%%%%%%%%%%%%%%%%');

% INPUT TO THE PROGRAM

fact = input('Type the fact within a single quote=');
% Type the assumed fact within a single quote
disp('The assumed fact is')
disp(fact);
disp('%%%%%%%%%%%%%%%%%%%%%%%%%%%%%%%%%%%%%%%%');

% BACKWARD CHAINING OF FACTS

switch fact
case {''I get 1000 golden eggs' and 'a luxurious house''};
disp('Start from rule no.4');
fact_4='I will be happy';                                      % Rule No.4

switch fact_4
case {'I will be happy'};
```

```
disp('I will be happy IF');
disp('They take care of my business');
disp('%%%%%%%%%%%%%%%%%%%%%%%%%%%%%%%%%%%%%%%%');

fact_3='They take care of my business';           % Rule No.3
end

switch fact_3
case{'They take care of my business'}
disp('They take care of my business IF')
disp('I have two children');
disp('%%%%%%%%%%%%%%%%%%%%%%%%%%%%%%%%%%%%%%%%');
fact_2='I have two children';                     % Rule No.2
end

switch fact_2
case{'I have two children'};
disp('I have two children IF')
disp('I marry');
disp('%%%%%%%%%%%%%%%%%%%%%%%%%%%%%%%%%%%%%%%%');
fact_1='I marry';                                 % Rule No.1
end

switch fact_1
case{'I marry'};
disp('I marry IF')
disp(''I get 1000 golden eggs' and 'a luxurious house'');   % Assumed fact
disp('%%%%%%%%%%%%%%%%%%%%%%%%%%%%%%%%%%%%%%%%');
end

end % End of the switch loop for the input assumed fact

% FINAL CONCLUSION

disp('Therfore the assumed fact');
disp(fact);
disp('deduces or establishes');
disp(fact_4);
```

2. ***Forward chaining***: The forward chaining reasoning mechanism goes forward from the starting point, via the conclusions generated at each step. Suppose we want to prove that 'I will be happy', assuming we know that 'I get 1000 golden eggs' and 'a luxurious house'.

| | |
|---|---|
| Is this fact known? | → No |
| Which facts do we know? | → 'I get 1000 golden eggs' and 'a luxurious house'. |
| What facts follow from it? | → 'I marry' from Rule (1) |
| Is this what we want to prove? | → No |
| What facts follow from this? | → 'I have two children' from Rule (2) |
| Is this what we want to prove? | → No |
| What facts follow from this? | → 'They take care of my business' from Rule (3) |
| Is this what we want to prove? | → No |

What facts follow from this? → 'I will be happy' from Rule (4)
Is this what we want to prove? → Yes

Thus, we established from 'I get 1000 golden eggs' and 'a luxurious house' that 'I marry'. From 'I marry', we established that 'I have two children'. From 'I have two children', we established 'they take care of my business'. Finally, from 'they take care of my business', we established that 'I will be happy', which was our goal. The reasoning mechanism used here is called forward chaining. It is best used to solve problems in which data is to be used as the starting point for problem-solving. A combination of forward chaining and backward chaining can be used to get to problem solutions quickly when dealing with large search spaces. This search strategy can be applied when solving complex problems.

The following MATLAB code demonstrates the use of forward chaining in a simple expert system program.

### MATLAB Program 1.4

```
%%%%%%%%%%%%%%%%%%%%%%%%%%%%%%%%%%%%%%%%
% DEMONSTRATING FORWARD CHAINING METHOD
%%%%%%%%%%%%%%%%%%%%%%%%%%%%%%%%%%%%%%%%

% Note: This expert program works only for the assumed fact
% It will give erroneous results for other facts

% CLEARING ALL PREVIOUS DATA

clear workspace
clear all
clc
format long

disp('Given facts');
disp('%%%%%%%%%%%%%%%%%%%%%%%%%%%%%%%%%%%%%%%%');

fact = ''I get 1000 golden eggs' and 'a luxurious house'';   % Assumed fact
fact_1 = ''I marry'';                                         % Rule No.1
fact_2 = ''I have two children'';                             % Rule No.2
fact_3 = ''They take care of my business'';                   % Rule No.3
fact_4 = ''I will be happy'';                                 % Rule No.4

% DISPLAYING THE GIVEN FACTS

disp('fact');disp(fact);
disp('fact_1');disp(fact_1);
disp('fact_2');disp(fact_2);
disp('fact_3');disp(fact_3);
disp('fact_4');disp(fact_4);
disp('%%%%%%%%%%%%%%%%%%%%%%%%%%%%%%%%%%%%%%%%');

% INPUT TO THE PROGRAM

fact=input('Type the fact within a single quote=');
% Type the assumed fact within a single quote
disp('The assumed fact is')
disp(fact);
disp('%%%%%%%%%%%%%%%%%%%%%%%%%%%%%%%%%%%%%%%%');
```

```
% FORWARD CHAINING OF FACTS

switch fact
case {''I get 1000 golden eggs' and 'a luxurious house''};
disp('Start from rule no.1');
disp('IF'I get 1000 golden eggs' and 'a luxurious house'');
disp('I marry');
disp('%%%%%%%%%%%%%%%%%%%%%%%%%%%%%%%%%%%%%%%%');
fact_1='I marry';                                              % Rule No.1

switch fact_1
case {'I marry'};
disp('IF I marry');
disp('I have two childern');
disp('%%%%%%%%%%%%%%%%%%%%%%%%%%%%%%%%%%%%%%%%');
fact_2='I have two children';                                  % Rule No.2
end

switch fact_2
case {'I have two children'};
disp('IF I have two children');
disp('They take care of my business');
disp('%%%%%%%%%%%%%%%%%%%%%%%%%%%%%%%%%%%%%%%%');
fact_3='They take care of my business';                        % Rule No.3
end

switch fact_3
case{'They take care of my business'};
disp('IF They take care of my business')
disp('I will be happy');                                       % Rule No.4
disp('%%%%%%%%%%%%%%%%%%%%%%%%%%%%%%%%%%%%%%%%');
fact_4='I will be happy';
end

end       % End of the switch loop for the input assumed fact

% FINAL CONCLUSION

disp('Therfore the assumed fact');
disp(fact);
disp('deduces or establishes');
disp(fact_4);
```

### 1.7.4 Expert System Knowledge Base

The different stages in the development of an expert KB are shown in Fig. 1.9. The process of building an expert system is called *knowledge engineering* and is carried out by a *knowledge engineer*. The knowledge engineer must be a qualified person in computer science and must know how to build an expert system. This person makes a decision about the format of representing the knowledge in the KB and helps the programmers to write the code. *Knowledge engineering* is the acquisition of knowledge from a human expertise or from any other source.

The job of the knowledge engineer is given as follows:

- Creates a platform with the human expert in order to extract the knowledge from him
- Codes all the knowledge in a structured format contained in the KB

- Evaluate the expert system with the human expert
- Process continues till the expertise is fully satisfied

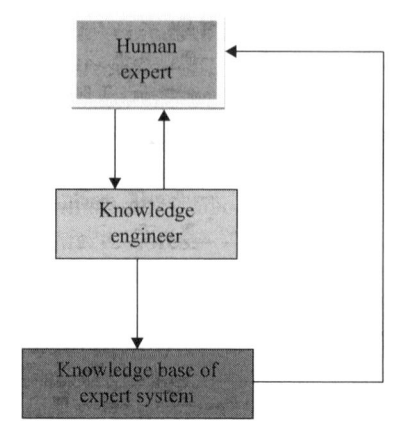

**Fig. 1.9** Stages in building knowledge base

Generally, the limitation in the development of expert system is due to lack of general knowledge. It should be noted that programming expert system with shallow knowledge with empirical and heuristic knowledge than with deep knowledge based on the basic structures, functions, and behaviours of objects does not guarantee to succeed the same way as an algorithm that gives a guaranteed solution to a problem.

### 1.7.5 Basic Activities of an Expert System

Many different types of problems are solved by expert system. However, their basic activities can be grouped into different categories as given in Table 1.3. In this section, we define each of these activities, describing the type of data typically involved [27].

Expert systems infer situation description by performing *interpretation* using sensor data. Interpretation is carried out directly with real data than the coded representation of the problem in hand. For example, both visual detection and speech recognition system use natural inputs such as visual images and audio signals respectively to infer features and meaning. However, the difficulty comes in terms of handling data that are noisy, sparse, incomplete, unreliable, or erroneous. Therefore, special techniques are needed for extracting and processing the aforementioned data.

*Prediction* is performed by expert systems to infer the likely consequences of given situations. *Diagnosis* is performed by expert systems using situation descriptions, behaviour characteristics, or knowledge about the component design to infer probable causes of system malfunctions. *Designing* is performed by expert systems developing configurations of objects based on a set of problem constraints. *Planning* is performed by expert systems with design actions. They decide on an entire course of action before acting.

**Table 1.3** General categories of expert system application

| Category | Problem addressed |
|---|---|
| Interpretation | Inferring situation descriptions from sensor data |
| Prediction | Inferring the likely consequences of given situations |
| Diagnosis | Inferring system malfunctions from observations |
| Design | Configuring objects under constraints |
| Planning | Designing actions |
| Monitoring | Comparing observations to expected outcomes |
| Debugging | Prescribing remedies for malfunctions |
| Repair | Executing plans to administer prescribed remedies |
| Instruction | Diagnosing, debugging, and repairing |
| Control | Governing overall system behaviour |

*Monitoring* is performed by expert systems by comparing actual system behaviour to expected behaviour. *Debugging* is performed by expert system by finding remedies for malfunctions. Repairing is performed by expert systems by following a plan to administer some prescribed remedy. *Instruction* is performed by expert systems by diagnosing, debugging, and repairing system behaviour. *Control* is performed by expert systems by adaptively governing overall system behaviour.

The previously mentioned applications are well addressed and successfully solved using expert system [28].

### 1.7.6 Verification, Validation, and Design of Expert Systems

*Verification* ensures that an expert system is developed correctly which does not contain technical errors. *Validation* demonstrates the exactness of the final product satisfying the needs of a user in solving the problem. Therefore, verification process should check the robustness of the program by looking into redundant rules, conflicting rules, subsumed rules, unnecessary IF conditions, unreachable IF conditions, and circular rule chains in the process of expert system development. These conditions are explained here [27, 29].

**Redundant rules**: Two rules are redundant if their IF parts are equivalent and one or more conclusions are also equivalent.

IF
(NOT (Very high? Load demand))
(NOT (Very low? Water available))          Rule (1)
THEN
(assert (Type of plant? Thermal))
IF
(NOT (OR) (Very high? Load demand)
(Very low? Water available)                Rule (2)
THEN
(assert (Type of plant? Thermal))

# 40 Soft Computing with MATLAB Programming

Here both the rules (1) and (2) contain 'Water available is NOT Very low' in their IF parts. In addition, the conclusion 'Type of plant is thermal'. Therefore both the rules are considered to be redundant.

The following MATLAB code illustrates redundant rules in a simple expert system program.

## MATLAB Program 1.5

```
%%%%%%%%%%%%%%%%%%%%%%%%%%%%%%%
% DEMONSTRATING REDUNDANT RULES
%%%%%%%%%%%%%%%%%%%%%%%%%%%%%%%

% CLEARING ALL PREVIOUS DATA

clear workspace
clear all
clc
format long

% DEFINING THE KNOWLEDGE

disp('If the load demand is greater than or equal to 800MW,');
disp('Then the load demand is very high');
disp('If the water avilabiltiy is lesser than or equal to 25m');
disp('Then the water availability is very low');

% INPUT TO THE PROGRAM

MW=input('Give the load demand between (200MW to 900MW) =');
% Give the mega watt limit of the input load demand
hgt=input('Give the water availability level(10m to 110m) =');
% Give the height of the water level

disp('%%%%%%%%%%');
disp('Verifying the conditions');

if MW>=800,
 disp('The load demand is very high');
else
disp('The load demand is not very high');
end disp('%%%%%%%%%%');

if hgt<=25,
disp('The water avilability is very low');
else
disp('The water availabiliy is not very low');
end disp('%%%%%%%%%%');

% RULE NO.1

if (MW>=800)~=1,                    % Load demand is not every high
disp('The type of plant is thermal');
end

if (hgt<=25)~=1,                    % Water available is not very low
disp('The type of plant is thermal');
end
```

% RULE NO.2

```
if ((MW>=800)|(hgt<=25))~=1,
% Load demand is not every high (OR) Water available is not very low
disp('The type of plant is thermal');
end
```

***Conflicting rules***: Two rules are conflicting if they succeed in the same situation but with conflicting conclusions.

IF
(is? Generation Hydel)
THEN
(assert (Cost? Generation low))
THEN
(assert (is? Generation conventional))

The following MATLAB code illustrates redundant rules in a simple expert system program.

## MATLAB Program 1.6

```
%%%%%%%%%%%%%%%%%%%%%%%%%%%%%%%
% DEMONSTRATING CONFLICTING RULES
%%%%%%%%%%%%%%%%%%%%%%%%%%%%%%%

% CLEARING ALL PREVIOUS DATA

clear workspace
clear all
clc
format long

% DISPLAYING FACTS

disp('Defining Facts ');           % Defining facts
fact_1 = 'Generation is Hydel';
fact_2 = 'Cost of the Generation is low';
fact_3 = 'Generation is conventional';
disp('%%%%%%%%%%%%%%%%%%%%%%%%%');
disp(fact_1);disp(fact_2);disp(fact_3);
disp('%%%%%%%%%%%%%%%%%%%%%%%%%');

% INPUT TO THE PROGRAM

fact=input('Type the fact =');     % Type fact_1
disp('The succeeding fact is ');
disp(fact);
disp('%%%%%%%%%%%%%%%%%%%%%%%%%');

disp('Conclusion');                % Display the conclusion

% RULE NO.1

if fact==fact_1,                           % If generation is hydel
disp('Cost of the generation is low');     % Then the cost of generation is low
end
```

```
% RULE NO.2

if fact==fact_1,                        % If generation is hydel
 disp('Generation is conventional');    % Then the generation is conventional
end

% CONCLUSIONS

disp('%%%%%%%%%%%%%%%%%%%%%%%%%');
disp('Two different conclusions are obtained');
disp('Therefore the rules are confilicting');
```

***Subsumed rules***: Two rules are subsumed if they have the same conclusions, but one contains additional constraints in situations in which it succeeds.

IF
(is? Load demand medium)        Rule (1)
THEN
(is? System reliable)
IF
((is? Load demand medium)
(is ? Spinning reserve high ))    Rule (2)
THEN
(is? System reliable)

The following MATLAB code illustrates subsumed rules in a simple expert system program.

## MATLAB Program 1.7

```
%%%%%%%%%%%%%%%%%%%%%%%%%%%%%%
% DEMONSTRATING SUBSUMMED RULES
%%%%%%%%%%%%%%%%%%%%%%%%%%%%%%

% CLEARING ALL PREVIOUS DATA

clear workspace
clear all
clc
format long

% DISPLAYING FACTS

disp('Defining Facts ');              % Defining facts
fact_1 = 'Load demand is medium';
fact_2 = 'System is reliable';
fact_3 = 'Spinning reserve is high';

disp('%%%%%%%%%%%%%%%%%%%%%%%%%');
disp('fact_1');disp(fact_1);
disp('fact_2');disp(fact_2);
disp('fact_3');disp(fact_3);
disp('%%%%%%%%%%%%%%%%%%%%%%%%%');
```

```matlab
% INPUT TO THE PROGRAM

disp('Type fact_1');
input_A=input('Type the first input(input_A) =');   % Type fact_1
disp('Type fact_3');
input_B=input('Type the second input(input_B) =');  % Type fact_3

disp('%%%%%%%%%%%%%%%%%%%%%%%%%%%%');
disp('The succeeding fact is ');
disp(fact_1);
disp('%%%%%%%%%%%%%%%%%%%%%%%%%%%%');

disp('Conclusion1');                 % Display the conclusion1 for Rule(1)

% RULE NO.1

if input_A==fact_1,                  % Rule(1) if the load demand is medium
    disp('System is reliable');      % Then the system is reliable
end

disp('%%%%%%%%%%%%%%%%%%%%%%%%%%%%');
disp('The succeeding fact with additional constraint (i.e.,input_B)is ');
disp(fact_1);disp(fact_3);
disp('%%%%%%%%%%%%%%%%%%%%%%%%%%%%');

disp('Conclusion2');                 % Display the conclusion2 for Rule(2)

% RULE NO.2

if input_A==fact_1,
if input_B==fact_3,
% Rule(2) if the load demand is medium and spinning reserve is high
    disp('System is reliable');      % Then the system is reliable
end
end

% CONCLUSIONS

disp('%%%%%%%%%%%%%%%%%%%%%%%%%%%%');
disp('Same conclusions are obtained for the succeeding input_A')
disp('and the succeeding input_A with additional constraints(i.e.,input_B)');
disp('Therefore the rules are subsummed')
```

***Unnecessary IF conditions***: Two rules contain unnecessary IF conditions if they have the same conclusions.

    IF
    (is? Load demand medium)          Rule (1)
    THEN
    (is? System reliable)
    IF
    (NOT (is? Load demand is very high)      Rule (2)
    THEN
    (is? System reliable)

The following MATLAB code illustrates the unnecessary IF conditions in a simple expert system program.

## MATLAB Program 1.8

```matlab
%%%%%%%%%%%%%%%%%%%%%%%%%%%%%%%%%%%%%%%%
% DEMONSTRATING UNNECESSARY IF CONDITIONS
%%%%%%%%%%%%%%%%%%%%%%%%%%%%%%%%%%%%%%%%

% CLEARING ALL PREVIOUS DATA

clear workspace
clear all
clc
format long

% DISPLAYING THE FACTS

disp('Defining Facts');     % Defining facts
fact_1 = 'Load demand is medium';
fact_2 = 'Load demand is very high';
fact_3 = 'System is reliable';
fact_4 = 'System is not reliable';
disp('fact_1');disp(fact_1);
disp('fact_2');disp(fact_2);
disp('fact_3');disp(fact_3);
disp('fact_4');disp(fact_4);

% DEFINING THE KNOWLEDGE

disp('%%%%%%%%%%%%%%%%%%%%');
disp('Defining the conditions');
disp('%%%%%%%%%%%%%%%%%%%%%%%%%%%%%%%%%%%%%%%%')
disp('If the load demand is less than 800MW,');
disp('Then the load demand is medium(fact_1)');
disp('%%%%%%%%%%%%%%%%%%%%%%%%%%%%%%%%%%%%%%%%')
disp('If the load demand is greater than or equal to 800MW,');
disp('Then the load demand is very high (fact_2)');
disp('%%%%%%%%%%%%%%%%%%%%%%%%%%%%%%%%%%%%%%%%')

% INPUT TO THE PROGRAM

MW=input('Give the load demand between (200MW to 900MW) =');
% Give the mega watt limit of the input load demand

disp('%%%%%%%%%%%%%%%%%%%%%%%%%');
disp('Verifying the conditions');

if MW<800,                  % Defining threshold levels of the load demand
disp('The load demand is medium');
else
disp('The load demand is very high');
end
disp('%%%%%%%%%%%%%%%%%%%%%%%%%');

% RULE NO.1

disp('Conclusion 1')
if MW<800,                  % If the load demand is medium
disp('If the load demand is medium');
```

```
disp(fact_3);
else                         % If the load demand is not medium
disp('If the load demand is not medium');
disp(fact_4);
end

% RULE NO.2

disp('Conclusion 2')
if (MW>800)~=1,              % If the load demand is not very high
disp('If the load demand is not very high');
disp(fact_3);
else                         % If the load demand is very high
disp('If the load demand is very high');
disp(fact_4);
end

% CONCLUSIONS

disp('Both the if conditions gives the same meaning');
disp('Also the conclusion drawn is the same');
disp('Therefore the rules consist of unnecessary if conditions');
if MW<800
disp('Demonstration is as per the book content for Rule No.1 and Rule No.2');
else
disp('Concept is right but demonstration is not as per the book content for
Rule No.1 and Rule No.2');
end
```

***Unreachable IF conditions*****:** If there is no match for an IF condition, then it is called as unreachable IF condition.

IF
(is? Load demand high)                             Rule (1)
THEN
(is? Load demand high demand)

The following MATLAB code illustrates the unreachable IF conditions in a simple expert system program.

## MATLAB Program 1.9

```
%%%%%%%%%%%%%%%%%%%%%%%%%%%%%%%%%%%%%%
% DEMONSTRATING UNREACHABLE IF CONDITIONS
%%%%%%%%%%%%%%%%%%%%%%%%%%%%%%%%%%%%%%

% CLEARING ALL PREVIOUS DATA

clear workspace
clear all
clc
format long

% DISPLAYING THE FACTS

disp('Defining Facts');
fact_1 = 'Load demand is high';
fact_2 = 'Load demand is high demand';
```

```
disp('fact_1');disp(fact_1);
disp('fact_2');disp(fact_2);

% DEFINING THE KNOWLEDGE

disp('%%%%%%%%%%%%%%%%%%%%%%%');
disp('Defining the conditions');
disp('%%%%%%%%%%%%%%%%%%%%%%%%%%%%%%%%%%%%%%%%%%%%%')
disp('IF the load demand is greater than or equal to 700MW,');
disp('Then the load demand is high (fact_1)');
disp('%%%%%%%%%%%%%%%%%%%%%%%%%%%%%%%%%%%%%%%%%%%%%')
disp('IF the load demand is greater than or equal to 800MW,');
disp('Then the load demand is high demand (fact_2)');
disp('%%%%%%%%%%%%%%%%%%%%%%%%%%%%%%%%');

% INPUT TO THE PROGRAM

disp('Enter a value greater than 800MW for demonstration');
MW=input('Give the load demand between (200MW to 900MW) =');
% Give the mega watt limit of the input load demand

disp('%%%%%%%%%%%%%%%%%%%%%%%%%%');
disp('Verifying the conditions');
disp('IF the load demand value given as input is >=700MW');

if MW>=700,                             % Defining threshold levels of the load demand
disp('The load demand is high');
end
disp('%%%%%%%%%%%%%%%%%%%%%%%%%%%%%');

disp('IF the load demand value given as input is >=800MW');
% Defining threshold levels of the load demand
if MW>=800,
disp('The load demand is high demand');
end
disp('%%%%%%%%%%%%%%%%%%%%%%%%%%%%%'); disp('');
disp('IF the given input is >=800');

% RULE NO.1

disp('Conclusion')
disp('IF the load demand value is >=700MW');
disp('i.e. IF the load demand is high')    % IF condition
if MW>=700,                                 % If the load demand is high
disp('Then the load demand is high demand');
disp(fact_2);                               % Resultant output
end

% CONCLUSIONS

disp('We are not sure whether the load demand is high or ''the load
demand is high demand''');
disp('Therefore the IF condition is not giving its correct conclusion');
disp('And hence unreachable if condition');

if MW>=800
disp('IF load value is given >=800MW')
```

```
disp('Demonstration is as per the book content for Rule No.1');
else
disp('IF load value is <800MW')
disp('Eroneous result will be displayed')
end
```

***Circular rule chains***: A set of rules is circular if their chaining in the set makes a cycle.

    IF
    (is? Load demand medium)      Rule (1)
    THEN
    (is? System reliable)
    IF
    (is? System reliable)      Rule (2)
    THEN
    (is? Load demand medium)

The following MATLAB code illustrates the circular rule chains in a simple expert system program.

## MATLAB Program 1.10

```
%%%%%%%%%%%%%%%%%%%%%%%%%%%%%%%%%%%%
% DEMONSTRATING CIRCULAR RULE CHAINS
%%%%%%%%%%%%%%%%%%%%%%%%%%%%%%%%%%%%

% CLEARING ALL PREVIOUS DATA

clear workspace
clear all
clc
format long

% DISPLAYING THE FACTS

disp('Defining Facts ');                    % Given facts
fact_1 = 'Load demand medium';
fact_2 = 'System is reliable';
disp('%%%%%%%%%%%%%%%%%%%%%%%%%%%%%%');
disp('fact_1');disp(fact_1);
disp('fact_2');disp(fact_2);
disp('%%%%%%%%%%%%%%%%%%%%%%%%%%%%%%');

% INPUT TO THE PROGRAM

disp('Type fact_1 for demonstration');      % Give the input fact fact_1
disp('Otherwise demonstration of circular rule chain is not possible');
disp('%%%%%%%%%%%%%%%%%%%%%%%%%%%%%%');
fact=input('Give the input fact=');

% CIRCULAR CHAINING OF FACTS

% RULE NO.1

while fact==fact_1                          % If load demand is medium
 disp('IF load demand is medium');          % Rule No.1
```

```
fact=fact_2;                                    % Resultant output
disp('System is reliable');                     % Displaying the output
disp('%%%%%%%%%%%%%%%%%%%%%%%%%%%%%');

% RULE NO.2

while fact==fact_2                              % If system is reliable
disp('IF system is reliable');                  % Rule No.2
fact=fact_1;                                    % Resultant output
disp('Load demand is medium');                  % Displaying the output
disp('%%%%%%%%%%%%%%%%%%%%%%%%%%%%%%%%%%%%%%%%%');
end

pause(1); % Pausing 1 second for slow display of events
disp('Press tab Ctrl C to stop circling of IF conditions');
% Action to be taken for stopping the program
disp('%%%%%%%%%%%%%%%%%%%%%%%%%%%%%%%%%%%%%%%%%');
end
```

### 1.7.6.1 Completeness of Verification and Validation

The expert program will be complete only with validation and testing which can be performed by looking into unreferenced attribute values, illegal attribute values, dead end IF conditions, dead end goals, and unreachable conclusions.

- *Unreferenced attribute values*: Unreferenced attribute values refer to an object's attributes that are not covered by any of the *IF conditions* among the possible values in the program.
- *Illegal attribute values*: If a rule refers to an attribute value that is not in the set of legal values during the execution of the program, it is called an illegal attribute value.
- *Dead end IF conditions*: The attributes of an *IF condition* should be obtained from a user or any of the *IF condition* values in the expert program. If this *IF condition* is not satisfied, then it is called dead end *IF condition*.
- *Dead end goals*: The attributes of the goals of the program should be obtained from a user or any of the conclusions from any one of the rules in the program. If it does not satisfy the aforementioned program, then the goal is known as dead end goal.
- *Unreachable conclusions*: If the conclusion does not have any matches in the database, then the condition is called unreachable conclusion.
- *The impact of confidence factors*: In order to make the validation procedure stringent and handle the complexity of the program confidence factors (*cfs*) [28] are used. A *confidence factor* indicates the amount uncertainty in a rule in the KB of the expert system. In general, if the value of $cf = +1.0$, the condition indicates that the rule or user response is definitely true. Similarly, if $cf = -1.0$, then it is false. However, if $cf = 0.0$, then the truth of the rule or user response is not known. The following section summarizes the impact of confidence factors in the debugging process of an expert program.

- **Redundant rules under uncertainty**: The procedure for verifying the redundancy remains the same even if confidence factors are used in the program. However, if confidence factors are used in the KB, then redundant rules can generate serious problems. This situation arises when a redundant rule is fired resulting in multiple counting of the same information. Therefore the weight value given to the associated conclusion is increased erroneously.
- **Conflicting rules under uncertainty**: The verifying process with conflicting rules remains same with uncertainty or while using the confidence factors. Sometimes if confidence factors are involved, there is a possibility of the same condition leading to different actions. This situation of conflicting rules is indicated by the verification procedure. However, the knowledge engineer may combine the conflicting rules or ignore the outcome to sort out this bug.
- **Subsumed rules under uncertainty**: When subsumed rules are used with confidence factor, one does not have to remove rules that are subsumed to sort out any of the problems. While debugging the program, the knowledge engineer ensures to build up rules such that the more restrictive rule provides added weight to the conclusions reached by the less restrictive one. Let us try to illustrate this case from the two rules listed as follows. Rule (1) is technically subsumed by Rule (2).

  IF
  (is? Load demand medium)                Rule (1)
  THEN
  (is? System reliable) (cf = 0.6)
  IF
  ((is? Load demand medium)               Rule (2)
  (is? Spinning reserve high))
  THEN
  (is? System reliable) (cf = 0.7)

  By leaving both these rules in the KB, the weight provided to the conclusion 'System is reliable' is increased if both are fired. That is, the fact 'Spinning reserve high' evidently gives extra weight to the conclusion of Rule (2).
- **Unnecessary IF conditions under uncertainty**: The reasoning of *unnecessary IF conditions* with confidence factor is similar to that of subsumed rules. For example, Rules (1) and (2) have an *unnecessary IF condition* only if either of the rules are deterministic or if the rules have the same confidence factor.

  IF
  (is? Load demand medium)                Rule (1)
  THEN
  (is? System reliable) (cf)

IF
((is? Load demand medium)  Rule (2)
(NOT (is? Spinning reserve high))
THEN
(is? System reliable) (cf)

However, in case of confidence factors having different values, the certainty of the conclusion is changed. The conclusion 'System is reliable' is understood differently based on the values of the second condition of Rule (2).

- **Circular rules under uncertainty**: A cycle of the execution is broken in case of circular rules employing confidence factors. If the value of confidence factor of loop falls below a threshold level (i.e., say 0.2), then the loop is broken.
- **Unreferenced attribute values and illegal attribute values under uncertainty**: The verification process of the unreferenced and illegal attribute values with and without certainty is similar in obtaining same conclusions.
- **Unreachable conclusions under uncertainty**: Detecting an unreachable conclusion becomes more complex under uncertainty. Even though the condition of a particular conclusion matches a conclusion in any of the rules in the program, it becomes unreachable.
- **Dead end goals and dead end IF conditions under uncertainty**: Detecting the dead end IF conditions and goals will be complicated by the use of confidence factors. For instance, a dead end goal may occur even though its condition appears as the conclusion of another rule. This may happen if the confidence factor of the other rule is less than the threshold level.

IF
(is? Load demand medium)  Rule (1)
THEN
(is? System reliable) (cf)
IF
(is? System reliable)  Rule (2)
THEN
goal = yes (cf)

Let us try to illustrate based on the rule set given earlier. Here the assumption is that no query is associated with the conditions of Rule (2). Now if the only rule in which 'System is reliable' appears as a conclusion is Rule (1), and if the attenuated confidence factor of Rule (1) is less than the threshold level, the goal in Rule (2) will be in a dead end condition. The same problem would exist if a chain of rules led to the conclusion 'System is reliable', and the resultant confidence factor for the chain was less than the threshold value. Similarly, detection of a dead end IF condition is complicated. If the attenuated confidence factor for Rule (1) in the previous rule set was less than the threshold level, the conditions of Rule (2) would be in a dead end condition.

## 1.7.7 Expert System Tools

The choice of the expert system tool is vital which drives much of the development process. Most of the expert system tools have sharp distinction between the KB and inference engines. Sometimes, we may expect inference engine to have more number of utilities which may be easier for developing an expert system than simply using a programming language. Since many products according to their design recommend an inbuilt building process, we should ensure that the selected tool indeed fits the proposed application.

### 1.7.7.1 Nature of Expert System Tools

The nature of the expert system tools is to simplify the job during its development phase [27]. These tools range from very high to low level programming languages. We can divide expert system tools into four major categories as shown in Fig. 1.10. We have to know the differences between programming languages used for expert system development and knowledge-engineering languages before going into other details. An artificial language developed to control and direct the operation of a computer is called a *programming language*. A kind of programming language is a *knowledge-engineering language* (KEL). Knowledge-engineering languages are built to construct and debug expert systems. They offer certain facilities for developing expert programs with more flexibility and are user friendly than ordinary programming languages. The strength of KELs lies in knowledge representation and the manipulation of knowledge.

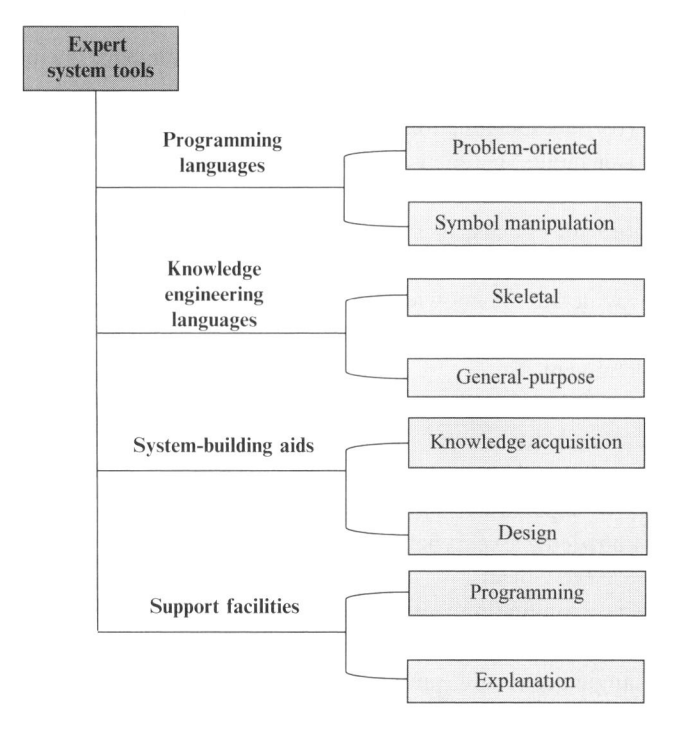

**Fig. 1.10** Main categories of tools available for expert systems

### 1.7.7.2 Programming Languages Used for Expert Systems

The problem-oriented languages or symbol manipulation languages are generally used programming languages for developing expert system [29]. Problem-oriented languages are used for particular classes of problems. For example, COBOL was designed for business, FORTRAN for scientific, and GPSS for simulation. Symbolic manipulation languages are used for AI applications. For example, Lisp has mechanisms for manipulating symbols in the form of list structures. A list is simply a collection of items enclosed within parentheses, where each item can be either a symbol or another list.

Programming languages like Lisp offer great flexibility to the expert system builder but are not user friendly while developing KB. However, KELs offer little flexibility as the knowledge engineer is indirectly forced to use the control scheme defined by the ready-made inference engine.

### 1.7.7.3 Knowledge Engineering Languages

A knowledge engineering language is a sophisticated tool for developing expert systems. It is the language used to define the various kinds of knowledge artefacts available in the different products of the *knowledge ware solution*. It can come with four different flavours as: mathematical engineering language, core engineering language, advanced engineering language, and extensible language. The *mathematical engineering language* groups the language operators and the numerical functions (maths, measures, etc.) necessary to express the sets of equations used to valuate parameters in knowledge advisor.

The *core engineering language* has the following language elements such as (a) keywords for control structures, like the 'if... then... else' conditional statement in rules and (b) Specific functions such as the ones dedicated to messages and prompts for user inputs, geometry construction or strings, and lists manipulation (c) Additional operators, like the '=>' operator, which corresponds to a kind of 'imply' keyword for checks. It is used in the following knowledge artefacts that are related to the update process through their parameters such as formulas, rules, and checks provided in the knowledge advisor product. *The advanced engineering language* takes over most of the operators, keywords, and functions from the core engineering language.

Certain applications aim at creating design objects enriched by a knowledge type. This advanced language can manipulate them as knowledge objects through tightly integrated knowledge artefacts such as (a) actions and reactions in knowledge advisor, (b) expert rules in knowledge expert, (c) knowledge expert behaviour, and (d) knowledge expert patterns. It also provides a full set of functionalities such as knowledge objects: basic attributes and methods, search capabilities, value pointers manipulation, and applications-specific services (constructors). Finally, the extensible language contains the applicative packages available in core engineering languages to add functions in the user development domain with user functions to create interactively new functions that may be used within advanced engineering language.

### 1.7.7.4 System-building Aids

The programs that facilitate the acquisition and representation of the domain expert's knowledge and the design needs of the expert system can be called as system-building aids. They are divided into two main groups: design aids and knowledge acquisition aids. For example, the software AGE provides the design aids. It helps the knowledge engineer design and builds an expert system. It constitutes user-friendly building blocks that can be assembled to form portions of an expert system. Similarly, TEIRESIAS software developed by Stanford University (1970) is a nice example of a knowledge acquisition aid. This software tool facilitates the knowledge transfer from a domain expert to a KB. It conducts dialogue in a restrictive subset of natural language English. It helps the user to debug effectively by analysing the rules and recommends suggestions regarding their completeness and consistency [29].

### 1.7.7.5 Support Facilities

The support facilities consist of tools for helping with programming, such as debugging aids and KB editors, and tools that enhance the capabilities of the finished system, such as built-in input/output (I/O) and explanation mechanisms. These facilities are usually available as part of a KEL and are designed to work specifically with that language. These are typical components of an expert system supporting environment.

### 1.7.7.6 Debugging Methods

Tracing facility and break packages are some of the features that are present in most of the programming and KELs. *Tracing* provides the user with a trace or display of system operation. It shows the list of names fired by the rules or the names of all the sub-routines that are called. *Break package* guides the user as to when to stop the program execution before some recurring error, thereby examining the current values in the database during the program run.

### 1.7.7.7 I/O Facilities

Various tools handle I/O communication in an expert system in different ways. Some facilities run time knowledge acquisition in which the tool itself makes the user converse with the running expert system. Expert systems handle I/O facility by providing a set of powerful commands or procedures which makes the writing of I/O routines easy.

### 1.7.7.8 Explanation Facilities

Expert systems are generally user friendly that explain the users how to reach a specific conclusion. However, not all expert systems may have the same degree of software support for explanation. *Respective reasoning* is one of the common types of support facility for explanation system which helps the system reaching a particular conclusion. If the user needs to know the response of the system for a particular question, the system may describe the rule that led to the question, or display the part of the chain or sequence of rules that led to the conclusion.

## 1.7.8 Expert System-building Tools

Expert system-building tools can be grouped in a number of ways. If all the representation techniques available in a tool are considered, then the commercially available expert system tools are divided into five general types as follows:

1. Inductive tools
2. Simple-rule-based tools
3. Structured-rule-based tools
4. Hybrid tools
5. Domain-specific tools

**Inductive tools**

The software that generates rules from examples or facts is called inductive tools. Large inductive tools run on mainframes and PCs while small inductive tools run only on personal computers. These tools are built from experiments conducted in machine learning. Minicomputers and personal computers are used while developing inductive tools. Large number of examples for the machine's information base is fed into these tools by the developer. A program within the software converts the examples that are fed into rules and determines the order the system that will follow when questioning the user.

**Simple rule-based tools**

Simple-rule-based tools consist of IF-THEN rules for knowledge representation. Personal computer provides them a platform to execute these rules. The simple-rule-based tools are found to be very effective in developing expert system containing fewer than 500 rules. The rules are simple in contrast to structured-rule systems. The limitation observed are with certain editing features which are available in structured-rule-based systems.

**Structured-rule-based tools**

Structured-rule-based tools facilitate with context trees, multiple instantiation, confidence factors, and more powerful editors in developing the KB. Separate rule sets with IF-THEN rule arrangement is possible which looks like separate KBs. The information inherited from one set of rules is obtained while examining the other rule set. Structured-rule-based tools are mostly preferred when large number of rules are involved and if the rules need to be sub-divided into sets.

**Hybrid tools**

The most complex expert systems development platform constitutes the hybrid tools. Mid-size hybrid tools offer number of conditions for knowledge representations and run on personal computers. They use object-oriented programming techniques for representing elements of every problem as objects. Facts and IF-THEN rules are contained in an object. These tools are capable of building an expert system which contains 500 to several thousand rules. They have graphically oriented interfaces.

*Knowbel* is an example of hybrid tool that supports representation and organization concepts. It offers a logic programming system facilitating the developer with an inference mechanism for a particular application. Most of the hybrid tools lack narrow focus to build specific knowledge system and are considered as research tools rather than practical tools to rapidly prototype an expert system.

**Domain-specific tools**
The building platforms for expert system that facilitate a particular domain are called domain-specific tools. They incorporate any of the techniques listed earlier, and thus be classified among any of the previous categories. They offer special development and user interfaces in a particular domain considerably faster than the aforecited types For example, *HYCONES II* is a domain-specific tool that enables the construction of hybrid connectionist systems for solving classification problem.

## 1.7.9 Expert System Shells

Expert system shell provides a platform for designing an expert system. Knowledge engineer is guided with an efficient and user-friendly software environment while building an expert system. It facilitates an environment for both the developer and the client for which the expert system is developed within the shell or exported to a compatible computer [26].

Nowadays, excellent commercial expert system shells are available in which hardly anyone builds an expert system from ground zero. These shells provide good debugging and value-checking aids. It also offers a mechanism for handling uncertainty both from the developer and from the end user side. The important factor that should be considered before building an expert system is to ensure the shells with the components that support all the requirements of the system to be built. They include the already explained basic components given as follows:

- Inference engine
- KB
- User-system interface
- Explanation facility
- Knowledge acquisition facility

All these five components must be in the proper place and must work together to obtain desired results in the expert system that is built (Martin & Oxman, 1988). However, the actual shell components provided by the various shell producers may vary. They may differ in functionality and these variations may exist due to the

- vendor's intended market,
- vendor's view of what is needed,

- vendor's background and capabilities,
- product's age, and
- targeted level of the knowledge engineer's experience.

### 1.7.9.1 Commercial Packages of Expert System Shells

Expert system shells may sometimes compared to DBMS (database management systems) products. Most industries buy commercial *off-the-shelf DBMS* products such as information management systems (IMS) and object-relational database management system (Oracle RDBMS) and use it according to their own data. The shell contains all the generic expert system logic required to build an expert system. An expert system with 300 rules will take over a year to develop from scratch, but take less than 3 months to develop with a shell.

Most of the expert system shells commercially available can run on mainframe, mini, and personal computers depending on the applications. The features of a few commercial shells based on the personal computer are presented in Table 1.4.

**Table 1.4** Commercial expert system packages

| Name | Company | System | Language |
|---|---|---|---|
| 1ST CLASS | 1st Class Expert Systems, Inc. | IBM PC | Microsoft Pascal |
| ART | Inference Corporation | Sun, VAX, Lisp Machine, IBM PC | Lisp, C |
| PC PLUS | Texas Instrumentation | IBM PC, Compaq PC | PC Scheme |
| GURU | Micro Database Systems, Inc. | IBM PC | C |
| EXSYS | Exsys, Inc. | IBM PC, SUN, Apple Macintosh, VAX | C |
| KES | Software Architecture and Engineering, Inc. | IBM PC, SUN, VAX, Apollo | C |

## 1.7.10 Application of Expert Systems

In the future, expert system technology will be applied to many different application areas. Let us take a look at how these systems are classified (Martin & Oxman, 1988).

*Product-specific systems*
- Commodity-based
- System developed from a single design to be embedded in a mass-marketed product
- Examples include vehicles, home appliances, instruments, and office machines

*Service-specific systems*
- Generic task based
- Systems designed to be employed by many users doing the same task
- Examples include computer system use advisor and database access assistant

*Organization-specific systems*
- Corporate goal based
- Systems designed for a single organization's use
- Examples include intelligent customer services assistant, expert configuration system, and intelligent proposal generation assistant

*Task-specific systems*
- Personal workstations
- Systems developed to assist a single, key knowledge worker
- Examples include an intelligent assistant for job shop scheduling, an intelligent sales manager's assistant, and an intelligent assistant for a system programmer

### 1.7.11 Future Scope of Expert Systems

The aforementioned applications areas prove that expert system technology enables the development of large number of new products. The future expert system products will be intelligent enough and may appear in the market as:

- Intelligent technical manuals
- Intelligent repair manuals
- Intelligent process controllers
- Intelligent monitoring systems
- Intelligent training systems

Though most of the expert system products run on computer-based systems and if space is an issue, then these computing resources do not offer viable solutions. Recently Bell laboratories have produced an inference engine and a KB on a custom CMOS chip. They claim that this expert system chip can perform 80,000 fuzzy logical inferences per second. We can expect to see more chip-based expert systems and components in the market in the future. These chips will certainly make it easy to deliver expert system components to commodities like digitally controlled microwave ovens. In future, expert system will be developed with programming techniques involving intelligent systems and other soft computing techniques.

## 1.8 COMPARISON AMONG INTELLIGENT SYSTEMS

Normally, the intelligent systems have wider application in various fields. It should be noted that the suitability of any kind of applications depends upon how effective these intelligent techniques are implemented for a specific application. However, in Table 1.5 we have given a comparison of intelligent systems for a limited number of applications which may give an idea of its applicability.

After going through this table, we will be getting some idea to choose the exact intelligent agent for a particular task. Depending on the problem that we are required to solve, we may adapt the suitable solution techniques.

**Table 1.5** Comparison of different intelligent systems based on their applications

| Application | Expert system | Fuzzy system | Neural network | Genetic algorithm | Swarm intelligence |
|---|---|---|---|---|---|
| Diagnosis | ♦ | | | | |
| Optimisation problem | | | | ♦ | ♦ |
| Prediction | | | ♦ | | |
| Control applications | | ♦ | | | |
| Load forecasting | | | ♦ | | |
| Air sonar target recognition | | | ♦ | | |
| Mobile robot navigation | | ♦ | | | |
| To tune fuzzy controller performance | | | | ♦ | ♦ |
| Classification of soil | | | ♦ | | |
| Hot extrusion of steel | | | ♦ | | |
| Composite laminates | | | | ♦ | ♦ |

## SUMMARY

- Soft computing differs from conventional (hard) computing in that, it is tolerant of imprecision, uncertainty, partial truth, and approximation.
- Systems such as biological neural systems and fuzzy logic systems relate the human way of thinking and interpretation.
- Systems such as genetics and evolutionary systems relate to a biological process in which the systems improve with time.
- Swarm intelligence (SI) systems such as ant colony optimisation (ACO), particle swarm optimisation (PSO), artificial bee colony (ABC), cuckoo search algorithm (CSA), gravitational search algorithms (GSA), etc., mimic the intelligent behaviour involved in animals, birds, insects, microorganisms, or any individual living in groups to solve complex problems in a more efficient manner.
- Expert system and its application are not currently very popular in engineering applications mainly due to advancement in varieties of soft computing techniques. Whereas, expert system may complement soft computing techniques for practical and field engineering application.
- Expert systems are intelligent computer programs that use expertise knowledge and inference schemes for solving problems, thereby emulating the decision-making like a human expert.

## EXERCISES

### Part A  Short-answer Questions

1. What is soft computing?
2. 'Conventional computing fails to give solution in certain applications'. Justify with some examples.
3. Give few examples of intelligent systems.
4. What is an artificial neural network?
5. Why artificial neural network is called an intelligent network?
6. Name a few of the second-generation neural network models.
7. How are third-generation neural networks different from second-generation neural networks?
8. List out the strength and weakness of artificial neural network?
9. How is neuro-computing different from conventional computing?
10. What is meant by fuzzy logic system? Give examples.
11. How is fuzzy logic system different from crisp systems?
12. List out the characteristic features proposed by Zadeh.
13. Name a few fuzzy logic applications with examples.
14. Why fuzzy logic is misconceived as an imprecise logic?

15. 'Behavior of fuzzy logic is deterministic'. Justify.
16. What is the difference between possibility and fuzzy theories?
17. 'Fuzzy logic is no better alternative to linear control'. Justify?
18. What is intuitionist fuzzy logic? How is it different from fuzzy logic?
19. What are metaheuristic algorithms? Give examples.
20. Name few evolutionary algorithms.
21. What is a genetic algorithm?
22. What is the difference between genetic algorithm and genetic programming?
23. What is evolutionary programming?
24. How are simulated annealing, hill climbing, and tabu search heuristic techniques different from GAs and EP?
25. What is the significant difference between genetic algorithm and evolutionary programming?
26. What are the limitations of genetic algorithms?
27. What are the differences between evolutionary strategy and evolutionary programming?
28. Why the solution obtained using GAs and EP is non-deterministic?
29. Name few software packages of genetic algorithm that are available in the market.
30. What are swarm intelligent systems?
31. What is swarm intelligence according to Eric Bonabeau?
32. How is artificial intelligence different from swarm intelligence?
33. List out the strength and weakness of swarm intelligence techniques.
34. What are expert systems?
35. What do you understand by the knowledge base editor in an expert system?
36. What is knowledge acquisition facility?
37. What is an inference engine?
38. What is the explanation for a sub-system?
39. What do you understand by 'self-training' in expert system?
40. List out the major errors that occur while developing an expert system.
41. What is rule-based expert system? Give an example.
42. What do you understand by the term 'chunk' in rule-based expert system?
43. What is backward chaining and forward chaining in rule-based expert system?
44. List out some examples using backward chaining or rules in expert system.
45. List out some examples using forward chaining or rules in expert system.
46. What is knowledge engineering?
47. List out the job performed by a knowledge engineer.
48. List out the various categories of expert system application.
49. What is verification and validation in expert system?
50. What are redundant rules? Give an example.
51. What are conflicting rules? Give an example.
52. What are subsumed rules? Give an example.
53. What are unnecessary IF conditions? Give an example.
54. What are unreachable IF conditions? Give an example.
55. What are circular rule chains? Give an example.
56. What is the difference between an unreferenced and an illegal attribute value?
57. What are dead end IF conditions?
58. What is a confidence factor in an expert system?
59. What is the significant difference between a programming and knowledge-engineering language?
60. Name some programming language used for building an expert system.
61. List out the five general types of expert system tools.
62. List out some of the commercial packages of expert system available in the market.

## Part B  Long-answer Questions

1. How is soft computing different from hard computing? Explain.
2. Explain the development of the three generations of neural networks.
3. Discuss in detail the misconceptions in fuzzy logic.
4. Explain the strength and weakness of swarm intelligent techniques.
5. Explain the architecture of an expert system with the help of block diagrams.
6. Discuss the concept of consistency and completeness testing of expert systems.
7. Consider the rule bases presented below. Perform backward chaining to get to the goal. (Let goal = good job.)

    R1: IF
       marks = good
    THEN
       test A = yes
    R2: IF
       test A = yes
    AND
       test B = no
    THEN
       job = good company
    R3: IF
       job = good company
    THEN
       marks = good

8. Consider the rule bases presented below. Perform forward chaining to get to the goal. (Let goal = goal; assume a user prompt for attribute A only.)

    R1: IF
       A = X
    AND
       B = Y
    THEN
       D = V
    R2: IF
       F = W
    THEN
       goal = no
    R3: IF
       D = V
    THEN
       B = Z

9. Consider the following rule base. Perform backward chaining to get to the goal, the final attribute of which is 'status'.

    R1: IF
       temperature is high
    THEN
       pressure is high
    R2: IF
       pressure is high
    AND
       fluid level is high
    THEN
       status is dangerous
    R3: IF
       chiller is on
    THEN
       temperature is high

R4: IF
    status is dangerous
    THEN
    chiller is on

10. Briefly explain expert system tools.
11. Describe the main application of expert system.

## Part C  Practical Exercises

1. Develop a MATLAB Program for Part B, Q. 9, using backward chaining and also forward chaining of rules.
2. Identify a person other than yourself who is considered either an expert or someone who is very knowledgeable. Interview this expert and discuss how well this person's expertise would be modelled by an expert system using IF-THEN rules.
3. Write 10 non-trivial rules expressing the knowledge of the expert in Part C, Q. 2.
4. Write a MATLAB Program that will give your expert's (of Part C, Q. 2) advice. [*Hint:* Include test results to show that each of the 10 rules (of part C, Q. 3) gives the correct advice. For ease of programming, you may allow the user to provide the necessary input through a menu.]
5. Develop a MATLAB Program demonstrating subsumed rules with uncertainty for the example given in the section on 'Completeness of verification and validation'. (*Hint:* Use confidence factors.)

## REFERENCES

[1] Haykin, Simon, *Neural Networks: A Comprehensive Foundation*, MacMillan Publishing Company, 1994.
[2] Zurada, Jacek M., *Introduction to Artificial Neural Systems*, West Publishing Company, St. Paul, Minnesota, 1992.
[3] Warren McCulloch and Walter Pitts, 'Logical Calculus of Ideas Immanent in Nervous Activity', *Bulletin of Mathematical Biophysics* Vol. 5, pp. 115–133, 1943.
[4] Hebb, D. O., *The Organization of Behavior: A Neuropsychological Theory*, Psychology Press, New edition, United Kingdom, 2002.
[5] Rosenblatt, Frank, The Perceptron: A Perceiving and Recognizing Automaton. Report 85-460-1, Cornell Aeronautical Laboratory, 1957.
[6] Minsky, Marvin and Seymour Papert, *Perceptrons: An Introduction to Computational Geometry*, The MIT Press, Cambridge MA, 1972.
[7] Werbos, Paul John, *The Roots of Backpropagation: From Ordered Derivatives to Neural Networks and Political Forecasting*, Wiley Publishers, United States of America, January 1994.
[8] David J. Chalmers, 'The Conscious Mind: In Search of a Fundamental Theory (Philosophy of Mind)', Oxford Paperbacks, 12 March 1998.
[9] Collins English Dictionary—Complete & Unabridged, 10th Edition, United Kingdom, 2009.
[10] Zadeh, Lotfi A., 'Fuzzy sets', *Information and Control*, Vol.8, pp. 338–353, 1965.
[11] Lotfi A. Zadeh, *Fuzzy Logic for the Management of Uncertainty*, John Wiley & Sons, Inc., New York, NY, USA, 1992.
[12] Assilian, S. and E. H. Mamdani 1974, '*Fourth IFAC/IFIP International Conference on Digital Computer Applications to Process Control*', Lecture Notes in Economics and Mathematical Systems, Vol. 93, pp. 13–24; Learning Control Algorithms in Real Dynamic Systems.
[13] Mamdani, E. H., and S. Assilian, 'An Experiment in Linguistic Synthesis with a Fuzzy Logic Controller', *International Journal of Man-Machine Studies*, Vol. 7, Issue 1, pp. 1–13. January, 1975 .
[14] Yen, John, Reza Langari, Fuzzy logic: Intelligence, Control, and Information, Prentice-Hall, Inc., 1 December 1998.
[15] Atanassov, Krassimir T., *Intuitionistic fuzzy sets;* 31 August 1986; Fuzzy sets and Systems; Vol. 20, No. 1, North-Holland, pp. 87–96.
[16] Thomas Baeck, D., Fogel, B., and Z. Michalewicz, *Evolutionary Computation 1: Basic Algorithms and Operators*, CRC Press, 2000.
[17] Mitchell, Melanie, *An Introduction to Genetic Algorithm*, MIT Press, United States of America, 1998.
[18] Thomas Back , David B. Fogel, Zbigniew Michalewicz, Handbook of Evolutionary Computation, Oxford University Press; Lslf edition ,1997.

[19] Grefenstette, J. J. (Ed.) (1993). Special Track on Genetic Algorithms, IEEE Expert, IEEE Press.
[20] Koza, J. R., *Genetic Programming: A Paradigm for Genetically Breeding Populations of Computer Programs to Solve Problems,* Stanford University Computer Science Department technical report STAN-CS-90-1314, 1990.
[21] Negnevitsky, Michael, *Artificial Intelligence,* Pearson Education India, Second Edition, India, 2008.
[22] Apostolakis, Georgios, Evolutionary Aseismic Design of Self-centering Post-tensioned Energy Dissipating Steel, ProQuest, 2006.
[23] Back, Thomas, Computer Science Department University of Dortmund, *Evolutionary Algorithms in Theory and Practice: Evolution Strategies, Evolutionary Programming, Genetic Algorithms: Evolution Strategies, Evolutionary Programming, Genetic Algorithms,* Oxford University Press, United States of America, 1995.
[24] Fogel, L. J., A. J. Owens and M. J. Walsh, 'Intelligent - Decision making through a simulation of evolution,' *IEEE Trans. Of the Professional Technical Group on Human Factors in Electronics,* Vol. 6, Issue 1, 1965.
[25] Beni, G., and J. Wang, Swarm Intelligence in Cellular Robotic Systems, *Proceedings of NATO Advanced Workshop on Robots and Biological Systems,* Tuscany, Italy, June 26–30, 1989.
[26] Dorigo, Marco, Vittorio Maniezzo, and Alberto Colorni, Ant System: Optimization by a Colony of Cooperating Agents 1996/2, Systems, Man, and Cybernetics, Part B: Cybernetics, IEEE Transactions, Vol. 26, Issue 1, pp. 29–41.
[27] Waterman, Donald Arthur, *A Guide to Expert Systems, Volume 2 of Teknowledge Series in Knowledge Engineering Series,* Addison-Wesley Publishing Company, United States of America, 1986.
[28] Ignizio, James P., *An Introduction To Expert Systems,* Mcgraw-Hill College; Har/Dis edition, United States of America, 1 January 1991.
[29] Martin, James, and Oxman, *Steven Building Expert Systems: A Tutorial*, Prentice Hall, United States of America, May 1988.

# e-References

1. http://www.ideas.youe-hut.com/ideas/janine-benyus-quotes/ (last accessed on 9/7/2014)
2. http://www.webopedia.com/TERM/N/neural_network.html (last accessed 9/7/2014)
3. http://searchnetworking.techtarget.com/definition/neural-network posted by Margaret Rouse (last accessed on 9/7/2014)
4. http://www.britannica.com/EBchecked/topic/752951/Frank-Rosenblatt (last accessed 9/7/2014)
5. http://www.investopedia.com/terms/f/fuzzy-logic.asp (last accessed on 9/9/2014)
6. https://www.calvin.edu/~pribeiro/othrlnks/Fuzzy/history.htm (last accessed on 09/07/2014)
7. interview with Eric Bonabeau on emergent swarm technologies, http://lilarajiva.wordpress.com/2007/07/29/eric-bonabeau-on-swarm-intelligence/ (last accessed 9/7/2014)
8. http://www.agesoftware.com/ (last accessed on 8/9/2014)

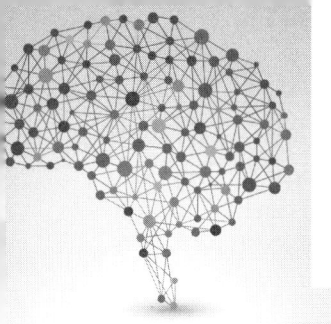

# 2 Artificial Neural Networks—First Generation

*'I praise you because I am fearfully and wonderfully made; your works are wonderful, I know that full well'*

A Psalm of King David (139:14)

## LEARNING OBJECTIVES

*After reading this chapter, the reader will be able to:*

- Understand the concept of biological neural networks (NNs)
- Interpret neuronal communication
- Understand the evolution of artificial NNs from biological NNs
- Explain the concept of McCulloch-Pitts NN and perceptron NNs
- Analyse the fundamentals of Adaline and Madaline NNs

## 2.1 INTRODUCTION TO NEURAL NETWORKS

When we see dancing peacocks, croaking frogs in a forest, and dark clouds in the sky, we say 'it may rain'. When we see a huge crowd and police personnel near a highway, we say 'it must be an accident or it must be the presence of a politician'. When we hear 'NEWS', we can expand it as North–East–West–South, or when we say 'OK', it is understood as 'Oral Correct'. If we give a hint, a person may be able to answer a particular question. *Memory, Association, Training,* and *Outcome* are some of the fundamental terms that can be correlated with respect to the aforementioned statements and can be connected with the working of a human brain.

Brain is the central organ of the human body. It is extremely complex and sophisticated. The functions of the brain were discovered by the ancient Egyptians and Greeks in 400 BC. It was Hippocrates who first discovered that brain played an important role in sensation and intelligence. Neurons are considered to be the smallest unit in the brain. Neurons develop at the rate of 250,000 neurons per minute during early pregnancy. Humans continue to make new neurons throughout life in response to mental activity. Information travels at different speeds within different types of neurons. Not all neurons are the same. There are a few different types within the body and transmission along these different kinds can be as slow as 0.5 m/sec or as fast as 120 m/sec.

The average number of thoughts that humans are believed to experience each day is 70,000. Approximately 85,000 neocortical neurons are lost each day in the human brain. Fortunately, this goes unnoticed due to the built-in redundancies and the fact that even after 3 years this loss adds up to less than 1 per cent of the total available neurons in the human brain. In addition, new neuronal connections sprout between cells to meet demands as long as the environment challenges or stimulates. If one asks what artificial neural network (ANN) is, it can be defined in a simple language as *an information processing system that mimics certain performance characteristics of the biological neural systems of the brain.*

## 2.2 BIOLOGICAL INSPIRATION

Nervous systems possess global architectures of variable complexity, but all are composed of similar building blocks, the neural cells or neurons. Human brain belongs to central nervous system. Figure 2.1 shows the cerebral cortex of a human brain. Each sub-area of the cerebral cortex is concerned with different functions such as primary sensory area, sensory association area, visual association area, area of language comprehension and formation, and so on. These can perform different functions, which in turn leads to a very variable morphology. Sometimes one wonders that if each of the sub-areas of the neural region of the cerebral cortex is modelled, then each area's neural network (NN) model can be a unique one.

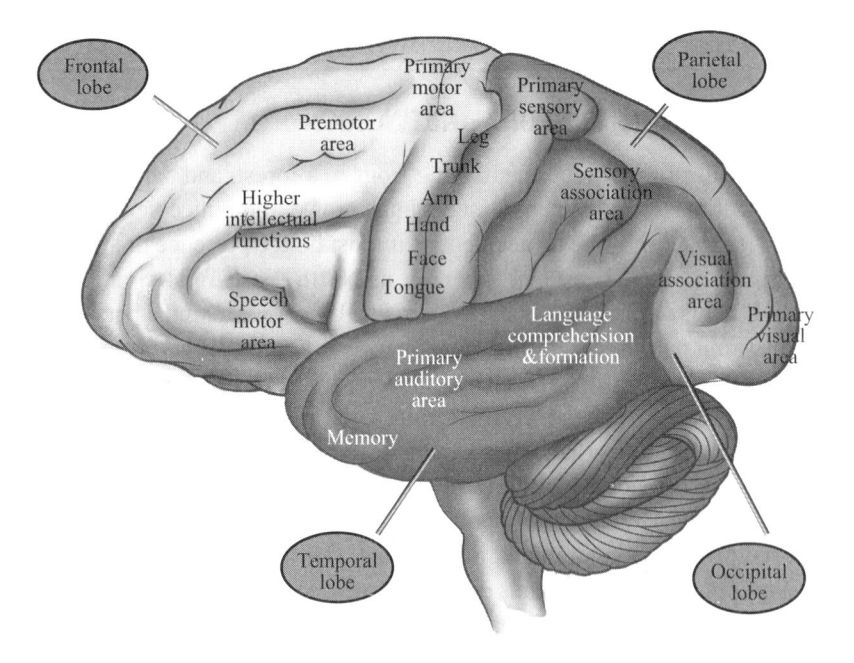

**Fig. 2.1** Cerebral cortex of a human brain

If we analyse the human cortex under a microscope, we can find several different types of neurons. The human brain contains about 10 to 100 billion nerve cells or *neurons*. On an average, each neuron is connected to other neurons through about 10,000 *synapses* (actual figures vary greatly, depending on the local neuroanatomy). Synapses are the interface between neurons where transfer of information takes place. Figure 2.2 shows neurons snarled in the cortex of the brain.

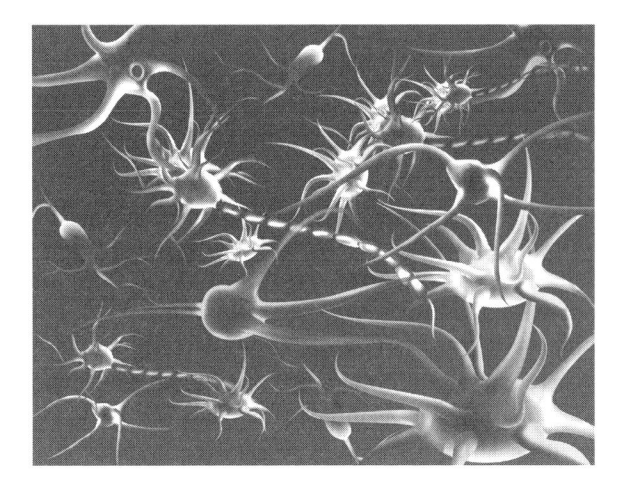

**Fig. 2.2** Tangled neurons in the cortex of the brain

Also when billions of neurons are linked, they look like a neural forest (Fig. 2.3), where the neurons communicate to each other and intelligence starts evolving, which performs different functions in the human brain.

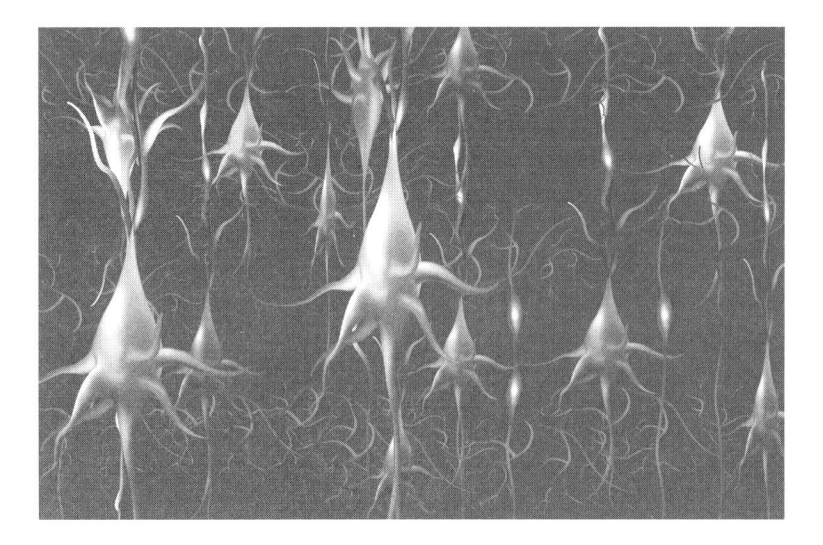

**Fig. 2.3** A neural forest (vertical organization of neurons in the visual cortex of human brain)

## 2.2.1 Comparison between Brain and Computer

The brain has been compared to different inventions. In the past, the brain was compared to a water clock and a telephone switchboard. These days, the favourite invention that the brain is compared to is a computer. Once, in a class, a question was raised to students, that is, which one is more powerful—a computer or a brain. Immediately, most of the students in the class replied that it is human brain and reasoned that computer is, in fact, invented by the human brain. Immediately, a simple mathematical problem $9^{9^{999}}$ was placed before them and they were asked to find the solution without using a calculator or computer. The students were flustered and with a puzzled look on their faces. Again, some argued that the computer is better than the brain and some argued that the brain is better than the computer. Finally, a consensus emerged and all the students responded, 'Perhaps, it is best to say that the brain is better at doing some jobs and the computer is better at doing other jobs'. This is logically correct; however, it is good to explore the differences and similarities between the two.

Human intelligence has the remarkable ability of creating links between ideas. However, it is weak at storing information and on which knowledge is based. The natural strength of computers is roughly the opposite and, thus, are powerful allies of the human intellect. Human knowledge bank, the brain, stores information in abstract concepts. When we come in contact with a new concept, we add new links.

Knowledge structures are not affected by the failure of the hardware (50,000 neurons die each day in an adult brain, but our concepts and ideas do not necessarily deteriorate). We are capable of storing apparently contradictory ideas. Unless a new idea is reinforced, it will eventually die out. Strong links between our emotions and knowledge is another distinguishing characteristic of human brain. Our knowledge is closely tied to our pattern-recognition capabilities. We are able to change our minds and change our internal networks of knowledge. To illustrate the information stored in a computer (let us try to look at a section of the 11th edition of *Concise Oxford English Dictionary* [2008]), it is an ambitious attempt to organize all human knowledge in a single hierarchy. It allows multiple classifications. It takes time to understand but it is successful in view of the vast scope of the material it covers. Such data structures provide a formal methodology for representing a broad class of knowledge and are easily stored and manipulated by the computer.

Human brain is in the order of 10 billion to 100 billion neurons. Each neuron has thousands of synaptic connections. There is a speculation that certain long-term memories are chemically coded in neuron cell bodies. Therefore, if the capacity of each neuron is 1,000 bits, then the brain has the capacity of $10^{14}$ bits. If we assume an average redundancy factor of $10^4$ that gives us $10^{10}$ bits per concept, then it is $10^6$ concepts per human brain. It has been estimated that a 'master' of a particular domain of knowledge has mastered about 50,000 concepts, which is about 5 per cent of the total capacity, according to the aforecited estimate.

The human brain uses a type of circuitry that is very slow. For tasks such as vision, language, or motor control, the brain is more powerful than 1,000 supercomputers. For certain simple tasks, such as multiplying digital numbers, it is less powerful than the 4-bit microprocessor found in an old model calculator. The brain is wired to learn its interaction with the world, re-programming itself over the time. Computers do not learn easily by experiences. However, a human child starts out listening to understand spoken language, learns to speak, and can perform written language. Computers start with the ability to generate written language, learning to understand it, speak with synthetic voices, and understand continuous human speech. Let us try to look at the game of chess of *Man Versus Machine*. In 1990, IBMs *Deep Thought* chess computer (initially called Chipset run in SUN 4/160 Workstation) is easily defeated by then reigning champion Garry Kasparov in a two-game match in New York. *Deep Thought* can evaluate 720,000 moves per second. However, the Project continued at IBM's T.J. Watson Research Centre. Improvements are seen every year and it has developed 30 Power Two Super Chip Processors capable of 200 million positions/second (Kasparov with 3 positions/second). The new version of Deep Thought has been re-named to *Deep Blue* in February 1993. On 11 May 1997, the machine won the second six-game match against the world champion by two wins to one with three draws. Kasparov accused IBM of cheating and demanded a re-match, but IBM refused and dismantled Deep Blue. The computer has no use of psychology. Its strengths are the strengths of a machine and it has a database of opening games played by grandmasters over the last 100 years. It does not think, but reacts. It does only one specific job. Deep Blue relies on computational power and a search and evaluation function.

Let us understand this concept by an example. The African elephants are considered to be an endangered species. These elephants move as a herd with smaller one to the elder one and they care for each other. The huge old tuskers are killed for ivory. When older elephants are killed for ivory, the young elephants have no one to guide and they fight and kill each other. The reasons may be that the experience and knowledge accumulated by the older elephants is not properly transferred to their next generations. Therefore, when the experience of grandmasters over the last 100 years is stored in the computer for evaluating the chess move, the World Chess Champion is not able to beat the computer. Therefore it is rightly said, 'experience is knowledge, and knowledge is power'.

## 2.3 BIOLOGICAL NEURAL NETWORKS TO ARTIFICIAL NEURAL NETWORKS

In human brain, the grey matter consists of neuron cell bodies and dendrites; and the white matter (myelin) consists of axon tracts. The neurons receive signals and produce a response. The general structure of a biological neuron is shown in Fig. 2.4.

The branches to the left are the transmission channels for incoming information and are called 'dendrites'. Dendrites receive the signals at the contact regions with other cells called the *synapses*. Organelles in the body of the cell produce all the necessary chemicals for the continuous working of the neuron. The mitochondria, shown in Fig. 2.4, can be thought of as part of the energy supply of the cell, since they produce chemicals that are consumed by other cell structures. The output signals are transmitted by the axon, of which each cell has at most one.

The four elements (i.e., dendrites, synapses, cell body, and axon) are the minimal structure we will adopt from the biological model. Artificial neurons for computing will have input channels, a cell body, and an output channel. Synapses will be simulated by contact points between the cell body and input or output connections; a weight will be associated with these points. The simplified diagram of the biological neuron is shown in Fig. 2.5.

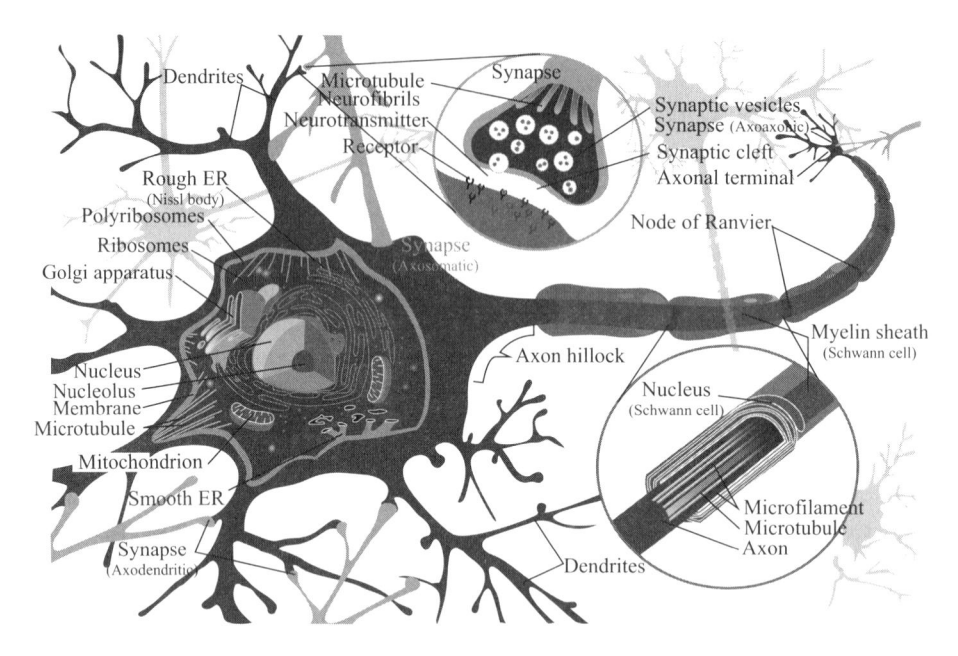

**Fig. 2.4** A biological neuron

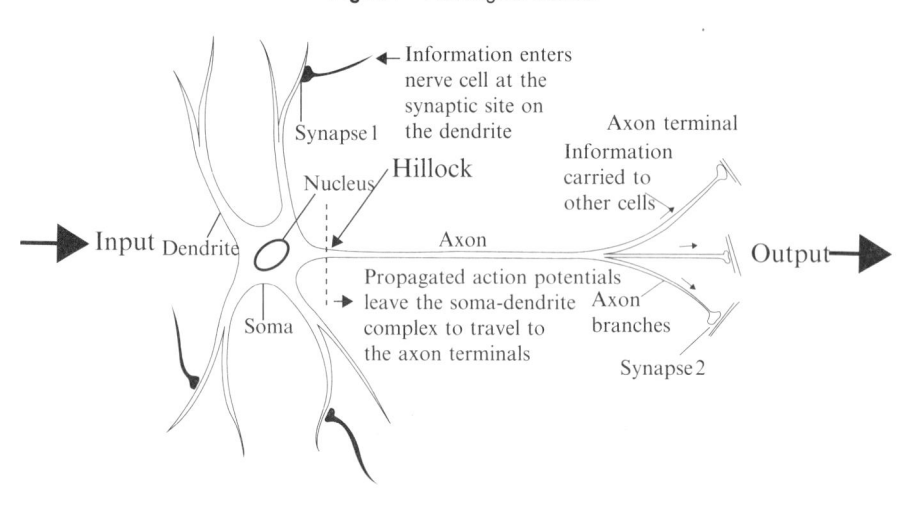

**Fig. 2.5** Simplified diagram of biological neuron

## 2.3.1 Information Processing at the Neurons and Synapses

The direction of the signal impulses is shown in Fig. 2.6. It should be noted that the information processed in a neuron is *unidirectional*. The neuron will not fire its signal just a little bit. Therefore, the law for a neuron is that *either it fires or it does not*. Synapses are the junctions where the transfer of information (synaptic transmission) takes place from one neuron to the other.

The synaptic transmission takes place through chemical substances called *neurotransmitters*. The bulging terminal end of the axon contains synaptic vesicles or sacs that contain these chemicals. The receptor sites are of the dendrites that

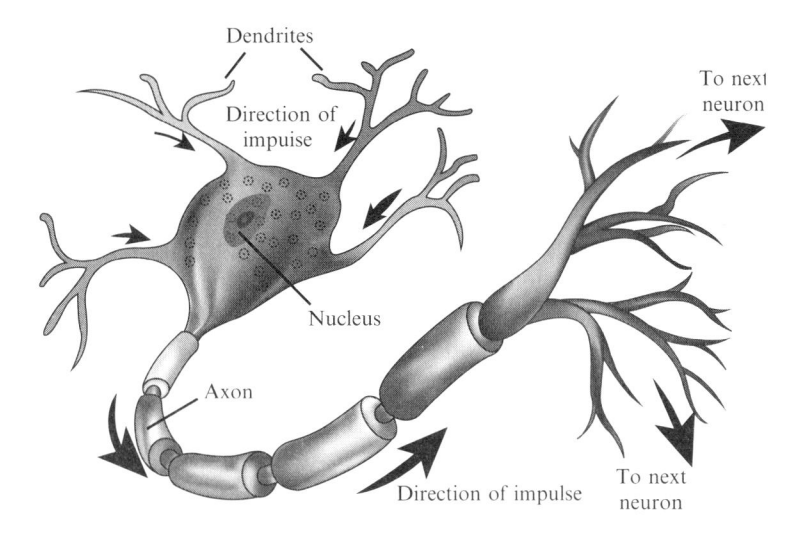

**Fig. 2.6** Direction of impulse

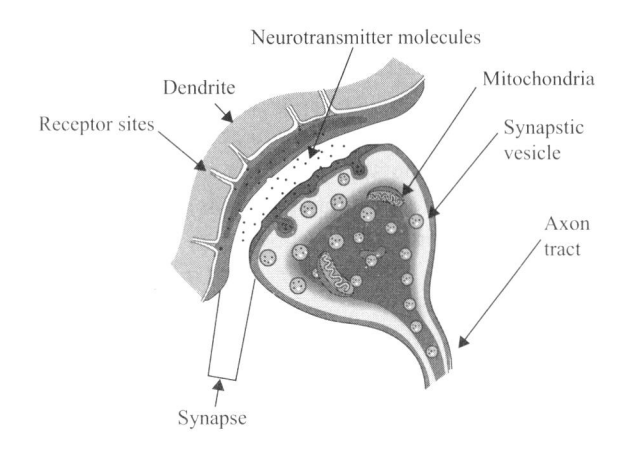

**Fig. 2.7** Synaptic transmission

receive these neurotransmitter molecules. Both the receptor sites and the terminal end of the axon do not touch each other, as shown in Fig. 2.7.

When an electric impulse arrives at a synapse, the synaptic vesicles fuse with the cell membrane (Fig. 2.7). The neurotransmitters flow into the synaptic gap and some attach themselves to the ionic channels. If the transmitter is of the right kind, the ionic channels are opened and more ions can now flow from the exterior to the interior of the cell. The cell's potential is altered in this way. If the potential in the interior of the cell is increased, this helps to prepare an action potential and the synapse causes an excitation of the cell. If negative ions are transported into the cell, the probability of starting an action potential is decreased for some time and we are dealing with an inhibitory synapse.

Synapses determine a direction for the transmission of information. Signals flow from one cell to the other in a well-defined manner. The binding between neurotransmitters and receptor sites is often expressed as a *lock-and-key* relationship because neurotransmitters fit particular receptor sites in the same way that a key fits a specific lock. First, a neurotransmitter is released by a presynaptic vesicle and crosses the synapse, where it binds to a post-synaptic receptor. This chemical event (transmitter binding to receptor sites) initiates a series of electrical events. Neurotransmitter molecules have specific shapes and receptor molecules have binding sites. When they bind to receptors, neurotransmitters open channels in the nerve membrane that allow ions to flow in and out of the neuron. These effects are responsible for the changes in membrane potential necessary to transmit messages between neurons and along nerve fibres.

A single neuron activity depends upon the potential difference that exists between the interior of the neuron cell and its surrounding, and is called *membrane potential*. By altering the permeability of the membrane to sodium and potassium ions, this voltage can be affected. Signals arriving at synapses cause chemicals known as *neurotransmitters* to be released and these cross the synapse and alter the permeability of the receiving neuron's membrane. If the change in membrane permeability is large enough, then the neuron *fires*, by producing a rapid change (a 'spike') in its membrane potential. This is known as an *action potential*, and the action potential (neuronal spike) then travels down the axon, away from the cell body.

A *spike* is generated when the *membrane potential* is greater than its threshold. Hence, we can forget all the sub-threshold activity and concentrate on *spikes (action potentials)*, which are the signals sent to other neurons. Only spikes are important since other neurons receive them (signals). Neurons communicate with spikes. Information is coded in spikes. Although it seems funny to predict and fiction-like, it is true that *if we are able to manage and control the spikes we can decipher human brain*. It should be noted that neurons fire only when stimulus is bigger than some threshold. In addition, firing does not get bigger as stimulus increases. This is illustrated in Fig. 2.8.

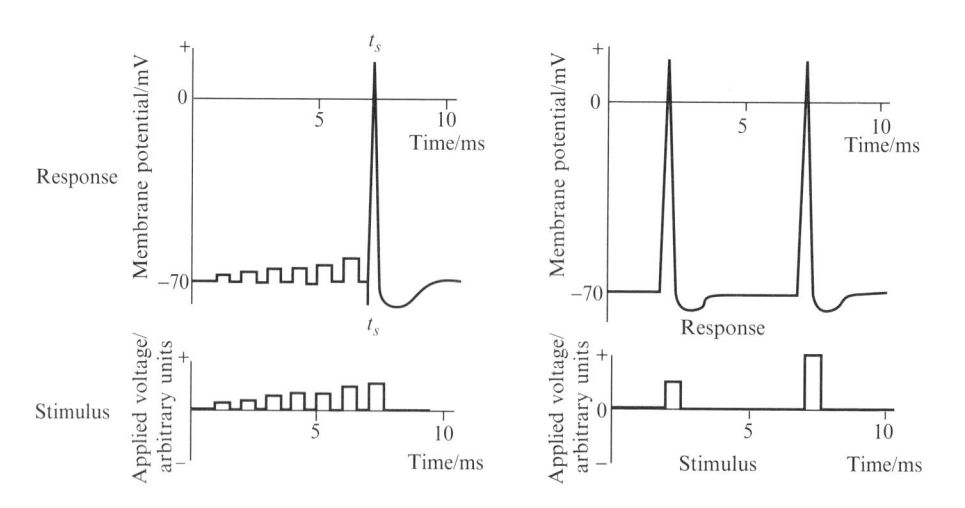

**Fig. 2.8** Neuronal firing [1]

The following are some of the facts about input and output of the neurons:

1. Synapses can be *excitory* or *inhibitory*.
2. These differ in the kind of transmitter released.
3. Signals arriving at an excitory synapse tend to cause the receiving neuron to fire.
4. Signals arriving at an inhibitory synapse tend to inhibit the receiving neuron from firing.
5. The cell body and synapses (by a complicated chemical/electrical process) essentially compute the difference between the incoming excitory and inhibitory inputs (spatial and temporal summation).
6. When this difference is large enough (compared to the neuron's threshold), the neuron will fire.
7. If the excitory spikes arrive at its synapses in a faster rate, then the firing of the neuron will be faster.
8. Similarly, if the inhibitory spikes arrive at its synapses in a faster rate, then the firing of the neuron is inhibited immediately.

The structural representation of biological neural networks (BNNs) is shown in Fig. 2.9. This helps us to understand the evolving of ANN.

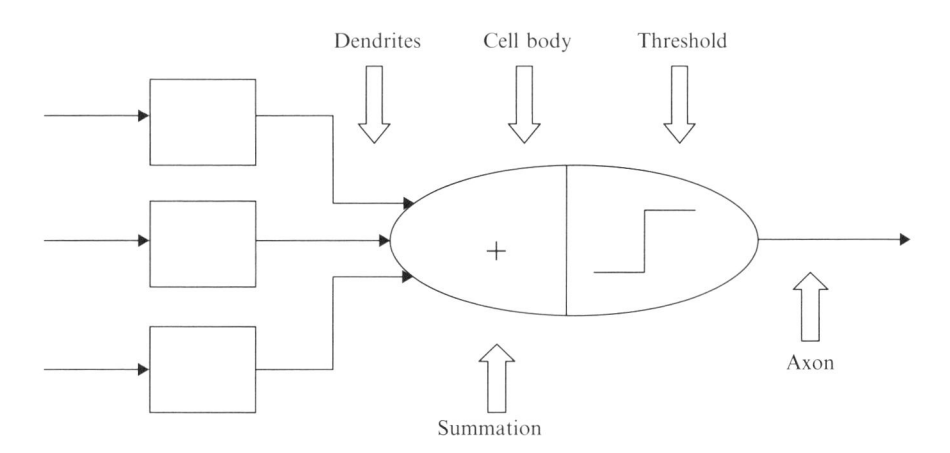

**Fig. 2.9** Structural representation of BNN

When creating a functional model of the biological neuron, there are three basic components of importance. First, the synapses of the neuron are modelled as weights. The strength of the connection between an input and a neuron is noted by the value of the weight. Negative weight values reflect inhibitory connections, whereas positive values designate excitatory connections [2]. The next two components model the actual activity within the neuron cell. An adder sums up all the inputs modified by their respective weights. This activity is referred to as linear combination. A bias term is another weight whose weight value is always equal to unity, which helps in the process of initial learning. Finally, an activation function controls the amplitude of the output of the neuron. An acceptable range of output is usually between 0 and 1, or −1 and 1. A simple ANN model is shown in Fig. 2.10. From this model, the internal activity of the neuron can be shown to be as follows:

$$sum_k = \sum_{j=0}^{n} W_{kj} I_j + b_k \tag{2.1}$$

The output of the neuron $O_k$ would therefore be the outcome of some activation function on the value of $sum_k$. Table 2.1 gives the difference in terms used in both BNN and ANN.

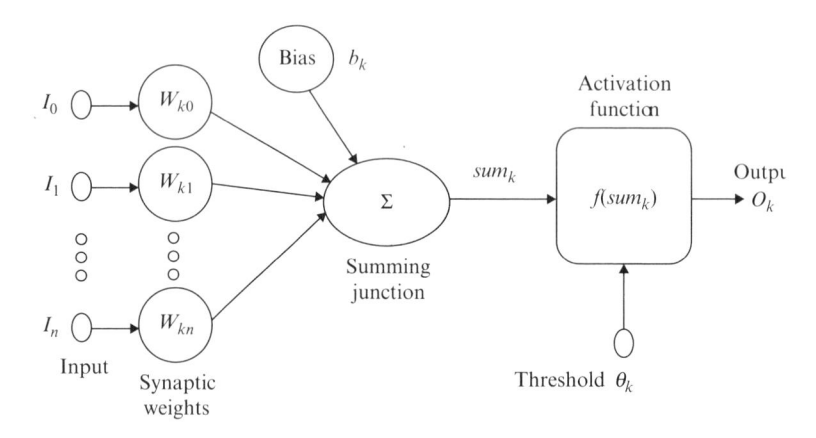

**Fig. 2.10** A simple ANN

**Table 2.1** Terminologies used for ANN and BNN

| ANN | Unit | Connections | Weights | Unit's output | Transfer (activation) function |
|---|---|---|---|---|---|
| BNN | Neuron | Synaptic interactions | Synaptic efficacies | Activity of axon | Influences of synapses on axon |

Some of the assumptions of ANN are as follows:

1. Information processing occurs at many simple elements called neurons.
2. Signals are passed between neurons over connection links.
3. Each connection link has an associated weight, which, in a typical neural net, multiplies the signal transmitted.
4. Each neuron applies an activation function to its net input (sum of weighted input signals) to determine its output signal.
5. Bias may be added to the net sum for better learning process.

Some of the major developments in the field of ANNs have been listed in Table 2.2.

Table 2.2  Development of ANNs

| Year/Author/ANN model | Functions |
|---|---|
| 1943, Warren McCulloch and mathematician Walter Pitts, McCulloch-Pitts ANN model | Solves simple logic functions such as AND, OR, NOT, etc. |
| 1949, Donald Hebb, Hebb rule | Explains the adaptation of neurons in the brain during the learning process. |
| 1959, Bernard Widrow and Marcian Hoff, Adaline and Madaline networks | Adaline was developed to recognize binary patterns so that if it was reading streaming bits from a phone line, it could predict the next bit. Madaline was the first neural network applied to a real-world problem, using an adaptive filter that eliminates echoes on phone lines. |
| 1960, Rosenblatt, Perceptron | Perceptron, a classification algorithm that makes its predictions based on a linear predictor function combining a set of weights with the feature vector describing a given input. |
| 1962, Widrow and Hoff, Widrow-Hoff rule | Leaning procedure for the adjustments of weights based on error. i.e., minimizes the squared error between the desired output and neuron's activation value. |
| 1969, Minsky and Papert, Perceptrons | An important analysis on perceptron that showed that a perceptron could not learn to evaluate the logical function of exclusive-OR (XOR). |
| 1982, John Hopfield, Hopfield NN | Hopfield NNs are recurrent ANNs and serve as content-addressable memory systems with binary threshold units. It is also used in optimisation applications. |
| 1982, Kohonen, Kohnonen NN or self-organizing maps | Self-organizing maps different from other ANNs in the sense that they use a neighbourhood function to preserve the topological properties of the input space. They are used as classification through unsupervised learning. |
| 1986, Rumelhart, Hinton and Williams, Backpropogation NN | Backpropagation NN (BPN) is a common method of training ANNs so as to minimize the objective function. It is a supervised learning method, and is a generalization of the delta rule. |
| 1988, Broomhead and Lowe, Radial basis function | A radial basis function (RBF) network is an ANN that uses radial basis functions as activation functions. It is a linear combination of radial basis functions. They are used in function approximation, time series prediction, and control. |
| 1988, L.O. Chang and L. Yang, Cellular NN | Cellular NNs (CNNs) are a parallel computing paradigm similar to NNs, with the difference that communication is allowed between neighbouring units only. Typical applications include image processing, analysing 3D surfaces, solving partial differential equations, reducing non-visual problems to geometric maps, modelling biological vision, and other sensory-motor organs. |
| 1990, Vapnik, Support vector machines | A support vector machine (SVM) is a concept in statistics and computer science for a set of related supervised learning methods that analyse data and recognize patterns, used for classification and regression analysis. The standard SVM takes a set of input data and predicts, for each given input, which of the two possible classes forms the input, making the SVM a non-probabilistic binary linear classifier. |

(*Continued*)

**Table 2.2** (Continued)

| Year/Author/ANN model | Functions |
|---|---|
| 2001, Wulfram Gerstner, Spiking NNs | Spiking NNs (SNNs) fall into the third generation of NN models, increasing the level of realism in a neural simulation. In addition to neuronal and synaptic state, SNNs also incorporate the concept of time into their operating model. The idea is that neurons in the SNN do not fire at each propagation cycle (as it happens with typical multi-layer perceptron networks), but rather fire only when a membrane potential—an intrinsic quality of the neuron related to its membrane electrical charge—reaches a specific value. When a neuron fires, it generates a signal which travels to other neurons which, in turn, increase or decrease their potentials in accordance with this signal. |
| Future-generation hybrid ANN models | Hybrid ANN models are used as sequential, embedded, and auxiliary hybrid models involving soft computing technologies such as fuzzy systems, meta heuristic algorithms, and expert systems. |

## 2.4 CLASSIFICATION OF ANNs

The development of NNs dates back to 1940 when McCulloch and Pitts tried a simple mathematical model of a neuron that can solve simple logic functions. Later, with the progress in the learning and generalization with its advantages in application to non-linear problems, the progress by which this soft computing technology has penetrated in all kinds of science and engineering problems is remarkable. The progress in the NNs is seen towards the extent of minimizing the difference between the actual biological neural models and mathematical models.

The history of the ANN has been tabulated in Table 2.2. With available ANN models that exist in the literature, there are so many ways that ANNs may be classified based on setting different criteria, and there is no limit. However, the classification of ANN can be simplified by classifying them based on their characteristics such as network architecture (a pattern of connections between the neurons), training/learning (method of determining weights), and activation function. It should be noted that Chapter 4 discusses different types of NNs based on the ANN developments as first-generation, second-generation, and third-generation NNs.

### 2.4.1 Neural Network Architecture

It is convenient to visualize neurons as arranged in layers. In addition, it can be understood that neurons in the same layer behave in the same manner. The key factors in determining the behaviour of a neuron are its activation function and the pattern of weighted connections over which it sends and receives signals. Within each layer, neurons usually have the same activation function and the same pattern of connections to other neurons [2]. However, based on the number of layers and the pattern of connections, the NNs can be classified as follows:

## Single-layer Neural Network

A single-layer net has one layer of connection weights. Often, the units can be distinguished as input units, which receive signals from the outside world, and output units, from which the response of the net can be read. In the typical single-layer net, as shown in Fig. 2.11, the input units are fully connected to output units but are not connected to other input units, and the output units are not connected to other output units. By contrast, the Hopfield net architecture (Fig. 2.12) is an example of a single-layer net in which all units function as both input and output units.

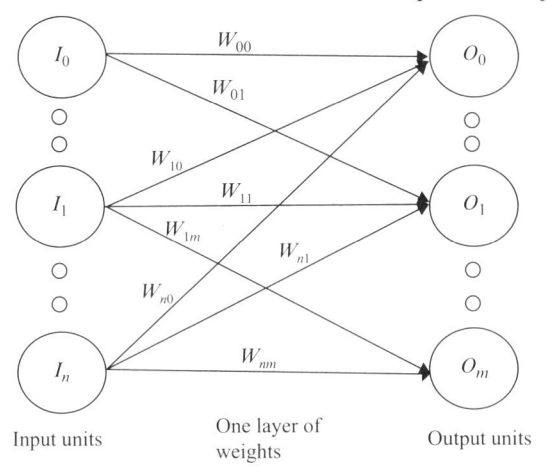

**Fig. 2.11** Single-layer NN

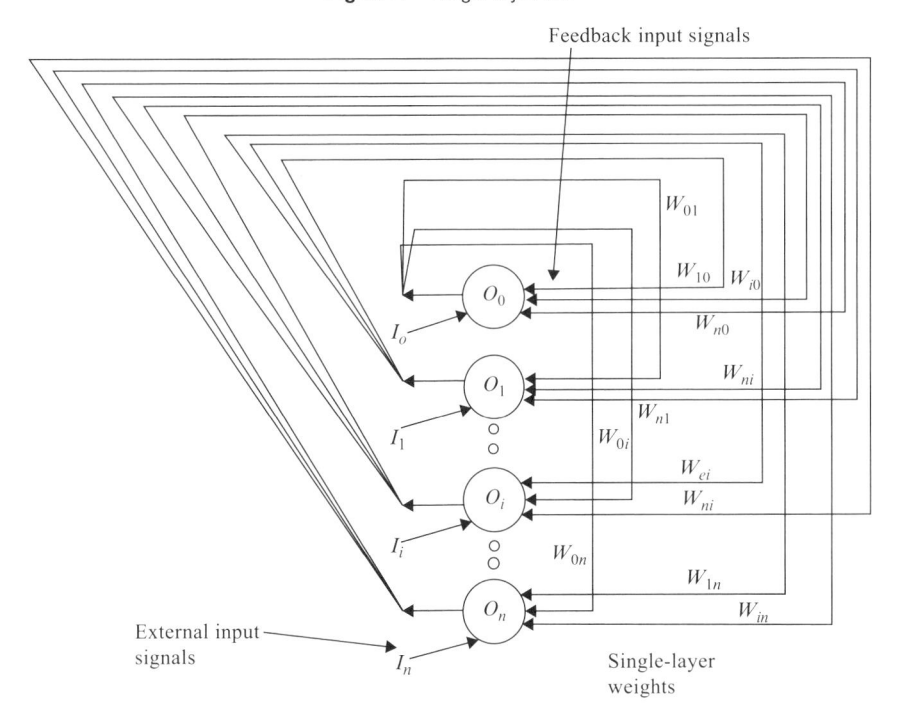

**Fig. 2.12** Hopfield recurrent NN

## Multi-layer Neural Network

A multi-layer net is a net with one or more layers (or levels) of nodes (the so-called hidden units) between the input units and the output units. Typically, there is a layer of weights between two adjacent levels of units (input, hidden or output). Multi-layer nets or multi-layer perceptrons (Fig. 2.13) can solve more complicated problems than single-layer nets but training may be more difficult. However, in some cases, training may be more successful, because it is possible to solve a problem that a single-layer net cannot be trained to perform correctly at all.

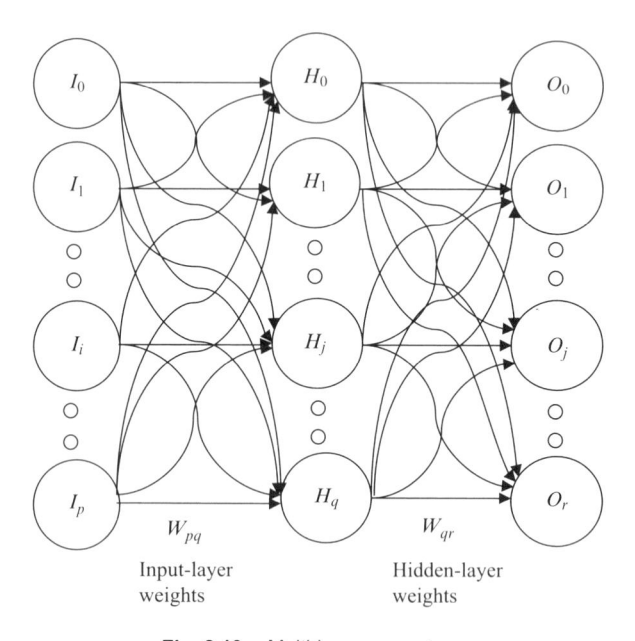

**Fig. 2.13** Multi-layer perceptrons

## Competitive Neural Network

A competitive layer forms a part of large number of NNs. Typically, the interconnections between neurons in the competitive layer of these competitive NNs are rarely shown in the architectural diagrams. An example of the architecture for a competitive layer is shown in Fig. 2.14. The competitive connections have weights of $-\alpha$. The operation is based on winner-takes-all competition. One example for the competitive NN is the one developed by Lippman in 1987, which is called MAXNET.

It should be noted that based on the direction of the data flow, the NN can be again classified as *feed-forward NNs* and *feed-back NNs* or recurrent NNs.

In feed-forward NNs, the data flow starts from the input units to output units. The data flow is possible through multiple layers and no feedback connections are present from the output units to the inputs of the units of the same layer or the previous layer units. An example for this is a simple feed-forward BPN (Fig. 2.13).

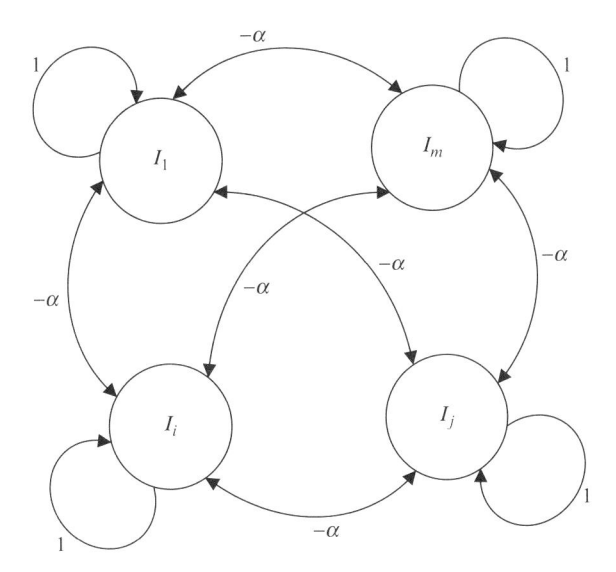

**Fig. 2.14** MAXNET

However, if there are feedback connections, the NN is called 'recurrent neural network'. An example for this type of network is the Hopfield NN (Fig. 2.12). It should be noted that this recurrent NN should have at least one neuron with feedback. In addition, a self-feedback occurs when the output of a neuron is fed back to itself.

## 2.4.2 Learning/Training

It is a common saying that 'practice makes a man perfect'. Therefore, for any system to be perfect, it needs to learn and get trained. Learning can happen through interactions between two entities such as a system interacting with an environment. The way an ANN learns can be classified as follows:

**Supervised Learning**

The supervised learning, as the name suggests, takes place with supervision or under a strategy to correct the learning process for achieving the desired target. Let us understand the concept of 'supervised learning' by the means of an example.

After the formulation of the theory of relativity $E = mc^2$, Albert Einstein went around Germany to lecture on the theory. His driver accompanied him everywhere, and hence was made to attend all his lectures. One day, the driver proposed to deliver a lecture on Einstein's behalf. Since the driver had attended most of his lectures, Einstein accepted the proposal. In his next lecture, the role play got exchanged, with Einstein taking his driver's place in the lecture hall, and his driver delivering a lecture on the theory of relativity. The speech part went well, but answering the queries raised by the audience became the challenging part. When the questions started pouring, the smart driver appearing unperturbed replied:

'These are too simple for a person like me to respond. My driver, sitting right there (pointing towards Einstein), will be more than happy to clarify all your doubts!'

The analogy is that the driver had the target or ambition to deliver a lecture like Einstein. He practised and corrected, trained himself to behave, talk, and adopt the body language of Einstein. The driver is related to the input source and his ambition is related to the target data. The driver should practice or learn in such a way as to reduce the imperfection or error between his actual performance and the target performance to deliver the lecture like Einstein.

In another example, the supervised learning can be related in the way parents correcting their children to bring them up or train them to inculcate good habits. Here, the children are the source and inculcating good habits is the target to be achieved. The parents can be related to the learning rules or training algorithms. The supervised learning method is illustrated in Fig. 2.15.

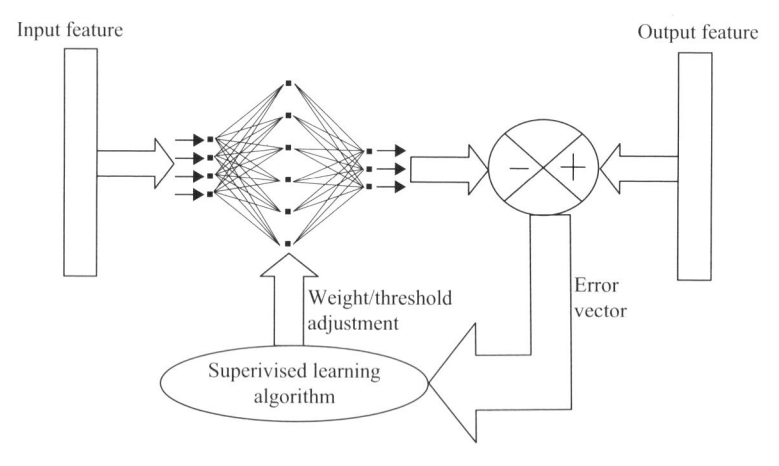

**Fig. 2.15** Supervised learning method

In Fig. 2.15, the NN is given by a source (input feature) and a target data (desired). The learning is carried out by an algorithm to minimize the error difference (error vector) between the actual output (output feature) and target output. It should be noted that, when learning occurs, the weights are modified. This type of learning can also be considered like a closed-loop feedback system, where the error is the feedback signal. A feed-forward BPN is an example for this type of learning.

## Unsupervised Learning

Contrary to the unsupervised NN, the learning takes place even if the target feature is not given. For a teacher, during the start of the course work for every new batch of students, it is really a puzzle to observe the way the students cluster among themselves while sitting in the classroom. The students from the same region, same state, and same language groups sat close to each other. In addition, sometimes the students who have similar characteristics sat close to each other; perhaps it was comfortable for them to learn and interact within their own social group.

The same holds true for an unsupervised learning, where the learning starts to occur within the similar kind of patterns.

Similar kinds of input features produce similar kind of output features. Therefore, an output unit is trained to respond to clusters of pattern within the input. In this paradigm, the system is supposed to discover statistically salient features of the input population. Unlike the supervised learning paradigm, there is no *a priori* set of categories into which the patterns are to be classified; rather the system must develop its own representation of the input stimuli. Unsupervised Hebb learning is an example for this type of learning.

**Reinforced Learning**

Reinforced learning reinforces either of the supervised or unsupervised learning method. To understand this, let us take a day-to-day example. Generally in primary schools, the students are made to stand in a straight line in their respective position in the morning assembly. Other than the respective class position, the class teacher remains standing to monitor the situation. When the assembly session is over, all the students move in a reinforced line to their respective classrooms. If someone drifts from the straight line path, a hidden cane from the class teacher would hit the legs of the student immediately. This would automatically reinforce the straight line.

Here the teacher, who is the external factor, grades the behaviour of the students to go in a line. Based on the response, a penalty (beating by a cane) or a bonus (encouraging the students) will adjust the situation in order and thereby performing better. This type of learning may be considered an intermediate form of the aforesaid two types of learning. Here, the learning machine does some action on the environment and gets a feedback/response from the environment. The learning system grades its action good (rewarding) or bad (punishable) based on the environmental response and accordingly adjusts its network parameters. Generally, parameter adjustment is continued until an equilibrium state occurs, following which there will be no more changes in its parameters. The self-organizing neural learning (Kohonen NN) may be categorized under this type of learning.

### 2.4.3 Training and Testing Modes

The performance of an NN can be understood by its training and testing modes. The different modes of operation of NNs are presented in Fig. 2.16.

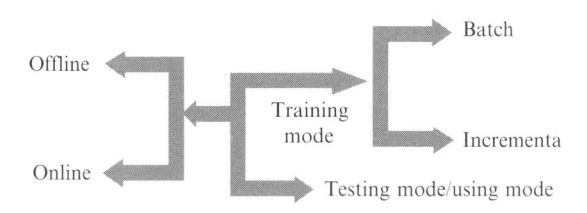

**Fig. 2.16** Modes of operation

In the *training mode,* the neuron can be trained to fire (or not) for particular input patterns. In the *using mode/testing,* when a test input pattern is given at the input, its associated output becomes the current output. In the *batch training mode,* updation of weights is done as a sum over all the training set. In the *incremental training mode,* updation of weights is done after each pattern is presented. These modes of operation can be understood from common experiences in our school days. Let us assume each student is an input pattern to be trained. The students are taught in the class by their teachers for a particular term and their performance is evaluated by the conduct in an examination. Teachers teaching the students can be related to the *training mode* and the examination for the students can be related to the *using mode* or testing mode. Batch training mode can be thought of as a teacher training a batch of 100 students in a class simultaneously, where the process of learning is taking place together for all the students.

Therefore in NN training, all the patterns are simultaneously trained by updating the weights related to all patterns simultaneously. However, the same teacher when training each of the individual students in a tuition class can be compared to incremental training. This is why in NN training, each of the individual patterns is trained sequentially and weights are updated sequentially.

The selection of the modes of training is based on the trade-off between the time taken for training and accuracy in training error. In the *offline mode,* training is carried out with the available data of a system from the past. Once the updated weights are set after training, it will not be changed in the system operation mode. In the *online mode,* a system learns in operation mode where the weights are updated even after the completion of training (requires more complex network architecture).

### 2.4.4 Activation/Transfer Function

To understand the functioning of activation or a transfer function, let us consider the simple NN with inputs and weights as in Fig. 2.10. The Eq. (2.1) gives the ($sum_k$) of the input signals $I_j$ multiplied with the weights of the network ($W_{kj}$). The activation function denoted by $f(sum_k)$ defines the output of the neuron by comparing with the threshold value $\theta_k$.

The sigmoid activation function, whose graph is s-shaped, is the common form of activation function used in the construction of ANNs. It is defined as a strictly increasing function that exhibits a graceful balance between linear and non-linear behaviour. The sigmoid function passes negative information when the output is less than the threshold $\theta_k$ and positive information when the output is greater than the threshold $\theta_k$. More commonly, the activation function is a continuous function that varies gradually between two asymptotic values, typically 0 and 1, or −1 and +1. The commonly used activation function is the logistic function, one of the sigmoidal activation functions shown in Fig. 2.17, and is represented by the Eq. (2.2):

$$f(sum_k) = \frac{1}{1+e^{-s \times (sum_k)}} \qquad (2.2)$$

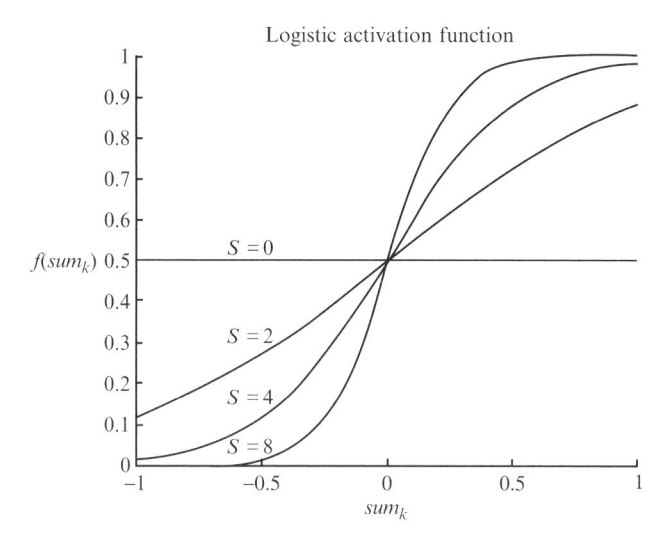

**Fig. 2.17** Logistic activation function

where 's' is a slope parameter of the sigmoid function that adjusts the abruptness of this function as it changes between the two asymptotic values. By varying the parameters, we can obtain sigmoid functions of different slopes.

The transfer functions can even be developed based on the research applications [8]. Some of the standard common transfer functions that are used often are given in Table 2.3.

**Table 2.3** List of standard and common activation function

| Function | Equation |
|---|---|
| Identity function (purelin) | $f(sum_k) = sum_k$ for all $sum_k$ |
| Binary step function | $f(sum_k) = \begin{cases} 1 & \text{if } sum_k \geq \theta_k \\ 0 & \text{if } sum_k < \theta_k \end{cases}$ |
| Binary sigmoid (logsig) | $f(sum_k) = \dfrac{1}{1 + \exp(-s \times sum_k)}$ |
| Bipolar sigmoid function (tansig) | $f(sum_k) = \dfrac{1 - \exp(-s \times sum_k)}{1 + \exp(-s \times sum_k)}$ |
| Hard limit (hardlim) | $f(sum_k) = \begin{cases} 1 & \text{if } sum_k \geq 0 \\ 0 & \text{if } sum_k < 0 \end{cases}$ |
| Symmetrical hard limit (hardlims) | $f(sum_k) = \begin{cases} 1 & \text{if } sum_k > 1 \\ sum_k & \text{if } 0 \leq sum_k \leq 1 \\ 0 & \text{if } sum_k < 0 \end{cases}$ |

*(Continued)*

**Table 2.3** (Continued)

| Function | Equation |
|---|---|
| Saturating linear (satlin) | $f(sum_k) = \begin{cases} 1 & \text{if } sum_k \geq 0 \\ -1 & \text{if } sum_k < 0 \end{cases}$ |
| Symmetric saturating linear (satlins) | $f(sum_k) = \begin{cases} 1 & \text{if } sum_k > 1 \\ sum_k & \text{if } -1 \leq sum_k \leq 1 \\ -1 & \text{if } sum_k < -1 \end{cases}$ |

Radial basis functions are special class of activation functions used in RBF NNs, which are extremely efficient as universal function approximators. These activation functions can take many forms but are usually found as one of the three functions as given in Table 2.4.

**Table 2.4** Radial basis/specialized activation functions

| Function | Equation |
|---|---|
| Gaussian | $f(sum_k) = \exp\left(-\dfrac{\|sum_k - c_k\|^2}{2\sigma^2}\right)$ |
| Multiquadratics | $f(sum_k) = \sqrt{\|sum_k - c_k\|^2 + a^2}$ |
| Inverse multiquadratics | $f(sum_k) = \left(\|sum_k - c_k\|^2 + a^2\right)^{-1/2}$ |

*Note:* Where $c_k$ is the vector representing the function centre and $a$ and $\sigma$ are parameters affecting the spread of the radius

Support vector machines can effectively utilize a class of activation functions that includes both sigmoids and RBFs. In this case, the input is transformed to reflect a decision boundary hyper-plane based on a few training inputs called *support vectors x*. The activation function for the hidden layer of these machines is referred to as the *inner product kernel* and is given as $K(sum_k, x) = f(sum_k)$.

The support vectors are represented as the centres in RBFs with the kernel equal to the activation function, but they take a unique form in the perceptron as:

$$f(sum_k) = \tanh\left(\beta_1 + \beta_0 \sum_j sum_{kj} x_j\right) \tag{2.3}$$

where $\beta_1$ and $\beta_0$ must satisfy certain conditions for convergence. These machines can also accept arbitrary-order polynomial activation functions,

where:
$$f(sum_k) = \left(1 + \sum_j sum_{kj} x_j\right)^p \tag{2.4}$$

## 2.5 FIRST-GENERATION NEURAL NETWORKS

The first generation of ANNs consisted of McCulloch-Pitts threshold neurons [3], a conceptually very simple model: a neuron sends a binary 'high' signal if the sum of its weighted incoming signals rises above a threshold value. Even though these neurons can only give digital output, they have been successfully applied in powerful ANNs such as multi-layer perceptrons and Hopfield nets. For example, any function with Boolean output can be computed by a multi-layer perceptron with a single hidden layer; these networks are called 'universal for digital computations'. Although McCulloch-Pitts threshold neurons are the earlier ones, these models help in understanding the performance of neuron for simple logic functions, which will be discussed in the following sections.

### 2.5.1 McCulloch and Pitts Neuron Model

McCulloch and Pitts's neuron model did not have the features of the present-day NNs. However, it enabled the development of the third-generation NNs which are in the research and development phase and are very much closer to its biological counterparts. The following are the assumptions involved in this model:

(a) McCulloch neurons have a binary output of either 'one' or 'zero'. If the firing of neuron takes place, then the neuron has an activation of 'one' and if it does not fire, then the neuron has an activation of 'zero'.
(b) McCulloch neurons are connected via the connection links called the 'weight path'. Each of the weight paths has some values and is often considered as the strength of the NNs.
(c) If the weight value on the path is positive, then the connection path is excitatory; or else, it is inhibitory. Same weight values are kept for the excitatory connections.
(d) A threshold level is present in each of the neuron. If the net input passing through the neuron is greater than the threshold level, then the neuron fires an output. However, the threshold value $\theta_k$ should satisfy the constraint given in Eq. (2.5) such that the inhibition is absolute.
(e) The time taken for a signal to pass through a connection link is a one-time step.

The architecture of a simple McCulloch-Pitts neuron is shown in Fig. 2.18. The excitatory connections has $w > 0$ and the inhibitory connection has weight values as $-v$ and $v > 0$. Here, $n$ units have excitatory connections and $m$ connections have inhibitory connections. The output '$O$' of the McCulloch-Pitts neuron is given by the activation function as in Eq. (2.5). Here, $sum_k$ is the total weighted net input and $\theta_k$ is the threshold level of the neuron.

$$f(sum_k) = \begin{cases} 1 & \text{if } sum_k \geq \theta_k \\ 0 & \text{if } sum_k < \theta_k \end{cases} \quad (2.5)$$

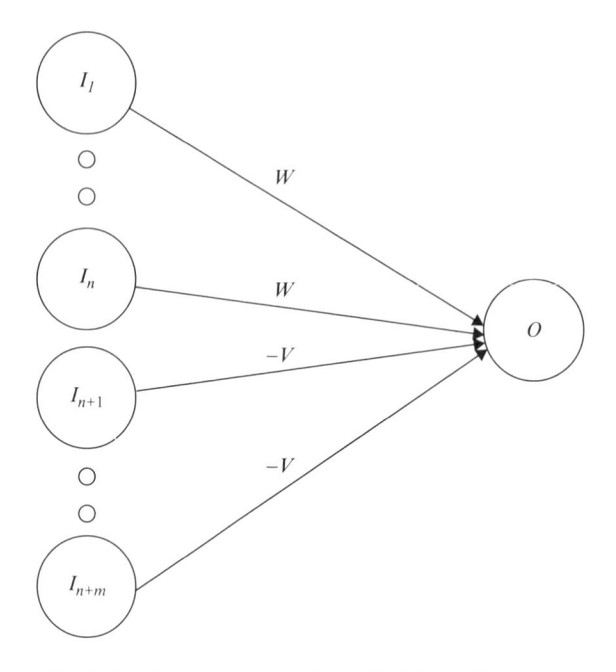

**Fig. 2.18** Architecture of a simple McCulloch-Pitts neuron

The threshold value of the McCulloch-Pitts NN should be set, such that it satisfy the inequality constraint given in Eq. (2.6).

$$\theta_k > n \times w - p \tag{2.6}$$

Let us try to solve some simple Boolean AND and OR logic functions. Let us consider two binary inputs and the value of the threshold $\theta_k$ be fixed as 2. In addition, the weight values connecting the two inputs to the output neuron be '1' for AND logic and '2' for 'OR logic. The following are the truth table of AND and OR logic function performed on a 2-input, 1-output McCulloch-Pitts NN and is illustrated in Fig. 2.19 and Table 2.5.

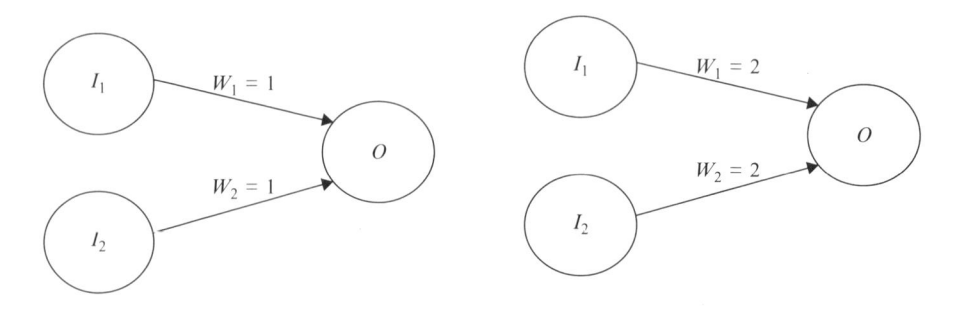

**Fig. 2.19** AND-OR logics performed by McCulloch-Pitts neuron

Table 2.5 AND-OR logics performed using McCulloch-Pitts NN

| Input-1($I_1$) | Input-2($I_2$) | AND logic weights ($W_1=1, W_2=1$) $sum_k$ | OR logic weights ($W_1=2, W_2=2$) $sum_k$ | Compare $sum_k$ and $\theta_k = 2$ using Eq. (2.5) | AND logic Output (O) | OR logic Output (O) |
|---|---|---|---|---|---|---|
| 0 | 0 | 0 | 0 | | 0 | 0 |
| 0 | 1 | 1 | 2 | | 0 | 1 |
| 1 | 0 | 1 | 2 | | 0 | 1 |
| 1 | 1 | 2 | 4 | | 1 | 1 |

## 2.5.2 Learning Rules: Hebbian and Delta

Learning begins once we start using the brain. Has anyone ever taught us 'how' to think? It might seem like an odd question but, if we think about it for a moment, we start learning. When we start thinking in the right direction, learning is effective. Hence, thinking in the right direction is a learning strategy or a learning rule.

Learning is a process by which the free parameters of an NN are adapted through a process of stimulation by the environment in which the network is embedded. The type of the learning is determined by the manner in which the parameter changes take place [4].

One might have noticed that different students learn the same concept in different ways. The same holds for the NNs. All through the years, different types of algorithms involving different schemes of adjusting weights and other network parameters have evolved for the effective training of ANN. However, the following section deals with some of the learning methods that are commonly used in the training of NNs.

### 2.5.2.1 Hebbian Learning Rule

In 1949, Donald Olding Hebb, a Canadian psychologist, came up with postulates on the function of neurons in the psychological processes such as learning. He has been described as the father of neuropsychology and NNs. In his famous book *The Organization of Behavior*, Hebb discussed in detail about the human behaviour connected with the biological function of the brain [5]. His hypothesis has been popularly called Hebbian theory and has been well adopted as Hebbian learning in the training of ANN. In *The Organization of Behavior*, the theory defines: 'When an axon of cell A is near enough to excite cell B and repeatedly or persistently takes part in firing it, some growth process or metabolic change takes place in one or both cells such that A's efficiency, as one of the cells firing B, is increased'.

This is often paraphrased as 'neurons that fire together wire together' and has been commonly referred to as Hebb's Law. This reminds two old proverbs that says, 'Good company makes a person good, and bad company makes a person bad', and 'Birds of the same feather flock together'. This comes in the purview of how we associate with others. However, association is the fundamental philosophy in the school of behavioural psychology.

To remember certain things such as formulas, hard concept, or a portion from a book, we try to associate or relate it with some other things. For example, to calculate the resistance of a resistor, we have to remember the painted colour codes around the resistor body that correspond to some integer value. It has been remembered by phrasing it as 'BB ROY of Great Britain has a Very Good Wife' corresponds to various lines of colour codes that are allotted to a specific value in the resistor as B-Black 0, B-Brown 1, R-Red 2, O-Orange 3, Y-Yellow 4, G-Green 5, B-Blue 6, V-Violet 7, G-Grey 8, and W-White 9.

However, the Hebbian learning pattern can be explained by a *stimulus* and a *response* with the Ivan Pavlov's experiment on behavioural pattern observed on training a dog to salivate while ringing the bell whenever food was presented [6]. Here the dog salivates whenever the food is synchronized with the ringing of the bell. This procedure is repeated for quite a number of times. However, at some instants when the bell rings and the food is not placed, the dog still starts to salivate. Thus, the dog is conditioned to salivate even if the food is not placed before it. Here, two types of inputs are paired. That is, *conditional stimulus* and *unconditional stimulus* corresponds to the ringing of the bell and the presentation of the food to the dog, respectively. The *desired response* or target is to make the dog to salivate.

The Hebb rule strengthens the association between the two input stimulus and the output response by modifying the weights with a learning factor ($\eta$). The learning factor directs the number of times the stimulus and the response to occur together before an association is made. The Hebb rule given later in Eq. (2.7) is an unsupervised learning rule.

$$w_{jk}(t) = w_{jk}(t-1) + \eta \times O_k(t) \times I_j(t) \qquad (2.7)$$

Where, $j$ and $k$ are the indices of input and output units, and $t$ is the iteration number. Here, let us try to demonstrate the Hebb rule. The aforementioned experiment can be illustrated with an example using a hard limit activation function (Table 2.3). Consider a simple NN as shown in Fig. 2.20. Let us represent '1' for a condition to happen and '0' for a condition that does not happen. The condition can be a stimulus or a response. Now let us repeat the process step-wise by presenting the inputs and, based upon the response, the weights are updated as per Eq. 2.7. Here $W_0 = 1$ and bias ($b$) = $-0.5$ is fixed and is not allowed to change during the training phase. The bias is set such that the network will respond (i.e., $O = 1$) even if the unconditional stimulus (presentation of food) is present or absent. In addition, the value of $W_0$ should be greater than the bias value. Let the value of the learning factor, $\eta = 1$. If the inputs are $I_0 = 1$ and $I_1 = 1$, then both the presentation of food and the ringing of the bell occurs together. If $I_0 = 0$ and $I_1 = 1$, then the food is presented and the bell rings. The steps involved in the training process are tabulated in Table 2.6.

Table 2.6  Demonstration of unsupervised Hebb Rule

| $t=0$ | $I_0$ | $I_1$ | $W_0=1$ | $W=0$ | Sum calculation $(W_0 \times I_0(t) + W(t-1) \times I_1(t) - b)$ | Compare sum and $\theta = 0$ using hardlimit function | Response (O) | Weight update ($W$) using Eq. (2.7) $w_{jk}(t) = w_{jk}(t-1) + \eta \times O_k(t) \times I_j(t)$ |
|---|---|---|---|---|---|---|---|---|
| 1 | 0 | 1 | $W_0=1$ | $W(0)=0$ | $(1 \times 0 + 0 \times 1) - 0.5 = -0.5$ | $-0.5 < \theta$ | $O(1)=0$ | $W(1) = 0 + 1 \times 0 \times 1 = 0$ |
| 2 | 1 | 1 | $W_0=1$ | $W(1)=0$ | $(1 \times 1 + 0 \times 1) - 0.5 = 0.5$ | $0.5 > \theta$ | $O(2)=1$ | $W(2) = 0 + 1 \times 1 \times 1 = 1$ |
| 3 | 0 | 1 | $W_0=1$ | $W(2)=1$ | $(1 \times 0 + 1 \times 1) - 0.5 = 0.5$ | $0.5 > \theta$ | $O(3)=1$ | $W(3) = 1 + 1 \times 1 \times 1 = 2$ |

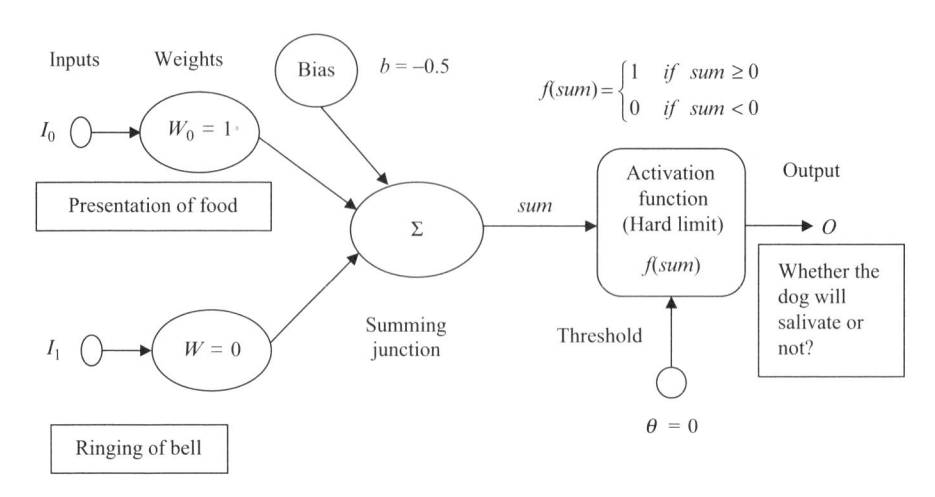

**Fig. 2.20** A simple Hardlimit NN

During the first iteration ($t = 1$), one of the input stimuli (presentation of food, $I_0 = 0$) is not present and the response seen is that the dog did not salivate, $O = 0$. In the second iteration, when both the input stimulus are present (presentation of food, $I_0 = 1$; ringing the bell, $I_1 = 1$), it is observed that the dog has salivated, $O = 1$. Now it should be noted from the third iteration that, even in the absence of the input stimuli (presentation of food, $I_0 = 0$), the dog is made to salivate by obtaining the desired response, $O = 1$. It is really interesting to observe that the absence of an input stimuli does not hinder the output response and makes the network function intelligently even in case of missing data. A good day-to-day example of partial input data can be how we may recognize our college-day friends even after 20 years when the facial and physical appearance may change.

### 2.5.2.2 Variations of Hebbian Learning

The previous Hebbian rule which is given in Eq. (2.7) has certain limitations. When we continue presenting the input patterns for more number of iterations, there is a problem with regard to the weight values becoming arbitrarily large. In addition, there is no mechanism to control the decrease of weights. Therefore to overcome the limitation, Hebb rule with a decay factor $\gamma$ is proposed and is given in Eq. (2.8).

$$\begin{aligned} w_{jk}(t) &= w_{jk}(t-1) + \eta \times O_k(t) \times I_j(t) - \gamma \times w_{jk}(t-1) \\ &= (1-\gamma)w_{jk}(t-1) + \eta \times O_k(t) \times I_j(t) \end{aligned} \quad (2.8)$$

Here, $\gamma$ is a constant which is positive and lesser than unity. When $\gamma$ becomes zero, the learning law becomes the standard one which is same as in Eq. (2.7). However, when $\gamma$ becomes unity, the rule quickly forgets the past inputs and memorizes the present input patterns. This procedure keeps the weight updating within the boundary limits. Suppose the change in weights is replaced by the desired output with the difference between the desired and the actual output, then a new kind of learning rule called delta learning rule emerges.

### 2.5.2.3 Delta Learning Rule

In 1960, Widrow and Hoff (1960) developed the delta learning rule as an iterative learning technique for Adaline (i.e., a single neuron computation). This rule is applied only to problems whose input patterns are linearly independent, but not orthogonal. However, the delta rule will give the least square solution when the input patterns are not linearly independent [8]. The initial delta rule when developed for a single output unit is computed such that it will minimize the difference between the *weighted sum* that is given into the output unit and target value or desired output. Here, the error is minimized over all the training patterns. The error reduction is carried out by each input vector, one at a time. Let us consider a single neuron with $n$ number of units. Let $I$ be the input vector with $n$ number of elements and $D$ is the desired output. Let $j$ be the index of the input elements and $W$ is the weights from input units to the output unit $O$. Then the weighted sum of the inputs that is passing into the output unit is given as:

$$sum = \sum_{j=1}^{n} I_j W_j \qquad (2.9)$$

The squared error (SE) for an input vector $I$ is given as in Eq. (2.10)

$$E = (D - sum)^2 \qquad (2.10)$$

where $E$ is a function of all of the weights and $W_j, j = 1, 2, 3\ldots n$. The direction of the error ($E$) is given by the gradient of $E$ of the vector consisting of the partial derivatives of $E$ with respect to each of the weights. The gradient $\partial E / \partial W_{j=1..n}$ gives the direction of the increase in error and the opposite direction of the gradient $-\partial E / \partial W_{j=1..n}$ gives the direction of the decrease in error. The error $E$ can be reduced by adjusting the weights $W_{j=1..n}$ in the opposite direction of the gradient. We know $sum = \sum_{j=1}^{n} I_j W_j$, therefore

$$\partial E / \partial W_{j=1..n} = -2 \times (D - sum) \times \partial(sum) / \partial W_{j=1..n}$$
$$= -2 \times (D - sum) \times I_{j=1..n} \qquad (2.11)$$

Therefore, for a given learning rate of $\eta$, the error $E$ will be reduced by modifying the weights according to the delta rule given in Eq. (2.12)

$$\Delta W_{j=1..n} = \eta \times (D - sum) \times I_{j=1..n} \qquad (2.12)$$

The delta rule for more than one unit is considered by having $m$ number of output units and let $k$ be the index of the output elements. Now, the SE for an input vector $I$ is given as in Eq. (2.13).

$$E = \sum_{k=1}^{m}(D_j - sum_k)^2 \qquad (2.13)$$

Similar to the derivation of the delta rule for a single-layer output unit, the error $E$ can be reduced by adjusting the weights $W_{jk}, j=1,..n; k=1,...m.$ in the opposite direction of the gradient $-\partial E / \partial W_{jk}, j=1,..n; k=1,...m$ or $-\partial E / \partial W_{jk}$. Now the gradient to be adjusted with weights can be derived as follows:

$$\partial E / \partial W_{jk} = \partial E / \partial W_{jk} \sum_{k=1}^{m}(D_k - sum_k)^2$$
$$= \partial E / \partial W_{jk} \times (D_k - sum_k)^2 \qquad (2.14)$$

It should be noted that the weights $W_{jk}$ influence the error at the output units $O_k$ and is given by Eq. (2.15),

$$O_k = \sum_{j=1}^{n} I_j W_{jk} \qquad (2.15)$$

Therefore,

$$\partial E / \partial W_{jk} = -2 \times (D_k - sum_k) \times \partial(sum_k) / \partial W_{jk}$$
$$= -2 \times (D_k - sum_k) \times I_j$$

Therefore, for a given learning rate of $\eta$, the error $E$ will be reduced by modifying the weights according to the delta rule given as:

$$\Delta W_{jk} = \eta \times (D_k - sum_k) \times I_k \qquad (2.16)$$

However, the aforecited delta rule can be modified by minimizing the difference between the actual value of the output unit and target value or desired output and is known as *extended delta rule*. Now, the SE for an input vector $I$ is given as:

$$E = \sum_{k=1}^{m}(D_j - O_k)^2 \qquad (2.17)$$

Now the gradient to be adjusted with weights can be derived as:

$$\partial E / \partial W_{jk} = \partial E / \partial W_{jk} \sum_{k=1}^{m}(D_k - O_k)^2$$
$$= \partial E / \partial W_{jk} \times (D_k - O_k)^2 \qquad (2.18)$$

Here, the weights $W_{jk}$ influence the error at the output units $O_k$. The actual value in the outputs is given by $O_k = f(sum_k)$. Therefore,

$$\partial E / \partial W_{jk} = -2 \times (D_k - O_k) \times \partial (sum_k) / \partial W_{jk}$$
$$= -2 \times (D_k - O_k) \times I_j \times f'(sum_k) \quad (2.19)$$

Now the error $E$ is reduced by modifying the weights according to the extended delta rule and is given by Eq. (2.20)

$$\Delta W_{jk} = \eta \times (D_k - O_k) \times I_k \times f'(sum_k) \quad (2.20)$$

This extended delta rule which is a supervised one is most commonly used in various kinds of BPNs.

## 2.6 PERCEPTRON NETWORK

In 1957, Frank Rosenblatt developed the perceptron at Cornell Aeronautical Laboratory, USA. A perceptron is sometimes called a linear classifier since it can classify an input into one of two possible outputs. A simple perceptron is a single-layer feed-forward NN that uses a supervised learning rule for training. However, multiple layer perceptrons that belong to the second-generation NN are available. There are different kinds of perceptrons that have emerged and are discussed by Frank Rosenblatt [9], Marvin Minsky [10], and Seymour Papert [11].

However, the initial perceptron has three layers in its architecture as sensory neurons, associator neurons, and a response neuron which is sometimes considered to be analogous of a retina model. The perceptron developed by Block in 1962 has sensory neurons connected to the associator units by connection links with fixed weights with value +1, 0, or −1 assigned at random. The transfer function for each associator units is a binary step function with arbitrary fixed threshold. Therefore, the signal sent from the associator units to the output unit is either 1 or 0. The transfer function used in the output neuron of the perceptron is given in Eq. (2.21).

$$f(sum_k) = \begin{cases} 1 & if\ sum_k > \theta_k, \\ 0 & if\ -\theta_k \leq sum_k \leq \theta_k \\ -1 & if\ sum_k < -\theta_k \end{cases} \quad (2.21)$$

The preceptron rule modifies the weights from the associator units to the output unit (response neuron). The rule compares whether the actual output is equal to the target value. If not, it considers an error has occurred. Then the weights will be updated as in Eq. (2.22).

$$W_j(t) = W_j(t-1) + \eta \times D_k \times I_j \quad (2.22)$$

However, if error has not occurred, then there will be no updation of weights. Training will continue till there is no error. It is not necessary that the weights continue to modify correctly to all the input patterns and there are limitations for its convergence. It should be noted the original perceptron has been modified based on the *perceptron learning rule convergence theorem* [12]. Therefore, the assumption of a binary input is not conditional and only the weights from the associator units to the output unit need to be modified. The perceptron NN (Fig. 2.21) as a classifier can be illustrated with a flow chart given in Fig. 2.22.

The network classifies each input pattern into a particular class or group. Whether the input pattern belongs to a class or not depends on the positive or negative response of the output unit. In this perceptron classifier, any binary or bipolar input patterns can be considered with a bipolar target, fixed threshold value $\theta_k$ and an adjustable bias during training process. It should be noted that the positive and negative response region is decided based on a *undecided region* (i.e., $-\theta_k \leq sum_k \leq \theta_k$). Here, a plane separates the two response regions instead of a line. Let us try to train a simple perceptron network to behave like an AND function for two binary inputs and a bipolar output.

Let the initial weight and bias values be $W_1 = 1$, $W_2 = 0$ and $b_k = 0$. In addition, let the fixed threshold value for the activation be $\theta_k = 0.5$. The results of the updated weights and the output response obtained for every epoch (one complete set of training pattern) are tabulated in Table 2.7.

Once the training mode is over, the input patterns of the AND functions can be tested to check whether the perceptron behave like an AND logic function for the given input. The final weights and biases after training is found to $W_1 = 2$, $W_2 = 3$, and $b_k = -4$. Two line Eqs (2.25 and 2.26) for positive and negative response can be obtained from Eqs (2.23 and 2.24) which forms the undecided band. This can be plotted in a two-dimensional plot for two inputs $I_1$ and $I_2$ as in Fig. 2.23.

$$W_1 \times I_1 + W_2 \times I_2 + b_k > \theta_k \tag{2.23}$$

$$W_1 \times I_1 + W_2 \times I_2 + b_k < -\theta_k \tag{2.24}$$

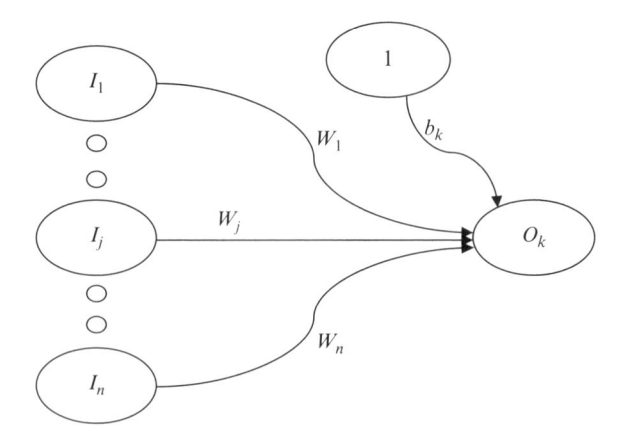

**Fig. 2.21** A simple perceptron as a classifier

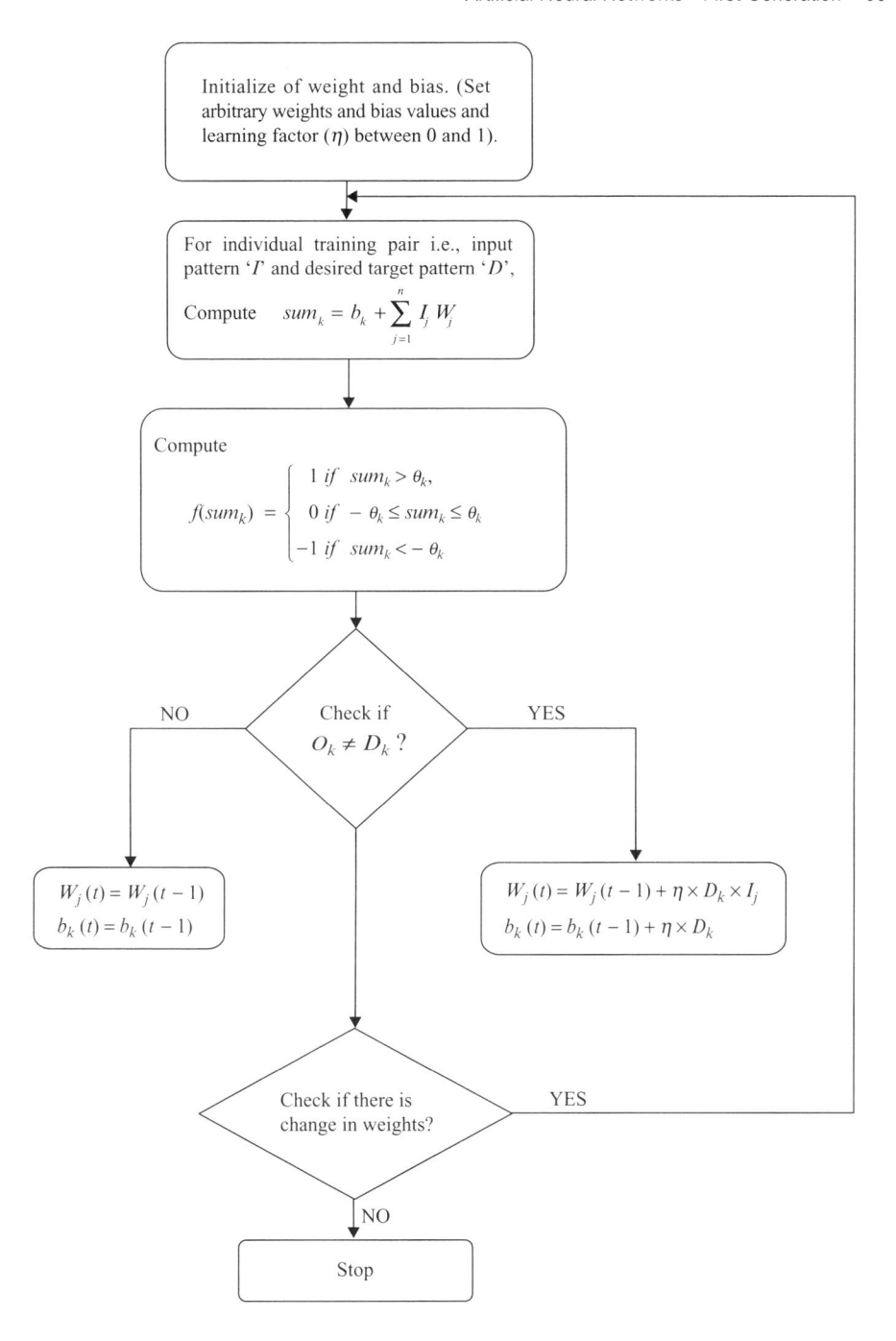

```
┌─────────────────────────────────┐
│ Initialize of weight and bias.  │
│ (Set arbitrary weights and bias │
│ values and learning factor (η)  │
│ between 0 and 1).               │
└─────────────────────────────────┘
                │
                ▼
┌─────────────────────────────────┐
│ For individual training pair    │
│ i.e., input pattern 'I' and     │
│ desired target pattern 'D',     │
│ Compute $sum_k = b_k + \sum_{j=1}^{n} I_j W_j$ │
└─────────────────────────────────┘
                │
                ▼
┌─────────────────────────────────┐
│ Compute                         │
│            ⎧ 1  if $sum_k > \theta_k$,       │
│ $f(sum_k)$ = ⎨ 0  if $-\theta_k \le sum_k \le \theta_k$ │
│            ⎩ -1 if $sum_k < -\theta_k$       │
└─────────────────────────────────┘
                │
                ▼
         Check if $O_k \ne D_k$?
    NO ◄────────┴────────► YES
     │                       │
     ▼                       ▼
┌──────────────┐   ┌──────────────────────────┐
│ $W_j(t) = W_j(t-1)$ │   │ $W_j(t) = W_j(t-1) + \eta \times D_k \times I_j$ │
│ $b_k(t) = b_k(t-1)$ │   │ $b_k(t) = b_k(t-1) + \eta \times D_k$ │
└──────────────┘   └──────────────────────────┘
         │                  │
         └────────┬─────────┘
                  ▼
         Check if there is    YES
         change in weights? ──────►(back to top)
                  │ NO
                  ▼
                Stop
```

**Fig. 2.22** Flow chart of a perceptron algorithm

$$2 \times I_1 + 3 \times I_2 - 4 > 0.5 \text{ Line 1 (Positive region)} \quad (2.25)$$

$$2 \times I_1 + 3 \times I_2 - 4 < -0.5 \text{ Line 2 (Negative region)} \quad (2.26)$$

Table 2.7 Computation of step-by-step training process for AND logic function

| Input (I) | | $sum_{k=1}$ | $O_{k=1}$ | $D_{k=1}$ | Weights (W) | | Bias |
|---|---|---|---|---|---|---|---|
| $I_1$ | $I_2$ | | Output response | Desired target | $W_1 = 1$ | $W_2 = 0$ | $b_k = 0$ |
| 1 | 1 | 1 | 1 | 1 | 0 | 1 | 0 |
| 1 | 0 | 0 | 0 | −1 | −1 | 1 | −1 |
| 0 | 1 | 0 | 0 | −1 | −1 | 0 | −2 |
| 0 | 0 | −2 | −1 | −1 | −1 | 0 | −2 |
| 1 | 1 | −3 | −1 | 1 | 0 | 1 | −1 |
| 1 | 0 | −1 | −1 | −1 | 0 | 1 | −1 |
| 0 | 1 | 0 | 0 | −1 | 0 | 0 | −2 |
| 0 | 0 | −2 | −1 | −1 | 0 | 0 | −2 |
| 1 | 1 | −2 | −1 | 1 | 1 | 1 | −1 |
| 1 | 0 | 0 | 0 | −1 | 0 | 1 | −2 |
| 0 | 1 | −1 | −1 | −1 | 0 | 1 | −2 |
| 0 | 0 | −2 | −1 | −1 | 0 | 1 | −2 |
| 1 | 1 | −1 | −1 | 1 | 1 | 2 | −1 |
| 1 | 0 | 0 | 0 | −1 | 0 | 2 | −2 |
| 0 | 1 | 0 | 0 | −1 | 0 | 1 | −3 |
| 0 | 0 | −3 | −1 | −1 | 0 | 1 | −3 |
| 1 | 1 | −2 | −1 | 1 | 1 | 2 | −2 |
| 1 | 0 | −1 | −1 | −1 | 1 | 2 | −2 |
| 0 | 1 | 0 | 0 | −1 | 1 | 1 | −3 |
| 0 | 0 | −3 | −1 | −1 | 1 | 1 | −3 |
| 1 | 1 | −1 | −1 | 1 | 2 | 2 | −2 |
| 1 | 0 | 0 | 0 | −1 | 1 | 2 | −3 |
| 0 | 1 | −1 | −1 | −1 | 1 | 2 | −3 |
| 0 | 0 | −3 | −1 | −1 | 1 | 2 | −3 |
| 1 | 1 | 0 | 0 | 1 | 2 | 3 | −2 |
| 1 | 0 | 0 | 0 | −1 | 1 | 3 | −3 |
| 0 | 1 | 0 | 0 | −1 | 1 | 2 | −4 |
| 0 | 0 | −4 | −1 | −1 | 1 | 2 | −4 |
| 1 | 1 | −1 | −1 | 1 | 2 | 3 | −3 |
| 1 | 0 | −1 | −1 | −1 | 2 | 3 | −3 |
| 0 | 1 | 0 | 0 | −1 | 0 | 0 | −4 |
| 0 | 0 | −4 | −1 | −1 | 2 | 2 | −4 |
| 1 | 1 | 0 | 0 | 1 | 3 | 3 | −3 |
| 1 | 0 | 0 | 0 | −1 | 2 | 3 | −4 |
| 0 | 1 | −1 | −1 | −1 | 2 | 3 | −4 |
| 0 | 0 | −4 | −1 | −1 | 2 | 3 | −4 |

(Continued)

**Table 2.7** (Continued)

| Input ($I$) | | $sum_{k=1}$ | $O_{k=1}$ Output response | $D_{k=1}$ Desired target | Weights ($W$) | | Bias |
|---|---|---|---|---|---|---|---|
| $I_1$ | $I_2$ | | | | $W_1 = 1$ | $W_2 = 0$ | $b_k = 0$ |
| 1 | 1 | 1 | 1 | 1 | 2 | 3 | −4 |
| 1 | 0 | −2 | −1 | −1 | 2 | 3 | −4 |
| 0 | 1 | −1 | −1 | −1 | 2 | 3 | −4 |
| 0 | 0 | −4 | −1 | −1 | 2 | 3 | −4 |

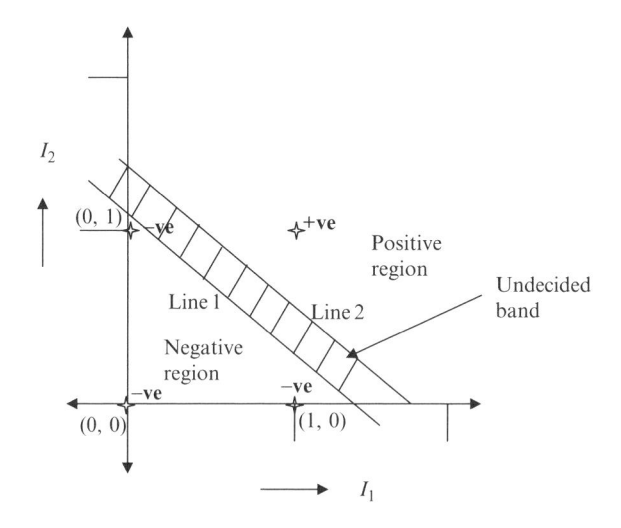

**Fig. 2.23** Decision boundaries of AND function after successful training

Similarly, the computation of step-by-step training process is carried out for OR function and the results are presented in Table 2.8. Both AND and OR logic function is run for 10 epochs. It is found there is no weight modification seen after the presentation of 2nd pattern of 9th epoch and of 3rd pattern of the 4th epoch for AND and OR logic, respectively.

**Table 2.8** Computation of step-by-step training process for OR logic function

| Input ($I$) | | $sum_{k=1}$ | $O_{k=1}$ Output response | $D_{k=1}$ Desired target | Weights ($W$) | | Bias |
|---|---|---|---|---|---|---|---|
| $I_1$ | $I_2$ | | | | $W_1 = 1$ | $W_2 = 0$ | $b_k = 0$ |
| 1 | 1 | 1 | 1 | 1 | 0 | 0 | 0 |
| 1 | 0 | 0 | 0 | 1 | 0 | 0 | 0 |
| 0 | 1 | 2 | 1 | 1 | 1 | 1 | 1 |
| 0 | 0 | 1 | 1 | −1 | 1 | 1 | 0 |
| 1 | 1 | 2 | 1 | 1 | 1 | 1 | 0 |
| 1 | 0 | 1 | 1 | 1 | 1 | 1 | 0 |

(Continued)

**Table 2.8** (Continued)

| Input (*I*) | | sum$_{k=1}$ | $O_{k=1}$ Output response | $D_{k=1}$ Desired target | Weights (*W*) | | Bias |
|---|---|---|---|---|---|---|---|
| $I_1$ | $I_2$ | | | | $W_1 = 1$ | $W_2 = 0$ | $b_k = 0$ |
| 0 | 1 | 1 | 1 | 1 | 1 | 1 | 0 |
| 0 | 0 | 0 | 0 | −1 | 1 | 1 | −1 |
| 1 | 1 | 1 | 1 | 1 | 1 | 1 | −1 |
| 1 | 0 | 0 | 0 | 1 | 2 | 2 | 0 |
| 0 | 1 | 1 | 1 | 1 | 2 | 1 | 0 |
| 0 | 0 | 0 | 0 | −1 | 2 | 1 | −1 |
| 1 | 1 | 2 | 1 | 1 | 2 | 1 | −1 |
| 1 | 0 | 1 | 1 | 1 | 2 | 1 | −1 |
| 0 | 1 | 0 | 0 | 1 | 2 | 2 | 0 |
| 0 | 0 | 0 | 0 | −1 | 2 | 2 | −1 |
| 1 | 1 | 3 | 1 | 1 | 2 | 2 | −1 |
| 1 | 0 | 1 | 1 | 1 | 2 | 2 | −1 |
| 0 | 1 | 1 | 1 | 1 | 2 | 2 | −1 |
| 0 | 0 | −1 | −1 | −1 | 2 | 2 | −1 |
| 1 | 1 | 3 | 1 | 1 | 2 | 2 | −1 |
| 1 | 0 | 1 | 1 | 1 | 2 | 2 | −1 |
| 0 | 1 | 1 | 1 | 1 | 2 | 2 | −1 |
| 0 | 0 | −1 | −1 | −1 | 2 | 2 | −1 |
| 1 | 1 | 3 | 1 | 1 | 2 | 2 | −1 |
| 1 | 0 | 1 | 1 | 1 | 2 | 2 | −1 |
| 0 | 1 | 1 | 1 | 1 | 2 | 2 | −1 |
| 0 | 0 | −1 | −1 | −1 | 2 | 2 | −1 |
| 1 | 1 | 3 | 1 | 1 | 2 | 2 | −1 |
| 1 | 0 | 1 | 1 | 1 | 2 | 2 | −1 |
| 0 | 1 | 1 | 1 | 1 | 2 | 2 | −1 |
| 0 | 0 | −1 | −1 | −1 | 2 | 2 | −1 |
| 1 | 1 | 3 | 1 | 1 | 2 | 2 | −1 |
| 1 | 0 | 1 | 1 | 1 | 2 | 2 | −1 |
| 0 | 1 | 1 | 1 | 1 | 2 | 2 | −1 |
| 0 | 0 | −1 | −1 | −1 | 2 | 2 | −1 |

A MATLAB code has been presented with detailed comments in the following steps to test the previously mentioned logic and can further be generalized for multiple input-output patterns.

## MATLAB Program 2.1

### Part A: Main program

```
%%%%%%%%%%%%%%%%%%%%%%%%%%%%%%%%%%%%%%%%%%%%%%%%%%
% SOLVING AND / OR LOGIC FUNCTIONS USING A PERCEPTRON NEURAL NETWORK
%%%%%%%%%%%%%%%%%%%%%%%%%%%%%%%%%%%%%%%%%%%%%%%%%%

% CLEARING ALL PREVIOUS DATA

clear workspace
clear all
clc
format long

% GET THE INPUT PATTERNS (I) AND THE DESIRED TARGET PATTERNS (D)

% AND FUNCTION

% I=[1 1; 1 0; 0 1; 0 0];      % Two input 4 binary patterns
% D=[1;-1;-1;-1];              % Single output 4 bipolar pattern

% OR FUNCTION

I=[1 1; 1 0; 0 1; 0 0];        % Two input 4 binary patterns
D=[1; 1; 1; -1];               % Single output 4 bipolar pattern

% INITIALIZATION OF THE NETWORK PARAMETERS

w=[0 1];   % Initial weights between input units to the output unit

b=[0];                         % Initial bias value
eta=1;                         % Learning factor
teta=0.5;                      % Threshold value of the activation function
epoch=10;                      % Maximum number of ireration

np=4;                          % No of input and output patterns
nj=2;                          % No of input units
mk=1;                          % No of output units

% TRAINING MODE

for iter=1:epoch,
disp('Epoch number');
disp(iter);
for p=1:np
disp('Pattern number');
disp(p);
for k=1:mk
sumk(k,1)=0;                   % Initialize the sum
out(k,1)=0;                    % Initialize the sum
for n=1:nj
sumk(k,1)=sumk(k,1)+I(p,n).*w(1,n);
% Calculating the weighted sum for the first input pattern
end
disp('The weighted sum to be sent into the output unit k');
sumk(k,1)=sumk(k,1)+b(k,1)     % Weighted sum inclusive of bias value
disp('The output response at output unit k');
out(k,1)=bifun(sumk(k,1),teta) % Applying activation function for output response
end
```

```matlab
% CHECKING IF WEIGHT AND BIAS UPDATION IS NECESSARY OR NOT?

for k=1:mk
disp('Check whether the output response and target response are same');
disp('The desired target response needed at output unit k');
disp(D(p,k));
disp('The actual output response at output unit k');
disp(out(k,1));
if out(k,1)~=D(p,k),
for n=1:nj
disp('Weight modification is necessary since there is an error');
disp('Since the actual output is not equal to the desired target value');
disp('The weight values');
disp(n)

% UPDATION OF WEIGHTS AND BIASES

w(1,n)=w(1,n)+eta.*D(p,k).*I(p,n) % Weight updation
end
disp('The bias value');
b(k,1)=b(k,1)+eta.*D(p,k)        % Bias updation
else
disp('Weight modification is not necessary since there is an error');
disp('Since the actual ouput is equal to the desired target value');
for n=1:nj
disp('The weight values');
disp(n)
w(1,n)=w(1,n)                    % No weight updation
end
disp('The bias value');
b(k,1)=b(k,1)                    % No bias updation
end
end
end
disp('Please press a tab to continue');
pause
end
disp('End of the training phase and maximum epoch is reached');

% TESTING MODE

disp('Testing mode started');
disp('To check whether the perceptron behaves like a AND function');
I=input('Give the any possible 2 binary input as 1 x 2 matrix format =');
p=1;                             % Here only one test pattern is given for testing
for k=1:mk
sumk(k,1)=0;                     % Initialize the sum
out(k,1)=0;                      % Initialize the sum
for n=1:nj
sumk(k,1)=sumk(k,1)+I(p,n).*w(1,n);
% Calculating the weighted sum for the first input pattern
end
disp('The weighted sum to be sent into the output unit k');
sumk(k,1)=sumk(k,1)+b(k,1)       % Weighted sum inclusive of bias value
disp('The output response at k output unit');
out(k,1)=bifun(sumk(k,1),teta)
% Applying activation function for output response
end
disp('If the test output is correct for the all given input patterns');
disp('Then the aim of the perceptron network is successful');
disp('Congrats you have understood the working of perceptron');
disp('You can also try to run the matlab code for OR logic')
disp('if you have completed AND logic experiment by commenting')
```

```
disp('AND input/output training patterns and uncommenting')
disp('OR input/output training patterns')
```

**Part B: Sub-programs (Subroutine functions)**

OBJECTIVE FUNCTION

```
function[out] = bifun(sumk,teta)

% ACTIVATION FUNCTION THAT GIVES BINARY/BIPOLAR OUTPUT

out=0;
if sumk>teta,              % If sumk greater than threshold value
out=1;                     % Then the output response is one
end
if-teta<=sumk<=teta,
% If sumk is between the negative and positive threshold value
out=0;                     % Then the output response is zero
end
if sumk<-teta,             % If sumk greater than negative threshold value
out=-1;                    % Then the output response is negative one
end
```

## 2.6.1 Perceptron Linear Separability

In a two-dimensional space, if two sets of points can be separated by a single line, then the sets satisfy the property of *linear seperability* [7]. Let us see some example of a set of four points in a two-dimensional space as illustrated in Fig. 2.24.

In Fig. 2.24, plots A, B, and C can be easily separated by a single line and are able to classify the four points into two classes as positive and negative regions. However, there are scatter of points which cannot be separated by a single line.

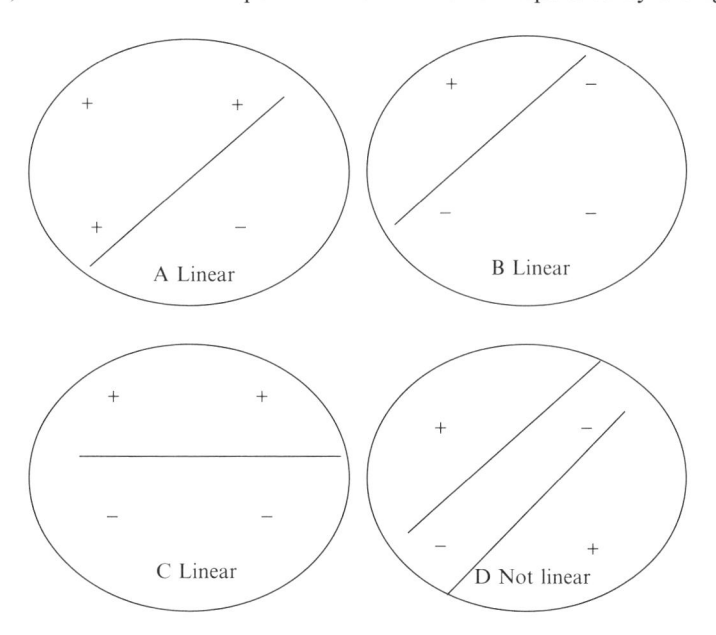

**Fig. 2.24** Illustration of linear seperability

They do not satisfy the property of linear seperability as in plot D of Fig. 2.24. However, those scatter of points can be separated by two lines forming a plane.

The perceptron we have discussed in the previous section for AND/OR logic problem, have the ability to satisfy the property of linear seperability. However, it cannot solve for the classification of XOR problem. Let us consider the truth table of 2-binary input/1-bipolar output of AND, OR, NAND, NOR, and XOR logic tabulated in Table 2.9.

**Table 2.9** Truth table of AND, OR, NAND, NOR, and XOR logic

| Binary inputs ($I$) | | Bipolar outputs | | | | |
|---|---|---|---|---|---|---|
| | | AND | OR | NAND | NOR | XOR |
| $I_1$ | $I_2$ | $O_1$ | $O_1$ | $O_1$ | $O_1$ | $O_1$ |
| 1 | 1 | 1 | 1 | −1 | −1 | −1 |
| 1 | 0 | −1 | 1 | 1 | −1 | 1 |
| 0 | 1 | −1 | 1 | 1 | −1 | 1 |
| 0 | 0 | −1 | −1 | 1 | 1 | −1 |

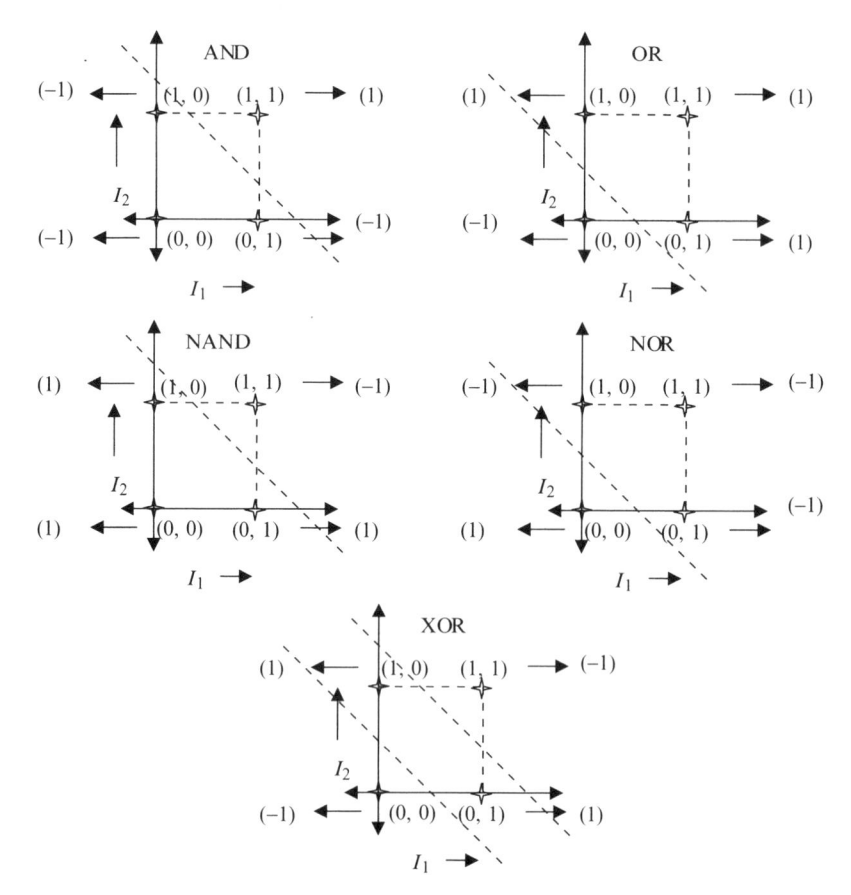

**Fig. 2.25** Illustration of linear seperability for AND, OR, NAND, NOR, and XOR logic

From Fig. 2.25, it is obvious that XOR problem cannot be classified into any of the two classes. It is possible for the perceptron to get trained and behave such as AND, OR, NAND, and NOR logics, but it is impossible for the XOR problem. This can be verified by using MATLAB Program 2.1 by properly giving the input and target patterns for the logics presented in Fig. 2.25.

Therefore, it can be concluded that, single-layer perceptron cannot solve problems which do not possess the property of linear seperability. This is the problem that has been reported by Minsky and Papert in 1969. Due to this problem, there is slight stagnation in the initial development of NNs. However, after the BPN modelled by Rumelhart, Hinton and Williams in 1986, the neural applications has penetrated into all fields of engineering and science.

## 2.7 ADALINE NETWORK

Professor Bernard Widrow and his student Ted Hoff at Stanford University in 1960 developed a single-layer neuron called Adaline (adaptive linear neuron). Adaline uses bipolar inputs and output. The weights and bias are adjusted based on delta rule or least mean squares (LMS) or Widrow-Hoff rule.

Adaline differs from McCulloch-Pitts only in with the modification of weights according to the weighted sum of the inputs $sum_k$. In addition, Adaline differs from the standard perceptron with respect to the passage of $sum_k$ into the activation or transfer function and the output response is used for the modification of weights. It should be noted that the Adaline has only one output unit and activation function is the identity function (Table 2.3).

The learning rule minimizes the mean SE and the activation function output same as the weighted sum of the inputs (since the transfer function is a linear one). However, Adaline network can also be used as a classifier with bivalent activation function using binary inputs and bipolar outputs. The architecture of the Adaline is similar to the perceptron as in Fig. 2.21. The flow chart of the Adaline algorithm is shown in Fig. 2.26.

Heicht-Nielsen [13] suggested the setting of learning factor by finding the correlation matrix $C_M$ of the input row vectors $I(p)$, where $I$ is the input vector of pattern $P$. The $C_M$ is given in Eq. 2.27.

$$C_M = \frac{1}{P} \sum_{p=1}^{P} I(p)^T I(p) \qquad (2.27)$$

He suggested that $\eta <$ one-half of the eigenvalue of $C_M$. However, for a single neuron, the range of the learning rate is within $0.1 \le n \times \eta \le 1$.

A MATLAB Program 2.2 is given as follows to check the modification of weights and bias during training. The program can be exercised with different learning factors, input, and output patterns.

## Flow chart of an Adaline algorithm

- Initialize weight/bias values as small random values. Set learning rate ($\eta$) within $0.1 \leq n \times n \leq 1$, and the tolerance limit of weight change

- For each bipolar training pair ie, input pattern 'I' and desired target pattern 'D',
  Compute $sum_k = b_k + \sum_{j=1}^{n} I_j W_j$

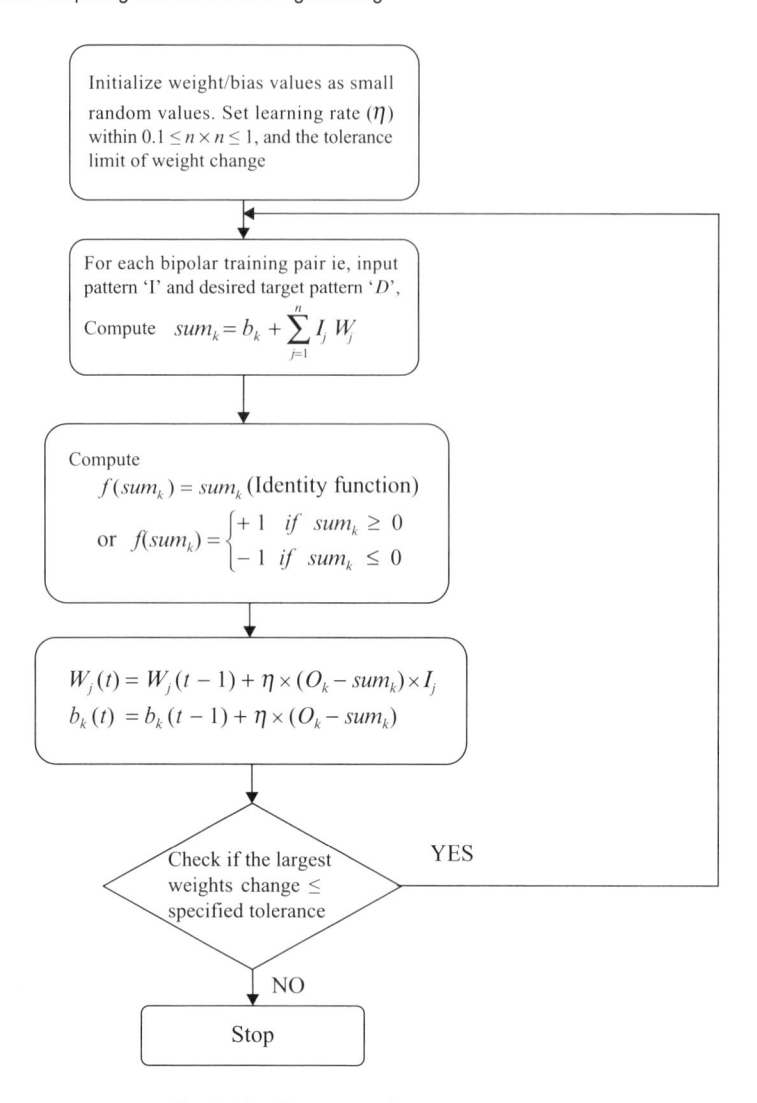

- Compute
  $f(sum_k) = sum_k$ (Identity function)
  or $f(sum_k) = \begin{cases} +1 & if \ sum_k \geq 0 \\ -1 & if \ sum_k \leq 0 \end{cases}$

- $W_j(t) = W_j(t-1) + \eta \times (O_k - sum_k) \times I_j$
  $b_k(t) = b_k(t-1) + \eta \times (O_k - sum_k)$

- Check if the largest weights change $\leq$ specified tolerance
  - YES → (loop back)
  - NO → Stop

**Fig. 2.26** Flow chart of an Adaline algorithm

## MATLAB Program 2.2

### Part A: Main program

```
%%%%%%%%%%%%%%%%%%%%%%%%%%%%%%%%%%%%%%
% WEIGHT AND BIAS UPDATION FOR AN ADALINE NEURON
%%%%%%%%%%%%%%%%%%%%%%%%%%%%%%%%%%%%%%

% CLEARING ALL PREVIOUS DATA

clear workspace
clear all
clc
format long
```

```
% GETS THE INPUT PATTERNS (I) AND THE DESIRED TARGET PATTERNS (D)

I=[1 1;1-1;-1 1;-1-1];          % Two input 4 bipolar patterns
D=[1;-1;-1;-1];                 % Single output 4 bipolar pattern

% INITIALIZATION OF THE NETWORK PARAMETERS

w=randn(1,2);
% Initializing small random weights values between input units to the output unit
b=randn(1);                     % Initializing small random bias value
toll=0.4;
% Maximum tolerance of change in weights that is allowed to take place
eta=0.2;                        % Learning factor
maxepoch=100;                   % Maximum number of epochs
np=4;                           % No of input and output patterns
nj=2;                           % No of input units
mk=1;                           % No of output units

% TRAINING MODE

t=1;
wrec=w;                         % Storing the initial weights
brec=b;                         % Storing the initial bias value
for iter=1:maxepoch,
% For the maximum number of epochs to be trained
disp('Epoch number');
disp(iter);
for p=1:np
t=t+1;
disp('Pattern number');
disp(p);
for k=1:mk
sumk(k,1)=0;                    % Initialize the sum
out(k,1)=0;                     % Initialize the output
for n=1:nj
sumk(k,1)=sumk(k,1)+I(p,n).*w(1,n); % Calculating the weighted sum
end
disp('The weighted sum to be sent into the output unit k');
sumk(k,1)=sumk(k,1)+b(k,1)      % Weighted sum inclusive of bias value
disp('The output response at output unit k');
out(k,1)=identityfun(sumk(k,1))
% Applying linear activation function for output response
end

% WEIGHT UPDATION

for k=1:mk
for n=1:nj
disp('The weight values');
w(1,n)=w(1,n)+eta.*(D(p,k)sumk(k,1)).*I(p,n) % Weight updation

% EVALUATING THE CHANGE IN WEIGHT

delw=w(1,n)-wrec(t-1,n);
% Change in weights with respect to previous weight
end
disp('The weight values');
w                               % Displaying the weight values
wrec(t,:)=w;                    % Recording the weight values
disp('The bias value');
b(k,1)=b(k,1)+eta.*(D(p,k)sumk(k,1))  % Bias updation
brec(t,1)=b;                    % Recording the bias values
```

```
end
end

% STOPPING CRITERIA

if delw>toll
% Checking if the weight change is less than the tolerance
break
end
end

disp('No of epochs trained');
disp(iter);
disp('End of the training phase due to large weight change');
disp('or the maximum epoch has reached');
disp('Modification of weights and bias from the first epoch')
disp('      W1              W2              b');
disp([wrec brec])
% Displaying the recorded weights and bias values
```

### Part B: Subprograms (Subroutine functions)

OBJECTIVE FUNCTION

```
function[out] = identity(sumk,teta)

% ACTIVATION FUNCTION THAT GIVE LINEAR OUTPUT

out=sumk
```

## 2.8 MADALINE NETWORK

Many Adalines (many adaptive linear neuron) arranged in a multi-layer networks constitute the Madaline network (Figs 2.27 and 2.21)

A simple Madaline is shown in Fig. 2.27. The Madaline has two inputs $I_1$ and $I_2$ connected through weights $W_{11}$, $W_{12}$, $W_{21}$, and $W_{22}$. Two hidden Adalines $H_1$ and $H_2$ are connected to the output unit through fixed weights $Z_1$ and $Z_2$. The hidden

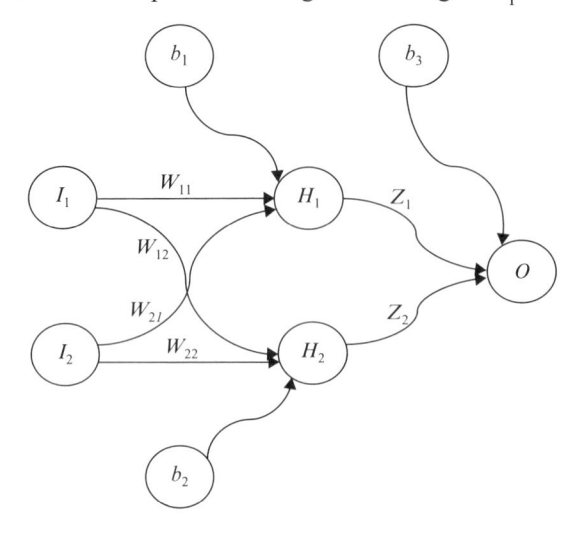

**Fig. 2.27** 2-Input/2-Hidden/1-Output units/2-Layer Madaline network

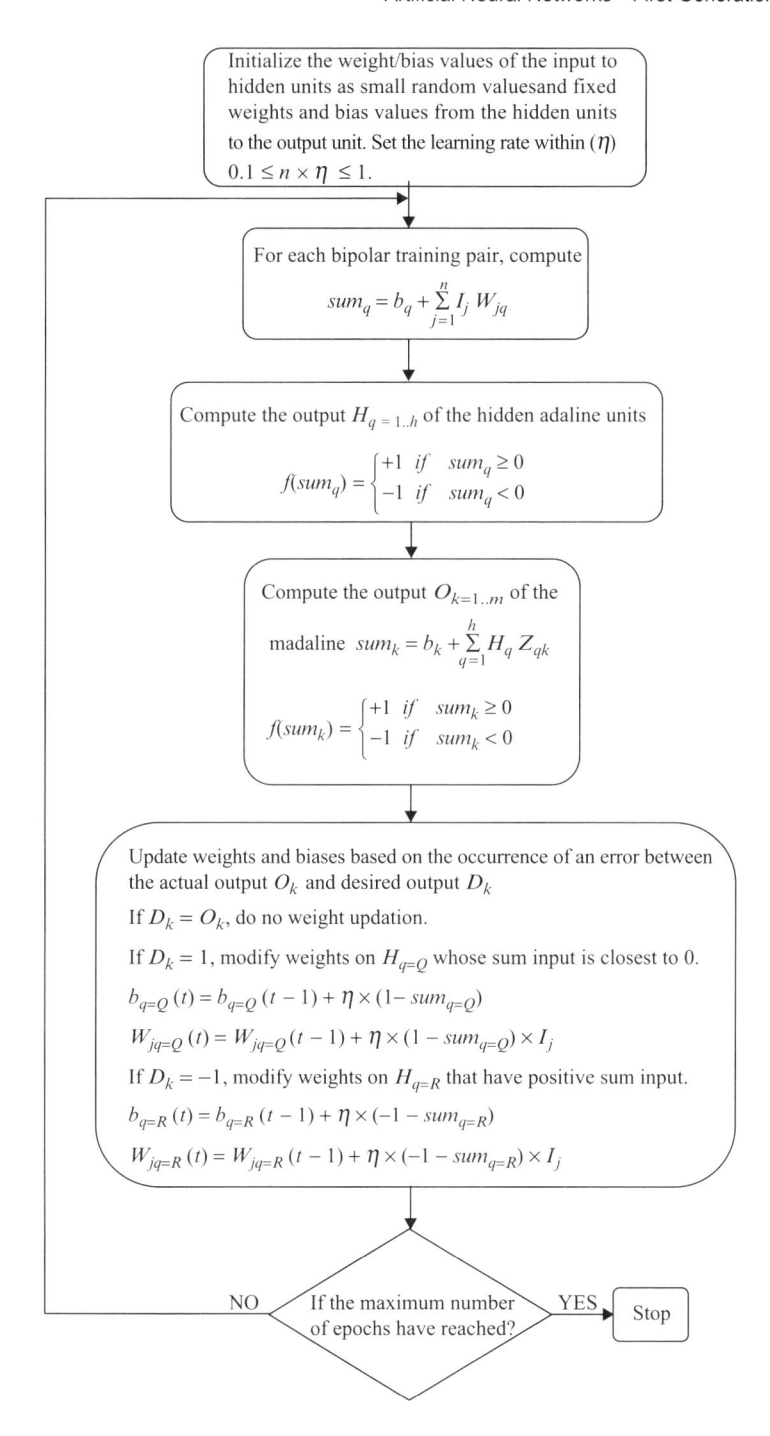

```
┌─────────────────────────────────────────┐
│ Initialize the weight/bias values of the input to │
│ hidden units as small random values and fixed │
│ weights and bias values from the hidden units │
│ to the output unit. Set the learning rate within ($\eta$) │
│ $0.1 \leq n \times \eta \leq 1$. │
└─────────────────────────────────────────┘
                    │
                    ▼
┌─────────────────────────────────────────┐
│ For each bipolar training pair, compute │
│ $sum_q = b_q + \sum_{j=1}^{n} I_j W_{jq}$ │
└─────────────────────────────────────────┘
                    │
                    ▼
┌─────────────────────────────────────────┐
│ Compute the output $H_{q=1..h}$ of the hidden adaline units │
│ $f(sum_q) = \begin{cases} +1 & if \ sum_q \geq 0 \\ -1 & if \ sum_q < 0 \end{cases}$ │
└─────────────────────────────────────────┘
                    │
                    ▼
┌─────────────────────────────────────────┐
│ Compute the output $O_{k=1..m}$ of the │
│ madaline $sum_k = b_k + \sum_{q=1}^{h} H_q Z_{qk}$ │
│ $f(sum_k) = \begin{cases} +1 & if \ sum_k \geq 0 \\ -1 & if \ sum_k < 0 \end{cases}$ │
└─────────────────────────────────────────┘
                    │
                    ▼
┌─────────────────────────────────────────┐
│ Update weights and biases based on the occurrence of an error between │
│ the actual output $O_k$ and desired output $D_k$ │
│ If $D_k = O_k$, do no weight updation. │
│ If $D_k = 1$, modify weights on $H_{q=Q}$ whose sum input is closest to 0. │
│ $b_{q=Q}(t) = b_{q=Q}(t-1) + \eta \times (1 - sum_{q=Q})$ │
│ $W_{jq=Q}(t) = W_{jq=Q}(t-1) + \eta \times (1 - sum_{q=Q}) \times I_j$ │
│ If $D_k = -1$, modify weights on $H_{q=R}$ that have positive sum input. │
│ $b_{q=R}(t) = b_{q=R}(t-1) + \eta \times (-1 - sum_{q=R})$ │
│ $W_{jq=R}(t) = W_{jq=R}(t-1) + \eta \times (-1 - sum_{q=R}) \times I_j$ │
└─────────────────────────────────────────┘
                    │
                    ▼
         NO  ◇ If the maximum number ◇  YES  → Stop
              of epochs have reached?
```

**Fig. 2.28** Flow chart of Madaline NN

units increase the network capabilities not available in a single-layer NN. For example, linear inseparable problems can be solved using Madaline network. Here, the output of the Adaline units consists of non-linear activation function.

Table 2.10 Training results for every Epoch for XOR logic

| Input | | $sum_k$ | | Hidden Adalines output | | $sum_{k=1}$ | $O_{k=1}$ | $D_{k=1}$ | Weights (W) $Z_1 = 0.5, Z_2 = 0.6$ | | | | Bias (Bh) | |
|---|---|---|---|---|---|---|---|---|---|---|---|---|---|---|
| $I_1$ | $I_2$ | $sum_{q=1}$ | $sum_{q=2}$ | $H_{q=1}$ | $H_{q=2}$ | | | | $W_{11}=$ 0.1 | $W_{12}=$ 0.2 | $W_{12}=$ 0.3 | $W_{12}=$ 0.4 | $b_{q=1}=$ 0.5 | $b_{q=2}=$ 0.5 |
| 1 | 1 | 0.90 | 1.10 | 1 | 1 | 1.60 | 1 | −1 | −1.23 | −1.27 | −1.03 | −1.07 | −0.83 | −0.97 |
| 1 | −1 | −1.03 | −1.17 | −1 | −1 | −0.60 | −1 | 1 | 0.19 | −1.27 | −2.45 | −1.07 | 0.59 | −0.97 |
| −1 | 1 | −2.05 | −0.77 | −1 | −1 | −0.60 | −1 | 1 | 0.19 | −2.51 | −2.45 | 0.17 | 0.59 | 0.27 |
| −1 | −1 | 2.85 | 2.61 | 1 | 1 | 1.60 | 1 | −1 | 2.89 | 0.02 | 0.25 | 0.27 | −2.11 | −2.26 |
| 1 | 1 | 1.03 | 0.455 | 1 | 1 | 1.60 | 1 | −1 | 1.47 | −1.00 | −1.17 | 1.68 | −3.52 | −3.28 |
| 1 | −1 | −0.88 | −5.95 | −1 | −1 | −0.60 | −1 | 1 | 2.79 | −1.00 | −2.49 | 1.68 | −2.21 | −3.28 |
| −1 | 1 | −7.48 | −0.60 | −1 | −1 | −0.60 | −1 | 1 | 2.79 | −2.12 | −2.49 | 2.80 | −2.21 | −2.16 |
| −1 | −1 | −2.50 | −2.83 | −1 | −1 | −0.6 | −1 | 1 | 2.79 | −2.12 | −2.49 | 2.80 | −2.21 | −2.16 |
| 1 | 1 | −1.91 | −1.48 | −1 | −1 | −0.6 | −1 | 1 | 2.79 | −2.12 | −2.49 | 2.80 | −2.21 | −2.16 |
| 1 | −1 | 3.07 | −7.07 | 1 | −1 | 0.4 | 1 | −1 | 2.79 | −2.12 | −2.49 | 2.80 | −2.21 | −2.16 |
| −1 | 1 | −7.48 | 2.76 | −1 | 1 | 0.6 | 1 | −1 | 2.79 | −2.12 | −2.49 | 2.80 | −2.21 | −2.16 |
| −1 | −1 | −2.50 | −2.83 | −1 | −1 | −0.6 | −1 | 1 | 2.79 | −2.12 | −2.49 | 2.80 | −2.21 | −2.16 |
| 1 | 1 | −1.91 | −1.48 | −1 | −1 | −0.6 | −1 | 1 | 2.79 | −2.12 | −2.49 | 2.80 | −2.21 | −2.16 |
| 1 | −1 | 3.07 | −7.07 | 1 | −1 | 0.4 | 1 | −1 | 2.79 | −2.12 | −2.49 | 2.80 | −2.21 | −2.16 |
| −1 | 1 | −7.48 | 2.76 | −1 | 1 | 0.6 | 1 | −1 | 2.79 | −2.12 | −2.49 | 2.80 | −2.21 | −2.16 |
| −1 | −1 | −2.50 | −2.83 | −1 | −1 | −0.6 | −1 | 1 | 2.79 | −2.12 | −2.49 | 2.80 | −2.21 | −2.16 |

Widrow and Hoff [14] proposed the original Madline called MRI (Madaline Rule One). Here, the weights from the hidden Adalines are adjusted keeping the output units weights fixed. However in 1987, Widrow, Winter, and Baxter proposed another Madaline, called MRII (Madaline Rule Two), where the weights in the net are modified during training.

Let us try to illustrate MRI with 2-Input/2-Hidden/1-Output units for solving a XOR problem using the flow chart given in Fig. 2.28. Therefore, here $n = 2$, $h = 2$, and $m = 1$ where $j$, $q$, and $k$ are the indices of the input, hidden, and output units, respectively. $Q$ and $R$ are the specific indices which meet the required conditions.

A MATLAB Program 2.3 is given to solve the XOR problem for bipolar patterns.

## MATLAB Program 2.3

### Part A: Main program

```
%%%%%%%%%%%%%%%%%%%%%%%%%%%%%%%%%%%%%%%%%%%%%%
% MADALINE RULE-I (MRI) FOR SOLVING XOR PROBLEM
%%%%%%%%%%%%%%%%%%%%%%%%%%%%%%%%%%%%%%%%%%%%%%

% CLEARING ALL PREVIOUS DATA

clear workspace
clear all
clc
format short

% INPUT/OUTPUT BIPOLAR PATTERNS FOR XOR PROBLEM

P=4;                        % Number of training pairs (index-p)
n=2;                        % Number of input units (index-j)
h=2;                        % Number of hidden adaline units (index-q)
m=1;                        % Number of output adaline units (index-k)
I=[1,1;1,-1;-1,-1,-1];      % Input patterns
D=[-1;1,1,-1];              % Desired target patterns
eta=0.7;                    % Learning rate
Z=[0.5;0.6];
% Fixed weights from hidden adalines to output adaline
Bm=0.5;                     % Fixed bias for the output adaline
W=[0.1,0.2;0.3,0.4];        % Initial weights from input to hidden
Bh=[0.5;0.5];               % Initial bias for hidden adalines

maxepoch=input('Number of epochs to be carried out =');
% Enter 4 to get the tabulated results as in Table 2.10
display('Initial weights');    % Displaying the initial weights
display(W);
display('Initial bias values'); % Displaying the initial bias
display(Bh);
for iter=1:maxepoch
for p=1:P
sumh=zeros(h,1);            % Initializing the sum variable to zero
H=zeros(h,1);               % Initializing the hidden output variable to zero

% CALCULATING WEIGHTED SUM INCLUSIVE OF BIAS FOR THE HIDDEN ADALINE OUTPUTS

for q=1:h,
for j=1:n,
```

```matlab
sumh(q)=sumh(q)+I(p,j)*W(j,q);  % Weighted sum without bias
end
sumh(q)=sumh(q)+Bh(q);          % Weighted sum with bias
H(q)=bipolarfun(sumh(q));       % Applying activation function for output response
end
display('Weighted sum to the hidden adaline units');
display(sumh)
display('Output of the hidden adaline units')
display(H)
summ=zeros(m,1);                % Initializing the sum variable to zero
O=zeros(m,1);                   % Initializing the madaline output unit to zero

% CALCULATING WEIGHTED SUM INCLUSIVE OF BIAS FOR THE OUTPUT ADALINE

for k=1:m,
for q=1:h,
summ(k)=summ(k)+H(q,k)*Z(q,k);  % Weighted sum without bias
end
summ(k)=summ(k)+Bm(k);          % Weighted sum with bias
O(k)=bipolarfun(summ(k));
% Applying activation function for output response
end
display('Weighted sum to the output adaline units');
display(summ)
display('Output of the output adaline units')
display(O)

% CHECKING IF WEIGHT UPDATION FROM INPUT TO HIDDEN ADALINE IS NECESSARY

for k=1:m,
if D(p,k)==O(k),
% If desired target is matching with actual output,no weight and bias updation
disp('No need of weight updation since the desired target and output are matching');
end
end

for k=1:m,

if D(p,k)~=O(k),
% If the desired target value is not equal to the actual output
if D(p,k)==1,                   % If the desired target value is equal to one
disp('Desired target=1')
disp('Need weight updation since the desired target and output are not matching');

% FINDING THE Q$^{TH}$ HIDDEN UNIT WHOSE WEIGHTED SUM INPUT IS CLOSEST TO ZERO

dist=(sumh-O).^2;
% Square distance from the weighted sum inputs of the hidden adaline units
% to zero
Q=find(dist==min(dist));
% Finding the index of the hidden units whose sum input is closest to zero
for j=1:n
W(j,Q(1,1))=W(j,Q(1,1))+eta*(1-sumh(Q(1,1)))*I(p,j);  % Modification of weights
end
Bh(Q(1,1))=Bh(Q(1,1))+eta*(1-sumh(Q(1,1)));           % Modification of bias values
end
end

if D(p,k)~=O(k),
% If the desired target value is not eqaul to the actual output
```

```
if D(p,k)==-1,
% If the desired target value is equal to negative one
disp('Desired target=-1');
disp('Need weight updation since the desired target and output are not
matching');
R=find(sumh>0);
% Finding the index for which R$^{th}$ hidden units weighted sum inputs are positive
siz=size(R);
rz=siz(1,1);
% Rowsize or Number of hidden adaline unit whose weighted sum inputs are positive
for r=1:rz,
for j=1:n
W(j,R(r))=W(j,R(r))+eta*(-1-sumh(R(r)))*I(p,j);      % Modification of weights
end
Bh(R(r))=Bh(R(r))+eta*(-1-sumh(R(r)));
% If the desired target value is equal to negative one
end
end
end

disp('No of patterns completed')
disp(p);
disp('Modified weights between input to hidden adalines');
disp(W);
disp('Bias values between input to hidden adalines');
disp(Bh);
disp('Please press the tab to continue....');
disp('Next pattern will be given as input');
pause
end
disp('No of epochs completed');
disp(iter)
disp(' Weights between input to hidden adalines');
disp(W);
disp('Bias values between input to hidden adalines');
disp(Bh);
disp('Please press the tab to continue....');
pause
if iter==maxepoch,
disp('Maximum epochs reached and program terminates here')
end
end

% TESTING MODE

disp( 'Testing mode started');
I=input( 'Give the bipolar test input pattern in 1 x 2 matrix format =' )
sumh=zeros(h,1);               % Initializing the sum variable to zero
H=zeros(h,1);
% Initializing the hidden adaline output units to zero

% CALCULATING WEIGHTED SUM INCLUSIVE OF BIAS AND THE HIDDEN ADALINE OUTPUT

for q=1:h,
for j=1:n,
sumh(q)=sumh(q)+I(1,j)*W(j,q);   % Weighted sum without bias
end
sumh(q)=sumh(q)+Bh(q);           % Weighted sum with bias
H(q)=bipolarfun(sumh(q));
```

```
% Applying activation function for the hidden adaline output end
display('Weighted sum to the hidden adaline units');
display(sumh)
display('Output of the hidden adaline units')
display(H)
summ=zeros(m,1);          % Initializing the sum variable to zero
O=zeros(m,1);             % Initializing the madaline output unit to zero

% CALCULATING WEIGHTED SUM INCLUSIVE OF BIAS AND THE HIDDEN ADALINE OUTPUT

for k=1:m,
for q=1:h,
summ(k)=summ(k)+H(q,k)*Z(q,k); % Weighted sum without bias
end
summ(k)=summ(k)+Bm(k);    % Weighted sum wiht bias
O(k)=bipolarfun(summ(k)); % Output of the madaline unit
display('Weighted sum to the output adaline units');
display(summ)
display('Output of the output adaline units')
display(O)
end

disp('If the test output is correct for the all given input patterns');
disp('Then the aim of the madaline network for solving XOR problem is
successful');
disp('Congrats you have understood the working of madaline');
disp('You can also try to run the matlab code for AND,OR,NAND,NOR logic')
```

The initial weight and bias values between input to hidden Adaline units are $W_{11} = 0.1$, $W_{12} = 0.2$, $W_{21} = 0.3$, $W_{22} = 0.4$, and $b_1 = 0.5$, $b_2 = 0.5$, respectively. In addition, the fixed weights and bias values from hidden Adalines to an output Adaline unit is $Z_{11} = 0.5$, $Z_{21} = 0.6$, and $b_3 = 0.5$, respectively. The learning rate $\eta$ is kept as 0.7. The algorithm is run for a maximum of 4 epochs. The training is successful and the weights and bias values did not change from the 4th pattern of 2nd epoch. Once the training mode is over, all the 2-input bipolar input patterns are tested, and the output of the XOR logic is verified. Now, the Madaline network behaves like XOR logic. The earlier mentioned MATLAB code (MATLAB Program 2.3) has been presented with detailed comments to test this logic, and it can further be generalized for multiple input-output patterns.

## 2.9 ILLUSTRATIVE PROBLEMS

**Example 2.1**

Consider a single-layer perceptron having 2 inputs and 1 output. Let threshold be 0.5, learning rate be 0.6, bias be $-2$ and weight values $w_1 = 0.3$ and $w_2 = 0.7$. Given the input patterns in the table, compute the value of the output and train using perceptron learning rule for one epoch.

Table 2.11  Source/Target pattern

| $x_1$ | $x_2$ | D |
|---|---|---|
| 1 | 1 | 1 |
| 1 | 0 | 1 |
| 0 | 1 | −1 |
| 0 | 0 | 1 |

**Solution:** *Taking first training pattern*
$sum_1 = x_1 \times w_1 + x_2 \times w_2 + b = 1 \times 0.3 + 1 \times 0.7 - 2 = -1$
From Eq. 2.21, the output is given by
$O_1 = f(sum_1) = f(-1) = -1$
Since $T \ne O_1$, we need to change the weight values
$w_1(t) = w_1(t-1) + \eta \times D \times I_1 = 0.3 + 0.6 \times 1 \times 1 = 0.9$
$w_2(t) = w_2(t-1) + \eta \times D \times I_2 = 0.7 + 0.6 \times 1 \times 1 = 1.3$
$b(t) = b(t-1) + \eta \times D = -2 + 0.6 \times 1 = -1.4$

*Taking second training pattern*
$sum_1 = x_1 \times w_1 + x_2 \times w_2 + b = 1 \times 0.9 + 0 \times 1.3 - 1.4 = -0.5$
The output is given by
$O_1 = f(sum_1) = f(-0.5) = 0$
Since $T \ne O_1$, we need to change the weight values
$w_1(t) = w_1(t-1) + \eta \times D \times I_1 = 0.9 + 0.6 \times 1 \times 1 = 1.5$
$w_2(t) = w_2(t-1) + \eta \times D \times I_2 = 1.3 + 0.6 \times 1 \times 1 = 1.9$
$b(t) = b(t-1) + \eta \times D = -1.4 + 0.6 \times 1 = -0.8$

*Taking the third training pattern*
$sum_1 = x_1 \times w_1 + x_2 \times w_2 + b = 0 \times 1.5 + 1 \times 1.9 - 0.8 = 1.1$
The output is given by
$O_1 = f(sum_1) = f(1.1) = 1$
$T \ne O_1$, so
$w_1(t) = w_1(t-1) + \eta \times D \times I_1 = 1.5 + 0.6 \times -1 \times 1 = 0.9$
$w_2(t) = w_2(t-1) + \eta \times D \times I_2 = 1.9 + 0.6 \times -1 \times 1 = 1.3$
$b(t) = b(t-1) + \eta \times D = -0.8 - 0.6 \times 1 = -1.4$

*Taking the fourth training pattern*
$sum_1 = x_1 \times w_1 + x_2 \times w_2 + b = 0 \times 0.9 + 0 \times 1.3 - 1.4 = -1.4$
The output is given by
$O_1 = f(sum_1) = f(-1.4) = -1$
$T \ne O_1$, so
$w_1(t) = w_1(t-1) + \eta \times D \times I_1 = 0.9 + 0.6 \times 1 \times 1 = 1.5$
$w_2(t) = w_2(t-1) + \eta \times D \times I_2 = 1.3 + 0.6 \times 1 \times 1 = 1.9$
$b(t) = b(t-1) + \eta \times D = -1.4 + 0.6 \times 1 = -0.8$

### Example 2.2

Compute for the 1st pattern of the XOR network as in Table 2.10.

**Solution:** Given that $w_{11} = 0.1$, $w_{12} = 0.2$, $w_{21} = 0.3$, $w_{22} = 0.4$, $b_1 = b_2 = 0.5$, $z_{11} = 0.5$, $z_{21} = 0.6$, $b_3 = 0.5$, $\eta = 0.7$

*Taking the first pattern*
$sum_{q=1} = w_{11} \times I_1 + w_{21} \times I_2 + b_1 = 0.1 \times 1 + 0.3 \times 1 + 0.5 = 0.9$
$sum_{q=2} = w_{12} \times I_1 + w_{22} \times I_2 + b_2 = 0.2 \times 1 + 0.4 \times 1 + 0.5 = 1.1$
$H_1 = f(sum_{q=1}) = f(0.9) = 1$, $H_2 = f(sum_{q=2}) = f(1.1) = 1$
$sum_{k=1} = z_{11} \times H_1 + z_{21} \times H_2 + b_3 = 0.5 \times 1 + 0.6 \times 1 + 0.5 = 1.6$

$O_{k=1} = f(sum_{k=1}) = f(1.6) = 1$

As $O_{k=1} \neq D_{k=1}$, the input to hidden weight values need to be changed

$w_{11}(new) = w_{11}(old) + \eta \times (-1 - sum_{q=1}) \times I_1 = 0.1 + 0.7 \times (-1-0.9) \times 1 = -1.23$
$w_{12}(new) = w_{12}(old) + \eta \times (-1 - sum_{q=2}) \times I_1 = 0.2 + 0.7 \times (-1-1.1) \times 1 = -1.27$
$w_{21}(new) = w_{21}(old) + \eta \times (-1 - sum_{q=1}) \times I_2 = 0.3 + 0.7 \times (-1-0.9) \times 1 = -1.03$
$w_{22}(new) = w_{22}(old) + \eta \times (-1 - sum_{q=2}) \times I_2 = 0.4 + 0.7 \times (-1-1.1) \times 1 = -1.07$

Updating the bias,

$b_1(new) = b_1(old) + \eta \times (-1 - sum_{q=1}) = 0.5 + 0.7 \times (-1-0.9) = -0.83$
$b_2(new) = b_2(old) + \eta \times (-1 - sum_{q=2}) = 0.5 + 0.7 \times (-1-1.1) = -0.97$

### Example 2.3

A single input, single output neuron has a weight of 5 and a bias of −3. What is the net input to the transfer function if it is given an input of 1? What will be the output if the transfer function is bipolar sigmoid given slope $s = 0.5$?

**Solution:** From Eq. 2.2, the net input to the transfer function is
$sum_k = 5 \times 1 - 3 = 2$
The output is given by

$$f(sum_k) = \frac{1}{(1 + \exp(-s \times sum_k))}$$

$f(sum_k) = 1/(1 + \exp(-0.5 \times 2)) = 0.731$

### Example 2.4

A 2-input single-output NN has weight values [1.3 2.7] and bias of 1.6. It is given an input $[3.1\ 2.4]^T$. What is the output if the identity function is used as the transfer function?

**Solution:** From Table 2.3, $f(sum_k) = sum_k$ for all $sum_k$
$sum_k = 1.3 \times 3.1 + 2.7 \times 2.4 + 1.6 = 12.11$
The output is given by
$f(sum_k) = sum_k = 12.11$

### Example 2.5

For the network in Question 2.4, consider a symmetric saturating linear function to be used as activation. What will be the output if the input is $[-6\ 4.1]^T$?

**Solution:** $sum_k = 1.3 \times (-6) + 2.7 \times 4.1 + 1.6 = 4.87$
The output is given by
$f(sum_k) = 1$ as $sum_k > 1$

### Example 2.6

A 3-input 2-output NN has the weight values $w_{11} = 0.6$, $w_{12} = 1.1$, $w_{21} = 0.7$, $w_{22} = 0.5$, $w_{31} = 0.8$, and $w_{32} = 0.2$. It is given an input of $[0.3\ 0.7\ 1.6]^T$. What is the output of the NN if the binary step function is used? Assume a threshold of 1.5.

**Solution:** Since there are 2 output units, $k = 1, 2$
Refer Table 2.3,
$sum_{k=1} = w_{11} \times I_1 + w_{21} \times I_2 + w_{31} \times I_3 = 0.6 \times 0.3 + 0.7 \times 0.7 + 0.8 \times 1.6 = 1.95$
$sum_{k=2} = w_{12} \times I_1 + w_{22} \times I_2 + w_{32} \times I_3 = 1.1 \times 0.3 + 0.5 \times 0.7 + 0.2 \times 1.6 = 1$
The output is given by
$f(sum_{k=1}) = 1$ as $sum_{k=1} > 1.5$ (threshold)
$f(sum_{k=2}) = 0$ as $sum_{k=2} < 1.5$ (threshold)

### Example 2.7

For the data given in Example 2.6, find the output if bipolar sigmoid function is used as the activation function. Assume slope $s = 1.1$.

**Solution:** The outputs are given by
$f(sum_{k=1}) = (1 - \exp(-s \times sum_{k=1}))/(1 + \exp(-s \times sum_{k=1}))$
$= (1 - \exp(-1.1 \times 1.95))/(1 + \exp(-1.1 \times 1.95)) = 0.79$
$f(sum_{k=2}) = (1 - \exp(-s \times sum_{k=2}))/(1 + \exp(-s \times sum_{k=2}))$
$= (1 - \exp(-1.1 \times 1))/(1 + \exp(-1.1 \times 1)) = 0.5$

### Example 2.8

For the data given in Example 2.1, perform the learning using Hebbian rule for the first two input patterns using a decay factor of 0.3. Use hardlimit as the activation function. Assume the desired response $D$ to have binary rather than bipolar values.

**Solution:** Taking first training pattern
$sum_1 = -1$
Since we are using the hardlimit function, the output is given by
$O_1 = f(sum_1) = f(-1) = 0$
Using the Hebbian rule with decay factor in Eq. 2.8,
$w_1(t) = (1 - \gamma) \times w_1(t - 1) + \eta \times O_1(t) \times I_1 = (1 - 0.3) \times 0.3 + 0.6 \times 0 \times 1 = 0.21$
$w_2(t) = (1 - \gamma) \times w_2(t - 1) + \eta \times O_1(t) \times I_2 = (1 - 0.3) \times 0.7 + 0.6 \times 0 \times 1 = 0.49$
$b(t) = (1 - \gamma) \times b(t - 1) + \eta \times O_1(t) = (1 - 0.3) \times (-2) + 0.6 \times 0 = -1.4$

*Taking second training pattern*
$sum_1 = x_1 \times w_1 + x_2 \times w_2 + b = 1 \times 0.21 + 0 \times 0.49 - 1.4 = -1.19$
The output is given by
$O_1 = f(sum_1) = f(-1.19) = 0$
Since $T \neq O_1$, we need to change the weight values
$w_1(t) = (1 - \gamma) \times w_1(t - 1) + \eta \times O_1(t) \times I_1 = (1 - 0.3) \times 0.21 + 0.6 \times 0 \times 1 = 0.147$
$w_2(t) = (1 - \gamma) \times w_2(t - 1) + \eta \times O_1(t) \times I_2 = (1 - 0.3) \times 0.49 + 0.6 \times 0 \times 1 = 0.343$
$b(t) = (1 - \gamma) \times b(t - 1) + \eta \times O_1(t) = (1 - 0.3) \times (-1.4) + 0.6 \times 0 = -0.98$

### Example 2.9

For the data given in Example 2.6, find the value of the output if a binary sigmoid is used as a transfer function. In addition, find the new weights if the delta learning rule is used. Assume the desired output to be $[1.5 \ 1.2]^T$, $\eta = 0.6$, and $s = 0.5$.

**Solution:** The outputs are given by

$O_1 = f(sum_{k=1}) = 1/(1 + \exp(-s \times sum_{k=1})) = 1/(1 + \exp(-0.5 \times 1.95)) = 0.7261$
$O_2 = f(sum_{k=2}) = 1/(1 + \exp(-s \times sum_{k=2})) = 1/(1 + \exp(-0.5 \times 1)) = 0.6224$

Differentiating the bipolar sigmoid gives us

$f'(sum_k) = s \times \exp(-s \times sum_k)/(1 + \exp(-s \times sum_k))^2$

From Eq. 2.20

$\Delta w_{11} = \eta \times (D_1 - O_1) \times I_1 \times f'(sum_{k=1})$
$= 0.6 \times (1.5 - 0.7261) \times 0.3 \times 0.5 \times \exp(-0.5 \times 1.95)/(1 + \exp(-0.5 \times 1.95))^2$
$= 0.0138$

$\Delta w_{12} = \eta \times (D_2 - O_2) \times I_1 \times f'(sum_{k=2})$
$= 0.6 \times (1.2 - 0.6224) \times 0.3 \times 0.5 \times \exp(-0.5 \times 1)/(1 + \exp(-0.5 \times 1))^2 = 0.0122$

$\Delta w_{21} = \eta \times (D_1 - O_1) \times I_2 \times f'(sum_{k=1})$
$= 0.6 \times (1.5 - 0.7261) \times 0.7 \times 0.5 \times \exp(-0.5 \times 1.95)/(1 + \exp(-0.5 \times 1.95))^2 = 0.0323$

$\Delta w_{22} = \eta \times (D_2 - O_2) \times I_2 \times f'(sum_{k=2})$
$= 0.6 \times (1.2 - 0.6224) \times 0.7 \times 0.5 \times \exp(-0.5 \times 1)/(1 + \exp(-0.5 \times 1))^2 = 0.0285$

$\Delta w_{31} = \eta \times (D_1 - O_1) \times I_3 \times f'(sum_{k=1})$
$= 0.6 \times (1.5 - 0.7261) \times 1.6 \times 0.5 \times \exp(-0.5 \times 1.95)/(1 + \exp(-0.5 \times 1.95))^2$
$= 0.0738$

$\Delta w_{32} = \eta \times (D_2 - O_2) \times I_3 \times f'(sum_{k=2})$
$= 0.6 \times (1.2 - 0.6224) \times 1.6 \times 0.5 \times \exp(-0.5 \times 1)/(1 + \exp(-0.5 \times 1))^2 = 0.0651$

$w_{11}(new) = w_{11}(old) + \Delta w_{11} = 0.6 + 0.0138 = 0.6138$
$w_{12}(new) = w_{12}(old) + \Delta w_{12} = 1.1 + 0.0122 = 1.1122$
$w_{21}(new) = w_{21}(old) + \Delta w_{21} = 0.7 + 0.0323 = 0.7323$
$w_{22}(new) = w_{22}(old) + \Delta w_{22} = 0.5 + 0.0285 = 0.5285$
$w_{31}(new) = w_{31}(old) + \Delta w_{31} = 0.8 + 0.0738 = 0.8738$
$w_{32}(new) = w_{32}(old) + \Delta w_{32} = 0.2 + 0.0651 = 0.2651$

**Example 2.10**

Find out the undecided band for the perceptron OR from the results obtained in Table 2.8.

**Solution:** At the end of training, the weights and bias are

$w_1 = 2, w_2 = 2$ and $b = -1$

The threshold for the network is set at 0.5
The positive region is given by

$2 \times I_1 + 2 \times I_2 - 1 > 0.5$

The negative region is given by

$2 \times I_1 + 2 \times I_2 - 1 < -0.5$

The region between these two planes is the undecided band

i.e., $2 \times I_1 + 2 \times I_2 - 1 < 0.5, 2 \times I_1 + 2 \times I_2 - 1 > -0.5$
or $2 \times I_1 + 2 \times I_2 < 1.5, 2 \times I_1 + 2 \times I_2 > 0.5$

# SUMMARY

- Artificial neural network is an information processing system that mimics certain performance characteristics of the biological neural systems of the brain.
- When billions of neurons are linked, they form a neural forest where the neurons talk to each other and intelligence starts evolving that performs different functions in a human brain.
- The four elements of a biological neuron (i.e., dendrites, synapses, cell body, and axon) are the minimal structure adopted for the artificial neuron model. Artificial neurons for computing will have an input channel, a cell body, and an output channel; and synapses will be simulated by contact points between the cell body and input or output connections, and also a weight will be associated with these points.
- The classification of ANN is fundamentally based on their characteristics such as network architecture (a pattern of connections between the neurons), training/learning (method of determining weights), and activation function.
- In feed-forward neural networks, the data flow starts from the input units to output units. However, if there are feedback connections, the neural network is called 'recurrent neural network', such as the Hopfield neural network.
- The way an ANN learns can be classified as: (i) supervised learning (i.e., takes place with supervision or under a strategy to correct the learning process for achieving the desired target), (ii) unsupervised learning (i.e., takes place even if the target feature is not given), and (iii) reinforced learning (i.e., reinforces either of the supervised or unsupervised learning method).
- In the *offline mode,* training is carried out with the available data of a system from the past. Whereas, in the *online mode,* a system learns in operation mode where the weights are updated even after the completion of training.
- The sigmoid activation function, whose graph is *s*-shaped, is the common form of activation function used in the construction of artificial neural networks. It is defined as a strictly increasing function that exhibits a graceful balance between linear and non-linear behaviour.
- The Hebb rule strengthens the association between the two input stimulus and the output response by modifying the weights with a learning factor.
- McCulloch neurons have a binary output of either 'one' or 'zero'. If the firing of neuron takes place, then the neuron has an activation of 'one' and if it does not fire, then the neuron has an activation of 'zero'.
- The Madaline has two inputs $I_1$ and $I_2$ connected through weights $W_{11}$, $W_{12}$, $W_{21}$, and $W_{22}$. Two hidden Adalines $H_1$ and $H_2$ are connected to the output unit through fixed weights $Z_1$ and $Z_2$. The hidden units increase the network capabilities not available in a single-layer neural network.

# EXERCISES

## Part A Short-answer Questions

1. Define 'artificial neural network'.
2. What is a 'neuron'?
3. What is the 'grey matter' in the BNN?
4. What are the three main entities of BNN?
5. What is a 'dendrite'?
6. What is the function of 'axonal tract'?
7. What is the direction of the signal impulses in the neurons?
8. State the law of neuron.
9. What are 'neurotransmitters'? Give examples.
10. What are 'synaptic vesicles'?
11. What is 'action potential'?
12. What is 'membrane potential'?
13. Sketch the structural representation of a BNN.
14. What is a 'bias ANN model'?
15. What are weights in ANN related in BNN?
16. How is activation function in ANN related in BNN?
17. Given a four-input neuron with the following parameters: $b = 1$, $W = [3\ 2\ 2\ 3]$, and $p = [3\ 4\ 5\ 6]^T$. Calculate the neuron output for satlins, poslin, satlin, purelin, hardlim, and hardlims.

18. How are ANN classified?
19. Give examples of single-layer NN and competitive NN.
20. What do you understand by 'supervised learning' in ANN?
21. What do you understand by 'unsupervised learning' in ANN?
22. What do you understand by 'reinforced learning' in ANN?
23. List out the training and testing modes of ANN.
24. What is meant by 'online training' and 'offline training' of ANN?
25. What is a 'sigmoid activation function'?
26. What is 'purelin'?
27. What is 'hardlimit function'?
28. Demonstrate the operation of AND and OR logics using McCulloch-Pitts neuron.
29. State 'Hebb's law'.
30. Define 'delta learning rule'.
31. What is a 'perceptron neural network'?
32. Define 'linear seperability'.
33. What is an 'Adaline neural network'?
34. What is a 'Madaline neural network'?

## Part B Long-answer Questions

1. Compare the strengths and weaknesses of a human brain with respect to a computer.
2. Explain BNN with a neat sketch.
3. Elaborately discuss the neuronal communication that takes place at synapse with necessary diagrams.
4. Write short notes on classification of ANNs.
5. Give a detailed account of Adaline and Madaline networks.
6. Solve the following AND function having binary input and binary targets using learning rule. Given training data are:

| Input | | | Target |
|---|---|---|---|
| $X_1$ | $X_2$ | 1 | |
| 1 | 1 | 1 | 1 |
| 1 | 0 | 1 | 0 |
| 0 | 1 | 1 | 0 |
| 0 | 0 | 1 | 0 |

Use learning rate (0.8), threshold value ($\theta = 0.5$), initial weights, and bias ($w_1 = 2$, $w_2 = 1$, $b = -3$). The output of the neuron is 1 when the sum potential is greater than and is $-1$ when lesser than $-\theta$, otherwise it is zero.

Check whether the problem is solvable within six iterations. If solvable, give the boundary equation for positive and negative response.

1. Can XOR problem be solved using perceptron? If not, give the reasons.
2. Apply the perceptron learning algorithm to classify the following three-dimensional unipolar binary patterns before augmentation:

$$\text{Class A}: \{x\} = \{(0, 0, 0), (1, 1, 1)\}$$
$$\text{Class B}: \{x\} = \{(0, 0, 1), (0, 1, 1)\}$$

In addition, draw a figure of the perceptron obtained, with its connections, weights, threshold and transfer characteristic specified.

3. Give the algorithm of Madaline network. Discuss its potential in solving an XOR problem which is linearly inseparable.

## Part C Practical Exercises

1. Develop a MATLAB Program using perceptron algorithm to check whether the following patterns are linearly separable or not.

| Input | | | Target | |
|---|---|---|---|---|
| $X_1$ | $X_2$ | $X_3$ | $Y_1$ | $Y_2$ |
| 1 | 1 | 1 | 1 | 1 |
| 1 | 0 | 0 | 0 | 1 |
| 0 | 1 | 1 | 1 | 0 |
| 0 | 0 | 0 | 0 | 0 |

2. Check whether the above patterns converge or train successfully with Madaline algorithm by writing a MATLAB Program.

## REFERENCES

[1] http://www.codeproject.com/Articles/16419/AI-Neural-Network-for-beginners-Part-of.
[2] Haykin, Simon, O, *Neural Networks and Learning Machines*, Prentice Hall; 3 edition, 18 November, 2008.
[3] McCulloch, W., and W. Pitts 1943, 'A logical calculus of the ideas immanent in nervous activity', Bulltin of Mathematical Biophysics, volume 7, pp. 115–133.
[4] Mendel, J. M., and R. W. McLaren 1970 'Reinforcement-learning control and pattern recognition systems', Mathematics in Science and Engineering, Volume 66, pp. 287–318, Elsevier Publication.
[5] Hebb, D. O, *The Organization of Behavior: A Neuropsychological Theory*, Psychology Press, 2002.
[6] Pavlov, I. P., *Conditional Reflexes*. Dover Publications, New York, 1960.
[7] Anderson, James A., *An Introduction to Neural Networks*, MIT Press, 1995.
[8] Rumelhart, D. E., and J. L. McClelland, PDP Research Group, Parallel distributed processing: Explorations in the microstructure of cognition (V1 and V2) MIT press, 1986.
[9] Rosenblatt, Frank, *Principles of Neurodynamics*. Spartan Books, Washington, DC, 1962.
[10] Minsky, M. L. and Papert, S. A., *Perceptrons*. MIT Press, Cambridge, MA, 1969.
[11] Marvin Minsky Seymour Papert, Neurocomputing: foundations of research, MIT Press Cambridge, MA, USA, 1988.
[12] Rojas, Raul, *Neural Networks - A Systematic Introduction*, Springer-Verlag, Berlin, New York, 1996.
[13] Hecht Nielsen, Robert, *Neurocomputing*, Addison-Wesley, 1990.
[14] Widrow, B., and M. E. Hoff, Jr., Adaptive switching circuits, 1960 IRE WESCON Convention Record, Part 4, IRE, New York, 96–104, 1960.

## e-Reference

1. http://sciencespin.com/articles/21-featured/61-unravelling-the-mysterious-brain/. (Last accessed 09/7/2014).

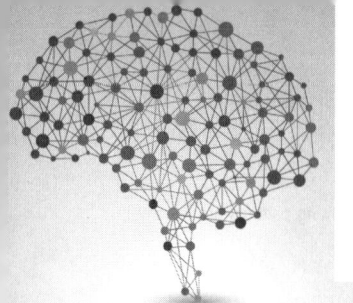

# 3 Artificial Neural Networks—Second Generation

*'Experience is knowledge and understanding knowledge is intelligence'*

Narayana Prasad Padhy

### LEARNING OBJECTIVES

*After reading this chapter, the reader will be able to:*

- Explain the backpropagation neural networks
- Learn the working of Kohonnen neural networks
- Understand the concept of learning vector quantization (LVQ) network
- Familiarize with Hamming NNs and Hopfield NNs
- Explain the fundamentals of bi-directional associative memory
- Elaborate on adaptive resonance theory (ART) networks
- Discuss the functioning of Boltzmann machine
- Understand concepts of radial basis NNs and support vector machines
- Conduct electrical load forecasting using MATLAB NN toolbox

## 3.1 INTRODUCTION TO SECOND-GENERATION NEURAL NETWORKS

Neurons of the second generation do not use a step or threshold function to compute their output signals but a continuous activation function, making them suitable for analog input and output. Commonly used examples of activation functions are the sigmoid and hyperbolic tangents.

Typical examples of neural networks (NNs) consisting of neurons of these types are feed-forward and recurrent NNs. These are more powerful than their first-generation predecessors: when equipped with a threshold function at the output layer of the network, they are universal for digital computations and do so with fewer neurons than a network of the first generation [1]. In addition, they can approximate any analog function arbitrarily well, making these networks universal for analog computations.

## 3.2 BACKPROPAGATION NEURAL NETWORKS

Backpropagation is a systematic method for training multiple- (three or more) layer artificial neural networks (ANNs) [2]. The elucidation of this training algorithm by Rumelhart, in 1986, was the key step in making NNs practical in many real-world situations. However, Rumelhart was not the first to develop the backpropagation algorithm. In 1972, it was developed independently by D. Parker [3], and earlier in 1974 by P. Werbos [4].

However, backpropagation algorithm is a generalization of the Widrow-Hoff error correction rule as discussed in Chapter 2. Nevertheless, the backpropagation algorithm was critical to the advances in NNs because of the limitations of the one-layer and two-layer networks. Indeed, backpropagation played a critically important role in the resurgence of the NN field in the mid-1980s. Today, it is estimated that 80 per cent of all applications utilize this backpropagation algorithm in one form or the other.

Prior to the development of backpropagation, attempts to use perceptrons with more than one layer of weights were frustrated by what was called the 'weight assignment problem'; i.e., how one allocates the error at the output layer between the two (or more) layers of weights when there is no firm mathematical foundation for doing so. This problem plagued the NN field for over two decades and was cited by Minsky and Papert as one of the criticisms of multi-layer perceptrons [5].

Ironically, this need not have been the case because Amari, in 1960s, developed a method for allocating weights that was not widely disseminated [6]. Even more ironic is the fact that Rosenblatt's method of using a random distribution of the weight values in the middle neuron layer and adjusting only the weights for the output neuron layer has been shown to provide adequate training of the network in most cases [7].

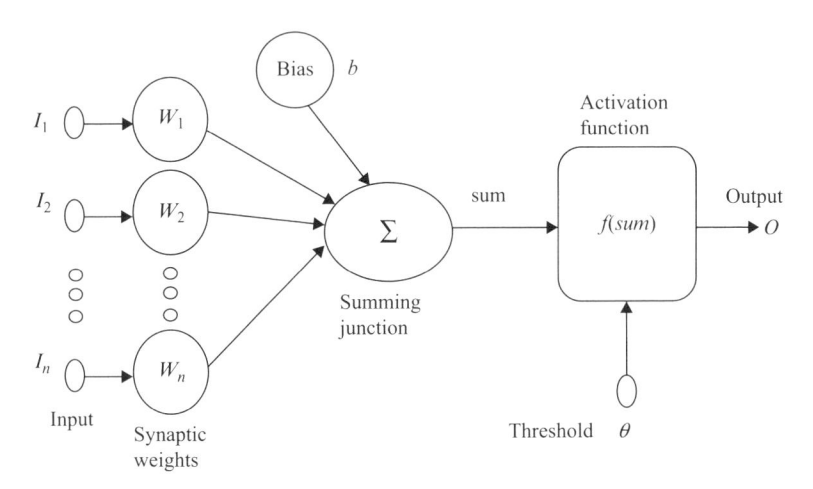

**Fig. 3.1** A simple neuron with many inputs

Let us consider a typical neuron as shown in Fig. 3.1 with inputs $I_{j=1,...n}$, weights $W_{j=1,...n}$, a summation function in the left half of the neuron, and a non-linear activation function in the right half. The summation of the weighted inputs designated by *sum* is given by,

$$sum = I_1 W_1 + I_2 W_2 + ..... + I_n W_n + b = \sum_{j=1}^{n} I_j W_j + b \tag{3.1}$$

The typical sigmoidal function as the non-linear activation function is used and is given by,

$$f(sum) = \frac{1}{(1+e^{-s\times sum})} = (1+e^{-s\times sum})^{-1} \qquad (3.2)$$

This sigmoidal function is a logistic function which monotonically increases from a lower limit (0 or −1) to an upper limit (+1) as *sum* increases. The values vary between 0 and 1, with a value of 0.5 when I is zero. An examination of Fig. 3.2 shows that the derivative (slope) of the curve asymptotically approaches zero as the input *sum* approaches minus infinity and plus infinity, and it reaches a maximum value of $s/4$ when *sum* equals zero as shown in Fig. 3.2.

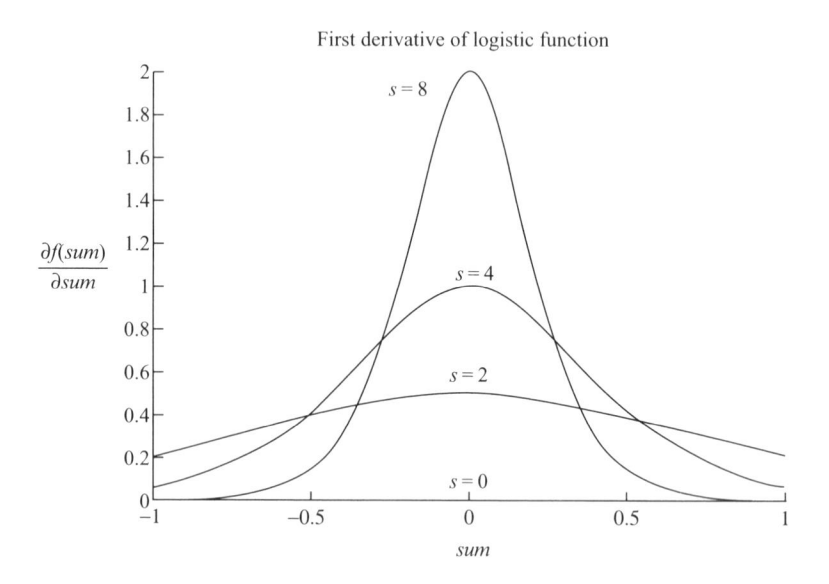

**Fig. 3.2** First derivative logistic function

Since this derivative function will be utilized in backpropagation, let us reduce it to its most simple form. If we take a derivative of the Eq. (3.3), we get,

$$\frac{\partial f(sum)}{\partial sum} = (-1)(1+e^{-s\times sum})^{-2} e^{-s\times sum}(-s)$$

$$= s \times e^{-s\times sum}(1+e^{-s\times sum})^{-2} = s \times e^{-s\times sum} f^2(sum) \qquad (3.3)$$

If we solve Eq. (3.2) for $e^{-s\times sum}$, substitute it into Eq. (3.3), and simplify, we get,

$$\frac{\partial f(sum)}{\partial sum} = s \times \frac{1-f(sum)}{f(sum)} f^2(sum) = s \times [1-f(sum)] \times [f(sum)]$$

$$= s \times (1-f) \times f \qquad (3.4)$$

where $f(sum)$ has been simplified by $f$ by dropping $(sum)$.

Multi-layer networks have greater representational power than single-layer networks only if non-linearities are introduced. The logistic function provides the necessary non-linearity. While applying backpropagation algorithm, any non-linear function can be used if it is differentiable everywhere and monotonically increasing with sum. Sigmoidal functions, including logistic, hyperbolic tangent, and arctangent functions, meet these requirements.

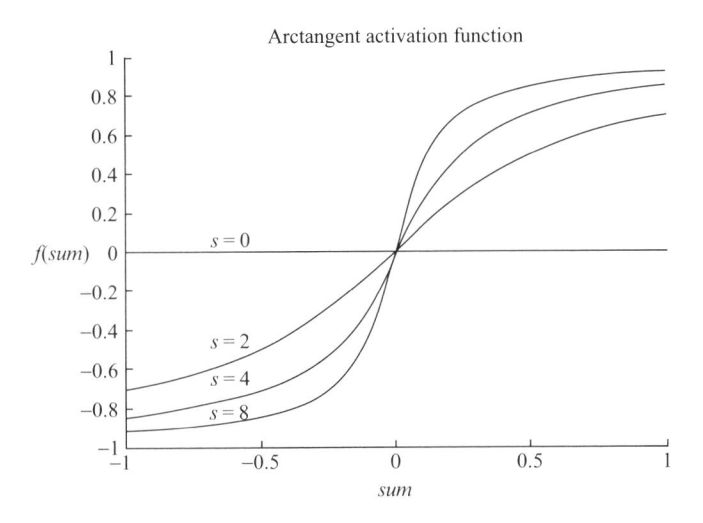

**Fig. 3.3** Arctangents activation function

The arctangent function, denoted as $\tan^{-1}$, has the form,

$$f(sum) = \frac{2}{\pi}\tan^{-1}(s \times sum) \tag{3.5}$$

Where the factor $2/\pi$ reduces the amplitude of the arctangent function so that it is restricted to the range $-1$ to $+1$. The constant $s$ determines the rate at which the function changes between the limits of $-1$ and $+1$ and to the slope of the function at the origin is $2s/\pi$. The $s$ value influences the shape of the arctangent function in the same way that $s$ influences the logistic function in Fig. 3.2. The arctangent function has the same sigmoidal shape shown in Fig. 3.3. The derivative is as follows:

$$\frac{\partial f(sum)}{\partial sum} = \frac{2}{\pi}\left[\frac{s}{1+s^2 sum^2}\right] \tag{3.6}$$

Equation (3.6) would be used in place of Eq. (3.4) if the arctangent replaced the logistic activation function.

The hyperbolic tangent function has the form:

$$f(sum) = \tan h(s \times sum) = \frac{e^{s \times sum} - e^{-s \times sum}}{e^{s \times sum} + e^{-s \times sum}} \tag{3.7}$$

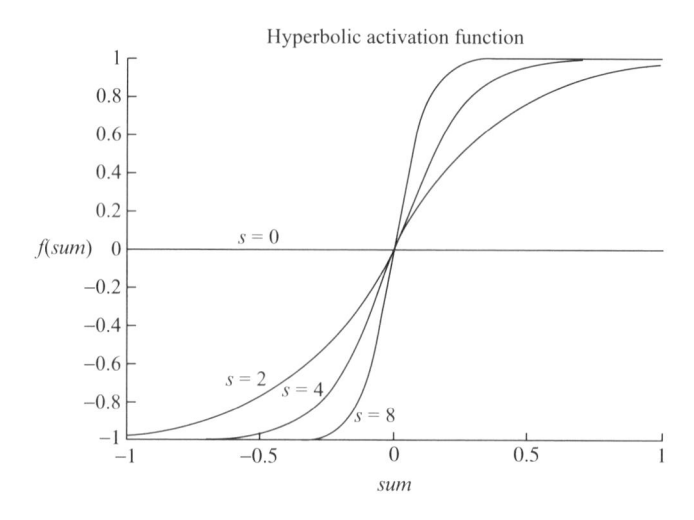

Fig. 3.4 Hyperbolic tangent activation function

The shape of the hyperbolic tangent function is shown in Fig. 3.4. Its derivative is as follows:

$$\frac{\partial f(sum)}{\partial sum} = s \times \sec h^2(s \times sum) \qquad (3.8)$$

The slope of $f(sum)$ at the origin is $4s$ and it determines the rate at which the function changes between the limits of $-1$ and $+1$ in the same general way that $s$ influences the shape of the logistic function as in Fig. 3.2.

The use of a sigmoidal function provides a form of 'automatic gain control'; that is, for small values of $sum$ near zero, the slope of the input-output curve is steep, producing a high gain, since all sigmoidal activation functions have derivatives with bell shapes of the type as shown in Fig. 3.2. As the magnitude of $sum$ becomes greater in a positive or negative direction, the gain decreases. Hence, large signals can be accommodated without saturation as given in Fig. 2.17.

## 3.2.1 Backpropagation Training for Multi-layer Neural Network

Before discussing the details of the backpropagation process, let us consider the benefits of the middle layer(s) in an ANN. A network with only two layers (input and output) can only represent the input with whatever representation already exists in the input data [8], [9]. Hence, if the data are discontinuous or non-linearly separable, the innate representation is inconsistent and the mapping cannot be learned.

The network is composed of a hierarchy of processing units, organized in a series of two or more mutually exclusive sets of neurons or layers. This mainly consists of the input layer, output layer, and a hidden layer between the two. Weights connect each unit in one layer only to those in the next higher layer.

The output of the unit is scaled by the value of the connecting weight, and it is fed forward to provide a portion of the activation for the units in the next higher layer.

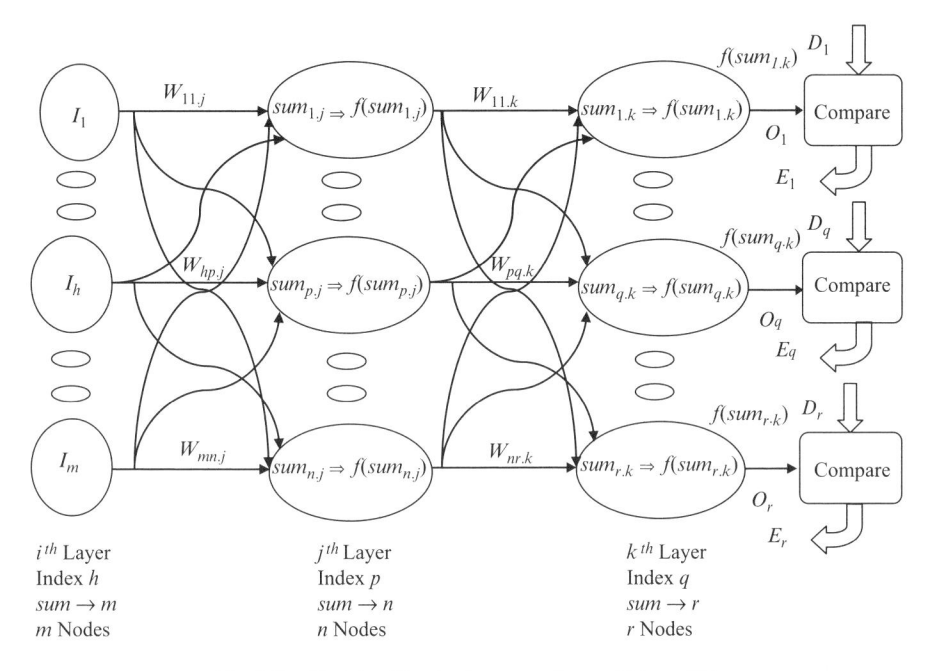

Fig. 3.5 Sketch of the backpropagation multi-layer NN

Let us consider the three-layer network shown in Fig. 3.5, where all activation functions are logistic functions. It is important to note that backpropagation can be applied to an ANN with any number of hidden layers. The training objective is to adjust the weights so that the application of a set of inputs produces the desired outputs. To accomplish, this network is usually trained with a large number of input-output pairs. The training procedure is given as follows:

*Step 1*: Generate the weights randomly to small random values (both positive and negative) to ensure that the network is not saturated by large values of weights (if all weights start at equal values and the desired performance requires unequal weights, the network would not train at all).
*Step 2:* Choose a training pair from the training set.
*Step 3:* Apply the input vector to network input.
*Step 4:* Calculate the network output.
*Step 5:* Calculate the error, the difference between the network output and the desired output.
*Step 6:* Adjust the weights of the network in a way that minimizes this error.
*Step 7:* Repeat steps 2–6 for each pair of input-output in the training set until the error for the entire system is acceptably low.

Training of a backpropagation neural network (BPNN) involves two passes. In the forward pass, the input signals moves forward from the network input to the output. In the backward pass, the calculated error signals propagate backward through the network, where they are used to adjust the weights. The calculation of the output is carried out, layer by layer, in the forward direction. The output of one layer is the input to the next layer like feedback. In the reverse pass, the weights of the output neuron layer are adjusted first since the target value of each output neuron is available to guide the adjustment of the associated weights using the delta rule. Next, we adjust the weights of the middle layers. As the middle-layer neurons have no target values, it makes the problem complex.

Hence, the training is more complicated, because the error must be propagated back through the network, including the non-linear functions, layer by layer. The number of hidden units depends on the number of input units. Kolomogorov's theorem defines that any function of $n$ variables may be represented by the superposition of a set of $2n + 1$ univariate functions to derive the upper bound for the required number of hidden units as one greater than twice the number of input units [10]. That is, you will not require more than twice the number of hidden units as you have the inputs [11]. When choosing the number of hidden units $h$:

- Never choose $h$ to be more than twice the number of input units.
- You can load $p$ patterns of $I$ elements into $log_2 p$ hidden units. So never use more. If we need good generalization, use considerably less.
- Ensure that we must have at least $1/e$ times as many training examples as we have weights in our network. Here '$e$' is the error limit.
- Feature extraction requires fewer hidden units than inputs.
- Learning many examples of disjointed inputs requires more hidden units than inputs.
- The number of hidden units required for a classification task increases with the number of classes in the task. Large networks require longer training times.

## 3.2.2 Calculation of Weights for Output-layer Neurons

Let us consider the details of the backpropagation learning process for the weights of the output layer. When neuron $j$ is located in the output layer of the network, it is supplied with a desired response of its own. Figure 3.6 suggests training of neurons leading to the output layer designated by the subscript $k$ with neurons $p$ and $q$, outputs $f(sum_{p.j})$ and $f(sum_{q.k})$, input weights $W_{hp.j}$ and $W_{pq.k}$, and a target value $D_q$. The notation $(sum)$ in $f(sum_{q.k})$ will be dropped for convenience.

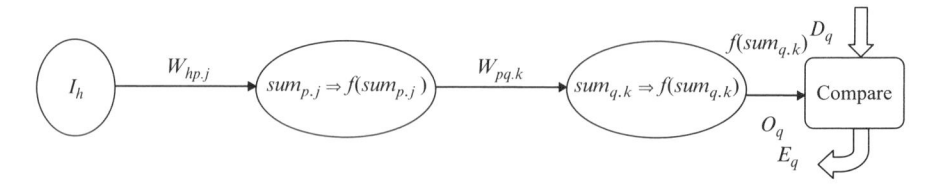

**Fig. 3.6** Representation of neurons for output-layer neurons weight

The output $f(sum_k)$ or $O_q$ of the neuron in layer $k$ is subtracted from its target value and squared to produce the square error signal, which for a layer $k$ neuron is,

$$E = E_q = [D_q - f_{q.k}] \quad (3.9)$$

This is because only one output error is involved. Hence,

$$E^2 = E_q^2 = [D_q - f_{q \cdot k}]^2 \tag{3.10}$$

According to delta rule, the change in a weight is proportional to the rate of change of the square error with respect to that weight, that is,

$$\Delta W_{pq \cdot k} = -\eta_{p \cdot q} \frac{\partial E_q^2}{\partial W_{pq \cdot k}} \tag{3.11}$$

where $\eta_{p \cdot q}$ is constant of proportionality called 'learning rate'. To evaluate this partial derivative, the chain rule of differentiation is used:

$$\frac{\partial E_q^2}{\partial W_{pq \cdot k}} = \frac{\partial E_q^2}{\partial f_{q \cdot k}} \frac{\partial f_{q \cdot k}}{\partial sum_{q \cdot k}} \frac{\partial sum_{q \cdot k}}{\partial W_{pq \cdot k}} \tag{3.12}$$

Each of these terms is evaluated in turn. The partial derivative of Eq. (3.10) with respect to $f_{q \cdot k}$ gives,

$$\frac{\partial E_q^2}{\partial f_{q \cdot k}} = -2\left[D_q - f_{q \cdot k}\right] \tag{3.13}$$

We know from Eq. (3.4),

$$\frac{\partial f_{q \cdot k}}{\partial sum_{qk}} = s \times f_{q \cdot k}\left[1 - f_{q \cdot k}\right] \tag{3.14}$$

We see that $sum_{q \cdot k}$ is the sum of the weighted inputs from the middle layer, that is,

$$sum_{q \cdot k} = \sum_{p=1}^{n} W_{pq \cdot k} f_{p \cdot j} \tag{3.15}$$

Taking the partial derivative with respect to $W_{pq \cdot k}$ gives,

$$\frac{\partial sum_{q \cdot k}}{\partial W_{pq \cdot k}} = f_{p \cdot j} \tag{3.16}$$

Since we are dealing with one weight, only one term of the summation of Eq. (3.15) survives. Substituting the previous equations into Eq. (3.12) gives,

$$\frac{\partial E_q^2}{\partial W_{pq \cdot k}} = -2 \times s \times \left[D_q - f_{q \cdot k}\right] f_{q \cdot k} \left[1 - f_{q \cdot k}\right] f_{p \cdot j} = \chi_{pq \cdot k} f_{p \cdot j} \tag{3.17}$$

where $\chi_{pq \cdot k}$ is defined as,

$$\chi_{pq \cdot k} \equiv -2 \times s \times \left[D_q - f_{q \cdot k}\right] f_{q \cdot k} \left[1 - f_{q \cdot k}\right] \tag{3.18}$$

Substituting Eq. (3.17) into Eq. (3.11) gives,

$$\Delta W_{pq \cdot k} = -\eta_{p \cdot q} \frac{\partial E_q^2}{\partial W_{pq \cdot k}} = -\eta_{p \cdot q} X_{pq \cdot k} f_{p \cdot j} \qquad (3.19)$$

$$W_{pq \cdot k}(t+1) = W_{pq \cdot k}(t) - \eta_{p \cdot q} X_{pq \cdot k} f_{p \cdot j} \qquad (3.20)$$

where $t$ is the number of the iteration involved.

An identical process is performed for each weight of the output layer to give the adjusted values of the weights. The error term $X_{pq \cdot k}$ is used to adjust the weights of the output-layer neurons using Eqs (3.19) and (3.20). In Eq. (3.19), we have calculated an error that has to be propagated back through the network.

This error exists because of the wrong outputs generated by the output neurons. These are due to their own incorrect weights and the middle-layer neurons generate the wrong output. To overcome from this situation, we backpropagate the errors for each output-layer neuron, using the same interconnections and weights as the middle layer used to transmit its outputs to the output layer.

When a weight between a middle-layer neuron and an output-layer neuron is large and the output-layer neuron has a very large error, the weights of the middle-layer neurons may be assigned a very large error, even if that neuron has a very small output, and thus could not have contributed much to the output error. By applying the derivative of the squashing function, this error is moderated, and only small to moderate changes are made to the middle-layer weights because of the bell-shaped curve of the derivative function.

### 3.2.3 Calculation of Weights for Hidden-layer Neurons

When $p^{th}$ neuron is located in the hidden layer of the network, there is no specified desired response for that neuron [12], [13]. The error signal for a hidden neuron would have to be determined recursively in terms of the error signals of all the neurons to which the hidden neuron is directly connected. Since the hidden layers have no target vectors, the problem of adjusting the weights of the hidden layers is a major issue faced by researchers in this field for years until BPNN was put forth.

Backpropagation trains hidden layers by propagating the adjusted error back through the network, layer by layer, adjusting the weight of each layer as it goes. The equations for the hidden layer are the same as for the output layer except that the error term $X_{hp \cdot j}$ must be generated without a target vector. We must compute $X_{hp \cdot j}$ for each neuron in the middle layer that includes contributions from the errors in each neuron in the output layer to which it is connected.

Let us consider a single neuron in the hidden layer just before the output layer, designated with the subscript $p$. In the forward pass, this neuron propagates its output values to the $q$ neurons in the output layer through the interconnecting weights $W_{pq \cdot k}$. During training, these weights operate in reverse order, passing the value of $X_{pq \cdot k}$ from the output layer back to the hidden layer. Each of these weights is multiplied by the value of the neuron through which it connects in the output layer. Summing all such products produces the value of $X_{hp \cdot j}$, needed for the hidden-layer neuron.

The arrangement in Fig. 3.7 shows the errors that are backpropagated to produce the change in $W_{hp \cdot j}$. Since all error terms of the output layer are involved, the partial derivative involves a summation over the $r$ outputs.

$i^{th}$ Layer  
Index $h$  
$sum \rightarrow m$  
$m$ Nodes

$j^{th}$ Layer  
Index $p$  
$sum \rightarrow n$  
$n$ Nodes

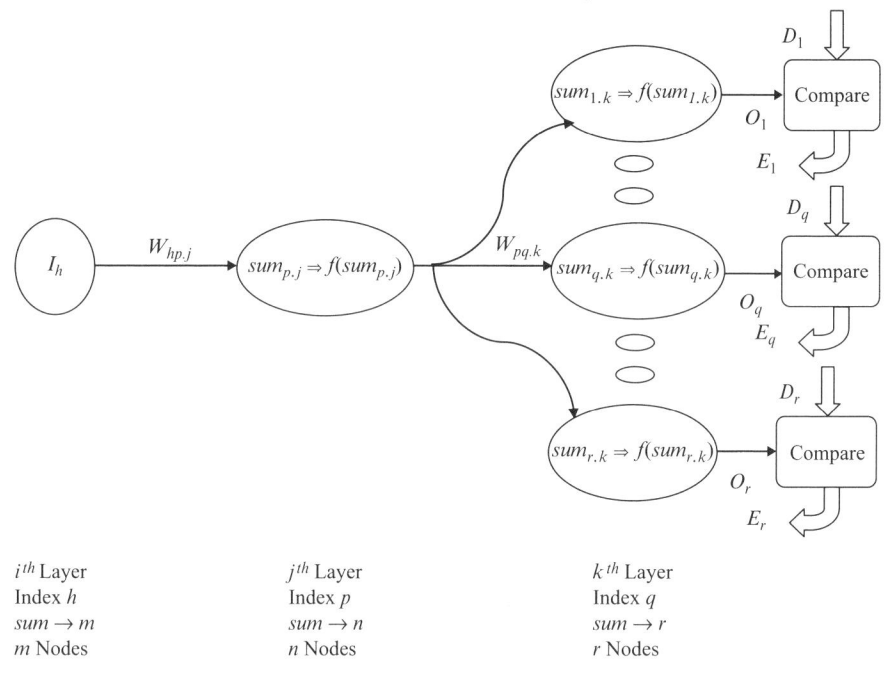

$k^{th}$ Layer  
Index $q$  
$sum \rightarrow r$  
$r$ Nodes

**Fig. 3.7** Weight updation of a middle (hidden)-layer neuron

The procedure for calculating $X_{hp \cdot j}$ is substantially the same as calculating $X_{pq \cdot k}$. Let us start with the derivative of the square error with respect to the weight for the middle layer that is to be adjusted. Then, in a manner analogous to Eq. (3.21), the delta rule training gives,

$$\Delta W_{hp \cdot j} = -\eta_{h \cdot p} \frac{\partial E^2}{\partial W_{hp \cdot j}} = -\eta_{h \cdot p} \sum_{q=1}^{r} \frac{\partial E^2}{\partial W_{hp \cdot j}} \quad (3.21)$$

Where, the total mean square $E^2$ is now defined by,

$$E^2 = \sum_{q=1}^{r} E_q^2 = \sum_{q=1}^{r} \left[ D_q - f_{q \cdot k} \right]^2 \quad (3.22)$$

since several output errors may be involved. The learning constant $\eta$ is usually, but not necessarily, equal to $\eta_{p \cdot q}$.

Again, we can evaluate the last term of Eq. (3.12) using the chain rule of differentiation, which gives,

$$\frac{\partial E^2}{\partial W_{hp \cdot j}} = \sum_{q=1}^{r} \frac{\partial E_q^2}{\partial f_{q \cdot k}} \frac{\partial f_{q \cdot k}}{\partial sum_{q \cdot k}} \frac{\partial sum_{q \cdot k}}{\partial f_{p \cdot j}} \frac{\partial sum_{p \cdot j}}{\partial sum_{p \cdot j}} \frac{\partial sum_{p \cdot j}}{\partial W_{hp \cdot j}} \quad (3.23)$$

where,

$$\frac{\partial E^2}{\partial f_{q \cdot k}} = -2(D_q - f_{q \cdot k}) = -2E_q \qquad (3.24)$$

$$\frac{\partial f_{q \cdot k}}{\partial sum_{q \cdot k}} = s \times f_{q \cdot k}(1 - f_{q \cdot k}) \qquad (3.25)$$

and

$$sum_{q \cdot k} = \sum_{p=1}^{n} W_{pq \cdot k} f_{p \cdot j} \qquad (3.26)$$

Taking the partial derivative of Eq. (3.26) with respect to $f_{p \cdot j}$ gives,

$$\frac{\partial sum_{q \cdot k}}{\partial f_{p \cdot j}} = W_{pq \cdot k} \qquad (3.27)$$

The summation over $p$ disappears because only one connection is involved. Changing subscripts on Eq. (3.25) to correspond to the middle layer gives,

$$\frac{\partial f_{p \cdot j}}{\partial sum_{p \cdot j}} = s \times f_{p \cdot j} \left[ 1 - f_{p \cdot j} \right] \qquad (3.28)$$

Changing subscripts on Eq. (3.26) and substituting the $i^{th}$-layer input $I_h$ for the $j^{th}$-layer input $f_{p \cdot j}$ gives,

$$sum_{p \cdot j} = \sum_{h=1}^{m} W_{hp \cdot j} I_h \qquad (3.29)$$

Taking the partial derivative of Eq. (3.29) gives,

$$\frac{\partial sum_{p \cdot j}}{\partial W_{hp \cdot j}} = I_h \qquad (3.30)$$

Again, the summation over $h$ disappears because only one connection is involved. Substituting Eqs (3.24, 3.25, 3.27, 3.28, and 3.30) in Eq. (3.23) gives,

$$\frac{\partial E^2}{\partial W_{hp \cdot j}} = \sum_{q=1}^{r} (-2) \times s \times (D_q - f_{q \cdot k}) \left[ f_{q \cdot k}(1 - f_{q \cdot k}) \right] W_{pq \cdot k} \times s \times \left[ f_{p \cdot j}(1 - f_{p \cdot j}) \right] I_h$$

$$= \sum_{q=1}^{r} \chi_{pq \cdot k} W_{pq \cdot k} \frac{\partial f_{p \cdot j}}{\partial sum_{p \cdot j}} I_h \qquad (3.31)$$

If we define $\chi_{hp \cdot j}$ as

$$\chi_{hp \cdot j} \equiv \chi_{pq \cdot k} W_{pq \cdot k} \frac{\partial f_{p \cdot j}}{\partial sum_{p \cdot j}} \qquad (3.32)$$

then Eq. (3.31) becomes,

$$\frac{\partial E^2}{\partial W_{hp \cdot j}} = \sum_{q=1}^{r} \chi_{hp \cdot j} I_h \qquad (3.33)$$

Since the change in weights is proportional to the negative of the rate of change of the square error with respect to that weight, then, substitution of Eq. (3.33) into Eq. (3.21) gives,

$$\Delta W_{hp \cdot j} = -\eta_{h \cdot p} \frac{\partial E^2}{\partial W_{hp \cdot j}} = -\eta_{h \cdot p} \sum_{q=1}^{r} \chi_{pq \cdot k} W_{pq \cdot k} \frac{\partial f_{p \cdot j}}{\partial I_{p \cdot j}} I_h \qquad (3.34)$$

and hence,

$$W_{hp \cdot j}(t+1) = W_{hp \cdot j}(t) - \eta_{h \cdot p} I_h \sum_{q=1}^{r} \chi_{hp} \qquad (3.35)$$

If there is more than one middle layer of neurons, this process moves through the network, layer by layer to the input, adjusting the weights as it goes. When finished, a new training input is applied and the process starts the whole process again. It continues until an acceptable error is reached. At that point, the network is trained.

### 3.2.4 Factors Influencing Backpropagation Training

Factors that influence backpropagation training are as follows:

### Bias

Networks with biases can represent relationships between inputs and outputs more easily than networks without biases [14]. For example, neurons without a bias will always have a net input to the transfer function of zero when all of its inputs are zero. However, a neuron with a bias can learn to have any net transfer function input under the same conditions by learning an appropriate value for the bias. Adding a bias (a + 1 input with a training weight, which can be either positive or negative) to each neuron is usually desirable to offset the origin of the activation function. This produces an effect equivalent to adjusting the threshold of the neuron and often permits more rapid training. The weight of the bias is trainable just like any other weight except that the input is always +1.

### Momentum

Another technique to reduce training time is the use of momentum because it enhances the stability of the training process. Momentum is used to keep the training process going in the same general direction analogous to the way the momentum of a moving object behaves [15], [16]. In backpropagation with momentum, the weight change is a combination of the current gradient and the previous gradient.

This is a modification of gradient descent whose advantages arise when training data are very different from the majority of the data. It is desirable to use a small learning rate to avoid a major disruption of the direction of learning when a very unusual pair of training pattern is presented.

Convergence is sometimes faster if a momentum term is added to the weights update formulas. This involves adding a term to the weight adjustment that is proportional to the amount of the previous weight change. In effect, the previous adjustment is 'remembered' and used to modify the next change in weights. Hence, Eq. (3.20) now becomes,

$$\Delta W_{pq \cdot k}(t+1) = -\eta_{pq} X_{pq \cdot k} f_{p \cdot j} + \mu \Delta W_{pq \cdot k}(t) \qquad (3.36)$$

Where $\mu$ is the momentum coefficient (typically about 0.9). The new values of the weight then becomes equal to the previous value of the weight plus the weight change of Eq. (3.20), which includes the momentum terms. Equation (3.36) now becomes,

$$W_{pq \cdot k}(t+1) = W_{pq \cdot k}(t) + \Delta W_{pq \cdot k}(t+1) \qquad (3.37)$$

This process works well in many problems but not so well in others. There are a substantial number of advanced algorithms or other procedures that have been proposed as means of speeding up the training of BPNNs. Sejnowski and Rosenberg [17] proposed a similar momentum method that used exponential smoothing. However, the results were mixed. In some cases it improved the speed of the training, whereas in other cases it did not.

Parker [18] proposed a method called the 'second-order' backpropagation that used the second derivative to produce a more accurate estimation of the correct weight change. The computational requirements were greater and were generally viewed as not being cost-effective compared to other methods. It was, however, clear that higher-order (greater than 2) backpropagation systems were not effective. Stornetta and Huberman (1987) pointed out that the 0–1 range of sigmoidal function is not optimal for binary inputs. Since the magnitude of a weight adjustment is proportional to the output level of the neuron from which it originates, a level of 0 results in no modification.

With binary inputs, half of the outputs (on the average) will be zero, and weights do not train. The proposed solution was to change the input range of the activation function from −1/2 to +1/2 by adding a bias of −1/2. They demonstrated that for binary functions this procedure reduces the training time by 30–50 per cent. Nowadays, a more common method of accomplishing this is to use the arctan or hyperbolic tangent activation function.

Despite some spectacular results, it is clear that the main problem of backpropagation is the long and sometimes uncertain training time. Some ANNs have been known to require days or weeks of training, and in some cases the network simply will not train at all. This may be the result of a poor choice of training coefficients or perhaps the initial random distribution of the weights. However, in most cases, failure to train is usually due to local minima or network paralysis, where training virtually ceases due to operation in the flat region of the sigmoid function.

Let us try to understand the updating of weights through backpropagation in a simple feed-forward NN as in Fig. 3.8. Here all the neurons have the same logistic function and the slope ($s$) is set to 1 with the learning rate ($\eta$) 0.5 for both the hidden- and output-layer weight upgradation. The weight and bias upgradation for 1 epoch is handworked in the following section.

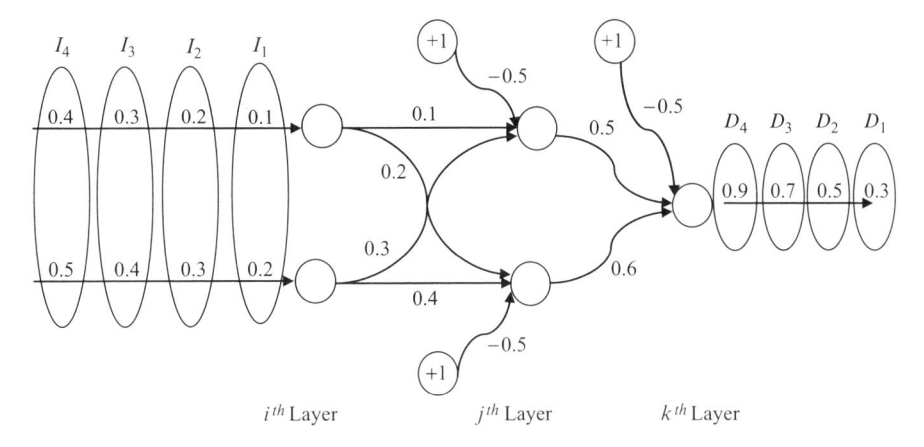

Fig. 3.8  Illustration of weight upgradation for simple BPNN

The change in weights and bias values from output layer to hidden layer is given by the Eqs 3.38 and 3.39, respectively, and has been tabulated in Table 3.1. It is also handworked for one epoch to have clear understanding.

$$\Delta W_{pq \cdot k} = -\eta_{p \cdot q}\left(-2 \times s \times \left(D_q - f_{q \cdot k}\right) f_{q \cdot k}\left(1 - f_{q \cdot k}\right) f_{p \cdot j}\right) \quad (3.38)$$

$$\Delta b_{q \cdot k} = -\eta_{p \cdot q}\left(-2 \times s \times \left(D_q - f_{q \cdot k}\right) f_{q \cdot k}\left(1 - f_{q \cdot k}\right) \times 1\right) \quad (3.39)$$

Similarly, the change in weights and bias values from input layer to hidden layer is given by the Eqs 3.40 and 3.41, respectively.

$$\Delta W_{hp \cdot j} = -\eta_{h \cdot p}\left[\sum_{q=1}^{r}(-2) \times s \times (D_q - f_{q \cdot k})\left[f_{q \cdot k}(1 - f_{q \cdot k})\right] W_{pq \cdot k}\right.$$
$$\left. \times s \times \left[f_{p \cdot j}(1 - f_{p \cdot j})\right] I_h\right] \quad (3.40)$$

$$\Delta b_{p \cdot j} = -\eta_{h \cdot p}\left[\sum_{q=1}^{r}(-2) \times s \times (D_q - f_{q \cdot k})\left[f_{q \cdot k}(1 - f_{q \cdot k})\right] W_{pq \cdot k}\right.$$
$$\left. \times s \times \left[f_{p \cdot j}(1 - f_{p \cdot j})\right] \times 1\right] \quad (3.41)$$

The handworked portion for one epoch is given here.

The subscripts $h$, $p$, $q$ and the indices $m$, $n$, and $r$ are considered as given in Fig. 3.5. Here, $m = 2$, $n = 2$, and $r = 1$. In this illustration, momentum term $(\mu) = 0$. Here, the target patterns are the sum of the input elements of each pattern.

**Epoch No. 1/Pattern No. 1**

$$I_1 = 0.1, \; I_2 = 0.2$$

**Table 3.1** Upgradation of weights and biases

| $I_1$ | $I_2$ | $sum_{1,j}$ | $sum_{2,j}$ | $f_{1,j}$ | $f_{2,j}$ | $sum_{k=1}$ | $f_{1,k}$ | $D_{1,k}$ | $W_{11,k}$ | $W_{12,k}$ | $b_{1,k}$ | $W_{11,j}$ | $W_{12,j}$ | $W_{21,j}$ | $W_{22,j}$ | $b_{1,j}$ | $b_{2,j}$ |
|---|---|---|---|---|---|---|---|---|---|---|---|---|---|---|---|---|---|
| 0.10 | 0.20 | −0.43 | −0.40 | 0.39 | 0.40 | −0.06 | 0.49 | 0.30 | 0.48 | 0.58 | −0.55 | 0.10 | 0.20 | 0.30 | 0.40 | −0.51 | −0.51 |
| 0.20 | 0.30 | −0.40 | −0.35 | −0.40 | 0.41 | −0.11 | 0.47 | 0.50 | 0.49 | 0.58 | −0.54 | 0.10 | 0.20 | 0.30 | 0.40 | −0.51 | −0.51 |
| 0.30 | 0.40 | −0.36 | −0.29 | 0.41 | 0.44 | −0.09 | 0.48 | 0.70 | 0.51 | 0.61 | −0.48 | 0.10 | 0.20 | 0.30 | 0.40 | −0.50 | −0.50 |
| 0.40 | 0.50 | −0.31 | −0.22 | 0.42 | 0.45 | 0.003 | 0.50 | 0.90 | 0.55 | 0.65 | −0.38 | 0.11 | 0.21 | 0.31 | 0.41 | −0.49 | −0.48 |
| 0.10 | 0.20 | −0.41 | −0.38 | 0.40 | 0.41 | 0.10 | 0.53 | 0.30 | 0.53 | 0.63 | −0.44 | 0.11 | 0.21 | 0.31 | 0.41 | −0.49 | −0.49 |
| 0.20 | 0.30 | −0.38 | −0.33 | 0.41 | 0.2 | 0.04 | 0.51 | 0.50 | 0.53 | 0.63 | −0.44 | 0.11 | 0.21 | 0.31 | 0.41 | −0.49 | −0.49 |
| 0.30 | 0.40 | −0.34 | −0.27 | 0.42 | 0.43 | 0.05 | 0.51 | 0.70 | 0.55 | 0.65 | −0.40 | 0.11 | 0.21 | 0.31 | 0.41 | −0.49 | −0.49 |
| 0.40 | 0.50 | −0.29 | −0.20 | 0.43 | 0.45 | 0.13 | 0.53 | 0.90 | 0.59 | 0.69 | −0.30 | 0.11 | 0.22 | 0.32 | 0.42 | −0.48 | −0.47 |
| 0.10 | 0.20 | −0.40 | −0.37 | 0.40 | 0.41 | 0.21 | 0.55 | 0.30 | 0.56 | 0.67 | −0.37 | 0.11 | 0.21 | 0.31 | 0.42 | −0.48 | −0.48 |
| 0.20 | 0.30 | −0.37 | −0.31 | 0.41 | 0.42 | 0.14 | 0.54 | 0.50 | 0.56 | 0.66 | −0.38 | 0.11 | 0.21 | 0.31 | 0.42 | −0.49 | −0.48 |
| 0.30 | 0.40 | −0.33 | −0.25 | 0.42 | 0.44 | 0.15 | 0.54 | 0.70 | 0.57 | 0.68 | −0.34 | 0.11 | 0.22 | 0.32 | 0.42 | −0.48 | −0.48 |
| 0.40 | 0.50 | −0.28 | −0.18 | 0.43 | 0.46 | 0.22 | 0.56 | 0.90 | 0.61 | 0.72 | −0.25 | 0.12 | 0.22 | 0.32 | 0.43 | −0.47 | −0.46 |

*Hidden-layer units weighted sum and output*

$$sum_{1 \cdot j} = (0.1 \times 0.1 + 0.2 \times 0.3) + 1 \times -0.5 = -0.43$$

$$f(sum_{1 \cdot j}) = \frac{1}{\left(1 + e^{\left(-1 \times sum_{1 \cdot j}\right)}\right)} = 0.3941$$

$$sum_{2 \cdot j} = (0.1 \times 0.2 + 0.2 \times 0.4) + 1 \times -0.5 = -0.40$$

$$f(sum_{2 \cdot j}) = \frac{1}{\left(1 + e^{\left(-1 \times sum_{2 \cdot j}\right)}\right)} = 0.4013$$

*Output-layer unit weighted sum and output*

$$sum_{1 \cdot k} = (0.3941 \times 0.5 + 0.4013 \times 0.6) + 1 \times -0.5 = -0.0621$$

$$f(sum_{1 \cdot k}) = \frac{1}{\left(1 + e^{\left(-1 \times sum_{1 \cdot j}\right)}\right)} = 0.4845$$

*Change in weights in the output layer*

$$\Delta W_{11 \cdot k} = -0.5 \times \left(-2 \times 1 \times (0.3 - 0.4845) \times 0.4845 \times (1 - 0.4845) \times 0.3941\right)$$
$$= -0.0182$$

$$\Delta W_{21 \cdot k} = -0.5 \times \left(-2 \times 1 \times (0.3 - 0.4845) \times 0.4845 \times (1 - 0.4845) \times 0.4013\right)$$
$$= -0.0185$$

*Change in bias in the output layer*

$$\Delta b_{1 \cdot k} = -0.5 \times \left(-2 \times 1 \times (0.3 - 0.4845) \times 0.4845 \times (1 - 0.4845) \times 1\right) = -0.0461$$

*Change in weights in the input layer*

$$\Delta W_{11 \cdot j} = -0.5 \sum_{q=1}^{r=1} \begin{bmatrix} (-2) \times 1 \times (0.3 - 0.4845) \times [0.4845 \times (1 - 0.4845)] \times 0.5 \times 1 \\ \times [0.3941 \times (1 - 0.3941)] \times 0.1 \end{bmatrix}$$
$$= -0.0006$$

$$\Delta W_{12 \cdot j} = -0.5 \sum_{q=1}^{r=1} \begin{bmatrix} (-2) \times 1 \times (0.3 - 0.4845) \times [0.4845 \times (1 - 0.4845)] \times 0.6 \times 1 \\ \times [0.3941 \times (1 - 0.3941)] \times 0.1 \end{bmatrix}$$
$$= -0.0007$$

$$\Delta W_{21 \cdot j} = -0.5 \sum_{q=1}^{r=1} \begin{bmatrix} (-2) \times 1 \times (0.3 - 0.4845) \times [0.4845 \times (1 - 0.4845)] \times 0.5 \times 1 \\ \times [0.4013 \times (1 - 0.4013)] \times 0.2 \end{bmatrix}$$
$$= -0.0011$$

$$\Delta W_{22 \cdot j} = -0.5 \sum_{q=1}^{r=1} \begin{bmatrix} (-2) \times 1 \times (0.3 - 0.4845) \times [0.4845 \times (1 - 0.4845)] \times 0.6 \times 1 \\ \times [0.4013 \times (1 - 0.4013)] \times 0.2 \end{bmatrix}$$
$$= -0.0013$$

*Change in bias in the input layer*

$$\Delta b_{1 \cdot j} = -0.5 \sum_{q=1}^{r=1} \begin{bmatrix} (-2) \times 1 \times (0.3 - 0.4845) \times [0.4845 \times (1 - 0.4845)] \times 0.5 \times 1 \\ \times [0.3941 \times (1 - 0.3941)] \times 1 \end{bmatrix}$$
$$= -0.0055$$

$$\Delta b_{2 \cdot j} = -0.5 \sum_{q=1}^{r=1} \begin{bmatrix} (-2) \times 1 \times (0.3 - 0.4845) \times [0.4845 \times (1 - 0.4845)] \times 0.6 \times 1 \\ \times [0.4013 \times (1 - 0.4013)] \times 1 \end{bmatrix}$$
$$= -0.0066$$

*New weights in the output layer*

$$W_{11 \cdot k}(t+1) = 0.5 - 0.0182 = 0.4818$$
$$W_{21 \cdot k}(t+1) = 0.6 - 0.0185 = 0.5815$$

*New bias in the output layer*

$$b_{1 \cdot k} = -0.5 - 0.0461 = -0.5461$$

*New weights in the input layer*

$$W_{11 \cdot j} = 0.1 - 0.0006 = 0.0994$$
$$W_{12 \cdot j} = 0.2 - 0.0007 = 0.1993$$
$$W_{21 \cdot j} = 0.3 - 0.0011 = 0.2989$$
$$W_{22 \cdot j} = 0.4 - 0.0013 = 0.3987$$

*New bias in the input layer*

$$b_{1 \cdot j} = -0.5 - 0.0055 = -0.5055$$
$$b_{2 \cdot j} = -0.5 - 0.0066 = -0.5066$$

**Epoch No. 1/Pattern No. 2**

$$I_1 = 0.2, \ I_2 = 0.3$$

*Hidden-layer units weighted sum and output*

$$sum_{1 \cdot j} = (0.2 \times 0.0994 + 0.3 \times 0.2989) + 1 \times -0.5055 = -0.3959$$

$$f(sum_{1 \cdot j}) = \frac{1}{\left(1 + e^{\left(-1 \times sum_{1 \cdot j}\right)}\right)} = 0.4023$$

$$sum_{2 \cdot j} = (0.2 \times 0.1993 + 0.3 \times 0.3987) + 1 \times -0.5066 = -0.3472$$

$$f(sum_{2 \cdot j}) = \frac{1}{\left(1 + e^{\left(-1 \times sum_{2 \cdot j}\right)}\right)} = 0.4141$$

*Output-layer unit weighted sum and output*

$$sum_{1 \cdot k} = (0.4023 \times 0.4818 + 0.4141 \times 0.5815) + 1 \times -0.5461 = -0.1114$$

$$f(sum_{1 \cdot k}) = \frac{1}{\left(1 + e^{\left(-1 \times sum_{1 \cdot j}\right)}\right)} = 0.4722$$

*Change in weights in the output layer*

$$\Delta W_{11 \cdot k} = -0.5 \times \left(-2 \times 1 \times (0.5 - 0.4722) \times 0.4722 \times (1 - 0.4722) \times 0.4023\right) = 0.0028$$

$$\Delta W_{21 \cdot k} = -0.5 \times \left(-2 \times 1 \times (0.5 - 0.4722) \times 0.4722 \times (1 - 0.4722) \times 0.4141\right) = 0.0029$$

*Change in bias in the output layer*

$$\Delta b_{1 \cdot k} = -0.5 \times \left(-2 \times 1 \times (0.5 - 0.4722) \times 0.4722 \times (1 - 0.4722) \times 1\right) = 0.0069$$

*Change in weights in the input layer*

$$\Delta W_{11 \cdot j} = -0.5 \sum_{q=1}^{r=1} \left[ \begin{array}{l} (-2) \times 1 \times (05 - 0.4722) \times [0.4722 \times (1 - 0.4722)] \times 0.4818 \times 1 \\ \times [0.4023 \times (1 - 0.4023)] \times 0.2 \end{array} \right]$$

$$= -0.0001607$$

$$\Delta W_{12 \cdot j} = -0.5 \sum_{q=1}^{r=1} \left[ \begin{array}{l} (-2) \times 1 \times (0.5 - 0.4722) \times [0.4722 \times (1 - 0.4722)] \times 0.5815 \times 1 \\ \times [0.4141 \times (1 - 0.4141)] \times 0.2 \end{array} \right]$$

$$= -0.0001957$$

$$\Delta W_{21 \cdot j} = -0.5 \sum_{q=1}^{r=1} \left[ \begin{array}{l} (-2) \times 1 \times (0.5 - 0.4722) \times [0.4722 \times (1 - 0.4722)] \times 0.4818 \times 1 \\ \times [0.4023 \times (1 - 0.4023)] \times 0.3 \end{array} \right]$$

$$= 0.0002411$$

$$\Delta W_{22 \cdot j} = -0.5 \sum_{q=1}^{r=1} \left[ \begin{array}{l} (-2) \times 1 \times (0.5 - 0.4722) \times [0.4722 \times (1 - 0.4722)] \times 0.5815 \times 1 \\ \times [0.4141 \times (1 - 0.4141)] \times 0.3 \end{array} \right]$$

$$= 0.0002936$$

*Change in bias in the input layer*

$$\Delta b_{1 \cdot j} = -0.5 \sum_{q=1}^{r=1} \left[ \begin{array}{l} (-2) \times 1 \times (0.5 - 0.4722) \times [0.4722 \times (1 - 0.4722)] \times 0.4818 \times 1 \\ \times [0.4023 \times (1 - 0.4023)] \times 1 \end{array} \right]$$

$$= 0.0008037$$

$$\Delta b_{2 \cdot j} = -0.5 \sum_{q=1}^{r=1} \begin{bmatrix} (-2) \times 1 \times (0.5 - 0.4722) \times [0.4722 \times (1 - 0.4722)] \times 0.5818 \times 1 \\ \times [0.4141 \times (1 - 0.4141)] \times 1 \end{bmatrix}$$

$$= 0.0009787$$

*New weights in the output layer*

$$W_{11 \cdot k}(t+1) = 0.4818 + 0.0028 = 0.4846$$

$$W_{21 \cdot k}(t+1) = 0.5815 + 0.0029 = 0.5844$$

*New bias in the output layer*

$$b_{1 \cdot k} = -0.5461 + 0.0069 = -0.5391$$

*New weights in the input layer*

$$W_{11 \cdot j} = 0.0994 - 0.0001607 = 0.0996$$

$$W_{12 \cdot j} = 0.1993 - 0.0001957 = 0.1995$$

$$W_{21 \cdot j} = 0.2989 - 0.0002411 = 0.2991$$

$$W_{22 \cdot j} = 0.3987 - 0.0008037 = 0.3990$$

*New bias in the input layer*

$$b_{1 \cdot j} = -0.5055 - 0.0008037 = -0.5047$$

$$b_{2 \cdot j} = -0.5 - 0.0066 = -0.5066$$

**Epoch No. 1/Pattern No. 3**

$$I_1 = 0.3, \ I_2 = 0.4$$

*Hidden-layer units weighted sum and output*

$$sum_{1 \cdot j} = (0.3 \times 0.0996 + 0.4 \times 0.2991) + 1 \times -0.5047 = -0.3552$$

$$f(sum_{1 \cdot j}) = \frac{1}{\left(1 + e^{(-1 \times sum_{1 \cdot j})}\right)} = 0.4121$$

$$sum_{2 \cdot j} = (0.3 \times 0.1995 + 0.4 \times 0.3990) + 1 \times -0.5066 = -0.2862$$

$$f(sum_{2 \cdot j}) = \frac{1}{\left(1 + e^{(-1 \times sum_{2 \cdot j})}\right)} = 0.4289$$

*Output-layer unit weighted sum and output*

$$sum_{1 \cdot k} = (0.4121 \times 0.4846 + 0.4289 \times 0.5844) + 1 \times -0.5391 = -0.0887$$

$$f(sum_{1 \cdot k}) = \frac{1}{\left(1 + e^{(-1 \times sum_{1 \cdot j})}\right)} = 0.4778$$

*Change in weights in the output layer*

$$\Delta W_{11 \cdot k} = -0.5 \times (-2 \times 1 \times (0.7 - 0.4778) \times 0.4778 \times (1 - 0.4778) \times 0.4121) = 0.0228$$

$$\Delta W_{21 \cdot k} = -0.5 \times (-2 \times 1 \times (0.7 - 0.4778) \times 0.4778 \times (1 - 0.4778) \times 0.4289) = 0.0238$$

*Change in bias in the output layer*

$$\Delta b_{1 \cdot k} = -0.5 \times (-2 \times 1 \times (0.7 - 0.4778) \times 0.4778 \times (1 - 0.4778) \times 1) = 0.0554$$

*Change in weights in the input layer*

$$\Delta W_{11 \cdot j} = -0.5 \sum_{q=1}^{r=1} \begin{bmatrix} (-2) \times 1 \times (0.7 - 0.4778) \times [0.4778 \times (1 - 0.4778)] \times 0.4846 \times 1 \\ \times [0.4121 \times (1 - 0.4121)] \times 0.3 \end{bmatrix}$$
$$= 0.0020$$

$$\Delta W_{12 \cdot j} = -0.5 \sum_{q=1}^{r=1} \begin{bmatrix} (-2) \times 1 \times (0.7 - 0.4778) \times [0.4778 \times (1 - 0.4778)] \times 0.5844 \times 1 \\ \times [0.4289 \times (1 - 0.4289)] \times 0.3 \end{bmatrix}$$
$$= 0.0024$$

$$\Delta W_{21 \cdot j} = -0.5 \sum_{q=1}^{r=1} \begin{bmatrix} (-2) \times 1 \times (0.7 - 0.4778) \times [0.4778 \times (1 - 0.4778)] \times 0.4846 \times 1 \\ \times [0.4121 \times (1 - 0.4121)] \times 0.4 \end{bmatrix}$$
$$= 0.0026$$

$$\Delta W_{22 \cdot j} = -0.5 \sum_{q=1}^{r=1} \begin{bmatrix} (-2) \times 1 \times (0.7 - 0.4778) \times [0.4778 \times (1 - 0.4778)] \times 0.5844 \times 1 \\ \times [0.4289 \times (1 - 0.4289)] \times 0.4 \end{bmatrix}$$
$$= 0.0032$$

*Change in bias in the input layer*

$$\Delta b_{1 \cdot j} = -0.5 \sum_{q=1}^{r=1} \begin{bmatrix} (-2) \times 1 \times (0.7 - 0.4778) \times [0.4778 \times (1 - 0.4778)] \times 0.4846 \times 1 \\ \times [0.4121 \times (1 - 0.4121)] \times 1 \end{bmatrix}$$
$$= 0.0065$$

$$\Delta b_{2 \cdot j} = -0.5 \sum_{q=1}^{r=1} \begin{bmatrix} (-2) \times 1 \times (0.7 - 0.4778) \times [0.4778 \times (1 - 0.4778)] \times 0.5844 \times 1 \\ \times [0.4289 \times (1 - 0.4289)] \times 1 \end{bmatrix}$$
$$= 0.0079$$

*New weights in the output layer*

$$W_{11 \cdot k}(t+1) = 0.4846 + 0.0228 = 0.5075$$

$$W_{21 \cdot k}(t+1) = 0.5844 + 0.0238 = 0.6082$$

*New bias in the output layer*

$$b_{1 \cdot k} = -0.5391 - 0.0554 = -0.4837$$

*New weights in the input layer*

$$W_{11,j} = 0.0996 + 0.0020 = 0.1016$$
$$W_{12,j} = 0.1995 - 0.0024 = 0.2019$$
$$W_{21,j} = 0.2991 + 0.0026 = 0.3017$$
$$W_{22,j} = 0.3990 + 0.0032 = 0.4021$$

*New bias in the input layer*

$$b_{1,j} = -0.5047 + 0.0065 = -0.4021$$
$$b_{2,j} = -0.5066 + 0.0079 = -0.4977$$

**Epoch No. 1/Pattern No. 4**

$$I_1 = 0.4, \quad I_2 = 0.5$$

*Hidden-layer units weighted sum and output*

$$sum_{1,j} = (0.4 \times 0.1016 + 0.5 \times 0.3017) + 1 \times -0.4021 = -0.3067$$

$$f(sum_{1,j}) = \frac{1}{\left(1 + e^{(-1 \times sum_{1,j})}\right)} = 0.4239$$

$$sum_{2,j} = (0.4 \times 0.2019 + 0.5 \times 0.4021) + 1 \times -0.4977 = -0.2159$$

$$f(sum_{2,j}) = \frac{1}{\left(1 + e^{(-1 \times sum_{2,j})}\right)} = 0.4462$$

*Output-layer unit weighted sum and output*

$$sum_{1,k} = (0.4239 \times 0.5075 + 0.4462 \times 0.6082) + 1 \times -0.4837 = 0.0028$$

$$f(sum_{1,k}) = \frac{1}{\left(1 + e^{(-1 \times sum_{1,j})}\right)} = 0.5007$$

*Change in weights in the output layer*

$$\Delta W_{11,k} = -0.5 \times (-2 \times 1 \times (0.9 - 0.5007) \times 0.5007 \times (1 - 0.5007) \times 0.4239) = 0.0423$$

$$\Delta W_{21,k} = -0.5 \times (-2 \times 1 \times (0.9 - 0.5007) \times 0.5007 \times (1 - 0.5007) \times 0.4462) = 0.0445$$

*Change in bias in the output layer*

$$\Delta b_{1,k} = -0.5 \times (-2 \times 1 \times (0.9 - 0.5007) \times 0.5007 \times (1 - 0.5007) \times 1) = 0.0998$$

*Change in weights in the input layer*

$$\Delta W_{11,j} = -0.5 \sum_{q=1}^{r=1} \begin{bmatrix} (-2) \times 1 \times (0.9 - 0.5007) \times [0.5007 \times (1 - 0.5007)] \times 0.5075 \times 1 \\ \times [0.4239 \times (1 - 0.4239)] \times 0.4 \end{bmatrix}$$
$$= 0.0049$$

$$\Delta W_{12.j} = -0.5 \sum_{q=1}^{r=1} \begin{bmatrix} (-2) \times 1 \times (0.9 - 0.5007) \times [0.5007 \times (1 - 0.5007)] \times 0.6082 \times 1 \\ \times [0.4462 \times (1 - 0.4462)] \times 0.4 \end{bmatrix}$$
$$= 0.0060$$

$$\Delta W_{21.j} = -0.5 \sum_{q=1}^{r=1} \begin{bmatrix} (-2) \times 1 \times (0.9 - 0.5007) \times [0.5007 \times (1 - 0.5007)] \times 0.5075 \times 1 \\ \times [0.4239 \times (1 - 0.4239)] \times 0.5 \end{bmatrix}$$
$$= 0.0062$$

$$\Delta W_{22.j} = -0.5 \sum_{q=1}^{r=1} \begin{bmatrix} (-2) \times 1 \times (0.9 - 0.5007) \times [0.5007 \times (1 - 0.5007)] \times 0.6082 \times 1 \\ \times [0.4462 \times (1 - 0.4462)] \times 0.5 \end{bmatrix}$$
$$= 0.0075$$

*Change in bias in the input layer*

$$\Delta b_{1.j} = -0.5 \sum_{q=1}^{r=1} \begin{bmatrix} (-2) \times 1 \times (0.9 - 0.5007) \times [0.5007 \times (1 - 0.5007)] \times 0.5075 \times 1 \\ \times [0.4239 \times (1 - 0.4239)] \times 1 \end{bmatrix}$$
$$= 0.0124$$

$$\Delta b_{2.j} = -0.5 \sum_{q=1}^{r=1} \begin{bmatrix} (-2) \times 1 \times (0.9 - 0.5007) \times [0.5007 \times (1 - 0.5007)] \times 0.6082 \times 1 \\ \times [0.4462 \times (1 - 0.4462)] \times 1 \end{bmatrix}$$
$$= 0.0150$$

*New weights in the output layer*
$$W_{11.k}(t+1) = 0.5075 + 0.0423 = 0.5498$$
$$W_{21.k}(t+1) = 0.6082 + 0.0445 = 0.6527$$

*New bias in the output layer*
$$b_{1.k} = -0.4837 + 0.0998 = -0.3839$$

*New weights in the input layer*
$$W_{11.j} = 0.1016 + 0.0049 = 0.1065$$
$$W_{12.j} = 0.2019 + 0.0060 = 0.2079$$
$$W_{21.j} = 0.3017 + 0.0062 = 0.3079$$
$$W_{22.j} = 0.4021 - 0.0075 = 0.4096$$

*New bias in the input layer*
$$b_{1.j} = -0.4021 + 0.0124 = -0.4858$$
$$b_{2.j} = -0.4977 + 0.0150 = -0.4827$$

*Sum Squared Error (Epoch No. 1)*

$$sse = \left( \sum_{Pattern\ Number(PN)=1}^{4} \left( \sum_{q=1}^{r=1} \left(D_q - f_{q.k}\right)^2 \right) \right)$$

$$= (0.3 - 0.4845)^2 + (0.5 - 0.4722)^2 + (0.7 - 0.4778)^2 + (0.9 - 0.5007)^2$$

$$= 0.2436$$

The training should be carried out for more number of epochs to reduce the sum squared error, and thereby the accuracy of the test output will be improved. A MATLAB Program 3.1, Part A is given to demonstrate and test the previously given patterns. In this program, parameters are initialized uncommenting Part A and commenting Part B. The convergence plot (Fig. 3.9) is given as follows after training for 10,000 epochs with a sum squared error of $7.6902e^{-004}$. The final weights and bias values that are obtained after training is given here in Table 3.2.

Table 3.2 Final weights and biases after 10,000 epochs

| Output-layer weights and bias | | | Input-layer weights and biases | | | | | |
|---|---|---|---|---|---|---|---|---|
| $W_{11.k}$ | $W_{12.k}$ | $b_{1.k}$ | $W_{11.j}$ | $W_{12.j}$ | $W_{21.j}$ | $W_{22.j}$ | $b_{1.j}$ | $b_{2.j}$ |
| 3.6357 | 4.9436 | −2.3061 | 2.3589 | 3.1077 | 2.4296 | 3.0606 | −1.7930 | −2.9714 |

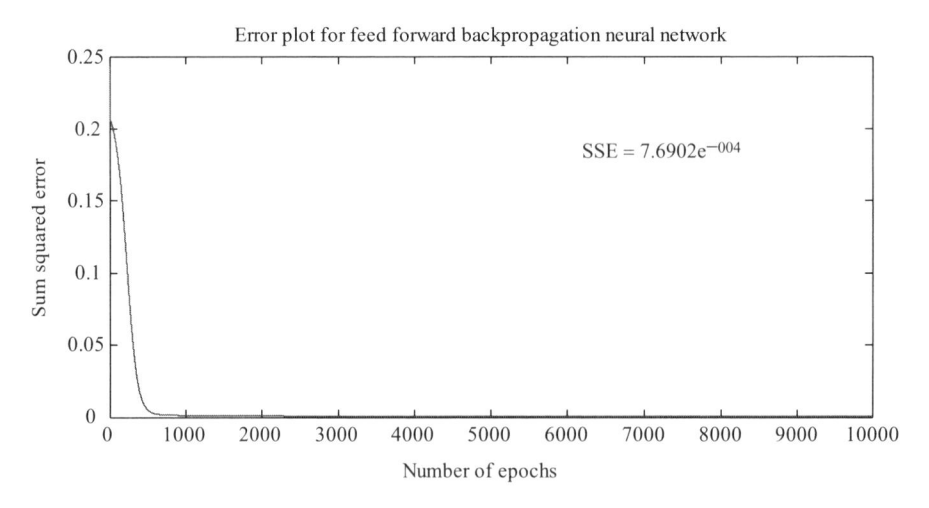

Fig. 3.9 Error convergence plot

After the training is over, the following are the results that are tabulated in Table 3.3 for various test inputs.

During the testing mode, the test inputs are given from the input patterns already present in the training set, and the output results obtained are closer to the desired one.

Table 3.3 Test results

| Test input | | Desired output | Actual/predicted output |
|---|---|---|---|
| $I_1$ | $I_2$ | $f_{1,k}$ | $D_{1,k}$ |
| 0.1 | 0.2 | 0.3000 | 0.3071 |
| 0.2 | 0.3 | 0.5000 | 0.4855 |
| 0.3 | 0.4 | 0.7000 | 0.7162 |
| 0.4 | 0.5 | 0.9000 | 0.8878 |
| 0.4 | 0.3 | 0.7000 | 0.7159 |
| 0.2 | 0.5 | 0.7000 | 0.7165 |
| 0.18 | 0.32 | 0.5000 | 0.4856 |
| 0.367 | 0.438 | 0.8050 | 0.8196 |
| 0.463 | 0.333 | 0.7960 | 0.8117 |
| 0.345 | 0.543 | 0.8880 | 0.8806 |

Here, the desired target patterns are basically kept as the summation of the elements of the input pattern. Even if we give a typical or simillar kind of input pattern not present in the training set, still the NN is capable of giving an output which is closer to the desired target pattern. This shows the adaptablity of the NN for similar kind of input patterns that are not present in the training process.

The overall working range of elements that are considered is between 0.1 and 0.9, and the desired target patterns are set such that it should not go beyond 0.9. Also, it should be noted that the logistic sigmoidal function can produce an output between 0 and 1. The accuracy of the output can be increased, when more input patterns are considered, by properly tuning the NN training parameter and by selecting optimal network architecture.

Let us try another example to illustrate the BPNN for a two-input binary patterns to behave like AND, OR, XOR, NAND, and NOR logic simultaneously. The network is given in Fig. 3.10. The numbers of hidden layers are set as one with four hidden units. It should be noted that the inputs and output patterns need not necessarily be discrete but also can be continous values. The initial weights and biases are set randomly.

Let us try to use logistic functions for both the hidden and output-layer units. The output values that will be obtained are between 0 and 1. Since the desired target units are binary, during testing mode the output unit has to produe a binary value. Therefore, we will pass the output through a binary logic to produce a binary output and test for all input patterns to ascertain that BPNN is able to perform AND, OR, XOR, NAND, and NOR logic simultaneously. The binary logic will give a digital output as one if the continous output of the network is greater than 0.5, otherwise the output is zero.

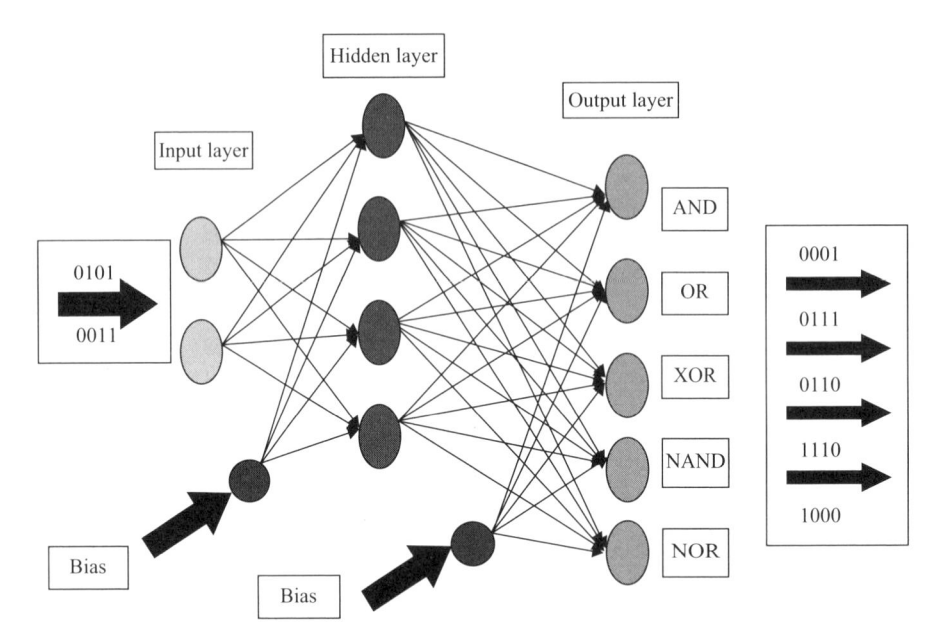

**Fig. 3.10** Backpropagation neural network with 2-input/5-output units

The MATLAB Program 3.1, Part B, can be used to demonstrate the aforementioned application. In this program, parameters are initialized uncommenting Part B and commenting Parts A and C. The same program can be used to train and test to check whether the network behaves in the aforementioned manner.

### 3.2.5 Character Recognition Using Backpropagation Neural Network

Character recognition is a trivial task for humans; however to make a computer program that does that is extremely difficult. Recognizing patterns is just one of those things that humans do well and computers do not. The main reason may be the many sources of variability. Noise, for example, consists of random changes to a pattern, particularly near the edges and a character with much noise may be interpreted as a completely different character by a computer program.

Another source of confusion is the high level of abstraction; there are thousands styles of type in common use and a character recognition program must recognize most of these to be of any use. There exist several different techniques for recognizing characters. One distinguishes characters by the number of loops in a character and the direction of their concavities. Another common technique uses BPNN for character recognition.

In this section, alphabets from A to Z are used for training, and have been tested with error incorporated in the test pattern. The alphabet is represented using a $7 \times 5$ matrix (Fig. 3.11) of 35 binary bits as shown here:

A = [00100010101000110001111111000110001], B = [11110100011000111110100011000111110]
C = [01110100011000010000100001000101110], D = [11110100011000110001100011000111110]

E = [11111100001000111101000010000111111], F = [11111100001000111101000010000111111]
G = [01110100011000100001011110001011110], H = [10001100011000111111100011000110001]
I = [01110001000010000100001000010001110], J = [11111001000010000100001001010001000]
K = [10001100101010011000101001001010001], L = [10000100001000010000100001000011111]
M = [10001110111010110001100011000110001], N = [10001110011100110101100111001110001]
O = [01110100011000110001100011000101110], P = [11110100011000111110100001000010000]
Q = [01110100011000110001101011001001101], R = [11110100011000111110101001001010001]
S = [01110100010100000100000101000101110], T = [11111001000010000100001000010000100]
U = [10001100011000110001100011000101110], V = [10001100011000110001100011000101000100]
W = [10001100011000110001101011101110001], X = [10001100010101000100010101000110001]
Y = [10001100010101000100001000010000100], Z = [11111000010001000100010001000011111]

```
     A        B        C        D        E        F
  0 0 1 0 0  1 1 1 1 0  0 1 1 1 0  1 1 1 1 0  1 1 1 1 1  1 1 1 1 1
  0 1 0 1 0  1 0 0 0 1  1 0 0 0 1  1 0 0 0 1  1 0 0 0 0  1 0 0 0 0
  1 0 0 0 1  1 0 0 0 1  1 0 0 0 0  1 0 0 0 1  1 0 0 0 0  1 0 0 0 0
  1 0 0 0 1  1 1 1 1 0  1 0 0 0 0  1 0 0 0 1  1 1 1 1 0  1 1 1 1 0
  1 1 1 1 1  1 0 0 0 1  1 0 0 0 0  1 0 0 0 1  1 0 0 0 0  1 0 0 0 0
  1 0 0 0 1  1 0 0 0 1  1 0 0 0 1  1 0 0 0 1  1 0 0 0 0  1 0 0 0 0
  1 0 0 0 1  1 1 1 1 0  0 1 1 1 0  1 1 1 1 0  1 1 1 1 1  1 0 0 0 0

     G        H        I        J        K        L
  0 1 1 1 0  1 0 0 0 1  0 1 1 1 0  1 1 1 1 1  1 0 0 0 1  1 0 0 0 0
  1 0 0 0 1  1 0 0 0 1  0 0 1 0 0  0 0 1 0 0  1 0 0 1 0  1 0 0 0 0
  1 0 0 0 0  1 0 0 0 1  0 0 1 0 1  0 0 1 0 0  1 0 1 0 0  1 0 0 0 0
  1 0 0 0 0  1 1 1 1 1  0 0 1 0 0  0 0 1 0 0  1 1 0 0 0  1 0 0 0 0
  1 0 1 1 1  1 0 0 0 1  0 0 1 0 0  0 0 1 0 0  1 0 1 0 0  1 0 0 0 0
  1 0 0 0 1  1 0 0 0 1  0 0 1 0 0  1 0 1 0 0  1 0 0 1 0  1 0 0 0 0
  0 1 1 1 0  1 0 0 0 1  0 1 1 1 0  0 1 0 0 0  1 0 0 0 1  1 1 1 1 1

     M        N        O        P        Q        R
  1 0 0 0 1  1 0 0 0 1  0 1 1 1 0  1 1 1 1 0  0 1 1 1 0  1 1 1 1 0
  1 1 0 1 1  1 1 0 0 1  1 0 0 0 1  1 0 0 0 1  1 0 0 0 1  1 0 0 0 1
  1 0 1 0 1  1 1 0 0 1  1 0 0 0 1  1 0 0 0 1  1 0 0 0 1  1 0 0 0 1
  1 0 0 0 1  1 0 1 0 1  1 0 0 0 1  1 1 1 1 0  1 0 0 0 1  1 1 1 1 0
  1 0 0 0 1  1 0 0 1 1  1 0 0 0 1  1 0 0 0 0  1 0 1 0 1  1 0 1 0 0
  1 0 0 0 1  1 0 0 1 1  1 0 0 0 1  1 0 0 0 0  1 0 0 1 0  1 0 0 1 0
  1 0 0 0 1  1 0 0 0 1  0 1 1 1 0  1 0 0 0 0  0 1 1 0 1  1 0 0 0 1

     S        T        U        V        W        X
  0 1 1 1 0  1 1 1 1 1  1 0 0 0 1  1 0 0 0 1  1 0 0 0 1  1 0 0 0 1
  1 0 0 0 1  0 0 1 0 0  1 0 0 0 1  1 0 0 0 1  1 0 0 0 1  1 0 0 0 1
  0 1 0 0 0  0 0 1 0 0  1 0 0 0 1  1 0 0 0 1  1 0 0 0 1  0 1 0 1 0
  0 0 1 0 0  0 0 1 0 0  1 0 0 0 1  1 0 0 0 1  1 0 0 0 1  0 0 1 0 0
  0 0 0 1 0  0 0 1 0 0  1 0 0 0 1  1 0 0 0 1  1 0 1 0 1  0 1 0 1 0
  1 0 0 0 1  0 0 1 0 0  1 0 0 0 1  0 1 0 1 0  1 1 0 1 1  1 0 0 0 1
  0 1 1 1 0  0 0 1 0 0  0 1 1 1 0  0 0 1 0 0  1 0 0 0 1  1 0 0 0 1

     Y        Z
  1 0 0 0 1  1 1 1 1 1
  1 0 0 0 1  0 0 0 0 1
  0 1 0 1 0  0 0 0 1 0
  0 0 1 0 0  0 0 1 0 0
  0 0 1 1 0  0 1 0 0 0
  0 0 1 0 0  1 0 0 0 0
  0 0 1 0 0  1 1 1 1 1
```

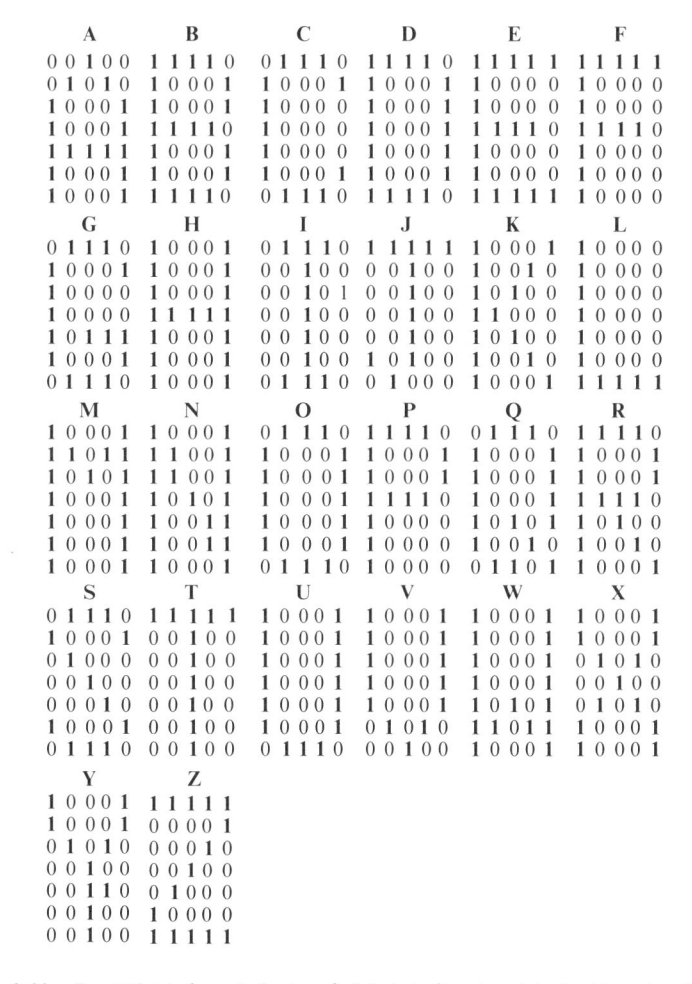

**Fig. 3.11** $7 \times 5$ Matrix format display of alphabets (input and desired target patterns)

The forward BPNN is designed with 35 input and output units. The hidden-layer neurons are choosen by trial and error method. The training set consists of 26 patterns. All other network and training parameters are carefully chosen to reduce the sums squared error. Since we use sigmoidal logistic function for all neurons, during the testing mode, the actual output of the NN is passed through a binary logic to get binary output. The binary logic will give a digital output as 1 if the continous output of the network is greater than 0.5, otherwise the output is 1.

Once the training is carried out succesfully with less sum squared error, the newwork is tested to recognize the patterns with and without error. The accuracy of the predicted output depends upon the increased epochs of training and selection of suitable network parameters. However, there are limitations that correspond to BPNN and the limitations of the learning rules that used for training. The accuracy of the output can be increased by increasing the number of elements in the training patterns since they should have atleast a minimal difference between individual training patterns. This will enable the network to generalize and train effectively.

The MATLAB Program 3.1, Part C, can be used to demonstrate the aforecited application. In this program, parameters are initialized uncommenting Part C and commenting Parts A and B. The readers can use the following program to train and test to check whether the network behaves in the aforementioned manner. The convergence error plot during the training mode for 10,000 epochs is given in Fig. 3.12.

The network can be tested with the same input patterns used in the training set (i.e., input patterns withput error) and also with the input patterns with error as shown in Fig. 3.13. It should be noted, in the testing mode, the network is able to correctly recognize similar test patterns with an error. One of the sample testing mode result is presented in Fig. 3.14.

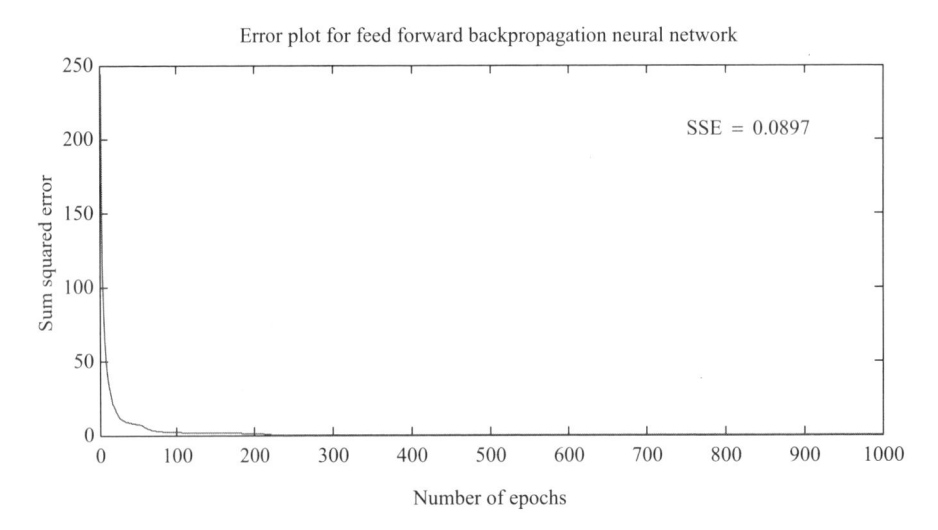

**Fig. 3.12** Error convergence plot

## Artificial Neural Networks—Second Generation

```
     A            B            C            D            E            F
_1_ 0 1 0 0   1 1 1 1 0    0 1 1 1 0    1 1 1 1 0    1 1 1 1 1    1 1 1 1 1
 0 1 0 1 0   1 0 _1_ 0 1   1 0 0 0 1    1 0 0 0 1    1 0 0 0 0    1 0 _1_ 0 0
 1 0 0 0 1   1 0 0 0 1    1 0 0 0 0    1 0 0 0 1    1 0 0 0 0    1 0 0 0 0
 1 0 0 0 1   1 1 1 1 0    1 0 0 0 0    1 0 0 0 1    1 1 1 1 0    1 1 1 1 0
 1 1 1 1 1   1 0 0 0 1    1 0 0 0 0    1 0 0 0 1    1 0 0 0 0    1 0 0 0 0
 1 0 0 0 1   1 0 0 0 1    1 0 0 0 1    1 0 0 0 1    1 0 0 0 _1_  1 0 0 0 0
 1 0 0 0 1   1 1 1 1 0    0 1 1 _0_ 0  1 _0_ 1 1 0   1 1 1 1 1    1 0 0 0 0

     G            H            I            J            K            L
 0 1 1 1 0   1 0 0 0 1    0 1 1 _0_ 0  1 1 1 1 1    1 0 0 0 1    1 0 0 0 0
 1 0 0 0 1   1 0 0 0 1    0 0 1 0 0    0 0 1 0 _1_  1 0 0 1 0    1 0 0 0 0
 1 0 _1_ 0 0 1 0 0 0 0    0 0 1 0 0    0 0 1 0 0    1 0 1 0 0    1 _1_ 0 0 0
 1 0 _0_ 0 0 1 _0_ 1 1 1  0 0 1 0 0    0 0 1 0 0    1 1 0 0 0    1 0 0 0 0
 1 0 1 1 1   1 0 0 0 1    0 0 1 0 0    0 0 1 0 0    1 0 1 0 0    1 0 0 0 0
 1 0 0 0 1   1 0 0 0 1    0 0 1 0 0    1 0 1 0 0    1 0 0 1 0    1 0 0 0 0
 0 1 1 1 0   1 0 0 0 1    0 1 1 1 0    0 1 0 0 0    1 0 _1_ 0 1  1 1 1 1 1

     M            N            O            P            Q            R
 1 0 0 0 1   1 0 0 0 1    0 1 1 1 0    1 1 1 1 0    0 1 1 1 0    1 1 1 1 0
 1 1 0 1 1   1 1 0 0 1    1 0 0 0 1    1 0 _1_ 0 1  1 0 _1_ 0 1  1 0 0 0 1
 1 0 1 0 1   _0_ 1 0 0 1  1 0 _1_ 0 1  1 0 0 0 1    1 0 0 0 1    _0_ 0 0 0 1
 1 0 0 0 1   1 0 1 0 1    1 0 0 0 1    1 1 1 1 0    1 0 0 0 1    1 1 1 1 0
 1 0 0 0 1   1 0 0 1 1    1 0 0 0 1    1 0 0 0 0    1 0 1 0 1    1 0 1 0 0
 _0_ 0 0 0 1 1 0 0 1 1    1 0 0 0 1    1 0 0 0 0    1 0 0 1 0    1 0 0 1 0
 1 0 0 0 1   1 0 0 0 1    0 1 1 1 0    1 0 0 0 0    0 1 1 0 1    1 0 0 0 1

     S            T            U            V            W            X
 0 1 _0_ 1 0 1 1 1 1 1    1 0 0 0 1    1 0 0 0 1    1 0 0 0 1    1 0 0 0 1
 1 0 0 0 1   0 0 1 0 0    1 0 _1_ 0 1  1 0 0 0 1    1 0 0 0 1    1 0 0 0 1
 0 1 0 0 0   0 0 1 0 0    1 0 0 0 1    1 0 0 0 1    1 0 0 0 1    0 1 0 1 0
 0 0 1 0 0   0 0 1 0 0    1 0 0 0 1    1 0 _1_ 0 1  1 0 0 0 1    0 0 1 0 0
 0 0 0 1 0   _1_ 0 1 0 0  1 0 0 0 1    1 0 0 0 1    1 0 1 0 1    0 1 0 1 0
 1 0 0 0 1   0 0 1 0 0    1 0 0 0 1    0 1 0 1 0    1 1 0 1 _0_  1 0 0 0 1
 0 1 1 1 0   0 0 1 0 0    0 1 1 1 0    0 0 1 0 0    1 0 0 0 _1_  1 0 0 0 _0_

     Y            Z
 1 0 0 0 1   1 1 1 1 1
 1 0 _1_ 0 1 1 0 _1_ 0 1
 0 1 0 1 0   0 0 _0_ 1 0
 0 0 1 0 0   0 0 1 0 0
 0 0 1 0 0   0 1 0 0 0
 0 0 1 0 0   1 0 0 0 0
 0 0 1 0 0   1 1 1 1 1
```

**Fig. 3.13** Input test patterns with error

```
         A                                              A
 _1_ 0 1 0 0                                       0 0 1 0 0
  0 1 0 1 0                                        0 1 0 1 0
  1 0 0 0 1                                        1 0 0 0 1
  1 0 0 0 1                                        1 0 0 0 1
  1 1 1 1 1                                        1 1 1 1 1
  1 0 0 0 1                                        1 0 0 0 1
  1 0 0 0 1                                        1 0 0 0 1
```

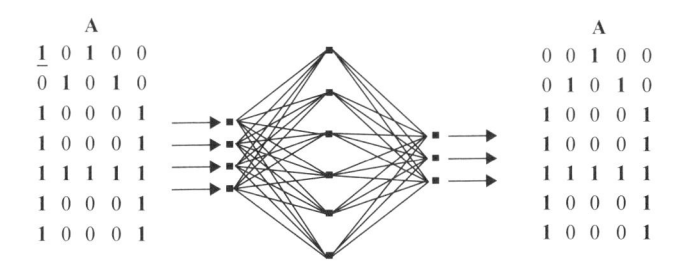

**Fig. 3.14** Testing mode for a sample pattern A with error

## MATLAB Program 3.1

### Part A: Main program

```
%%%%%%%%%%%%%%%%%%%%%%%%%%%%%%%%%%%%%%%%%%
% BACK PROPOGATION NEURAL NETWORK ALGORITHM
%%%%%%%%%%%%%%%%%%%%%%%%%%%%%%%%%%%%%%%%%%

clear workspace
clear all
clc
format short
tic

%%%%%%%%%%%%%%%%%%%%%%%%%% START %%%%%%%%%%%%%%%%%%%%%%%%%%%%%%%%%%

%%%%%%%%%%%%%%%%%%%%%%%%%%%%%%%%%%%%%%%%%%
% PART-A DEMONSTRATION OF UPGRADATION OF WEIGHTS
%%%%%%%%%%%%%%%%%%%%%%%%%%%%%%%%%%%%%%%%%%

source=[0.10 0.20 0.3 0.4;
        0.20 0.30 0.4 0.5];
target=[0.3 0.5 0.7 0.9];
mxpt=4;                     % No of patterns
epoch=100;                  % Maximum number of epochs
m=2;                        % Number of input nodes
n=2;                        % Number of hidden nodes
r=1;                        % Number of output nodes
etaj=0.5;                   % Learning coefficient
etak=0.5;                   % Learning Coefficient
mew=1;                      % Momentum factor
s=1;                        % Slope

% INITIALIZATION OF WEIGHTS AND BIAS VALUES

Wj=[0.1 0.2;0.3 0.4];       % Initial weights
bj=[-0.5;-0.5];             % Initial bias
Wk=[0.5;0.6];               % initial weights
bk=[-0.5];                  % Initial bias

%%%%%%%%%%%%%%%%%%%%%%%%%%%END%%%%%%%%%%%%%%%%%%%%%%%%%%%%%%%%%%%%

%%%%%%%%%%%%%%%%%%%%%%%%%%%START%%%%%%%%%%%%%%%%%%%%%%%%%%%%%%%%%%

%%%%%%%%%%%%%%%%%%%%%%%%%%%%%%%%%%%%%%%%%%%%%%%%%%%%%%%%%%%%%%%%%%
% PART-B TRAINING AND TESTING OF AND,OR,XOR,NAND AND NOR LOGIC FUNCTIONS
%%%%%%%%%%%%%%%%%%%%%%%%%%%%%%%%%%%%%%%%%%%%%%%%%%%%%%%%%%%%%%%%%%

% BINARY INPUT (TWO INPUT NODE) [INPUT PATTERNS]

source=[1 0 1 0;
        1 1 0 0];

% BINARY OUTPUT (FIVE OUTPUT NODE)[DESIRED TARGET PATTERNS]

target=[1 0 0 0;            % BINARY AND LOGIC OUTPUT
        1 1 1 0;            % BINARY OR LOGIC OUTPUT
        0 1 1 0;            % BINARY XOR LOGIC OUTPUT
        0 1 1 1;            % BINARY NAND LOGIC OUTPUT
        0 0 0 1];           % BINARY NOR LOGIC OUTPUT
```

```
mxpt=4;                 % No of patterns
epoch=1000;             % Maximum number of epochs
m=2;                    % Number of input nodes
n=4;                    % Number of hidden nodes
r=5;                    % Number of output nodes
etaj=0.5;               % Learning coefficient
etak=0.5;               % Learning Coefficient
mew=1;                  % Momentum factor
s=1;                    % Slope
Wj=randn(m,n);          % Initializing weights from input layer to hidden layer
Wk=randn(n,r);          % Initializing weights from hidden layer to output layer
bj=randn(n,1);          % Bias value
bk=randn(r,1);          % Bias value

%%%%%%%%%%%%%%%%%%%%%%%%%% END %%%%%%%%%%%%%%%%%%%%%%%%%%%%%%%%%%%

%%%%%%%%%%%%%%%%%%%%%%%%%% START %%%%%%%%%%%%%%%%%%%%%%%%%%%%%%%%%

%%%%%%%%%%%%%%%%%%%%%%%%%%%%%%%%%%%%%%%%%%%%%%%
% PART-C CHARACTER RECOGNITION WITH A-Z ALPHABETS
%%%%%%%%%%%%%%%%%%%%%%%%%%%%%%%%%%%%%%%%%%%%%%%

       % A B C D E F G H I J K L M N O P Q R S T U V W X Y Z
data=[1 1 0 1 1 1 0 1 0 1 1 1 1 0 1 0 1 0 1 1 1 1 1 1 1 1;
      0 1 1 1 1 1 1 0 1 1 0 0 0 0 1 1 1 1 1 1 0 0 0 0 0 1;
      1 1 1 1 1 1 1 0 0 1 0 0 0 0 1 1 1 1 0 1 0 0 0 0 0 1;
      0 1 1 1 1 1 1 1 0 1 0 0 1 0 0 1 0 0 1 1 1 0 0 0 0 1;
      0 0 0 0 1 1 0 1 0 1 1 0 1 1 0 0 0 0 1 1 1 1 1 1 1 1;
      0 1 1 1 1 1 1 1 0 0 1 1 1 1 1 1 1 1 0 1 1 1 1 1 1 0;
      1 0 0 0 0 0 0 0 0 0 0 1 1 0 0 0 0 0 0 0 0 0 0 0 0 0;
      0 1 0 0 0 1 0 0 1 1 0 0 0 0 1 1 0 0 1 1 0 0 0 1 1 1;
      1 0 0 0 0 0 0 0 0 0 1 0 1 0 0 0 0 0 0 0 0 0 0 0 0 0;
      0 1 1 1 0 0 1 1 0 1 0 0 1 1 1 1 1 1 0 1 1 1 1 1 1 1;
      1 1 1 1 1 1 1 1 0 0 1 1 1 0 1 1 1 1 0 0 1 1 1 0 0 0;
      0 0 0 0 0 0 0 0 0 0 0 1 0 0 0 0 1 0 0 0 0 0 1 1 0 0;
      0 0 0 0 0 1 0 1 1 1 0 1 0 1 0 0 0 1 0 0 0 0 0 0 0 0;
      0 0 0 0 0 0 0 0 0 1 0 0 0 0 0 0 0 0 0 0 0 0 0 1 1 1;
      1 1 0 1 0 0 0 1 0 0 0 0 1 1 1 1 1 1 0 0 1 1 1 0 0 0;
      1 1 1 1 1 1 1 1 0 0 1 1 1 1 1 1 0 0 0 1 1 1 0 0 0 0;
      0 1 0 0 1 1 0 0 0 1 0 0 0 0 1 0 1 0 0 0 0 0 0 0 0 0;
      0 1 0 0 1 1 0 1 1 1 0 0 0 1 0 1 1 1 0 1 0 1 0 1 1 1;
      0 1 0 0 1 1 0 1 0 0 0 0 0 0 0 1 0 0 0 0 0 0 0 0 0 0;
      1 0 0 1 0 0 0 1 0 0 0 0 1 1 1 0 1 0 0 1 1 1 0 0 0 0;
      1 1 1 1 1 1 1 1 0 0 1 1 1 1 1 1 1 0 1 1 1 1 0 0 0 0;
      1 0 0 0 0 0 0 0 0 0 0 0 0 0 0 0 0 0 0 0 0 0 0 1 0 1;
      1 0 0 0 0 0 1 0 1 1 1 0 0 0 0 1 1 0 1 0 0 1 0 1 0 0;
      1 0 0 0 0 0 1 0 0 0 0 0 1 0 0 0 0 1 0 0 0 0 1 0 0 0;
      1 1 0 1 0 0 1 1 0 0 0 0 1 1 1 0 0 0 1 1 1 0 0 0 0 0;
      1 1 1 1 1 1 1 1 0 1 1 1 0 1 1 1 1 1 0 1 0 1 1 0 1 1;
      0 0 0 0 0 0 0 0 0 0 0 0 0 0 0 0 0 0 0 0 1 1 0 0 0 0;
      0 0 0 0 0 0 0 1 1 0 0 0 0 0 0 0 0 1 0 0 0 0 1 0 1 0;
      0 0 0 0 0 0 0 0 1 0 0 1 0 0 1 1 0 0 1 1 0 0 0 0 0 0;
      1 1 1 1 1 0 1 1 0 0 0 1 1 1 0 0 0 1 0 1 0 0 1 0 0 0;
      1 1 0 1 1 1 0 1 0 0 1 1 1 0 1 0 1 0 0 0 0 1 1 0 1;
      0 1 1 0 1 0 1 0 1 1 0 1 0 0 1 0 1 0 1 0 0 0 0 0 0 1;
      0 1 1 1 0 1 0 1 0 1 1 0 0 1 0 0 1 1 1 1 0 0 0 1 1;
      0 1 0 1 1 0 1 0 1 0 0 1 0 0 1 0 1 0 0 0 0 1;
      1 0 0 0 1 0 0 1 0 0 1 1 1 1 0 0 1 1 0 0 0 0 1 0 0 1]];
```

```matlab
% BINARY INPUT [INPUT PATTERNS]

source=data;

% BINARY OUTPUT [DESIRED TARGET PATTERNS]

target=data;
mxpt=26;                % No of patterns (26 Alphabets)
epoch=1000;             % Maximum number of epochs
m=35;                   % Number of input nodes (7 x 5 matrix alphabet)
n=20;                   % Number of hidden nodes
r=35;                   % Number of output nodes
etaj=0.5;               % Learning coefficient
etak=0.5;               % Learning coefficient
mew=1;                  % Momentum factor
s=1;                    % Slope
Wj=randn(m,n);          % Initializing weights from input layer to hidden layer
Wk=randn(n,r);          % Initializing weights from hidden layer to output layer
bj=randn(n,1);          % Bias value
bk=randn(r,1);          % Bias value

%%%%%%%%%%%%%%%%%%%%%%%%%%% END %%%%%%%%%%%%%%%%%%%%%%%%%%%%%%%%%%%%%%

% TRAINING MODE

for iter=1:epoch,
disp('Epoch Number');
disp(iter);
for pt=1:mxpt,
disp('Pattern Number');
disp(pt);
I=source(:,pt);
D=target(:,pt);
sumj=zeros(n,1);
outj=zeros(n,1);
sumk=zeros(r,1);
outk=zeros(r,1);

% CALCULATING WEIGHTED SUM AND OUTPUT INCLUSIVE OF BIAS FOR THE HIDDEN LAYER UNITS

for p=1:n,
for h=1:m,
sumj(p)=sumj(p)+I(h)*Wj(h,p);
end
sumj(p)=sumj(p)+bj(p);
outj(p)=logistic(sumj(p),s);
end
disp('Hidden layer units weighted sum and output')
disp(sumj);
disp(outj);

% CALCULATING WEIGHTED SUM AND OUTPUT INCLUSIVE OF BIAS FOR THE OUTPUT LAYER UNITS

for q=1:r,
for p=1:n,
sumk(q)=sumk(q)+outj(p)*Wk(p,q);
end
sumk(q)=sumk(q)+bk(q);
outk(q)=logistic(sumk(q),s);
end
disp('Output layer units weighted sum and output')
disp(sumk);
disp(outk);
```

% CALCULATION OF CHANGE IN WEIGHTS AND BIAS FROM HIDDEN UNIT TO OUTPUT UNITS

```
delWk=zeros(n,r);
delbk=zeros(r,1);
for q=1:r,
for p=1:n,
foutk(q)=logistic(sumk(q),s);
foutj(p)=logistic(sumj(p),s);
delWk(p,q)=-etak*-2*s*((D(q)-foutk(q))*foutk(q)*(1-foutk(q))*foutj(p))
 +mew.*delWk(p,q);
 end
delbk(q,1)=-etak*-2*s*((D(q)-foutk(q))*foutk(q)*(1-foutk(q))*1) +mew.*delbk(q,1);
end
disp('Change in weights in the output layer')
disp(delWk);
disp('Change in bias in the output layer')
disp(delbk);
```

% CALCULATION OF CHANGE IN WEIGHTS AND BIAS FROM HIDDEN UNITS TO INPUT UNITS

```
delWj=zeros(m,n);
delbj=zeros(n,1);
for h=1:m,
for p=1:n,
foutk(q)=logistic(sumk(q),s);
foutj(p)=logistic(sumj(p),s);
delsumj=0;
delsumjb=0;

for q=1:r,
delsumj=delsumj+(-2.*s.*(D(q)-foutk(q)).*foutk(q).*(1-foutk(q)).
*Wk(p,q).*foutj(p).*(1-foutj(p)).*I(h));
end
delsumjb=delsumjb+(-2.*s.*(D(q)-foutk(q)).*foutk(q).*(1-foutk(q)).
*Wk(p,q).*foutj(p).*(1-foutj(p)).*1);
delWj(h,p)=-etaj*delsumj+mew.*delWj(h,p);
delbj(p,1)=-etaj*delsumjb+mew.*delbj(p,1);
end
end
disp('Change in weights in the input layer')
disp(delWj);
disp('Change in bias in the input layer')
disp(delbj);
```

% UPGRADATION OF WEIGHTS AND BIASES

```
Wk=Wk+mew*delWk;            % Output layer weight modification
bk=bk+mew*delbk;            % Output layer bias modification
Wj=Wj+mew*delWj;            % Hidden layer weight modification
bj=bj+mew*delbj;            % Hidden layer bias modification
disp('New weights in the output layer')
disp(Wk);
disp('New bias in the output layer')
disp(bk);
disp('New weights in the input layer')
disp(Wj);
disp('New bias in the input layer')
disp(bj);
error(:,pt)=(D-foutk').^2;
end
erepoch(iter)=sum(sum(error));    % Sum Squared Error
disp('Sum Squared Error')
disp(erepoch(iter))
```

```
figure(1);
plot(erepoch)
title('Error plot for feed forward backpropagation neural network');
xlabel('Number of epochs');
ylabel('Sum squared error');
end
disp('The total time taken for training:');
toc

% TESTING MODE

disp('Testing mode started')
disp('Simulating a input test pattern');
disp('Please press the tab to continue..')
pause

%%%%%%%%%%%%%%%%%%%%%%%%%%%%START%%%%%%%%%%%%%%%%%%%%%%%%%%%%%%%%%%%%

%%%%%%%%%%%%%%%%%%%%%%%%%%%%
% PART-C (WITHOUT ERROR)
%%%%%%%%%%%%%%%%%%%%%%%%%%%%

disp( 'Input test patterns')
disp('1  2  3  4  5  6  7  8  9  10 11 12 13 14 15 16 17 18 19 20 21 22 23 24 25 26')
disp('A  B  C  D  E  F  G  H  I  J  K  L  M  N  O  P  Q  R  S  T  U  V  W  X  Y  Z')

disp(num2str(source));

%%%%%%%%%%%%%%%%%%%%%%%%%%%%%%% END %%%%%%%%%%%%%%%%%%%%%%%%%%%%%%%%%%

%%%%%%%%%%%%%%%%%%%%%%%%%%%%%%START%%%%%%%%%%%%%%%%%%%%%%%%%%%%%%%%%%%

%%%%%%%%%%%%%%%%%%%%%%%%%%
% PART-C (WITH ERROR)
%%%%%%%%%%%%%%%%%%%%%%%%%%

disp('Input test patterns with error');
source_err=source;
source_err(1,1)=1;source_err(8,2)=1;source_err(34,3)=0;
source_err(32,4)=0;source_err(30,5)=1;source_err(8,6)=1;
source_err(13,7)=1;source_err(17,8)=0;source_err(3,9)=0;
source_err(10,10)=1;source_err(33,11)=1;source_err(14,12)=1;
source_err(26,13)=0;source_err(11,14)=0;source_err(13,15)=1;
source_err(8,16)=1;source_err(8,17)=1;source_err(16,18)=0;
source_err(3,19)=0;source_err(21,20)=1;source_err(8,21)=1;
source_err(18,22)=1;source_err(30,23)=0;source_err(35,24)=0;
source_err(8,25)=1;source_err(8,26)=1;
disp('1  2  3  4  5  6  7  8  9  10 11 12 13 14 15 16 17 18 19 20 21 22 23 24 25 26')
disp('A  B  C  D  E  F  G  H  I  J  K  L  M  N  O  P  Q  R  S  T  U  V  W  X  Y  Z')
disp(num2str(source_err));
disp('Desired target patterns');
disp('1  2  3  4  5  6  7  8  9  10 11 12 13 14 15 16 17 18 19 20 21 22 23 24 25 26')
disp('A  B  C  D  E  F  G  H  I  J  K  L  M  N  O  P  Q  R  S  T  U  V  W  X  Y  Z')
disp(num2str(target));
source=source_err;
pt=input('Enter the test pattern number = ');
disp('Pattern Number');
disp(pt);
I=source(:,pt);
D=target(:,pt);

%%%%%%%%%%%%%%%%%%%%%%%%%%%%% END %%%%%%%%%%%%%%%%%%%%%%%%%%%%%%%%%%%%
```

%%%%%%%%%%%%%%%%%%%%%%%%%% START%%%%%%%%%%%%%%%%%%%%%%%%%%%%%%%%%%%

%%%%%%%%%%%%%
% PART-A & B
%%%%%%%%%%%%%

```
disp('For Part A,If you want to select the test pattern from the input patterns enter
1 else enter 2');
disp('For Part B,you have to compulsorily choose 1');
select=input('Give input either 1 or 2  =');
if select==1
disp('Input test patterns');
disp('(1)  (2)  (3)  (4)');
disp(source);
disp('Desired target patterns');
disp(target);
pt=input('Enter the test pattern number  = ');
disp('Pattern Number');
disp(pt);
I=source(:,pt);
D=target(:,pt);
end

if select==2,
I=input('Enter a test pattern (2 x 1 matrix format)  = ');
D=sum(I);
end
sumj=zeros(n,1);
outj=zeros(n,1);
sumk=zeros(r,1);
outk=zeros(r,1);
```

%%%%%%%%%%%%%%%%%%%%%%%%%%% END%%%%%%%%%%%%%%%%%%%%%%%%%%%%%%%%%%%%

% CALCULATION OF WEIGHTED SUM AND OUTPUT INCLUSIVE OF BIAS FOR THE HIDDEN LAYER UNITS

```
for p=1:n,
for h=1:m,
sumj(p)=sumj(p)+I(h)*Wj(h,p);
end
sumj(p)=sumj(p)+bj(p);
outj(p)=logistic(sumj(p),s);
end
disp('Hidden layer units weighted sum and output')
disp(sumj);
disp(outj);
```

% CALCULATION WEIGHTED SUM AND OUTPUT INCLUSIVE OF BIAS FOR THE OUTPUT LAYER UNITS

```
for q=1:r,
for p=1:n,
sumk(q)=sumk(q)+outj(p)*Wk(p,q);
end
sumk(q)=sumk(q)+bk(q);
outk(q)=logistic(sumk(q),s);
end
disp('Output layer units weighted sum')
disp(sumk);
disp('Actual Output');
disp(outk);
```

%%%%%%%%%%%%%
% PART-A & B
%%%%%%%%%%%%%

%%%%%%%%%%%%%%%%%%%%%%%%%%%START%%%%%%%%%%%%%%%%%%%%%%%%%%%%%%%%

```
if select==1
disp('Desired - Actual');
disp([target(:,pt) outk]);
end
if select==2
disp(' Desired - Actual');
disp([sum(I) outk]);
end
```
%%%%%%%%%%%%%%%%%%%%%%%%%%% END %%%%%%%%%%%%%%%%%%%%%%%%%%%%%%%%

%%%%%%%%%%%%%%%%%%%%%%%%%%%START%%%%%%%%%%%%%%%%%%%%%%%%%%%%%%%%

%%%%%%%%%%%%%%%%%%%%%%%%%
% PART-C (WITHOUT ERROR)
%%%%%%%%%%%%%%%%%%%%%%%%%

```
disp('Target character')
disp(num2str(dispalp(target,pt)));
disp('Output character')
disp(num2str(dispalp(outk>0.5,1)));
```

%%%%%%%%%%%%%%%%%%%%%%%%%%% END %%%%%%%%%%%%%%%%%%%%%%%%%%%%%%%%

%%%%%%%%%%%%%%%%%%%%%%%%%%%START%%%%%%%%%%%%%%%%%%%%%%%%%%%%%%%%

%%%%%%%%%%%%%%%%%%%%%%%%%
% PART-C (WITH ERROR)
%%%%%%%%%%%%%%%%%%%%%%%%%

```
disp('Input character')
disp(num2str(dispalp(source_err,pt)));
disp('Target character')
disp(num2str(dispalp(target,pt)));
disp('Output character')
disp(num2str(dispalp(outk>0.5,1)));
```

%%%%%%%%%%%%%%%%%%%%%%%%%%% END %%%%%%%%%%%%%%%%%%%%%%%%%%%%%%%%

## Part B: Sub-programs (Sub-routine functions)

### OBJECTIVE FUNCTION

```
function [out] = logistic(sum,s)
```

% ACTIVATION FUNCTION THAT GIVE CONTINOUS VALUE BETWEEN 0 AND 1

```
out=1./(1+exp(-s*sum));
```

### DISPLAY FUNCTION

```
function [out]=dispalp(data,a)
```

% DISPLAY OF ALPHABET IN A MATRIX FORMAT

```
k=0;
for i=1:7,
for j=1:5,
k=k+1;
out(i,j)=data(k,a);
end
end
```

## 3.3 KOHONEN NEURAL NETWORK

In 1989, Finnish professor Teuvo Kohonen had developed a topological structure analogous to a typical NN with competitive units or cluster units in network layers [19]. This topology uses an unsupervised learning procedure to produce a two-dimensional discretized representation of the input space of the training samples, called a 'map'. Therefore, this network is called 'self-organizing map' or simply a Kohonen neural network (KNN). Kohnonen NN creates a competition among cluster units similar to a property observed in the brain but not in other ANNs. Stephen Grossberg in 1976 developed a Grossberg network which takes the motivation from the biological human visual system which is also a self-organizing one but continuous-time [20]. However, the KNN is widely used for clustering applications.

Clustering progresses by checking the closeness of the input patterns with the weight vector associated with each of the cluster units. A cluster unit is considered as a winner if the Euclidean distance (ED) between the weight vector associated with it and the given input pattern is the minimum when compared among the other neighbourhood cluster units. The weights associated with the winner cluster unit and neighbour cluster units are updated. The neighbours are the cluster units nearer to the winner cluster unit and can be considered based on a measure of geometrical boundary. Figures 3.15 and 3.16 give the architecture and the flow chart of the KNN, respectively.

### 3.3.1 Illustration on Clustering of Bipolar Input Patterns

Let us try to cluster 4 bipolar patterns into 2 clusters. The handworked portion for one epoch is given later. The subscripts $h$ and $k$ and the indices $m$ and $n$ are considered as given in Fig. 3.15. Here, $n = 4$ and $m = 2$ and topological parameter $R = 0$ (for simplifying the illustration). Let the learning rate be $\eta = 0.9$ and will geometrically decrease 0.5 times of $\eta$ for every epoch. The 4 bipolar input patterns, initial weights, and initial learning rate $\eta$ are given as follows:

$$I = \begin{bmatrix} 1 & 1 & 1 & -1 \\ -1 & -1 & -1 & 1 \\ 1 & -1 & -1 & -1 \\ -1 & -1 & 1 & 1 \end{bmatrix} \begin{matrix} (I_1) \\ (I_2) \\ (I_3) \\ (I_4) \end{matrix}$$

$$W = \begin{bmatrix} 0.2 & 0.8 \\ 0.6 & 0.4 \\ 0.5 & 0.7 \\ 0.9 & 0.3 \end{bmatrix}_{n \times m}$$

$$\eta = 0.9$$

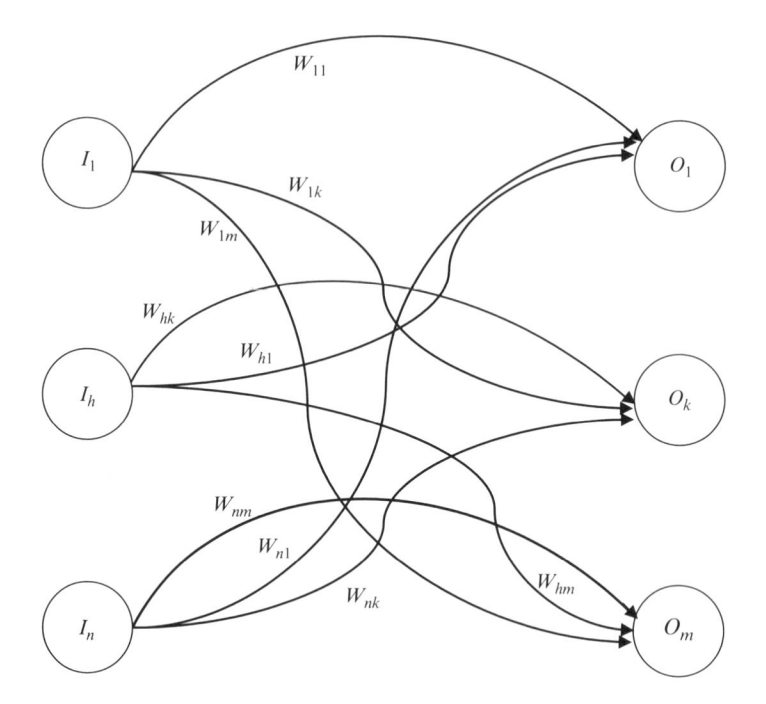

**Fig. 3.15** Architecture of KNN

**Epoch No. 1/Pattern No. 1**
*Calculation of ED*

$$ED(1) = \sum_{h=1:n} \left(w_{h1} - I_h\right)^2$$

(Cluster $k = 1$)
$ED(1) = (0.2 - 1)^2 + (0.6 - 1)^2 + (0.5 - 1)^2 + (0.9 - (-1))^2 = 4.6600$
(Cluster $k = 2$)
$ED(2) = (0.8 - 1)^2 + (0.4 - 1)^2 + (0.7 - 1)^2 + (0.3 - (-1))^2 = 2.1800$

The winner cluster unit is $K = 2$ because $ED$ is minimum (i.e., the input vector is closest to the 2$^{nd}$ output cluster unit). Therefore, the weights connected to the winner cluster unit 2 should be updated.

*Weight updation*

$w_{hk=2}(new) = w_{hk=2}(old) + 0.9 \times \left(I_1 - w_{hk=2}(old)\right)$
$w_{12} = 0.8 + 0.9 \times (1 - 0.8) = 0.9800$
$w_{22} = 0.4 + 0.9 \times (1 - 0.4) = 0.9400$
$w_{32} = 0.7 + 0.9 \times (1 - 0.7) = 0.9700$
$w_{42} = 0.3 + 0.9 \times (-1 - 0.3) = -0.8700$

Artificial Neural Networks—Second Generation 155

```
┌─────────────────────────────────────────┐
│ Initialize the random weight values.    │
│ Give the topological parameter R        │
│ (geometric measure of the neighbourhood │
│ boundary), and set the learning rate    │
│ ($\eta$) within $0.1 \leq n \times \eta \leq 1$. │
└─────────────────────────────────────────┘
                    │
                    ▼
┌─────────────────────────────────────────┐
│ For each input pattern $I_h$ training   │
│ pair compute the Euculidean distance    │
│ for each output cluster unit $k$,       │
│                                         │
│     $ED(k) = \underset{h=1:n}{\Sigma}(w_{hk} - I_h)^2$ │
│                                         │
│ Get the winner cluster unit index $K$   │
│ for which the ED is minimum.            │
└─────────────────────────────────────────┘
                    │
                    ▼
┌─────────────────────────────────────────┐
│ Update the weights for all the $k$      │
│ units within the neighbourhood boundary │
│ of the winner $K$. Then                 │
│                                         │
│ $w_{hk}(t+1) = w_{hk}(t) - \eta \times (x_h - w_{hk}(t))$ │
│                                         │
│ Update the learning rate $\eta$.        │
│ Decrease the topological parameter $R$  │
│ at specified times after the completion │
│ of an epoch.                            │
└─────────────────────────────────────────┘
                    │
         NO         ▼
    ◄──────── ◇ If the maximum number of ◇
              ◇ epochs have reached?     ◇
                    │
                    │ YES
                    ▼
                 ┌──────┐
                 │ Stop │
                 └──────┘
```

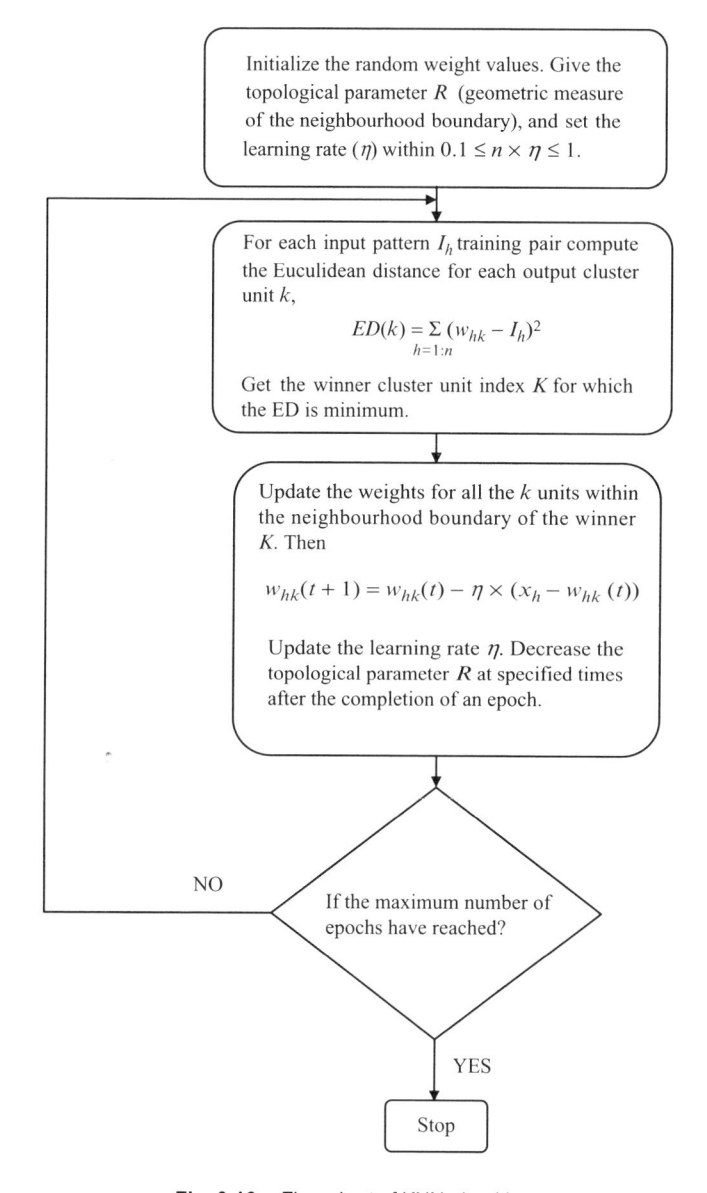

**Fig. 3.16** Flow chart of KNN algorithm

$$W = \begin{bmatrix} 0.2 & 0.98 \\ 0.6 & 0.94 \\ 0.5 & 0.97 \\ 0.9 & -0.87 \end{bmatrix}$$

**Epoch No. 1/Pattern No. 2**

$$ED(1) = \underset{h=1:n}{\Sigma}\left(w_{h1} - I_h\right)^2$$

(Cluster $k = 1$)

$ED(1) = (0.2 - (-1))^2 + (0.6 - (-1))^2 + (0.5 - (-1))^2 + (0.9 - 1)^2 = 6.2600$

(Cluster $k = 2$)

$ED(2) = (0.98 - (-1))^2 + (0.94 - (-1))^2 + (0.97 - (-1))^2 + (-0.87 - 1)^2 = 15.0618$

The winner cluster unit is $K = 1$ because $ED$ is minimum (i.e., the input vector is closest to the 1$^{st}$ output cluster unit). Therefore, the weights connected to the winner cluster unit 1 should be updated.

### Weight updation

$w_{hk=1}(new) = w_{hk=1}(old) + 0.9 \times (I_2 - w_{hk=1}(old))$

$w_{11} = 0.2 + 0.9 \times (-1 - 0.2) = -0.8800$

$w_{21} = 0.6 + 0.9 \times (-1 - 0.6) = -0.8400$

$w_{31} = 0.5 + 0.9 \times (-1 - 0.5) = -0.8500$

$w_{41} = 0.0 + 0.9 \times (-1 - 0.9) = 0.9900$

$$W = \begin{bmatrix} -0.88 & 0.98 \\ -0.84 & 0.94 \\ -0.85 & 0.97 \\ 0.99 & -0.87 \end{bmatrix}$$

### Epoch No. 1/Pattern No. 3

$ED(1) = \sum_{h=1:n} (w_{h1} - I_h)^2$

(Cluster $k = 1$)

$ED(1) = (-0.88 - 1)^2 + (-0.84 - (-1))^2 + (-0.85 - (-1))^2 + (0.99 - (-1))^2 = 7.5426$

(Cluster $k = 2$)

$ED(2) = (0.98 - 1)^2 + (0.94 - (-1))^2 + (0.97 - (-1))^2 + (-0.87 - (-1))^2 = 7.6618$

The winner cluster unit is $K = 1$ because $ED$ is minimum (i.e., the input vector is closest to the 1$^{st}$ output cluster unit). Therefore, the weights connected to the winner cluster unit 1 should be updated.

### Weight updation

$w_{hk=1}(new) = w_{hk=1}(old) + 0.9 \times (I_3 - w_{hk=1}(old))$

$w_{11} = -0.88 + 0.9 \times (1 - (-0.88)) = 0.8120$

$w_{21} = -0.84 + 0.9 \times (-1 - (-0.84)) = -0.9840$

$w_{31} = -0.85 + 0.9 \times (-1 - (-0.85)) = -0.9850$

$w_{41} = 0.99 + 0.9 \times (-1 - 0.99) = -0.8010$

$$W = \begin{bmatrix} 0.8120 & 0.98 \\ -0.984 & 0.94 \\ -0.985 & 0.97 \\ -0.801 & -0.87 \end{bmatrix}$$

## Epoch No. 1/Pattern No. 4

$$ED(1) = \sum_{h=1:n} \left(w_{h1} - I_h\right)^2$$

(Cluster $k = 1$)

$ED(1) = (0.81 - (-1))^2 + (-0.984 - (-1))^2 + (-0.985 - 1)^2 + (-0.801 - 1)^2 = 10.4674$

(Cluster $k = 2$)

$ED(2) = (0.98 - (-1))^2 + (0.94 - (-1))^2 + (0.97 - 1)^2 + (-0.87 - 1)^2 = 11.1818$

The winner cluster unit is $K = 1$ because $ED$ is minimum (i.e., the input vector is closest to the 1st output cluster unit). Therefore, the weights connected to the winner cluster unit 1 should be updated.

### *Weight updation*

$w_{hk=1}(new) = w_{hk=1}(old) + 0.9 \times \left(I_4 - w_{hk=1}(old)\right)$
$w_{11} = -0.812 + 0.9 \times (-1 - 0.812)) = -0.8188$
$w_{21} = -0.984 + 0.9 \times (-1 - (-0.984)) = -0.9984$
$w_{31} = 0.985 + 0.9 \times (1 - (-0.985)) = 0.8015$
$w_{41} = 0.801 + 0.9 \times (1 - (-0.801)) = 0.8199$

$$W = \begin{bmatrix} 0.8188 & 0.98 \\ -0.9984 & 0.94 \\ -0.8015 & 0.97 \\ -0.8199 & -0.87 \end{bmatrix}$$

One epoch is completed. Now the learning rate will geometrically decrease 0.5 times of $\eta$ for every epoch. Therefore, the learning rate will be 0.45 for the starting of the second epoch.

After 1000 epochs, the learning rate and weights are found to be $\eta = 8.3994e - 302$.

$$W = \begin{bmatrix} -0.9794 & 0.9977 \\ -0.9998 & -0.0148 \\ 0.2130 & -0.0114 \\ 0.9795 & -0.9852 \end{bmatrix}$$

It is found that the clustering has become stagnant even after the second epoch and has been constant till 1,000 epochs. The final resultant of the input patterns clustered is given as follows:

## Result

Pattern 1- (1 1 1 −1) and Pattern 3- (1 −1 −1 −1) belong to the second cluster, whereas Pattern 2- (−1 −1 −1 1) and Pattern 4- (−1 −1 1 1) belong to the first cluster. This can be verified with the final updated weights and by calculating the ED. Each of the input patterns can be checked to find the winner cluster unit. It is obvious that the winner cluster unit output will be the corresponding input pattern whose ED is minimum.

## Verification

Pattern 1- (1 1 1 −1)

$$ED(k) = \sum_{h=1:n} \left(w_{hk} - I_h\right)^2$$

(Cluster $k = 1$)

$ED(1) = (-0.9794 - 1)^2 + (-0.9998 - 1)^2 + (0.2130 - 1)^2 + (0.9795 - (-1))^2$
$= 12.4550$

(Cluster $k = 2$)

$ED(2) = (0.9977 - 1)^2 + (-0.0148 - 1)^2 + (0.0114 - 1)^2 + (-0.9852 - (-1))^2$
$= 2.0074$

Since the winner cluster output unit is $K = 2$, the Pattern 1 belongs to the second cluster.

Pattern 2- (−1 −1 −1 1)

(Cluster $k = 1$)

$ED(1) = (-0.9794 - (-1))^2 + (-0.9998 - (-1))^2 + (0.2130 - (-1))^2 + (0.9795 - 1)^2$
$= 1.4722$

(Cluster $k = 2$)

$ED(2) = (0.9977 - (-1))^2 + (-0.0148 - (-1))^2 + (0.0114 - (-1))^2 + (-0.9852 - 1)^2$
$= 9.9254$

Since the winner cluster output unit is $K = 1$, the Pattern 2 belongs to the first cluster.

Pattern 3- (1 −1 −1 −1)

(Cluster $k = 1$)

$ED(1) = (-0.9794 - 1)^2 + (-0.9998 - (-1))^2 + (0.2130 - (-1))^2 + (0.9795 - (-1))^2$
$= 9.3078$

(Cluster $k = 2$)

$ED(2) = (0.9977 - 1)^2 + (-0.0148 - (-1))^2 + (0.0114 - (-1))^2 + (-0.9852 - (-1))^2$
$= 1.9938$

Since the winner cluster output unit is $K = 2$, the Pattern 1 belongs to the second cluster.

Pattern 4- (−1 −1 1 1)
(Cluster $k = 1$)

$$ED(1) = (-0.9794 - (-1))^2 + (-0.9998 - (-1))^2 + (0.2130 - 1)^2 + (0.9795 - 1)^2$$
$$= 0.6202$$

(Cluster $k = 2$)

$$ED(2) = (0.9977 - (-1))^2 + (-0.0148 - (-1))^2 + (0.0114 - 1)^2 + (-0.9852 - 1)^2$$
$$= 9.8798$$

Since the winner cluster output unit is $K = 1$, the Pattern 2 belongs to the first cluster. The simulation of 1,000 epochs can be carried out using the MATLAB Program 3.2, Part A. In this program, parameters are initialized commenting Part B and uncommenting Part A. The KNN program can be used to train and test so as to check whether the network is able to validate the illustration.

### 3.3.2 Clustering of Numerical Characters

This application aims to cluster 25 binary patterns representing numerals from 1 to 9. They are represented by $9 \times 7$ matrix format. The 25 patterns are shown in Fig. 3.17. The objective is to cluster the 25 patterns into 9 groups. Each of the input patterns are represented as binary input vectors as given in the Part B of the MATLAB Program 3.2. Here, $n = 25$, $m = 2$, initial topological parameter $R = 4$ and the initial learning rate be $\eta = 0.6$. Let the learning rate be $\eta = 0.9$ and will geometrically decrease 0.5 times of $\eta$ for every epoch. Also, the topological parameter $R$ (geometrical radius) will be decreased by subtracting a small value of 0.2 for every epoch. The value of $R$ should be rounded off to obtain an integer value.

It should be understood that the boundary area of updating of weights corresponding to the winner cluster unit is dependent on $R$. If the value of $R$ becomes zero during the iteration process, then the updating of weights will be carried out for the connections available solely to the winner cluster unit. The simulation of 1,000 epochs can be carried out using the MATLAB Program 3.2. In this program, parameters are initialized uncommenting Part B and commenting Part A. The readers can simulate and cluster the 25 binary patterns into 9 groups.

The simulation is conducted for 10 trial runs. The differences in the clustering pattern are due to the randomness involved during the initialization of weights. It is observed from Table 3.4 that same kinds of patterns are grouped into the same cluster in all the trials. However, there are some patterns that are slightly different from each other which are changing its groups in every trial.

The reason for not being able to get clustered is due to the less variation of demarcation of the $ED$ among the groups. It is to be noted, that on every trial, only 6 clusters are formed and depends upon the nature of the patterns which have the same kind of characteristic features. The frequency of the patterns that are grouped among the 10 trials gives an overall clarity about the clustering behaviour of the input patterns using KNN and is given in Table 3.5.

| 1a [1] | 1b [2] | 1c [3] | 2a [4] | 2b [5] | 2c [6] |
|---|---|---|---|---|---|
| 0 0 0 1 0 0 0 | 0 0 0 1 0 0 0 | 0 0 0 1 0 0 0 | 1 1 1 1 1 1 1 | 1 1 1 1 1 1 1 | 0 1 1 1 1 0 0 |
| 0 0 0 1 0 0 0 | 0 0 1 1 0 0 0 | 0 0 1 1 0 0 0 | 0 0 0 0 0 0 1 | 1 0 0 0 0 0 1 | 1 0 0 0 0 1 0 |
| 0 0 0 1 0 0 0 | 0 0 0 1 0 0 0 | 0 1 0 1 0 0 0 | 0 0 0 0 0 0 1 | 0 0 0 0 0 0 1 | 0 0 0 0 0 0 1 |
| 0 0 0 1 0 0 0 | 0 0 0 1 0 0 0 | 0 0 0 1 0 0 0 | 0 0 0 0 0 0 1 | 0 0 0 0 0 0 1 | 0 0 0 0 0 0 1 |
| 0 0 0 1 0 0 0 | 0 0 0 1 0 0 0 | 0 0 0 1 0 0 0 | 1 1 1 1 1 1 1 | 1 1 1 1 1 1 1 | 0 0 0 0 0 1 0 |
| 0 0 0 1 0 0 0 | 0 0 0 1 0 0 0 | 0 0 0 1 0 0 0 | 1 0 0 0 0 0 0 | 1 0 0 0 0 0 0 | 0 0 0 0 1 0 0 |
| 0 0 0 1 0 0 0 | 0 0 0 1 0 0 0 | 0 0 0 1 0 0 0 | 1 0 0 0 0 0 0 | 1 0 0 0 0 0 0 | 0 0 0 1 0 0 0 |
| 0 0 0 1 0 0 0 | 0 0 0 1 0 0 0 | 0 0 0 1 0 0 0 | 1 0 0 0 0 0 0 | 1 0 0 0 0 0 1 | 0 0 1 0 0 0 0 |
| 0 0 0 1 0 0 0 | 0 0 1 1 1 0 0 | 1 1 1 1 1 1 1 | 1 1 1 1 1 1 1 | 1 1 1 1 1 1 1 | 1 1 1 1 1 1 1 |

| 3a [7] | 3b [8] | 3c [9] | 4a [10] | 4b [11] | 4c [12] |
|---|---|---|---|---|---|
| 1 1 1 1 1 1 1 | 1 1 1 1 1 1 1 | 1 1 1 1 1 1 1 | 0 0 0 0 0 1 0 | 0 1 0 0 0 1 0 | 0 0 0 1 0 1 0 |
| 0 0 0 0 0 0 1 | 1 0 0 0 0 0 1 | 0 0 0 0 0 1 0 | 0 0 0 1 0 1 0 | 0 1 0 0 0 1 0 | 0 0 1 0 0 1 0 |
| 0 0 0 0 0 0 1 | 0 0 0 0 0 0 1 | 0 0 0 0 1 0 0 | 0 0 1 0 0 1 0 | 0 1 0 0 0 1 0 | 0 0 1 0 0 1 0 |
| 0 0 0 0 0 0 1 | 0 0 0 0 0 0 1 | 0 0 0 1 0 0 0 | 0 1 0 0 0 1 0 | 0 1 0 0 0 1 0 | 0 1 0 0 0 1 0 |
| 1 1 1 1 1 1 1 | 0 1 1 1 1 1 1 | 0 0 1 0 0 0 0 | 1 0 0 0 0 1 0 | 0 1 0 0 0 1 0 | 0 1 0 0 0 1 0 |
| 0 0 0 0 0 0 1 | 0 0 0 0 0 0 1 | 0 1 1 1 1 1 0 | 1 1 1 1 1 1 1 | 0 1 1 1 1 1 1 | 1 1 1 1 1 1 1 |
| 0 0 0 0 0 0 1 | 0 0 0 0 0 0 1 | 0 0 0 0 0 0 1 | 0 0 0 0 0 1 0 | 0 0 0 0 0 1 0 | 0 0 0 0 0 1 0 |
| 0 0 0 0 0 0 1 | 1 0 0 0 0 0 1 | 0 0 0 0 0 1 0 | 0 0 0 0 0 1 0 | 0 0 0 0 0 1 0 | 0 0 0 0 0 1 0 |
| 1 1 1 1 1 1 1 | 1 1 1 1 1 1 1 | 1 1 1 1 1 1 0 | 0 0 0 0 0 1 0 | 0 0 0 0 0 1 0 | 0 0 0 0 0 1 0 |

| 5a [13] | 5b [14] | 6a [15] | 6b [16] | 6c [17] | 7a [18] |
|---|---|---|---|---|---|
| 1 1 1 1 1 1 1 | 1 1 1 1 1 1 1 | 0 0 1 1 1 1 0 | 1 1 1 1 1 1 1 | 1 1 1 1 1 1 1 | 1 1 1 1 1 1 1 |
| 1 0 0 0 0 0 0 | 1 0 0 0 0 0 0 | 0 1 0 0 0 0 1 | 1 0 0 0 0 0 0 | 1 0 0 0 0 0 1 | 0 0 0 0 0 0 1 |
| 1 0 0 0 0 0 0 | 1 0 0 0 0 0 0 | 1 0 0 0 0 0 0 | 1 0 0 0 0 0 0 | 1 0 0 0 0 0 0 | 0 0 0 0 0 0 1 |
| 1 0 0 0 0 0 1 | 1 1 1 0 0 0 0 | 1 0 0 0 0 0 0 | 1 0 0 0 0 0 0 | 1 0 0 0 0 0 0 | 0 0 0 0 0 1 0 |
| 1 1 1 1 1 1 1 | 0 0 0 0 1 0 0 | 1 1 0 1 1 0 0 | 1 1 1 1 1 1 1 | 1 1 1 1 1 1 1 | 0 0 0 0 1 0 0 |
| 0 0 0 0 0 0 1 | 0 0 0 0 0 1 0 | 1 0 0 0 1 0 | 1 0 0 0 0 0 1 | 1 0 0 0 0 0 1 | 0 0 0 1 0 0 0 |
| 0 0 0 0 0 0 1 | 0 0 0 0 0 0 1 | 1 0 0 0 0 0 1 | 1 0 0 0 0 0 1 | 1 0 0 0 0 0 1 | 0 0 0 1 0 0 0 |
| 0 0 0 0 0 0 1 | 1 0 0 0 0 1 0 | 1 0 0 0 0 1 0 | 1 0 0 0 0 0 1 | 1 0 0 0 0 0 1 | 0 0 1 0 0 0 0 |
| 1 1 1 1 1 1 1 | 0 1 1 1 1 0 0 | 0 1 1 1 1 0 0 | 1 1 1 1 1 1 1 | 1 1 1 1 1 1 1 | 0 1 0 0 0 0 0 |

| 7b [19] | 7c [20] | 8a [21] | 8b [22] | 9a [23] | 9b [24] |
|---|---|---|---|---|---|
| 1 1 1 1 1 1 1 | 0 0 1 1 1 1 1 | 1 1 1 1 1 1 1 | 0 1 1 1 1 1 0 | 1 1 1 1 1 1 1 | 1 1 1 1 1 1 1 |
| 0 0 0 0 0 0 1 | 0 0 0 0 0 0 1 | 1 0 0 0 0 0 1 | 1 0 0 0 0 0 1 | 1 0 0 0 0 0 1 | 1 0 0 0 0 0 1 |
| 0 0 0 0 0 0 1 | 0 0 0 0 0 0 1 | 1 0 0 0 0 0 1 | 1 0 0 0 0 0 1 | 1 0 0 0 0 0 1 | 1 0 0 0 0 0 1 |
| 0 0 0 0 0 0 1 | 0 0 0 0 0 1 0 | 1 0 0 0 0 0 1 | 1 0 0 0 0 0 1 | 1 0 0 0 0 0 1 | 1 0 0 0 0 0 1 |
| 0 0 0 0 0 0 1 | 0 0 0 0 1 0 0 | 1 1 1 1 1 1 1 | 0 1 1 1 1 1 0 | 1 1 1 1 1 1 1 | 1 1 1 1 1 1 1 |
| 0 0 0 0 0 0 1 | 0 0 0 1 0 0 0 | 1 0 0 0 0 0 1 | 1 0 0 0 0 0 1 | 0 0 0 0 0 0 1 | 0 0 0 0 0 0 1 |
| 0 0 0 0 0 0 1 | 0 0 0 1 0 0 0 | 1 0 0 0 0 0 1 | 1 0 0 0 0 0 1 | 0 0 0 0 0 0 1 | 0 0 0 0 0 0 1 |
| 0 0 0 0 0 0 1 | 0 0 0 1 0 0 0 | 1 0 0 0 0 0 1 | 1 0 0 0 0 0 1 | 0 0 0 0 0 0 1 | 1 0 0 0 0 0 1 |
| 0 0 0 0 0 0 1 | 0 0 0 1 0 0 0 | 1 1 1 1 1 1 1 | 0 1 1 1 1 1 0 | 1 1 1 1 1 1 1 | 1 1 1 1 1 1 1 |

| 9c [25] |
|---|
| 0 1 1 1 1 1 0 |
| 1 0 0 0 0 0 1 |
| 1 0 0 0 0 0 1 |
| 1 0 0 0 0 0 1 |
| 0 1 1 1 1 1 0 |
| 0 0 0 0 0 0 1 |
| 0 0 0 0 0 0 1 |
| 1 0 0 0 0 0 1 |
| 0 1 1 1 1 1 0 |

**Fig. 3.17** Input test patterns for clustering

**Table 3.4** Test results

| Group | 1 | 2 | 3 | 4 | 5 | 6 | 7 | 8 | 9 |
|---|---|---|---|---|---|---|---|---|---|
| Trial No. 1 | – | 10,11,12 | 1,2,3,6,9,18,20 | 4,14,15 | – | 19 | 5,13,16,17,21,22,23,24,25 | – | 7,8 |
| Trial No. 2 | 10,11,12 | 4,15 | 1,2,3,6,9,18,20 | 7 | – | 5,13,16,17,21,22,23,24,25 | 8,14,19 | – | – |
| Trial No. 3 | 8,14 | 15,19 | 5,13,16,17,21,22,23,24,25 | – | 4,7 | – | – | 10,11,12 | 1,2,3,6,9,18,20 |
| Trial No. 4 | – | 8 | – | 4,7,14,15,19 | – | 10,11,12 | 5,13,16,17,21,22,23,24,25 | – | 1,2,3,6,9,18,20 |
| Trial No. 5 | – | 10,11,12 | 4,15 | – | 7,8 | 5,13,16,17,21,22,23,24,25 | – | 14,19 | 1,2,3,6,9,18,20 |
| Trial No. 6 | 1,2,3,6,9,18,20 | – | – | – | 5,13,16,17,21,22,23,24,25 | 10,11,12 | 4,19 | 14,15 | 7,8 |
| Trial No. 7 | 10,11,12 | 7,8,19 | – | 14 | – | 1,2,3,6,9,18,20 | 5,13,16,17,21,22,23,24,25 | 4,15 | — |
| Trial No. 8 | 7 | – | – | 15 | – | 4,8,14,19 | 10,11,12 | 5,13,16,17,21,22,23,24,25 | 1,2,3,6,9,18,20 |
| Trial No. 9 | – | 7,8 | – | 1,2,3,6,9,18,20 | 4 | 14,15,19 | 5,13,16,17,21,22,23,24,25 | 10,11,12 | — |
| Trial No. 10 | 8,14 | 19 | – | 10,11,12 | – | – | 5,13,16,17,21,22,23,24,25 | 1,2,3,6,9,18,20 | 4,7,15 |

**Table 3.5** Frequency of occurrence of significant clustered groups (Out of 10 trials)

| Groups | 10,11,12 | 1,2,3,6,9,18,20 | 5,13,16,17,21,22,23,24,25 | 7,8 | 4,15 | 8,14 | 7 | 19 |
|---|---|---|---|---|---|---|---|---|
| Frequency | 10 | 10 | 10 | 4 | 3 | 2 | 2 | 2 |

## MATLAB Program 3.2

### Part A: Main program

```
%%%%%%%%%%%%%%%%%%%%%%%%%%%%%%%%
% KOHONEN NEURAL NETWORK ALGORITHM
%%%%%%%%%%%%%%%%%%%%%%%%%%%%%%%%

clear workspace
clear all
clc
format short
```

## 162 Soft Computing with MATLAB Programming

```
% Part-A Start

%%%%%%%%%%%%%%%%%%%%%%%%%%%%%%%%%%%%%
% PART-A CLUSTERING OF BIPOLAR VECTORS
%%%%%%%%%%%%%%%%%%%%%%%%%%%%%%%%%%%%%
in=[1   1   1 -1;
   -1  -1  -1  1;
    1  -1  -1 -1;
   -1  -1   1  1];

% Part-A End

% Part-B Start

%%%%%%%%%%%%%%%%%%%%%%%%%%%%%%%%%%%%%%%%%%%%%%%%%%%%%%
% PART-B CLUSTERING OF A-Z ALPHABETS INTO m- GROUPS OR CLUSTERS
%%%%%%%%%%%%%%%%%%%%%%%%%%%%%%%%%%%%%%%%%%%%%%%%%%%%%%

 In=[0001000000100000010000001000000100000010000001000000100000010000001000;%1a
     0001000001100000010000001000000100000010000001000000100000010000011100;%1b
     0001000001100001010000001000000100000010000001000000100000010001111111;%1c
     1111111000000100000010000001111111100000010000001000000100000011111111;%2a
     1111111000000100000010000001111111100000010000001000000100000011111111;%2b
     0111100100000100000010000001000000100000010000001000000100001111111111;%2c
     1111111000000100000010000001111111100000010000001000000100000011111111;%3a
     1111111000000100000010000010111111100000010000001100000011000011111111;%3b
     1111111000000100000010000010000011111000000010000010111111100;%3c
     0000010000101000100100100010100001011111110000010000001000000010;%4a
     0100010010001001000100100100100010011111110000010000001000000010;%4b
     0001010001001000100100100100100010111111110000010000001000000010;%4c
     1111111000000100000010000001111111000000010000001000000100000011111111;%5a
     1111111000000100000011100000000100000001000000110000100111100;%5b
     0011100100000110000001000000110110010000101000001100001001111100;%6a
     1111111000000100000010000001111111000000110000011000001111111111;%6b
     1111111000001100000010000001111111000000110000011000001111111111;%6c
     1111111000000100000010000010000010000001000000100000010000100000;%7a
     1111111000000100000010000010000010000001000000100000010000001;%7b
     0011110000001000000100000010000010000001000000100000010000001000;%7c
     1111111000001100000110000011111111000001100000011000001111111111;%8a
     0111101000001100000110000010111110100000110000001100000010111110;%8b
     1111111000001100000110000011111111000000100000001000000011111111;%9a
     1111111000001100000110000011111111000000100000001100000011111111;%9b
     0111101000001100000110000010111110000000010000001100000010111110]%9c

% Part-B End

% INITIALIZATION OF PARAMETERS

% Part-A Start

m=2;                % No of clusters or group
mxpt=4;             % No of patterns to be clustered
epoch=1000;         % Maximum number of epochs
R=0;                % Boundary radius of the neighbourhood (should be less than m)
n=4;                % No of elements in the input pattern
eta=0.9;            % Learning coefficient
W=[0.2 0.8;0.6 0.4;0.5 0.7;0.9 0.3]; % Initial weights

% Part-A End

% Part B-Start
```

```
m=9;              % No of clusters or group
mxpt=25;          % No of patterns to be clustered
epoch=1000;       % Maximum number of epochs
R=4;   % Boundary radius of the neighbourhood (should be less than or equal to m)
n=54;             % No of elements in the input pattern
eta=0.6;          % Learning coefficient
W=rand(n,m);

% Part-B End

for iter=1:epoch,
for pt=1:mxpt,
disp('Epoch Number');
disp(iter);
disp('Pattern Number');
disp(pt);
I=in(pt,:);

% CALCULATING EUCLIDEAN DISTANCE WITH RESPECT TO OUTPUT CLUSTER UNITS

for k=1:m,
ED(k,1)=0;
for h=1:n,
ED(k,1)=ED(k,1)+(W(h,k)-I(1,h)).^2;
end
end

% FINDING THE WINNER CLUSTER UNIT AT THE OUTPUT LAYER

arr=sort(ED);
[r c]=size(ED);
aa=0;
for i=1:r,
[a1 b1]=find(arr(i,1)==ED);
[r1 c1]=size(a1);
for ii=1:r1
aa=aa+1;
a(aa,1)=a1(ii,1);
end
end
disp('The winner output cluster unit of each pattern');
disp(a(1,1));

% STORING THE INPUT PATTERNS AND ITS GROUP

store(pt,:)=[pt   a(1,1)];

if R>0
for j=1:R,
for h=1:n
W(h,a(j,1))=W(h,a(j,1))+eta*(I(1,h)-W(h,a(j,1)));
end
end
end
if R==0
for h=1:n
W(h,a(1,1))=W(h,a(1,1))+eta*(I(1,h)-W(h,a(1,1)));
end
end
end
```

```
% DECREASING THE LEARNING RATE AND TOPOLOGICAL PARAMETER

eta=0.5*eta;
if R>0
R=R-1;
End

% Part-A Start

disp('Weights after the completion of each epoch');
disp(W);

% Part-A End
end
disp('Pattern-Group')
disp(store)
```

## 3.4 LEARNING VECTOR QUANTIZATION

Learning vector quantization (LVQ) network, developed by Kohonen in 1989, is a supervised NN where the input vectors are trained for a specific class or group already mapped in the training set [21]. The architecture (Fig. 3.18) of the LVQ is similar to the KNN where the number of output units is equal to the number of available classes but without a topological structure which is assumed for the output units. Therefore, the weight updation is carried out only for the weight vector for which the input vector corresponds to the output unit. A reference input vector is selected for a specific class.

All the reference input vectors together constitute the initial weights. However, random weights are also initialized in some of the variant LVQ network.

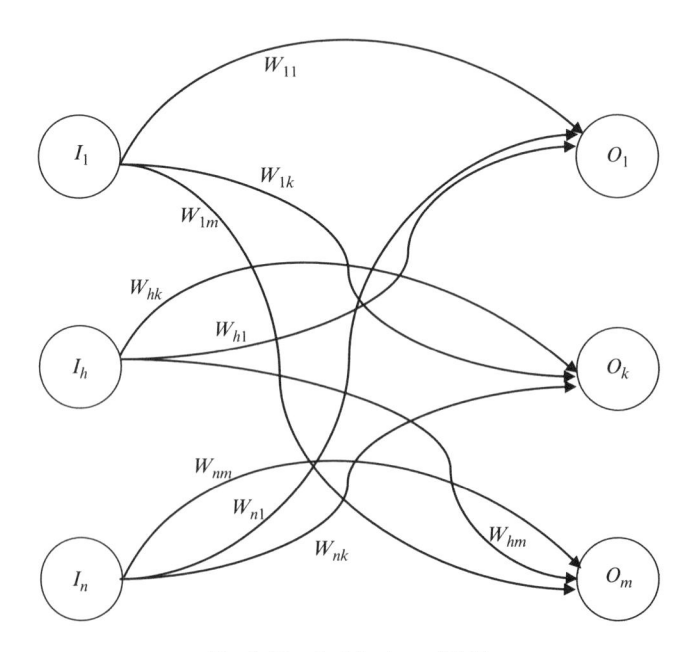

**Fig. 3.18** Architecture of LVQ

The training is carried out in such a way as to minimize the *ED* between the input vector and the weights of the corresponding output unit. Once the training is over, the LVQ network will be able to classify the input vector to the already mapped output unit that has the weight vector or the reference vector closest to the input vector (Fig. 3.19).

```
Initialize the input vector as reference vector
i.e., initial weight values and set the learning
rate (η) within 0.1 ≤ n × η ≤ 1.
               │
               ▼
For each input pattern I_h training pair compute
the Euclidean distance between input vector and
weight vector for each output cluster unit k,
        ED (k) = Σ (w_{hk} − I_h)²
               h=1:n
Find the unit index k for which the ED is
minimum.
               │
               ▼
Update the weights for the k^{th} output unit by
comparing target class (T) with the Output
class (O_k).
If T = O_k, then
  w_{hk} (t + 1) = w_{hk}(t) + η × (x_h − w_{hk} (t))
If T ≠ O_k, then
  w_{hk} (t + 1) = w_{hk} (t) − η × (x_h − w_{hk} (t))
Reduce the learning rate
               │
               ▼
       ◇ If the maximum number of
         epochs have reached?
         NO → loop back
         YES ↓
            Stop
```

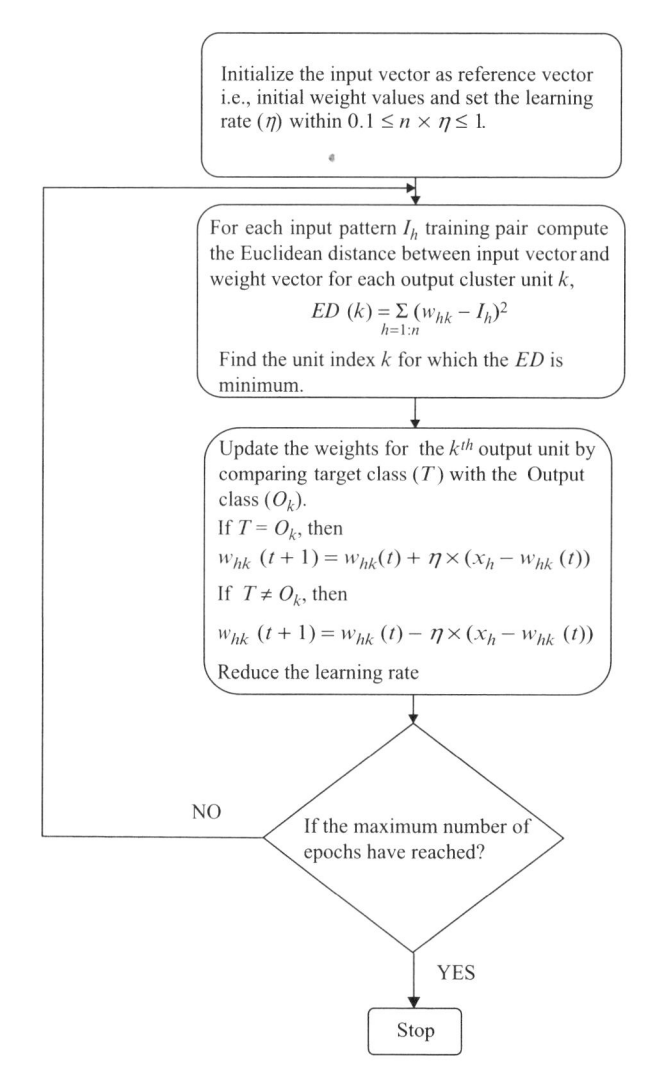

**Fig. 3.19** Flow chart of LVQ algorithm

## 3.4.1 Clustering of Bipolar Input Patterns in LVQ

Let us try to cluster 6 bipolar patterns into 2 clusters. The handworked portion for one epoch is given later. Here, $n = 4$ and $m = 2$ and learning rate be $\eta = 0.9$ and will geometrically decrease 0.5 times of $\eta$ for every epoch. The 6 bipolar input patterns ($I$), output patterns ($T$), initial weights ($W$), and initial learning rate $\eta$ are given as follows:

$$I = \begin{bmatrix} 1 & 1 & 1 & -1 \\ -1 & -1 & -1 & 1 \\ 1 & -1 & -1 & -1 \\ -1 & -1 & 1 & 1 \\ -1 & 1 & 1 & 1 \\ -1 & 1 & -1 & -1 \end{bmatrix} \begin{matrix}(I_1)\\(I_2)\\(I_3)\\(I_4)\\(I_5)\\(I_6)\end{matrix}$$

$$T = \begin{bmatrix} 1 \\ 2 \\ 2 \\ 1 \\ 1 \\ 2 \end{bmatrix}_{n \times m} \quad W = \begin{bmatrix} 1 & -1 \\ 1 & -1 \\ 1 & -1 \\ -1 & 1 \end{bmatrix}_{n \times m}$$

$\eta = 0.9$

The first input vector that belongs to the Class 1 and the second input vector that belongs to the Class 2 are selected as reference vector that constitute the initial weight vector ($W$). However, the selection of the reference vector is arbitrary.

**Epoch No. 1/Pattern No. 1**
*Calculation of ED*

$$ED(1) = \sum_{h=1:n} \left(w_{h1} - I_h\right)^2$$

(Cluster $k = 1$)

$ED(1) = (1-1)^2 + (1-1)^2 + (1-1)^2 + ((-1)-(-1))^2 = 0$

(Cluster $k = 2$)

$ED(2) = ((-1)-1)^2 + ((-1)-1)^2 + ((-1)-1)^2 + (1-(-1))^2 = 16$

The class represented by output unit is 1 (i.e., $O_2 = 1$ because $ED(1)$ is minimum). But the given target class is 1 (i.e., $T = 1$). Therefore, the weights connected to cluster unit 1 should be updated. Since $T = O_2$.

*Weight updation*

$w_{hk=1}(new) = w_{hk=1}(old) + 0.9 \times \left(I_1 - w_{hk=1}(old)\right)$
$w_{11} = 1 + 0.9 \times (1-1) = 1$
$w_{21} = 1 + 0.9 \times (1-1) = 1$
$w_{31} = 1 + 0.9 \times (1-1) = 1$
$w_{41} = (-1) + 0.9 \times (-1-(-1)) = -1$

$$W = \begin{bmatrix} 1 & -1 \\ 1 & -1 \\ 1 & -1 \\ -1 & 1 \end{bmatrix}$$

**Epoch No. 1/Pattern No. 2**

$$ED(1) = \sum_{h=1:n} \left(w_{h1} - I_h\right)^2$$

(Cluster $k = 1$)

$ED(1) = (1-(-1))^2 + (1-(-1))^2 + (1-(-1))^2 + ((-1)-1)^2 = 16$

(Cluster $k = 2$)

$ED(2) = (-1-(-1))^2 + (-1-(-1))^2 + (-1-(-1))^2 + (1-1)^2 = 0$

The class represented by output unit is 2 (i.e., $O = 2$ because $ED$ (2) is minimum). The given target class is 2 (i.e., $T = 2$). Therefore, the weights connected to cluster unit 2 should be updated. Since $T = O_2$.

*Weight updation*

$w_{hk=2}(new) = w_{hk=2}(old) + 0.9 \times \left(I_2 - w_{hk=2}(old)\right)$
$w_{12} = -1 + 0.9 \times (-1-(-1)) = -1$
$w_{22} = -1 + 0.9 \times (-1-(-1)) = -1$
$w_{32} = -1 + 0.9 \times (-1-(-1)) = -1$
$w_{42} = 1 + 0.9 \times (1-1) = 1$

$$W = \begin{bmatrix} 1 & -1 \\ 1 & -1 \\ 1 & -1 \\ -1 & 1 \end{bmatrix}_{n \times m}$$

**Epoch No. 1/Pattern No. 3**

$$ED(1) = \sum_{h=1:n} \left(w_{h1} - I_h\right)^2$$

(Cluster $k = 1$)

$ED(1) = (1-1)^2 + (1-(-1))^2 + (1-(-1))^2 + (-1-(-1))^2 = 8$

(Cluster $k = 2$)

$$ED(2) = (-1-1)^2 + (-1-(-1))^2 + (-1-(-1))^2 + (1-(-1))^2 = 8$$

The class represented by output unit is both 1 and 2 (i.e., $O = 1, 2$) because $ED$ (1) equals to $ED$ (2). The given target class is 2 (i.e., $T = 2$). Therefore, the weights connected to both the output 1 and 2 should be updated. Since $T \neq O_1$ and $T = O_2$.

*Weight updation*

$$w_{hk=1}(new) = w_{hk=1}(old) - 0.9 \times (I_3 - w_{hk=1}(old))$$
$$w_{11} = 1 - 0.9 \times (1-1) = 1$$
$$w_{21} = 1 - 0.9 \times (-1-1) = 2.8$$
$$w_{31} = 1 - 0.9 \times (-1-1) = 2.8$$
$$w_{41} = -1 - 0.9 \times (-1-(-1)) = -1$$

$$w_{hk=2}(new) = w_{hk=2}(old) + 0.9 \times (I_3 - w_{hk=2}(old))$$
$$w_{12} = -1 + 0.9 \times (1-(-1)) = 0.8$$
$$w_{22} = -1 + 0.9 \times (-1-(-1)) = -1$$
$$w_{32} = -1 + 0.9 \times (-1-(-1)) = -1$$
$$w_{42} = 1 + 0.9 \times (-1-1) = -0.8$$

$$W = \begin{bmatrix} 1 & 0.8 \\ 2.8 & -1 \\ 2.8 & -1 \\ -1 & -0.8 \end{bmatrix}$$

**Epoch No. 1/Pattern No. 4**

$$ED(1) = \sum_{h=1:n} (w_{h1} - I_h)^2$$

(Cluster $k = 1$)

$$ED(1) = (1-(-1))^2 + (2.8-(-1))^2 + (2.8-1)^2 + (-1-1)^2 = 25.68$$

(Cluster $k = 2$)

$$ED(2) = (0.8-(-1))^2 + (-1-(-1))^2 + (-1-1)^2 + (-0.8-1)^2 = 10.48$$

The class represented by output unit is 2 (i.e., $O = 2$), because $ED$ (2) is minimum. The given target class is 1 (i.e., $T = 1$). Therefore, the weights connected to cluster unit 2 should be updated. Since, $T \neq O_2$.

*Weight updation*

$$w_{hk=2}(new) = w_{hk=2}(old) - 0.9 \times (I_4 - w_{hk=2}(old))$$
$$w_{12} = 0.8 - 0.9 \times (-1-0.8) = 2.42$$

$w_{22} = -1 - 0.9 \times (-1 - (-1)) = -1$
$w_{32} = -1 - 0.9 \times (1 - (-1)) = -2.8$
$w_{42} = -0.8 - 0.9 \times (1 - (-0.8)) = -2.42$

$$W = \begin{bmatrix} 1 & 2.42 \\ 2.8 & -1 \\ 2.8 & -2.8 \\ -1 & -2.42 \end{bmatrix}$$

**Epoch No. 1/Pattern No. 5**

$ED(1) = \sum_{h=1:n} (w_{h1} - I_h)^2$

(Cluster $k = 1$)

$ED(1) = (1-(-1))^2 + (2.8-1)^2 + (2.8-1)^2 + (-1-1)^2 = 14.48$

(Cluster $k = 2$)

$ED(2) = (2.42-(-1))^2 + (-1-1)^2 + (-2.8-1)^2 + (-2.42-1)^2 = 41.8328$

The class represented by output unit is 1 (i.e., $O = 1$), because $ED(1)$ is minimum. The given target class is 1 (i.e., $T = 1$). Therefore, the weights connected to cluster unit 1 should be updated. Since $T = O_1$.

***Weight updation***

$w_{hk=1}(new) = w_{hk=1}(old) + 0.9 \times (I_5 - w_{hk=1}(old))$
$w_{11} = 1 + 0.9 \times (-1 - 1) = -0.8$
$w_{21} = 2.8 + 0.9 \times (1 - 2.8) = 1.18$
$w_{31} = 2.8 + 0.9 \times (1 - 2.8) = 1.18$
$w_{41} = -1 + 0.9 \times (1 - (-1)) = 0.8$

$$W = \begin{bmatrix} -0.8 & 2.42 \\ 1.18 & -1 \\ 1.18 & -2.8 \\ 0.8 & -2.42 \end{bmatrix}$$

**Epoch No. 1/Pattern No. 6**

$ED(1) = \sum_{h=1:n} (w_{h1} - I_h)^2$

(Cluster $k = 1$)

$ED(1) = (-0.8-(-1))^2 + (1.18-1)^2 + (1.18-(-1))^2 + (0.8-(-1))^2 = 8.0648$

(Cluster $k = 2$)

$ED(2) = (2.42 - (-1))^2 + (-1 - 1)^2 + (-2.8 - (-1))^2 + (-2.42 - (-1))^2 = 20.95$

The class represented by output unit is 1 (i.e., $O = 1$), because $ED(1)$ is minimum. The given target class is 2 (i.e., $T = 2$). Therefore, the weights connected to cluster unit 1 should be updated. Since, $T \ne O_1$.

### *Weight updation*

$w_{hk=1}(new) = w_{hk=1}(old) - 0.9 \times (I_6 - w_{hk=1}(old))$

$w_{11} = -0.8 - 0.9 \times (-1 - (-0.8)) = -0.62$

$w_{21} = 1.18 - 0.9 \times (1 - 1.18) = 1.342$

$w_{31} = 1.18 - 0.9 \times (-1 - 1.18) = 3.142$

$w_{41} = 0.8 - 0.9 \times (-1 - 0.8) = 2.42$

$$W = \begin{bmatrix} -0.62 & 2.42 \\ 1.342 & -1 \\ 3.142 & -2.8 \\ 2.42 & -2.42 \end{bmatrix}$$

One epoch is completed. Now, the learning rate will geometrically decrease 0.5 times of $\eta$ for every epoch. Therefore, the learning rate will be 0.45 for the starting of the second epoch.

After 1000 epochs, the learning rate and weights are found to be $\eta = 8.3994e - 302$.

$$W = \begin{bmatrix} -0.4760 & -0.3775 \\ 0.3906 & -0.2086 \\ 1.0822 & -1.0691 \\ 0.5451 & -0.4139 \end{bmatrix}$$

It is found that the clustering has become stagnant even after the second epoch and has been constant till 1000 epochs. The final resultant of the input patterns classified is given as follows:

### *Result*

Pattern 1- (1 1 1 −1), Pattern 4- (−1 −1 1 1), and Pattern 5- (−1 1 1 1) belong to the Class 1, whereas Pattern 2- (−1 −1 −1 1), Pattern 3- (1 −1 −1 −1), and Pattern 6- (−1 1 −1 −1) belong to the Class 2. This can be verified with the final updated weights and calculating the $ED$. Each of the input patterns can be checked to find the winner cluster unit. It is obvious that the winner cluster unit output will be the corresponding input pattern whose $ED$ is minimum.

*Verification*
Pattern 1- (1 1 1 −1)
$$ED(k) = \sum_{h=1:n} (w_{hk} - I_h)^2$$
(Output unit $k = 1$)
$ED(1) = (-0.476 - 1)^2 + (0.3906 - 1)^2 + (1.0822 - 1)^2 + (0.5451 - (-1))^2 = 4.9440$
(Output unit $k = 2$)
$ED(2) = (-0.3775 - 1)^2 + (-0.2086 - 1)^2 + (-1.0691 - 1)^2 + (-0.4139 - (-1))^2$
    $= 7.9829$
Since the winner cluster output unit is $K = 1$, the Pattern 1 belongs to the first cluster or Class 1.
Pattern 2- (−1 −1 −1 1)
(Cluster $k = 1$)
$ED(1) = (-0.476 - (-1))^2 + (0.3906 - (-1))^2 + (1.0822 - (-1))^2 + (0.5451 - 1)^2$
    $= 6.7508$
(Output unit $k = 2$)
$ED(2) = (-0.3775 - (-1))^2 + (-0.2086 - (-1))^2 + (-1.0691 - (-1))^2$
    $+ (-0.4139 - 1)^2 = 3.0177$
Since the winner cluster output unit is $K = 1$, the Pattern 2 belongs to the first cluster or Class 1.
Pattern 3- (1 −1 −1 −1)
(Output unit $k = 1$)
$ED(1) = (-0.476 - 1)^2 + (0.3906 - (-1))^2 + (1.0822 - (-1))^2 + (0.5451 - (-1))^2$
    $= 10.8352$
(Output unit $k = 2$)
$ED(2) = (-0.3775 - 1)^2 + (-0.2086 - (-1))^2 + (-1.0691 - (-1))^2$
    $+ (-0.4139 - (-1))^2 = 2.8721$
Since the winner cluster output unit is $K = 2$, the Pattern 3 belongs to the second cluster or Class 2.
Pattern 4- (−1 −1 1 1)
(Output unit $k = 1$)
$ED(1) = (-0.476 - (-1))^2 + (0.3906 - (-1))^2 + (1.0822 - 1)^2 + (0.5451 - 1)^2$
    $= 2.4220$
(Output unit $k = 2$)
$ED(2) = (-0.3775 - (-1))^2 + (-0.2086 - (-1))^2 + (-1.0691 - 1)^2$
    $+ (-0.4139 - 1)^2 = 7.2941$
Since the winner cluster output unit is $K = 1$, the Pattern 4 belongs to the first cluster or Class 1.

Pattern 5- (−1 1 1 1)
(Output unit $k = 1$)

$$ED(1) = (-0.476-(-1))^2 + (0.3906-1)^2 + (1.0822-1)^2 + (0.5451-1)^2 = 0.8596$$

(Output unit $k = 2$)

$$ED(2) = (-0.3775-(-1))^2 + (-0.2086-1)^2 + (-1.0691-1)^2 + (-0.4139-1)^2$$
$$= 8.1285$$

Since the winner cluster output unit is $K = 1$, the Pattern 5 belongs to the first cluster or Class 1.

Pattern 6- (−1 1 −1 −1)
(Output unit $k = 1$)

$$ED(1) = (-0.476-(-1))^2 + (0.3906-1)^2 + (1.0822-(-1))^2 + (0.5451-(-1))^2$$
$$= 7.3688$$

(Output unit $k = 2$)

$$ED(2) = (-0.3775-(-1))^2 + (-0.2086-1)^2 + (-1.0691-(-1))^2$$
$$+ (-0.4139-(-1))^2 = 2.1965$$

Since the winner cluster output unit is $K = 2$, the Pattern 6 belongs to the second cluster or Class 2.

The simulation of 1,000 epochs can be carried out using the MATLAB Program 3.3. In this program, parameters are initialized commenting Part B and uncommenting Part A. The readers can use the following program to train and test to check whether the network behaves in the aforesaid manner.

### 3.4.2 Classification of Numerical Characters

This application aims to cluster 25 binary patterns representing numerals from 1 to 9. They are represented by $9 \times 7$ matrix format. The 25 patterns are already shown in Fig. 3.17. The objective is to cluster the 25 patterns into 9 groups. Each of the input patterns are represented as binary input vectors as given in the Part B of the MATLAB Program 3.3. Here, $n = 25$, $m = 2$, and the initial learning rate be $\eta = 0.6$. The learning rate will geometrically decrease 0.5 times of $\eta$ for every epoch.

The simulation of 1,000 epochs can be carried out using the MATLAB Program 3.3. In this program, parameters are initialized uncommenting Part B and commenting Part A. The readers can simulate and classify the 25 binary patterns into 9 groups. After the training, all input patterns considered are tested for classification. The results are presented in Table 3.6 given at specific epoch. The results infer that the input patterns 1, 2, 3, 6, 7, 8, 10, 11, 12, 13, 14, 15, 18, 19, 20, 17, 22, 23, 24, and 25 have learned to classify correctly. However, the patterns 5, 9, 16, 4, and 21 (Underlined patterns in Table 3.6) are not able to classify correctly. Improvements can be made by trial and error approach by optimal choice of reference vectors, representation of the input vector elements (binary or bipolar), the number of training patterns in a training set, learning parameter, and the number of elements in an input vector.

Table 3.6  Test results

| Class | 1 | 2 | 3 | 4 | 5 | 6 | 7 | 8 | 9 |
|---|---|---|---|---|---|---|---|---|---|
| 5th epoch | 1,2,3 | 6 | 4,7,8 | 9,10,11,12 | 13,16 | 15 | 14,18,19,20 | 22 | 5,17,21, 23,24, 25 |
| 10th epoch | 1,2,3 | 6 | 4,5,7,8 | 10,11,12 | 13,14,16 | 15 | 9,18,19,20 | 22 | 17,21, 23,24, 25 |
| 20th epoch | 1,2,3 | 6 | 5,7,8 | 9,10,11,12 | 13,16 | 15 | 14,18,19,20 | 17,22 | 4,21,23, 24, 25 |
| 50th epoch | 1,2,3 | 6 | 5,7,8 | 10,11,12 | 13,14,16 | 15 | 9,18,19,20 | 17,22 | 4,21, 23,24, 25 |
| 100th epoch | 1,2,3 | 6 | 5,7,8 | 10,11, 12 | 9,13,14,16 | 15 | 18, 19,20 | 17,22 | 4,21, 23, 24, 25 |

## MATLAB Program 3.3

### Part A: Main program

```
%%%%%%%%%%%%%%%%%%%%%%%%%%%%%%%%%%%%%%%%%%%%%
% LEARNING VECTOR QUANTIZATIONNETWORK ALGORITHM
%%%%%%%%%%%%%%%%%%%%%%%%%%%%%%%%%%%%%%%%%%%%%

clear workspace
clear all
clc
format short

% Part-A Start

%%%%%%%%%%%%%%%%%%%%%%%%%%%%%%%%%%%%%%%%%%%%
% PART-A CLASSIFICATION OF BIPOLAR VECTORS
%%%%%%%%%%%%%%%%%%%%%%%%%%%%%%%%%%%%%%%%%%%%
in=[1  1  1 -1;
   -1 -1 -1  1;
    1 -1 -1 -1;
   -1 -1  1  1;
   -1  1  1  1;
   -1  1 -1 -1];

% Part-A End

% Part-B Start

%%%%%%%%%%%%%%%%%%%%%%%%%%%%%%%%%%%%%%%%%%%%%%%%%%%%%%%%%
% PART-B CLASSIFICATION OF 1-9 NUMBERS   INTO 9- GROUPS OR CLASSES
%%%%%%%%%%%%%%%%%%%%%%%%%%%%%%%%%%%%%%%%%%%%%%%%%%%%%%%%%
in=[000100000010000001000000100000010000001000000100000010000001000;%1a
    000100000110000001000000100000010000001000000100000010000011100;%1b
    000100000110000101000000100000001000000100000010000111111;%1c
    111111100000010000001000000111111110000001000000100000011111111;%2a
    111111100000010000001000000111111110000001000000100000011111111;%2b
    011100010000100000001000000100000010000001000000100001111111;%2c
    111111100000010000001000000111111110000001000000100000011111111;%3a
```

```
    11111111000001000001000001011111100000010000001100000111111111;%3b
    11111110000010000010000010000010000011110000000100000101111100;%3c
    00000100001010001001001000101000010111111100000100000010000010;%4a
    01000100100010010001001000100100010011111110000010000001000010;%4b
    00010100010010001001001000100100010111111110000010000001000010;%4c
    11111111000000100000001000000111111100000001000000100000011111111;%5a
    11111111000000100000011100000000100000001000000110000100111100;%5b
    00111100100001100000010000001101100100001010000011000010111100;%6a
    11111111000001000001000001111111100000011000001100000111111111;%6b
    11111111000001100000010000001111111110000011000001100001111111;%6c
    11111110000001000001000001000001000001000001000001000001000000;%7a
    11111110000001000001000001000001000001000001000001000010000001;%7b
    00111110000001000001000001000001000001000001000001000001000000;%7c
    11111111000001100000110000011111111110000011000001100001111111;%8a
    01111101000001100000110000010111110100000110000011000010111110;%8b
    11111111000001100000110000011111111110000001000000100000011111111;%9a
    11111111000001100000110000011111111100000001000001100001111111;%9b
    01111101000001100000110000010111110000000100000011000010111110];%9c

% Part-B End

% INITIALIZATION OF PARAMETERS

% Part-A Start

m=2;            % No of clusters or group
mxpt=4;         % No of patterns to be clustered
epoch=1000;     % Maximum number of epochs
R=0;            % Boundary radius of the neighbourhood (should be less than m)
n=4;            % No of elements in the input pattern
eta=0.9;        % Learning coefficient
W= in(1:2,:)';  % Initial weights

% Part-A End

% Part B-Start

m=9;            % No of clusters or group
mxpt=25;        % No of patterns to be clustered
epoch=1000;     % Maximum number of epochs
R=4;            % Boundary radius of the neighbourhood (should be less than or equal to m)
n=54;           % No of elements in the input pattern
eta=0.6;        % Learning coefficient
W=[in(1:3:14,:)' in(15:3:22,:)' in(23,:)'];   % Initial weights

% Part-B End

for iter=1:epoch,
for pt=1:mxpt,
disp('Epoch Number');
disp(iter);
disp('Pattern Number');
disp(pt);
I=in(pt,:);

% CALCULATING EUCLIDEAN DISTANCE WITH RESPECT TO OUTPUT CLUSTER UNITS

for k=1:m,
ED(k,1)=0;
for h=1:n,
ED(k,1)=ED(k,1)+(W(h,k)-I(1,h)).^2;
end
end
```

```
% FINDING THE WINNER CLUSTER UNIT AT THE OUTPUT LAYER

arr=sort(ED);
[r c]=size(ED);
aa=0;
for i=1:r,
[a1 b1]=find(arr(i,1)==ED);
[r1 c1]=size(a1);
for ii=1:r1
aa=aa+1;
a(aa,1)=a1(ii,1);
end
end
disp('The winner output cluster unit of each pattern');
disp(a(1,1));

% STORING THE INPUT PATTERNS AND ITS GROUP

store(pt,:)=[pt a(1,1)];

% UPDATING THE WEIGHT VECTOR

for h=1:n
if T(pt)== a(1,1)
W(h,a(1,1))=W(h,a(1,1))+eta*(I(1,h)-W(h,a(1,1)));
elseif T(pt)~= a(1,1)
W(h,a(1,1))=W(h,a(1,1))-eta*(I(1,h)-W(h,a(1,1)));
end
end
end
end

% DECREASING THE LEARNING RATE

eta=0.5*eta;

% Part-A Start

disp('Weights after the completion of each epoch');
disp(W);

% Part-A End

end
disp('Pattern-Group')
disp(store)
```

## 3.5 HAMMING NEURAL NETWORK

Lippmann [22] modelled a two-layer bipolar network called Hamming neural network (HNN). The first layer is the Hamming net and the second layer is the MAXNET. The first layer is a feed-forward type network which classifies the input patterns based on minimum Hamming distance (HD). The HD between any two vectors is the number of components in which the vectors differ. For example, let $I$ (1−11111) and $S$ (11−1−111) be the two fixed length bipolar vectors whose HD $(I, S)$ is equal to 3. If $I$ and $S$ are bipolar components, then the scalar product of $I$ and $S$ is given by:

$$I'S = [n - \text{HD}(I, S)] - \text{HD}(I, S) \qquad (3.42)$$

If $n$ is the number of components in the vectors, then $[n-\text{HD}(I, S)]$ are the number of components in which the vectors agree.

$$I^t S = n - 2\text{HD}(I, S) \tag{3.43}$$

Let $I$ be the input vector and $S$ be the vector that represents the patterns placed on a cluster (stored vector) or a can be considered as a standard pattern. For a two-layer classifier of bipolar vector, the strongest response of a neuron indicates that the minimum HD exists between the two vectors $I$ and $S$, respectively. For setting up the weights and bias, the Eq. 3.43 can be written as:

$$\text{HD}(I, S) = I^t \cdot S/2 + n/2 \tag{3.44}$$

If the weights are fixed to one half of the standard vector $S/2$ and bias to $n/2$, then the network will be able to find the input vector $I$, closest to the standard vector $S$. This is done by finding the output unit with the largest net input.

The Hamming net uses MAXNET in the second layer as a subnet to find the unit with the largest net input. The second layer operates as recurrent recall network which suppresses all the outputs except the initially obtained maximum output of the first layer. Therefore, MAXNET is a competition network which is used as a subnet to pick the cluster unit whose input is the largest. The architecture of the HNN is shown in Fig. 3.20. The flow chart for the Hamming net together with the MAXNET (as provided in Chapter 2, Fig. 2.14) is given in Fig. 3.21.

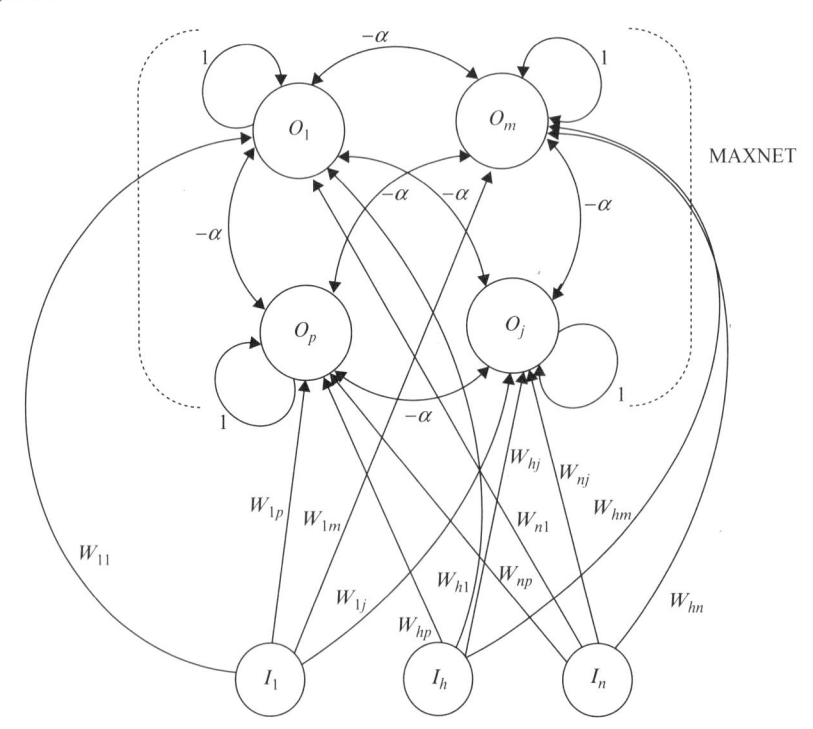

**Fig. 3.20** Hamming neural network with MAXNET

```
┌─────────────────────────────────────────────────────┐
│ Read the number of input units (n), number of       │
│ output units (m), total number of input vectors (T) │
│ and stored vectors (S(j)),                          │
│ where, S(j) = (S₁(j)..(Sₕ(j))..(Sₙ(j)), h = 1,..n   │
│ and j = 1,..m                                       │
│ Initialize weight as $W_{hj} = \frac{S_h(j)}{2}$     │
│ and bias as $B_j = \frac{n}{2}$                      │
└─────────────────────────────────────────────────────┘
```

For each input vector $I_i$, $i = 1$

Compute the net input $O_j$
$$O_j = B_j + \sum_{h=1}^{n} I_{ih} W_{hj}, j = 1,..m$$

if $i < T$ — NO → Stop (Hamming Net)

$i = i + 1$

YES

Set the weights for MAXNET as $0 < \alpha < \frac{1}{m}$, i.e, $w_{pj} = \begin{cases} 1 & if\ p = j; \\ -\alpha & p \neq j; \end{cases}$

The activation function for the MAXNET is given as follows:
$$f(sum_j) = \begin{cases} sum_j & if\ sum_j > 0 \\ 0 & otherwise \end{cases}$$

Initialize the inputs to the MAXNET as $O_j(t) = O_j, j = 1,..m$ and set $t = 0$.

$t = t + 1$

$O_j(t) = O_j(t+1)$

Check if only one non-zero input exists? — NO →

Update the inputs $O_j$ for each unit, $j = 1,..m$,
$O_j(t+1) = f(sum_j)$, where,
$sum_j = O_j(t) - \alpha \times \sum_{p \neq j} O_p(t)$

YES

Stop (MAXNET)
(The non-zero input of the MAXNET is the winner and is the best match for the input $I_i$, i.e., $I_i$ is closer to $S(j)$, the stored vector). Continue for the next input vector.

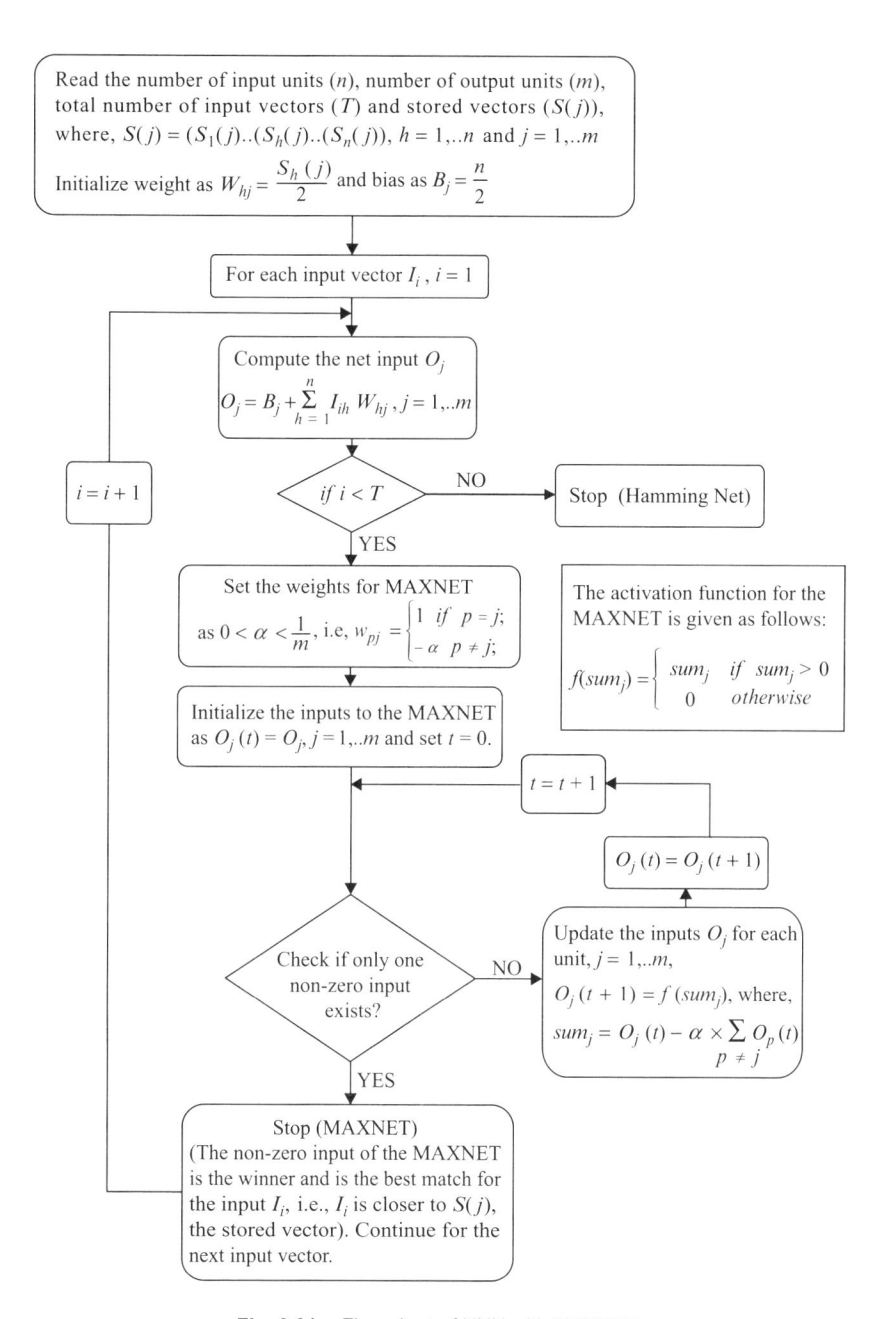

**Fig. 3.21** Flow chart of HNN with MAXNET

## 3.5.1 Illustration on Finding the Best Match with Standard Vector

Let us try to cluster 4 bipolar patterns and find the patterns closest to 2 standard bipolar patterns $S(1) = (1\ 1\ -1\ -1\ 1\ 1)$ and $S(2) = (-1\ -1\ 1\ -1\ 1\ 1)$. The handworked portion for one epoch is given here. The subscripts $h$ and $j$ and the indices $n$ and $m$ are considered as given in Fig. 3.20. Here $n = 6$, $m = 2$ and $I = 4$. The 4 bipolar input patterns ($I$), initial weights ($W$), and bias ($B$) are given as follows:

$$I = \begin{bmatrix} 1 & 1 & 1 & -1 & 1 & 1 \\ -1 & -1 & -1 & 1 & 1 & -1 \\ 1 & -1 & -1 & -1 & 1 & 1 \\ -1 & -1 & 1 & 1 & 1 & -1 \end{bmatrix}_{T \times n} \begin{matrix} (I_1) \\ (I_2) \\ (I_3) \\ (I_4) \end{matrix}$$

$$W = \begin{bmatrix} 0.5 & -0.5 \\ 0.5 & -0.5 \\ -0.5 & 0.5 \\ -0.5 & -0.5 \\ 0.5 & 0.5 \\ 0.5 & 0.5 \end{bmatrix}_{n \times m}$$

$$B = [3\ 3]$$

The net input to each output unit of the first layer for all the 4 input paterns is calculated from $O_j = B_j + \sum_{h=1}^{n} I_{ih} W_{hj}, j = 1,..m$

Pattern 1- (1 1 1 −1 1 1)
*Computation in the first layer*

$O_1(0) = 3 + 1 \times 0.5 + 1 \times 0.5 + 1 \times (-0.5) + (-1) \times (-0.5) + 1 \times 0.5 + 1 \times 0.5 = 5$
$O_2(0) = 3 + 1 \times -0.5 + 1 \times -0.5 + 1 \times 0.5 + (-1) \times (-0.5) + 1 \times 0.5 + 1 \times 0.5 = 4$

*Computation in the second layer (MAXNET)*

**t = 0**

$$w_{pj} = \begin{bmatrix} 1 & 0.25 \\ 0.25 & 1 \end{bmatrix}$$

$O_1(0+1) = f(O_1(0) - 0.25 \times (4)) = 4;\ O_2(0+1) = f(O_2(0) - 0.25 \times (5)) = 2.75$
$O_1(0) = 4; O_2(0) = 2.75$

**t = 1**

$O_1(1+1) = f(O_1(1) - 0.25 \times (2.75)) = 3.3125;\ O_2(1+1) = f(O_2(1) - 0.25 \times (4)) = 1.75$
$O_1(2) = 3.2125; O_2(2) = 1.75$

**t = 2**
$O_1(2+1) = f(O_1(2) - 0.25 \times (1.75)) = 2.8750;$
$O_2(2+1) = f(O_2(2) - 0.25 \times (3.3125)) = 0.9219$
$O_1(3) = 2.8750; O_2(3) = 0.9219$

**t = 3**
$O_1(3+1) = f(O_1(3) - 0.25 \times (0.9219)) = 2.6445;$
$O_2(3+1) = f(O_2(3) - 0.25 \times (2.8750)) = 0.2031$
$O_1(4) = 2.6445; O_2(4) = 0.2031$

**t = 4**
$O_1(4+1) = f(O_1(4) - 0.25 \times (0.2031)) = 2.5938;$
$O_2(4+1) = f(O_2(4) - 0.25 \times (2.6445)) = 0$

Since $sum_2 = -0.4580 < 0$, $f(sum_2) = 0$
Here, the non-zero input unit $j=1$ of the MAXNET is the winner, i.e, $I_1$ (1 1 1 −1 1 1) is closer to S(1) = (1 1 −1 −1 1 1).

Pattern 2- (−1 −1 −1 1 1 −1)
*Computation in the first layer*

$O_1(0) = 3 + (-1) \times 0.5 + (-1) \times 0.5 + (-1) \times (-0.5) + 1 \times (-0.5) + 1 \times 0.5 + (-1) \times 0.5 = 2$
$O_2(0) = 3 + (-1) \times -0.5 + (-1) \times -0.5 + (-1) \times 0.5 + 1 \times (-0.5) + 1 \times 0.5 + (-1) \times 0.5 = 3$

*Computation in the second layer (MAXNET)*
**t = 0**
$O_1(0+1) = f(O_1(0) - 0.25 \times (3)) = 1.25; O_2(0+1) = f(O_2(0) - 0.25 \times (2)) = 2.5$
$O_1(1) = 1.25; O_2(1) = 2.5$

**t = 1**
$O_1(1+1) = f(O_1(1) - 0.25 \times (2.5)) = 0.625;$
$O_2(1+1) = f(O_2(1) - 0.25 \times (1.25)) = 2.1875$
$O_1(2) = 0.625; O_2(2) = 2.1875$

**t = 2**
$O_1(2+1) = f(O_1(2) - 0.25 \times (2.1875)) = 0.0781;$
$O_2(2+1) = f(O_2(2) - 0.25 \times (0.625)) = 2.0312$
$O_1(3) = 0.0781; O_2(3) = 2.0312$

**t = 3**
$O_1(3+1) = f(O_1(3) - 0.25 \times (2.0312)) = 0;$
$O_2(3+1) = f(O_2(3) - 0.25 \times (0.0781)) = 2.0117$
Since $sum_1 = -0.4297 < 0$, $f(sum_1) = 0$

Here, the non-zero input unit $j = 2$ of the MAXNET is the winner, i.e, $I_2$ (−1 −1 −1 1 1 −1) is closer to $S(2) = $ (−1 −1 1 −1 1 1).

Pattern 3- (1 −1 −1 −1 1 1)
*Computation in the first layer*

$O_1(0) = 3 + 1 \times 0.5 + (-1) \times 0.5 + (-1) \times (-0.5) + (-1) \times (-0.5) + 1 \times 0.5 + 1 \times 0.5 = 5$

$O_2(0) = 3 + 1 \times -0.5 + (-1) \times -0.5 + (-1) \times 0.5 + (-1) \times (-0.5) + 1 \times 0.5 + 1 \times 0.5 = 4$

*Computation in the second layer (MAXNET)*

**t = 0**

$O_1(0 + 1) = f(O_1(0) - 0.25 \times (4)) = 4$ ; $O_2(0 + 1) = f(O_2(0) - 0.25 \times (5)) = 2.75$

$O_1(1) = 4; O_2(1) = 2.75$

**t = 1**

$O_1(1 + 1) = f(O_1(1) - 0.25 \times (2.75)) = 3.3125$ ;

$O_2(1 + 1) = f(O_2(1) - 0.25 \times (4)) = 1.75$

$O_1(2) = 3.2125; O_2(2) = 1.75$

**t = 2**

$O_1(2 + 1) = f(O_1(2) - 0.25 \times (1.75)) = 2.8750$ ;

$O_2(2 + 1) = f(O_2(2) - 0.25 \times (3.3125)) = 0.9219$

$O_1(3) = 2.8750; O_2(3) = 0.9219$

**t = 3**

$O_1(3 + 1) = f(O_1(3) - 0.25 \times (0.9219)) = 2.6445$ ;

$O_2(3 + 1) = f(O_2(3) - 0.25 \times (2.8750)) = 0.2031$

$O_1(4) = 2.6445; O_2(4) = 0.2031$

**t = 4**

$O_1(4 + 1) = f(O_1(4) - 0.25 \times (0.2031)) = 2.5938$ ;

$O_2(4 + 1) = f(O_2(4) - 0.25 \times (2.6445)) = 0$

Since $sum_2 = -0.4580 < 0, f(sum_2) = 0$

Here, the non-zero input unit $j = 2$ of the MAXNET is the winner, i.e., $I_3$ (1 −1 −1 −1 1 1) is closer to $S(1) = $ (1 1 −1 −1 1 1).

Pattern 4- (−1 −1 1 1 1 −1)
*Computation in the first layer*

$O_1(0) = 3 + (-1) \times 0.5 + (-1) \times 0.5 + 1 \times (-0.5) + 1 \times (-0.5) + 1 \times 0.5 + (-1) \times 0.5 = 1$

$O_2(0) = 3 + (-1) \times -0.5 + (-1) \times -0.5 + 1 \times 0.5 + 1 \times (-0.5) + 1 \times 0.5 + (-1) \times 0.5 = 4$

*Computation in the second layer (MAXNET)*

**t = 0**

$O_1(0+1) = f(O_1(0) - 0.25 \times (4)) = 0$; $O_2(0+1) = f(O_2(0) - 0.25 \times (1)) = 3.75$

Since $sum_1 = 0 \leq 0$, $f(sum_1) = 0$

Here, the non-zero input unit $j = 2$ of the MAXNET is the winner, i.e., $I_2$ (−1 −1 1 1 1 −1) is closer to $S(2) = (-1 -1\ 1\ -1\ 1\ 1)$.

The simulation can be carried out using the MATLAB Program 3.4. In this program, parameters are initialized commenting Part B and uncommenting Part A. The readers can use the following program to check the network behaving as per the previous illustration.

### 3.5.2 Character Recognition through Clustering of Numerical Characters

This application aims to recognize the closest match of the input test pattern of an alphabet with an error. Here, the representation of an alphabet is by a matrix of $7 \times 5$ bipolar elements.

It can be understood from Figs 3.11 and 3.13 with a small alteration, where 0 should be changed to −1. Figure 3.11 represents the standard patterns (26 alphabets from A to Z) that will store as half of its value as weights in the Hamming network, whereas Fig. 3.12 will be given as test input pattern with an error. The simulation can be carried out using the MATLAB Program 3.4. In this program, parameters are initialized commenting Part A and uncommenting Part B. Although HNN can be used for clustering of patterns, this application tries to recognize the input patterns with an error and finds the closest match. Here, $n = 35$, $m = 26$ (number of cluster units), and $T = 26$ (number of input patterns). Some of the sample simulation results are given in Fig. 3.22.

| (A) | (I) | (K) | (Z) |
|---|---|---|---|
| The input | The input | The input | The input |
| 1 0 1 0 0 | 0 1 0 1 0 | 1 0 0 0 1 | 1 1 1 1 1 |
| 0 1 0 1 0 | 0 0 1 0 0 | 1 0 0 1 0 | 0 0 1 0 1 |
| 1 0 0 0 1 | 0 0 1 0 0 | 1 0 1 0 0 | 0 0 0 1 0 |
| 1 0 0 0 1 | 0 0 1 0 0 | 1 1 0 0 0 | 0 0 1 0 0 |
| 1 1 1 1 1 | 0 0 1 0 0 | 1 0 1 0 0 | 0 1 0 0 0 |
| 1 0 0 0 1 | 0 0 1 0 0 | 1 0 0 1 0 | 1 0 0 0 0 |
| 1 0 0 0 1 | 0 1 1 1 0 | 1 0 1 0 1 | 1 1 1 1 1 |
| is closer to | is closer to | is closer to | is closer to |
| 0 0 1 0 0 | 0 1 1 1 0 | 1 0 0 0 1 | 1 1 1 1 1 |
| 0 1 0 1 0 | 0 0 1 0 0 | 1 0 0 1 0 | 0 0 0 0 1 |
| 1 0 0 0 1 | 0 0 1 0 0 | 1 0 1 0 0 | 0 0 0 1 0 |
| 1 0 0 0 1 | 0 0 1 0 0 | 1 1 0 0 0 | 0 0 1 0 0 |
| 1 1 1 1 1 | 0 0 1 0 0 | 1 0 1 0 0 | 0 1 0 0 0 |
| 1 0 0 0 1 | 0 0 1 0 0 | 1 0 0 1 0 | 1 0 0 0 0 |
| 1 0 0 0 1 | 0 1 1 1 0 | 1 0 0 0 1 | 1 1 1 1 1 |

**Fig. 3.22** Simulation results of HNN for character recognition

**182** Soft Computing with MATLAB Programming

The display of the output in the MATLAB Program 3.4 is presented in binary format to have visual clarity than in bipolar format. It should be noted that the actual results for the Hamming network are obtained in bipolar form. All the alphabets (A–Z) with an error are able to match with their own counterpart. The accuracy of the algorithm increases with the increasing HD or difference between the input pattern and the stored pattern. It can be improved by having larger size of matrix format.

## MATLAB Program 3.4

### Part A: Main program

```
%%%%%%%%%%%%%%%%%%%%%%%%%%%%%%%%%%
% HAMMING NEURAL NETWORK ALGORITHM
%%%%%%%%%%%%%%%%%%%%%%%%%%%%%%%%%%

clear workspace
clear all
clc
format short

%%%%%%%%%%%%%%%%%%%%%%%%%%%%%%%%%%%%%%%%%%%%%%%%%%%%%%%%%%%%%%%%%%%%
% PART-A DEMONSTRATION OF HAMMING NEURAL NETWORK FOR ILLUSTRATION
%%%%%%%%%%%%%%%%%%%%%%%%%%%%%%%%%%%%%%%%%%%%%%%%%%%%%%%%%%%%%%%%%%%%

% START A

% data= [1  1 -1 -1  1  1;         % Patterns that can be stored as weights
%       -1 -1  1 -1  1  1];

% test_data=[1  1  1 -1  1  1;
%           -1 -1 -1  1  1 -1;
%            1 -1 -1 -1  1  1;
%           -1 -1  1  1  1 -1];
% Input test patterns to be checked for the closeness of the stored paterns
% in=6;                             % Number of input nodes
% ou=2;                             % Number of clusters to be formed
% END A

%%%%%%%%%%%%%%%%%%%%%%%%%%%%%%%%%%%%%%%%%%%%%%%%%%%%%%%%%%%%%%%%%%%%%%%
% PART-B HAMMING NEURAL NETWORKS FOR FINDING THE BEST MATCH (A-Z ALPHABETS)
%%%%%%%%%%%%%%%%%%%%%%%%%%%%%%%%%%%%%%%%%%%%%%%%%%%%%%%%%%%%%%%%%%%%%%%

% START B

in=35;                              % Number of input nodes
ou=26;                              % Number of clusters to be formed

% STANDARD ALPHABETICAL VECTORS WITHOUT ERROR
     %  A  B  C  D  E  F  G  H  I  J  K  L  M  N  O  P  Q  R  S  T  U  V  W  X  Y  Z
dat=[-1  1 -1  1  1  1 -1  1 -1  1  1  1  1 -1  1 -1  1 -1  1  1  1  1  1  1  1  1;
     -1  1  1  1  1  1  1  1 -1  1 -1 -1 -1 -1  1  1  1  1  1 -1 -1 -1 -1 -1 -1  1;
      1  1  1  1  1  1 -1  1 -1 -1 -1 -1  1  1  1  1  1  1 -1 -1 -1 -1 -1 -1 -1  1;
     -1  1  1  1  1  1 -1  1 -1 -1 -1 -1  1  1  1  1  1  1 -1 -1 -1 -1 -1 -1 -1  1;
     -1 -1 -1 -1  1  1 -1  1 -1  1  1 -1 -1 -1 -1 -1 -1  1  1  1  1  1  1  1  1;
     -1  1  1  1  1  1  1 -1 -1  1  1  1  1  1  1  1  1  1 -1  1  1  1  1  1  1 -1;
      1 -1 -1 -1 -1 -1 -1 -1 -1 -1  1 -1 -1 -1 -1 -1 -1 -1 -1 -1 -1 -1 -1 -1 -1 -1;
     -1 -1 -1 -1 -1 -1 -1 -1  1  1 -1 -1 -1 -1 -1 -1 -1  1 -1 -1 -1 -1 -1 -1 -1 -1;
```

## Artificial Neural Networks—Second Generation 183

```
         1 -1 -1 -1 -1 -1 -1 -1 -1 -1  1 -1  1 -1 -1 -1 -1 -1 -1 -1 -1 -1 -1 -1 -1 -1;
        -1  1  1  1 -1 -1  1  1 -1 -1 -1 -1  1  1  1  1  1  1  1 -1  1  1  1  1  1  1;
         1  1  1  1  1  1  1 -1 -1  1  1  1  1  1  1  1  1 -1  1  1  1  1  1 -1 -1 -1;
        -1 -1 -1 -1 -1  1  1  1 -1 -1 -1 -1  1 -1 -1 -1 -1 -1  1 -1 -1 -1 -1  1  1 -1;
        -1 -1 -1 -1 -1 -1 -1  1  1  1 -1  1 -1 -1 -1 -1 -1  1 -1 -1 -1 -1  1 -1 -1 -1;
        -1 -1 -1 -1 -1 -1 -1 -1 -1 -1 -1 -1 -1 -1 -1 -1 -1 -1 -1 -1 -1  1  1  1  1  1;
         1  1 -1  1 -1 -1 -1  1 -1 -1 -1 -1  1  1  1  1  1 -1 -1  1  1  1 -1 -1 -1 -1;
         1  1  1  1  1  1  1  1 -1 -1  1  1  1  1  1  1  1 -1 -1  1  1  1 -1 -1 -1 -1;
        -1  1 -1 -1  1  1 -1  1 -1  1 -1 -1 -1 -1  1 -1  1 -1 -1 -1 -1 -1 -1 -1 -1 -1;
        -1  1 -1 -1  1  1  1  1  1  1 -1 -1 -1  1 -1  1 -1  1  1 -1 -1 -1  1  1  1  1;
        -1  1 -1 -1  1  1 -1  1 -1 -1 -1 -1 -1  1 -1  1 -1 -1 -1 -1 -1 -1 -1 -1 -1 -1;
         1 -1 -1  1 -1 -1 -1  1 -1 -1 -1 -1  1  1  1 -1  1 -1 -1 -1  1  1  1 -1 -1 -1;
         1  1  1  1  1  1  1  1 -1 -1  1  1  1  1  1  1  1 -1 -1  1  1  1 -1 -1 -1 -1;
         1 -1 -1 -1 -1 -1 -1 -1 -1 -1 -1 -1 -1 -1 -1 -1 -1 -1 -1 -1 -1 -1 -1  1 -1  1;
         1 -1 -1 -1 -1 -1  1 -1  1  1  1 -1 -1 -1 -1  1  1 -1  1 -1 -1  1 -1  1 -1 -1;
         1 -1 -1 -1 -1 -1  1 -1 -1 -1 -1 -1  1 -1 -1 -1  1 -1 -1 -1  1 -1 -1  1 -1 -1;
         1  1 -1  1 -1 -1  1  1 -1 -1 -1 -1  1  1  1  1 -1 -1 -1  1  1  1 -1 -1 -1 -1;
         1  1  1  1  1  1  1  1 -1  1  1  1  1  1  1  1  1 -1  1 -1  1  1  1 -1  1  1;
        -1 -1 -1 -1 -1 -1 -1 -1 -1 -1 -1 -1 -1 -1 -1  1 -1 -1 -1 -1 -1  1  1 -1 -1 -1;
        -1 -1 -1 -1 -1 -1 -1  1  1 -1 -1 -1 -1 -1 -1 -1 -1 -1 -1  1 -1 -1 -1 -1  1 -1;
        -1 -1 -1 -1 -1 -1 -1 -1  1 -1 -1  1 -1 -1  1  1 -1 -1 -1  1 -1 -1 -1 -1 -1 -1;
         1  1  1  1 -1 -1  1  1 -1 -1 -1 -1  1  1  1 -1 -1  1 -1  1  1  1 -1 -1 -1 -1;
         1  1 -1  1  1  1 -1  1 -1 -1  1  1  1  1 -1  1 -1  1 -1 -1 -1  1  1 -1  1  1;
        -1  1  1  1  1 -1  1 -1  1  1 -1 -1  1 -1  1 -1  1 -1  1 -1 -1 -1 -1 -1  1  1;
        -1  1  1  1  1 -1  1 -1  1  1 -1 -1  1 -1  1  1  1  1  1  1 -1 -1  1  1  1  1;
        -1  1  1  1  1 -1  1 -1  1  1 -1 -1  1 -1  1  1  1 -1 -1 -1 -1  1  1  1  1  1;
         1 -1 -1  1 -1 -1  1 -1 -1  1  1  1  1 -1 -1  1  1 -1 -1 -1 -1  1  1 -1  1  1];
data=dat';
```

% STANDARD ALPHABETICAL VECTORS WITH ERROR

```
         %A  B  C  D  E  F  G  H  I  J  K  L  M  N  O  P  Q  R  S  T  U  V  W  X  Y  Z
test_dat= [1  1 -1  1  1  1 -1  1 -1  1  1  1  1 -1  1 -1  1 -1  1  1  1  1  1  1  1  1;
          -1  1  1  1  1  1  1 -1  1  1 -1 -1 -1 -1  1  1  1  1  1  1 -1 -1 -1 -1 -1  1;
           1  1  1  1  1  1  1 -1 -1  1 -1 -1 -1 -1  1  1  1  1 -1  1 -1 -1 -1 -1 -1  1;
          -1  1  1  1  1  1  1 -1  1  1 -1 -1 -1 -1  1  1  1  1  1  1 -1 -1 -1 -1 -1  1;
          -1 -1 -1 -1  1  1 -1  1 -1  1  1 -1  1  1 -1 -1 -1 -1 -1  1  1  1  1  1  1  1;
          -1  1  1  1  1  1  1 -1 -1  1  1  1  1  1  1 -1  1  1  1 -1  1  1  1  1  1 -1;
           1 -1 -1 -1 -1 -1 -1 -1 -1 -1 -1  1  1 -1 -1 -1 -1 -1 -1 -1 -1 -1 -1 -1  1 -1;
          -1  1 -1 -1 -1  1 -1 -1  1  1 -1 -1 -1 -1  1  1 -1 -1  1  1 -1 -1 -1  1  1  1;
           1 -1 -1 -1 -1 -1 -1 -1 -1  1 -1  1 -1 -1 -1 -1 -1 -1 -1 -1 -1 -1 -1 -1 -1 -1;
          -1  1  1  1 -1 -1  1  1 -1  1 -1 -1  1  1  1  1  1  1 -1  1  1  1  1  1  1  1;
           1  1  1  1  1  1  1 -1 -1  1  1  1 -1  1  1  1  1 -1 -1  1  1  1 -1 -1 -1 -1;
          -1 -1 -1 -1 -1 -1 -1 -1 -1 -1 -1 -1 -1 -1 -1  1  1 -1 -1  1 -1 -1  1  1 -1 -1;
          -1 -1 -1 -1 -1 -1 -1  1 -1  1  1  1 -1  1 -1 -1 -1 -1 -1 -1 -1 -1 -1  1  1 -1;
          -1 -1 -1 -1 -1 -1 -1 -1 -1  1 -1 -1 -1 -1 -1 -1 -1 -1 -1 -1 -1 -1 -1  1  1  1;
           1  1 -1  1 -1 -1  1  1 -1 -1 -1 -1  1  1  1  1  1  1 -1 -1  1  1  1 -1 -1 -1;
           1  1  1  1  1  1  1  1 -1 -1  1  1  1  1  1  1  1 -1 -1  1  1  1 -1 -1 -1 -1;
          -1  1 -1 -1  1  1 -1 -1 -1  1 -1 -1 -1 -1  1 -1  1 -1 -1 -1 -1 -1 -1 -1 -1 -1;
          -1  1 -1 -1  1  1  1  1  1  1 -1 -1 -1  1 -1  1 -1  1  1 -1 -1 -1  1  1  1  1;
          -1  1 -1 -1  1  1 -1  1 -1 -1 -1 -1 -1  1 -1  1 -1 -1 -1 -1 -1 -1 -1 -1 -1 -1;
           1 -1 -1  1 -1 -1 -1  1 -1 -1 -1 -1  1  1  1 -1  1 -1 -1 -1  1  1  1 -1 -1 -1;
           1  1  1  1  1  1  1  1 -1 -1  1  1  1  1  1  1  1 -1 -1  1  1  1 -1 -1 -1 -1;
           1 -1 -1 -1 -1 -1 -1 -1 -1 -1 -1 -1 -1 -1 -1 -1 -1 -1 -1 -1 -1 -1 -1  1 -1  1;
           1 -1 -1 -1 -1 -1  1 -1  1  1  1 -1 -1 -1 -1  1  1 -1  1 -1 -1  1 -1  1 -1 -1;
           1 -1 -1 -1 -1 -1  1 -1 -1 -1 -1 -1  1 -1 -1 -1  1 -1 -1 -1  1 -1 -1  1 -1 -1;
           1  1 -1  1 -1 -1  1  1 -1 -1 -1 -1  1  1  1  1 -1 -1 -1  1  1  1 -1 -1 -1 -1;
           1  1  1  1  1  1  1  1 -1  1  1  1  1  1  1  1  1 -1  1 -1  1  1  1 -1  1  1;
          -1 -1 -1 -1 -1 -1 -1 -1 -1 -1 -1 -1 -1 -1 -1 -1 -1 -1 -1  1  1 -1 -1 -1 -1 -1;
          -1 -1 -1 -1 -1 -1 -1 -1  1  1 -1 -1 -1 -1 -1 -1 -1 -1 -1  1 -1 -1 -1 -1  1 -1;
          -1 -1 -1 -1 -1 -1 -1 -1  1 -1 -1  1 -1 -1  1  1 -1 -1 -1  1 -1 -1 -1 -1 -1 -1;
           1  1  1  1  1 -1  1  1 -1 -1 -1  1  1 -1 -1 -1  1 -1  1 -1 -1  1 -1 -1 -1 -1;
```

```
                1  1 -1  1  1  1 -1  1 -1 -1  1  1  1  1 -1  1 -1  1 -1 -1 -1 -1  1  1 -1  1;
               -1  1  1 -1  1 -1  1 -1  1  1 -1  1 -1 -1  1 -1  1 -1  1 -1  1 -1 -1 -1 -1  1;
               -1  1  1  1  1 -1  1 -1  1  1 -1  1 -1 -1  1 -1  1 -1  1  1  1  1 -1 -1  1  1;
               -1  1 -1  1  1 -1  1 -1  1 -1 -1  1 -1 -1  1 -1 -1 -1  1 -1  1 -1 -1 -1 -1  1;
                1 -1 -1 -1  1 -1 -1  1 -1 -1  1  1  1  1 -1 -1  1  1 -1 -1 -1 -1  1 -1 -1  1];

test_data=test_dat';
% END B

temp=size(test_data);
pat=temp(1,1);                    % Getting the number of patterns from the test data
w=zeros(size(data));              % Defining the matrix space of the weights

% INITIALIZING OF WEIGHTS AND BIASES


for i=1:ou,
for j=1:in,
w(i,j)=data(i,j)/2;               % Setting the non-changing weights
end
b(1,i)=in/2;                      % Setting the non-changing bias
end

for k=1:pat,                      % For each of the input test pattern
disp('Test pattern no');
disp(k);
net_ou=zeros(1,ou);               % Defining the matrix space for output unit

% COMPUTING THE NET INPUT TO EACH OUTPUT UNIT

for i=1:ou,
for j=1:in,
net_ou(1,i)=net_ou(1,i)+test_data(k,j)*w(i,j);
end
net_ou(1,i)=b(1,i)+net_ou(1,i);   % Adding the bias for the total net input
end
disp('The net input to each output unit');
disp(net_ou);

% CALLING THE MAXNET OF THE SECOND LAYER

rec(k,1)=maxnet(net_ou,50);
% Set the maximum iteration as 50 for the MAXNET stopping criterion
store(k,:)=[k rec(k,1)];
% Recording the winner node for each test input pattern
end


% DISPLAYING THE RESULTS

disp('Pattern - Group');
disp(store);
% START B
disp('Display of Results');
for d=1:ou,
disp('The input')
disp(num2str(dispalp(test_dat>0,d)));
% Dispalying the bipolar pattern into binary pattern for display clarity
disp('is closer to');
disp(num2str(dispalp(dat>0,store(d,2))));
```

% Dispalying the bipolar pattern into binary pattern for display clarity
end
% END B

## Part B: Sub-programs (Sub-routine functions)

%%%%%%%%%%%%%%%%%%%%%%
% MAXNET NEURAL NETWORK
%%%%%%%%%%%%%%%%%%%%%%

```
function [win_node] = maxnet(net_ou,epoch)    % Getting the winner node
temp=size(net_ou);    % Getting the output unit matrix space from the input
m=temp(1,2);

% INITIALIZATION OF WEIGHTS

% START A
% e=0.3;                              % Weights selected between 0 and 0.5 (Illustration)
% END A

% START B
e=(ran(0,1/m,1,1));                   % Weights selected between 0 and 1/m randomly
% END B

% UPDATION OF THE INPUTS OF THE MAXNET

for iter=1:epoch
input=zeros(size(net_ou));
% Defining the matrix space for input units of MAXNET
for j=1:m,
input(1,j)=linearout(net_ou(1,j)-(e*(sum(net_ou)-net_ou(1,j))));
end
net_ou=input;                         % Updating the inputs
disp('The updated input of the MAXNET');
disp(iter);
disp(net_ou);
end

[a b]=find(net_ou==max(net_ou));      % Finding the non-zero input unit(winner unit)
disp('The output values of the cluster units using MAXNET are');
disp(net_ou);
disp('The winner cluster node is');
win_node=b(1,1);
disp(win_node);
```

OBJECTIVE FUNCTION (MAXNET)

```
function [out_neuron] = linearout(x) % Calling function for MAXNET

% LINEAR THRESHOLD FUNCTION OF MAXNET

if x>0,
out_neuron=x;
else
out_neuron=0;
end
```

```
% RANDOM VALUE GENERATION FUNCTION

function [weights] = ran(a,b,m,n)

% GENERATION RANDOM MATRIX(m X n) WEIGHTS BETWEEN a and b

weights=zeros(m,n);                 % Defining matrix space
for i=1:m,
for j=1:n,
weights(i,j)=(a + (b - a) * rand);
end
end
```

DISPLAY FUNCTION

```
function [out]=dispalp(data,a)

% DISPLAY OF ALPHABET IN A MATRIX FORMAT

k=0;
for i=1:7,
for j=1:5,
k=k+1;
out(i,j)=data(k,a);                 % Output display for a 7 X 5 matrix data
end
end
```

## 3.6 HOPFIELD NEURAL NETWORK

In 1982, John Hopfield developed a form of recurrent ANN [23]. It served as a content-addressable memory systems (special type of computer memory used in certain very high speed searching applications) with binary threshold units. A content-addressable memory system allows the recall of data on the degree of similarity between the input patterns and the patterns stored in memory. Hopfield neural networks and bi-directional associative memeory (BAM) are some of the examples of a class of networks called associative memory neural networks (AMNNs) which will discussed later in this chapter.

Associative memory neural networks are single-layer networks in which the weights are determined for the network to store a set of pattern associations. Each association is an input ($I$)-output ($O$) vector pair. If the input vector ($I$) is same as that of the output vector ($O$) associated, then the NN is called as Auto-AMNN. If $I$s and $O$s are different, then the NN is called 'Hetero-AMNN'. The architecture of the AMNNs is either feed-forward or recurrent in nature. The input-output patterns can be suitably represented as ON and OFF signals. The patterns can be of binary or bipolar kind of representation. Hebb rule is one of the most common methods of determining weights for an AMNN. It can be used for both binary and bipolar patterns.

Hopfield added feedback connections to the network (the outputs are fed back into the inputs) and found that these connections enabled the networks capable of performing interesting behaviours which can hold memories. The network is fully interconnected where each unit is connected to every other unit. However, the network has symmetric weights with no self-connections.

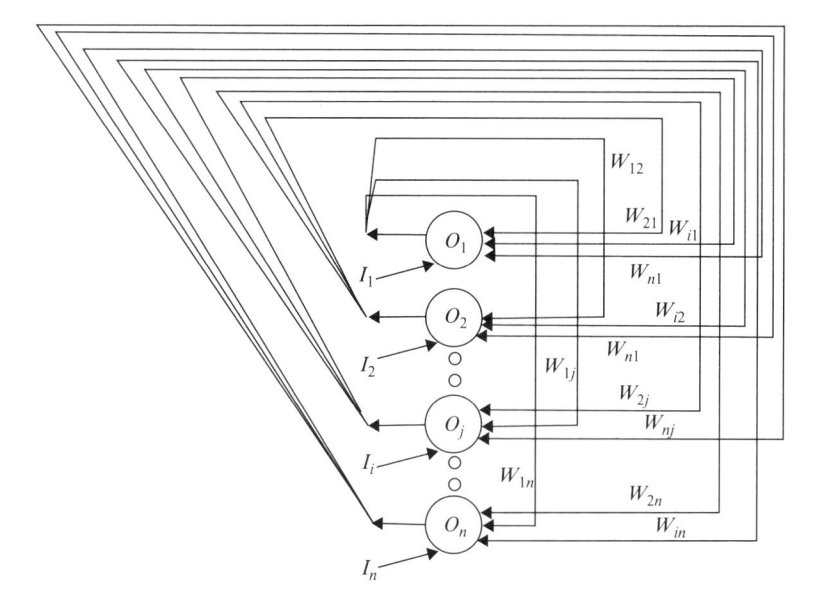

**Fig. 3.23** Hopfield neural network

In the Hopfield network, only one unit updates its activations at a time based on the signals it receives from the other unit. Also, each unit continues to receive an external signal in addition to the signal from other units in the net. These networks are guaranteed to converge to a local minimum, but convergence to one of the stored patterns is not guaranteed since oscillations may occur.

However, the asynchronous updating of the units allows an energy function called 'Lyapunov function' which can enable the network to converge to a stable set of activations but again to certain extent only depending upon the application. The architecture of the Hopfield network is shown in Figs 3.23 and 2.12 The flow chart of the Hopfield neural network handling discrete input vectors is shown in Fig. 3.24.

### 3.6.1 Illustration of Settlement of Stable Input Patterns

Let us try to test 3 binary input patterns and find the patterns that settle or converge to any one of the 2 standard binary patterns $S(1) = (1\ 1\ 1\ 1\ 0\ 0)$ and $S(2) = (0\ 1\ 1\ 1\ 1\ 1)$. The handworked portion for one epoch is given later. The subscripts $h, i, j,$ and $k$ with the indices $P, T,$ and $n$ are considered as given in Fig. 3.23. Here, $P = 2$, $T = 3$, and $n = 6$. The 3 binary input patterns ($I$) are given as follows:

$$I = \begin{bmatrix} 1 & 1 & 1 & 0 & 1 & 0 \\ 0 & 1 & 0 & 1 & 1 & 1 \\ 0 & 0 & 1 & 1 & 1 & 1 \end{bmatrix}_{T \times n} \begin{matrix} (I_1) \\ (I_2) \\ (I_3) \end{matrix}$$

***Initialization of weights as per Hebb rule for binary numbers***
The weight of the binary patterns that has to be stored in the Hopfield neural network is given as follows:

## 188 Soft Computing with MATLAB Programming

```
Read the number of input units (n), total number of
input vectors (T) and stored vectors S(h), where,
S(h) = (S_1(h)..S_i(h)..S_n(h)), h = 1,...P. Initialize the
weight values as per Hebb rule for binary/bipolar
paterns. Set initial input signal O_j, j = 1,..n for the net
equal to external signal I_{ki}, k = 1,..T, i = 1,..n.
    i.e, O_j = I_i, j = i
```

↓

For each input pattern $I_k$

↓

Set $k = 1$ and select the input units $j = 1,...n$ of the net in a random order (asynchronous updation of units). Compute the net input of the units.

$$O_{k,net\_j} = I_{ki} + \sum_{j=1,i=1}^{n} O_{kj} W_{ji}, j \neq i$$

$k = k + 1$

↓

Compute the output signal from $O_{net\_j}$

$$O_{kj} \begin{cases} 1 & if\ O_{k,net\_j} > \theta_j \\ O_{kj} & if\ O_{k,net\_j} = \theta_j \\ 0 & if\ O_{k,net\_j} < \theta_j \end{cases}$$

Update the value of $O_j$ to all other units

↓

Check whether the input pattern got settled or converged? — NO

↓ YES

If $k = T$ — NO

↓ YES

Stop

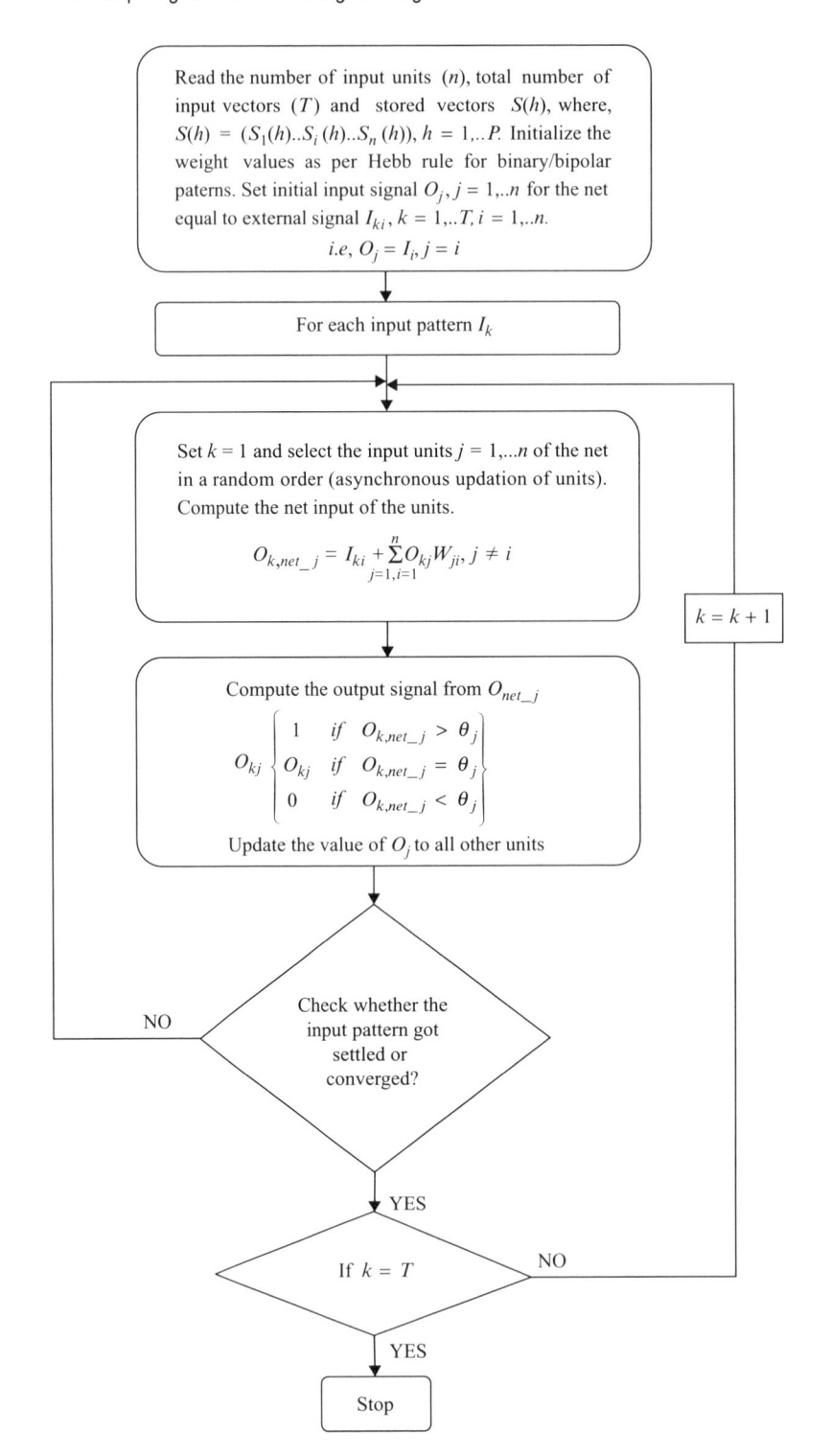

**Fig. 3.24** Flow chart of Hopfield neural network

$$W_{ij} = \sum_{h=1}^{P} (2S_i(h) - 1) \times (2S_j(h) - 1), \text{ where } i = 1,...n, j = 1,...n \text{ and } i \neq j \quad (3.45)$$
$$W_{ij} = 0 \quad \text{for } i = j$$

Suppose, the patterns to be handled are bipolar, then the weights can be initialized as,

$$W_{ij} = \sum_{h=1}^{P} S_i(h) \times S_j(h), \text{ where } i = 1,...n, j = 1,...n \text{ and } i \neq j \quad (3.46)$$
$$W_{ij} = 0 \quad \text{for } i = j$$

Here the weights are initialized as,

$$W_{ij} = \sum_{h=1}^{2} (2S_i(h) - 1) \times (2S_j(h) - 1), \text{ where } i = 1,...6, j = 1,...6 \text{ and } i \neq j$$
$$W_{ij} = 0 \quad \text{for } i = j$$

when $h = 1$          when $h = 2$

$W_{11} = 0$          $W_{11} = 0$

$W_{12} = ((2 \times 1) - 1) \times ((2 \times 1) - 1) = 1$      $W_{12} = ((2 \times 0) - 1) \times ((2 \times 1) - 1) = -1$

$\vdots$          $\vdots$

$W_{65} = ((2 \times 0) - 1) \times ((2 \times 0) - 1) = 1$      $W_{65} = ((2 \times 1) - 1) \times ((2 \times 1) - 1) = 1$

$W_{66} = 0$          $W_{66} = 0$

$$W_{ij} = \begin{bmatrix} 0 & 1 & 1 & 1 & -1 & -1 \\ 1 & 0 & 1 & 1 & -1 & -1 \\ 1 & 1 & 0 & 1 & -1 & -1 \\ 1 & 1 & 1 & 0 & -1 & -1 \\ -1 & -1 & -1 & -1 & 0 & 1 \\ -1 & -1 & -1 & -1 & 1 & 0 \end{bmatrix}_{h=1} + \begin{bmatrix} 0 & -1 & -1 & -1 & -1 & -1 \\ -1 & 0 & 1 & 1 & 1 & 1 \\ -1 & 1 & 0 & 1 & 1 & 1 \\ -1 & 1 & 1 & 0 & 1 & 1 \\ -1 & 1 & 1 & 1 & 0 & 1 \\ -1 & 1 & 1 & 1 & 1 & 0 \end{bmatrix}_{h=2}$$

$$= \begin{bmatrix} 0 & 0 & 0 & 0 & -2 & -2 \\ 0 & 0 & 2 & 2 & 0 & 0 \\ 0 & 2 & 0 & 2 & 0 & 0 \\ 0 & 2 & 2 & 0 & 0 & 0 \\ -2 & 0 & 0 & 0 & 0 & 2 \\ -2 & 0 & 0 & 0 & 2 & 0 \end{bmatrix}_{n \times n}$$

*Note*: The input signal should be set to the external signal, $O = I$.

Pattern 1- (1 1 1 0 1 0)

Let the order of the asynchronous updation of units be [4 3 6 5 1 2].

*Computing the net input to the units* ($k = 1$)

$O_{1,net\_4} = 0 + (1 \times 0) + (1 \times 2) + (1 \times 2) + (0 \times 0) + (1 \times 0) + (0 \times 0) = 4$

$O_{14} = 1, \because O_{1,net\_4} > 0, O_1 = (1\ 1\ 1\ \underline{1}\ 1\ 0)$

$O_{1,net\_3} = 1 + (1 \times 0) + (1 \times 2) + (1 \times 0) + (1 \times 2) + (1 \times 0) + (0 \times 0) = 5$

$O_{13} = 1, \because O_{1,net\_3} > 0, O_1 = (1\ 1\ \underline{1}\ 1\ 1\ 0)$

$O_{1,net\_6} = 0 + (1 \times -2) + (1 \times 0) + (1 \times 0) + (1 \times 0) + (1 \times 2) + (0 \times 0) = 0$

$O_{16} = 0, \because O_{1,net\_6} = 0, O_1 = (1\ 1\ 1\ \underline{1}\ 1\ 0)$

$O_{1,net\_5} = 1 + (1 \times -2) + (1 \times 0) + (1 \times 0) + (1 \times 0) + (1 \times 0) + (0 \times 2) = -1$

$O_{15} = 0, \because O_{1,net\_5} < 0, O_1 = (1\ 1\ 1\ \underline{1}\ 0\ 0)$

$O_{1,net\_1} = 1 + (1 \times 0) + (1 \times 0) + (1 \times 0) + (1 \times 0) + (0 \times -2) + (0 \times -2) = 1$

$O_{11} = 1, \because O_{1,net\_1} > 0, O_1 = (1\ 1\ 1\ \underline{1}\ 0\ 0)$

$O_{1,net\_2} = 1 + (1 \times 0) + (1 \times 0) + (1 \times 2) + (1 \times 2) + (0 \times 0) + (0 \times 0) = 5$

$O_{12} = 1, \because O_{1,net\_2} > 0,$

$O_1 = (1\ 1\ 1\ \underline{1}\ 0\ 0) \rightarrow S(1) = (1\ 1\ 1\ 1\ 0\ 0),$ Converged

Pattern 2- (0 1 0 1 1 1)
Let the order of the asynchronous updation of units be [3 1 6 4 2 5].
*Computing the net input to the units* ($k = 2$)

$O_{2,net\_3} = 0 + (0 \times 0) + (1 \times 2) + (0 \times 2) + (1 \times 2) + (1 \times 0) + (1 \times 0) = 4$

$O_{23} = 1, \because O_{2,net\_3} > 0, O_2 = (0\ 1\ \underline{1}\ 1\ 1\ 1)$

$O_{2,net\_1} = 0 + (0 \times 0) + (1 \times 0) + (0 \times 0) + (1 \times 0) + (1 \times -2) + (1 \times -2) = -4$

$O_{21} = -1, \because O_{2,net\_1} < 0, O_2 = (0\ 1\ \underline{1}\ 1\ 1\ 1)$

$O_{2,net\_6} = 1 + (0 \times -2) + (1 \times 0) + (1 \times 0) + (1 \times 0) + (1 \times 2) + (1 \times 0) = 3$

$O_{26} = 1, \because O_{2,net\_6} > 0, O_2 = (0\ 1\ \underline{1}\ 1\ 1\ 1)$

$O_{2,net\_4} = 1 + (0 \times 0) + (1 \times 2) + (1 \times 2) + (1 \times 0) + (1 \times 0) + (1 \times 0) = 5$

$O_{24} = 1, \because O_{2,net\_4} > 0, O_2 = (0\ 1\ \underline{1}\ 1\ 1\ 1)$

$O_{2,net\_2} = 1 + (0 \times 0) + (1 \times 0) + (1 \times 2) + (1 \times 2) + (1 \times 0) + (1 \times 0) = 5$

$O_{22} = 1, \because O_{2,net\_2} > 0, O_2 = (0\ 1\ \underline{1}\ 1\ 1\ 1)$

$O_{2,net\_5} = 0 + (0 \times -2) + (1 \times 0) + (1 \times 0) + (1 \times 0) + (1 \times 0) + (1 \times 2) = 3$

$O_{25} = 1, \because O_{2,net\_5} > 0,$

$O_2 = (0\ 1\ \underline{1}\ 1\ 1\ 1) \rightarrow S(2) = (0\ 1\ 1\ 1\ 1\ 1),$ Converged

Pattern 3- (0 0 1 1 1 1)
Let the order of the asynchronous updation of units be [4 2 1 6 5 3].
*Computing the net input to the units* ($k = 3$)

$O_{3,net\_4} = 1 + (0 \times 0) + (0 \times 2) + (1 \times 2) + (1 \times 0) + (1 \times 0) + (1 \times 0) = 3$

$O_{34} = 1, \because O_{3,net\_4} > 0, O_3 = (0\ 0\ 1\ \underline{1}\ 1\ 1)$

$O_{3,net\_2} = 0 + (0 \times 0) + (0 \times 0) + (1 \times 2) + (1 \times 2) + (1 \times 0) + (1 \times 0) = 4$

$O_{32} = 1, \because O_{3,net\_2} > 0, O_3 = (0\ \underline{1}\ 1\ 1\ 1\ 1)$

$O_{3,net\_1} = 0 + (0 \times 0) + (1 \times 0) + (1 \times 0) + (1 \times 0) + (1 \times -2) + (1 \times -2) = -4$

$O_{31} = 0, \because O_{3,net\_1} < 0, O_3 = (0\ \underline{1}\ 1\ 1\ 1\ 1)$

$O_{3,net\_6} = 1 + (0 \times -2) + (1 \times 0) + (1 \times 0) + (1 \times 0) + (1 \times 2) + (1 \times 0) = 3$

$O_{36} = 1, \because O_{3,net\_6} > 0, O_3 = (0\ \underline{1}\ 1\ 1\ 1\ 1)$

$O_{3,net\_5} = 1 + (0 \times -2) + (1 \times 0) + (1 \times 0) + (1 \times 0) + (1 \times 0) + (1 \times 2) = 3$

$O_{35} = 1, \because O_{3,net\_5} > 0, O_3 = (0\ \underline{1}\ 1\ 1\ 1\ 1)$

$O_{3,net\_3} = 1 + (0 \times 0) + (1 \times 2) + (1 \times 0) + (1 \times 2) + (1 \times 0) + (1 \times 0) = 5$

$O_{33} = 1, \because O_{3,net\_3} > 0,$

$O_3 = (0\ \underline{1}\ 1\ 1\ 1\ 1) \rightarrow S(2) = (0\ 1\ 1\ 1\ 1\ 1)$, Converged

Since all the input test patterns had settled to any one of the stored binary patterns, the iteration process of the algorithm has reached its stoppage criterion. The simulation can be carried out using the MATLAB Program 3.5. In this program, parameters are initialized commenting Part B and uncommenting Part A. The readers can use the MATLAB Program 3.5 to check the network behaving as per the earlier illustration. However, the readers should note that the same format of the model calculation may not be observed since randomness is introduced in the asynchronous updation of weights. Also, on certain occasions, the manner in which the input test patterns get settled may vary by choosing a different stored pattern.

### 3.6.2 Character Recognition through Stabilization of Input Test Patterns

The Hopfield network can be used for pattern recognition to identify the standard pattern associated with the input test pattern. Here, three alphabets (A, B, and C) are the standard patterns shown in Fig. 3.25a. The representation of an alphabet is by a matrix of $7 \times 5$ binary elements.

The simulation can be carried out using the MATLAB Program 3.4. In this program, parameters are initialized commenting Part A and uncommenting Part B. In our analysis, the same patterns (A, B, and C) with errors [shown in Fig. 3.25b, c] are given as input patterns to the Hopfield network.

*Results analysis*
When A, B, and C are stored as standard patterns and A′, B′, and C′ are given as input test patterns, the input patterns are able to settle to any one of the stored patterns. The simulation results obtained for two sample trial runs are shown in Fig. 3.26.

|     (A)     |     (B)     |     (C)     |
|:-----------:|:-----------:|:-----------:|
| 0 0 1 0 0   | 1 1 1 1 0   | 0 1 1 1 0   |
| 0 1 0 1 0   | 1 0 0 0 1   | 1 0 0 0 1   |
| 1 0 0 0 1   | 1 0 0 0 1   | 1 0 0 0 0   |
| 1 0 0 0 1   | 1 1 1 1 0   | 1 0 0 0 0   |
| 1 1 1 1 1   | 1 0 0 0 1   | 1 0 0 0 0   |
| 1 0 0 0 1   | 1 0 0 0 1   | 1 0 0 0 1   |
| 1 0 0 0 1   | 1 1 1 1 0   | 0 1 1 1 0   |

A = [00100010101000110001111111000110001], B = [11110100011000111110100011000111110]
C = [01110100011000010000100001000101110],

**(a) Stored Patterns**

|     (A′)    |     (B′)    |     (C′)    |
|:-----------:|:-----------:|:-----------:|
| <u>1</u> 0 1 0 0 | 1 1 1 1 0 | 0 1 1 1 0 |
| 0 1 0 1 0   | 1 0 <u>1</u> 0 1 | 1 0 0 0 1 |
| 1 0 0 0 1   | 1 0 0 0 1   | 1 0 0 0 0 |
| 1 0 0 0 1   | 1 1 1 1 0   | 1 0 0 0 0 |
| 1 1 1 1 1   | 1 0 0 0 1   | 1 0 0 0 0 |
| 1 0 0 0 1   | 1 0 0 0 1   | 1 0 0 0 1 |
| 1 0 0 0 1   | 1 1 1 1 0   | 0 1 1 <u>0</u> 0 |

A′ = [<u>1</u>0100010101000110001111111000110001], B′ = [111101<u>0</u>1011000111110100011000111110]
C′ = [0111010001100001000010000100010110<u>0</u>],

**(b) Test input patterns with single element errors**

|    (A‴)    |    (B‴)    |    (C‴)    |
|:----------:|:----------:|:----------:|
| <u>1</u> <u>1</u> 1 0 0 | 1 1 1 1 0 | <u>1</u> 1 1 1 0 |
| 0 1 0 1 0  | 1 0 <u>1</u> <u>1</u> 1 | 1 0 0 0 1 |
| 1 0 0 0 1  | 1 0 0 0 1  | 1 0 0 0 0 |
| 1 0 0 0 1  | 1 1 1 1 0  | 1 0 0 0 0 |
| 1 1 1 1 1  | 1 0 <u>1</u> 0 1 | 1 0 <u>1</u> 0 0 |
| 1 0 0 0 1  | 1 0 0 0 1  | 1 0 0 0 1 |
| 1 0 <u>1</u> 0 1 | 1 1 1 1 0 | 0 1 1 <u>0</u> 0 |

A‴ = [<u>11</u>100010101000110001111111000110<u>101</u>], B‴ = [111101<u>0</u>1<u>1</u>1000111110101<u>0</u>1011000111110]
C‴ = [<u>1</u>1110100011000010000101001000101100],

**(c) Test input patterns with three element errors**

**Fig. 3.25** Binary patterns for character recognition

It is observed that the test patterns, even though gets converged, gets settled to any one of the standard pattern. In the first sample trial run, all the input test patterns A′, B′, and C′ have correctly settled to A, B, and C, respectively. However, in the second sample trial run, the input test patterns A′, B′, and C′ have settled to A, B, and B instead of A, B, and C. This is due to the asynchronous updation (random order) of activation units of the Hopfield network.

In another analysis, when the patterns A‴, B‴, and C‴ are given as inputs to the Hopfield network, they have settled to A, B, and B instead of A, B, and C. Even though there are three erroneous positions in the input test patterns, the network is still able to settle correctly for A‴ and B‴. Here, the network has converged and all the test patterns are able to get settled with any one of the stored patterns. The simulation results are shown in Fig. 3.27.

In another case study, an additional stored pattern D = [1111010001100011000 01100011000111110] is incorporated as weights in the network. Then 3 patterns

The input (A')   The input (B')   The input (C')          The input (A')   The input (B')   The input (C')

1̲ 0 1 0 0        1 1 1 1 0        0 1 1 1 0               1̲ 0 1 0 0        1 1 1 1 0        0 1 1 1 0
0 1 0 1 0        1 0 1̲ 0 1        1 0 0 0 1               0 1 0 1 0        1 0 1̲ 0 1        1 0 0 0 1
1 0 0 0 1        1 0 0 0 1        1 0 0 0 0               1 0 0 0 1        1 0 0 0 1        1 0 0 0 0
1 0 0 0 1        1 1 1 1 0        1 0 0 0 0               1 0 0 0 1        1 1 1 1 0        1 0 0 0 0
1 1 1 1 1        1 0 0 0 1        1 0 0 0 0               1 1 1 1 1        1 0 0 0 1        1 0 0 0 0
1 0 0 0 1        1 0 0 0 1        1 0 0 0 1               1 0 0 0 1        1 0 0 0 1        1 0 0 0 1
1 0 0 0 1        1 1 1 1 0        0 1 1 0̲ 0               1 0 0 0 1        1 1 1 1 0        0 1 1 0̲ 0

settles to (A)   settles to (B)   settles to (C)          settles to (A)   settles to (B)   settles to (B)

0 0 1 0 0        1 1 1 1 0        0 1 1 1 0               0 0 1 0 0        1 1 1 1 0        1 1 1 1 0
0 1 0 1 0        1 0 0 0 1        1 0 0 0 1               0 1 0 1 0        1 0 0 0 1        1 0 0 0 1
1 0 0 0 1        1 0 0 0 1        1 0 0 0 0               1 0 0 0 1        1 0 0 0 1        1 0 0 0 1
1 0 0 0 1        1 1 1 1 0        1 0 0 0 0               1 0 0 0 1        1 1 1 1 0        1 1 1 1 0
1 1 1 1 1        1 0 0 0 1        1 0 0 0 0               1 1 1 1 1        1 0 0 0 1        1 0 0 0 1
1 0 0 0 1        1 0 0 0 1        1 0 0 0 1               1 0 0 0 1        1 0 0 0 1        1 0 0 0 1
1 0 0 0 1        1 1 1 1 0        0 1 1 1 0               1 0 0 0 1        1 1 1 1 0        1 1 1 1 0

        (Trial-1)                                                  (Trial-2)

**Fig. 3.26** Simulation results for test input patterns with single element errors


The input (A''')  The input (B''')  The input (C''')      The input (A')   The input (B')   The input (C')

1̲ 1 1 0 0        1 1 1 1 0        1̲ 1 1 1 0               1̲ 0 1 0 0        1 1 1 1 0        0 1 1 1 0
0 1 0 1 0        1 0 1̲ 1 1        1 0 0 0 1               0 1 0 1 0        1 0 1̲ 0 1        1 0 0 0 1
1 0 0 0 1        1 0 0 0 1        1 0 0 0 0               1 0 0 0 1        1 0 0 0 1        1 0 0 0 0
1 0 0 0 1        1 1 1 1 0        1 0 0 0 0               1 0 0 0 1        1 1 1 1 0        1 0 0 0 0
1 1 1 1 1        1 0 1̲ 0 1        1 0 1̲ 0 0               1 1 1 1 1        1 0 0 0 1        1 0 0 0 0
1 0 0 0 1        1 0 0 0 1        1 0 0 0 1               1 0 0 0 1        1 0 0 0 1        1 0 0 0 1
1 0 1̲ 0 1        1 1 1 1 0        0 1 1 0̲ 0               1 0 0 0 1        1 1 1 1 0        0 1 1 0̲ 0

settles to (A)   settles to (B)   settles to (B)          settles to (A)   settles to (B)   settles to (`')

0 0 1 0 0        1 1 1 1 0        1 1 1 1 0               0 0 1 0 0        1 1 1 1 0        1 1 1 1 0
0 1 0 1 0        1 0 0 0 1        1 0 0 0 1               0 1 0 1 0        1 0 0 0 1        1 0 0 0 1
1 0 0 0 1        1 0 0 0 1        1 0 0 0 1               1 0 0 0 1        1 0 0 0 1        1 0 0 0 1
1 0 0 0 1        1 1 1 1 0        1 1 1 1 0               1 0 0 0 1        1 1 1 1 0        1 0 0 0 0
1 1 1 1 1        1 0 0 0 1        1 0 0 0 1               1 1 1 1 1        1 0 0 0 1        1 0 0 0 1
1 0 0 0 1        1 0 0 0 1        1 0 0 0 1               1 0 0 0 1        1 0 0 0 1        1 0 0 0 1
1 0 0 0 1        1 1 1 1 1        1 1 1 1 0               1 0 0 0 1        1 1 1 1 0        1 1 1 1 0

**Fig. 3.27** Simulation results                **Fig. 3.28** Simulation results

(A', B', and C') are given as input to the network and the simulation results are given in Fig. 3.28. Here, the third test pattern C' is not able to settle to any of the patterns (A, B, C, or D). The third test pattern C' is oscillatory and could not stabilize to any of the pattern.

During the computational process, maximum number of iterations will be set, and if the input pattern is not able to stabilize, it will come out of the loop. Therefore, in Hopfield network, we cannot guarantee that the solution will always converge. It also depends upon the storage capacity of the discrete patterns. John Hopfield suggested that if $n$ is the number of units in the net, then the number of binary patterns that can be stored and recalled in the net is approximately equal to $N_{binary\_patterns} \approx 0.15 \times n$. Abu-Mostafa et al, [24] suggested that if $n$ is the number of units in the net, then the number of bipolar patterns that can be stored and recalled in the net is approximately equal to $N_{bipolar\_patterns} \approx \dfrac{n}{2\log_2 n}$.

## MATLAB Program 3.5

### Part A: Main program

```
%%%%%%%%%%%%%%%%%%%%%%%%%%%%%%%%%%
% HOPFIELD NEURAL NETWORK ALGORITHM
%%%%%%%%%%%%%%%%%%%%%%%%%%%%%%%%%%

clear workspace
clear all
clc
format short

%%%%%%%%%%%%%%%%%%%%%%%%%%%%%%%%%%%%%%%%%%%%%%%%%%%%%%%%%%%%%%%%%%%%
% PART-A DEMONSTRATION OF HOPFIELD NEURAL NETWORK FOR AN ILLUSTRATION
%%%%%%%%%%%%%%%%%%%%%%%%%%%%%%%%%%%%%%%%%%%%%%%%%%%%%%%%%%%%%%%%%%%%

% START A

% data=[1 1 1 1 0 0;              % Patterns that can be stored as weights
%       0 1 1 1 1 1];
% test_data=[1  1  1  0  1  0;    % Input test patterns to be checked for the
%                                 % association of the stored paterns
%            0  1  0  1  1  1;    % Here the number of components present in
%                                 % both the stored vector and the
%            0  0  1  1  1  1];   % input test vector should be same

% END A

%%%%%%%%%%%%%%%%%%%%%%%%%%%%%%%%%%%%%%%%%%%%%%%
% PART-B CHARACTER RECOGNITION WITH ABCD ALPHABETS
%%%%%%%%%%%%%%%%%%%%%%%%%%%%%%%%%%%%%%%%%%%%%%%

% START B

% STANDARD BINARY PATTERNS THAT ARE TO BE STORED IN THE NETWORK

% Uncomment the data if 3 patterns A, B & C are considered as standard patterns

data= [0 0 1 0 0 0 1 0 1 0 1 0 0 0 1 1 0 0 0 1 1 1 1 1 1 0 0 0 1 1 0 0 0 1; %A
       1 1 1 1 0 1 0 0 0 1 1 0 0 0 1 1 1 1 1 0 1 0 0 0 1 1 0 0 0 1 1 1 1 0; %B
       0 1 1 1 0 1 0 0 0 1 1 0 0 0 0 1 0 0 0 0 1 0 0 0 0 1 0 0 0 1 0 1 1 1 0]; %C

% Uncomment if 4 patterns A, B, C & D are considered as standard patterns

% data= [0 0 1 0 0 0 1 0 1 0 1 0 0 0 1 1 0 0 0 1 1 1 1 1 1 0 0 0 1 1 0 0 0 1; %A
%        1 1 1 1 0 1 0 0 0 1 1 0 0 0 1 1 1 1 1 0 1 0 0 0 1 1 0 0 0 1 1 1 1 0; %B
%        0 1 1 1 0 1 0 0 0 1 1 0 0 0 0 1 0 0 0 0 1 0 0 0 0 1 0 0 0 1 0 1 1 1 0; %C
%        1 1 1 1 0 1 0 0 0 1 1 0 0 0 1 1 0 0 0 1 1 0 0 0 1 1 0 0 0 1 1 1 1 1 0]; %D

% Uncomment the test input data if A', B' & C' are considered

test_data= [1 0 1 0 0 0 1 0 1 0 1 0 0 0 1 1 0 0 0 1 1 1 1 1 1 0 0 0 1 1 0 0 0 1; %A'
            1 1 1 1 0 1 0 1 0 1 1 0 0 0 1 1 1 1 1 0 1 0 0 0 1 1 0 0 0 1 1 1 1 0; %B'
            0 1 1 1 0 1 0 0 0 1 1 0 0 0 0 1 0 0 0 0 1 0 0 0 0 1 0 0 0 1 0 1 1 0 0]; %C'

% Uncomment the test input data if A', B' & C' are considered

% test_data= [1 1 1 0 0 0 1 0 1 0 1 0 0 0 1 1 0 0 0 1 1 1 1 1 1 0 0 0 1 1 0 1 0 1; %A'''
%             1 1 1 1 0 1 0 1 1 1 1 0 0 0 1 1 1 1 1 0 1 0 1 0 1 1 0 0 0 1 1 1 1 0; %B'''
%             1 1 1 1 0 1 0 0 0 1 1 0 0 0 0 1 0 0 0 0 1 0 1 0 0 1 0 0 0 1 0 1 1 0 0]; %C'''

% END B
```

```
% INITIALIZES THE WEIGHTS AS PER HEBB RULE

[r c]=size(data);
% Getting the matrix format of the binary patterns to be stored as weights
W=zeros(c,c);          % Defining the space for the weight matrix
for s=1:r,
for i=1:c,
for j=1:c
if i~=j,
W(i,j)=W(i,j)+((2*data(s,i)-1)*(2*data(s,j)-1));
else
W(i,j)=0;
end
end
end
end
disp('The initialized weights as per hebb rule for binary patterns');
disp(W);

% SETTING THE INPUT SIGNAL EQUAL TO EXTERNAL SIGNAL

O=test_data;

% COMPUTING THE NET INPUT OF THE UNITS

[r1 c1]=size(test_data);
store=zeros(r1,c1);    % Recording the input patterns settling to the stored pattern
O_net=zeros(r1,c1);    % Defining the matrix space for output units for all input patterns
for k=1:r1,
disp('The input pattern number');
disp(k);
iter=0;
% Initializing the iteration count to know the iterations taken by an input pattern to settle
converged=0;           % Initializing the convergence flag to zero
max_iter=100;
% If the input test pattern does not get settled even after 100 iterations, it will come
% out of loop
while converged==0;
% Iterations continue(Oscilations occur) till the kth test input pattern will
% become same (converged=1) as any of the stored pattern
iter=iter+1;
disp('Iteration No');
disp(iter);
Od=randperm(c1);       % Define the asynchronous order of units
disp('The order of the asynchronous updation of units')
disp(Od);
for j=1:c1,
sum=0;
for i=1:c1
sum=sum+O(k,i)*W(i,Od(1,j));
end
O_net(k,Od(1,j))=test_data(k,Od(1,j))+sum;
disp('The net input to the units');
disp(O_net(k,Od(1,j)));

% COMPUTES AND UPDATES THE OUTPUT SIGNAL FROM THE NET INPUT TO THE UNITS

O(k,Od(1,j))=h_bin_fun(O_net(k,Od(1,j)),0);
% Threshold value is generally kept as zero
```

```
end
for t=1:r,
if (all(O(k,:)==data(t,:)))==1;
converged=1;
store(k,:)=O(k,:);
break
end

if iter>max_iter,
converged=1;
store(k,:)=O(k,:);
disp('The input test pattern');
disp(k);

% START A

% disp(test_data(k,:));

% END A

% START B

disp(num2str(dispalp_h(test_data(k,:))));

% END B

disp('is oscilatory and cannot be settled to its counterpart');
break
end
end

end
end

% DISPLAYING THE RESULTS

% START

% disp('The final settled patterns');
% disp(num2str(O));
% disp('The test data');
% disp(num2str(test_data));
% disp('The stored patterns');
% disp(num2str(data));

% END A

% START B

disp('Display of results');
for d=1:k,
disp('The input')
disp(num2str(dispalp_h(test_data(d,:))));
% Dispalying the bipolar pattern into binary pattern for display clarity
disp('settles to');
disp(num2str(dispalp_h(store(d,:))));
% Dispalying the bipolar pattern into binary pattern for display clarity
end

% END   B
```

## Part B: Sub-programs (Sub-routine functions)

```
function out = h_bin_fun(a, r)

% THRESHOLD FUNCTION

out(a>r) = 1;
out(a==r) = a;
out(a<r) = 0;
 end

DISPLAY FUNCTION

function [out]=dispalp_h(data)

%  DISPLAY OF ALPHABET IN A MATRIX FORMAT

k=0;
for i=1:7,
for j=1:5,
k=k+1;

out(i,j)=data(1,k);        % Output display for a 7 X 5 matrix data
end
end
```

## 3.7 BI-DIRECTIONAL ASSOCIATIVE MEMORY

Bart Kosko [25] published a paper in *IEEE* transaction of 'System Man and Cybernetics' titled *Bi-directional Associative Memories*. In his paper, Kosko introduced the bi-directional, forward and backward information flow, in neural nets to produce a two-way associative search. There are now several versions of BAM; however, BAM has the properties of two-layer non-linear feedback NNs.

Here, heteroassociative information is encoded in a BAM by summing correlation weights matrices obtained from the associative pairs of the the binary or bipolar patterns. The architecture of BAM consists of two layers of neurons, connected by bi-directional weights and is shown in Fig. 3.29. The flow chart of BAM is given in Fig. 3.30.

The weights of BAM are initialized based on the Hebb rule. Let us suppose $\{S(h) \Leftrightarrow T(k)\}$ are associated $P$ paired patterns that should be stored as weights by summing the correlation weights of all the paired patterns. Then the bi-directional weights for the $P$ paired binary patterns are given as,

$$W_{ij} = \sum_{p=1}^{P}(2S_i(k)-1) \times (2T_j(k)-1), \text{where } i=1,...n, j=1,...m \quad (3.47)$$

The bi-directional weights for the $P$ paired bipolar patterns are given as,

$$W_{ij} = \sum_{p=1}^{P} S_i(k) \times T_j(k), \text{where } i=1,...n, j=1,...m \quad (3.48)$$

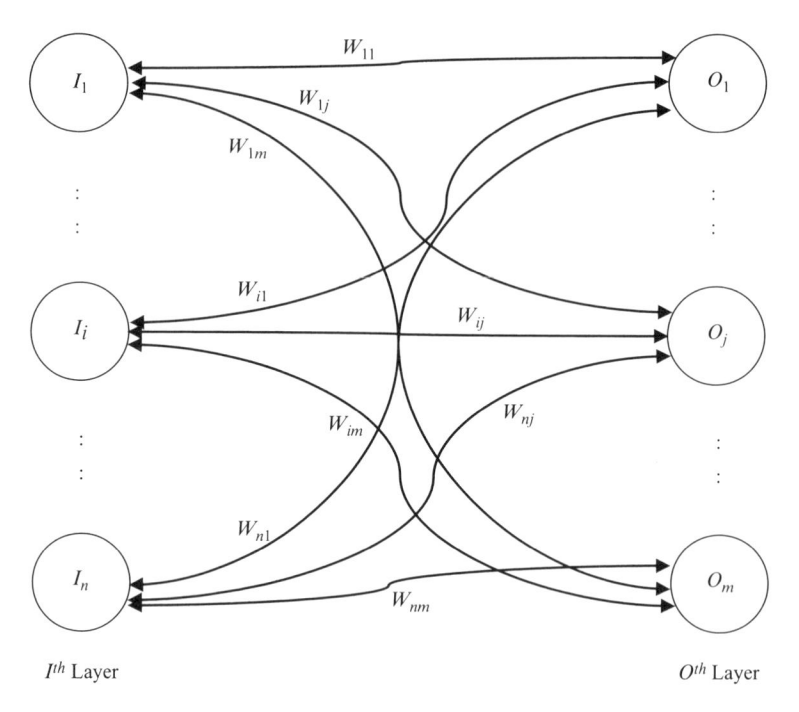

**Fig. 3.29** Bi-directional AMNN

BAM is similar to the Hopfield network in that they are both forms of associative memory. However, Hopfield nets return patterns of the same size.

The activation functions of the $I^{th}$ and $O^{th}$ layers for the binary vectors are given by:

$$I_{tj} = \begin{cases} 1 & if \ I_{t,net\_i} > \theta_i \\ I_{ti} & if \ I_{t,net\_i} = \theta_i \\ 0 & if \ I_{t,net\_i} < \theta_i \end{cases} \tag{3.49}$$

$$O_{tj} = \begin{cases} 1 & if \ O_{t,net\_j} > \theta_j \\ O_{tj} & if \ O_{t,net\_j} = \theta_j \\ 0 & if \ O_{tk,net\_j} < \theta_j \end{cases} \tag{3.50}$$

Similarly for the bipolar vectors,

$$I_{tj} = \begin{cases} 1 & if \ I_{t,net\_i} > \theta_i \\ I_{ti} & if \ I_{t,net\_i} = \theta_i \\ -1 & if \ I_{t,net\_i} < \theta_i \end{cases} \tag{3.51}$$

$$O_{tj} = \begin{cases} 1 & if \ O_{t,net\_j} > \theta_j \\ O_{tj} & if \ O_{t,net\_j} = \theta_j \\ -1 & if \ O_{tk,net\_j} < \theta_j \end{cases} \tag{3.52}$$

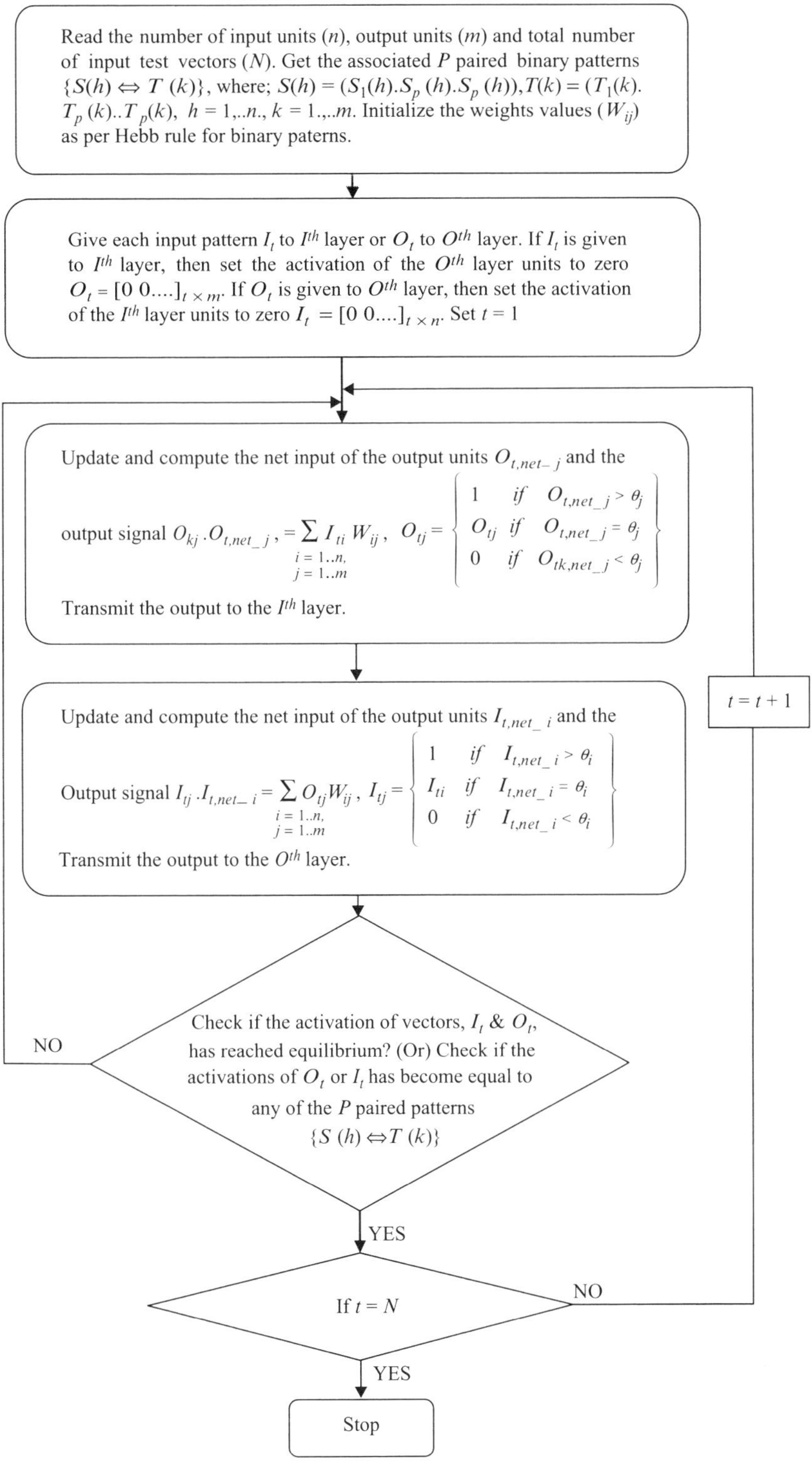

Read the number of input units ($n$), output units ($m$) and total number of input test vectors ($N$). Get the associated $P$ paired binary patterns $\{S(h) \Leftrightarrow T(k)\}$, where; $S(h) = (S_1(h).S_p(h).S_p(h)), T(k) = (T_1(k).T_p(k)..T_p(k),\ h = 1,..n.,\ k = 1.,..m$. Initialize the weights values ($W_{ij}$) as per Hebb rule for binary paterns.

↓

Give each input pattern $I_t$ to $I^{th}$ layer or $O_t$ to $O^{th}$ layer. If $I_t$ is given to $I^{th}$ layer, then set the activation of the $O^{th}$ layer units to zero $O_t = [0\ 0....]_{t \times m}$. If $O_t$ is given to $O^{th}$ layer, then set the activation of the $I^{th}$ layer units to zero $I_t = [0\ 0....]_{t \times n}$. Set $t = 1$

↓

Update and compute the net input of the output units $O_{t,net\_j}$ and the output signal $O_{kj}$. $O_{t,net\_j} = \sum_{\substack{i=1..n,\\ j=1..m}} I_{ti} W_{ij}$, $O_{tj} = \begin{cases} 1 & \text{if } O_{t,net\_j} > \theta_j \\ O_{tj} & \text{if } O_{t,net\_j} = \theta_j \\ 0 & \text{if } O_{tk,net\_j} < \theta_j \end{cases}$

Transmit the output to the $I^{th}$ layer.

↓

Update and compute the net input of the output units $I_{t,net\_i}$ and the Output signal $I_{tj}$. $I_{t,net\_i} = \sum_{\substack{i=1..n,\\ j=1..m}} O_{tj} W_{ij}$, $I_{tj} = \begin{cases} 1 & \text{if } I_{t,net\_i} > \theta_i \\ I_{ti} & \text{if } I_{t,net\_i} = \theta_i \\ 0 & \text{if } I_{t,net\_i} < \theta_i \end{cases}$

Transmit the output to the $O^{th}$ layer.

↓

Check if the activation of vectors, $I_t$ & $O_t$, has reached equilibrium? (Or) Check if the activations of $O_t$ or $I_t$ has become equal to any of the $P$ paired patterns $\{S(h) \Leftrightarrow T(k)\}$

NO → (loop back, $t = t+1$)
YES ↓

If $t = N$
NO → (loop back)
YES ↓

Stop

**Fig. 3.30** Flow chart of BAM

The value of the threshold $\theta$ is generally taken as 0 for binary vectors. However, an optimal value of $\theta$ can be selected for bipolar vectors. Bart Kosko [25] also introduced continous BAM for binary patterns, where the activation function of BAM units is a logistic function whose activation is continous in the range of [0 1]. Here the net weighted sum to the BAM units is calculated incorporating a bias value.

### 3.7.1 Illustration of Settlement of Stable Input Patterns

Let us have 2 paired binary standard patterns to be stored in BAM and test 4 binary test patterns.

A = [00100010101000110001111111000110001] is paired with 1 = [01]
B = [11110100011000111101000110001111110] is paired with 2 = [10]

*Binary test patterns*
A = [00100010101000110001111111000110001]
B = [11110100011000111101000110001111110]
A′ = [<u>1</u>0100010101000110001111111000110001]
B′ = [1111010<u>1</u>011000111101000110001111110]

The handworked portion for one epoch is given later. The subscripts and indices are considered as given in Fig. 3.29. Here, $P = 2$, $N = 4$, $n = 35$, and $m = 2$. Let the initial activation of the $I^{th}$ and $O^{th}$ layers of BAM be set as follows:

$$I = \begin{bmatrix} 0010001010 & 1000110001 & 1111110001 & 10001 \\ 1111010001 & 1000111110 & 1000110001 & 11110 \\ 1010001010 & 1000110001 & 1111110001 & 11110 \\ 1111010101 & 1000111110 & 1000110001 & 11110 \end{bmatrix}_{N \times n} \begin{matrix} (I_1) \\ (I_2) \\ (I_3) \\ (I_4) \end{matrix}$$

$$O = \begin{bmatrix} 0 & 0 \\ 0 & 0 \\ 0 & 0 \\ 0 & 0 \end{bmatrix}_{N \times m} \begin{matrix} (O_1) \\ (O_2) \\ (O_3) \\ (O_4) \end{matrix}$$

The $P$ paired binary patterns are stored as weights using Hebb rule.

$$S = \begin{bmatrix} 00100010101000110001111111000110001 \\ 11110100011000111101000110001111110 \end{bmatrix}_{P \times n} \quad T = \begin{bmatrix} 01 \\ 10 \end{bmatrix}_{P \times m}$$

Here the weights are initialized as,

$$W_{ij} = \sum_{p=1}^{2} (2S_i(k) - 1) \times (2T_j(k) - 1), \text{ where } i = 1,\ldots 35, j = 1,..2$$

$$W_{ij}^{Transpose} = \begin{bmatrix} 2 & 2 & 0 & 2 & 0 & 2 & -2 & 0 & -2 & 2 & 0 & 0 & 0 & 0 & 0 & 2 & 2 \\ -2 & -2 & 0 & -2 & 0 & -2 & 2 & 0 & 2 & -2 & 0 & 0 & 0 & 0 & 0 & -2 & -2 \\ 2 & -2 & 0 & -2 & -2 & -2 & 0 & 0 & 0 & 0 & 0 & 0 & 2 & 2 & 2 & -2 \\ -2 & 2 & 0 & 2 & 2 & 2 & 0 & 0 & 0 & 0 & 0 & 0 & -2 & -2 & -2 & 2 \end{bmatrix}$$

Pattern 1- [00100010101000110001111111000110001]
*Computing the net input to the output units (t = 1)*

$O_{t,net\_1} = I_{1^{st}\ row \times 35} \times W_{35 \times 1^{st}\ column} = -14$

$O_{1,1} = 0, \because O_{1,net\_1} < 0,$

$O_{t,net\_2} = I_{1^{st}\ row \times 35} \times W_{35 \times 2^{nd}\ column} = 14$

$O_{1,2} = 1, \because O_{1,net\_2} > 0,$

$O = \begin{bmatrix} 0 & 1 \\ 0 & 0 \\ 0 & 0 \\ 0 & 0 \end{bmatrix}_{N \times m} \begin{matrix} (O_1) \\ (O_2) \\ (O_3) \\ (O_4) \end{matrix}$

*Computing the net input to the input units (t = 1)*

$I_{t,net\_1} = O_{1^{st}\ row \times 2} \times W_{2 \times 1^{st}\ row} = -2$

$I_{1,1} = 0, \because I_{1,net\_1} < 0,$

$I_{t,net\_2} = O_{1^{st}\ row \times 2} \times W_{2 \times 2^{nd}\ row} = -2$

$I_{1,2} = 0, \because I_{1,net\_2} < 0,$

$\vdots$

$I_{t,net\_35} = O_{1^{st}\ row \times 2} \times W_{2 \times 35^{th}\ row} = 2$

$I_{1,35} = 1, \because I_{1,net\_35} > 0,$

$I_{t=1,net\_n} = [-2\ -2\ 0\ -2\ 0\ -2\ 2\ 0\ 2\ -2\ 0\ 0\ 0\ 0\ 0\ -2\ -2\ -2\ 2\ 0\ 2$
$\qquad 2\ 2\ 0\ 0\ 0\ 0\ 0\ 0\ -2\ -2\ -2\ 2]_{1 \times n}$

$I_{t=1,n} = [0\ 0\ 0\ 0\ 0\ 1\ 0\ 1\ 0\ 0\ 0\ 0\ 0\ 0\ 0\ 0\ 0\ 1\ 0\ 1\ 1\ 1\ 0\ 0\ 0\ 0\ 0$
$\qquad 0\ 0\ 0\ 0\ 1]_{1 \times n}$

On checking the equilibrium state, the activation of the output unit $O_{1,m} = [0\ 1]$ has already become equal to the $T_{1,m} = [0\ 1]$. Therefore, A = [00100010101000 110001111111000110001], the input test pattern ($t = 1$) has converged and A is associated with 1 = [0 1].

Pattern 2- [11110100011000111101000110001111110]
*Computing the net input to the output units (t = 2)*

$O_{t,net\_1} = I_{2^{nd}\ row \times 35} \times W_{35 \times 1^{st}\ column} = 22$

$O_{2,1} = 1, \because O_{2,net\_1} > 0,$

$O_{t,net\_2} = I_{2^{nd}\ row \times 35} \times W_{35 \times 2^{nd}\ column} = -22$

$O_{2,2} = 0, \therefore O_{1,net\_2} < 0,$

$$O = \begin{bmatrix} 0 & 1 \\ 1 & 0 \\ 0 & 0 \\ 0 & 0 \end{bmatrix}_{N \times m} \begin{matrix} (O_1) \\ (O_2) \\ (O_3) \\ (O_4) \end{matrix}$$

*Computing the net input to the input units (t = 2)*

$I_{t,net\_1} = O_{2^{nd}\ row \times 2} \times W_{2 \times 1^{st}\ row} = 2$

$I_{2,1} = 1, \therefore I_{2,net\_1} > 0,$

$I_{t,net\_2} = O_{2^{nd}\ row \times 2} \times W_{2 \times 2^{nd}\ row} = 2$

$I_{2,2} = 1, \therefore I_{2,net\_2} > 0,$

$\vdots$

$I_{t,net\_35} = O_{2^{nd}\ row \times 2} \times W_{2 \times 35^{th}\ row} = -2$

$I_{2,35} = 0, \therefore I_{2,net\_35} < 0,$

$I_{t=2,net\_n} = [2\ 2\ 0\ 2\ 0\ 2\ -2\ 0\ -2\ 2\ 0\ 0\ 0\ 0\ 0\ 2\ 2\ 2\ -2\ 0\ -2\ -2\ -2$
$\qquad\qquad 0\ 0\ 0\ 0\ 0\ 0\ 0\ 2\ 2\ 2\ -2]_{1 \times n}$

$I_{t=2,n} = [1\ 1\ 0\ 1\ 0\ 1\ 0\ 0\ 0\ 1\ 0\ 0\ 0\ 0\ 0\ 1\ 1\ 1\ 0\ 0\ 0\ 0\ 0\ 0\ 0\ 0\ 0\ 0$
$\qquad\qquad 0\ 0\ 1\ 1\ 1\ 0]_{1 \times n}$

On checking the equilibrium state, the activation of the output unit $O_{2,m} = [1\ 0]$ has already become equal to the $T_{2,m} = [1\ 0]. \therefore$, B = [11110100011000111111010 0011000111110], the input test pattern ($t = 2$) has converged and B is associated with 2 = [1 0].

Pattern 3- [10100010101000110001111111000110001]
*Computing the net input to the output units (t = 3)*

$O_{t,net\_1} = I_{3^{rd}\ row \times 35} \times W_{35 \times 1^{st}\ column} = -12$

$O_{3,1} = 0, \therefore O_{3,net\_1} < 0,$

$O_{t,net\_2} = I_{3^{rd}\ row \times 35} \times W_{35 \times 2^{nd}\ column} = 12$

$O_{3,2} = 1, \therefore O_{3,net\_2} > 0,$

$$O = \begin{bmatrix} 0 & 1 \\ 1 & 0 \\ 0 & 1 \\ 0 & 0 \end{bmatrix}_{N \times m} \begin{matrix} (O_1) \\ (O_2) \\ (O_3) \\ (O_4) \end{matrix}$$

Artificial Neural Networks—Second Generation    203

*Computing the net input to the input units* ($t = 3$)

$I_{t,net\_1} = O_{3^{rd}\ row \times 2} \times W_{2 \times 1^{st}\ row} = -2$

$I_{3,1} = 0, \because I_{3,net\_1} < 0,$

$I_{t,net\_2} = O_{3^{rd}\ row \times 2} \times W_{2 \times 2^{nd}\ row} = -2$

$I_{3,2} = 0, \because I_{3,net\_2} < 0,$

$\vdots$

$I_{t,net\_35} = O_{3^{rd}\ row \times 2} \times W_{2 \times 35^{th}\ row} = 2$

$I_{3,35} = 1, \because I_{3,net\_35} > 0,$

$I_{t=3,net\_n} = [-2\ -2\ 0\ -2\ 0\ -2\ 2\ 0\ 2\ -2\ 0\ 0\ 0\ 0\ 0\ -2\ -2\ -2\ 2\ 0$
$\qquad\qquad\ \ 2\ \ 2\ 2\ \ 0\ 0\ \ 0\ 0\ 0\ 0\ \ 0\ -2\ -2\ -2\ 2\ ]$

$I_{t=3,n} = [0\ 0\ 0\ 0\ 0\ 1\ 0\ 1\ 0\ 0\ 0\ 0\ 0\ 0\ 0\ 0\ 0\ 1\ 0\ 1\ 1\ 1\ 0\ 0\ 0\ 0$
$\qquad\ \ 0\ 0\ 0\ 0\ 0\ 0\ 1]_{1 \times n}$

On checking the equilibrium state, the activation of the output unit $O_{3,m} = [0\ 1]$ has already become equal to the $T_{3,m} = [0\ 1]$. Therefore, A′ = [$\underline{1}$01000101010001 10001111111000110001], the input test pattern ($t = 3$) has converged and A′ is associated with 1 = [0 1].

Pattern 4- [1111010$\underline{1}$01100011111010001100011110]

*Computing the net input to the output units* ($t = 4$)

$O_{t,net\_1} = I_{4^{th}\ row \times 35} \times W_{35 \times 1^{st}\ column} = 22$

$O_{4,1} = 1, \because O_{4,net\_1} > 0,$

$O_{t,net\_2} = I_{4^{th}\ row \times 35} \times W_{35 \times 2^{nd}\ column} = -22$

$O_{4,2} = 0, \because O_{4,net\_2} < 0,$

$O = \begin{bmatrix} 0\ 1 \\ 1\ 0 \\ 0\ 1 \\ 1\ 0 \end{bmatrix}_{N \times m} \begin{matrix} (O_1) \\ (O_2) \\ (O_3) \\ (O_4) \end{matrix}$

*Computing the net input to the input units* ($t = 4$)

$I_{t,net\_1} = O_{4^{th}\ row \times 2} \times W_{2 \times 1^{st}\ column} = 2$

$I_{4,1} = 1, \because I_{4,net\_1} > 0,$

$I_{t,net\_2} = O_{4^{th}\ row \times 2} \times W_{2 \times 2^{nd}\ column} = 2$

$I_{4,2} = 1, \because I_{4,net\_2} > 0,$

$\vdots$

$I_{t,net\_35} = O_{4^{th}\ row \times 2} \times W_{2 \times 35^{th}\ column} = -2$

$I_{4,35} = 0, \therefore I_{4,net\_35} < 0,$

$I_{t=4,net\_n} = [2\ 2\ 0\ 2\ 0\ 2\ -2\ 0\ -2\ 2\ 0\ 0\ 0\ 0\ 0\ 2\ 2\ 2\ -2\ 0\ -2\ -2$
$\qquad\qquad -2\ 0\ 0\ 0\ 0\ 0\ 0\ 2\ 2\ 2\ -2]_{1 \times n}$

$I_{t=4,n} = [1\ 1\ 0\ 1\ 0\ 1\ 0\ 0\ 0\ 1\ 0\ 0\ 0\ 0\ 0\ 1\ 1\ 1\ 0\ 0\ 0\ 0\ 0\ 0\ 0\ 0$
$\qquad\quad 0\ 0\ 0\ 1\ 1\ 1\ 0]_{1 \times n}$

On checking the equilibrium state, the activation of the output unit $O_{4,m} = [1\ 0]$ has already become equal to the $T_{4,m} = [1\ 0]$. Therefore, B′ = [11110101̲0110001 11110100011000111110], the input test pattern ($t = 4$) has converged and B′ is associated with 2 = [1 0].

Since all the input test patterns had settled to any one of the stored binary patterns, the iteration process of the algorithm has reached its stoppage criterion. It should be noted that the input test patterns (A′ and B′) with a single error element are able to associate to their counterparts (1 and 2) correctly. The simulation can be carried out using the MATLAB Program 3.5. In this program parameters are initialized commenting Part B and uncommenting Part A. The readers can use the following program to check the network behaving as per the previous illustration.

### 3.7.2 BAM for Character Mapping

BAM can be used for mapping two unrelated patterns through hetero association. Let us consider two pairs of binary patterns as shown in Fig. 3.31. In this analysis, the number of elements present in the pair of patterns is larger than the one discussed in the illustration. Eight binary test patterns are given to BAM. Here A′, B′; A″, B″; and A‴, B‴ are input test patterns with single, double, and triple element errors. The following are the test patterns given to BAM:

A = [0 0 1 0 0 0 1 0 1 0 1 0 0 0 1 1 0 0 0 1 1 1 1 1 1 0 0 0 1 1 0 0 0 1]
B = [1 1 1 1 0 1 0 0 0 1 1 0 0 0 1 1 1 1 1 0 1 0 0 0 1 1 0 0 0 1 1 1 1 1 0]
A′ = [1̲ 0 1 0 0 0 1 0 1 0 1 0 0 0 1 1 0 0 0 1 1 1 1 1 1 0 0 0 1 1 0 0 0 1]
B′ = [1 1 1 1 0 1 0 1̲ 0 1 1 0 0 0 1 1 1 1 1 0 1 0 0 0 1 1 0 0 0 1 1 1 1 1 0]
A″ = [1̲ 0 1 0 0 0 1 0 1 0 1 0 0 0 1 1 0 0 0 1 1 1 0̲ 1 1 1 0 0 0 1 1 0 0 0 1]
B″ = [1 1 1 1 0 1 0 1̲ 0 1 1 0 0 0 1 1 1 1 1 0 1 0 0 0 1 1 0 0 0 1 1 0̲ 1 1 0]
A‴ = [1̲ 1 1 0 0 0 1 0 1 0 1 0 0 0 1 1 0 0 0 1 1 1 0̲ 1 1 1 0 0 0 1 1 0 1̲ 0 1]
B‴ = [1 1 1 1 0 1 0 1̲ 0 1 1 0 0 0 1 1 1 1 1 0 1 0 1̲ 0 1 1 0 0 0 1 1 0̲ 1 1 0]

The simulation can be carried out using the MATLAB Program 3.6. In this program, parameters are initialized commenting Part A and uncommenting Part B. The result shows that all the input test patterns are correctly mapped to its associated counterpart [i.e., (A,1), (B,2), (A′,1), (B′,2), (A″,1), (B″,2), (A‴,1), and (B‴,2)].

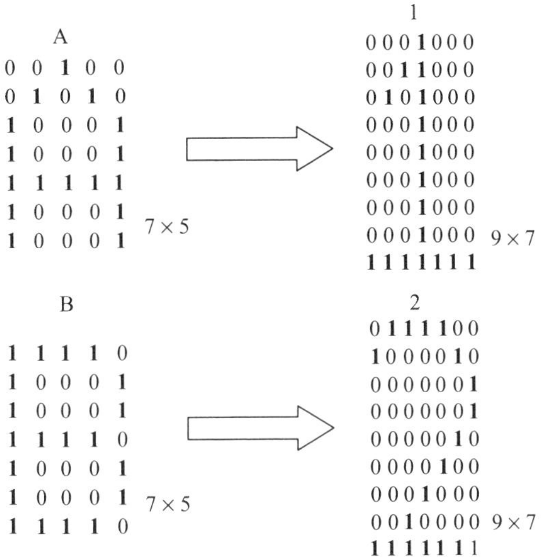

```
               A                    1
          0 0 1 0 0            0 0 0 1 0 0 0
          0 1 0 1 0            0 0 1 1 0 0 0
          1 0 0 0 1            0 1 0 1 0 0 0
          1 0 0 0 1   ⟹        0 0 0 1 0 0 0
          1 1 1 1 1            0 0 0 1 0 0 0
          1 0 0 0 1            0 0 0 1 0 0 0
          1 0 0 0 1  7×5       0 0 0 1 0 0 0
                               0 0 0 1 0 0 0   9×7
                               1 1 1 1 1 1 1

               B                    2
                               0 1 1 1 1 0 0
          1 1 1 1 0            1 0 0 0 0 1 0
          1 0 0 0 1            0 0 0 0 0 0 1
          1 0 0 0 1   ⟹        0 0 0 0 0 0 1
          1 1 1 1 0            0 0 0 0 0 1 0
          1 0 0 0 1            0 0 0 0 1 0 0
          1 0 0 0 1  7×5       0 0 0 1 0 0 0
          1 1 1 1 0            0 0 1 0 0 0 0   9×7
                               1 1 1 1 1 1 1
```

**Fig. 3.31** Paired binary patterns

## MATLAB Program 3.6

### Part A: Main program

```
%%%%%%%%%%%%%%%%%%%%%%%%%%%%%%%%%%%%%%
% BI-DIRECTIONAL ASSOCIATIVE MEMORY (BAM)
%%%%%%%%%%%%%%%%%%%%%%%%%%%%%%%%%%%%%%

clear workspace
clear all
clc
format short


%%%%%%%%%%%%%%%%%%%%%%%%%%%%%%%%%%%%%%
% PART-A DEMONSTRATION OF BAM FOR ILLUSTRATION
%%%%%%%%%%%%%%%%%%%%%%%%%%%%%%%%%%%%%%


% START A

% source=[0 0 1 0 0 0 1 0 1 0 1 0 0 0 1 1 0 0 0 1 1 1 1 1 1 1 0 0 0 1 1 0 0 0 1;
%         1 1 1 1 0 1 0 0 0 1 1 0 0 0 1 1 1 1 1 0 1 0 0 0 1 1 0 0 0 1 1 1 1 1 0];

% target=[0 1;
%         1 0];

% test_input=[0 0 1 0 0 0 1 0 1 0 1 0 0 0 1 1 0 0 0 1 1 1 1 1 1 1 0 0 0 1 1 0 0 0 1; %A
%             1 1 1 1 0 1 0 0 0 1 1 0 0 0 1 1 1 1 1 0 1 0 0 0 1 1 0 0 0 1 1 1 1 1 0; %B
%             1 0 1 0 0 0 1 0 1 0 1 0 0 0 1 1 0 0 0 1 1 1 1 1 1 1 0 0 0 1 1 0 0 0 1; %A'
%             1 1 1 1 0 1 0 1 0 1 1 0 0 0 1 1 1 1 1 0 1 0 0 0 1 1 0 0 0 1 1 1 1 1 0]; %B'
% END A


%%%%%%%%%%%%%%%%%%%%%%%%%%%%%%%%%%%
% PART-B BAM FOR CHARACTER MAPPING
%%%%%%%%%%%%%%%%%%%%%%%%%%%%%%%%%%%


% START B
```

```
source=[0 0 1 0 0 0 1 0 1 0 1 0 0 0 1 1 0 0 0 1 1 1 1 1 1 1 0 0 0 1 1 0 0 0 1;  %A
        1 1 1 1 0 1 0 0 0 1 1 0 0 0 1 1 1 1 1 0 1 0 0 0 1 1 0 0 0 1 1 1 1 1 0]; %B

target=[0 0 0 1 0 0 0 0 0 1 1 0 0 0 0 1 0 1 0 0 0 0 0 0 1 0 0 0 0 0 0 1 0 0 0 0 0
        0 1 0 0 0 0 0 0 1 0 0 0 0 0 0 1 0 0 0 1 1 1 1 1 1 1;   % 1
        0 1 1 1 1 0 0 1 0 0 0 0 1 0 0 0 0 0 0 0 0 1 0 0 0 0 0 0 1 0 0 0 0 0 1 0 0 0
        0 0 1 0 0 0 0 0 0 1 0 0 0 0 0 1 0 0 0 0 1 1 1 1 1 1 1]; % 2

test_input=[0 0 1 0 0 0 1 0 1 0 1 0 0 0 1 1 0 0 0 1 1 1 1 1 1 1 0 0 0 1 1 0 0 0 1; % A
            1 1 1 1 0 1 0 0 0 1 1 0 0 0 1 1 1 1 1 0 1 0 0 0 1 1 0 0 0 1 1 1 1 1 0; % B
            1 0 1 0 0 0 1 0 1 0 1 0 0 0 1 1 0 0 0 1 1 1 1 1 1 1 0 0 0 1 1 0 0 0 1; % A'
            1 1 1 1 0 1 0 1 0 1 1 0 0 0 1 1 1 1 1 0 1 0 0 0 1 1 0 0 0 1 1 1 1 1 0; % B'
            1 0 1 0 0 0 1 0 1 0 1 0 0 0 1 1 0 0 0 1 1 1 0 1 1 1 0 0 0 1 1 0 0 0 1; % A''
            1 1 1 1 0 1 0 1 0 1 1 0 0 0 1 1 1 1 1 0 1 0 0 0 1 1 0 0 0 1 1 0 1 1 0; % B''
            1 1 1 0 0 0 1 0 1 0 1 0 0 0 1 1 0 0 0 1 1 1 0 1 1 1 0 0 0 1 1 0 1 0 1; % A'''
            1 1 1 1 0 1 0 1 0 1 1 0 0 0 1 1 1 1 1 0 1 0 1 0 1 1 0 0 0 1 1 0 1 1 0]; % B'''

% END B

% INITIALIZES THE WEIGHTS AS PER HEBB RULE

[r c]=size(source);
% Getting the matrix format of the binary pattern to be stored as weights
[r1 c1]=size(target);
[r2 c2]=size(test_input);
W=zeros(c,c1);          % Defining the space for the weight matrix
O=zeros(r2,c1);         % Setting the zero activations to the output layer
for p=1:r
for i=1:c,
for j=1:c1
W(i,j)=W(i,j)+((2*source(p,i)-1)*(2*target(p,j)-1));
end
end
end
disp('The initialized weights as per hebb rule for binary patterns');
disp(W);

% DEFINING THE MATRIX SPACE FOR THE VARIABLES

sum_ot=zeros(r2,c1);
out_t=zeros(r2,c1);
sum_it=zeros(r2,c2);
in_t=zeros(r2,c2);

for t=1:r2,
disp('Present the t-th input binary pattern with a TAB');
disp(t);

disp(num2str(dispalp_b_ip(test_input(t,:))));
I(t,:)=test_input(t,:);   % Presenting the input pattern to the input layer
pause
iter=0;
% Initializing the iteration count to know the iterations taken by an input
% pattern to settle
converged=0;            % Initializing the convergence flag to zero
max_iter=100;
% If the input test pattern does not get settled even after 100 iterations,
% it will come out of loop

while converged~=1,
% Iterations continue(Oscilations occur) till the tth test input pattern will
% become same(converged=1) as any of the stored pattern
```

```
iter=iter+1;
disp('Iter No:');
disp(iter);

% COMPUTES AND UPDATES THE OUTPUT SIGNAL FROM THE NET INPUT TO THE OUTPUT UNITS
  (OUTPUT LAYER)

for p=1:c1,
for h=1:c2,
sum_ot(t,p)=sum_ot(t,p)+I(t,h).*W(h,p);
% Calculation of net weighted sum to the output units
end
out_t(t,p)=b_bin_fun(sum_ot(t,p),0);
% Calculating the activation of the output units
end
disp('Output layer units weighted sum');
disp(num2str(sum_ot));
disp('Output layer units output');
O(t,:)=out_t(t,:);
disp(num2str(out_t));

% COMPUTES AND UPDATES THE INPUT SIGNAL FROM THE NET INPUT TO THE INPUT UNITS
  (INPUT LAYER)

for h=1:c2,
for p=1:c1,
sum_it(t,h)=sum_it(t,h)+O(t,p).*W(h,p);
% Calculation of net weighted sum to the input units
end
in_t(t,h)=b_bin_fun(sum_it(t,h),0);
% Calculating the activation of the input units
end
disp('Input layer units weighted sum');
disp(num2str(sum_it));
disp('Input layer units output');
I(t,:)=in_t(t,:);
disp(num2str(in_t));

% EQULIBRIUM  CHECK

for p=1:r1,
if (all(O(t,:)==target(p,:))|all(I(t,:)==test_input(t,:)))==1,
% If the activations of the input layer units (or)-
converged=1;     % the output layer units has become equal to any of the P paired patterns

disp('Equilibrium has reached')
break
end
end

if iter>max_iter,
converged=1;
disp('The input test pattern is not able to reach equilibrium')
end

end

disp('The binary output of the converged output pattern');

% START A

% disp((num2str(O(t,:))));

% END A
```

```
% START B

disp(num2str(dispalp_b_op(O(t,:))));

% END B

disp('is related to the test input test pattern displayed below');
disp(num2str(dispalp_b_ip(test_input(t,:))));

end
```

**Part B: Sub-programs (Sub-routine functions)**

```
% THRESHOLD FUNCTION

function out = b_bin_fun(a, r)
out(a>r) = 1;
out(a==r) = a;
out(a<r) = 0;

% DISPLAY FUNCTION FOR INPUT ACTIVATION UNITS

function [out]=dispalp_b_ip(data)

% DISPLAY OF ALPHABET IN A MATRIX FORMAT

k=0;
for i=1:7,
for j=1:5,
k=k+1;
out(i,j)=data(1,k);      % Output display for a 7 X 5 matrix data
end
end

% DISPLAY FUNCTION FOR INPUT ACTIVATION UNITS

function [out]=dispalp_b_op(data)

% DISPLAY OF ALPHABET IN A MATRIX FORMAT

k=0;
for i=1:9,
for j=1:7,
k=k+1;
out(i,j)=data(1,k);      % Output display for a 9 X 7 matrix data
end
end
```

## 3.8 ADAPTIVE RESONANCE THEORY NEURAL NETWORKS

Carpenter and Stephen Grossberg [27] proposed adaptive resonance theory (ART) neural networks (ART-NN). These NNs are widely used for clustering applications. There are some problems faced by the competitive NNs which do not always form stable clusters. They are oscillatory when more input patterns are presented. Also, there is no guarantee that, as more inputs are applied to an NN used for clustering purpose, the weight matrix will eventually converge and be stable. The learning instability occurs because of the network's adaptability (or plasticity), which causes prior learning to be eroded by more recent learning.

Therefore, the challenge lies in developing a network that is receptive to significant new patterns and still remains stable. Adaptive resonance theory is designed to overcome the problems occurring in learning stability by a modified type of competitive learning called ART. There are three types of ART networks, namely, ART-1 (1986) that can cluster only binary inputs; ART-2 (1987) that can handle gray-scale inputs; and ART-3 (1989) that can handle analog inputs better by overcoming the limitations of ART-2. This chapter discusses the basic operations of ART and then briefs the procedure of clustering of binary patterns using ART-1 NNs.

The key innovation of ART is the use of a degree of expectations called vigilance parameter. Vigilance parameter is the user-specified value to decide the degree of similarity essential for the input patterns to be assigned to a cluster unit. As each input is presented to the network, it is compared with the prototype vector for a match (based on vigilance parameter). If the match between the prototype and the input vector is not adequate, a new prototype or a cluster unit is selected. In this way, previous learned memories (prototypes) are not eroded by new learning. The basic ART learning is an unsupervised one. The term 'resonance' in ART is the state of the network when a class of a prototype vector very closely matches to the current input vector, and leads to a state which permits learning. During this resonant state, the weight updation takes place.

The basic architecture of ART (Fig. 3.32) consists of three layers, namely, input processing layer ($L_1$) for processing the given inputs, output layer ($L_2$) with the cluster units, and reset layer ($R$) which decides the degree of similarity of patterns placed on the same cluster by a reset mechanism. The input processing layer is further divided into input layer ($L_{1S}$) and input interface layer ($L_{1I}$). The bottom-up weights ($u_{ij}$) are connected between the input interface layer to the output-layer

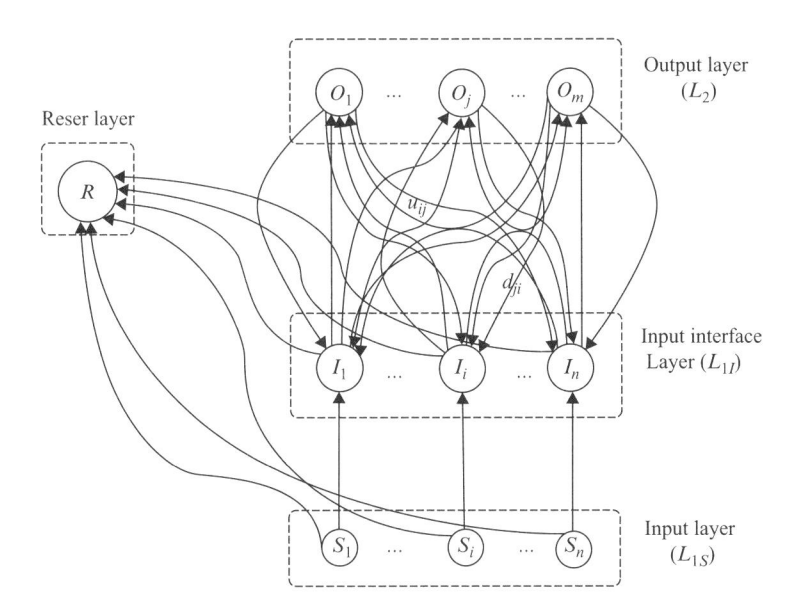

**Fig. 3.32** Architecture of ART-1

and the top-down weights ($d_{ji}$) are connected between the output layer and the interface layer.

The output layer is a competitive layer or a recognition region where the cluster units participates to check the closeness of the input patterns. The interface layer is usually called the 'comparison region', where it gets an input vector and transfers it to its best match in the recognition region. The best match is the single neuron in the competitive layer whose set of weights closely matches the input vector. The reset layer compares the strength of the recognition match to the vigilance parameter. If the vigilance threshold is met, then the training or the updation of weights takes place, else the firing of the recognition neuron is inhibited until a new input vector is applied.

The operation of the ART-1 can be understood by presenting a binary input vector $S_p$ to the input layer $L_{1S}$ and the information is passed to its corresponding units in the input interface layer $L_{1I}$. Now the interface units transmit the information to the output layer $L_2$ cluster units through the bottom-up weights $u_{ij}$. The output units compete to become a winner. The operation is similar to MAXNET where the largest net input to the output unit usually becomes the winner and the activation becomes 1. All the other output units will have an activation of 0. Let the winning cluster unit's index be set to capital $J$. If there is a tie, then the index $j$, which is the smallest one, can be considered as the winner. Now the winner unit $J$ will be allowed to learn the input pattern.

Therefore, the information about the winner is sent from the output layer $L_2$ to the interface layer $L_{1S}$ through the top-down weights $d_{ji}$. The interface unit's activations will be maintaining a value 1; if a unit receives a non-zero signal simulataneously from the input layer $L_{1S}$ and the output layer $L_2$. Now, the norm of the vector $I$ of the comparison region gives the number of components for which the top-down weight vector $d_{ji}$ for the winning unit $J$ and the input vector $S_p$ are same as 1. The value of $\|I\|$ gives an estimate of the degree of the match. The learning will occur only if the match is acceptable to the user-specified value of 'degree of expectations' called vigilance parameter $v$. The verdict for learning is carried out by calculating the ratio between the $\|I\|$ and $\|S_p\|$. The updation of the weights ($u_{ij}$ & $d_{ji}$) is carried out if $\|I\| / \|S_p\| \geq v$.

Suppose, $\|I\| / \|S_p\| < v$, then the current winner unit is rejected and is inhibited in this learning trial. A learning trial is the presentation of one pattern. Now the activations of the interface layer units are reset to zero. The same input binary vector $S_p$ is yet again allowed to send its signal to the interface units and the same procedure takes place except the inhibited units in the output layer are not allowed to participate in the competition. This procedure is repeated until a cluster unit is accepted or all the units in the output layer are inhibited.

Now, a decision has to be taken by the user if all the output-layer units are inhibited. The user can have any of the following decisions:

(a) Reduce the value of the vigilance parameter allowing less matched patterns to be placed on the same cluster units which may be inhibited during earlier learning trial
(b) Addition of more number of cluster units
(c) Specify the current input pattern as the one that cannot be clustered

The aforesaid scheme of learning trials is carried out for all the $P$ input patterns $S_{p=1...P}$. The flow chart of the ART-1 algorithm is given in Fig. 3.33. The success

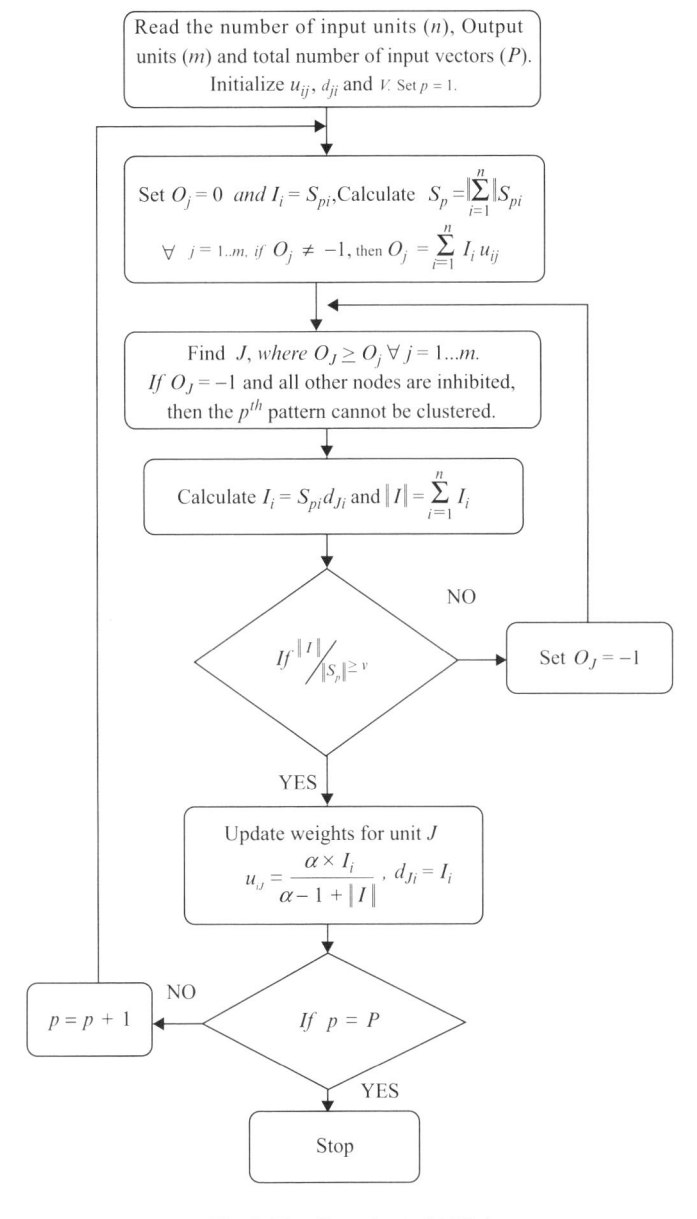

```
┌─────────────────────────────────────────────┐
│ Read the number of input units (n), Output  │
│ units (m) and total number of input vectors │
│ (P). Initialize u_ij, d_ji and V. Set p = 1.│
└─────────────────────────────────────────────┘
                      │
                      ▼
┌─────────────────────────────────────────────┐
│ Set O_j = 0 and I_i = S_pi, Calculate       │
│   S_p = Σ|S_pi|                             │
│   ∀ j = 1..m, if O_j ≠ −1, then             │
│   O_j = Σ I_i u_ij                          │
└─────────────────────────────────────────────┘
                      │
                      ▼
┌─────────────────────────────────────────────┐
│ Find J, where O_J ≥ O_j ∀ j = 1...m.        │
│ If O_J = −1 and all other nodes are         │
│ inhibited, then the p^th pattern cannot be  │
│ clustered.                                  │
└─────────────────────────────────────────────┘
                      │
                      ▼
┌─────────────────────────────────────────────┐
│ Calculate I_i = S_pi d_Ji and ‖I‖ = Σ I_i   │
└─────────────────────────────────────────────┘
                      │
                      ▼
             ◇ If ‖I‖/‖S_p‖ ≥ v ◇ ── NO ──▶ [ Set O_J = −1 ]
                  │ YES
                  ▼
┌─────────────────────────────────────────────┐
│ Update weights for unit J                   │
│   u_iJ = (α × I_i)/(α − 1 + ‖I‖),  d_Ji = I_i│
└─────────────────────────────────────────────┘
                      │
                      ▼
             ◇ If p = P ◇ ── NO ──▶ [ p = p + 1 ]
                  │ YES
                  ▼
               [ Stop ]
```

**Fig. 3.33** Flow chart of ART-1

of the algorithm depends upon the selection of proper parameter values. The vigilance parameter $v$ can have a value between 0 and 1. The top-down weights $d_{ji}$ can be set to 1. The bottom-up weights $u_{ij}$ can be set as:

$$0 < u_{ij} < \frac{\alpha}{\alpha - 1 + n}, \text{ where } \alpha > 1 \tag{3.53}$$

Whenever a new learning trial starts by the presentation of a binary pattern, all the inhibitions set in the previous learning trial will be reset by setting the activation of the entire output cluster unit to 0. It should also be noted that whenever the activation of the inhibited cluster unit is set to $-1$, all the weights and signals related to that inhibited unit will be non-negative. Therefore, a unit with a negative activation will never have the largest activation and cannot become a winner.

## 3.9 BOLTZMAN MACHINE NEURAL NETWORKS

In 1983, Geoffrey Hinton and Terry Sejnowski developed a stochastic recurrent NN called Boltzman machine neural networks (BMNNs) [28]. It is a network of symmetrically connected, neuron-like units that make stochastic decisions about whether to be ON or OFF. Boltzmann machines have a simple learning algorithm that allows them to discover interesting features that represent complex regularities in the training data. Sometimes, BMNN can be understood as an extension of discrete Hopfield networks since both have the commonalities of weights being symmetric, random asynchronous updation of unit's activation, and units have no self-feedback. In a BMNN, the randomized local updation and Hebbian learning has been replaced by a powerful stochastic learning scheme. The update of activations in the Hopfield network is determininstic wheras it is stochastic in BMNN. Hidden layer of units are present in a BMNN which is not present in a Hopfield network.

Boltzmann machines can be generally used in two different ways. The first one is related to optimisation where the weights represent the constraints and the quantity to be optimised. Here, the stochastic dynamics of the Boltzmann machine allow the samples to settle to an optimal state reaching equilibrium. The other way is to learn a set of sample vectors by updating the weights in order to generate these vectors with a high probability. Each update is again based on settling of vector states to equilibrium. The settling of sample states to reach an equilibrium state is carried out by simulated annealing technique which is stochastic in nature. In this section, BMNN is explained for learning input and output patterns and derives the explanation from the work carried out by Ackley, Hinton, and Sejnowski in 1985 for solving an 'encoder problem'.

The architecture of the BMNN is shown in Fig. 3.34 which consists of two layers of visible units and one layer of hidden units. The visible units are the interface between the network and the environment. The number of visible

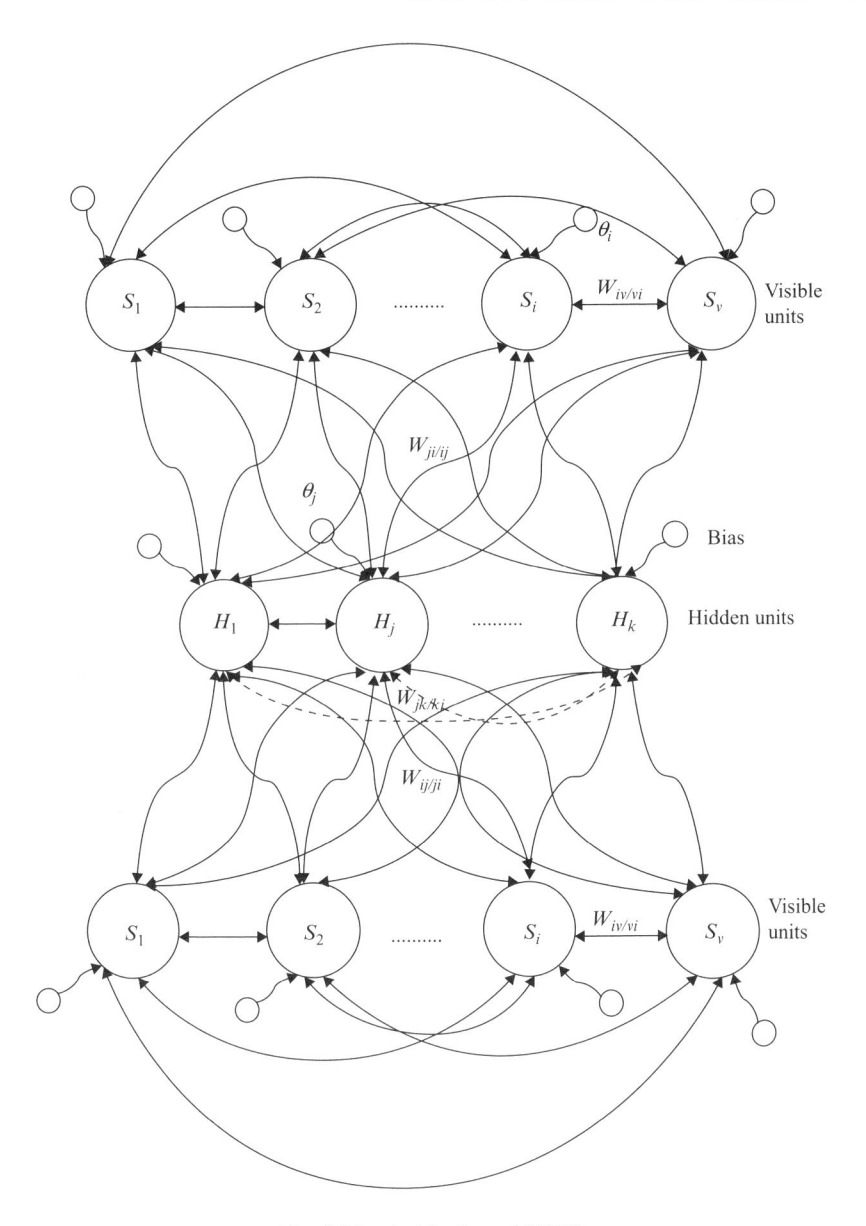

**Fig. 3.34** Architecture of BMNN

units in the visible layer is the same which makes the symmetry of the Boltzman network. The interconnections between units have bi-directional links and the link weights are symmetric having the same strength. A threshold value $\theta$ called a bias is associated with each unit.

Every individual unit in BMNN will have any one of the two states, namely, ON or OFF. It can be either 1 or 0 (binary resperentation); or 1 or −1 (bipolar respresentation) depending upon the problem domain. This state of the unit is a function of probabilistic function of the states of its neighbouring units and the weights on its links to them. A unit being ON or OFF can be considered as the acceptance or rejection of a hypothesis of the problem domain.

Here, the global state or the equilibrium state of the whole network can be represented by 'energy' (E) of the state. The energy of any global configuration of a BMNN can be defined as:

$$E = -\sum_{r<s} w_{rs} S_r S_s + \sum_r \theta_r S_r \qquad (3.54)$$

Where, $w_{rs}$ is the strength of connection between units $r$ and $s$; $S_r$ is 1 if the unit $r$ is ON or 0 if the unit $r$ is OFF; and $\theta_r$ is the threshold of $r^{th}$ unit.

The rejection or acceptance of a hypothesis for the $r^{th}$ unit is determined by an 'energy gap' ($\Delta E_r$) given as:

$$\Delta E_r = \sum_r w_{rs} S_r - \theta_r \qquad (3.55)$$

The rule for minimizing an energy continuted by the $r^{th}$ unit can be ON; if it's total net input obtained by summing up of the signals from the neighbouring units of the system exceeds its threshold. Generally an NN that uses deterministic algorithms like gradient descent methods get struck in local minima that are not globally optimal.

A simple scheme for not getting trapped in the local minima is allowing the states to occasionally jump to configurations of higher energy. This can be achieved by the property of simulated annealing concept available in the thermodynamic systems. The scheme of gradually decreasing the temperature $T$ is called simulated annealing [29]. It is analogous to the physical annealing process used to produce a strong metal with a regular crystalline structure. During annealing, a molten metal is cooled gradually in order to avod imperfections in the crystalline structure of the metal due to freezing.

If the energy gap between ON and OFF states of the $r^{th}$ unit is $\Delta E_r$, then regardless of the previous state, set $S_k = 1$ with a probability given as,

$$P_r = \frac{1}{(1+e^{-\Delta E_r/T})} \qquad (3.56)$$

where, $T$ is a parameter that acts like temperature. The probability $P_r$ of the $r^{th}$ unit becoming 1 (i.e., $S_k = 1$), increases at lower values of $T$ and vice versa. However, the learning mechanism of the Boltzman machine is influenced by the proper selection of parameter values such as weights ($w_{ij}$), threshold values ($\theta_j$), learning rate or the fixed-size weight adjustment, temperature ($T$), and the time taken to calculate two types of probabilities $P(V^\alpha)$ and $P'(V^\alpha)$. $P(V^\alpha)$ is the probability of the $\alpha^{th}$ state of the visible units when their states are determined by the environment and $P'(V^\alpha)$ is the corresponding probability when the network is running freely with no environmental input.

The flow chart of the annealing schedule and determining the activation of units are given in Figs 3.35 and 3.36, respectively, and will be called in the main

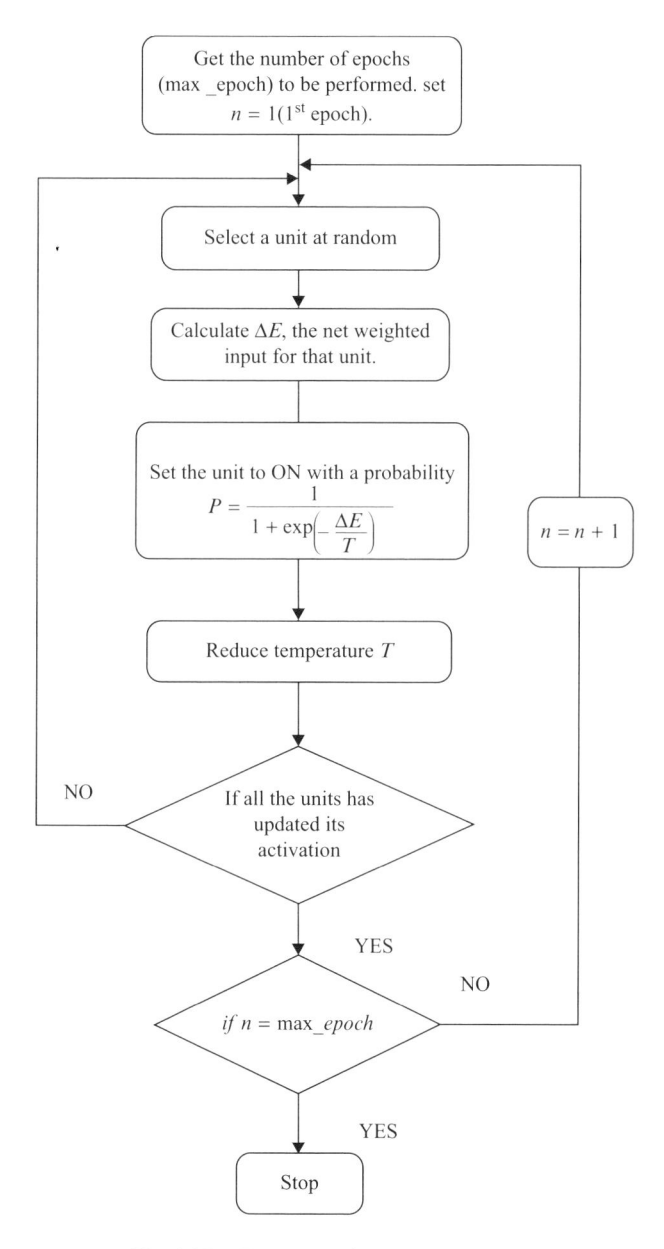

**Fig. 3.35** Flow chart of annealing schedule

```
                    ┌─────────────────────────────┐
                    │ Get the number of epochs    │
                    │ (max_epoch) to be performed.│
                    │ Set n = 1(1st epoch).       │
                    └─────────────────────────────┘
                                 │
                                 ▼
                    ┌─────────────────────────────┐
                    │   Select a unit at random   │
                    └─────────────────────────────┘
                                 │
                                 ▼
                    ┌─────────────────────────────┐
                    │ Calculate ΔE, the net       │
                    │ weighted input for that unit│
                    └─────────────────────────────┘
                                 │
                                 ▼
                    ┌─────────────────────────────┐
                    │ Set the unit to ON with a   │
                    │ probability                 │
                    │      P = 1/(1+exp(-ΔE/T))   │
                    └─────────────────────────────┘
```

*(Flow chart follows — see Fig. 3.36)*

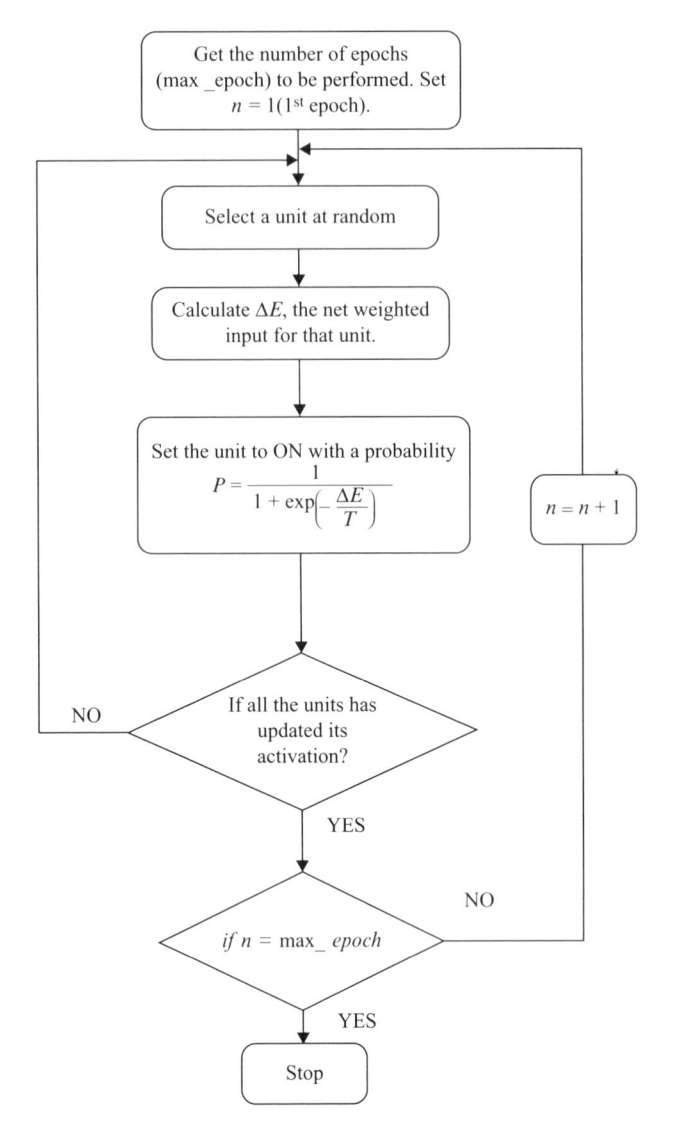

**Fig. 3.36** Flow chart for determining activation

flow chart of the Boltzmann learning which is given in Fig. 3.37. Once the learning is over, a test pattern can be given as input and tested.

In the Boltzman learning of training patterns, an epoch is considered to be the same number of activation updates of the unclamped units (hidden units in this algorithm). This allows that each of the unclamped units has one chance to update its activation. The binary states (0 or 1) of the source and target training patterns are clamped or fixed for every presentation in the corresponding input-output layer of the visible units. For example, if the 1st source-target training pair is [$S$ (1 0 0 0): $T$ (1 0 0 0)], then the binary states of $S$ vector and target vector are fixed correspondingly to the input and output of the visible units, respectively. The training vectors are to be considered as the environmental vectors.

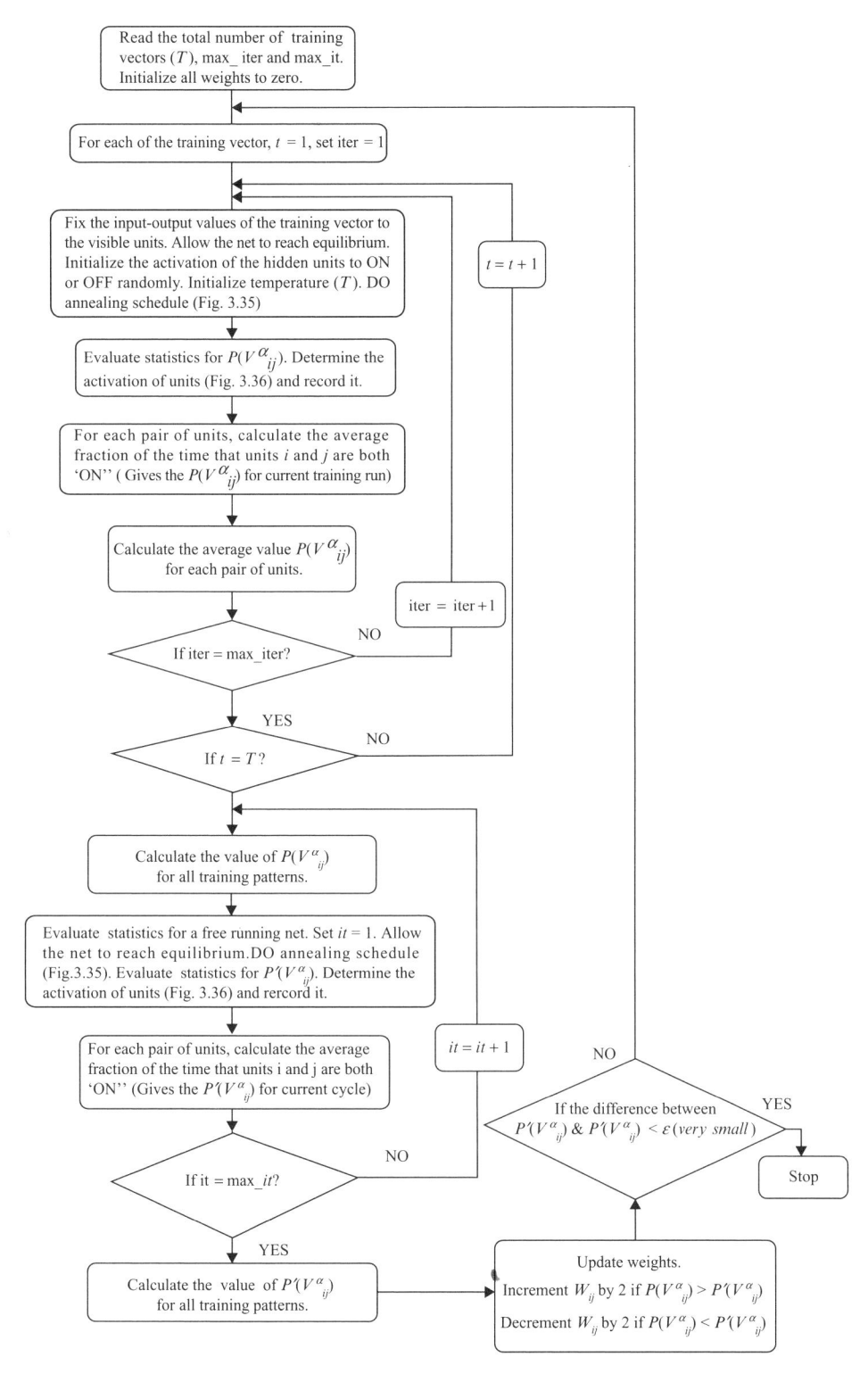

# Artificial Neural Networks—Second Generation 217

**Fig. 3.37** Flow chart for Boltzman learning

## 3.10 RADIAL BASIS FUNCTION NEURAL NETWORKS

The development of radial basis function neural networks (RBFNN) has started in the start of 1990 [30], [31], [32]. It has evolved during the time when feed-forward multi-layer perceptron NNs are widely used in different fields of engineering applications. The architecture of the RBFNN (Fig. 3.38) is similar to feed-forward networks with a single hidden layer strictly.

The hidden-layer unit incorporates the specialised activation function (Table 2.4) called RBFs. These functions produce localized, bounded, and radially symmetric activations that decreases the distance from the function's centres. However, the sigmoidal function used in backpropagation feed-forward NN produces global and unbounded activations.

Figure 3.38 shows an RBFNN. The bell-shaped curves in the hidden nodes indicate that each hidden-layer node represents a bell-shaped RBF that is centred on a vector in the feature space. There are no weights on the lines from the input units to the hidden units. The input vector is fed to each of the $j^{th}$ radial basis hidden units. The output of the $k^{th}$ unit of the RBF network is given in Eq. (3.57).

$$O_k = B_o + \sum_{j=1}^{h} w_{jk} \times H_j \qquad (3.57)$$

where $H_j$ is the radial basis output of the $j^{th}$ hidden unit and is given by Eq. (3.58).

$$H_j = f\left(\left\|I - c_j\right\|\right) \qquad (3.58)$$

Here $c \in R$ belongs to the centre of the RBF which has radius $r$.
Given the vector (3.59) on $R^n$,

$$I = [I_1, ..I_i ... I_n]' \qquad (3.59)$$

the Euclidean norm on this space measures the size of the vector and is given by Eq. (3.60).

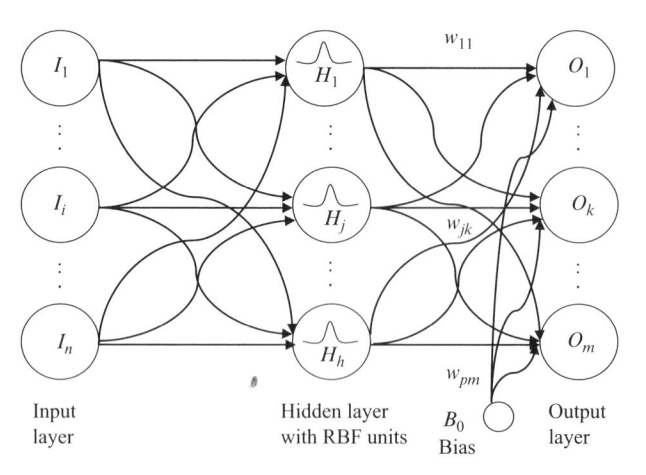

**Fig. 3.38** Architecture of RBFNN

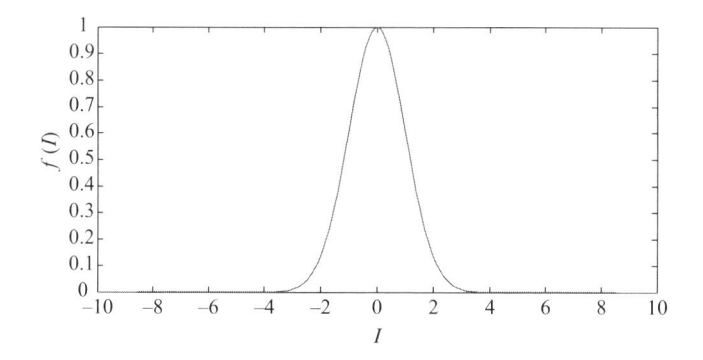

**Fig. 3.39** Gaussian RBF with centre $c = 0$ and radius $r = 1$

$$\|I\| = \left(\sum_{i=1}^{n} I_i^2\right)^{\frac{1}{2}} = (I'I)^{\frac{1}{2}} \qquad (3.60)$$

The non-linear function $f$ is an RBF. Commonly, Gaussian function is used and is given in Eq. (3.61). It is obvious that the Gaussian RBF monotonically decreases with distance from the centre as shown in Fig. 3.39.

$$f(x) = e^{\frac{-\|I_i - c_j\|^2}{r^2}} \qquad (3.61)$$

where,
$$x_i = \|I_i - c_{ij}\|$$

The training of the RBFNN is similar to the BPNN. The most popular approach to update both the center $C_{ij}$ and $W_{jk}$ is through gradient descent learning. If the input and the target vector are given as in Eq. (3.62),

$$I = [I_1,..I_i...I_n]'$$
$$T = [T_1,..T_k...T_m] \qquad (3.62)$$

the mean square error function is minimized by adjusting the output-layer weights ($w_{jk}$), and is given by $E$ as in Eq. (3.63).

$$E = \frac{1}{m}\sum_{k=1}^{m}(T_k - O_k)^2 \qquad (3.63)$$

Substituting Eq. (3.64),

$$E = \frac{1}{m}\sum_{k=1}^{m}\left(T_k - \left(B_0 + \sum_{j=1}^{h} w_{jk} \times H_j\right)\right)^2 \qquad (3.64)$$

The update rule for the updation of weights from the hidden layer to the output layer and centre learning is given by Eqs (3.65) and (3.66),

$$w_{jk}(t+1) = w_{jk}(t) - \eta_2 \times \frac{\partial E}{\partial w_{jk}} \qquad (3.65)$$

$$c_{ij}(t+1) = c_{ij}(t) - \eta_1 \times \frac{\partial E}{\partial c_{ij}} \qquad (3.66)$$

where, $\eta_1$ and $\eta_2$ are the learning factors or the step size for the centre and weight updation, respectively; and $t$ is the iteration number.

Differentiating $E$ w.r.t. $w_{jk}$ gives the gradient of the error function $E$ and can be written as,

$$\frac{\partial E}{\partial w_{jk}} = \left(\frac{\partial E}{\partial O_k}\right) \times \left(\frac{\partial O_k}{\partial w_{jk}}\right) = \left(\left(\frac{-2}{m}\right)\sum_{k=1}^{m}(T_k - O_k)\right) \times \left(\frac{H_j}{h}\right) \qquad (3.67)$$

Substituting Eq. (3.67) in Eq. (3.65) we get,

$$w_{jk}(t+1) = w_{jk}(t) - \eta_2 \times \left(\left(\frac{-2}{m}\right)\sum_{k=1}^{m}(T_k - O_k)\right) \times \left(\frac{H_j}{h}\right) \qquad (3.68)$$

Considering all the $P$ training patterns, the Eq. (3.68) becomes,

$$w_{jk}(t+1) = w_{jk}(t) + \left(\left(\frac{2 \times \eta_2}{h \times m}\right)\sum_{p=1}^{P}\sum_{k=1}^{m}(T_k^p - O_k^p)\right) \times H_j^p$$

Now, for centre learning, differentiate $E$ w.r.t. $c_{ij}$ and the gradient can be written as,

$$\frac{\partial E}{\partial c_{ij}} = \left(\frac{\partial E}{\partial O_k}\right) \times \left(\frac{\partial O_k}{\partial H_j}\right) \times \left(\frac{\partial H_j}{\partial c_{ij}}\right) \qquad (3.69)$$

From Eqs (3.67) and (3.57), we get,

$$\left(\frac{\partial E}{\partial O_k}\right) = \left(\left(\frac{-2}{m}\right)\sum_{k=1}^{m}(T_k - O_k)\right) \qquad (3.70)$$

$$\left(\frac{\partial O_k}{\partial H_j}\right) = w_{jk} \qquad (3.71)$$

We can write the third term of Eq. (3.69) as

$$\left(\frac{\partial H_j}{\partial c_{ij}}\right) = \left(\frac{\partial H_j}{\partial x_i}\right) \times \left(\frac{\partial x_i}{\partial c_{ij}}\right) \qquad (3.72)$$

Now,

$$\left(\frac{\partial H_j}{\partial x_i}\right) = -\frac{x_i}{\left(\frac{r}{2h}\right)} \times H_j \qquad (3.73)$$

and

$$\left(\frac{\partial x_i}{\partial c_{ij}}\right) = \frac{\partial\left(\sum_{j=1}^{h}(I_i - c_{ij})^2\right)^{\frac{1}{2}}}{\partial c_{ij}} = -\frac{(I_i - c_{ij})}{x_i} \quad (3.74)$$

Substituting (3.73) and (3.74) in (3.72) we get,

$$\left(\frac{\partial H_j}{\partial c_{ij}}\right) = \left(-\frac{2h \times x_i \times H_j}{r}\right) \times \left(-\frac{(I_i - c_{ij})}{x_i}\right) \quad (3.75)$$

Substituting (3.70), (3.71), and (3.75) in Eq. (3.69) we get,

$$\frac{\partial E}{\partial c_{ij}} = \left(\left(\frac{-2}{m}\right)\sum_{k=1}^{m}(T_k - O_k)\right) \times w_{jk} \times \left(-\frac{2h \times H_j}{r}\right) \times -(I_i - c_{ij}) \quad (3.76)$$

Substituting Eq. (3.76) in Eq. (3.66), we get,

$$c_{ij}(t+1) = c_{ij}(t) + \eta_1 \times \left(\frac{4h}{m \times r}\right) \times \left(\sum_{k=1}^{m}(T_k - O_k)\right) \times w_{jk} \times (I_i - c_{ij}) \quad (3.77)$$

If centre learning method is not present in RBFNN training, there are unsupervised techniques such as fixed centres selected at random, orthogonal least sqares and k-means clustering, etc. The simplest and quickest approach is setting the RBF parameters to have their centres fixed at $M$ points selected at random from the $N$ data points, and to set all their widths to be equal and fixed at an appropriate size for the distribution of data points. The orthogonal least square method involves the sequential addition of new basis functions, each centred on one of the data points.

If we already have $L$ such basis functions, there remain $N - L$ possibilities for the next, and we can determine the output weights for each of those $N - L$ potential networks. Then the $L + 1th$ basis function which leaves the smallest residual sum squared output error is chosen, and then we go on to choose the next basis function. This sounds not worthwhile, but if we construct a set of orthogonal vectors in the space $S$ spanned by the vectors of hidden unit activations for each pattern in the training set, we can calculate directly the data point that should be chosen for the next basis function at each stage, and the output-layer weights can be determined at the same time. To get a good generalization, we can use validation/cross validation to stop the process when an appropriate number of data points have been selected as centres.

A better approach is to use clustering techniques to find a set of centres that accurately reflects the distribution of the data point. The $k$-means clustering algorithm picks the number $K$ of centres in advance, and then follows a simple re-estimation procedure to partition the data points $\{I^P\}$ into $K$ disjoint sub-sets $S_j$ containing $N_j$ data points to minimize the sum squared clustering function.

$$f_c = \sum_{j=1}^{K} \sum_{p \in S_j} \left\| I^p - c_j \right\|^2 \qquad (3.78)$$

where, $c_j$ is the mean/centroid of the data points in set $S_j$ and is given as,

$$\mu_j = \frac{1}{N_j} \sum_{p \in S_j} I^p \qquad (3.79)$$

Once the basis centres have been determined in this way, the widths can be set according to the variances of the points in the corresponding cluster. RBF networks have been successfully applied to a large diversity of applications like interpolation, chaotic time-series modelling, system identification, control engineering, speech recognition, and image restoration.

## 3.11 SUPPORT VECTOR MACHINES

A support vector machine (SVM) [33] is a learning algorithm typically used for classification problems (text categorization, handwritten character recognition, image classification, etc.). Work on SVMs began in the 1960s, but recent developments in the 1990s have made SVMs much more useful for application to real-world problems. It has been derived from the statistical learning theory by Vapnik and Chervonenkis [34].

It can be first realized as a classifier where a decision plane separates between a set of objects having different class memberships. The simplest example is a linear classifier (i.e., a classifier that separates a set of objects into their respective groups with a line). However, most classification tasks are not that simple, and often more complex structures are needed in order to make an optimal separation, i.e., correctly classify new objects (test cases) on the basis of the examples that are available (training cases).

Classification tasks based on drawing separating lines to distinguish between objects of different class memberships are known as 'hyper plane classifiers'. Therefore, instead of minimizing the training error as in conventional supervised NNs, the SVM tries to minimize the upper bound of the generalization error and maximizes the margin between a separating hyper plane and the training data. The goal of the SVM is to optimise 'generalization', the ability to correctly classify unseen data. It addresses problems seen in other learning algorithms such as errors due to local minima, overfitting, and an inconveniently large number of tunable parameters.

The SVM can be trained just like an ANN. It maps training data in the 'input space' into a high dimensional 'feature space'. It determines a linear decision boundary in the feature space by constructing the 'optimal separating hyperplane' distinguishing the classes. This allows the SVM to achieve a non-linear boundary in the input space. The 'support vectors' (SVs) are those points in the input space which best define the boundary between the classes.

Let us try to illustrate the concept of SVM though an example. Consider a two-class problem which is linearly seperable. The two classes can be separated

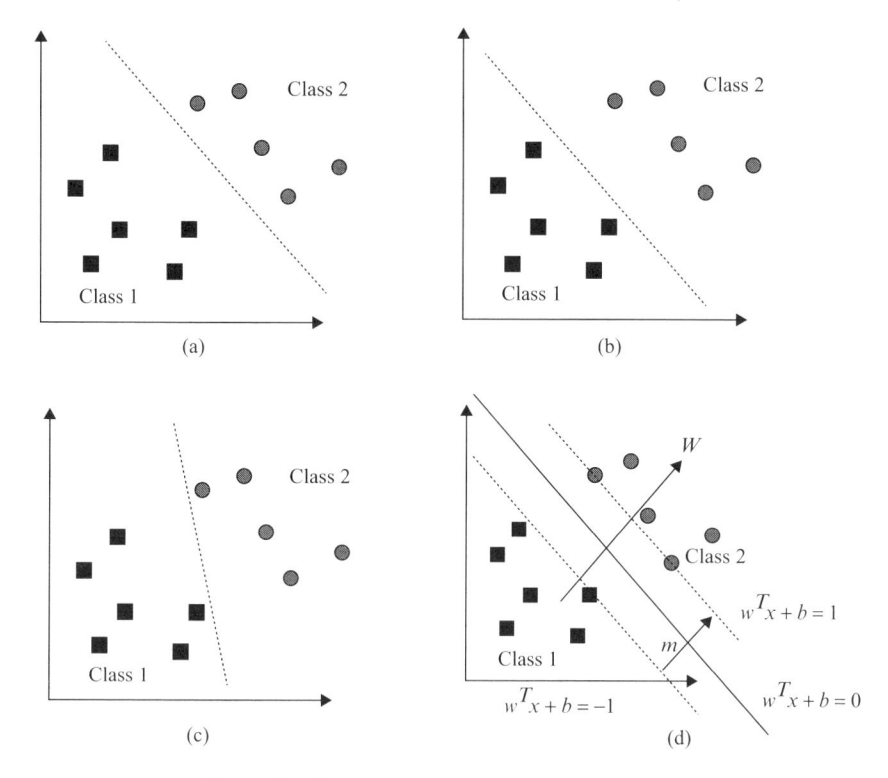

**Fig. 3.40** Decision boundaries between two classes

by many decision boundaries as shown in Fig. 3.40 a, b, and d. However, there is an ambiguity to choose the one that is the best, which is the bottom line that need to be solved. The decision boundary should be as far way from the data of both the classes as possible. Therefore, the margin 'm' as shown in Fig. 3.40(d) between the two classes has to be maximized, thereby evolving to an optimisation problem.

Let $x = \{x_1,...x_i,...,x_n\}$ be a set of points in a domain that has to be classified. Let $y_i \in \{1,-1\}$ be the class label of $x_i$. The decision boundary should classify all the points correctly as $y_i(w^T x_i + b) \geq 1, \forall i$. Here, $w$ and $b$ are the weights and biases or the coefficients of a decision boundary. Now the finding of the solution to the constrained optimisation problem as in Eq. (3.80) becomes the training part of the SVM.

$$\text{Minimize } \frac{1}{2}\|w\|^2 \tag{3.80}$$

Subject to
$$y_i(w^T x_i + b) \geq 1, \forall i \tag{3.81}$$

The minimization problem can be transformed into dual as,

$$\text{Maximize } w(\alpha) = \sum_{i=1}^{n} \alpha_i - \frac{1}{2} \sum_{i=1, j=1}^{n} \alpha_i \alpha_j y_i y_j x_i^T x_j \tag{3.82}$$

Subject to
$$\alpha_i \geq 0 \tag{3.83}$$

$$\sum_{i=1}^{n} \alpha_i y_i = 0$$

This is quadratic programming (QP) problem, where the the opimal value of $\alpha_i$ can be recovered. Therefore, $w$ can be recovered by Eq. (3.84).

$$w = \sum_{i=1}^{n} \alpha_i y_i x_i \tag{3.84}$$

If the characteristics of the solution are observed, many of the $\alpha_i$ are found to be zeros. The weights $w$ will finally become a linear combination of a small number of data. Now $x_i$ with non-zero $\alpha_i$ can be called support vector (SV). This can be understood from the geometric interpretation shown in Fig. 3.41. The decision boundary is determined only by the SV. If $t_j$ be the indices of the $s$ SV and $j = 1,....,s$, then $w$ can be written as in Eq. (3.85).

$$w = \sum_{j=1}^{s} \alpha_{t_j} y_{t_j} x_{t_j} \tag{3.85}$$

Once the weights are finalized or the training is over, a new set of data $z$ can be tested for classification. This can be carried out by computing the Eq. (3.86),

$$w^T z + b = \sum_{j=1}^{s} \alpha_{t_j} y_{t_j} \left( x_{t_j}^T z \right) + b \tag{3.86}$$

The test data $z$ will be classified to class 1 if the computed sum is positive, and to class 2 otherwise; the geometrical interpretation of the previous illustration is as shown in Fig. 3.41.

There are theoritical upper bounds on the error on the unseen data for SVM. The larger the margin, the smaller the bound. The smaller the number of SVs, the smaller the bound. It is to be noted that in both training and testing, the data are computed as an inner product of $x^T$ and $y$ (i.e, $x^T y$). This is important for generalization when the

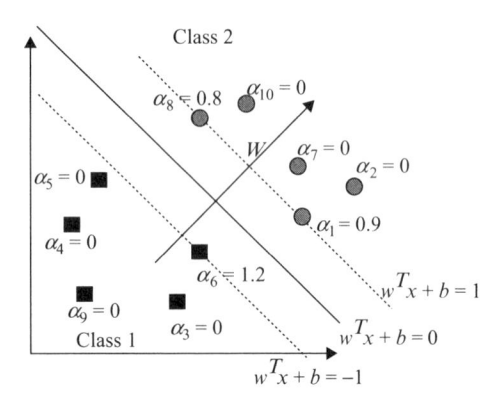

**Fig. 3.41** Decision boundaries with $\alpha_i$ coefficients

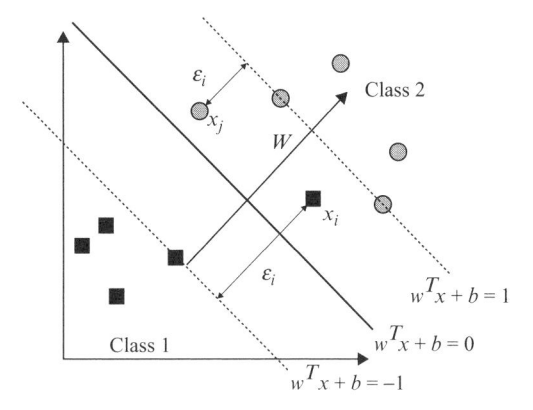

**Fig. 3.42** Decision boundaries with $\varepsilon_i$ for linearly inseperable classes

problem is linearly inseperable. Suppose, if the set of points in a domain is insepa‑rable by a straight line, then an error $\varepsilon_i$ can be incorporated (Fig. 3.42) during clas‑sification which belongs to a field of soft margin hyperplane decision boundaries.

Let us define $\varepsilon_i = 0$, if there is no error for $x_i$. The error coefficients can be incorporated as slack variables for defining the boundaries in an optimisation problem. The equation for boundaries incorporating $\varepsilon_i$ is given in Eqs 3.87–3.89.

$$w^T z + b \geq 1 - \varepsilon_i \qquad y_i = 1 \qquad (3.87)$$

$$w^T z + b \leq -(1 - \varepsilon_i) \qquad y_i = -1 \qquad (3.88)$$

$$\varepsilon_i \geq 0 \qquad \forall i \qquad (3.89)$$

Now the classification problem can be formulated as an optimisation problem as,

$$\text{Minimize } \frac{1}{2}\|w\|^2 + C \sum_{i=1}^{n} \varepsilon_i \qquad (3.90)$$

Subject to $y_i\left(w^T x_i + b\right) \geq 1 - \varepsilon_i, \quad \varepsilon_i \geq 0$ (3.91)

The minimization problem can be transformed into dual as in Eq. (3.92).

$$\text{Maximize } w(\alpha) = \sum_{i=1}^{n} \alpha_i - \frac{1}{2} \sum_{i=1, j-1}^{n} \alpha_i \alpha_j y_i y_j x_i^T x_j \qquad (3.92)$$

Subject to $C \geq \alpha_i \geq 0$ (3.93)

$$\sum_{i=1}^{n} \alpha_i y_i = 0 \qquad (3.94)$$

This is QP problem, where the optimal value of $\alpha_i$ can be recovered. Therefore, $w$ can be recovered by,

$$w = \sum_{j=1}^{s} \alpha_{t_j} y_{t_j} x_{t_j} \qquad (3.95)$$

It should be noted that the only difference with the linear separable case is the presence of an upper bound C on $\alpha_i$. Now the real challenge is to find a way to extend the SV to non-linear decision boundary problems. The best way to do so is to transform $x_i$ to a higher dimensional space by transforming the input space $x_i$ to a feature space $\phi(x_i)$ (Fig. 3.43). Sometimes, one may argue that the need for transformation as the linear operation in the feature space is equivalent to non-linear operation in input space. It is also possible to classify easily as in an XOR problem if a proper transformation method is readily available. However, the real issue of these transformations comes with very high computation burden and it is very hard to get a good estimate.

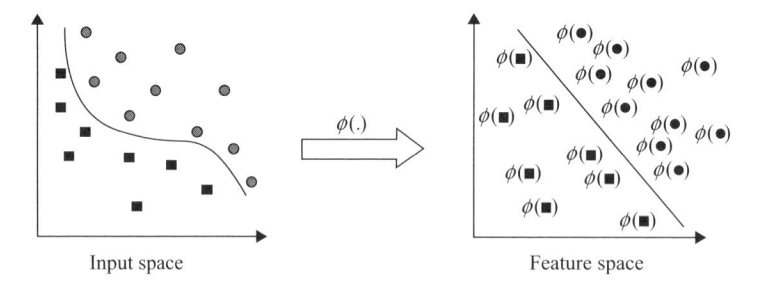

**Fig. 3.43** Transformation from input space to feature space

Support vector machines solve the aforecited two issues by kernel mapping for efficient computation and by minimizing $\|w\|^2$, it can lead to a good classifier. Kernel mapping use $\phi(x_i)$ to map the input space to a feature space using a class of functions called 'kernels'.

A kernel $K(x, y)$ is a real valued function $K : X \times X \to \Re$ for which there exists a function $\phi : X \to Z$, where Z is a real vector space, with the property $K(x, y) = \langle \phi(x), \phi(y) \rangle$, and is known as the kernel trick. The kernel $K(x, y)$ acts as dot product in space Z. In the SVM literature, X and Z are called input space and feature space, respectively. For example, let us define the kernel function $K(x, y)$ as in Eq. (3.96).

$$K(x, y) = (1 + x_1 y_1 + x_2 y_2)^2 \tag{3.96}$$

Consider the following transformation.

$$\phi\left(\begin{bmatrix} x_1 \\ x_2 \end{bmatrix}\right) = (1, \sqrt{2}x_1, \sqrt{2}x_2, x_1^2, x_2^2, \sqrt{2}x_1 x_2) \tag{3.97}$$

$$\phi\left(\begin{bmatrix} y_1 \\ y_2 \end{bmatrix}\right) = (1, \sqrt{2}y_1, \sqrt{2}y_2, y_1^2, y_2^2, \sqrt{2}y_1 y_2) \tag{3.98}$$

$$\left\langle \phi\left(\begin{bmatrix} x_1 \\ x_2 \end{bmatrix}\right), \phi\left(\begin{bmatrix} y_1 \\ y_2 \end{bmatrix}\right) \right\rangle = (1 + x_1 y_1 + x_2 y_2)^2 \tag{3.99}$$

$$= K(x, y)$$

The inner product can be computed by K without going through the map $\phi(.)$. In practice, we specify K, there by specifying $\phi(.)$ indirectly, instead of choosing $\phi(.)$. Intuitively, $K(x, y)$ represents our desired notion of similarity between data $x$ and $y$ and this is from our prior knowledge. $K(x, y)$ need to satisfy a theorem called 'Mercer theorem' [35] for $\phi(.)$ to exist. Some of the examples of kernel functions are given as follows:

Polynomial kernel with degree $d$

$$K(x, y) = (x^T y + 1)^d \qquad (3.100)$$

Radial basis function kernel with width $\sigma$

$$K(x, y) = \exp(-\|x - y\|^2 / (2\sigma^2)) \qquad (3.101)$$

Although SVM is a two-class classifier, it can be used for solving multi-class classification by suitably modifying the QP technique. More commonly, the data set is divided into two parts, suitably in different ways, and a separate SVM is trained for each way of division. Finally, multi-class classification is done by combining the output of all the SVM classifiers. To summarize, reduction of the classification problem to the computation of a linear decision function is done by SVM. It trains the NN in the absence of local optimisation through QP. It is capable of providing a computationally efficient decision function (sparse solution).

## 3.12 ELECTRICAL LOAD FORECASTING USING MATLAB NEURAL NETWORK TOOLBOX

Electrical load forecasting [36] is the process by which the electrical load at a future time is predicted based on past values of load as well as weather, economic, and demographic factors. Load forecasting is an important tool for institutions such as electric utilities, Independent System Operators ISOs, financial institutions, and transmission planning.

There are three types of load forecasting. They are short-term, medium-term, and long-term load forecasting. Short-term load forecasts cover a period of an hour to several days, medium-term load forecasts from a week to several months, and long-term forecasts from a period of one year to several years.

Load demand depends on several factors such as time, weather, end user, connected loads, and demographic and economic conditions. The load profile depends on the hour of the day, the day of the week, and the month of the year. The load profile follows a particular pattern throughout the day, increasing during work times, evening, and extreme weather periods and decreasing during night and early morning. The load pattern will also show a correspondence between similar days of the week. The load consumed during weekends will be lower than that on weekdays. The load patterns on holidays will be different to those of normal weekdays and must be considered separately. Seasonal variation in load can also be observed. The load in tropical regions during summer months will be greater due to increased cooling demand as well as in temperate regions during winter months due to heating demand.

Weather patterns also affect load profile. Temperature and humidity are the two most important factors affecting load profile. Wind speed affects load but to a lesser extent. The other weather-dependent factors that can be considered include precipitation, air pressure, solar irradiation, heat index, and wind chill index.

The types of end users are residential, industrial, and commercial. Each type of end user has a different pattern of electricity usage but is broadly similar within each group. Therefore, power utilities tend to differentiate each type of user when deciding on dispatch and tariff.

There are several methods to perform electrical load forecasting. They are similar-day approach, regression models, time series, expert systems, fuzzy logic, and NNs. Similar-day approach tries to predict the load using load patterns from similar days, weather patterns, and time periods. Regression methods are used to find models that relate the load with weather, day type, and type of customer.

Time-series methods assume that data have an internal structure, such as autocorrelation, trend, and seasonal variation. Auto regressive moving average (ARMA) and auto regressive integrated moving average (ARIMA) are two commonly used methods in time-series analysis. Auto regressive moving average is used for stationary processes while ARIMA is used for non-stationary processes. Auto regressive moving average and ARIMA consider only time and load as the input factors. But, as the load also depends on weather, another method called ARIMA with exogenous variables (ARIMAX) is commonly used in load forecasting as it is able to account for weather.

Expert systems make use of rules that are developed by experts in the field of load forecasting which are then converted to computer programs by software developers working closely with the experts. The forecast program may end up containing up to thousands of rules.

Fuzzy logic is a method of computation where the inputs can be imprecise and noisy. The inputs can take on any state between completely true and completely false with any degree of variability in between. This method avoids the need to form a mathematical model between the input and output and avoids the need to have extremely noise-free inputs. A properly designed fuzzy system can give very accurate forecasting results.

Neural networks for load forecasting have been researched extensively since 1990. Neural networks are essentially functions that represent outputs as a non-linear function of input. Neural networks are modelled on the operation of neurons present in the nervous system of animals. The set of inputs are considered to be nodes that form a layer which can then have connections to outputs through an intermediary or hidden layer of nodes. For load forecasting, the types of NNs (Hopfield, BPNN, BMNN) need to be selected. The number of input and output nodes and layers, the connectivity between layers, whether connections are uni- or bi-directional, and the format of the data (binary, bipolar, or continuous) must also be determined. Currently, the most common type of NN in use is the BPNN with continuous valued functions and supervised learning.

We shall perform similar-day short-term electrical load forecasting using the data mentioned in the coming section. In similar-day load forecast, the load and weather data from similar days of the week are used to predict the load profile for the same day for the next week.

The training is carried out for data between 1 December 2010 and 24 December 2010. The training data are split into seven groups with each group containing data from a particular weekday. Then, seven different NNs are trained, one for each weekday, with the seven different training data sets. The trained NN is tested using data over a period of one week from 25 December 2010 to 31 December 2010.

The graph in Fig. 3.44 shows the variation of load in MW over the month of December 2010. As can be seen, the load profile of each day shows a similar pattern. The load has a sinusoidal type variation with two peaks occurring at 7:00 A.M. in the morning and at 7:00 P.M. evening.

The next graph shows the variation of temperature values in degree Celsius with each hour in a day for the whole month.

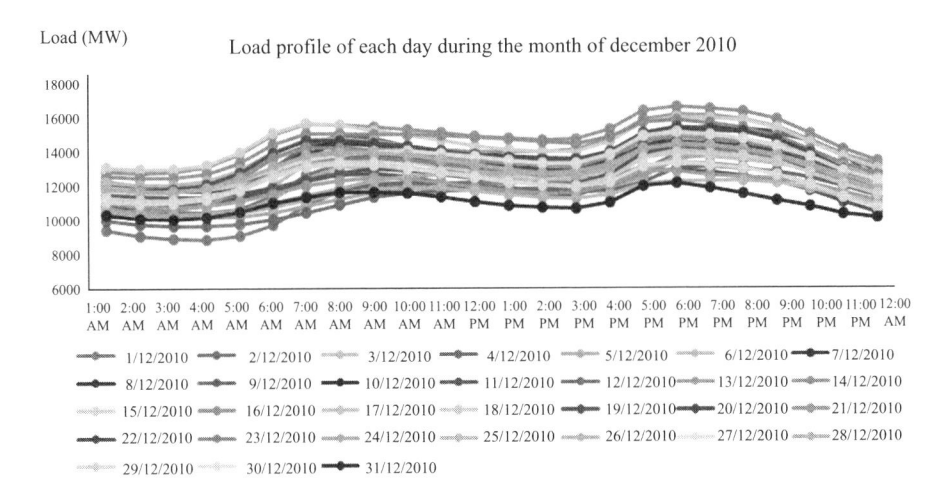

**Fig. 3.44** Historical load data
*Source:* It is an open resource; http://www.pjm.com/markets-and-operations/energy/real-time/loadhryr.aspx

From Fig. 3.45, it can be seen that the temperature varies about 7°C in a day with the maximum temperatures occurring between 7 P.M. and 9 P.M.

The inputs consists of 60 parameters representing the current days average hourly load value for 24 hours, the average hourly temperature for 24 hours, the current and previous day's maximum and minimum temperature, precipitation, wind speed, and humidity. The input also consists of day value with numbers from 1 to 7 representing each day of the week and 8 representing a holiday and the month number from 1 to 12 representing the months from January to

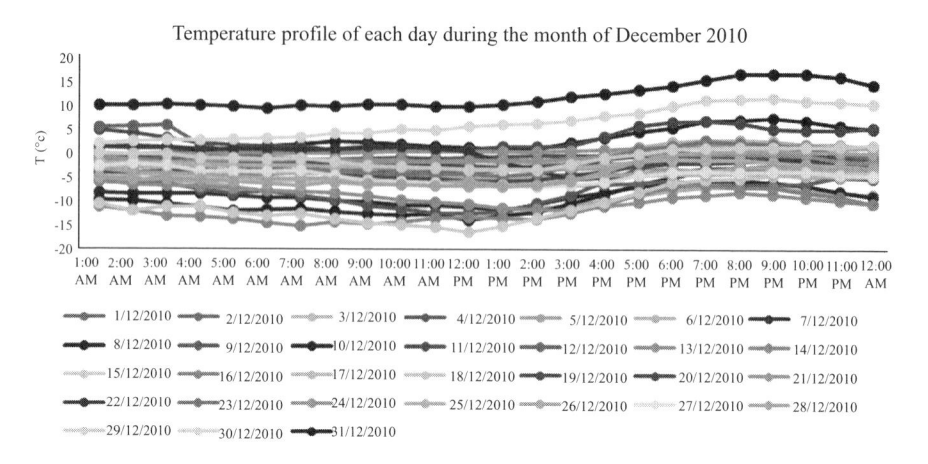

**Fig. 3.45** Historical temperature data
Source: It is an open resource; http://www7.ncdc.noaa.gov/CDO/georegion

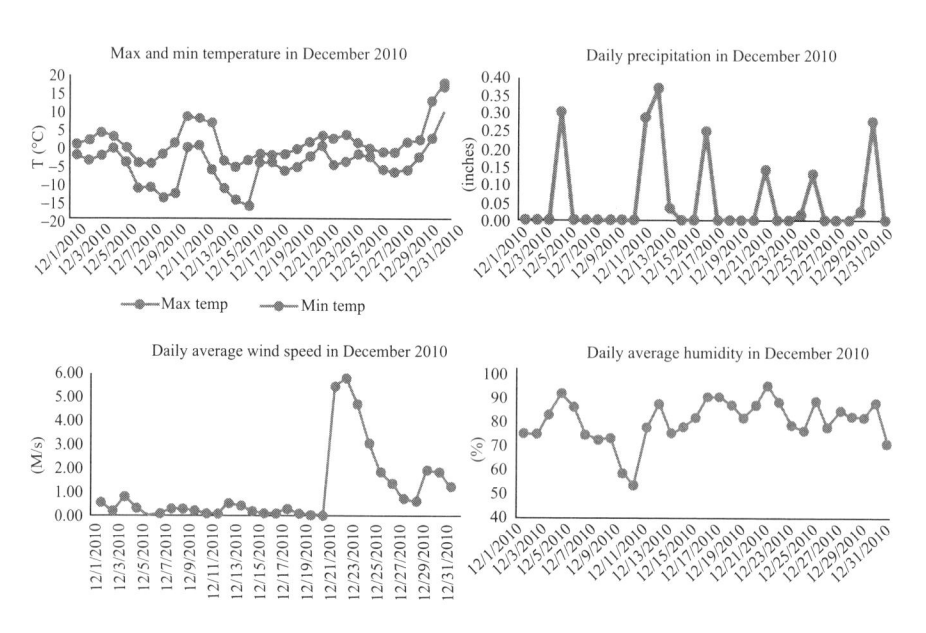

**Fig. 3.46** Historical weather data
Source: It is an open resource; http://www7.ncdc.noaa.gov/CDO/georegion

December. The output will be the next day's predicted average hourly load value for 24 hours.

The data are normalized between −1 and 1 by choosing a positive dividing factor that is higher than the magnitudes of the maximum and minimum data points. The load data from each point are divided by 20,000, the temperature values are divided by 50, precipitation divided by 5, wind speed by 20, humidity by 100, day value by 10, and month value by 20.

The MATLAB NN toolbox is used to apply various NN principles for the purposes of function approximation and classification. The NN toolbox consists of several inbuilt libraries that implement the different types of NNs such as perceptron, feed-forward backpropagation, Hopfield, radial basis, and self-organizing maps. For ease of use, the NN toolbox also comes with a GUI that lets the user to specify parameters such as the input and target vectors, type of network, the transfer function of each layer, the learning rate, and so on. The following gives a description of the GUI and its usage.

The NN toolbox GUI is displayed by typing 'nntool' in the command prompt '>>' in the MATLAB command window. This GUI window is shown in Fig. 3.47.

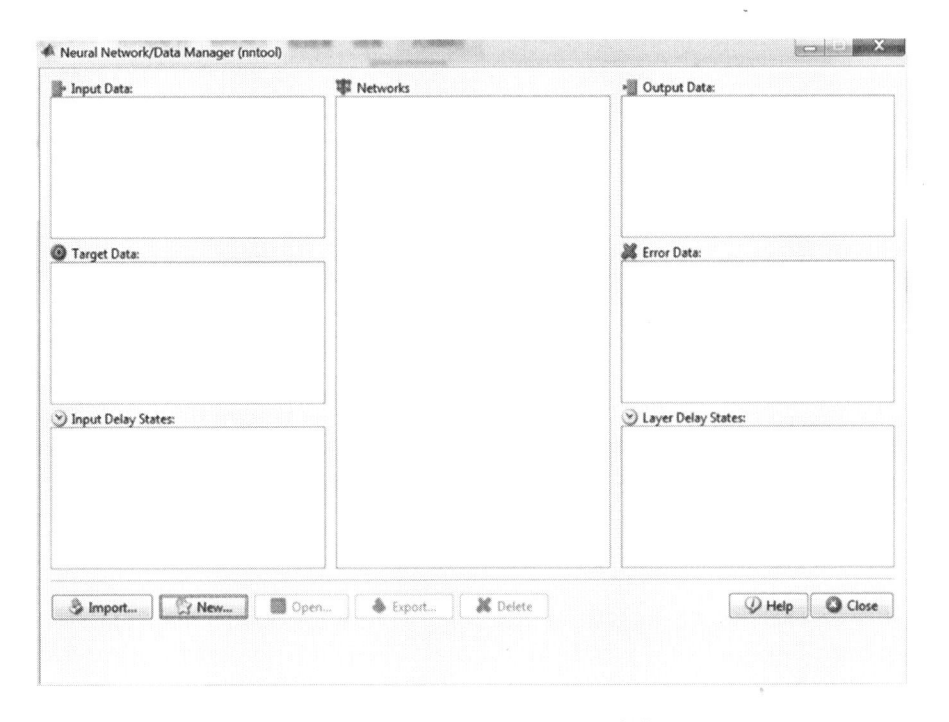

**Fig. 3.47** Neural network toolbox GUI

Let us carry out similar-day approach training for Sunday. The procedure for similar-day training on other days will follow the same steps as detailed. In this example, the training input data are stored in the matrix variable 'input_sun', training output in 'output_sun', test input data in 'test_in_sun', and test output data in 'test_out_sun' in the workspace. The data must be in the form of a matrix where number of rows is equal to number of input (or output) parameters and the number of columns must be equal to number of data samples.

Run the NN tool using the command nntool. The first step is to import the data in the workspace into nntool GUI. Clicking import opens the 'Import to network/data manager' window. This is shown in Fig. 3.48.

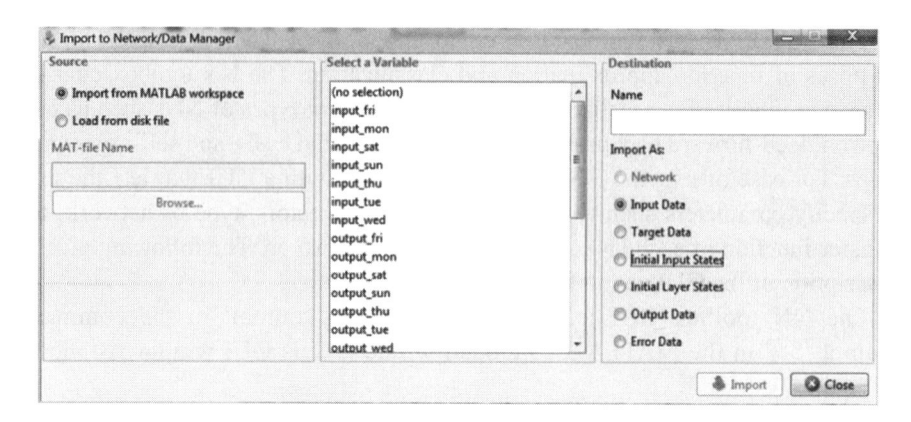

Fig. 3.48 Neural network data manager GUI

In this example, the data are stored in workspace. For this reason, select 'import from MATLAB workspace', select the variable 'input_sun', and in destination, click 'Input Data' in the 'Import as' section. Perform the same operation with 'output_sun' assigning it to 'Target Data'. Do the same assigning 'test_in_sun' to Input data and 'test_out_sun' to target data. Then close the window. If the data are stored in a .mat or .dat file in hard disk, then click the 'Load from disk file', and use the 'Browse' button to navigate to the data file and select it.

In the nntool GUI, click 'New'. The 'Create network or data' window is displayed. This window is used to create the NN architecture as well as specify the training input and output data. Give a name to the network (e.g., network_sun). In network type, give the type of network that is required. In this example, let us select 'Feed forward backprop' for feed-forward BPNN. In input data, select the variable 'input_ sun', target data, select 'output_sun'. For training function, select 'TRAINGD' for gradient descent algorithm and select 'MSE' as performance function.

Here, we are considering a three-layer network with one hidden and one output layer. Therefore, in number of layers, select 2 for hidden and output layer. In 'properties for', select 'Layer 1' for the hidden layer and specify the number of hidden nodes and the transfer function. Select 'Layer 2' for the output layer and select the transfer function. In this example, the number of hidden nodes is taken as 90 and the transfer function of the hidden layer is 'TANSIG' for tansigmoid and output layer is 'LOGSIG' for logsigmoid. The window will be as shown in Fig. 3.49. Click 'Create' and then click 'Close'.

In the nntool GUI (Fig. 3.47), under the section 'Networks', click the created network and then click Open. Select the tab 'Train'. Under 'Training Info', select the Inputs as 'input_sun' and Targets as 'output_sun'. The training parameters tab allows the user to specify the number of epochs, learning rate (lr) and minimum gradient.

The NN toolbox also performs validation during the training. Validation is the process by which a part of the training data is segregated before training occurs and used to check the error in prediction of the NN at the end of each epoch during the training. If the error in predicted output during validation during the

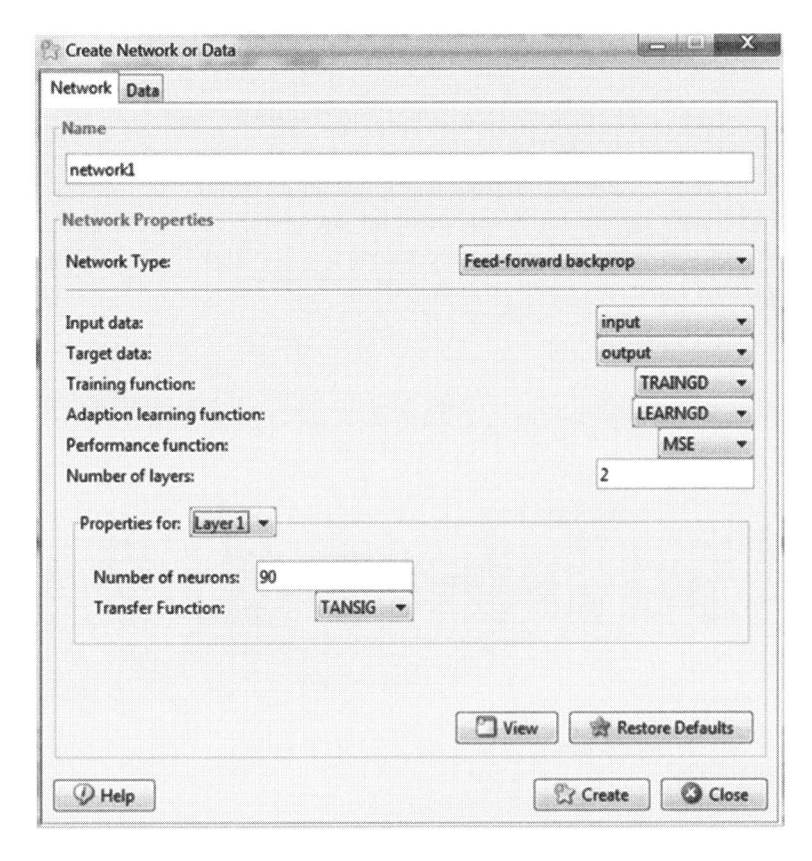

Fig. 3.49  GUI for creating the network

Fig. 3.50  GUI for Network1

current epoch is greater than the previous epoch for a number of iterations (given by max_fail), then the training is stopped even if the error in the gradient descent, usually mean squared error, is decreasing. The parameter max_fail can be set in the training parameters tab. This is shown in Fig. 3.50.

Click the 'Train Network' button to begin training of the NN. A window will be displayed showing the current status of the training as shown in Fig. 3.51. The real-time progress of the training can be seen in this window. This window also has three functions under the 'Plots' section marked as 'Performance', 'Training State',

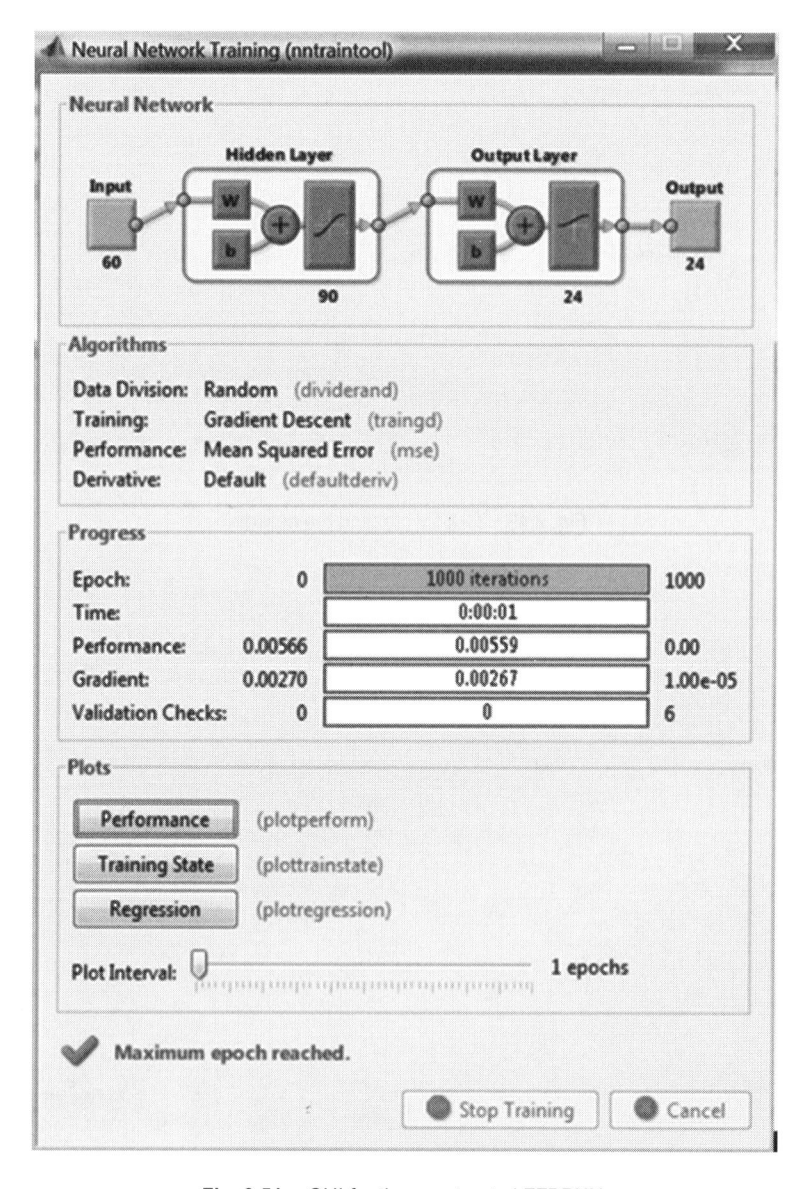

Fig. 3.51  GUI for the constructed FFBPNN

and 'Regression'. The 'Performance' button displays a window which shows the mean squared error with epoch. 'Training state' shows the gradient of the error as well as the number of validation checks performed with each epoch. 'Regression' gives a scatter plot with actual values on the $x$ axis and predicted values on the $y$ axis. It also draws the line of best fit of the scatter plot. This line will have a slope of 1 if the actual and predicted values match, as all the scatter points will lie on this line. The performance and training state of the training are updated in real time as the training progresses.

The NN is said to be trained when the weight values are optimised such that the sum squared error of the training data is below a certain threshold or the number of validation checks have exceeded a set point. The suitability of the NN for load forecasting can be known only by testing it against data not in the training set.

In order to test the NN, go back to the network properties in Fig. 3.50 and select the Simulate tab. Under Simulation Data, select 'test_in_sun' as Inputs. Mark the Supply Targets check box. Then, select 'test_out_sun' as Targets. Click 'Simulate Network'. The output of the simulation will be stored in the nntool GUI under the Output Data section. In order to analyze the simulated output data, it can be exported to the MATLAB workspace. In order to export the simulated output data to workspace, click 'Export' button in nntool GUI to display the 'Export' from 'Network/Data Manager' window. Select the simulated output data variable and press 'Export'. The data will now be saved to the workspace. The 'Export' from window is shown in Fig. 3.52.

In order to estimate the deviation in the predicted load from the actual value, mean absolute percentage error (MAPE) is used as a measure of accuracy. MAPE is given by,

$$\text{MAPE}(\%) = \frac{100}{n} \times \sum_{i=1}^{n} \left| \frac{A_i - F_i}{A_i} \right| \qquad (3.102)$$

where $A_i$ and $F_i$ are the actual and forecasted values, respectively, and $n$ is the number of samples.

In this example, the actual outputs are stored in 'test_out_sun' and the predicted outputs are stored in 'network_sun_outputs'. The actual and expected outputs are still in normalized form. Therefore, they are multiplied with the dividing factor of 20,000 to obtain the actual value in MW. The procedure to find the MAPE can be carried out through MATLAB commands as given in Tables 3.7 and 3.8.

The graph in Fig. 3.53 shows the variation between actual versus expected load for 24 hours on 26 December 2010, which is a Sunday.

Figure 3.54 shows the variation of MAPE from 25 December 2010 to 31 December 2010.

This forecasting application can be extended in a way similar to various forecasting applications like weather forecasting, financial forecasting, market forecasting, business forecasting, population forecasting, etc., by getting the historical data. Various NN models available in the MatLab ANN toolbox can also be used.

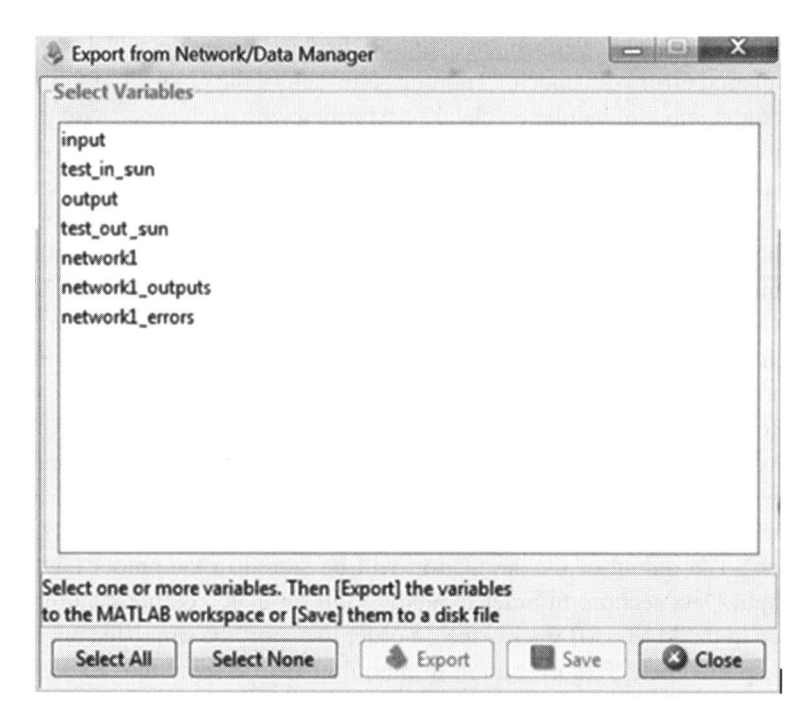

Fig. 3.52  GUI for exporting the result to workspace

Table 3.7  MATLAB commands to find MAPE

| | |
|---|---|
| delta = abs(test_out-network1_outputs); | % this calculates the absolute value of the error between |
| | % each of the actual and predicted values |
| pterr = (delta./test_out)*100; | % to calculate the percentage error for each data point |
| mape = sum(sum(pterr))/numel(pterr) | % sum(sum(pterr)) calculates the sum of the percentage |
| | % errors over all test hours and all test days. This is divided |
| | % by numel(pterr) which gives the total number of elements |
| | % in pterr |

Table 3.8  Actual and expected load obtained for each test day

| Test date | Day of the week | Hour | Actual load (MW) | Expected load (MW) | MAPE |
|---|---|---|---|---|---|
| 25/12/2010 | Saturday | 1 | 10545.57 | 11482.75 | 11.0869 |
| | | 2 | 10299.00 | 11727.95 | |
| | | 3 | 10191.14 | 11281.68 | |
| | | 4 | 10222.42 | 11453.65 | |
| | | 5 | 10379.57 | 11750.09 | |
| | | 6 | 10688.57 | 12355.75 | |
| | | 7 | 11108.71 | 12732.14 | |
| | | 8 | 11492.85 | 13294.01 | |

(*Continued*)

Table 3.8 (Continued)

| Test date | Day of the week | Hour | Actual load (MW) | Expected load (MW) | MAPE |
|---|---|---|---|---|---|
| | | 9 | 11741.85 | 13107.88 | |
| | | 10 | 11818.71 | 13325.13 | |
| | | 11 | 11774.00 | 12855.65 | |
| | | 12 | 11639.28 | 12404.66 | |
| | | 13 | 11411.42 | 12468.43 | |
| | | 14 | 11230.85 | 12319.84 | |
| | | 15 | 11156.00 | 12253.77 | |
| | | 16 | 11398.57 | 12674.44 | |
| | | 17 | 12023.00 | 13246.92 | |
| | | 18 | 12209.42 | 13917.11 | |
| | | 19 | 12193.71 | 13834.42 | |
| | | 20 | 12183.57 | 13704.45 | |
| | | 21 | 12062.85 | 13477.47 | |
| | | 22 | 11748.28 | 12520.34 | |
| | | 23 | 11227.85 | 12130.04 | |
| | | 24 | 10743.57 | 11271.68 | |
| 26/12/2010 | Sunday | 1 | 10416.71 | 11293.24 | 3.4829 |
| | | 2 | 10276.00 | 10656.59 | |
| | | 3 | 10237.42 | 10982.70 | |
| | | 4 | 10321.28 | 10437.48 | |
| | | 5 | 10544.71 | 10686.74 | |
| | | 6 | 10925.14 | 10883.81 | |
| | | 7 | 11385.71 | 12294.61 | |
| | | 8 | 11805.85 | 12669.82 | |
| | | 9 | 12227.85 | 12911.29 | |
| | | 10 | 12473.85 | 12325.30 | |
| | | 11 | 12577.42 | 12483.49 | |
| | | 12 | 12637.57 | 12298.30 | |
| | | 13 | 12626.28 | 12161.96 | |
| | | 14 | 12635.57 | 11949.23 | |
| | | 15 | 12735.00 | 11928.18 | |
| | | 16 | 13174.85 | 12565.11 | |
| | | 17 | 14056.85 | 13691.64 | |
| | | 18 | 14293.71 | 14150.36 | |
| | | 19 | 14221.00 | 13782.62 | |

(Continued)

**Table 3.8** (Continued)

| Test date | Day of the week | Hour | Actual load (MW) | Expected load (MW) | MAPE |
|---|---|---|---|---|---|
| | | 20 | 14028.57 | 13647.43 | |
| | | 21 | 13650.42 | 13789.69 | |
| | | 22 | 13120.71 | 13194.03 | |
| | | 23 | 12483.85 | 12506.40 | |
| | | 24 | 11978.28 | 11427.89 | |
| 27/12/2010 | Monday | 1 | 11689.00 | 11712.12 | 4.4234 |
| | | 2 | 11597.28 | 11063.67 | |
| | | 3 | 11607.57 | 11186.62 | |
| | | 4 | 11806.85 | 11454.09 | |
| | | 5 | 12270.42 | 12701.35 | |
| | | 6 | 12901.28 | 13779.17 | |
| | | 7 | 13436.42 | 14490.74 | |
| | | 8 | 13741.14 | 14268.77 | |
| | | 9 | 13919.57 | 14239.79 | |
| | | 10 | 13950.71 | 14208.96 | |
| | | 11 | 13807.00 | 13983.43 | |
| | | 12 | 13612.00 | 13855.91 | |
| | | 13 | 13384.85 | 13790.45 | |
| | | 14 | 13206.42 | 13738.40 | |
| | | 15 | 13222.14 | 13725.03 | |
| | | 16 | 13704.71 | 14408.92 | |
| | | 17 | 14800.57 | 15664.42 | |
| | | 18 | 15051.57 | 15999.89 | |
| | | 19 | 14902.14 | 15634.66 | |
| | | 20 | 14667.42 | 15460.64 | |
| | | 21 | 14185.28 | 15056.67 | |
| | | 22 | 13532.85 | 14514.81 | |
| | | 23 | 12772.57 | 13534.83 | |
| | | 24 | 12167.71 | 13104.11 | |
| 28/12/2010 | Tuesday | 1 | 11801.71 | 12606.79 | 10.5397 |
| | | 2 | 11610.71 | 12239.56 | |
| | | 3 | 11613.42 | 12755.02 | |
| | | 4 | 11808.42 | 13029.15 | |
| | | 5 | 12319.00 | 13785.32 | |
| | | 6 | 13071.00 | 14401.69 | |

(*Continued*)

Table 3.8 (Continued)

| Test date | Day of the week | Hour | Actual load (MW) | Expected load (MW) | MAPE |
|---|---|---|---|---|---|
| | | 7 | 13654.85 | 15241.25 | |
| | | 8 | 13830.71 | 14843.63 | |
| | | 9 | 13824.14 | 15349.87 | |
| | | 10 | 13705.00 | 15227.16 | |
| | | 11 | 13439.57 | 14521.01 | |
| | | 12 | 13131.00 | 14114.48 | |
| | | 13 | 12863.85 | 14361.36 | |
| | | 14 | 12644.28 | 14060.87 | |
| | | 15 | 12558.42 | 14619.45 | |
| | | 16 | 12915.00 | 15183.71 | |
| | | 17 | 14008.00 | 15667.37 | |
| | | 18 | 14335.85 | 15672.32 | |
| | | 19 | 14238.42 | 15779.06 | |
| | | 20 | 14042.28 | 15566.71 | |
| | | 21 | 13634.42 | 15550.27 | |
| | | 22 | 13000.00 | 14045.59 | |
| | | 23 | 12234.85 | 13135.32 | |
| | | 24 | 11629.28 | 13108.45 | |
| 29/12/2010 | Wednesday | 1 | 11260.28 | 13035.54 | 12.4594 |
| | | 2 | 11101.14 | 12924.62 | |
| | | 3 | 11075.28 | 11920.35 | |
| | | 4 | 11264.57 | 12170.75 | |
| | | 5 | 11794.14 | 12820.96 | |
| | | 6 | 12561.71 | 14023.82 | |
| | | 7 | 13168.71 | 14856.35 | |
| | | 8 | 13325.14 | 15289.95 | |
| | | 9 | 13247.85 | 14396.68 | |
| | | 10 | 13043.71 | 14831.96 | |
| | | 11 | 12775.71 | 14043.11 | |
| | | 12 | 12466.14 | 14177.82 | |
| | | 13 | 12211.42 | 13990.05 | |
| | | 14 | 11992.42 | 13603.93 | |
| | | 15 | 11910.57 | 13902.05 | |
| | | 16 | 12355.28 | 14456.96 | |
| | | 17 | 13487.85 | 14727.08 | |

(Continued)

Table 3.8  (Continued)

| Test date | Day of the week | Hour | Actual load (MW) | Expected load (MW) | MAPE |
|---|---|---|---|---|---|
| | | 18 | 13811.85 | 15851.22 | |
| | | 19 | 13740.71 | 15665.09 | |
| | | 20 | 13605.71 | 14971.58 | |
| | | 21 | 13249.57 | 14638.04 | |
| | | 22 | 12645.71 | 14482.11 | |
| | | 23 | 11950.28 | 13657.86 | |
| | | 24 | 11377.28 | 12310.27 | |
| 30/12/2010 | Thursday | 1 | 11045.57 | 12528.62 | 13.8869 |
| | | 2 | 10934.42 | 11762.13 | |
| | | 3 | 10951.42 | 11722.74 | |
| | | 4 | 11174.28 | 12560.62 | |
| | | 5 | 11691.85 | 12963.30 | |
| | | 6 | 12450.42 | 14191.89 | |
| | | 7 | 13017.85 | 14667.59 | |
| | | 8 | 13192.14 | 14967.94 | |
| | | 9 | 13139.00 | 14294.94 | |
| | | 10 | 12951.57 | 14223.37 | |
| | | 11 | 12682.42 | 14101.75 | |
| | | 12 | 12398.28 | 14640.50 | |
| | | 13 | 12152.00 | 13879.94 | |
| | | 14 | 11946.28 | 13568.28 | |
| | | 15 | 11838.14 | 13493.89 | |
| | | 16 | 12143.42 | 14762.35 | |
| | | 17 | 13066.85 | 15569.98 | |
| | | 18 | 13284.14 | 15263.78 | |
| | | 19 | 13128.42 | 15365.38 | |
| | | 20 | 12916.42 | 14573.73 | |
| | | 21 | 12547.14 | 14745.65 | |
| | | 22 | 11944.71 | 14479.46 | |
| | | 23 | 11229.85 | 12900.98 | |
| | | 24 | 10606.42 | 11990.45 | |
| 31/12/2010 | Friday | 1 | 10982.14 | 12094.95 | 14.277 |
| | | 2 | 10747.71 | 11825.30 | |

(Continued)

Table 3.8 (Continued)

| Test date | Day of the week | Hour | Actual load (MW) | Expected load (MW) | MAPE |
|---|---|---|---|---|---|
| | | 3 | 10660.71 | 11807.20 | |
| | | 4 | 10753.42 | 12013.83 | |
| | | 5 | 11062.85 | 12772.84 | |
| | | 6 | 11519.42 | 13745.78 | |
| | | 7 | 11957.71 | 14609.13 | |
| | | 8 | 12262.71 | 14678.06 | |
| | | 9 | 12418.71 | 14276.58 | |
| | | 10 | 12371.14 | 14028.99 | |
| | | 11 | 12157.85 | 13868.56 | |
| | | 12 | 11865.85 | 13580.93 | |
| | | 13 | 11615.42 | 13384.52 | |
| | | 14 | 11470.71 | 13178.94 | |
| | | 15 | 11491.28 | 12974.29 | |
| | | 16 | 11892.00 | 13514.17 | |
| | | 17 | 12758.71 | 14700.79 | |
| | | 18 | 12755.57 | 14787.62 | |
| | | 19 | 12522.71 | 14370.90 | |
| | | 20 | 12421.42 | 14478.06 | |
| | | 21 | 12282.28 | 13840.83 | |
| | | 22 | 11986.71 | 13433.03 | |
| | | 23 | 11493.42 | 12700.37 | |
| | | 24 | 10958.57 | 12282.46 | |

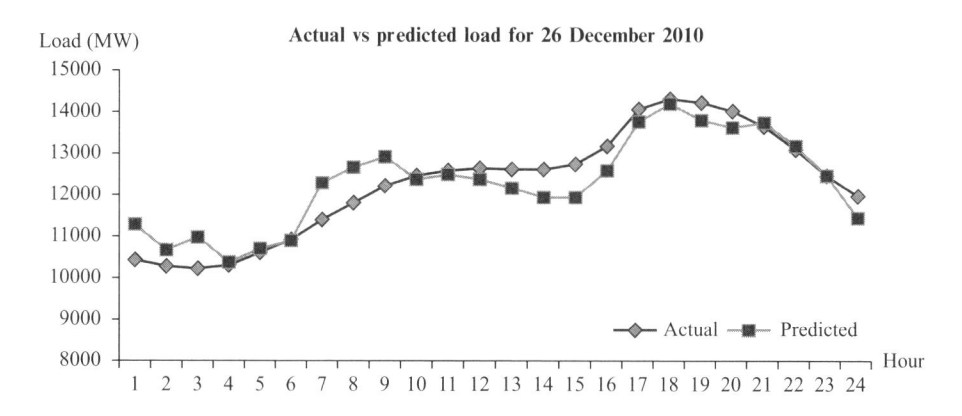

Fig. 3.53 Actual vs forecasted load

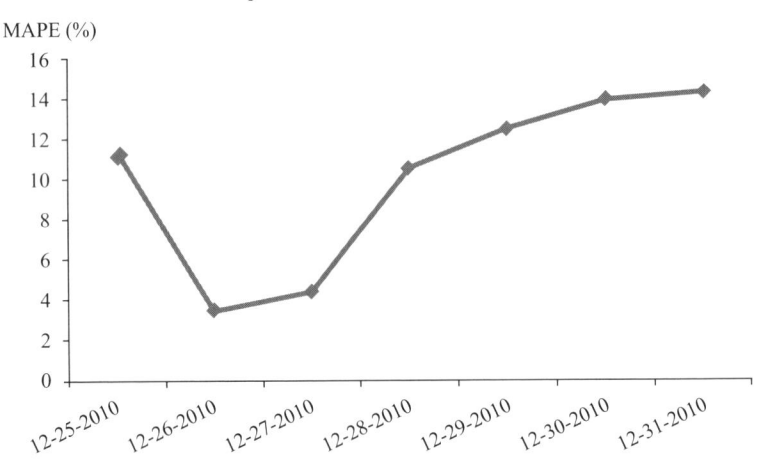

**Fig. 3.54** Mean absolute percentage error

## 3.13 ILLUSTRATIVE PROBLEMS

**Problem 3.1** _____

A single-layer neural network has the weights $w = [0.2\ 0.5\ 0.66\ 0.45]^T$ with bias $b = 0.3$. It is given an input of $I = [0.5\ 0.8\ 0.1\ 0.36]$. Find the net input to the output node.

*Solution:* From Eq. 3.1,
$$sum = I_1 W_1 + I_2 W_2 + \ldots + I_n W_n = 0.5 \times 0.2 + 0.8 \times 0.5 + 0.1 \times 0.66 + 0.36 \times 0.45 + 0.3 = 1.028$$

**Problem 3.2** _____

From the data in Problem 3.1, find the output if the sigmoidal activation function is used.

*Solution:*
Take $s = 0.3$ (Slope)
$f(sum) = 1/(1 + \exp(-s \times sum)) = 1/(1 + \exp(-0.3 \times 1.028)) = 0.5765$

**Problem 3.3** _____

Find the value of the derivative of the output w.r.t. sum for the data in problem 3.1 (Assume $s = 0.3$)

*Solution:* $f'(sum) = (d/d(sum))f(sum) = s \times (1-f) \times f = 0.3 \times (1 - 0.5765) \times 0.5765 = 0.0732$

**Problem 3.4** _____

A two-input, single-output, two-layer feed-forward neural network has the hidden-layer weights $w_{hp,j} = [0.3\ 0.4;\ 0.2\ 0.8;\ 0.1\ 0.6]$ and output-layer weights

$w_{pq,k} = [0.22\ 0.47\ 0.36]$. The bias values are $b_j = 0.5$ and $b_k = 0.45$. Consider a sigmoidal function with $s = 0.2$ as activation function. What is the output of the neural network if the input is $I = [0.5\ 0.2]^T$?

**Solution:** The hidden-layer net input is given by,

$sum_{1,j} = 0.3 \times 0.5 + 0.4 \times 0.2 = 0.23$
$sum_{2,j} = 0.2 \times 0.5 + 0.8 \times 0.2 = 0.26$
$sum_{3,j} = 0.1 \times 0.5 + 0.6 \times 0.2 = 0.17$

The hidden-layer output is given by,

$f(sum_{1,j}) = 1/(1 + \exp(-0.2 \times 0.23)) = 0.5115$
$f(sum_{2,j}) = 1/(1 + \exp(-0.2 \times 0.26)) = 0.513$
$f(sum_{3,j}) = 1/(1 + \exp(-0.2 \times 0.17)) = 0.5084$

The output-layer net input is given by,

$sum_{1,k} = 0.22 \times 0.5515 + 0.47 \times 0.513 + 0.36 \times 0.5084 = 0.5366$

The output-layer output is given by,

$f(sum_{1,k}) = 1/(1 + \exp(-0.2 \times 0.5366)) = 0.5268$

**Problem 3.5**

For Problem 3.4, find the output if an arctangent function is used as transfer function.

**Solution:** The hidden-layer output is given by,

$f(sum_{1,j}) = (2/\pi) \times \tan^{-1}(s \times sum_{1,j}) = (2/\pi) \times \tan^{-1}(0.2 \times 0.23) = 0.0292$
$f(sum_{2,j}) = (2/\pi) \times \tan^{-1}(s \times sum_{2,j}) = (2/\pi) \times \tan^{-1}(0.2 \times 0.26) = 0.033$
$f(sum_{3,j}) = (2/\pi) \times \tan^{-1}(s \times sum_{2,j}) = (2/\pi) \times \tan^{-1}(0.2 \times 0.17) = 0.0216$

The output-layer net input is given by,

$sum_{1,k} = 0.22 \times 0.0292 + 0.47 \times 0.033 + 0.36 \times 0.0216 = 0.0297$

The output-layer output is given by,

$f(sum_{1,k}) = (2/\pi) \times \tan^{-1}(s \times sum_{1,k}) = (2/\pi) \times \tan^{-1}(0.2 \times 0.0297) = 0.00378$

**Problem 3.6**

For Problem 3.4, find the output if the transfer function is a hyperbolic transfer function.

**Solution:** The hidden-layer output is given by,

$f(sum_{1,j}) = \tanh(s \times sum_{1,j}) = \tanh(0.2 \times 0.5115) = 0.1019$
$f(sum_{2,j}) = \tanh(s \times sum_{2,j}) = \tanh(0.2 \times 0.513) = 0.1022$
$f(sum_{3,j}) = \tanh(s \times sum_{3,j}) = \tanh(0.2 \times 0.5084) = 0.1013$

The output-layer net input is given by,

$sum_{1,k} = 0.22 \times 0.1019 + 0.47 \times 0.1022 + 0.36 \times 0.1013 = 0.1069$

The output-layer output is given by,

$f(sum_{1,k}) = \tanh(s \times sum_{1,k}) = \tanh(0.2 \times 0.1069) = 0.0213$

## Problem 3.7

For the data given in Problem 3.4, find the change in weights using gradient descent method given target is 0.7 and $\eta = 0.6$.

**Solution:** From Eq. 3.18,

$$\chi_{pq,k} = -2 \times 0.2 \times (0.7 - 0.5268) \times 0.5268 \times (1 - 0.5268) = -0.0172$$

The change in output weights are given by Eq. 3.19,

$\Delta w_{11,k} = -0.6 \times -0.0172 \times 0.5115 = 0.0053$
$\Delta w_{12,k} = -0.6 \times -0.0172 \times 0.513 = 0.00531$
$\Delta w_{13,k} = -0.6 \times -0.0172 \times 0.5084 = 0.00526$

From Eq. 3.32,

$\chi_{h1,j} = \chi_{pq,k} \times w_{11,k} \times f(sum_{1,j}) \times (1 - f(sum_{1,j})) = -0.0172 \times 0.22 \times 0.5115$
$\quad \times (1 - 0.5115) = -0.000945$
$\chi_{h2,j} = \chi_{pq,k} \times w_{12,k} \times f(sum_{2,j}) \times (1 - f(sum_{2,j})) = -0.0172 \times 0.47 \times 0.513$
$\quad \times (1 - 0.513) = -0.002$
$\chi_{h3,j} = \chi_{pq,k} \times w_{13,k} \times f(sum_{3,j}) \times (1 - f(sum_{3,j})) = -0.0172 \times 0.36 \times 0.5084$
$\quad \times (1 - 0.5084) = -0.0015$

From Eq. 3.34,

$\Delta w_{11,j} = -0.6 \times 0.5 \times -0.000945 = 0.000283$
$\Delta w_{12,j} = -0.6 \times 0.2 \times -0.000945 = 0.000113$
$\Delta w_{21,j} = -0.6 \times 0.5 \times -0.002 = 0.0006$
$\Delta w_{22,j} = -0.6 \times 0.2 \times -0.002 = 0.00024$
$\Delta w_{31,j} = -0.6 \times 0.5 \times -0.0015 = 0.00045$
$\Delta w_{32,j} = -0.6 \times 0.2 \times -0.0015 = 0.00018$

## Problem 3.8

For the data given in Problem 3.4, find the change in weights in the next iteration of Problem 3.7 using a momentum factor $\mu = 0.7$.

**Solution:**

$w_{11,k}(new) = w_{11,k}(old) + \Delta w_{11,k} = 0.22 + 0.0053 = 0.2253$
$w_{12,k}(new) = w_{12,k}(old) + \Delta w_{12,k} = 0.47 + 0.00531 = 0.47531$
$w_{13,k}(new) = w_{13,k}(old) + \Delta w_{13,k} = 0.36 + 0.00526 = 0.36526$
$w_{11,j}(new) = w_{11,j}(old) + \Delta w_{11,j} = 0.3 + 0.000283 = 0.30028$
$w_{12,j}(new) = w_{12,j}(old) + \Delta w_{12,j} = 0.4 + 0.00011 = 0.40011$
$w_{21,j}(new) = w_{21,j}(old) + \Delta w_{21,j} = 0.2 + 0.0006 = 0.2006$
$w_{22,j}(new) = w_{22,j}(old) + \Delta w_{22,j} = 0.8 + 0.00024 = 0.80024$
$w_{31,j}(new) = w_{31,j}(old) + \Delta w_{31,j} = 0.1 + 0.00045 = 0.10045$
$w_{32,j}(new) = w_{32,j}(old) + \Delta w_{32,j} = 0.6 + 0.00018 = 0.60018$

The hidden-layer net input is given by,

$sum_{1,j} = 0.30028 \times 0.5 + 0.40011 \times 0.2 = 0.2301$
$sum_{2,j} = 0.2006 \times 0.5 + 0.80024 \times 0.2 = 0.2603$
$sum_{2,j} = 0.10045 \times 0.5 + 0.60018 \times 0.2 = 0.1702$

The hidden-layer output is given by,
$f(sum_{1,j}) = 1/(1 + \exp(-0.2 \times 0.2301)) = 0.5115$
$f(sum_{2,j}) = 1/(1 + \exp(-0.2 \times 0.2603)) = 0.513$
$f(sum_{3,j}) = 1/(1 + \exp(-0.2 \times 0.1702)) = 0.5085$

The output-layer net input is given by,
$sum_{1,k} = 0.22 \times 0.5515 + 0.47 \times 0.513 + 0.36 \times 0.5085 = 0.5367$

The output-layer output is given by,
$f(sum_{1,k}) = 1/(1 + \exp(-0.2 \times 0.5367)) = 0.52681$
$\chi_{pq,k} = -2 \times 0.2 \times (0.7 - 0.52681) \times 0.52681 \times (1-0.52681) = -0.0172$

The change in output weights are given by Eq. 3.36.
$\Delta w_{11,k} = -0.6 \times -0.0172 \times 0.5115 + 0.7 \times 0.0053 = 0.00898$
$\Delta w_{12,k} = -0.6 \times -0.0172 \times 0.513 + 0.7 \times 0.00531 = 0.00901$
$\Delta w_{13,k} = -0.6 \times -0.0172 \times 0.5085 + 0.7 \times 0.00526 = 0.00892$
$\chi_{h1,j} = \chi_{pq,k} \times w_{11,k} \times f(sum_{1,j}) \times (1 - f(sum_{1,j})) = -0.0172 \times 0.2253 \times 0.5115 \times (1 - 0.5115) = -0.000968$
$\chi_{h2,j} = \chi_{pq,k} \times w_{12,k} \times f(sum_{2,j}) \times (1 - f(sum_{2,j})) = -0.0172 \times 0.47531 \times 0.513 \times (1 - 0.513) = -0.002$
$\chi_{h3,j} = \chi_{pq,k} \times w_{13,k} \times f(sum_{3,j}) \times (1 - f(sum_{3,j})) = -0.0172 \times 0.36526 \times 0.5085 \times (1-0.5085) = -0.00157$
$\Delta w_{11,j} = -0.6 \times 0.5 \times -0.000968 + 0.7 \times 0.000283 = 0.000485$
$\Delta w_{12,j} = -0.6 \times 0.2 \times -0.000968 + 0.7 \times 0.000113 = 0.000195$
$\Delta w_{21,j} = -0.6 \times 0.5 \times -0.002 + 0.7 \times 0.0006 = 0.001$
$\Delta w_{22,j} = -0.6 \times 0.2 \times -0.002 + 0.7 \times 0.00024 = 0.0004$
$\Delta w_{31,j} = -0.6 \times 0.5 \times -0.00157 + 0.7 \times 0.00045 = 0.000786$
$\Delta w_{32,j} = -0.6 \times 0.2 \times -0.00157 + 0.7 \times 0.00018 = 0.00031$

## Problem 3.9

Consider a four-input two-cluster KNN with the weight values $w$ = [0.1 0.5; 0.7 0.3; 0.4 0.7; 0.2 0.9]. Two input patterns $I$ = [1 −1 1 1;1 −1 −1 −1] are given to the neural network. Calculate the *ED* to each cluster for each input pattern.

**Solution:** Euclidean distances of first input,
$ED(1) = (0.1 - 1)^2 + (0.7 - (-1))^2 + (0.4 - 1)^2 + (0.2 - 1)^2 = 4.7$
$ED(2) = (0.5 - 1)^2 + (0.3 - (-1))^2 + (0.7 - 1)^2 + (0.9 - 1)^2 = 2.04$
Euclidean distances of second input,
$ED(1) = (0.1 - 1)^2 + (0.7 - (-1))^2 + (0.4 - (-1))^2 + (0.2 - (-1))^2 = 7.1$
$ED(2) = (0.5 - 1)^2 + (0.3 - (-1))^2 + (0.7 - (-1))^2 + (0.9 - (-1))^2 = 8.44$

## Problem 3.10

In Problem 3.9, update the weights after the first input pattern is presented and then find and check the *ED*s of the second input pattern. Use a learning rate of 0.6.

**Solution:** Since cluster 2 is the winner cluster for the first input pattern, the weights corresponding to the second cluster are updated.

$w_{12}(new) = w_{12}(old) + 0.6 \times (I_1 - w_{12}(old)) = 0.5 + 0.6 \times (1 - 0.5) = 0.8$
$w_{22}(new) = w_{22}(old) + 0.6 \times (I_2 - w_{22}(old)) = 0.3 + 0.6 \times (-1 - 0.3) = 0.48$
$w_{32}(new) = w_{32}(old) + 0.6 \times (I_3 - w_{32}(old)) = 0.4 + 0.6 \times (1 - 0.4) = 0.76$
$w_{42}(new) = w_{42}(old) + 0.6 \times (I_4 - w_{42}(old)) = 0.9 + 0.6 \times (1 - 0.9) = 0.96$

Euclidean distances of second input,

$ED(1) = (0.1 - 1)^2 + (0.7 - (-1))^2 + (0.4 - (-1))^2 + (0.2 - (-1))^2 = 7.1$
$ED(2) = (0.8 - 1)^2 + (0.48 - (-1))^2 + (0.76 - (-1))^2 + (0.96 - (-1))^2 = 10.21$

### Problem 3.11

The input vectors to a Hamming net are given as $I = [1\ 1\ 1\ -1\ -1\ 1\ -1;\ 1\ -1\ -1\ 1\ 1\ 1\ 1;\ -1\ 1\ 1\ -1\ 1\ -1\ -1]$. Calculate the HD of this input set to $S = [1\ 1\ 1\ 1\ 1\ -1\ -1]$.

**Solution:** $HD(I_1, S) = 3$ since three components are different between $I_1$ and $S$.
Similarly, $HD(I_2, S) = 4$ and $HD(I_3, S) = 2$.

### Problem 3.12

Calculate the scalar product of $I$ and $S$. Choose $I$ and $S$ as in Problem 3.11.

**Solution:** Scalar product of $I_1$ and $S$, $I_1'S = n - 2\ HD(I_1, S) = 7 - 2 \times 3 = 1$
Similarly, $I_2'S = n - 2\ HD(I_2, S) = 7 - 2 \times 4 = -1$
$I_3'S = n - 2\ HD(I_3, S) = 7 - 2 \times 2 = 3$

### Problem 3.13

A Hamming network has the weights $w = [0.3\ -0.1;\ -0.5\ 0.7;\ 0.6\ -0.6]$ and bias $b = [1.3\ 0.5]$. It is given as input pattern of $I = [1\ -1\ -1]$. Determine its closeness to the bipolar standard patterns $S_1 = [-1\ -1\ -1]$ and $S_2 = [1\ 1\ 1]$. Take $\alpha = 0.3$.

**Solution:** Computation in the first layer,

$O_1(0) = 1.3 + 1 \times 0.3 + -1 \times -0.5 + -1 \times 0.6 = 1.5$
$O_2(0) = 0.5 + 1 \times -0.1 + -1 \times 0.7 + -1 \times -0.6 = 0.3$

Computation in the second layer, $t = 0$

$O_1(0+1) = f(1.5 - 0.3 \times 0.3) = 1.41,\ O_2(0+1) = f(0.3 - 0.3 \times 1.5) = f(-1.5) = 0$
$O_1(1) = 1.41,\ O_2(1) = 0$
$O_1$ has non-zero output; therefore, $S_1$ is the winner (i.e., $I$ is closer to $S_1$).

### Problem 3.14

A Hopfield network has the following standard binary patterns: $S = [1\ 1\ 1;\ 1\ 0\ 1;\ 1\ 0\ 0]$. Find the weight matrix.

**Solution:** Since binary patterns are used, we use Eq. (3.45) to find the weight values.
$h$ is the number of input patterns
when $h = 1$,
$w_{11} = 0$
$w_{12} = (2 \times 1 - 1) \times (2 \times 1 - 1) = 0$

Similarly, $w_{13} = w_{21} = w_{22} = w_{23} = w_{31} = w_{32} = w_{33} = 0$
when $h = 2$
$w_{11} = 0$
$w_{12} = (2 \times 1 - 1) \times (2 \times 0 - 1) = -1$
$w_{13} = (2 \times 1 - 1) \times (2 \times 1 - 1) = 1$
$w_{22} = 0$
$w_{23} = (2 \times 0 - 1) \times (2 \times 1 - 1) = -1$
$w_{33} = 0$. The weight matrix is a symmetric matrix. Therefore,
$w_{21} = w_{12} = -1$
$w_{31} = w_{13} = 1$
$w_{32} = w_{23} = -1$

when $h = 3$
$w_{11} = 0$
$w_{12} = -1$
$w_{13} = -1$
$w_{22} = 0$
$w_{23} = (2 \times 0 - 1) \times (2 \times 0 - 1) = 1$
$w_{33} = 0$
$w_{21} = w_{12} = -1$
$w_{31} = w_{13} = -1$
$w_{32} = w_{23} = 1$

Adding the same terms according to Eq. 3.45,
$w_{11} = 0, w_{22} = 0, w_{33} = 0$
$w_{12} = -1 + -1 = -2$
$w_{13} = 1 + -1 = 0$
$w_{21} = -1 + -1 = -2$
$w_{23} = -1 + 1 = 0$
$w_{31} = 1 + -1 = 0$
$w_{32} = -1 + 1 = 0$

## Problem 3.15

A bi-directional associative memory has the following paired binary patterns $S = [1 -1 -1; 1\ 1 -1]$ paired to $T = [1 -1; 1\ 1]$. Calculate the weight matrix.

*Solution:* As bipolar values are used, we can use Eq. 3.48,
$w_{11} = S_{11} \times T_{11} + S_{21} \times T_{12} = 1 \times 1 + 1 \times -1 = 0$
$w_{21} = S_{12} \times T_{11} + S_{22} \times T_{12} = -1 \times 1 + 1 \times -1 = -2$
$w_{31} = S_{13} \times T_{11} + S_{23} \times T_{12} = -1 \times 1 + -1 \times -1 = 0$
$w_{12} = S_{11} \times T_{21} + S_{21} \times T_{22} = 1 \times 1 + 1 \times 1 = 2$
$w_{22} = S_{12} \times T_{21} + S_{22} \times T_{22} = -1 \times 1 + 1 \times 1 = 0$
$w_{32} = S_{13} \times T_{21} + S_{23} \times T_{22} = -1 \times 1 + -1 \times 1 = -2$

Therefore, the weight values are $w = [0\ 2; -2\ 0; 0\ -2]$

## Problem 3.16

An ART1 network has 2 nodes in the input layer, interface layer, and output layer. The bottom-up weights are given by $u = [0.3\ 0.5;\ 0.2\ 0.6]$ and top-down weights are $d = [0.1\ 0.3;\ 0.6\ 0.1]$. Take $\alpha = 4$ and vigilance parameter $v = 0.3$. The network is given an input $S = [0.5\ 0.6]$. Find the cluster to which $S$ belongs.

**Solution:**

$I = S = [0.5\ 0.6]$
$\|S\| = 0.5 + 0.6 = 1.1$
$O_1 = I_1 u_{11} + I_2 u_{12} = 0.5 \times 0.3 + 0.6 \times 0.5 = 0.45$
$O_2 = I_1 u_{21} + I_2 u_{22} = 0.5 \times 0.2 + 0.6 \times 0.6 = 0.46$
$O_1 > O_2$, so output cluster 1 is selected
$I_1 = S_1 d_{11} = 0.5 \times 0.1 = 0.05$
$I_2 = S_2 d_{12} = 0.6 \times 0.3 = 0.18$
$\|I\| = I_1 + I_2 = 0.05 + 0.18 = 0.23$
$\|I\|/\|S\| = 0.23/1.1 = 0.209 < v$, the vigilance parameter
Cluster 2 is selected

Again, $I_1 = S_1 d_{21} = 0.5 \times 0.6 = 0.3$
$I_2 = S_2 d_{22} = 0.6 \times 0.1 = 0.06$
$\|I\| = I_1 + I_2 = 0.3 + 0.06 = 0.36$
$\|I\|/\|S\| = 0.36/1.1 = 0.327 > v$, the vigilance parameter
Therefore, $S$ is assigned to cluster 2

## Problem 3.17

For Problem 3.16, calculate the new updated weights.

**Solution:** As the cluster selected is 2, only the weights associated with it are updated
The new bottom-up weights are given by,
$u_{21} = \alpha \times I_1/(\alpha - 1 + \|I\|) = 4 \times 0.3 / (4 - 1 - 0.36) = 0.454$
$u_{22} = \alpha \times I_2/(\alpha - 1 + \|I\|) = 4 \times 0.06 / (4 - 1 - 0.36) = 0.091$

The top-down weights are given by,
$d_{21} = I_1 = 0.3;\ d_{22} = I_2 = 0.06$

## Problem 3.18

Consider an SVM whose SV is given by the equation $w^T x + b = 0$. What is the width of the SV margin?

**Solution:** The margin is given by $2/\|w\|$

## Problem 3.19

Prove that the kernel $K(x, y)$ is symmetric, where $x$ and $y$ represent input parameters.

**Solution:** $K(x, y) = \varphi(x)^T \varphi(y) = \varphi(y)^T \varphi(x)$ as $x$ and $y$ are input parameters and are single-column vectors
Therefore, $K(x, y) = K(y, x)$

## Problem 3.20

Given two input vectors $x = [0.3\ 0.6]$ and $y = [0.4\ 0.8]$, convert them into the mapped feature space given in Eq. 3.97.

*Solution:*

$\varphi(x) = (1, \sqrt{2}x_1, \sqrt{2}x_2, x_1^2, x_1^2, \sqrt{2}x_1x_2)$
$\varphi(x) = (1, 0.4242, 0.8485, 0.09, 0.36, 0.2545)$
$\varphi(y) = (1, 0.5656, 1.1313, 0.16, 0.64, 0.4525)$

## Problem 3.21

If an SVM has overfitted the training data, what would happen to the SVs?

*Solution:* Most, if not all, of the training data will become SVs. For a good generalization, only a relatively few points must become SVs.

## Problem 3.22

Suggest a suitable kernel for classifying two sets of data which can be separated by an S curve on the input space

*Solution:* A suitable kernel would be a cubic polynomial given by,

$$K(x, y) = (1 + x^T y)^3$$

A Gaussian kernel function can also be used.

## Problem 3.23

What are the general techniques that can be used to prevent overfitting of training data in SVM?

*Solution:* To prevent overfitting in SVM,
(a) decrease C in Eq. (3.90)
(b) use a smaller-degree polynomial as a kernel function
(c) try to get more training data

## SUMMARY

- The BPNN algorithm was critical to the advances in NNs because of the limitations of one-layer and two-layer networks of the first-generation networks. Indeed, backpropagation played a critically important role in the resurgence of the NN field in the mid-1980s.
- Prior to the development of backpropagation, attempts to use perceptrons with more than one layer of weights were frustrated by what was called the 'weight assignment problem' (i.e., how one allocates the error at the output layer between the two [or more] layers of weights when there is no firm mathematical foundation for doing so).
- Kolomogorov's theorem describes that any function of n variables may be represented by the superposition of a set of 2n+1 univariate functions to derive the upper bound for the required number of hidden units as one greater than twice the number of input units.
- A cluster unit is considered as a winner if the ED between the weight vector associated with it and the given input pattern is the minimum when compared among the other neighbourhood cluster units.
- Commonly and mostly used second-generation NNs are BPNNs, KNNs, LVQ network, HNNs, Hopfield neural networks, bi-directional associative memory, adaptive resonance theory (ART) networks, BMNN, radial basis neural networks, and SVMs.
- Learning vector quantization network, developed by Kohonen in 1989, is a supervised neural network where the input vectors are trained for a specific class or group already mapped in the training set.

- Lippmann [22] modelled a two-layer bipolar network called HNN. The first layer is the Hamming net and the second layer is the MAXNET. The first layer is a feed-forward type network which classifies the input patterns based on minimum HD. The HD between any two vectors is the number of components in which the vectors differ.
- Associative memory neural networks are single-layer nets in which the weights are determined for the network to store a set of pattern associations. Each association is an input ($I$)–output ($O$) vector pair. If the input vector ($I$) is the same as that of the output vector ($O$) associated, then the neural network is called as Auto-AMNN.
- The Hopfield network can be used for pattern recognition to identify the standard pattern associated with the input test pattern.
- Bi-directional associative memory can be used for mapping two unrelated patterns through hetero-association.
- The key innovation of ART is the use of a degree of expectations called 'vigilance parameter' (i.e., the user-specified value to decide the degree of similarity essential for the input patterns to be assigned to a cluster unit).
- An SVM is a learning algorithm typically used for classification problems (text categorization, handwritten character recognition, image classification, etc.). The simplest example is a linear classifier (i.e., a classifier that separates a set of objects into their respective groups with a line).
- Electrical load forecasting is the process by which the electrical load at a future time is predicted based on past values of load as well as weather, economic, and demographic factors. Load forecasting is an important tool for institutions such as electric utilities, ISOs, financial institutions, and transmission planning.

# EXERCISES

## Part A  Short-answer Questions

1. What are the features of the second-generation NN?
2. Why is backpropagation neural network so called?
3. What is a 'sigmoidal function'?
4. What is an 'arctangent function'?
5. Draw the output characteristic plot of a hyperbolic tangent function.
6. What is forward pass and backward pass in the training of BPNN?
7. How do you select the number of hidden-layer neurons according to Kolomogorov's theorem?
8. What is a 'momentum factor'?
9. What is sum squared error in neural network training?
10. Why KNN is called 'self-organizing map'?
11. How is a cluster unit considered to be a winner?
12. Sometimes some patterns keep changing their groups in every trial while clustering in KNN. Give reasons.
13. Why do we need a MAXNET in HNN?
14. What is a Hamming distance between two patterns (−1 1 1 1 1 −1) and (1 1 1 1 1 1)?
15. How are weights and bias values set in an HNN?
16. Why is Hopfield neural network also called a recurrent network?
17. What is meant by a 'content-addresable memory'?
18. How are units updated in the HNN (i.e., synchronous or asynchronous mode)? Does it affect the convergence?
19. Give the significance between auto-associative and hetero-associative neural networks?
20. How are the weights initialized in BAM?
21. What do you understand by 'resonance in ART networks'?
22. What is a vigilance parameter in ART networks?
23. How are the top-down weights and bottom-up weights set in an ART-1 network?
24. What is the common feature involved in HNN and BMNN?
25. What is the role of the principle of annealing in BMNN?
26. What is a 'radial basis function'?
27. How is SVM different from other neural networks?
28. What are 'support vectors'?
29. What is 'Validation' during training neural networks?

## Part B Long-answer Questions

1. Derive the generalized expression for the feed-forward BPNN with a neat sketch for its weight upgradation with linear function $\varphi(I) = I$ in both hidden-layer and sigmoidal function output layer.
2. Explain the weight updation process in a BPNN network in both hidden and output layers using sigmoidal function.
3. How can BPNN be used for character recognition problems? Explain with necessary illustrations.
4. Briefly explain the architecture of a BPNN with a neat sketch.

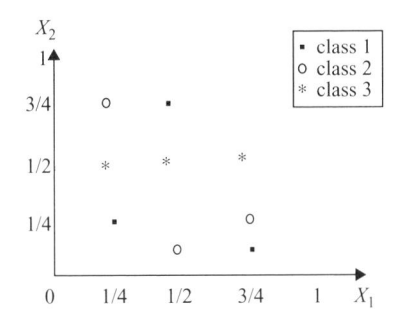

5. Design a feed-forward network for the example training set containing linearly non-separable patterns of three classes as shown in the following figure:
6. Explain the steps involved in clustering by KNN.
7. Discuss the architecture and algorithm of KNN with a neat sketch.
8. Explain the architecture and algorithm of an HNN.
9. How is HNN used in the character recognition problem? Illustrate with examples.
10. Explain the architecture and algorithm of the Hopfield neural network.
11. Discuss the weight updation procedure in Hopfield network.
12. What is a 'Boltzmann machine neural network'? Explain its architecture with a neat sketch. Also discuss the procedure involved in updation of weights.
13. Explain the procedures involved in the weight updation in SVM.

## Part C Practical Exercises

1. Develop a MATLAB Program using BPN algorithm to forecast the weather parameters using historical data. Test the model's suitability in forecasting applications.
2. Solve XOR problem using BPNN with the help of MATLAB Program.
3. Create a medical diagnosis ANN tool using BPNN.
4. Develop a grading model using KNN for clustering the marks of your class for a particular subject into five groups and grade it as S, A, B, C, and D. Modify the MATLAB Program already given in this chapter for implementation.
5. Develop a speech recognition model using BPNN.
6. Develop a MATLAB code for ART-1 network, radial basis neural network, and SVM.
7. Solve a travelling salesman problem using BMNN.
8. Solve a simple optimisation problem with a single variable using Hopfield network.

## REFERENCES

[1] Vreeken, Jilles, *Spiking Neural Networks, An Introduction*, Technical Report UU-CS, Issue 2003–008, Utrecht University: Information and Computing Sciences, 2003.
[2] Rumelhart, D.E., G. R. Hinton, and R. J. Williams, 'Learning internal representations by error propagation', in D. E. Rumelhart and J. L. McClelland (eds), Parallel Distributed Processing, MIT Press, Cambridge, MA, vol. 1, 1986.
[3] Parker, D., 'Learning logic', Invention Report, S81-64, File 1, Office of Technology Licensing, Stanford University, Palo Alto, CA., 1972.

[4] Werbos, P., 'Beyond Regression: New Tools for Prediction and Analysis in the Behavioral Sciences', PhD dissertation, Harvard University, Boston, MA, 1974.
[5] Papert, Seymour, Minsky, and Marvin Lee, *Perceptrons: an introduction to computational geometry*, MIT Press, Cambridge, Mass, 1988.
[6] Amari, S. 1972, 'Characteristics of random nets of analog neuron-like elements', 'IEEE Transactions on Systems, Man, and Cybernetics' SMC-2, pp. 643–647.
[7] Rosenblatt, F., *Principles of Neuro Dynamics: Perceptrons and the Theory of Brain Mechanisms*, Spartan Books, Washington, DC, 1961.
[8] Bose, N. K., and P. Liang, *Neural Network Fundamentals with Graphs, Algorithms and Applications*, Tata McGraw-Hill, New Delhi, 1998.
[9] Cichocki, A., *Neural Networks for Optimisation and Signal*, John Wiley, Chichester, 1996.
[10] Věra Kůrková, Kolmogorov's theorem and multilayer neural networks, Neural Networks, Elsevier Science Ltd, Oxford, UK, Volume 5 Issue 3, pp. 501–506, 1992.
[11] Hassoun, Mohamad H., *Fundamentals of Artificial Neural Networks*, MIT Press, 1995.
[12] Luo, Fa-Long and Rolf Unbehauen, *Applied Neural Networks for Signal Processing*, Cambridge University Press, Cambridge, 1997.
[13] Pao, Yoh-Han, *Adaptive Pattern Recognition and Neural Networks*, Addison-Wesley, Reading, MA, 1989.
[14] Schalkoff, Robert J., *Artificial Neural Networks*, McGraw-Hill International Edition, Singapore, 1997.
[15] Swingler, Kevin, *Applying Neural Networks a Practical Guide*, Academic Press, London, 1996.
[16] Tsoukalas, Lefteri H. and Robert E. Uhrig, *Fuzzy and Neural Approaches inv Engineering*, John Wiley, New York, 1996.
[17] Sejnowski, T. and C. Rosenberg 1987, Parallel networks that learn to pronounce English text', Complex Systems, Vol. 1, pp. 145–68.
[18] Parker, D., 'Optimal algorithms for adaptive networks: Second order Hebbian learning', *Proceedings of the First IEEE International Conference on Neural Networks, San Diego, CA*, vol. II, pp. 593–600, 1987.
[19] Professor Teuvo Kohonen, *Self-Organization and Associative Memory*, Springer Series in Information Sciences, Volume 8, 1989.
[20] Pattern Recognition by Self-organizing Neural Networks, Gail A. Carpenter, Stephen Grossberg, MIT Press, 1991.
[21] Kohonen, T., *'Improved Versions of Learning Vector Quantization'* International Joint Conference on Neural Networks, Vol. 1, San Diego, CA, pp. 545–550, 1990.
[22] Richard, P. Lippmann, *Introduction to Computing with Neural Nets*, IEEE ASSP Publisher, 1987.
[23] Hopfield, J. J., Neural networks and physical systems with emergent collective computational abilities, *Proceedings of the National Academy of Sciences of the USA*, vol. 79 no. 8 pp. 2554–2558, April 1982.
[24] Abu-Mostafa, Yaser S., (Author), Malik Magdon-Ismail, *Learning From Data*, AMLBook publisher, 2012.
[25] Bart Kosko, 'Bidirectional Associative Memories', IEEE Transactions On Systems, Man, and Cybernetics, Vol. 18, no.1, January/February 1988.
[26] Laurene Fausett, *Fundamentals of Neural Networks: Architectures, Algorithms and Applications*, Pearson Education India, 2006.
[27] Gail, A., Carpenter and Stephen Grossberg, Associative learning,adaptive pattern recognition and cooperative-competetive decision making by neu- neural networks. In H. Szu, editor. Hybrid and Optical Computing. SPIE, 1986.
[28] Geoffrey, E. Hinton and Terrence J., Sejnowski, Analyzing Cooperative Computation. In *Proceedings of the 5th Annual Congress of the Cognitive Science Society*, Rochester, New York, May 1983.
[29] Ackley, David H.; Hinton, Geoffrey E.; and Sejnowski, Terrence J. 1985, A learning algorithm for Boltzmann machines. Cognitive Science 9(1), pp. 147–169.
[30] Moody, J. and C. J. Darken 1989, 'Fast learning in networks of locally tuned processing units,' Neural Computation, Vol. 1, 281–294.
[31] Hush, D. R., and B. G. Horne1993, Signal Processing Magazine, IEEE, vol. 10, issue 1, pp. 8–39, 1283.
[32] Wasserman, P. D., *Advanced Methods in Neural Computing*, Van, Nostrand Reinhold, New York, pp. 155–161, 1993.
[33] Cortes, C.; and Vapnik, V 1995, Support-vector networks. Machine Learning, vol. 20, issue 3, p. 273.
[34] Vapnik, Vladimir N., *Statistical Learning Theory*. Wiley-Interscience, 1989.
[35] Mercer, J. 1909, 'Functions of positive and negative type and their connection with the theory of integral equations', *Philosophical Transactions of the Royal Society A* 209, pp. 441–458.
[36] Soliman, S. A., Ahmad Mohammad Al-Kandari, *Electrical Load Forecasting: Modeling and Model Construction*, Elsevier (26 May 2010).

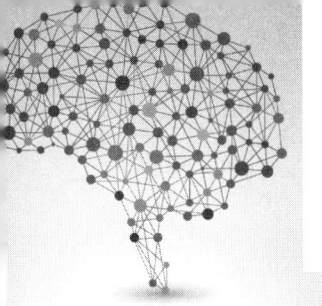

# 4 Artificial Neural Networks—Third Generation

*'We are what we think'*

*Buddha*

### LEARNING OBJECTIVES

*After reading this chapter, the reader will be able to:*
- Explain the third-generation models: spiking neural networks and pulsed neural networks
- Learn threshold-based firing models
- Discuss conductance-based response models
- Elaborate on the basic features of spike propagation algorithm
- Analyse electrical load forecasting using spike propagation algorithm

## 4.1 INTRODUCTION TO THIRD-GENERATION NEURAL NETWORKS

The first-generation neurons developed in the 1940s and 1950s did not involve any encoding of the temporal aspect of information processing [1]. They function as an integrate-and-fire units which will fired if the internal state (defined as the weighted sum of inputs to each neuron) reached a threshold. It does not consider the time when the threshold has exceeded.

The second-generation neurons developed from the 1950s to 1990s also do not concentrate on rate encoding and the internal state is defined in a similar manner of the first-generation neurons. However, they used a mathematically defined activation function having a continuous output using a smooth sigmoidal or radial basis function, instead of a fixed threshold value, for output determination [2].

It is a known fact that, Rumelhart's widely used backpropagation (BP) training algorithms [3], which has a continuous and differentiable activation function, was significantly more powerful than the one based on first-generation neurons and could solve complex pattern recognition problems [4]. However, the computational power of the neuron still did not reach its full potential because the temporal information about individual spikes is not represented. However, Spiking neurons have been developed and adapted for artificial neural networks (ANNs) to overcome this shortcoming by communicating via the precise timing of spikes or a sequence of spikes. In the literature, spiking neurons have been referred to as third-generation neurons.

## 4.2 INTRODUCTION TO SPIKES

Let us try to revisit a biological neural network as discussed in Chapter 2. Information is processed between neurons as neuronal signals. Here, sending and receiving end neuron are commonly referred as presynaptic neuron and post-synaptic neuron, respectively. Suppose we place a fine electrode close to the soma or axon, the neuronal signals can be observed. The voltage trace in a typical recording shows a sequence of short pulses, called action potentials or spikes.

A chain of pulses emitted by a single neuron is usually called a 'spike train', a sequence of stereotyped events which occur at regular or irregular intervals. The duration of an action potential is typically in the range of 1 to 2 ms with amplitude of about 100 mV. Examples of action potentials are shown in Fig. 4.1. Since all spikes of a given neuron look alike, the shape of the action potential does not carry any information. Rather, it is the number and the timing of spikes which matter.

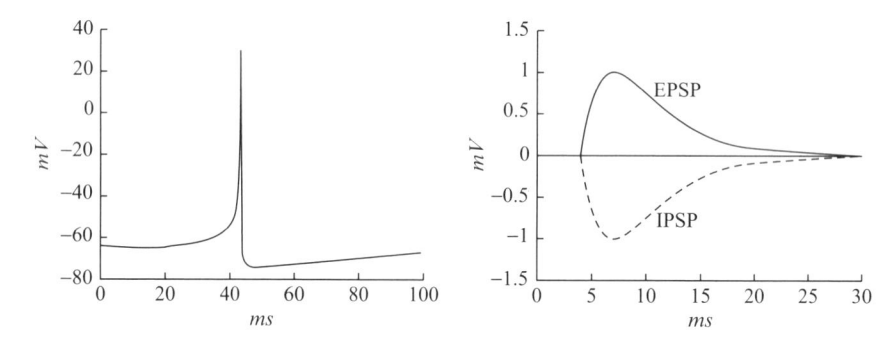

**Fig. 4.1** Action potentials (EPSP–Excitatory Post-Synaptic Potential; IPSP–Inhibitory Post-Synaptic Potential)

The potential difference between the interior of the cell (soma) and its surroundings is called the 'membrane potential'. This potential is directly affected by the post-synaptic potentials (PSPs) generated by the spikes received from pre-synaptic neurons. If the membrane potential reaches a threshold value, then an action potential (spike) is triggered and sent out through the axon and its branches to the post-synaptic neurons.

If the PSP is positive, it is said to be excitatory post-synaptic potential (EPSP) and if the change is negative, the synapse is inhibitory post-synaptic potential (IPSP). When the spike is transmitted through the axon, there exists an associated delay called 'axonal delay'. At rest, the cell membrane already has a strong negative polarization of about −65 mV [5]. An input at an EPSP reduces the negative polarization of the membrane and is therefore called 'depolarizing'. Likewise, an IPSP increases the negative polarization of the membrane even further and is called 'hyperpolarizing'. Single EPSPs have amplitudes in the range of 1 mV and the threshold for spike initiation is about 20–30 mV [6] above the resting potential.

Now, let us try to understand some of the parameters associated with a spike as in Fig. 4.1. A presynaptic neuron is denoted by $i$ and a post-synaptic neuron by $j$. The set of all the presynaptic neurons connected to a neuron $j$ is denoted as $\Sigma_j = \{i / i \text{ presynaptic to } j\}$. Similarly, the set of all the post-synaptic neurons connected to the neuron $i$ is denoted as $\Sigma_j = \{j / j \text{ postynaptic to } i\}$. The instant at which a neuron $j$ emits an action potential is called the firing time of the $j^{th}$ neuron. The firing time can be denoted as $t_j^{(f)}$, with $f$ varying from 1 to $n$. The spike train of neuron $j^{th}$ is then characterized by the set of firing times given by Eq. (4.1).

$$F_j = \{t_j^{(1)}, t_j^{(2)}, \ldots, t_j^{(n)}\} \quad (4.1)$$

where, $t_j^{(n)}$ is the most recent spike of neuron $j^{th}$ denoted by $\hat{t}$. The PSP is the response generated by a spike from the presynaptic neuron $i$ in the post-synaptic neurons $j^{th}$ and has the shape shown in Fig. 4.2. It is important to note that, due to interneuron distances and finite axonal transmission times, there may be a delay between the emission of a spike and the beginning of its corresponding PSP. Equation (4.2) gives a mathematical formulation for a generic PSP originated in neuron $j$ by a spike emitted by neuron $i$ [7].

$$\varepsilon_{ij}(t) = \left[ \exp\left(-\frac{t - t_i^{(f)}}{\tau_m}\right) - \exp\left(-\frac{t - t_i^{(f)} - \Delta_{ij}^{ax}}{\tau_s}\right) \right] \times H\left(t - t_i^{(f)} - \Delta_{ij}^{ax}\right) \quad (4.2)$$

The Eq. (4.2) can be also written as in Eq. (4.3).

$$\varepsilon_{ij}(t) = \left[ \frac{t - t_i^{(f)} - \Delta_{ij}^{ax}}{\tau} \exp\left(1 - \frac{t - t_i^{(f)} - \Delta_{ij}^{ax}}{\tau}\right) \right] \times H\left(t - t_i^{(f)} - \Delta_{ij}^{ax}\right) \quad (4.3)$$

Once the spike is generated, the membrane potential does not come back to its resting potential $P_{rest}$ immediately, but will go through a segment of elevated hyperpolarization lower than the $P_{rest}$. During the course of rising or falling of a spike from the $i^{th}$ neuron, there will be no generation of another spike simultaneously from the same neuron. The generation of another spike during this course is prevented due to absolute refractoriness effect. During this effect, the value of the action potential (i.e., after the generation of a spike) is found to be more negative and can be called spike after potential (SAP).

The SAP resist the generation of another spike from the $i^{th}$ neuron during the course of occurrence of a spike from the same neuron. This period of reduced sensitivity after a spike is called as the relative refractory period. Therefore, spiking is sequential emitted and two or more spikes cannot occur at the same time from the same neuron. Figure 4.3 shows the generation of the spike from the rest potential $P_{rest}$ and the variation of the membrane potential during and after the course of rising or falling of a spike. The membrane potential increases from the rest potential $P_{rest}$ and reaches the threshold $\theta$ and the range is denoted by $x$. The absolute refractory period and the relative refractory period is denoted by $y$ and $z$, respectively.

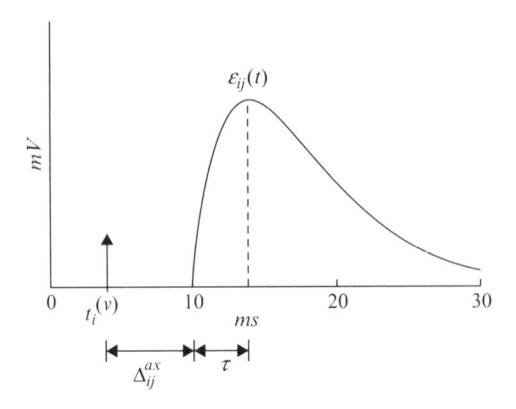

**Fig. 4.2** Typical shape of the EPSP (Eq. 4.3)

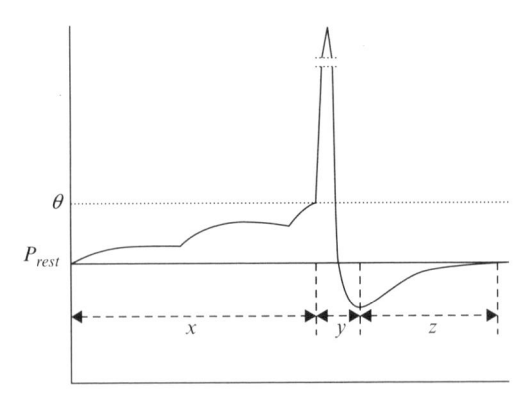

**Fig. 4.3** Variation of membrane potential

During mathematical modelling of spiking neurons, one should incorporate the neuro-computational features of real neurons. Some of the real cortical neuronal spiking responses are shown in Fig. 4.4.

Here, the responses of the 20 types of real (cortical) neurons during the injection of simple DC pulses is given and are briefed later.

(a) **Tonic spiking:** Spikes are fired by a neuron as long as the presence of the input current. This kind of behaviour can be observed in the three types of cortical neurons: regular spiking excitatory neurons (RS), low-threshold spiking neurons (LTS), and fast spiking inhibitory neurons (FS).
(b) **Phasic spiking:** At the onset of the input, the neuron fires only a single spike.
(c) **Tonic bursting:** When stimulated by the input current, the neuron fires periodic bursts of spikes. This kind of spiking behaviour can be observed in chattering neurons in cat neocortex. The frequency of the bursts may be as high as 50 Hz. It is believed that such kind of neuron contributes to the gamma-frequency oscillations in the brain.
(d) **Phasic bursting:** At the onset of the input, the neuron fires only a single burst.

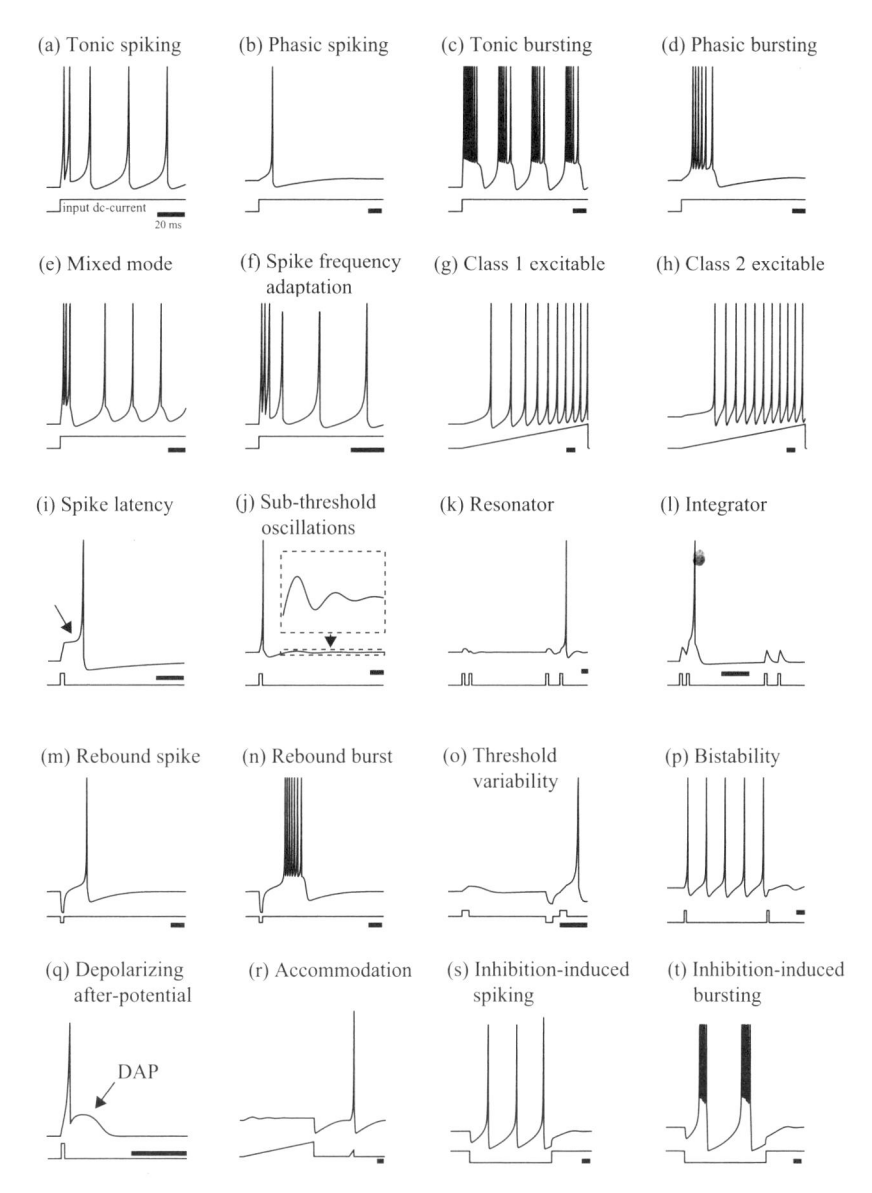

**Fig. 4.4** Neuronal responses for a simple spiking neuronal model
*Source:* Electronic version of this figure and reproduction permissions are freely available at; Eugene.Izhikevich@braincorporation.com

(e) **Mixed model:** The neuron fires a phasic burst at the onset of stimulation, and then switch to the tonic spiking mode. The intrinsically bursting excitatory neurons in mammalian neocortex may exhibit this behaviour.

(f) **Spike frequency adaptation:** The neuron fires tonic spikes with decreasing frequency. RS neurons usually exhibit adaptation of the inter spike intervals, when these intervals increase until a steady state of periodic firing is reached, whereas FS neurons show no adaptation.

(g) **Class 1 excitability:** Here, the frequency of tonic spiking depends on the strength of the input (i.e., the weaker is the DC current), and the lower will be the spike frequency. The frequency of tonic spiking of neocortical neurons may vary from 2 to 200 MHz.

(h) **Class 2 excitability:** The neuron is unable to fire low-frequency spike trains and will either fire a high-frequency spike train or will not fire at all.

(i) **Spike latency:** The neuron fires with a delay that depends on the strength of the stimulation. RS neurons in mammalian cortex can have latencies of tens of milliseconds.

(j) **Sub-threshold oscillations:** The neuron exhibits oscillatory potentials.

(k) **Frequency preference and resonance:** Due to the resonance phenomenon, a neuron having oscillatory potentials can respond selectively to the inputs having frequency content similar to the frequency of sub-threshold oscillations. Such neurons are called 'resonators'.

(l) **Integration and coincidence detection:** The neuron without oscillatory potentials acts as an integrator. The higher the frequency, the more likely it fires.

(m) **Rebound spike:** The neuron fires a post-inhibitory (rebound) spike when it receives, and then is released from an inhibitory input.

(n) **Rebound burst:** The neuron fires post-inhibitory bursts. It is believed that such bursts contribute to the sleep oscillations in the thalamo-cortical system.

(o) **Threshold variability:** A biological neuron has a variable threshold that depends on the prior activity of the neurons. Therefore, it may not fire in response to a single brief excitatory pulse, but will fire if a brief inhibitory input is applied just before the same excitatory pulse.

(p) **Bi-stability of resting and spiking states:** The neuron exhibits two stable modes of operation: resting and tonic spiking (or even bursting). The modes are switched by an excitatory or inhibitory pulse.

(q) **Depolarizing after-potentials:** After firing a spike, the membrane potential of a neuron may exhibit a prolonged after-hyperpolarization (AHP) or a prolonged depolarized after potential (DAP). In any case, such a neuron has shortened refractory period and becomes super excitable.

(r) **Accommodation:** The neuron loses its sensitivity to a strong but slowly increasing stimulus (*flat ramp*) and does not fire, although it may fire in response to a weak but fast increasing stimulus (*step ramp*).

(s) **Inhibition-induced spiking:** The neuron remains quiescent as long as there is no input, but fires when hyperpolarized by an inhibitory input or an injected current.

(t) **Inhibition-induced bursting:** Similar to the previous case, the neuron can fire tonic bursts of spikes in response to a steady hyperpolarization.

The previous output responses give clarity of the spiking behaviour of neurons.

## 4.3 SPIKE NEURON MODELS

It is an established fact that neural processing and information coding inside brain is done with the help of spike trains and not real valued signals. It was first proposed in 1952 by Hodgkin–Huxley [8]. These findings led to the proposal of more detailed models of biological neurons known as the 'spiking neuron models'. However, the exactness of the model poses a real challenge. If we really try to look from lower level of mechanism in the neural activity, then we have to start from the large number of ion channels due to sodium and potassium concentration levels, pores in the cell membrane which open and close depending on the voltage and the presence (or absence) of various chemical messenger molecules. In addition, one of the spiking neurons can be simulated through compartmental models, where each small segment of a neuron is described by a set of ionic equations, aim at a description of these processes.

On the other hand, when choosing a higher level of abstraction, there is no need to worry about the spatial structure of a neuron or about the exact ionic mechanisms. We only have to consider the neuron as a simple homogeneous unit, which generates spikes if the total excitation is sufficiently large, as with rate models. It is also clear that the choice of which model to use is a very important decision that must be based on what kind of phenomena or neuronal behaviour we wish to simulate. Based on the literature survey, spiking neuron models can be classified into three main classes, namely threshold-fire, conductance-based, and compartmental models [9].

The following sections briefly discuss these models.

### 4.3.1 Threshold-fire Models

The threshold-fire models are based on the temporal summation of all contributions to the membrane potential $u(t)$ received from all presynaptic neurons. If this contribution exceeds a threshold, then the post-synaptic neuron will fire. In the simplest case one assumes that the PSPs simply sum up linearly in the soma. In this section, we will discuss two of these models, the integrate-and-fire and the spike response model (SRM).

#### 4.3.1.1 Integrate-and-fire Models

The models consist of an RC circuit as shown in Fig. 4.5. The circuit is charged by an input current $I$. If the voltage across the capacitor $C$ reaches a threshold $\theta$, the circuit is shunted and a pulse is transmitted to other neurons (lower right). A pulse sent out by a presynaptic neuron and travelling on the presynaptic axon (left), is low-pass filtered first (middle) before it is fed as a current pulse $I(t - t_i^{(f)})$ into the integrate-and-fire circuit. The voltage response of the RC circuit to the presynaptic pulse is the PSP $\varepsilon(t - t_i^{(f)})$. The driving current is divided into two components, one for charging the capacitor and the other for going through the resistor, therefore the equation can be written as in (4.4).

**260** Soft Computing with MATLAB Programming

$$I(t) = \frac{u(t)}{R} + C\frac{du}{dt} \quad (4.4)$$

If the time constant $\tau_m = RC$ (the membrane time constant) is incorporated in the Eq. (4.4), we can write the modified equation as in (4.5).

$$\tau_m \frac{du}{dt} = -u(t) + RI(t) \quad (4.5)$$

Here the voltage $u(t)$ across the capacitor $C$ can be related to the membrane potential of a neuron.

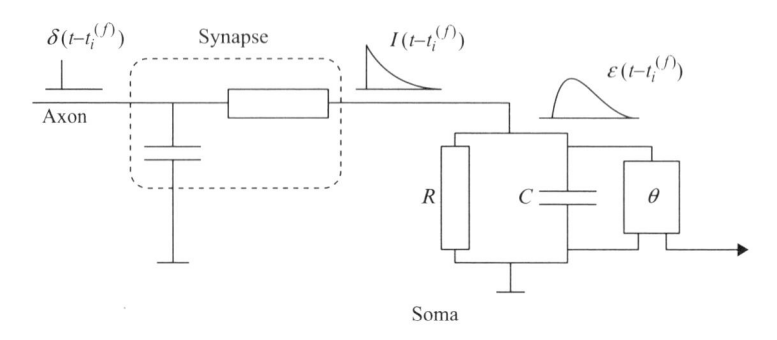

**Fig. 4.5** Integrate-and-fire neuronal model

The Eq. (4.5) is a first-order linear differential equation and cannot describe full neuronal spiking behaviour. Therefore, it has to be supplemented by a threshold condition. A pulse will be emitted at $t \cong t^{(f)}$ when the threshold has attained a value of $\theta$ (i.e., when $u\{t^{(f)}\} \cong \theta$). The shape of the spike is not described explicitly but only the firing time $t^{(f)}$ is used. Immediately after $t^{(f)}$, the potential is reset to $P_{rest}$ and the integration starts over again from this point. The reset potential is defined by Eq. (4.6)

$$\lim_{t \to t^{(f)}; t > t^{(f)}} u(t) = P_{rest} \quad (4.6)$$

The behaviour of the integrate-and-fire neuronal model can be understood by the Eqs (4.5 and 4.6). Let us give a constant input current $I_0$ at a rest potential $P_{rest} \cong 0$ to the integrate–and–fire neuron. Integrating Eq. (4.6) with the initial condition $u(t^{(1)}) \cong P_{rest} \cong 0$, we get the following:

$$u(t) \cong RI_0 \left[1 - e\left(-\frac{t - t^{(1)}}{\tau_m}\right)\right] \quad (4.7)$$

Let us assume that a spike occurred $t \cong t^{(1)}$ and no further spike will occur as long as $u(t) < \theta$. If $t \cong t^{(2)}$, then the spike will be generated. Therefore, the condition $u(t^{(2)}) = \theta$, or $\theta \cong RI_0 \left[1 - e\left(-\frac{t^{(2)} - t^{(1)}}{\tau_m}\right)\right]$ has to be satisfied. Let $T = t^{(2)} - t^{(1)}$, then we get the following result:

$$T \cong \tau_m \ln \frac{RI_0}{RI_0 - \theta} \tag{4.8}$$

The neuron will continuously fire with a period $T$ as long the constant current $I_0$ is given as input. In order to quantify, an absolute refractoriness $\Delta^{abs}$ is added to the period $T$. Therefore, the frequency in this case is the mean firing rate $f$ and is given as follows:

$$f = \left[ \Delta^{abs} + \tau_m \ln \frac{RI_0}{RI_0 - \theta} \right]^{-1} \tag{4.9}$$

### 4.3.1.2 Spike Response Model (SRM)

Let the state of a typical neuron $j$ be described by as single variable $u_j(t)$. If $u_j(t)$ crosses below $\left(\frac{du}{dt} > 0\right)$, a threshold $\theta$ at a moment $t_j^{(v)}$, then a spike is generated. As already mentioned in (4.1), the set of all firing times of neuron $j$ is denoted as follows:

$$F_j = \{t_j^{(v)}; 1 \leq v \leq n\} = \{t | u_j(t) = \theta\} \tag{4.10}$$

There are two different processes influencing the value of the state variable $u_j(t)$. The first processes can be seen as the contribution of all presynaptic neurons $i \in \Gamma_j$, which form the neuron response to presynaptic spikes. It is given by Eq. (4.11).

$$h(t) = \sum_{i \in \Gamma_j} \sum_{t_i^{(v)} \in \Gamma_j} W_{ij} \in_{ij} \left( t - \hat{t}_j, t - t_i^{(v)} - \Delta_{ij}^{ax} \right) + I_j^{ext} \tag{4.11}$$

where $W_{ij}$ is the synaptic efficacy, $I_j^{ext}$ is an external excitation, and $\in_{ij}$ is the PSP, as shown in Fig. 4.3 and Eqs (4.2) and (4.3). The post-synaptic can either be EPSP or IPSP. In most cases, $\Delta^{ax}$ is neglected and does not appear in the equations. To make it clear, let $s \cong t - t_j^v - \Delta_{ij}^{ax}$.

The second process is the reset of $u_j(t)$ till it reaches $P_{rest}$, including the negative overshoot which typically follows a spike during the refractory period. This term describes the response of neuron $j$ to its own spikes and is modelled by a response kernel $\eta_j \left( t - \hat{t}_j \right)$, which is a function only of the last firing time of $j(\hat{t}_j)$. More formally, all previous firing times of $j$ should be considered, as in $\sum \eta_j \left( t - t_j^{(v)} \right)$, but the approach adopted earlier does not alter the results. Suppose, if the linear response of the membrane potential is considered as the driving current $I^{ext}$, the expression for the last term of Eq. (4.11) is the given by the Eq. (4.12).

$$\int_0^\infty x(t - \hat{t}_j, s) I^{ext}(t - s) ds \tag{4.12}$$

The total PSP is also given by the Eq. (4.13).

$$h(t\,|\,\hat{t}_j) \cong \sum_j W_{ij} \sum_{t_j^{(v)}} \in_{ij}(t-\hat{t}_j,s) + \int_0^\infty x(t-\hat{t}_j,s)I^{ext}(t-s)ds \quad (4.13)$$

The dependence of the elapsed time after the generation of the last spike at $\hat{t}_j$ is due to the opening of many ion channels so that the membrane resistance is reduced.

The state $u_j(t)$ of a typical neuron $j$ at time $t$ is given by the linear superposition of all contributions and can be written as in Eq. (4.14).

$$u_j(t) \cong \eta(t-\hat{t}_j) + h(t\,|\,\hat{t}_j) \quad (4.14)$$

In addition to the use of $\eta$ kernel, refractoriness can be also modelled by an increase in the threshold after a spike so that $\theta \to \theta(t-\hat{t}_j)$. If the objective is preventing the neuron from firing, an increase in the threshold is equivalent to the hyper polarization of the membrane potential and is called 'dynamic threshold' (Fig. 4.6).

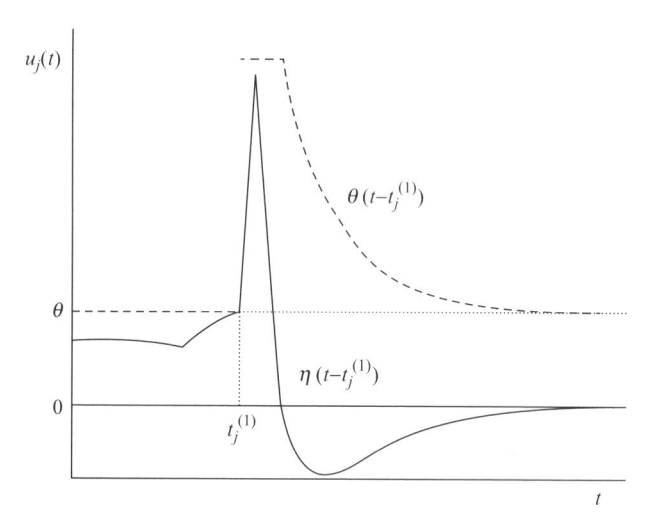

**Fig. 4.6** Membrane potential due to dynamic threshold [5]

A simplified $SRM_0$ can be constructed with little modifications to the complete model and is shown in Fig. 4.7. Here, the spike is replaced by a $\delta$-pulse and $\Delta^{ax} \cong 0$. First let us suppose that $\in_{ij}$ is the same for all presynaptic neurons and independent of the first argument $t-\hat{t}_j$. Then, if the kernel $x$ is also kept independent of the first argument, the Eq. (4.14) can be rewritten as follows:

$$u_j(t) \cong \eta(t-\hat{t}_j) + \sum_j W_{ij} \sum_{t_j^{(v)}} \in_0(s) + \int_0^\infty k_0(s)I^{ext}(t-s)ds \quad (4.15)$$

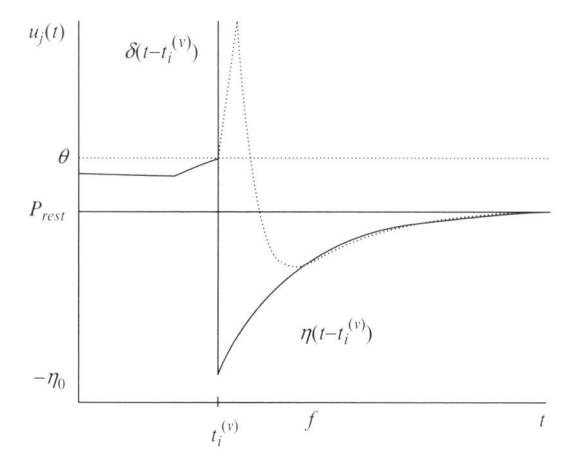

**Fig. 4.7** Simplified model [5]

It can be established that the SRM, with the appropriate kernels, is equivalent to the integrate-and-fire model; furthermore, with a different choice of kernels, the SRM also approximates the Hodgkin-Huxley equations with time-dependent input.

### 4.3.2 Conductance-based Response Model

This model mimics the intricate behaviour of ionic channels (Fig. 4.8). As these channels open and close, their conductance value changes accordingly, yielding a set of differential equations describing the process. The variations among the models in this class are mostly due to the choice of which channels to use and the parameters of the resulting differential equations. This section will be focussed on the classic model of Hodgkin-Huxley.

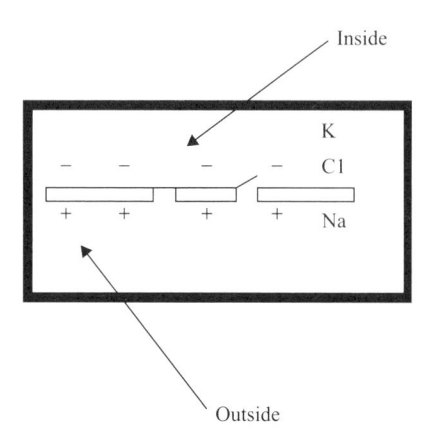

**Fig. 4.8** Ionic channels (opening and closing)

The Hodgkin-Huxley model (Fig. 4.9) is generally accepted as the classic description of a conductance model. Hodgkin and Huxley [8], based on their experiments with the giant axon of the squid, found three types of ionic current,

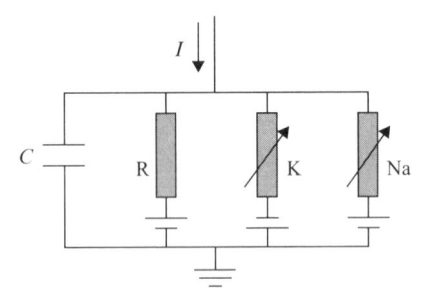

**Fig. 4.9** Hodgkin-Huxley representation

namely sodium (Na), potassium (K) and a leak current. The first two types are controlled by specific voltage dependent ion channels. The third type takes care of other channels and consists mainly of $Cl^{-1}$.

The representation Hodgkin-Huxley is shown as an RC-circuit model. The cell membrane is a good insulator and acts as a capacitor. Besides the capacitor, there are three resistances, one for each ion channel considered in the model. The potassium and sodium channels are voltage dependent. The different ion concentration, inside and outside the cell, yields the '*Nernst Potential*' that is represented by the batteries. The total current ($I$) must be equal to the sum of the currents of the branches and can be given by the Eq. (4.16).

$$I(t) \cong I_c(t) + \sum_{ch} I_{ch}(t) \tag{4.16}$$

since $I_c = C\dfrac{du}{dt}$

$$C\frac{du}{dt} = -\sum_{ch} I_{ch} + I(t) \tag{4.17}$$

Characterizing each channel by its conductance (or resistance), the leak conductance ($g_L$) is constant and the other two ($g_K$ and $g_{Na}$) are time and voltage dependent. Furthermore, considering that a channel is either open or closed, three more variables were added [10], yielding Eq. (4.18) for the sum of the three currents.

$$\sum_{ch} I_{ch} \cong g_{Na} m^3 h(u - E_{Na}) + g_K n^4 (u - E_K) + g_L (u - E_L) \tag{4.18}$$

If the channels are open always, then the currents could be defined simply by $I_x \cong g_X u$. Then the Eq. (4.18) can be written as given here:

$$C\frac{du}{dt} = -g_{Na} m^3 h(u - E_{Na}) + g_K n^4 (u - E_K) + g_L (u - E_L) \tag{4.19}$$

The three new variables are given by the following differential equations:

$$\frac{dm}{dt} = \alpha_m(u)(1 - m) - \beta_m(u)m \tag{4.20}$$

$$\frac{dn}{dt} = \alpha_m(u)(1-n) - \beta_m(u)n \qquad (4.21)$$

$$\frac{dh}{dt} = \alpha_h(u)(1-h) - \beta_h(u)h \qquad (4.22)$$

The typical parameters for the aforementioned equations for $\alpha_X$ and $\beta_X$ are given here in Table 4.1.

Table 4.1 (Values of $\alpha_X$ and $\beta_X$)

| X | $\alpha_X$ (u/mV) | $\beta_X$ (u/mV) |
|---|---|---|
| m | $(2.5 - 0.1u)/[\exp(2.5 - 0.1u) - 1]$ | $4\exp(-u/18)$ |
| h | $0.07\exp(-u/20)$ | $[1/[\exp(3 - 0.1u) + 1]$ |
| n | $(0.1 - 0.01 u)/[\exp(1 - 0.1u) - 1]$ | $0.125\exp(-u/80)$ |

The functions $-\alpha_X$ and $\beta_X$ are shown in Table 4.1 which are empirical equations from the adaptations made to fit the experimental data. Equations (4.19, 4.20, 4.21, and 4.22) define the Hodgkin-Huxley model.

### 4.3.2.1 Compartment Models

The complexity of a biological neuron is better captured by compartment models, which take into account the spatial structure of the dendritic tree and also model the synaptic transmission at a greater level of detail. With this approach, it is possible to consider other ion currents, beyond the $Na^+$ and $K^+$ currents incorporated in the Hodgkin-Huxley model ($Ca^{2+}$ and Ca-mediated K currents which are related to neuronal adaptation.

It is obvious that in biological neurons, the dendrites receive synaptic inputs from other neurons. These inputs activate ion channels in the dendrites, which create PSPs that are propagated to the cell body (soma), where voltage-activated ion channels may create action potentials to its terminal branches, in which they form synapses connecting to other neurons.

The basic idea of compartmental models is to divide these components into smaller uniform components or compartments. Each compartment is then modelled with equations describing the equivalent electrical circuit. The use of appropriate differential equations for each compartment enables the simulation of their behaviour as well as their interactions with other compartments. This notion of an equivalent electrical circuit for a small piece of cellular membrane is the basis for all compartmental models.

An equivalent circuit for neural compartment model is shown in Fig. 4.10, where $u$ is the membrane potential, which appears across the membrane capacitance $C$. It may cause a current flow through the axial resistance $R_a$ (or $R_a'$) into or out the compartment when there is a difference $u - u''$ (or $u - u'$) between the two compartments. The resistor $G_{ch}$ crossed by an arrow represents a generic variable channel conductance, specific to a particular ion combination. The corresponding

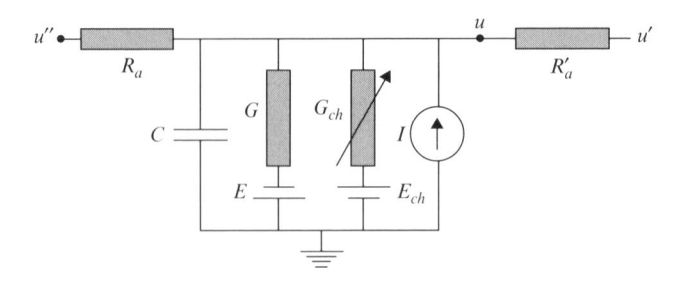

Fig. 4.10 Equivalent circuit of a neural compartment model

equilibrium potential is represented by the battery in series with the conductance. The other resistor is the leakage conductance $G$, and the associated equilibrium potential $E$ is typically close to $P_{rest}$. The current $I$ represents an external input. The resulting differential equation is given as follows:

$$C\frac{du}{dt} \cong (E-u)G + \sum_{ch}(E_{ch}-u)G_{ch} + \frac{(u'-u)}{R'_a} + \frac{(u''-u)}{R_a} + I \quad (4.23)$$

Equation (4.23) describes a linear compartmental model. Other more complex compartmental models would also contain non-linear conductance for various ionic currents, or could model synaptic currents at a greater level of detail.

### 4.3.2.2 Rate Models

The rate models, also known as *sigmoidal units*, are the most traditional and widely used models for the analysis of learning and memory in artificial neural networks (ANNs). As already mentioned, the first choice to be made before the construction of a neuronal model happens to be the level of abstraction; and, therefore, the complexity of the model. The class of rate models, first proposed in [11], represents the highest abstraction level, as they neglect the pulse structure of the neuronal systems and the neural activity is described only in terms of spike rate. A good example of rate model is the Perceptron.

The response $r_j$ of a neuron $j$ is also a rate and depends on a sigmoidal function. The input to this function is the summation of all the excitations applied to $j$ (i.e., all the output rates of the presynaptic neurons $i \in \Gamma_j$)

$$r_j = g\left(\sum_{i \in \Gamma_j} W_{ij} r_i\right) \quad (4.24)$$

where $w_{ij}$ is the synaptic strength between neurons $i$ and $j$. Equation (4.24) is the starting point of standard neural network (NN) theory. The dependence of a sigmoidal function may be explained by the Eq. (4.25).

$$r_j(p) = \begin{cases} \dfrac{Mp^0}{\sigma^n + p^n} & \text{for } p \geq 0 \\ 0 & \text{for } p < 0 \end{cases} \quad (4.25)$$

The Eq. (4.25) is known as Naka-Rushton function [12], which relates the stimulus intensity $p$, the net PSP, to the response or spike rate of a neuron observed in several visual areas such as lateral geniculate, striate cortex, and middle temporal cortex. In Eq. (4.25), $r$ is the spike rate response to the stimulus $p$; M is the maximum spike rate for very intense stimuli; sigma ($\sigma$) determines the point (semi-saturation point) where $r(p)$ reaches half of its maximum; and $n$ determines the maximum slope of the function.

## 4.4 ELECTRICAL LOAD FORECASTING USING SPIKE RESPONSE MODEL

Forecasting is an important tool used in various applications such as weather variables, stock market prices, electricity trading prices, and so on. Therefore, a large number of forecasting methods are available in the literature. Generally, forecasting methods are classified into two types: (1) classical and (2) non-conventional methods. The classical methods include the time series models and causal models. The non-conventional methods consist of ANNs, fuzzy logic inference methods, expert systems, etc. However, in this section, we use spiking NN with SRM for electrical load forecasting.

### 4.4.1 Temporal Encoding in Spiking Neural Networks

Neural coding refers to the scheme by which information is represented in the form of spike trains. The methods of encoding real values include temporal encoding, rate encoding and population encoding [13]. However, the actual coding scheme employed in human brain is still not certain and is an issue of discussion. In rate coding, information is encoded by instantaneous firing probability. Population coding is the scheme in which information is encoded in the activity of a given population of neurons firing within a window of time. Bialek et al. [14] can be referred for more details on several coding schemes.

In this work, temporal neural coding scheme applicable to time series modelling and forecasting task is proposed to exploit the correlated temporal events hidden in the time series. The method of encoding the real values in the temporal encoding scheme include inter spike interval or time to next spike and probability based encoding [12]. The temporal coding scheme employed in this study uses the precise time of spikes, which is continuously fed into the network (Fig. 4.11).

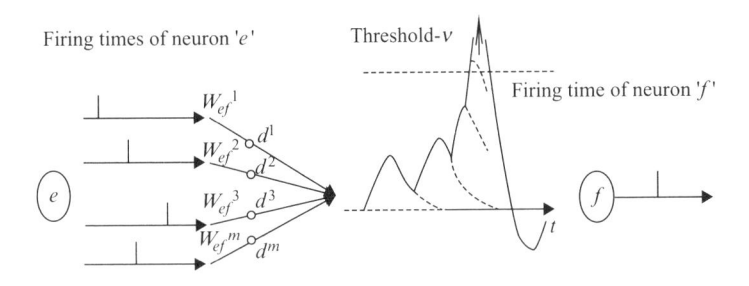

**Fig. 4.11** Multiple synaptic connections between two neurons

The input and the output of a spiking neuron are described by a series of firing times known as the spike train. One firing time means, the instant the neuron has fired a pulse. The potential of a spiking neuron is modelled by a dynamic variable and works as an integrator of the incoming spikes. Newer spikes contribute more to the net action potential than the older spikes. If this integrated sum of the incoming spikes is greater than a predefined threshold level, then the neuron fires a spike. This makes spiking neural network (SNN) a dynamic system, in contrast with the second-generation sigmoid NNs which are static, and enables it to perform computation on temporal patterns in a very natural biological manner. Though its likeness is closer to the conventional feed-forward BPNN, the difference lies in having many numbers of connections between individual neurons of successive layers as in (Fig. 4.12).

Formally, between any two neurons 'e' and 'f', input neuron 'e' receives a set of spikes with firing times $t_e$. The output neuron 'f' fires a spike only when membrane potential exceeds its threshold value ($\tau$). The relationship between the input spikes and the internal state variable is described as the SRM. The internal state variable $x_f(t)$ is described by the spike response function $\varepsilon(t)$ weighted by the synaptic efficacy. That is, the weight between the two neurons is given as in the following equation:

$$x_f(t) = \sum_{k=1}^{m} Y_e^k W_{ef}^k \qquad (4.26)$$

where, $W_{ef}^k$ is the weight of the sub-connection $k$, $m$ is the number of synaptic terminals between any two neurons of successive layers and $Y$ gives the un-weighted contribution of all spikes to the synaptic terminal. $Y$ is given as follows:

$$Y_e^k(t) = \varepsilon(t - t_e - d^k) \qquad (4.27)$$

where, $d^k$ is the delay between the two nodes in the $k^{th}$ synaptic terminal. $e(t)$ is the spike response function shaping the PSP of a neuron, as given here:

$$\varepsilon(t) = \begin{cases} \frac{t}{\tau} e^{1-\frac{t}{\tau}} & t \geq 0 \\ 0 & t < 0 \end{cases} \qquad (4.28)$$

where, $\tau$ is the membrane potential decay time constant.

Bohte (2002) developed the spike propagation algorithm for a network of spiking neurons that encode information in the timing of individual spikes. The learning algorithm is based on the error BP algorithm of the sigmoidal NNs.

### 4.4.2 Spike Propagation Algorithm

The architecture of a three-layer feed-forward SNN is shown in Fig. 4.12. The step-by-step procedure of the spike propagation algorithm is given here.

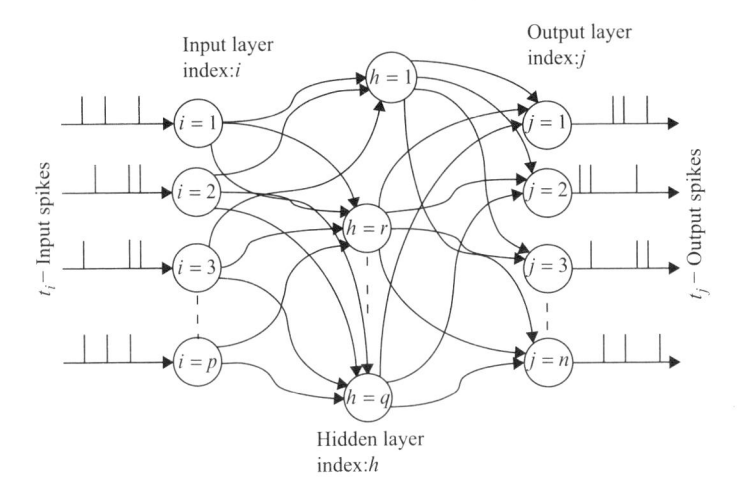

**Fig. 4.12** Architecture of a multi-layer SNN

**Step 1:** Prepare initial dataset normalized between 0 & 1.
**Step 2:** Generate the weights to small random values. Initialize the SNN parameters such as membrane potential decay time constant ($\tau$) and learning rate ($\alpha$).
**Step 3:** For the proposed SNN architecture, input layer ($i$), hidden layer ($h$), and output layer ($o$), do the steps 4 – 8 '$itt$' times ($itt$ = no. of iterations). The network indices represents the number of neurons, where, $p$ = number of neurons in the input layer; $q$ = number of neurons in the hidden layer; $n$ = number neurons in the output layer; and $m$ = number of synaptic terminals between any two neurons of successive layers.
**Step 4:** For each pattern in the training set, apply the input vector to the network input.
**Step 5:** Calculate the internal state variable of the hidden-layer neurons, which is given by Eq. (4.29).

$$x_h(t) = \sum_{i=1}^{p} \sum_{k=1}^{m} Y_i^k W_{ih}^k \qquad (4.29)$$

**Step 6:** Calculate the network output which is given by Eq. (4.30).

$$x_j(t) = \sum_{h=1}^{q} \sum_{k=1}^{m} Y_h^k W_{hj}^k \qquad (4.30)$$

**Step 7:** Calculate the error, the difference between the actual spike time and the desired spike time which is given in Eq. (4.31).

$$E = 0.5 \times \sum_{j=1}^{n} \left(t_j^a - t_j^d\right)^2 \qquad (4.31)$$

where, $t_j^a$ is the actual output spike, $t_j^d$ is the desired output spike, and $n$ is the neurons in the output layer.

**Step 8:** Adjust weights of the network in such a way that minimizes the error ($E$). Then repeat steps 4 – 8 for each pair of input and output vectors of the training set until the error for the entire system is acceptably low. The equations representing the change in weights are given here.

The change in weights from hidden layer to output layer is given as follows:

$$\Delta W_{hj}^{k} = -\alpha \delta_j Y_{hj}^{k}\left(t_j^a\right) \tag{4.32}$$

The change in weight from input (i) to hidden-layer (h) is given here:

$$\Delta W_{ih}^{k} = -\alpha \delta_h Y_{ih}^{k}\left(t_h^a\right) \tag{4.33}$$

where,

$$\delta_j = \frac{t_j^d - t_j^a}{\sum_{k,h} W_{hj}^{k} \left(\dfrac{\partial Y_{hj}^{k}\left(t_j^a\right)}{\partial t_j^a}\right)} \tag{4.34}$$

where,

$$\delta_h = \frac{\sum_{j=1}^{n} \delta_j \sum_{k} W_{hj}^{k} \left(\dfrac{\partial Y_{hj}^{k}\left(t_j^a\right)}{\partial t_h^a}\right)}{\sum_{k,i} W_{ih}^{k} \left(\dfrac{\partial Y_{ih}^{k}\left(t_j^a\right)}{\partial t_h^a}\right)} \tag{4.35}$$

However, to obtain reliable results from the proposed methodology, the control parameters must be set accordingly. The setting of various control parameters is generalized and explained in detail in the next section.

### 4.4.3 Control Parameter Setting

The proposed SNN has the following adjustable parameters: Number of hidden nodes ($h$), weights ($W_{ih}$ and $W_{hj}$), learning rate ($\alpha$) and decay time constant ($\hat{o}$). As with many other forecast methods, the accuracy of the proposed SNN is dependent on the appropriate adjustment of its parameters. Mean square error (MSE) is considered as the performance index for adjustment of the control parameters. The range for each of the parameter is selected in some neighbourhood.

Initially, training samples are constructed for setting the control parameters. Keeping the other parameters constant, within the selected neighbourhood, the weights from input to hidden layer and hidden to output layer are varied and the training process is stopped when MSE obtained is minimum. Now with the weights being set, and keeping all other parameters constant, the number of hidden-layer neurons is varied. The number of neurons in the hidden layer determines the network's learning capabilities. The selection of the number of hidden neurons is a very essential issue in network design.

A network with too few hidden neurons will not be capable of accurately modelling electrical load demand. In addition, too many hidden neurons may force the network to memorize the training data. The performance of such a network may be poor when different data is applied to it. In addition, the hidden-layer size affects the training time. Therefore, optimal number of hidden-layer neurons are selected and varied within the given neighbourhood and training is carried out till least MSE is obtained.

The number of synaptic connections is another important parameter for obtaining reliable results from the network. The number of connections between two neurons is varied for each trial. The setting for which least MSE is obtained is selected. For the feed-forward network, the delay value in each synaptic connection is increased in steps of few milliseconds (e.g., 5 ms). However, it is not necessary that the delay in each terminal should be same. The next parameter to be set with respect to the order of precedence is the decay time constant value ($\tau$) which depends on the coding interval ($\Delta t$). The coding interval ($\Delta t$) is the difference between the minimum value and maximum value of the normalized input spikes, which is once again problem dependent. Training is performed for values both greater and lesser than $\Delta t$. For optimal convergence, the most reliable results are obtained for values of time constant larger than or equal to the coding interval (Bohte, 2002).The last parameter to be tuned is the learning rate $\alpha$. It is found that for high values of $\alpha$, the probability of convergence of the algorithm is decreased. Therefore, small values are considered.

### 4.4.4 Implementation of SNN for STLF

The power demand of consumers varies in accordance with their activities. The result of this variation in demand can be observed from the load in a power station which is never constant and varies with respect to time. In this work, it is assumed that no two days can have same load profile but can have similar characteristic features. Therefore, to forecast load, the input and target data must be correlated in accordance with their consumption profile. Based on mapping of input and target data, two cases are formulated and investigated in this section. They are similar-day correlation and day-ahead correlation.

However, in this application similar-day correlation approach is carried out. In addition, the real-time load demand database for the implementation of the proposed forecasting model is obtained from Australian Energy Market Operator (AEMO). The real-time hourly historical demand for the region Victoria is also obtained from AEMO.

In a similar day approach, the activities of the consumers are found to be similar on the same weekdays. Here, load pattern of similar days are correlated for training the historical load data. For example, load profile on Monday of the previous week is correlated to Monday of the present week. Hence, when a test input is fed into the SNN, a week-ahead consumption profile is forecasted. The load profile for similar days is shown in Figs 4.13 and 4.14. It is observed from these two figures that, though the load curves are not exactly same, they look similar.

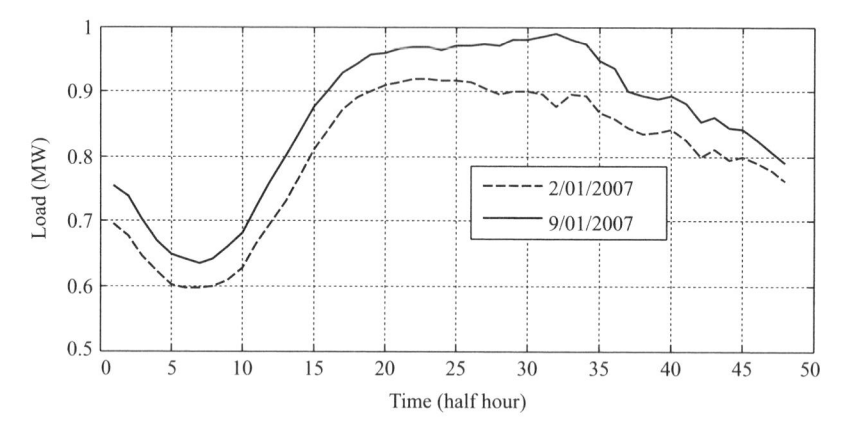

**Fig. 4.13** January 2007 (Victoria)

*Source*: It is an open resource; *www.aemo.com.*

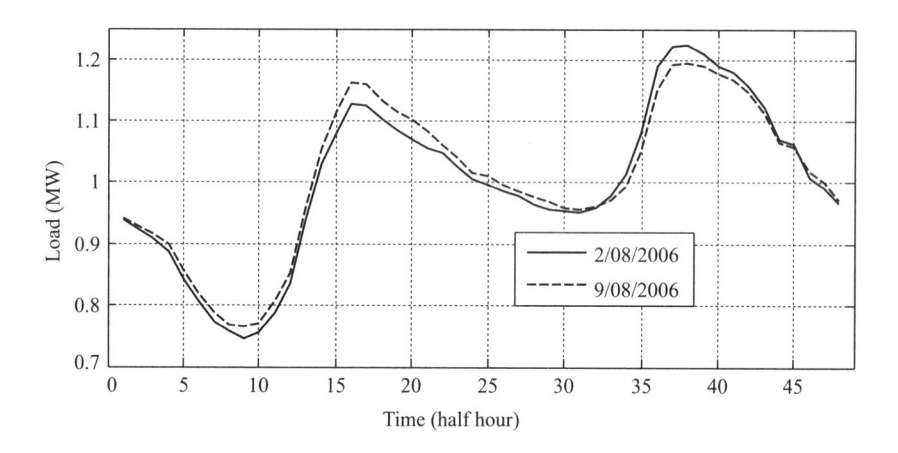

**Fig. 4.14** August 2006 (Victoria)

*Source*: It is an open resource; *www.aemo.com.*

The implementation of the proposed model is divided into two phases. The block diagram in Fig. 4.15 consists of 2 SNNs sequentially. $E_1$ and $E_2$ represent the training errors of SNN1 and SNN2, respectively. In Phase 2, the forecasted temperature values are given as input to SNN2 to forecast the load pattern.

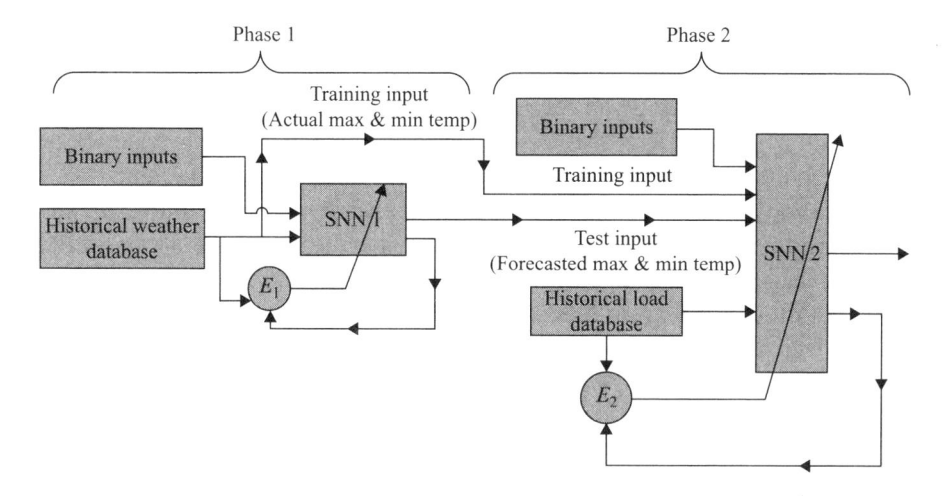

**Fig. 4.15** Block diagram of the proposed SNNSTLF engine

## Phase 1

In Phase 1, using SNN1, a day-ahead hourly temperature profile is forecasted. The input data consists of hourly temperatures of the previous 2 days (12 neurons), hourly humidity values of the previous 2 days (12 neurons), maximum solar radiation of the previous day (1 neuron) and the corresponding month encoded in binary form. The 12 months in the yearly calendar are encoded in binary form (0001 to 1100). For example, if the binary representation is 0010, it represents month of July (4 neurons). The target values consist of the corresponding hourly temperatures on the day of forecast (6 neurons). Therefore, SNN1 consists of 29 input nodes 6 output nodes, respectively.

Training is carried out for four times with the input data divided into 4 parts of a day consisting of 24 hrs. The first part consists of hourly weather variables from 12 A.M to 5 A.M. Similarly, the other three parts consist of data for the remaining time horizon. For each of the four input formats, the temperatures for six hours are forecasted. Thus, all the 24 hourly temperatures are forecasted. The maximum and the minimum temperatures of the forecasted day is recorded and used as test input for SNN2.

The aforecited scheme of testing and training in Phase 1 is carried out for the city of Melbourne in Victoria. The same procedure is repeated for the city of Geelong in Victoria. The objective of the forecast engine is to forecast the electrical load for the state of Victoria in Australia. Therefore, to have accurate forecast result, the weather data for two cities are considered in Phase 1. Finally, the maximum and the minimum forecasted temperatures for the 2 cities is recorded which will be acting as 4 test inputs for SNN2 in Phase 2.

The best combination of parameters for SNN1 is $W_{ih} \in (1, 2)$, $W_{hj} \in (2, 3)$, $h = 15$, $k = 12$, $\tau = 7$ ms and $\alpha = 0.001$. The cross-correlation analysis between temperature and humidity is shown in Fig. 4.16. It enables us to choose the number of input variables with time lag which affect the other variables as well. As seen in Fig. 4.16, the cross-correlation coefficients obtained for the first five time lags are quiet significant. Therefore, humidity values of the previous two days are chosen as inputs to the forecasting model.

A similar analysis performed on the maximum temperature and maximum solar radiation is shown in Fig. 4.17. It is found that the coefficient obtained for a zero time lag is comparatively higher than other coefficients (coefficients obtained for other time lags). Therefore, solar radiation of the previous day is taken as an input variable for the SNN2 model. The form of cross-correlation function (XCF) adopted here follows that of Box, Jenkins, and Reinsel, specifically [15].

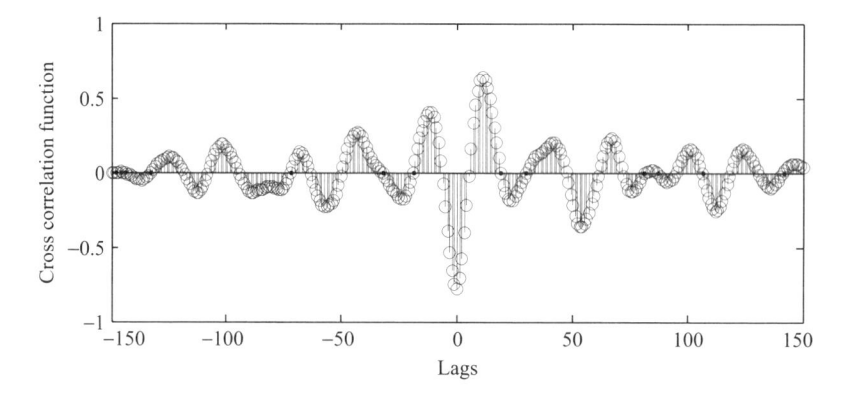

**Fig. 4.16** Cross-correlation function between temperature and humidity

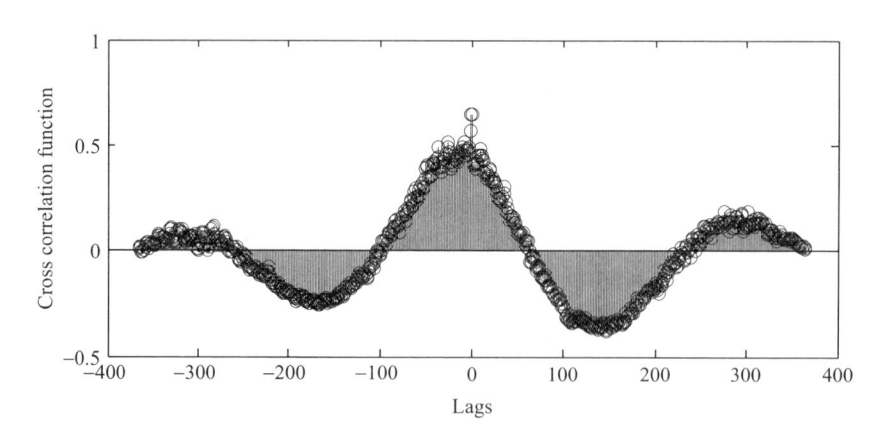

**Fig. 4.17** Cross-correlation function between temperature and solar radiation

## Phase 2

In Phase 2, a day-ahead half hourly load profile is forecasted. For example, if the load pattern of Monday is given as test input, the load pattern of Tuesday is forecasted. For producing accurate load forecasts, the best combination of input variables is required. Here in this work, apart from historical load data, the factors which have significant impact on the consumption pattern such as day of the week, weather variables, holiday effect, and so on are chosen as inputs to the network.

The topology of SNN2 included the following variables as inputs:

One day half hourly lagged load: (48 neurons)

One day lagged temperature values (minimum and maximum values): (4 neurons)

Forecasted temperature values obtained from Phase 1 (minimum and maximum values): (4 neurons)

Maximum and minimum demand in the last 24 hrs: (2 neurons)

Average temperature value in the last seven days: (2 neurons)

Day of the week is encoded in binary form: (001 to 111). For example, if the binary representation is 010, it represents Tuesday (3 neurons).

Month number: (0001 to 1100) (4 neurons)

Holiday effect: (0–holiday; 1–working day) (1 neuron)

The corresponding target training data consists of half hourly load on the day of forecast. Therefore, the SNN2 model has 68 input neurons and 48 output neurons, respectively. It is observed that the following set of control parameters provided the best results during the training of the SNN2 model: $W_{ih} \in (2, 3)$, $W_{hj} \in (1, 2)$, $h = 10$, $k = 8$, $\tau = 5\ ms$, and $\alpha = 0.0006$.

### 4.4.5 Performance Evaluation

The accuracy of the results in this case study is evaluated based on three error indices. They are: mean absolute percentage error (MAPE), normalized mean square error (NMSE), and Error Variance (EV).

The MAPE is defined by the following equation:

$$MAPE = \frac{1}{NH} \sum_{i=1}^{NH} \left| \frac{P_i - A_i}{A_i} \right| \quad (4.36)$$

The NMSE [16] is defined as follows:

$$NMSE = \left[ \frac{1}{\Delta^2 NH} \sum_{i=1}^{NH} (P_i - A_i)^2 \right] \quad (4.37)$$

where,

$$\Delta = \frac{1}{NH - 1} \sum_{i=1}^{NH} (A_i - A_{Ave})^2 \quad (4.38)$$

EV [17] is defined as

$$\sigma^2 = \frac{1}{NH} \sum_{i=1}^{NH} \left( \left| \frac{P_i - A_i}{A_i} \right| - MAPE \right)^2 \quad (4.39)$$

where, $P_i$ and $A_i$ are the $i^{th}$ predicted and actual values respectively, $A_{Ave}$ is the mean of the actual value, and $NH$ is the total number of predictions.

### 4.4.6 Results and Discussions

The real-time dataset which is obtained from AEMO website from January 2004 to October 2008 is used for training the SNNSTLF engine. The data from AEMO website from October 2008 to March 2009 is used to test the proposed model. The average mean absolute error (MAE) and MAPE obtained for each month from October 2008 to March 2009 are tabulated in Table 4.2 [18].

Table 4.2 Monthly performance comparisons

| Month | SNNSTLF (Forecasted temperature as input) | |
|---|---|---|
| | MAE | MAPE |
| Oct-2008 | 123.56 | 2.11 |
| Nov-2008 | 118.58 | 2.06 |
| Dec-2008 | 119.25 | 2.09 |
| Jan-2009 | 129.26 | 2.10 |
| Feb-2009 | 111.54 | 1.92 |
| Mar-2009 | 109.56 | 1.90 |
| Average | 118.62 | 2.03 |

The MAPE and MAE computed when actual and forecasted temperature values are fed as inputs to SNN2 model are presented in Table 4.3.

Table 4.3 Monthly average performance comparisons

| Month | SNNSTLF (Forecasted temperature as input to SNNSTLF) | |
|---|---|---|
| | MAE | MAPE |
| Dec-2008 | 119.25 | 2.09 |
| Jan-2009 | 129.26 | 2.10 |
| Feb-2009 | 111.54 | 1.92 |
| Mar-2009 | 109.56 | 1.90 |
| Average | 113.62 | 2.00 |

A comparative analysis using EV and NMSE is tabulated in Table 4.4.

Table 4.4 EV and NMSE for test data

| Month | SNNSTLF (Forecasted temperature as input to SNNSTLF) | |
|---|---|---|
| | EV | NMSE |
| Dec-2008 | 0.172 | 0.0689 |
| Jan-2009 | 0.198 | 0.0784 |
| Feb-2009 | 0.185 | 0.0526 |
| Mar-2009 | 0.182 | 0.0537 |

It is observed from Table 4.4 that the EV and NMSE obtained are less when actual historical temperature values are fed as inputs to the SNNSTLF engine. However, the values obtained for the two cases do not differ by a large value.

The results computed in Tables 4.3 and 4.4 indicate that the performance of the forecast engine for the months of February and March is much better than the results obtained for the month of January. This is mainly attributed to the abnormal high peak loads occurring due to the high temperatures in the month of January.

To understand the influence of weather variables on load pattern, SNN2 is trained and tested using solely the historical load data. The results evaluated on each week day for the months of January and February is tabulated in Tables 4.5 and 4.6, respectively. The MAPE and maximum absolute percentage error (Max. APE) calculated with the incorporation of weather variables for all the Mondays in January is 74 per cent and 8.94 per cent less when the weather variables are excluded.

Error analysis carried out for the month of February is presented in Table 4.6. It is found that the average MAPE (incorporating temperature) obtained for

Table 4.5  Performance evaluation on all weekdays (Jan 2009)

| Day | Influence of weather variables | | | |
|---|---|---|---|---|
| | Including temperatures | | Excluding temperatures | |
| | MAPE | Max. APE | MAPE | Max. APE |
| Monday | 2.08 | 8.15 | 8.03 | 8.95 |
| Tuesday | 2.02 | 7.46 | 8.07 | 8.07 |
| Wednesday | 2.00 | 7.23 | 6.92 | 9.35 |
| Thursday | 2.04 | 8.45 | 7.36 | 8.31 |
| Friday | 2.03 | 8.25 | 6.49 | 9.23 |
| Saturday | 2.21 | 8.78 | 9.81 | 19.37 |
| Sunday | 2.28 | 9.15 | 10.83 | 24.65 |

Table 4.6  Performance evaluation on all weekdays (Feb 2009)

| Day | Influence of weather variables | | | |
|---|---|---|---|---|
| | Including temperatures | | Excluding temperatures | |
| | MAPE | Max. APE | MAPE | Max. APE |
| Monday | 1.94 | 8.45 | 5.95 | 9.65 |
| Tuesday | 1.96 | 7.26 | 5.98 | 7.52 |
| Wednesday | 1.87 | 7.33 | 5.78 | 9.17 |
| Thursday | 1.82 | 7.33 | 5.78 | 9.17 |
| Friday | 1.90 | 8.18 | 6.07 | 8.28 |
| Saturday | 1.95 | 8.84 | 9.21 | 15.37 |
| Sunday | 2.03 | 8.38 | 9.62 | 19.28 |

all Mondays in February is 6 per cent less than the average MAPE obtained in January. The MAPE and the Max. APE computed for Saturdays and Sundays are higher than the other weekdays for both January and February. The MAPE and the Max. APE for other typical week days (Tuesday to Friday) are presented in Tables 4.5 and 4.6.

From the aforementioned analysis, it is concluded that the accuracy of the temperature forecasts will indirectly enhance the performance of the load forecasting model.

The actual load pattern and the forecasted half-hourly day-ahead demand profile, when forecasted temperatures are considered as inputs to the proposed SNNSTLF are presented in Figs 4.18, 4.19, 4.20, and 4.21. In Figs 4.18 and 4.19, the MAPE calculated is 2.12 per cent and 2.04 per cent, respectively. In Fig. 4.18, the MAPE obtained for the first 12 hrs (24 observations) is found to be 1.91 per cent and it is 2.33 per cent for the remaining time horizon.

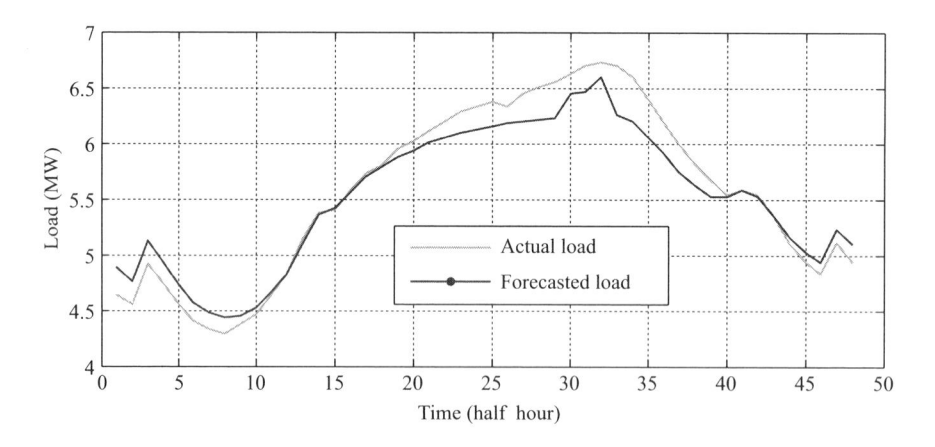

**Fig. 4.18** Performance on 5 January 2009

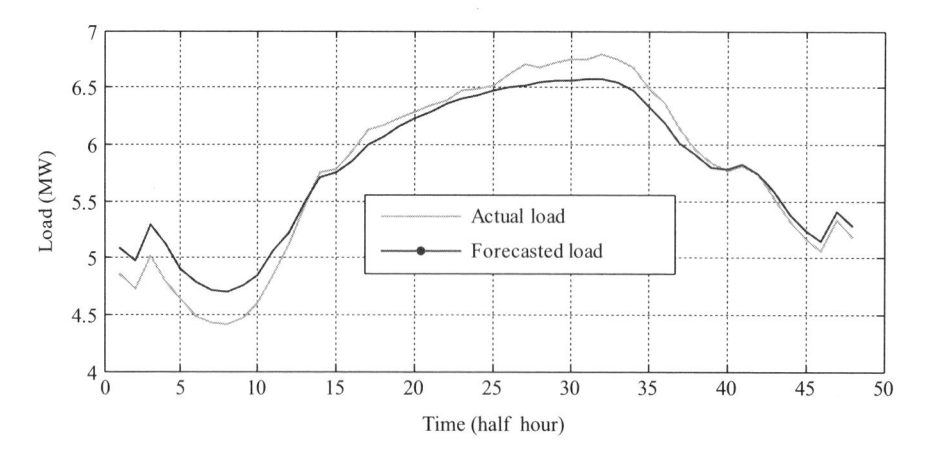

**Fig. 4.19** Performance on 12 January 2009

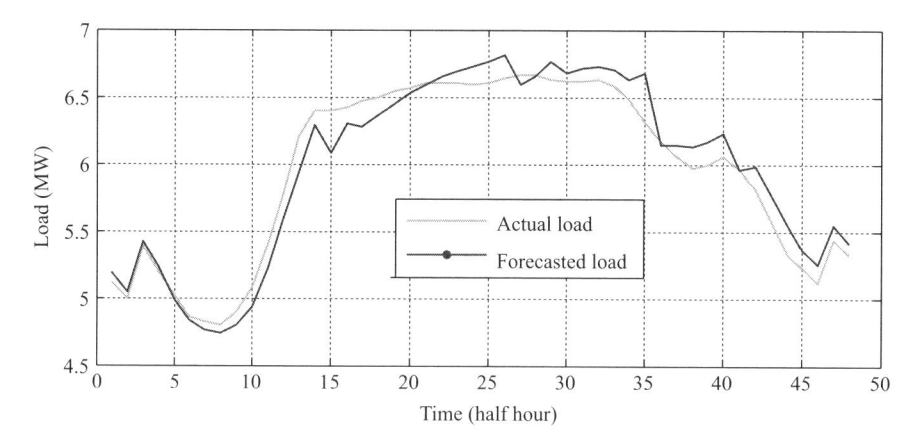

**Fig. 4.20** Performance on 25 February 2009

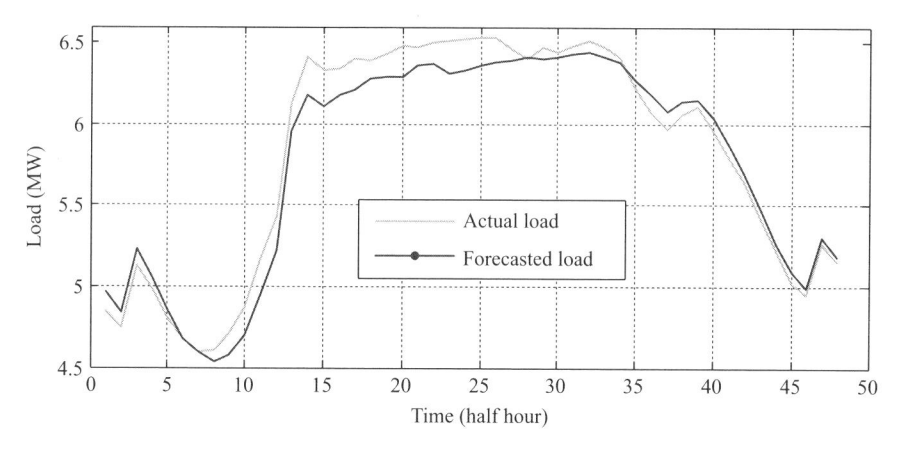

**Fig. 4.21** Performance on 23 March 2009

The actual peak demand is 6,600 MW where as the forecasted peak demand is 6,515 MW. The average error obtained (Fig. 4.19) is 2.03 per cent, 1.94 per cent, and 2.03 per cent for the first 8 hrs (16 observations), for the next 8 hrs, and for the remaining time horizon, respectively.

The MAPE computed for one day-ahead forecasts in Figs 4.20 and 4.21 is 2.01 per cent and 1.92 per cent, respectively. The minimum absolute error obtained for the one-day-ahead forecasts in Figs 4.20 and 4.21 is 0.002 MW. The Max. APE obtained in Figs 4.20 and 4.21 is 4.23% and 4.01%, respectively.

In Fig. 4.22, the forecasted load curves with and without the weather variables are plotted. It is obvious that the forecasted curve including the weather variables follows the actual load pattern more closely than the other curve (without weather variables). It indicates that the percentage error in the forecasted curve is significantly reduced when the weather variables are incorporated in SNN2. The variations of the absolute percentage error are shown in Fig. 4.23. All the load values in

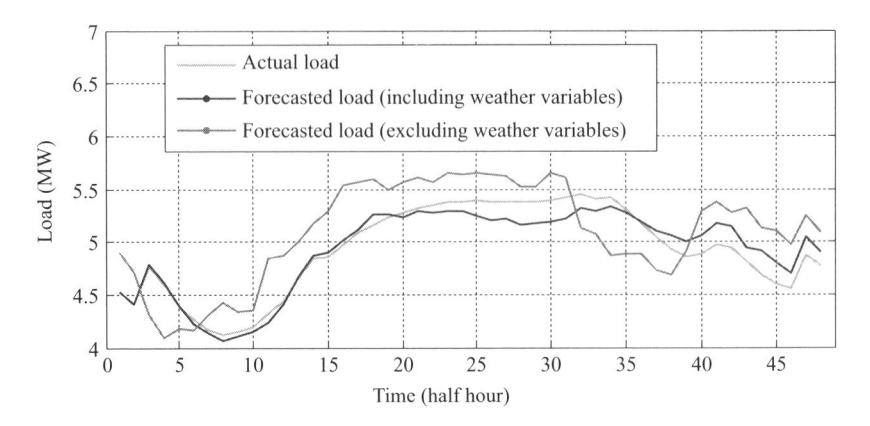

**Fig. 4.22** Performance on 3rd January 2009

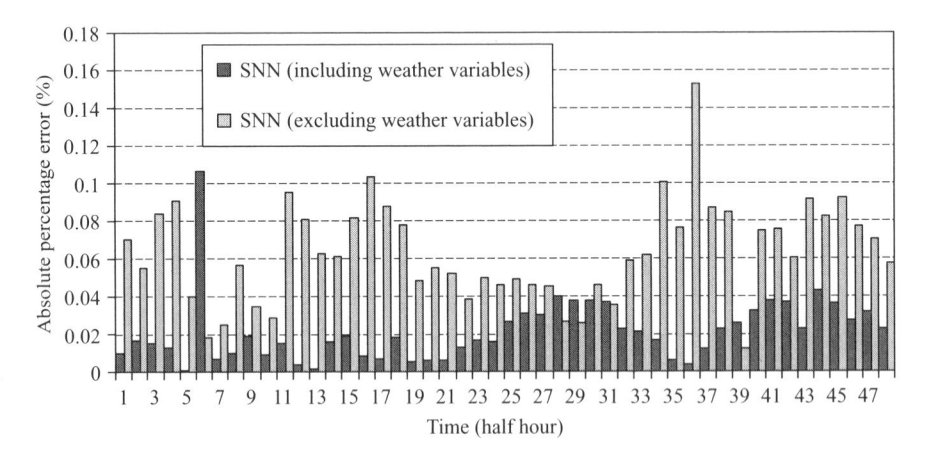

**Fig. 4.23** Performance on 3rd January 2009

Figs 4.19, 4.20, 4.21, and 4.22 are scaled by a factor of 1,000 (i.e., if the load is 6,500 MW, it is scaled to 6.5).

This application uses SNN, which can capture the inherent dynamics of the time series system. The accurate week-ahead forecasts can help in carrying out scheduling operations of the electrical generators, whereas the one day-ahead forecasts help in making the final corrections in the scheduling operations.

## SUMMARY

- Spiking neural networks, also called 'pulsed neural network', differentiates itself from the second-generation neural networks where the information is encoded and decoded by a series of trains of pulses (i.e., action potential).
- Spikes are chain of pulses emitted by a single neuron, which is usually a sequence of stereotyped events which occur at regular or irregular intervals.
- Spiking neuron models can be classified into three main classes: (i) threshold fire, (ii) conductance-based, and (iii) compartmental models.

- Spike response neural network model is used to forecast electrical load and is presented to validate its engineering application.
- The area of neural network is under active research and seems to have a bright future, and may be more suitable in most of the applications where the second-generation neural network has tread successfully.

## EXERCISES

### Part A Short-answer Questions

1. What are the features of the second-generation neural network?
2. What is a 'spike train'?
3. What is 'excitatory post-synaptic potential'?
4. What is meant by 'inhibitory post-synaptic potential'?
5. Define 'spike after potential'.
6. Define 'resting potential'.
7. What is meant by: (a) tonic spiking and (b) tonic bursting?
8. What is 'phasic spiking' and 'phasic bursting'?
9. Define Class I and Class II excitability.
10. What is 'spike latency'?
11. What do you understand by 'rebound spike' and 'rebound burst'?
12. How is 'spiking neuron models' classified?
13. What is a 'threshold-firing model'?
14. What are 'compartment models'?
15. What are 'rate models'?
16. What is a 'spike response model'?

### Part B Long-answer Questions

1. Discuss in detail about the real cortical neuronal spiking responses during the injection of simple DC pulses.
2. Explain the process of information between neurons in terms of spikes with relevant sketches.
3. Explain the different threshold-fire models in detail.

    Write short notes on:

    (a) Conductance-based response model

    (b) Compartment models
4. Explain the spike propagation algorithm with relevant sketches.

### Part C Practical Exercises

1. Develop a MATLAB Program for spike propagation algorithm for character recognition.
2. Create a medical diagnosis MATLAB tool using spike propagation algorithm.

## REFERENCES

[1] Vreeken, J., *Spiking Neural Networks, an Introduction*, Technical Report UU-CS, 1–5, 2003.

[2] Maass, Wolfgang and Christopher M. Bishop, *Pulsed Neural Networks*, MIT Press, Cambridge, MA, London, 2001.

[3] Rumelhart, D. E., G. E. Hinton, and R. J. Williams, Learning internal representations by error propagation, in Rumelhart D. E., and McClelland J. L. (eds), *Parallel Distributed Processing*, MIT Press, Cambridge, MA, Vol. 1, 318–362, 1986.

[4] Warren, McCulloch, and Walter Pitts, A logical calculus of ideas immanent in nervous activity, *Bulletin of Mathematical Biophysics*, Vol. 5, Issue 4, 115–133, 1943.

[5] Gerstner, Wulfram and Werner M. Kistler, *Spiking Neuron Models: Single Neurons, Populations, Plasticity*, Cambridge University Press, Cambridge, 2002.

[6] Gasparini, Sonia, Michele Migliore, and Jeffrey C. Magee, On the initiation and propagation of dendritic spikes in CA1, *The Journal of Neuroscience*, Vol. 24, Issue, 49, 11046–11056, 2004.

[7] Gerstner, Wulfram, and Werner M. Kistler, Richard Naud and Liam Paninski, Neuronal dynamics. *From Single Neurons to Networks and Models of Cognition*, Cambridge University Press, Cambridge, 2014.

[8] Hodgkin, A. L. and A. F. Huxley, A quantitative description of membrane current and its application to conduction and excitation in nerve, *The Journal of Physiology*, Vol. 117, Issue 4, 500–544, 1952.

[9] Maass, Wolfgang and Christopher M. Bishop, *Pulsed Neural Networks*, MIT Press, 2001 [Online Publication].

[10] Tanaka, Masao, Taishin Nomura, and Yoshiyuki Asai, *Harnessing Biological Complexity: An Introduction to Computational Physiology*, Volume 1 of A First Course in 'In Silico Medicine', Springer Science & Business Media, 2010.

[11] McCulloch, W., and W. Pitts 1943, 'A logical calculus of the ideas immanent in nervous activity', *Bulltin of Mathematical Biophysics*, vol 7, pp. 115–133.

[12] Rotstein, Horacio G., and Farzan Nadim, *Neurons and Neural Networks: Computational Models*, John Wiley & Sons, 2001.

[13] Sharma, V. and D. Srinivasan, A spiking neural network based on temporal encoding for electricity price time series forecasting in deregulated markets, *International Conference on Neural Networks (IJCNN)*, 2010.

[14] Bialek, W., F. Rieke., R. R. Steveninck, and D. Warland, Reading a neural code, *Science*, Vol. 252, 1854–1857, 1991.

[15] Box, G. E. P., G. M. Jenkins, and G. C. Reinsel, *Time Series Analysis: Forecasting and Control*, Third edition, Prentice-Hall, Upper Saddle River, NJ, 1994.

[16] Amjady, Nima, Farshid Keynia and Hamidreza Zareipour, Short-term wind power forecasting using ridgelet neural network, *Electric Power Systems Research*, Vol. 81, Issue 12, 2099–2107, 2011.

[17] Amjady, Nima, Farshid Keynia and Hamidreza Zareipour, Short-term load forecasts of microgrids by a new bi-level prediction strategy, *IEEE Transactions on Smart Grid*, Vol. 1, Issue 3, 286–294, 2010.

[18] Kulkarni, S., S. P. and Simon, K. Sundareswaran, A spiking neural network (SNN) forecast engine for short-term electrical load forecasting. *Applied Soft Computing*, Elsevier Publications, Vol. 13, Issue 8, 3628–3635, 2013.

## e-References

1. Bohte S. M., (2002) Spiking Neural Networks, (Doctoral dissertation), (Available online) homepages.cwi.nl/~sbohte/publication/phdthesis.pdf

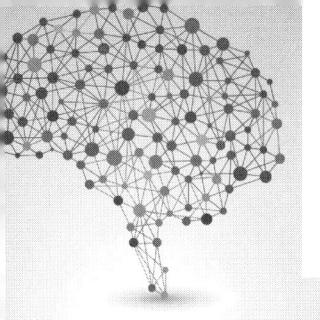

# 5 Fuzzy Logic

*'Life is really simple, but we insist on making it complicated.'*
*Confucius*

### LEARNING OBJECTIVES

*This chapter will enable the reader to:*
- Learn the concept of fuzzy logic and its day-to-day utility
- Explain the functions of fuzzy arithmetic and operations
- Draw the structure of a fuzzy system
- List the applications of fuzzy logic systems
- Understand MATLAB implementation of fuzzy logic
- Comprehend recent trends in fuzzy technology

## 5.1 INTRODUCTION TO FUZZY LOGIC

The Bollywood blockbuster movie '3 Idiots' has a sequence of play in which a professor asks Aamir Khan (an engineering student) the definition of a machine. The answer comes '*Sir, a machine is anything reduces human effort.*' To elaborate, Aamir supplies an array of examples including fan, calculator, mobile phone, and a zipper (showing its up-down motion)! Unsatisfied with this simple answer, the professor poses the same question to another student who answers '*Sir, machines are any combination of bodies so connected that their relative motions are constraint., and by means force and motion may be transmitted and modified as the screw in its nut or a lever range turnabout a fulcrum or a pulley by its pivot etc. especially a construction more or less complex consisting of a combination of moving parts or simple mechanical elements as wheels, levers, cams etc.*' This rather complicated definition gets a nod of appreciation from the professor!

Sometimes, if we think wisely, the complex things can be made simple. In a similar manner, fuzzy logic takes into account that real world is complex and there are uncertainties; everything cannot have absolute values and follow a linear function. It is similar to human thinking and interpretation and gives meaning to expressions such as beautiful, cold, bigger, and so on.

Fuzzy logic was introduced in 1965 by Lofti A. Zadeh, a professor in the University of California, Berkeley. It is a controversial theory ever since its launch as it emphasizes on imprecision of data. Even though there was a strong resistance, numerous papers got published using fuzzy logic and fuzzy logic got accepted as emerging technology since the 1980s.

L.A. Zadeh [1] refers fuzzy logic approach as having a fundamental trade-off between precision and cost which can be called *'principle of incompatibility'*. He points that, one has to pay a higher cost for higher precision. Therefore, the cost of modelling and investigating complex systems can be very high to be sensible. Prof. Zadeh illustrates the trade-off with an example of parking a car. Usually, a driver may take less than half a minute to park his vehicle in the marked parking area. Suppose, if we ask the driver to park the vehicle such that the outside wheel should precisely be within 0.01 mm from the side lines of the parking space, and the wheels are within 1 degree from a specific angle, how much time the driver needs to park the car? Sometimes, in that situation we may try longer and finally give up. Here, a parallel can be drawn such that the cost involved is the time taken for parking, and therefore, the cost will increase as precision increases. This trade-off can be extended not only for car parking, but also can be applied to other events. The event may be a well-defined engineering problem, control system, fabrication of chip, assembling a mobile phone, getting appointment with a doctor, building a house, getting a movie ticket, etc., where fuzzy logic can be put in use.

Fuzzy logic generalizes classical two-valued logic for reasoning uncertainty. In a broad sense, it refers all the theories and technologies that employ fuzzy sets. The source of fuzziness is the imprecision involved in designing and using symbols, words and interpretation. Consider a switch has two positions ON and OFF. It can be represented as 0 or 1 in a two-valued logic. Consider tossing a coin it can give two results HEAD or TAIL. Head can be represented as 1 and tail can be represented as 0. Now, let us consider representing a student's mark out of 100. It can be represented by a set $\{0, 1, 2, \ldots 100\}$.

But, if you try to represent his performance in the exam, then the fuzziness comes. If the student scores 60 per cent, you may say that the student's performance is good; the first examiner may say the performance is average; the second examiner may say the performance is mediocre; and the student's friend may say his performance is excellent. Therefore, there is an inability to express the performance of a student in a precise manner. The concept of fuzzy logic helps us to tackle the uncertainty and vagueness associated with the event.

Consider parents looking for a bride for their son. They can express their expectations as follows:

Height = 163 cm
Weight = 52 kg
Education = 90.8 % in B.E.
Colour = (R = 165 G = 42 B = 42)
Hair length = 60 cm.

Eye dimensions:

Axial length along the visual axis: 21–27 mm
Vertical diameter: 23 mm
Horizontal diameter: 23.5 mm
Circumference at the equator: 73.5 mm

Rather, they can express their expectation as tall, average built, educated, elegant with beautiful eyes. Here, the precision of the data is not so important. Fuzzy logic aims to reduce difficulties in developing and analysing complex systems by conventional mathematical modelling tools. It also aims to incorporate human reasoning (approximation, analogies, and selective memory) in dealing with vague concepts which do not have sharp boundaries.

Consider a man in a vehicle showroom wants to purchase a car with a cash amount of ₹1 lakh as his budget. The attributes he has in his mind may include a car having five seats, and the top speed being 120 km/hr. In the showroom, the man finds 3 five-seater cars. The top speeds of three cars are 110 km/hr, 120 km/hr, and 200 km/hr, with a cost of ₹0.9 lakh, ₹1.8 lakh, and ₹1.9 lakh, respectively. The man can buy the car with 120 km/hr for ₹1.8 lakh. We would rather suggest him to take the car with 110 km/hr instead of paying extra money of ₹80,000. The fundamental principle of fuzzy logic is to develop cost effective approximate solution to complex problems by exploiting the tolerance of impression. The following section helps us to understand the nature of fuzziness involved in human interpretation.

## 5.2 HUMAN LEARNING ABILITY, IMPRECISION, AND UNCERTAINTY

When any person encounters a problem he/she, tries to gather various information for solving the problem. The information may be acquired from a set of inputs to achieve his target. The inputs may be in the form of measurements, suggestions from experts or friends, websites, books, television, or a radio.

These inputs are often as follows:

1. Distorted
2. Incomplete
3. Imprecise or vague

The intelligence of human beings is far superior, adaptive, and successful than many existing systems pertaining to mathematical models. Uncertainties prevail in many situations in day-to-day life. The ability of the human intelligence to process the distorted, incomplete, vague information, and achieving the goal is remarkable and amazing [2].

Human intelligence does not require precise numerical information and statistics as inputs; yet, they are capable in performing highly adapting control. Human reasoning has the capability to accept the partial truth to get the desired output.

Human learning ability makes him unique when compared to any advanced technical system. The following are the factors influencing human learning abilities:

1. Generalization
2. Association (memory mapping)
3. Information loss (memory loss or forgetfulness)

Human beings do not store information statistically. Rather, the brain absorbs certain salient features in the information. When a new situation is encountered the brain, it gives a solution generally by recalling its past stored information (experience) and inferring a suitable solution to the present situation. It should be noted that the previous stored information in the memory may not be the experience of his/her own. He/she can get the information from others. The past experience may also be irrelevant to the present problem. We try to generalize data and store only important data. Human intelligence stores only relevant and important data as time advances where unimportant information are deleted from the memory. This is the most important property that enables learning.

In engineering applications, or in any real-world application, instruments are used to measure variables. These measurements are subjected to a large degree of uncertainty. Our inability to measure variables very close to its true value is termed as *inexactness*. The cause of inexactness may be due to instrument error or human error (e.g., parallax error). *Precision* of measurement refers to number of numerical digits used to represent the measured output. *Accuracy* is the term which explains how close the instrument reading is closer to the true value.

## 5.3 UNDECIDABILITY

Ambiguity that originates from the inability to distinguish between various states of an event is termed as *Undecidability*. Here, we are unable to make a choice between states. Consider two wiremen A and B, working in a house which is situated at the first floor. They have switched off the main switch and started working together to sort out the wiring issues in the house. Finally, they had identified a probable fault. Their conversation goes on related to the mains and is given here:

*A* (*Keeping the wire in hand*)*:* Go down and switch 'ON' the main when I say OK.

*B* (Immediately climbs down the stairs and stands near the main box waiting for the command).

*A:* Remember; Switch 'ON' the mains when I say 'OK' OK?

Let us try to guess the response of B. The probable actions may be from any of the two options. The first option is to reply 'I remember your command'. The second option is to switch 'ON' the mains immediately after receiving the command 'OK'.

Consider a young man looking for a bride. Let us assume that he gets two alliance proposals. The first proposal is from a woman without an employment, and the other proposal is from a woman employed in a private consulting agency. Let us also consider the two females are equally competent in physical and moral values. Now let us try to analyse the dilemma faced by the young man looking into the pros and cons in each of the proposal to marry.

If he chooses the unemployed woman, he can have timely food, good care for him; his children will have good motherly care spending most of the time for raising children. In addition, she may be able to share and sort out most of the responsibilities within the house. On the other hand, marrying an employed woman will increase the financial status of the family; wife may not depend on him for her financial needs; time spent together and in raising children will decrease; and a lot of compromises need to be considered in terms of work sharing within the house. It may include preparation of food, washing of clothes, looking after the kids, and other activities related within the house which depend upon the nature of the job both are employed in.

Therefore, the young man may not settle to a decision and may continuously even after months considering all the variables. Fuzzy logic may help in drawing a line in taking a decision between the two proposals even if the variables are imprecise and vague in nature.

## 5.4 PROBABILITY THEORY VS POSSIBILITY THEORY

Among all concepts and techniques in fuzzy logic, possibility theory is the one that is most often confused with probability theory. Possibility and probability measure two kinds of uncertainty. Probability theory attempts to explain events occurring in a random space. Representation of probability requires the knowledge about the solution space [3].

For example, while tossing a coin, the possible solution space is {Head, Tail} (i.e., the probability of getting a head or tail is 0.5 and has equal chances). Let us try to consider a newly opened foreign restaurant. It may be difficult to predict the colour of the variety of rice served in the restaurant. The reason is that the solution space is not small. In fact, we do not know the solution space. However, *possibility theory complements probability theory if the knowledge about the solution space is incomplete.*

Let us try to illustrate possibility with a different example. Imagine you are working in a plant to predict the temperature. When a person asks about the temperature of a particular day, your answer may be any one of the following:

*Answer 1*: Temperature ranges from 24°C to 34°C.
*Answer 2*: Temperature is more or less medium.

Both the answers impose a constraint (based on our perception) on the possible temperature on that particular day. The *first answer* imposes a crisp constraint. This implies that the temperature cannot be less than 24°C and cannot be greater than 34°C. The *second answer* imposes an imprecise constraint on the temperature of that particular day. Unlike the answer within an interval, the second response does not have sharp well-defined boundaries between the possible temperatures and the impossible ones. However, it suggests that a certain temperature is more possible than the other one.

When we assign a fuzzy set, a variable whose value we do not know exactly introduces an *imprecise constraint* on the variables value. We call such a constraint a *possibility distribution*, because it specifies the degree of possibility for the variable to take a certain value. The constraint imposed by an internal value assignment is a special kind of possibility distribution. The concept of possibility distribution generalizes the notion of interval value to smooth the boundary between the possible values and the impossible values so that possibility becomes a matter of degree. We use $\Pi(x)$ to denote the possibility distribution of variable $x$.

Possibility measures the degree of ease for a variable to take a value, whereas probability measures the likelihood for a variable to take a value. Hence, they deal with two different types of uncertainty. *Possibility theory handles imprecision and probability theory handles likelihood of occurrence.* This fundamental difference leads to different mathematical properties of their distributions. Being a measure of occurrence, the probability distribution of a variable must add up exactly 1. The possibility distribution is not subject to this restriction since a variable can have multiple possible values.

The notion of non-interactiveness in possibility theory is analogous to the concept of independence in probability theory. If two random variables $x$ and $y$ are independent, their joint probability distribution is the product of their individual distributions. Similarly, if two linguistic variables are non-interactive, their joint possibility distribution is formed by combining their individual possibility distributions through a fuzzy conjunction operator. Basically, two variables are non-interactive if they do not have an impact on each other. Even though possibility and probability are different, they are related in a way. If it is impossible for a variable $x$ to take a value $x_i$, it is also improbable for $x$ to have the value $x_i$, that is,

$$\Pi_x(x_i) = 0 \Rightarrow P_x(x_i) = 0$$

In general, possibility can serve as an upper bound on probability: $P_x(x_i) \leq \Pi_x(x_i)$. The distributions between probability and possibility are given in Table 5.1.

Table 5.1 Probability versus possibility

| Probability distribution | Possibility distribution |
| --- | --- |
| $0 < P(x) < 1$ | $0 < \Pi(x) < 1$ |
| $p(x, y) = p(x) \times p(y)$ if $x$ and $y$ are independent $\int p(x) \, dx = 1$ | $\Pi(x, y) = \Pi(x) \vee \Pi(y)$ if $x$ and $y$ are non-interacting. |

It should be noted that the possibilities and probabilities can be combined to handle problems in which both kinds of uncertainty exist. *However to conclude, fuzzy set theory can define set membership as a possibility distribution. In addition, fuzzy logic measures the degree to which an outcome belongs to an event, whereas probability measures the likelihood of an event to occur.*

## 5.5 CLASSICAL SETS AND FUZZY SETS

We know a *crisp set* is a collection of distinct (precisely defined) elements. In classical set theory, a crisp set can be a superset containing other crisp sets. A superset will represent the universe of discourse if it defines the boundaries in which all elements reside. In any given situation, a new element can be tested to see whether it belongs to any set. This query is mathematically represented by the characteristic function.

Fuzziness is a property of language. Its main source is the imprecision involved in defining and using symbols. Consider an example, the set of members with height less than 5 ft in a particular family [1]. In a set theory, the set of members may be established by pointing to every member in that family asking the question, 'Are you less than 5 feet?'. In classical set theory we are allowed to use only two answers: Yes or No. Let us code Yes as 1 and No as 0.

Thus, our answers will be in the pair {0, 1}. If the answer is 1, an element belongs to a set; if the answer is 0, it does not. In the end we collect all the members whose label is 1 and obtain the set of members in that family. Suppose we ask the question, 'How many members in a family are of short height?'. Again we could point to every member and say, 'Your height is short'.

The answer here too could artificially be restricted to {0, 1}. Now it is a set not uniquely defined. It all depends on what we mean by the *word function*. Word function has many shades of meaning and can be used in many different ways. Their meaning and use may vary with different persons, circumstances, and purposes; it depends on the specifics of a situation. We say therefore that the set of members of short height is a fuzzy set, in the sense that we may not have crisply defined criteria for deciding membership into the set. Fuzziness is a feature of their representation in a milieu of symbols and is generally a property of models, computational procedures, and language. A *fuzzy set* is a collection of distinct elements with a varying degree of relevance or inclusion [4].

### 5.5.1 Representation of a Classical Set

Classical set as already mentioned is a collection of objects of any kind. They can be represented as list method, rule method, and characteristic function method. The examples of these methods are given in Table 5.2.

Table 5.2  Classical set representation

| Method | Examples |
|---|---|
| **List method**<br>Listing of objects in a set parenthesis. | $N = \{1, 2, 3, \ldots 100\}$<br>$A = \{\text{Madras, Madurai, Roorkee, Mumbai}\}$ |
| **Rule method**<br>The set is defined by property or rule satisfied by every object within the set parenthesis. | $N = \{x \mid f(x)\}$<br>$N = \{f(3)\} = \{3, 6, 9, \ldots\}$<br>$A = \{\text{Densely populated city}\}$ |
| **Characteristic function method**<br>The set is defined by a function termed as characteristic function denoted as $\mu$. The characteristic function declares whether the element is a member of the set or not. | $A = \{\text{Pigeon, Horse, Trichy, 5, 6}\}$<br>$x \in A$ implies that $x$ is a member of set $A$<br>$x \notin A$ implies that $x$ is not a member of set $A$.<br>$\mu_A(x) = \begin{cases} 1 \text{ for } x \in A \\ 0 \text{ for } x \notin A \end{cases}$ |

Consider an example of grading system, where *S, A, B, C, D, E,* and *F* are grades awarded to the students in exams. Grade awarded for the students scoring from 90 to 100 will be *S*. Grade awarded to students scoring from 80 to 89 will be *A*. Subsequent grades will be allotted as per the following set definitions:

$S = \{x \mid 90 \leq x \leq 100\}$
$A = \{x \mid 80 \leq x \leq 89\}$
$B = \{x \mid 70 \leq x \leq 79\}$
$C = \{x \mid 60 \leq x \leq 69\}$
$D = \{x \mid 50 \leq x \leq 59\}$
$E = \{x \mid 40 \leq x \leq 49\}$
$F = \{x \mid 0 \leq x \leq 39\}$

Also, the grades can be represented with the help of a graph as in Fig. 5.1. It can be noticed that the range of marks within 70 and 79 have a value $=1$ and all remaining elements will have $\mu_B(x) = 0$. That is, $69 \notin B$ whose characteristic function $\mu_B(x) = 0$; $71 \in B$ whose characteristic function $\mu_B(x) = 1$.

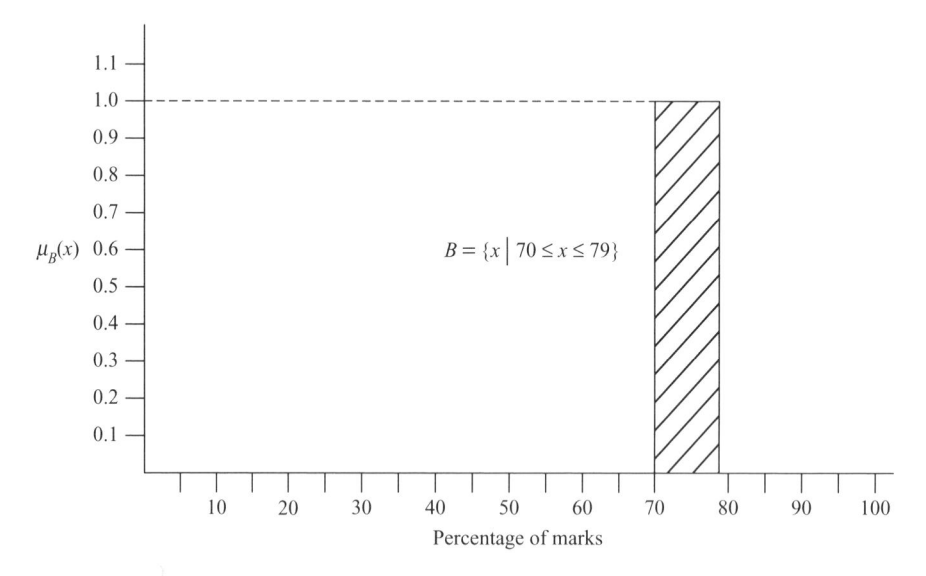

**Fig. 5.1** Representation of classical set $B$ and its characteristic function

## 5.5.2 Representation of a Fuzzy Set

Crisp set rises and falls abruptly making its elements totally disjoint with one another [5]. However, such strict categorization does not exist when considering human reasoning. Consider the following statement:

*Rahul scored* high *in the T20 match.*

Let us try to distinguish between high and low score using crisp set. The assumption is that the runs scored above 50 are considered high. However, if a batsman scores 49 runs, according to crisp set theory his score is not high. However, the human intelligence will not accept 49 runs as low and 50 runs as a good score. Human perception about the good score continuously varies. Consider the truth associated with the aforementioned statement if the batsman's score is 10 runs. Then it is definitely not a good score. However, 40 runs can be accepted as good. Hence, in a fuzzy set theory, membership function $\mu_{Good}(x)$ for 10 runs is 0.1 and 40 runs is 0.8. This membership function describes the amount of truth in the statement. Figure 5.2 shows the fuzzy membership values for a range of runs scored by the batsman in a graph.

The curve in the graph represents the line of human thinking process. Representation of a physical variable as a continuous curve is called *fuzzy set* or *membership function*. The numerical value is termed as *Degree of membership* or *Truth function*.

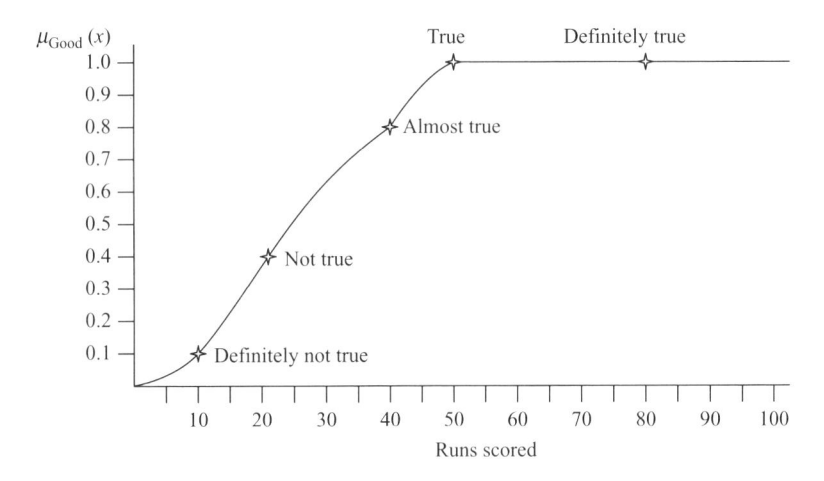

**Fig. 5.2** Membership function

Let us try to classify the 'batsman scores' into three categories such as 'good score', 'average score', and 'bad score'. The membership function of the three categories is represented as $\mu_{Good}(x)$, $\mu_{Avg}(x)$, and $\mu_{Bad}(x)$. They can be represented as shown in Fig. 5.3.

Many degrees of membership are allowed in fuzzy sets. A number between 0 and 1 indicates the degree of membership to a set in the interval {0, 1} [6]. The point of departure for fuzzy sets is simply the generalization of the valuation set from the pair of numbers {0, 1} to all numbers found in the interval {0, 1}.

When the valuation set is expanded, the nature of the characteristic function is altered which is known as *membership function* and is denoted by $\mu_A(x)$. The membership function can take intermediate values between 1 and 0 and is often indicated using square brackets [0, 1]. Since the interval {0, 1} contains infinite numbers, infinite degrees of membership are possible.

$$\mu_A(x): X \rightarrow \{0, 1\} \quad (5.1)$$

Thus referring to Eq. (5.1), we say that a membership function maps every element of the universe of discourse $X$ to the interval {0, 1}. In general, fuzzy sets are denoted in two ways. If $X$ is the universe of discourse and $x$ is a particular element of $X$, then a fuzzy set $A$ is defined on $X$ and may be written as a collection of ordered pairs, as given here:

$$A = \{(x, \mu_A(x))\}, \quad x \in X \quad (5.2)$$

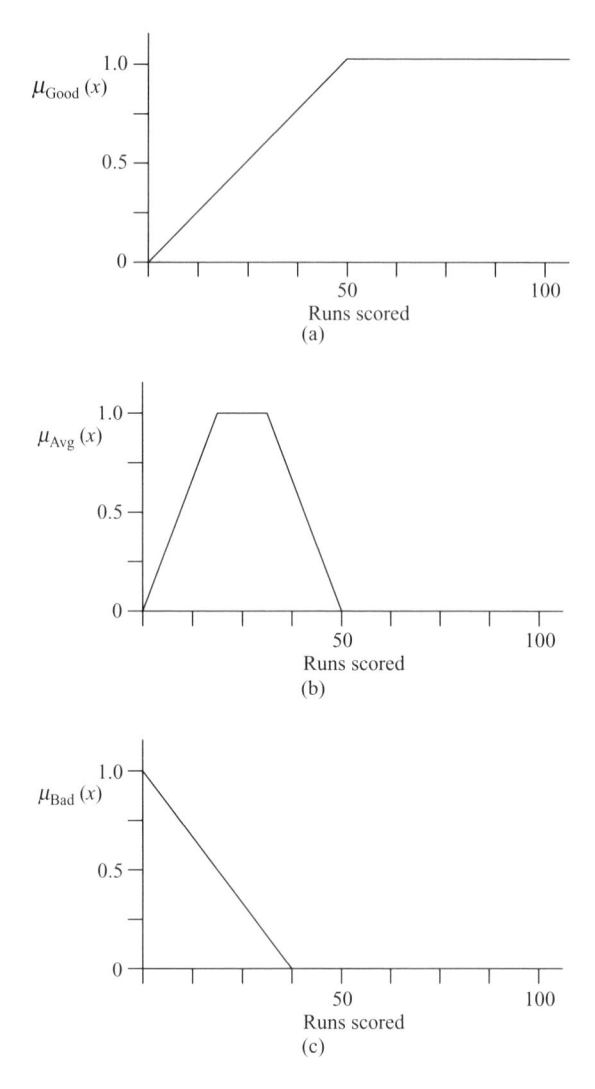

**Fig. 5.3** (a) Membership of good score (b) Membership of average score (c) Membership of bad score

where, each pair $(x, \mu_A(x))$ is called a *singleton*. Here, $x$ is followed by its membership in $A$ (i.e., $\mu_A(x)$.

In a classical set theory, the characteristic function only distinguishes between belonging to a set and not belonging to it. If we re-define the crisp set $A$ as $A = \{x\}$, then we only include the elements with characteristic functions that are equal to 1. In crisp sets, a singleton is simply the element $x$ by itself whereas in fuzzy sets, a singleton is composed of two terms: $x$ and $\mu_A(x)$.

A singleton can also be represented as $\mu_A(x)/x$, that is, by putting the membership function first, followed by the marker '/', which is not division but indicates the separation of the function from x. Singletons whose membership value in a fuzzy set is 0 may be omitted (i.e., optional). Let us try to illustrate a set of small integers $A$ defined (subjectively) over the universe of discourse of positive integers. Then the set $A$ may be given by the collection or union of all singletons $\mu_A(x_i)/x_i$ as in Eq. (5.3) [7].

$$A = \{(1, 1.0), (2, 1.0), (3, 0.75), (4, 0.5), (5, 0.3), \\ (6, 0.3), (7, 0.1), (8, 0.1)\} \tag{5.3}$$

The fuzzy set $A$ can also be represented as follows:

$$A = \sum_{x_i \in X} \mu_A(x_i)/x_i \tag{5.4}$$

In this alternative notation, the set of small integers mentioned earlier can be written like this:

$$A = \mu_A(1)/1 + \mu_A(2)/2 + \mu_A(3)/3 + \mu_A(4)/4 + \mu_A(5)/5 \\ + \mu_A(6)/6 + \mu_A(7)/7 + \mu_A(8)/8 \\ = 1.0/1 + 1.0/2 + 0.75/3 + 0.5/4 + 0.3/5 + 0.3/6 \\ + 0.1/7 + 0.1/8$$

For a continuous universe of discourse, we write as follows:

$$A = \int_x \mu_A(x)/x \tag{5.5}$$

where, the integral sign represents the union of all $\mu_A(x)/x$ singletons.

For example, the fuzzy set $A$ for a set of small numbers can be defined over the set of non-negative real numbers through a continuous membership function, which may be written such as this:

$$\mu_A(x) = \frac{1}{1 + \left(\dfrac{x}{6}\right)^2} \tag{5.6}$$

From Eq. (5.5), the fuzzy set $A$ is written as follows:

$$A = \int_{x \geq 0} \mu_A(x)/x = \int_{x \geq 0} \left[\frac{1}{1 + \left(\dfrac{x}{6}\right)^2}\right]/x \tag{5.7}$$

The membership function of fuzzy set $A$ is shown in Fig. 5.4. The difference between crisp sets and fuzzy sets can be understood based on their characteristic and membership functions.

### 5.5.3 Basic Properties of Fuzzy Sets

A system has several input and output variables. Each variable has its own maximum and minimum values. These variables may be composed of multiple, overlapping fuzzy sets, where each fuzzy set describe a portion of the variable's

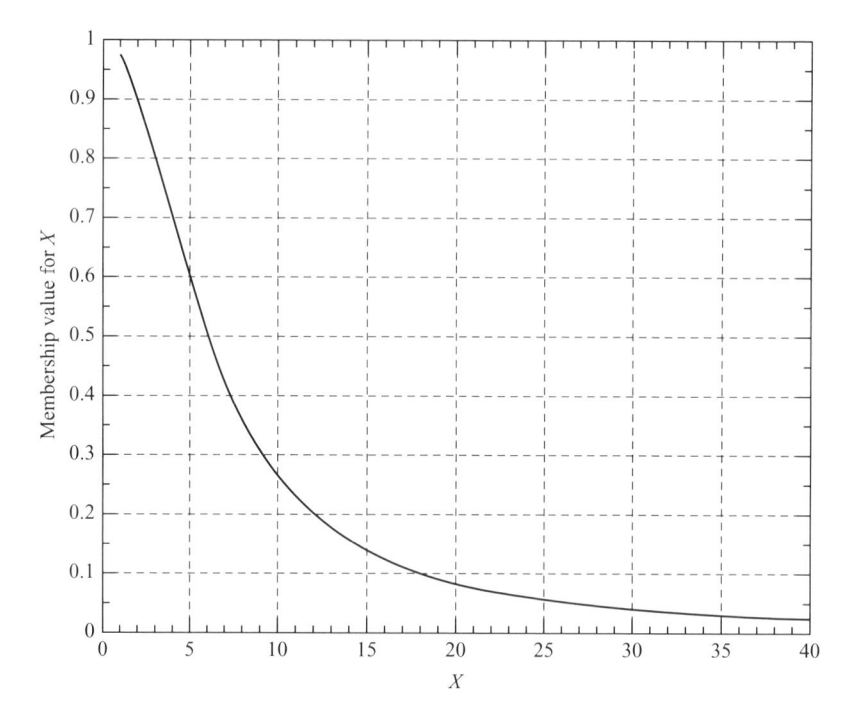

**Fig. 5.4** Membership diagram function for fuzzy set A = {small numbers}

range of space. Let us try to categorize the model of 'batsman scores' again into 'good score', 'average score', and 'bad score' as shown in Fig. 5.5.

The complete range of the model variable is called *universe of discourse*. Universe of discourse is associated with the system variable (score) and not with a particular fuzzy set (Good Score, Average Score, or Bad Score).

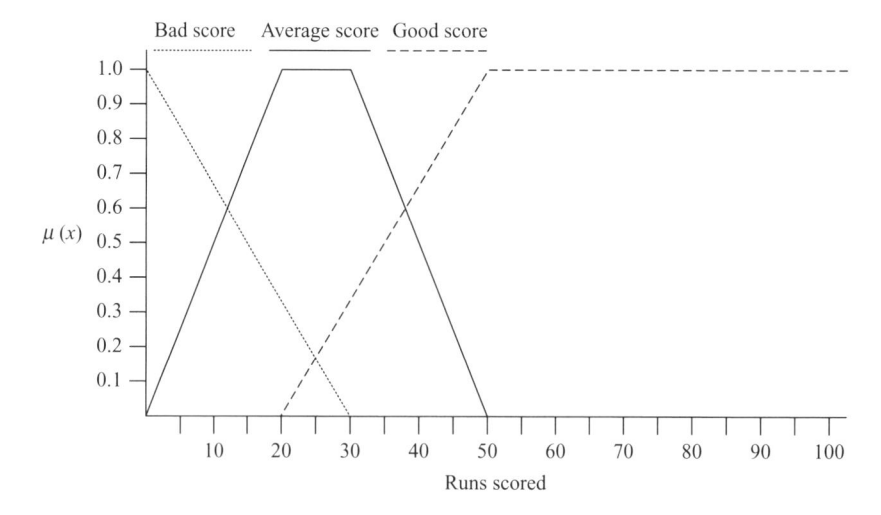

**Fig. 5.5** Membership function of overlapping fuzzy sets

Let the *universe of discourse* of the model variable score be between 0 to 100 runs. The range of values covered by a particular fuzzy set is termed as *domain of fuzzy set*. The *domain of fuzzy set* is set of elements whose degree of membership in the fuzzy set is greater than zero. The domain of fuzzy sets for Good Score, Average Score and Bad Score are 20 to 100, 0 to 50, and 0 to 30, respectively.

They can be represented within the parenthesis as Good Score = $\{20, 100\}$, Average Score = $\{0, 50\}$, and Bad Score = $\{0, 30\}$. The domain is selected to represent the operating range of value for the fuzzy set. The domain has both upper and lower end, the scope of value associated with fuzzy set may be closed-ended or open-ended. For example, fuzzy sets bad score and average score are close ended. The fuzzy set good score is open-ended such that the batsman's score can go beyond 100 as well. However, we terminate the domain at this point.

### 5.5.3.1 Non-convex and Convex Fuzzy Sets

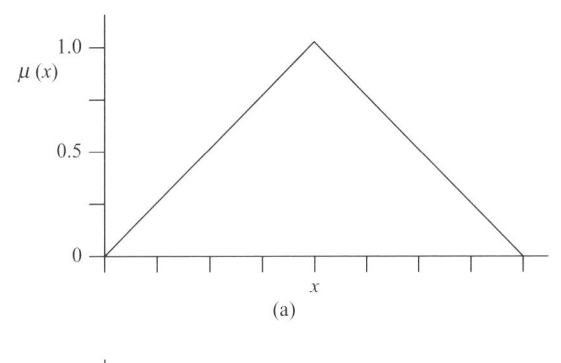

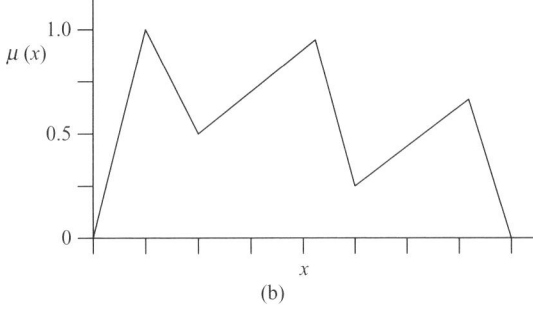

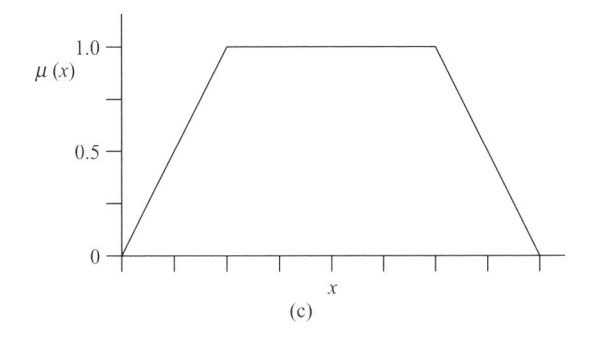

**296** Soft Computing with MATLAB Programming

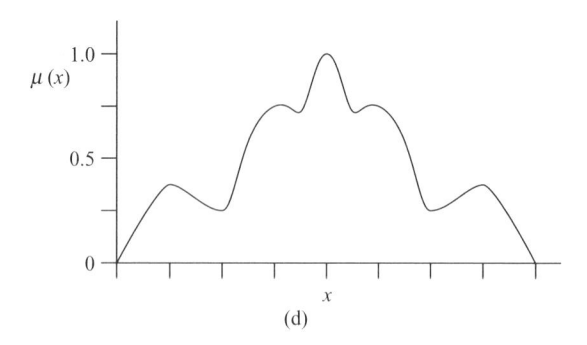

(d)

**Fig. 5.6** (a) Convex fuzzy set (b) Non-convex fuzzy set (c) Convex fuzzy set (d) Non-convex set

Non-convex fuzzy sets are fuzzy sets in which membership grade alternately increases and decreases on the domain. Fuzzy sets in which membership grades do not alternately increase and decrease are called convex fuzzy set. Some of the examples of convex and non-convex fuzzy sets are shown in Fig. 5.6.

It should be noted that the membership function defines the fuzzy set having a range of values in the horizontal axis. However, the only constraint a membership function is in the vertical axis that must be scaled between 0 and 1. The function can take any shape and depend upon the requirement of the designer. Some of the commonly used fuzzy sets are shown in Fig. 5.7. The characteristic equation is also given with respect to each fuzzy set. The points $a$, $b$, $c$, and $d$ in Fig. 5.7 represent the design parameters of the membership function.

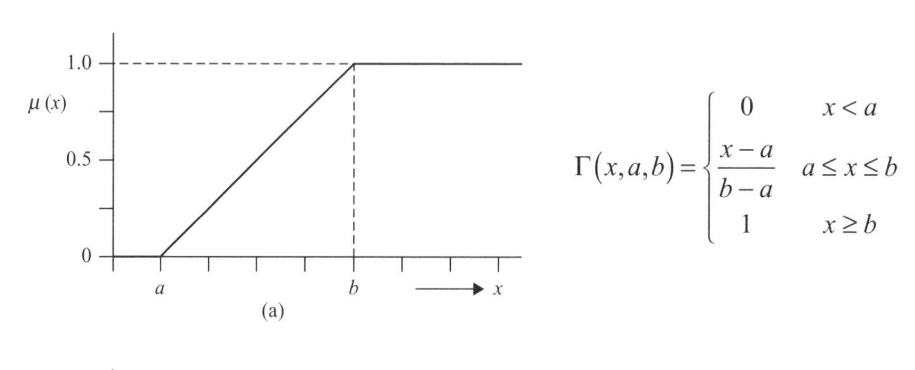

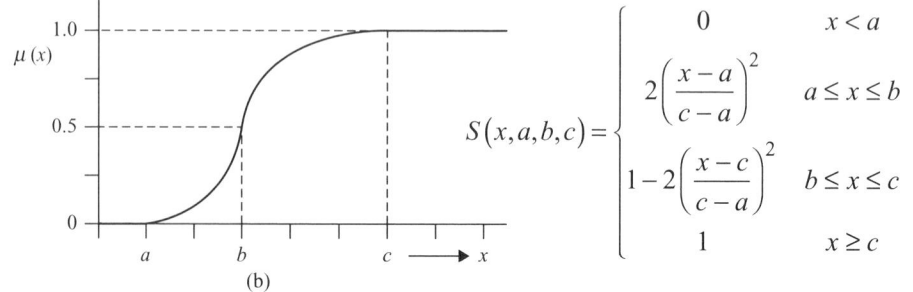

$$\Gamma(x,a,b) = \begin{cases} 0 & x < a \\ \dfrac{x-a}{b-a} & a \leq x \leq b \\ 1 & x \geq b \end{cases}$$

(a)

$$S(x,a,b,c) = \begin{cases} 0 & x < a \\ 2\left(\dfrac{x-a}{c-a}\right)^2 & a \leq x \leq b \\ 1 - 2\left(\dfrac{x-c}{c-a}\right)^2 & b \leq x \leq c \\ 1 & x \geq c \end{cases}$$

(b)

$$G(x,a,b) = e^{-b(a-x)^2}$$

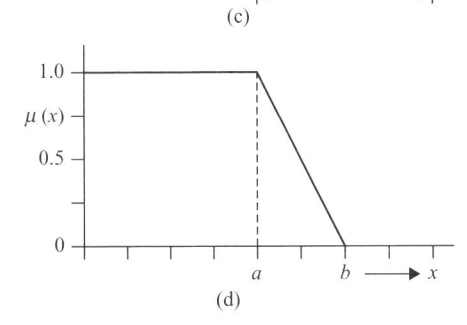

(c)

$$L(x,a,b) = \begin{cases} 1 & x < a \\ \dfrac{b-x}{b-a} & a \leq x \leq b \\ 0 & x \geq b \end{cases}$$

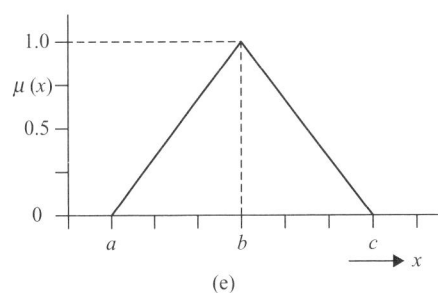

(d)

$$\lambda(x,a,b,c) = \begin{cases} 0 & x < a \\ \dfrac{x-a}{b-a} & a \leq x \leq b \\ \dfrac{c-x}{c-b} & b \leq x \leq c \\ 0 & x \geq c \end{cases}$$

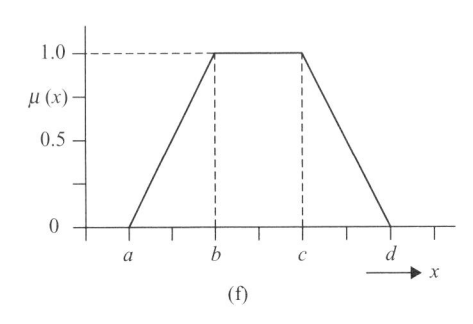

(e)

$$\Pi(x,a,b,c,d) = \begin{cases} 0 & x < a \\ \dfrac{x-a}{b-a} & a \leq x \leq b \\ 1 & b < x < c \\ \dfrac{d-x}{d-c} & c \leq x \leq d \\ 0 & x \geq d \end{cases}$$

(f)

**Fig. 5.7** Function fuzzy sets (a) Γ – Linearly expressed gamma membership function (b) S – Sigmoidal membership function (c) G – Gaussian membership function (d) L – L membership function (e) λ – Triangle membership function (f) Π – Trapezoidal membership function

## 5.6 FUZZY SET OPERATIONS

Analytical solutions are required when operations of two or three fuzzy sets describe the uncertainties of a given problem. The following are some of the important set operations that can be carried out using fuzzy sets:

1. Intersection of fuzzy sets
2. Union of fuzzy sets
3. Complement of fuzzy sets

The applications of aforecited operations in decision-making are explained and illustrated in the following sections.

## 5.6.1 Intersection of Fuzzy Sets

Intersection of two fuzzy sets contains the elements that are common to both the sets and is also equivalent to logical AND operation. In fuzzy logic, this operation is performed by taking the minimum of the truth membership functions. If $A$ and $B$ are two fuzzy sets having a membership values of $\mu_A(x)$ and $\mu_B(x)$, then the intersection of these two fuzzy sets is given by the Eq. (5.8).

$$\mu_A(x) \wedge \mu_B(x) = \min\{\mu_A(x), \mu_B(x)\} \qquad (5.8)$$

Let us try to illustrate with an example. Consider parents looking for a bridegroom for their daughter. They want to their daughter to be married within a stipulated period of time. The preference of their daughter is that the bridegroom should be tall and earning a higher salary. They decided that the bridegroom should be definitely greater than 6.4 feet and his salary should be greater than ₹ 20,000. Let us assume that the very essential qualifications such as character and family background are all already satisfied. Based on the available information, the height and the salary of the available candidates are tabulated in Table 5.3. Suppose they are very particular about their preference in satisfying both the conditions thereby taking crisp decision, there are no candidates available for their daughter.

However, if they are flexible enough to take an intelligent decision for their daughter, then the fuzzy logic decision can help them in their decision-making.

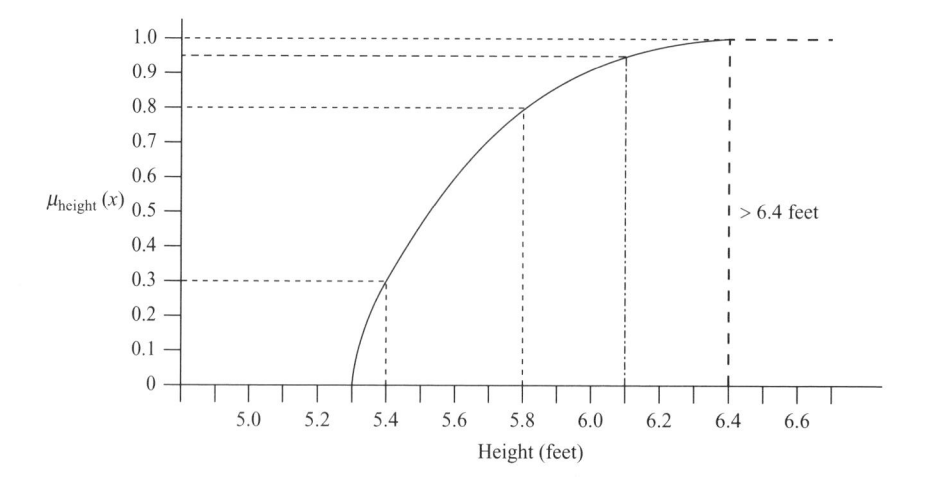

**Fig. 5.8** Membership function (Height)

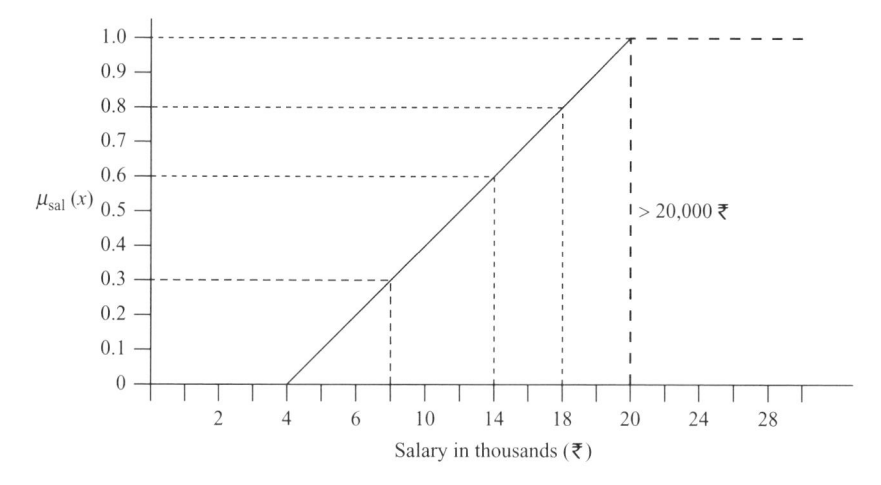

**Fig. 5.9** Membership function (Salary)

**Table 5.3** Bridegroom details—I

| Name | Height (ft) | Salary (₹) | $\mu_{height}(x)$ | $\mu_{sal}(x)$ | $\mu_{height}(x) \wedge \mu_{sal}(x)$ |
|---|---|---|---|---|---|
| Banerji | 6.1 | 8,000 | 0.95 | 0.3 | 0.3 |
| Gupta | 6.4 | 4,000 | 1 | 0 | 0 |
| Vetri | 5.8 | 14,000 | 0.8 | 0.6 | **0.6** |
| Vinoth | 5.4 | 18,000 | 0.3 | 0.8 | 0.3 |
| Raja | 5.0 | 20,000 | 0 | 1 | 0 |

Let the characteristic function for tallness is given by $\mu_{height}(x)$ and the characteristic function for the salary is given by $\mu_{sal}(x)$. The membership function chosen by for tallness and salary is shown in Figs 5.8 and 5.9, respectively. When the intersection operation of two fuzzy set is performed as per Eq. (5.8), then there are three out of five candidates who are eligible. However, the one who had the high truth value is Vetri.

Even though there are no suitable candidates in the crisp decision mechanism, the best decision within the stipulated period, the daughter's parents can decide to propose Vetri for their daughter. Therefore, from Table 5.3, we can conclude that Vetri is the likely person to be selected who is found to be best with both the attributes preferred by their daughter (i.e., tallness and salary). It should be noted that suitable membership function for the right variable should be selected for any application. However, this depends upon the designer's experience and his preference.

Suppose, let us try to analyse if we change the membership functions for the illustrated example. Now the membership function chosen for salary and tallness is shown in Figs 5.10 and 5.11, respectively. The final results are tabulated in Table 5.4. Here, Banerji with a truth value of 0.65 is the winner. Vetri is not

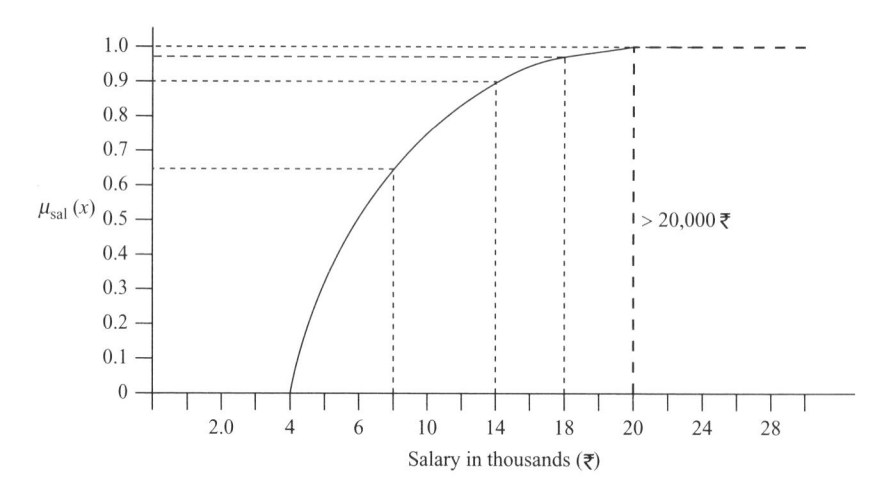

**Fig. 5.10** Membership function (Salary)

selected in this case. Now looking at the attributes of Banerji and Vetri, Banerji is taller than Vetri, but earns lesser than Vetri. Therefore in the first illustration, the ramping membership function chosen (Fig. 5.9) for salary gives more weightage to its variable. Therefore, Vetri is selected.

However, in the second illustration, the ramping membership function chosen (Fig. 5.11) for tallness gives more weightage to its variable (height). Therefore, Banerji is selected. If the daughter's preference is tallness, then she can marry Banerji. However, if the daughter's preference is higher salary, then she can marry Vetri. Therefore, the fuzzy designer should select the right choice of membership function based on the preferences.

Suppose, if the preference between the two inputs tallness and salary is same, then let us try to illustrate by choosing the same functions. In the third illustration we use the ramping function, by considering Figs 5.9 and 5.11 for salary and

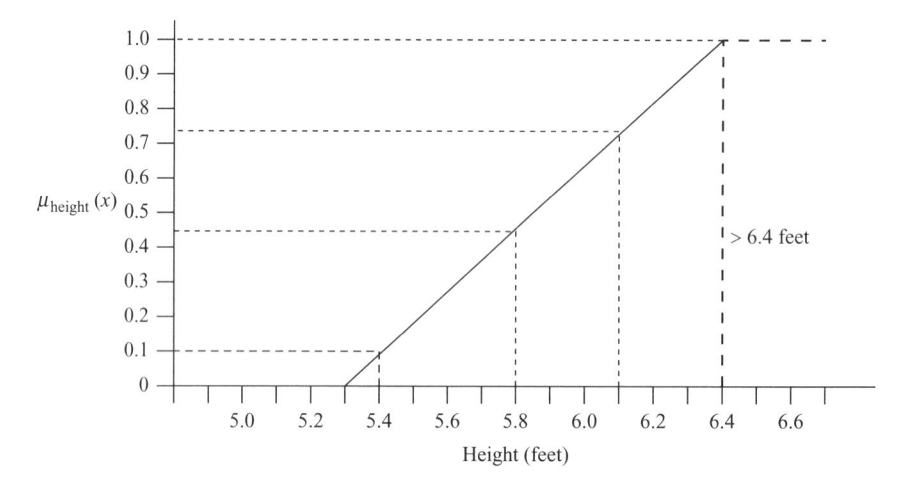

**Fig. 5.11** Membership function (Height)

Table 5.4  Bridegroom details—II

| Name | Height (ft) | Salary (₹) | $\mu_{height}(x)$ | $\mu_{sal}(x)$ | $\mu_{height}(x) \wedge \mu_{sal}(x)$ |
|---|---|---|---|---|---|
| Banerji | 6.1 | 8,000 | 0.73 | 0.65 | **0.65** |
| Gupta | 6.4 | 4,000 | 1 | 0 | 0 |
| Vetri | 5.8 | 14,000 | 0.45 | 0.9 | 0.45 |
| Vinoth | 5.4 | 18,000 | 0.1 | 0.97 | 0.1 |
| Raja | 5.0 | 20,000 | 0 | 1 | 0 |

height, respectively. The results are tabulated in Table 5.5. In the fourth illustration we use the curved function, by considering Figs 5.8 and 5.10 for height and salary, respectively. The results are tabulated in Table 5.6.

The results from Tables 5.5 and 5.6, clearly suggest that Vetri is the right choice if the preference level between two input variable remains the same.

Table 5.5  Bridegroom details—III

| Name | Height (ft) | Salary (₹) | $\mu_{height}(x)$ | $\mu_{sal}(x)$ | $\mu_{height}(x) \wedge \mu_{sal}(x)$ |
|---|---|---|---|---|---|
| Banerji | 6.1 | 8,000 | 0.73 | 0.3 | 0.3 |
| Gupta | 6.4 | 4,000 | 1 | 0 | 0 |
| Vetri | 5.8 | 14,000 | 0.45 | 0.6 | **0.45** |
| Vinoth | 5.4 | 18,000 | 0.1 | 0.8 | 0.1 |
| Raja | 5.0 | 20,000 | 0 | 1 | 0 |

Table 5.6  Bridegroom details—IV

| Name | Height (ft) | Salary (₹) | $\mu_{height}(x)$ | $\mu_{sal}(x)$ | $\mu_{height}(x) \wedge \mu_{sal}(x)$ |
|---|---|---|---|---|---|
| Banerji | 6.1 | 8,000 | 0.95 | 0.65 | 0.65 |
| Gupta | 6.4 | 4,000 | 1 | 0 | 0 |
| Vetri | 5.8 | 14,000 | 0.8 | 0.9 | **0.8** |
| Vinoth | 5.4 | 18,000 | 0.3 | 0.97 | 0.3 |
| Raja | 5.0 | 20,000 | 0 | 1 | 0 |

## 5.6.2 Union of Fuzzy Sets

Union of two fuzzy sets contains all the elements belonging to both the sets and is equivalent to logical OR operation. In fuzzy logic, this operation is performed by taking the maximum of the truth membership functions. If $A$ and $B$ are two fuzzy sets having a membership values of $\mu_A(x)$ and $\mu_B(x)$, then the union of these two fuzzy sets is given by Eq. (5.9).

$$\mu_A(x) \vee \mu_B(x) = \max\{\mu_A(x), \mu_B(x)\} \qquad (5.9)$$

Let us try to illustrate the intersection by the selection of players. Assume that there is a requirement of quality fast bowlers and quality batsmen in the T20 cricket tournament. The committee decided to select at least five players based on their requirement. Fast bowlers are can be characterized by the speed of bowling. However, the quality of the batsman can be characterized by their average scores in past tournaments. The selection committee decides that any speed greater than 135 km/hr will be considered for the fast bowlers.

Therefore, the membership value of the fast bowlers should become unity after 140 km/hr. Similarly, the committee decided to select any batsman whose average score is greater than 50 runs. Therefore, the membership value of the quality batsman should become unity after 50 runs. Let the characteristic function for the fast bowlers and quality batsman be given by $\mu_{f\_bowlers}(x)$ and $\mu_{q\_batsman}(x)$, respectively. The membership function chosen for the fast bowlers and the quality of batsman is given in Figs. 5.12 and 5.13, respectively. The details of the candidate players are given in Table 5.7.

Cricket players can be oriented more towards as a batsman or a bowler. Therefore, if the committee prefers to select the players based on quality fast bowlers or quality batsmen, then fuzzy OR (union) is used. However, if the selection committee feels to select all-round players who can bowl and also bat, then fuzzy AND (intersection) operation should be performed. In this illustration, let us assume the selection committee prefers to select the players who are more oriented towards being a quality batsman or a quality bowler. Therefore, fuzzy union operation has to be performed.

The fuzzy union operation can be performed as per Eq. (5.9) and the results are tabulated in Table 5.7. If the committee is very strict, they cannot have five players as per requirement.

Table 5.7 Details of the cricket players

| Name | Bowling speed (km/hr) | Average score (runs) | $\mu_{f\_bowlers}(x)$ | $\mu_{q\_batsman}(x)$ | $\mu_{f\_bowlers}(x) \vee \mu_{q\_batsman}(x)$ |
|---|---|---|---|---|---|
| Anil | 120 | 45 | 0.75 | 0.7 | 0.75 |
| Venkatesh | 130 | 15 | 0.9 | 0 | 0.9 |
| Sachin | 70 | 60 | 0 | 1 | 1 |
| Rahul | 50 | 65 | 0 | 1 | 1 |
| Raina | 90 | 35 | 0.33 | 0 | 0.33 |
| Robin | 55 | 40 | 0 | 0.38 | 0.38 |
| Abai | 140 | 25 | 1 | 0 | 1 |
| Balaji | 135 | 20 | 1 | 0 | 1 |

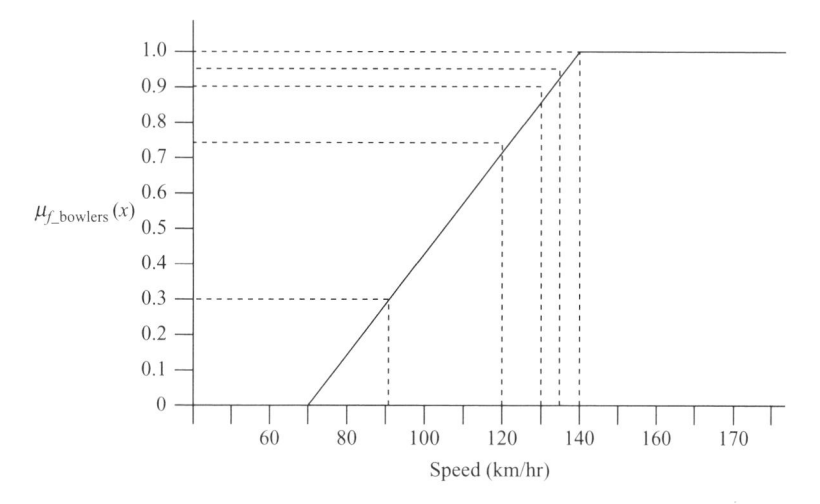

**Fig. 5.12** Membership function (Fast bowler)

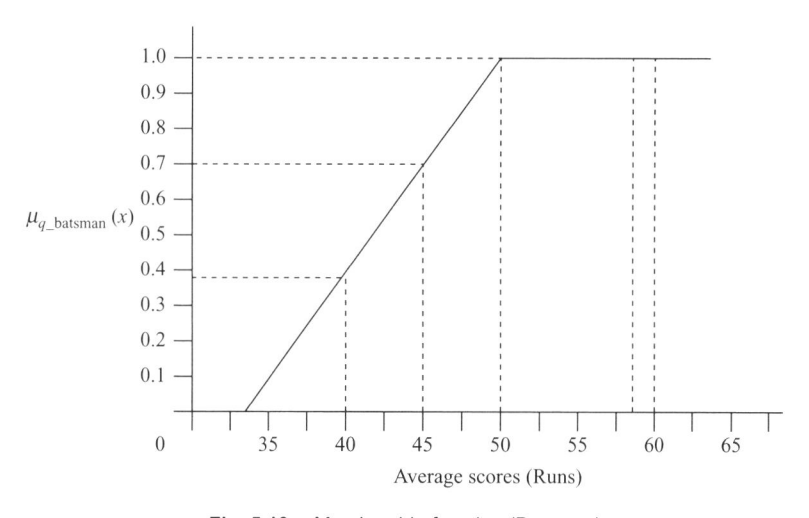

**Fig. 5.13** Membership function (Batsman)

Moreover, the crisp decision-making will help in selecting only four players. The genuine chance of Venkatesh will be lost. However, fuzzy provide a win-win situation for both Venkatesh and the selection committee. Since, the truth value of Venkatesh is '0.9', very closer to the threshold level '1' of pass value; he can be selected as the total requirement of the committee in five players.

## 5.6.3 Complement of Fuzzy Sets

The complement of a fuzzy set consists of the elements from universe which are not present in the set. This is equivalent to logical NOT operation. In fuzzy logic, this operation is performed by subtracting the membership value from one. If $A$ is a fuzzy set having membership values of $\mu_A(x)$, then the complement of the fuzzy set $A$ is given by the Eq. (5.10).

$$\mu_{\bar{A}}(x) = 1 - \mu_A(x) \tag{5.10}$$

Let us try to illustrate with the eliminating process of a singing competition. The selection is based on the marks given by three judges who are well versed in music. The singers getting more marks will be selected. The singers getting low marks will be eliminated (NOT selected). The maximum mark awarded is 100. The pass mark is 75. The committee will select the candidate who gets more than 75, but also decided to consider the candidates scoring beyond 50 marks if the required number of selected candidates are not obtained.

Now, if the rules of the competition are to eliminate three participants out of six, then the complement of fuzzy set operation can be performed. If the selection characteristic function is $\mu_{goodmarks}(x)$ or $\mu_{selection}(x)$, then the elimination characteristic function is the complement of the selection characteristic function and can be represented as $\mu_{badmarks}(x)$ or $\mu_{elimination}(x)$.

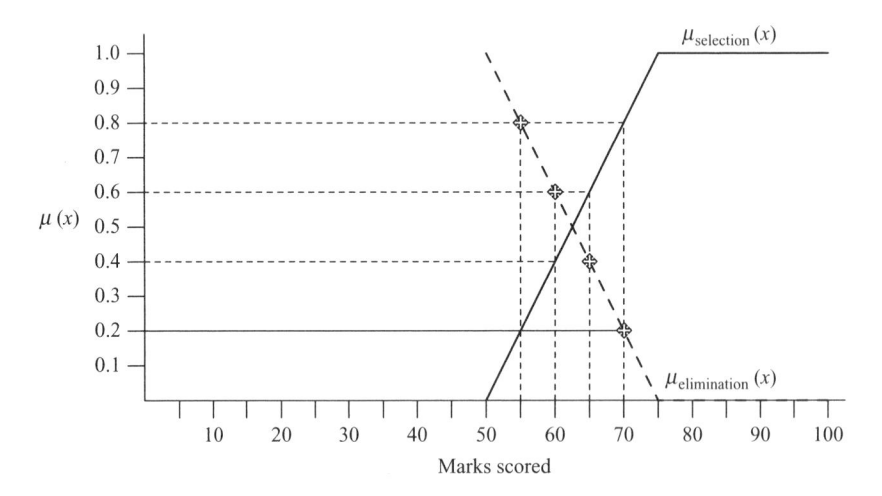

**Fig. 5.14** Membership function

The elimination characteristics function is given as follows:

$$\mu_{elimination}(x) = 1 - \mu_{selection}(x) \tag{5.11}$$

The membership functions for selection and elimination are shown in Fig. 5.14. Let the marks and the truth value of selection and elimination of scored by the 6 participants are given in Table 5.8. The results clearly suggest Ganga, Vanitha, and Mary are the candidates to be eliminated.

It should be noted that the aforesaid operations such as intersection, i.e., min($\wedge$) and union, i.e., max($\wedge$) can also be operated on entire sets. For example, if we want to find the smallest element $\mu$ out of a list of elements $(\mu_1, \mu_2, ...., \mu_n)$, then the same can be obtained as in Eq. (5.12).

$$\mu = \wedge(\mu_1, \mu_2, ...., \mu_n) \tag{5.12}$$

Table 5.8 Details of the participant marks

| Name | Marks (Max 100) | $\mu_{selection}(x)$ | $\mu_{elimination}(x)$ |
|---|---|---|---|
| Lakshmi | 75 | 1 | 0 |
| Fatheema | 70 | 0.8 | 0.2 |
| Vanitha | 60 | 0.4 | 0.6 |
| Parvathy | 80 | 1 | 0 |
| Mary | 65 | 0.6 | 0.4 |
| Ganga | 55 | 0.2 | 0.8 |

The Eq. (5.12) can also be written as Eqs (5.12) and (5.13).

$$\mu = \mu_1 \wedge \mu_2 \wedge \mu_3, ...\mu_n \tag{5.12}$$

$$\mu = \bigwedge_{k=1}^{n} (\mu_k) \tag{5.13}$$

## 5.6.4 Important Terminologies in Fuzzy Set Operations

The fuzzy set often gets its terminologies based on the membership values it possesses. Some of the terminologies and other fuzzy set operations are given in this section.

### (a) Empty fuzzy set

A fuzzy set $A$ is said to be an empty set if it has no members and its membership function is zero everywhere in its universe of discourse $U$ and can be written as Eq. (5.14).

$$A \equiv \emptyset \text{ if } \mu_A(x) = 0, \forall_x \in U \tag{5.14}$$

where '$\forall_x \in U$' is shorthand notation indicating 'for any element $x$ in $U$'.

### (b) Normal fuzzy set

A fuzzy set $A$ is said to be normal if it has a membership function that includes at least one singleton equal to unity in its universe of discourse $U$, thereby satisfying the Eq. (5.15).

$$\mu_A(x_0) = 1 \tag{5.15}$$

If there is no singleton equal to unity, then the fuzzy set is called *subnormal*.

### (c) Equal fuzzy sets

If the membership functions of any two fuzzy sets $A$ and $B$ are equal everywhere in the universe of discourse, then the two fuzzy sets are said to be equal, thereby satisfying the Eq. (5.16).

$$A \equiv B \text{ if } \mu_A(x) = \mu_B(x) \tag{5.16}$$

### (d) Fuzzy set support
A fuzzy set $A$ is supported only if the crisp set of all $x \in U$ such that the membership values are non-zero, which is given here:

$$\mu_A(x) > 0 \tag{5.17}$$

### (e) Product of fuzzy sets
Let us define any two fuzzy sets $A$ and $B$ defined on the same universe of discourse $X$. Then the product of the fuzzy set $A$ and $B$ produces a new fuzzy set, with its membership function value equal to the algebraic product of the membership function of $A$ and $B$ as in Eq. (5.18).

$$\mu_{A \cdot B}(x) \equiv \mu_A(x) \cdot \mu_B(x) \tag{5.18}$$

The product of the two fuzzy sets can be generalized to any number of fuzzy sets on the same universe of discourse. The algebraic product is the multiplication of the possibility values between each corresponding singleton.

### (f) Fuzzy set multiplication by a crisp number
The membership function of a fuzzy set $A$ is multiplied by the crisp number '$b$' to obtain a new fuzzy set whose membership function $\mu_{bA}(x)$ is given in Eq. (5.19).

$$\mu_{bA}(x) \equiv b\, \mu_A(x) \tag{5.19}$$

### (g) Power of a fuzzy set
If $\alpha$ is set as the power of a fuzzy set $A$, then a new fuzzy set $A^\alpha$ has a membership function value as given by Eq. (5.20).

$$\mu_{A^\alpha}(x) \equiv [\mu_A(x)]^\alpha \tag{5.20}$$

The power of a fuzzy set is an important concept in fuzzy representation of linguistic variables which will be discussed in the upcoming sections.

## 5.6.5 Properties of Fuzzy Sets

Most of the properties of the crisp set operations that also hold for fuzzy set operations are listed in Part A. In addition, there are properties in crisp sets that do not hold for fuzzy sets and properties specific to fuzzy sets are discussed in Part B. Let $A$, $B$, and $C$ be the fuzzy sets that are defined over a common universe of discourse $U$. The complement of a set can be represented by a bar over it.

**Part A**
   *Double negation law*

$$(\bar{A}) = A \tag{5.21}$$

   *Idempotency*

$$A \cup A = A \tag{5.22}$$

$$A \cap A = A \tag{5.22}$$

## Commutativity

$$A \cap B = B \cap A \quad (5.23)$$
$$A \cup B = B \cup A \quad (5.24)$$

## Associative property

$$(A \cup B) \cup C = A \cup (B \cup C) \quad (5.25)$$
$$(A \cap B) \cap C = A \cap (B \cap C) \quad (5.26)$$

## Distributive property

$$A \cup (B \cap C) = (A \cup B) \cap (A \cup C) \quad (5.25)$$
$$A \cap (B \cup C) = (A \cap B) \cup (A \cap C) \quad (5.27)$$

## Absorption

$$A \cap (A \cup B) = A \quad (5.28)$$
$$A \cup (A \cap B) = A \quad (5.29)$$

## De Morgan's laws

$$\overline{A \cup B} = \overline{A} \cap \overline{B} \quad (5.30)$$
$$\overline{A \cap B} = \overline{A} \cup \overline{B} \quad (5.31)$$

It should be noted that all the previously mentioned properties can be represented with the membership functions of the sets involved in the operations such as intersection, union, and complement. For example, the Eqs (5.25) and (5.30) that refers Associative Property and De Morgan's law can be written as in Eqs (5.32) and (5.33), respectively.

$$(\mu_A(x) \vee \mu_B(x)) \vee \mu_C(x) = \mu_A(x) \vee (\mu_B(x) \vee \mu_C(x)) \quad (5.32)$$

$$\overline{\mu_A(x) \vee \mu_B(x)} = \overline{\mu_A(x)} \wedge \overline{\mu_B(x)} \quad (5.33)$$

## Part B

Some of the properties that are not valid for fuzzy sets but valid for crisp sets are given as follows:

### Law of contradiction

$$A \cap \overline{A} = \emptyset \text{ (Empty fuzzy set)} \quad (5.34)$$

### Law of excluded middle

$$A \cup \overline{A} = U \text{ (Universe of discourse)} \quad (5.35)$$

Some of the properties that are specific only for fuzzy sets, but not valid for crisp sets are given as follows:

### Intersection of a fuzzy set with an empty set

$$A \cap \emptyset = \emptyset \text{ (Empty fuzzy set)} \quad (5.36)$$

(Or)

$$\mu_A(x) \wedge 0 = 0 \quad (5.37)$$

***Union of a fuzzy set with an empty set***

$$A \cup \emptyset = A \text{ (Empty fuzzy set)} \quad (5.38)$$

(Or)

$$\mu_A(x) \vee 0 = \mu_A(x) \quad (5.39)$$

***Intersection of a fuzzy set with Universe of discourse***

$$A \cap U = A \quad (5.40)$$

(Or)

$$\mu_A(x) \wedge 1 = \mu_A(x) \quad (5.41)$$

***Union of a fuzzy set with Universe of discourse***

$$A \cup U = U \text{ (Universe of discourse)} \quad (5.42)$$

(Or)

$$\mu_A(x) \vee 1 = 1 \quad (5.43)$$

It should be noted that the universe of discourse is also a fuzzy set having membership function that equals 1 everywhere (i.e., $\mu_U(x) = 1 \; \forall_x \in U$).

### 5.6.6 Fuzzy Arithmetics

Fuzzy set operations such as union, intersection, and complement can be applied to a fuzzy set using fuzzy numbers (membership function values). In addition, arithmetic operations such as addition, subtraction, multiplication, and division can be performed with fuzzy numbers using $\alpha$ cut or extension principle method which are discussed in the succeeding sections.

#### 5.6.6.1 Extension Principle (Discrete Fuzzy Set)

The extension principle is a mathematical tool for extending crisp mathematical notions and operations to the milieu of fuzziness. The extension principle suggests that fuzzifying the parameters of a function yields fuzzy outputs.

Consider a function $y = f(x)$ that maps elements $x_1, x_2, \ldots x_n$ of a universe of discourse $X$ to another universe of discourse $Y$. If the input argument is a fuzzy set $A$ on the universe of discourse of $X$, then the fuzzy output must obey the extension principle $B = f(A)$. Now the elements in the universe of discourse $Y$ become such as this:

$$y_1 = f(x_1) \quad (5.44a)$$

$$y_2 = f(x_2) \quad (5.44b)$$

$$\vdots$$

$$y_n = f(x_n) \quad (5.44c)$$

Now suppose that we have a fuzzy set A defined on $x_1, x_2, \ldots x_n$, then $A$ is given by Eq. (5.45).

$$A = \mu_A(x_1)/x_1 + \mu_A(x_2)/x_2 \ldots + \mu_A(x_n)/x_n \qquad (5.45)$$

We then ask the question, if the input to our function f becomes fuzzy then the output must be fuzzy. In other words, is there an output fuzzy set $B$ that can be computed by inputting $A$ to $f$?. The extension principle tells us that there is indeed such an output fuzzy set $B$ and it is given by Eq. (5.46).

$$B = f(A) = \mu_A(y_1)/f(x_1) + \mu_A(y_2)/f(x_2) \ldots + \mu_A(y_n)/f(x_n) \qquad (5.46)$$

where every single image of $x_i$ under f that is $y_i = f(x_i)$ becomes fuzzy to a degree determined by the membership value. In many-to-one mapping, which is often the case, the singleton with maximum membership value is selected. Thus for a certain $y_0$ we may have more than one $x$; let us say $x_1$ and $x_2$ are mapping to $y_0$. Hence, we have to decide which of the two membership values, $\mu_A(x_1)$ or $\mu_A(x_2)$, we should take as membership value of $y_0$. According to extension principle the maximum of the membership values of these elements in the fuzzy set $A$ to be chosen as the grade of membership of $y_0$ to the set $B$ which is given by Eq. (5.47).

$$\mu_B(y_0) = \mu_A(x_1) \vee \mu_A(x_2) \qquad (5.47)$$

The extension principle also can be generalized for several variables, from different universe of discourses.

**(a) Addition**

The extension principle is used to obtain the fuzzy set $C$ on $z = f(x, y)$. Suppose that we have two fuzzy numbers, $A$ and $B$, defined over $x$ and $y$ (the universe of discourse of real numbers). According to the extension principle, their sum is a fuzzy set on $z$ denoted as $C$, whose membership function is as follows:

$$\mu_C(z) \equiv \bigvee_{z=x+y} \left[ \mu_A(x) \wedge \mu_B(y) \right] \qquad (5.48)$$

The aforesaid equation tells us that to compute the grade of membership of a certain crisp number $z$ to the fuzzy number $C$, we take the maximum of the minima of the grades of membership of all pairs $x$ and $y$ which add up to $z$. Let us see how this concept is going to work in the following example.

Let us compute the sum $C$ of two fuzzy numbers $A = 3$ and $B = 6$, which is defined here:

$A = 3 = 0.3/1 + 0.7/2 + 1.0/3 + 0.7/4 + 0.3/5 + 0/6$
$B = 6 = 0.2/4 + 0.6/5 + 1.0/6 + 0.6/7 + 0.2/8 + 0/9$

Now, let us take another look at the previous equation. It calls for taking the maximum of pairs of singletons that add up to a certain $z$. For example, let us suppose $z = 8$. There are different ways to get $z = 8$; adding $y = 7$ and $x = 1$, adding

$y = 6$ and $x = 2$, adding $y = 5$ and $x = 3$, and so on. The following are minimum membership value of the pairs satisfying 8:

$\mu_A(6) \wedge \mu_B(2) = 0.0 \wedge 0.0 = 0.0$
$\mu_A(5) \wedge \mu_B(3) = 0.3 \wedge 0.0 = 0.0$
$\mu_A(4) \wedge \mu_B(4) = 0.7 \wedge 0.2 = 0.2$
$\mu_A(3) \wedge \mu_B(5) = 1.0 \wedge 0.6 = 0.6$
$\mu_A(2) \wedge \mu_B(6) = 0.7 \wedge 1.0 = 0.7$
$\mu_A(1) \wedge \mu_B(7) = 0.3 \wedge 0.6 = 0.3$
$\mu_A(0) \wedge \mu_B(8) = 0.0 \wedge 0.2 = 0.0$

Next, we take the maximum of these numbers, which in this case is 0.7; this is the maximum with respect to $z = 8$.

$$\mu_{A+B}(8) = [(0.0) \vee (0.0) \vee (0.2) \vee (0.6) \vee (0.7) \vee (0.3)]$$
$$= 0.7$$

This is the grade of membership of $z = 8$ to the sum $C = A + B$. We repeat this procedure for all possible addition values varies from 2 to 15. The final membership function of $C$ is given as follows:

$$C = 0/4 + 0.2/5 + 0.3/6 + 0.6/7 + 0.7/8 + 1.0/9 + 0.7/10 + 0.6/11$$
$$+ 0.3/12 + 0.2/13 + 0/14 + 0/15$$

It has been found that the maximum value corresponds to 9(3 + 6). The steps involved in the arrival of the fuzzy set $C$ are presented in the Table 5.9.

**(b) Subtraction**

To define the difference of fuzzy numbers $A$ and $B$, the extension principle is used by fuzzifying a function $z = x - y$. Fuzzification means that we define fuzzy sets on the universes of discourse where the crisp elements $x$ and $y$ are found. As a result, $z$ gets fuzzified as well; that is, there is a fuzzy set $C$ over the universe of discourse of the $z$'s, which is the result of fuzzifying the function $z = f(x, y) = x - y$. The membership function of $C = A - B$ can be computed from Eq. (5.49).

$$\mu_{A-B}(z) \equiv \vee_{z=x-y} \left[ \mu_A(x) \wedge \mu_B(y) \right] \qquad (5.49)$$

**(c) Multiplication**

We can define the product of $A$ and $B$ through the extension principle by fuzzifying the function $z(x, y) = x \cdot y$. The extension principle tells us that their product is a fuzzy set on $z$, denoted as $A \cdot B$, whose membership function is as follows:

$$\mu_{A \cdot B}(z) \equiv \vee_{z=x \cdot y} \left[ \mu_A(x) \wedge \mu_B(y) \right] \qquad (5.50)$$

Also multiplying a fuzzy set by a crisp number is discussed and is given in Section 5.6.4 of Eq. (5.19).

**(d) Division**

We can find the quotient of $A$ and $B$ through the extension principle by fuzzifying the function $z(x, y) = x \div y$, where $x$ and $y$ are crisp elements of the universe of discourse of $A$ and $B$. The extension principle tells us that $A \div B$ is a fuzzy set with membership function, as shown here:

$$\mu_{A \div B}(z) \equiv \bigvee_{z=x \div y} \left[ \mu_A(x) \wedge \mu_B(y) \right] \qquad (5.51)$$

Table 5.9  Fuzzy addition

| Sum $z = x+y$ | Possible combinations | | $\mu_A(x)$ | $\mu_B(y)$ | $\min(\mu_A(x), \mu_B(y))$ | $\max(\min(\mu_A(x), \mu_B(y)))$ |
|---|---|---|---|---|---|---|
| | x | y | | | | |
| 15 | 6 | 9 | 0 | 0 | 0 | 0 |
| 14 | 6 | 8 | 0 | 0.2 | 0 | 0 |
| | 5 | 9 | 0.3 | 0 | 0 | |
| 13 | 6 | 7 | 0 | 0.6 | 0 | 0.2 |
| | 5 | 8 | 0.3 | 0.2 | 0.2 | |
| | 4 | 9 | 0.7 | 0 | 0 | |
| 12 | 6 | 6 | 0 | 1.0 | 0 | 0.3 |
| | 5 | 7 | 0.3 | 0.6 | 0.3 | |
| | 4 | 8 | 0.7 | 0.2 | 0.2 | |
| | 3 | 9 | 1.0 | 0 | 0 | |
| 11 | 6 | 5 | 0 | 0.6 | 0 | 0.6 |
| | 5 | 6 | 0.3 | 1.0 | 0.3 | |
| | 4 | 7 | 0.7 | 0.6 | 0.6 | |
| | 3 | 8 | 1.0 | 0.2 | 0.2 | |
| | 2 | 9 | 0.7 | 0 | 0 | |
| 10 | 6 | 4 | 0 | 0.2 | 0 | 0.7 |
| | 5 | 5 | 0.3 | 0.6 | 0.3 | |
| | 4 | 6 | 0.7 | 1.0 | 0.7 | |
| | 3 | 7 | 1.0 | 0.6 | 0.6 | |
| | 2 | 8 | 0.7 | 0.2 | 0.2 | |
| | 1 | 9 | 0.3 | 0 | 0 | |
| 9 | 6 | 3 | 0 | 0 | 0 | 1.0 |
| | 5 | 4 | 0.3 | 0.2 | 0.2 | |
| | 4 | 5 | 0.7 | 0.6 | 0.6 | |
| | 3 | 6 | 1.0 | 1.0 | 1.0 | |
| | 2 | 7 | 0.7 | 0.6 | 0.6 | |
| | 1 | 8 | 0.3 | 0.2 | 0.2 | |
| | 0 | 9 | 0 | 0 | 0 | |

(Continued)

Table 5.9 (Continued)

| Sum $z = x+y$ | Possible combinations | | $\mu_A(x)$ | $\mu_B(y)$ | $\min(\mu_A(x), \mu_B(y))$ | $\max(\min(\mu_A(x), \mu_B(y)))$ |
|---|---|---|---|---|---|---|
| | x | y | | | | |
| 8 | 6 | 2 | 0 | 0 | 0 | 0.7 |
| | 5 | 3 | 0.3 | 0 | 0 | |
| | 4 | 4 | 0.7 | 0.2 | 0.2 | |
| | 3 | 5 | 1.0 | 0.6 | 0.6 | |
| | 2 | 6 | 0.7 | 1.0 | 0.7 | |
| | 1 | 7 | 0.3 | 0.6 | 0.3 | |
| | 0 | 8 | 0 | 0.2 | 0 | |
| 7 | 6 | 1 | 0 | 0 | 0 | 0.6 |
| | 5 | 2 | 0.3 | 0 | 0 | |
| | 4 | 3 | 0.7 | 0 | 0 | |
| | 3 | 4 | 1.0 | 0.2 | 0.2 | |
| | 2 | 5 | 0.7 | 0.6 | 0.6 | |
| | 1 | 6 | 0.3 | 1.0 | 0.3 | |
| | 0 | 7 | 0 | 0.6 | 0 | |
| 6 | 6 | 0 | 0 | 0 | 0 | 0.3 |
| | 5 | 1 | 0.3 | 0 | 0 | |
| | 4 | 2 | 0.7 | 0 | 0 | |
| | 3 | 3 | 1.0 | 0 | 0 | |
| | 2 | 4 | 0.7 | 0.2 | 0.2 | |
| | 1 | 5 | 0.3 | 0.6 | 0.3 | |
| | 0 | 6 | 0 | 1.0 | 0 | |
| 5 | 5 | 0 | 0.3 | 0 | 0 | 0.2 |
| | 4 | 1 | 0.7 | 0 | 0 | |
| | 3 | 2 | 1.0 | 0 | 0 | |
| | 2 | 3 | 0.7 | 0 | 0 | |
| | 1 | 4 | 0.3 | 0.2 | 0.2 | |
| | 0 | 5 | 0 | 0.6 | 0 | |
| 4 | 4 | 0 | 0.7 | 0 | 0 | 0 |
| | 3 | 1 | 1.0 | 0 | 0 | |
| | 2 | 2 | 0.7 | 0 | 0 | |
| | 1 | 3 | 0.3 | 0 | 0 | |
| | 0 | 4 | 0 | 0.2 | 0 | |

### 5.6.6.2 Alpha-cuts and Resolution Principle

A level fuzzy set has membership values greater than $\alpha$, where $\alpha$ lies between 0 and 1. For any given fuzzy set $A$, we can associate a collection of crisp sets known as α-cuts (alpha-cuts) or level sets of $A$. An α-cut is a crisp set consisting of elements of $A$ which belong to the fuzzy set at least to a degree α. α-cuts are indispensable in performing arithmetic operations with fuzzy sets that represent various qualities of numerical data. It should be noted that α-cuts are crisp, not fuzzy, sets.

The α-cuts of a fuzzy set $A$ denoted as $A^\alpha$ is the crisp set comprised of the elements $x$ of a universe of discourse $U$ for which the membership function of $A$ is greater than or equal to α; that is,

$$A^\alpha = \{x \in U \mid \mu_A(x) \geq \alpha\} \tag{5.52}$$

where α is a parameter in the range $0 < \alpha \leq 1$; the vertical bar '|' in the previous equation is shorthand for 'such that'. We can also fuzzify the new set depending on the computational objective. In practical terms, an α cut can be viewed as a lower-bound threshold for possibility. Accordingly, a membership function after being subjected to an α cut represents a set smaller than its original size in terms of the number of singletons.

For example, consider the following set $A$ of small integers:

$$A = 1.0/1 + 1.0/2 + 0.75/3 + 0.5/4 + 0.3/5 + 0.3/6 + 0.1/7 + 0.1/8$$

The 0.5-cut of $A$ is simply the crisp set $A^{0.5} = (1, 2, 3, 4)$ or it can be represented as follows:

$$A^\alpha = 1.0/1 + 1.0/2 + 0.75/3 + 0.5/4$$

The *resolution principle* offers an alternative way of representing membership to a fuzzy set through its α-cuts and is given here:

$$\mu_A(x) = \vee [\alpha \times \mu A^\alpha(x)] \ \forall_{\alpha \to [0\ 1]} \tag{5.53}$$

In Eq. (5.52) α varies from 0 to 1. It also indicates that the membership function of $A$ is the union of all α cuts, after each crisp set $\mu_{A\alpha}(x)$ is multiplied by α. This approach yields an approximate representation of the membership function because some of the fuzzy logic singletons are converted into crisp singletons.

### 5.6.6.3 Alpha-cut Method (Discrete Fuzzy Set)

The alpha-cut method for discrete fuzzy set is carried out by performing arithmetic operations within the boundary elements present between fuzzy sets and the solutions that depend on the boundary values of the discrete fuzzy function.

#### (a) Addition

When two fuzzy numbers $A$ and $B$ are added, a new fuzzy number $C = A + B$ is computed and it is uniquely described when we obtain its membership function, $\mu_C(z) \equiv \mu_{A+B}(z)$, with $z$ being the crisp sum of $x$ and $y$, the elements of the universe of discourse of $A$ and $B$. The addition of $A$ and $B$ may be defined in terms of addition of the α-cuts of the two numbers as follows:

$$A + B = \left[a_1^{(\alpha)}, a_2^{(\alpha)}\right] + \left[b_1^{(\alpha)}, b_2^{(\alpha)}\right] \tag{5.54}$$

where $[a_1^{(a)}, a_2^{(a)}]$ is the collection of intervals representing the fuzzy number $A$, and $[b_1^{(a)}, b_2^{(a)}]$ is the collection of intervals representing the fuzzy number $B$. Intervals are added by adding their corresponding left and right endpoints.

$$A + B = \left[ a_1^{(\alpha)} + a_1^{(\alpha)}, b_2^{(\alpha)} + b_2^{(\alpha)} \right] \tag{5.55}$$

**(b) Subtraction**

Using $\alpha$-cut representation the difference $C$ of two fuzzy numbers $A$, $B$ may be defined as follows:

$$A - B = \left[ a_1^{(\alpha)}, a_2^{(\alpha)} \right] - \left[ b_1^{(\alpha)}, b_2^{(\alpha)} \right] \tag{5.56}$$

where $[a_1^{(\alpha)}, a_2^{(\alpha)}]$ is the collection of closed intervals representing $A$, and $[b_1^{(\alpha)}, b_2^{(\alpha)}]$ is the collection of closed intervals representing $B$. Two intervals are subtracted by subtracting their left and right endpoints.

$$A - B = \left[ a_1^{(\alpha)} - b_1^{(\alpha)}, a_2^{(\alpha)} - b_2^{(\alpha)} \right] \tag{5.57}$$

**(c) Multiplication**

The multiplication of two numbers $A$, $B$ can be represented using the $\alpha$-cut representation, and is defined as follows:

$$A \cdot B = \left[ a_1^{(\alpha)}, a_2^{(\alpha)} \right] \cdot \left[ b_1^{(\alpha)}, b_2^{(\alpha)} \right] \tag{5.58}$$

In general, the product of two intervals is a new interval whose left endpoint is the product of the left endpoints of the two intervals and the right endpoint is the product of the right endpoints of the two intervals.

So,
$$A \cdot B = \left[ a_1^{(\alpha)} \cdot b_1^{(\alpha)}, a_2^{(\alpha)} \cdot b_2^{(\alpha)} \right] \tag{5.59}$$

**(d) Division**

Similarly the division of two fuzzy numbers $A$ and $B$ in terms of their $\alpha$-cut representation is as follows:

$$A \div B = \left[ a_1^{(\alpha)}, a_2^{(\alpha)} \right] \div \left[ b_1^{(\alpha)}, b_2^{(\alpha)} \right] \tag{5.60}$$

Hence, provided that $b_2^{(\alpha)} \neq 0$ and $b_1^{(\alpha)} \neq 0$, the quotient of $A$, $B$ is given such as this:

$$A \div B = \left[ \frac{a_1^{(\alpha)}}{b_2^{(\alpha)}}, \frac{a_2^{(\alpha)}}{b_1^{(\alpha)}} \right] \tag{5.61}$$

### 5.6.6.4 Alpha-cut Method (Continuous Fuzzy Set)

In most of the discrete arithmetic operations, the solutions basically depends on the boundary values of the discrete fuzzy function and free from all types of mathematical complexity. However, the accuracy of the operations can be improved by assuming continuous fuzzy functions instead of discrete functions.

The membership functions of two fuzzy numbers $A, B$ are defined as follows:

$$\mu_A(x) = \begin{cases} 0 & x \leq 6 \\ x-6 & 6 \leq x \leq 7 \\ -x+8 & 7 \leq x \leq 8 \\ 0 & x \geq 8 \end{cases} \quad (5.62)$$

and

$$\mu_B(x) = \begin{cases} 0 & x \leq 3 \\ x-3 & 3 \leq x \leq 4 \\ -x+5 & 4 \leq x \leq 5 \\ 0 & x \geq 5 \end{cases} \quad (5.63)$$

To simplify matters, consider the left and right side of each membership function separately. There is one equation for the left side and another for the right side of the membership function of $A$, and likewise for $B$. Thus, we have a total of four equations to parameterize. Let us take the left side of $A$, $\mu_{A^l}(x) = x - 6$ and write it in terms of $\alpha$. We note that the value of $\alpha$ is the same as the value of the membership function at the left endpoint $a_1^{(\alpha)}$ of an $\alpha$-cut and $a_1^{(\alpha)}$ is the value of $x$ at that point. We have the following for the left side of A:

$$\alpha = a_1^{(\alpha)} - 6 \Rightarrow a_1^{(\alpha)} = \alpha + 6 \quad (5.64)$$

where $a_1^{(\alpha)}$ is the left endpoint of the 'slice' of $A$ at level $\alpha$.

Similarly for the right side of $A$, we parameterize the right endpoint $a_2^{(\alpha)}$ of each $\alpha$-cut in terms of $\alpha$ as given here:

$$\alpha = -a_2^{(\alpha)} + 8 \Rightarrow a_2^{(\alpha)} = -\alpha + 8 \quad (5.65)$$

Using Eqs (5.64) and (5.65) the $\alpha$-cut representation of $A$ is written as follows:

$$A = [a_1^{(\alpha)}, a_2^{(\alpha)}] = [\alpha + 6, -\alpha + 8] \quad (5.66)$$

The membership function of the number $B$ is parameterized in terms of $\alpha$ in a similar fashion. We express the left endpoint $b_1^{(\alpha)}$ in terms of $\alpha$ by the following equation:

$$\alpha = b_1^{(\alpha)} - 3 \Rightarrow b_1^{(\alpha)} = \alpha + 3 \quad (5.67)$$

The right endpoint $b_2^{(\alpha)}$ is given as a function of $\alpha$ such as this:

$$\alpha = -b_2^{(\alpha)} + 5 \Rightarrow b_2^{(\alpha)} = -\alpha + 5 \quad (5.68)$$

From the aforegiven results, the following is the representation of $B$:

$$B = [b_1^{(\alpha)}, b_2^{(\alpha)}] = [\alpha + 3, -\alpha + 5] \quad (5.69)$$

## (a) Addition
From the $\alpha$-cut representations of $A$ and $B$, we find their summation by adding their corresponding intervals at each $\alpha$, that is,

$$\begin{aligned}C = A + B &= [a_1(\alpha) + b_1(\alpha), a_2(\alpha) + b_2(\alpha)]\\ &= [(\alpha + 6) + (\alpha + 3), (-\alpha + 8) + (-\alpha + 5)]\\ &= [2\alpha + 9, -2\alpha + 13]\end{aligned} \quad (5.70)$$

Therefore, $C$ is given as follows:

$$C = [c_1(\alpha), c_2(\alpha)] = [2\alpha + 9, -2\alpha + 13] \quad (5.71)$$

We note that the left and right endpoints of $C$ are functions of $\alpha$. To express the fuzzy number $C$ in terms of a membership function, we derive equations for the left and right side of $C$. The left endpoint $c_1(\alpha) = x$ and recalling that $\alpha = \mu_{C^L}(x)$, where $\mu_{C^L}(x)$ is the left-side membership function for $C$, which is given here:

$$x = 2\mu_{C^L}(x) + 9 \Rightarrow \mu_{C^L}(x) = (x - 9)/2 \quad (5.72)$$

In a similar manner we obtain an equation for $\mu_{C^R}(x)$, the right side of the membership function of $C$, and solve it to obtain the membership function of the right side, that is,

$$x = -2\mu_{C^R}(x) + 13 \Rightarrow \mu_{C^R}(x) = (x - 13)/2 \quad (5.73)$$

From the earlier mentioned results, we obtain the following:

$$\mu_C(x) = \begin{cases} 0 & x \leq 9 \\ (x-9)/2 & 9 \leq x \leq 11 \\ -(x-13)/2 & 11 \leq x \leq 13 \\ 0 & x \geq 13 \end{cases} \quad (5.74)$$

## (b) Subtraction
Similarly, the following equation is for subtraction:

$$\begin{aligned}C = A - B &= [a_1(\alpha) - b_2(\alpha), a_2(\alpha) - b_1(\alpha)]\\ &= [(\alpha + 6) - (-\alpha + 5), (-\alpha + 8) - (\alpha + 3)]\\ &= [2\alpha + 1, -2\alpha + 5]\end{aligned} \quad (5.75)$$

Therefore, $C$ is as follows:

$$C = [c_1(\alpha), c_2(\alpha)] = [2\alpha + 1, -2\alpha + 5] \quad (5.76)$$

Now we have the following result:

$$x = 2\mu_{C^L}(x) + 1 \Rightarrow \mu_{C^L}(x) = (x - 1)/2 \quad (5.77)$$

In a similar manner, we obtain an equation for $\mu_{C^R}(x)$, the right side of the membership function of $C$, and solve it to obtain the membership function of the right side, that is,

$$x = 2\mu_{C^R}(x) + 5 \Rightarrow \mu_{C^R}(x) = -(x-5)/2 \quad (5.78)$$

From Eqs (5.76) and (5.77) we obtain this:

$$\mu_C(x) = \begin{cases} 0 & x \leq 1 \\ (x-1)/2 & 1 \leq x \leq 3 \\ -(x-5)/2 & 3 \leq x \leq 5 \\ 0 & x \geq 5 \end{cases} \quad (5.79)$$

### (c) Multiplication

Similarly for multiplication and division, let us assume the following membership functions $A$ and $B$:

$$\mu_A(x) = \begin{cases} 0 & x \leq 7 \\ x-7 & 7 \leq x \leq 8 \\ -x+9 & 8 \leq x \leq 9 \\ 0 & x \geq 9 \end{cases} \quad (5.80)$$

and

$$\mu_B(x) = \begin{cases} 0 & x \leq 4 \\ x-4 & 4 \leq x \leq 5 \\ -x+6 & 5 \leq x \leq 6 \\ 0 & x \geq 6 \end{cases} \quad (5.81)$$

The left and right endpoints of $A_1$ are provided here:

$$\alpha = (a_1^{(\alpha)}) - 7 \Rightarrow a_1^{(\alpha)} = (\alpha+7) \quad (5.82)$$

and

$$\alpha = -(a_2^{(\alpha)}) + 9 \Rightarrow a_2^{(\alpha)} = (9-\alpha) \quad (5.83)$$

Using Eqs (5.82) and (5.83), we obtain $A$ as shown here:

$$A_1 = [a_1^{(\alpha)}, a_2^{\alpha}] = [(\alpha+7), (9-\alpha)]$$

Similarly, we parameterize the membership function of $B_1$ and write its left and right endpoints at each $\alpha$ such as the following:

$$\alpha = (b_1^{(\alpha)} - 4) \Rightarrow b_1^{(\alpha)} = (\alpha+4) \quad (5.84)$$

and

$$\alpha = (b_2^{(\alpha)}) + 6 \Rightarrow b_2^{(\alpha)} = (6-\alpha) \quad (5.85)$$

Thus, from Eqs (5.84) and (5.85), the interval representation of $B$ is as follows:

$$B_1[b_1^{(\alpha)}, b_2^{(\alpha)}] = [(\alpha+4)(6-\alpha)] \quad (5.86)$$

Having the endpoints of $A$ and $B$ in terms of $\alpha$, we multiply the two numbers and obtain the following:

$$C = A_1 \cdot B_1 = [a_1^{(\alpha)} \cdot b_1^{(\alpha)}, a_2^{(\alpha)} \cdot b_2^{(\alpha)}]$$
$$= [(\alpha + 7)(\alpha + 4), (9 - \alpha)(6 - \alpha)]$$
$$= [\alpha^2 + 11\alpha + 28, \alpha^2 - 15\alpha + 54] \quad (5.87)$$

The interval representation of $C$ is as follows:

$$C = [c_1^{(\alpha)}, c_2^{(\alpha)}] = [\alpha^2 + 11\alpha + 28, \alpha^2 - 15\alpha + 54]$$

where the left and right endpoints in Eq. (5.87) are functions of $\alpha$. We can obtain the membership function of $C$ as well. The equation for the left-side membership function $\mu_{C^L}(x)$ is obtained by setting $c_1^{(\alpha)} = x$ and recalling that $\alpha = \mu_{C^L}(x)$. Thus, we obtain an equation involving $\mu_{C^L}(x)$, which is given here:

$$(\mu_{C^L}(x))^2 + 11\mu_{C^L}(x) + 28 - x = 0 \quad (5.88)$$

Solving the previous quadratic equation for $\mu_{C^L}(x)$, we obtain two solutions and accept only the value of $\mu_{C^L}(x)$ in [0,1], ignoring the other one. The result is given as follows:

$$\mu_{C^L}(x) = -11/2 + 1/2 \left( \sqrt{121 - 4(28 - x)} \right) \quad (5.89)$$

Similarly, we obtain an equation for $\mu_{C^R}(x)$, the right side of the membership function of $C$, and solve it, keeping the solution which is within [0,1]. The result is

$$\mu_{C^R}(x) = 15/2 - 1/2 \left( \sqrt{225 - 4(54 - x)} \right) \quad (5.90)$$

The following is the membership function of $C$:

$$\mu_C(x) = \begin{cases} 0, & x \leq 28 \\ -11/1 + 1/2\left(\sqrt{121 - 4(28 - x)}\right) & 28 \leq x \leq 40 \\ 15/2 - 1/2\left(\sqrt{225 - 4(54 - x)}\right) & 40 \leq x \leq 54 \\ 0 & x \geq 54 \end{cases} \quad (5.91)$$

It should be noted that $C$ has its peak point at crisp 40 and therefore may be considered a fuzzy number 40. *It should also be noted that multiplying two fuzzy numbers results in a new number whose shape has been considerably changed, no longer having a triangular membership function with linear sides but in this case parabolic sides. Multiplication in general has the effect of 'fattening' the lower part of the membership functions involved.*

### (d) Division
Let us find $C = A \div B$ using interval division. Here,

$$A_1 = [a_1^{(\alpha)}, a_2^{(\alpha)}] = [(\alpha + 7), (9 - \alpha)] \quad (5.92)$$

$$B_1 = [b_1^{(\alpha)}, b_2^{(\alpha)}] = [(\alpha + 4), (6 - \alpha)] \quad (5.93)$$

Since the result of $A_1/B_1$ is a fraction, the modified new membership function is

$$\mu_B(x) = \begin{cases} 0 & x \leq 3 \\ x-3 & 3 \leq x \leq 4 \\ -x+5 & 4 \leq x \leq 5 \\ 0 & x \geq 5 \end{cases} \quad (5.94)$$

$$B_1 = [b_1^{(\alpha)}, b_2^{(\alpha)}] = [(\alpha+3), (5-\alpha)] \quad (5.95)$$

Thus their quotient $C = A \div B$ is obtained using the following equations:

$$C = A \div B = \left[ \frac{a_1^{(\alpha)}}{b_2^{(\alpha)}}, \frac{a_2^{(\alpha)}}{b_1^{(\alpha)}} \right] \quad (5.96)$$

$$= \left[ \frac{\alpha+7}{5-\alpha}, \frac{9-\alpha}{\alpha+3} \right] \quad (5.97)$$

The $\alpha$-cut representation of $C$ is as follows:

$$C = [c_1^{(\alpha)}, c_2^{(\alpha)}] = \left[ \frac{\alpha+7}{5-\alpha}, \frac{9-\alpha}{\alpha+3} \right] \quad (5.98)$$

where the left and right endpoints are functions of $\alpha$. The equation of the left side is obtained by setting $c_1^{(\alpha)} = x$ and recalling that $\alpha = \mu_{C^L}(x)$, where, $\mu_{C^L}(x)$ is the left-side membership function for $C$. The following is the result:

$$\mu_{C^L}(x) = \frac{5x-7}{1+x} \quad (5.99)$$

Similarly, we obtain an equation for $\mu_{C^R}(x)$, right side of the membership function of $C$, and solve it to obtain

$$\mu_{C^R}(x) = \frac{9-3x}{1+x} \quad (5.100)$$

The following is the analytical description of the membership function $C$:

$$\mu_C(x) = \begin{cases} 0, & x \leq 7/5 \\ \dfrac{5x-7}{x+1}, & 7/5 \leq x \leq 2 \\ \dfrac{9-3x}{x+1}, & 2 \leq x \leq 3 \\ 0 & x \geq 3 \end{cases} \quad (5.101)$$

It should be noted from equation $(A \div B)$ that the quotient is a new fuzzy number that no longer has a triangular shape with linear sides.

### 5.6.6.5 Higher Order Arithmetic Operations

It has been observed that, if the membership function of the variables ($A$ and $B$) are linear, then $A + B$, $A - B$, and $A/B$ will also be linear, but $a_1^{(\alpha)}$ and $a_2^{(\alpha)}$ of $A \times B$ will be of second order. Now, for example, if $A$, $B$, $C$, and $D$ are different fuzzy numbers and if we want to calculate $A \times B \times C \times D$. Then $a_1^{(\alpha)}$ and $a_2^{(\alpha)}$ will be of fourth order, and so on. Finally, the complexity increases proportionally with the number of multiplication. Similarly, it is also true for higher order divisions.

From the previous discussion, it has been found that if the membership functions are non-linear or for higher order arithmetic operations, it is not easy to carry out arithmetic operations. Hence in the first step, it has been assumed that the membership functions of the variables are at least linear and if not, then it has to be expressed in terms of approximate linear function. However, in case of multiplication and division, mathematical complexity (i.e., the order of $\alpha$ in $a_1^{(\alpha)}$) is proportional to the order of multiplication and division. Hence, generation of suitable membership function becomes difficult.

Now, the fuzzy numbers are expressed as follows:

$A = [a_1^{(\alpha)}, a_2^{(\alpha)}] = [\alpha + 7, -\alpha + 9]$
$B = [b_1^{(\alpha)}, b_2^{(\alpha)}] = [\alpha + 4, -\alpha + 6]$
$A_1 = [a_1^{(\alpha)}, a_2^{(\alpha)}] = [4(\alpha + 1), -4(\alpha - 3)]$
$B_1 = [b_1^{(\alpha)}, b_2^{(\alpha)}] = [2\alpha, -4(\alpha - (3/2))]$

If we are interested to calculate $AB\, A_1 B_1$, then the value of $a_1^{(\alpha)}$ and $a_2^{(\alpha)}$ of the product will be of fourth order and hence it is suggested that in each level of multiplication, convert the quadratic function into its approximate linear using the following formula and proceed for the next step of operation.

$$Ax^2 + bx + c = \left(ax^{\max} + b\right)x + c \tag{5.102}$$

where $x^{\max}$ is the maximum value of $x$.

Now,

$$\begin{aligned} AB &= [(\alpha + 7)(\alpha + 4), (-\alpha + 9)(-\alpha + 6)] \\ &= [12\alpha + 28, -14\alpha + 54] \end{aligned} \tag{5.103}$$

$$\begin{aligned} AB\, A_1 &= [(\alpha + 7)(\alpha + 4)(4(\alpha + 1)), (-\alpha + 9)(-\alpha + 6)(-4(\alpha - 3))] \\ &= [208\alpha + 112, -328\alpha + 648] \end{aligned} \tag{5.104}$$

$$\begin{aligned} AB\, A_1 B_1 &= [(\alpha + 7)(\alpha + 4)(4(\alpha + 1))(2\alpha), (-\alpha + 9)(-\alpha + 6) \\ &\quad (-4(\alpha - 3))(-4(\alpha - (3/2)))] \\ &= [640\alpha, -3248\alpha + 3888] \end{aligned} \tag{5.105}$$

The membership function of the product is given here:

$$\mu_{ABA_1 B_1}(x) = \begin{cases} 0 & x < 7/5 \\ x/640 & 0 \leq x \leq 640 \\ (3888 - x)/3248 & 640 \leq x \leq 3888 \\ 0 & x > 3888 \end{cases} \tag{5.106}$$

The number $ABA_1 B_1$ described by equations $(ABA_1 B_1)$ has its peak at crisp 640, and therefore it can be considered as a fuzzy number 640 (as expected, since $8 \times 5 \times 8 \times 2 = 640$).

## 5.7 FUZZY RELATIONS

Classical relationship represents the presence or absence of correlation and interaction between the elements of two or more crisp sets. Here, only two degrees of relationship is possible: 'Completely Related' and 'Non-Related'. However, a fuzzy relation generalizes the aim of binary classical relation into one that allows partial membership. It is developed by allowing relationship between elements of two or more sets to take an infinite number of degrees of relation between extreme of 'Completely Related' and 'Non-Related'. It converts relation into matter of degree [8].

**Example 5.1**

Consider a patient meeting a doctor. The symptoms are S = $\{s_1, s_2, s_3\}$ = {Headache, Vomiting, Back pain}. Given the symptoms the disease may be D = $\{d_1, d_2, d_3, d_4, d_5\}$ = {Eye Problem, Nervous Disorder, Fever, Stomach Upset, Sprain}. First we need to establish how the symptoms are related to a disease and the membership grades given by the doctor for the relation as shown in Fig. 5.15. Find out the fuzzy relation matrix for the same.

The arrow in Fig. 5.15 indicates that the symptom is related with the problem. The numeric value on the arrow indicates that the grade of membership of the symptom with the problem (degree of association of symptom with the problem).

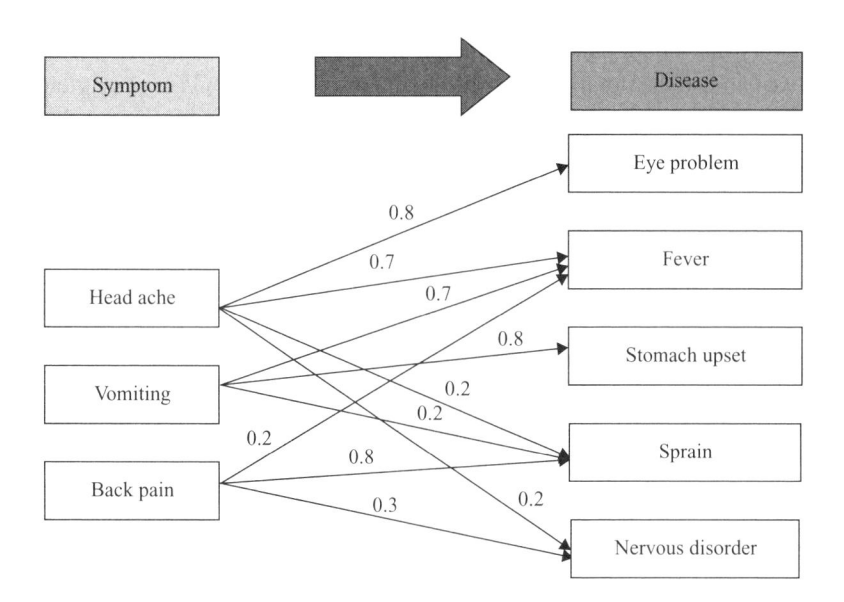

**Fig. 5.15** Fuzzy relation between symptom and disease

**Solution:** For the preceding example, the fuzzy relation $R$ can be expressed as $S \times D$ matrix.

$$R = \begin{array}{c|ccccc} S \diagdown D & d_1 & d_2 & d_3 & d_4 & d_5 \\ \hline s_1 & 0.8 & 0.7 & 0 & 0.2 & 0.2 \\ s_2 & 0 & 0.7 & 0.8 & 0 & 0.2 \\ s_3 & 0 & 0.2 & 0 & 0.8 & 0.3 \end{array}$$

Fuzzy relations are fuzzy sets defined on Cartesian products. Fuzzy sets have one universe of discourse, whereas fuzzy relations have higher dimensional universe of discourse. Fuzzy relations also map elements of one universe, say $X$, to those of another universe, say $Y$, through the Cartesian product of the two universes. The 'strength' of the relation between ordered pairs of the two universes is not measured with the characteristic function, but rather with a membership function expressing various 'degrees' of strength of the relation on the unit interval [0, 1]. Hence, a fuzzy relation $R$ is a mapping from the Cartesian space $X \times Y$ to the interval [0, 1], where the strength of the mapping is expressed by the membership function of the relation for ordered pairs from the two universes or $\mu_R(x, y)$.

Let $A$ be a fuzzy set on universe $X$ and $B$ be a fuzzy set on universe $Y$; then the Cartesian product between fuzzy sets $A$ and $B$ will result in a fuzzy relation $R$, which is contained within the full Cartesian product space, or

$$A \times B = R \subset X \times Y \tag{5.107}$$

where the fuzzy relation $R$ has a membership function as given here:

$$\mu_R(x, y) = \mu_{A \times B}(x, y) = \min(\mu_A(x), \mu_B(y)) \tag{5.108}$$

where every individual pair $(x, y)$ belongs to the Cartesian product $X \times Y$. Alternatively, we can use the notation to form the union of all $\mu_R(x, y)/(x, y)$ singletons of $X \times Y$. For a discrete Cartesian product, we would have the following result:

$$R = \sum_{(x_i, y_j) \in X \times Y} \mu_R(x_i, y_j)/(x_i, y_j) \tag{5.109}$$

Whereas, for a continuous Cartesian product we have the following result:

$$R = \int_{X \times Y} \mu_R(x, y)/(x, y) \tag{5.110}$$

The same notation is used for any $n$-array fuzzy relation.

An alternative way of representing them is by the membership matrix (of an $n \times m$ binary fuzzy relation) is given by the following equation:

$$R = \begin{bmatrix} \mu_R(x_1, y_1) & \mu_R(x_1, y_2) & \cdots & \mu_R(x_1, y_n) \\ \mu_R(x_2, y_1) & \mu_R(x_2, y_2) & \cdots & \mu_R(x_2, y_n) \\ \vdots & \vdots & & \vdots \\ \mu_R(x_m, y_1) & \mu_R(x_m, y_2) & \cdots & \mu_R(x_m, y_n) \end{bmatrix} \tag{5.111}$$

**Example 5.2**

Consider a speeding car which has two variables 'Speed' and 'Fuel Supply' which can be measured by speedometer and fuel gauge. The range of speed is defined by universe of discourse $S = [s_1, s_2, s_3]$. The range of variable fuel supply is defined by the universe of discourse $F = [f_1, f_2, f_3, f_4]$. Consider that $S$ can be classified into two fuzzy sets ('$A$ = Normal Speed', '$B$ = High Speed') and F can be classified into two fuzzy sets ('$C$ = Optimum Supply', '$D$ = Excess Supply'). Here, fuzzy sets $A$ and $B$ are defined on universe of discrete speed $S = [s_1, s_2, s_3]$ and $C$ is defined on universe of discrete fuel supply $F = [f_1, f_2, f_3, f_4]$. Speed-Fuel Supply pairs associated with efficient performance of the speeding car can be achieved by Cartesian product of $B$ and $C$.

*Solution:*

Let,
$$B = 0/s_1 + 0.6/s_2 + 1/s_3$$
$$C = 0.4/f_1 + 1/f_2 + 0.5/f_3 + 0/f_4$$

Then the Cartesian product $R$ can be given by $B \times C$

*Note:* $B$ can be represented by a column of size $3 \times 1$ and $C$ can be represented by a row vector of size $1 \times 4$.

$$R = B \times C = \begin{bmatrix} 0 \\ 0.6 \\ 1 \end{bmatrix} \times \begin{bmatrix} 0.4 & 1 & 0.5 & 0 \end{bmatrix} = \begin{bmatrix} 0 & 0 & 0 & 0 \\ 0.4 & 0.6 & 0.5 & 0 \\ 0.4 & 1 & 0.5 & 0 \end{bmatrix}$$

### 5.7.1 Operations on Fuzzy Relations

If $R$ and $S$ are fuzzy relations on the Cartesian space $X \times Y$, then the following operations apply for the membership values for various set operations:

**(a) Union**

The union operation of two fuzzy relations $R$ and $S$ is given as follows:

$$\mu_{R \vee S}(x, y) = \max(\mu_R(x, y), \mu_S(x, y)) \qquad (5.112)$$

**(b) Intersection**

The intersection operation of two fuzzy relations $R$ and $S$ is given here:

$$\mu_{R \wedge S}(x, y) = \min(\mu_R(x, y), \mu_S(x, y)) \qquad (5.113)$$

**(c) Complement**

The complement operation of the fuzzy relations $R$ is given as follows:

$$\mu_{\overline{R}}(x, y) = 1 - \mu_R(x, y) \qquad (5.114)$$

**(d) Containment**

The containment operation of the fuzzy relations $R$ and $S$ is given as follows:

$$R \subset S \Rightarrow \mu_R(x, y) \leq \mu_S(x, y) \qquad (5.115)$$

## 5.8 FUZZY COMPOSITION

Fuzzy compositions can combine fuzzy relations defined on different Cartesian products with each other in a number of different ways. A more complex form of relation is called 'composition of fuzzy relation', where the associations among fuzzy sets are of concern in addition to associations among the elements of each fuzzy set [9]. Composition acts as a bridge that allows us to connect one product space to another, provided that there is a common boundary. For a given two fuzzy relations—one in $X \times Y$ and another on $Y \times Z$—if we want to associate directly elements of $X$ with elements of $Z$, the set $Y$ is the common boundary. Composition results in a new relation that directly relates $X$ to $Z$.

Our main task in composition is to compute the grades of membership of the pairs $(x, z)$ in the composed relation, namely $\mu(x, z)$. Fuzzy algorithms are mathematically equivalent to fuzzy relations and the problem of inference or evaluating them with specific inputs is mathematically equivalent to composition. There are several types of composition. By far the most common in engineering applications is max-min composition, but we will also look at max-star, max-product, and max-average. In general, different types of compositions result in different composed relations.

### 5.8.1 Max-Min Composition

Given the relation matrices of the relation $R$ and $S$, the max-min composition is defined as $T = R \text{ o } S$. The max-min composition of two fuzzy relations uses the familiar operators of fuzzy sets, max ($\vee$) and min ($\wedge$). Suppose that we have two fuzzy relations ($R_1(x,y)$ and $R_2(y,z)$) defined over the Cartesian products $X \times Y$ and $Y \times Z$, respectively. The max-min composition of $R_1$ and $R_2$ is a new relation $R_1$ o $R_2$ defined on $X \times Z$ such as this:

$$R_1 \text{ o } R_2 \equiv \int_{x \times z} \vee_y \left[ \mu_{R_1}(x, y) \wedge \mu_{R_2}(y, z) \right] / (x, z) \quad (5.116)$$

where the symbol 'o' stands for max-min composition of relations $R_1$ and $R_2$. From the prior expression, we see that the grade of membership of each $(x, z)$ pair in the new relation is as given here:

$$\mu_{R_1 \text{ o } R_2}(x, z) = \vee_y \left[ \mu_{R_1}(x, y) \wedge \mu_{R_2}(y, z) \right] \quad (5.117)$$

where the outer maximum is taken with respect to the elements $y$ of the common boundary. The composition operations are very similar to multiplication in matrix algebra.

### 5.8.2 Max-Star Composition

Multiplication, summation, or some other binary operations (*) can be used in place of min ($\wedge$) while still performing maximization with respect to $y$. This type of composition of two fuzzy relations is generally known as the 'max-star' or 'max-* composition'. If '*' is an associative operation which is monotonically non-decreasing in each argument, then the max-star composition corresponds essentially to the max-min composition.

Suppose that we have two fuzzy relations $R_1$ and $R_2$ defined over the Cartesian products $X \times Y$ and $Y \times Z$, respectively. The max-* composition of $R_1$ and $R_2$ is the new relation, which is given here:

$$R_1 * R_2 \equiv \int_{x \times z} \vee_y \left[ \mu_{R_1}(x, y) \times \mu_{R_2}(y, z) \right] / (x, z) \qquad (5.118)$$

We see from the previous equation that the membership function of the new relation is given here:

$$\mu_{R_1 * R_2}(x, z) = \vee_y \left[ \mu_{R_1}(x, y) \times \mu_{R_2}(y, z) \right] \qquad (5.119)$$

When the Cartesian product is discrete, the integral sign has to be replaced by summation.

### 5.8.3 Max-Product Composition

In max-product composition we use product (·) in place of (*) of max-star composition. Thus the max-product composition of two relations $R_1$ and $R_2$ is as follows:

$$R_1 \cdot R_2 \equiv \int_{x \times z} \vee_y \left[ \mu_{R_1}(x, y) \cdot \mu_{R_2}(y, z) \right] / (x, y) \qquad (5.120)$$

For discrete product spaces we use the summation sign in the prior equation. The membership function of the composed relation is given such as this:

$$\mu_{R_1 \cdot R_2}(x, y) = \vee_y \left[ \mu_{R_1}(x, y) \cdot \mu_{R_2}(y, z) \right] \qquad (5.121)$$

### 5.8.4 Max-Average Composition

In the max-average composition of fuzzy relations we use the arithmetic sum $\langle + \rangle$ divided by 2 in place of (*) of max-star composition. Thus the max-average composition of $R_1$ with $R_2$ is a new relation $R_1 \langle + \rangle R_2$, which is given as follows:

$$R_1 \langle + \rangle R_2 \equiv \int_{x \times z} \vee_y \left[ \frac{1}{2} \left( \mu_{R_1}(x, y) + \mu_{R_2}(y, z) \right) \right] / (x, z) \qquad (5.122)$$

with the membership function

$$\mu_{R_1 \langle + \rangle R_2}(x, z) = \vee_y \left[ \frac{1}{2} \left( \mu_{R_1}(x, y) + \mu_{R_2}(y, z) \right) \right] \qquad (5.123)$$

**Example 5.3**

Let us try to analyse the usage of fuzzy composition for the necessary requirements of an engineering student for the future to get a good life partner, beautiful house, increased lifespan, and increase in happiness coefficient. The following are the conditions and relations in order to achieve this:

(a) If a student studies well, physically fit with good character, he/she may get a good job, be highly respected, have good health, and have good bank balance.
(b) If he/she may get a good job, be highly respected, have good health and good bank balance, then he/she may have a good life partner, beautiful house, increased lifespan and increase in happiness quotient.

Figure 5.16 gives the relationship with the strength or degree of membership grades between various entities.

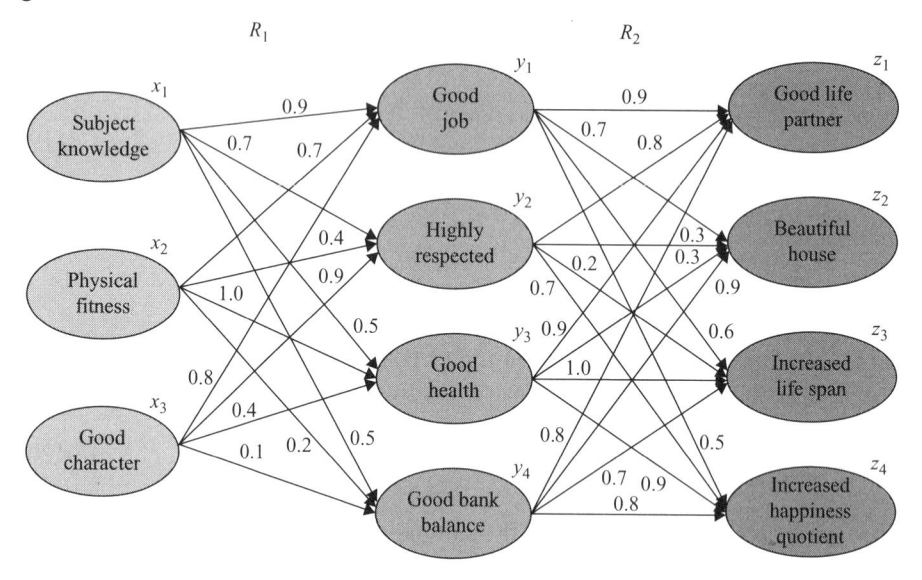

**Fig. 5.16** Relation diagram

Let us determine max-min, max-product, and max-average composition of fuzzy relations. We have two relations $R_1$ and $R_2$, and we want to compute a new relation various fuzzy composition techniques. The relations to be composed are described by the following membership tables:

| $R_1$ | $y_1$ | $y_2$ | $y_3$ | $y_4$ |
|---|---|---|---|---|
| $x_1$ | 0.9 | 0.7 | 0.5 | 0.5 |
| $x_2$ | 0.7 | 0.4 | 1.0 | 0.2 |
| $x_3$ | 0.8 | 0.9 | 0.4 | 0.1 |

| $R_2$ | $z_1$ | $z_2$ | $z_3$ | $z_4$ |
|---|---|---|---|---|
| $y_1$ | 0.9 | 0.7 | 0.6 | 0.5 |
| $y_2$ | 0.8 | 0.3 | 0.2 | 0.7 |
| $y_3$ | 0.9 | 0.3 | 1.0 | 0.9 |
| $y_4$ | 0.8 | 0.9 | 0.7 | 0.8 |

**Max-Min composition:**

To find the new relation $R = R_1 \circ R_2$ we use max-min composition, namely,

$$\mu_{R_1 \circ R_2}(x,z) = \vee_y \left[ \mu_{R_1}(x,y) \wedge \mu_{R_2}(y,z) \right] \quad (5.124)$$

First, we fix $x$ and $z$ (e.g., $x = x_1$ and $z = z_1$), and vary $y$. Next, we evaluate the following pairs of minima:

$\mu_{R_1}(x_1, y_1) \wedge \mu_{R_2}(y_1, z_1) = 0.9 \wedge 0.9$
$\mu_{R_1}(x_1, y_2) \wedge \mu_{R_2}(y_2, z_1) = 0.7 \wedge 0.8$
$\mu_{R_1}(x_1, y_3) \wedge \mu_{R_2}(y_3, z_1) = 0.5 \wedge 0.9$
$\mu_{R_1}(x_1, y_4) \wedge \mu_{R_2}(y_4, z_1) = 0.5 \wedge 0.8$

We take the maximum of all these terms and obtain the value of the $(x_1, z_1)$ element of the relation, namely,

$$\mu_{R_1 \circ R_2}(x_1, z_1) = (0.9 \vee 0.7 \vee 0.5 \vee 0.5) = 0.9$$

In a similar manner, we determine the grades of membership for all other pairs and finally we have composed the relation as shown in the following:

$$R = R_1 \circ R_2$$

| $R_1 \circ R_2$ | $z_1$ | $z_2$ | $z_3$ | $z_4$ |
|---|---|---|---|---|
| $x_1$ | 0.9 | 0.7 | 0.6 | 0.7 |
| $x_2$ | 0.9 | 0.7 | 1.0 | 0.9 |
| $x_3$ | 0.8 | 0.7 | 0.7 | 0.7 |

**Max-Product composition:**

To find the new relation $R = R_1 \cdot R_2$ we use max-product composition, namely,

$$\mu_{R_1 \cdot R_2}(x, z) = \vee_y \left[ \mu_{R_1}(x, z) \cdot \mu_{R_2}(y, z) \right] \qquad (5.125)$$

Let us now compose these two relations using max-product composition. That is, again we fix $x$ and $z$, and vary $y$ (e.g., $x = x_1$, $z = z_1$, and $y = y_I$ for $I = 1,\ldots 5$). We form and evaluate the products within the relation tables. That is,

$$\mu_{R_1}(x_1, y_1) \wedge \mu_{R_2}(y_1, z_1) = 0.9 \times 0.9 = 0.81$$
$$\mu_{R_1}(x_1, y_2) \wedge \mu_{R_2}(y_2, z_1) = 0.7 \times 0.8 = 0.56$$
$$\mu_{R_1}(x_1, y_3) \wedge \mu_{R_2}(y_3, z_1) = 0.5 \times 0.9 = 0.45$$
$$\mu_{R_1}(x_1, y_4) \wedge \mu_{R_2}(y_4, z_1) = 0.5 \times 0.8 = 0.40$$

We take the maximum of all these terms and obtain the value of the $(x_1, z_1)$ element of the relation, namely,

$$\mu_{R_1 \cdot R_2}(x_1, z_1) = (0.81 \vee 0.56 \vee 0.45 \vee 0.40) = 0.81$$

which coincidentally evaluates to $\mu_{R_1 \cdot R_2}(x_1, z_1) = 0.81$. This is one of the elements in the relation table given below. Similarly, we obtain the membership of all other pairs and finally we get the membership table of the composition as $R_1 \cdot R_2$.

| $R_1 \cdot R_2$ | $z_1$ | $z_2$ | $z_3$ | $z_4$ |
|---|---|---|---|---|
| $x_1$ | 0.81 | 0.63 | 0.54 | 0.49 |
| $x_2$ | 0.63 | 0.49 | 1.0 | 0.9 |
| $x_3$ | 0.72 | 0.36 | 0.48 | 0.63 |

**Max-Average composition:**

For the max-average composition of the two relations, again we fix $x$ and $z$, and vary $y$, in order to find the max with respect to $y$ for each $(x, z)$ pair. Thus, first we form and evaluate the sums as follows:

$$\mu_{R_1}(x_1, y_1) \wedge \mu_{R_2}(y_1, z_1) = 0.9 + 0.9 = 1.8$$
$$\mu_{R_1}(x_1, y_2) \wedge \mu_{R_2}(y_2, z_1) = 0.7 + 0.8 = 1.5$$
$$\mu_{R_1}(x_1, y_3) \wedge \mu_{R_2}(y_3, z_1) = 0.5 + 0.9 = 1.4$$
$$\mu_{R_1}(x_1, y_4) \wedge \mu_{R_2}(y_4, z_1) = 0.5 + 0.8 = 1.3$$

Thus, membership of the $(x_1, z_1)$ pair is

$$\mu_{R_1 \langle + \rangle R_2}(x_1, z_1) = \tfrac{1}{2}[1.8 \vee 1.5 \vee 1.4 \vee 1.3] = 0.9.$$

In a similar manner, the membership function for each pair is computed, and finally we get the max-average composition of the two relations as in the following relation table.

| $R_1 \langle + \rangle R_2$ | $z_1$ | $z_2$ | $z_3$ | $z_4$ |
|---|---|---|---|---|
| $x_1$ | 0.9 | 0.8 | 0.75 | 0.7 |
| $x_2$ | 0.95 | 0.7 | 0.65 | 0.95 |
| $x_3$ | 0.85 | 0.75 | 0.7 | 0.8 |

We observe from the tables of the composed relations that max-min, max-product, and max-average compositions of $R_1$ and $R_2$ may result in different relations. From the fuzzy composition results, we can understand the degree or strength of relation between $(x, z)$ pairs with the help of newly obtained membership grades.

## 5.9 NATURAL LANGUAGE AND FUZZY INTERPRETATIONS

The natural language that we use often use includes the primary terms. A collection of these primary terms will form phrases, of our natural language. The primary terms can be called as atomic terms as in the literature. Examples of some atomic terms are *slow, medium, young, beautiful, angry, cold, temperature,* etc. The collection of atomic terms can form compound terms. Examples of compound terms are *very cold, medium speed, young lady, fairly beautiful picture,* etc. [10].

Let us define an atomic term, as an element $\delta$, in the universe of natural language $U$. In addition, let $A$ be a fuzzy set in the universe of interpretations $I$, which represents the precise meaning for the term $\delta$. Here the natural language can be mapped from a set of atomic terms defined in $U$ to a set of interpretations $I$. That is, each of the atomic terms in $U$ corresponds to a fuzzy set $A$ in $I$ which is represented by as shown in Fig. 5.17.

The fuzzy set $A$ gives the fuzziness while mapping the atomic term with the interpretations and is given by the Eq. (5.126).

$$\mu_M(\delta, x) = \mu_A(x) \qquad (5.126)$$

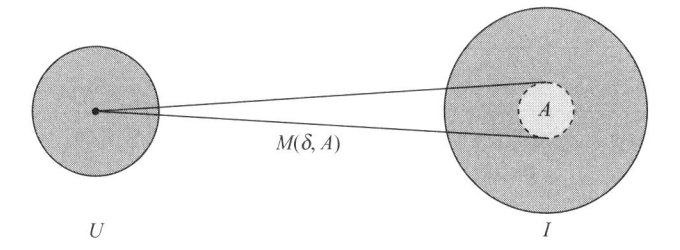

Fig. 5.17 Mapping of an atomic term to interpretations

**Example 5.4**

Consider an atomic term 'Low' ($\delta$) and we want to interpret this linguistic atom in terms of temperature, $T$ by a membership function that expresses the term 'Low'. The membership function for the fuzzy set $A$ is one of the interpretation of the term low expressed as a function of temperature.

To convert the primary terms to membership values, we use function whose form is adjusted through a finite set of parameters as given in Eq. (5.127).

$$\mu_A(\delta, T) = \frac{1}{1 + u(T - v)^w} \quad (5.127)$$

The parameters $u$, $v$ and $w$ are used to vary the overall shape of the membership function, $\mu_A(\delta, T)$. If the values of $u = 0.0005$, $v = 30$ (Low), 60 (Medium), 90 (High), and $w = 2.4$. The temperature range which is also the universe of discourse ranges from 0° to 120°. The membership function for the atomic term 'Low' will be getting its interpretation from Eq. (5.126), when $v$ is set as 30. Similarly, if we want to get the interpretation of the atomic term 'Medium' and 'High', we can get it from Eq. (5.126) by adjusting the shape of the membership curve by setting the value of $v = 60$ and $v = 90$, respectively. The membership function is plotted for the Eq. (5.126) for 'Low', 'Medium', and 'High' which is shown in Fig. 5.18.

Based on the earlier example, it is clear that we can call '$\delta$' a natural language variable whose value is defined by the fuzzy set $\mu_\delta(x)$. Therefore, the value of the linguistic variable will be one and the same with its interpretation.

Let us define two primary terms, $\alpha$ and $\beta$, on the universe $U$. Then the interpretation of the compound value defined on universe $I$ can be defined by the following set operations as given in Eqs (5.128, 5.129, and 5.130).

$$\alpha \text{ or } \beta \Rightarrow \mu_{\alpha \text{ or } \beta}(x) = \max(\mu_\alpha(x), \mu_\beta(x)) \quad (5.128)$$

$$\alpha \text{ and } \beta \Rightarrow \mu_{\alpha \text{ and } \beta}(x) = \min(\mu_\alpha(x), \mu_\beta(x)) \quad (5.129)$$

$$\text{Not } \alpha \Rightarrow \mu_{\bar{\alpha}}(x) = 1 - \mu_\alpha(x) \quad (5.130)$$

### 5.9.1 Linguistic Modifiers

Linguistic modifiers modifies or encloses the primary terms with adjectives (nouns) or adverbs (verbs) such as very, more or less, almost, mostly, small,

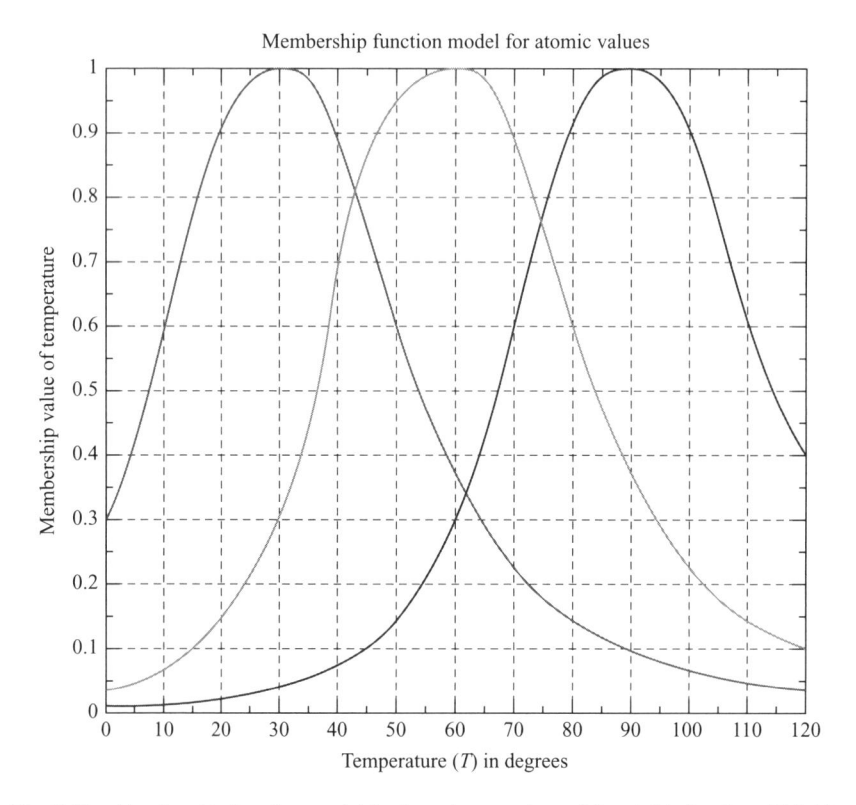

**Fig. 5.18** Membership function model for the primary values of 'Low', 'Medium', and 'High'

approximately, fairly, slightly, indeed, over, under, and so on. These enclosures, linguistic modifiers, modify the meaning of the primary term from its original interpretation. The changes that happen when the primary terms are used with linguistic modifier can be understood from the following example.

If the basic linguistic term '$\delta$' is defined as $\delta = \int_I \mu_\delta(x)/x$, then the Table 5.10 lists few of the modifiers and the membership function when the primary terms are subjected to linguistic modifiers. Based on the modification of the primary terms, the process of the modifiers is classified into three types of operation, which are as follows:

(a) Concentration
(b) Dilation
(c) Intensification

### 5.9.1.1 Concentration

Concentrations tend to concentrate or reduce the fuzziness of the elements in a fuzzy set by reducing the degree of membership of all elements that are only 'partly' in the set. The less the membership value an element in a set possesses, the more it is reduced in membership through concentration.

**Table 5.10** Linguistic modifiers

| Primary terms with modifiers | Modification | Membership function |
|---|---|---|
| Very $\delta$ | $\delta^2$ | $\int_I \dfrac{[\mu_\delta(x)]^2}{x}$ |
| Very very $\delta$ | $\delta^4$ | $\int_I \dfrac{[\mu_\delta(x)]^4}{x}$ |
| More or less $\delta$<br>Slightly $\delta$ | $\delta^{1/2}$ | $\int_I \dfrac{[\mu_\delta(x)]^{\frac{1}{2}}}{x}$ |
| Plus $\delta$ | $\delta^{1.25}$ | $\int_I \dfrac{[\mu_\delta(x)]^{1.25}}{x}$ |
| Minus $\delta$ | $\delta^{0.75}$ | $\int_I \dfrac{[\mu_\delta(x)]^{0.75}}{x}$ |
| Over $\delta$ | $1-\delta,\ x \geq x_{max}$<br>$0,\ x < x_{max}$ | $-\int_I \dfrac{\mu_\delta(x)}{x},\ x \geq x_{min}$<br>$0,\ x > x_{min}$ |
| Under $\delta$ | $1-\delta,\ x \leq x_{min}$<br>$0,\ x > x_{min}$ | $-\int_I \dfrac{\mu_\delta(x)}{x},\ x \leq x_{max}$<br>$0,\ x < x_{max}$ |
| Indeed $\delta$ | $2\delta^2,\ 0 \leq \delta \leq 0.5$<br>$1 - 2[1-\delta]^2,\ 0.5 \leq \delta \leq 1.0$ | $2\int_I \left[\dfrac{\mu_\delta(x)}{x}\right]^2$<br>$0 \leq \int_I \left[\dfrac{\mu_\delta(x)}{x}\right] \leq 0.5$<br>$1 - 2\left[1 - \int_I \left[\dfrac{\mu_\delta(x)}{x}\right]\right]^2$<br>$0.5 \leq \int_I \left[\dfrac{\mu_\delta(x)}{x}\right] \leq 1.0$ |

Let us consider the same membership function for the linguistic term 'Low' as discussed in the Example 5.4. The membership function for 'Low' is given in Eq. (5.131).

$$\mu_A(\text{Low}, T) = \dfrac{1}{1 + 0.0005(T-30)^{2.4}} \qquad (5.131)$$

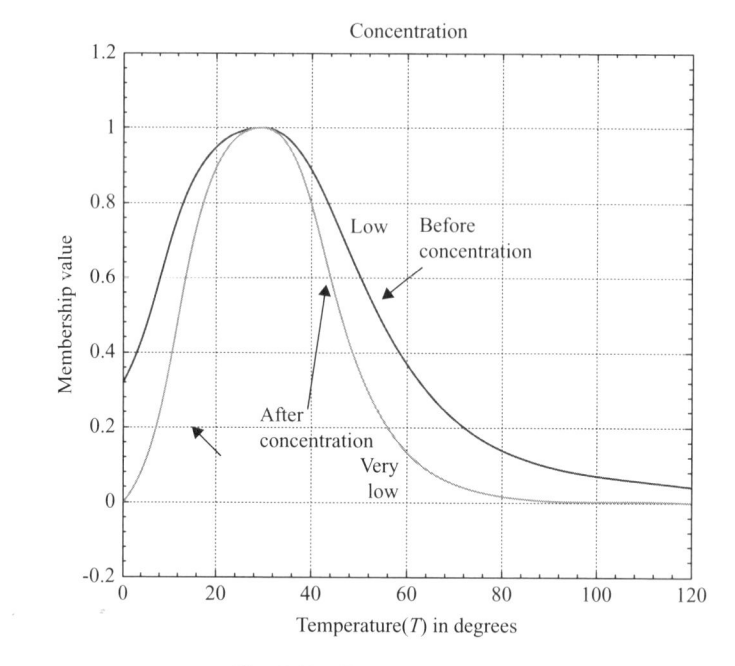

**Fig. 5.19** Fuzzy concentration

When we say 'Very Low', the modified membership function becomes like this:

$$\mu_A(\text{Very Low}, T) = \left[\frac{1}{1 + 0.0005(T - 30)^{2.4}}\right]^2 \tag{5.132}$$

The membership function after fuzzy concentration is shown in Fig. 5.19. A membership value of 0.9 is reduced by 10 per cent to a value of 0.81, but a membership value of 0.1 is reduced by an order of magnitude to 0.01. The decrease is simply an expression of the properties of the membership value itself. If the membership value is $0 \leq \mu \leq 1$, then $\mu \geq \mu^2$.

### 5.9.1.2 Dilation

Dilation tends to dilate or increase the fuzziness of the elements in a fuzzy set by increasing the degree of membership of all elements that are only 'partly' in the set. The less the membership value an element in a set possesses, the less it is reduced in membership through dilation.

When we say 'Slightly Low', the modified membership function becomes such as given here:

$$\mu_A(\text{Slightly Low}, T) = \left[\frac{1}{1 + 0.0005(T - 30)^{2.4}}\right]^{0.5} \tag{5.133}$$

A membership value of 0.9 is increased by 11 per cent to a value of 0.81, but a membership value of 0.1 is increased by an order of magnitude to 0.01. The membership function after fuzzy dilation is shown in Fig. 5.20.

![Fig. 5.20 Fuzzy dilation graph showing membership value vs Temperature with Before dilation and After dilation curves labeled Slightly low and Low]

**Fig. 5.20** Fuzzy dilation

### 5.9.1.3 Intensification

This property of the linguistic modifier is found to have a property which is a combination of both fuzzy concentration and fuzzy intensification. This property increases the degree of membership of those elements in the set whose membership values are greater than 0.5 and decreases the degree of membership of those elements in the set whose membership values are lesser than 0.5, respectively.

If the membership function for 'Low' is given as follows:

$$\mu_A(\text{Low}, T) = \frac{1}{1 + 0.005(T-30)^{2.0}} \tag{5.134}$$

then the modified membership function for 'Indeed Low', becomes

$$\mu_A(\text{Indeed Low}, T) = \begin{cases} 2 \times \left[\dfrac{1}{1+0.005(T-30)^{2.0}}\right]^2 \\ \qquad 0 \le \left[\dfrac{1}{1+0.005(T-30)^{2.0}}\right] \le 0.5 \\ 1 - 2\left[1 - \left[\dfrac{1}{1+0.005(T-30)^{2.0}}\right]\right]^2 \\ \qquad 0.5 \le \left[\dfrac{1}{1+0.005(T-30)^{2.0}}\right] \le 1.0 \end{cases} \tag{5.135}$$

The membership function after fuzzy intensification is shown in Fig. 5.21.

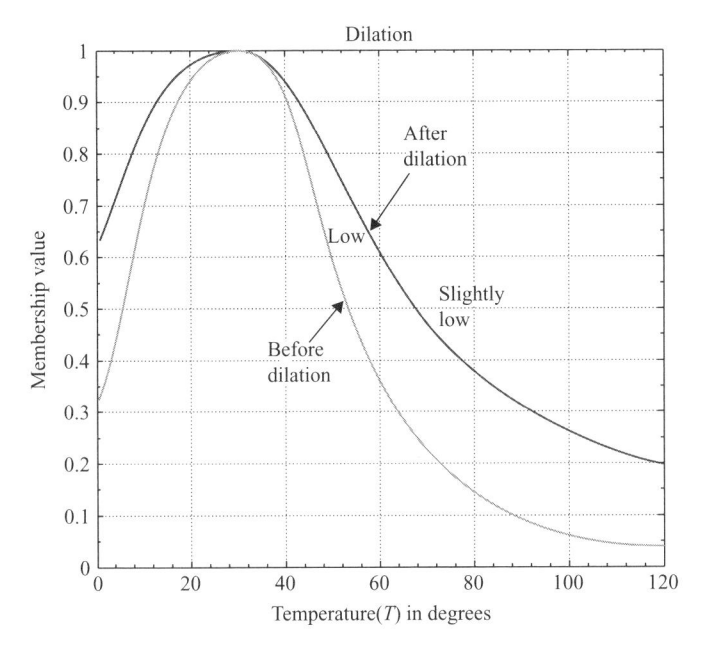

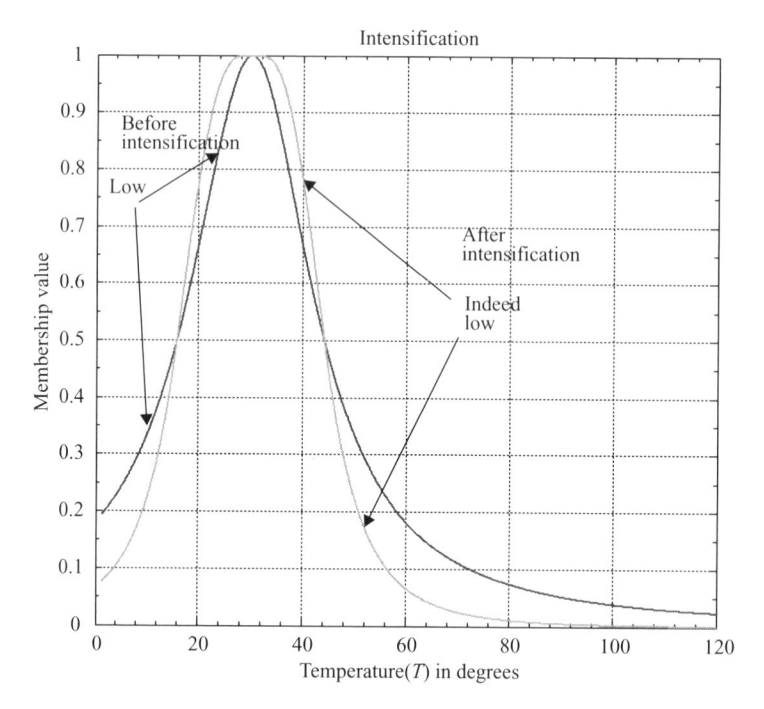

**Fig. 5.21** Fuzzy intensification

## 5.9.2 Logical Operations using Linguistic Modifiers

It is possible to perform logical operations using the linguistic modifiers, but the order of precedence needs to be followed to avoid confusion. This problem can be resolved by properly using the parentheses by the rule that use 'association to the right'. The precedence of operation should be 'NOT' in the first, 'AND' in the second, and 'OR' in the third. For example, if we have a compound terms 'plus very minus very low', then following the rule 'association to the right' while using the parentheses we get 'Plus (very (minus (very (low))))'. We will also look into few examples with the logical operations on linguistic terms.

### Example 5.5

Let the universe of integers, $U = \{1, 2, 3, 4, 5\}$. The primary linguistic terms are 'Low' and 'High' which is mapped onto U. The fuzzy set for 'Low' and 'High' are given as follows:

$$\text{'Low'} = \left\{ \frac{1}{1} + \frac{0.8}{2} + \frac{0.6}{3} + \frac{0.4}{4} + \frac{0.2}{5} \right\}$$

$$\text{'High'} = \left\{ \frac{0.2}{1} + \frac{0.4}{2} + \frac{0.6}{3} + \frac{0.8}{4} + \frac{1}{5} \right\}$$

Find the linguistic modified fuzzy set.

*Solution:*

(a) 'Very Low'
$$\Rightarrow (\text{'Low'})^2$$
$$= \left\{ \frac{1}{1} + \frac{0.64}{2} + \frac{0.36}{3} + \frac{0.16}{4} + \frac{0.04}{5} \right\}$$

(b) 'Not Very Low'
$$\Rightarrow \text{Not (Very (Low))}$$
$$\Rightarrow 1 \text{ 'Very Low'}$$
$$= \left\{ \frac{0}{1} + \frac{0.36}{2} + \frac{0.64}{3} + \frac{0.84}{4} + \frac{0.96}{5} \right\}$$

(c) 'Not Very Low And Not Very Very High'
$$\Rightarrow \text{'(Not (Very (Low))) And (Not (Very (Very (High))))'}$$
$$= \left\{ \frac{0.36}{2} + \frac{0.64}{3} + \frac{0.84}{4} + \frac{0.96}{5} \right\} \cap \left\{ \frac{1}{1} + \frac{1}{2} + \frac{0.9}{3} + \frac{0.6}{4} \right\}$$
$$= \left\{ \frac{0.36}{2} + \frac{0.64}{3} + \frac{0.6}{4} \right\}$$

(d) 'Intensively Low'
$$\Rightarrow \text{Fuzzy Intensification}$$
$$= \left\{ \frac{1-2(1-1)^2}{1} + \frac{1-2(1-0.8)^2}{2} + \frac{1-2(1-0.6)^2}{3} + \frac{2(0.4)^2}{4} + \frac{2(0.2)^2}{5} \right\}$$
$$= \left\{ \frac{1}{1} + \frac{0.92}{2} + \frac{0.68}{3} + \frac{0.32}{4} + \frac{0.08}{5} \right\}$$

## 5.10 STRUCTURE OF FUZZY INFERENCE SYSTEM

A fuzzy system may be a SISO system or MIMO system. In a fuzzy inference system, as shown in Fig. 5.22, crisp inputs are converted into fuzzy variables for further processing. The crisp values of inputs are called fuzzy singleton. Fuzzified inputs will be passed through a rule base and the output is identified using fuzzy implication method. The fuzzy-based output will be then converted into crisp output using de-fuzzification techniques.

### 5.10.1 Fuzzification

In conventional systems or real-world problems, the inputs will be a numeric value. This numeric value is called crisp value or fuzzy singleton. The process of converting the crisp values to fuzzy variable is called 'fuzzification'. This is the process of converting fuzzy singleton into a membership grade in one or more fuzzy sets. Let us illustrate with the runs scored by a cricketer in a T20 match.

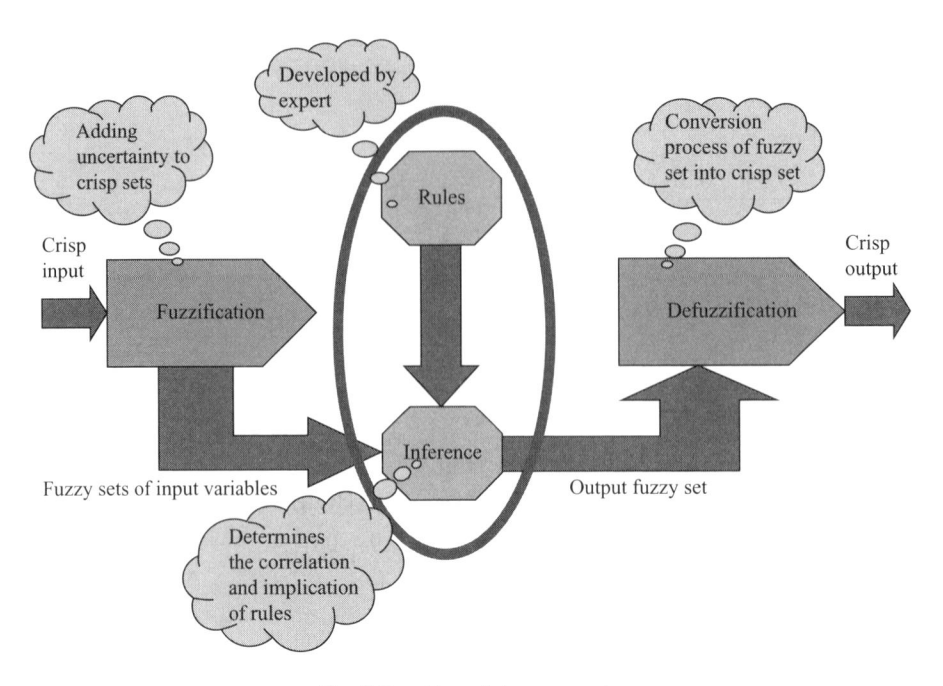

**Fig. 5.22** Fuzzy inference system

Here, runs scored are described by three fuzzy sets, namely 'Low Score', 'Average Score', and 'Good Score'. Let the three categories of the fuzzy set be represented by the membership diagram as shown in Fig. 5.23. Let us consider a batsman scores 45 in a particular match (i.e., $x = 45$). This crisp value has a membership grade in the fuzzy set of 'Average Score' and 'Good Score' with a degree of $\mu_{Average}(45) = 0.25$ and $\mu_{Good}(45) = 0.8$, respectively. Thus the crisp value 45 is fuzzified to membership grades in one or more fuzzy sets through the process of fuzzification.

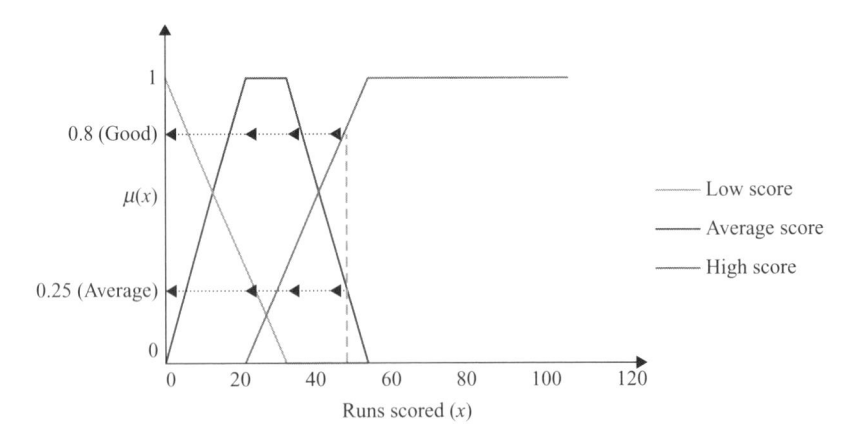

**Fig. 5.23** Membership diagram for low score, average score, and high score

## 5.10.2 Fuzzy Propositions

As in our ordinary informal language, a 'sentence' is used in logical reasoning. A sentence having only 'true (1)' and 'false (0)' as its truth value is called propositions which belongs to classical proportional logic. However in fuzzy logic, a fuzzy proposition can have its truth value in the interval [0, 1]. If we represent a proposition as a variable, the variable can have a truth value and the variable is called proposition variable or logic variable. Propositions are generally expressed in the form $x$ and $P$ where $x$ is a symbol of a subject and $P$ is a predicate that characterizes the property. In classical logic $x$ is an element of universal set $X$, while $P$ is a function on $X$, which for each value of $x$ forms a proposition. $P(x)$ is called predicate; it becomes true or false for any particular value of $x$.

The truth of fuzzy proposition is a matter of degree. This truth value is used in correlation and inferring the output fuzzy solution space. The final output is created by combining the collection of fuzzy propositions based on the truth of each fuzzy proposition.

Suppose a proposition $P$ is assigned to fuzzy set $F$; then the truth value of a proposition is denoted by the following equation:

$$T(P) = \mu_F(x), \text{ where } 0 \leq \mu_F \leq 1 \tag{5.136}$$

$T(P)$ indicates the degree of truth for the proposition $P: x \in F$ is equal to the membership grade of $x$ in the fuzzy set $F$.

Fuzzy propositions can be classified into the following four types:

(a) Unconditional and unqualified propositions
(b) Unconditional and qualified propositions
(c) Conditional and unqualified propositions
(d) Conditional and qualified propositions

### 5.10.2.1 Unconditional and Unqualified Propositions

The canonical form of fuzzy propositions of this type $P$ is expressed by the sentence

$P: \mathcal{V}$ is $F$,

E.g., temperature of 45° is high

where, $\mathcal{V}$ is a variable that takes values $v$ from some universal set $V$, and $F$ is a fuzzy set on $V$ that represents a fuzzy predicate, such as tall, expensive, low, normal, and so on.

Given a particular value for $\mathcal{V}$ (say, $v$), this value belongs to $F$ with membership grade $F(v)$. This membership grade is then interpreted as the degree of truth $T(P)$, of proposition $P$. That is, $T(P) = F(v)$ for each given particular value $v$ of variable $\mathcal{V}$ in proposition $P$. This means that $T$ is in effect a fuzzy set on [0, 1], which assigns the membership grade $F(v)$ to each value $v$ of variable $\mathcal{V}$.

In some fuzzy propositions, values of variable $\mathcal{V}$ are assigned to individuals in a given set $I$. That is, variable $\mathcal{V}$ becomes a function $\mathcal{V}: I \to V$ where $\mathcal{V}(i)$ is the value of $\mathcal{V}$ for individual $i$ in $V$. The canonical form must then be modified to the following form:

$P: \mathcal{V}(i)$ is $F$, where $i \in I$

### 5.10.2.2 Unconditional and Qualified Propositions

Propositions $P$ of this type are characterized by the canonical form

$P: \mathcal{V}$ is $F$, is $S$,

E.g., temperature of 65° is high is very true

where, $S$ is the fuzzy truth qualifier. In general, the degree of truth, $T(P)$, of any truth-qualified proposition $P$ is given for each $v \in V$ by the following equation:

$$T(P) = S(F(v)) \qquad (5.137)$$

### 5.10.2.3 Conditional and Unqualified Propositions

Propositions $P$ of this type are expressed by the following canonical form:

$P$: IF $\mathcal{X}$ is $A$, THEN $\mathcal{Y}$ is $B$,

E.g., IF the temperature is high, THEN it is hot

where $\mathcal{X}$ and $\mathcal{Y}$ are variables whose values are in sets $X$, $Y$, respectively, and $A$, $B$ are fuzzy sets on $X$, $Y$, respectively.

These propositions may also be viewed as propositions of the form

$\langle \mathcal{X}, \mathcal{Y} \rangle$ is $R$,

where, $R$ is a fuzzy set on $X \times Y$ that is determined for each $x \in X$ and each $y \in Y$.

### 5.10.2.4 Conditional and Qualified Propositions

Propositions $P$ of this type can be characterized by the canonical form

$P$: IF $\mathcal{X}$ is $A$, THEN $\mathcal{Y}$ is $B$ is $S$,

E.g., IF the temperature is high, THEN it is hot is true.

where, $\mathcal{X}$ and $\mathcal{Y}$ are variables whose values are in sets $X$, $Y$, respectively, and $A$, $B$ are fuzzy sets on $X$, $Y$, respectively. In addition, $S$ is the fuzzy truth qualifier.

## 5.10.3 Fuzzy Connectives

The linguistic variables are combined by various connectives such as negation, disjunction, conjunction, and implication. However, this section discusses few of the connectives that can be used to combine various fuzzy propositions to derive the final output fuzzy solution space. Table 5.11 lists some of the connectives and its usage when combining fuzzy propositions if $P$ and $Q$ are fuzzy propositions with their truth values.

The $P$ and $Q$ are related with an implication operator by antecedent and consequent, respectively, just like the crisp set where '$\Rightarrow$' represents the IF/THEN statement. The following examples illustrate the usage of the connectives with the propositions.

**Table 5.11** Fuzzy connectives

| Symbol | Connective | Usage | Definition |
|---|---|---|---|
| − | Negation | $\bar{P}$ | $1 - T(P)$ |
| ∨ | Disjunction | $P \vee Q$ | $\max(T(P), T(PP))$ |
| ∧ | Conjunction | $P \wedge Q$ | $\min(T(P), T(Q))$ |
| ⇒ | Implication | $P \Rightarrow Q$ | $\bar{P} \vee Q = \max(1 - T(P), T(Q))$ |

**Example 5.6**

Let $P$ and $Q$ be the propositions with their truth values as given here:
  $P$: Mary is efficient, $T(P) = 0.8$
  $Q$: Ram is efficient, $T(P) = 0.65$
  Find out the truth value of the following fuzzy propositions that uses fuzzy connectives.

*Solution:*

(i) $\bar{P}$: Mary is not efficient
  $T(P) = 1 - T(P) = 1 - 0.8 = 0.2$

(ii) $P \wedge Q$: Mary is efficient and so is Ram
  $T(P \wedge Q) = \min(T(P), T(Q))$
    $= \min(0.8, 0.65)$
    $= 0.65$

(iii) $P \vee Q$: Either Mary or Ram is efficient
  $T(P \vee Q) = \max(T(P), T(Q))$
    $= \max(0.8, 0.65)$
    $= 0.65$

(iv) $P \Rightarrow Q$: IF Mary is efficient THEN so is Ram
  $T(P \Rightarrow Q) = T(\bar{P} \vee Q)$
    $\bar{P} \vee Q = \max(1 - T(P), T(Q))$
    $= \max(0.2, 0.65)$
    $= 0.65$

## 5.10.4 Fuzzy Implication Relations

Fuzzy implication attempts to correlate the semantic meaning of the antecedent (partial truth in input variable) with the semantics of the consequent (output fuzzy set), and generates a solution. The functional tie between the degrees of truth in related fuzzy regions is called the *method of implication*.

Most of the conditional statements describe the dependence of one or more linguistic variable on another. Let us consider a generic IF/THEN conditional statement involving two linguistic terms.

  IF $x$ is $A$ THEN $y$ is $B$ (5.138)

Here, the linguistic terms take the values $x$ and $y$ for $A$ and $B$, respectively. Consider $A$ is input fuzzy set and $B$ is output fuzzy set. Many methods can be formulated to calculate the following fuzzy relation:

$$R = A \times B \tag{5.139}$$

$R$ can be viewed as a fuzzy set with the following two-dimensional membership function:

$$\mu_R(x, y) = \Psi(\mu_A(x), \mu_B(y))$$

where, $\Psi$ is the fuzzy implication function, it performs the task of transforming the membership degrees of $x$ in $A$ and $y$ in $B$ into those of $(x, y)$ in $A \times B$.

Various types of implication operators are available and few of them have been listed in the Table 5.12.

Suppose we consider conditional statements with 'IF/THEN' and 'ELSE' as follows:

IF $x$ is $A_1$ THEN $y$ is $B_1$ ELSE
IF $x$ is $A_2$ THEN $y$ is $B_2$ ELSE  (5.140)
......

IF $x$ is $A_n$ THEN $y$ is $B_n$

Table 5.12  Fuzzy implication operators with the interpretation of ELSE

| Implication operator ($\Psi$) | Usage $\mu_R(x,y) = \Psi(\mu_A(x), \mu_B(y))$ | Interpretation of 'ELSE' |
|---|---|---|
| Zadeh max-min | $(\mu_A(x) \wedge \mu_B(y)) \vee (1 - \mu_A(x))$ | AND($\wedge$) |
| Mamdani min | $\mu_A(x) \wedge \mu_B(y)$ | OR($\vee$) |
| Larsen product | $\mu_A(x) \bullet \mu_B(y)$ | OR($\vee$) |
| Arithmetic | $1 \wedge (1 - \mu_A(x) + \mu_B(y))$ | AND($\wedge$) |
| Boolean | $(1 - \mu_A(x)) \vee \mu_B(y)$ | AND($\wedge$) |
| Bounded product | $0 \vee (\mu_A(x) + \mu_B(y) - 1)$ | OR($\vee$) |
| Drastic product | $\mu_A(x)$, if $\mu_B(y) = 1$ <br> $\mu_B(y)$, if $\mu_A(x) = 1$ <br> $0$, if $\mu_A(x) < 1$ & $\mu_B(y) < 1$ | OR($\vee$) |
| Standard sequence | $1$, if $\mu_A(x) \leq \mu_B(y)$ <br> $0$, if $\mu_A(x) > \mu_B(y)$ | AND($\wedge$) |
| Gougen | $1$, if $\mu_A(x) \leq \mu_B(y)$ <br> $\dfrac{\mu_B(y)}{\mu_A(x)}$, if $\mu_A(x) > \mu_B(y)$ | AND($\wedge$) |
| Godelian | $1$, if $\mu_A(x) \leq \mu_B(y)$ <br> $\mu_B(y)$, if $\mu_A(x) > \mu_B(y)$ | AND($\wedge$) |

If the 'IF/THEN' rules are defined over the same product space and are connected by the connective 'ELSE', then operation can be interpreted either as union or intersection depending on the implication operator used for the individual rules. Table 5.12 also lists the interpretation of 'ELSE' for various implications.

## 5.10.5 Fuzzy Inference Procedures

There are various inference mechanisms to evaluate fuzzy linguistic descriptions. Inference is a technique by which a set of facts or postulates $F_1, F_2 \ldots F_n$ is given and a goal $G$ needs to be derived. The important fuzzy inference methods are as follows:

(a) Generalized modus ponens (GMP)
(b) Generalized modus tollens (GMT)

### 5.10.5.1 Generalized Modus Ponens (GMP)

In a raw sense, generalized modus ponens (GMP) means 'the way that affirms by affirming'. It is one of the accepted mechanisms for the construction of deductive proofs that includes the 'rule of definition' and the 'rule of substitution'. *Modus ponens* allows one to eliminate a conditional statement from a logical proof (the antecedents). Lengthy strings of 33 symbols and rules can be eliminated by using modus ponens. Hence, modus ponens is also called as 'rule of detachment'.

Consider a rule 'IF temperature is high, THEN AC is ON'.

It should be noted that another rule is hidden inside this rule. The hidden rule that can be understood is 'IF temperature is NOT high, THEN AC is NOT ON'; however, it is not explicitly described.

These sentences have terms that involve only a simple IF/THEN rule with known implication relation $R(x, y)$ and a fuzzy value $A'$ approximately matching the antecedent of the rule. Generalized modus ponens allows us to compute or infer the consequent $B'$.

Now consider an IF/THEN rule with fuzzy terms $A$ and $B$ (i.e. 'IF $X$ is $A$, THEN $Y$ is $B$'). The requisite for us is to know the consequent of $Y$ if the input of the system is $A'$. Based on the inference, the output of the system will be $B'$ (i.e. 'If $x$ is $A'$ and $y$ is $B'$').

However, GMP is a standard technique that allows us to evaluate the rule and infer a value for performance.

Generalized modus ponens is generally explained such as this:

IF $x$ is $A$ THEN $y$ is $B$

$$\Rightarrow \frac{x \text{ is } A' \quad \text{(Analytically Known)}}{y \text{ is } B' \quad \text{(Analytically Unknown)}}$$

Here $A, B, A'$ and $B'$ are all fuzzy terms. Every linguistic statement that is above the line is analytically known, but the linguistic term that is below the line analytically is unknown.

To compute the membership function of $B'$, we use max-min composition (max-product can also be used) of fuzzy set $A'$ with $R(x, y)$, that is,

$$B' = A' \circ R(x, y) \qquad (5.141)$$

In terms of membership function

$$\mu_{B'}(y) \equiv \vee_{x}\left[\mu_{A'}(x) \wedge \mu(x, y)\right] \qquad (5.142)$$

Or

$$\mu_{B'}(y) = \max(\min(\mu_{A'}(x), \mu_R(x, y))) \qquad (5.143)$$

### 5.10.5.2 Generalized Modus Tollens (GMT)

In a raw sense, generalized modus tollens (GMT) means 'the way that denies by denying'. In GMT, a rule and a fuzzy value approximately matching its consequent are given. Therefore, it is desired to infer the antecedent.

Now consider an IF/THEN rule with fuzzy terms $A$ and $B$ (i.e., 'IF $X$ is $A$, THEN $Y$ is $B'$). The requisite for us is to know the antecedent of $X$, if the output of the system is $B'$. That is, $A'$ can be inferred by knowing $B'$ using GMT.

Generalized modus tollens is generally defined as follows:

IF $x$ is $A$ THEN $y$ is $B$

$$\Rightarrow \frac{y \text{ is } B' \text{ (Analytically Known)}}{x \text{ is } A' \text{ (Analytically Unknown)}}$$

To compute the membership function of $A'$, we use max-min composition (max-product can also be used) of fuzzy set $B'$ with $R(x, y)$, that is,

$$A' = R(x, y) \circ B' \qquad (5.144)$$

In terms of membership function

$$\mu_{A'}(y) \equiv \vee_{x}\left[\mu_R(x, y) \wedge \mu_{B'}(x)\right] \qquad (5.145)$$

Or

$$\mu_{A'}(y) = \max(\min(\mu_R(x, y), \mu_{B'}(x))) \qquad (5.146)$$

**Example 5.7**

Apply GMP with the fuzzy Mamdani Min implication operator and max-average composition for the following statements. Deduce the time taken for consumption when the food is 'very good'.

*Given:*

If the food is 'good', time taken for consumption is 'slow'
The food is 'very good'
The fuzzy set for 'good' and 'slow' is given as follows:

$$\text{good} = \left\{\frac{0.5}{2} + \frac{1.0}{3} + \frac{0.5}{4}\right\}$$

$$\text{slow} = \left\{\frac{0.33}{5} + \frac{0.67}{6} + \frac{1.0}{7} + \frac{0.67}{8} + \frac{0.33}{9}\right\}$$

The universe of discourse for the 'condition of the food' $X$ and 'time taken for the consumption' $Y$ is as follows:

$X = \{1\ 2\ 3\ 4\ 5\ 6\}$
$Y = \{1\ 2\ 3\ 4\ 5\ 6\ 7\ 8\ 9\ 10\}$

**Solution:** Here, the fuzzy set for 'very good' is not given. Therefore we use linguistic modifiers to get the fuzzy set for 'very good'.

$$\text{very good} = (\text{good})^2 = \left\{\frac{0.25}{2} + \frac{1.0}{3} + \frac{0.25}{4}\right\}$$

As per the GMP,

Using Mamdani min implication operator, we get the implication relation between 'good' and 'slow'.

$$\Psi(\mu_{(good)}(x), \mu_{(slow)}(y)) = \mu_{(good)}(x) \wedge \mu_{(slow)}(y)$$

$$\Rightarrow \Psi(\mu_{(good)}(x), \mu_{(slow)}(y)) = \begin{bmatrix} 0 \\ 0.5 \\ 1 \\ 0.5 \\ 0 \\ 0 \end{bmatrix} [0\ 0\ 0\ 0\ 0.33\ 0.67\ 1\ 0.67\ 0.33\ 0]$$

$$= \begin{bmatrix} 0 & 0 & 0 & 0 & 0 & 0 & 0 & 0 & 0 & 0 \\ 0 & 0 & 0 & 0 & 0.33 & 0.5 & 0.5 & 0.5 & 0.33 & 0 \\ 0 & 0 & 0 & 0 & 0.33 & 0.67 & 1 & 0.67 & 0.33 & 0 \\ 0 & 0 & 0 & 0 & 0.33 & 0.5 & 0.5 & 0.5 & 0.33 & 0 \\ 0 & 0 & 0 & 0 & 0 & 0 & 0 & 0 & 0 & 0 \\ 0 & 0 & 0 & 0 & 0 & 0 & 0 & 0 & 0 & 0 \end{bmatrix}$$

The time for consumption when the food is 'very good' is $B'$.

$B' = A' \circ R(x, y)$

$$= [0\ 0.25\ 1\ 0.25\ 0\ 0] \circ \begin{bmatrix} 0 & 0 & 0 & 0 & 0 & 0 & 0 & 0 & 0 & 0 \\ 0 & 0 & 0 & 0 & 0.33 & 0.5 & 0.5 & 0.5 & 0.33 & 0 \\ 0 & 0 & 0 & 0 & 0.33 & 0.67 & 1 & 0.67 & 0.33 & 0 \\ 0 & 0 & 0 & 0 & 0.33 & 0.5 & 0.5 & 0.5 & 0.33 & 0 \\ 0 & 0 & 0 & 0 & 0 & 0 & 0 & 0 & 0 & 0 \\ 0 & 0 & 0 & 0 & 0 & 0 & 0 & 0 & 0 & 0 \end{bmatrix}$$

$= [0\ 0\ 0\ 0\ 0.665\ 0.835\ 1\ 0.835\ 0.665\ 0]$ (Using max-average composition)

Here, $B'$ is a measure of the degree of similarity between input $A'$ and the antecedent of the rule $A$. The membership function of $B'$ is basically the membership function of $B$ at a height equal to the degree that $A'$ matches $A$. This value is called *degree of fulfilment* (DOF). In this example, the DOF = 1.

**Example 5.8**

Apply GMT with the Larsen Product implication operator and max-min composition for the following statements. Deduce the 'condition of the food' when the time taken consumption of food is 'Average'.

*Given*:

If the food is 'good', then time taken for consumption is 'slow'
The time taken for consumption is 'average'
The fuzzy sets for 'good', 'slow' and 'average' is given here:

$$\text{good} = \left\{ \frac{0.5}{2} + \frac{1.0}{3} + \frac{0.5}{4} \right\}$$

$$\text{slow} = \left\{ \frac{0.33}{5} + \frac{0.67}{6} + \frac{1.0}{7} + \frac{0.67}{8} + \frac{0.33}{9} \right\}$$

$$\text{average} = \left\{ \frac{0.625}{5} + \frac{0.85}{6} + \frac{1.0}{7} + \frac{0.85}{8} + \frac{0.625}{9} \right\}$$

The universe of discourse for the 'condition of the food' $X$ and 'time taken for the consumption' $Y$ is given here:

$X = \{1\ 2\ 3\ 4\ 5\ 6\}$
$Y = \{1\ 2\ 3\ 4\ 5\ 6\ 7\ 8\ 9\ 10\}$

**Solution:** As per the GMT

Using Larsen product implication operator, we get the implication relation between 'good' and 'slow'.

$$\Psi(\mu_{(good)}(x), \mu_{(slow)}(y)) = \mu_{(good)}(x) \bullet \mu_{(slow)}(y) \Rightarrow R(x, y)$$

$$\Rightarrow \Psi(\mu_{(good)}(x), \mu_{(slow)}(y)) = \begin{bmatrix} 0 \\ 0.5 \\ 1 \\ 0.5 \\ 0 \\ 0 \end{bmatrix} \begin{bmatrix} 0 & 0 & 0 & 0 & 0.33 & 0.67 & 1 & 0.67 & 0.33 & 0 \end{bmatrix}$$

$$= \begin{bmatrix} 0 & 0 & 0 & 0 & 0 & 0 & 0 & 0 & 0 & 0 \\ 0 & 0 & 0 & 0 & 0.165 & 0.335 & 0.5 & 0.335 & 0.165 & 0 \\ 0 & 0 & 0 & 0 & 0.33 & 0.67 & 1 & 0.67 & 0.33 & 0 \\ 0 & 0 & 0 & 0 & 0.165 & 0.335 & 0.5 & 0.335 & 0.165 & 0 \\ 0 & 0 & 0 & 0 & 0 & 0 & 0 & 0 & 0 & 0 \\ 0 & 0 & 0 & 0 & 0 & 0 & 0 & 0 & 0 & 0 \end{bmatrix}$$

The 'condition of food' $A'$ when the time taken for consumption is 'average' is

$$A' = R(x,y) \circ B'$$

$$= \begin{bmatrix} 0 & 0 & 0 & 0 & 0 & 0 & 0 & 0 & 0 & 0 \\ 0 & 0 & 0 & 0 & 0.165 & 0.335 & 0.5 & 0.335 & 0.165 & 0 \\ 0 & 0 & 0 & 0 & 0.33 & 0.67 & 1 & 0.67 & 0.33 & 0 \\ 0 & 0 & 0 & 0 & 0.165 & 0.335 & 0.5 & 0.335 & 0.165 & 0 \\ 0 & 0 & 0 & 0 & 0 & 0 & 0 & 0 & 0 & 0 \\ 0 & 0 & 0 & 0 & 0 & 0 & 0 & 0 & 0 & 0 \end{bmatrix} \circ \begin{bmatrix} 0 \\ 0 \\ 0 \\ 0 \\ 0.625 \\ 0.85 \\ 1 \\ 0.85 \\ 0.625 \\ 0 \end{bmatrix}$$

$$= \begin{bmatrix} 0 \\ 0.5 \\ 1 \\ 0.5 \\ 0 \\ 0 \end{bmatrix} \text{(Using max-min composition)}$$

Here $A'$ is found and the following fuzzy set is obtained:

$$A' = \left\{ \frac{0.5}{2} + \frac{1.0}{3} + \frac{0.5}{4} \right\}$$

**Example 5.9**

Apply GMP with Larsen product implication for evaluating IF/THEN rule. The antecedent and consequent variables of rule 'IF $x$ is $A$ THEN $y$ is $B$' is given in Figs 5.24 and 5.25. If the singleton membership function $A'$ is as shown in Fig. 5.26, then find $B'$ using GMP. Use max-min composition.

$$A = \left\{ \frac{0}{-6} + \frac{0}{-5} + \frac{0}{-4} + \frac{0.14}{-3} + \frac{0.28}{-2} + \frac{0.42}{-1} + \frac{0.52}{0} + \frac{0.7}{1} + \frac{0.85}{2} + \frac{1.0}{3} + \frac{0.66}{4} \right.$$
$$\left. + \frac{0.35}{-5} + \frac{0}{-6} \right\}$$

$$B = \left\{ \frac{0}{-6} + \frac{0.34}{-5} + \frac{0.67}{-4} + \frac{1.0}{-3} + \frac{0.67}{-2} + \frac{0.34}{-1} + \frac{0}{0} + \frac{0}{1} + \frac{0}{2} + \frac{0}{3} + \frac{0}{4} + \frac{0}{-5} + \frac{0}{-6} \right\}$$

$$A' = \left\{ \frac{0}{-6} + \frac{0}{-5} + \frac{0}{-4} + \frac{0}{-3} + \frac{0}{-2} + \frac{0}{-1} + \frac{0}{0} + \frac{0}{1} + \frac{0}{2} + \frac{0}{3} + \frac{0.7}{4} + \frac{0}{-5} + \frac{0}{-6} \right\}$$

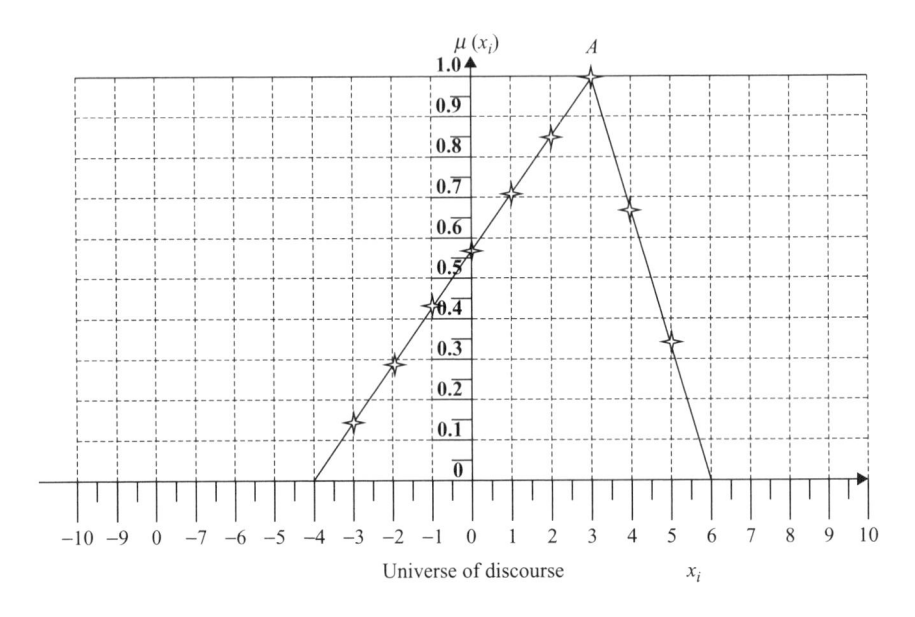

**Fig. 5.24** Membership diagram for A

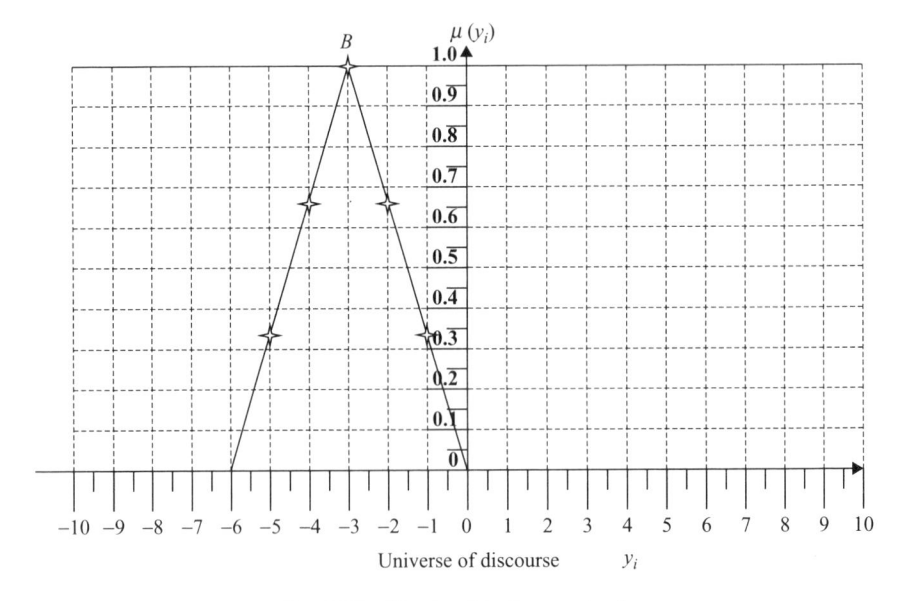

**Fig. 5.25** Membership diagram for B

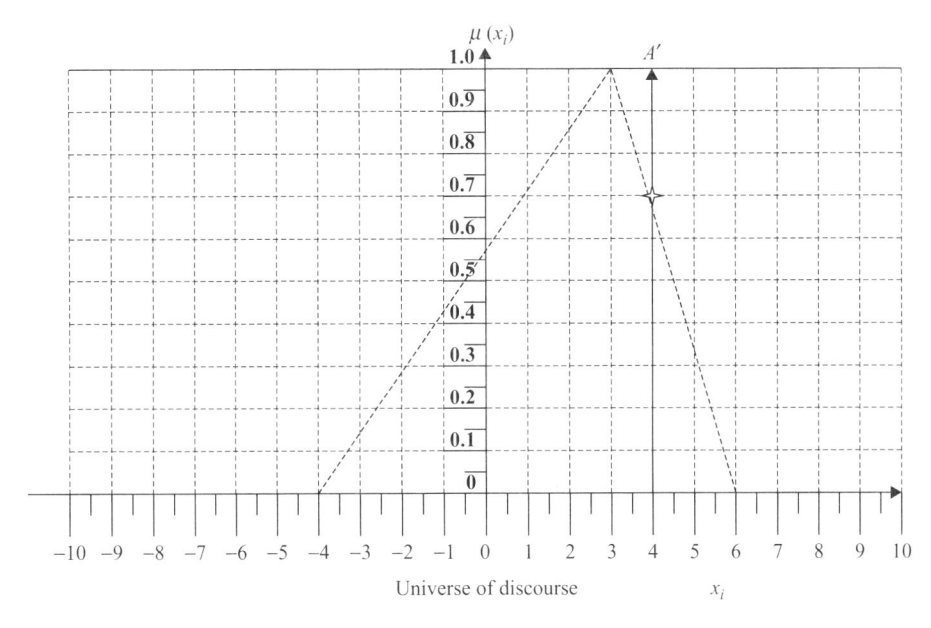

**Fig. 5.26** Membership diagram for A′

**Solution:** As per the GMT, using Larsen Product implication operator, we get the implication relation between 'A' and 'B'.

$$\Psi(\mu_{(A)}(x), \mu_B(y)) = \mu_{(A)}(x) \bullet \mu_{(B)}(y) \Rightarrow R(x, y)$$

$$= \begin{bmatrix} 0 \\ 0 \\ 0 \\ 0.14 \\ 0.28 \\ 0.42 \\ 0.52 \\ 0.7 \\ 0.85 \\ 1 \\ 0.66 \\ 0.35 \\ 0 \end{bmatrix} \begin{bmatrix} 0 & 0.34 & 0.67 & 1 & 0.67 & 0.34 & 0 & 0 & 0 & 0 & 0 & 0 & 0 \end{bmatrix}$$

$$= \begin{bmatrix} 0 & 0 & 0 & 0 & 0 & 0 & 0 & 0 & 0 & 0 & 0 & 0 & 0 \\ 0 & 0 & 0 & 0 & 0 & 0 & 0 & 0 & 0 & 0 & 0 & 0 & 0 \\ 0 & 0 & 0 & 0 & 0 & 0 & 0 & 0 & 0 & 0 & 0 & 0 & 0 \\ 0 & 0.0476 & 0.0938 & 0.1400 & 0.0938 & 0.0476 & 0 & 0 & 0 & 0 & 0 & 0 & 0 \\ 0 & 0.0952 & 0.1876 & 0.2800 & 0.1876 & 0.0952 & 0 & 0 & 0 & 0 & 0 & 0 & 0 \\ 0 & 0.1428 & 0.2814 & 0.4200 & 0.2814 & 0.1428 & 0 & 0 & 0 & 0 & 0 & 0 & 0 \\ 0 & 0.1768 & 0.3484 & 0.5200 & 0.3484 & 0.1768 & 0 & 0 & 0 & 0 & 0 & 0 & 0 \\ 0 & 0.2380 & 0.4690 & 0.7000 & 0.4690 & 0.2380 & 0 & 0 & 0 & 0 & 0 & 0 & 0 \\ 0 & 0.2890 & 0.5695 & 0.8500 & 0.5695 & 0.2890 & 0 & 0 & 0 & 0 & 0 & 0 & 0 \\ 0 & 0.3400 & 0.6700 & 1.000 & 0.6700 & 0.3400 & 0 & 0 & 0 & 0 & 0 & 0 & 0 \\ 0 & 0.2244 & 0.4422 & 0.6600 & 0.4422 & 0.2244 & 0 & 0 & 0 & 0 & 0 & 0 & 0 \\ 0 & 0.1190 & 0.2345 & 0.3500 & 0.2342 & 0.1190 & 0 & 0 & 0 & 0 & 0 & 0 & 0 \\ 0 & 0 & 0 & 0 & 0 & 0 & 0 & 0 & 0 & 0 & 0 & 0 & 0 \end{bmatrix}$$

$B' = A' \circ R(x, y)'$ (Using max-min composition)

$$= \begin{bmatrix} 0 & 0 & 0 & 0 & 0 & 0 & 0 & 0 & 0 & 0 & 0.7 & 0 & 0 \end{bmatrix} \circ$$

$$\begin{bmatrix} 0 & 0 & 0 & 0 & 0 & 0 & 0 & 0 & 0 & 0 & 0 & 0 & 0 \\ 0 & 0 & 0 & 0 & 0 & 0 & 0 & 0 & 0 & 0 & 0 & 0 & 0 \\ 0 & 0 & 0 & 0 & 0 & 0 & 0 & 0 & 0 & 0 & 0 & 0 & 0 \\ 0 & 0.0476 & 0.0938 & 0.1400 & 0.0938 & 0.0476 & 0 & 0 & 0 & 0 & 0 & 0 & 0 \\ 0 & 0.0952 & 0.1876 & 0.2800 & 0.1876 & 0.0952 & 0 & 0 & 0 & 0 & 0 & 0 & 0 \\ 0 & 0.1428 & 0.2814 & 0.4200 & 0.2814 & 0.1428 & 0 & 0 & 0 & 0 & 0 & 0 & 0 \\ 0 & 0.1768 & 0.3484 & 0.5200 & 0.3484 & 0.1768 & 0 & 0 & 0 & 0 & 0 & 0 & 0 \\ 0 & 0.2380 & 0.4690 & 0.7000 & 0.4690 & 0.2380 & 0 & 0 & 0 & 0 & 0 & 0 & 0 \\ 0 & 0.2890 & 0.5695 & 0.8500 & 0.5695 & 0.2890 & 0 & 0 & 0 & 0 & 0 & 0 & 0 \\ 0 & 0.3400 & 0.6700 & 1.000 & 0.6700 & 0.3400 & 0 & 0 & 0 & 0 & 0 & 0 & 0 \\ 0 & 0.2244 & 0.4422 & 0.6600 & 0.4422 & 0.2244 & 0 & 0 & 0 & 0 & 0 & 0 & 0 \\ 0 & 0.1190 & 0.2345 & 0.3500 & 0.2342 & 0.1190 & 0 & 0 & 0 & 0 & 0 & 0 & 0 \\ 0 & 0 & 0 & 0 & 0 & 0 & 0 & 0 & 0 & 0 & 0 & 0 & 0 \end{bmatrix}$$

$B' = \begin{bmatrix} 0 & 0.2244 & 0.4422 & 0.6600 & 0.4422 & 0.2244 & 0 & 0 & 0 & 0 & 0 & 0 & 0 \end{bmatrix}$

$$B' = \left\{ \frac{0}{-6} + \frac{0.2244}{-5} + \frac{0.4422}{-4} + \frac{0.6600}{-3} + \frac{0.4422}{-2} + \frac{0.2244}{-1} + \frac{0}{0} + \frac{0}{1} + \frac{0}{2} + \frac{0}{3} + \frac{0}{4} + \frac{0}{-5} + \frac{0}{-6} \right\}$$

The final membership diagram for $B'$ is given in Fig. 5.27.

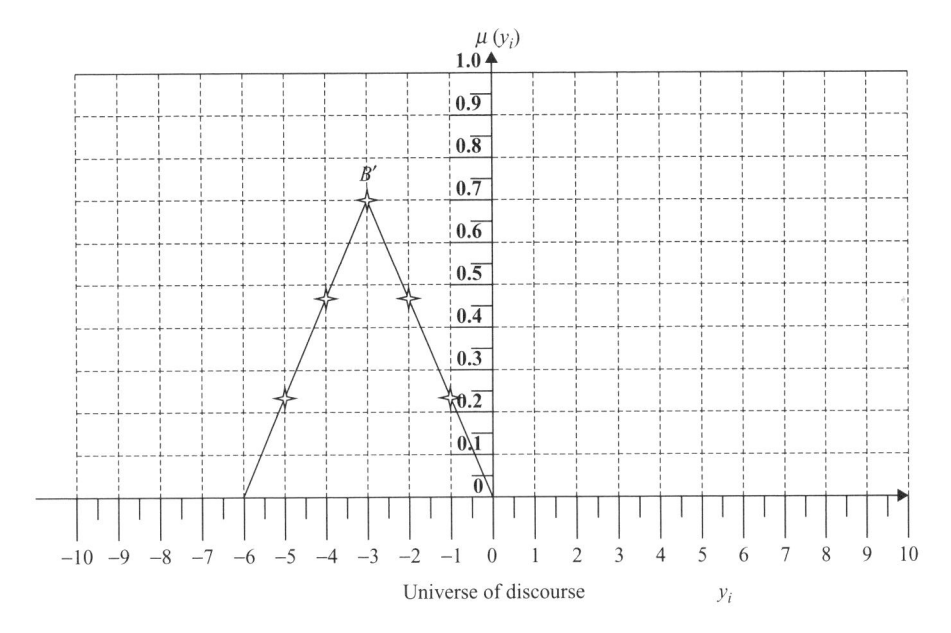

**Fig. 5.27** Membership diagram for $B'$

### 5.10.6 Fuzzy Inference Algorithms

Fuzzy inference algorithms are procedures that perform evaluation of fuzzy IF/THEN rules. In general, past experience or knowledge forms the core competency in generating rules. These rules are then simply represented with IF/THEN and ELSE statements such as the following:

IF $x$ is $A_1$ THEN $y$ is $B_1$ ELSE

IF $x$ is $A_2$ THEN $y$ is $B_2$ ELSE

……

IF $x$ is $A_n$ THEN $y$ is $B_n$

**Case I: IF/THEN rules with connective AND/OR**
Consider an IF/THEN rule of the form.

$$\text{IF } x_1 \text{ is } A_1 \text{ AND } x_2 \text{ is } A_2 \text{ AND } ….. \text{ AND } x_n \text{ is } A_n \text{ THEN } y \text{ is } B \quad (5.147)$$

where $x_1,……, x_n$ are antecedent linguistic variables with $A_1,…..,A_m$ being their corresponding fuzzy values and $y$ is the consequent linguistic variable with B as its fuzzy value. In the antecedent side, we can use the connective AND to logical model by using either using min or as an arithmetic product. Therefore, we can combine the propositions in the antecedent side either through min ($\wedge$) or through product (.) and use an appropriate implication operator $\Psi$, and thus Eq. (5.147) can be denoted as Eq. (5.148).

$$\mu(x_1, x_2, ……, x_n, y) = \Psi[\mu_{A1}(x_1) \wedge \mu_{A2}(x_2) \wedge …… \wedge \mu_{An}(x_n), \mu_B(y)] \quad (5.148)$$

In case AND is logically modelled as product, then Eq. (5.147) can be denoted as Eq. (5.149):

$$\mu(x_1, x_2, \ldots, x_n, y) = \Psi[\mu_{A1}(x_1) \cdot \mu_{A2}(x_2) \cdot \ldots \cdot \mu_{An}(x_n), \mu_B(y)] \quad (5.149)$$

Similarly if OR is the connective, then we use max ($\vee$) or sum (+).

**Case II: Nested IF/THEN Rules**

Consider an IF/THEN rule which involves $n$ nested fuzzy implications, such that each nested part is having one antecedent variable.

$$\text{IF } x_1 \text{ is } A_1 \text{ THEN (if } x_2 \text{ is } A_2 \text{ THEN } \ldots \text{ (IF } x_n \text{ is } A_n \text{ THEN } y \text{ is B)}\ldots) \quad (5.150)$$

The representation of a multivariate fuzzy implication is carried out by means of repeated application of an implication operator, once for each nested IF/THEN rule as in Eq. (5.149):

$$\mu(x_1, x_2, \ldots, x_n, y) = \Psi[\mu_{A1}(x_1), \Psi[\mu_{A2}(x_2) \ldots \Psi[\mu_{An}(x_n), \mu_B(y)]\ldots] \quad (5.151)$$

**Case III: IF/THEN rules with connective ELSE**

Consider an IF/THEN rule which involves $n$ variables $x_1, \ldots, x_n$ on the antecedent side of the $i^{th}$ IF/THEN rule taking values $A_{1i}, \ldots, A_{np}$ ($i = 1, \ldots, p$) and only one consequent linguistic variable $y$, taking values $B_1, B_2, \ldots, B_q$.

IF $x_1$ is $A_{11}$ AND $x_2$ is $A_{21}$ AND....AND $x_{1n}$ is $A_{n1}$ THEN $y$ is $B_1$ ELSE
IF $x_1$ is $A_{12}$ AND $x_2$ is $A_{22}$ AND....AND $x_n$ is $A_{n2}$ THEN $y$ is $B_2$ ELSE
.........
IF $x_1$ is $A_{1p}$ AND $x_2$ is $A_{2p}$ AND....AND $x_{1n}$ is $A_{np}$ THEN $y$ is $B_q$ ELSE  (5.152)

The aggregation of all the statements is analytically described by the following algorithmic relation of the form:

$$R_\Sigma (x_1, x_2, \ldots, x_n, y)$$
$$= \int (x_1, x_2, \ldots, x_n, y) \, \mu_\alpha(x_1, x_2, \ldots, x_n, y)/(x_1, x_2, \ldots, x_n, y) \quad (5.153)$$

and when discrete fuzzy sets are used, we obtain the following result:

$$R_\Sigma (x_{1i}, x_{2i}, \ldots, x_{ni}, y_i)$$
$$= \sum_{(x_1, x_2, \ldots, x_{ni}, y_j)} \mu_\Sigma (x_{1i}, x_{2i}, \ldots, x_{ni}, y_j)/(x_{1i}, x_{2i}, \ldots, x_{ni}, y_j) \quad (5.154)$$

Once the algorithmic relation is known, GMP or GMT can be used as an inference procedure.

### 5.10.7 De-fuzzification

De-fuzzification is the process of converting the fuzzy set into a crisp value (i.e., to get a crisp number $u^*$ representative of $\mu(u)$). Generally, the membership functions are sampled to find the membership grade used in the fuzzy logic equations(s) to define an outcome region, thereby deducing the crisp output.

The crisp output is the result of the implication and aggregation steps of the fuzzy output, which is the union of all the outputs of individual rule. The crisp output can be sent as a control signal for any decision-making application. The efficiency of the decision depends very much on the de-fuzzification process. Several de-fuzzification techniques have been suggested over the years. However, the following de-fuzzification techniques will be discussed in this section:

(a) Max-membership (height method)
(b) Centre of area (COA) or centre of gravity or centroid method
(c) Weighted average method
(d) Mean of maxima (middle of maxima)
(e) Centre of sums
(f) Centre of largest area (COLA)
(g) First of maxima
(h) Last of maxima

### 5.10.7.1 Max-Membership (Height Method)

This method defines the maximum value or the peak of the membership function as the de-fuzzified crisp output. The crisp output $u^*$ is the intersecting point in the horizontal axis when a vertical line is drawn between the peak point in the fuzzy membership diagram. The peak point is the maximum value of all the $\mu(u)$ representing the fuzzy set as shown in Fig. 5.28. Since for a fuzzy $A$, the height of the fuzzy set $A$ (i.e., h ($A$)) is the largest membership grade obtained by any element in that set which is also equal to maximum value of all the $\mu_A(u)$ representing the fuzzy set, the crisp output $u^*$ is given by the Eq. (5.155).

$$u^* = \max(\mu_A(u_i)), \text{where}, \ i = 1....N \qquad (5.155)$$

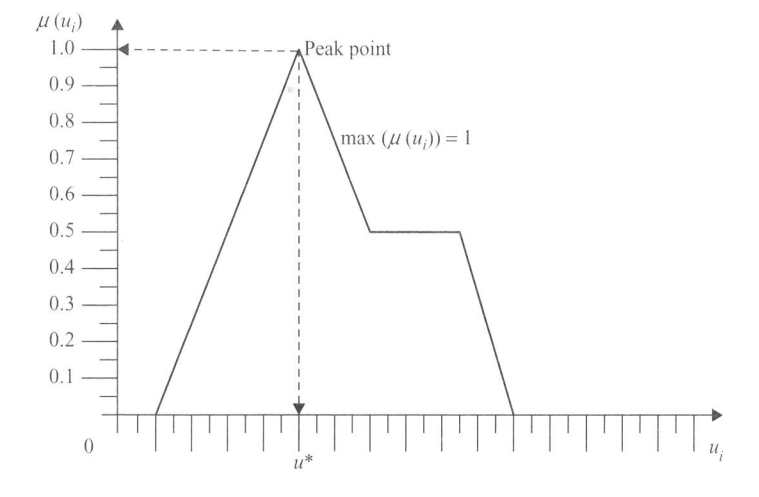

**Fig. 5.28** Max-membership de-fuzzification method

The domain range of evaluation is carried out over (discrete) values of the universe of discourse $u_i$ sampled at $N$ points.

### 5.10.7.2 Centre of Area (COA) De-fuzzification

In centre of area (COA) de-fuzzification, the crisp value u is taken to be the geometrical centre of the output fuzzy value $\mu_{OUT}(u)$, where $\mu_{OUT}(u)$ is formed by taking the union of all the contributions of rules whose DOF is greater than zero. The centroid methods are based on finding a balance point of a property that can be the total geometric figure which represents the area of each fuzzy set. Let us assume we have a discretized universe of discourse. The de-fuzzified output is defined as follows:

$$u^* = \frac{\sum_{i=1}^{N} u_i \mu_{OUT}(u_i)}{\sum_{i=1}^{N} \mu_{OUT}(u_i)} \quad (5.156)$$

where the summation is carried out over (discrete) values of the universe of discourse $u$ sampled at $N$ points. Centre of area takes into account the area of the resultant membership function. If the areas of two or more contributing rules overlap, COA does not take into account the overlapping area. Approximation embedded in Eq. (5.156) will be justified when the membership function is defined as a fuzzy set comprising singleton. Otherwise the approximation is determined by the number of summations. The membership function $\mu_{OUT}(u)$ represents the fuzzy set of the final output of one linguistic or fuzzy variable, and u is the location of each singleton on the universe of discourse.

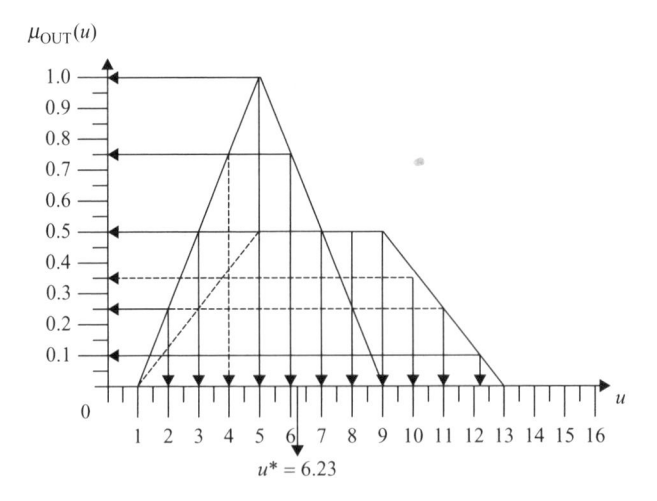

**Fig. 5.29** Centre of area method

From Fig. 5.29, we can calculate the crisp out $u^*$ as follows:

$$u^* = \frac{\begin{array}{c}(2\times 0.25 + 3\times 0.5 + 4\times 0.75 + 5\times 1 + 6\times 0.75 + 7\times 0.5 + \\ 8\times 0.5 + 9\times 0.5 + 10\times 0.35 + 11\times 0.25 + 12\times 0.1)\end{array}}{\begin{array}{c}(0.25 + 0.5 + 0.75 + 1 + 0.75 + 0.5 + \\ 0.5 + 0.5 + 0.35 + 0.25 + 0.1)\end{array}}$$

$$u^* = 6.23$$

### 5.10.7.3 Weighted Average Method

Whenever the fuzzy outputs are symmetrical in nature, the weighted average method is used. The de-fuzzified output is defined as follows:

$$u^* = \frac{\sum_{j=1}^{Z} \overline{z}_j \mu_{\text{OUT}}(\overline{z}_j)}{\sum_{j=1}^{Z} \mu_{\text{OUT}}(\overline{z}_j)} \quad (5.157)$$

$$\overline{z}_j = \frac{1}{N}\sum_{i=1}^{N} u_i \quad (5.158)$$

Here, Z is the number of symmetrical fuzzy output and $\overline{z}_j$ is the average or mean of the fuzzy symmetrical output. N is the number of samples considered in each of the fuzzy symmetrical output. Let us calculate the crisp output for the fuzzy symmetrical membership plot given in Fig. 5.30. In this figure, two symmetrical parts $z_1$ and $z_2$ are present.

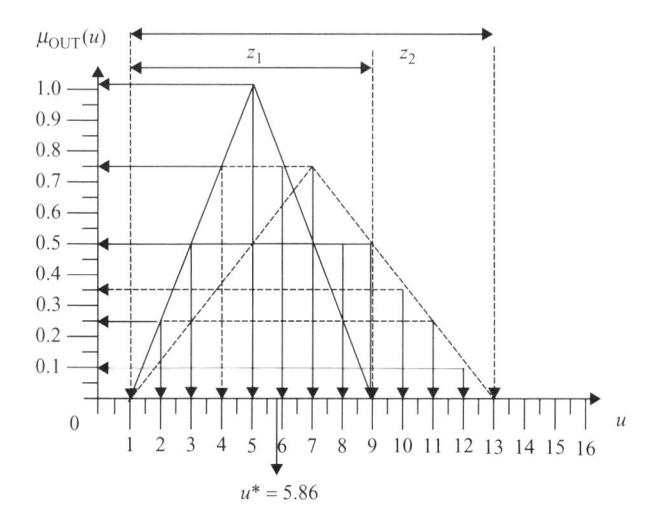

**Fig. 5.30** Weighted average method

From Fig. 5.30, we can calculate the crisp out $u^*$ as follows:

$$\bar{z_1} = \frac{(2+3+4+5+6+7+8)}{7} = 5$$

$$\mu_{OUT}(\bar{z_1} = 5) = 1$$

$$\bar{z_2} = \frac{(2+3+4+5+6+7+8+9+10+11+12)}{11} = 7$$

$$\mu_{OUT}(\bar{z_2} = 7) = 0.75$$

$$u^* = \frac{(5 \times 1) + (7 \times 0.75)}{(1 + 0.75)} = 5.86$$

Since the method is limited to symmetrical membership functions, the values $\bar{z_1}$ and $\bar{z_2}$ are the means of their respective shapes.

#### 5.10.7.4 Mean of Maxima (MOM)

One simple way to de-fuzzify the output is to take the crisp value with the highest degree of membership in $\mu_{OUT}(u)$. When we have more than one element in the universe of discourse with maximum value, the mean value of the maximum is taken or we can randomly select one of them. Suppose that we have $M$ such maxima in a discrete universe of discourse. The crisp output can be obtained by the following equation:

$$u^* = \frac{1}{M} \sum_{m=1}^{M} u_m \qquad (5.159)$$

where, $u_m$ is the $m^{th}$ element in the universe of discourse, the membership function of $\mu_{OUT}(u)$ is at the maximum value, and $M$ is the total number of such elements. From Fig. 5.33, we can calculate the crisp out $u^*$ such as this:

$$u^* = \frac{(9+10)}{2} = 9.5$$

#### 5.10.7.5 Centre of Sums (COS)

This method involves the algebraic sum of individual output fuzzy sets, say $C_1$ and $C_2$, instead of their union. In general the overlapping area is counted once in COA method. However, in centre of sums (COS), we take into account the overlapping areas of multiple rules more than once, a variant of COA called COS. This method is faster when compared to COA de-fuzzification technique. The de-fuzzification output is defined as follows:

$$u^* = \frac{\sum_{i=1}^{N} u_i \sum_{k=1}^{n} \mu_{C'_k}(u_i)}{\sum_{i=1}^{N} \sum_{k=1}^{n} \mu_{C'_k}(u_i)} \qquad (5.160)$$

where, $\mu_{C'_k}(u_i)$ is the membership value at the sample $u_i$ of the universe of discourse that results from the firing of the $k^{th}$ rule.

From Fig. 5.31, we can calculate the crisp out $u^*$ by the following process:

$$u^* = \frac{\sum_{i=1}^{N=11} u_i \sum_{k=1}^{n=2} \mu_{C'_k}(u_i)}{\sum_{i=1}^{N=11} \sum_{k=1}^{n=2} \mu_{C'_k}(u_i)}$$

$$u^* = \frac{\begin{bmatrix}(2 \times 0.25)+(3 \times 0.5)+(4 \times 0.75)+(5 \times 1)+(6 \times 0.75)+(7 \times 0.5)+(8 \times 0.25)\end{bmatrix} + \\ \begin{bmatrix}(2 \times 0.1)+(3 \times 0.25)+(4 \times 0.35)+(5 \times 0.5)+(6 \times 0.5)+(7 \times 0.5)+(8 \times 0.5) \\ +(9 \times 0.5)+(10 \times 0.35)+(11 \times 0.25)+(12 \times 0.1)\end{bmatrix}}{\begin{bmatrix}0.25+0.5+0.75+1+0.75+0.5+0.5+0.25\end{bmatrix} + \\ \begin{bmatrix}0.1+0.25+0.35+0.5+0.5+0.5+0.5+0.5+0.35+0.25+0.1\end{bmatrix}}$$

$$u^* = \frac{46.95}{8.4} = 5.59$$

Here, the overlapping area is counted twice.

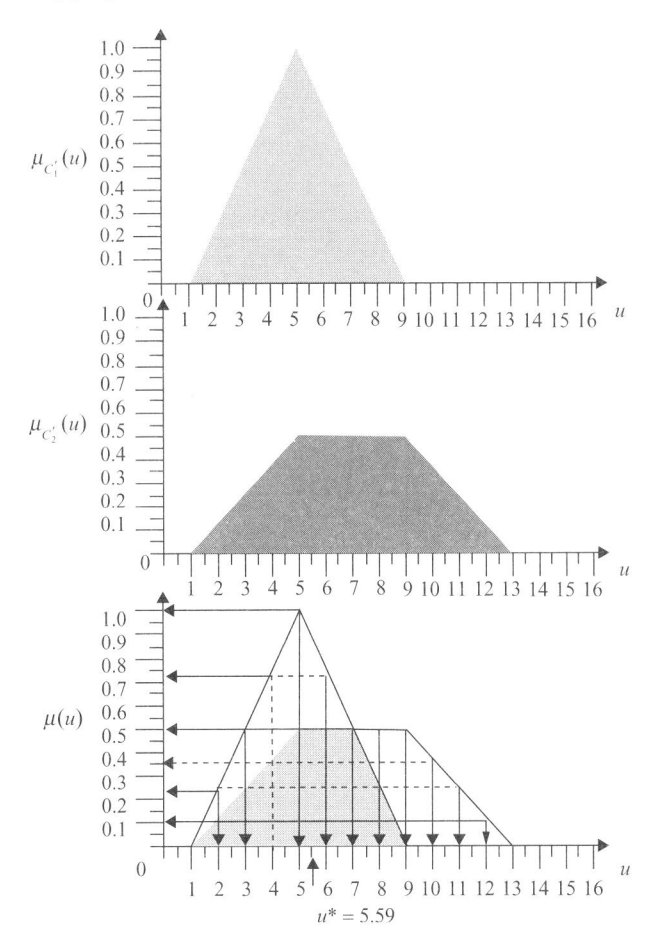

**Fig. 5.31** Centre of sums

## 5.10.7.6 Centre of Largest Area (COLA)

In this method, the fuzzy output should have at least two convex regions. Then the de-fuzzified value $u^*$ of the output of centre of largest area (COLA) is calculated using COA for the convex fuzzy sub-region with the largest area. Consider Fig. 5.32 which has two convex regions $C_1$ and $C_2$.

$C_L$ is the convex sub-region that has the largest area making up fuzzy output. This condition applies in the case when the overall fuzzy output is non-convex; and in the case when fuzzy output is convex, $u^*$ is the same quantity as determined by the COA as there is only one convex region. The de-fuzzified output is defined as

$$u^* = \frac{\sum_{i=1}^{N} u_i \mu_{C_L}(u_i)}{\sum_{i=1}^{N} \mu_{C_L}(u_i)} \qquad (5.161)$$

From Fig. 5.27, we can calculate the crisp out $u^*$ as given here:

$$u^* = \frac{(1 \times 0.4 + 2 \times 0.4 + 3 \times 0.5 + 4 \times 0.5 + 5 \times 0.8 + 6 \times 0.8 + 7 \times 0.1)}{(0.4 + 0.4 + 0.5 + 0.5 + 0.8 + 0.8 + 0.1)}$$

$$u^* = 4.06$$

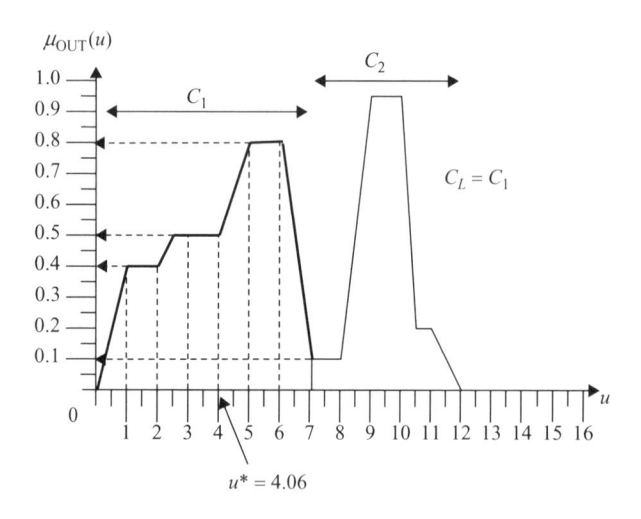

**Fig. 5.32** Centre of largest area

## 5.10.7.7 First of Maxima

In this method, the clipped fuzzy set $C_i$ having highest membership grade $\mu_{C_m}(u)$ is first identified from Eq. (5.162).

$$\mu_{C_m}(u) = \max(\mu_{C_i}(u)), \; i = 1....N_c \qquad (5.162)$$

where, $N_c$ is the number of clipped fuzzy sets.

Then the smallest value of the variable within the domain of this clipped fuzzy set with highest membership grade is taken as $u^*$ and is given by the following:

$$u^* = \min(u_i) \tag{5.163}$$

Such that

$$u_{First} \leq u_i^* \leq u_{Last} \tag{5.164}$$

where, $u_{First}$ and $u_{Last}$ are the values corresponding to the $\min(u_i|\mu(u_i) = \mu_{Cm}(u))$ and $\max(u_i|\mu(u_i) = \mu_{Cm}(u))$, respectively.

Let us consider the fuzzy output set shown in Fig. 5.33. Here, $N_c = 6$, $m = 6$, $u_{First} = 9$ and $u_{Last} = 10$. Finally the de-fuzzified output is given as $u^* = \min(u_i) = 9$.

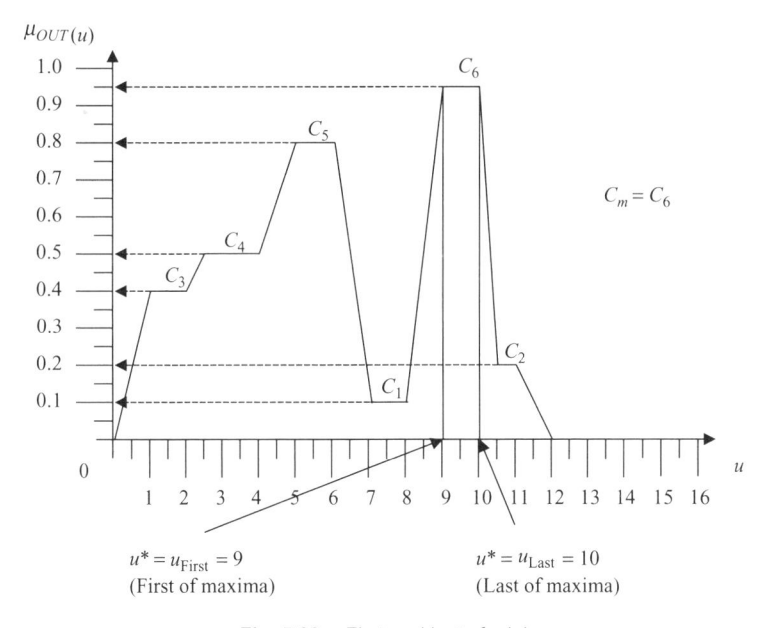

**Fig. 5.33** First and last of minima

### 5.10.7.8 Last of Maxima

This method is similar to the first of maxima. Here, in the same manner, the clipped fuzzy set $C_i$ having highest membership grade $\mu_{C_m}(u)$ is first identified from Eq. (5.162).

Then the largest value of the variable within the domain of this clipped fuzzy set with highest membership grade is taken as $u^*$ and is given by the Eq. (5.165).

$$u^* = \max(u_i) \tag{5.165}$$

Such that

$$u_{First} \leq u_i^* \leq u_{Last} \tag{5.166}$$

where, $u_{\text{First}}$ and $u_{\text{Last}}$ are the values corresponding to the $\max(\mu_{C_m}(u))$ and $\min(\mu_{C_m}(u))$, respectively.

Let us consider the same fuzzy output set shown in Fig. 5.33. Here, $N_C = 6$, $m = 6$, $u_{\text{First}} = 9$ and $u_{\text{Last}} = 10$. Finally the de-fuzzified output is given as $u^* = \max(u_i) = 10$.

### 5.10.8 Assessment of de-fuzzification Methods

After discussing various de-fuzzification techniques, there arises a question of using the right choice of de-fuzzification techniques at the right place. Hellendoorn and Thomas [11] have suggested some five criteria such that an ideal de-fuzzification technique should satisfy. It should be noted that none of the de-fuzzification techniques satisfy all the five criteria. However, the right choice of the de-fuzzification techniques for a particular application can be selected only by understanding the trade-off between these criteria.

**Criterion No. 1: Continuity**

A small change in the input of the fuzzy system should not result in a large change in the output. That is, if $I$ and $(I + \nabla I)$ are the two inputs to a fuzzy system whose de-fuzzified crisp outputs are $u_I^*$ and $u_{(I+\nabla I)}^*$, then $\left| u_I^* - u_{(I+\nabla I)}^* \right| \cong |\nabla|$.

**Criterion No. 2: Disambiguity**

A de-fuzzification method for a given fuzzy system should always result in a unique value of the crisp output $u^*$ (i.e., there should not be any ambiguity in the de-fuzzified value). However, this criterion is not satisfied by the COLA method. Suppose the two convex regions as in Fig. 5.34 is of equal area, then there is an ambiguity in selecting the de-fuzzified output $u^*$.

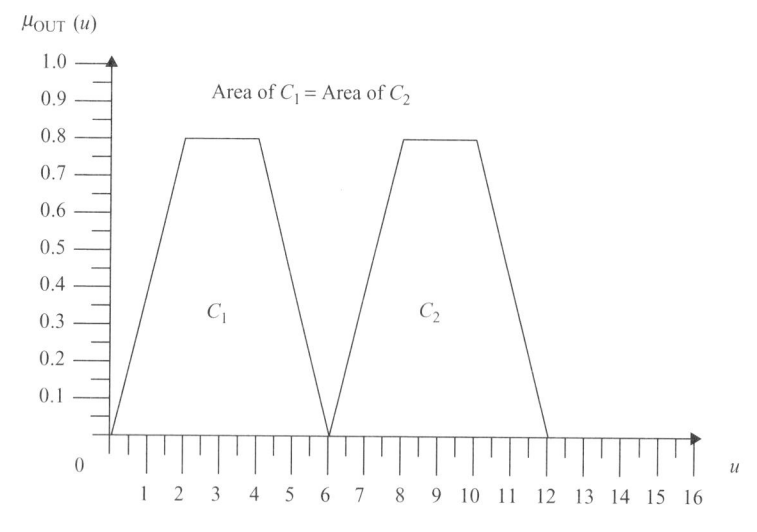

**Fig. 5.34** Equal area fuzzy outputs ($C_1$ and $C_2$)

## Criterion No. 3: Plausibility

A de-fuzzification method for a given fuzzy system is said to be plausible if the de-fuzzified output $u^*$ lies in the middle of the fuzzy-supported region and also $u^*$ should have the highest membership value in the clipped fuzzy set. The COA and COS satisfy this criterion to a larger extent compared to other de-fuzzification methods. In Fig. 5.35, the fuzzy outputs satisfy the plausibility criterion.

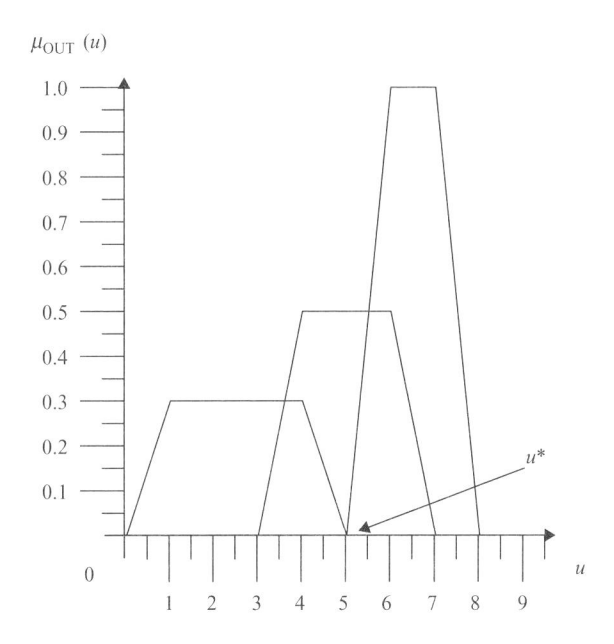

**Fig. 5.35** Fuzzy outputs that satisfy the plausibility criterion

## Criterion No. 4: Computational Complexity

The computational complexity is directly related to the time taken for processing a de-fuzzified output. When comparing all the methods that have been discussed in this section, Max-membership (height method) is the fastest method followed by first of maxima, last of maxima and middle of maxima. Centre of largest area is slower, but COS method is still slower. Computational burden is highest with COA method. The processing time in the de-fuzzification technique is very important in case of online process control.

## Criterion No. 5: Weighting Methods

The weighting methods weigh the contribution of each fuzzy output support region or the clipped fuzzy set in obtaining the de-fuzzified output, $u^*$. Generally in the case of COA, COS, and Max-membership (height method), the calculation of $u^*$ is very much dependent on each of the fuzzy output support region. However, this property is not found in other methods.

The merits and demerits of fuzzy logic are defined as follows:

**Merits**

1. The user interface is convenient, easier, and easy interpretation.
2. Linear parameterized systems can be employed to validate non-linear systems.
3. Redundancy of the system can be verified from the rule base itself.
4. Integral control schemes can be developed by combining fuzzy set with regular algorithms.
5. Fuzzy logic can be incorporated into existing conventional controllers to fine-tune the controller capabilities.

**Demerits**

1. When the number of inputs is more, the design of rule base becomes too complex.
2. The memory space required to store information of Cartesian product is very high.
3. Tuning of fuzzy-based system is monotonous and time-consuming.
4. Fuzzy PID-like controller does not outperform the conventional controllers.
5. Many actual implementations are similar to lookup table.

## 5.11 ILLUSTRATIVE PROBLEMS

**Problem 5.1**

Perform the following fuzzy arithmetic operation $C = A + B$ through extension principle by fuzzifying the function $z(x, y) = x + y$ for the given fuzzy set.

$$A = 0/0 + 0.2/1 + 0.4/2 + 0.6/3 + 0.8/4 + 1/5$$
$$B = 1/0 + 0.8/1 + 0.6/2 + 0.4/3 + 0.2/4 + 0/5$$

*Solution:*

$$\mu_{A+B}(z) = \vee_{z=x+y} [\mu_A(x) \wedge \mu_B(y)]$$

| Sum $z = x+y$ | Possible combination | | $\mu_A(x)$ | $\mu_B(y)$ | $\min(\mu_A(x), \mu_B(y))$ | $\max(\min(\mu_A(x), \mu_B(y)))$ |
|---|---|---|---|---|---|---|
| | x | y | | | | |
| 10 | 5 | 5 | 1 | 0 | 0 | 0 |
| 9 | 5 | 4 | 1 | 0.2 | 0.2 | 0.2 |
| | 4 | 5 | 0.8 | 0 | 0 | |
| 8 | 5 | 3 | 1 | 0.4 | 0.4 | 0.4 |
| | 4 | 4 | 0.8 | 0.2 | 0.2 | |
| | 3 | 5 | 0.6 | 0 | 0 | |

*(Continued)*

(Continued)

| Sum $z = x+y$ | Possible combination | | $\mu_A(x)$ | $\mu_B(y)$ | min($\mu_A(x)$, $\mu_B(y)$) | max(min($\mu_A(x)$, $\mu_B(y)$)) |
|---|---|---|---|---|---|---|
| | x | y | | | | |
| 7 | 5 | 2 | 1 | 0.6 | 0.6 | 0.6 |
| | 4 | 3 | 0.8 | 0.4 | 0.4 | |
| | 3 | 4 | 0.6 | 0.2 | 0.2 | |
| | 2 | 5 | 0.4 | 0 | 0 | |
| 6 | 5 | 1 | 1 | 0.8 | 0.8 | 0.8 |
| | 4 | 2 | 0.8 | 0.6 | 0.6 | |
| | 3 | 3 | 0.6 | 0.4 | 0.4 | |
| | 2 | 4 | 0.4 | 0.2 | 0.2 | |
| | 1 | 5 | 0.2 | 0 | 0 | |
| 5 | 5 | 0 | 1 | 1 | 1 | 1 |
| | 4 | 1 | 0.8 | 0.8 | 0.8 | |
| | 3 | 2 | 0.6 | 0.6 | 0.6 | |
| | 2 | 3 | 0.4 | 0.4 | 0.4 | |
| | 1 | 4 | 0.2 | 0.2 | 0.2 | |
| | 0 | 5 | 0 | 0 | 0 | |

$C = A + B = C(z) = \{1/5 + 0.8/6 + 0.6/7 + 0.4/8 + 0.2/9 + 0/10\}$

## Problem 5.2

Perform the following fuzzy arithmetic operation $D = A - B$ through extension principle by fuzzifying the function $z(x, y) = x - y$ for the previously given instance in Problem 5.1 fuzzy set.

**Solution:**

$$\mu_{D=A-B}(z) = \vee_{z=x-y} [\mu_A(x) \wedge \mu_B(y)]$$

| Difference $z = x - y$ | Possible combination | | $\mu_A(x)$ | $\mu_B(y)$ | min($\mu_A(x)$, $\mu_B(y)$) | max(min($\mu_A(x)$, $\mu_B(y)$)) |
|---|---|---|---|---|---|---|
| | x | y | | | | |
| 5 | 5 | 0 | 1 | 1 | 1 | 1 |
| 4 | 5 | 1 | 1 | 0.8 | 0.8 | 0.8 |
| | 4 | 0 | 0.8 | 1 | 0.8 | |
| 3 | 5 | 2 | 1 | 0.6 | 0.6 | 0.8 |
| | 4 | 1 | 0.8 | 0.8 | 0.8 | |
| | 3 | 0 | 0.6 | 1 | 0.6 | |

(Continued)

(Continued)

| Difference $z = x - y$ | Possible combination | | $\mu_A(x)$ | $\mu_B(y)$ | $\min(\mu_A(x), \mu_B(y))$ | $\max(\min(\mu_A(x), \mu_B(y)))$ |
|---|---|---|---|---|---|---|
| | x | y | | | | |
| 2 | 5 | 3 | 1 | 0.4 | 0.4 | 0.6 |
| | 4 | 2 | 0.8 | 0.6 | 0.6 | |
| | 3 | 1 | 0.6 | 0.8 | 0.6 | |
| | 2 | 0 | 0.4 | 1 | 0.4 | |
| 1 | 5 | 4 | 1 | 0.2 | 0.2 | 0.6 |
| | 4 | 3 | 0.8 | 0.4 | 0.4 | |
| | 3 | 2 | 0.6 | 0.6 | 0.6 | |
| | 2 | 1 | 0.4 | 0.8 | 0.4 | |
| | 1 | 0 | 0.2 | 1 | 0.2 | |
| 0 | 5 | 5 | 1 | 0 | 0 | 0.4 |
| | 4 | 4 | 0.8 | 0.2 | 0.2 | |
| | 3 | 3 | 0.6 | 0.4 | 0.4 | |
| | 2 | 2 | 0.4 | 0.6 | 0.4 | |
| | 1 | 1 | 0.2 | 0.8 | 0.2 | |
| | 0 | 0 | 0 | 1 | 0 | |
| −1 | 4 | 5 | 0.8 | 0 | 0 | 0.4 |
| | 3 | 4 | 0.6 | 0.2 | 0.2 | |
| | 2 | 3 | 0.4 | 0.4 | 0.4 | |
| | 1 | 2 | 0.2 | 0.6 | 0.2 | |
| | 0 | 1 | 0 | 0.8 | 0 | |
| −2 | 3 | 5 | 0.6 | 0 | 0 | 0.2 |
| | 2 | 4 | 0.4 | 0.2 | 0.2 | |
| | 1 | 3 | 0.2 | 0.4 | 0.2 | |
| | 0 | 2 | 0 | 0.6 | 0 | |
| −3 | 2 | 5 | 0.4 | 0 | 0 | 0.2 |
| | 1 | 4 | 0.2 | 0.2 | 0.2 | |
| | 0 | 3 | 0 | 0.4 | 0 | |
| −4 | 1 | 5 | 0.2 | 0 | 0 | 0 |
| | 0 | 4 | 0 | 0.2 | 0 | |
| −5 | 0 | 5 | 0 | 0 | 0 | 0 |

$D = A - B = D(z) = \{0/-5 + 0/-4 + 0.2/-3 + 0.2/-2 + 0.4/-1 + 0.4/0 + 0.6/1 + 0.6/2 + 0.8/3 + 0.8/4 + 1/5\}$

## Problem 5.3

Perform the following fuzzy arithmetic operation $E = A \times B$ through extension principle by fuzzifying the function $z(x, y) = x \times y$ for the given in Problem 5.1 fuzzy set.

**Solution:**

$$\mu_{E=A\times B}(z) = \vee_{z=x\times y}[\mu_A(x) \wedge \mu_B(y)]$$

| Product $z = x \times y$ | Possible combination $x$ | $y$ | $\mu_A(x)$ | $\mu_B(y)$ | min($\mu_A(x), \mu_B(y)$) | max(min($\mu_A(x), \mu_B(y)$)) |
|---|---|---|---|---|---|---|
| 25 | 5 | 5 | 1 | 0 | 0 | 0 |
| 20 | 5 | 4 | 1 | 0.2 | 0.2 | 0.2 |
|    | 4 | 5 | 0.8 | 0 | 0 |  |
| 15 | 5 | 3 | 1 | 0.4 | 0.4 | 0.4 |
|    | 3 | 5 | 0.6 | 0 | 0 |  |
| 12 | 4 | 3 | 0.8 | 0.4 | 0.4 | 0.4 |
|    | 3 | 4 | 0.6 | 0.2 | 0.2 |  |
| 10 | 5 | 2 | 1 | 0.6 | 0.6 | 0.6 |
|    | 2 | 5 | 0.4 | 0 | 0 |  |
| 8  | 4 | 2 | 0.8 | 0.6 | 0.6 | 0.6 |
|    | 2 | 4 | 0.4 | 0.2 | 0.2 |  |
| 6  | 3 | 2 | 0.6 | 0.6 | 0.6 | 0.6 |
|    | 2 | 3 | 0.4 | 0.4 | 0.4 |  |
| 5  | 5 | 1 | 1 | 0.8 | 0.8 | 0.8 |
|    | 1 | 5 | 0.2 | 0 | 0 |  |
| 4  | 4 | 1 | 0.8 | 0.8 | 0.8 | 0.8 |
|    | 1 | 4 | 0.2 | 0.2 | 0.2 |  |
| 3  | 2 | 2 | 0.4 | 0.6 | 0.4 | 0.6 |
|    | 3 | 1 | 0.6 | 0.8 | 0.6 |  |
| 2  | 1 | 3 | 0.2 | 0.4 | 0.2 | 0.4 |
|    | 2 | 1 | 0.4 | 0.8 | 0.4 |  |
| 1  | 1 | 2 | 0.2 | 0.6 | 0.2 | 0.2 |
|    | 1 | 1 | 0.2 | 0.8 | 0.2 |  |
| 0  | 5 | 0 | 1 | 1 | 1 | 1 |
|    | 4 | 0 | 0.8 | 1 | 0.8 |  |
|    | 3 | 0 | 0.6 | 1 | 0.6 |  |
|    | 2 | 0 | 0.4 | 1 | 0.4 |  |
|    | 1 | 0 | 0.2 | 1 | 0.2 |  |
|    | 0 | 1 | 0 | 0.8 | 0 |  |
|    | 0 | 2 | 0 | 0.6 | 0 |  |
|    | 0 | 3 | 0 | 0.4 | 0 |  |
|    | 0 | 4 | 0 | 0.2 | 0 |  |
|    | 0 | 5 | 0 | 0 | 0 |  |

$E = A \times B = E(z) = \{1/0 + 0.2/1 + 0.4/2 + 0.6/3 + 0.8/4 + 0.8/5 + 0.6/6 + 0.6/8 + 0.6/10 + 0.4/12 + 0.4/15 + 0.2/20 + 0/25\}$

## Problem 5.4

Perform the following fuzzy arithmetic operation $F = A/B$ through extension principle by fuzzifying the function $z(x, y) = x/y$ for the given in Problem 5.1 fuzzy set.

**Solution:**

$$\mu_{F=A/B}(z) = \vee_{z = x/y} [\mu_A(x) \wedge \mu_B(y)]$$

| Division $z = x/y$ | Possible combination | | $\mu_A(x)$ | $\mu_B(y)$ | $\min(\mu_A(x), \mu_B(y))$ | $\max(\min(\mu_A(x), \mu_B(y)))$ |
|---|---|---|---|---|---|---|
| | x | y | | | | |
| 5 | 5 | 1 | 1 | 0.8 | 0.8 | 0.8 |
| 4 | 4 | 1 | 0.8 | 0.8 | 0.8 | 0.8 |
| 3 | 3 | 1 | 0.6 | 0.8 | 0.6 | 0.6 |
| 2 | 4 | 2 | 0.8 | 0.6 | 0.6 | 0.6 |
| | 2 | 1 | 0.4 | 0.8 | 0.4 | |
| 1 | 5 | 5 | 1 | 0 | 0 | 0.4 |
| | 4 | 4 | 0.8 | 0.2 | 0.2 | |
| | 3 | 3 | 0.6 | 0.4 | 0.4 | |
| | 2 | 2 | 0.4 | 0.6 | 0.4 | |
| | 1 | 1 | 0.2 | 0.8 | 0.2 | |
| | 0 | 0 | 0 | 1 | 0 | |
| 0 | 0 | 1 | 0 | 0.8 | 0 | 0 |
| | 0 | 2 | 0 | 0.6 | 0 | |
| | 0 | 3 | 0 | 0.4 | 0 | |
| | 0 | 4 | 0 | 0.2 | 0 | |
| | 0 | 5 | 0 | 0 | 0 | |

$F = A/B = F(z) = \{0/0 + 0.4/1 + 0.6/2 + 0.6/3 + 0.8/4 + 0.8/5\}$

## Problem 5.5

Consider the linguistic variable 'speed'. Let the term 'high' be defined by this equation:

$$\mu_{high}(x) = \begin{cases} e^{-b(a-x)^2} & \text{if } 50 \leq x \leq 1 \\ 0 & \text{elsewhere} \end{cases}$$

Determine the membership functions of the terms 'very high speed', 'Not very high speed', and 'more or less high speed'.

**Solution:**

$\mu_{very\ high}(x) = (e^{-b(a-x)^2})^2$

$\mu_{not\ very\ high}(x) = 1 - (e^{-b(a-x)^2})^2$

$\mu_{more\ or\ less\ high}(x) = (e^{-b(a-x)^2})^{0.5}$

## Problem 5.6

Let $x$ be a linguistic variable that measures a company's employee performance, which takes values from the universe of discourse $U = \{1, 2, 3, 4, 5, 6, 7, 8, 9, 10\}$. Suppose the term set of $x$ includes Excellent, Good, Fair, and Bad. The membership functions of these linguistic labels are listed as follows:

$\mu_{\text{Excellent}} = \{(8,0.3), (9,0.5), (10,1)\}$
$\mu_{\text{Good}} = \{(6,0.2), (7,0.6), (8,0.8), (9,1), (10,1)\}$
$\mu_{\text{Fair}} = \{(3,0.4), (4,0.6), (5,0.9), (6,0.9), (7,0.5), (8,0.1)\}$
$\mu_{\text{Bad}} = \{(1,1), (2,0.8), (3,0.7), (4,0.4)\}$

Construct the membership functions of the following compound sets:

(i) Not bad but not very good
(ii) Good but not excellent

**Solution:** The membership function of linguistic label 'Not bad but Not very good' can be framed as follows:

(i) Not bad but not very good

$\mu_{\text{Not bad but Not very good}} = \mu_{\text{Not bad}} \wedge \mu_{\text{Not very good}} = (1 - \mu_{\text{Bad}}) \wedge (1 - \mu_{\text{Very good}})$

$\mu_{\text{Very Good}} = (\mu_{\text{Good}})^2$

$\mu_{\text{Very Good}} = \{(6,0.04), (7,0.36), (8,0.64), (9,1), (10,1)\}$

$\mu_{\text{Not very good}} = 1 - \mu_{\text{Very good}}$
$= \{(1,1), (2,1), (3,1), (4,1), (5,1), (6,0.96), (7,0.64), (8,0.36), (9,0), (10,0)\}$

$\mu_{\text{Not bad}} = 1 - \mu_{\text{Bad}}$
$= \{(1,0), (2,0.2), (3,0.3), (4,0.6), (5,1), (6,1), (7,1), (8,1), (9,1), (10,1)\}$

$\mu_{\text{Not bad but Not very good}} = \mu_{\text{Not Bad}} \wedge \mu_{\text{Not very good}}$
$= \{(1,0), (2,0.2), (3,0.3), (4,0.6), (5,1), (6,0.96), (7,0.64), (8,0.36), (9,0), (10,0)\}$

(ii) $\mu_{\text{Good but Not excellent}} = \mu_{\text{Good}} \wedge \mu_{\text{Not excellent}} = \mu_{\text{Good}} \wedge (1 - \mu_{\text{Excellent}})$

$\mu_{\text{Not excellent}} = 1 - \mu_{\text{Excellent}}$
$= \{(1,1), (2,1), (3,1), (4,1), (5,1), (6,1), (7,1), (8,0.7), (9,0.5), (10,0)\}$

$\mu_{\text{Good but Not excellent}} = \mu_{\text{Good}} \wedge \mu_{\text{Not excellent}}$
$= \{(1,0), (2,0), (3,0), (4,0), (5,0), (6,0.2), (7,0.6), (8,0.7), (9,0.5), (10,0)\}$

## Problem 5.7

Let R and S be two fuzzy relations defined here:

$$R = \begin{array}{c} \\ x_1 \\ x_2 \end{array} \begin{array}{c} \begin{array}{ccc} y_1 & y_2 & y_3 \end{array} \\ \left[ \begin{array}{ccc} 0.0 & 0.2 & 0.8 \\ 0.3 & 0.6 & 1.0 \end{array} \right] \end{array}$$

$$S = \begin{array}{c} \\ y_1 \\ y_2 \\ y_3 \end{array} \begin{array}{c} z_1 \quad z_2 \quad z_3 \\ \begin{bmatrix} 0.3 & 0.7 & 1.0 \\ 0.5 & 1.0 & 0.6 \\ 1.0 & 0.2 & 0.0 \end{bmatrix} \end{array}$$

Compute the result of R o S using max-min composition.

**Solution:** Max-Min Composition:

$\mu_R(x_1, y) \wedge \mu_S(y, z_1) = \{0.0, 0.2, 0.8\} \Rightarrow V(\mu_R(x_1, y) \wedge \mu_S(y, z_1))$
$= \mu_{RoS}(x_1, z_1) = 0.8$
$\mu_R(x_1, y) \wedge \mu_S(y, z_2) = \{0.0, 0.2, 0.2\} \Rightarrow V(\mu_R(x_1, y) \wedge \mu_S(y, z_2))$
$= \mu_{RoS}(x_1, z_2) = 0.2$
$\mu_R(x_1, y) \wedge \mu_S(y, z_3) = \{0.0, 0.2, 0.0\} \Rightarrow V(\mu_R(x_1, y) \wedge \mu_S(y, z_3))$
$= \mu_{RoS}(x_1, z_3) = 0.2$
$\mu_R(x_2, y) \wedge \mu_S(y, z_1) = \{0.3, 0.5, 1.0\} \Rightarrow V(\mu_R(x_2, y) \wedge \mu_S(y, z_1))$
$= \mu_{RoS}(x_2, z_1) = 1.0$
$\mu_R(x_2, y) \wedge \mu_S(y, z_2) = \{0.3, 0.6, 0.2\} \Rightarrow V(\mu_R(x_2, y) \wedge \mu_S(y, z_2))$
$= \mu_{RoS}(x_2, z_2) = 0.6$
$\mu_R(x_2, y) \wedge \mu_S(y, z_3) = \{0.3, 0.6, 0.0\} \Rightarrow V(\mu_R(x_2, y) \wedge \mu_S(y, z_3))$
$= \mu_{RoS}(x_2, z_3) = 0.6$

| R o S | $z_1$ | $z_2$ | $z_3$ |
|---|---|---|---|
| $x_1$ | 0.8 | 0.2 | 0.2 |
| $x_2$ | 1.0 | 0.6 | 0.6 |

**Problem 5.8**

Compute the result of R · S using max-product composition for Problem 5.7.

**Solution:** Max-Product Composition:

$\mu_R(x_1, y) \wedge \mu_S(y, z_1) = \{0.00, 0.10, 0.80\} \Rightarrow V(\mu_R(x_1, y) \wedge \mu_S(y, z_1))$
$= \mu_{R \cdot S}(x_1, z_1) = 0.8$
$\mu_R(x_1, y) \wedge \mu_S(y, z_2) = \{0.00, 0.20, 0.16\} \Rightarrow V(\mu_R(x_1, y) \wedge \mu_S(y, z_2))$
$= \mu_{R \cdot S}(x_1, z_2) = 0.2$
$\mu_R(x_1, y) \wedge \mu_S(y, z_3) = \{0.00, 0.12, 0.00\} \Rightarrow V(\mu_R(x_1, y) \wedge \mu_S(y, z_3))$
$= \mu_{R \cdot S}(x_1, z_3) = 0.12$
$\mu_R(x_2, y) \wedge \mu_S(y, z_1) = \{0.09, 0.30, 1.00\} \Rightarrow V(\mu_R(x_2, y) \wedge \mu_S(y, z_1))$
$= \mu_{R \cdot S}(x_2, z_1) = 1.0$
$\mu_R(x_2, y) \wedge \mu_S(y, z_2) = \{0.21, 0.60, 0.20\} \Rightarrow V(\mu_R(x_2, y) \wedge \mu_S(y, z_2))$
$= \mu_{R \cdot S}(x_2, z_2) = 0.6$
$\mu_R(x_2, y) \wedge \mu_S(y, z_3) = \{0.30, 0.36, 0.00\} \Rightarrow V(\mu_R(x_2, y) \wedge \mu_S(y, z_3))$
$= \mu_{R \cdot S}(x_2, z_3) = 0.36$

| R·S | $z_1$ | $z_2$ | $z_3$ |
|---|---|---|---|
| $x_1$ | 0.8 | 0.2 | 0.12 |
| $x_2$ | 1.0 | 0.6 | 0.36 |

### Problem 5.9

Solve the following fuzzy relation equations by Mamdani Max-Min composition:
If rainfall is 'High', drought is 'Low'. Deduce the drought level when rainfall is very high.
Let High (rainfall) = {0.5/2 + 0.8/3 + 1/4} and Low (drought) = {1/1 + 0.6/2 + 0.2/3}.
The universe discourse for the 'rainfall rate' is $X$ and 'drought level' is $Y$ as

$$X = \{1, 2, 3, 4\}, Y = \{1, 2, 3\}.$$

**Solution:** Here the fuzzy set for 'very high' is not given. Therefore we use linguistic modifiers to get the fuzzy set for 'very high'.

$$\text{very high} = (\text{high})^2 = \{0.25/2 + 0.64/3 + 1/4\}$$

As per GMP, using Mamdani Min implication operator, we get the implication relation between 'High' and 'Low'.

$$\Psi(\mu_{High}(x), \mu_{Low}(y)) = \mu_{High}(x) \wedge \mu_{Low}(y)$$

$$\mu_{R(High, Low)}(x, y) = \begin{bmatrix} 0.0 \\ 0.5 \\ 0.64 \\ 1 \end{bmatrix} \begin{bmatrix} 1 & 0.6 & 0.2 \end{bmatrix} = \begin{bmatrix} 0.0 & 0.0 & 0.0 \\ 0.5 & 0.5 & 0.2 \\ 0.64 & 0.6 & 0.2 \\ 1 & 0.6 & 0.2 \end{bmatrix}$$

The drought when the rainfall is 'very high' is

$$B' = A \circ R(x, y) = \begin{bmatrix} 0.0 & 0.25 & 0.64 & 1 \end{bmatrix} \circ \begin{bmatrix} 0 & 0 & 0 \\ 0.5 & 0.5 & 0.2 \\ 0.64 & 0.6 & 0.2 \\ 1 & 0.6 & 0.2 \end{bmatrix} = \begin{bmatrix} 1 & 0.6 & 0.2 \end{bmatrix}$$

$$\mu_{Verylow} = \{1/0 + 0.6/1 + 0.2/2\} \text{ (Using max-min composition)}$$

### Problem 5.10

Solve the Problem 5.9 by Zadeh max-min composition.

**Solution:** Here the fuzzy set for 'very high' is not given. Therefore we use linguistic modifiers to get the fuzzy set for 'very high'.

$$\text{very high} = (\text{high})^2 = \{0.25/2 + 0.64/3 + 1/4\}$$

As per GMP, using Zadeh min implication operator, we get the implication relation between 'High' and 'Low'.

$$\Psi(\mu_{High}(x), \mu_{Low}(y)) = (\mu_{High}(x) \wedge \mu_{Low}(y)) \vee (1 - \mu_{High}(x))$$

$$\mu_{High}(x) \wedge \mu_{Low}(y) = \begin{bmatrix} 0.0 \\ 0.5 \\ 0.64 \\ 1 \end{bmatrix} \begin{bmatrix} 1 & 0.6 & 0.2 \end{bmatrix} = \begin{bmatrix} 0.0 & 0.0 & 0.0 \\ 0.5 & 0.5 & 0.2 \\ 0.64 & 0.6 & 0.2 \\ 1 & 0.6 & 0.2 \end{bmatrix}$$

$$(1 - \mu_{High}(x)) = \begin{bmatrix} 1 \\ 0.5 \\ 0.36 \\ 0 \end{bmatrix}$$

$$(\mu_{High}(x) \wedge \mu_{Low}(y)) \vee (1 - \mu_{High}(x)) = \begin{bmatrix} 0.0 & 0.0 & 0.0 \\ 0.5 & 0.5 & 0.2 \\ 0.64 & 0.6 & 0.2 \\ 1 & 0.6 & 0.2 \end{bmatrix} \vee \begin{bmatrix} 1.0 \\ 0.5 \\ 0.36 \\ 0.0 \end{bmatrix}$$

$$= \begin{bmatrix} 1 & 1 & 1 \\ 0.5 & 0.5 & 0.5 \\ 0.64 & 0.6 & 0.36 \\ 1 & 0.6 & 0.2 \end{bmatrix}$$

The drought when the rainfall is 'very high' is

$$B' = A \circ R(x, y) = \begin{bmatrix} 0.0 & 0.25 & 0.64 & 1 \end{bmatrix} \circ \begin{bmatrix} 1 & 1 & 1 \\ 0.5 & 0.5 & 0.5 \\ 0.64 & 0.6 & 0.36 \\ 1 & 0.6 & 0.2 \end{bmatrix} = \begin{bmatrix} 1 & 0.6 & 0.36 \end{bmatrix}$$

$\mu_{VeryLow} = \{1/0 + 0.6/1 + 0.36/2\}$ (Using max-min composition)

## Problem 5.11

Determine the relation between two given fuzzy sets by using Larsen product implication operation:

$$A = \{(0.2, 1)\ (0.5, 2)\ (0.8, 3)\ (1, 4)\} \quad B = \{(1, 1)\ (0.6, 2)\ (0.2, 3)\}$$

**Solution:**

$$R(x, y) = \mu_A(x) \bullet \mu_B(y) = \begin{bmatrix} 0.2 \\ 0.5 \\ 0.8 \\ 1 \end{bmatrix} \begin{bmatrix} 1 & 0.6 & 0.2 \end{bmatrix} = \begin{bmatrix} 0.2 & 0.12 & 0.04 \\ 0.5 & 0.3 & 0.1 \\ 0.8 & 0.48 & 0.16 \\ 1 & 0.6 & 0.2 \end{bmatrix}$$

## Problem 5.12

Determine the relation between two given fuzzy sets by using Arithmetic implication operation:

$$A = \{(0.2, 1)\ (0.5, 2)\ (0.8, 3)\ (1, 4)\}\ B = \{(1, 1)\ (0.6, 2)\ (0.2, 3)\}$$

**Solution:**

$$R(x, y) = 1 \wedge (1 - \mu_A(x) + \mu_B(y)) = 1 \wedge \left(1 - \begin{bmatrix} 0.2 \\ 0.5 \\ 0.8 \\ 1 \end{bmatrix} + [1\ \ 0.6\ \ 0.2]\right) = \begin{bmatrix} 0 & 0.2 & 0.6 \\ 0.0 & 0 & 0.3 \\ 0.0 & 0 & 0 \\ 0 & 0 & 0 \end{bmatrix}$$

## Problem 5.13

Determine the relation between two given fuzzy sets by using Boolean implication operation:

$$A = \{(0.2, 1)\ (0.5, 2)\ (0.8, 3)\ (1, 4)\}\ B = \{(1, 1)\ (0.6, 2)\ (0.2, 3)\}$$

**Solution:**

$$R(x, y) = (1 - \mu_A(x)) \vee \mu_B(y) = \begin{bmatrix} 0.8 \\ 0.5 \\ 0.2 \\ 0 \end{bmatrix} \vee [1\ \ 0.6\ \ 0.2] = \begin{bmatrix} 1 & 0.8 & 0.8 \\ 1 & 0.6 & 0.5 \\ 1 & 0.6 & 0.2 \\ 1 & 0.6 & 0.2 \end{bmatrix}$$

## Problem 5.14

Determine the relation between two given fuzzy sets by using bounded product implication operation:

$$A = \{(0.2, 1)\ (0.5, 2)\ (0.8, 3)\ (1, 4)\}\ B = \{(1, 1)\ (0.6, 2)\ (0.2, 3)\}$$

**Solution:**

$$R(x, y) = 0 \vee (\mu_A(x) + \mu_B(y) - 1) = 0 \vee \left(\begin{bmatrix} 0.2 \\ 0.5 \\ 0.8 \\ 1 \end{bmatrix} + [1\ \ 0.6\ \ 0.2] - 1\right) = \begin{bmatrix} 0.2 & 0 & 0 \\ 0.5 & 0.1 & 0 \\ 0.8 & 0.4 & 0 \\ 1 & 0.6 & 0.2 \end{bmatrix}$$

## Problem 5.15

Determine the relation between two given fuzzy sets by using drastic product implication operation:

$$A = \{(0.2, 1)\ (0.5, 2)\ (0.8, 3)\ (1, 4)\}\ B = \{(1, 1)\ (0.6, 2)\ (0.2, 3)\}$$

**Solution:**

$$R(x, y) = \begin{cases} \mu_A(x) & \text{if } \mu_B(y) = 1 \\ \mu_B(y) & \text{if } \mu_A(x) = 1 \\ 0 & \text{if } \mu_A(x) < 1 \text{ \& } \mu_B(y) < 1 \end{cases}$$

$$R(x, y) = \begin{bmatrix} 0.2 \\ 0.5 \\ 0.8 \\ 1 \end{bmatrix} \begin{bmatrix} 1 & 0.6 & 0.2 \end{bmatrix} = \begin{bmatrix} 0.2 & 0 & 0 \\ 0.5 & 0 & 0 \\ 0.8 & 0 & 0 \\ 1 & 0.6 & 0.2 \end{bmatrix}$$

## Problem 5.16

Determine the relation between two given fuzzy sets by using standard sequence implication operation:

$A = \{(0.2, 1)\ (0.5, 2)\ (0.8, 3)\ (1, 4)\}\ B = \{(1, 1)\ (0.6, 2)\ (0.2, 3)\}$

**Solution:**

$$R(x, y) = \begin{cases} 1 & \text{if } \mu_A(x) \le \mu_B(y) \\ 0 & \text{if } \mu_A(x) > \mu_B(y) \end{cases}$$

$$R(x, y) = \begin{bmatrix} 0.2 \\ 0.5 \\ 0.8 \\ 1 \end{bmatrix} \begin{bmatrix} 1 & 0.6 & 0.2 \end{bmatrix} = \begin{bmatrix} 1 & 1 & 1 \\ 1 & 1 & 0 \\ 1 & 0 & 0 \\ 1 & 0 & 0 \end{bmatrix}$$

## Problem 5.17

Determine the relation between two given fuzzy sets by using Gougen implication operation:

$A = \{(0.2, 1)\ (0.5, 2)\ (0.8, 3)\ (1, 4)\}\ B = \{(1, 1)\ (0.6, 2)\ (0.2, 3)\}$

**Solution:**

$$R(x, y) = \begin{cases} 1 & \text{if } \mu_A(x) \le \mu_B(y) \\ \dfrac{\mu_B(y)}{\mu_A(x)} & \text{if } \mu_A(x) > \mu_B(y) \end{cases}$$

$$R(x, y) = \begin{bmatrix} 0.2 \\ 0.5 \\ 0.8 \\ 1 \end{bmatrix} \begin{bmatrix} 1 & 0.6 & 0.2 \end{bmatrix} = \begin{bmatrix} 1 & 1 & 1 \\ 1 & 1 & 0.4 \\ 1 & 0.75 & 0.25 \\ 1 & 0.6 & 0.2 \end{bmatrix}$$

## Problem 5.18

Determine the relation between two given fuzzy sets by using Godelian implication operation:

$$A = \{(0.2, 1) (0.5, 2) (0.8, 3) (1, 4)\} \quad B = \{(1, 1) (0.6, 2) (0.2, 3)\}$$

**Solution:**

$$R(x, y) = \begin{cases} 1 & \text{if } \mu_A(x) \leq \mu_B(y) \\ \mu_B(y) & \text{if } \mu_A(x) > \mu_B(y) \end{cases}$$

$$R(x, y) = \begin{bmatrix} 0.2 \\ 0.5 \\ 0.8 \\ 1 \end{bmatrix} \begin{bmatrix} 1 & 0.6 & 0.2 \end{bmatrix} = \begin{bmatrix} 1 & 1 & 1 \\ 1 & 1 & 0.2 \\ 1 & 0.6 & 0.2 \\ 1 & 0.6 & 0.2 \end{bmatrix}$$

## Problem 5.19

Choose the least cost and good quality from given fuzzy set of four products.

$P_1 = \{0.5/C + 0.75/Q\}$, $P_2 = \{0.2/C + 0.9/Q\}$, $P_3 = \{0.8/C + 0.3/Q\}$, and $P_4 = \{0.7/C + 0.4/Q\}$

**Solution:**

| Products | $\mu_{Cost}(x)$ | $\mu_{Quality}(y)$ | $\mu_{Cost}(x) \wedge \mu_{Quality}(y)$ |
|---|---|---|---|
| $P_1$ | 0.5 | 0.75 | 0.5 |
| $P_2$ | 0.2 | 0.9 | 0.2 |
| $P_3$ | 0.8 | 0.3 | 0.3 |
| $P_4$ | 0.7 | 0.4 | 0.4 |

Product $P_1$ is satisfying both in cost and quality.

## Problem 5.20

The fuzzy set for 'Smooth' linguistic variable is given as Smooth = $\{1/1 + 0.8/2 + 0.6/3 + 0.4/4 + 0.2/5\}$. Determine the linguistic variable 'Very smooth' and 'Not very smooth'.

**Solution:**
Smooth = $\{1/1 + 0.8/2 + 0.6/3 + 0.4/4 + 0.2/5\}$
Very smooth = $\{1/1 + 0.64/2 + 0.36/3 + 0.16/4 + 0.04/5\}$
Not very smooth = $\{0/1 + 0.36/2 + 0.64/3 + 0.84/4 + 0.96/5\}$

## Problem 5.21

The fuzzy set for 'Clever' linguistic variable is given as Clever = $\{1/1 + 0.75/2 + 0.5/3 + 0.25/4 + 0/5\}$. Determine the linguistic variable 'Slightly clever' and 'Very very clever'.

## Solution:
Clever = {1/1 + 0.75/2 + 0.5/3 + 0.25/4 + 0/5}
Slightly clever = {1/1 + 0.866/2 + 0.707/3 + 0.5/4 + 0/5}
Very very clever = {1/1 + 0.31/2 + 0.0625/3 + 0.0039/4 + 0/5}

## Problem 5.22

The mobile characteristics are defined as speed and cost. The fuzzy set for 'High Speed' and 'Costly' linguistic variables are given as High speed = {1/1 + 0.8/2 + 0.5/3 + 0.3/4 + 0.1/5} and Costly = {0/1 + 0.2/2 + 0.4/3 + 0.7/4 + 0.9/5}, respectively. Determine the linguistic variable 'Slightly Costly', 'Very high speed', and 'Not very high speed and Not costly'.

## Solution:
High speed = {1/1 + 0.8/2 + 0.5/3 + 0.3/4 + 0.1/5}
Costly = {0/1 + 0.2/2 + 0.4/3 + 0.7/4 + 0.9/5}
Slightly costly = {0/1 + 0.44/2 + 0.63/3 + 0.836/4 + 0.948/5}
Very high speed = {1/1 + 0.64/2 + 0.25/3 + 0.09/4 + 0.01/5}
Not very high speed and Not costly = 'Not very high speed' and 'Not costly'
=> {0/1 + 0.36/2 + 0.75/3 + 0.91/4 + 0.99/5} ∧ {1/1 + 0.8/2 + 0.6/3 + 0.3/4 + 0.1/5}
= {0/1 + 0.36/2 + 0.6/3 + 0.3/4 + 0.1/5}

## Problem 5.23

Perform the intersection, union, and negation fuzzy operation for given fuzzy set $A$ = {(0.95, 1) (0.8, 2) (0.6, 3) (0.55, 4) (0.3, 5)} and $B$ = {(0.25, 2) (0.5, 3) (0.75, 4) (0.9, 5) (1, 6)}.

## Solution:
$\mu_A(x) \wedge \mu_B(y)$ = {(0, 1) (0.25, 2) (0.5, 3) (0.55, 4) (0.3, 5) (0, 6)}
$\mu_A(x) \vee \mu_B(y)$ = {(0.95, 1) (0.8, 2) (0.6, 3) (0.75, 4) (0.9, 5) (1, 6)}
$1 - \mu_A(x)$ = {(0.05, 1) (0.2, 2) (0.4, 3) (0.45, 4) (0.7, 5) (1, 6)}
$1 - \mu_B(x)$ = {(1, 1) (0.75, 2) (0.5, 3) (0.25, 4) (0.1, 5) (0, 6)}

## Problem 5.24

Solve the following fuzzy relation equation by max-min composition.

$$R \circ \begin{bmatrix} 0.5 & 0.3 & 0.2 \\ 0.2 & 0.5 & 0.8 \\ 0.4 & 0.7 & 0.4 \end{bmatrix} = \begin{bmatrix} 0.4 & 0.5 & 0.3 \end{bmatrix}$$

## Solution:
Let R be relation between x and y => R(x, y)
3 × 3 matrix represent the relation between y and z => S(y, z)
1 × 3 matrix represent the relation between x and z => T(x, z)
Therefore universe of discourse is X = {1}, Y = {1, 2, 3}, Z = {1, 2, 3}

To find the $R(x, y) = \vee \{T(x, z) \wedge S(z, y)\} = \begin{bmatrix} 0.4 & 0.5 & 0.3 \end{bmatrix} \begin{bmatrix} 0.5 & 0.3 & 0.2 \\ 0.2 & 0.5 & 0.8 \\ 0.4 & 0.7 & 0.4 \end{bmatrix}$
$= \begin{bmatrix} 0.4 & 0.5 & 0.5 \end{bmatrix}$

## Problem 5.25

Find the de-fuzzified value for the given fuzzy set by centroid method.

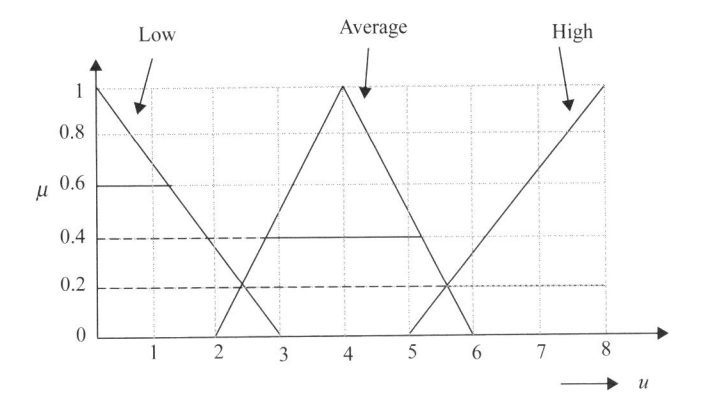

**Solution:**

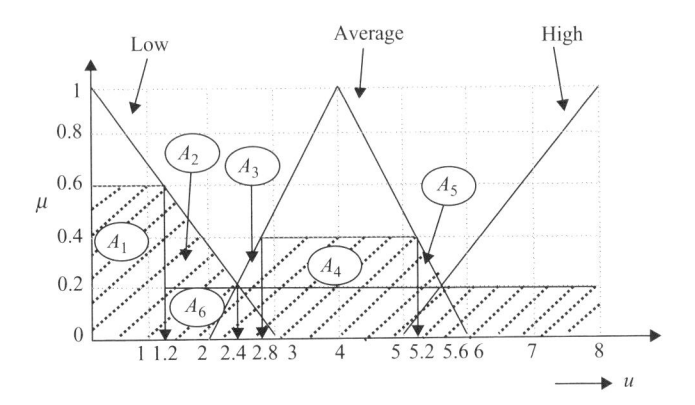

$$u^* = \frac{\text{Area under shaded portion} \times \text{centre}}{\text{Area under shaded portion}}$$

| Shaded portion | Area | Centre | Area × centre |
|---|---|---|---|
| $A_1$ | 1.2 × 0.6 = 0.72 | 0.6 | 0.72 × 0.6 = 0.432 |
| $A_2$ | 0.5 × 1.2 × 0.4 = 0.24 | 1.6 | 0.24 × 1.6 = 0.384 |
| $A_3$ | 0.5 × 0.4 × 0.2 = 0.04 | 2.67 | 0.04 × 2.67 = 0.1067 |
| $A_4$ | 2.4 × 0.4 = 0.96 | 4 | 0.96 × 4 = 3.84 |
| $A_5$ | 0.5 × 0.8 × 0.4 = 0.16 | 5.46 | 0.16 × 5.46 = 0.8736 |
| $A_6$ | 1.6 × 0.2 = 0.32 | 2 | 0.32 × 2 = 0.64 |
| Sum | 2.44 | | 6.2763 |

$u^* = 6.2763/2.44 = 2.572$

## Problem 5.26

Find the de-fuzzified value for the previous fuzzy set by centre of sum method.

*Solution:*

$$u^* = \frac{\sum_{i=1}^{N=8} u_i \sum_{k=1}^{n=3} \mu_{ck}(u_i)}{\sum_{i=1}^{N=8} \sum_{k=1}^{n=3} \mu_{ck}(u_i)}$$

$$u^* = \frac{[(1\times 0.6)+(1.2\times 0.6)+(2\times 0.33)]+[(2.8\times 0.4)+(3\times 0.4)+(4\times 0.4)+(5\times 0.4)]}{[0.6+0.6+0.33]+[0.4+0.4+0.4+0.4+0.4]+[0.2+0.2+0.2+0.2]}$$

$$+[(5.6\times 0.2)+(6\times 0.2)+(7\times 0.2)+(8\times 0.2)]$$

$$u^* = 15.3/4.33 = 3.53$$

## Problem 5.27

Find the de-fuzzified value for earlier mentioned fuzzy set by weighted average method.

*Solution:* Average linguistic label is having largest area

$$u^* = \frac{\sum_{i=1}^{N=3} z_i \mu_{cm}(z_i)}{\sum_{i=1}^{N=3} \mu_{cm}(z_i)} \qquad z_j = \frac{1}{N}\sum_i^N u_i$$

$$z_1 = \frac{1}{4}(0+1+1.2+2) = 0.55, \quad z_2 = \frac{1}{5}(2.8+3+4+5+5.2) = 4$$

$$z_3 = \frac{1}{4}(5.6+6+7+8) = 6.65$$

$$u^* = \frac{(0.55\times 0.6)+(4\times 0.4)+(6.65\times 0.2)}{(0.6+0.4+0.2)} = \frac{3.26}{1.2} = 2.716$$

## Problem 5.28

Find the de-fuzzified value for the previously given fuzzy set by centre of largest area method.

*Solution:* Average linguistic label is having largest area

$$u^* = \frac{\sum_{i=1}^{N=3} u_i \mu_{cm}(u_i)}{\sum_{i=1}^{N=3} \mu_{cm}(u_i)}$$

$$u^* = \frac{[(2.8\times 0.4)+(3\times 0.4)+(4\times 0.4)+(5\times 0.4)+(5.2\times 0.4)]}{[0.4+0.4+0.4+0.4+0.4]}$$

$$u^* = 8/2 = 4$$

## Problem 5.29

Find the de-fuzzified value for the previous fuzzy set by mean of maxima method.

**Solution:** Maximum value occur between 0 to 1.2

$$u^* = \frac{1}{M}\sum_{i=1}^{M} U_m$$

$$u^* = \frac{(0+1.2)}{2} = 0.6$$

## Problem 5.30

Find the de-fuzzified value for aforegiven fuzzy set by first of maxima and last of maxima method.

**Solution:** The first maximum value occurs at 0

$$u^* = 0$$

The last of maxima value occurs at 1.2

$$u^* = 1.2$$

## SUMMARY

- Probability measures the likelihood of event to occur, whereas fuzzy logic measures degree to which an outcome belongs to an event.
- A crisp set is a collection of distinct (precisely defined) elements.
- A fuzzy set is a collection of distinct elements with a varying degree of relevance or inclusion.
- The fuzzy designer should select the right choice of membership function based on the preferred inputs.
- Extension principle and alpha-cut methods can be used for fuzzy arithmetic operation.
- Fuzzy relations are fuzzy sets defined on Cartesian products.
- Fuzzy compositions can combine fuzzy relations defined on different Cartesian products with each other in a number of different ways.
- Linguistic modifiers modify the meaning of the primary term from its original interpretation.
- A fuzzy proposition can have its truth value in the interval [0, 1].
- The two important fuzzy inference methods are generalized modus ponens (GMP) and generalized modus tollens (GMT).
- De-fuzzification is the process of converting the fuzzy set into a crisp value. In this chapter, eight de-fuzzification techniques are discussed.

## EXERCISES

1. Determine the intersection and unions of the following fuzzy sets.
   A = {(3, 1) (4, 0.2) (5, 0.3) (6, 0.4) (7, 0.6) (8, 0.8) (10, 1) (12, 0.8) (14, 0.6)}
   B = {(2, 0.4) (3, 0.6) (4, 0.8) (5, 1) (6, 0.8) (7, 0.6) (8, 0.4)}
   C = {(2, 0.4) (4, 0.8) (5, 1) (7, 0.6)}.

2. Determine which fuzzy sets, defined by the following functions, are fuzzy numbers.

   (i) $A(x) = \begin{cases} \sin(x) & \text{for } 0 \le x \le \pi \\ 0 & \text{otherwise} \end{cases}$

   (ii) $B(x) = \begin{cases} x & \text{for } 0 \le x \le 1 \\ 0 & \text{otherwise} \end{cases}$

(iii) $C(x) = \begin{cases} 1 & \text{for } 0 \leq x \leq 10 \\ 0 & \text{otherwise} \end{cases}$

(iv) $D(x) = \begin{cases} 1 & \text{for } x = 5 \\ 0 & \text{otherwise} \end{cases}$

3. Which of the following fuzzy sets are fuzzy numbers?

(a) $\tilde{A} = \{(x, \mu_{\tilde{A}}(x)) | x \in R\}$

where

$$\mu_{\tilde{A}}(x) = \begin{cases} \left(1 + \left(\dfrac{5-x}{2}\right)^2\right)^{-1} & x \leq 5 \\ \left(1 + \left|\dfrac{2(x-5)}{3}\right|\right)^{-1} & x \geq 5 \end{cases}$$

(b) $\tilde{B} = \{(x, \mu_{\tilde{B}}(x)) | x \in R^+\}$

where

$$\mu_{\tilde{B}}(x) = \begin{cases} x & x \in [0,1] \\ 1 & x \in [1,2] \\ 3-x & x \in [2,3] \end{cases}$$

(c) $\tilde{C} = \{(0, .4), (1, 1), (2, .7)\}$.

4. Consider the linguistic variable 'Age'. Let the term old be defined as follows:

$$\mu_{old}(x) = \begin{cases} 0 & \text{if } x \in [0, 40] \\ \left(1 + \left(\dfrac{x-40}{5}\right)^{-2}\right)^{-1} & \text{if } x \in (40, 100] \end{cases}$$

Determine the membership functions of the terms 'very old,' 'not very old,' and 'more or less old.'

5. Let the term *true* of the linguistic variable 'Truth' be characterized by the membership function.

$$T(v; \alpha, \beta, \gamma) = \begin{cases} 0 & \text{if } v \leq \alpha \\ 2\left(\dfrac{v-\alpha}{\gamma-\alpha}\right)^2 & \text{if } \alpha \leq v \leq \beta \\ 1 - 2\left(\dfrac{v-\gamma}{\gamma-\alpha}\right)^2 & \text{if } \beta \leq v \leq \gamma \\ 1 & \text{if } v \geq \gamma \end{cases}$$

Draw the membership function of 'true'. Determine the membership functions of 'rather true' and 'very true'. What is the membership function of 'false' = not 'true' and what of 'very false'?

6. Consider the fuzzy sets A and B defined on the interval $X = [0,5]$ of real numbers, by the following membership grade functions:

$$\mu_A(x) = x/(x+1), \quad \mu_B(x) = 2^{-x}$$

Determine the mathematical formulae and graphs of the membership grade function of each of the following sets:

(i) $A^C \cdot B^C$

(ii) $A \cup B$.

(iii) $(A \cup B)^C$

(iv) $A \cap U B$.

7. Prove the Fuzzy DeMorgan laws:
   (a) $A \cap B = \left(A^c \cup B^c\right)^c$
   (b) $A \cup B = \left(A^c \cap B^c\right)^c$
8. Let us assume that $A =$ 'x considerable larger than 10' and $B =$ 'x approximately'. Then find $A \cap B$ and $A \cup B$.
9. Determine mathematical formulae and graphs of the membership grade functions of each of the following sets:
   (i) $A^c, B^c, C^c$
   (ii) $A \cup B, A \cup C, B \cup C$
   (iii) $A \cap B, A \cap C, B \cap C$
   (iv) $A \cup B \cup C, A \cap B \cap C$
10. Let $X = [1, 10]$, $A =$ small integers, $B =$ integers close to 4. Then find $A \cap B$.
11. Prove: $M(A) + M(B) = M(A \cap B) + M(A \cap B)$.
12. Prove: $E(A) = E(A^c) = E(A \cap A^c) = E(A \cap A^c)$.
13. Let the membership grade functions of fuzzy sets $A$, $B$, and $C$ defined in Q.3 on the universal set $X = [0,10]$ and let $\xi(x) = x^2$ for all $x \in X$. Use the extension principle to derive $\xi(A), \xi(B), \xi(C)$. Given a fuzzy set $D$ defined on $\{0, 1\ 4, 9, 16, \ldots, 100\}$ by
    $$\mu_D(x) = 0.5/4 + 0.6/16 + 0.7/25 + 1/100$$
    Find $\xi^{-1}(D)$.
14. Let $A = \{(-1, 0.5)\ (0, 0.8)\ (1, 1)\ (2, 0.4)\}$ by applying extension principle. Find
    $B = \Psi(A)$, where $\Psi(x) = x_2$.
15. Let $A$ and $B$ be fuzzy sets defined on the universal set $X = Z$, whose membership functions are given as follows:
    $A(x) = 0.5/(-1) + 1/0 + 0.5/1 + 0.3/2$ and
    $B(x) = 0.5/2 + 1/3 + 0.5/4 + 0.3/5$.
    Let a function $f: X_{XX} \to X$ be defined for all $x_1, x_2 \in X$ by $f(x_1, x_2) = x_1 \cdot x_2$. Calculate $f(A, B)$.
16. Let $f$ be defined by $f(a) = e^a$ for all $a \in [0, 1]$. Determine the fuzzy intersection, fuzzy union, fuzzy implication, and fuzzy complement generated by $f$.
17. Let the universe $X = \{1, 2, 3, 4, 5\}$ and 'small integers' be defined as $\tilde{A} = \{(1, 1), (2, 0.5)\ (3, 0.4)\ (4, 0.2)\}$. Let the fuzzy relation $\tilde{R}$: 'almost equal' be defined as follows:

|   | 1 | 2 | 3 | 4 |
|---|---|---|---|---|
| 1 | 1 | .8 | 0 | 0 |
| 2 | .8 | .1 | .8 | 0 |
| 3 | 0 | .8 | 1 | .8 |
| 4 | 0 | 0 | .8 | 1 |

What is the membership function of the fuzzy set $B =$ 'rather small integers' if it is interpreted as the composition $\tilde{A} \circ \tilde{R}$?

18. Given are two fuzzy sets $A$ and $B$ whose membership functions are as follows:
    $A = 0.2/x_1 + 0.8/x_2 + 1/x_3$
    $B = 0.5/y_1 + 0.8/y_2 + 0.6/y_3$
    Determine $R$ such that $A \circ R = B$.
19. Let $A = \{(3, 0.5)\ (5, 1)\ (7, 0.6)\}$ and $B = \{(3, 1)\ (5, 0.6)\}$
    then find (i) $A \times B$ (ii) $A^2$ (iii) $A + B$ (iv) $A \ominus B$ (v) $A \times B$
20. Let $\tilde{R}_1$ and $\tilde{R}_2$ be defined by the following relational matrices respectively.

|       | $y_1$ | $y_2$ | $y_3$ | $y_4$ | $y_5$ |
|-------|-------|-------|-------|-------|-------|
| $x_1$ | .1    | .2    | 0     | 1     | .7    |
| $x_2$ | .3    | .5    | 0     | .2    | 1     |
| $x_3$ | .8    | 0     | 1     | .4    | .3    |

|       | $z_1$ | $z_2$ | $z_3$ | $z_4$ |
|-------|-------|-------|-------|-------|
| $y_1$ | .9    | 0     | .3    | .4    |
| $y_2$ | .2    | 1     | .8    | 0     |
| $y_3$ | .8    | 0     | .7    | 1     |
| $y_4$ | .4    | .2    | .3    | 0     |
| $y_5$ | 0     | 1     | 0     | .8    |

Compute the min-max composition $\tilde{R}_1 \cdot \tilde{R}_2(x,z)$.

21. A linguistic description is composed of a single rule 'if $x$ is $A$ then $y$ is $B$' where
    $A = 0.33/6 + 0.67/7 + 1.0/8 + 0.67/9 + 0.33/10$.
    $B = 0.33/1 + 0.67/2 + 1.0/3 + 0.67/4 + 0.33/5$.
    If $A^1 = 0.5/5 + 1.0/6 + 0.5/7$, then determine $B^1$ using the implication relation of the rule modelled through max-min implication operator.

22. In the field of computer networking, there is an imprecise relationship between the level of use of a network communication bandwidth and the latency experienced in peer-to-peer communications. Let $X$ be a fuzzy set of use levels (in terms of the percentage of full bandwidth used) and $Y$ be a fuzzy set of latencies with the following membership functions:
    $X = \{0.2/10 + 0.5/20 + 0.8/40 + 1.0/60 + 0.6/80 + 0.1/100\}$
    $Y = \{0.3/0.5 + 0.6/1 + 0.9/1.5 + 1.0/4 + 0.6/8 + 0.3/20\}$
    (a) Find the Cartesian product represented by the relation $R = X \times Y$.

    Now suppose we have a second fuzzy set of bandwidth usage given here:
    $Z = \{0.3/10 + 0.6/20 + 0.7/40 + 0.9/60 + 1/80 + 0.5/100\}$
    Find $S = Z_{1\times 6} \cdot R_{6\times 6}$
    (b) Using max-min composition
    (c) Using max-product composition

23. Let $A = \{(x_1, 0.2), (x_2, 0.7), (x_3, 0.4)\}$ and $B = \{(y_1, 0.5), (y_2, 0.6)\}$ be two fuzzy sets defined on the universes of discourses $X = \{x_1, x_2, x_3\}$ and $Y = \{y_1, y_2\}$, respectively. Then find the relation $A \times B$.

24. $X = \{x_1, x_2, x_3\}$, $Y = \{y_1, y_2\}$, and $Z = \{z_1, z_2, z_3\}$. And relations $R$ and $S$ are given as follows:

$$R(X, Y) = \begin{bmatrix} 0.5 & 0.1 \\ 0.2 & 0.9 \\ 0.8 & 0.6 \end{bmatrix}$$

$$S(Y, Z) = \begin{bmatrix} 0.6 & 0.4 & 0.7 \\ 0.5 & 0.8 & 0.9 \end{bmatrix}$$

Find $R \circ S$ using all compositions.

25. Solve the following fuzzy relation equations for the max-min composition.

(i) $R \cdot \begin{bmatrix} 0.9 & 0.6 & 1 \\ 0.8 & 0.8 & 0.5 \\ 0.6 & 0.4 & 0.6 \end{bmatrix} = [0.6 \ 0.6 \ 0.5]$,

(ii) $R \cdot \begin{bmatrix} 0.5 & 0.4 & 0.6 & 0.7 \\ 0.2 & 0 & 0.6 & 0.8 \\ 0.1 & 0.4 & 0.6 & 0.7 \\ 0 & 0.3 & 0 & 1 \end{bmatrix} = \begin{bmatrix} 0.2 & 0.4 & 0.5 & 0.7 \\ 0.1 & 0.2 & 0.2 & 0.2 \end{bmatrix}$

(iii) $\begin{bmatrix} 0.6 & 0.4 \\ 0.8 & 0.2 \end{bmatrix} Ro = [0.8 \ 1]$

26. Perform max-min composition for the following.

$$\mu(x,y) = \begin{pmatrix} 0 \\ 0.25 \\ 0.5 \\ 0.75 \\ 1 \\ 0.75 \\ 0.5 \\ 0.25 \\ 0 \\ 0 \end{pmatrix} \circ [0 \ 0.25 \ 0.5 \ 0.75 \ 1 \ 1 \ 0.75 \ 0.5 \ 0.25 \ 0]$$

27. In a simple vision recognition system, we may want to locate specific objects within a scene containing many objects. Let $X$ be a universe of general, well-known objects such as $X$ = {car, boat, house, bike, tree, mountain}, and let $Y$ be a universe of simple geometric shapes such as $Y$ = {square, octagon, triangle, circle, ellipse} We now define simple fuzzy set of objects, such as those for 'car' and 'square'.

   $A$ = car = {1.0/car + 0.4/boat + 0.1/house + 0.6/bike + 0.1/tree + 0/mountain}
   $B$ = square = {1.0/square + 0.5/octagon + 0.4/triangle + 0/circle + 0.1/ellipse}

   (a) Find the relation between 'car' and 'square'.
   Now suppose we define another fuzzy set of objects, called 'shapes with corners' as
   $S$ = 'Shapes with corners' = {0.6/square + 0.9/octagon + 0.4/triangle + 0/circle + 0.2/ellipse}
   Using an appropriate composition operation, find the fuzzy set $T$ = 'objects using corners' using the following:
   (a) Max-min composition
   (b) Max-product composition

28. Perform the following operations on intervals.
   (a) [2,3] + [3,4]
   (b) [1,2] × [1, 3]
   (c) [ 4, 6 ] ÷ [ 1, 2]
   (d) [ 3, 5] − [ 4, 5]

29. Carry out fuzzy arithmetic operations of the following linguistically defined terms.
   $a$ = very close to 3
   $b$ = more or less equal to 7
   using both alpha-cut and extension principles.

30. Carry out fuzzy addition $(a + b)$ to the following linguistically defined terms:
   $a = 4$
   $b$ = about 8
   using alpha-cut principle.

31. Perform the fuzzy arithmetic operations on the following membership grade functions.

   $$A(x) = \begin{cases} 0 & \text{for } x \leq -1 \text{ and } x > 3 \\ (x+1)/2 & \text{for } -1 < x \leq 1 \\ (3-x)/2 & \text{for } 1 < x \leq 3 \end{cases}$$

   $$B(x) = \begin{cases} 0 & \text{for } x \leq -1 \text{ and } x > 5 \\ (x-1)/2 & \text{for } 1 < x \leq 3 \\ (5-x)/2 & \text{for } 3 < x \leq 5 \end{cases}$$

32. Find MIN $(A, B)(x)$ and MAX $(A, B)(x)$?

   $$A(x) = \begin{cases} 0 & \text{for } x \leq -2 \text{ and } x > 4 \\ (x+2)/3 & \text{for } -2 < x \leq 1 \\ (4-x)/3 & \text{for } 1 < x \leq 4 \end{cases}$$

$$B(x) = \begin{cases} 0 & \text{for } x \leq -2 \text{ and } x > 3 \\ (x-1) & \text{for } 1 < x \leq 2 \\ (3-x) & \text{for } 2 < x \leq 3 \end{cases}$$

33. Consider,

$$A(x) = \begin{cases} 0 & \text{for } x \leq 3 \text{ and } x > 5 \\ x-3 & \text{for } 3 < x \leq 4 \\ 5-x & \text{for } 4 < x \leq 5 \end{cases}$$

$$B(x) = \begin{cases} 0 & \text{for } x \leq 12 \text{ and } x > 32 \\ (x-12)/8 & \text{for } 12 < x \leq 20 \\ (32-x)/12 & \text{for } 20 < x \leq 32 \end{cases}$$

$A \cdot X = B$ then find $X$ with alpha-cut method?

34. Let $A$, $B$ be two fuzzy numbers whose membership functions are given as follows:

$$A(x) = \begin{cases} (x+2)/2 & \text{for } -2 < x \leq 0 \\ (2-x)/2 & \text{for } 0 < x \leq 2 \\ 0 & \text{Otherwise,} \end{cases}$$

$$B(x) = \begin{cases} (x-2)/2 & \text{for } 2 < x \leq 4 \\ (6-x)/2 & \text{for } 4 < x \leq 6 \\ 0 & \text{Otherwise,} \end{cases}$$

Calculate the fuzzy numbers $A + B$, $A - B$, $B - A$, $A \times B$, $A/B$, MIN $(A, B)$, and MAX $(A, B)$.

35. Let $A$, $B$, and $C$ be three fuzzy numbers with following membership functions:

$$A(x) = \begin{cases} (x+2)/2 & \text{for } -2 < x \leq 0 \\ (2-x)/2 & \text{for } 0 < x \leq 2 \\ 0 & \text{Otherwise,} \end{cases}$$

$$B(x) = \begin{cases} (x-2)/2 & \text{for } 2 < x \leq 4 \\ (6-x)/2 & \text{for } 4 < x \leq 6 \\ 0 & \text{Otherwise,} \end{cases}$$

$$C(x) = \begin{cases} (x-6)/2 & \text{for } 6 < x \leq 8 \\ (10-x)/2 & \text{for } 8 < x \leq 10 \\ 0 & \text{Otherwise,} \end{cases}$$

Solve the following equations for $X$:
(i) $A + X = B$  (ii) $B \times X = C$

36. The voltage drop across an element in a series circuit is equal to the series current multiplied by the elements impedance. The current $I$, impedance $R$, and Voltage $V$ are presumed to be fuzzy variables. Membership functions for the current and the impedance are as follows:
$I = \{0/0 + 0.8/0.5 + 1/1 + 0.8/1.5 + 0/2\}$
$R = \{0.5/500 + 0.9/750 + 1/1000 + 0.9/1250 + 0.5/1500\}$
Find the arithmetic product for $V = I \cdot R$ using the extension principle.

37. For fluids, the product of the pressure ($P$) and the volume ($V$) of the fluid is a constant for a given temperature (i.e., $PV$ = constant).
Assume that at a given temperature, a fluid of fuzzy volume
$V_1 = \{0.0/0.5 + 0.5/0.75 + 1.0/1.0 + 0.5/1.25 + 0.0/1.5\}$
is under a fuzzy pressure.
$P_1 = \{0.0/0.5 + 0.5/1.75 + 1.0/2.0 + 0.5/2.25 + 0.0/2.5\}$
(a) Using the extension principle, determine the pressure $P_2$ if the volume is reduced to
$V_2 = \{0.0/0.4 + 0.5/0.45 + 1.0/0.5 + 0.5/0.55 + 0.0/0.6\}$

(b) Develop analogous continuous membership functions for the fuzzy pressure $P_1$ and volume $V_1$ and solve for pressure $P_2$ and plot the resulting membership function.
(c) Explain why $P_2 \cdot V_2$ would not be the same as $P_1 \cdot V_1$.

38. Given a fuzzy set A, describing pressure P is higher than 15 units, through the membership function and fuzzy set B, describing pressure P is approximately equal to 17 units. Find the membership function of the fuzzy set C, describing pressure P is higher than 15 units and approximately equal to 17 units and also plot it.
$\mu_A(x) = 1/1 + (x - 15)^{-2}$ for $x > 15$ and 0 for $x \le 15$
$\mu_B(x) = 1/1 + (x - 17)^4$

39. Consider the fuzzy numbers A and B described by the following membership functions: and

$$\mu_A(x) = \begin{cases} 0, & 0 \le 7 \\ x - 7 & 7 \le x \le 8 \\ x + 9 & 8 \le x \le 9 \\ 0 & x \ge 9 \end{cases}$$

$$\mu_A(x) = \begin{cases} 0, & 0 \le 4 \\ x - 4 & 4 \le x \le 5 \\ x + 6 & 5 \le x \le 6 \\ 0 & x \ge 6 \end{cases}$$

40. Given $\mu_A(x) = 1/1 + 2x$,
$\mu_B(x) = (1/1 + 2x)\, 1/2$
Calculate (a) $\mu_{A \cup B}(x)$ (b) $\mu_{A \cap B}(x)$ (c) $\mu^{\wedge}_{A+B}$.

41. Let sets of values of variables x and y be $X = \{x_1, x_2, x_3\}$ and $Y = \{y_1, y_2\}$, respectively. Assume that a proposition 'if x is A, Then y is B' is given, where $A = 0.5/x_1 + 1/x_2 + 0.6/x_3$ and $B = 1/y_1 + 0.4/y_2$. Then given a fact expressed by the proposition 'x is A`', where $A` = 0.6/x_1 + 0.9/x_2 + 0.7/x_3$. By using generalized modus ponens, derive a conclusion in the form of 'y is B'.

42. Consider a fuzzy conditional and qualified proposition
P: If x is A then y is B is very true
where $A = 1/x_1 + 0.5/x_2 + 0.7/x_3$, $B = 0.6/y_1 + 1/y_2$ and S stands for very true; let $S(a) = a^2$ for all $a \in [0, 1]$. Given a fact 'x is A' where $A` = 0.9/x_1 + 0.6/x_2 + 0.7/x_3$, then calculate B` as 'y is B`'.

43. Consider the following IF/THEN rules:
 (i) IF is $A_1$, THEN y is $B_1$
 (ii) IF is $A_2$, THEN y is $B_2$
where $Aj \in f(X)$, $Bi \in f(Y)$ ($j = 1,2$) are fuzzy sets,
 $A_1 = 1/x_1 + 0.9/x_2 + 0.1/x_3$; $A_2 = 0.9/x_1 + 1/x_2 + 0.2/x_3$.
 $B_1 = 1/y_1 + 0.2/xy_2$; $B_2 = 0.2/y_1 + 0.9/y_2$.
Given the fact 'x is A'', where $A' = 0.8/x_1 + 0.9/x_2 + 0.1/x_3$, use the method of interpolation to calculate the conclusion B`.

44. Considering a rule such as IF X is A THEN Y is A., where A is given as follows:
$A(x) = 0/0 + 0.5/1 + 1/2 + 1/3 + 0.5/4 + 0/5$
What would be the ratio of the effects produced by modifying this membership function to $A'(x) = 0/0 + 0.33/1 + 0.66/2 + 1/3 + 0.5/4 + 0/5$?

45. If
$A(x) = 0/1 + 0.25/2 + 0.5/3 + 0.75/4 + 1/5 + 0.75/6 + 0.5/7 + 0.25/8 + 0/9 + 0/10$
$B(x) = 0/1 + 0.25/2 + 0.5/3 + 0.75/4 + 1/5 + 1/6 + 0.75/7 + 0.5/8 + 0.25/9 + 0/10$
$A'(x) = 1.0/4$
Then find B'(x).

46. Use correlation-minimum encoding to construct the FAM matrix M from the fit-vector pair (A, B) if $A = (.6\ 1\ .2\ .9)$ and $B = (.8\ .3\ 1)$. Is (A, B) a bi-directional fixed point? Pass $A' = (.2\ .9\ .3\ .2)$ through M and $B' = (.9\ .5\ 1)$ through $M^T$. Do the re-called fuzzy sets differ from B and A?

47. Three variables of interest in power transistors are the amount of current that can be switched, the voltage can be switched, and the cost. The following membership functions for power transistors were developed from a hypothetical components catalogue:

Average current (in amps) = $I$ = {0.4/0.8 + 0.7/0.9 + 1/1 + 0.8/1.1 + 0.6/1.2}
Average voltage (in volts) = $V$ = {0.2/30 + 0.8/45 + 1/60 + 0.9/75 + 0.7/90}
Note how the membership values in each set taper off faster towards the lower voltage and currents. These two fuzzy sets are related to the 'power' of the transistor. Power in electronics is defined by an algebraic operation $P = VI$, but let us work with a general Cartesian relationship between the voltage and current (i.e., simply with $P = V \times I$).
Keep in mind that the Cartesian product is different from the arithmetic product. The Cartesian product expresses the relationship between $Vi$ and $Ij$, where $Vi$ and $Ij$ are individual elements in fuzzy sets $V$ and $I$.
(a) Find the fuzzy Cartesian product $P = V \times I$.
Now let us define a fuzzy set for the cost $C$ in dollars of a transistor, for example,
$C$ = {0.4/0.5 + 1/0.6 + 0.5/0.7}
(b) Using a fuzzy Cartesian product, find $T = I \times C$. What would this relation $T$ represent physically?
(c) Using max-min composition, find $E = P \cdot T$. What would this relation $E$ represent physically?
(d) Using max-product composition, find $E = P \cdot T$. What would this relation $E$ represent physically?

48. Let us say we build a temperature controller, but instead of building a thermostatic system that controls temperature to a desired specific value of, say, 72°F or 85°F, we would like to indicate linguistic comfort ranges such as 'slightly cold' and 'not too hot'. The membership functions for the atomic terms defined on a universe of temperatures in degree Fahrenheit are as follows.
'Hot' = {0/50 + 0/60 + 0.1/70 + 0.5/80 + 0.9/90 + 1/100}
'Cold' = {1/50 + 0.9/60 + 0.3/70 + 0/80 + 0/90 + 0/100}
Find the membership functions for
(a) Not very hot
(b) Slightly cold or slightly hot
(c) Not very cold and not very hot

49. Amplifier capacity on a normalized universe, say [0, 100], can be described linguistically by fuzzy variables like these:
'Powerful' = {0/1 + 0.4/10 + 0.8/50 + 1/100}
'Weak' = {1/1 + 0.9/10 + 0.3/50 + 0/100}
Find the membership functions for the following linguistic phrases used to describe the capacity of various amplifiers:
(a) Powerful and not weak
(b) Very powerful or very weak
(c)V ery, very powerful and not weak

50. This problem discusses the voltages generated internally in switching power supplies. Embedded systems are often supplied 120 V AC for power. A 'power supply' is required to convert this to a useful voltage (quite often +5 V DC). Some power supply designs employ a technique called 'switching.' This technique generates the appropriate voltages by storing and releasing the energy between inductors and capacitors. This problem characterizes two linguistic variables, high and low voltage, on the voltage range of 0 to 200 V AC.
'High' = {0/0 + 0/25 + 0/50 + 0.1/75 + 0.2/100 + 0.4/125 + 0.6/150 + 0.8/175 + 1/200}
'Medium' = {0.2/0 + 0.4/25 + 0.6/50 + 0.8/75 + 1/100 + 0.8/125 + 0.6/150 + 0.4/175 + 0.2/200}
Find the membership functions for the following phrases:
(a) Not very high
(b) Slightly medium and very high
(c) Very, very high or very, very medium

51. Let $X$ = {a, b, c, d} and $Y$ = {1, 2, 3, 4}
$A$ = {(a, 0) (b, 0.8) (c, 0.6) (d, 1)}, $B$ = {(1, 0.2) (2, 1) (3, 0.8) (4, 0)}
$C$ = {(1, 0) (2, 0.4) (3, 1) (4, 0.8)}
Determine the implication relations
(i) IF $x$ is A THEN $y$ is B
(ii) IF $x$ is A THEN $y$ is B ELSE $y$ is C

52. Zadeh's consequent conjunction syllogism schematizes such as this:
$Q_1$ As are Bs
$Q_2$ As are Cs
Therefore: $Q$ As are Bs and Cs
Show that if $Q_1 = S(A, B)$ and $Q_2 = S(A, C)$, then the fuzzy quantifier Q obeys max(0, $Q_1 + Q_2 - 1$) Q min($Q_1, Q_2$).

53. Applying the fuzzy modus ponens rule to deduce rotation is quite slow, as given here:
    (i) If the temperature is high, then the rotation is slow.
    (ii) The temperature is very high.
    Let $H$ (high), $VH$ (very high), $S$ (slow), and $QS$ (quite slow) indicate the associated fuzzy sets as follows:
    For $X = \{30, 40, 50, 60, 70, 80, 90, 100\}$, the set of temperature and $Y = \{10, 20, 30, 40, 50, 60\}$, the set of rotations per minute.
    $H = \{(70, 1) (80, 1) (90, 0.3)\}$, $VH = \{(90, 0.9) (100, 1)\}$, $QS = \{(10, 1) (20, 0.8)\}$, and $S = \{(30, 0.8) (40, 1) (50, 0.6)\}$

54. $A_1$, $A_2$, and $A_3$ are three fuzzy sets as shown in the following figures. Illustrate the aggregation of the aforementioned three sets and then de-fuzzify by: (i) centroid method, (ii) centre of sums method, and (iii) mean of max method.

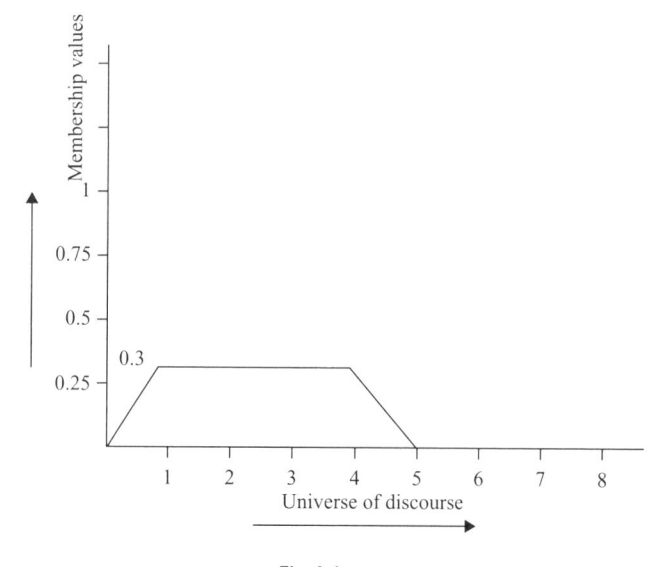

Fig. A.1

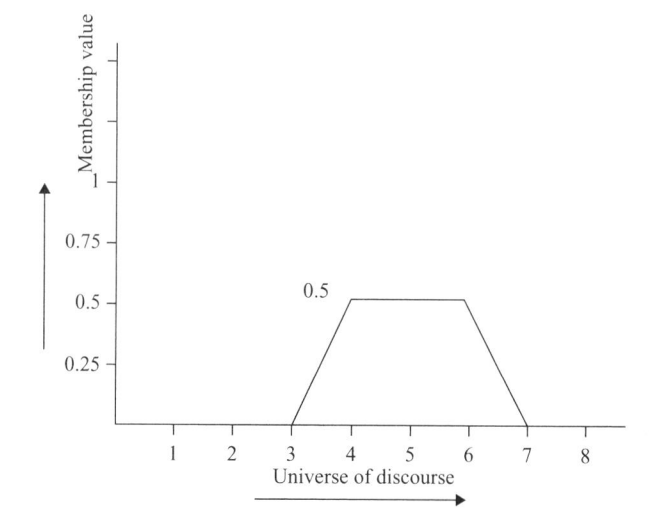

Fig. A.2

**384** Soft Computing with MATLAB Programming

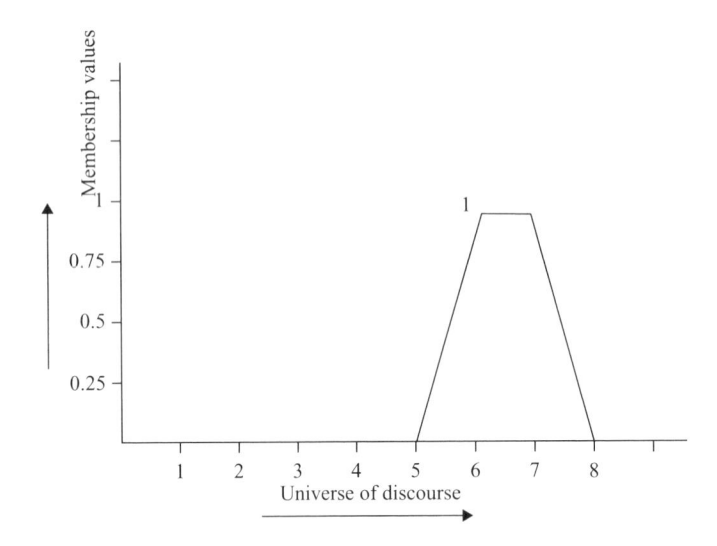

**Fig. A.3**

55. Consider a fuzzy inference system given by the following rules.
    (i) IF colour is Dark AND Texture is soft THEN Fruit quality is rotten.
    (ii) IF colour is Light OR Texture is Hard THEN fruit quality is ripe.
    The membership functions for dark, light, soft, hard, rotten, and ripe are expressed by the following fuzzy sets.
    $A_{dark}(x) = 0/1 + 0.25/2 + 0.5/3 + 0.75/4 + 1/5 + 0.75/6 + 0.5/7 + 0.25/8 + 0/9$.
    $A_{light}(x) = 0/6 + 0.25/7 + 0.5/8 + 0.75/9 + 1/10 + 0.75/11 + 0.5/12 + 0.25/13 + 0/14$.
    $A_{soft}(x) = 0/1 + 0.25/2 + 0.5/3 + 0.75/4 + 1/5 + 0.75/6 + 0.5/7 + 0.25/8 + 0/9$
    $A_{hard}(x) = 0/6 + 0.25/7 + 0.5/8 + 0.75/9 + 1/10 + 0.75/11 + 0.5/12 + 0.25/13 + 0/14$.
    $A_{rotten}(x) = 0/0 + 0.25/0.25 + 0.5/1 + 0.75/1.5 + 1/2 + 0.75/2.5 + 0.5/3 + 0.25/3.5 + 0/4$
    $A_{ripe}(x) = 0/3 + 0.25/3.5 + 0.5/4 + 0.75/4.5 + 1/5 + 0.75/5.5 + 0.5/6 + 0.25/6.5 + 0/7$
    Evaluate the antecedent membership functions for the inputs colour = 3 and Texture = 6 using the max-min composition operator.

56. How would you characterize the membership functions *Temperature high* and *Temperature medium* if 100 people agreed *Temperature high* to be between 20° and 45°, and 25 people agreed *Temperature medium* to be between 15° and 25° in the context of outdoor weather? How would you incorporate the number of agreement votes into the membership function design?

## REFERENCES

[1] Yen, John and Reza Langari, *Fuzzy Logic: Intelligence, Control, and Information*, Pearson Education, Singapore, 1999.
[2] Cox, Earl and O'Hagan, Michael, *The Fuzzy Systems Handbook: A Practitioner's Guide to Building, Using, and Maintaining Fuzzy Systems* (2nd ed.), Morgan Kaufmann, Burlington, October 28 1998.
[3] Yager, Ronald R., *Fuzzy Set and Possibility Theory Recent Developments*, Pergamon Press, New York, 1982.
[4] Zadeh, Lotfi A., 'Fuzzy logic', IEEE Computer, Vol. 21, Issue 4, pp. 83–93, 1988.
[5] Zadeh, Lotfi A., 'Fuzzy Sets', Information and Control, Vol. 8, pp. 338–353, 1965.
[6] Berkan, Riza C. and Sheldon L. Trubatch, *Fuzzy System Design Principles*, Wiley-IEEE Press, New York, 1997.
[7] Tsoukalas, Lefteri H. and Robert E. Uhrig, *Fuzzy and Neural Approaches in Engineering*, John Wiley, New York, 1996.
[8] Ross, Timothy J., *Fuzzy Logic with Engineering Applications*, McGraw-Hill, New York, 1995.
[9] Zimmermann, J., *Fuzzy Set Theory and its Applications*, Kluwer Academic Publishers, Boston, 1991.
[10] Zadeh, Lotfi A., A computational approach to fuzzy quantifiers in natural languages, *Computer and Mathematics*, Vol. 9, Issue 1, pp. 149–184, 1983.
[11] Hellendoorn, Hans and Christoph Thomas, Defuzzification in fuzzy controllers, *Journal of Intelligent and Fuzzy Systems*, Vol. 1, Issue 2, pp. 109–123, 1993.

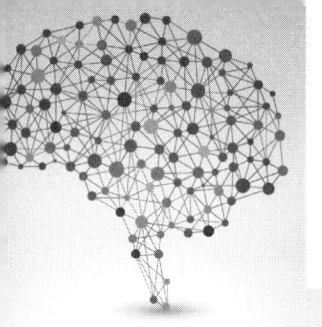

# 6 Fuzzy Logic Applications

*'Remember, to learn and not to do is really not to learn. To know and not to do is really not to know.'*

Stephen R. Covey,
The 7 Habits of Highly Effective People

### LEARNING OBJECTIVES

*After reading this chapter, the reader will be able to:*

- Discuss the procedures involved in designing a fuzzy logic controller
- Learn how to implement a fuzzy logic-based control (FLBC)
- Analyse the processing of fuzzy decision-making
- Explain the MATLAB implementation of fuzzy applications
- Describe the role of FIS editor and Simulink block sets in the implementation process
- Familiarize with the hybrid techniques in fuzzy logic systems

## 6.1 INTRODUCTION TO FUZZY LOGIC APPLICATIONS

Fuzzy logic finds itself with impressive applications in engineering and decision-making problems than just considering it as an interesting mathematics. Whenever accurate decisions are not possible, due to the conventional complexity in understanding the system parameters, an optimal, flexible, and smooth decision can be met out from fuzzy decision-making process. However, the main applications of fuzzy logic in engineering are in the area of control systems.

A control system controls the desired output response of the system by controlling its related parameters through various means. In most of the places, conventional control system can be replaced by fuzzy logic-based control (FLBC) system. Though it is a bit of an overloaded statement, FLBC surely simplifies the design of many more complicated systems. In addition, it should be noted that fuzzy logic is not the answer to everything, so it must be used appropriately. Suppose a closed loop or proportional integral derivative (PID) controller works well, then there is no need for an FLBC. Sometimes while designing a complex system, tuning of PID constants or designing schemes may be unmanageable where fuzzy logic gets its opportunity to excel.

## 6.2 FUZZY CONTROLLERS

Some of the most successful applications of FLBC systems are carried out by synergizing the capability of fuzzy control with conventional controllers such as the PID controller [1]. When we proceed to the implementation part, the following are the two questions that need to be kept in mind:

(a) How can one apply a control strategy as a fuzzy linguistic description?
(b) What are the decisive factors drawn in fuzzy algorithmic synthesis and study?

This section illustrates the basic ideas of fuzzy linguistic description to control using ideas derived from Chapter 5, than the replacement or enhancement of PID controllers. However, before entering into the FLBC, let us refresh the concept of a simple PID controller. Figure 6.1 shows the block diagram of a conventional PID controller.

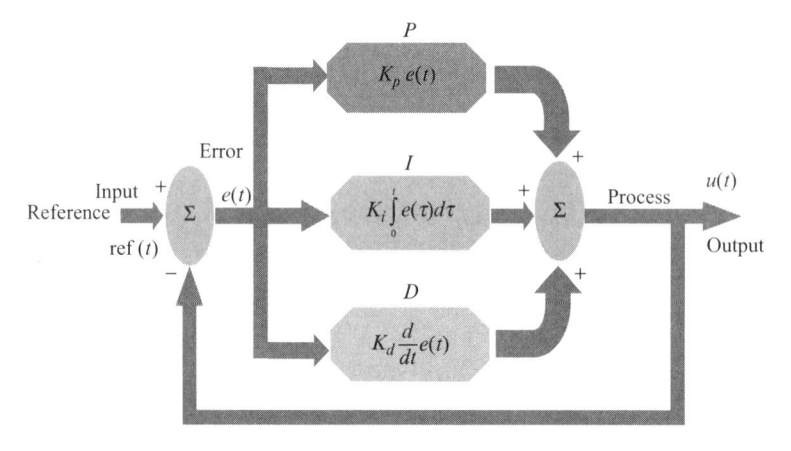

**Fig. 6.1** Block diagram of conventional PID controller

Proportional integral derivative controllers are the most widely used controllers in industrial applications. The control relation associated with PID controllers is given in Eq. (6.1).

$$u(t) = K_p e(t) + K_i \int_{t=0}^{t} e(\tau)d\tau + K_d \frac{d}{dt} e(t) \qquad (6.1)$$

where,
$u(t)$ is the output of the controller
$K_p$ is the proportional gain constant
$K_i$ is the integral gain constant
$K_d$ is the derivative gain constant
$e(t)$ is error between the output $e(t)$ and the reference ref($t$)
$t$ is the time or instantaneous time
$\tau$ is the integration variable

The first term in Eq. (6.1) is called proportional term where the output of the controller $u(t)$ is changed in proportion to the error $e(t)$, which is the percentage deviation from the reference point ref($t$). The second term is called the integral term where the present controller's output $u(t)$ depends on the history of errors that has existed.

The reset constant or the integral constant $K_i$ expresses the scaling between error $e(t)$ and controller output $u(t)$. A large value of $K_i$ means a small error produces a large rate of change of $u(t)$ and vice versa. The third term is the derivative term where the controller's output is dependent on the rate of change of error. Derivative mode tends to minimize oscillation of the system and prevent overshooting. The combination of these three modes is called *proportional integral derivative* (PID) control which is a powerful combination of control modes applied commonly in various engineering control application.

Figure 6.2 shows the block diagram of an FLBC. The central part of a fuzzy controller is a linguistic description prescribing approximate action for a given condition. Fuzzy linguistic descriptions involve associations of fuzzy variables and procedures for inferencing. However, in a conventional PID controller, the model represents the physical system or process being controlled.

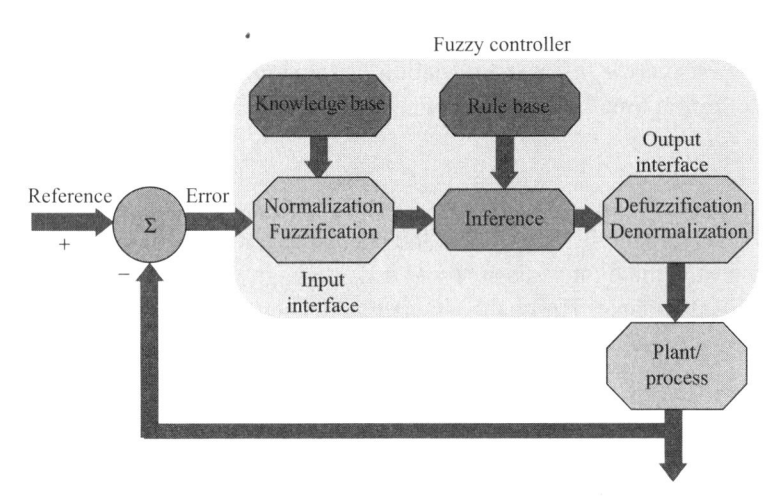

**Fig. 6.2** Block diagram of FLBC

In fuzzy controllers, we seek to incorporate expertise in the control algorithm. Therefore, a fuzzy controller can be viewed as a real-time expert system modelling of the thinking process that an expert might go through in the course of influencing the process.

The basic structure of a fuzzy controller consists of five principle elements: (i) fuzzification module (fuzzifier), (ii) knowledge base, (iii) rule base, (iv) inference engine, and (v) de-fuzzification module (de-fuzzifier). If there are design parameters of any of the five elements that are automatically adjusted, then the fuzzy controller is adaptive. If the design parameters are fixed, the fuzzy controller is non-adaptive. The fuzzification module transforms the crisp values of the control inputs into fuzzy values which are compatible with the fuzzy set representation in the rule base, whereas defuzzification module converts fuzzified output to crisp output.

The inference engine decides the fuzzification strategy that involves composition based or individual rule-firing-based approach. The knowledge base holds the plant's database. It also provides all the information and necessary definitions for the fuzzification process such as membership functions, fuzzy set representation of the input-output variables, and the mapping functions between the physical and fuzzy domain. The input and output interface handling fuzzification and de-fuzzification process also handle various signal processing such as normalization, scaling, smoothing, and quantization.

The operation of fuzzy controllers takes place in discrete time intervals. As in conventional digital control, the rules are evaluated at regular intervals. However, several rules are executed simultaneously within the same time interval. Let $k$ be the subscript to indicate the discrete time, i.e., $t = t_k$.

## 6.2.1 Antecedent/Consequent Variables

Generally in the FLBC, the IF/THEN rules are framed such that the antecedent variable is the error 'e' and the consequent is the directly manipulated variables. The variables are defined on the universe of discourse respective to that variable.

Let the crisp error 'e' be the deviation of some measured variable $V_m$ from a reference 'ref' at time $t = t_k$ and is defined as follows:

$$e(k) = ref - V_m(k) \tag{6.2}$$

Not only the variable 'e' is used, but the change in error $\Delta e$ or $\Delta error$ between two consecutive time intervals at '$t = k$' and '$t = k-1$', is also commonly used as an antecedent variable. The change in error is defined as follows:

$$\Delta e(k) \equiv e(k) - e(k-1) \tag{6.3}$$

Sometimes, the rate of change of error is considered as the antecedent variable and is defined as follows:

$$\Delta^2 e(k) \equiv \Delta e(k) - \Delta e(k-1) \tag{6.4}$$

In cases where the historical errors are an important component, the integral effect of all the past errors are considered as the antecedent variable and is defined as the sum of errors $\bar{e}(k)$ and is given by the Eq. (6.5).

$$\bar{e}(k) \equiv \sum_{i=1}^{k} e_i \tag{6.5}$$

In some cases, actual state variables, indirectly measured variables such as reliability, performance, and so on, may be used instead of error. All these things are possible which are based on the availability of parameters such that they can be estimated in a timely and reliable manner [2].

The directly manipulated variable 'u' can be defined on the universe of discourse of a crisp manipulated variable. In most of the cases, the change in output $\Delta u$ is more often used as the consequent variable. $\Delta u$ represents the amount of change of the control variable '$u$' at time $t = k$. Therefore, if the de-fuzzified output at time $k$ is $\Delta u \times (k)$, then the overall crisp output of the controller will be such as this:

$$u(k) \equiv u(k-1) + \Delta u \times (k) \qquad (6.6)$$

## 6.2.2 IF/THEN Rules and Inference

As discussed in Chapter 5, fuzzy rule base is the vital control part of the system. It is developed based on the expertise input expressed as a set of IF/THEN rules which consist of the antecedents and consequents are associated with linguistic variables. In most of the cases, the antecedent and consequent variables are selected on the same universe of discourse and have fuzzy values of the same type. If the values of all the variables are scaled on a common ground, the speed and considerable saving in memory are achieved during computer implementation. With the availability of various fuzzy logic (FL) tools and development shells, the performance of the controller can be easily investigated.

Let us try to illustrate the fuzzy values error, $\Delta error$ and $\Delta u$ as shown in Fig. 6.3 in connection with a fuzzy controller that follows the derivative mode of a conventional controller [3, 4].

The common fuzzy values are as follows:

ML ⇒ Minus Large, MM ⇒ Minus Medium, MS ⇒ Minus Small, ZE ⇒ Zero Error, PS ⇒ Plus Small, PM ⇒ Plus Medium, PL ⇒ Plus Large.

All variables share the same universe of discourse ranging between −10 and +10 as shown in Fig. 6.3. In computer implementations, fuzzy values are usually quantized and stored in memory in the form of a lookup table as shown in Table 6.1.

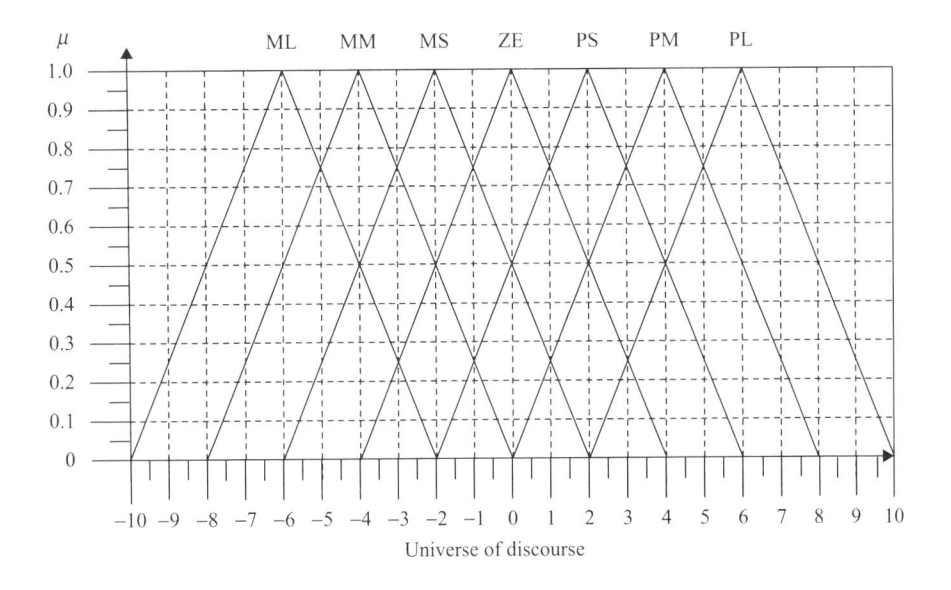

**Fig. 6.3** Scaled fuzzy values of error, $\Delta error$ and $\Delta u$ variables

**Table 6.1** Quantified fuzzy values in lookup table of size 7 × 19

| | -9 | -8 | -7 | -6 | -5 | -4 | -3 | -2 | -1 | 0 | 1 | 2 | 3 | 4 | 5 | 6 | 7 | 8 | 9 |
|---|---|---|---|---|---|---|---|---|---|---|---|---|---|---|---|---|---|---|---|
| ML | 0.25 | 0.5 | 0.75 | 1 | 0.75 | 0.5 | 0.25 | 0 | 0 | 0 | 0 | 0 | 0 | 0 | 0 | 0 | 0 | 0 | 0 |
| MM | 0 | 0 | 0.25 | 0.5 | 0.75 | 1 | 0.75 | 0.5 | 0.25 | 0 | 0 | 0 | 0 | 0 | 0 | 0 | 0 | 0 | 0 |
| MS | 0 | 0 | 0 | 0 | 0.25 | 0.5 | 0.75 | 1 | 0.75 | 0.5 | 0.25 | 0 | 0 | 0 | 0 | 0 | 0 | 0 | 0 |
| ZE | 0 | 0 | 0 | 0 | 0 | 0 | 0.25 | 0.5 | 0.75 | 1 | 0.75 | 0.5 | 0.25 | 0 | 0 | 0 | 0 | 0 | 0 |
| PS | 0 | 0 | 0 | 0 | 0 | 0 | 0 | 0 | 0.25 | 0.5 | 0.75 | 1 | 0.75 | 0.5 | 0.25 | 0 | 0 | 0 | 0 |
| PM | 0 | 0 | 0 | 0 | 0 | 0 | 0 | 0 | 0 | 0 | 0.25 | 0.5 | 0.75 | 1 | 0.75 | 0.5 | 0.25 | 0 | 0 |
| PL | 0 | 0 | 0 | 0 | 0 | 0 | 0 | 0 | 0 | 0 | 0 | 0 | 0.25 | 0.5 | 0.75 | 1 | 0.75 | 0.5 | 0.25 |

In this case, the fuzzy values are stored in a $7 \times 19$ table, with every row in the table representing a quantized fuzzy value. The fuzzy algorithm of a controller that follows a derivative mode is comprised by the given IF/THEN rules as in Rule Set (6.7). Each individual rule which consists of two antecedent variables and one consequent variable can be arranged in a table form (Table 6.2), which is called *fuzzy associative memory* (FAM) matrix.

**Table 6.2** Fuzzy associative memory

| $\Delta$ error / error | ML | MM | MS | ZE | PS | PM | PL |
|---|---|---|---|---|---|---|---|
| ML |   |   |   | PL |   |   |   |
| MM |   |   |   | PM |   |   |   |
| MS |   |   |   | PS |   |   |   |
| ZE | PL | PM | PS | ZE | MS | MM | ML |
| PS |   |   |   | MS |   |   |   |
| PM |   |   |   | MM |   |   |   |
| PL |   |   |   | ML |   |   |   |

Rule 1:  IF error is ML  AND  $\Delta$error is ZE  THEN  $\Delta u$ is PL   ELSE
Rule 2:  IF error is MM  AND  $\Delta$error is ZE  THEN  $\Delta u$ is PM   ELSE
Rule 3:  IF error is MS  AND  $\Delta$error is ZE  THEN  $\Delta u$ is PS   ELSE
Rule 4:  IF error is ZE  AND  $\Delta$error is ZE  THEN  $\Delta u$ is ZE   ELSE
Rule 5:  IF error is PS  AND  $\Delta$error is ZE  THEN  $\Delta u$ is MS  ELSE
Rule 6:  IF error is PM  AND  $\Delta$error is ZE  THEN  $\Delta u$ is MM ELSE
Rule 7:  IF error is PL  AND  $\Delta$error is ZE  THEN  $\Delta u$ is ML  ELSE  (6.7)
Rule 8:  IF error is ZE  AND  $\Delta$error is ML  THEN  $\Delta u$ is PL   ELSE
Rule 9:  IF error is ZE  AND  $\Delta$error is MM THEN  $\Delta u$ is PM   ELSE
Rule 10: IF error is ZE  AND  $\Delta$error is MS  THEN  $\Delta u$ is PS   ELSE
Rule 11: IF error is ZE  AND  $\Delta$error is PS  THEN  $\Delta u$ is MS  ELSE
Rule 12: IF error is ZE  AND  $\Delta$error is PM  THEN  $\Delta u$ is MM ELSE
Rule 13: IF error is ZE  AND  $\Delta$error is PL  THEN  $\Delta u$ is ML

Blank boxes in the table indicate that there is no rule present for the particular combination of antecedent variables. In case of more than two antecedent variables, a tabular representation needs further dimensions.

From Chapter 5, we know that fuzzy control algorithms are evaluated or inferred using *generalized modus ponens* (GMP). Generalized modus ponens is generally a data-driven inferencing mechanism and analytically involves the composition of fuzzy relations, frequently max-min composition. In general, GMP transforms the consequent by a degree that corresponds to the degree to which the antecedent part of a fuzzy rule is satisfied which is known as degree of fulfilment (DOF). Here, the fuzzy rule is dictated by the choice of the implication operator. Let us focus on how such transformation can be used in a fuzzy control application.

For the IF/THEN fuzzy rules given in Rule Set (6.7), implication operator discussed in Chapter 5 can be used with the connective ELSE that can be analytically modelled as either $OR(\vee)$ or $AND(\wedge)$, again depending on the implication operator. The inputs to a fuzzy controller are usually crisp numbers. In addition, in the case of uncertainty, fuzzy inputs can also be considered, and thereby the crisp numbers can be fuzzified.

### 6.2.2.1 Illustration of Mamdani Min Implication Operator

Let us try to illustrate a control action that involves rules $Rule_3$, $Rule_4$, and $Rule_{11}$ of Rule Set (6.7). Here, Mamdani min implication operator is used, therefore the connective ELSE is interpreted as OR. Let the instantaneous time be $t = k$, at which the crisp error $e'$ and crisp change in error $\Delta e'$ are given to these rules as in Fig. 6.4.

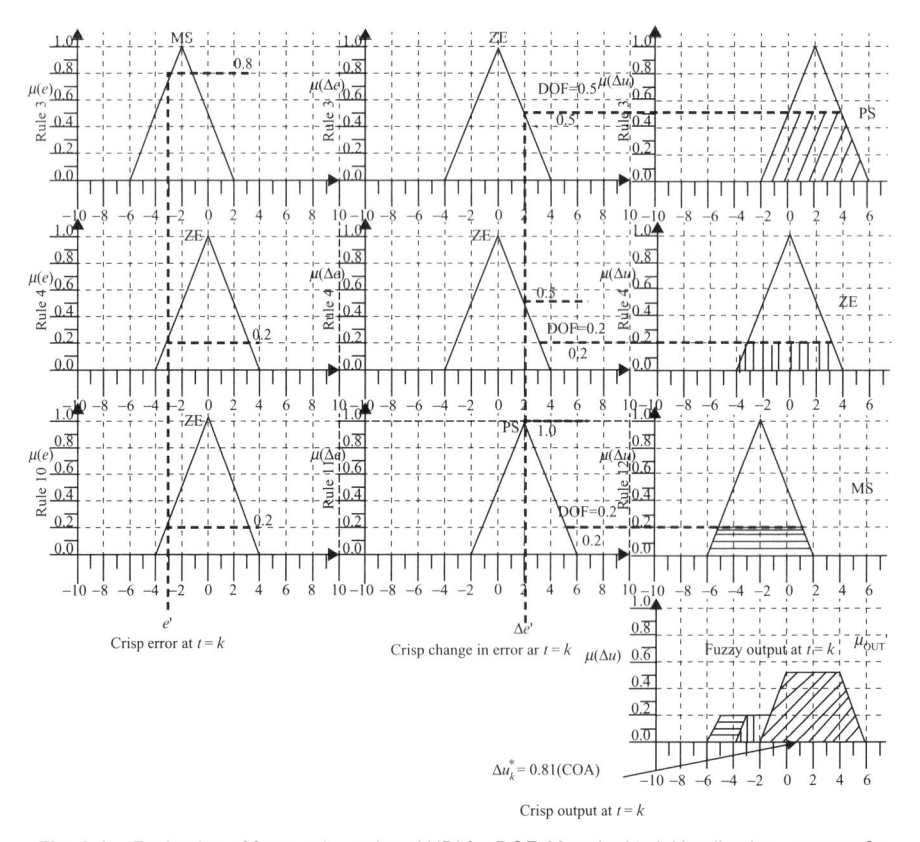

**Fig. 6.4** Evaluation of fuzzy rules using 'AND' for DOF, Mamdani 'min' implication operator for implication relation and 'OR' for ELSE

It should be noted that the DOF should not be equal to zero when the rule is executed. For example, in Rule$_3$ the crisp error $e'$ shown has a 0.8 degree of membership to MS, whereas the crisp change in error $\Delta e'$ has a 0.5 degree of membership to ZE. Thus the DOF of rule Rule$_3$ at this particular time is given as follows:

$$\text{DOF}_3 = \mu_{MS}(e') \wedge \mu_{ZE}(\Delta e') = 0.8 \wedge 0.5 = 0.5 \qquad (6.8)$$

Here, the antecedent part connective 'AND' is interpreted as min ($\wedge$) and the consequent part PS will be transformed in accordance with DOF$_3$ as in Eq. (6.8).

When Mamdani Min is used, the transformation is accomplished by clipping PS at the highest of DOF$_3$ as shown in Fig. 6.4. Thus Rule$_3$ contributes $\mu_{PS}(\Delta u)$, the shaded part of the consequent value to the total fuzzy output. Similarly, the DOF of Rule$_4$ and Rule$_{11}$ is given as Eqs (6.9) and (6.10) respectively.

$$\text{DOF}_4 = \mu_{ZE}(e') \wedge \mu_{ZE}(\Delta e') = 0.2 \wedge 0.5 = 0.2 \qquad (6.9)$$

$$\text{DOF}_{11} = \mu_{ZE}(e') \wedge \mu_{PS}(\Delta e') = 0.2 \wedge 1.0 = 0.2 \qquad (6.10)$$

They contribute $\mu_{ZE}(\Delta u)$ and $\mu_{MS}(\Delta u)$ as shaded parts for the consequent part as shown in Fig. 6.4. However, we assumed that the rest of the rules of Rule Set (6.7) are not executed (i.e., they contribute a zero output). $\mu_{OUT}(\Delta u)$ is the complete shaded part shown at the lower part of Fig. 6.4. Finally the 'OR' connective for ELSE combines all the consequent fuzzy output as the union of the individual rules as given in Eq. (6.11).

$$\mu_{OUT}(\Delta u) = \mu_{PS}(\Delta u) \vee \mu_{ZE}(\Delta u) \vee \mu_{MS}(\Delta u) \qquad (6.11)$$

Once the fuzzy output shaded area is obtained, the de-fuzzification process for $\mu_{OUT}(\Delta u)$ is carried out to obtain a crisp value $\Delta u_k^*$ which can be used as input to the plant/process. If centre of area (COA) method is used as the de-fuzzification method, then the crisp output is given as follows:

$$u_k^* = \frac{\sum_{i=1}^{N=11}\begin{pmatrix} -5\times 0.2 - 4\times 0.2 - 3\times 0.2 - 2\times 0.2 - 1\times 0.2 + 0\times 0.5 + \\ 1\times 0.5 + 2\times 0.5 + 3\times 0.5 + 4\times 0.5 + 5\times 0.2 \end{pmatrix}}{\sum_{i=1}^{N=11}\begin{pmatrix} 0.2 + 0.2 + 0.2 + 0.2 + 0.2 + \\ 0.5 + 0.5 + 0.5 + 0.5 + 0.5 + 0.2 \end{pmatrix}} = 0.81 \quad (6.12)$$

The answer may vary for different de-fuzzification methods and has already been discussed in Chapter 5.

### 6.2.2.2 Illustration of Larsen Product Implication Operator

Let us now illustrate for the same rules considered in Section 6.2.2.1. Here we use *Larsen product* as the fuzzy implication operator with the arithmetic product for combining the antecedent variables. Finally the 'OR' connective for ELSE combines all the consequent fuzzy output as the union of the individual rules.

The graphical fuzzy output with the shaded area is shown in Fig. 6.5. It is observed that the $\mu_{OUT}(\Delta u)$ is bit different from the total fuzzy output obtained using Mamdani Min shown in Fig. 6.4. Similarly, it should be understood that if other fuzzy implication operators are used, then the fuzzy output would produce different transformations in shape for the antecedent fuzzy value and, hence, a different $\mu_{OUT}(\Delta u)$.

The DOF for Rule$_3$, Rule$_4$, and Rule$_{11}$ is given as Eqs (6.13), (6.14), and (6.15), respectively.

$$\text{DOF}_3 = \mu_{MS}(e') \cdot \mu_{ZE}(\Delta e') = 0.8 \cdot 0.5 = 0.40 \tag{6.13}$$

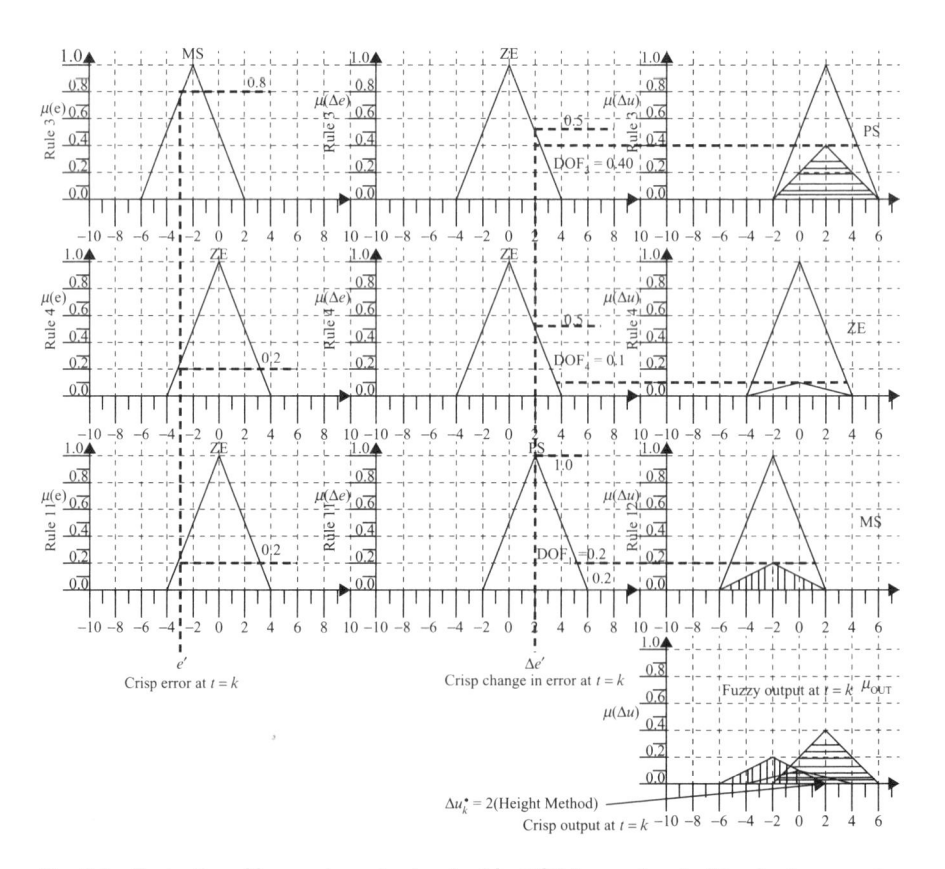

**Fig. 6.5** Evaluation of fuzzy rules using 'product' for DOF, Larsen 'product' implication operator for implication relation, and 'OR' for ELSE.

$$\text{DOF}_4 = \mu_{ZE}(e') \bullet \mu_{ZE}(\Delta e') = 0.2 \bullet 0.5 = 0.10 \qquad (6.14)$$

$$\text{DOF}_{11} = \mu_{ZE}(e') \bullet \mu_{PS}(\Delta e') = 0.2 \bullet 1.0 = 0.20 \qquad (6.15)$$

Finally, the total fuzzy output is the union of the three outputs, since we interpret the connective ELSE as OR($\vee$) which is given by the Eq. (6.16).

$$\mu_{OUT}(\Delta u) = \mu_{PS}(\Delta u) \wedge \mu_{ZE}(\Delta u) \vee \mu_{MS}(\Delta u) \qquad (6.16)$$

Once the output fuzzy shaded area is obtained, we can de-fuzzify the fuzzy output using any of the methods discussed in Chapter 5. If we use the height or max-membership method, then $\Delta u_k^* = 2.0$.

Historically, knowledge about PID controllers has evolved to a large extent. Therefore, it will be useful to emulate various forms and combinations of the PID controller by fuzzy rules. If a fuzzy controller emulates a conventional PID mode of control, then the controller would consist of rules having the following form:

$$\text{IF} \quad \text{error is } A \quad \text{AND} \quad \Delta\text{error is } B \quad \text{THEN} \quad u \text{ is } C \qquad (6.17)$$

A PI-like fuzzy controller would have rules of the following form:

$$\text{IF} \quad \text{error is } A \quad \text{AND} \quad \Delta\text{error is } B \quad \text{THEN} \quad \Delta u \text{ is } C \qquad (6.18)$$

whereas a P-like controller would have rules such as this:

$$\text{IF} \quad \text{error is } A \quad \text{THEN} \quad u \text{ is } C \qquad (6.19)$$

The rule form of PID-like fuzzy controller is as follows:

$$\text{IF error is } A \text{ AND } \Delta\text{error is } B \text{ AND } \overline{\text{error}} \text{ is } C \text{ THEN } u \text{ is } D \quad (6.20)$$

where $\overline{\text{error}}$ is the sum of errors.

Though we have used implication operators such as Mamdani Min or Larsen product, sometimes it is advantageous in considering crisp or special membership functions. There are fuzzy controllers that use rules where the output variable is given in terms of a functional relation of the inputs such as *Sugeno* or TSK form of fuzzy rules. Such rules are of the following form:

$$\text{IF} \quad x_1 \text{ is } A_1 \quad \text{AND} \quad x_2 \text{ is } A_2 \quad .... \quad \text{THEN} \quad u = f(x_1, x_2, .., x_n) \qquad (6.21)$$

where, $f$ is a function of the inputs $x_1, x_2, ..., x_n$. If $f(x_1, x_2, ..., x_n)$ is a constant, then the Eq. (6.21) constitutes a *zero-order Sugeno controller*. If $f(x_1, x_2, ..., x_n)$ is a first-order polynomial, the Eq. (6.21) constitutes a *first-order Sugeno controller*.

A PI-like fuzzy controller with TSK rules is of the following form:

$$\text{IF } \text{error is SMALL} \quad \text{AND} \quad \Delta\text{error is MEDIUM } .... \text{ THEN}$$
$$u = 2 \times \text{error} + 3 \times \Delta\text{error} \qquad (6.22)$$

Non-linear systems can be modelled well using Sugeno fuzzy models by interpolating multiple linear models. They are well suited to mathematical analysis and provide themselves to adaptive techniques, whereas Mamdani rules are more perceptive and better suited to human way of linguistic description.

### 6.2.3 Fuzzy Decision-making

In this section, a generalized fuzzy decision system for recruiting candidates in an industry environment is modelled and solved. The essential qualifications and the basic requirements for the job are stated imprecisely. A requirement fuzzy subset is formulated. For the interviewed candidates, the experts give their opinion linguistically. The various factors considered while evaluating a candidate are appearance, qualification, communication skills (CS), intelligent quotient (IQ), problem-solving approach, alertness, age, and experience. It is proposed to construct a fuzzy decision set which will indicate the relative merits of all the candidates interviewed. The indices of fuzziness of various expert opinions are measured and compared. A fuzzy opinion matrix is formed, and the existing statistical decision-making methods are extended in order to derive a fuzzy decision set, from which the candidate with the highest grade of membership is to be selected.

When the management considers alternative elements within a database for decision-making purposes, some means for evaluating alternative record formats representing combinations of data elements are required. A decision-making problem is deterministic if the management's objectives and the data elements are precisely known. If they are not precisely known, it is very difficult to determine the relative importance of different data elements or integrate a large volume of data to help decision-making. The fuzzy decision-making approach can be utilized effectively to tackle this problem of imprecisely stated information. The fuzzy approach is based on the premise that the key elements in human thinking are not just numbers but can be approximated to tables of fuzzy sets, or, in other words, classes of objects in which the transition from membership to non-membership is gradual rather than abrupt.

In the recruitment problem, it has been assumed that the experts in the interview committee have stated their opinion about the candidates linguistically. A relationship is formed between the basic requirements for the job (objectives) and the experts' opinion about the candidates (data elements) using fuzzy subset representation. The steps involved in the development of the fuzzy decision system are systematically explained later.

#### 6.2.3.1 Statement of the Recruitment Problem

An organization is seeking a candidate for a particular job. It desires to evaluate the candidates with respect to various factors, namely qualification, CS, experience, IQ, etc. The required qualifications and other desirable factors have been stated imprecisely (Table 6.3).

**Table 6.3** Prescribed requirements for the job

| Requirements | Fuzzy values |
|---|---|
| • Qualification | • MSc or equivalent |
| • Communication skills | • More than average |
| • IQ | • Average |
| • Problem-solving approach | • Should be very good |
| • Alertness | • Should be high |
| • Age | • Young |
| • Experience | • Must have enough |
| • Appearance | • Good looking |

The candidates with the following qualifications are eligible to apply for the job:
(1) BSc, (2) BSc and PGDCA, (3) MSc, (4) MSc and PGDCA, (5) MPhil, (6) PhD

The following linguistic terms have been considered for CS, IQ, and problem-solving approach:
(1) Excellent (E), (2) Very good (VG), (3) Good (G), (4) Average (AV), (5) Fair (F), (6) Bad (B)

For alertness and experience, the following fuzzy terms have been considered:
(1) Very high, (2) High, (3) Medium, (4) Low, (5) Very low, (6) Nil

For age and appearance, the following linguistic terms have been used:
(1) Very, very young, (2) Very young, (3) Young, (4) Old, (5) Very old, (6) Very, very old

and (1) Excellent, (2) Good looking, (3) Smart, (4) Average, (5) Fair, (6) Not good
The fuzzy subset representation for the basic requirements is as follows:

Qualification: $1/0.2 + 2/0.4 + 3/0.8 + 4/1 + 5/0.6 + 6/0.2$
Communication skills: $1/1.0 + 2/1.0 + 3/1.0 + 4/1.0 + 5/0.8 + 6/0.2$
IQ: $1/1.0 + 2/1.0 + 3/1.0 + 4/1.0 + 5/0.8 + 6/0.2$
Problem-solving approach: $1/1.0 + 2/1.0 + 3/0.9 + 4/0.7 + 5/0.4 + 6/0.0$
Alertness: $1/1.0 + 2/1.0 + 3/0.8 + 4/0.6 + 5/0.4 + 6/0.0$
Experience: $1/0.4 + 2/0.8 + 3/1.0 + 4/0.6 + 5/0.4 + 6/0.2$
Age: $1/0.6 + 2/1.0 + 3/1.0 + 4/0.8 + 5/0.4 + 6/0.2$
Appearance: $1/1.0 + 2/1.0 + 3/0.8 + 4/0.5 + 5/0.3 + 6/0.1$

The fuzzy subset representation for the various deciding factors is as follows:

*Qualification*
(1) BSc: $1/1.0 + 2/0.8 + 3/0.6 + 4/0.2 + 5/0.2 + 6/0.2$
(2) BSc and PGDCA: $1/0.8 + 2/1.0 + 3/0.6 + 4/0.4 + 5/0.2 + 6/0.2$

(3) MSc: 1/0.2 + 2/0.4 + 3/1.0 + 4/0.6 + 5/0.4 + 6/0.2
(4) MSc and PGDCA: 1/0.2 + 2/0.6 + 3/0.8 + 4/1.0 + 5/0.4 + 6/0.2
(5) MPhil: 1/0.0 + 2/0.2 + 3/0.4 + 4/0.6 + 5/1.0 + 6/0.4
(6) PhD: 1/0.0 + 2/0.0 + 3/0.2 + 4/0.4 + 5/0.8 + 6/1.0

*Communication skills, IQ, and problem-solving approach*
(1) Excellent: 1/1.0 + 2/0.8 + 3/0.6 + 4/0.4 + 5/0.2 + 6/0.0
(2) Very good: 1/0.8 + 2/1.0 + 3/0.6 + 4/0.4 + 5/0.2 + 6/0.0
(3) Good: 1/0.6 + 2/0.8 + 3/1.0 + 4/0.6 + 5/0.4 + 6/0.2
(4) Average: 1/0.4 + 2/0.6 + 3/0.8 + 4/1.0 + 5/0.6 + 6/0.2
(5) Fair: 1/0.2 + 2/0.4 + 3/0.6 + 4/0.8 + 5/1.0 + 6/0.4
(6) Bad: 1/0.0 + 2/0.2 + 3/0.4 + 4/0.6 + 5/0.8 + 6/1.0

*Alertness and experience*
(1) Very high: 1/1.0 + 2/0.8 + 3/0.4 + 4/0.2 + 5/0.6 + 6/0.0
(2) High: 1/0.8 + 2/1.0 + 3/0.6 + 4/0.4 + 5/0.2 + 6/0.0
(3) Medium: 1/0.4 + 2/0.6 + 3/1.0 + 4/0.4 + 5/0.2 + 6/0.0
(4) Low: 1/0.0 + 2/0.2 + 3/0.6 + 4/1.0 + 5/0.8 + 6/0.2
(5) Very low: 1/0.0 + 2/0.0 + 3/0.4 + 4/0.8 + 5/1.0 + 6/0.4
(6) Nil: 1/0.0 + 2/0.0 + 3/0.0 + 4/0.2 + 5/0.4 + 6/1.0

*Age*
(1) Very, very young: 1/1.0 + 2/0.8 + 3/0.4 + 4/0.2 + 5/0.0 + 6/0.0
(2) Very young: 1/0.8 + 2/1.0 + 3/0.6 + 4/0.2 + 5/0.0 + 6/0.0
(3) Young: 1/0.2 + 2/0.6 + 3/1.0 + 4/0.4 + 5/0.2 + 6/0.0
(4) Old : 1/0.2 + 2/0.4 + 3/0.6 + 4/1.0 + 5/0.2 + 6/0.0
(5) Very old: 1/0.0 + 2/0.0 + 3/0.2 + 4/0.4 + 5/1.0 + 6/0.4
(6) Very, very old: 1/0.0 + 2/0.0 + 3/0.0 + 4/0.4 + 5/0.8 + 6/1.0

*Appearance*
(1) Excellent: 1/1.0 + 2/0.8 + 3/0.6 + 4/0.4 + 5/0.2 + 6/0.0
(2) Good looking: 1/0.8 + 2/1.0 + 3/0.8 + 4/0.6 + 5/0.4 + 6/0.2
(3) Smart: 1/0.4 + 2/0.6 + 3/1.0 + 4/0.6 + 5/0.4 + 6/0.2
(4) Average: 1/0.4 + 2/0.4 + 3/0.6 + 4/1.0 + 5/0.6 + 6/0.2
(5) Fair: 1/0.0 + 2/0.2 + 3/0.2 + 4/0.6 + 5/1.0 + 6/0.4
(6) Not good: 1/0.0 + 2/0.2 + 3/0.4 + 4/0.6 + 5/0.8 + 6/1.0

With these fuzzy subset representations, a decision system has been developed using the fuzzy distance approach and the fuzzy opinion matrix approach to select a suitable candidate.

### 6.2.3.2 Fuzzy Distance Approach

Once the requirement set and the experts opinion about the candidate have been stated linguistically, the fuzzy hamming distance between the requirement set and the opinion set for each candidate with respect to each factor is estimated. The following matrix shows the fuzzy opinion of six experts about all the candidates with respect to their CS:

$$\begin{array}{c} & \begin{array}{cccccc} c_1 & c_2 & c_3 & c_4 & c_5 & c_6 \end{array} \\ \begin{array}{c} e_1 \\ e_2 \\ e_3 \\ e_4 \\ e_5 \\ e_6 \end{array} & \left[ \begin{array}{cccccc} E & G & F & VG & B & G \\ VG & AV & B & VG & AV & VG \\ G & AV & B & VG & AV & VG \\ G & AV & B & E & B & E \\ G & F & A & G & F & G \\ VG & VG & F & G & G & G \end{array} \right] \end{array}$$

The fuzzy set representations of these linguistic terms have been already stated. The overall opinion about each candidate can be obtained by considering the relevant column for that candidate. For example, for candidate 1, the overall opinion of the experts using intersection of fuzzy sets with respect to CS is as follows:

$$O = 1/0.6 + 2/0.8 + 3/0.6 + 4/0.4 + 5/0.2 + 6/0.0$$

The requirement set for CS is given as follows:

$$R = 1/1.0 + 2/1.0 + 3/1.0 + 4/1.0 + 5/0.8 + 6/0.2$$

The fuzzy hamming distance [5] between the earlier-given two sets is given here:

$$d(O,R) = \sum_{i=1}^{6} |\mu_O(x_i) - \mu_R(x_i)| = 2.4 \quad (6.23)$$

Similarly, a fuzzy distance set is formed for all the candidates with respect to CS and is given as follows:

$$\begin{array}{c} & \begin{array}{cccccc} c_1 & c_2 & c_3 & c_4 & c_5 & c_6 \end{array} \\ f_{CS} = [ & 2.4 & 3.2 & 3.2 & 2.4 & 3.2 & 2.4 \ ] \end{array}$$

After considering the other factors, the following fuzzy distance matrix has been formed:

$$\begin{array}{c} & \begin{array}{cccccc} c_1 & c_2 & c_3 & c_4 & c_5 & c_6 \end{array} \\ \begin{array}{r} Qualification \\ Communication\ skill \\ IQ \\ Alertness \\ Experience \\ Age \\ Appearance \\ Problem\text{-}solving\ approach \end{array} & \left[ \begin{array}{cccccc} 2.4 & 2.0 & 2.4 & 2.0 & 2.4 & 2.4 \\ 2.4 & 3.2 & 3.2 & 2.4 & 3.2 & 2.4 \\ 2.4 & 3.8 & 3.2 & 2.4 & 3.2 & 3.8 \\ 2.2 & 2.6 & 3.4 & 1.6 & 2.4 & 3.4 \\ 1.8 & 1.8 & 2.6 & 1.2 & 2.0 & 3.2 \\ 3.6 & 2.6 & 3.0 & 2.6 & 2.8 & 2.8 \\ 1.5 & 2.1 & 1.9 & 2.1 & 2.7 & 2.1 \\ 1.4 & 2.2 & 3.2 & 1.4 & 2.2 & 1.8 \end{array} \right] \end{array}$$

If the fuzzy opinion set is very close to the requirement set, the hamming distance will be very less. A vector that contains the minimum-distance values for each candidate with respect to all the factors is constructed.

$$V = [\underset{c_1}{1.4} \quad \underset{c_2}{1.8} \quad \underset{c_3}{1.9} \quad \underset{c_4}{1.2} \quad \underset{c_5}{2.0} \quad \underset{c_6}{1.8}]$$

From this minimum-distance vector, it can be observed that $c_4$ has the least minimum distance, which implies that his qualifications and other capabilities resemble the requirement set. Therefore, candidate 4 is selected.

## 6.3 MATLAB Implementation of Fuzzy Logic Applications

The MATLAB implementations of FL applications have been discussed in the following sections. The implementation has been carried out using MATLAB codes and also FL tool box.

### 6.3.1 Automatic Fuzzy Acceleration Controller

Let us design an automatic fuzzy acceleration controller for a car. The input to the acceleration system is the relative speed/velocity of the car and the distance perceived by the driver between the car and a vehicle travelling in front of the car. The output is the amount of acceleration or deceleration (braking) required to given such that the process is automatic.

*Inputs*: Distance, Relative velocity
*Outputs*: Acceleration, Deceleration (Brake)

The range or the universe of discourse assumed for both the input and output variables are given in Table 6.4.

Table 6.4  Universe of discourse (Assumed)

| Variable | Range |
| --- | --- |
| Distance | 0 to infinity |
| Relative velocity | −50 to 50 |
| Acceleration | 0 to 120 km/hr |
| Brake | 0 to 100% |

Before going to the fuzzy inference system (FIS) editor in the FL tool box, let us first choose the membership function for each variable.

**Distance:**
The input variable 'Distance' can be classified into Low Distance, Average Distance, Safe Distance, and Very Large Distance. Membership functions of these fuzzy sets are shown in Fig. 6.6.

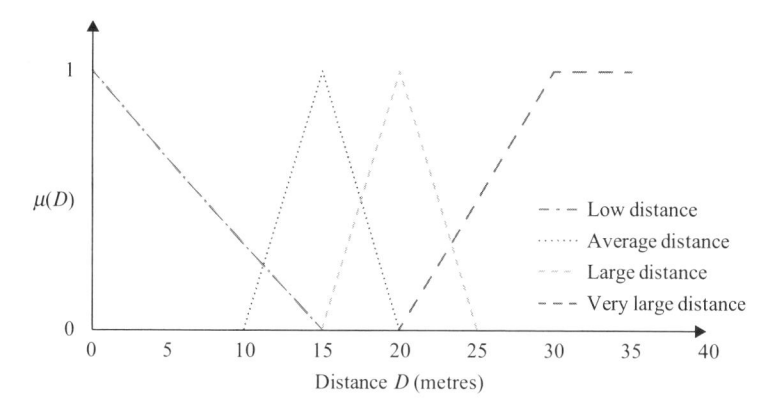

**Fig. 6.6** Membership diagram for the variable 'Distance'

**Relative velocity:**
Relative velocity between the car and the vehicle will increase positively, if the vehicle in the front moves faster than the car. Relative velocity will increase negatively, if the vehicle in the front moves backward or it moves slower than the car or it is standing still and the car is moving forward. The fuzzy sets associated with the relative velocity are Large Negative, Zero, and Large Positive, as given in Fig. 6.7.

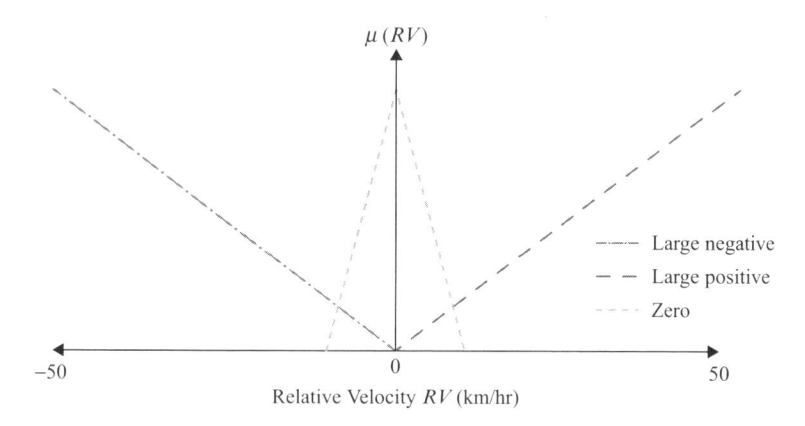

**Fig. 6.7** Membership diagram for the variable 'Relative Velocity'

**Acceleration:**
Acceleration varies from 0 to 120 km/hr$^2$. It can be classified into fuzzy sets of Low Acceleration, Average Acceleration, and Large Acceleration. The membership function of the fuzzy sets is given in Fig. 6.8.

**Braking/Deceleration:**
Braking varies from 0 to 100 per cent. It can be classified into fuzzy sets of Low Braking, Medium Braking, and High Braking. The membership function of the fuzzy sets is shown in Fig. 6.9.

The aforecited information of the variables should be properly entered in the FIS editor of the FL toolbox as given in the following steps:

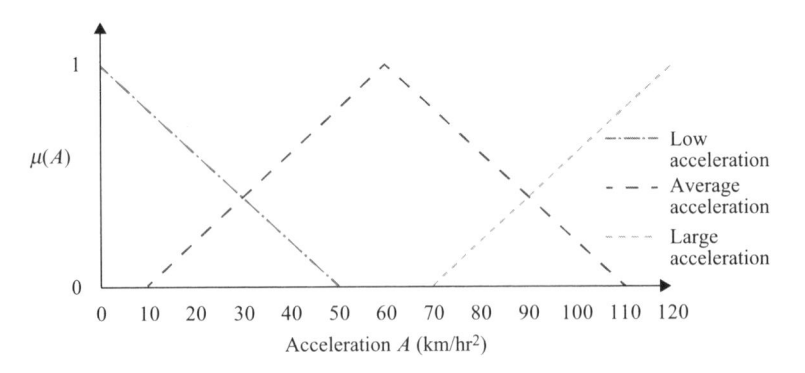

**Fig. 6.8** Membership diagram for the variable 'Acceleration'

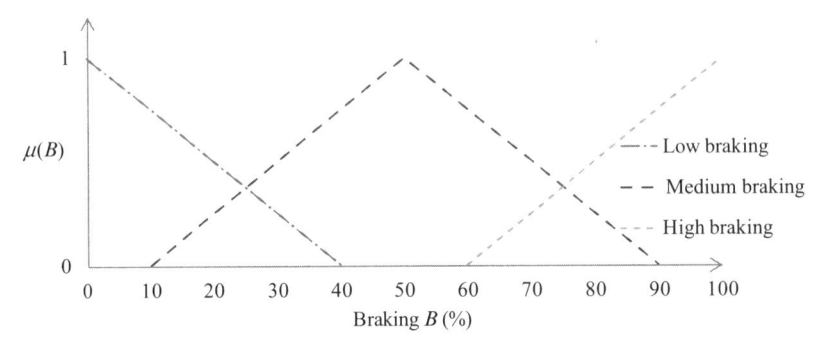

**Fig. 6.9** Membership diagram for the variable 'Braking'

**Step 1:** Open FIS editor in MATLAB by typing the command 'fuzzy' in the prompt of the command window. Then specify the current variable name as 'Distance' as in the graphical user interface (GUI) Fig. 6.10.

**Step 2:** Double-click on the Distance Input figure (yellow colour) and open the membership function editor. Then edit the membership function.

**Step 3:** Give the range for each of the fuzzy set membership function such as Average, Large, and Very Large as in Fig. 6.11.

**Step 4:** Repeat the same procedure for all the membership functions of all input and output variables.

**Step 5:** Now, we can define the rule base to be entered in the FIS editor. The rules can be framed as follows:

1. If (Distance is Low) and (Relative Velocity is Large_negative) then (Acceleration is Low Acceleration)(Brake is High)
2. If (Distance is Low) and (Relative Velocity is Large_Positive) then (Acceleration is Low Acceleration)
3. If (Distance is Average) and (Relative Velocity is Large_negative) then (Acceleration is Low Acceleration)(Brake is Medium)

Similarly, $n$ number rules for all combination of inputs can be made.

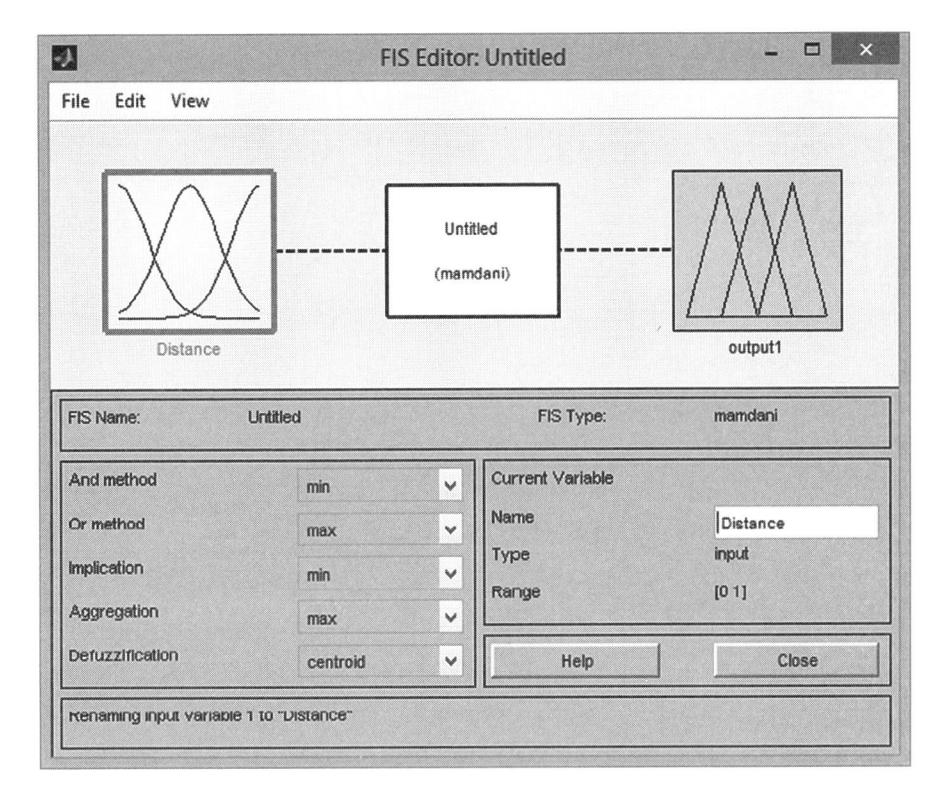

**Fig. 6.10** Specifying 'Distance' in the FIS editor

**Editing the rule base:**
In FIS editor, select Edit and then select Rules. Then the rule editor is opened for us to create the fuzzy rule base as shown in Fig 6.12.

**Step 6:** Select input states and corresponding output states. The fuzzy operation to be carried out such as AND, OR, or NOT are selected by clicking Add rule. Weights for each rule can be specified. Close the rule editor after editing all the rules.

**Step 7:** Once the rules are created, then the variation between input and output variables can be observed with the help of the Surface Viewer. Surface viewer can be navigated from FIS editor by selecting View and then selecting Surface (Figs 6.12 and 6.13).

## 6.3.2 Selection of a Bridegroom for a Bride

Consider a similar kind of example of selection of a groom that has been discussed in Chapter 5. Here, the parent searches for a bridegroom for their daughter. The girl's height is 165 cm and her present age is 23. The parents believe that the right choice would be some guy having approximately same height or taller than her. They want to make sure that the groom should be employed and his work timings should be defined. The daughter's father is adamant in his belief that 'If a man's work timing is low, then he may be a lazy'. However, the daughter's mother says,

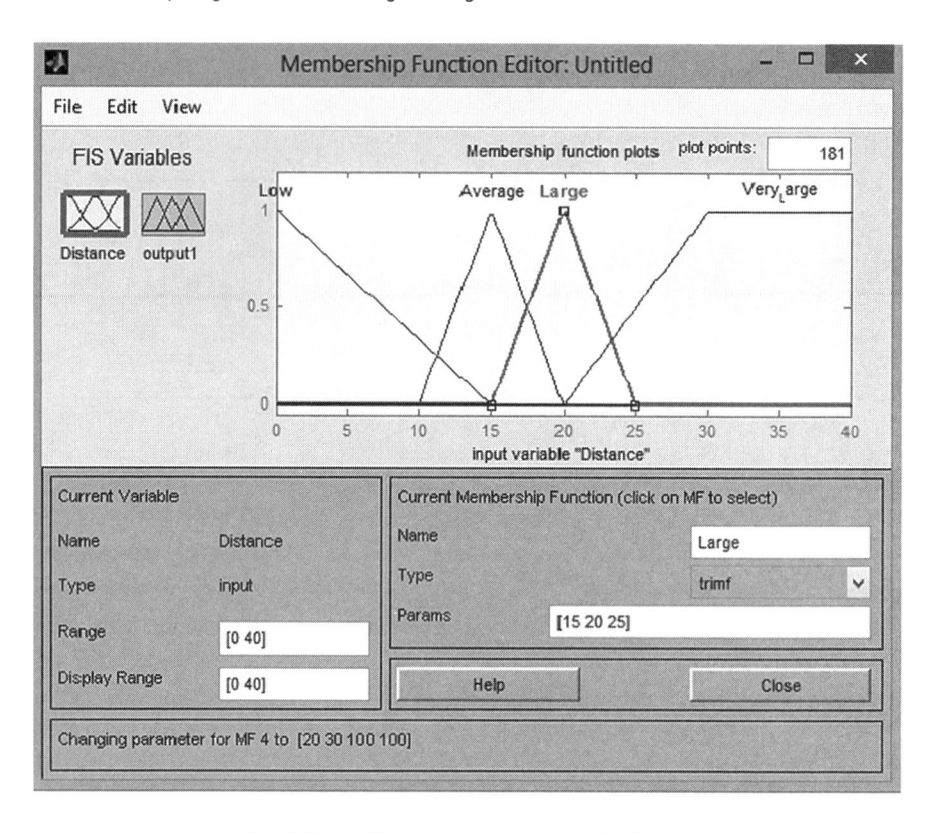

Fig. 6.11 Editing of membership function 'Large'

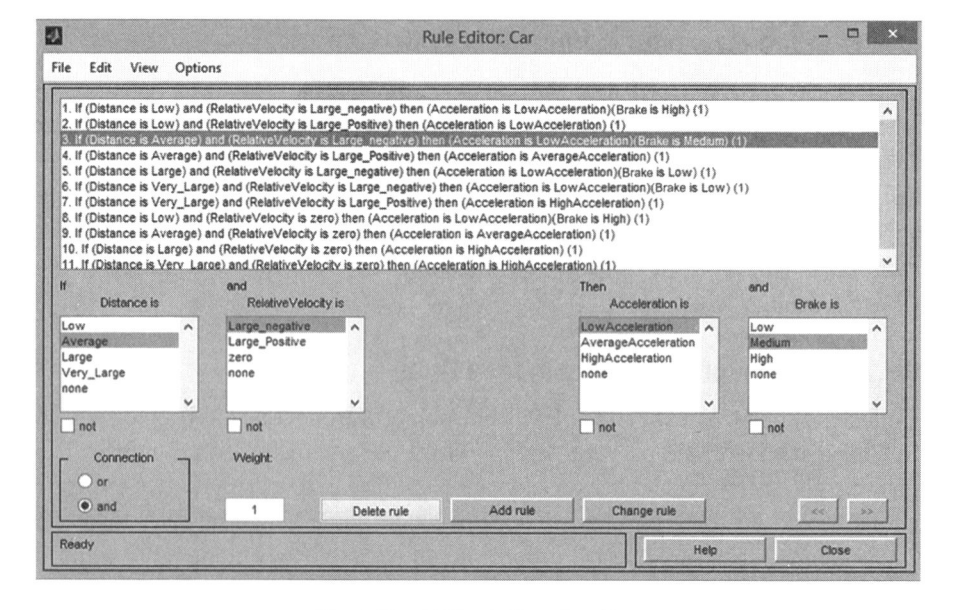

Fig. 6.12 Editing in the rule editor

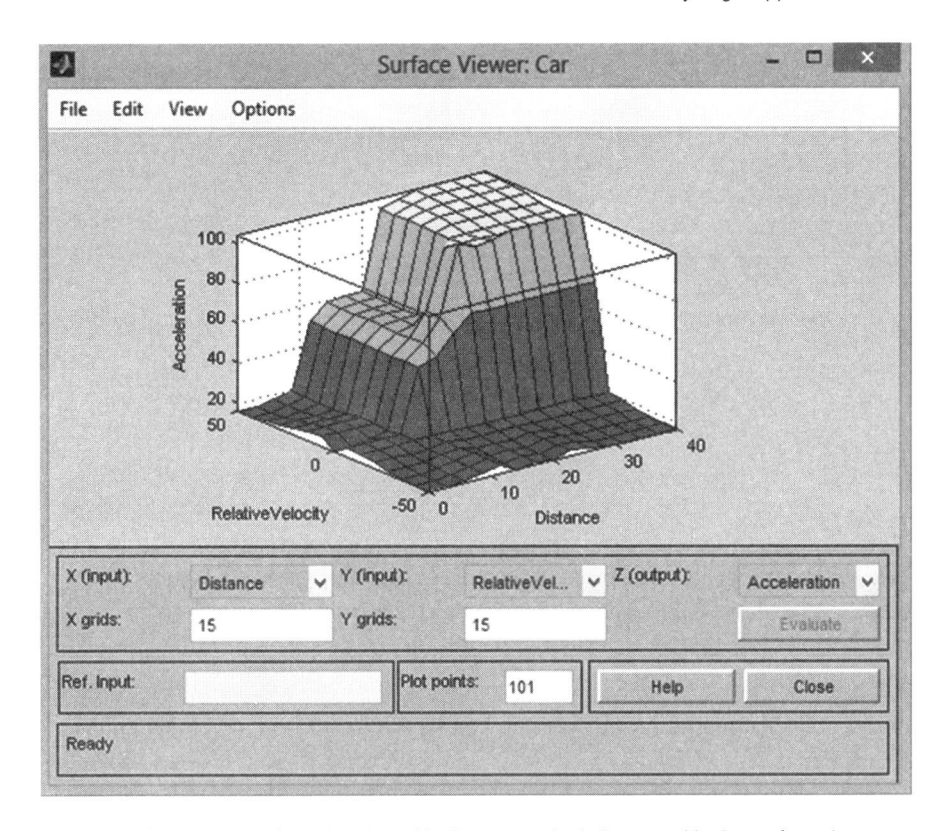

**Fig. 6.13** Variation of acceleration with distance and relative speed in the surface viewer

'Don't work so much, however, that you need to re-introduce yourself to your family'. Therefore, they decided to search for a groom with respect to height, working hours of at least 7 hr a day, and around the age of their daughter. They have three profiles, as given in Table 6.5, from their relatives such that the basic qualities such as human values, family background, and so on are fulfilled by all of them.

The input variables to the fuzzy systems are Height, Working Hours, and Age.

Table 6.5  Bridegroom profiles

| Name | Height (cm) | Working time (hours)/ Profession | Age |
|---|---|---|---|
| Raman | 179 | 9 (Teacher) | 24 |
| Rajesh | 189 | 6 (Real estate agent) | 35 |
| Ravi | 155 | 18 (Software engineer) | 21 |

These inputs can be classified into fuzzy sets as in Table 6.6.

Table 6.6  Fuzzy domain classification of input variables

| Input variable | Range | Fuzzy sets | Domain of fuzzy set |
| --- | --- | --- | --- |
| Height, cm | 50–200 | Short | 50–160 |
| | | Tall | 150–185 |
| | | Very tall | 180–200 |
| Working hours, hr/day | 0–24 | Low | 0–6 |
| | | Moderate | 4–10 |
| | | Very high | 9–24 |
| Age, yr | 18–40 | Low | 18–23 |
| | | Average | 20–26 |
| | | High | 25–40 |

**Step 1:** Let us define the membership function of each fuzzy set over the input variable range given in Table 6.6 (universe of discourse) (Figs 6.14, 6.15, and 6.16).
**Step 2:** Define the membership function of output

Let the output variable be fitness or likelihood of the candidate. Based on the fitness, the selection of a candidate can be classified into Poor, Average, and Good (Fig. 6.17).

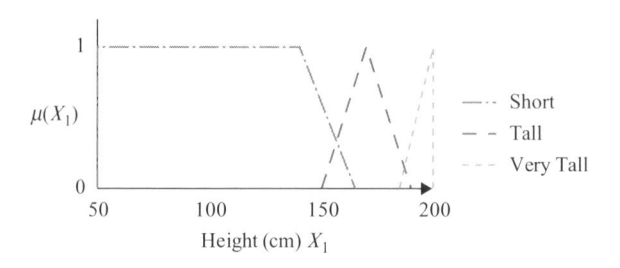

**Fig. 6.14**  Membership function of 'Height'

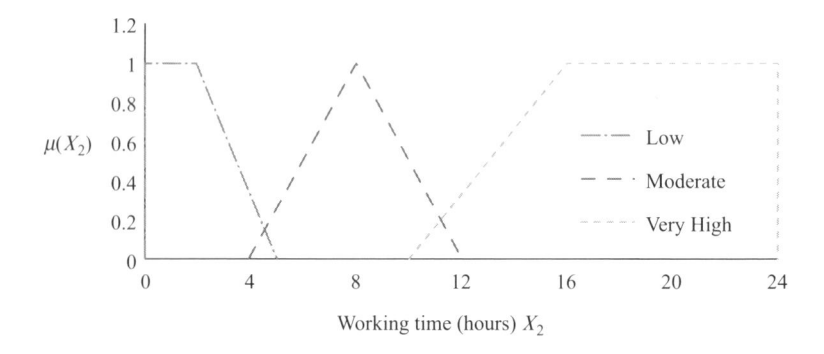

**Fig. 6.15**  Membership function of 'Working Time'

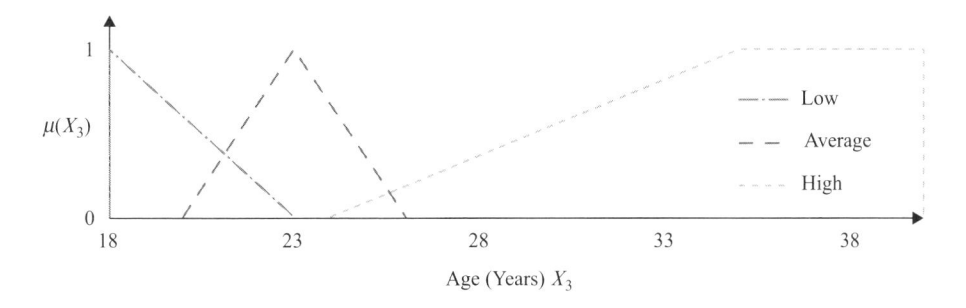

**Fig. 6.16** Membership function of 'Age'

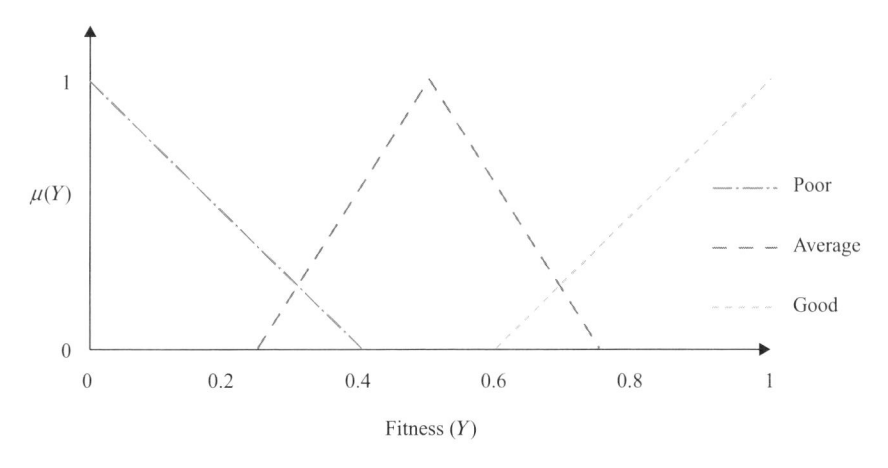

**Fig. 6.17** Membership function of 'Fitness'

**Step 3:** Enter the input and output variables in the FIS editor as in Fig. 6.18.
**Step 4:** Form the fuzzy rule base.

Rule base of this selection process can be framed with IF/THEN/ELSE terms. In this scenario, moderate working time, height = 170 cm, and age = 23 are considered as the best selection. Hence, we can frame rules accordingly as follows:

1. IF Height is Tall AND Working Time is Moderate AND Age is Average, then Fitness is Good.
2. IF Height is NOT Tall AND Working Time is NOT Moderate AND Age is NOT Average, then Fitness is Poor.
3. IF Height is NOT Tall OR Working Time is NOT Moderate OR Age is NOT Average, then Fitness is Average.

Similarly, $n$ number rules for all combination of inputs can be made.

**Step 5:** Enter the rules in the MATLAB FIS Rule editor as in Fig. 6.19.
**Step 6:** Evaluate the available bridegrooms.

The value of the membership function of all the grooms in each fuzzy set is given in Table 6.7.

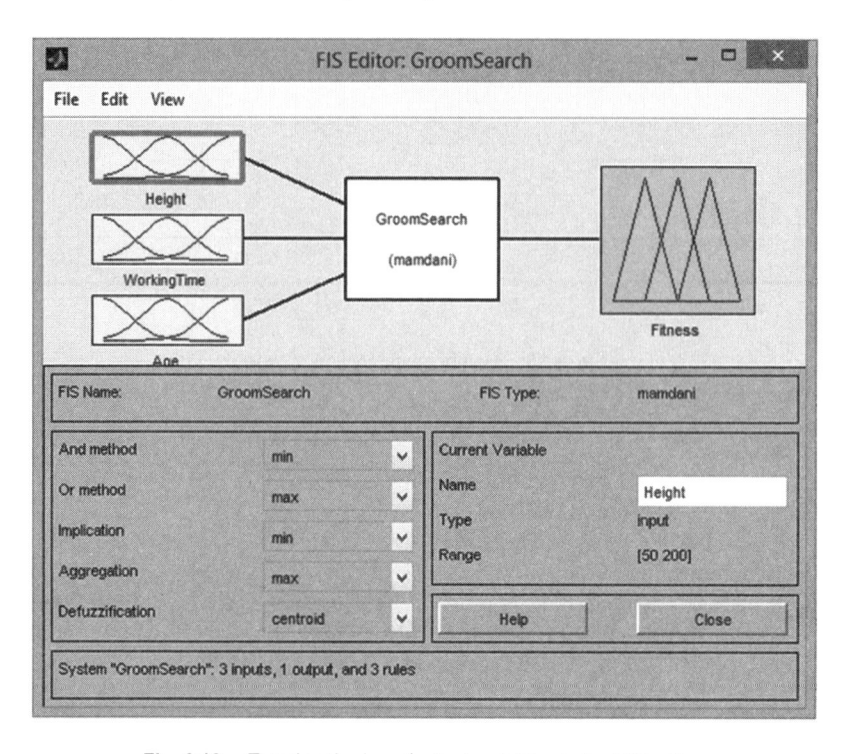

Fig. 6.18 Entering the input/output variables in the FIS editor

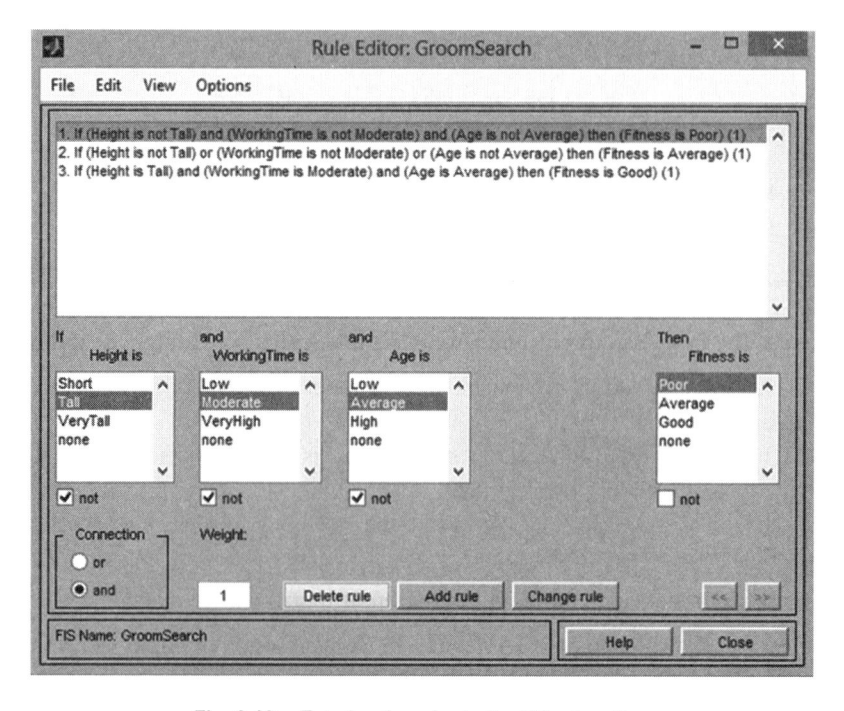

Fig. 6.19 Entering the rules in the FIS rule editor

Table 6.7  Membership function of the grooms

| Name | Height | | | Working hours | | | Age | | |
|---|---|---|---|---|---|---|---|---|---|
| | Short | Tall | Very tall | Low | Moderate | Very high | Low | Average | High |
| Raman | – | 0.55 | – | – | 0.78 | – | – | 0.35 | 1 |
| Rajesh | – | 0.08 | 0.18 | – | 0.5 | – | – | – | 1 |
| Ravi | 0.4 | 0.22 | – | – | – | 1 | 0.4 | 0.325 | – |

| To evaluate grooms we can use the following code in MATLAB |
|---|
| *In FIS* |
| Save the FIS as 'GroomSearch' and Export to work space. This will add a variable Groomsearch to workspace. |
| *In workspace* |
| BridegroomData = [179 10 25;189 6 35;155 18 21] |
| BridegroomData = |
| 179   10   25 |
| 189    6   35 |
| 155   18   21 |
| >> Selection = evalfis (BridegroomData, GroomSearch) |
| Selection = |
| 0.5096 |
| 0.3871 |
| 0.3437 |

The selection fitness values for the grooms are presented in Table 6.8.

Table 6.8  Selection fitness for each groom

| Name | Selection fitness |
|---|---|
| Raman | 0.5096 |
| Rajesh | 0.3871 |
| Ravi | 0.3437 |

According to the selection fitness, Raman is found to be the best compared with other available grooms.

## 6.3.3 Selection of Cricket Players from a Group of Players

Consider that a selection committee is selecting a team for a T-20 Cricket tournament. The information about the cricket players is given to the selectors as in Table 6.9.

Table 6.9  Profile of cricket players

| S. No. | Name | Total runs | Highest score | Batting average | Wickets | Stumpings |
|---|---|---|---|---|---|---|
| 1 | Tendul | 18426 | 200 | 44.83 | 154 | 0 |
| 2 | Rahal David | 10768 | 153 | 39.15 | 4 | 14 |
| 3 | M Alaudin | 9378 | 153 | 36.92 | 12 | 0 |
| 4 | SC Gangal | 11221 | 183 | 40.95 | 100 | 0 |
| 5 | Yuvaraja | 8119 | 139 | 36.9 | 108 | 0 |
| 6 | Kumblu | 903 | 26 | 10.37 | 334 | 0 |
| 7 | Seyag | 7995 | 219 | 35.37 | 94 | 0 |
| 8 | Srinathan | 883 | 53 | 10.63 | 315 | 0 |
| 9 | Harbhajulu | 1166 | 49 | 13.25 | 255 | 0 |
| 10 | N Kamil Devan | 3783 | 175 | 23.79 | 253 | 0 |
| 11 | M Dani | 7085 | 183 | 51.34 | 1 | 65 |
| 12 | A sadoja | 5359 | 119 | 37.47 | 20 | 0 |
| 13 | ZB Khan | 753 | 34 | 11.58 | 269 | 0 |
| 14 | AB Agarikan | 1269 | 95 | 14.58 | 288 | 0 |
| 15 | Prasad | 221 | 19 | 6.9 | 196 | 0 |
| 16 | Rana | 4068 | 116 | 36.98 | 19 | 0 |
| 17 | Shastori | 3108 | 109 | 29.04 | 129 | 0 |
| 18 | Gambhil | 5238 | 150 | 39.68 | 0 | 0 |
| 19 | Srikkanth | 4091 | 123 | 29.01 | 25 | 0 |
| 20 | Mongli | 1272 | 69 | 20.19 | 0 | 44 |
| 21 | Sindhu | 4413 | 134 | 37.08 | 0 | 0 |
| 22 | Robin | 2336 | 100 | 25.95 | 69 | 0 |
| 23 | Prabhakar | 1858 | 106 | 24.12 | 157 | 0 |
| 24 | Vengkar | 3508 | 105 | 34.73 | 0 | 0 |
| 25 | Kalif | 2753 | 111 | 32.01 | 0 | 0 |
| 26 | Parhan | 1544 | 83 | 23.39 | 173 | 0 |
| 27 | Nelra | 140 | 24 | 5.83 | 155 | 0 |
| 28 | Gavaskaro | 3092 | 103 | 35.13 | 1 | 0 |
| 29 | Kamabali | 2477 | 106 | 32.59 | 1 | 0 |
| 30 | Kolin | 4054 | 183 | 49.43 | 2 | 0 |
| 31 | Kimore | 563 | 42 | 13.09 | 0 | 27 |
| 32 | Shalma | 2065 | 114 | 30.82 | 8 | 0 |
| 33 | VV Lachumanan | 2338 | 131 | 30.76 | 0 | 0 |
| 34 | M Amar | 1924 | 102 | 30.53 | 46 | 0 |
| 35 | SV Manju | 1994 | 105 | 33.23 | 1 | 0 |
| 36 | Binny | 629 | 57 | 16.12 | 77 | 0 |

(Continued)

**Table 6.9** (Continued)

| S. No. | Name | Total runs | Highest score | Batting average | Wickets | Stumpings |
|---|---|---|---|---|---|---|
| 37 | Patel | 74 | 15 | 6.72 | 86 | 0 |
| 38 | Josli | 584 | 61 | 17.17 | 69 | 0 |
| 39 | Kumar | 292 | 54 | 13.9 | 77 | 0 |
| 40 | Madan bob | 401 | 53 | 19.09 | 73 | 0 |
| 41 | R Soroja | 1028 | 78 | 30.23 | 70 | 0 |
| 42 | Shama | 456 | 101 | 24 | 67 | 0 |
| 43 | Mahinderan | 49 | 8 | 12.25 | 66 | 0 |
| 44 | Rudra pratap | 104 | 23 | 10.4 | 69 | 0 |
| 45 | Dinesh M | 1230 | 159 | 27.95 | 14 | 0 |
| 46 | Y Palan | 810 | 123 | 27 | 33 | 0 |
| 47 | Ishanth | 61 | 13 | 5.08 | 76 | 0 |
| 48 | Raju | 32 | 8 | 4 | 63 | 0 |
| 49 | Sreejith | 44 | 10 | 4 | 75 | 0 |
| 50 | K Karthik | 1008 | 79 | 27.24 | 0 | 5 |

**Task for the selection committee**

[1] **Objective:** Select the 11 best players out of the available 50 players for the tournament ahead
[2] **Constraints:**
   (a) The playing squad should comprise of five batsmen, two all-rounders, one wicket keeper, and three bowlers
   (b) The performance of the players has to be judged based on total matches played, total runs scored, highest score, current performance, wickets, etc.
[3] **Input variables:**
   (a) Total score
   (b) Highest score
   (c) Batting average
   (d) Number of wickets taken
   (e) Number of stumping
[4] **Output variables:**
   (a) Batsman
   (b) Bowler
   (c) Wicketkeeper
   (d) All-rounder

**Key steps in fuzzy-based decision-making system using MATLAB**

1. Create a FIS using fuzzy prototype MATLAB commands.
2. Create membership function for both input and output variables and feed into FIS.
3. Form the rule base and evaluate the player performance using FIS.
4. Select the players according to maximum truth value.

The following section presents the detailed implementation part of the fuzzy-based decision-making system for the selection of the required cricket players.

The input variables available for the fuzzy system are the individual player's Total Score, Highest Score, Batting Average, Number of Wickets Taken, and Number of Stumping. The output variables are Batsman, Bowler, Wicketkeeper, and All-Rounder. Let us try to solve the problem in phases using MATLAB Programming.

**Step 1:** Add the player information by using following commands in MATLAB.

```
clear;                  % clear all prior variables
clc;                    % clear the command window
playerName = [
    {'Tendul'},...
    {'Rahal David'},...
    {'M Alaudin'},...
    {'SC Gangal'},...
         :
         :
         :
    {'K Karthik'}
    ];
% Input the player data
% Column1= Total Runs
% Column2= Highest Score
% Column3= Average Score
% Column4= Wickets Taken
% Column5= No of Stumpings
playerData = [
    18426   200  44.83   154  0
    10768   153  39.15     4  14
     9378   153  36.92    12  0
                   :
                   :
                   :
     1008    79  27.24     0  5];
```

**Step 2:** Create a new FIS in MATLAB using the function prototype.

```
playersel = newfis('team', 'mamdani', 'min', 'max', 'min', ...
                    'max', 'centroid');
% Example=newfis(fisName,fisType,and Method,or Method,implication
Method,...
%              aggregation Method,defuzzification Method)
```

**Step 3:** Create input variables.

```
playersel = addvar(playersel, 'input', 'totalruns', [0 20000]);
% Input No.1
% Argument 1 : fis name
% Argument 2 : specify if input or output
% Argument 3 : input name
% Argument 4 : span of crisp data values to be considered(Domain of
the fuzzy set)
playersel = addvar(playersel, 'input', 'highscore', [0 300]); %Input
No.2
playersel = addvar(playersel, 'input', 'bataverage', [0 70]); %Input
No.3
playersel = addvar(playersel, 'input', 'wickets', [0 500]); %Input
No.4
playersel = addvar(playersel, 'input', 'stumped', [0 70]); %Input
No.5
```

Each of the input variables has its own range (universe of discourse) and can be classified into fuzzy sets as in Table 6.10.

**Table 6.10** Fuzzy domain classification of input variables

| Input variable | Range | Fuzzy sets | Domain of fuzzy set |
| --- | --- | --- | --- |
| Total runs | 0–20,000 | Low | 0–200 |
| | | Average | 1000–6000 |
| | | High | 5000–20,000 |
| Highest score | 0–300 | Low | 0–40 |
| | | Average | 30–110 |
| | | High | 80–300 |
| Batting average | 0–70 | Low | 0–20 |
| | | Average | 15–45 |
| | | High | 30–70 |
| Wickets | 0–500 | Low | 0–60 |
| | | Average | 50–250 |
| | | High | 200–500 |
| Stumpings | 0–70 | Low | 0–30 |
| | | Average | 20–50 |
| | | High | 40–70 |

**Step 4:** Determine the membership function of each fuzzy set for the corresponding input variables. For example, the membership function for the input variable 'Total Runs' as Low, Average, and High is shown in Fig. 6.20.

**Step 5:** The information regarding membership functions of variable total runs can be fed into FIS through the following MATLAB commands.

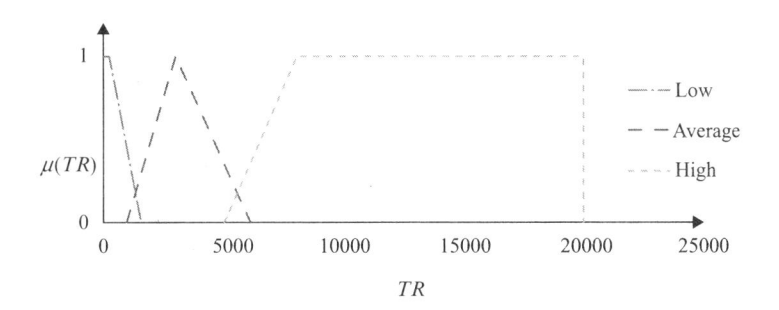

**Fig. 6.20** Membership function for 'Total Runs'

```
% Create membership functions for the input No1.(total runs scored)
playersel = addmf(playersel, 'input', 1, 'low', 'trapmf', [0 0 200 1500]);
% Argument 1 : fis name
% Argument 2 : specify if input or output member     function
% Argument 3 : input label. here, matches is the first input defined
%              and so has a label number 1
% Argument 4 : member function name
% Argument 5 : shape of member function. trimf stands for triangular
%              member
% Function and trapmf stands for trapezoidal member function
% Argument 6 : lower bound, max point and upper bound of member
%              Function

playersel = addmf(playersel, 'input', 1, 'avg', 'trimf', [1000 3000
6000]);
playersel = addmf(playersel, 'input', 1, 'high', 'trapmf', [5000 8000
20000 20000]);
```

**Step 6:** Similarly, describe membership function for all the input variables.

```
% Create membership functions for catches taken(Input No 2)
playersel = addmf(playersel, 'input', 2, 'low', 'trapmf', [0 0 20 40]);
playersel = addmf(playersel, 'input', 2, 'avg', 'trimf', [30 70 110]);
playersel = addmf(playersel, 'input', 2, 'high', 'trapmf', [80 150 300
300]);

% Create membership functions for batting average(Input No 3)
playersel = addmf(playersel, 'input', 3, 'low', 'trapmf', [0 0 10 20]);
playersel = addmf(playersel, 'input', 3, 'avg', 'trimf', [15 30 45]);
playersel = addmf(playersel, 'input', 3,'high', 'trapmf', [30 40 70 70]);

% Create membership functions for wickets taken(Input No 4)
playersel = addmf(playersel, 'input', 4, 'low', 'trapmf', [0 0 20 60]);
playersel = addmf(playersel, 'input', 4, 'avg', 'trimf', [50 150 250]);
playersel = addmf(playersel, 'input', 4, 'high', 'trapmf', [200 400 500
500]);

% Create membership functions for stumped(Input No 5)
playersel = addmf(playersel, 'input', 5, 'low', 'trapmf', [0 0 5 30]);
playersel = addmf(playersel, 'input', 5, 'avg', 'trimf', [20 35 50]);
playersel = addmf(playersel, 'input', 5, 'high', 'trapmf', [40 60 70 70]);
```

**Step 7:** Similarly, describe the membership function for all the output variables.

A cricket player can be classified into various categories such as opening batsman, middle order batsman, hard hitter, spin bowler, fast bowler, wicketkeeper, fielder, all-rounder, and so on. For simplicity let us classify the players as batsman, bowler, wicketkeeper, and all-rounder. Therefore, the output of the fuzzy decision-making system is batsman (Fig. 6.21), bowler, all-rounder, and wicketkeeper.

```
Playersel = addvar(playersel, 'output', 'batsman', [0 1]);
playersel = addvar(playersel, 'output', 'allround', [0 1]);
playersel = addvar(playersel, 'output', 'wktkeeper', [0 1]);
playersel = addvar(playersel, 'output', 'bowler', [0 1]);
```

**Step 8:** Define the membership functions for the output variables.

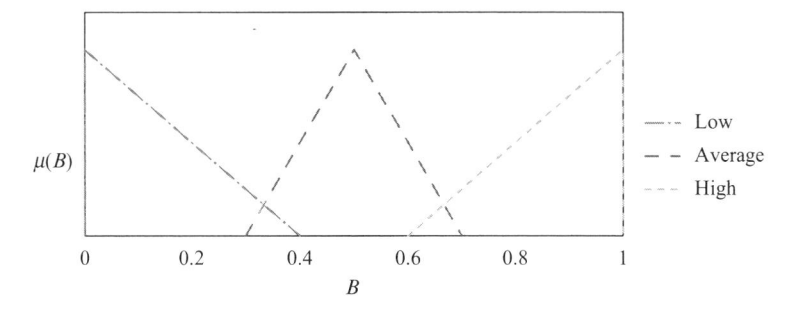

**Fig. 6.21** Membership function for 'Batsman'

Each player will have a degree of association in each output variable. For example, bowler would bat at some occasions and a batsman would have bowled at conditions when there was demand. Each output can be classified into fuzzy sets as Low, Average, and High. Each output can be given a range from 0 to 1. An individual having 0 in Batsman is a poor batsman and an individual having 1 in Batsman is a good batsman. Hence, the fuzzy set can be classified as follows:

1. Low (Poor batting attributes)
2. Average (Average batting attributes)
3. High (Good batting attributes)

A similar kind of fuzzy set explanation can be given to all the output variables.

**Step 9:** The information regarding membership functions of all output variables can be fed into FIS through following MATLAB commands:

```
% Create membership functions for output batsman selection
playersel = addmf(playersel, 'output', 1, 'low', 'trimf', [0 0 0.4]);
playersel = addmf(playersel, 'output', 1, 'avg', 'trimf', [0.3 0.5 0.7]);
playersel = addmf(playersel, 'output', 1, 'high', 'trimf', [0.6 1 1]);

% Create membership functions for output allround selection
playersel = addmf(playersel, 'output', 2, 'low', 'trimf', [0 0 0.4]);
playersel = addmf(playersel, 'output', 2, 'avg', 'trimf', [0.3 0.5 0.7]);
playersel = addmf(playersel, 'output', 2, 'high', 'trimf', [0.6 1 1]);

% Create membership functions for output wktkeeper selection
playersel = addmf(playersel, 'output', 3, 'low', 'trimf', [0 0 0.4]);
playersel = addmf(playersel, 'output', 3, 'avg', 'trimf', [0.3 0.5 0.7]);
playersel = addmf(playersel, 'output', 3, 'high', 'trimf', [0.6 1 1]);

% Create membership functions for output bowler selection
playersel = addmf(playersel, 'output', 4, 'low', 'trimf', [0 0 0.4]);
playersel = addmf(playersel, 'output', 4, 'avg', 'trimf', [0.3 0.5 0.7]);
playersel = addmf(playersel, 'output', 4, 'high', 'tipmf', [0.6 1 1]);
```

**Step 10:** Form the rule base as in Table 6.11.

Connect the input variables with output variables using the rule base. A rule base consists of IF/THEN statements. Each rule will have an antecedent. It may be AND or OR. Consider Rule 3 of Table 6.11.

Table 6.11 Formation of rule base

| S. No. | Total score | Highest runs | Batting average | Wickets | Stump-ings | Batsman | All rounder | Wicket-keeper | Bowler |
|---|---|---|---|---|---|---|---|---|---|
| 1 | LOW(1) | HIGH(3) | AVG(2) | LOW(1) | LOW(1) | LOW(1) | AVG(2) | LOW(1) | LOW(1) |
| 2 | AVG(2) | AVG(2) | AVG(2) | LOW(1) | LOW(1) | AVG(2) | LOW(1) | LOW(1) | LOW(1) |
| 3 | AVG(2) | HIGH(3) | AVG(2) | LOW(1) | LOW(1) | HIGH(3) | LOW(1) | LOW(1) | LOW(1) |
| 4 | AVG(2) | HIGH(3) | AVG(2) | LOW(1) | LOW(1) | HIGH(3) | LOW(1) | LOW(1) | LOW(1) |
| 5 | AVG(2) | HIGH(3) | HIGH(3) | LOW(1) | LOW(1) | HIGH(3) | LOW(1) | LOW(1) | LOW(1) |
| 6 | HIGH(3) | HIGH(3) | AVG(2) | AVG(2) | LOW(1) | HIGH(3) | LOW(1) | LOW(1) | AVG(2) |
| 7 | HIGH(3) | HIGH(3) | HIGH(3) | X | LOW(1) | HIGH(3) | LOW(1) | LOW(1) | LOW(1) |
| 8 | LOW(1) | AVG(2) | AVG(2) | LOW(1) | LOW(1) | LOW(1) | AVG(2) | LOW(1) | LOW(1) |
| 9 | AVG(2) | AVG(2) | AVG(2) | AVG(2) | LOW(1) | AVG(2) | AVG(2) | LOW(1) | AVG(2) |
| 10 | HIGH(3) | AVG(2) | AVG(2) | AVG(2) | LOW(1) | AVG(2) | AVG(2) | LOW(1) | AVG(2) |
| 11 | AVG(2) | HIGH(3) | AVG(2) | HIGH(3) | LOW(1) | HIGH(3) | HIGH(3) | LOW(1) | HIGH(3) |
| 12 | AVG(2) | AVG(2) | AVG(2) | HIGH(3) | LOW(1) | AVG(2) | HIGH(3) | LOW(1) | HIGH(3) |
| 13 | LOW(1) | LOW(1) | LOW(1) | X | AVG(2) | LOW(1) | LOW(1) | AVG(2) | LOW(1) |
| 14 | LOW(1) | LOW(1) | LOW(1) | X | HIGH(3) | LOW(1) | LOW(1) | HIGH(3) | LOW(1) |
| 15 | LOW(1) | AVG(2) | LOW(1) | X | AVG(2) | LOW(1) | LOW(1) | AVG(2) | LOW(1) |
| 16 | AVG(2) | AVG(2) | AVG(2) | X | AVG(2) | AVG(2) | LOW(1) | AVG(2) | LOW(1) |
| 17 | AVG(2) | AVG(2) | AVG(2) | X | HIGH(3) | AVG(2) | LOW(1) | HIGH(3) | LOW(1) |
| 18 | AVG(2) | HIGH(3) | AVG(2) | X | HIGH(3) | AVG(2) | LOW(1) | HIGH(3) | LOW(1) |
| 19 | HIGH(3) | HIGH(3) | AVG(2) | X | HIGH(3) | HIGH(3) | LOW(1) | HIGH(3) | LOW(1) |
| 20 | HIGH(3) | HIGH(3) | HIGH(3) | X | HIGH(3) | HIGH(3) | LOW(1) | HIGH(3) | LOW(1) |
| 21 | LOW(1) | LOW(1) | LOW(1) | AVG(2) | LOW(1) | LOW(1) | LOW(1) | LOW(1) | AVG(2) |
| 22 | LOW(1) | LOW(1) | LOW(1) | HIGH(3) | LOW(1) | LOW(1) | LOW(1) | LOW(1) | HIGH(3) |
| 23 | AVG(2) | LOW(1) | LOW(1) | AVG(2) | LOW(1) | LOW(1) | LOW(1) | LOW(1) | AVG(2) |
| 24 | AVG(2) | LOW(1) | LOW(1) | HIGH(3) | LOW(1) | LOW(1) | LOW(1) | LOW(1) | HIGH(3) |
| 25 | LOW(1) | AVG(2) | LOW(1) | AVG(2) | LOW(1) | LOW(1) | LOW(1) | LOW(1) | AVG(2) |
| 26 | LOW(1) | AVG(2) | LOW(1) | HIGH(3) | LOW(1) | LOW(1) | LOW(1) | LOW(1) | HIGH(3) |
| 27 | LOW(1) | LOW(1) | AVG(2) | AVG(2) | LOW(1) | LOW(1) | LOW(1) | LOW(1) | AVG(2) |
| 28 | LOW(1) | LOW(1) | AVG(2) | HIGH(3) | LOW(1) | LOW(1) | LOW(1) | LOW(1) | HIGH(3) |
| 29 | LOW(1) | AVG(2) | AVG(2) | AVG(2) | LOW(1) | LOW(1) | LOW(1) | LOW(1) | AVG(2) |
| 30 | LOW(1) | AVG(2) | AVG(2) | HIGH(3) | LOW(1) | LOW(1) | LOW(1) | LOW(1) | HIGH(3) |

**Rule 3**

| Total score | Highest runs | Batting average | Wickets | Stumpings | Batsman | All rounder | Wicket-keeper | Bowler |
|---|---|---|---|---|---|---|---|---|
| AVG(2) | HIGH(3) | AVG(2) | LOW(1) | LOW(1) | HIGH(3) | LOW(1) | LOW(1) | LOW(1) |

When the rule antecedent is 1, the rule may be formulated as '*If Total Score is 'Average' and Highest Runs is 'HIGH' and Batting Average is 'AVERAGE' and Wickets is 'LOW' and Stumpings is 'LOW', then Batsman is 'HIGH' and All Rounder is 'LOW' and Wicket keeper is 'LOW' and Bowler is 'LOW'*". If rule antecedent is 2, then OR operation will be carried out. Each rule can be given a weight ranging from 0 to 1. For adding Rule 3 in Table 6.11, we can use the following MATLAB command. This command consists of $m + n + 2$ number of columns. First m columns represent

ruleList = [2    3    2    1    1    3    1    1    1    1    1]

the input state (fuzzy set they belong to). '2' in the first column represents that the 'Total Run' is Average, and '3' in the second column represents that the 'Highest Runs' is High. The next n columns represent the output variables state. Column $m + n + 2$ (last column) represents whether 'AND' or 'OR' operation should be carried out between inputs. Column $m + n + 1$ represents the weight given to the rule.

**Step 11:** Add the rule base and evaluate the player data using FIS.

The rule base can be added to the FIS using the following MATLAB command.

```
% Add the rule base to the Fuzzy Inference System
playersel = addrule(playersel, ruleList);
% Evaluate the fis using the player data, member functions and rules
fuzzyOutput = evalfis(playerData, playersel);
```

The output of evaluation function will have output variables and likelihood of each player to be classified into the category in terms of membership function.

The best batsman can be picked by picking the one who has maximum truth function in the output batsman. As the numbers of batsmen in the squad will be five, the players with top five membership in the truth function $\mu_{Batsman}$ can be selected. The truth values obtained for individual players are presented in Table 6.12.

**Step 12:** Similarly, the best among each category can be picked and displayed using the following MATLAB code.

```
% Select one wicketkeeper and exclude him from further selection
[~,wicketkeeper] = max (outputCopy(:,3))
outputCopy(wicketkeeper,:) = zeros
% Select two all rounders and exclude from further selection
allrounder = zeros(2,1);
for i=1:2
    [~,allrounder(i)] = max (outputCopy(:,2));
    outputCopy(all rounder(i),:) = zeros;
end
```

```
% Select five batsmen and exclude from further selection
batsmen = zeros(5,1);
for i=1:5
    [~,batsmen(i)] = max (outputCopy(:,1));
    outputCopy(batsmen(i),:) = zeros;
end

% Select three bowlers and exclude from further selection
bowlers = zeros(3,1);
for i=1:3
    [~,bowlers(i)] = max (outputCopy(:,2));
    outputCopy(bowlers(i),:) = zeros;
end
% Display playing 11
disp('BATSMEN');
for i=1:5
    disp(playerName(batsmen(i)));
end
disp('ALLROUNDERS');
for i=1:2
    disp ( playerName(allrounder(i)));
end
disp('WICKET KEEPER');
disp (playerName(wicketkeeper));

disp('BOWLERS');
for i=1:3
    disp (playerName(bowlers(i)));
end
```

**Table 6.12** Truth values evaluated for individual player

| Player No. | $\mu_{Batsman}$ | $\mu_{Allrounder}$ | $\mu_{Wicketkeeper}$ | $\mu_{Bowler}$ |
|---|---|---|---|---|
| 1 | 0.8700 | 0.1300 | 0.1300 | 0.1368 |
| 2 | 0.8567 | 0.1433 | 0.1433 | 0.1433 |
| 3 | **0.8597** | **0.1403** | **0.1403** | **0.1403** |
| 4 | 0.8700 | 0.1300 | 0.1300 | 0.2429 |
| 5 | 0.8596 | 0.1404 | 0.1404 | 0.3052 |
| 6 | 0.1560 | 0.1560 | 0.1560 | 0.8440 |
| 7 | 0.8498 | 0.1502 | 0.1502 | 0.3109 |
| 8 | 0.1549 | 0.1549 | 0.1549 | 0.8451 |
| 9 | 0.1730 | 0.1730 | 0.1730 | 0.8270 |
| 10 | 0.8277 | 0.8277 | 0.1723 | 0.8277 |
| 11 | 0.8599 | 0.1401 | 0.8599 | 0.1401 |
| ⋮ | | | | |
| 50 | | | | |

**Step 13:** The selection made from the previous database using the fuzzy-based MATLAB Program is given in Table 6.13.

**Table 6.13** Selected players

| S. No. | Batsmen | All rounders | Wicketkeeper | Bowlers |
|---|---|---|---|---|
| 1 | Tendul | N Kamil Devan | M Dani | Shastori |
| 2 | SC Gangal | Y Palan | | Prabhakar |
| 3 | M Alaudin | | | Parhan |
| 4 | Yuvaraja | | | |
| 5 | VV Lachumanan | | | |

### 6.3.4 Illustration of Hydel Power Plant Operation Estimation

In a hydel power plant, water is collected in huge amount by constructing a dam across the river. The collected water in the dam stores energy as potential energy. The water from the dam is fed into a powerhouse situated below the dam. Due to the difference in the level of the head, between the dam and powerhouse, the potential energy in water is converted into kinetic energy as the water moves towards the powerhouse from the dam. The powerhouse consists of turbine and generator. The amount of power produced by the powerhouse can be controlled by varying the water flow rate. The water flow rate can be governed by a valve situated in the penstock (Fig. 6.22).

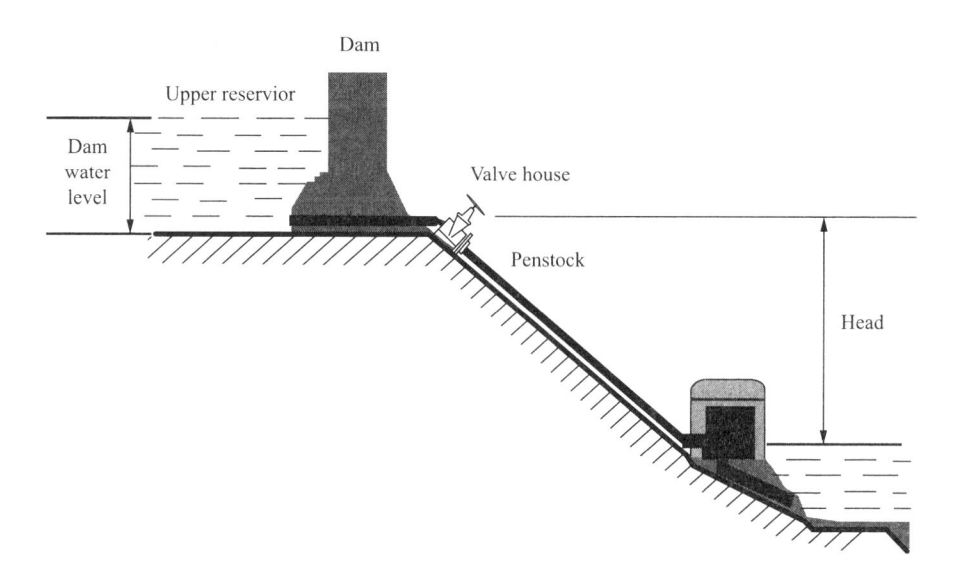

**Fig. 6.22** Sketch of a hydel power plant

Consider a hydel power plant with a dam of height 165 m. The dam is connected to an upstream that has a flow rate ranging from 0 to 3000 l/s. The safe water level of the dam is 130 m. An increase in water level will affect the stability of the dam. Decrease in water level will affect future water requirement. In order to maintain the water level within safe limits, the amount of water flowing out of the dam is regulated. The water flowing out of the dam is fed into the powerhouse. This variation in water flow rate in turn varies the power output of powerhouse.

Let us consider power output as the output variable, and the input variables influencing the power output are water flow rate entering into the dam and water level of the dam.

If the input water flow rate is slow and water level of dam is below a certain limit, the amount of water released from the dam is low. As the amount of water entering the powerhouse is low, the power generated from the plant is also low.

If the input water flow rate is slow and water level of dam is within the limits, then the power output of the plant is low. Similarly, if the input water flow rate is high and the water level in the dam is within the limits, then the power output of the plant is high. If the input water flow rate is high and water level of the dam is maximum, then the amount of water released from the dam is very high. At this very high water flow rate, the powerhouse should be bypassed in order to safeguard the equipments placed in the powerhouse. The power generated by the powerhouse at this condition is zero. From the aforementioned operations, we can infer that the hydel power plant is non-linear.

Consider three fuzzy sets describing the variable input water flow rate. These fuzzy sets are labelled as SLOW, MED, and FAST. Similarly, the other input variable water levels have three fuzzy sets with labels LOW, SAFE, and HIGH. The fuzzy membership representations of input variables are shown in Fig. 6.23.

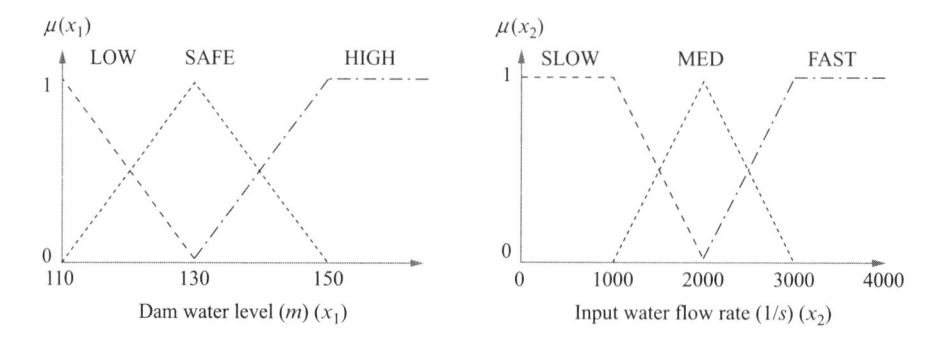

**Fig. 6.23** Fuzzy membership function for input variables

Note that there are two input variables and each input variable consists of three fuzzy sets. Therefore, there will be nine propositions. Thus in general, if $n$ is the number of fuzzy sets representing one input variable and $m$ is the number of fuzzy sets representing the second input variable, then the maximum number of propositions that can be written is $m \times n$. However, there may be some propositions which have no significance. Hence, they are not valid. Consider that the output variable power has three fuzzy sets with labels ZERO, MED, and HIGH (Fig. 6.24).

```
                μ(y)
                 ▲
          ZERO      MED       HIGH
         1 ┤
           │
           │
           │
           │
         0 └────────────────────────▶
           0         50         100
               Power output (MW) (y)
```

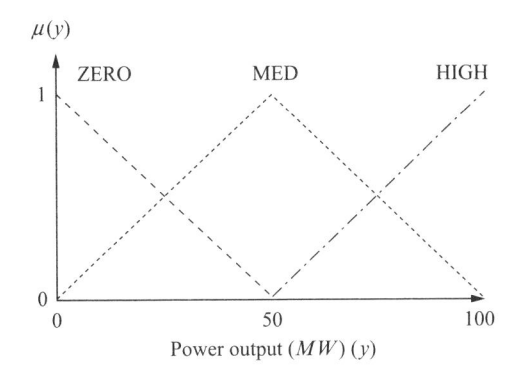

**Fig. 6.24**  Fuzzy membership function for input variables

The valid propositions for the example under consideration are as follows:

1. If (InputWaterFlowRate is SLOW) and (DamWaterLevel is LOW), then (PowerOutput is ZERO).
2. If (InputWaterFlowRate is SLOW) and (DamWaterLevel is SAFE) then (PowerOutput is ZERO).
3. If (InputWaterFlowRate is SLOW) and (DamWaterLevel is HIGH) then (PowerOutput is MED).
4. If (InputWaterFlowRate is MED) and (DamWaterLevel is LOW) then (Power Output is ZERO).
5. If (InputWaterFlowRate is MED) and (DamWaterLevel is SAFE) then (Power Output is MED).
6. If (InputWaterFlowRate is MED) and (DamWaterLevel is HIGH) then (Power Output is HIGH).
7. If (InputWaterFlowRate is FAST) and (DamWaterLevel is LOW) then (Power Output is MED).
8. If (InputWaterFlowRate is FAST) and (DamWaterLevel is SAFE) then (Power Output is HIGH).
9. If (InputWaterFlowRate is FAST) and (DamWaterLevel is HIGH) then (Power Output is ZERO).

When the number of fuzzy sets describing the input variable increases, the number of proposition also increases. Hence, writing all propositions is a tedious job. In order to avoid this difficulty, a matrix representation is followed. The matrix representation connecting input and output variable is called *fuzzy associative memory* (FAM) (Fig. 6.25).

| Flow Rate \ Water Level | LOW  | SAFE | HIGH |
|---|---|---|---|
| SLOW | ZERO | ZERO | MED  |
| MED  | ZERO | MED  | HIGH |
| FAST | MED  | HIGH | ZERO |

**Fig. 6.25**  Fuzzy associative memory

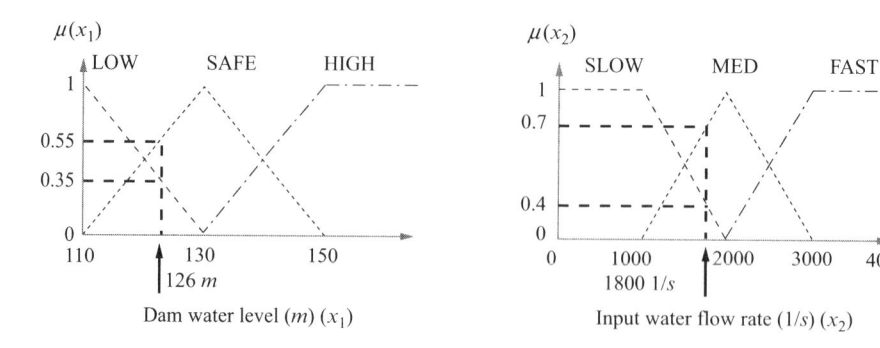

**Fig. 6.26** Triggering of the fuzzy rule

In fuzzy system the input variable is fuzzified. According to the fuzzified inputs the corresponding rules are evaluated. Deriving the consequent fuzzy set from the input fuzzy set and rules is called implication method. For the current example, let us use Mamdani min implication and min interpretation of AND (DOF).

For instance, consider the value of input water flow rate as 1800 l/s and the dam water level as 126 m (Fig. 6.26).

The numerical value of input is converted into fuzzy membership. The fuzzified values of 126 m dam water level are 0.35 LOW and 0.55 SAFE. The fuzzified values of 1,800 l/s Input water flow rate are 0.4 SLOW and 0.7 MED.

The fuzzy propositions which will be triggered for the previous input values are as follows:

1. If (InputWaterFlowRate is SLOW) and (DamWaterLevel is LOW) then (Power Output is ZERO).
2. If (InputWaterFlowRate is SLOW) and (DamWaterLevel is SAFE) then (Power Output is ZERO).
3. If (InputWaterFlowRate is MED) and (DamWaterLevel is LOW) then (Power Output is ZERO).
4. If (InputWaterFlowRate is MED) and (DamWaterLevel is SAFE) then (Power Output is MED).

| Flow rate \ Water level | LOW | SAFE | HIGH |
|---|---|---|---|
| SLOW | ZERO | ZERO | MED |
| MED | ZERO | MED | HIGH |
| FAST | MED | HIGH | ZERO |

**Fig. 6.27** Fuzzy associative memory

Figure 6.27 shows the triggered rules in the FAM. When the first rule is evaluated, the truth of the predicate is taken as minimum of membership grades of the two input fuzzy sets (0.4 SLOW and 0.35 LOW, i.e., AND (0.4, 0.35) = min {0.4, 0.35} = 0.35). Thus the consequent fuzzy set ZERO is selected with truth of 0.35.

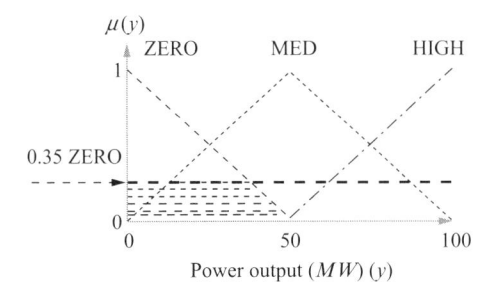

**Fig. 6.28** Fuzzy output of the first rule

In a similar manner, when the next rule is evaluated, 0.4 SLOW and 0.55 MED will select output fuzzy set ZERO with the truth value of 0.4 (min {0.4, 0.55}). Thus, depending upon the value of fuzzy singleton (Numerical value of the input variable), the truth of consequent fuzzy set is identified. Once the truth of consequent fuzzy set is identified, shaping of consequent fuzzy set is carried out using Mamdani min implication operator.

If Mamdani min is used for shaping the consequent fuzzy set, the consequent fuzzy set will be selected as shown in Fig. 6.28 (shaded portion). Here, the output fuzzy set ZERO is truncated at the truth level 0.35. The output fuzzy sets extracted from each triggered rule is given in Table 6.14.

**Table 6.14** Output fuzzy sets extracted from each triggered rule

| Rules to be executed | Output truth value | Output fuzzy set |
|---|---|---|
| If (InputWaterFlowRate is SLOW) and (DamWaterLevel is LOW) then (PowerOutput is ZERO). | 0.4 SLOW **AND** 0.35 LOW→0.35 ZERO. min{0.4, 0.35} = 0.35 | |
| If (InputWaterFlowRate is SLOW) and (DamWaterLevel is SAFE) then (PowerOutput is ZERO). | 0.4 SLOW **AND** 0.55 SAFE→0.4 ZERO. min{0.4, 0.55} = 0.4 | |

*(Continued)*

**Table 6.14** (Continued)

| Rules to be executed | Output truth value | Output fuzzy set |
|---|---|---|
| If (InputWaterFlowRate is MED) and (DamWaterLevel is LOW) then (PowerOutput is ZERO). | 0.7 MED **AND** 0.35 LOW→0.35 ZERO | $\mu(y)$ vs Power output (MW) ($y$): ZERO, MED, HIGH membership functions; ZERO truncated at 0.35 (0.35 ZERO). |
| If (InputWaterFlowRate is MED) and (DamWaterLevel is SAFE) then (PowerOutput is MED). | 0.7 MED **AND** 0.55 SAFE→0.55 MED | $\mu(y)$ vs Power output (MW) ($y$): ZERO, MED, HIGH membership functions; MED truncated at 0.55 (0.55 MED). |

The output fuzzy region will be the aggregated fuzzy regions that is obtained by combining the truncated fuzzy sets resulted due to execution of all valid proposition and is given Fig. 6.29. The process of obtaining numerical value of output from output fuzzy region is called as de-fuzzification. The commonly employed de-fuzzification method is COA and formula is given in Eq. (6.24).

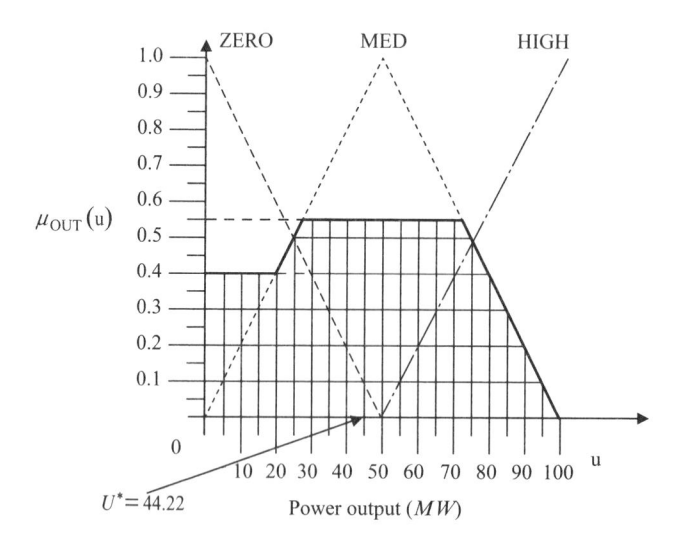

$U^* = 44.22$

**Fig. 6.29** Aggregated fuzzy output as shaded part

$$u^* = \frac{\sum_{i=1}^{N} u_i \mu_{\text{OUT}}(u_i)}{\sum_{i=1}^{N} \mu_{\text{OUT}}(u_i)} \qquad (6.24)$$

$$U^* = \frac{\begin{array}{c}(10 \times 0.4) + (20 \times 0.4) + (25 \times 0.5) + (27.5 \times 0.55) \\ +(50 \times 0.55) + (72.5 \times 0.55) + (80 \times 0.4) + (90 \times 0.2)\end{array}}{(0.4 + 0.4 + 0.5 + 0.55 + 0.55 + 0.4 + 0.2)} = \frac{157}{3.55} = 44.22 \quad (6.25)$$

In our example, the de-fuzzified output value considering the aforementioned truncated fuzzy set is 44.22 MW.

#### 6.3.4.1 MATLAB Implementation of Hydel Plant Output Estimation

The MATLAB implementation of hydel power plant output estimation can be carried out using FL tool box with the help of GUI called fuzzy inference system (FIS editor). The step-by-step procedure is given here:

**Step 1:** Type 'fuzzy' in MATLAB command window. This will open the GUI-FIS editor as in Fig. 6.30.

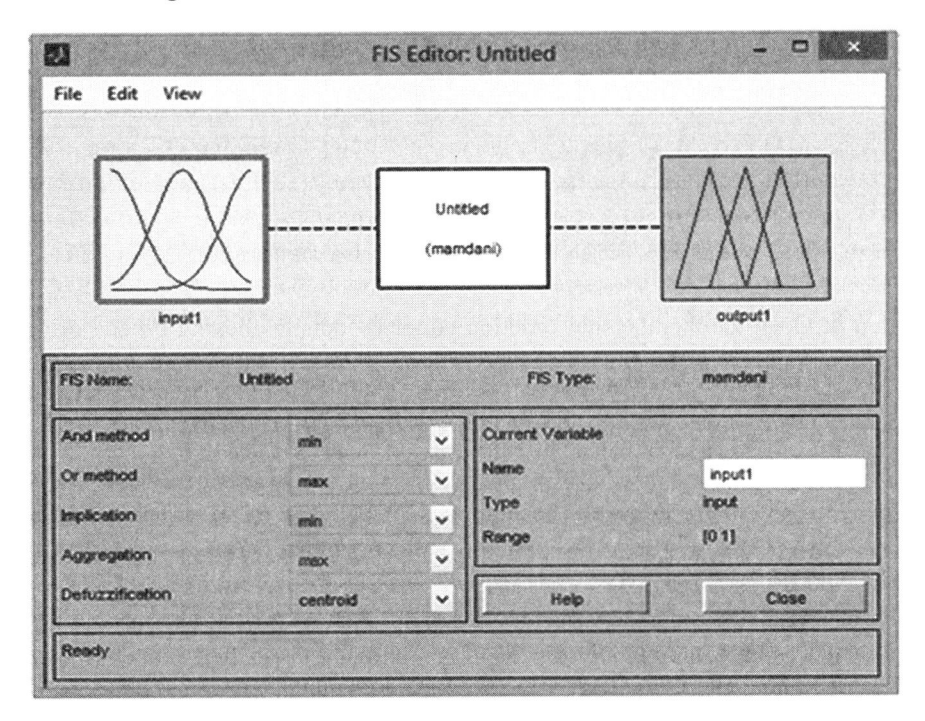

**Fig. 6.30** FIS editor

**Step 2:** Add required number of input variables by clicking EDIT/ADD VARIABLE/ INPUT (or) OUTPUT in the FIS editor. In our example, the number of inputs are 2 and the number of output is 1.

**Step 3:** Give names to the input and output variables in the Name box as in Fig. 6.31.

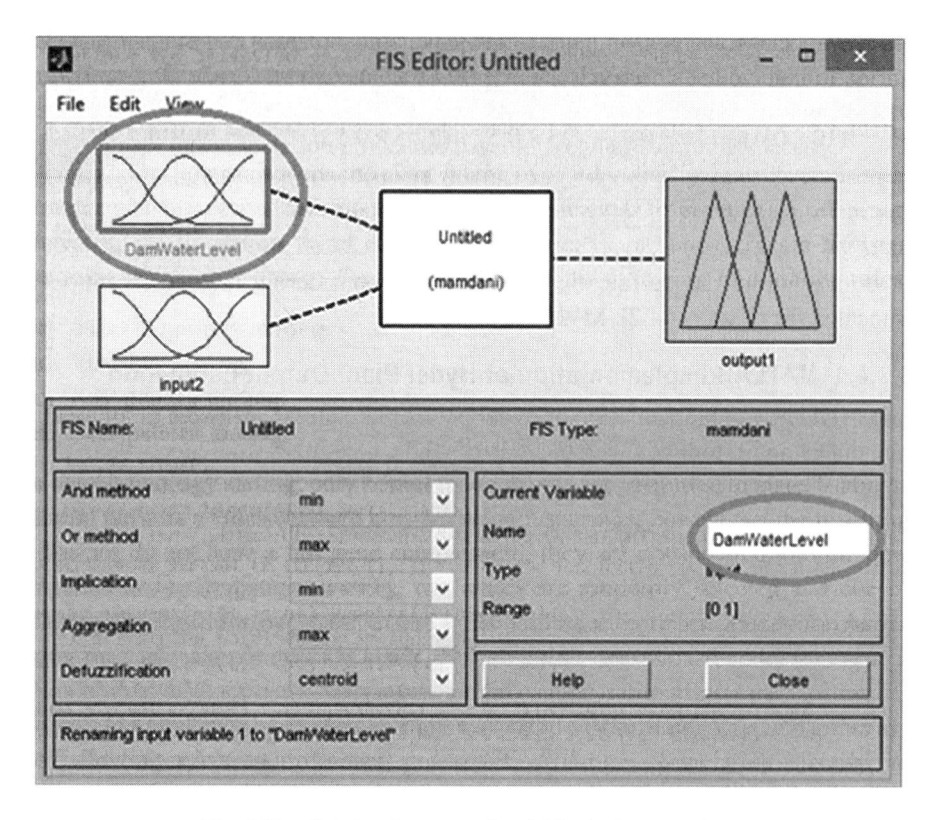

**Fig. 6.31** Entering the name of variables in the name box

**Step 4:** Open the membership function editor by double-clicking on any of the input variables or output variables. This will open the membership function editor as in Fig. 6.32.

**Step 5:** Configure the membership function of each variable.

(a) Click on the variable whose membership function needs to be configured. This will show the membership functions associated with the variable. By default each variable will have three membership functions with labels $MF_1$, $MF_2$, and $MF_3$ as in Fig. 6.33.
(b) Configure the range of variable.
(c) Click on any of the membership function. Configure Name, Type, and parameters associated. The types of MF may be trapezoidal, triangular, sigmoidal, etc. The parameters associated with MF are the edge points (Alpha cuts) (Fig. 6.34).
(d) After configuring the membership function of all the variables, close the membership function editor by clicking the cross button on the right top of the GUI.

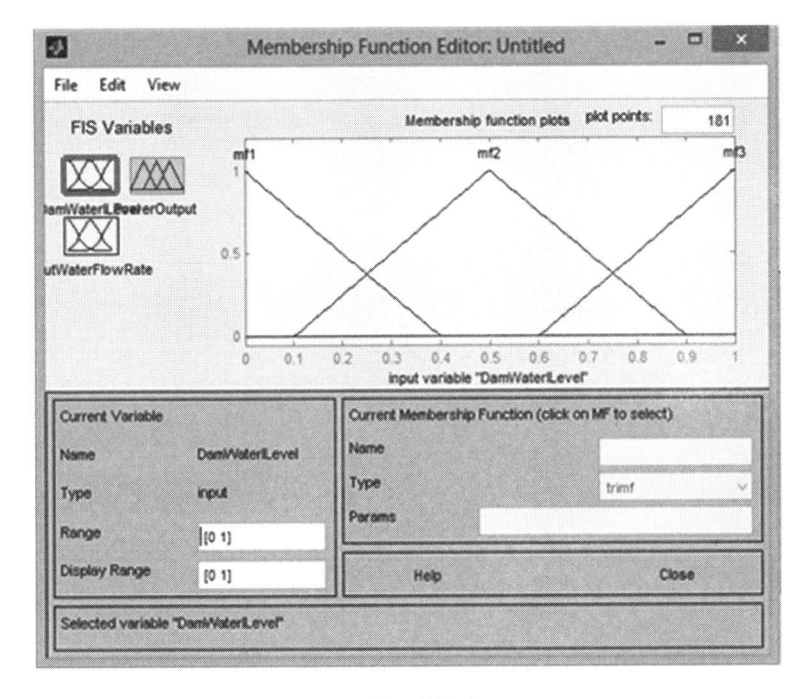

Fig. 6.32 MF editor

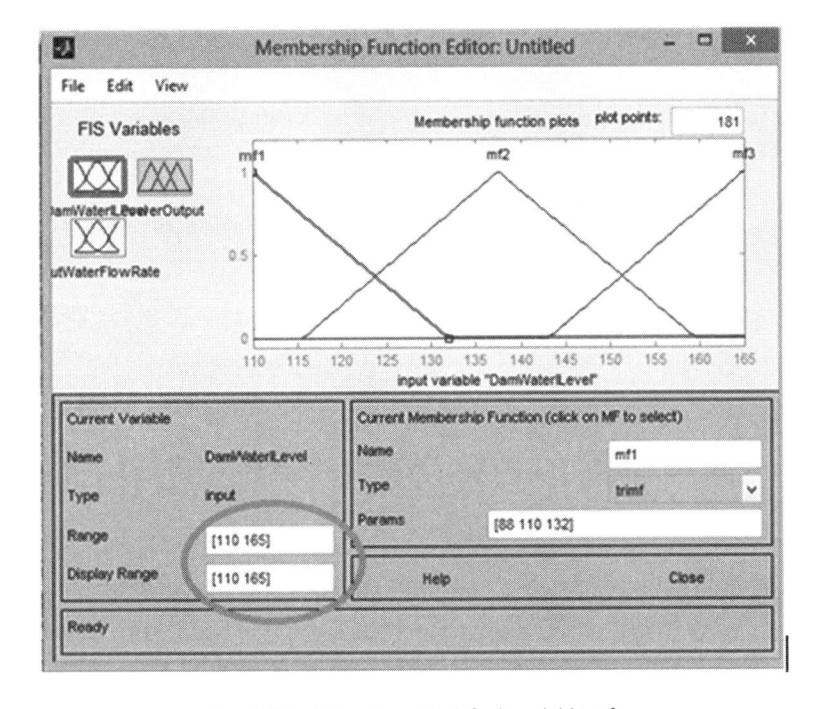

Fig. 6.33 MF editor with default variable mf$_1$

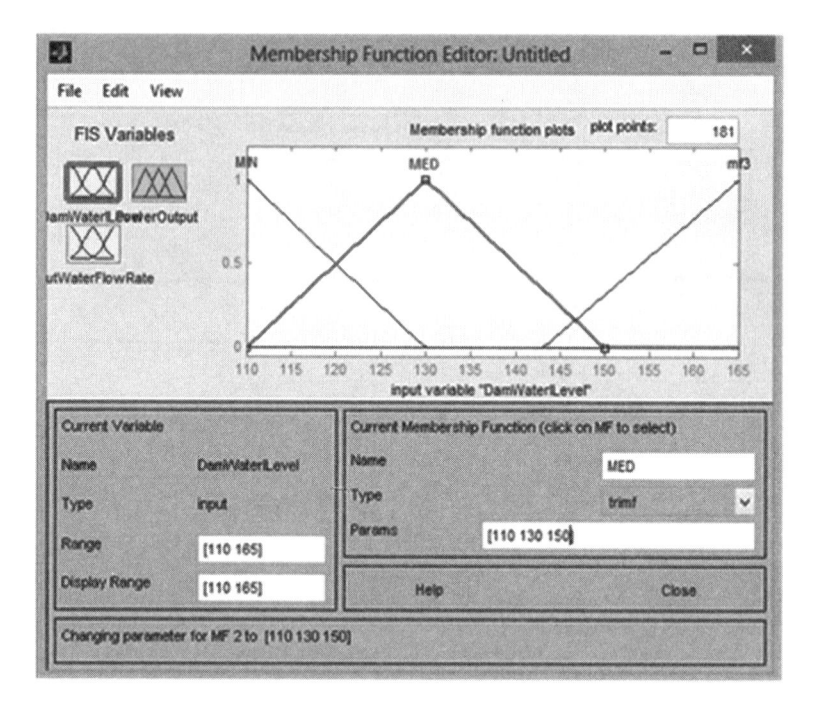

**Fig. 6.34** Configuration of a membership function 'MED'

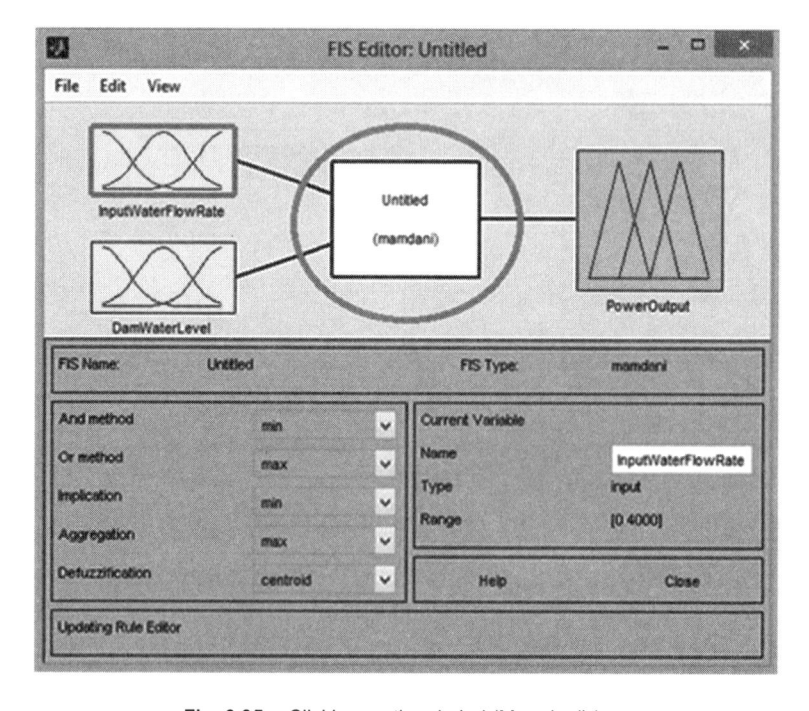

**Fig. 6.35** Clicking on the circled (Mamdani) box

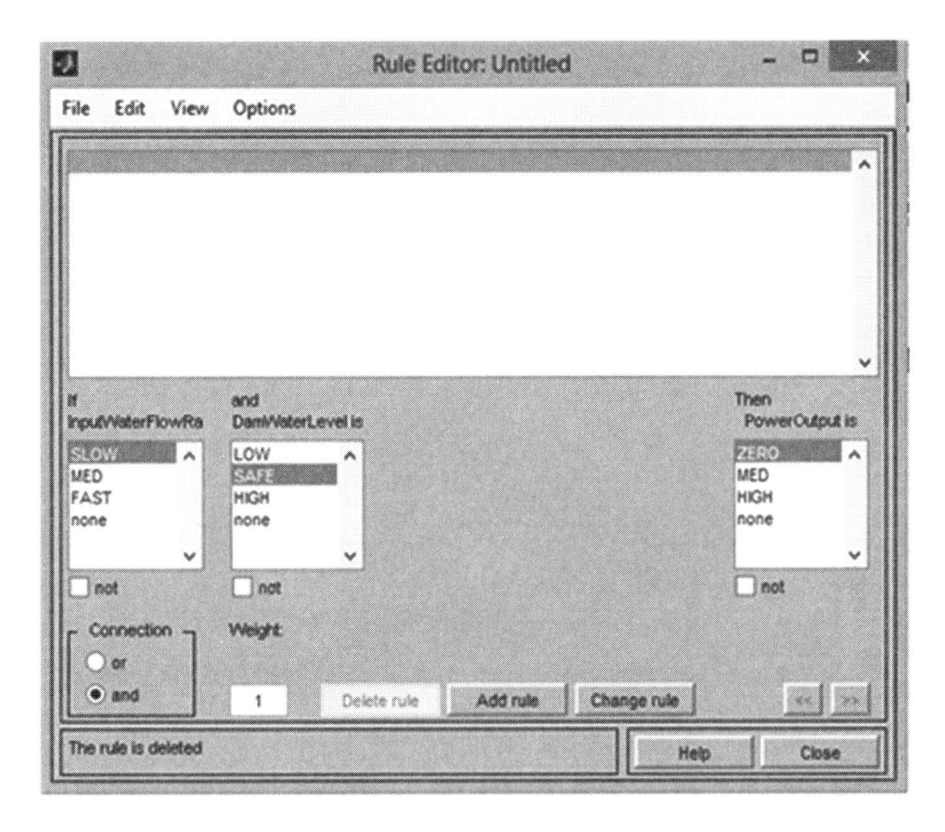

**Fig. 6.36** Opening of the rule editor

**Step 6:** Configure the rules as follows:

(a) Double-click on the 'mamdani' box in the FIS editor as in Fig. 6.35. This will open the rule editor as in Fig. 6.36.
(b) Select the input variable fuzzy sets, fuzzy operator (AND, OR, NOT), and fuzzy output set corresponding to the rule. Select a weight to the rule. Click on ADD RULE button to add the corresponding rule as in Fig. 6.37.
(c) Similarly, configure all the rules and close the rule editor as in Fig. 6.38.

**Step 7:** Save the FIS by clicking File/Export/To File. Give the name for the FIS as 'HydelPlantController'.

**Step 8:** View the Rule Viewer and Surface Viewer by clicking on view button as in Figs 6.39 and 6.40, respectively.

By using rule viewer, the value of the power output for various input values can be obtained. The surface viewer will show input-output relation graphically. In Fig. 6.39, all the nine rules are considered together and aggregated. Here, for an input flow rate of 2000 l/s and 82.5 m height of water level in the dam, the power output obtained is 16.2 MW. However, if we need to see the variation in the output for a continuous change in input, then it can be achieved by calling the saved FIS in Simulink block sets.

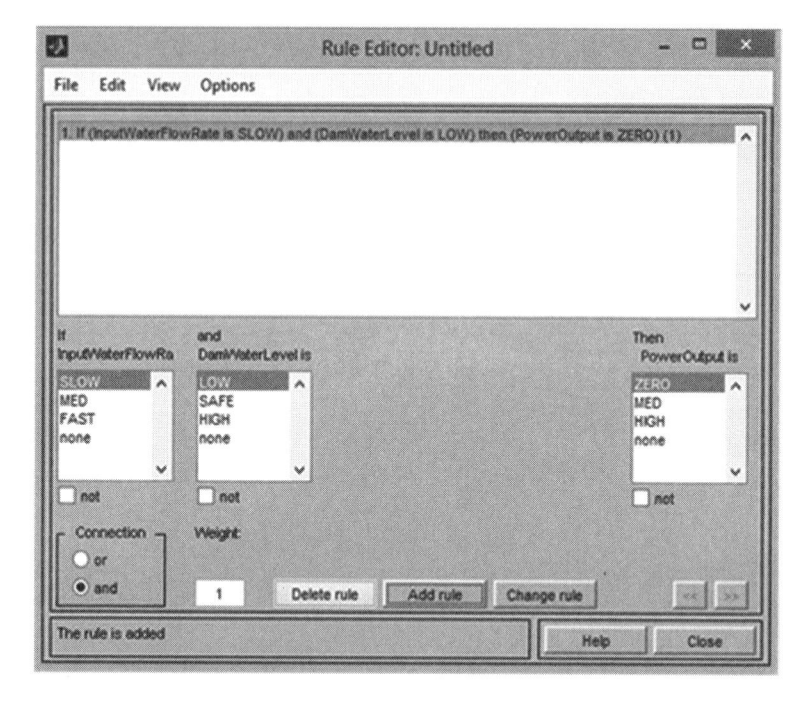

**Fig. 6.37** Entering the first rule

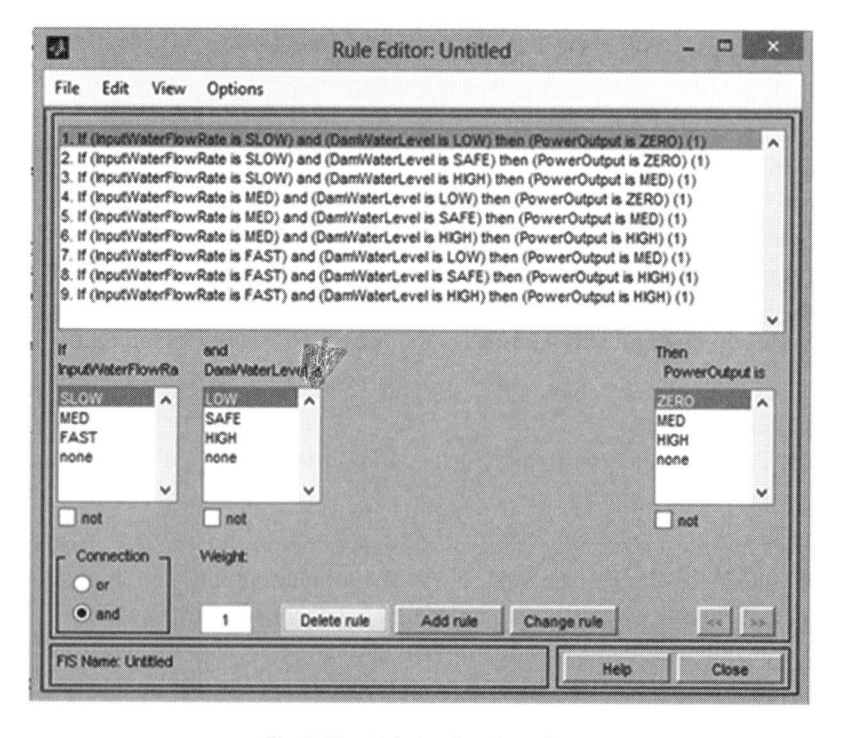

**Fig. 6.38** Entering the nine rules

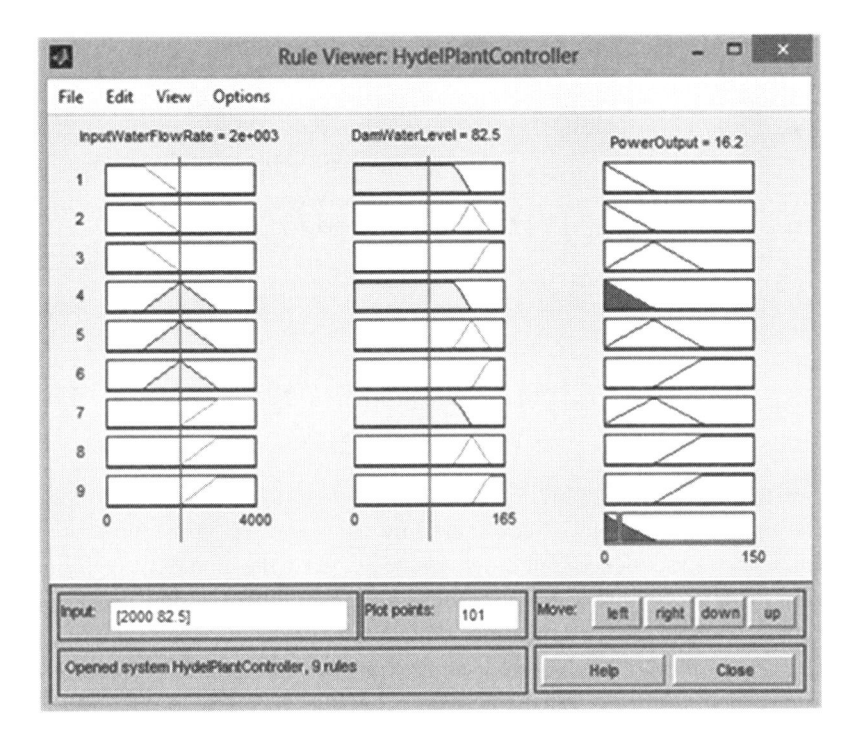

Fig. 6.39 Rule viewer

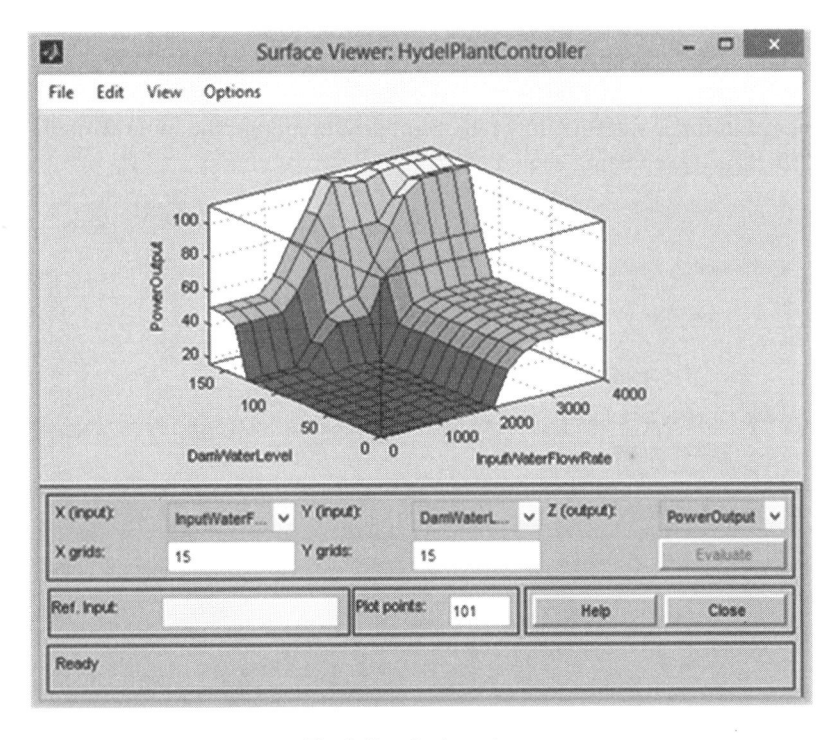

Fig. 6.40 Surface viewer

**432** Soft Computing with MATLAB Programming

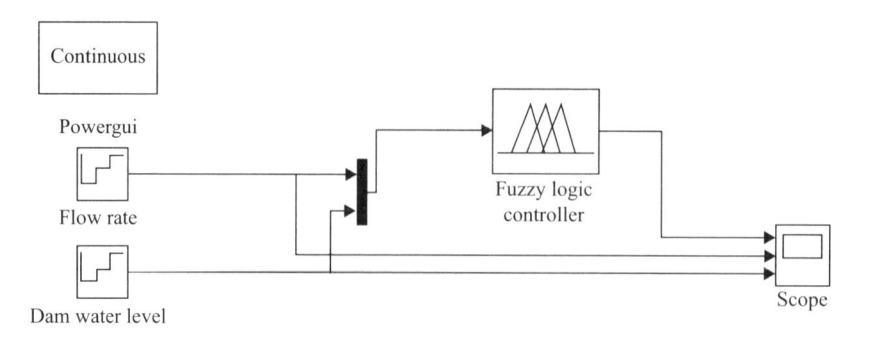

**Fig. 6.41** Fuzzy logic controller in the simulink mode

**Step 9:** Using Simulink, create a new model. Draw the following model with the Simulink block sets as given in Fig. 6.41.

(a) The input variable can be configured by using the repeating sequence stair. The repeating sequence stair block can be placed in the model by the following steps. Click on library browser button in Simulink window → Simulink toolbox → Sources → Repeating sequence stair.
(b) The vector of output values and sample time are configured by entering those values in the repeating sequence stair. Let the vector of output values for 'Flow Rate' be 50, 1500, and 2800 and the sampling time be 0.3 as shown in Fig. 6.42. In addition, the vector of output values for 'Dam Water Level' is [100 125 160] and the sampling time is 0.1 as in Fig. 6.43.

The output of the repeating sequence stair will have a magnitude of 50 for 0.3 sec, 1500 from 0.3 sec to 0.6 sec, and 2800 from 0.6 to 0.9 sec. This will simulate the change in input variable flow rate. Similarly, configure the input variable dam water level using repeating sequence stair.

**Fig. 6.42** Repeating sequence stair for flow rate

Fuzzy Logic Applications  433

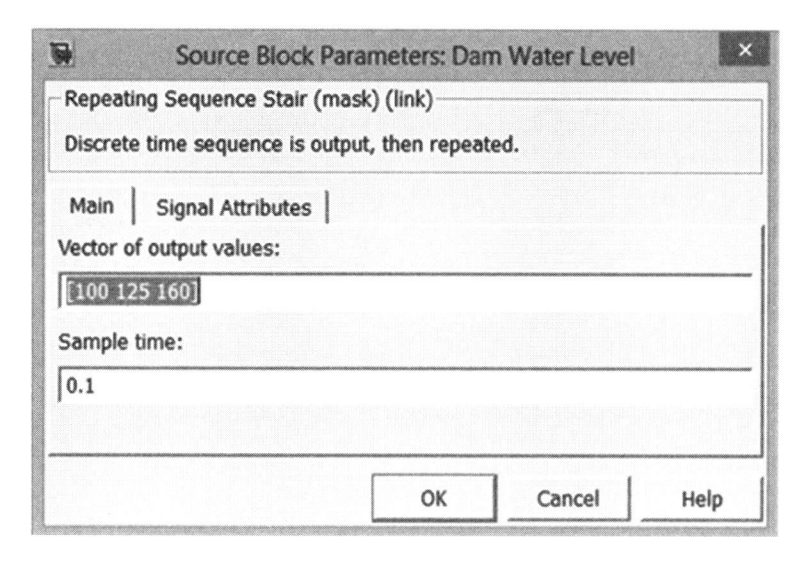

**Fig. 6.43** Repeating sequence stair for dam water level

(c) The HydelPlantController FIS can be called in to MATLAB by using FL controller block from the Simulink library browser → fuzzy logic toolbox → fuzzy logic controller.

(d) Double-click on the FL controller block and give the FIS file name between two single quotes as in Fig. 6.44.

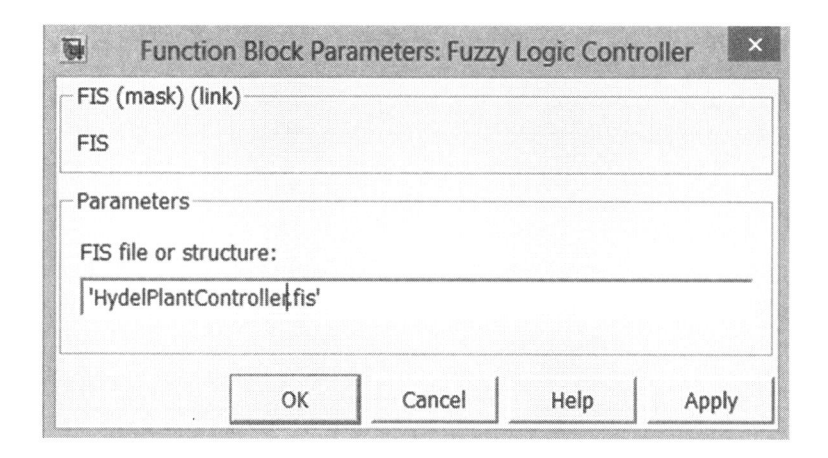

**Fig. 6.44** FIS file name

(e) The inputs of the FIS can be fed into FL controller by using multiplexer.

**Step 10:** Save the model and run it. The inputs and outputs of the hydel power plant operation estimator are given in Fig. 6.45. Here, the input variable of water flow rate varies every 0.3 sec and the input variable dam water level varies every 0.1 sec. The variations in output power generated by the hydel power plant for various values of input variables are clearly observed in Fig. 6.45.

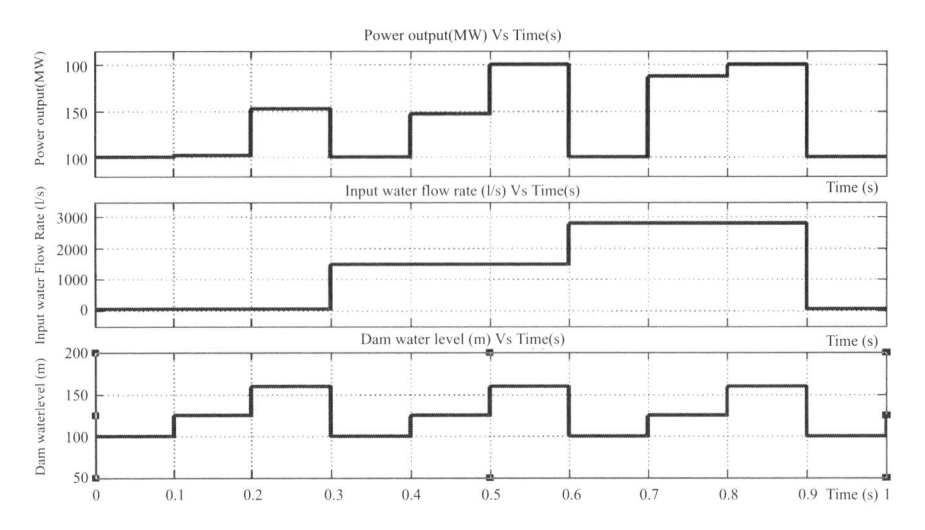

**Fig. 6.45** Power output variation of the hydel power plant

## 6.4 HYBRID TECHNIQUES

Hybrid techniques are the integration of various soft computing techniques that synergizes the strength and weakness of an individual technique with the other. Therefore, the overall performance of such techniques working in unison is increased. Here, we present a very brief introduction about such hybrid techniques with FL system in the following sections.

### 6.4.1 Neuro-Fuzzy Systems

Neuro-fuzzy systems incorporate elements from fuzzy systems and neural networks (NNs). Neural systems fail to reflect a type of imprecision that is associated with the lack of sharp transition from the occurrence of an event to its non-occurrence. Fuzzy theory can be introduced in the model of the neuron to deal with this imprecision. Neural networks are computational algorithms dealing with sensor data, and FL deals with reasoning. Incorporating FL into NN enables a system to deal with cognitive uncertainties in a way similar to humans. Fuzzy systems are not capable of learning, whereas NN can do. Neural networks lack flexibility, human interaction, or knowledge representation, which lies at the core of FL. Together FL and NN compromise each other. Neuro-fuzzy systems pursue the goal to design new architectures in which enhanced learning and improved knowledge representational capabilities can be incorporated. Commercial applications of FL obtained large success over the past years. This success resulted in products that solve tasks in a more intelligent and thereby efficient manner. The increased complexity of technical systems is handled by NNs that speed up the computation of complex rule-based systems.

In neuro-fuzzy systems, the dominant component is the fuzzy system, which is therefore regarded as fuzzy systems with the capability of neural adaptation [6]. Neuro-fuzzy systems apply the learning techniques to the membership function shapes by considering the usual FIS. In some cases, FL plays the role of an interface between an expert that possesses the knowledge to solve a certain problem, and NN processes and utilizes this knowledge. These systems can refine the rules obtained from experts by applying learning to the NN. Usually, expert knowledge is viewed as a preliminary knowledge, whereas learning by the network is regarded as a subsequent tuning and optimisation process. The prior approaches represent fuzzy systems that are enhanced by analytical learning and/or parallel processing abilities.

### 6.4.2 Fuzzy Genetic Algorithms

Fuzzy systems are not capable of learning whereas a GA can do. Genetic lacks flexibility, human interaction or knowledge representation, which lies at the core of FL. Fuzzy systems and NNs complement each other. Genetic algorithms can be used as a learning algorithm of the fuzzy systems.

Genetic algorithms have some parameters to be set, so fuzzy rules can be used to change these parameters during the searching process. A genetic fuzzy system (GFS) is a fuzzy system which has an evolutionary learning process. Widely used GFS systems are genetic fuzzy rule-based system where GA is employed to learn or tune the components of fuzzy systems.

## 6.5 INTUITIONISTIC FUZZY SETS

One of the demerits of fuzzy system is handling the ignorant knowledge. However, a new form of fuzzy sets that recently evolved is the intuitionistic fuzzy set (IFS) which was initially proposed by K Y Atanassovin 1986 [7].

The IFS theory is based on the following aspects:
- Extensions of corresponding definitions of fuzzy set objects
- Definitions of new objects and their properties

### Example 6.1

A Government passes a new bill in parliament for voting. The Bill is passed with 75 per cent vote of Member of Parliament (MP). Of the remaining, 15% (MPs) voted against the Bill and ten per cent demanded the discussion on the Bill for further correction. The Government announces that 'Bill passed in parliament'. Evaluate the truth value of this statement.

#### Solution
According to fuzzy set theory, Bill is supported by (0.75, 0.25).
$\mu_{supported}(\text{bill}) = 0.75$ and $\mu_{not\ supported}(\text{bill}) = \mu_{opposed}(\text{bill}) = 0.25$
However, the ten per cent of MPs neither supported nor opposed. Therefore
$\mu_{supported}(\text{bill}) = 0.75$, $\mu_{opposed}(\text{bill}) = 0.15$ and $\mu_{neither\ supported\ nor\ opposed}(\text{bill}) = 0.1$

The degree of uncertainty now is 0.1 and it corresponds to our ignorance of the boundaries of people who seek discussion. Therefore, the apparatus of IFSs gives us the most accurate answer to the question: (0.75, 0.15). It opens a new way of representing a fuzzy set that has membership function, non-membership function, and hesitation margin.

An IFS $A$ in E is defined as an object of the following form:

$$A = \{\langle x, \mu_A(x), \vartheta_A(x)\rangle \mid x \in E\}$$

where the functions

$$\mu_A: E \to [0,1]$$
$$\vartheta_A: E \to [0,1]$$

define the degree of membership and the degree of non-membership of the element $x \in E$, respectively, and for every $x \in E$:

$$0 \leq \mu_A(x) + \vartheta_A(x) \leq 1$$

The value of $\pi_A(x) = 1 - \mu_A(x) - \vartheta_A(x)$ is called the degree of non-determinacy (or uncertainty or hesitation margin) of the element $x \in E$ to the IFS $A$.

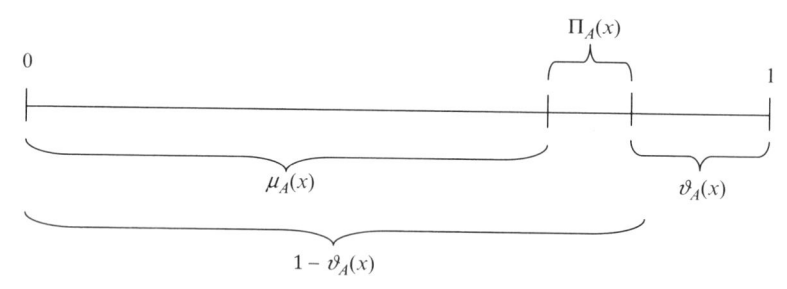

Obviously, each ordinary fuzzy set may be written as

$$A = \{\langle x, \mu_A(x), 1 - \mu_A(x)\rangle \mid x \in E\},$$

Clearly, in the case of ordinary fuzzy sets, $\pi_A(x) = 0$

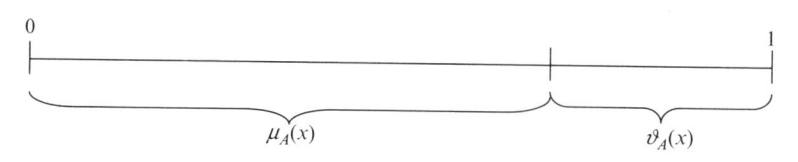

The following relations (mostly equalities) are valid for the three IFSs $A$, $B$, and $C$:

$$A \cap B = B \cap A,$$
$$A \cup B = B \cup A,$$
$$A + B = B + A,$$
$$A \cdot B = B \cdot A,$$
$$A \times B = B \times A,$$
$$(A \cap B) \cap C = A \cap (B \cap C),$$
$$(A \cup B) \cup C = A \cup (B \cup C),$$
$$(A + B) + C = A + (B + C),$$

$$(A \cdot B) \cdot C = A \cdot (B \cdot C),$$
$$(A \cap B) \cup C = (A \cup C) \cap (B \cup C),$$
$$(A \cap B) + C = (A + C) \cap (B + C),$$
$$(A \cap B) \cdot C = (A \cdot C) \cap (B \cdot C),$$
$$(A \cup B) \cap C = (A \cap C) \cup (B \cap C),$$
$$(A \cup B) + C = (A + C) \cup (B + C),$$
$$(A \cup B) \cdot C = (A \cdot C) \cup (B \cdot C),$$
$$(A + B) \cdot C = (A \cdot C) + (B \cdot C),$$
$$A \cap A = A,$$
$$A \cup A = A,$$

If $A$ and $B$ are two IFSs over $E$,

then a function $f_A$ will assign to $x \in E$ a point $f_A(x) \in F$ with the following coordinates:

$$\langle \vartheta_A(x), \mu_A(x) \rangle$$

then a function $f_{A \cap B}$ will assign to $x \in E$ a point $f_{A \cap B}(x) \in F$ with the following coordinates:

$$\langle \min(\mu_A(x), \mu_B(x)), \max(\vartheta_A(x), \vartheta_B(x)) \rangle$$

then a function $f_{A \cup B}$ will assign to $x \in E$ a point $f_{A \cup B}(x) \in F$ with the following coordinates:

$$\langle \max(\mu_A(x), \mu_B(x)), \min(\vartheta_A(x), \vartheta_B(x)) \rangle$$

then a function $f_{A+B}$ will assign to $x \in E$ a point $f_{A+B}(x) \in F$ with the following coordinates:

$$\langle \mu_A(x) + \mu_B(x) - \mu_A(x) \cdot \mu_B(\vec{x}), \vartheta_A(x) \cdot \vartheta_B(x) \rangle$$

then a function $f_{A.B}$ will assign to $x \in E$ a point $f_{A.B}(x) \in F$ with the following coordinates:

$$\langle \mu_A(x) \cdot \mu_B(x), \vartheta_A(x) + \vartheta_B(x) - \vartheta_A(x) \cdot \vartheta_B(x) \rangle$$

then a function $f_{A \times B}$ will assign to $x \in E$ a point $f_{A \times B}(x) \in F$ with the following coordinates:

$$\left\langle \frac{\mu_A(x) + \mu_B(x)}{2 \cdot \mu_A(x) \cdot \mu_B(x) + 1}, \frac{\vartheta_A(x) + \vartheta_B(x)}{2 \cdot (\vartheta_A(x) \cdot \vartheta_B(x) + 1)} \right\rangle$$

**Example 6.2**

Let $E = \{a, b, c, d, e\}$ and let the IFSs $A$ and $B$ have the forms.

*Solution*

$A = \{(a, 0.4, 0.3), (b, 0.2, 0.6), (c, 0.9, 0.0), (d, 0.0, 0.9), (e, 0.1, 0.8)\}$,
$B = \{(a, 0.6, 0.2), (b, 0.4, 0.3), (c, 0.4, 0.5), (d, 0.3, 0.6), (e, 1.0, 0.0)\}$.
$A = \{(a, 0.3, 0.4), (b, 0.6, 0.2), (c, 0.0, 0.9), (d, 0.9, 0.0), (e, 0.8, 0.1)\}$,
$A \cap B = \{(a, 0.4, 0.3), (b, 0.2, 0.6), (c, 0.4, 0.5), (d, 0.0, 0.9), (e, 0.1, 0.8)\}$,

$A \cup B = \{(a, 0.6, 0.2), (b, 0.4, 0.3), (c, 0.9, 0.0), (d, 0.3, 0.6), (e, 1.0,0.0)\}$,
$\overline{A} + B = \{(a, 0.76, 0.06), (b, 0.52, 0.18), (c, 0.94, 0.0), (d, 0.3, 0.54), (e, 1.0,0.0)\}$,
$A \cdot B = \{(a, 0.24, 0.44), (b, 0.08, 0.72), (c, 0.36, 0.5), (d, 0.0, 0.96), (e, 0.1,0.8)\}$,
$A \times B = \{(a, 0.403, 0.236), (b, 0.278, 0.38), (c, 0.478, 0.25), (d, 0.15, 0.487),$
$(e, 0.5,0.4)\}$,

## 6.6 ILLUSTRATIVE PROBLEMS

### Problem 6.1

Estimate the vote percentage (VP) of the candidate in election based on three input variables such as 'No. of times meeting with people (MP), No. of issues solved by candidate (IS), Party vote bank (PVB)'. Let each of the three input and output variables has three linguistic labels as 'Low, Average, High' within the same universe of discourse.

Aditya = $\{15/MP + 22/IS + 35/PVB\}$ and Guru = $\{8/MP + 18/IS + 12/PVB\}$. Assume the two candidates got 50 per cent overall vote.

**Solution:**

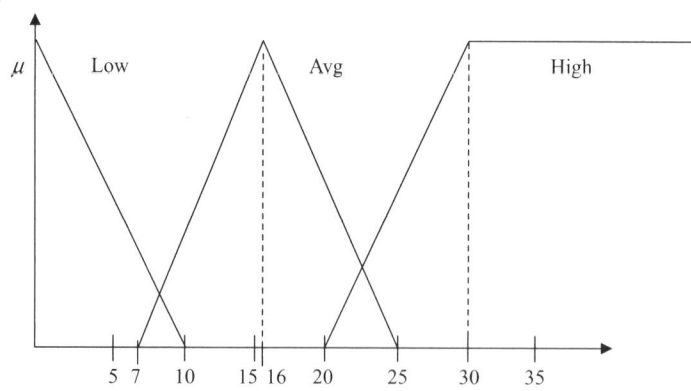

**Rules:**

| S. No. | MP | IS | PVB | VP |
|---|---|---|---|---|
| 1 | L | L | L/A | L |
| 2 | L | L | H | L |
| 3 | L | A | L | L |
| 4 | L | A | A/H | A |
| 5 | A | L | L | L |
| 6 | A | L | A/H | A |
| 7 | A | A | L | L |
| 8 | A | A | A/H | A |
| 9 | A | H | L | A |
| 10 | A | H | A/H | H |
| 11 | H | L | L | L |
| 12 | H | L | A/H | A |

| 13 | H | A | L | A |
| 14 | H | A | A | H |
| 15 | H | A/H | H | H |

(i) Aditya has crisp value as {15/MP + 22/IS + 35/PVB}

***Fuzzification:***
 MP = Avg (0.88)
 IS = Avg (0.33) and High (0.2)
 PVB = High (1)

***Rules implication:***
It fires the rules 8 and 10.
Rule 8: IF MP is Avg (0.88) and IS is Avg (0.33) and PVB is High (1) THEN VP is Avg
min(MP (0.88), IS (0.33), PVB (1)) => 0.33
Therefore VP is Avg (0.33)
Rule 10: IF MP is Avg (0.88) and IS is High (0.2) and PVB is High (1) THEN VP is High
min(MP (0.88), IS (0.2), PVB (1)) => 0.2
Therefore VP is High (0.2)

***De-fuzzification:***

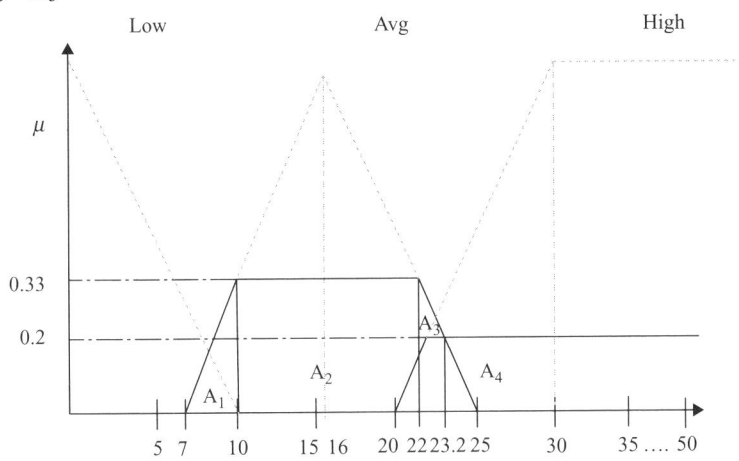

| Shaded area | Area | Centre | Area × Centre |
| --- | --- | --- | --- |
| $A_1$ | 0.5 × 3 × 0.33 = 0.495 | 9 | 0.495 × 9 = 4.455 |
| $A_2$ | 12 × 0.33 = 3.96 | 16 | 3.96 × 16 = 63.36 |
| $A_3$ | 0.5 × 1.2 × 0.13 = 0.078 | 22.4 | 0.078 × 22.4 = 1.7472 |
| $A_4$ | 28 × 0.2 = 5.6 | 36 | 5.6 × 36 = 201.6 |
| Sum | 10.133 | | 271.1622 |

VP* = 271.1622/10.133 = 26.76%

Therefore, Aditya will get 26.76 per cent vote in the election.

(ii) Guru has crisp value as {8/MP + 18/IS + 12/PVB}

**Fuzzification:**
MP = Low (0.2) and Avg (0.11)
IS = Avg (0.77)
PVB = Avg (0.55)

**Rules implication:**
It fires the rules 4 and 8
Rule 4: IF MP is Low (0.2) and IS is Avg (0.77) and PVB is Avg (0.55) THEN VP is Avg
min(MP (0.2), IS (0.77), PVB (0.55) ) => 0.2
Therefore VP is Avg (0.2)
Rule 8: IF MP is Avg (0.11) and IS is Avg (0.77) and PVB is Avg (0.55) THEN VP is Avg
min(MP (0.11), IS (0.77), PVB (0.55) ) => 0.11
Therefore VP is Avg (0.11)

**De-fuzzification:**

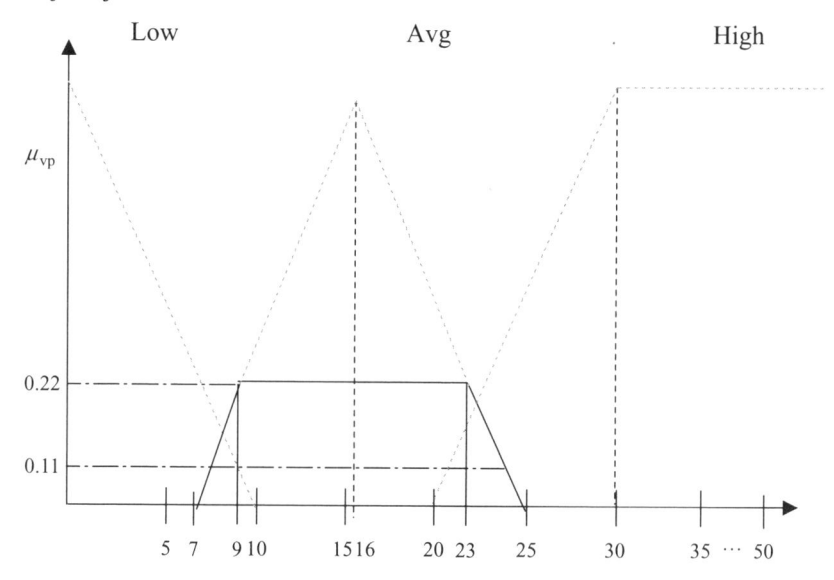

| Shaded area | Area | Centre | Area × Centre |
|---|---|---|---|
| $A_1$ | 0.5 × 2 × 0.22 = 0.22 | 8.33 | 0.22 × 8.33 = 1.8326 |
| $A_2$ | 14 × 0.22 = 3.08 | 16 | 3.08 × 16 = 49.28 |
| $A_3$ | 0.5 × 2 × 0.22 = 0.22 | 23.67 | 0.22 × 23.67 = 5.2067 |
| Sum | 3.52 | | 56.3193 |

VP* = 56.3193/3.52 = 16%

Therefore, Guru will get 16% vote in the election.

## Problem 6.2

A student wants to join a good college, which is evaluated by factors of Moderate fees, High Pass Percentage (PP), and Very old college (YO). The options are given as follows:

SBN = {1,00,000/fees + 88/PP + 25/YO}
TVE = {75,000/fees + 78/PP + 45/YO}
PVG = {65,000/fees + 72/PP + 35/YO}
RSE = {35,000/fees + 68/PP + 55/YO}
SPM = {1,25,000/fess + 70/PP + 30/YO}

Prepare priority list of colleges to help the student.

### Solution:

Membership function of college fee:

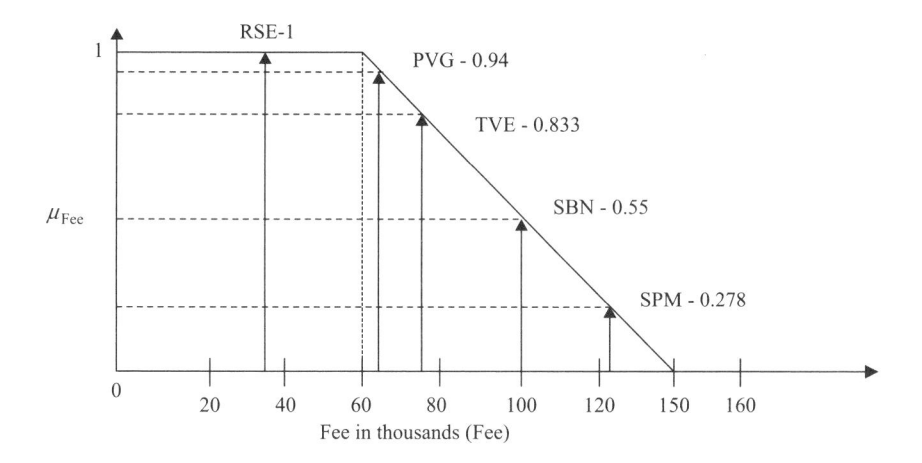

Membership function of pass percentage:

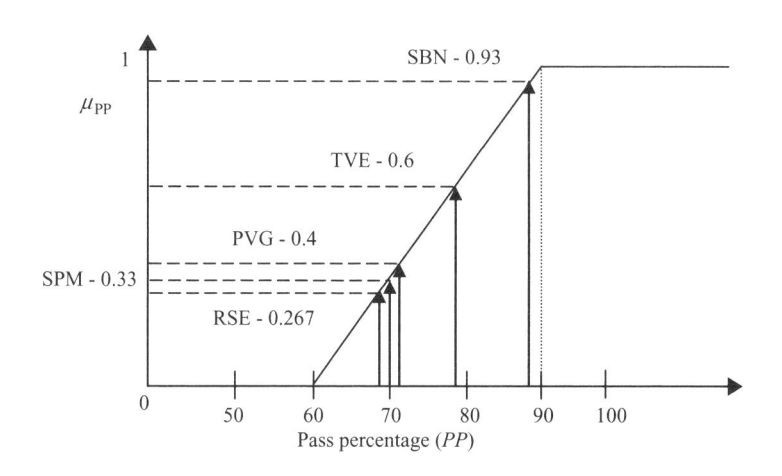

Membership function of years of old:

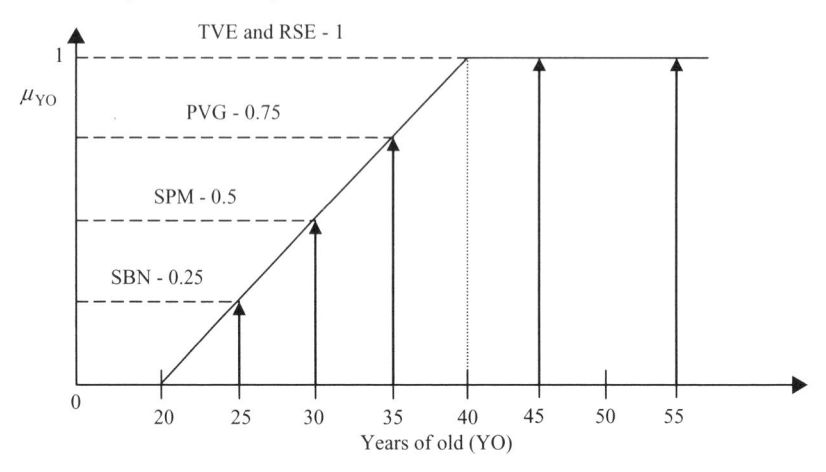

[Figure: Membership function μ_YO vs Years of old (YO). Levels marked: TVE and RSE - 1, PVG - 0.75, SPM - 0.5, SBN - 0.25; x-axis values: 20, 25, 30, 35, 40, 45, 50, 55]

Priority list is made by max-min composition.
SBN = {0.55/fees + 0.93/PP + 0.25/YO}
TVE = {0.83/fees + 0.6/PP + 1/YO}
PVG = {0.94/fees + 0.4/PP + 0.75/YO}
RSE = {1/fees + 0.267/PP + 1/YO}
SPM = {0.278/fess + 0.33/PP + 0.5/YO}
Perform min of $\{\mu_{fee}, \mu_{PP}, \mu_{YO}\}$
= {0.25/SBN + 0.6/TVE + 0.4/PVG + 0.267/RSE + 0.278/SPM}
Priority list = {TVE, PVG, SPM, RSE, SBN}

## SUMMARY

- Conventional control system can be replaced by fuzzy logic-based control (FLBC) system if design of more complicated systems can be simplified.
- The basic structure of a fuzzy controller consists of five principle elements: (i) fuzzification module (fuzzifier), (ii) knowledge base, (iii) rule base, (iv) inference engine, and (v) de-fuzzification module (de-fuzzifier).
- Fuzzy associative memory (FAM) matrix is a table form, where an individual rule consists of two antecedent variables and one consequent variable.
- A degree that corresponds to the degree to which the antecedent part of a fuzzy rule is satisfied is known as degree of fulfilment (DOF).
- Fuzzy inference system editor in MATLAB can be opened by typing the command 'fuzzy' in the prompt of the command window.
- A recent development in fuzzy logic system is intuitionistic fuzzy set (IFS) theory which is based on (1) extensions of corresponding definitions of fuzzy set objects and (2) definitions of new objects and their properties.

## EXERCISES

1. Show that the average squared re-construction error of the real-valued sequencer $x(0)...x(M-1)$ equals the average squared re-construction error of the transformed values:

$$\frac{1}{M}\sum_{m=0}^{M-1}[x(m)-\hat{x}(m)]^2 = \frac{1}{M}\sum_{u=0}^{M-1}\left|X(u)-\hat{X}(u)\right|^2$$

If $[X(0)... X(M-1)] = [x(0)... x(M-1)]\ U$. $U$ denotes a unitary matrix and $U^*$ denotes its complex conjugate transpose. Hence, $U^*U = I$, where I denotes the M-by-M identity matrix.

2. A1, A2, and A3 are three fuzzy sets as shown in figure. Illustrate the aggregation of these three fuzzy sets and then de-fuzzify by: (i) centroid method (ii) centre of sums method, and (iii) mean of max method.
3. Consider a fuzzy inference system given by the following rules:
   (i) IF colour is Dark AND Texture is soft THEN Fruit quality is rotten.
   (ii) IF colour is Light OR Texture is Hard THEN Fruit quality is ripe.

   The membership functions for Dark, Light, Soft, Hard, Rotten, and Ripe are expressed by the following fuzzy sets:
   $A_{dark}(x) = 0/1 + 0.25/2 + 0.5/3 + 0.75/4 + 1/5 + 0.75/6 + 0.5/7 + 0.25/8 + 0/9$.
   $A_{light}(x) = 0/6 + 0.25/7 + 0.5/8 + 0.75/9 + 1/10 + 0.75/11 + 0.5/12 + 0.25/13 + 0/14$.
   $A_{soft}(x) = 0/1 + 0.25/2 + 0.5/3 + 0.75/4 + 1/5 + 0.75/6 + 0.5/7 + 0.25/8 + 0/9$
   $A_{hard}(x) = 0/6 + 0.25/7 + 0.5/8 + 0.75/9 + 1/10 + 0.75/11 + 0.5/12 + 0.25/13 + 0/14$.
   $A_{rotten}(x) = 0/0 + 0.25/0.25 + 0.5/1 + 0.75/1.5 + 1/2 + 0.75/2.5 + 0.5/3 + 0.25/3.5 + 0/4$
   $A_{ripe}(x) = 0/3 + 0.25/3.5 + 0.5/4 + 0.75/4.5 + 1/5 + 0.75/5.5 + 0.5/6 + 0.25/6.5 + 0/7$

   Evaluate the antecedent membership functions for the inputs Colour = 3 and Texture = 6 using the max-min composition operator.
4. How would you characterize the membership functions *Temperature high* and *Temperature medium* if 100 people agreed *Temperature high* to be between 20° and 45°, and 25 people agreed *Temperature medium* to be between 15° and 25° in the context of outdoor weather? How would you incorporate the number of agreement votes into the membership function design?

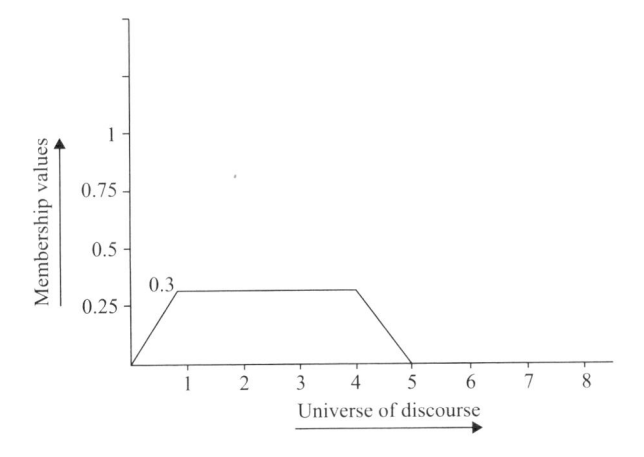

Fig. A1

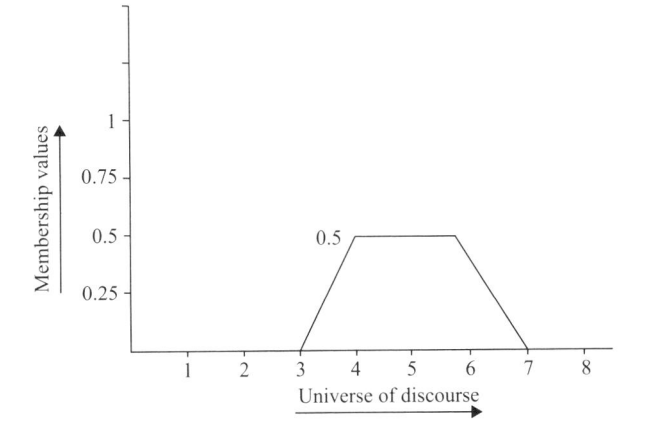

Fig. A2

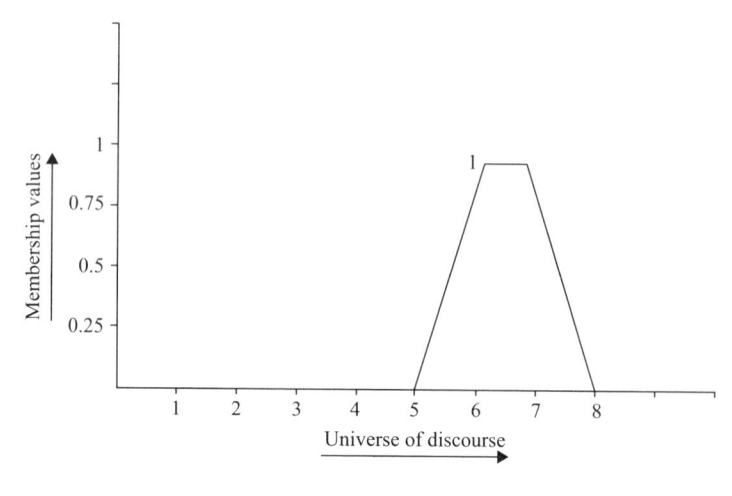

Fig. A3

## REFERENCES

[1] Lee, C.C., 'Fuzzy logic in control systems: Fuzzy logic controller. I', Systems, Man and Cybernetics, IEEE Transactions, Vol.20, Issue 2, Mar/Apr 1990, pp. 404–418.
[2] Tsoukalas, L.H., Berkan, R. C., Upadhyaya, B. R., and Kisner, R. A., 'Intelligent control using fuzzy logic in nuclear reactor systems', *Proceedings of ANS Topical Meeting - Advances in Mathematics, Computations and Reactor Physics, 8.2 2-1 - 8.2 2-12*, Pittsburgh, Pennsylvania, Apr 28–May 1, 1991.
[3] Sugeno, M., An introductory survey of fuzzy control, *Information Sciences*, Vol. 36, pp. 59–83, 1985.
[4] Mizumoto, M., Fuzzy controls under various reasoning methods, *Information Sciences*, Vol.45, pp. 129–141, 1988.
[5] Rajasekaran, S. and G.A. Vijayalakshmi Pai, *Neural Networks, Fuzzy Logic and Genetic Algorithms*, PHI, New Delhi, 2003.
[6] Detlef Nauck, Frank Klawonn, Rudolf Kruse, *Foundations of Neuro-Fuzzy Systems*, Wiley, 19-Sep-1997.
[7] Atanassov, K. T., Intuitionistic fuzzy sets, *Fuzzy sets and Systems*, Vol. 20, Issue1, pp. 87–96, 1986.

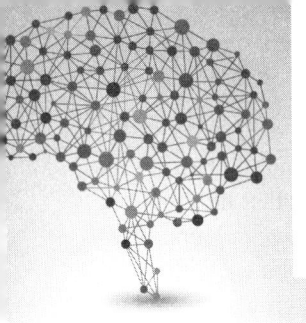

# 7 Genetic Algorithms and Evolutionary Programming

*'It is not the strongest of the species that survives, nor the most intelligent that survives. It is the one that is the most adaptable to change.'*

Charles Darwin

### LEARNING OBJECTIVES

*After reading this chapter, the reader will be able to:*

- Comprehend the fundamentals of the genetic algorithm (GA)
- Explain the different types of genetic representations and selection mechanisms
- Familiarize with the genetic operators and types of crossover and mutation
- Discuss the natural inheritance operators
- Solve the optimisation problems using GA with MATLAB codes
- Know the applications of GA and MATLAB Codes
- Understand the fundamentals of evolutionary programming (EP)
- Analyse the optimisation problem using EP
- Describe the machine learning classifier system

## 7.1 INTRODUCTION TO GENETIC ALGORITHMS

The science of genetics began with the applied and theoretical work of Gregor Mendel in the mid-nineteenth century. The importance of Mendel's work did not gain wide understanding until the 1890s, after his death, when other scientists working on similar problems re-discovered his research. Mendel traced the inheritance patterns of certain traits in pea plants and described them mathematically. Although this pattern of inheritance could only be observed for a few traits, Mendel's work suggested that heredity was particulate, not acquired, and that the inheritance patterns of many traits could be explained through simple rules and ratios. The process of those expressions of traits involves complex interactions between chromosomes where genetic information gets exchanged.

The complexity of the genetic process relates to a comic scene in a drama conducted in a village long back. In this scene, the father of a newborn carries the baby in front of the maternity ward of the village hospital. The man was screaming at his wife drawing the attention of the crowd. A tense and heated-up argument commenced between the couple. The ignorant husband in a loud voice claimed that the child born did not belong to them since it had a whitish complexion. He questioned how a whitish complexion child was born to a dark-complexioned couple. An elderly man intervened. He asked the husband about certain things he possessed. They were the betel leaves (green in colour), food-grade lime (white), and betel nut (black). The elderly man asked the tensed husband to chew all the three together and spit the contents out. He asked the husband that he should be careful to spit it out as it should certainly contain any of the three colours. However, everybody there knew that it was an impossible task. As you chew the three items and spit them out, it would be of red colour. Finally, the crowd cheered the elderly person as the ignorant man was convinced and returned happily to his wife. Though it looks hilarious, the insight present within the context definitely helps us to know the complexity involved in the genetic mechanism.

The traits are the physical expressions of genes that are present in a simple living cell. A simple animal cell (Fig. 7.1) is a complex of many small 'factories' working together. At the centre of this all is the cell nucleus. The nucleus (Fig. 7.2) contains the chromosomes. The genetic information is preserved in chromosomes as DNA strands (Fig. 7.3).

A simple Hebrew proverb quotes 'Whoever teaches his son teaches not alone his son but also his son's son, and so on, to the end of generations'. As the knowledge is transferred from one generation to next generation, the best-of-best information is evolved with time. Richard Dawkins, a renowned biologist, argues that the tall trees that exist in the mountains today were only a foot tall in the early ages of evolution. Sometimes it is beyond belief, but this fact can be justified and explained using *natural evolution* and *natural selection*. Suppose, during the early ages, by genetic processing one tree had produced an offspring an inch taller than the other trees; that offspring enjoyed more sunlight and rain and attracted

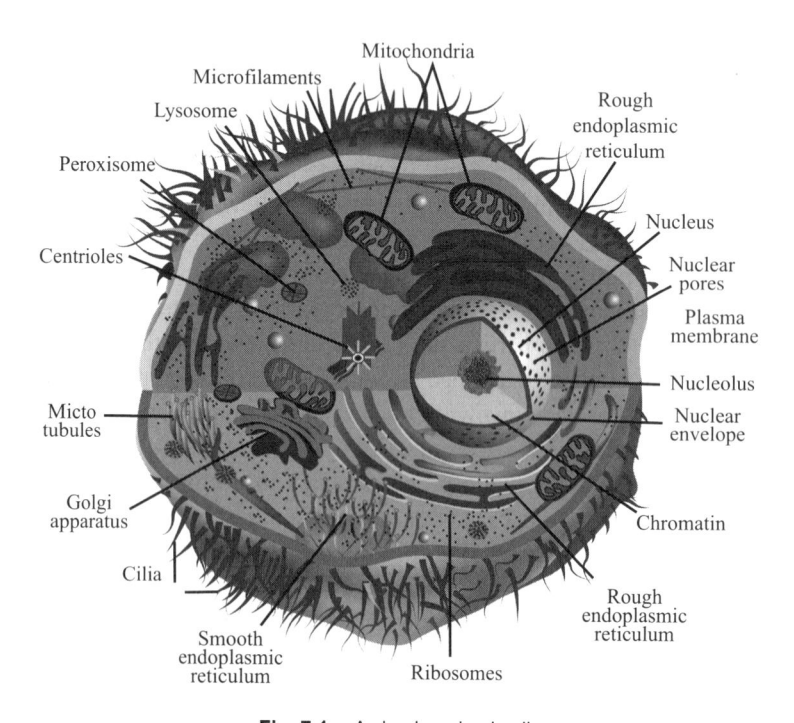

**Fig. 7.1** A simple animal cell

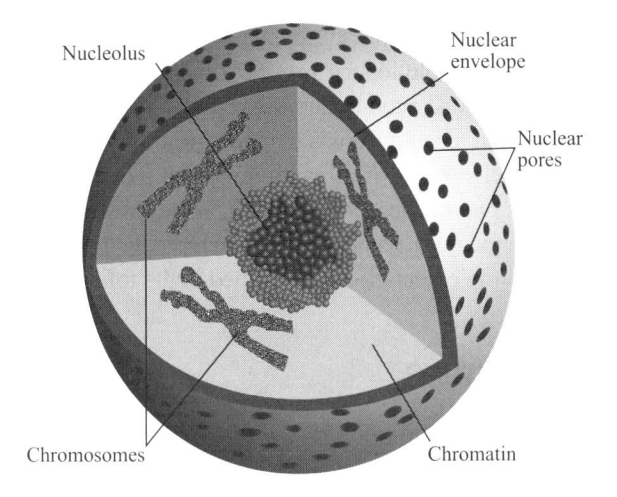

**Fig. 7.2** A cell nucleus

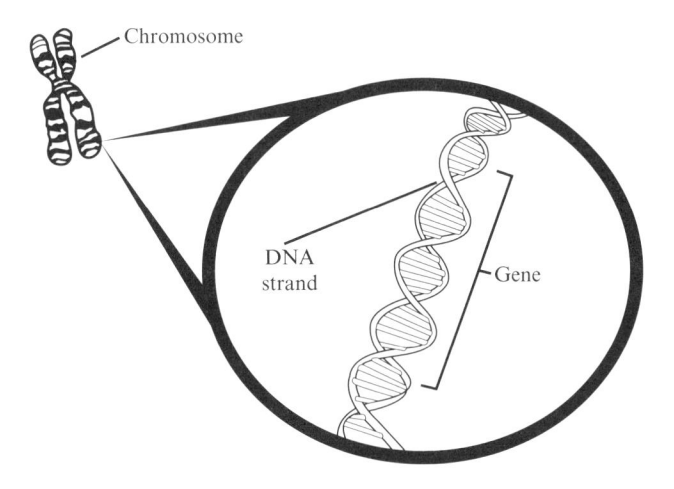

**Fig. 7.3** Chromosome and gene

more insects for pollination than all other trees. Now suppose this lucky offspring happened to be blessed with an increased lifespan and more importantly produced several tall offspring like itself. This situation proves the proposition of the 'survival of the fittest' by Darwin. Using this theory, achieving desirable outcomes for an objective and seeking the best solution in the form of the global minimum is a challenge ahead to every researcher and scientist. Genetic algorithms and evolutionary programming have provided solutions for many of the problems faced today; some are yet to be solved.

The genetics-based mechanism of problem-solving was first conceived by Professor John Holland of the University of Michigan, Ann Arbor, in 1965 [1]. Genetic algorithms owe their popularity as solutions in various search and optimisation problems to their global perspective, widespread applicability, and inherent parallelism. The simulation of the natural evolutionary process of organisms results in stochastic optimisation techniques called evolutionary algorithms, which can often outperform conventional optimisation techniques when applied to difficult real-world problems. At present, three parallel streams of research are being pursued: GAs, EP, and evolution strategies (ESs). Out of these streams, GA is the most widely known type of evolutionary algorithm today. The analogy between biological evolution and the computational GA with its implementation is explained in the following sections [2].

## 7.2 GENETIC ALGORITHMS

The GA is a randomized search and optimisation technique guided by the principle of natural genetic systems. In recent years, there has been a great deal of interest in GAs and their application to various engineering fields. The GA is also being applied to a wide range of optimisation and learning problems in many domains. Genetic algorithms also lend themselves well to power system optimisation problems, since they are known to exhibit robustness, require no auxiliary information, and can offer significant advantages in solution methodologies and optimisation performance. Genetic algorithms solve problems using principles inspired by natural population genetics. They maintain populations of knowledge structures that represent candidate solutions, and let those populations evolve over time through competition and controlled variation.

The main advantage of the GA formulation is that fairly accurate results may be obtained using a very simple algorithm. The GA has become increasingly popular in recent years in science and engineering disciplines. It is a method of finding a good answer to a problem, based on the feedback received from its repeated attempts at a solution. The *objective* or *fitness* function is a judge of the GA's attempts. Genetic algorithms do not know how to derive a problem's solution, but they do know, from the objective function, how close they are to a better solution.

In the biological world, the problem is evolutionary survival, and a particular gene represents one possible solution to survival within a competitive environment. In the digital world, the stated problem varies from one application program to another, as does the objective function. Genetic algorithms are optimisation algorithms based on the principle of biological evolution. They are unlike many conventional search algorithms in the sense that they simultaneously consider many points in the search space. They work not with the parameters themselves but with strings of numbers representing the parameter set, and they use probabilistic rules to guide their search. By considering many points in the search space simultaneously, they reduce the chances of converging to local minima.

The GA maintains a set of possible solutions (population) represented as a string of, typically, binary numbers (0/1). New strings are produced in each and every generation by the repetition of a two-step cycle. This involves first decoding each individual string and assessing its ability to solve the problem. Each string is assigned fitness values, depending on how well it has performed in an environment.

In the second stage, the fittest string is preferentially chosen for re-combination, which involves the selection of two strings, and the switching of the segments to the right of the meeting point of the two strings. This is called *crossover*. Another genetic operator is *mutation*. It is used to maintain genetic diversity within a small population of strings. There is a small probability that any bit in a string will be flipped from its present value to its opposite (e.g., 0 to 1); this prevents certain bits from becoming fixed at a specific value due to every string in the population having the same value, often causing premature convergence to a non-optimal solution. An additional common feature of the GA is the automatic inclusion of the best performing string of the parent generation in the new offspring generation. This procedure prevents a good string from being lost by the probabilistic nature of reproduction and speeds convergence to a good solution.

Until some kind of stopping criteria are reached, GA goes through the following cycle: Evaluate, Select and Mate, and Mutate. One criterion is to let the GA run for a certain number of cycles. A second one is to allow the GA to run until a reasonable solution is found. Although GA seems to be a good method for solving optimisation problems, sometimes the solution obtained is only a near-global optimum solution.

The idea behind GAs is to do what nature does. Before we take a closer look at the structure of a GA, let us have a quick look at the history of genetics. Genetic algorithms use vocabulary borrowed from natural genetics. We will talk about individuals (or *genotypes* and *structures*) in a population; quite often these individuals are called *strings* or *chromosomes*. Chromosomes are made of units—*genes* (also *features*, *characters*, or *decoders*)—arranged in linear succession; every gene controls the inheritance of one or more characters. The genes of certain characters are located at certain places in a chromosome, which are called *loci* (string positions). Any feature of an individual (e.g., hair colour) can manifest itself in different ways—the gene is thus said to have several states, called *alleles* (feature values).

Each genotype (a single chromosome) represents a potential solution to a problem (the meaning of a particular chromosome (i.e., its *phenotype*) is defined externally by the user); an evolution process run on a population of chromosomes corresponds to a search through a space of potential solutions. Such a search requires the balancing of two (apparently conflicting) objectives: exploiting the best solutions and exploring the search space. Random search is a typical example of a strategy that explores the search space without exploiting the promising regions of the space. Genetic algorithms are a class of general-purpose (domain-independent) search methods, which strike a remarkable balance between the exploration and exploitation of the search space.

A GA performs a multi-directional search by maintaining a population of potential solutions and encouraging information formation and exchange between these directions. The population undergoes a simulated evolution; at each generation the relatively 'good' solutions reproduce and the relatively 'bad' solutions die. To distinguish between different solutions, an objective (evaluation) function is used, which plays the role of the selection process in the biological environment.

A GA starts with an initial set of random solutions, the population. Each individual in the population is a chromosome, representing a solution to the problem.

A chromosome is a string structure, typically a concatenated list of binary digits representing a coding of the control parameters of a given problem. The chromosomes evolve through successive iterations called *generations*. The chromosomes of each generation are evaluated using some measure of fitness. To create the next generation, new chromosomes called offspring are formed by either (a) merging two chromosomes from the current generation using a crossover operator or (b) modifying a chromosome using a mutation operator. A new generation is formed by selecting, according to the fitness value, some of the parents and offspring, and rejecting others in order to keep the population size constant. Suitable chromosomes having higher survival probabilities are selected. Normally, the roulette-wheel selection approach is used. After several generations, the algorithm converges to the best chromosome, which hopefully represents the optimal or near-optimal solution to the problem. Genetic algorithms have quite successfully been applied to optimisation problems such as wire routing, scheduling, adaptive control, game playing, cognitive modelling, transportation problems, travelling salesman problems (TSPs), optimal control problems, database query optimisation, and so on.

Post 1990s, the significance of optimisation has grown even further—many important large-scale combinatorial optimisation problems and highly constrained engineering problems can only be solved approximately on present-day computers. Genetic algorithms aim at solving such complex problems. They belong to the class of probabilistic algorithms; yet they are very different from random algorithms, as they combine elements of directed and stochastic search. Thus, GAs are also more robust than existing directed search methods. Another important property of such genetics-based search methods is that they maintain a population of potential solutions; all other methods process a single point of the search space at a time.

There is a large class of interesting problems for which no reasonably fast algorithm has been developed. Many of these problems are optimisation problems that arise frequently in various applications. Given such a difficult optimisation problem, it is often possible to find an efficient algorithm whose solution is approximately optimal. For certain complex optimisation problems, one can use probabilistic algorithms as well—these algorithms do not guarantee the optimum value, but by randomly choosing a sufficient number of 'witnesses', the probability of error may be made as small as desired. There are a lot of important practical optimisation problems for which such high-quality algorithms have become available. Moreover, many other large-scale combinatorial optimisation problems can be solved approximately on present-day computers.

In general, any abstract task to be accomplished can be thought of as solving a problem, which, in turn, can be perceived as a search through a space of potential solutions. Since we are after *the best* solution, we can view this task as an optimisation process. For small spaces, classical exhaustive methods usually suffice; for large spaces special artificial intelligence techniques must be employed. Genetic algorithms are among such techniques; they are stochastic algorithms whose search methods would model natural phenomena such as genetic inheritance and Darwinian strife for survival.

Genetic algorithms differ from other optimisation and search procedures in the following ways:

- Many real-life problems cannot be solved in polynomial amount of time using deterministic algorithms.
- Sometimes near-optimal solutions that can be generated quickly, using GAs, are more desirable than optimal solutions which require a large amount of time.
- Using GAs, problems can be modelled as optimisation problems.
- Genetic algorithms work with a coding of the parameter set, not the parameters themselves. Therefore, they can easily handle integral or discrete variables.
- Genetic algorithms search among a population of points, not a single point. Hence, they can provide globally optimal solutions.
- Genetic algorithms use only objective function information, not derivatives or other auxiliary knowledge. Therefore, they can deal with the non-smooth, non-continuous, and non-differentiable functions, which actually exist in a practical optimisation problem.
- Genetic algorithms use probabilistic transition rules, not deterministic rules.

## 7.3 PROCEDURES OF GAs

Figure 7.4 shows the generalized flow chart for GAs.

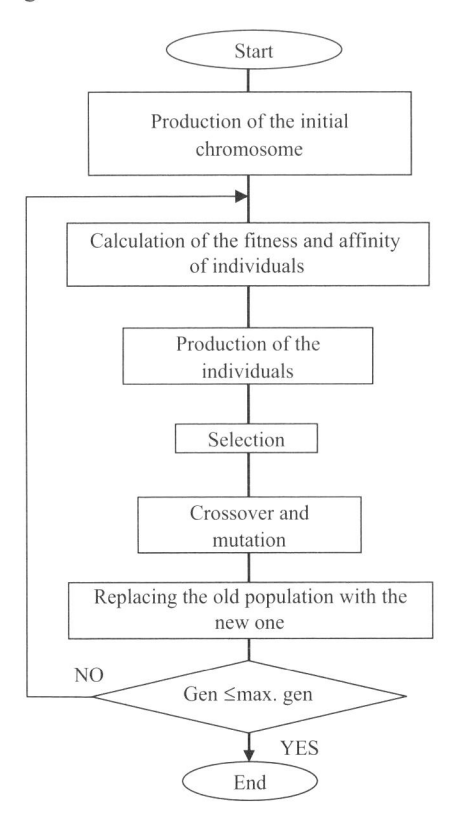

**Fig. 7.4** Flow chart for the GA

A GA (like any evolution program) for a particular problem must have the following five components:

(a) A genetic representation for the potential solutions to the problem.
(b) A way to create an initial population of potential solutions.
(c) An evaluation function that plays the role of the environment, rating solutions in terms of their 'fitness'.
(d) Genetic operators that alter the composition of the offspring.
(e) Values for various parameters that the GA uses (population size, probabilities of applying genetic operators, etc.).

Let us note first that, without any loss of generality, we can assume the problem to a maximization problem. If the optimisation problem is to minimize a function $f$, this is equivalent to maximizing a function $g$, where $g = -f$, which is given as follows:

$$\text{Min}\{f(x)\} = \max\{g(x)\} = \max\{-f(x)\} \tag{7.1}$$

Moreover, we can assume that the objective function $f$ takes only the positive values in its domain; otherwise we can add some positive constant $C$ to $g$ as given in the following:

$$\text{Max}\{g(x)\} = \max\{g(x) + C\} \tag{7.2}$$

Now suppose we wish to maximize a function of $k$ variables, $f(x_1, \ldots, x_k): R^k \to R$. Suppose further that each variable $x_i$ can take values from a domain $D_i = [a_i, b_i] \subseteq R$, and $f(x_1, \ldots, x_k) > 0$ for all $x_i \in D_i$. We wish to optimise the function $f$ with some required precision; say, up to six decimal places for the variables. It is clear that to achieve such precision, each domain $D_i$ must be cut into $(b_i - a_i) \times 10^6$ equal-sized ranges. Let $m_i$ be the smallest integer such that $(b^i - a^i) \times 10^6 \leq 2^{m_i} - 1$. Then, a representation having each variable $x_i$ coded as a binary string of length $m_i$ clearly satisfies the precision requirement. Additionally, the following formula interprets each such string:

$$X_i = a_i + \text{decimal}(1001\ldots001_2) \cdot b_i - a_i/2^{m_i} - 1 \tag{7.3}$$

where decimal(string$_2$) represents the decimal value of that binary string.

Each chromosome (a potential solution) is represented by a binary string of length $\sum_{i=1}^{k} m_i$. The first $m_1$ bits map onto a value in the range $[a_1, b_1]$, the next group of $m_2$ bits map onto a value in the range $[a_2, b_2]$, and so on; the last group of $m_k$ bits map onto a value in the range $[a_k, b_k]$. The problem is genetically represented with the help of binary strings. Let us also discuss briefly the different types of representations in the following section.

## 7.3.1 Genetic Representations

Representing or encoding the problem in hand when applying a GA is a vital task. Encoding can be defined as the chromosomal representation of the problem.

When GA was initially introduced, the binary string encoding technique was used. However, when it came to industrial and other scientific applications, applying GA directly using binary strings became a problem, because it was not natural coding. During the past decade, various types of encoding techniques, such as real number coding for constrained optimisation problems and integer coding for combinatorial optimisation problems, have evolved. It is also possible to represent genes using arrays, trees, lists, etc. It is necessary to ensure that a suitable representation of solutions with meaningful and problem-specific genetic operators is considered. In the following, we discuss some representation schemes [3], [4].

### 7.3.1.1 Binary Representation

*Binary coding*

Binary representation consists of binary coding and Gray coding (Table 7.1). In binary coding, the strings are made up of 1s and 0s (i.e., 11110010101011). The length of the string is determined by the precision desired for the solution. Any integer can be converted into binary code by continuously dividing it by 2, as shown here:

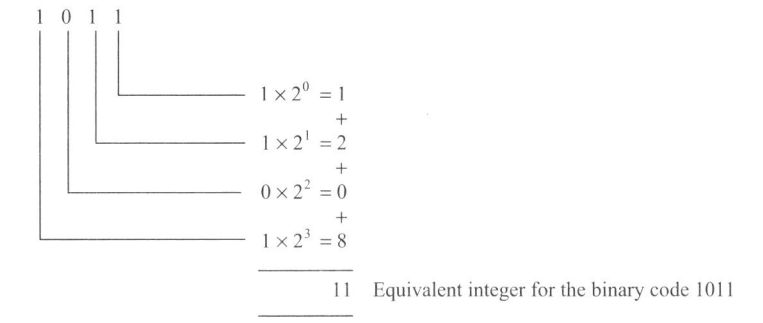

```
2 | 11     Remainder
2 |  5        1
2 |  2        1
   |  1       0    Binary equivalent of 11 is 1011
```

```
1 0 1 1
        └── 1 × 2⁰ = 1
                   +
      └──── 1 × 2¹ = 2
                   +
    └────── 0 × 2² = 0
                   +
  └──────── 1 × 2³ = 8
            ─────────
                11    Equivalent integer for the binary code 1011
```

Let us consider two variables $(X_1\ X_2)$ as (1100 1010). Each variable has both an upper and a lower limit, which can be represented as $X_i^l \le X_i \le X_i^u$. Each variable is a four-bit string that can be represented by an integer between 0 and 15 (16 elements) (i.e., the binary representations of $X_i^l$ and $X_i^u$ are (0000) and (1111)). Therefore, an $n$-bit string can be represented by any integer in the range 0 to $2^n - 1$, which consists of $2^n$ integers. The equivalent value for any four-bit string can be obtained as follows:

$$X_i = X_i^l + \frac{X_i^u - X_i^l}{(2^{n_i} - 1)} \times (decoded\ value\ of\ string) \qquad (7.4)$$

Suppose $X_i^l = 5$ and $X_i^u = 20$ and the four-bit string is $X_i = 1010$, then it can be decoded as follows:

$$D_i = 1010 = 2^3 \times 1 + 2^2 \times 0 + 2^1 \times 1 + 2^0 \times 0 = 10$$

$$X_i = 2 + \frac{(20-5)}{(2^4-1)} \times 10 = 12$$

The precision attained with a four-bit string is equal to 1/16th of the search space. Whenever the length of a string is increased by adding a digit (0 or 1) to it, the precision increases exponentially to $1/2^{(\text{string length})}$ (i.e., for a length $n_i$, the obtainable accuracy in the variable approximation is $\frac{(X_i^u - X_i^l)}{2^{n_i}}$). It is not mandatory that all variables should be coded in equal sub-string length. Thus, the coding of the corresponding variable $X_i$ can be done using Eq. (7.4). If $p$ is the precision required for a continuous variable, then the string length $S_l$ should be equal to:

$$S_1 = \log_2\left[\frac{X^u - X^l}{p}\right]$$

It is also not necessary that the variable $X_i$ should be equally distributed; it can be applied using a linear mapping rule. For example,

$\{0000, 0001, ..., 1111\}_{(\text{binary coding})} \rightarrow \{0, 1, ..., 15\}_{(\text{decoded value})}$
$\rightarrow \{0, 10, 20, 30, 45, 60, 70, 80, 90, -10, -20, -30, -45, -60, -70, -80\}_{(\text{fibre angle})}$

Here, the values are not uniformly distributed, but the function value at a point $X$ can be evaluated by substituting $X$ in the given fitness function.

*Gray coding*
The Gray coding representation, which also consists of bits 0 and 1 in a chromosomal string, has the property that any two points next to each other in the problem space differ by one bit only (i.e., an increase of one step in the parameter value corresponds to a change of a single bit in the code).

Table 7.1 Binary and gray codes

| Binary | 0000 | 0001 | 0010 | 0011 | 0100 | 0101 | 0110 | 0111 | 1000 | 1001 | 1010 | 1011 | 1100 | 1101 | 1110 | 1111 |
|---|---|---|---|---|---|---|---|---|---|---|---|---|---|---|---|---|
| Gray | 0000 | 0001 | 0011 | 0010 | 0110 | 0111 | 0101 | 0100 | 1100 | 1101 | 1111 | 1110 | 1010 | 1011 | 1001 | 1000 |

### 7.3.1.2 Octal Representation

Dividing an integer by '8' codes the integer into an octal string, which consists of a group of digits taking values from 0 to 7. For example, the integer 1506 can be coded in the following way:

```
8 | 1506     Remainder
8 | 188        2
8 |  23        4
8 |   2        7
      0        2         Octal equivalent of 1506 is 2742
```

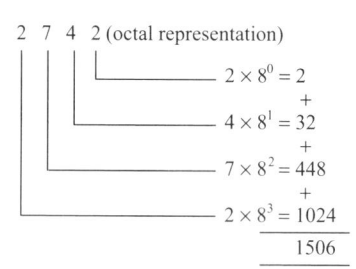

2 7 4 2 (octal representation)
- $2 \times 8^0 = 2$
- $+$
- $4 \times 8^1 = 32$
- $+$
- $7 \times 8^2 = 448$
- $+$
- $2 \times 8^3 = 1024$

1506   Equivalent integer for the octal code 2742

Here, the four-bit octal string for two points $X_1$ and $X_2$ as $(X_1^l, X_2^l)$ and $(X_1^u, X_2^u)$ variables can take integer values from 0 to 4095, that is, $X_i^l$ and $X_i^u$ correspond to (0000 0000) and (7777 7777), respectively, and the precision of the variable approximation is $\dfrac{(X_i^u - X_i^l)}{8^{n_i}}$.

### 7.3.1.3 Hexadecimal Representation

Dividing an integer by '16' codes the integer into a hexadecimal string, which consists of a group of digits taking values from 0 to 9, A, B, C, D, E, and F. Here, the four-bit hexadecimal string for two points $X_1$ and $X_2$ as $(X_1^l, X_2^l)$ and $(X_1^u, X_2^u)$ variables can take integer values from 0 to 65,535, corresponding to (0000 0000) to (FFFF FFFF), and the precision of the variable approximation is $\dfrac{(X_i^u - X_i^l)}{(16^{n_i})}$. For example, the integer 96856 can be hexadecimally coded as follows:

```
16 | 96856     Remainder
16 |  6053        8
16 |   378        5
16 |    23       10 (A)
16 |     1        7
         0        1     Hexadecimal equivalent of 96856 is 17A58
```

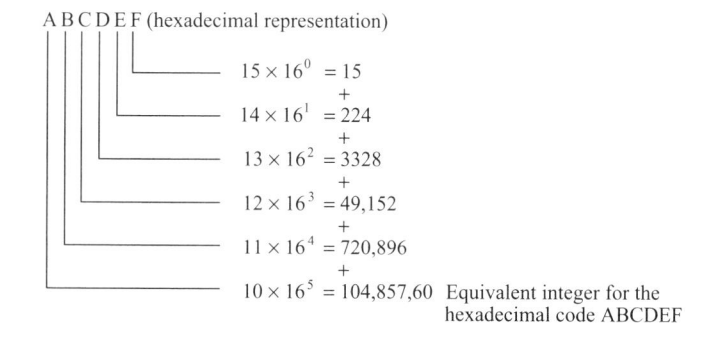

A B C D E F (hexadecimal representation)
- $15 \times 16^0 = 15$
- $+$
- $14 \times 16^1 = 224$
- $+$
- $13 \times 16^2 = 3328$
- $+$
- $12 \times 16^3 = 49,152$
- $+$
- $11 \times 16^4 = 720,896$
- $+$
- $10 \times 16^5 = 104,857,60$   Equivalent integer for the hexadecimal code ABCDEF

From these representations, it is clear that encoding to any base $b$ can be achieved. Bits of length $n_i$ can represent integers from 0 to $\left(b^{n_i}-1\right)$ and hence (0000 0000) and $((b-1)(b-1)(b-1)(b-1)\ (b-1)(b-1)(b-1)(b-1))$ would represent the points $X_1$ and $X_2$ as $\left(X_1^l, X_2^l\right)$ and $(X_1^u, X_2^u)$, respectively. The decoded value of the $b$-bit string $S_i$ is calculated as $\sum_{k=0}^{k=n_i-1} b^k s_k$. The precision of the variable approximation is given as $(X_i^u - X_i^l)/b^{n_i}$.

### 7.3.1.4 Floating-point Representation

In this representation, each chromosomal string is represented as a vector of floating-point numbers, of the same length as the solution vector. Each element is forced to be within the desired range, and the operators are carefully designed to preserve this requirement. The required precision in this approach depends on the problem being solved and is better compared to binary representation.

Even though the accuracy of binary representation is achieved by incorporating more bits, the execution of the algorithm slows down. Floating-point representation is capable of representing larger domains, whereas an increase in domain size decreases the precision in fixed binary length representation.

### 7.3.1.5 Tree Representation

The minimum spanning tree (MST) formulation method finds a significant role in most combinatorial optimisation problems. The extensions of the MST are generally NP-hard problems for which polynomial-time solutions do not exist. The complexity involved in using MSTs to solve problems lead researchers to opt for GAs. A spanning tree is a minimal set $E$ of edges that connects all the vertices in the set $V$; therefore, at least one spanning tree can be found in a graph $G$. An MST, denoted as $T^*$, is a spanning tree for which the total weight of all degrees is minimal. It is formulated as follows:

$$T^* = \min_T \sum_{e_{ij} \in E} w_{ij} \qquad (7.5)$$

where $T$ is the set of spanning trees of the undirected graph $G = (V, E)$, $V = \{v_1, v_2, \ldots, v_n\}$ is a finite set of vertices representing terminals, $E = \{e_{ij} | e_{ji} = (v_i, v_j), v_i, v_j \in V\}$ is a finite set of edges representing connections between the terminals, and $W = \{w_{ij} | w_{ji} = w(v_i, v_j), w_{ij} > 0, v_i, v_j \in V\}$ represents the weights of an edge, associated with a positive real number for distance, cost, and so on.

In order to implement a GA, the encoding of the MST is very critical, since any chromosome should represent a tree. The main categories of tree encoding are shown in Fig. 7.5. The encoding of the tree should be efficient enough to maintain a representation of all possible trees using the same number of genetic codes. The form of representation should be suitable for evaluating the fitness function and the constraints, and should possess the quality of locality (i.e., small changes in the representation should make small changes in the tree [3]).

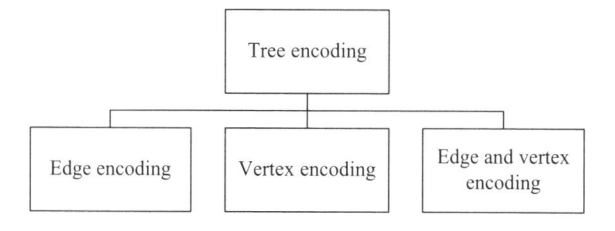

# Genetic Algorithms and Evolutionary Programming

**Fig. 7.5** Classification of tree encoding

## Edge encoding

Let us assume that $K$ is the number of edges in a graph and $k$ is the index for each edge (i.e., $E = \{e_k\}$, $k = 1, 2, \ldots, K$). Here, a bit string represents a candidate solution by indicating the edges used in a spanning tree, which is depicted in Fig. 7.6.

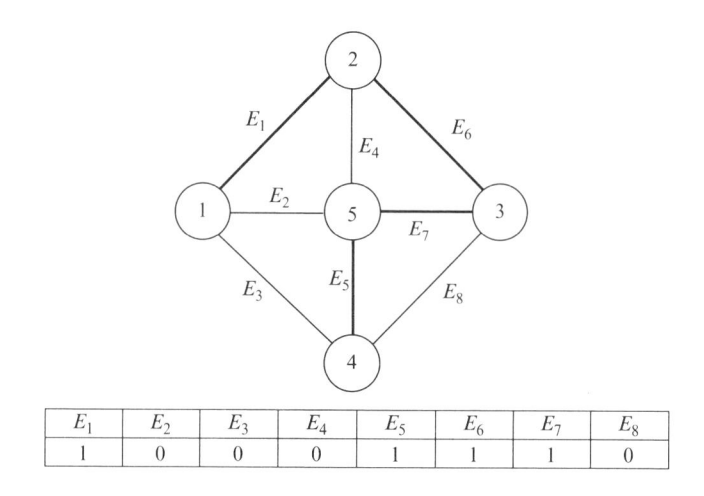

| $E_1$ | $E_2$ | $E_3$ | $E_4$ | $E_5$ | $E_6$ | $E_7$ | $E_8$ |
|---|---|---|---|---|---|---|---|
| 1 | 0 | 0 | 0 | 1 | 1 | 1 | 0 |

**Fig. 7.6** Representation of the edges of a spanning tree

## Vertex encoding

Caley's theorem of graphical enumerations gives $n^{n-2}$ distinct labelled trees for a complete graph with $n$ vertices. Prüfer proved this theorem by establishing a one-to-one correspondence between such trees and the set of all strings of $n - 2$ digits. Here, $(n - 2)$-digit permutation is uniquely represented for a tree where each digit is an integer between 1 and $n$ inclusively. This permutation is known as the *Prüfer number*. The representation can be explained by considering a labelled tree $T$. The first step is to find the smallest labelled leaf vertex $i$. Let $j$ be the first digit in the encoding, as the vertex $j$ incident on vertex $i$ is uniquely determined. The encoding process is built by adding digits to the right; the final code can be read from left to right. Then, the vertex $i$ and the edge from $i$ to $j$ are removed and the tree is left with $n-1$ vertices. The previous steps are continued till only one edge is left. Finally, a Prüfer number is obtained for the encoding, with $n-2$ digits between 1 and $n$ inclusively.

Figure 7.7 shows the Prüfer number corresponding to a spanning tree on a six-vertex complete graph. Here in this spanning tree the leaf vertex with the smallest label is the vertex 2. The only vertex adjacent to vertex 2 is vertex 3. Hence, the first digit of the Prüfer number becomes 3, and then vertex 2 and the edge (2, 3) are removed. This process is continued till the edge (1, 6) is left. Thus, a four-digit Prüfer number is obtained.

When decoding is done for the Prüfer number $P = \{3\ 3\ 1\ 1\}$, the vertices 2, 4, 5, and 6 are eligible; let $\bar{P} = \{2, 4, 5, 6\}$. Here, vertex 2 is the eligible vertex with the smallest label and 3 is the leftmost digit in $P$. Therefore, the edge (2, 3) is added to the tree, and vertex 2 and the leftmost digit in the Prüfer number, 3, are removed, respectively, from $\bar{P}$ and $P$. Now $\bar{P} = \{4, 5, 6\}$ and $P = \{3\ 1\ 1\}$; vertex 4 is the eligible vertex with the smallest label and the 3 is the leftmost digit in $P$. Therefore, the edge (4, 3) is added to the tree, and vertex 4 and the digit 3 are removed, respectively, from $\bar{P}$ and $P$. Now $\bar{P} = \{5, 6\}$ and $P = \{1\ 1\}$. This process is continued till all the digits of the Prüfer number are decoded.

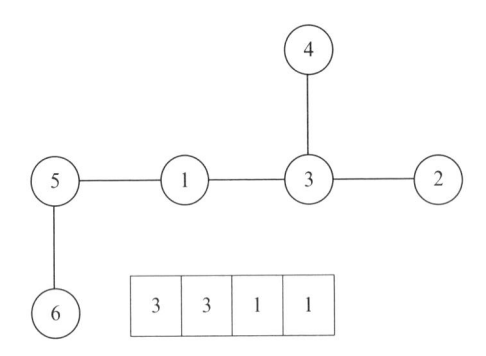

**Fig. 7.7** Representation of a tree and the Prüfer number

### Edge and vertex encoding

Palmer developed edge and vertex coding, which is also known as *link- and node-biased encoding*. In this scheme, the chromosome has bias values corresponding to each node and link; these values are integers ranging from 0 to 255. The encoding is based on Prim's MST algorithm on the modified cost matrix $C' = [C'_{ij}]$.

$$c'_{ij} = c_{ij} + p_1 b_{ij} c_{max} + p_2 (b_i + b_j) c_{max} \tag{7.6}$$

where $c_{max}$ is the maximum link cost in the graph, $b_{ij}$ is the link bias corresponding to the edge from node $i$ to node $j$, and $b_i$ is the node bias associated with node $i$. $p_1$ and $p_2$ are the control parameters. Based on the modified cost matrix, a tree is generated using Prim's algorithm. The limitations of this type of representation are the requirement of a very long code, the use of a conventional MST algorithm to generate a tree, and the unavailability of certain types of information such as the degree, connection, and so on (Fig. 7.8).

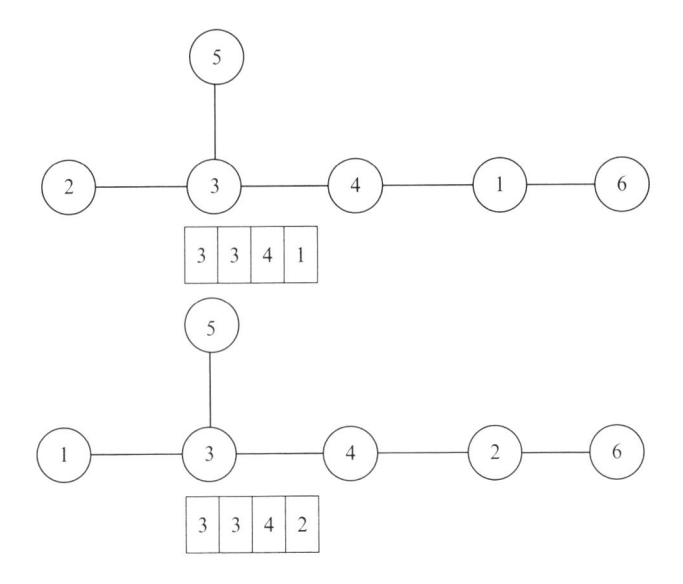

**Fig. 7.8** Illustration of Prüfer numbers 3341 and 3342

### 7.3.1.6 Permutation Representation

This representation is perhaps the most natural representation of a travelling salesman tour or the TSP, where cities are listed in the order in which they are visited. The search space for this representation is the set of permutations of the cities. For example, in an eight-city TSP [3], 3-5-8-1-4-2-6-7 can be represented as [3 5 8 1 4 2 6 7]. This representation is also known as the *path* or *order representation*.

### 7.3.1.7 Random Keys Representation

This representation is also used for the TSP problem. Here the solution is encoded with random numbers from the interval (0, 1). These values are used as sorting keys to decode the solution. For example, in an eight-city TSP, [0.45 0.68 0.91 0.11 0.62 0.34 0.74 0.89] can be represented as 3-5-8-1-4-2-6-7, where the position $i$ in the list represents city $i$. The random number in position $i$ determines the visiting order of city $i$ in a TSP tour. The random keys have been sorted in ascending order. Random keys eliminate the infeasibility of the offspring by representing the solution in a soft manner. This representation is applicable to many problems including machine scheduling, resource allocation, vehicle routing, and the quadratic assignment problem.

### 7.3.1.8 Other Representations

There are still a lot of different types of representations available. For example, job shop scheduling (JSP), which has lot of precedence constraints on operations, requires a different type of representation scheme; its representation is more complex than that of the TSP. In the last few years, different types of representations have evolved for JSP, such as the (a) operation-based, (b) job-based, (c) preference-list-based, (d) job-pair-relation-based, (e) priority-rule-based, (f) disjunctive-graph-based, (g) completion-time-based, (h) machine-based, and (i) random keys representations.

There are also representations like grammatical encoding for the evolution of network architectures. Hence, it is very important to choose the most suitable code for a particular problem so as to get a good optimal solution. To discuss all the representations available for different types of problems is not an easy task; we have, however, studied some of the most important representation schemes available, which can be extended or modified to solve many problems.

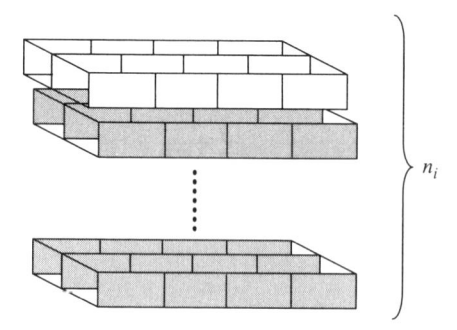

**Fig. 7.9** Depiction of populations

To initialize a population (Fig. 7.9), we can simply set some 'pop_size' number of chromosomes randomly in a bit-wise fashion. However, if we do have some knowledge about the distribution of potential optima, we may use such information to arrange the set of initial potential solutions. The rest of the algorithm is straightforward: in each generation, we evaluate each chromosome (using the function $f$ on the decoded sequences of variables), select a new population with respect to the probability distribution based on fitness values, and alter the chromosomes in the new population using mutation and crossover operators. After some generations, when no further improvement is observed, the best chromosome represents an (possibly the global) optimal solution. Often, we stop the algorithm after a fixed number of iterations, depending on the speed and resource criteria.

For the selection process (selection of a new population with respect to the probability distribution based on fitness values), a roulette wheel with slots sized according to fitness values is used. The fitness values are then calculated using the function $eval(v_i)$ for each chromosome $v_i$ ($i = 1, \ldots,$ pop_size). The total fitness of the population is given by the following:

$$F = \sum_{i=1}^{pop\_size} eval(v_i) \quad (7.7)$$

The probability of selection for each chromosome $v_i$ ($i = 1, \ldots,$ pop_size) is as follows:

$$p_i = eval(v_i)/F \quad (7.8)$$

and the cumulative probability is given here:

$$q_i = \sum_{j=1}^{i} p_i \quad (7.9)$$

The selection process is based on spinning the roulette wheel pop_size times, each time selecting a single chromosome for a new population in the following way.

- Generate a random (float) number $r$ from the range $[0, z]$.
- If $r < q_1$, select the first chromosome ($v_1$); otherwise, select the *i*th chromosome $v_i$ ($2 \leq i \leq$ pop_size) such that $q_{i-1} < r \leq q_i$.

Obviously, some chromosomes would be selected more than once. The best chromosomes get duplicated, the average stay even, and the worst die off. Hence, with the help of roulette-wheel selection, we understand that selection, which has been derived from Darwinian natural selection, provides the driving force in a GA. However, there are different types of selection issues and schemes, which will be explained in the following section.

## 7.3.2 Selection

There are three basic issues involved in the selection phase: (a) sampling space, (b) sampling mechanism, and (c) selection probability. Their significant influence in the selection procedure is discussed in the following sections [5].

### 7.3.2.1 Sampling Space

A new population is created for the next generation with the help of the selection procedure based on either all parents and offspring or some of them. During this process, there arises the problem of sampling space. Two important factors that affect the sample space are the size and constitution of the parents and offspring. Suppose the population size (pop_size) and the offspring size (off_size) in each generation are considered, then the regular sampling space has a size equal to pop_size and contains all the offspring but only some of the parents. On the other hand, the size of the enlarged sampling space is equal to the sum of pop_size and off_size, and it consists of all the parents and offspring.

*Regular sampling space*
In his original work on GAs, Holland proposed the replacement of parents by their offspring soon after they give birth; this is known as *generational replacement* [1]. If this procedure is followed, there is every chance of losing high-quality chromosomes. Hence, in order to overcome this limitation, several replacement strategies have evolved in the last few decades. Holland suggested that when an offspring is produced, it replaces a randomly chosen chromosome of the current population. A *crowding strategy* has been proposed by K.A. de Jong in which one parent chromosome is selected to die after the offspring is produced [6]. The dying parent is chosen in such a way that its resemblance is close to the new offspring produced with the help of a bit-by-bit similarity count mechanism to measure resemblance.

In Holland's work, selection is referred to for the purpose of choosing parents for re-combination; that is, a new population is formed by replacing parents with their offspring, called the *reproductive plan*. According to Grefenstette and Baker's work, selection is based on the probabilistic mechanism [7], [8]. Michalewicz gave a detailed explanation of how parents in each generation are replaced by their offspring using roulette-wheel selection [9], which has already been explained. Figure 7.10 gives an idea of the selection procedure based on regular sampling space.

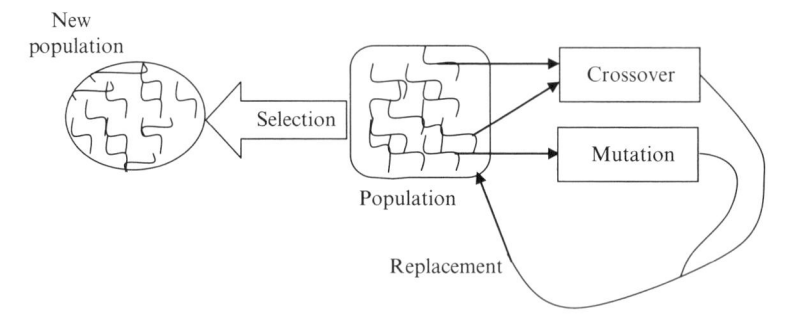

**Fig. 7.10** Selection based on regular sampling space

*Enlarged sampling space*
The enlarged sampling space offers both the parents and offspring an equal chance to compete for survival in the next generation. A $(\mu + \lambda)$ selection strategy, in which $\mu$ parents and $\lambda$ offspring are involved, is used in ESs. Back and Hoffmeiste introduced this technique in GAs, in which $\mu$ of the best offspring and parents are selected to be parents in the next generation. Another ES is $(\mu, \lambda)$ selection, in which $\mu$ best offspring are selected as parents for the next generation and $\mu < \lambda$ is maintained. These methods are deterministic in nature and can be achieved using the probabilistic method.

Most selection procedures are based on the regular sampling space, but implementation is easier in an enlarged sampling space. This approach is illustrated in Fig. 7.11. One of the benefits of this approach is improved performance of the GA through increased crossover and mutation rates, even though the high rate will lead to more random perturbation.

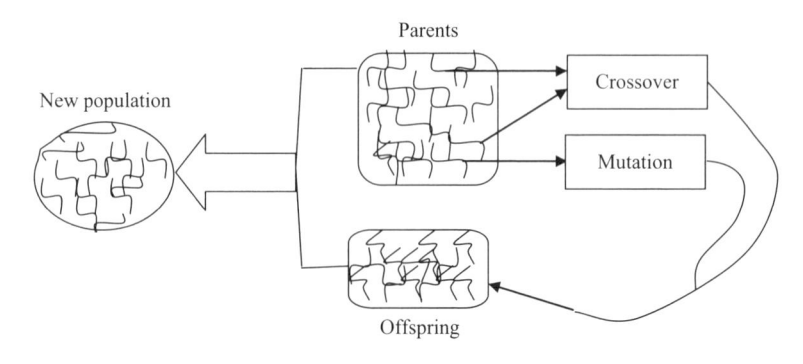

**Fig. 7.11** Selection based on enlarged sampling space

### 7.3.2.2 Sampling Mechanism

This mechanism deals with the selection of chromosomes from the sampling space, which can be achieved using three basic approaches, namely, (a) stochastic sampling, (b) deterministic sampling, and (c) mixed sampling.

*Stochastic sampling*

Most early work is based on this approach. The common feature of the methods in this class is that the selection phase determines the actual number of copies each chromosome receives based on its survival probability. Here the selection phase is divided into two parts. In the first part the chromosome's expected value is determined and in the second part the expected value is converted into the number of offspring. A chromosome's expected value is a real number indicating the average number of offspring the chromosome should receive. The sampling procedure is used to convert the real expected value into the number of offspring. The best known example of this type of selection is Holland's proportionate selection or roulette-wheel selection, where the basic idea is to determine the selection probability, called *survival probability*, for each chromosome proportionate to its fitness value.

Baker proposed stochastic universal sampling, which uses a single wheel spin. The wheel is constructed in the form of a roulette wheel, with the number of equally spaced markers equal to the population size. The expected value $e_k$ = pop_size × $P_k$. The basic idea is to keep the expected number of copies of each chromosome in the next generation while preventing the duplication of chromosomes in the population. In this approach, the domination of super-chromosomes is prevented by keeping many copies of the other chromosomes in the population; this also prevents premature convergence to local minima. The approach also maintains the diversity of the population, so that the constant generation pool can contain more information for genetic search. If the duplicated chromosomes are discarded, the size of the population formed with the remaining parents and offspring may be less than the pre-determined size, pop_size; in this case, the initial procedure is repeated, thereby completing the population pool.

*Deterministic sampling*

The selection of the best pop_size chromosomes from the sampling space is the significant feature of this approach. The $(\mu + \lambda)$ and $(\mu, \lambda)$ selection procedures belong to this class of methods. Both these approaches prohibit duplicate chromosomes from entering the population during selection. Most combinatorial problems are solved preferring this approach.

Truncation selection and block selection, which belong to this category, rank all chromosomes by evaluating their fitness values and select the best ones as parents. In truncation selection, a threshold $T$ is defined such that $T\%$ best chromosomes are selected and each one receives nearly $100/T$ copies. Block selection is almost similar to truncation selection, as for a given population size, one simply gives $s$ copies to the pop_size/$s$ best chromosomes. They become identical when $s$ = pop_size/$T$.

Elitist selection, which belongs to this class, ensures that the best chromosome is passed on to the next generation, if not selected by any other selection method. Deterministic sampling proposed by Brindle is based on the 'expected number'. Here $p_k = f_k / \Sigma f_j$ is called the selection probability for each chromosome. The expected number of each chromosome is calculated as $e_k = p_k \times \text{pop\_size}$. Each chromosome is allocated samples according to the integer part of the expected number, and then the population is sorted according to the fractional parts of the expected number. The remainder of chromosomes needed to fill in is drawn from the top of the sorted list.

Steady-state selection is a modified version of the generational replacement approach, where instead of replacing the entire set of parents by their offspring; the $n$ worst old chromosomes are replaced with $n$ offspring. Syswerda called this *steady-state reproduction*. Michalewicz gave a stochastic version of this approach, called *modGA*, where the parent chromosomes that are replaced by their offspring are picked up according to their probability of survival.

*Mixed sampling*

This mechanism mixes the features of the random and deterministic selection procedures. Tournament selection is an example of this approach, which has been proposed by Goldberg et al. This method chooses a team or group of chromosomes randomly and selects the best one from this set for reproduction. The number of chromosomes in the group is called the *tournament size*. Generally, a tournament size of 2 is considered, known as a binary tournament. Wetzel suggests stochastic tournament selection, where selection probabilities are based on calculating normally, and successive pairs of chromosomes are drawn using roulette-wheel selection. Once a pair of chromosomes is found, the best fit among them is inserted in the new population.

Remainder stochastic sampling, proposed by Brindle, is a modified version of deterministic sampling, where each chromosome is allocated samples according to the integer part of the expected number. Then, a competition is conducted among the chromosomes based on the fractional parts of the expected number for the remaining places in the population.

### 7.3.2.3 Selection Probability

The selection of chromosomes for the new generation is a vital issue, based on certain criteria. The selection probability of the proportional selection method is proportional to the fitness of the chromosomes; that is, in early generations, the selection process is dominated by a few super-chromosomes, and in later generations, when the population is largely converged, the competition among the chromosomes reduces and a random-search behaviour emerges. To overcome this limitation, the scaling and ranking mechanism is used. The scaling mechanism maps the raw objective function values to some positive real values, and the survival probability for each chromosome is determined according these values. The ranking method uses a ranking of the chromosomes, ignoring the actual objective function values, to determine their survival probabilities.

Fitness scaling is used to maintain a reasonable differential between the relative fitness ratings of chromosomes and to prevent the domination of super-chromosomes, in order to meet the requirement of limiting the competition early on but stimulating it later. Scaling of the objective function, according to De Jong, is a commonly accepted practice when several scaling mechanisms have been proposed. Goldberg and Michalewicz have formulated an appropriate expression for fitness scaling. Let $f'_k$ be the scaled fitness obtained from the raw fitness $f_k$, which can be an objective function value for chromosome $k$ and be expressed as given in the following:

$$f'_k = g(f_k) \qquad (7.10)$$

where, the function $g(\cdot)$ transforms the raw fitness into scaled fitness.

The function $g(\cdot)$ may take different forms to yield different scaling techniques, such as linear scaling, sigma truncation, power law scaling, logarithmic scaling, and so on. These scaling methods can be generally classified into two classes, namely (a) static scaling and (b) dynamic scaling. In static scaling, the mapping relationship between the scaled fitness and the raw fitness is constant; in dynamic scaling, the mapping relationship varies according to certain factors.

The variation in dynamic scaling is achieved in two ways. In the first case, the scaling parameters are adaptively adjusted to the scatter situation of the fitness values in each generation in order to maintain constant selective pressure (the degree to which better individuals are favoured). In the second case, scaling parameters are dynamically changed along with increasing the number of generations, with the aim of increasing the selective pressure accordingly.

## *Linear scaling*

In this type of scaling, the fitness values of all chromosomes are adjusted so that the best chromosome gets a fixed number of expected offspring and is, thus, prevented from duplicating. The linear function $g(\cdot)$ transforms raw fitness into scaled fitness according to the following expression:

$$f'_k = a f_k + b \qquad (7.11)$$

where the parameters are normally selected such that the average chromosomes receive one offspring copy on average, and the best one receives the specified number of copies. Here, negative fitness values are a limitation, which has to be dealt properly.

## *Dynamic linear scaling*

In this type of scaling, the parameter $b$ in the expression $f'_k = a f_k + b$ can be varied with the generation. Thus the expression changes to $f'_k = a f_k + b_t$. The parameter $b_t$ takes the minimal raw fitness value of the current population such that it is equal to $-f_{min}$.

## *Sigma truncation*

Forrest proposed this technique to overcome the limitation of negativity in the fitness values occurring in linear scaling. Sigma truncation also incorporates problem-dependent information into mapping. The function g(·) can be expressed as follows:

$$f'_k = f_k - (\bar{f} - c\sigma) \tag{7.12}$$

where, $c$ is a small integer, $\sigma$ is the standard deviation of the population, and $\bar{f}$ is the average raw fitness. The possible negative scaled fitness $f'_k$ is set to zero. The selection pressure is related to the scatter of the fitness values in the population. The scaling factor is set as the difference between the mean and the standard deviation, which is based on observation. Chromosomes below this score are assigned a fitness value of zero. This scaling method helps to overcome the large scattering of fitness values caused by poor chromosomes, thereby reducing the selection pressure.

### Power law scaling

Gillies proposed this technique, in which the g(·) takes the form of some specified power of the raw fitness. The expression is given as follows:

$$f'_k = f_k^\alpha \tag{7.13}$$

where $\alpha$ is problem-dependent. The gap of scaled fitness between the best and the worst chromosome increases with the value of $\alpha$. The gap approaches zero when $\alpha$ approaches zero and the sampling becomes a random search. When the value of $\alpha$ is greater than 1, the gap is increased and the sampling is allocated to fitter chromosomes. It is also important to note that there is a need for the range of $\alpha$ to be dynamically adjusted. Another way of expressing power law scaling is given here:

$$f'_k = (af_k + b)^\alpha \tag{7.14}$$

### Logarithmic scaling

Fitzpatrick and Grefenstette proposed this method, which is used to map the objective function for a minimization problem. The function g(·) can be expressed in the following logarithmic form:

$$f'_k = b - \log(f_k) \tag{7.15}$$

where $b > \log(f_k)$.

### Windowing

Hancock proposed this technique, where he introduced the modification of the baseline of the fitness function. Suppose the two chromosomes have fitness values of 2 and 1, respectively; the first will get twice as many offspring as the second [10]. If the original function is modified by adding 1 to all the values, the two chromosomes will score 3 and 2; the ratio changes to 1.5, and this mere modification has a significant effect on the rate of progress. The main idea behind this technique is to have fitness-proportional selection in order to maintain an effective constant selection pressure. The expression for the function g(·) is given as follows:

$$f'_k = f_k - f_w \tag{7.16}$$

where $w$ is known as the window size and is typically of the order of 2–10 and $f_w$ is the worst value observed in the $w$ most recent generations. This technique can be viewed as a kind of linear scaling.

## *Normalizing*
Gen and Cheng [3] proposed this technique, which can be treated as a kind of dynamic scaling method. If $f_{max}$ and $f_{min}$ are the best and the worst raw fitness values in current population, then for the maximization problem the function $g(\cdot)$ can be expressed as given in the following:

$$f'_k = \frac{f_k - f_{min} + \lambda}{f_{max} - f_{min} + \lambda} \quad (7.17)$$

It can be viewed as a normalized special windowing method where the window size is 1. $\lambda$ is a small positive real number which is usually restricted within the open interval (0, 1). For the minimization problem, the following equation is given:

$$f'_k = \frac{f_{max} - f_k + \lambda}{f_{max} - f_{min} + \lambda} \quad (7.18)$$

The main reason for using this transformation is to prevent the equation from zero division and to make it possible to adjust the selection behaviour from fitness-proportional selection to pure random selection.

## *Boltzman selection*
In this type of scaling method for proportional selection, the function $g(\cdot)$ can be expressed as follows:

$$f'_k = e^{f_k/T} \quad (7.19)$$

Here the selection pressure is low when the control parameter $T$ is high.

## *Ranking*
Baker proposed the concept of ranking selection for GAs in order to overcome the scaling problem. This is a direct fitness-based approach. Here the population is sorted from the best to the worst, and the selection probability is assigned according to the ranking. The two types of commonly used ranking are linear ranking and exponential ranking. Suppose $p_k$ is the selection probability for the $k$th chromosome in the ranking of the population, the linear ranking takes the following form:

$$P_k = q - (k-1)r \quad (7.20)$$

where the parameter $q$ is the probability for the best chromosome. If $q_0$ is the probability for the worst chromosome, the parameter $r$ can be determined as follows:

$$r = \frac{q - q_0}{pop\_size - 1} \quad (7.21)$$

The intermediate chromosomes' fitness values are decreased from $q$ to $q_0$ proportional to their rank. When $q_0$ is 0, it provides the maximum selective pressure.

Exponential ranking was proposed by Michalewicz and its selection probability is given as follows:

$$p_k = q(1-q)^{k-1} \qquad (7.22)$$

A large value of $q$ indicates that the selective pressure is also large. Hancock proposed the following exponential ranking method:

$$p_k = q^{k-1} \qquad (7.23)$$

where $q$ is typically about 0.99. The best chromosome has a fitness value equal to 1 and the worst one receives $q^{pop\_size-1}$.

Selection based on the process of evolution can also be classified into the following three categories according to Neo-Darwinism:

- Stabilizing selection
- Directional selection
- Disruptive selection

Stabilizing selection is also called as *normalizing selection* because it tends to remove chromosomes with extreme values. Directional selection has the effect of either increasing or decreasing the mean value of the population. Disruptive selection tends to eliminate chromosomes with moderate values. Most selection methods are based on directional selection.

Gen, Liu, and Ida proposed a stabilizing selection method where chromosomes are ranked from the best to the worst according to their raw fitness values. After ranking, three preference parameters $p_1$, $p_0$, and $p_2$ ($0 < p_1 < p_0 < p_2 < 1$) are defined, which are used to determine three critical chromosomes with ranks $u_1$, $u_0$, and $u_2$, respectively, such that $u_1 = |p_1 \times pop\_size|$, $u_0 = |p_0 \times pop\_size|$, and $u_2 = |p_2 \times pop\_size|$. Finally, the chromosome with the rank $u_1$ is assigned a fitness value of $e^{-1} \approx 0.37$, that with the rank $u_0$ is assigned a fitness value of 1, and that with the rank $u_2$ is assigned a fitness value of $2 - e^{-1} \approx 1.63$. For a chromosome $k$ with rank $u$, the relation between the rank and the exponential fitness $f_k$ is the following:

$$f_k = \begin{cases} \exp\left[-\dfrac{u-u_0}{u_1-u_0}\right], & u < u_0 \\ 2 - \exp\left[-\dfrac{u-u_0}{u_2-u_0}\right], & u \geq u_0 \end{cases} \qquad (7.24)$$

This is shown in Fig. 7.12. It is clear that the preference parameters $p_1$ and $p_2$ are used to designate the chromosomes with extreme values, which are to be eliminated.

Kuo and Hwang proposed a method based on disruptive selection. The method adopts a non-monotonic fitness function that is different from the traditional fitness function. They gave the concept of the normalized-by-mean fitness function as follows:

$$f'_k = |f_k - \bar{f}| \qquad (7.25)$$

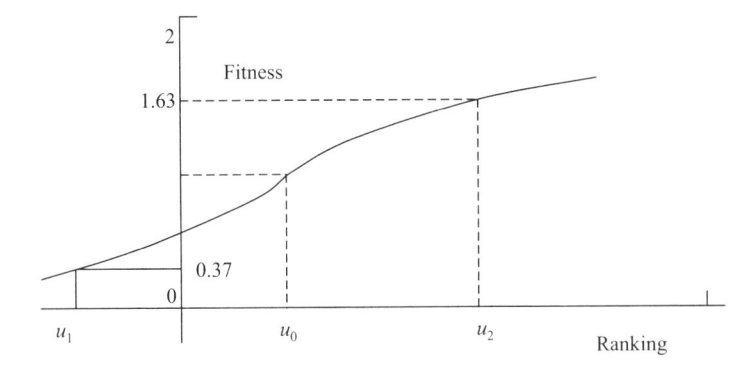

**Fig. 7.12** Relation between the rank $u$ and the exponential fitness $f_k$

This function is a kind of non-monotonic function. This method gives a higher probability to both the best and the worst chromosome. After the selection we can apply the re-combination operator, crossover (Fig. 7.13), to the individuals in the new population. As mentioned earlier, one parameter of the genetic system is the probability of crossover $p_c$. This probability gives us the expected number $p_c$, the pop_size of chromosomes which undergo the crossover operation.

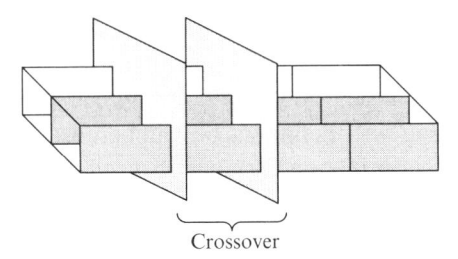

**Fig. 7.13** Illustration of two points crossing

This method proceeds in the following way:

- For each chromosome in the new population, generate a random (float) number $r$ from the range [0, 1].
- If $r < p_c$, select the given chromosome for crossover.
- Mate the selected chromosomes randomly: for each pair of coupled chromosomes, generate a random integer 'pos' from the range $[1, m-1]$ ($m$ is the total length of a chromosome; i.e., the number of bits in it). The number *pos* indicates the position of the crossing point. Two chromosomes

$$(b_1 b_2 \ldots b_{pos} b_{pos+1} \ldots b_m)$$

and

$$(c_1 c_2 \ldots c_{pos} c_{pos+1} \ldots c_m)$$

are replaced by a pair of their offspring:

$$(b_1 b_2 \ldots b_{pos} c_{pos+1} \ldots c_m)$$

and

$$(c_1 c_2 \ldots c_{pos} b_{pos+1} \ldots b_m)$$

We have discussed a general form of the crossover operation here. The following section discusses other genetic operators.

### 7.3.3 Genetic Operators

The crossover operator is a core genetic operator; it is considered as an axle for the generation of new offspring with strong characteristic features of new genetic information obtained as a result of the exchange of genetic material among the individuals of the chromosomal population. It can generally be classified into three main categories: conventional operators, arithmetical operators, and direction-based operators [3, 4, 5, 16].

#### 7.3.3.1 Conventional Binary Crossover

Binary crossover involves binary numbers. In this section, we discuss different types of binary crossover operations.

*Single-point crossover*

In this type of crossover, a single site is randomly selected along the span of the mated strings and bits next to the crossover site are exchanged as shown in Fig. 7.14. The only crossover point is at the third segment (from the bottom of the chromosomal string) of the parent. In this crossover operation, the crossover site, which is at a single point, is not known, since it is selected randomly. If an appropriate site is chosen, good child strings are produced. However, the quality of the offspring will definitely be hampered if the selected site does not exchange genetic information for the enhanced result of the child string's performance.

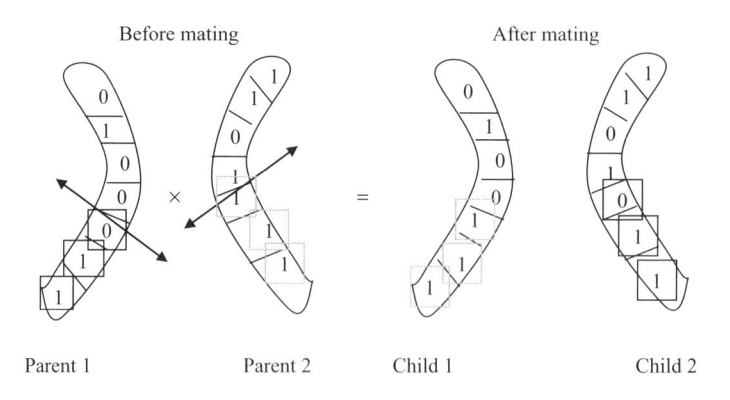

**Fig. 7.14** Single-point crossover

*Double-point Crossover*

Two random sites are chosen in this crossover operation. This crossover can be understood with the help of Fig. 7.15. The crossover points in the parent chromosomal string are at the second and fifth segments from its lower bottom.

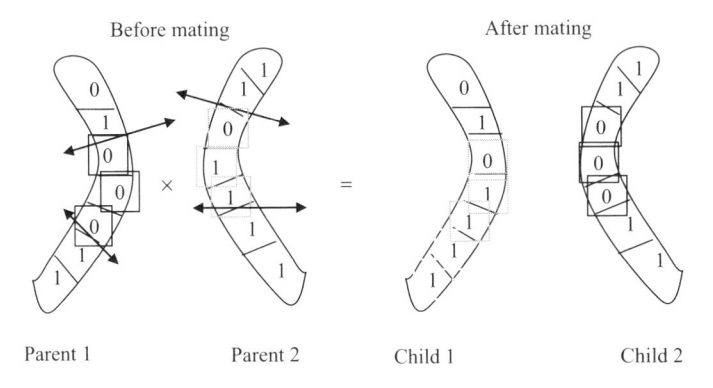

**Fig. 7.15** Double-point crossover

*Multiple-point crossover*
In the multiple-point crossover operation, the crossover operation takes place at even- and odd-numbered sites. In the case of even-numbered crossover sites, the chromosomal string is viewed as a ring with no beginning or end, and the crossover sites are selected around the circle at random (Fig. 7.16). In the case of odd-numbered crossover sites, the crossover point is chosen at the beginning of the string (see Fig. 7.17).

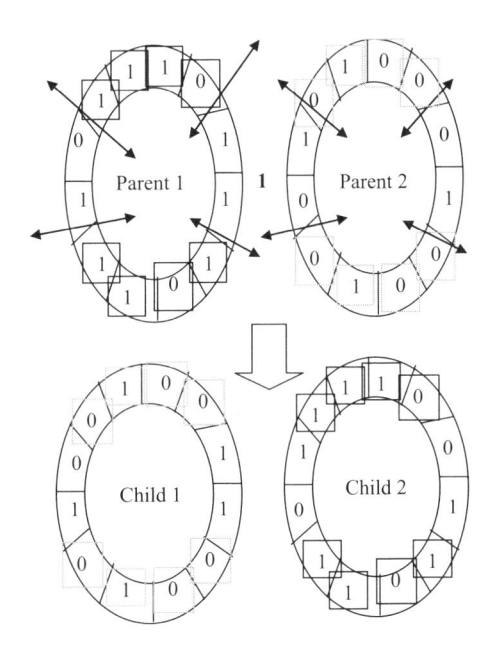

**Fig. 7.16** Multiple-point crossover: even-numbered crossover site

*Uniform crossover*
Uniform crossover is achieved as a result of exchanging bits from two individual parent chromosomes and maintaining a probability of 0.5 to produce offspring,

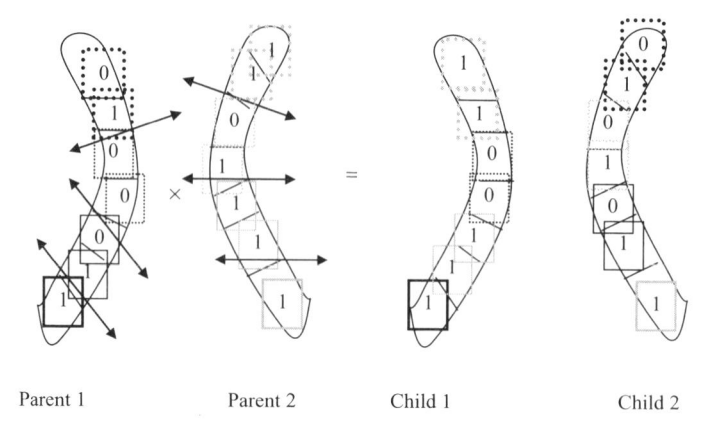

**Fig. 7.17** Multiple-point crossover: odd-numbered crossover site

which is shown in Fig. 7.18. In the uniform crossover operation, one can also observe a masking type of operation on the basis of a mask string generated randomly. Figure 7.19 shows the generation of a maskable binary string. Here, the first binary digit is 1, so the gene from the first parent chromosome is copied to the first child; simultaneously the gene from the second parent chromosome is copied to the second child. Conversely, when the second digit of the mask string is 0, the gene from the second parent chromosome is copied to the first child; simultaneously the gene from the first parent chromosome is copied to the second child. The number of crossing points is not fixed but is on the average equal to half the chromosomal length.

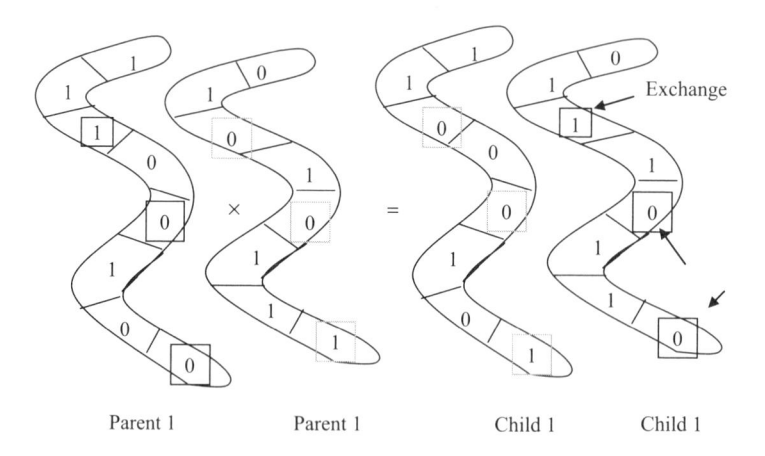

**Fig. 7.18** Uniform crossover

### *Matrix crossover*

The crossover operations discussed previously are one-dimensional in nature. In the case of matrix crossover, two-dimensional array vectors are used. Here, the

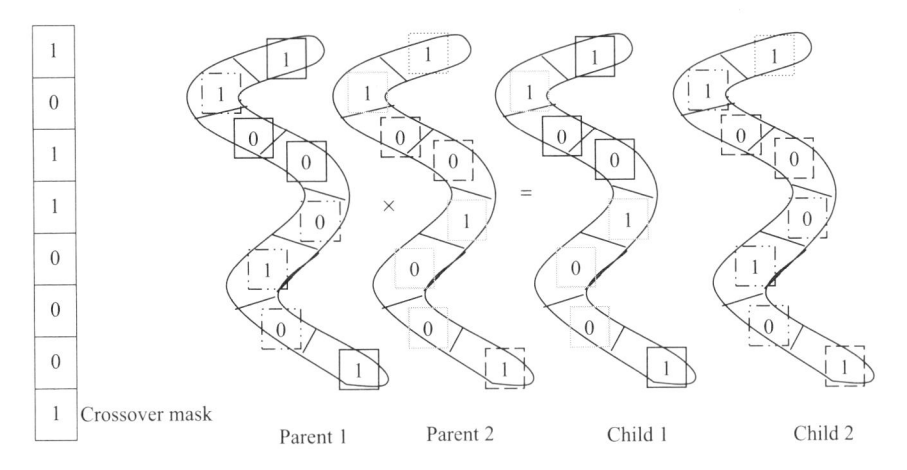

**Fig. 7.19** Masking-based uniform crossover

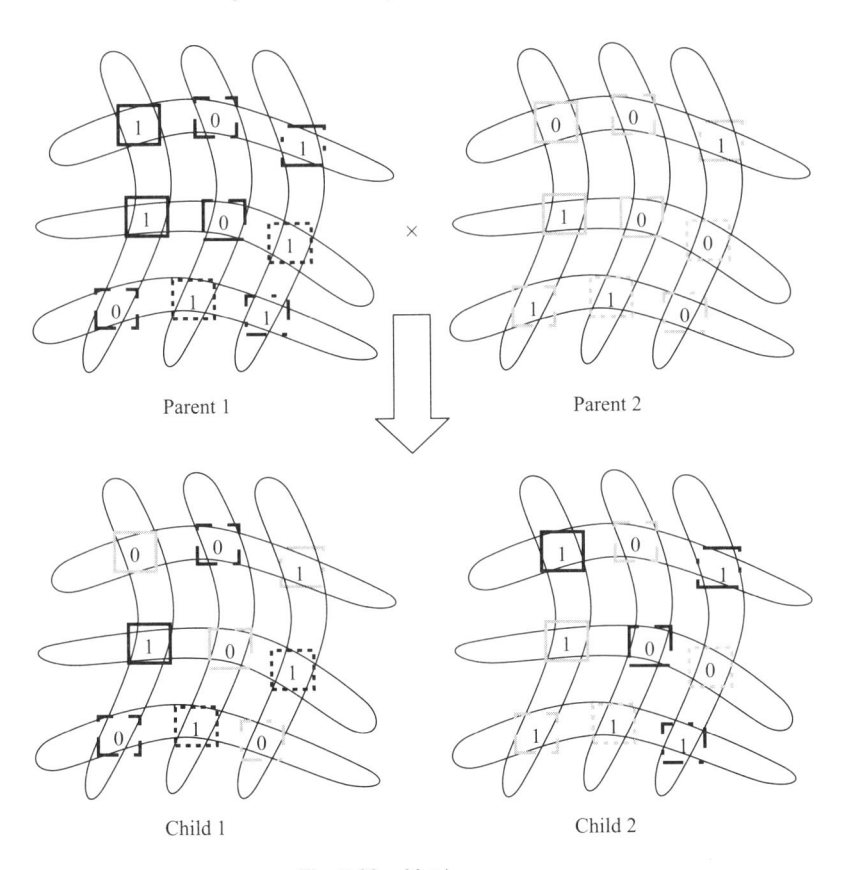

**Fig. 7.20** Matrix crossover

rows and columns of the crossover sites are chosen randomly. Thus, two crossover sites, both row-wise and column-wise, will divide into three layers horizontally and vertically. Select any region between two layers, either vertically or horizontally, and then exchange the information in the region between the mated populations.

This is illustrated in Fig. 7.20. Appropriate selection of crossover operators ensures that the search space is proper.

*Random crossover*

This crossover operation creates offspring randomly within a hyper-rectangle defined by the parent points. One of its basic types is the *flat crossover*. In this operation, an offspring is produced by uniformly picking a value for each gene from a range of values, the upper and lower limits of which correspond to the parent genes. Another type of random crossover is the *blend crossover*, which incorporates more variance by picking values that lie between two points containing the two parents [4].

*Permutation-based crossover operations*

These crossover operators have been developed mainly for combinatorial optimisation problems such as the TSP, machine scheduling, resource allocation, vehicle routing, and quadratic assignment problems. These operators function based on two main approaches: the canonical and the heuristic. In the canonical approach, the crossover can be seen as an extension of the double-point or multiple-point crossover of binary strings. This approach is based on the blind random mechanism and there is no guarantee that an offspring produced by this method is better than its parents. The application of heuristics in crossover tends to generate improved offspring [3].

*Partial-mapped crossover*

Goldberg and Lingle [11] proposed this method, which adopts a repairing procedure known as *relationship mapping* in order to prevent illegal duplication of genes. Partial-mapped crossover can be considered an extension of double-point crossover. Figure 7.21 shows two individual parent chromosomal strings, parent 1 and parent 2. Two positions along each of these strings are randomly and uniformly selected. In the figure, the two sub-strings 4-6-5-3 and 5-1-2-9 are selected and

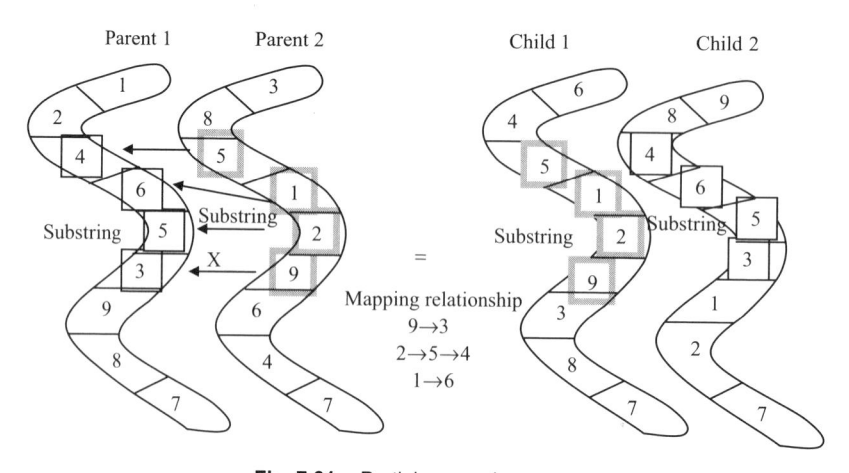

**Fig. 7.21** Partial-mapped crossover

exchanged between the parent chromosomes. Now, when 4-6-5-3 is inserted in the place of sub-string 5-1-2-9 of parent 2, the second parent string becomes 3-8-**4-6-5-3**-6-4-7, where the illegal duplication of 3, 4, and 6 is observed and the nodes 1, 2, and 9 are missing. In order to legalize the compulsory presence of all the available nodes, a mapping relationship repair mechanism is adopted, shown in Fig. 7.21. Now, to produce child 1, '1' in parent 1 is changed to '6' according to their relationship. This procedure is continued only for all the related nodes, keeping the swapped sub-string unchanged. For producing child 2, the changes $3 \rightarrow 9$, $6 \rightarrow 1$, and $4 \rightarrow 2$ should be made in the illegal parent 2 string to obtain 9-8-**4-6-5-3**-1-2-7.

*Order crossover (OX)*
Davis proposed this method, which is an extension of partial-mapped crossover with a different repairing procedure. In this method, a sub-string is selected randomly from one of the parents and copied exactly to the same positions in the child string as shown in Fig. 7.22.

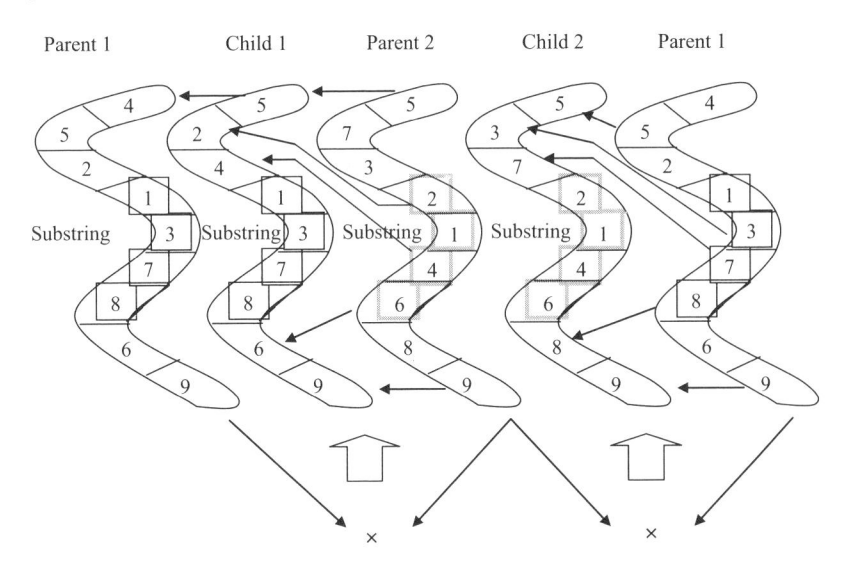

**Fig. 7.22** Order crossover

Here, the nodes 1, 3, 7, and 8 of parent 1 are copied to child 1. Now, those nodes of parent 2 which are already present in child 1 are deleted. Hence, starting from the bottom of the parent 2 string and going to the top, the nodes 9, 6, 4, 2, and 5 are deleted; these are filled in the empty segments of the child 1 string from the bottom to the top. The same procedure is repeated to produce child 2.

*Position-based crossover (OX)*
Syswerda proposed position-based crossover [12]. It can be considered a variation of order crossover and also a sort of uniform crossover. A set of randomly selected positions from one parent is considered and the corresponding nodes are transferred to the same positions of its child string. In Fig. 7.23, 5, 1, 8, and 6 from parent 1 are

copied to child 1. Now, those nodes of parent 2 which are already present in child 1 are deleted. Thus, starting from the bottom of the parent 2 string and going to the top, the nodes 9, 4, 2, 3, and 7 are deleted, these are filled in the empty segments of child 1 from bottom to top. The same procedure is repeated to produce child 2 (Fig. 7.23).

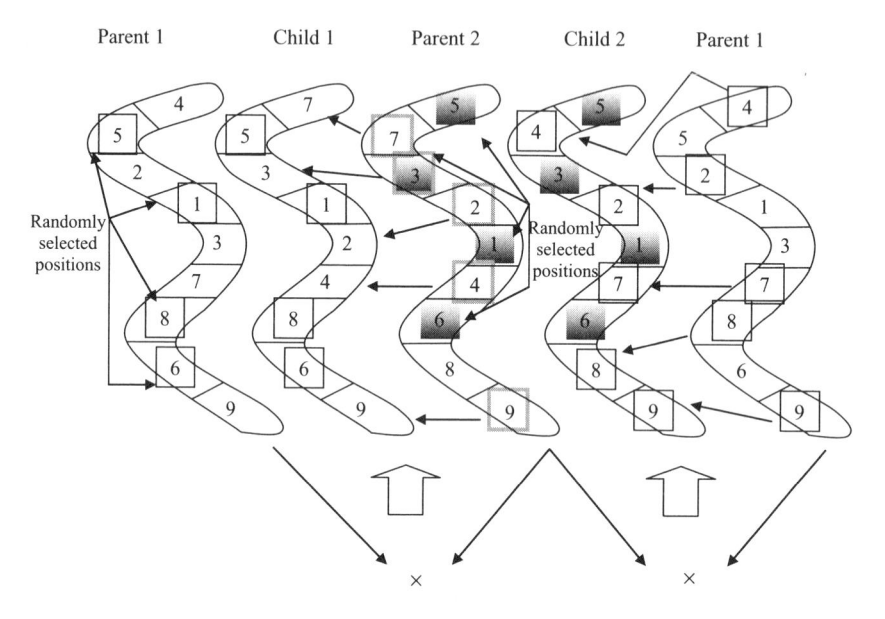

**Fig. 7.23** Position-based crossover

*Order-based crossover*
Syswerda also proposed order-based crossover, which is a slight variation of position-based crossover. In this method also, a set of randomly selected positions from one parent is considered (5, 1, 8, and 6 from parent 1; see Fig. 7.24). Now, the nodes selected from parent 1 are deleted from parent 2. The remaining nodes 9, 4, 2, 3, and 7 of parent 2 are transferred to its child 1 string, maintaining the same locations. The selected nodes of parent 1—5, 1, 8, 6—are then filled from bottom to top in the empty segments of the child 1 string. The same procedure is repeated to produce child 2.

*Cycle crossover (CX)*
Oliver, Smith, and Holland [13] proposed this crossover. Here, the nodes to be selected from a parent are defined by a cycle according to the corresponding position between the parents as shown in Fig. 7.25. The nodes (4, 5, 8, 7, 6) selected from parent 1, involved in the cycle, are transferred to its child 1 string, maintaining the same locations as the parent itself. Now, the nodes selected from parent 1 are deleted from parent 2. The remaining nodes 3, 2, 1, and 9 of parent 2 are transferred to its child 1 string, maintaining the same locations.

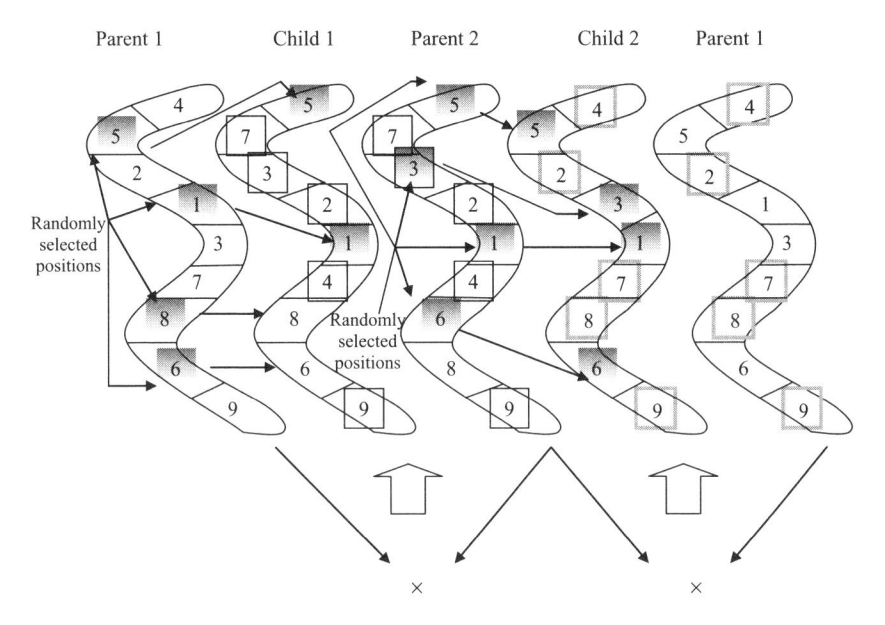

**Fig. 7.24** Order-based crossover

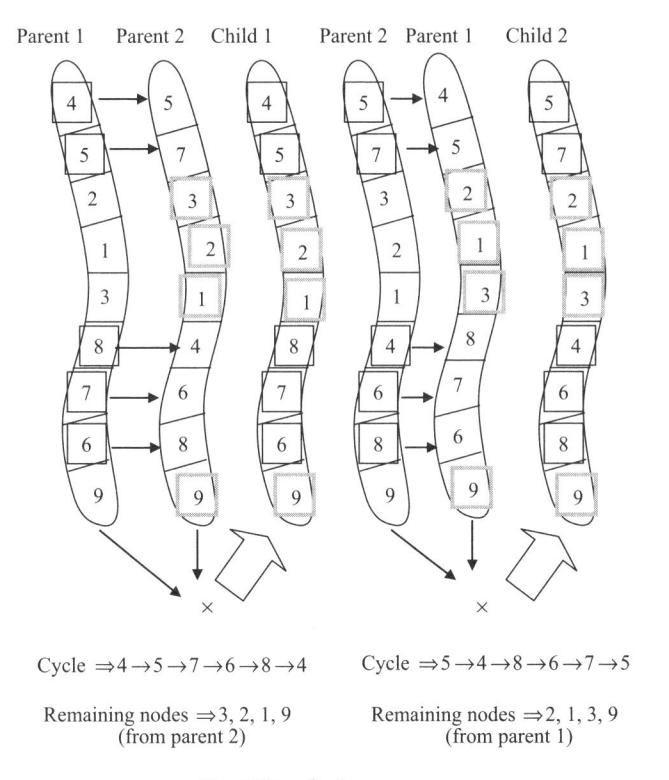

Cycle $\Rightarrow 4 \to 5 \to 7 \to 6 \to 8 \to 4$

Remaining nodes $\Rightarrow 3, 2, 1, 9$
(from parent 2)

Cycle $\Rightarrow 5 \to 4 \to 8 \to 6 \to 7 \to 5$

Remaining nodes $\Rightarrow 2, 1, 3, 9$
(from parent 1)

**Fig. 7.25** Cycle crossover

## Sub-tour exchange crossover

Yamamura, Ono, and Kobayashi [14] proposed this crossover method. Here, a substring is selected from each of the crossing parents. The sub-strings contain only the common nodes, which are exchanged between the parents, producing child strings as shown in Fig. 7.26.

## Heuristic crossover

In the heuristic approach, a random node is picked at the start. Then, its shortest edge that does not lead to a cycle is selected. If two edges lead to a cycle, then a random node is picked up again and the aforementioned process is continued till all the nodes are checked and a new offspring is produced. This approach is very efficient compared to other permutation operators.

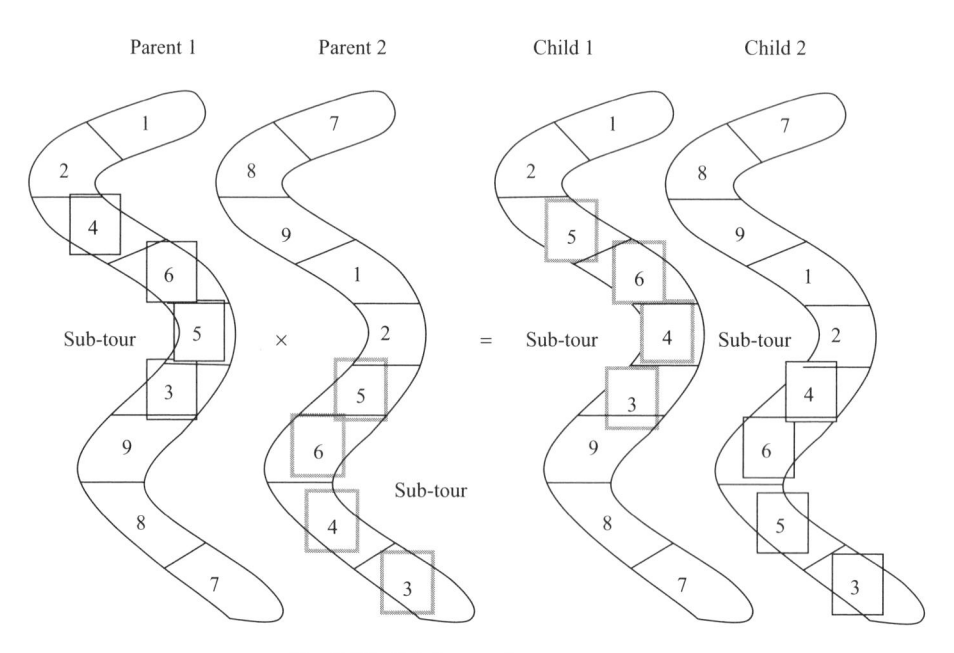

**Fig. 7.26** Sub-tour exchange crossover

### 7.3.3.2 Arithmetic Crossover

Arithmetic crossover is achieved by the principle of convex set theory. Here, the weighted average of two vectors $X_1$ and $X_2$ is calculated as $\alpha X_1 + \beta X_2$, where the multipliers are restricted by the relation $\alpha + \beta = 1$, such that $\alpha > 0$ and $\beta > 0$. If the non-negativity condition on the multipliers is dropped, the combination is an *affine combination*; if the multipliers are simply required to be in real space $S$, the combination is a *linear combination*. The crossover operation is defined in the following as a combination of two chromosomal vectors:

$$X'_1 = \alpha X_1 + \beta X_2 \qquad (7.26)$$
$$X'_2 = \alpha X_2 + \beta X_1 \qquad (7.27)$$

Based on the restriction of multipliers, three kinds of crossover are obtained. These are (a) convex crossover, (b) affine crossover, and (c) linear crossover. The most generally used one is the convex operator. A convex operator called *average* or *intermediate* crossover is used for the special case $\alpha = \beta = 0.5$. The affine crossover is used for the special case $\alpha = 1.5$ and $\beta = -0.5$. When one of the multipliers is assigned a random real number in the interval $[-n, 1+n]$, the *extended intermediate* crossover operator is used. In the case of linear crossover, the multipliers are strictly restricted as follows: $\alpha + \beta \leq 2$, where $\alpha > 0$ and $\beta > 0$.

Figure 7.27 shows the convex, affine, and linear regions for two parents $X_1$ and $X_2$, represented in two-dimensional space. Each region specifies the collection of the particular type of arithmetical crossover combination. The offspring generated with convex crossover lie within the solid line, those with affine crossover lie on both the solid and dashed lines, and those with linear crossover cover the whole space.

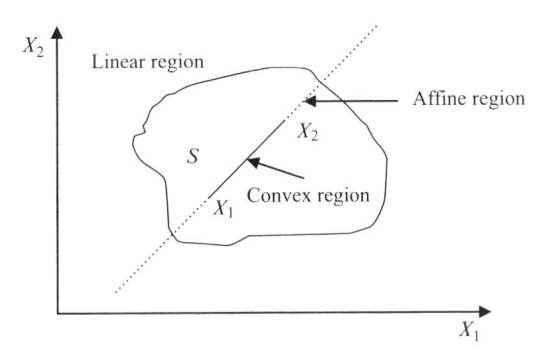

**Fig. 7.27** Arithmetic crossover

### 7.3.3.3 Directional Crossover

In this type of crossover operation, problem-specific knowledge is introduced into genetic operations in order to produce improved offspring. The directional crossover operator uses the objective function for determining the direction of genetic search and generates an offspring $X'$ from two parents $X_1$ and $X_2$ according to the following rule:

$$X' = R(X_2 - X_1) + X_2 \tag{7.28}$$

where, $R$ is a random number between 0 and 1. It is assumed that the parent $X_2$ is not worse than $X_1$ (i.e., $f(X_2) \geq f(X_1)$) for maximization problems) and vice versa (i.e., $f(X_2) \geq f(X_1)$ for minimization problems).

The next operator, mutation, is performed on a bit-by-bit basis. Another parameter of the genetic system, probability of mutation $(p_m)$, gives us the expected number of mutated bits, $P_m \times l \times \text{pop\_size}$. Here $l$ is the bit length of the chromosomal string and pop_size is the total number of chromosomal strings available in the population. Every bit (in all chromosomes in the whole population) has an equal chance of undergoing mutation (i.e., changing from 0 to 1 or vice versa). Hence, we proceed in the following way for each chromosome in the current (i.e., after crossover) population and for each bit within the chromosome:

- Generate a random (float) number $r$ from the range [0, 1].
- If $r < p_m$, mutate the bit.

Even though mutation is performed on a bit-by-bit basis, there are still different types and ways of implementing the mutation operator.

### 7.3.4 Mutation

Mutation is generally classified as (a) uniform, (b) boundary, and (c) non-uniform mutation [15].

#### 7.3.4.1 Uniform Mutation

In this mutation scheme, a gene (real number) is selected with the help of a randomly selected real number within a specific range. Let us consider a chromosome $X^t = [X_1, X_2, ..., X_m]$. A random number is selected such that $k \in [1, n]$ and an offspring $X^{t+1} = [X_1, ..., X'_k, ..., X_m]$ is produced, where $X'_k$ is a random value generated according to uniform probability distribution from the range $[X_k^L, X_k^U]$. Here $X_k^L$ and $X_k^U$, respectively, are the lower and upper bounds on the variable $X_k$ and can be determined using domain constraints. This range can be calculated dynamically from the set of inequality constraints.

#### 7.3.4.2 Boundary Mutation

The replacement of gene $X'_k$ by either $X_k^L$ or $X_k^U$, each with equal probability, is known as boundary mutation. Also, instead of lower and upper bounds, the range can be formed as $[X_{k-1}, X_{k+1}]$; this variation is called *plain mutation*.

#### 7.3.4.3 Non-uniform Mutation

This operator is capable of making fine adjustments to the system. Let us consider the same chromosomal vector $X^t = [X_1, X_2, ... X_m]$ and assume that $X'_k$ is the element selected for this mutation from the set of genes in the chromosome and that the resultant chromosome is $X^{t+1} = [X_1, ..., X'_k, ...X_m]$, where $k \in [1, n]$. Here,

$$X'_k = \begin{cases} X_k + \Delta(t, X_k^U - X_k) & \text{if the random digit is 0} \\ X_k - \Delta(t, X_k - X_k^L) & \text{if the random digit is 1} \end{cases} \quad (7.29)$$

The function $\Delta(t, Y)$ returns a value in the range $[0, y]$ such that the probability of $\Delta(t, Y)$ being close to 0 increases as $t$ increases. This property causes this operator initially (when $t$ is small) to search the space uniformly, and very locally at later stages. The function $\Delta(t, Y) = Y(1 - r^{(1 - t/T)^b})$ is used to determine the element to be selected. Here, $r$ is a random number from [0, 1], $T$ is the maximal generation number, and $b$ is a system parameter determining the degree of non-uniformity.

Mutation can be implemented by programming logic using the (a) one's complement operator, (b) logical bit-wise operator, (c) shift operator, and (d) masking operator [4].

## Genetic Algorithms and Evolutionary Programming

### One's complement operator

This operator is known as a *unary operator* (~). It causes the bits of its operand to be inverted (i.e., '1' becomes '0' and '0' becomes '1'). This operator always precedes its operand. Figure 7.28 shows two variables $X$ and $Y$ represented by $C$ with a chromosomal string length of eight bits. The one's complement operator mutates $C$ to give $C^m$.

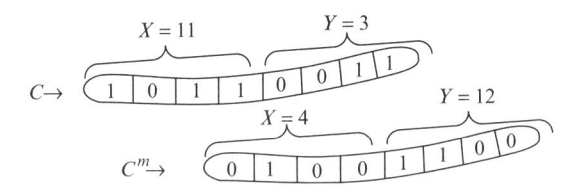

**Fig. 7.28** One's complement operator

### Logical bit-wise operator

This operator can be further classified into the (a) bit-wise AND, (b) bit-wise exclusive($X$)-OR, and (c) bit-wise OR operators. To use these operators, a two-integer operand is needed. They can be used instead of the crossover operator. When working with two operands, the operands are compared on a bit-by-bit basis. The operation of these operators can be understood from Table 7.2.

**Table 7.2** Truth table showing the operation of logical bit-wise operators

| X | Y | AND(X, Y) | XOR(X, Y) | OR(X, Y) |
|---|---|-----------|-----------|----------|
| 0 | 0 | 0 | 0 | 0 |
| 0 | 1 | 0 | 1 | 1 |
| 1 | 0 | 0 | 1 | 1 |
| 1 | 1 | 1 | 0 | 1 |

*Bit-wise AND operator* A bit-wise AND operator returns 1 if the corresponding bits of both the operands are 1, otherwise it returns 0. Figure 7.29 shows the parent chromosomes $P_X$ and $P_Y$ being mutated to get the child chromosome $C_{XY}$.

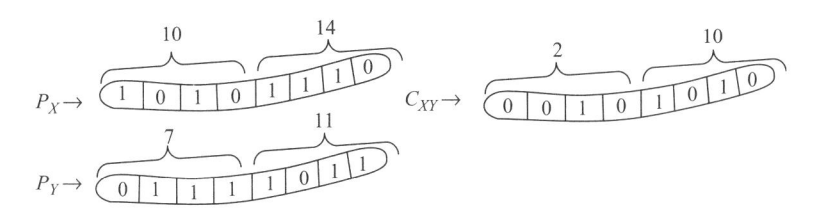

**Fig. 7.29** The bit-wise AND operator

*Bit-wise XOR operator* The bit-wise XOR operator returns 1 if one of the bits is 1 and the other is 0, otherwise it returns 0 (Fig. 7.30).

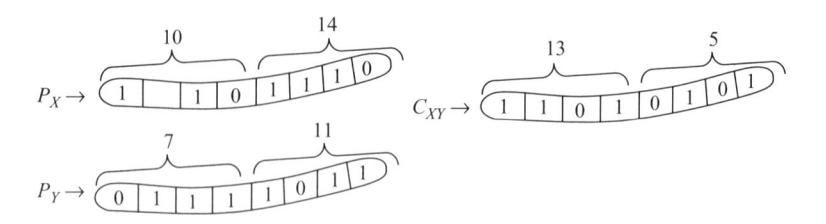

**Fig. 7.30** The bit-wise XOR operator

*Bit-wise OR operator* This operator returns 1 if one or more bits are 1, otherwise it returns a 0 (Fig. 7.31).

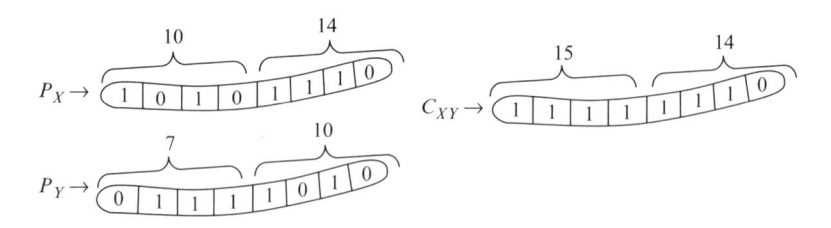

**Fig. 7.31** The bit-wise OR operator

## Shift operator
The shift operator is again divided into two types: the shift left (<<) and shift right (>>) operators. Each operator operates on a single variable but requires two operands. The first operand is an integer type that indicates the bit pattern to be shifted either to the left or to the right and the second operand indicates the number of displacements to be made. The constraint that has to be taken care of is that the value of the second operand cannot exceed the number of bits associated with the word size of the first operand.

## Shift left operator (<<)
The shift left operator shifts all the bits of the first operand to the left by the number of positions indicated by the second operand. The leftmost bits (i.e., the overflow bits) in the original bit pattern are lost. The rightmost bit positions that become vacant are filled with zeros (Fig. 7.32).

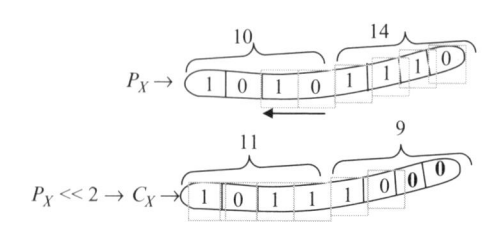

**Fig. 7.32** Shift left operator

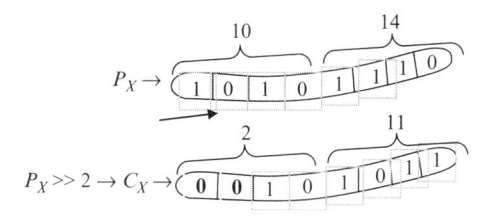

**Fig. 7.33** Shift right operator

*Shift right operator (>>)*
The shift right operator causes all the bits in the first operand to be shift to the right by the number of positions indicated by the second operand. The rightmost bits (i.e., the underflow bits) in the original bit pattern are lost. The leftmost bit positions that become vacant are then filled with zeros (Fig. 7.33).

*Masking operator*
This operator transforms a given bit pattern into another bit pattern with the help of the logical bit-wise operation. The original bit pattern is one of the operands in the bit-wise operation. The second operand called the *mask* is a specially selected bit pattern that brings about the desired transformation. In Fig. 7.34, if we use the AND operator for $P_X$ and the given mask table, we get $C_X$ as shown. Different kinds of masking operations exist. For example, a portion of a given bit pattern can be copied to a new word while the remainder of the new word is filled with zeros. Thus, the selected bit pattern of the original bit pattern will be masked off from the final result.

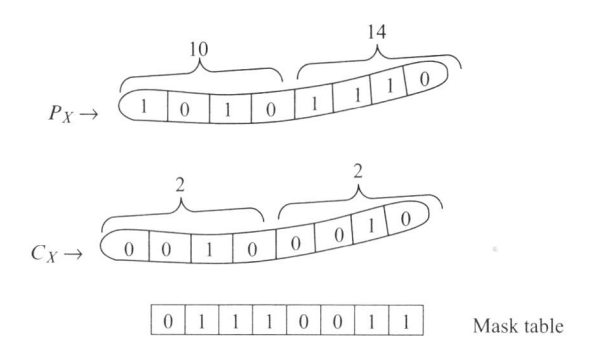

**Fig. 7.34** Masking operator

There are some other types of mutation too, especially for the permutation representation, which is useful in combinatorial problems, such as the TSP, machine scheduling problems, transportation problems, and quadratic assignment problems. Some of these mutation schemes, that is, inversion, insertion, displacement, and reciprocal exchange mutation, are discussed here.

*Inversion*
In inversion mutation, two positions within a chromosome are randomly selected first. Then the sub-string between these two positions is inverted as shown in Fig. 7.35.

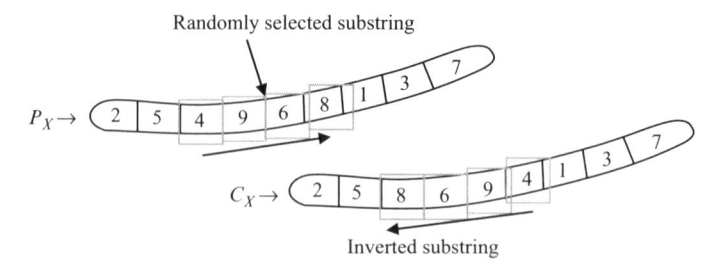

**Fig. 7.35** Inversion mutation

## Insertion
In insertion mutation, a node is selected at random and then inserted in a random position as shown in Fig. 7.36.

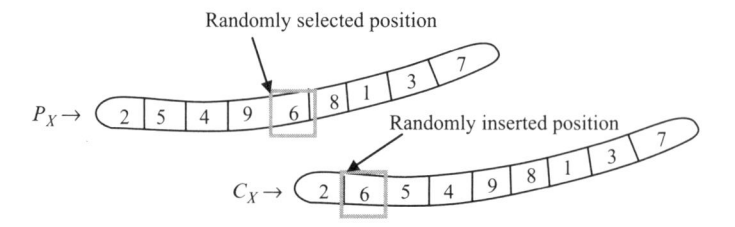

**Fig. 7.36** Insertion mutation

## Displacement
Displacement mutation selects a sub-string at random and inserts it in a random position as illustrated in Fig. 7.37. Insertion can be viewed as a special case of displacement in which the sub-string contains only one node.

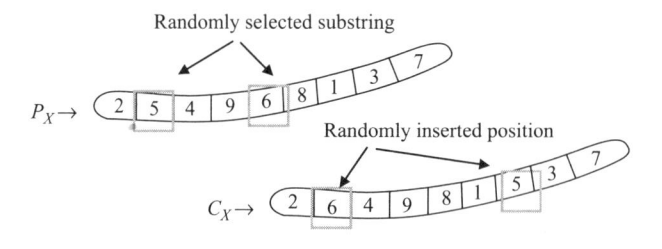

**Fig. 7.37** Displacement mutation

## Reciprocal exchange
Reciprocal exchange mutation selects two positions at random and then swaps the nodes in these positions as shown in Fig. 7.38.

### 7.3.4.4 Heuristic Mutation
Cheng and Gen proposed heuristic mutation. It is based on the neighbourhood technique, which can produce improved offspring. Here, a set of chromosomes transformable from a given chromosome by exchanging no more than $N$ genes is

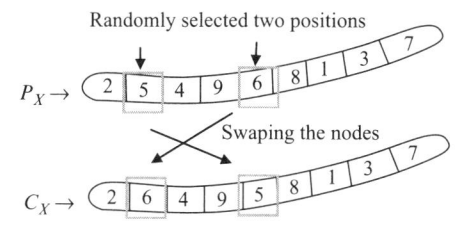

**Fig. 7.38** Reciprocal exchange

regarded as the neighbourhood. The best-valued chromosome among those in the neighbourhood is considered as the offspring produced by this mutation. Let us consider a chromosome $P_X$ to be mutated. Now all the possible permutations of the selected genes are produced for generating all the possible neighbours, as shown in Fig. 7.39. After evaluating all the neighbours, the best neighbour is selected, and it becomes the offspring obtained with this mutation.

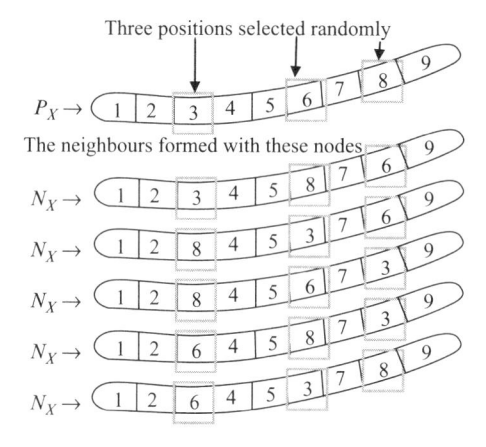

**Fig. 7.39** Heuristic mutation

## 7.3.5 Natural Inheritance Operators

Even though GAs largely use three basic operators, namely, reproduction, crossover, and mutation, these are not the only genetic operators available; there are other advanced operators and techniques in genetic search which can help to improve GAs further. Let us briefly discuss these operators in the following sections [5].

### 7.3.5.1 Dominance

Some of the earliest examples of practical GA applications contained diploid genotypes and the dominance mechanism. In the diploid form, a genotype (the genetic composition of an organism contained in a genome or chromosome) carries one or more pairs of chromosomes (homologous chromosomes), each containing information on the same function. Keeping two genes that decode the same function looks unnecessary, but *diploidy* provides a mechanism for remembering alleles and allele combinations that were previously useful, and dominance provides an operator to shield these memorized alleles from harmful selection in a hostile environment.

The concept of dominance can be understood as follows. Let us consider a diploid chromosomal structure where different letters represent different alleles (different gene function values). In Fig. 7.40, let the different letters represent different alleles. Each position of a letter represents one allele; the capital and lower case forms represent the alternative alleles at that position. In nature, each allele might represent different phenotypic characteristics. For example, the allele $B$ might represent the brown-eyed gene and the allele $b$ might represent the blue-eyed gene.

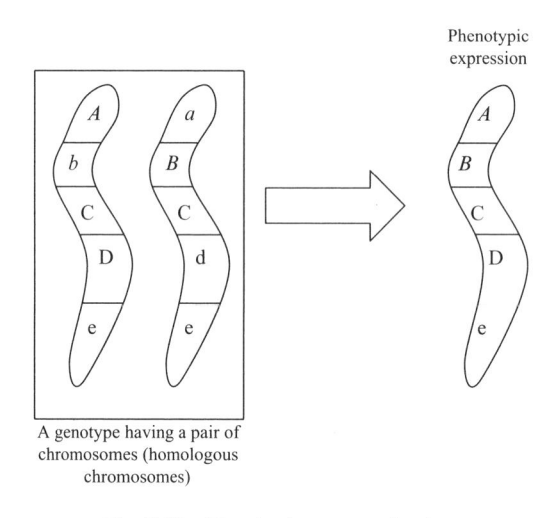

**Fig. 7.40** The dominance mechanism

The diploid chromosome is not much different from the haploid chromosome (single-stranded). However, it is obvious that the phenotypic (the environmentally and genetically determined traits of an organism actually observed) expression cannot have both brown and blue eyes at the same time. Hence, the primary mechanism for eliminating this conflict is to use a genetic operator called dominance. At a locus, it has been observed that a *dominant* allele dominates the other alternative alleles that are recessive at that locus. That is, an allele is dominant if it is *expressed*. In this example, if all the capital letters are dominant and all the lower case letters are recessive, it is observed at each locus that the dominant gene is always expressed and the recessive gene is expressed only when it shows up in the company of another recessive gene. In other words, the dominant allele is expressed when it is heterozygous (mixed, $Aa \rightarrow A$) or homozygous (pure, $CC \rightarrow C$) and the recessive allele is expressed only when it is homozygous ($ee \rightarrow e$).

### 7.3.5.2 Inversion

In the inversion mechanism, a string is selected from the chromosome and the bits at two randomly selected sites are inverted (Fig. 7.41). Frantz proposed two different forms of inversion: linear inversion and linear + end inversion. Linear

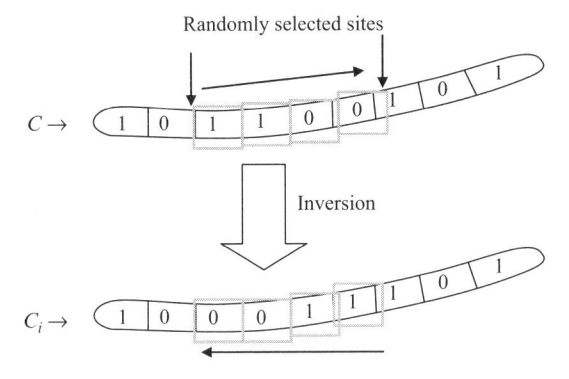

**Fig. 7.41** The inversion mechanism

inversion is a simple two-point inversion. Linear + end inversion performs linear inversion with a specified probability (0.75). If linear inversion is not performed, end inversion would be performed with equal probability (0.125) at either the left or right end of the string. In end inversion, the left or right end of the string is picked as one inversion point, and a second inversion point is picked uniformly at random from points farther away than one-half of the string length. D.R. Frantz proposed linear + end inversion in order to minimize the tendency for linear inversion to disrupt the alleles located near the centre of the string disproportionately to those located near the ends [16].

Both the inversion types discussed earlier can be used in two modes, namely, the continuous inversion and the mass inversion mode. In the continuous inversion mode, inversion is applied with a specified inversion probability ($p_i$) to each individual as the individual is created. In the mass inversion mode, no inversion takes place until a new population is created, and thereafter one-half of the population undergoes identical inversion (using the same two inversion points). The motive of mass inversion is to eliminate the creation of non-interacting sub-populations, which accompanies strict homologous mating.

### 7.3.5.3 Deletion

Deletion takes place at randomly selected sites; the information contained in the gene is permanently lost, as shown in Fig. 7.42.

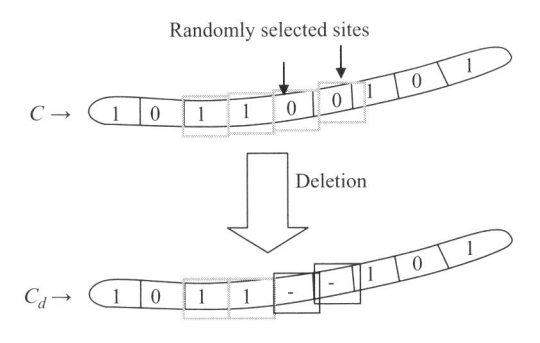

**Fig. 7.42** Deletion

### 7.3.5.4 Intrachromosomal Duplication

Deletion and intrachromosomal duplication can co-exist as shown in Fig. 7.43. Any two or three bits are deleted at random and the previous bits are duplicated.

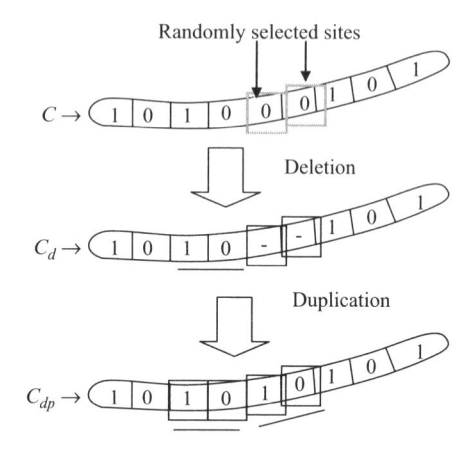

**Fig. 7.43** Intra-chromosomal duplication

### 7.3.5.5 Re-generation

In re-generation, genes from two crossover sites are deleted and re-generated randomly as shown in Fig. 7.44.

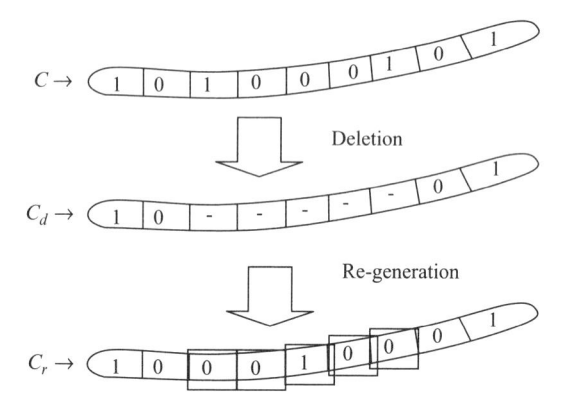

**Fig. 7.44** Re-generation

### 7.3.5.6 Segregation

In this type of mutation, the bits of the parent chromosomes are segregated and then crossed over to produce offspring, as shown in Fig. 7.45.

### 7.3.5.7 Translocation

Translocation can be viewed as an intrachromosomal crossover operator. To implement such an operator in an artificial setting, alleles are tagged with their gene names and their intended meaning is identified when the translocation operator shuffles them from chromosome to chromosome.

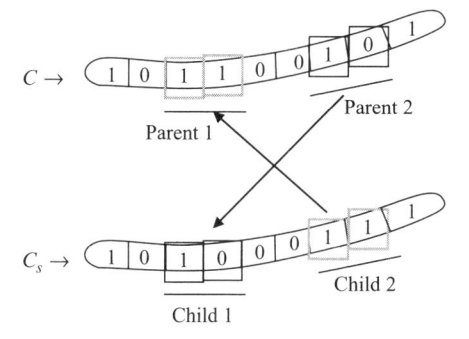

**Fig. 7.45** Segregation

### 7.3.5.8 Niche and Speciation

The survival strategy of an organism (grazing, hunting on the ground/in trees, etc.). Species in different niches (e.g., one eating plants, the other eating insects) may co-exist side-by-side without competition. If two species occupying the same niche are brought together, there will be competition, and eventually the weaker of the two species will become extinct. Hence, the diversity of species depends on them occupying a diversity of niches or being geographically separated.

In evolutionary computations, we often want to maintain diversity in the population. Sometimes, a fitness function may be known to be multi-modal and we might want to locate all the peaks. In such a case, we may consider each peak in the fitness function to be analogous to a niche.

The process of developing a new species is called *speciation*. The most common form of speciation occurs when a species is geographically separated from the main population long enough for its genes to diverge due to differences in selection pressures or genetic drift. Eventually, the genetic differences are great enough for the sub-population to become a new species.

### 7.3.5.9 Migration

The migration operator was proposed by Frantz and is also known as the *complement* operator. This operator complements roughly a third of the bits of selected individuals in a population. These individuals are called *immigrants* and are permitted to enter the subsequent generation. The motive of this operator is to maintain diversity in the population. The limitation of this approach is that the desired diversity is achieved at a high cost and thereby decreased performance.

### 7.3.5.10 Sharing

The sharing mechanism is used to determine the neighbourhood and degree of sharing for each string in the population. Suppose, for a given individual, the degree of sharing is determined by summing the sharing function values contributed by all other strings in the population. Strings close to an individual require a high degree of sharing, close to 1, and strings far away from the individual require a very low degree of sharing, close to 0. Since an individual is very close to itself, its sharing function is 1. Once the total degree of sharing is determined, an individual's derated fitness is calculated by taking the potential fitness (the unshared value) and dividing it by the cumulative degree of sharing. Thus if many individuals belong to the same neighbourhood, they contribute to each other's share count, thereby derating each other's fitness values. Thus, the sharing mechanism limits the uncontrolled growth of a particular species within a population.

### 7.3.5.11 Mating

Mating is an inheritance mechanism where two individual parent chromosomal strings exchange useful information between themselves to produce an offspring. However, the limitation faced during this process is the naive crosses between homologous pairs of strings. Frantz has proposed the following four mating rules:

(a) Strict homology mating
(b) Viability mating
(c) Any-pattern mating
(d) Best-pattern mating

In strict homology mating, only homologous strings are permitted to mate. Viability mating permits a cross between non-homologous strings; however, if the resulting offspring do not have a full gene complement, they are not inserted into the new population. In any-pattern mating, two mates are randomly selected and one of them is chosen to be the *prime ordering*. The other string is mapped to the prime ordering and a simple cross is made. The mapping operation thereby guarantees the viability of the cross. Best-pattern mating is the same as any-pattern mating except that the better of the two strings is chosen to determine the prime ordering.

Following selection, crossover, and mutation, the new population is ready for its next evaluation. This evaluation is used to build the probability distribution, that is, construct a roulette wheel with slots sized according to the current fitness values. The rest of the evolution is just cyclic repetition of the previous steps.

## 7.4 WORKING OF GAs

Let us understand the working of GAs with the following examples.

**Example 7.1**

In this example, we discuss the basic features of a GA for optimising a simple one-variable function using both Binary (Case 1) and Continuous GA (Case 2). The function is defined as follows and shown in Fig. 7.46[9]:

$$f(x) = x \times \sin(10\pi \times x) + 1.0 \tag{7.30}$$

### 7.4.1 Binary or Discrete GA (Case 1)

*Solution:*
*Assumptions*
Number of population = 20
Decimal point accuracy (DPA) = 6
Probability of crossover = 0.2

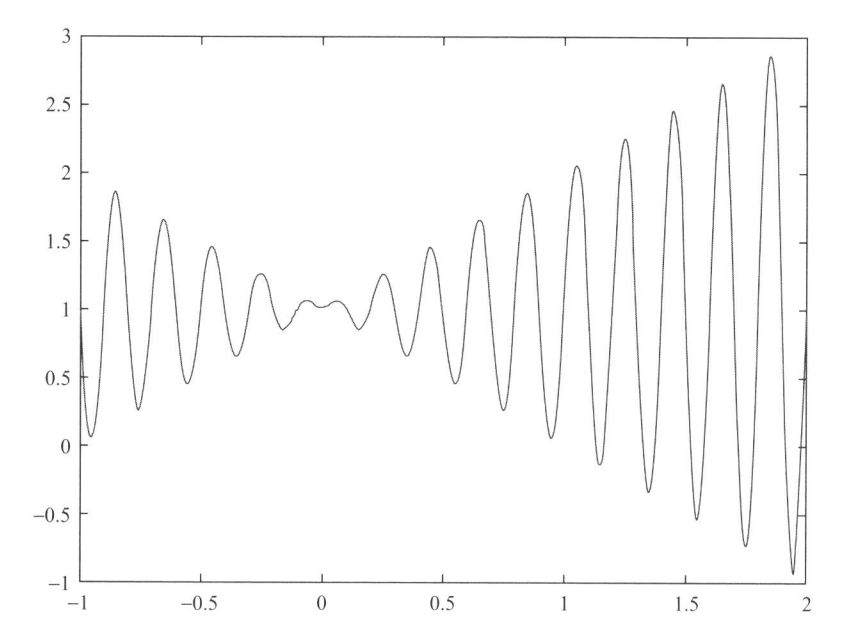

**Fig. 7.46** Plot of the function $f(x) = x \times \sin(10\pi \times x) + 1.0$

Probability of mutation = 0.01
Number of generations = 1
Lower bound range of the variable = −1
Upper bound range of the variable = 2
Domain length (DL) = 3(Upper bound − Lower bound)

*Steps*

(a) Calculate the two extremes of the boundary value
(b) Boundary value = DL × $(10)^{DPA}$
(c) Number of bits = $\dfrac{(\text{Log (DL)} + \text{DPA} \times \text{Log (10)})}{\text{Log (2)}}$

- Note: Round the number of bits to the next successive integer value (22)

(d) Initial population selected randomly as in Table 7.3
(e) The program has been run for one trial and for 100 epochs. The minimum of the function is obtained and the convergence of the solution is shown in Fig. 7.47. The previous program can be modified and improved.

Convert the binary string first to corresponding decimal value, then actual value of the variable '*X*' is found (Table 7.3) using the following formula:

Actual value = Lower bound + (Relative value × DL)/(2^Bit length − 1);

- Here the objective function is same as the fitness function.

(f) Selections of stings are achieved by ranking method (Table 7.4).

**Table 7.3** Generation of initial population

| Binary string (Initial population) | Relative value (X) | Actual value (X) | Objective function / Fitness value |
|---|---|---|---|
| 100111011001110010101101 | 2582317 | 0.8470 | 1.8396 |
| 111010000011101011011110 | 3804894 | 1.7215 | 1.6715 |
| 011110100001110100100 | 2000804 | 0.4311 | 1.2960 |
| 111110111010001011010101 | 4122805 | 1.9489 | 2.9464 |
| 101110000000001101010101 | 3014869 | 1.1564 | 2.1102 |
| 011100011110101010100011 | 1866403 | 0.3350 | 1.2655 |
| 001110111000111110100 | 975860 | −0.3020 | 0.9988 |
| 110001100100111001100 | 3249052 | 1.3239 | 1.6164 |
| 000010011010010011100 | 158012 | −0.8870 | 0.8597 |
| 101110011100100001100 | 3043864 | 1.1771 | 1.5096 |
| 010010110010010001011 | 1231127 | −0.1194 | 0.9608 |
| 111001000001011000111 | 3736974 | 1.6729 | 1.9469 |
| 100110110011111101111 | 2543582 | 0.8193 | 1.2663 |
| 011010111001011001001 | 1762707 | 0.2608 | 1.2320 |
| 011100001110010111000 | 1849712 | 0.3230 | 1.1414 |
| 000010100000100100001 | 164418 | −0.8824 | 0.7566 |
| 010101101101010000000 | 1422592 | 0.0175 | 1.0048 |
| 000101110000100111000 | 377456 | −0.7300 | 0.5217 |
| 111000100010111011101 | 3705787 | 1.6506 | 2.6500 |
| 111011101011001010100 | 3910824 | 1.7972 | 1.0135 |

Strings are sorted in ascending order according to fitness value. Ranking is kept according to our objective and experience. Here ten ranks are given accordingly. Percentage of ranked strings copied to total population according to ranks. (1% 3% 5% 7% 9% 11% 13% 15% 17% 19%) = 100%. This method helps the weaker strings to take part in the next generation and there by search for new strings and avoid getting trapped in the local minimum.

**Table 7.4** New populations of strings

| Fitness value sorted in ascending order | Corresponding binary strings | Number of strings copied to the next generation | New population of strings |
|---|---|---|---|
| 0.5217 | 0 0 0 1 0 1 1 1 0 0 0 0 1 0 0 1 1 1 0 0 0 0 | 0 | 0 0 0 0 1 0 1 / 0 0 0 0 0 1 0 0 1 0 0 0 0 1 0 |
| 0.7566 | 0 0 0 0 1 0 1 0 0 0 0 0 1 0 0 1 0 0 0 0 1 0 | 1 | 0 0 0 0 1 0 0 / 1 1 0 1 0 0 1 0 0 1 1 1 1 0 0 |
| 0.8597 | 0 0 0 0 1 0 0 1 1 0 1 0 0 1 0 0 1 1 1 1 0 0 | 1 | 0 1 0 0 1 0 1 1 0 0 1 0 0 1 0 0 0 1 0 1 1 1 |
| 0.9608 | 0 1 0 0 1 0 1 1 0 0 1 0 0 1 0 0 0 1 0 1 1 1 | 1 | 0 0 1 1 1 0 1 1 1 / 0 0 0 1 1 1 1 1 1 0 1 0 0 |
| 0.9988 | 0 0 1 1 1 0 1 1 1 0 0 0 1 1 1 1 1 1 0 1 0 0 | 2 | 0 0 1 1 1 0 1 1 1 / 0 0 0 1 1 1 1 1 1 0 1 0 0 |
| 1.0048 | 0 1 0 1 0 1 1 0 1 1 0 1 0 1 0 0 0 0 0 0 0 0 | 2 | 0 1 0 1 0 1 1 0 1 1 0 1 0 1 0 0 0 0 0 0 0 0 |
| 1.0135 | 1 1 1 0 1 1 1 0 1 0 1 1 0 0 1 0 1 0 1 0 0 0 | 3 | 0 1 0 1 0 1 1 0 1 1 0 1 0 1 0 0 0 0 0 0 0 0 |
| 1.1414 | 0 1 1 1 0 0 0 0 1 1 1 0 0 1 0 1 1 1 0 0 0 0 | 3 | 1 1 1 0 1 1 1 0 1 0 1 1 0 0 1 0 1 0 1 0 0 0 |
| 1.2320 | 0 1 1 0 1 0 1 1 1 0 0 1 0 1 1 0 0 1 0 0 1 1 | 3 | 1 1 1 0 1 1 1 0 1 0 1 1 0 0 1 0 1 0 1 0 0 0 |
| 1.2655 | 0 1 1 1 0 0 0 1 1 1 1 0 1 0 1 0 1 0 0 0 1 1 | 4 | 1 1 1 0 1 1 1 0 1 0 1 1 0 0 1 0 1 0 1 0 0 0 |
| 1.2663 | 1 0 0 1 1 0 1 1 0 0 1 1 1 1 1 1 0 1 1 1 1 0 | | 0 1 1 1 0 0 0 0 1 1 1 0 0 1 0 1 1 1 0 0 0 0 |
| 1.2960 | 0 1 1 1 1 0 1 0 0 0 0 1 1 1 1 0 1 0 0 1 0 0 | | 0 1 1 1 0 0 0 0 1 1 1 0 0 1 0 1 1 1 0 0 0 0 |
| 1.5096 | 1 0 1 1 1 0 0 1 1 0 0 1 0 0 0 0 1 1 0 0 0 | | 0 1 1 1 0 0 0 0 1 1 1 0 0 1 0 1 1 1 0 0 0 0 |
| 1.6164 | 1 1 0 0 0 1 1 0 0 1 0 0 1 1 1 0 0 1 1 1 0 0 | | 0 1 1 0 1 0 1 1 1 0 0 1 0 1 1 0 0 1 0 0 1 1 |
| 1.6715 | 1 1 1 0 1 0 0 0 0 0 1 1 1 0 1 1 0 1 1 1 1 0 | | 0 1 1 0 1 0 1 1 1 0 0 1 0 1 1 0 0 1 0 0 1 1 |
| 1.8396 | 1 0 0 1 1 1 0 1 1 0 0 1 1 1 0 0 1 0 1 1 0 1 | | 0 1 1 0 1 0 1 1 1 0 0 1 0 1 1 0 0 1 0 0 1 1 |
| 1.9469 | 1 1 1 0 0 1 0 0 0 0 0 1 0 1 1 0 0 0 1 1 1 0 | | 0 1 1 1 0 0 0 1 1 1 1 0 1 0 1 0 1 0 0 0 1 1 |
| 2.1102 | 1 0 1 1 1 0 0 0 0 0 0 0 0 0 1 1 0 1 0 1 0 1 | | 0 1 1 1 0 0 0 1 1 1 1 0 1 0 1 0 1 0 0 0 1 1 |
| 2.6500 | 1 1 1 0 0 0 1 0 0 0 1 0 1 1 1 0 1 1 1 0 1 1 | | 0 1 1 1 0 0 0 1 1 1 1 0 1 0 1 0 1 0 0 0 1 1 |
| 2.9464 | 1 1 1 1 1 0 1 1 1 0 1 0 0 0 1 0 1 1 0 1 0 1 | | 0 1 1 1 0 0 0 1 1 1 1 0 1 0 1 0 1 0 0 0 1 1 |

Generation 1

Best objective value = 0.5217

$X = -0.7300$

g. Number of strings participating in crossover = Number of population × Probability of crossover (1st, 2nd, 4th, 5th)

$$= 4 \ (20 \times 0.20)$$

Two strings are chosen randomly two times and single-point random crossover is done.

1st and 2nd string crossed
4th and 5th string crossed

h. Number of bits to be mutated = Number of population × Bit length × Probability of mutation

$$= 5$$

i.e., $(20 \times 22 \times 0.01)$

(Round 4.4 to the next nearest integer)

The mutation positions randomly chosen in row/column-wise
(16,2) – (3,14) – (15,6) – (2,20) – (1,21)
that is, after crossover, select 5 random positions (Table 7.5) of bits and replace 'one if zero' or 'zero if one'.

**Table 7.5** New populations of strings

| Binary strings after crossover | New population of strings |
|---|---|
| 0000101/110100100111100 | 0000101110100100111110 |
| 0000100/000001001000010 | 0000100000001001000110 |
| 0100101100100100010111 | 0100101100100000010111 |
| 0011101111/0001111110100 | 0011101110001111110100 |
| 0011101111/0001111110100 | 0011101110001111110100 |
| 0101011011010100000000 | 0101011011010100000000 |
| 0101011011010100000000 | 0101011011010100000000 |
| 1110111010110010101000 | 1110111010110010101000 |
| 1110111010110010101000 | 1110111010110010101000 |
| 1110111010110010101000 | 1110111010110010101000 |
| 0111000011100101110000 | 0111000011100101110000 |
| 0111000011100101110000 | 0111000011100101110000 |
| 0111000011100101110000 | 0111000011100101110000 |
| 0110101110010110010011 | 0110101110010110010011 |
| 0110101110010110010011 | 0110111110010110010011 |
| 0110101110010110010011 | 0010101110010110010011 |
| 0111000111101010100011 | 0111000111101010100011 |
| 0111000111101010100011 | 0111000111101010100011 |
| 0111000111101010100011 | 0111000111101010100011 |
| 0111000111101010100011 | 0111000111101010100011 |

i. The same procedure is repeated from (e) to (h) and the best fitness value so far obtained and the corresponding value of the variable $X$ is saved. After a required number of generations, the optimum value using GA is obtained. The results and convergence will vary depending upon GA parameters.

# MATLAB Program 7.1

## Part A

```
%%%%%%%%%%%%%%%%%%%%%%%%%%%%%%%%%%%%%%%%%%%%%%%%%%%%%%%%
% OPTIMISATION OF A SINGLE VARIABLE FUNCTION USING BINARY GA
%%%%%%%%%%%%%%%%%%%%%%%%%%%%%%%%%%%%%%%%%%%%%%%%%%%%%%%%

% CLEARING ALL PREVIOUS DATA

clear workspace             % Clears all previous variables in the work space
clear all                   % Clears all variables
clear figure                % Clear previous figures
tic                         % Start time

% INITIALIZATION OF PARAMETERS

n_pop=100;                  % Number of population
accu=6;                     % Decimal point accuracy
pr_cr=0.20;                 % Probability of crossover
pr_mu=0.01;                 % Probability of mutation
D=1;                        % Number of variables
epochs=1000;                % Number of generations
xmin=-1;xmax=2;             % Boundary limits of the variable x
dl=xmax-xmin;               % Domain Length
er=dl*10^accu;
% Number of solution points within the domain as per required decimal accuracy
bl=(log(dl)+accu*log(10))/log(2);   % Calculation of string length
lbl=fix(bl);                % Left bit length
rbl=lbl+1;    % Right bit length(er should lie between 2^lbl and 2^rbl)
pop_str=round(rand(n_pop,rbl*D));   % Initial of population of strings randomly

% CALCULATING THE FITNESS VALUE FOR THE ABOVE POPULATION OF STRINGS

for gen=1:epochs            % GA cycle starts
rx=[bi2de(pop_str(:,1:rbl),'left-msb')];  % Relative value of x
ax=xmin+(rx*dl)/(2^rbl-1);  % Actual value of x

% EVALUATION OF SUBSTITUTING ACTUAL VLAUE OF X IN OBJECTIVE FUNCTION

for i=1:n_pop,
x=ax(i,1);
fit(i,1)=sinfun(x);         % Here both fitness and objective function is same
end

% SELECTING STRINGS AND MAITAIN POPULATION ACCORDING TO RANKING METHOD

tempa=sort(fit);
% Sorting of fitness function and store in a temporary variable
for i=1:n_pop,
[a b]=find(tempa(i,1)==fit(:,1));
sort_str(i,:)=pop_str(a(1,1),:);
% Strings sorted in accending order according to fitness values
end

% CAPTURING THE GLOBAL BEST OPTIMUM OF THE OBJECTIVE FUNCTION

Currentbest(1,gen)=tempa(1,1);    % Iteration or generation best
Current_best=tempa(1,1);
Globalbest(1,gen)=min(Currentbest);  % Minimum best so far obtained is the global best
if Currentbest(1,gen)<=Globalbest,
```

```
% Record the best as global best If the iteration best is <=previous global best
[aa bb]=find(tempa(1,1)==fit(:,1));
Global_best=fit(aa,1);
value_x=ax(aa,:);
end
disp(gen);                      % Display the generation/iteration number
Global_best=min(Currentbest);

% RANKING BASED SELECTION OF STRINGS

% Ranking is kept according to our objective and experience. Here ten ranks are
% given accodingly
% Percentage of ranked strings copied to total population according to ranks
% [1% 3% 5% 7% 9% 11% 13% 15% 17% 19%]=100%

per=[1 3 5 7 9 11 13 15 17 19];   % Percentage of ranked string copied(or REPRODUCED)
for j=1:10,                       % 10 sets of percentage of strings selected
cnt(j,1)=(per(1,j)/100)*n_pop;
end
cnt=round(cnt);      % Rounding to integer value if decimal places are available

% COPIED RANKED STRINGS AND MAINTAINING THE POPULATION POOL

sel=0;
for ii=1
for jj=1:cnt(ii,1),   % Each set of percentage of strings copied into the population
sel=sel+1;
sel_str(sel,:)=sort_str(ii,:);
% Storing of strings based on their ranks and percentage fixed
end
end
[r c]=size(sel_str);
if r<n_pop,
% Correction has to be made if the selected population size is not maintained
dif=n_pop-r;
for h=1:dif,
sel_str(sel+1,:)=sort_str(ii+1,:);
end
else
final_str=sel_str(1:n_pop,:);
end

% CROSSOVER OPERATION (RANDOM POINT CROSSOVER)

no_strpar=round(pr_cr*n_pop);
% Number of strings participating in the crossover operation
if rem(no_strpar,2)==1,
% Checking if all the selected strings has partcipated crossover operation
 no_strpar=no_strpar-1;
end
cnts=0;
while cnts<no_strpar;
for g=1:n_pop;
if rand(1,1)<pr_cr;
% Selection of strings done based on roulette wheel concept by generating a random number
cnts=cnts+1;
sel_cr_str(1,cnts)=g;    % String number is selected according to probability crossover
if cnts==no_strpar
break
end
```

```
end
end
end

% BINARY CROSSING OPERATION IN PROGRESS

for t=1:no_strpar,
if rem(t,2)==0,
cpnt=round(ra(2,length(final_str(t,:))-1));      % Selecting crossover point randomly
varstr1=final_str(sel_cr_str(1,t-1),:);          % Mate 1
varstr2=final_str(sel_cr_str(1,t),:);            % Mate 2
varstr_1=[varstr1(1,1:cpnt) varstr2(1,cpnt+1:D*rbl)];   % After crossing-1st Child chromosome
varstr_2=[varstr2(1,1:cpnt) varstr1(1,cpnt+1:D*rbl)];   % After crossing-2nd Child chromosome
final_str(sel_cr_str(1,t-1),:)=varstr_1;         % 1st Child chromosome string replaced in pool
final_str(sel_cr_str(1,t),:)=varstr_2;           % 2nd Child chromosome string replaced in pool
end
end

% BINARY MUTATION OPERATION

no_mut=ceil(pr_mu*n_pop*rbl*D);                  % Numberof bits to be mutated
for k=1:no_mut,
mpos=[ran(n_pop) ran(rbl*D)];                    % Random selection of mutation position
if (final_str(mpos(1,1),mpos(1,2))==1),          % Replacing "one if zero" or "zero if one"
final_str(mpos(1,1),mpos(1,2))=0;
else
final_str(mpos(1,1),mpos(1,2))=1;
end
end
pop_str=final_str;
end
x=[value_x(1,1)];
Total_time_taken=toc                             % Total time taken for the GA run

% CONVERGENCE PLOT AND DISPLAY OF RESULTS

plot(1:epochs,Globalbest,'-');
xlabel('Number of epochs');
ylabel('f(x)');
title('Convergence plot using binary GA')
disp('Global value of the objective function')
disp(Global_best)
disp('Global best variable');
disp(x);
```

## Part B: Sub programs (Subroutine functions)

<u>Objective Function</u>
```
function [out]=sinfun(x)
out=(x*sin(10*pi*x)+1.0);            % Objective function
```

<u>Generation of Random Number Between '1' And 'b' Function</u>
```
function [out] = ran(b)
a=1;
if nargin == 1
out = round(a + (b - a) * rand);     % Generating random number between 1 and b
end
```

<u>Genaration Of Random Number Between 'a' And 'b' Function</u>
```
function [out] = ra(a,b)
out = a + (b - a) * rand;            % Generating random number between a and b
```

## Result (One-trial convergence plot)

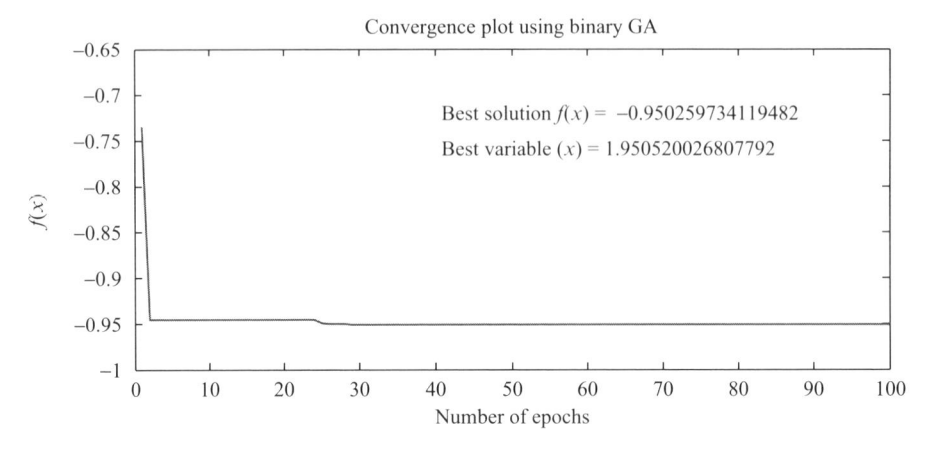

**Fig. 7.47** Convergence plot for minimization function

Best solution $f(x) = -0.950259734119482$
Best variable $(x) = 1.950520026807792$

## Observation

The program has been run for one trial and for 100 epochs. The minimum of the function is obtained and the convergence of the solution is shown in Fig. 7.47. The prior program can be modified and improved. The percentage of chromosome copied into the next generation can be reversed and convergence analysis can be carried out. The program may give different solutions for every trial run. However, after required number of iterations and proper tuning of GA control parameters, the program can give the best solution.

### 7.4.2 Real or Continuous GA (Case 2)

**Solution**

*Assumptions*

Number of generations (maxiter) = 1
Number of population (np) = 10
Number of variables (nv) = 1
Lower boundary value (varl) = −1
Upper boundary value (varh) = 2
Mutation rate (mutrate) = 0.1
Crossover rate = 0.5

*Steps*

**(a) Initialization**

- Number of mutation (nmut) to be carried out = Number of population × Mutation rate

$$= 10 \times 0.1 = 1$$

(*Note:* Round off to nearest integer if decimal places are present)

Number of matings (M) to be carried out = Number of population × Crossover rate
$$= 10 \times 0.5 = 5$$

(*Note:* Round off to nearest integer if decimal places are present)
Chromosomes are generated within boundary limits (pop)

**Table 7.6** Generation of population and evaluation

| Np = 10 (pop) | Cost | Cost in ascending order | Evaluation |
|---|---|---|---|
| −0.4691 | 1.3868 | 0.4697 | Current variable = 0.5605 |
| 0.1572 | 0.8468 | 0.5344 | Current Cost = 0.4697 |
| −0.5914 | 0.8424 | 0.8424 | Global variable = 0.5605 |
| 0.6454 | 1.6389 | 0.8468 | Global Cost = 0.4697 |
| 0.7796 | 0.5344 | 1.0027 | |
| 1.0580 | 2.0249 | 1.1820 | |
| 0.0991 | 1.0027 | 1.3868 | |
| 0.2772 | 1.1820 | 1.6389 | |
| 0.5605 | 0.4697 | 2.0249 | |
| 1.6327 | 2.3962 | 2.3962 | |

**(b) Evaluation of Population of Chromosomes (Table 7.6)**

- Calculate the cost of the objective function

  Substitute all the chromosome variables in the objective function (7.30). Here the fitness function is same as the objective function.

- Sort the cost in ascending order
- Capture the generation best variable with minimum cost
- Assign the current best value as the global best and global variable

**Table 7.7** Roulette-wheel selection

| Chromosomes in ascending order | Cost in ascending order | Normalisation | Probability | Cumulative probability | Random values generated for selection of mates No of matings(M) = 5 |
|---|---|---|---|---|---|
| 0.5605 | 0.4697 | 0.1000 | 0.2160 | 0.2160 | pick1 = 0.6777 |
| 0.7796 | 0.5344 | 0.1269 | 0.1790 | 0.3949 | 0.2345 |
| −0.5914 | 0.8424 | 0.2548 | 0.1405 | 0.5354 | 0.6190 |
| 0.1572 | 0.8468 | 0.2566 | 0.1154 | 0.6508 | 0.1389 |
| 0.0991 | 1.0027 | 0.3213 | 0.0950 | 0.7458 | 0.8430 |
| 0.2772 | 1.1820 | 0.3958 | 0.0771 | 0.8229 | pick2 = 0.0579 |
| −0.4691 | 1.3868 | 0.4808 | 0.0616 | 0.8844 | 0.9805 |
| 0.6454 | 1.6389 | 0.5855 | 0.0611 | 0.9456 | 0.7784 |
| 1.0580 | 2.0249 | 0.7458 | 0.0304 | 0.9760 | 0.4111 |
| 1.6327 | 2.3962 | 0.9000 | 0.0240 | 1.0000 | 0.2513 |

**Table 7.8** Crossover operation

| Selection of chromosomes for mating ma(Mate1) and pa(Mate2) | Random number generated for information mixing (R) | Crossover operation $M_1 \times M_2$ |
|---|---|---|
| Mate 1<br>5 (0.0991)<br>2 (0.7796) | 0.3451 | $M_1 - c_1 = 0.0991 - 0.3451 \times (0.0991 - 0.5605) = 0.2583$ (5)<br>$M_2 - c_2 = 0.5605 + 0.3451 \times (0.0991 - 0.5605) = \mathbf{0.4013}$ (1) |
| 4(0.1572)<br>1(0.5605)<br>**(0.4013)** | 0.4539 | $M_1 - c_1 = 0.7796 - 0.4539 \times (0.7796 - 1.6327) = \mathbf{1.1668}$ (2)<br>$M_2 - c_2 = 1.6327 + 0.4539 \times (0.7796 - 1.6327) = 1.2455$ (10) |
| 7(−0.4691)<br><br>Mate 1 | 0.8674 | $M_1 - c_1 = 0.1572 - 0.8674 \times (0.1572 - 0.2772) = 0.2613$ (4)<br>$M_2 - c_2 = 0.2772 + 0.8674 \times (0.1572 - 0.2772) = 0.1731$ (6) |
| 1(0.5605)<br>10(1.6327)<br>6(0.2772) | 0.1004 | $M_1 - c_1 = \mathbf{0.4013} - 0.1004 \times (\mathbf{0.4013} + 0.5914) = 0.3016$ (1)<br>$M_2 - c_2 = -0.5914 + 0.1004 \times (\mathbf{0.4013} + 0.5914) = -0.4917$ (3) |
| 3(−0.5914)<br>2(0.7796)<br>**(1.1668)** | 0.7801 | $M_1 - c_1 = -0.4691 - 0.7801 \times (-0.4691 - \mathbf{1.1668}) = 0.8071$ (7)<br>$M_2 - c_2 = \mathbf{1.1668} + 0.7801 \times (-0.4691 - \mathbf{1.1668}) = -0.1094$ (2) |

**(c) Roulette-wheel selection (Table 7.7)**

The selection of chromosome for crossover operation is carried out using roulette-wheel concept. The basic part of the selection process is to stochastically select from one generation to create the basis of the next generation. The requirement is that the fittest individuals have a greater chance of survival than weaker ones. This replicates nature in that fitter individuals will tend to have a better probability of survival and will go forward to form the mating pool for the next generation. Weaker individuals are not without a chance. In nature such individuals may have genetic coding that may prove useful to future generations. Here the chromosome is selected based on the probability of the chromosome and also incorporating randomness in the selection process. Thus information search through crossover operation has the property of exploitation and exploration which is very well explained in Chapter 8.

- The population of chromosomes are sorted in ascending order based on the cost. Therefore, the first chromosome is the one which has the least cost for a particular generation. Since negative cost is involved and also to get the probability of each chromosome, the cost of the corresponding to that chromosome has been normalized between 0.9 and 0.1. The best chromosome will be the one that has the minimum cost and should have more probability of selection.
- The nomalization is carried by using a line equation as given in the following Eq. (7.31):

$$\frac{x - x_1}{y - y_1} = \frac{y_2 - y_1}{x_2 - x_1} \quad (7.31)$$

Here $x_1 = 0.1$, $x_2 = 0.9$, $y_1 =$ Minimum cost of the population of chromosome and $y_2 =$ Maximum cost of the population of chromosome. If $y$ is the cost of a particular chromosome, then $x$ will give the normalized cost between 0.1 and 0.9.
- The probability of the $i^{th}$ chromosome in the pool of population size $n_p$ is calculated by the following Eq. (7.32):

$$prob = flip\left(\sum_{i=1}^{n_p}\left(\frac{Normalised\ cost\ of\ an\ individual\ chromosome\ (i)}{Sum\ of\ all\ the\ cost\ of\ the\ chromosomes\ present\ in\ the\ population(n_p)}\right)\right) \quad (7.32)$$

Flipping of the chromosome is carried out so that the best chromosome has the higher probability value of selection to mate. Then the cumulative probability or the probability distribution function (PDF) value is calculated for each individual chromosome and is given in Table 7.7.
- M number of random number is generated, between 0 and 1, for selecting Mate 1 and Mate 2 respectively. If the random number generated is made to fit between the upper and lower PDF value of the chromosomes respectively, then the chromosome corresponding to the upper PDF value is selected as a mate. For example (Table 7.2) let 0.6777 be the generated random number which is found to be between 0.7458 (upper PDF) and 0.6508 (lower PDF). Now the fifth chromosome 0.0991 in the population is selected for mating.

### (d) Crossover Operation (Table 7.8)

- Once the required number of chromosomes are selected and based on the number of crossover operation (i.e., 5), M random number between [0 1] is generated and is used in the crossover operation as in Section 7.3.3.2. Here the random number generated is the multiplier (R). If $X_1$ and $X_2$ are the two chromosome strings acting as Mate 1 and Mate 2, then crossover operation for real coded chromosome is carried out using the following equations.

$$X'_1 = X_1 - R \times (X_1 - X_2) \quad (7.33\ a)$$
$$X'_2 = X_2 + R \times (X_1 - X_2) \quad (7.33\ b)$$

- Once the corresponding parent chromosome is replaced with the newly generated child chromosome through crossover operation, the boundary limits of the chromosome variable has to be checked. If the chromosome variable is violating the boundary limits, then the replacement should not be considered.

### (e) Mutation Operation (Table 7.9)

- Select number of rows of the chromosomes randomly 'nmut' times.
- Replace the selected chromosomes with a new chromosome between the boundary limits. Here nmut = 1 and 3 is the selected random row position. Therefore the third row chromosome variable ($-0.4917$) is replaced by $-0.8745$.

Table 7.9  Mutation operation and new population for next generation

| Population after crossover | Random row selection nmut = 1 | Replace with a new chromosome between −1 and −2 | New population for next generation |
|---|---|---|---|
| 0.3016 | | 0.3016 | 0.3016 |
| −0.1094 | | −0.1094 | −0.1094 |
| −0.4917 | | **−0.8745 [−1 2]** | **−0.8745** |
| 0.2613 | | 0.2613 | 0.2613 |
| 0.2583 | 2.4567 (round to nearest integer value) 3 | 0.2583 | 0.2583 |
| 0.1731 | | 0.1731 | 0.1731 |
| 0.8071 | | 0.8071 | 0.8071 |
| 0.6454(8) | | 0.6454 | 0.6454 |
| 1.0580(9) | | 1.0580 | 1.0580 |
| 1.2455 | | 1.2455 | 1.2455 |

**(f) Termination Criterion**

- Once the required number of generation has reached the maximum generation/iteration, then the algorithm is stopped. Otherwise, repeat steps b to f.

## MATLAB Program 7.2

### Part A

```
%%%%%%%%%%%%%%%%%%%%%%%%%%%%%%%%%%%%%%%%%%%%%%%%%%%%%%%%%
% OPTIMISATION OF A SINGLE VARIABLE FUNCTION USING CONTINOUS GA
%%%%%%%%%%%%%%%%%%%%%%%%%%%%%%%%%%%%%%%%%%%%%%%%%%%%%%%%%

% CLEARING ALL PREVIOUS DATA

clear workspace           % Clears all previous variables in the work space
clear all                 % Clears  all variables
clear figure              % Clear previous figures

% INITIALIZATION OF PARAMETERS

maxit=1000;               % Maximum Number of iterations
np=75;                    % Initial population size
nv=1;                     % Number of variable
varl=-1;                  % Lower boundary value
varh=2;                   % Upper boundaray value

% CREATION AND EVALUATION OF THE INITIAL POPULATIONS

pop=(varh-varl)*rand(np,1)+varl;   % Chromosomes generated within boundary limits
it=0;                              % Set the iteration number
mutrate=0.05;                      % Set mutation rate
crossrate=0.8;                     % Crossover rate
nmut=round((np-1)*nv*mutrate);     % Total number of mutations
M=round(crossrate*np);             % Number of matings
cost=1+pop.*sin(10*pi.*pop);       % Evaluation of cost function for all population
[cost,ind]=sort(cost);             % Sorting the cost in accending order
```

```matlab
itervar=pop(ind(1,1));          % Capturing the generation best variable
pop=pop(ind(:,1),1);
% Arranging the chromosome according to ascending order of the cost
disp('Generation');
disp('1')                        % Display the generation number
disp('Current Variable');
disp(itervar);                   % Display the generation best variable
disp('Global Variable');
globvar(1)=itervar;
disp(globvar(1))                 % Display the global best variable so far obtained
minc(1)=cost(1,1);
itercost=minc(1);
disp('Current Cost');
disp(itercost);                  % Display the generation best cost
globcost(1)=minc(1);
disp('Global Cost')
disp(globcost(1,1));             % Display the global best cost so far obtained

% START OF GENERATION CYCLE

while it<maxit                   % Iterating through generations
it=it+1;                         % Incrementing generation counter

% ROULETTE WHEEL SELECTION SCHEME

norm_values = ((0.9-0.1)/(max(cost)-min(cost))).*((cost(:,1)-min(cost)))+0.1;
% Normalizing between 0.1 to 0.9
prob=flipud(norm_values(:,1)/sum(norm_values));   % Probability of each chromosome
pdf=[0 cumsum(prob(1:np))'];     % Probability distribution function
pick1=rand(1,M);    % First chromosome randomly picked up for crossover operation
pick2=rand(1,M);    % Second chromosome randomly picked up for crossover operation

% SELECTION OF CHROMOSOMES FOR MATING

ic=1;
while ic<=M
for id=1:np
if pick1(1,ic)<=pdf(id) & pick1(1,ic)>=pdf(id-1);
% Cheking the random number fit between upper pdf and lower pdf of  chromosome
ma(ic)=id-1;       % Index of the first chromosomes selected based on upper pdf(Mate 1)
end
if pick2(1,ic)<=pdf(id) & pick2(1,ic)>=pdf(id-1);
% Cheking the random number fit between upper pdf and lower pdf of  chromosome
pa(ic)=id-1;       % Index of the first chromosomes selected based on upper pdf(Mate 2)
end
end
ic=ic+1;
end

maposzero=find(ma<1);   % Preventing the Index of the Mate 1 chromosomes to become zero
if isempty(maposzero)~=1
ma(maposzero)=1;
end
paposzero=find(pa<1);   % Preventing the Index of the Mate 2 chromosomes to become zero
if isempty(paposzero)~=1
pa(paposzero)=1;
end

% REAL CODED CROSSOVER OPERATION

ix=1:np;
R=rand(1,M);             % Information mixing variable(random number multiplier)
```

```
ia=1;
while ia<=M
xy=pop(ma(ia),1)-pop(pa(ia),1);           % Mating of the first and second chromosome
pop(ix(ia),1)=pop(ma(ia),1);              % Mate 1
pop(ix(ia)+1,1)=pop(pa(ia),1);            % Mate 2
pop(ix(ia),1)=pop(ma(ia),1)-R(ia).*xy;    % Mate 1 replaced by 1st child chromosome
pop(ix(ia)+1,1)=pop(pa(ia),1)+R(ia).*xy;  % Mate 2 replaced by 2nd child chromosome
if isempty(find((pop>=varh)|(pop<=varl)))==1  % Checking for boundary limit violations
ia=ia+1;
end
end

% REAL CODED MUTATION OPERATION

mrow=sort(round(rand(1,nmut)*(np-1))+1);
% Random row selection of chromosome in the population
ii=1;
while ii<=nmut                            % No of times mutations must occur
pop(mrow(ii),1)=(varh-varl)*rand+varl;
% Replacing a new chromosome in the selected row position of the population
if isempty(find((pop>=varh)|(pop<=varl)))==1   % Checking for boundary limit violations
ii=ii+1;
end
end

% EVALUATION AND SORTING OF NEW POPULATION

cost=1+pop.*sin(10*pi.*pop);  % Evaluation of cost after crossover and mutation
[cost,ind]=sort(cost);        % Sorting the cost in accending order
itervar=pop(ind(1,1));        % Capturing the generation best variable
pop=pop(ind(:,1),1);          % Arranging the chromosome according to ascending order of the cost
itercost=cost(1,1);           % Capturing the generation best cost
minc(it+1)=itercost;          % Recording generation best for plotting
if itercost<globcost(it);     % Whether generation best cost is the global best cost?
globcost(it+1)=itercost;      % If YES, record global best cost for plotting
globvar(it+1)=itervar;        % Record the generation best variable as the global variable
else                          % If No
globcost(it+1)=globcost(it);  % Save the same previous global best cost for plotting
globvar(it+1)=globvar(it);    % Save the same previous global best variable for plotting
end

% CONVERGENCE PLOT AND DISPLAY OF RESULTS

disp('Generations')           % Display the generation number
disp(it);
disp('Current Variable')      % Display the generation best variable
disp(itervar);
disp('Current Cost')          % Display the generation best cost
disp('Global Variable');
disp(globvar(it+1));          % Display the global best variable so far obtained
disp('Global Cost');
disp(globcost(it+1));         % Display the global best cost so far obtained
figure                        % Display the figure
plot(2:it+1,minc(1,2:it+1),2:it+1,globcost(1,2:it+1));
% Plotting the iteration cost and the global cost convergence
title('Convergence plot using continous GA');          % Title label
xlabel('No of generations');ylabel('Cost of the function');  % X-Y label
end
```

## Result (One-trial convergence plot)

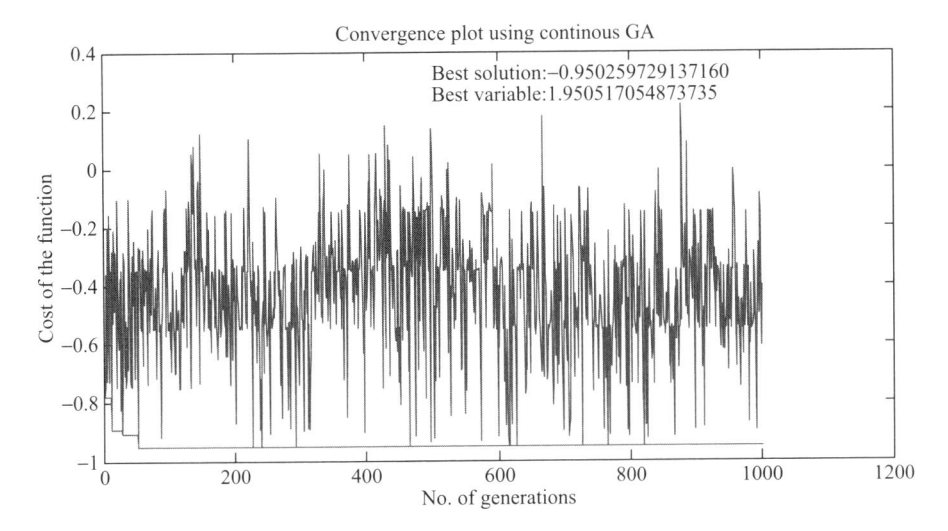

**Fig. 7.48** Convergence plot for minimization function

## Observation

The program has been run for one trial and for 1000 generations. Even though different costs are obtained in every generation, the best cost so far achieved is captured at every generation and plotted, which is the convergence plot. The minimum of the function is obtained and the convergence of the solution is shown in Fig. 7.48. The program may give different solutions for every trial run. However, after required number of iterations and proper tuning of GA control parameters, the program can give the best solution.

## 7.5 GENETIC ALGORITHM APPLICATIONS

Genetic algorithms have widely been used in radar and communication systems to synthesize multi-layer-radar-absorbing coating which maximizes the absorption of electromagnetic waves over a desired range of frequencies and incident angles, optimise weights in neural network (NN) training, adapt infinite impulse response (IIR) filters, obtain realistic solutions for inverse problems in geophysics, schedule problems, etc. In the following sections, we discuss some standard GA applications.

### 7.5.1 Travelling Salesman Problem

The TSP is one of the standard combinatorial optimisation problems. The application of the GA to TSP is a very interesting permutation-type problem where different types of crossovers and mutations have been tested. The problem is quite simple to understand: a salesman seeks the shortest tour through $n$ cities; that is, the travelling salesman must visit every city in his territory exactly once and then return to the starting point. Given the costs of travelling between all pairs of cities, his objective is to minimize the total cost for the entire tour. In the past, a lot of work has been done to solve the TSP optimally. The main objective is to reach the global optimum.

The TSP becomes more tough and time-consuming when the number of cities is increased, and determining the shortest tour proves to be a challenge. Scientists and researchers are trying different optimisation techniques and they have a very good reason to test their techniques on this problem. This problem is known as a *benchmark problem* because it exhibits all the aspects of a combinatorial optimisation problem. The GA community considers the TSP a challenge and is still working towards a global optimum solution, targeting quicker convergence by incorporating various modifications in the concepts of GAs. The main issues being focussed upon are the following [15], [4]:

- Determining the proper representation required to encode a tour
- Finding genetic operators applicable to building blocks while avoiding illegality
- Preventing premature convergence (i.e., getting trapped into local minima)
- Shortening the time required to produce the optimum result

The first and foremost challenge in solving the TSP is to represent the problem in such a way that the GA concept can be implemented on it. Even though there are many different representation schemes, which have already been discussed in the previous section, not every representation is suitable. To justify this statement, suppose that the binary representation is used. This representation requires special repair algorithms since a change in a single bit may result in an illegal tour. In such a case, any of permutation representations discussed earlier can be used. Now let us look at the flow chart for solving the TSP using a GA (Fig. 7.49).

Let the cost function for the simplest form of the TSP be just the distance travelled by the salesman for the given ordering $(x_n, y_n)$, where $n = 1 \ldots N$, as shown here:

$$\text{Cost} = \sum_{n=0}^{N} \sqrt{(x_n - x_{n+1})^2 + (y_n - y_{n+1})^2} \qquad (7.34)$$

where $(x_n, y_n)$ are the co-ordinates of the $n$th city visited. Let us fix the starting and the ending points at the origin, so $(x_0, y_0) = (x_{N+1}, y_{N+1})$, which is the origin (0, 0). Here, letting the starting city float provides greater possibilities of optimal solutions.

The problem is represented by integers ranging from 1 to $N$. Initially, each chromosome in the population will have its own sequence of city nodes. Here the *Position-based crossover* (*OX*) discussed earlier (see Fig. 7.23) proposed by syswerda is used. A single or a set of randomly selected positions from one parent chromosomal string is considered and the corresponding nodes are transferred to the same positions of its child string. Now, those nodes of second parent chromosome which are already present in child 1 are deleted. Thus, starting from the bottom of the second parent string and going to the top, the remaining nodes in the second parent string are used in filling the empty segments of child 1 from bottom to top. The same procedure is repeated to produce child 2. Thus, each offspring contains exactly one copy of each integer from 1 to N. The *reciprocal exchange* (see Section 7.3.4) mutation operator randomly chooses a string, selects two random sites within that string, and exchanges the integers at those sites.

**Table 7.10** Oliver 30 city problem

| City node | 1 | 2 | 3 | 4 | 5 | 6 | 7 | 8 | 9 | 10 | 11 | 12 | 13 | 14 | 15 |
|---|---|---|---|---|---|---|---|---|---|---|---|---|---|---|---|
| X-coordinate | 54 | 54 | 37 | 41 | 02 | 07 | 25 | 22 | 18 | 4 | 13 | 18 | 24 | 25 | 44 |
| Y-coordinate | 67 | 62 | 84 | 94 | 99 | 64 | 62 | 60 | 54 | 50 | 40 | 40 | 42 | 38 | 35 |
| City node | 16 | 17 | 18 | 19 | 20 | 21 | 22 | 23 | 24 | 25 | 26 | 27 | 28 | 29 | 30 |
| X-coordinate | 41 | 45 | 58 | 62 | 82 | 91 | 83 | 71 | 64 | 68 | 83 | 87 | 74 | 71 | 58 |
| Y-coordinate | 26 | 21 | 35 | 32 | 07 | 38 | 46 | 44 | 60 | 58 | 69 | 76 | 78 | 71 | 69 |

Let us assume $N = 30$ cities (Table 7.10). Therefore, if the starting and ending points are fixed, there are a total of $30!/2 = 1.326264299060955 \times 10^{32}$ possible combinations to check. The solving of TSP using GA can be understood by the following MATLAB Program.

Minimize cost
$$\sum_{n=0}^{N} \sqrt{(x_n - x_{n+1})^2 + (y_n - y_{n+1})^2}$$

Permutation representation of city nodes in each parent chromosome

Production of the initial Chromosomal population

Evaluation of cost

Selection of chromosomes for mating

Permutation crossover and mutation

Replace old population with new population

Test convergence of cost

Stop

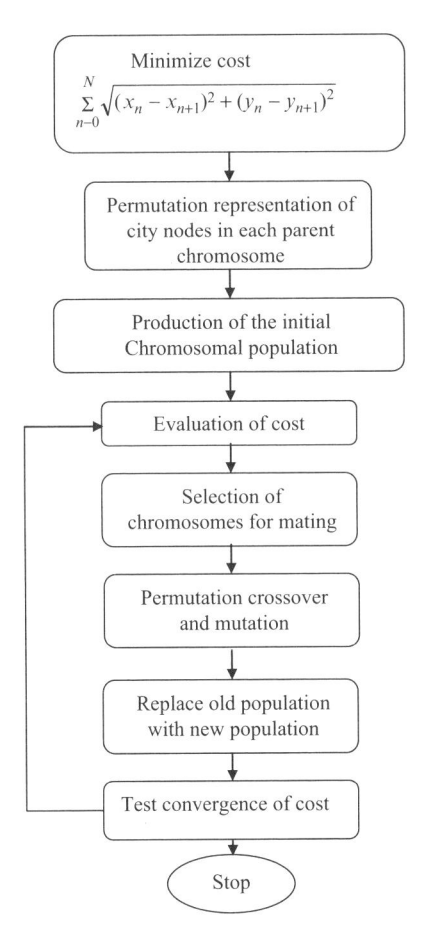

**Fig. 7.49** Flow chart of the TSP using a GA

## MATLAB Program 7.3

### Part A

```
%%%%%%%%%%%%%%%%%%%%%%%%%%%%%%%%%%%%%%%%%%%%%%%%%%%%%%%%%%%
% SOLVING TSP PROBLEM USING PERMUTATION GA FOR OILVER 30 CITY PROBLEM
%%%%%%%%%%%%%%%%%%%%%%%%%%%%%%%%%%%%%%%%%%%%%%%%%%%%%%%%%%%

% CLEARING ALL PREVIOUS DATA

clear all                       % Clears  all variables
clear figure                    % Clearprevious figures

% GLOBAL VARIABLES

global iga x y                  % Define global variables

% CITY LOCATIONS (X-Y CO-ORDINATES IN GRAPH)

x1=[54 54 37 41 02 07 25 22 18 4  13 18 24 25 44 41 45 58 62 82 91 83 71 
    64 68 83 87 74 71 58];
y1=[67 62 84 94 99 64 62 60 54 50 40 40 42 38 35 26 21 35 32 07 38 46 44 
    60 58 69 76 78 71 69];

% EUCLIDIAN DISTANCE BETWEEN CITIES

for i=1:Ncity
for j=1:Ncity
dist(i,j)=sqrt((x1(i)-x1(j))^2+(y1(i)-y1(j))^2);
% Calculating all the equilidian distances between any of the 2 city nodes
end
end

% GA INITILIAZATION PARAMETER

Npar=30;                        % No of variables
Ncity=npar;                     % No of variables is same as the number of city nodes
bestcost=999999;
% Set a very high value for the best tour cost that can act as reference for comparison
maxit=10000;                    % Maximum number of iterations
popsize=75;                     % Set population size
mutrate=0.1;                    % Set mutation rate
selection=0.9;                  % Crossover selection rate
M=round(selection*popsize);     % Number of matings
iga=0;                          % Generation counter initialized
for iz=1:popsize
pop(iz,:)=randperm(npar);       % Random population
end

% EVALUATION OF COST FOR THE INITIAL POPULATION OF CHROMOSOMES

for i=1:popsize    % Computing the tour cost for the chromosomal strings in the population
cost(i,1)=0;
x2=x1(pop(i,:));                % X-coordinate selected
y2=y1(pop(i,:));                % Y-coordinate selected
for k=1:30
if k~=30
D1=x2(k);
D2=x2(k+1);
E1=y2(k);
E2=y2(k+1);
else
```

```
D1=x2(k);
D2=x2(1);
E1=y2(k);
E2=y2(1);
end
cost(i,1)=cost(i,1)+sqrt((D1-D2)^2+(E1-E2)^2);
% Summation of all eculidean distances beween the cities of the chromosomal string
end
end

% SORTING AND GETTING THE MINIMUM COST STRING FOR THE INITIAL POPULATION

[cost,ind]=sort(cost);           % Sorting of in ascending order
pop=pop(ind,:);                  % Sorting population with lowest cost first
minc(1,1)=min(cost);             % Recording the minimum cost
if minc(1,1)<bestcost            % Checking the minimum cost is less than the best cost
globc(1,1)=minc(1,1);
% If, YES store the minimum cost in the global cost for plotting purpose
bestcost=minc(1,1);              % Store the minimum cost in the best cost for comparing purpose
beststr=pop(1,:);
% Capture the best string so far obtained,i.e, string corresponding to best cost
else
globc(1,1)=bestcost;             % If, NO retain the previous best cost as the global cost
end


% STARTING OF THE GA CYCLE

while iga<maxit
% Continue the cycle till the maximum iteration or stopping criteria is reached
 iga=iga+1;                      % Increments generation counter
disp('Iteration Number')
% Display the iteration/generation number as the algorithm runs
disp(iga)

% SELECTION OF CHROMOSOMES FOR CROSSOVER OPERATION

for i=1:M
% Selection of chromosomes  for M times ( Based on cross over selection rate)
pick1(1,i)=round(1+(M*(5/100)-1)*rand);
% Mate1 selection carried out randomly from the top 5% of the population
pick2(1,i)=round(1+(M*(5/100)-1)*rand);
% Mate2 selection carried out randomly  from the top 5% of the population
end

% POSITION BASED PERMUTATION CROSSOVER OPERATION

for ic=1:M                       % Crossover operation to be carried out for M times
 indx=2*(ic-1)+1;
% Index in the chromosome population where the new offspring should be placed
child1=zeros(1,Ncity);
% Defining the matrix space for new child 1 chromosomal string
child2=zeros(1,Ncity);
% Defining the matrix space for new child 2 chromosomal string
mate1=pop(pick1(1,M),:);
% Getting the mate 1 parent chromosome ( For a 5 city example Mate 1= [2 4 5 3 1])
mate2=pop(pick2(1,M),:);
% Getting the mate 2  parent chromosome (Let Mate 2= [4 5 3 1 2]
pos=[ran(1,Ncity)];
% Selection of a single random site for permutation crossover (Let pos=3)

for i=1:length(pos)
% One time(single site) process of modifying the elements in a string is carried out
```

```
child1(1,pos(i))=mate1(1,pos(i));     % child 1 = [ 0 0 5 0 0]
child2(1,pos(i))=mate2(1,pos(i));     % child 2 = [ 0 0 3 0 0]
end

temp1=mate2;                          % temp 1 = [4 5 3 1 2]
temp2=mate1;                          % temp 2 = [2 4 5 3 1]
xx=find(child1~=0);                   %   xx = 3
yy=find(child2~=0);                   %   yy = 3

npar=Ncity;                           % npar =5
for i=1:length(pos),                  % iter=1
for j=1:npar,                         % iter=5
if child1(xx(i))==temp1(j)            % iter (1 to 2 times)
temp1(j)=[];                          % temp1(2)=[ _ ], temp1=[4 3 1 2]
break
end
end
npar=length(temp1);
% npar=4 (This command will be useful when more random sites are selected)
end

npar=Ncity;                           % npar =5
for i=1:length(pos),                  % iter=1
for j=1:npar,                         % iter=5
if child2(yy(i))==temp2(j)            % iter (1 to 4 times)
temp2(j)=[];                          % temp2(4)=[ _ ] , temp2=[2 4 5 1]
break
end
end
npar=length(temp2);
% npar=4 (This command will be useful when more random sites are selected)
end

inx=1;iny=1;                          % Increment counter for child 1 (inx) and child 2 (iny)
for j=1:Ncity,                        % iter=5
if child1(j)==0,                      % child 1 = [0 0 5 0 0]
child1(j)=temp1(inx);                 % child 1 = [4 3 5 1 2]
inx=inx+1;
end
if child2(j)==0,                      % child 2 = [0 0 3 0 0]
child2(j)=temp2(iny);                 % child 2 = [2 4 3 5 1]
iny=iny+1;
end
end
pop(indx,:)=child1;
% If M=1, then indx=1, replace the new child1 with the old string
pop(indx+1,:)=child2;
% If M=1, then indx=2, replace the new child2 with the old string
end

% RECIPROCAL EXCHANGE MUTATION OPERATION

nmut=ceil(popsize*npar*mutrate);   % Number of mutations
for ic = 1:nmut                    % Mutation operation to be carried out for nmut times
row1=ceil(rand*(popsize-1))+1;
% Selection of the row of the population of chromosomal string randomly
% (For a 5 city example let the row selected be of the String [2 4 5 3 1])
col1=ceil(rand*npar);
% 1st position of random city node to be selected for the chromosomal row (let col1=1)
col2=ceil(rand*npar);
% 2nd position of random city node to be selected for the chromosomal row (let col2=4)
temp=pop(row1,col1);               % temp=[2]
pop(row1,col1)=pop(row1,col2);     % String [_4 5 3 1]→String [1 4 5 3 1]
pop(row1,col2)=temp;
```

```
% String [1 4 5 3_]→String [1 4 5 3 2]→temp=[2](New mutant string formed within population)
end

% EVALUATION OF COST FOR THE NEW POPULATION OF CHROMOSOMES

for i=1:popsize   % Computing the tour cost for the chromosomal strings in the population
cost(i,1)=0;
x2=x1(pop(i,:));                    % X-coordinate selected
y2=y1(pop(i,:));                    % Y-coordinate selected
for k=1:30
if k~=30
D1=x2(k);
D2=x2(k+1);
E1=y2(k);
E2=y2(k+1);
else
D1=x2(k);
D2=x2(1);
E1=y2(k);
E2=y2(1);
end
cost(i,1)=cost(i,1)+sqrt((D1-D2)^2+(E1-E2)^2);
% Summation of all eculidean distances beween the cities of the chromosomal string
end
end

% SORTING AND GETTING THE MINIMUM COST STRING FOR THE NEW POPULATION

part=pop; costt=cost;
[cost,ind]=sort(cost);              % Sorting of in ascending order
minc(1,iga)=min(cost);              % Recording the minimum cost
disp('Current Best Tour Cost');     % Displaying the current minimum tour cost
disp(min(cost));
pop=pop(ind,:);                     % Sorting population with lowest cost first
if minc(1,iga)<bestcost             % Checking the minimum cost is less than the best cost
globc(1,iga)=minc(1,iga);
% If ,YES store the minimum cost in the global cost for plotting purpose
bestcost=minc(1,iga);
% Store the minimum cost in the best cost for comparing purpose
beststr=pop(1,:);
% Capture the best string so far obtained,i.e, string corresponding to best cost
else
globc(1,iga)=bestcost; % If, NO retain the previous best cost as the global cost
disp('Global Best Tour Cost');      % Displaying the best cost so far obtained
disp(bestcost);
end
end                      % End of GA cycle

% CONVERGENCE PLOT AND DISPLAY OF RESULTS

disp('Best Tour String so far Obtained');
% Displaying the best string so far obtained
disp(beststr);
figure(1);                                % Initializing a 1st figure
plot(1:maxit,globc);   % Plotting the iteration cost and the global tour cost convergence
xlabel('Number of iterations');           % X label
ylabel('Total distance');                 % Y label
title('Convergence plot for the TSP solution')   % Title label

% DISPLAY OF TOUR MAP FOR OLIVER 30 CITY PROBLEM

figure(2);                                % Initializing  2nd figure
plot([x1(beststr(1,:)) x1(beststr(1,1))],[y1(beststr(1,:)) y1(beststr(1,1))],x1,y1,'o');
% Plotting the best tour map in a graph
```

```
xlabel('X-coordinates of the cities');    % X Label
ylabel('Y-coordinates of the cities');    % Y Label
title('Tour path-solution for the TSP');  % Title label
axis square
```

## Part B: Sub programs (Subroutine functions)

Generation of Random Number Between 'a' And 'b' Function

```
function [out] = ran(a,b)
out = a + (b - a) * rand;                 % Generating random number between a and b
```

### Observation

The program has been run for one trial and for 10,000 generations. The generation global best cost is plotted. The minimum of the TSP function is obtained and the convergence of the solution is shown in Fig. 7.49. The program may give different

### Result (One-trial convergence plot)

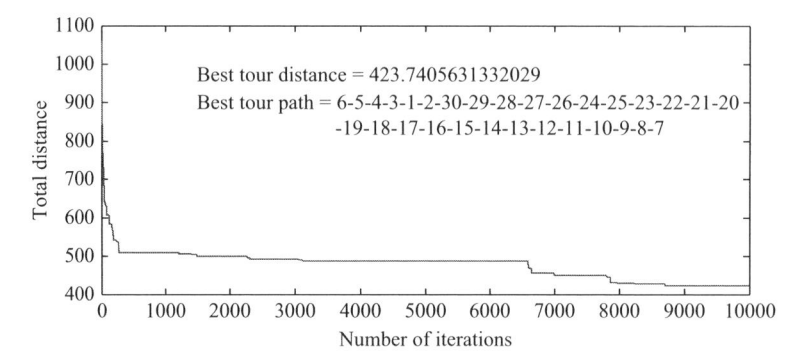

Best tour distance = 423.7405631332029
Best tour path = 6-5-4-3-1-2-30-29-28-27-26-24-25-23-22-21-20-19-18-17-16-15-14-13-12-11-10-9-8-7

**Fig. 7.49** Convergence plot for the TSP solution

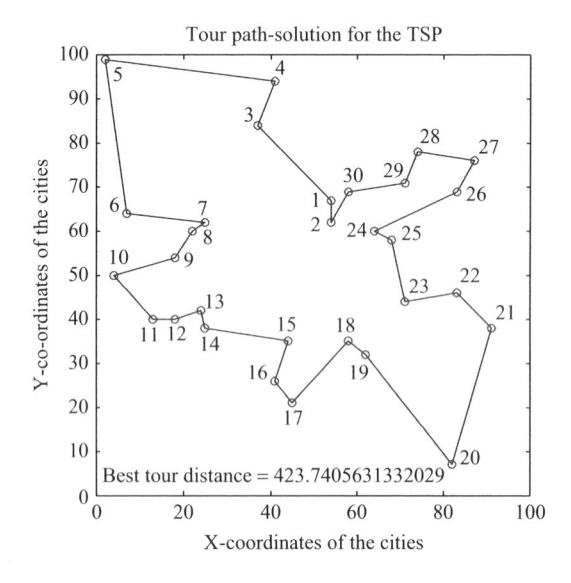

**Fig. 7.50** Oliver 30 city tour map in a graph

solutions for every trial run. However, after required number of iterations and proper tuning of GA control parameters, the program can give the best solution.

The results can be tried with various permutations crossover and permutation mutation operation discussed in Section 7.3.3. The GA parameter settings, the number of random crossover sites, and the number of generations can be varied to study the performances analysis. Other TSP benchmark problems can also be tested and evaluated. The tour map for the Oliver 30 city problem for the previous convergence of Fig. 7.49 is given in Fig. 7.50.

## 7.5.2 Economic Power Dispatch Problem

The fundamental requirement of power system economic load dispatch is to generate adequate quantity of electricity to meet the demand, at the possible lowest cost. In power system, minimizing the operation cost is very important. Economic Load Dispatch (ELD) is a method to schedule the power generator outputs with respect to the load demands, and to operate a power system most economically.

Traditional classical dispatch algorithms, (e.g., the Lagrangian multiplier method) require the incremental cost curves to be monotonically increasing or piece-wise linear [17]. The input/output characteristics of modern units are inherently highly non-linear (with valve-point effect, rate limits, etc) and having multiple local minimum points in the cost function. However, their characteristics are approximated to meet the requirements of classical dispatch algorithms leading to sub-optimal solutions and therefore, resulting in huge revenue loss over a period of time. Consideration of highly non-linear characteristics of the units requires highly robust algorithms to avoid getting stuck at local optima. The classical calculus-based techniques fail in solving these types of problems. Unlike the traditional algorithms, dynamic programming (DP) imposes no restrictions on the nature of the cost curves and hence solves inherently non-linear and discontinuous ELD problems. However, this method suffers from the curse of dimensionality or local optimality.

In this respect, stochastic search algorithms such as GA and EP may prove to be very efficient in solving highly non-linear ELD problems without any restrictions on the shape of the cost curves. Although heuristic methods do not always guarantee the global optimal solution, they provide a reasonable solution (sub-optimal or near-global optimal) in a short period of time. Recent research endeavours, therefore, have been directed towards application of these techniques.

### 7.5.2.1 Problem Formulation

The objective is to find the optimal solution, so that the minimum fuel cost is obtained subject to certain equality and inequality constraints. The problem may be expressed as a function which consists of the cost function and the constraints. In this work, equality constraint reflects a real power balance and the inequality constraint reflects the limit of real power generation.

Mathematically, the formulation may be given as follows:
Minimize,

$$F = \sum_{i=1}^{N} F_i(P_i) \; (\text{₹/hr}) \qquad (7.35)$$

where, $F_i(P_i)$ is the fuel cost function of generating unit $i$ and $P_i$ is the generation output of unit $i$ in MW.
Subject to:
(a) Power balance constraints is given as follows:

$$\sum_{i=1}^{N} P_i - P_D = 0 \qquad (7.36)$$

where, $P_D$ is the total real power demand in MW.
(b) Generating capacity constraints is given as follows:

$$P_i^{\min} \leq P_i \leq P_i^{\max} \text{ for } i = 1, 2, \ldots, N \qquad (7.37)$$

where, $P_i^{\min}$ and $P_i^{\max}$ are the minimum and maximum output generation of unit i.

The fuel cost function considering valve-point effect of the generating unit is given as follows:

$$F_i^*(P_i) = F_i(P_i) + \left| e_i \sin\left(f_i\left[P_i^{\min} - P_i\right]\right) \right| \qquad (7.38)$$

where

$$F_i(P_i) = a_i P_i^2 + b_i P_i + c_i \; (\text{₹/hr}) \qquad (7.39)$$

where $a_i$, $b_i$, $c_i$ are the fuel cost coefficients of unit $i$, and $e_i$ and $f_i$ are the fuel cost coefficients of unit $i$ with valve-point effect.

The aim of this section is to understand the application of both Binary GA and Continuous GA for economic dispatching of generating powers in a power system, satisfying the power balance constraint for system demand and total generating power, as well as the generating power constraints for all units. Therefore a simple three generating unit test system is considered and the details of the test system are given in Table 7.11.

Table 7.11  Units data for three generators (Total demand = 850 MW)

|        | $a_i$ | $b_i$ | $c_i$    | $P_i^{\max}$ | $P_i^{\min}$ |
|--------|-------|-------|----------|--------------|--------------|
| Unit 1 | 561   | 7.92  | 0.001562 | 600          | 100          |
| Unit 2 | 78    | 7.97  | 0.004820 | 200          | 50           |
| Unit 3 | 310   | 7.85  | 0.001940 | 400          | 100          |

### 7.5.2.2 Step-by-step Procedure of GA Applied to ELD Problem

To solve ELD problem by GA, the algorithm is formulated as follows:
1. Generate the initial population of generating powers randomly.
2. Compute the total production cost of the generating powers subject to the constraints in Eqs 7.36 and 7.37.

3. Compute the error ($\Delta P$) in satisfying the power balance constraint.
4. The objective is to minimize the cost and the $\Delta P$. Thus the fitness function is developed based on these two parameters.

$$\text{Fitness} = A\left[(1-\%\text{Cost})\right] + B\left[(1-\%\text{Error})\right] \quad (7.40)$$

where, $A, B (> 0)$: weighting coefficients

$$\text{Error} = \sum_{i=1}^{N} P_i - P_D \quad (7.41)$$

$$\%\text{Cost} = \frac{\text{Stringcost} - \text{Mincost}}{\text{Maxcost} - \text{Mincost}} \quad (7.42)$$

$$\%\text{Error} = \frac{\text{Stringerror} - \text{Minerror}}{\text{Maxerror} - \text{Minerror}} \quad (7.43)$$

String cost - String's cost of generation.
Mincost   - the minimum objective function value within the population.
Maxcost   - the minimum objective function value within the population.
Stringerror - String's error in meeting the power balance constraint.
Minerror   - the minimum constraint error within the population.
Maxerror   - the maximum constraint error within the population.

The total production cost and the error has to be minimized which leads to the maximization of fitness function.

1. Set the crossover probability and include the offspring in the next generation.
2. Set the mutation probability so that the random bits of the offspring flip from 0 to 1 and vice versa so that it gives characteristics that do not exist in the parent population.
3. This procedure is repeated for every unit's power value until the numbers of iterations are reached.
4. Output the solution and best fitness value.

The MATLAB codes for solving EDP using Binary GA and real or continuous coded GA are given in the following section as MATLAB Programs 7.4 and 7.5, respectively. Both Binary GA approach and real coded approach uses roulette-wheel-based selection scheme which is already discussed in the previous sections. To allow a faster convergence, some specialized techniques have been developed. One of these, called elitism, is a simple but very powerful idea. Here the fittest chromosome is retained from one generation to the other. This method enhances greatly the convergence of the GA.

With increase in the number of generations, the solution improves and reaches saturation after a point. To stop when the solution is no longer enhanced is a commonly used halting criterion. Another way is fixing the number of generations. In either case, the best solution found in final population is chosen as the

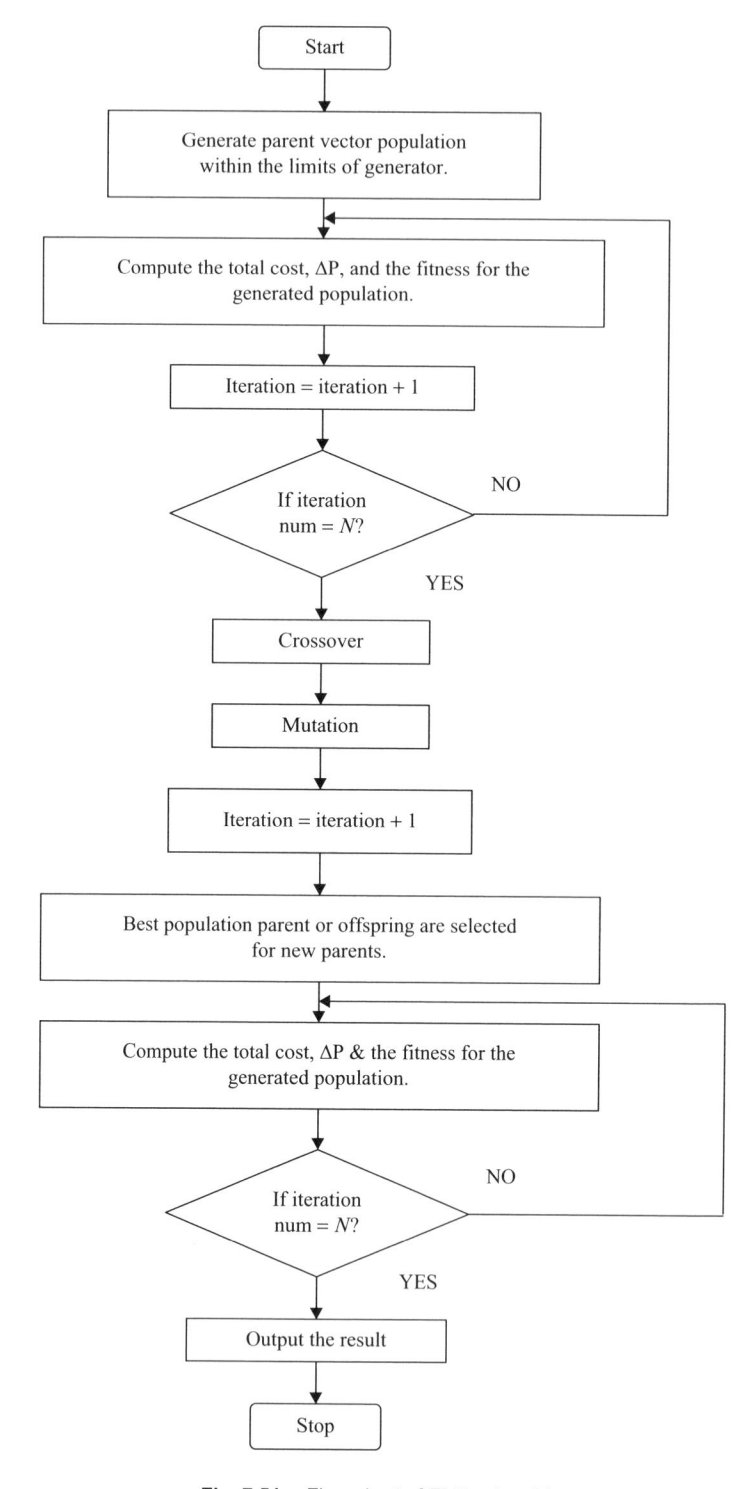

**Fig. 7.51** Flow chart of ELD using GA

optimal solution. The flow chart of the GA-based EDP is given in Fig. 7.51. The parameter settings for the following approach are carried out using trial and error approach. More trail runs are carried out to set these parameters.

## MATLAB Program 7.4

```
%%%%%%%%%%%%%%%%%%%%%%%%%%%%%%%%%%%%%%%%%%%%%%%%%%%%%%%%%%%
% SOLVING ED PROBLEM WITH VALVE POINT EFFECT USING BINARY GA
%%%%%%%%%%%%%%%%%%%%%%%%%%%%%%%%%%%%%%%%%%%%%%%%%%%%%%%%%%%

Part A

% CLEARING ALL PREVIOUS DATA

clc
clear workspace
clear all

% INITIALIZING GA PARAMETERS

format long
pop=500;            % Number of population
accu=8;             % Decimal point accuracy
p_cr=0.80;          % Probability of crossover
p_mu=0.09;          % Probability of mutation
no_gen=3;           % Number of generator variables
iter=1000;          % Setting the maximum number of iterations for halting criteria
Globfit=0.0001;     % Initializing the global best

% GETTING GENERATING SYSTEM AND UNIT DETAILS

PD=850;             % Total Load Demand
pmin=[150 100 50];  % Minimum power limit for each unit
pmax=[600 400 200]; % Maximum power limit for each unit
dl=pmax-pmin;       % Domain range (search space)
er=dl.*(10^accu);
% Number of solution points within the domain as per required decimal accuracy

% CALCULATING THE TOTAL NUMBER OF BITS IN A CHROMOSOMAL STRING

su=0;               % Initilization of count for the total no of generatots
for l=1:no_gen
bl(l)=(log(dl(l))+accu*log(10))/log(2);   % Calculation of the string length
lbl(l)=round(bl(l));    % Left bit length
rbl(l)=lbl(l)+1;    % Right bit length(er should lie between 2^lbl and 2^rbl)
su= su+rbl(l);
% Summation process of bits correponding to each of the generators
end
su;                 % Total number of bits for all the generators taken into account

% INITIALIZING THE RANDOM POPULATION OF BINARY CHROMOSOMAL STRINGS

pop_str=round(rand(pop,su));         % Generating random populations

% CONVERTING THE BINARY VALUE OF BITS INTO RELATIVE DECIMAL VALUE

realx=bin_real(pop_str,rbl,no_gen);  % Calling the subroutine function

% CONVERTING THE RELATIVE VALUE INTO ACTUAL VALUE WITHIN GENERATOR LIMITS

for m=1:pop
for j=1:no_gen
```

```
act_p(m,j)=pmin(j)+(realx(m,j)*dl(j))/(2^rbl(j)-1);
% Actual power dispatch of individual generators
end
end

% CHECKING THE POWER BALANCE CONSTRAINTS

for i=1:pop                    % To satisfy the power balance (PD=P1+P2+P3)
chromo=act_p(i,1:(no_gen-1));
% Here only 1st (P1) and 2nd (P2) generator variables are considered
Z(i,1)=PD-sum(chromo);
% Considering one variable P3=PD-(P1+P2) will definitely satify the constraint
if (Z(i,1)<=200)&(Z(i,1)>=50))  % Checking the constraint for the last variable (P3)
act_p(i,no_gen)=Z(i,1);         % Replacing P3 in the actual power dispatch matrix

last_var(i,1)=round(((Z(i,1)-pmin(no_gen))*(2^rbl(no_gen)-1))/(dl(no_gen)));
% Conversion of P3 into relative decimal value
pop_str(i,(su-rbl(no_gen)+1):su)=de2bi(last_var(i,1),rbl(no_gen),'left-msb');
% Replacing the P3 bit string in the population
end
end

% START OF GA CYCLE

for gen=1:iter
disp('Current Generation Cycle Number')
disp(gen);
[N,cl]=size(pop_str);          % Calculating the matrix size of the population
if (gen==1)
actn_str=act_p;    % Getting the actual power dispatch from the initial population
else
rlx=bin_real(pop_str,rbl,no_gen);  % Converting the binary string to decimal value
for ii=1:N
for jj=1:no_gen
actn_str(ii,jj)=pmin(jj)+(rlx(ii,jj)*dl(jj))/(2^rbl(jj)-1);
% Converting the relative decimal value to actual value of x
end
end
end

% EVALUATION OF COST AND ERROR (DIFFERENCE BETWEEN LOAD AND GENERATION)

for k=1:N
gen_str=actn_str( k,:);        % Getting the actual value of power dispatch
cost_gen(k,1)=obj(gen_str,pmin);
% Calling subroutine for calculation of generation cost
err(k,1)=abs(sum(gen_str)-PD); % Error in satisfying the load demand
end

% EVALUATION OF MIN/MAX COST AND MIN/MAX ERROR

min_cost=min(cost_gen);        % Minimum objective function value within the populatio
max_cost=max(cost_gen);        % Maximum objective function value within the populatio
min_err=min(err);              % Minimum constraint error within the population
max_err=max(err);              % Maximum constraint error within the population

% EVALUATION OF FITNESS FUNCTION

for n=1:N
per_cost(n,1)=(cost_gen(n,1)-min_cost)/(max_cost-min_cost);
% Calculation of percentage cost
per_err(n,1)=(err(n,1)-min_err)/(max_err-min_err);
% Calculation of percentage error
```

```
fit_fun(n,1)= 0.01*(1-per_cost(n,1))+0.1*(1-per_err(n,1));
% Fitness function calculation
end

% CAPTURING THE GLOBAL BEST OPTIMUM COST

[order_fita]=sort(fit_fun);   % Sorting the fitness value in ascending order
sort_str=pop_str(a,:);
% Strings are sorted in accending order according to fitness function
sort_genstr=actn_str(a,:);
% Actual power dispatch corresponding to the sorted string
sort_cost=cost_gen(a,:);
% Total generation cost corresponding to the sorted string
Currntbestfit(1,gen)= order_fit(N,1);
% Recording the best fitness value for each generation
disp('Current Best Fitness');   % Displaying the current best fitness value
disp(order_fit(N,1));
disp('Current Power Dispatch');
% Displaying the dispatch of the individual generators
disp(sort_genstr(N,:));
if Currntbestfit(1,gen)>= Globfit,
% If the cuurent best fitness value is better than previous one
beststr = pop_str(N,:);
% Capture the best string for the best fitness value obtained so far
load_gen = sort_genstr(N,:);
% Capturing the best load dispatch of generators so far obtained
Globfit=order_fit(N,1);         % Capturing the best fitness value so far obtained
bestcost=sort_cost(N,1);        % Capturing the best generation cost so far obtained
end
bestfit(gen,1)=Globfit;         % Recording the global best fitness value obtained so far
glob_cost(gen,1)=bestcost;
% Recording the global best generation cost obtained so far

% ROULETTE WHEEL SELECTION SCHEME

P = sum(fit_fun);
% Summing up the fitness value of the all the population of strings
selprob = fit_fun .* (1/P);
% Calculating the selection probability  for each of the string
rannum = rand(1,pop);
% Generating random number between 0 and 1 for each string of the population
for tt= 1: pop
% Maintaining the population size through roulette wheel selection scheme
u = rannum(1,tt);    % Getting the random number of the corresponding string
cumprob=0;           % Initializing the counter for calculating cummulative probability
for p = 1:N
cumprob = cumprob+selprob(p);
% Adding up the individual probability for calculating cummulative probability
if (u <= cumprob)
% Select the string if its random number value is less than its cummulative probability
final_str(tt,:)=pop_str(p,:);   % Selected strings through roulette wheel scheme
break;
end
end
end

% CROSSOVER OPERATION (RANDOM POINT CROSSOVER)

no_strpar=round(p_cr * pop);   % Number of strings selected for crossover operation
if rem(no_strpar,2)==1,        % Checking if even number of strings are selected
```

```
no_strpar=no_strpar-1;
end
cnts=0;
% Initializing the counter to check the required number of crossover operation
while cnts<no_strpar;
% Continue the selection of strings till the required number is over
for g=1:pop;
if rand(1,1)<p_cr;
% A string number is selected if a generated random value is less than crossover probability
cnts=cnts+1;                            % Increment the counter
sel_cr_str(1,cnts)=g;
% String number selected and recorded according to probability crossover
if cnts==no_strpar
% Continue process till the counter is equal to number of strings selected for crossover
break
end
end
end
end

% CROSSING IN PROGRESS

for t=1:no_strpar,
if rem(t,2)==0,
cpt=round(ara1(2,length(final_str(t,:))-1));
% Selecting the crossover point randomly within the string length
varstr1=final_str(sel_cr_str(1,t-1),:);    % Mate 1 selected
varstr2=final_str(sel_cr_str(1,t),:);      % Mate 2 selected
varstr_1=[varstr1(1,1:cpt) varstr2(1,cpt+1:su)];
% Child 1 string obtained after crossing
varstr_2=[varstr2(1,1:cpt) varstr1(1,cpt+1:su)];
% Child 2 string obtained after crossing
final_str(sel_cr_str(1,t-1),:)=varstr_1;   % Child 1 string replaced in pool
final_str(sel_cr_str(1,t),:)=varstr_2;     % Child 2 string replaced in pool
end
end

% MUTATION OPERATION IN PROGRESS

no_mut=ceil(p_mu*pop*su);                  % No of bits to be mutated
for k=1:no_mut,
mpos=[muta1(1,pop) muta1(1,su)];           % Random selection of mutation position
if (final_str(mpos(1,1),mpos(1,2))==1),    % Replacing "one if zero" or "zero if one"
final_str(mpos(1,1),mpos(1,2))=0;
else
final_str(mpos(1,1),mpos(1,2))=1;
end
end

% COMBINING THE PARENT BEST STRINGS WITH THE CHILD STRINGS BASED ON ELITISM

pop_str=[beststr(1,:); final_str];
end                                        % End of GA cycle

% DISPLAY OF RESULTS AND PLOTTING THE CONVERGENCE OF FITNESS FUNCTION

disp('Economic Dispatch of Generators'); % Display of power dispatch of each generating unit
disp(load_gen(1,:));
disp('Total Generation(MW)');            % Total generation to be met
disp(sum(load_gen(1,:)));
```

```
disp('Total Generation Cost');            % Total generation cost
disp(obj(load_gen(1,:),pmin))

% CONVERGENCE PLOT OF FITNESS FUNCTION

kl=(1:iter);                              % Scaling the-xaxis with the number of iteration
plot(kl,bestfit);                         % Plotting the best fitness value
xlabel('Number of generations')
ylabel('Fitness function')
title('Convergence plot of fitness function')
```

## Part B: Sub programs (Subroutine functions)

Objective Function

```
function [out]=obj(x,pmin)
global alpha beta c
% obj.m
% Total cost function to be minimised
% Ft = .001562*(x^2)+.00482*(y^2)+.00194*((z)^2)+7.92*x + 7.97*y +
% 7.85*(z)+949
alpha=[0.001562;0.00194;0.00482];         % Fuel cost coefficients of the generating units
beta=[7.92;7.85;7.97];                    % Fuel cost coefficients of the generating units
e=[300;150;200];
% Fuel cost coefficients of the generating units with valve point effects
f=[0.0315;0.063 ;0.042];
% Fuel cost coefficients of the generating units with valve point effects
x2= abs(sin((f.*(pmin-x)')));
w=(abs(e'*x2));
out = sum(beta.*(x')+alpha.*(x').^2)+949+w;   % Total generation cost
```

Conversion of binary string to real Value

```
function [realx] = bin_real(string, bit_mat, N)
% string is the binary population string
% bit_mat is the row vector containing bit length for each variable
% N is the number of Generating units
s=1;
for qq = 1:N
realx(:,qq)= bi2de(string(:,s:(s+bit_mat(qq)-1)),'left-msb');
s= s+bit_mat(qq);
end
```

Generation of integer random value between any two integer values

```
function [arg] = muta1(a,b)
arg = round(a + (b-a) * rand);
```

Generation of continous random value between any two values

```
function [out_1] = ara1(a,b)
out_1 = a + (b-a) * rand;
```

## Result (One-trial convergence plot)

**Convergence plot of fitness function**

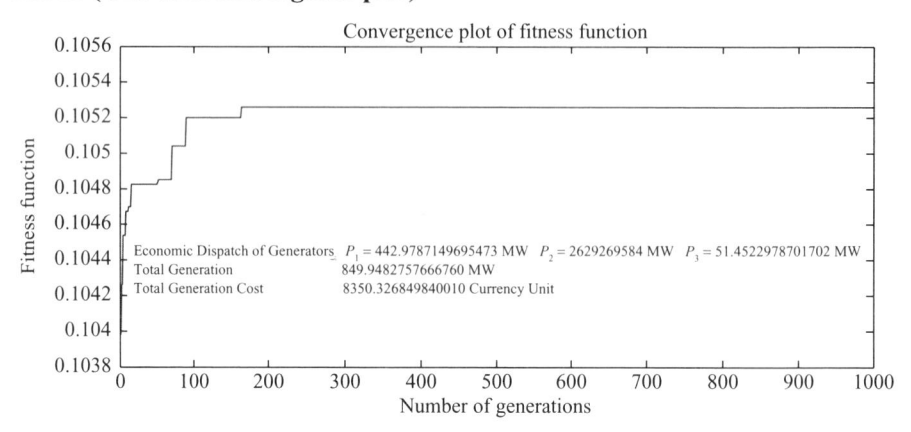

Economic Dispatch of Generators $P_1 = 442.9787149695473$ MW $P_2 = 2629269584$ MW $P_3 = 51.4522978701702$ MW
Total Generation 849.9482757666760 MW
Total Generation Cost 8350.326849840010 Currency Unit

**Fig. 7.52** Convergence plot of fitness function

## Observation

The convergence of the fitness value (Fig. 7.52) is seen increasing which means the total generation cost decreases relatively with less error. The program has been run for one trial and for 1000 generations. The accuracy of the solution and the reduction in total generation cost can be increased with proper tuning of GA control parameters such as population size, choosing the right selection scheme, crossover, mutation probability, and so on.

## MATLAB Program 7.5

```
%%%%%%%%%%%%%%%%%%%%%%%%%%%%%%%%%%%%%%%%%%%%%%%%%%%%%%%%%%%%%%%
% SOLVING ED PROBLEM WITH VALVE POINT EFFECT USING REAL CODED GA
%%%%%%%%%%%%%%%%%%%%%%%%%%%%%%%%%%%%%%%%%%%%%%%%%%%%%%%%%%%%%%%

% CLEARING ALL PREVIOUS DATA

clear workspace
clear all
clc
format long

% DEFINE GLOBAL VARIABLES

global alpha beta c

% IINITIALIZING OF GA PARAMETERS

pop=500;                % Number of population
p_cr=0.90;              % Probability of crossover
p_mu=0.09;              % Probability of mutation
D=3;                    % Total number of generator dispatch variables
iter=100;               % Setting the maximum number of iterations for halting criteria
Globfit=0.0001;         % Initializing the global best

% GETTING GENERATING SYSTEM AND UNIT DETAILS

pmin=[150 100 50];      % Minimum power limit for each unit
pmax=[600 400 200];     % Minimum power limit for each unit
pd = 850;               % Total Load Demand
```

```
% INITIALIZATION OF THE REAL VARIABLES

dl=pmax-pmin;              % Domain Length (Search Space)
aux_str=rand(pop,D);       % Generation of random initial population of strings
for i=1:D
aux_str(:,i)=pmin(i)+dl(i)*aux_str(:,i);
% Generator variables are converted within the upper and lower limits
end

% CHECKING THE CONSTRAINT FOR THE THIRD VARIABLE

for i=1:pop                       % To satisfy the power balance (PD=P1+P2+P3)
chrom = aux_str(i,1:(D-1));
% Here only 1st (P1) and 2nd (P2) generator variables are considered
Z(i,1)= pd - sum(chrom);
% Considering one variable P3=PD-(P1+P2) will definitely satify the constraint
if ((Z(i,1)<=200)&(Z(i,1)>=50));  % Checking the constraint for the last variable (P3)
aux_str(i,D)= Z(i,1);             % Replacing  P3 in the actual power dispatch matrix
end
end

% START OF GA CYCLE

for gen = 1:iter
disp('Current Generation Cycle Number')
disp(gen);
if gen==1
n_str=aux_str;         % Getting the actual power dispatch from the initial population
else
n_str=gen_str;
end
[N,cl]=size(n_str);    % Calculating the matrix size of the population

% EVALUATION OF COST AND ERROR (DIFFERENCE BETWEEN LOAD AND GENERATION)

for k=1:N
vec(k,:)=n_str(k, :);                    % Getting the actual value of power dispatch
cost_gen(k,1)=g_cost(vec(k,:),pmin);     % Calling subroutine for calculation of generation cost
error(k,1)=abs(sum(vec(k,:))-pd);        % Error in satisfying the load demand
end

% EVALUATION OF MIN/MAX COST AND MIN/MAX ERROR

Mincost=min(cost_gen);             % Minimum objective function value within the population
Maxcost=max(cost_gen);             % Maximum objective function value within the population
Minerr=min(error);                 % Minimum constraint error within the population
Maxerr=max(error);                 % Maximum constraint error within the population
for m=1:N
per_cost(m,1)=(cost_gen(m,1)-Mincost)/(Maxcost-Mincost);    % Calculation of percentage cost
per_err(m,1)=(error(m,1)-Minerr)/(Maxerr-Minerr);           % Calculation of percentage error
fitness(m,1)=5*(1-per_cost(m,1))+10*(1-per_err(m,1));       % Fitness function calculation
end

% SORTING THE FITNESS FUNCTION

[order_fit a] =sort(fitness);    % Sorting the fitness value in ascending order
sort_str=n_str(a,:);
% Strings represents the actual power dispatch corresponding to ascending to fitness function
sort_cost=cost_gen(a,:);         % Total generation cost corresponding to the sorted string
Currntbestfit(1,gen)= order_fit(N,1);
% Recording the best fitness value for each generation
disp('Current Best Fitness');    % Displaying the current best fitness value
```

```
disp(order_fit(N,1));
disp('Current Power Dispatch');   % Displaying the dispatch of the individual generators
disp(sort_str(N,:));

% CAPTURING THE GLOBAL BEST OPTIMUM COST

if Currntbestfit(1,gen)>= Globfit,
% If the current best fitness value is better  than previous one
beststr = sort_str(N,:);
% Capture the best string for the best fitness value obtained so far
load_gen = beststr;
% Capturing the best load dispatch of generators so far obtained
Globfit=order_fit(N,1);       % Capturing the best fitness value so far obtained
bestcost=sort_cost(N,1);      % Capturing the best generation cost so far obtained
end
bestfit(gen,1)=Globfit;       % Recording the global best fitness value obtained so far
glob_cost(gen,1)=bestcost;    % recording the global best generaion cost obtained so fart

% ROULETTE WHEEL SELECTION SCHEME

P = sum(fitness);      % Summing up the fitness value of the all the population of strings
selprob = fitness.*(1/P);  % Calculating the selection probability for each of the string
rannum = rand(1,pop);
% Generating random number between 0 and 1 for each string of the population
for tt= 1: pop
% Maintaining the population size through roulette wheel selection scheme
u = rannum(1,tt);              % Getting the random number of the corresponding string
cumprob=0;                     % Initializing the counter for calculating cumulative probability
for p = 1:N
cumprob = cumprob+selprob(p);
% Adding up the individual probability for calculating cumulative probability
if ( u <= cumprob)
% Select the string if its random number value is less than its cumulative probability
final_str(tt,:)=n_str(p,:);    % Selected strings through roulette wheel scheme
break;
end
end
end

% CROSSOVER OPERATION(RANDOM POINT CROSSOVER)

no_strpar=round(p_cr * pop);  % Number of strings selected for crossover operation
if rem(no_strpar,2)==1,       % Checking if even number of strings are selected
no_strpar=no_strpar-1;
end
cnts=0;   % Initializing the counter to check the required number of crossover operation
while cnts<no_strpar;
% Continue the selection of strings till the required number is over
for g=1:pop;
if rand(1,1)<p_cr;
% A string number is selected if a generated random value is less than crossover probability
cnts=cnts+1;                   % Increment the counter
n_str(1,cnts)=g;
% String number selected and recorded according to probability crossover
if cnts==no_strpar
% Continue process till the counter is equal to number of strings selected for crossover
break
end
end
end
end
```

```matlab
% CROSSING IN PROGRESS

for t=1:no_strpar,
if rem(t,2)==0,
varstr1=final_str(n_str(1,t-1),1:2);   % Mate 1 selected
varstr2=final_str(n_str(1,t),1:2);     % Mate 2 selected
R=rand(1,1);                           % Information mixing variable
xy=(varstr1-varstr2);
final_str(n_str(1,t-1),:)=[varstr1-R.*xy 850-sum(varstr1-R.*xy)];
% Child 1 string obtained after crossing & replaced in pool
final_str(n_str(1,t),:)=[varstr2+R.*xy 850-sum(varstr2+R.*xy)];
% Child 1 string obtained after crossing & replaced in pool
end
end

% MUTATION OPERATION IN PROGRESS

nomut=ceil(p_mu*pop*D);         % No of elements in string to be mutated
for k=1:nomut,
Mpos=[mut_on(1,pop) mut_on(1,D)];
% Random selection of mutation position (i.e row and column)
l=Mpos(1,2);                    % Getting the random generating unit selected
final_str(Mpos(1,1),Mpos(1,2))=pmin(l)+ dl(l)*(rand(1,1));
% Random value should be within the generators limits
end

for i=1:pop                     % To satisfy the power balance (PD=P1+P2+P3)
if ((Z(i,1)<=200)&(Z(i,1)>=50)) % Checking the constraint for the last variable (P3)
aux_str(i,D)= Z(i,1);           % Replacing P3 in the actual power dispatch matrix
end
chrom = aux_str(i,1:(D-1));
% Here only 1st (P1) and 2nd (P2) generator variables are considered
Z(i,1)= pd - sum(chrom);
% Considering one variable P3=PD-(P1+P2) will definitely satisfy the constraint
end

% COMBINING THE PARENTS BEST STRINGS WITH THE CHILD STINGS BASED ON ELITISM

gen_str=[final_str; beststr(1,:)];
end                             % End of GA cycle

% DISPLAY OF RESULTS AND PLOTTING THE CONVERGENCE OF FITNESS FUNCTION

disp('Economic Dispatch of Generators');
% Display of power dispatch of each generating unit
disp(load_gen(1,:));
disp('Total Generation(MW)');   % Total generation to be met
disp(sum(load_gen(1,:)));
disp('Total Generation Cost');  % Total generation cost
disp(g_cost(load_gen(1,:),pmin))

% CONVERGENCE PLOT OF FITNESS FUNCTION

kl=(1:iter);                    % Scaling the x-axis with the number of iteration
figure(1)
subplot(2,1,1),plot(kl,bestfit);   % Plotting the best fitness value
xlabel('Number of generations')
ylabel('Fitness function')
title('Convergence plot of fitness function')
subplot(2,1,2),plot(kl,glob_cost);  % Plotting the best fitness value
xlabel('Number of generations')
ylabel('Total generation cost')
title('Convergence plot of total generation cost')
```

## Part B: Sub programs (Subroutine functions)

CostFunction

```
% Total cost fuction with valve point effect
function [var]=g_cost( vec, pmin)
x=vec;
alpha=[0.001562;0.00194;0.00482];   % Fuel cost coefficients of the generating units
beta=[7.92;7.85;7.97];              % Fuel cost coefficients of the generating units
c=[561;310;78];                     % Constant
e=[300;200;150];
% Fuel cost coefficients of the generating units with valve point effects
f=[0.0315;0.042;0.063];
% Fuel cost coefficients of the generating units with valve point effects
p_min=pmin';
delp=p_min - vec';
var=sum(beta.*(x')+alpha.*(x').^2+abs(e.*sin(f.*delp)))+sum(c);   % Total cost
```

Generating a random number between a and b

```
function [ag] = mut_on(a,b)
ag = round(a + (b - a) * rand);
```

### Observation

The convergence of the fitness value is seen increasing which means the total generation cost decreases relatively with less error (Fig. 7.53). The program has been run for one trial and for 100 generations. The accuracy of the solution and the reduction in total generation cost can be increased with proper tuning of GA control parameters such as population size, choosing the right selection scheme, crossover and mutation probability, and so on.

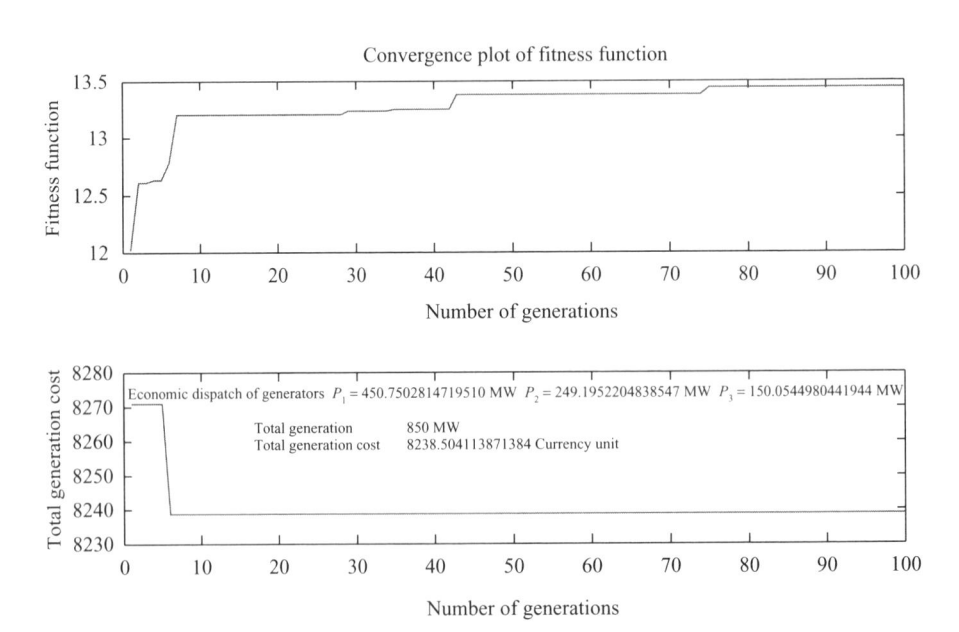

**Fig. 7.53** Convergence plot of fitness function/total generation cost

Economic dispatch of generators $P_1 = 450.7502814719510$ MW  $P_2 = 249.1952204838547$ MW  $P_3 = 150.0544980441944$ MW

Total generation 850 MW
Total generation cost 8238.504113871384 Currency unit

## 7.5.3 Optimisation of Weights in ANNs

The neuro-genetic hybrid algorithm uses the GA for the determination of the weights of the multi-layer feed-forward backpropagation neural network (BPNN). Conventional BPNNs use gradient descent learning for obtaining weights and have the limitation of getting stuck in local minima. Though a GA-based BPNN cannot guarantee convergence to the global minimum, it can produce acceptable solutions quickly, and has been implemented successfully in many areas. This mechanism can be understood with help of the following illustration [4].

The objective of BPNN training is to minimize the error criterion, which is given as follows:

$$E = \frac{1}{2}\sum(T_j - O_j)^2 \qquad (7.44)$$

where $T_j$ is the target output and $O_j$ is the output calculated by the network. It is important to devise a suitable code for the problem before executing the neuro-GA. Then the fitness function, which assigns merit to each of the individuals in the population, has to be formulated. This is followed by the sequence of weight determination of the BPNN using GA computation.

The coding strategy used is real (decimal) coding. Let us assume that the BPNN configuration has one input neuron, $m$ hidden neurons, and $n$ output neurons. The total number of weights in this NN is $(l+n)m$. For the representation of the code, each weight is considered to be a gene and a real number. Let $d$ be the gene length, which is the number of digits in the weight. Now, the string $S$ of decimal values represents the $(l+n)m$ weights; therefore, a string of length $L = (l+n)md$ is randomly generated. The string $S$ represents the weight matrices of the input–hidden and hidden–output layers in a linear form, arranged in row-major or column-major order as selected by the designer. Let $p$ chromosomes be generated for the initial population; this is also the population size.

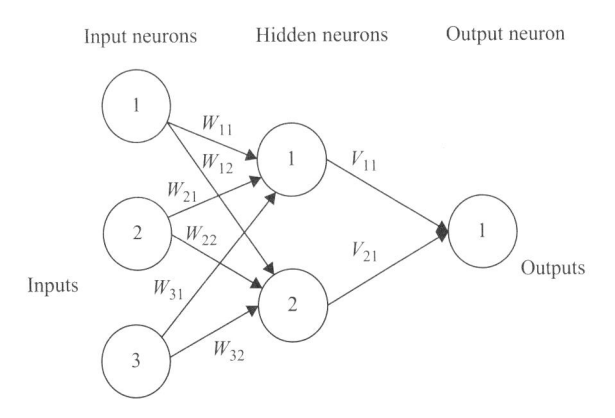

**Fig. 7.54** A BPNN with 3-2-1 configuration

Consider a 3-2-1 ($l$-$m$-$n$) BPNN architecture (Fig. 7.54). Therefore, the number of weights to be determined is $(l+n)m$, which is $(3+1) \times 2 = 8$. Let us now generate the initial population of $p$ chromosomes. The contents of a sample chromosome are given in Fig. 7.55. Here the number of digits of each gene is 5. Therefore the total length of the string is $8 \times 5 = 40$.

| $W_{11}$ | $W_{12}$ | $W_{21}$ | $W_{22}$ | $W_{31}$ | $W_{32}$ | $V_{11}$ | $V_{21}$ |
|---|---|---|---|---|---|---|---|
| Gene 0 | Gene 1 | Gene 2 | Gene 3 | Gene 4 | Gene 5 | Gene 6 | Gene 7 |
| 84321 | 46234 | 78901 | 32104 | 42689 | 63421 | 46421 | 87640 |
| 32478 | 76510 | 02461 | 84753 | 64753 | 14261 | 87654 | 87640 |

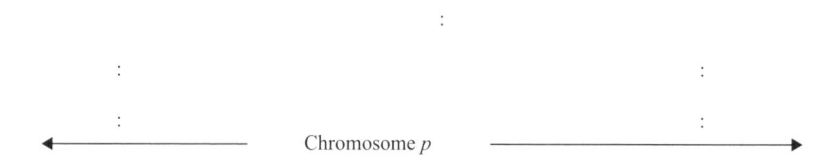

$\vdots$

$\longleftarrow$ Chromosome $p$ $\longrightarrow$

**Fig. 7.55** Representation of chromosomes generated randomly for BPNN weights

The next task is the determination of fitness values for the weights, which have to be decoded from the chromosomal strings. Let $x_1, x_2, ..., x_d, ..., x_L$ represent a chromosome and $x_{kd+1}, x_{kd+2}, ..., x_{(k+1)d}$ represent the $k$th gene ($k \geq 0$) in the chromosome. The actual weight $W_k$ is given as follows:

$$W_k = \begin{cases} + \dfrac{x_{kd+2} 10^{d-2} + x_{kd+3} 10^{d-3} + ... + x_{(k+1)d}}{10^{d-2}} & \text{if } 5 \leq x_{kd+1} \leq 9 \\ - \dfrac{x_{kd+2} 10^{d-2} + x_{kd+3} 10^{d-3} + ... + x_{(k+1)d}}{10^{d-2}} & \text{if } 0 \leq x_{kd+1} < 5 \end{cases} \quad (7.45)$$

Let us take chromosome 1 shown in Fig. 7.55 and extract the weights for the eight genes.

*Gene 0:84321* We know $k = 0$, $d = 5$, and $x_{(k+1)d}$, which is $x_1$, satisfies $5 \leq (x_1 = 8) \leq 9$

$$W_{11} = + \frac{4 \times 10^3 + 3 \times 10^2 + 2 \times 10 + 1}{10^3} = 4.321$$

Gene 1: *46234* Here $k = 1$, $d = 5$, and $x_{(k+1)d}$, which is $x_6$, satisfies $0 \leq (x_6 = 8) < 9$

$$W_{12} = - \frac{6 \times 10^3 + 2 \times 10^2 + 3 \times 10 + 4}{10^3} = -6.234$$

Similarly, we calculate the weights for other genes.

Gene 2: 78901 gives $W_{21} = +8.901$
Gene 3: 32104 gives $W_{22} = -2.104$

Gene 4: 42689 gives $W_{31} = -2.689$
Gene 5: 63421 gives $W_{32} = +3.421$
Gene 6: 46421 gives $V_{11} = -6.421$
Gene 7: 87640 gives $V_{21} = +7.640$

The next task is to calculate the fitness function. In the case of a BPNN, the algorithm to be trained must compulsorily have a set of input/target pairs such that the inputs are trained towards the target to be achieved. Suppose there are three sets of input/target pairs as given here:

$$[I_{11}, I_{21}] \to [T_{11}, T_{11}]$$
$$[I_{12}, I_{22}] \to [T_{12}, T_{22}]$$
$$[I_{13}, I_{23}] \to [T_{13}, T_{23}]$$

If $p = 50$ (the initial population of chromosomes), then it is understood that about 50 sets of weights from $W_{set1}, W_{set2}, \ldots, W_{set50}$ for the chromosomes $C_1, C_2, \ldots, C_{50}$ will be extracted using Eq. (7.45). To calculate the fitness values for a particular set of weights, the BPNN is trained for all the input instances given (i.e., the three input–output pairs given). Suppose the output is $O_1, O_2, O_3$, then the following is computed:

$$E_1 = (T_{11} - O_{11})^2 + (T_{21} - O_{21})^2$$
$$E_2 = (T_{12} - O_{12})^2 + (T_{22} - O_{22})^2$$
$$E_3 = (T_{13} - O_{13})^2 + (T_{23} - O_{23})^2$$

The root mean square of the error is given as follows:

$$E = \sqrt{\frac{(E_1 + E_2 + E_3)}{3}} \qquad (7.46)$$

The fitness $F_1$ for the first chromosome $C_1$ is given here:

$$F_1 = 1/E \qquad (7.47)$$

Similarly, the fitness values of all the $p$ chromosomes are determined, followed by the application of any of the mechanisms of selection, crossover, and mutation. Here, the fitness values for the chromosomal population $p_1$ are computed, the best individuals replicated, and reproduction carried out using any of the crossover operators to form the next generation $p_2$, new chromosomal population. This process evolves over successive generations, with the fitness value approaching the global optimum.

A population is said to have converged when 95 per cent of the individuals constituting the population share the same fitness value. At this stage, all the weights extracted from population $p_i$ ($i$ is the generation number) converge to one fitness value. These weights extracted from population $p_i$ are the final weights to be used by the BPNN. Now the BPNN is completely trained to receive any test inputs to be simulated.

## 7.6 APPLICABILITY OF GENETIC ALGORITHMS

The applicability of GAs refers to its fitness for solving a problem; they cannot be used in all situations. The much talked about parallelism can be adopted in GAs for computational reasons. Being confident of getting the right solution matters a lot; for this, the need for convergence proof has to be considered. In addition, the direction of future research should be known. The hybridization of GA with other techniques for better outcomes has to be looked at closely.

### 7.6.1 Parallel GA

In recent years, the price drop in off-the-shelf computer systems has enabled small institutions access to affordable super-computing. Thus, there has been considerable growth in research into inherently parallel problems and methods, which are well suited to cluster computing environments. One of the most promising developments in this regard has been that of parallel GAs. One of the motivation for the use of GAs to solve problems is that they are inherently parallel. In natural populations, thousands or even millions of individuals exist in parallel. This suggests a degree of parallelism that is directly proportional to the population size used in genetic search. In this section, different ways of exploiting parallelism in GAs are reviewed.

In parallel models, strings are mapped to processors in a particular way. Usually this is done in a way that maximizes parallelism while avoiding unnecessary processor communication. There is no standard methodology for incorporating parallel ideas into GAs; however, existing parallel implementations can be classified into three approaches, namely, (a) massively parallel GAs, (b) parallel island models, and (c) parallel hybrid GAs.

*Massively parallel GAs*
This approach uses a large number of processors ($\geq 2^{10}$). A single processor is assigned to an individual in the population. There are many possibilities of selection and mating in these models.

*Parallel island models*
This model assumes several sub-populations evolving in parallel. The approach involves the movement of an individual string from one sub-population to another and the crossover between individuals from different sub-populations.

*Parallel hybrid GAs*
In this approach, instead of a large number of processors as in massively parallel GAs, only a small number of processors are used. There is no one-to-one correspondence between the processors and the individuals. These GAs incorporate other heuristic algorithms like hill climbing for improving performance.

### 7.6.2 Convergence Proof of GA

There is no mathematical proof guaranteeing convergence in the case of GAs. However, it is possible to explain convergence criteria using the schema theorem, which has already been discussed. One criterion for convergence may be the following: when a fixed percentage (80% to 85%) of columns and rows in the population matrix becomes identical, it can be assumed that convergence has been attained.

In addition, knowing the right representation scheme for the problem in hand and the suitable selection, crossover, and mutation method, we can predict the convergence of a GA to some extent.

## 7.7 EVOLUTIONARY PROGRAMMING

Evolutionary programming is a technique used to search for the optimal solution to a problem by evolving a population of candidate solutions over a number of generations or iterations. The solution is evolved through mutation and competitive selection. The structure of an EP algorithm is shown in Fig. 7.56.

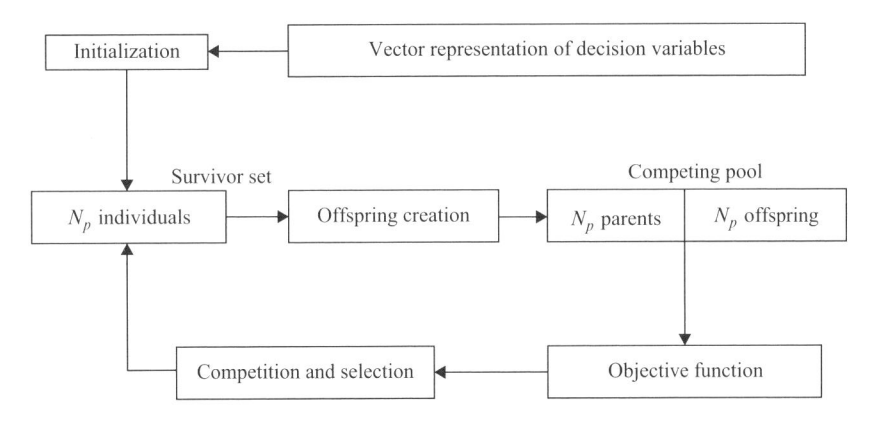

**Fig. 7.56** Structure of an EP algorithm

In this approach, the real-valued decision variables to be determined are represented by a trial $n$-dimensioned vector. Each vector is an individual of the population to be evolved. The major steps involved in this approach are the following.

### *Initialization*
An initial population of parent individuals ($PA_i$, $i = 1, 2, 3, ..., K$) is generated randomly within a feasible range in each dimension.

### *Mutation (Creation of offspring)*
Each parent vector $PA_i$ generates an offspring vector by adding a Gaussian random variable with a zero mean and pre-selected standard deviation to each individual of $PA_i$. The $K$ parents create $K$ offspring, thus resulting in $2K$ individuals in the competing pool.

### *Competition and selection*
Each individual in the competing pool is evaluated for its fitness. All individuals compete with each other for selection. The best $K$ individuals with the maximum

fitness values are retained to be parents in the next generation. The process of creating offspring and selecting those with maximum fitness is repeated until there is no appreciable improvement in the maximum fitness value or it has been repeated a prespecified number of times.

GA methods are used for encoding, decoding, and fitness function formulation. Evolutionary programming, on the other hand, is better for obtaining the global optimum, which relies on mutation rather than crossover. Due to inherent flexibilities in the fitness function and the ease of coding, the EP method produces the best solution with fewer generations.

Evolutionary programming is a probabilistic search technique which generates the initial parent vectors distributed uniformly in intervals within the limits and obtains the global optimum solution over a number of iterations. The main stages of this technique are initialization, creation of offspring vectors by mutation, and competition and selection of the best vectors in order to evaluate the best fitness solution.

## 7.8 WORKING OF EVOLUTIONARY PROGRAMMING

The implementation of the EP algorithm for the following objective function is given here:
*Minimize*

$$f(x) = 0.001562 P_1^2 + 0.00194 P_2^2 + 0.00482 P_3^2 + 7.92 P_1 \\ + 7.85 P_2 + 7.97 P_3 + 949 \ (₹/hr) \tag{7.48}$$

$$g(x, y) = 0$$
$$P_1 + P_2 + P_3 - 850 = 0$$
$$h(x, y) \leq \text{ or } \geq 0$$

subject to

$$150 \text{ MW} \leq P_1 \leq 600 \text{ MW}$$
$$100 \text{ MW} \leq P_2 \leq 400 \text{ MW}$$
$$50 \text{ MW} \leq P_3 \leq 200 \text{ MW}$$

### *Initialization*
The initial population ($k$ parent vectors) is generated after satisfying the constraints. The elements of the parent vectors ($P_j$) are the variables distributed uniformly between their minimum and maximum limits.

### *Mutation*
An offspring vector $P_i'$ is created from each parent vector by adding to it a Gaussian random variable with zero mean and standard deviation $\sigma_i$, denoted as $N(0, \sigma_i^2)$ in the following:

$$P_i' = P_i + N(0, \sigma_i^2) \text{ for } i = 1, 2, \ldots, n-1 \tag{7.49}$$

where

$$\sigma_i = \beta \sum_{i=1}^{n-1} (F_i/f_{\min})(P_i^{\max} - P_i^{\min}) \qquad (7.50)$$

$\beta$ is a scaling factor, $F_i$ is the function of $P_i$, and $f_{\min}$ is the value of $F_i$ with $P_i^{\min}$. The created offspring vector must satisfy the minimum and maximum limits of the variable $P_i$.

The constrained optimisation problem can be converted into an unconstrained optimisation problem using the penalty factor (PF) as given later. This becomes the fitness function in the EP method:

$$\text{Fitness function} = F + (\text{PF})\sum_{i=1}^{N} P_i - P_d \qquad (7.51)$$

The second term in the previous equation becomes zero during initialization, and is then occupied with a non-zero value after mutation only if the generated vector violates its limits. Therefore, the fitness function becomes simply $F$ and is computed for the offspring vectors in the same way as for the parent vectors.

Infeasible EP solutions can be produced if the mutation is high. This also contributes to the long execution time and poor convergence of EP algorithms. Conversely, if the value of the scaling factor $\beta$ is too small, the EP algorithm converges rapidly initially but fails to converge completely to the global optimum in later generations. The selection of the value of the scaling factor must, therefore, be such that it provides a suitably high initial mutation level and does not cool too rapidly so as to present complete convergence to the global optimum. A constant scaling factor is used in conventional EP; in the proposed EP method, step and non-linear scaling factors are used to obtain the best solution. The decrement step ($g$) for the step scaling factor is evaluated as follows:

$$g = (\beta_{\max} - \beta_{\min})/N_m(k) \qquad (7.52)$$

where $N_m(k)$ is the maximum number of generations.

*Competition and selection*
The parent trial vectors $P_i$ and the corresponding offspring $P'_i$ ($2k$ vectors) compete with each other for survival within the competing pool. The competition is based on the cost of the parent vectors $F_i(P_i)$ and the corresponding cost of the offspring vectors $F_i(P'_i)$ in this population. The vector having the minimum cost, whether a parent or an offspring, is selected to be the new parent for the next generation. Initialization and mutation are repeated until there is no appreciable improvement in the fitness value.

## 7.9 GENETIC ALGORITHM-BASED MACHINE LEARNING CLASSIFIER SYSTEM

The *learning mechanism of a machine* is a system that learns to perform necessary action by updating its knowledge with available information. A machine learning system consists of computer programs that help machines to construct new knowledge or improve their already existing knowledge with the help of heuristic approaches. In this section, machine learning systems based on evolutionary computational methodologies have been discussed.

### 7.9.1 Machine Learning Classifier System

The classifier systems in a machine learning classifier system (MLCS) are rule-based systems with general mechanisms for processing rules in parallel, adaptively generating new rules, and testing the effectiveness of existing rules. Classifier systems provide a framework in which a population of rules encoded as bit strings evolves on the basis intermittently given stimuli and reinforcement from its environment. The system learns to respond appropriately to the various stimuli presented. The rules in a classifier system form a population of individuals evolving over time. Figure 7.57 shows a classifier system.

A classifier system is most common in machine learning systems. It learns syntactically simple string rules called *classifiers* to guide its performance in an arbitrary environment. A classifier system is essentially a production rule system. Despite the explosion of rule-based expert systems, classifier systems are not preferred in learning situations, the reason being that they involve complex rule syntax. Moreover, during each matching cycle, the expert system activates a single rule, which creates a bottleneck. Classifier systems overcome this problem

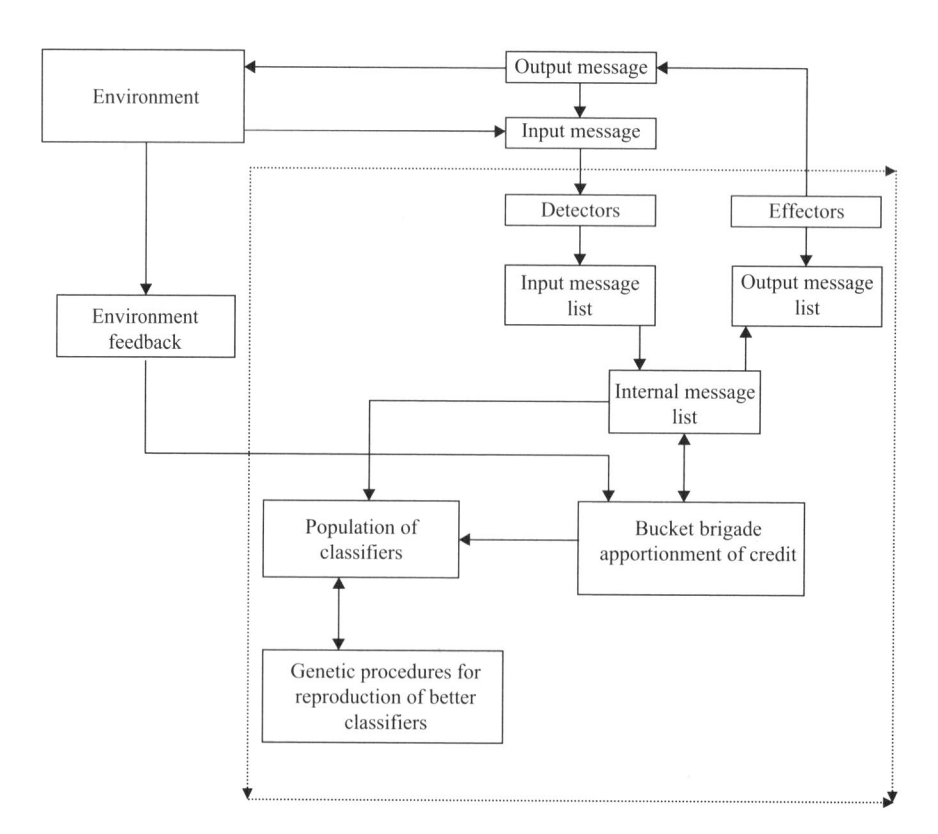

**Fig. 7.57** Machine learning classifier system

by allowing parallel activation of rules during a given matching cycle. Classifier systems depart from the mainstream by restricting a rule to the fixed-string-length representation. This has two benefits: first, all strings under the permissible alphabet are syntactically meaningful. Second, the fixed-string-length representation permits string operators of the genetic kind. This leaves the door propped open, ready for a GA search of the space of permissible rules.

A classifier system receives environmental information through sensors called *detectors*. This incoming *message* is decoded into some standard message format (may be one or more messages). These messages are posted to a finite-length *message list* from where they can in turn activate the classifiers from the *classifier store*. If activated, a classifier may then be chosen to send a message to the message list for the next cycle. These messages may then invoke other classifiers or cause an action to be taken through the system's action triggers called *effectors*.

Messages are bit strings of fixed length k defined as <message> :: = $\{0, 1\}^l$. Each classifier consists of a condition and an action part given as <classifier> :: = <condition> : <action>, where <condition> :: = $\{0, 1, \#, \$, \ldots\}^l$ (the symbols # and $ can be replaced by any variable). Each condition specifies a subset of the set of all messages and is also of length *k*. An action is a message that can be sent to the message list. Whether or not a candidate classifier will post its message is determined by the outcome of an activation function, which in turn depends on the evaluation of the classifier's value.

### 7.9.2 Working Principle of GA Machine Learning Classifier System

Machine learning is primarily devoted towards building computer programs that are able to construct new knowledge by using input information. The new knowledge can also be upgraded using the existing knowledge and genetic operators (crossover, mutation, etc.). A GA machine learning classifier system (GAMLCS) consists of the following:

- Performance system: detectors and effectors, message system (input, output, and internal message lists), rule system (population of classifiers)
- Apportionment of credit system (bucket brigade algorithm)
- Genetic procedures (reproduction of classifiers)

## 7.10 ILLUSTRATIVE PROBLEMS

**Problem 7.1** _____

Find the length of a binary string required to represent a variable '*X*', with a precision of 3 digits after a decimal point, where $15 \leq X \leq 50$.

**Solution:** Given that precision $p = 3$,

$$X^u = 50, X^l = 15,$$

Length of binary string required, $n = \log_2 \left[ \dfrac{X^u - X^l}{p} \right]$

$$= \log_2\left[\frac{50-15}{3}\right]$$
$$= \log_2(11.67)$$
$$= 3.54$$

So, the number of bits required = 4

**Problem 7.2**

Represent a variable '$X$' = 250 with a precision of 0.0001 using octal representation, where $200 \leq X \leq 326$.

**Solution:** Length of string required,
$$n = \log_8\left[\frac{X^u - X^l}{p}\right]$$
$$= \log_8\left[\frac{326-200}{4}\right]$$
$$= \log_8(31.5)$$
$$= 1.65$$

The number of bits required, $n = 2$

$$X = X^l + \frac{X^u - X^l}{8^n - 1} \times \text{(decode value of the string)}$$

Given that $X = 250$, $X^u = 326$, $X^l = 200$
Let Y be the equivalent decimal value of the string.

$$250 = 200 + \frac{326-200}{8^2 - 1}(Y)$$
$$\Rightarrow 250 = 200 + 2(Y)$$
$$\Rightarrow Y = 25$$
$$= [31] \text{ (in octal representation)}$$

**Problem 7.3**

Find the value of four-bit string '$X$' = 19A5 represented in Hexa decimal system, where
$$100 \leq X \leq 150$$

**Solution:** The length of string, $n = 4$
$$X^u = 150, X^l = 100$$

Decoded value of 19A5 in decimal = $16^0 \times 5 + 16^1 \times 10 + 16^2 \times 9 + 16^3 \times 1$
$$= 6565$$

The value of $X$ is given as follows:
$$X = X^l + \frac{X^u - X^l}{16^n - 1} \times \text{(decoded value of the string)}$$

$$X = 100 + \frac{150 - 100}{16^4 - 1} \times (6565)$$

$$= 100 + \frac{50}{65535} \times (6565)$$

$$= 100 + 5.0087$$

$$= 105.0087$$

## Problem 7.4

Generate the population in the next iteration using roulette-wheel criterion.

| Variable No. k | 1 | 2 | 3 | 4 | 5 |
|---|---|---|---|---|---|
| Fitness value $F_k$ | 3.5 | 4.6 | 5 | 2.8 | 1.8 |

**Solution:** pop-size = 5

Total fitness of population, $F = \sum_{k=1}^{\text{pop\_size}} F_k$

$$= 3.5 + 4.6 + 5.0 + 2.8 + 1.8$$

$$= 17.7$$

Probability of selecting $i^{\text{th}}$ chromosome, $P_i = \dfrac{F_i}{F}$

$$P_1 = \frac{F_1}{F} = 0.197$$

$$P_2 = \frac{F_2}{F} = 0.259$$

$$P_3 = \frac{F_3}{F} = 0.282$$

$$P_4 = \frac{F_4}{F} = 0.158$$

$$P_5 = \frac{F_5}{F} = 0.1016$$

Cumulative probability of each chromosome is calculated as follows:

$$q_1 = P_1 = 0.197$$
$$q_2 = P_2 + P_1 = 0.456.$$
$$q_3 = P_2 + P_1 + P_3 = 0.738$$
$$q_4 = P_2 + P_1 + P_3 + P_4 = 0.896$$
$$q_5 = P_2 + P_1 + P_3 + P_4 + P_5 = 0.9976$$

Selection of chromosomes for the next generation is presented here:

### 1st chromosome:
Generate a random number 'r'. Let $r = 0.52$

$$As\ q_2 \leq r \leq q_3,$$

The 3rd chromosome is selected as 1st chromosome in the next generation.

### 2nd chromosome:
Generate a random number r. Let $r = 0.63$

$$As\ q_2 \leq r \leq q_3$$

The 3rd chromosome is selected as 2nd chromosome in the next generation.

Similarly, the remaining chromosomes will be chosen by generating random numbers.

## Problem 7.5

For a minimization problem, find the scaled fitness values of given chromosomes using normalized technique.

| Chromosome k | 1 | 2 | 3 | 4 | 5 | 6 | 7 | 8 | 9 | 10 |
|---|---|---|---|---|---|---|---|---|---|---|
| Raw fitness $F_k$ | 12 | 45 | 33 | 27 | 50 | 24 | 42 | 36 | 15 | 30 |

**Solution:** For a minimization problem, the scaled fitness of $k^{th}$ chromosome is given here:

$$F_k^1 = \frac{f_{max} - f_k + \mu}{f_{max} - f_{min} + \mu}$$

where, $f_{max}$ and $f_{min}$ are the best and the worst raw fitness values, and $\mu$ is a random number.

$$Here, f_{max} = 50; f_{min} = 12$$
$$Let\ \mu = 0.5$$

The normalized fitness value of each chromosome is as follows:

$$f_1^1 = 1 \qquad f_6^1 = 0.6883$$
$$f_2^1 = 0.1428 \qquad f_7^1 = 0.22077$$
$$f_3^1 = 0.4545 \qquad f_8^1 = 0.3766$$
$$f_4^1 = 0.610 \qquad f_9^1 = 0.92207$$
$$f_5^1 = 0.012 \qquad f_{10}^1 = 0.53246$$

## Problem 7.6

Apply single-point crossover on the following binary strings and generate two offsprings.

$$A \rightarrow 0110100101$$
$$B \rightarrow 0100110010$$

*Solution:*
   Parent string 1: A = 0110/100101
   Parent string 2: B = 0100/110010
   Let us consider the 4th bit as the crossover site
   ⇒ Offspring 1: P = 0110110010
      Offspring 2: Q = 0100100101

**Problem 7.7** _____

For the aforementioned problem, generate offsprings using double-point crossover.

*Solution:*
   Parent string 1: A = 011/0100/101
   Parent string 2: B = 010/0110/010
   Let us consider 3rd and 7th bits as crossover sites
   ⇒ Offspring 1: P = 0110110101
      Offspring 2: Q = 0100100010

**Problem 7.8** _____

For the previous problem, generate offsprings using uniform crossover with mask technique.

*Solution:*
   Parent string 1: A = 0110100101
   Parent string 2: B = 0100110000
   Consider a crossover mask = 1101001010
   When the bit of mask string is '1', offspring 1 will get the information from parent 1 and offspring 2 gets the information from parent 2 and vice versa.
   ⇒ Offspring 1: P = 0100110000
      Offspring 2: Q = 0110100111

**Problem 7.9** _____

Apply both order crossover and position crossover on the two strings given below to generate two offsprings?
   A → 1 2 4 9 8 6 7 3 5
   B → 2 3 6 8 5 1 4 7 9

*Solution:*
**Order crossover:** Consider a sub-string which undergoes crossover as 4986 in parent A and 6851 in parent B.
   Parent A = 1 2 **4 9 8 6** 7 3 5
   Parent B = 2 3 **6 8 5 1** 4 7 9
   Offspring 1, P = 2 3 **4 9 8 6** 5 1 7
   Offspring 2, Q = 2 4 **6 8 5 1** 9 7 3

**Position crossover:** Randomly select four positions from parent strings. The underlined bits have been chosen.

Parent A = 1 **2** 4 9 **8** 6 **7** 3 **5**
Offspring 1, P = 3 **2** 6 1 **8** 4 **7** 9 **5**
Parent B = 2 **3** 6 8 **5** 1 4 **7** 9
Offspring 2, Q = 1 **3** 2 8 **5** 6 4 **7** 9

## Problem 7.10

Apply arithmetic crossover on the following four variable vectors $X_1, X_2$, with different weightage combinations.

$$X_1 = [1.5 \quad 2 \quad 3 \quad 5.6];$$
$$X_2 = [2 \quad 1.8 \quad 2.5 \quad 6];$$

*Solution:*
**Convex operator:** Assume $\alpha = 0.4, \beta = 0.6$ (where $\alpha + \beta = 1, \alpha > 0, \beta > 0$)
The offsprings are calculated as
Offspring 1: $X_1' = \alpha X_1 + \beta X_2$
= [(0.4×1.5+0.6×2), (0.4×2+0.6×1.8), (0.4×3+0.6×2.5), (0.4×5.6+0.6×6)];
= [1.8 1.88 2.7 5.84];
Offspring 2: $X_2' = \alpha X_1 + \beta X_2$
= [(0.6×1.5+0.4×2), (0.6×2+0.4×1.8), (0.6×3+0.4×2.5), (0.6×5.6+0.4×6)];
= [1.7 1.92 2.8 5.76]
**Affine operator:** Assume $\alpha = 1.2, \beta = -0.2$ (where $\alpha + \beta = 1, \alpha, \beta \, \varepsilon \, [-1,2]$)
The offsprings are calculated as follows:
Offspring 1: $X_1' = \alpha X_1 + \beta X_2$
= [(1.2×1.5−0.2×2),(1.2×2−0.2×1.8), (1.2×3−0.2×2.5), (1.2×5.6−0.2×6)];
= [1.4 2.04 3.1 5.52];
Offspring 2: $X_2' = \alpha X_1 + \beta X_2$
= [(−0.2×1.5+1.2×2),(−0.2×2+1.2×1.8), (0.2×3+1.2×2.5), (−0.2×3+ 1.2×2.5)];
= [2.1 1.76 2.4 6.08];
**Linear operator:** Assume $\alpha = 1.2, \beta = 0.4$ (where $\alpha + \beta \leq 2, \alpha > 0, \beta > 0$)
The offsprings are calculated as given here:
Offspring 1: $X_1' = \alpha X_1 + \beta X_2$
= [(1.2 × 1.5 + 0.4 × 2), (1.2 × 2 + 0.4 × 1.8), (1.2 × 3 + 0.4 × 2.5), (1.2 × 5.6 + 0.4 × 6)];
[2.6 3.12 4.6 9.12];
Offspring 2: $X_2' = \alpha X_1 + \beta X_2$
= [(0.4 × 1.5 + 1.2 × 2), (0.4 × 2 + 1.2 × 1.8), (0.4 × 3 + 1.2 × 2.5), (0.4 × 5.6 + 1.2 × 6)];
[3.0 2.96 4.2 9.44];

## Problem 7.11

In the problem of maximizing a function, $f(x) = 0.1x^2 + 2e^{-x} + 1$, determine an offspring 'X' from two parents 0.75 and 1.15 using directional crossover technique.

*Solution:* Let us consider the function value as the fitness value.
Let $X_1 = 0.75, X_2 = 1.15$.

Fitness value corresponds to $X_1$, $F_1 = f(1.15) = 1.7655$,
Fitness value corresponds to $X_2$, $F_2 = f(0.75) = 2.0009$
As $F_2 > F_1$; the offspring variable is calculated as given here:
Offspring 1: $X' = R(X_2 - X_1) + X_2$, where $R$ is a random number $\in [0,1]$
Let us consider $R = 0.35$
$\Rightarrow X' = 0.35(0.75 - 1.15) + 0.75$
$= 0.61$

## Problem 7.12

For the following binary strings, apply 1's compliment mutation operator with a probability of 40%.

A = (10001011)
B = (01001101)
C = (10101010)
D = (10101100)
E = (01100100)

**Solution:** Here, pop_size = 5
Probability of mutation, $p_m = 40\%$
$= 0.4$
Number of mutations to be performed, $N_m = 5 \times 0.4$
$= 2$
Randomly select two variables to be mutated.
Let 3rd (C) and 5th (E) variables be selected.

$$C = 10101010$$

3rd variable after mutation = 1's compliment of C
$$= 01010101$$

$$E = 01100100$$

5th variable after mutation = 1's compliment of E
$$= 10011011$$

## Problem 7.13

Transform the given binary string using different types of logical operators using mask string.

$$P \rightarrow 10101110$$

**Solution:** Let the masking operator, $Q = 01001100$ (which was randomly chosen)

**1. Bit-wise AND operator:**
$P = 10101110$
$P$ after mutation $= P \ \& \ Q = 00001100$

**2. Bit-wise OR operator:**
$P = 10101110$
$P$ after mutation $= P \ || \ Q = 11101110$

### 3. Bit-wise XOR operation:
$P = 10101110$
$P$ after mutation $= P \oplus Q = 11100010$

**Problem 7.14**

Generate a new string by applying inversion and insertion mutations operators on the following permutation represented string.

$$Q = [8 \quad 3 \quad 9 \quad 2 \quad 1 \quad 4 \quad 5 \quad 7]$$

*Solution:*
**Inversion:** Randomly select a sub-string and invert the string.
  Let us consider 2145 as the randomly selected sub-string.
  $Q = [8\ 3\ 9\ \mathbf{2\ 1\ 4\ 5}\ 7]$
  String after mutation $Q = [8\ 3\ 9\ \mathbf{5\ 4\ 1\ 2}\ 7]$
**Insertion:** Randomly select a node and insert at random position.
  Let us consider 5th node as the randomly selected node.
  $Q = [8\ 3\ 9\ 2\ \mathbf{1}\ 4\ 5\ 7]$
  String after mutation $Q = [8\ 3\ \mathbf{1}\ 9\ 2\ 4\ 5\ 7]$

**Problem 7.15**

Generate more numbers of improved offsprings by applying a heuristic mutation operator on the string given here.

$$P = [9 \quad 5 \quad 3 \quad 1 \quad 7 \quad 4 \quad 8 \quad 6 \quad 2]$$

*Solution:* Consider 2nd, 5th, and 8th positions randomly and the respective neighbourhoods are chosen as the improved transformations which are given as follows:

$$P = [9 \quad \mathbf{5} \quad 3 \quad 1 \quad \mathbf{7} \quad 4 \quad 8 \quad \mathbf{6} \quad 2]$$

The improved offsprings with these nodes are presented here:

$P_1 = [9\ \mathbf{5}\ 3\ 1\ \mathbf{6}\ 4\ 8\ \mathbf{7}\ 2]$
$P_2 = [9\ \mathbf{7}\ 3\ 1\ \mathbf{5}\ 4\ 8\ \mathbf{6}\ 2]$
$P_3 = [9\ \mathbf{7}\ 3\ 1\ \mathbf{6}\ 4\ 8\ \mathbf{5}\ 2]$
$P_4 = [9\ \mathbf{6}\ 3\ 1\ \mathbf{7}\ 4\ 8\ \mathbf{5}\ 2]$
$P_5 = [9\ \mathbf{6}\ 3\ 1\ \mathbf{5}\ 4\ 8\ \mathbf{7}\ 2]$

The best fitness value corresponding to these transformations will be considered for the next generation.

## SUMMARY

- The genetic algorithm (GA) is a randomized search and optimisation technique guided by the principle of natural genetic systems.
- Genetic algorithm goes through the four cycles: (i) evaluate, (ii) select, (ii) mate, and (iv) mutate.
- It is necessary to ensure that a suitable representation of solutions with meaningful and problem-specific genetic operators is considered. Three basic issues involved in the selection phase are: (a) sampling space, (b) sampling mechanism, and (c) selection probability.

- The crossover operator is a core genetic operator; it is considered as an axle for the generation of new offspring with strong characteristic features of new genetic information obtained as a result of the exchange of genetic material among the individuals of the chromosomal population.
- Mutation is the second important operator that maintains the diversity of the population of chromosomes from one generation to the next such that it tries to prevent the solution getting caught in the local optima.
- Evolutionary programming (EP) is a probabilistic search technique which generates the initial parent vectors distributed uniformly in intervals within the limits and obtains the global optimum solution over a number of iterations.
- The main stages of EP technique are initialization, creation of offspring vectors by mutation, and competition and selection of the best vectors in order to evaluate the best fitness solution.

## EXERCISES

### Part A Short-answer Questions

1. What are 'evolutionary algorithms'?
2. Why is it said that *genetic algorithms + data structures = evolution programs*?
3. Explain the terms natural genetics and natural selection.
4. Classify the applications of GAs.
5. How do GAs differ from conventional optimisation algorithms?
6. Arrange the following jumbled sequence of operations of a GA in order:
   encoding → solutions → crossover → offspring → new population
   → chromosomes → solutions → fitness computation → decoding
   → selection → evaluation → mutation
7. Define 'crossover rate' and 'mutation rate'.
8. Match the following:
   (a) Chromosome (string, individual)   (1) Position of gene
   (b) Genes (bits)                      (2) Encoded solution
   (c) Locus                             (3) Decoded solution
   (d) Alleles                           (4) Solution (coding)
   (e) Phenotype                         (5) Part of solution
   (f) Genotype                          (6) Values of genes
9. Explain exploitation and exploration in GA.
10. What do you understand by a 'schema'?
11. List out some crossover operations.
12. What is a 'roulette-wheel selection'?
13. What do you understand by 'tournament selection'?
14. What are 'parallel genetic algorithms'?
15. What is 'elitism in GAs'?
16. List out some low-level genetic operators.
17. What do you understand by inversion, deletion, duplication, and segregation?
18. What is a classifier system? Give an example.
19. Explain in detail how one can optimise the weights for training an artificial neural network.
20. How is GA different from evolutionary programming?

### Part B Long-answer Questions

1. Solve the following optimisation problems:
   (a) Maximize $F(X, Y) = X \sin(4\pi X) + Y \sin(20\pi X)$
       subject to
       $-3.0 \leq X \leq 12.1$
       $4.1 \leq Y \leq 5.8$
   (b) Minimize $F(X) = X \sin^2(10\pi X) + 1$
       subject to
       $-1 \leq X \leq 2$

2. Solve
$$4x + 2y = 8$$
$$3x + 4y = 12$$
subject to
$$-2 \leq x \leq 2$$
$$-1 \leq y \leq 3$$
Analyse the results by solving the problem numerically using the conventional method and find the difference when it is solved using GA.

3. Is it advisable to apply GAs for all kinds of optimisation problems? Justify your answer.

4. Solve the TSP for the famous Oliver 30 city problem using GA with Boltzman selection scheme.

5. Solve the TSP for the Burma 14 city problem using the uniform crossover operation with tournament selection. The data for the problem are given in the form of $(X, Y)$ co-ordinates on the graph of the positions of the cities from vertex:

| City No. | 1 | 2 | 3 | 4 | 5 | 6 | 7 | 8 | 9 | 10 | 11 | 12 | 13 | 14 |
|---|---|---|---|---|---|---|---|---|---|---|---|---|---|---|
| X | 16.47 | 16.47 | 20.09 | 22.39 | 25.23 | 22.00 | 20.47 | 17.20 | 16.30 | 14.05 | 16.53 | 21.52 | 19.41 | 20.09 |
| Y | 96.10 | 94.44 | 92.54 | 93.37 | 97.24 | 96.05 | 97.02 | 96.29 | 97.38 | 98.12 | 97.38 | 95.59 | 97.13 | 94.55 |

6. Figure 7.58 shows the mileages of the feasible links connecting nine offshore natural gas well heads with an inshore delivery point. Since well head 1 is closest to the shore, it is equipped with sufficient pumping and storage capacity to pump the output of the remaining eight wells to the delivery point. Using GA, determine the minimum pipeline network that links the well heads to the delivery point.

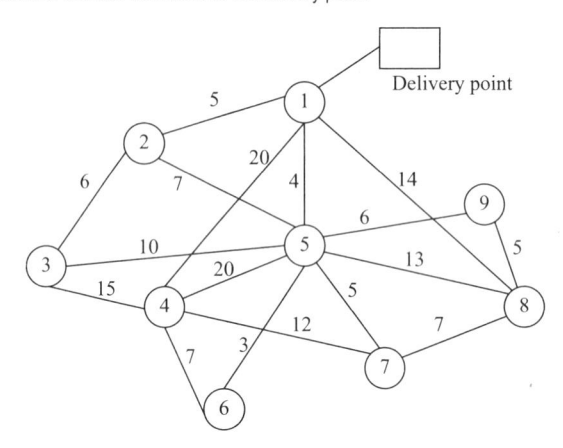

Fig. 7.58

7. Find the shortest highway route using any ant model between two cities. The network in Fig. 7.59 provides the possible routes between the starting city at node 1 and the destination city at node 8. The routes pass through intermediate cities designated by nodes 2 to 5.

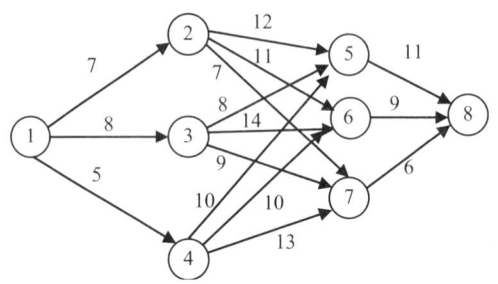

Fig. 7.59

8. Do you believe that running GA many times for the same problem guarantees convergence and the result is same after every particular $N^{th}$ generation? Give reasons.

## Part C  Practical Exercises

1. Using MATLAB Program decode the secret word $\rightarrow$ INDIA.

$$\sum_{n=1}^{\# letters} (guess[n] - answer[n])^2$$

where # letters is the number of letters in the word, guess[n] is the letter $n$ in the guess chromosome, and answer[n] is the letter $n$ in the answer. Let the value of each alphabet be an integer corresponding to its location in the alphabet (e.g., A = 1, B = 2, etc.). When the cost becomes zero, the secret word is identified by the GA.
   (a) How many generations does it take to decipher the code by generating random numbers?
   (b) How many generations does it take to decipher the code using GA?
   (c) By taking different cost functions and different secret words, try (a) and (b).
2. Five jobs are scheduled first on machine A, then on machine B, and finally on machine C. The time required for the completion of the jobs in the three machines is given in the following table.

| Jobs | Processing time (hr) | | |
|---|---|---|---|
| | Machine A | Machine B | Machine C |
| 1 | 8 | 3 | 8 |
| 2 | 3 | 4 | 7 |
| 3 | 7 | 5 | 6 |
| 4 | 2 | 2 | 9 |
| 5 | 5 | 1 | 10 |

   Using MATLAB and GA, find the sequence of jobs that minimizes the time required to complete all the jobs.
3. Solve unit commitment problem using GA with MATLAB.
4. Write a MATLAB Program to solve a simple optimistaion problem (1st question Part-B) using evolutionary programming technique.

## REFERENCES

[1] Holland, John Henry, *Adaptation in Natural and Artificial Systems: An Introductory Analysis with Applications to Biology, Control, and Artificial Intelligence*, University of Michigan Press, 1975.
[2] Onwubolu, Godfrey C., and  B. V., Babu, *New Optimization Techniques in Engineering*, Springer Science & Business Media, 21-Jan-2004.
[3] Gen, Mitsuo and Runwei Cheng, *Genetic Algorithms and Engineering Design*, New York, John Wiley, 1997.
[4] Rajasekaran, S., and G. A. Vijayalakshmi Pai,  *Neural Networks, Fuzzy Logic and Genetic Algorithms*, New Delhi, PHI, 2003.
[5] Goldberg, David E., *Genetic Algorithms in Search Optimization and Machine Learning*, Reading, MA, Addison-Wesley, 1989.
[6] de Jong, K. A., An Analysis of the Behavior of a Class of Genetic Adaptive Systems, PhD Thesis, Department of Computer and Communication Sciences, Ann Arbor, MI, University of Michigan, 1975.
[7] Baker, J. E., Adaptive selection measures for genetic algorithms, in John J. Grefenstette (ed.), *Proceedings of the 1st International Conference on Genetic Algorithms,* Pittsburgh, PA, USA, Lawrence Erlbaum, pp. 101–111, 1985.
[8] Baker, J. E., Reducing bias and inefficiency in the selection algorithm, in John J. Grefenstette (ed.), *Proceedings of the 1st International Conference on Genetic Algorithms,* Pittsburgh, PA, USA, Lawrence Erlbaum, pp. 14–21, 1987.
[9] Michalewicz, Zbigniew, *Genetic Algorithms + Data Structures = Evolution Programs*, New York, Springer, 1992.
[10] Hancock, P. J. B., An empirical comparison of selection methods in evolutionary algorithms, in T. C. Fogarty (ed.), *Evolutionary Computing: AISB Workshop*, Leeds, UK, Selected Papers, Lecture Notes in Computer Science, Vol. 865, pp. 80–94, 1994.

[11] Goldberg, David E. and R. Lingle, Alleles loci and the traveling salesman problem, in J. J. Grefenstette (ed.), *Proceedings of the 1st International Conference on Genetic Algorithms and their Applications,* Pittsburgh, PA, Hillsdale, NJ, Erlbaum, pp. 154–159, 1985.

[12] Syswerda, G., Scheduling optimization using genetic algorithms, in Davis, L. (ed.), *Handbook of Genetic Algorithms*, New York, Van Nostrand Reinhold, pp. 332–349, 1991.

[13] Oliver, I. M., D. J. Smith, and J. R. C. Holland, A study of permutation crossover operators on the travelling salesman problem, in Grefenstette, J. J. (ed.), *Genetic Algorithms and Their Applications: Proceedings of the Second International Conference,* Hillsdale, New Jersey, USA, Lawrence Erlbaum, pp. 224–230, 1987.

[14] Yamamura, M., T. Ono, and S. Kobayashi, Character preserving genetic algorithms for the travelling salesman problem, *Journal of Japan Society for Artificial Intelligence,* Vol. 6, pp. 1049–1059, 1992.

[15] Michalewicz, Z., A perspective on evolutionary computation, *Proceedings of the Workshop on Evolutionary Computation.* Armidale, Australia, University of New England, November 21–22, pp. 76–93, 1994.

[16] Frantz, D. R., 'Non-linearities in Genetic Adaptive Search', *Dissertation Abstracts International,* Vol. 33, Issue 11, pp. 5240B–5241B, 1972.

[17] Kothari, D. P., D. P. Kothari, and J. S. Dhillon, *Power System Optmisation,* PHI Learning Pvt. Ltd., 2012 – Electric power systems.

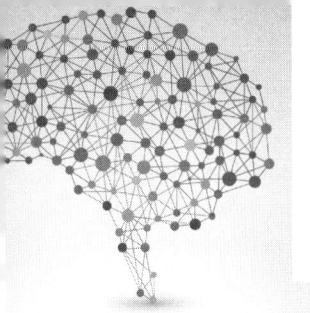

# 8 Swarm Intelligent System

*'We don't have control over randomness; but we get things done in a pseudo-random manner'*

Sishaj Pulikottil Simon

## LEARNING OBJECTIVES

*After reading this chapter, the reader will be able to:*

- Comprehend the fundamentals, background, and developments of swarm intelligence
- Describe ant colony systems with MATLAB codes
- Discuss particle swarm intelligent systems with MATLAB codes
- Analyse artificial bee colony systems with MATLAB codes
- Explain cuckoo search algorithm with MATLAB codes
- Learn engineering applications related to swarm intelligent systems

## 8.1 INTRODUCTION TO SWARM INTELLIGENCE

The success of any intelligent system depends upon the synergizing behaviour of the individual's actions. A famous Aristotle quote in support is, 'The whole is more than the sum of its parts'. The individual in a system can be artificial or natural agents. Unity in diversity is one such notion that is seen readily in swarm intelligence and helps the system to emerge and progress.

Swarm intelligence is the term used for the collective behaviour of a group (swarm) of animals as a single living creature, where via grouping and communication a *collective intelligence* emerges that actually results in more successful foraging for each individual in the group. Henry Ford said, 'Coming together is a beginning, keeping together is progress, and working together is success'. George Halas (American football Coach, 1895–1983) remarked: 'Many people flounder about in life because they do not have a purpose, an objective towards which to work'. Therefore, for any group to be successful, every entity in that group should have a purpose and then strive to achieve the collective goal.

Every living creature in the universe strives to survive according to the biological phenomenon observed in their natural habitat. *Optimal foraging policy* is one such phenomenon learned from these living creatures. *Foraging theory* is based on the assumption that animals search for and obtain nutrients in a way that maximizes their energy intake $E$ per unit time $T$ spent foraging [1]. Maximization of such a function provides nutrient sources to survive and additional time for other important activities (e.g., fighting, fleeing, mating, reproducing, sleeping, or shelter-building). Shelter-building and mate-finding activities sometimes bear similarities to foraging. Clearly, foraging is very different for different species. Foraging formulation is only meant to be a model that explains what optimal behaviour would be like.

The interaction of the individual agents in the group is very important for the synergizing activity. This can be illustrated with a simple example. Let us say that two candidates 'A' and 'B' are present in a group. 'A' has 2 objects (1 pencil and 1 rubber) and B has 2 objects (1 scale and 1 sharpener). 'A' has given two possessions to 'B' and similarly 'B' to 'A'. Now, the total number of ownership that both of them have is equal to 2. However, let us say that 'A' has 2 piece of information that 'B' does not know and similarly, 'B' has 2 piece of information that 'A' does not know. Once the information is shared among them through proper interaction, the total information that both 'A' and 'B' own is equal to four. Therefore, *information sharing* between entities in a group is vital for the success of the group. It depends mainly upon the type of information, method, and time of transfer.

The collective behaviour of the agents *natural or artificial* in a system should lead to the ultimate intelligence behaviour through proper converge. This depends on how the agents exploit a situation and explore in search of the best global outcome. Therefore, the search must involve two vital properties, namely *exploitation* and *exploration*, which directs the group towards the final goal. Exploitation and exploration enables a *probabilistic behaviour* and a *stochastic behaviour*, respectively in a group. The precise balance between these two phenomena helps the success of a particular group.

The stochastic behaviour comes from the real randomness involved in the swarm intelligent system by nature. However, two ways in which random numbers can be generated is through any physical phenomenon and through computational algorithms [2]. One way of generating random numbers is through certain random physical phenomenon such as radioactive decay, atmospheric noise, and thermal noise, which can be measured and through data acquisition can be used in a computer algorithm. In Linux-based system, random numbers are obtained from environment such as the timing of keystrokes and mouse movements of a user.

Another way of generating random numbers, that is, pseudo-random numbers, is through formulae that can produce a long sequence of numbers determined by a seed/fixed number or an initial key. If the seed is known, then nothing is random and is inherently predictable. However, it should be noted, the same sequence of numbers may be repeated again and again. Generally, the seed number may be kept as the time, the day or any date, etc. Again the random numbers generated are sometimes uniform through some probability distributions and sometimes totally unpredictable. Most of the time the random number used in the swarm intelligent algorithms is uniform to cover range of search domain. Therefore, the success of the swarm intelligent creatures to survive is through exploration (i.e., at random risk).

Most of the *social life forms* such as ants can achieve higher forms of foraging intelligence based on the swarm behaviour cooperating in groups. They live in a colony that is made up of more than one million members, workers, and soldiers that are all females. The male ants die after fertilizing the queen ant. The queen ant's only duty is to lay about 50,000 to 100,000 eggs a day. According to the Bible, the ants have a superior intelligence, which is almost second to man's? King Solomon (Bible-Proverbs 30:24–28) says, 'There are four things which are little upon the earth but they are exceeding wise: the ants are a people not strong, yet they prepare their meat in the summer….' The natural behaviour and qualities of ants should be appreciated. They are intelligent since they have good team work ethics, have sharing and helping character, have good communication among them, have good food/wealth management, have never-give-up attribute (hope), have goal orientation, have chosen always the best path, have the ability of learning from experience, have always preferred light, have an attribute on discipline, have been brisk and energetic always (no laziness), and finally they are the weakest individual but are the most successful creature on earth.

The biological behaviour of the swarm of ants taking the shortest route to find its food source (destination) from their nest (start) by a pheromone mediated chemical laid during its movement, forms the basis of ant colony intelligent system. Not only ants, but the survival strategies of the termites, *E. coli* bacteria, honey bees, bird flocking, fish schooling, cuckoo's habitat, fireflies, (Fig. 8.1) etc are also specialized and self-organized [3].

Swarm is not just related to social life forms, but also involves artificial or natural designs. There are systems that involve mass interactions due to gravitational forces, reactions occurring among the water drops in the riverbeds, self-propelled particles where a collection of particles that move with a constant speed but respond to a random perturbation, artificial immune systems where entities in the blood stream defend the body, charged particles interacting on some principles from physics and mechanics, etc.

*Self-organizing systems* are robust, reliable, and simple. The information or the knowledge stored is distributed in nature. The individual members in a swarm or agents follow very simple rules and there is no centralized control structure dictating how individual agents should behave. The behaviour has local interactions with certain degree of randomness between such agents. Certain important properties that can be observed are: (a) agents are assumed to be simple, (b) indirect agent communications, (c) global behaviour may be emergent, (d) behaviours are robust, and (e) individuals are not important.

When swarm operates, the information sharing is based on positive feedback, negative feedback, randomness, and has multiple interactions. The mathematical proofs for convergence are yet to be developed for most of the swarm-inspired systems. As natural systems itself are assumed to be perfect, the swarm intelligent systems are mimicked and modelled, thereby solving many of the scientific and engineering applications. The following section discusses the development and background of swarm intelligent systems.

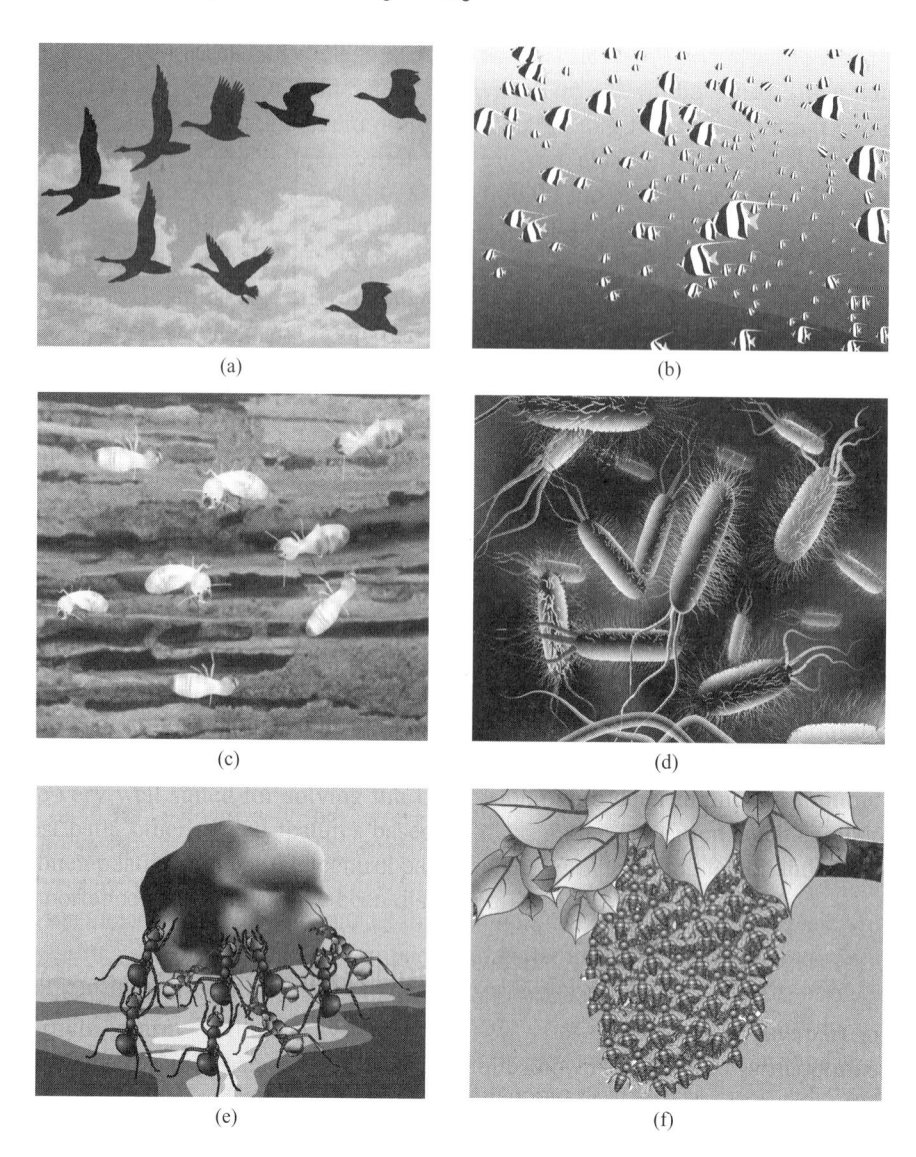

**Fig. 8.1** Social living beings (a) A flock of birds (b) A school of fish (c) Termites feeding on wood (d) Foraging E. coli bacteria (e) Group of ants working hard (f) A swarm of honeybees

## 8.2 BACKGROUND OF SWARM INTELLIGENT SYSTEMS

Table 8.1 lists history and developments of swarm intelligent systems. The success of any swarm intelligent system depends on its usefulness. Though there are many swarm intelligent techniques, few techniques that have evolved widely that had found acceptance are discussed in detail in the following sections.

Before going into the details, there is a question of how these techniques have to be implemented. Years back, during the start of the college days, there were senior-junior interaction sessions. In one such session, a student from the senior group challenged his juniors and put forth a question. *How can you measure the height of the building using a scale?* Although it looked a bit surprising, there were three answers:

Firstly, take the scale and go to the bottom of the building, and with a reference base $n$ times scale-by-scale go measuring till the top of the building.

Secondly, take the scale and go to the top of the building and drop the scale from the top. Note down the time taken ($t$) for the fall with the help of a stop clock. Now by using a physics equation $s = ut + 1/2\ a\ t^2$, the distance ($s$) which is the height of the building can be measured. (Here '$a$' is the acceleration due to gravity and '$u$' is the initial velocity.)

Thirdly, during a hot sunny day, take the scale and place it parallel to the wall and measure the shadow of the scale. With the help of similar triangle approach and Pythagoras theorem, the height of the building can be measured.

Table 8.1  List of swarm intelligent systems

| Swarm intelligent systems | Concept |
|---|---|
| Altruism algorithm<br>Waibel, M, Floreano, D and Keller, L (2011) | Altruism in a swarm of entities can, over time, evolve and result in more effective swarm behaviour. |
| Ant colony optimisation<br>M. Dorigo (1991) | Swarm of ants taking the shortest route to find its food source (destination) from its nest (start) by a pheromone mediated chemical laid during its movement. |
| Artificial bee colony algorithm<br>D. Karaboga (2005) | Simulates the foraging behaviour of honey bees. |
| Artificial immune systems<br>de Castro, Leandro N and Timmis, Jonathan (2002) | Inspired by specific immunological theories that explain the function and behaviour of the mammalian adaptive immune system. |
| Bacterial foraging techniques<br>Passino, K.M (2002) | Inspired by chemo tactic (foraging) behaviour of E. coli bacteria. |
| Charged system search<br>A. Kaveh and S. Talatahari (2010) | Utilizes the governing laws of Coulomb and Gauss from electrostatics and the Newtonian laws of mechanics. |
| Cuckoo search<br>Xin-She Yang and Suash Deb (2009) | Inspired by the obligate brood-parasitism of some cuckoo species by laying their eggs in the nests of other host birds (of other species). |
| Firefly algorithm<br>Xin-She Yang (2009) | Inspired by the flashing behaviour of fireflies. The primary purpose for a firefly's flash is to act as a signal system to attract other fireflies. |
| Gravitational search algorithm<br>Rashedi, E; Nezamabadi-Pour and H.; Saryazdi S (2009) | Constructed based on the law of gravity and the notion of mass interactions. |
| Intelligent water drops<br>Shah-Hosseini, H (2009) | Inspired by natural rivers and how they find almost optimal paths to their destination. |
| Particle swarm optimisation<br>Kennedy, J and Eberhart, R. (1995) | Inspired by the social behaviour of the movement of organisms in a bird flock or fish school. |
| River formation dynamics<br>P. Rabanal, I Rodriguez, and F. Rubio (2007) | Based on copying how water forms rivers by eroding the ground and depositing sediments. |

*(Continued)*

Table 8.1 (Continued)

| Swarm intelligent systems | Concept |
|---|---|
| Self-propelled particles Vicsek, T., Czivok, A., Ben-Jacob, E, and Cohen, I; Shochet, O. (1995) | Modelled as a collection of particles that move with a constant speed but respond to a random perturbation by adopting at each time increment the average direction of motion of the other particles in their local neighbourhood. |
| Stochastic diffusion search Bishop, J.M (1989) | Agent-based probabilistic global search and best suited to problems where the objective function can be decomposed into multiple-independent partial functions. Each agent maintains a hypothesis which is iteratively tested by evaluating a randomly selected partial objective function parameterized by the agent's current hypothesis. |

The analogy of a scale can be compared with any one of the swarm-based system. Since a particular swarm technique can used in different ways for solving the same problem, the success of any swarm intelligent technique depends on how best and suitably implemented for a particular application.

## 8.3 ANT COLONY SYSTEM

Ant algorithms were first proposed in the year 1991 as a multi-agent approach to solve difficult combinatorial optimisation problems such as TSP. There is currently a lot of ongoing activity in the scientific community to extend/apply ant-based algorithms to many different discrete optimisation problems. The application and experimental validation of these algorithms are being thoroughly researched owing to their capability to provide an almost global optimal solution to a given complex problem structure such as local search, image mapping and compression, database search, etc. Other than the examples enumerated earlier, there are many unexplored.

### 8.3.1 Biological Ant Colony System

To understand ant colony system, put a piece of sweet in your kitchen garden. Watch it for some time. Initially random ants are seen and after a while, a straight line of marching ants can be observed. They start carrying tiny bits of sweet individually and also like a united force. The discipline and the transport mechanism are amazing. This interesting behaviour of ant colonies is their foraging behaviour and, in particular, how ants can find shortest paths between food sources and their nest.

While walking from food sources to the nest and vice versa, ants deposit on the ground a chemical substance called pheromone, forming in this way a pheromone trail. The sketch shown in Fig. 8.2 gives a general idea of how real ants find the shortest path in four steps [4] as follows:

(a) Ants arrive at a decision point.
(b) Some ants choose the upper path and some the lower path. The choice is random.

(c) Since ants move at approximately constant speed, the ants which choose the lower, shorter path reach the opposite decision point faster than those which choose the upper, longer path.
(d) Pheromone accumulates at a higher rate on the shorter path. The number of dashed lines is approximately proportional to the amount of pheromone deposited by ants.

Ants can smell pheromone and, when choosing their path, they tend to choose, in probability, paths marked by strong pheromone concentrations. The pheromone trail allows the ants to find their way back to the food by their nest mates (Fig. 8.2).

The emergence of this shortest path selection behaviour can be explained in terms of autocatalysis (positive feedback) and differential path length (DPL) which uses a simple form of indirect communication mediated by pheromone laying, known as 'stigmergy' [5], [6] through the environment, either by physically changing or by depositing something on the environment (e.g., ants laying pheromone trail on the ground indirectly allows other ants to follow it to find its food source; deposits of soil pellets in termites colony stimulates the whole workers to accumulate more material through a positive feedback mechanism, since the accumulation of material reinforces the attractiveness of deposits through the diffusing pheromone emitted by the pellets). Also, the process whereby an ant is influenced towards a food source by another ant or by a chemical trail is called *recruitment*, and recruitment based solely on chemical trails is called 'mass recruitment'.

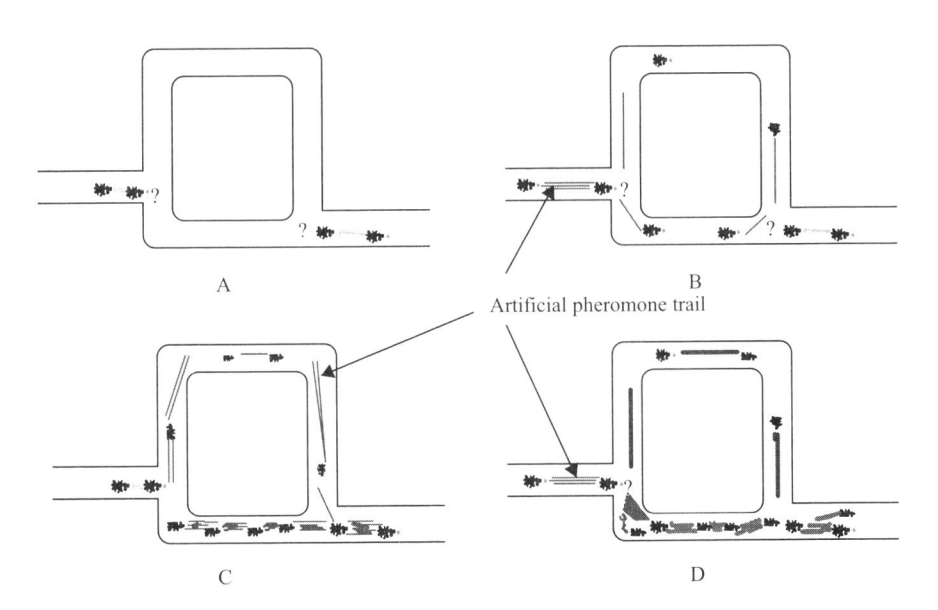

**Fig. 8.2** Real ants finding the shortest path

## 8.3.2 Artificial Ant Colony System

An artificial ant colony system (AACS) is a population-based heuristic algorithm on agents that simulate the natural behaviour of ants developing mechanisms of cooperation and learning which enables the exploration of the positive feedback between agents as a search mechanism.

In an AACS, the use of: (i) a colony of cooperating individuals, (ii) an artificial pheromone trail for local stigmergetic communication, (iii) a sequence of local moves to find shortest paths, and (iv) a stochastic decision policy using local information and no look ahead are the same as a real ant colony system, but artificial ants have also some characteristics which do not find their counterpart in real ants [7], [8]. They are mainly as follows:

(a) Artificial ants live in a discrete world and their moves consist of transitions from discrete states to discrete states.
(b) Artificial ants have an internal state. This private state contains the memory of the ant's past actions.
(c) Artificial ants deposit an amount of pheromone, which is a function of the quality of the solution found.
(d) Artificial ants timing in pheromone laying is problem-dependent and often does not reflect real ant's behaviour. For example, in many cases artificial ants update pheromone trails only after having generated a solution.
(e) To improve overall system efficiency, ant algorithms can be enriched with extra capabilities such as look ahead, local optimisation, backtracking, elitist approach, ranking-based, and so on that cannot be found in real ants.

## 8.3.3 Working of an Ant Colony System

Essentially, an ant colony search (ACS) algorithm performs a loop applying the following two basic procedures:

(a) A procedure specifying how ants construct or modify a solution for the problem in hand.
(b) A procedure for updating the pheromone trail.

The construction or modification of a solution is performed in a probabilistic way. The probability of adding a new term to the solution under construction is in turn a function of a problem-dependent heuristic and the amount of pheromone previously deposited in this trail. The pheromone trails are updated considering the evaporation rate and the quality of the current solution.

## 8.3.4 Probabilistic Transition Rule

In a simple ant colony optimisation (S–ACO) algorithm, the main task of each artificial ant, similarly to their natural counterparts, is to find the shortest path between a pair of nodes on a graph on which the problem representation is suitably mapped.

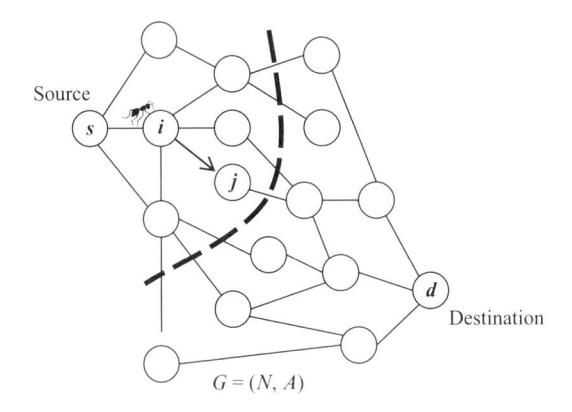

**Fig. 8.3** Ants build solutions from a source to destination node

Let $G = (N, A)$ be a connected graph with $n = |N|$ nodes. The S–ACO algorithm can be used to find a solution to the shortest path problem defined on the graph $G$, where a solution is a path on the graph connecting a source node 's' to a destination node 'd' shown in Fig. 8.3, and the path length is given by the number of loops in the path to each arc $(i, j)$ of the graph is associated with a variable $\tau_{ij}$ called *artificial pheromone trail*. At the beginning of the search process, a small amount of pheromone $\tau_0$ is assigned to all the arcs. Pheromone trails are read and written by ants. The amount (intensity) of pheromone trail is proportional to the utility, as estimated by the ants, of using that arc to build good solutions. Each ant applies a step-by-step constructive decision policy to build problem's solutions. At each node, local information, maintained on the node itself and/or on its outgoing arcs, is used in a stochastic way to decide the next node to move to.

The decision rule of an ant $k$ located in node $i$ uses the pheromone trails $\tau_{ij}$ to compute the probability with which it should choose node $j \in N_i$ as the next node to move to, where $N_i$ is the set of one-step neighbours of node $i$ given here:

$$p_{ij}^k = \begin{cases} \dfrac{T_{ij}}{\sum_{j \in N_i} T_{ij}} & \text{if } j \in N_i \\ 0 & \text{if } j \notin N_i \end{cases} \tag{8.1}$$

### 8.3.5 Pheromone Updating

While building a solution, ants deposit pheromone information on the arcs they use. In S–ACO, ants deposit a constant amount $\Delta\tau$ of pheromone. Consider an ant that at time $t$ moves from node $i$ to node $j$. It will change the pheromone value $\tau_{ij}$ as follows:

$$\tau_{ij}(t) \leftarrow \tau_{ij}(t) + \Delta\tau \tag{8.2}$$

By this rule, which simulates real ants' pheromone depositing on arc $(i, j)$, an ant using the arc connecting node $i$ to node $j$ increases the probability that ants will use the same arc in the future. As in the case of real ants, autocatalysis and DPL are at work to favour the emergence of short paths. To avoid a quick convergence of all the ants towards a sub-optimal path, an exploration mechanism is added: just as real pheromone trails, artificial pheromone trails evaporate. In this way, pheromone intensity decreases automatically, favouring the exploration of different arcs during the whole search process. The evaporation is carried out in a simple way, decreasing pheromone trails in an exponential way, $\tau = (1-\rho)\tau$, $\rho \in (0; 1)$ at each iteration of the algorithm. The way the pheromone is updated can be classified mainly into three types [9] as discussed here.

### Online Step-by-step Pheromone Update

When moving from node $i$ to neighbour node $j$, the ant can update the pheromone trail $\tau_{ij}$ on the arc $(i, j)$.

### Online Delayed Pheromone Update

Once a solution is built, the ant can re-trace the same path backward and update the pheromone trails on the traversed arcs.

### Offline Pheromone Update

Pheromone updates performed by global information available are called 'off-line pheromone updates'. Here, by observing the ant's behaviour and with the help of the global information like the shortest path the ant has taken or on the basis of the solution generated by ants, additional pheromone is deposited on the arcs enabling the ant search process from a non-local perspective.

## 8.3.6 Solution Evaluation

In ant colony optimisation (ACO) algorithms, solutions generated by ants provide feedback to direct the search of future ants entering the system. This is done by two mechanisms: *Implicit* and *Explicit solution evaluation*. In explicit solution evaluation, some measure of the quality of the solution generated is used to decide how much pheromone should be deposited by ant. In implicit solution evaluation, the ants exploit the DPL effect of real ants foraging behaviour (i.e., the fact that if the ant chooses a shorter path, then it is the first to deposit pheromone and to bias the search of forthcoming ants).

In geographically distributed problems like network problems, implicit solution evaluation based on the DPL effect can play an important role, where explicit solution is switched off by setting the amount of pheromone deposited by ants to a constant value independent of the cost of the path built by the ant, thus it is possible to find good solutions to network problems exploiting the DPL effect. It is also proved that coupling explicit and implicit solution evaluation by making the amount of pheromone deposited proportional to the cost of the solution generated improves the performance. The reason why the DPL effect can be exploited only in geographically distributed network problems is due to its efficiency since the distributed nature of nodes in routing problems allows more exploitation of DPL effect in a very natural way, without incurring on any additional computational cost. This is due to the de-centralized nature of the system and to inherently asynchronous (non-uniform movement of ants) nature of the dynamics of a real network. Asynchronous ants are not used in combinatorial optimisation problems due to the computational inefficiencies introduced and asynchronous ants can outweigh the gains due to the exploitation of the DPL effect.

## 8.4 WORKING OF ANT COLONY OPTIMISATION

The main steps of a simple schematic algorithm modelling the behaviour of real ant colonies can be given as follows:

BEGIN
    Initialize
    REPEAT
        Generate artificial ways for all artificial ants
        Compute the length of all artificial ways
        Update the amount of pheromone attached on the ways
        Keep the shortest or best path found up to now
    UNTIL (maxiteration or a criteria is satisfied)
END.

Let us understand the working of ant algorithms with the following examples.

### Example 8.1

In this example, we discuss the basic features of an ant algorithm for optimizing a simple one-variable function. Let us consider that the same function and the initial procedure are similar to the one discussed in Section 7.4.

$$\text{Min } f(x) = x \times \sin(10\pi \times x) + 1.0 \qquad (8.3)$$

Subject to

$$-1 \leq x \leq 3$$

**Representation**

An ant needs a search space to explore a best path. Here we construct a binary platform as shown in Fig. 8.4 [10]. Let the hypothetical ants are allowed to travel a binary path choosing a '1' or '0' with a pseudo-random probability. Each ant constructs a binary string and has to be evaluated. The binary vector is considered to represent real values of the variable $x$. The length of the vector depends on the required precisions, which, in this example, are six places after the decimal point.

The domain of the variable $x$ has length 3; the precision requirement implies that the range $[-1\ldots2]$ should be divided into at least $3 \times 1000000$ equal size ranges. This means that 22 bits are required as a binary vector:

$$2097152 = 2^{21} < 3000000 \leq 2^{22} = 4194304.$$

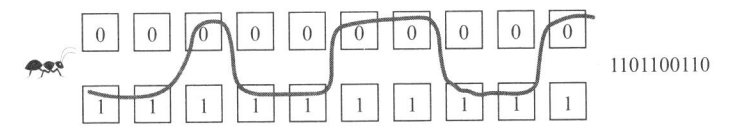

**Fig. 8.4** Ants build binary solutions from a source to destination node

The mapping from a binary string $(b_{21}\ b_{20}\ldots\ b_0)$ into a real number $x$ from the range $[-1\ldots2]$ is straightforward and is completed in the following two steps:

- Convert the binary string $(b_{21}\ b_{20}\ldots\ b_0)$ from the base 2 to base 10 and equal to $x'$.
- Find a corresponding real number:

$$x = -1.0 + x' \times (3/2^{22} - 1) \tag{8.4}$$

where $-1.0$ is the left boundary of the domain and 3 is the length of the domain.

For example, an ant constructed string be
(1000101110110101000111)
represent the number 0.637197, since
$x' = (1000101110110101000111)_2 = 2288967$
and
$x = -1.0 + 2288967 \times (3/4194303) = 0.637197$.

Of course, the binary ant constructed string (0000000000000000000000) and (1111111111111111111111) represent boundaries of the domain, $-1.0$ and 2.0, respectively.

**Ant search phase**

At the decision stage for the value of a bit, ants use only the pheromone information. Once an ant completes the decision process for the values of all bits in the string, it means that it has produced a solution to the problem.

**Evaluation function**

Evaluation function *eval* for binary vectors '$A$' is equivalent to the function $f$:

$$eval\ ('A') = f(x) \tag{8.5}$$

where the binary ant string '$A$' represents the real value $x$.

As noted earlier, the evaluation function plays the role of the environment, rating potential solutions in terms of their fitness. For example, let us consider three ant strings that are generated as follows:

$$A_1 = (1000101110110101000111),$$
$$A_2 = (0000001110000000010000),$$
$$A_3 = (1110000000111111000101),$$

Their corresponding real values are $x_1 = 0.637197$, $x_2 = -0.958973$, and $x_3 = 1.627888$, respectively. Consequently, the evaluation function would rate them as follows:

$$eval\ (A_1) = f(x_1) = 1.586345,$$
$$eval\ (A_2) = f(x_2) = 0.078878,$$
$$eval\ (A_3) = f(x_3) = 2.250650.$$

Clearly, the *Ant string* $A_2$ is the best of the three ant constructed paths, since its evaluation returns the lowest value. Here the solution is evaluated for the minimization problem and a numeric value showing the quality of the solution is calculated by using a function called the *evaluation function*.

An artificial pheromone to be attached to the sub-paths forming the solution is computed using this value. After all N ants in the colony have produced their solutions and the pheromone amount belonging to each solution has been calculated, the pheromones of sub-paths between the bits are updated. This is carried out by lowering the previous pheromone amounts and depositing the new pheromone amount on the paths.

**Pseudo-random Probability Function**
Assume that the probability of being preferred of the sub-path between 0 and 1 $(0 \rightarrow 1)$ at a stage is calculated. Then, the following equation is used:

$$P_{01}(t) = \frac{\tau_{01}}{\tau_{01} + \tau_{00}} \tag{8.6}$$

where, $P_{01}$ is the probability associated with the sub-path $(0 \rightarrow 1)$, and $\tau_{00}$ and $\tau_{01}$ are the artificial pheromones of the sub-paths $(0 \rightarrow 0, 0 \rightarrow 1)$.

The selection of a particular sub-path is done with certain degree of randomness. Here, the concept of exploitation and exploration is introduced. Let $q_0$ be a tuneable parameter that divides the decision on the solution knowledge into two parts. If $q_0 \leq rand\ value$ (*rand* value is a random number generated between 0 and 1), then the decision of ants for selecting a sub-path is purely done by the sub-path which has the maximum probability value and this process exploits the decision to the maximum. Otherwise if $q_0 > rand\ value$, the exploration process is carried out.

Here a pseudo-random selection is carried out. At a particular start position '0' an ant K has to choose a sub-path either '1' or '0'. Let us suppose, the probability associated with sub-paths '1' and '0' be $P_{01} = 0.4$ and $P_{02} = 0.8$, respectively. Now to introduce randomness in choosing a sub-path, a random value should be generated between 0 and 1. First check if *rand value* $\leq P_{01}$. If it is correct then select a sub-path $(0 \rightarrow 1)$. If it is not correct, check same generated random value (i.e., *rand value* $\leq P_{02}$, if it is correct, then select a sub-path $(0 \rightarrow 0)$. If it is not correct, again a new random value should be generated between 0 and 1 and the process has to be continued till a sub-path is selected.

**Pheromone Updating**
Artificial pheromone is computed by the following formula:

$$\Delta\tau_{01}^k(t, t+l) = \begin{cases} cons/g_b & \text{if the ant } k \text{ passes the sub-path } (0 \rightarrow 1), \\ 0 & \text{otherwise} \end{cases} \tag{8.7}$$

Here, $\Delta\tau_{01}^k$ is the pheromone attached to the sub-path $(0 \rightarrow 1)$ by the artificial ant $k$, $t$ is the unit step, $l$ is the length of the path (binary string length), *cons* is the pheromone deposition factor, $g_b$ is the best optimum fitness value obtained so far. $d_f \times g_b$ is the pheromone deposited which is a function of the solution obtained for the ants travelled so far.

## Pheromone evaporation

The pheromone amount of the sub-path $(0 - 1)$ at the time $(t + 1)$ is updated as follows:

$$\tau_{01}(t+l) = (1-\rho)\tau_{01}(t) + \Delta\tau_{01}(t, t+l) \tag{8.8}$$

where $\rho$ a coefficient is called the evaporation parameter of which the value is larger than 0 and less than 1.

## MATLAB Program 8.1

```
%%%%%%%%%%%%%%%%%%%%%%%%%%%%%%%%%%%%%%%%%%%%%%%%%%%%
% OPTIMISATION OF A SINGLE VARIABLE FUNCTION USING ACO
%%%%%%%%%%%%%%%%%%%%%%%%%%%%%%%%%%%%%%%%%%%%%%%%%%%%

clear all;              % Clears  all previous variables
xmin=-1;xmax=2;         % Boundary limits of  the variable x
accu=6;                 % Decimal accuracy
iphr=10^-6;             % Initial pheromone value
rho=0.5;                % Evaporation factor
cv= 0.001;              % A constant value so that denominator should not become zero
cons=1;                 % Deposition factor
qo=0.5;                 % Tunable parameter

% CALCULATION OF STRING LENGTH WITH REQUIRED DECIMAL ACCURACY

dl=xmax- xmin;          % Domain Length
er=dl*10^accu;          % Required  times the domain length to be divided to
                        % incorporating decimal accuracy
bl=(log(dl)+accu*log(10))/log(2);   % Calculation of string length
lbl=fix(bl);            % Left bit length
rbl=lbl+1;              % Right bit length(er should lie between
                        % 2^lbl and 2^rbl)
Tij=ones(2,rbl)*iphr;   % Initial trail available during the start of the problem
pos=[ones(1,rbl);zeros(1,rbl)];   % Binary positions either 0 or 1 an ant can select
m=1000;                 % m must be always greater than rbl i.e., Total number of ants taken
t=0;                    % Initializing the timer
s=1;                    % Counter
v=2*ones(m,rbl);        % Storing all the ants positions
aa=0;                   % Initializing the number of completed tour by an individual ant
for i=1:m,
deltij01=zeros(1,rbl);  % Initializing the zero pheromone change in the first
                        % path string (111111....)
deltij00=zeros(1,rbl);  % Initializing the zero pheromone change in the second
                        % path string(00000.....)
t = t + 1;
for j = s : i,
for k=1:(t+1) - j,
if k>=rbl+1,
break,
end
if v(j,k)==2

% CALCULATING THE TRANSITION PROBABILITY

densum=0;
for g=1:2,              % Calculating the denominator
densum=densum+(Tij(g,k));
end
prob=repmat(0,2,1);
for g=1:2,              % Calculating the denominator
```

```
prob(g,1)=Tij(g,k)/densum;    % Probability calculated for the kth ant
end
if (prob(1,1)==prob(2,1)),
prob(1,1)=prob(1,1)- 0.001;
end
q=rand(1,1);

% ACO PARTLY BY CUTTING EXPLORATION BY TUNABLE PARAMETER qo

if q<=qo,                     % Exploitation of decision knowledge for ant's selection
mx=max(prob);
for hd=1:2,
if prob(hd,1)==mx,
prob(hd,1)=1;
break
end
end
else

% ANTS CHOOSE SUB-PATH BASED ON PSEUDO RANDOM PROBABILITY FUNCTION

con=0;
while con==0,                 % Selection process of sub-path will be continuing till its finalised
p=rand(1);                    % Introducing the randomness into the probability of choosing a path
for hd=1:2,
if p<prob(hd,1)
con = 1;
prob(hd,1)=1;
break;
end
end
end
[e f]=find(1==prob(:,1));
v(j,k)=pos(e,k);              % Fixing the selected sub-path 1 or 0 in the
                              % constructed path string
end
end
end
if rem(t,rbl)==0,
s=s+1;
end
if s>1,
aa=aa+1;
rx(aa,1)=bi2de(v(aa,:),'left-msb');    % Relative value of  x
ax(aa,1)=xmin+(rx(aa,1)*dl)/(2^rbl-1); % Actual value of x
fit(aa,1)=ax(aa,1)*sin(10*pi*ax(aa,1))+1;  % Objective function to be
                              % minimised
[x y]=find(min(fit(:,1))==fit(:,1));   % Here fitness function is same as
                              % objective function
var4=[x y];
Ant_No=i;                     % Index of the current ant
disp('Best Solution');
disp(fit(var4(1,1),1));       % Display of best solution in the command window
disp('Best Variable (X)');
disp(ax(var4(1,1),1));        % Display of best variable in the command window
BSS(aa,1)=fit(var4(1,1),1);   % Storing the best solution value
D=v(1:(m-(rbl-1)),:);         % One complete cycle of all ants generated solutions

% COMPUTATION OF UPGRADATION OF ARTIFICIAL PHEROMONE
% (AFTER GENERATING THE SOLUTION BY K^th ANT)

for y=1:rbl,
if D(aa,y)==1,
deltij01(1,y)=deltij01(1,y)+cons/(ax(aa,1)+cv);
end
```

```
if D(aa,y)==0,
deltij00(1,y)=deltij00(1,y)+cons/(ax(aa,1)+cv);
end
deltij=[deltij01;deltij00];
Tij = (1-rho) * Tij + deltij;          % Upgradation of pheromone with evaporation
                                       % factor(rho)
end
end
end

% DISPLAY OF RESULTS

figure(1);
plot (1:aa,BSS); xlabel('Number of ants/iterations');
ylabel('f(x)');title('Convergence plot')
figure(2);
plot(1:aa,fit); xlabel('Number of ants/iterations');
ylabel('Individual ant''s solution');title('Solution obtained by each ant')
```

**Observation**

It should be noted that whenever a trial run is carried out, the result obtained will vary as the ant algorithm is heuristic in nature. However, after a required number of epochs, the solution converges and remains constant. It needs tuning of control parameters. More trial runs with more number of iterations have to be made to finalize a best solution.

Figures 8.5 and 8.6 give the convergence of the optimal solution obtained in one trial run using 1,000 ants/iterations. Lot of concepts can be introduced and modification can be made to the development of the previous program and good convergence behaviour can be obtained.

**Result (One-trial Convergence Plot)**

Best solution
−0.950235862520724

Best variable ($X$)
1.950361955252160

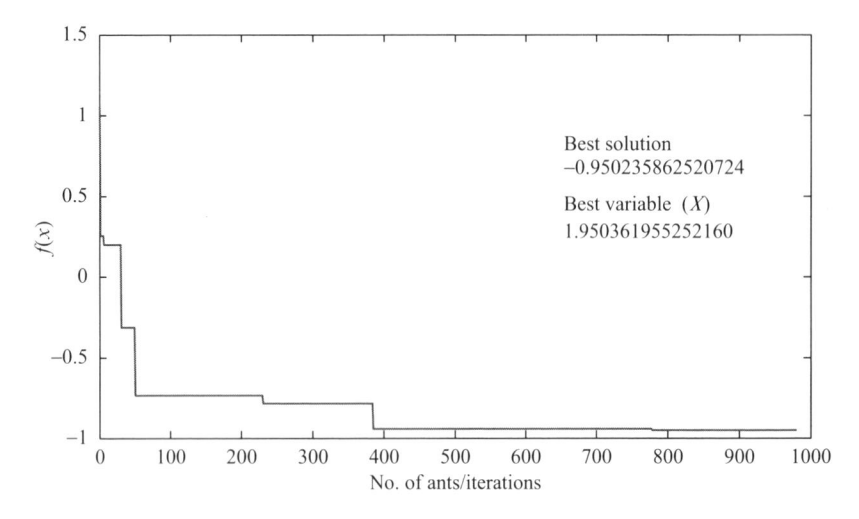

**Fig. 8.5** Convergence plot (a typical trial)

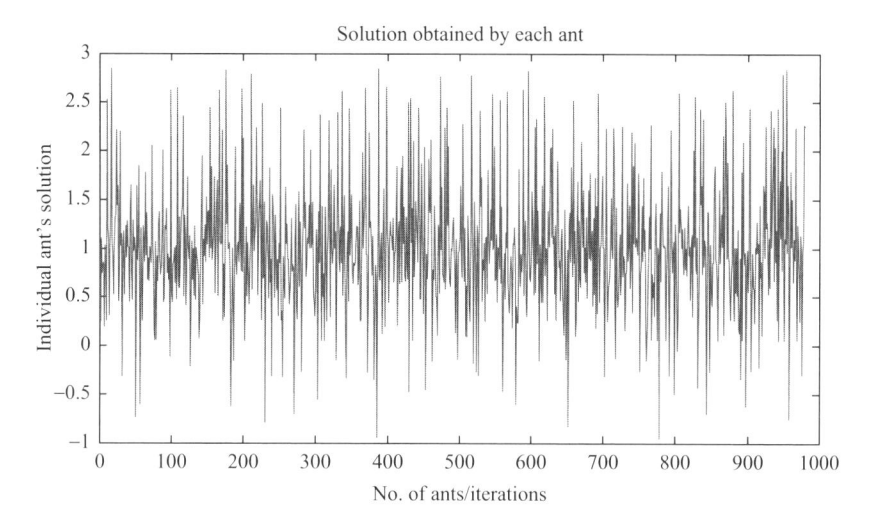

**Fig. 8.6** Convergence plot (A typical trial)

## 8.5 ANT COLONY OPTIMISATION ALGORITHM FOR TSP

The TSP is a hard combinatorial optimisation problem, and different types of ACO algorithms have already been reported for TSP by earlier researchers. Travelling salesman problem is also an appropriate problem for comparing and validating solutions, as the results using different approaches are already available for many standard test problems.

The ACO algorithms for TSP have two phases: *initialization phase* and *search-and-update phase*. During the initialization phase, ants are positioned on different towns or cities, and this phase remains similar to the implementation of well-established approaches for TSP using ACO. During the search-and-update phase, the positioned ants are allowed to search in the TSP solution space legally satisfying the TSP constraints, and there is a good amount of flexibility for implementing this phase.

Ant's movement is one of the important factors during the search-and-update phase. In this paper, we introduce an approach using serial ant system model for ant's movement during search-and-update phase. Simon et al. [11] proposed *Serial AS model*. The demonstration and its usefulness is validated by giving the experimental results for solution time needed to obtain near-optimal solutions for the well-known standard TSP benchmark problems, namely, Burma 14, Oliver 30, and Eilon 51.

### 8.5.1 Travelling Salesman Problem Formulation

Travelling salesman problem is the problem of a salesman who wants to find, starting from his hometown, and the shortest possible trip through a given set of customer cities and to return to its home town. More formally, it can be represented by a complete weighted graph $G = (N, A)$ with $N$ being the set of nodes representing the cities, and $A$ the set of arcs fully connecting the nodes $N$. Each arc is assigned a value $d_{r,s}$ which is the length of arc $(r, s) \in A$, that is, the distance between cities $i$ and $j$, with $(r, s) \in N$.

Travelling salesman problem is the problem of finding a minimal length Hamiltonian circuit of the graph, where an Hamiltonian circuit is a closed tour visiting exactly once each of the $n = N$ nodes of $G$. For symmetric TSPs, the distances between the cities are independent of the direction of traversing the arcs, that is, $d_{rs} = d_{sr}$ for every pair of nodes.

In the more general asymmetric TSP (ATSP), at least for one pair of nodes $(r, s)$ is such that $d_{rs} \neq d_{sr}$. In case of symmetric TSPs, Euclidean TSP instances are used in which the cities are points in the Euclidean space and the inter-city distances are available ACO algorithms for the TSP calculated using the Euclidean norm (i.e., $d_{rs} = [(x_r - x_s)^2 - (y_r - y_s)^2]^{1/2}$). However, here in this section we have considered only symmetric TSP problems.

### 8.5.2 Implementation of Ants in TSP Search Space

As mentioned in Section 8.2, there are many ways a particular swarm-based system can be used for solving an application. Similarly, ACO can be implemented in different methods for solving TSP. However, their potential varies based on the suitability of its implementation.

#### 8.5.2.1 Ant System Model with Elitist Ants

In this model, let $m$ be the total number of ants taken to solve the TSP. It is assumed that each ant is a simple agent that follows certain rules. Initially, each of the $m$ ants is placed on a randomly or uniformly chosen city, and then iteratively applies at each city a state transition rule.

Let us try to observe from Fig. 8.7 how an ant constructs a tour. At a city $r$, the ant chooses a still unvisited city $s$ probabilistically, biased by the pheromone trail strength $T_{rs}(t)$ on the arc between city $r$ and city $s$ and a locally available heuristic information, which is a function of the arc length. Ants probabilistically prefer cities, which are close and are connected by arcs with high pheromone trail strength. To construct a feasible solution each ant has a limited form of memory, called *tabu list*, in which the current partial tour is stored. The memory is used to determine at each construction step the set of cities which still has to be visited and to guarantee that a feasible solution is built.

Additionally, it allows the ant to re-trace its tour, once it is completed. After the ants have completed a tour, the pheromones are updated. This is typically done by first lowering the pheromone trail strengths by a constant factor, and then the ants are allowed to deposit pheromone on the arcs they have visited. The trail update is done in such a form that arcs contained in shorter tours and/or visited by many ants receive a higher amount of pheromone and are therefore chosen with a higher probability in the following iterations of the algorithm. In this sense, the amount of pheromone $T_{rs}(t)$ represents the learned desirability of choosing next city $s$ when an ant is at city $r$.

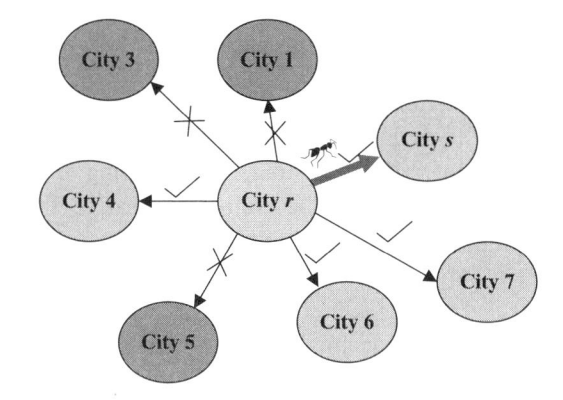

Fig. 8.7 Convergence plot (A typical trial)

In the case of ant system with elitist ants, we see that an elitist ant is the one which reinforces the edges belonging to $T$, the best tour found from the beginning of the trial, by a quantity $Q/L^+$, where $L^+$ is the length of $T^+$. At every cycle, elitist ants are added to the usual ants so that the edges belonging to $T^+$ gets an extra reinforcement $e \times Q/L^+$. The idea is that the pheromone trail of $T^+$, so reinforced, will direct the search of all the other ants in probability towards a solution composed of some edges of the best tour itself.

### 8.5.2.2 Touring Ant Colony Model

Hiroyasu, et al., presented the touring ant colony optimisation (TACO) algorithm. Karaboga, et al. [12] presented the modified TACO for designing digital IIR filters. Here, incorporating a frequency-based memory feature, limitation of premature convergence in TACO has been reduced. In the generalized TACO algorithm, a vector of design parameters, each of which is coded with a string of binary bits, represents each solution. Therefore, artificial ants search for the value of each bit in the string (i.e., they try to make a decision whether the value of a bit is a '0' or a '1'). This concept can be understood from Fig. 8.8.

At the decision stage for the value of a bit, ants use only the pheromone information. Once an ant completes the decision process for the values of all bits in the string, it means that it has produced a solution to the problem. This solution is evaluated for the problem and a numeric value showing the quality of the solution is calculated by using a function called the evaluation function. The concept of TACO is, however, attempted to TSP.

Let us consider the case of TSP which consists of three city nodes for simplicity. The number of bits for each city node has to be chosen optimally (say four).

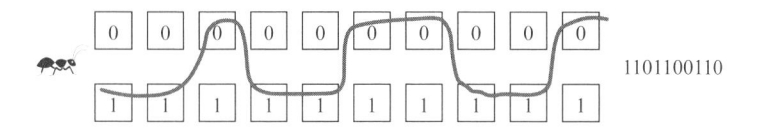

Fig. 8.8 An artificial path (Solution) found by an ant

However, here it is carried out by number of trials depending upon the size of the TSP. Therefore, the length of the fixed binary path for the ants' to travel is 12 bits, $(3 \times 4)$. Here, the ants that are positioned at the starting of the binary path have to choose either a '1' or a '0' during its travel. The ants are then allowed to travel as shown in Fig. 8.8. Each ant will be able to generate a string of 12 bits. The binary strings generated by each ant have to be evaluated to satisfy the TSP constraints for capturing the optimum. Suppose the binary string obtained is '101011100110' then the strings are grouped into three which is the total number of city nodes '1010' '1110' '0110'.

Each set is converted into decimal numbers and sorted from ascending to descending order. Then its position has to be noted which will give the travel path and the distance of the TSP is evaluated. Therefore, [10 (2) 14 (1) 6(3)] will give a TSP vector path of [(2 1) (1 3) (3 2)], which is the solution for the ant that travelled through the binary path.

### 8.5.2.3 Serial Ant System Model with Elitist Ants

In this proposed serial ant system (AS) model, initially an ant search space (ASS) is created for the ants to move on a platform. Here, each ant starts from the starting node only after its predecessor has reached the end stage. Let us consider a TSP with 4 city nodes. The TSP search space, also called ASS, is a $4 \times 4$ matrix space which is shown in Fig. 8.9. Let $m$ be the total number of ants taken initially. Each column of the matrix space contains 1 to $n$ city nodes for which each ant while travelling has to select one city node satisfying the TSP constraints.

The visited city node is stored in a tabu list as a memory. The tabu list helps to select the unvisited city while selecting the city node in each column of the matrix space. Once the ant visits all the city nodes the total sum of Euclidean distance is calculated which is the cost of the tour of that ant's journey. Therefore the tour of the first ant gives a TSP vector path of [(2 1) (1 3) (3 4) (4 2)]. The flow chart of the proposed model is given in Fig. 8.10.

The pheromone is initially kept low which is a constant. Initially, the first city that is selected by the ant is purely based on the pheromone deposits. After the visiting of the first city node the selection of the other city nodes are based on both the

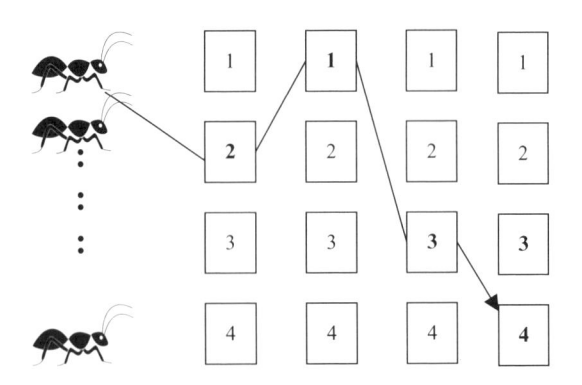

**Fig. 8.9** Ant search space (four city nodes)

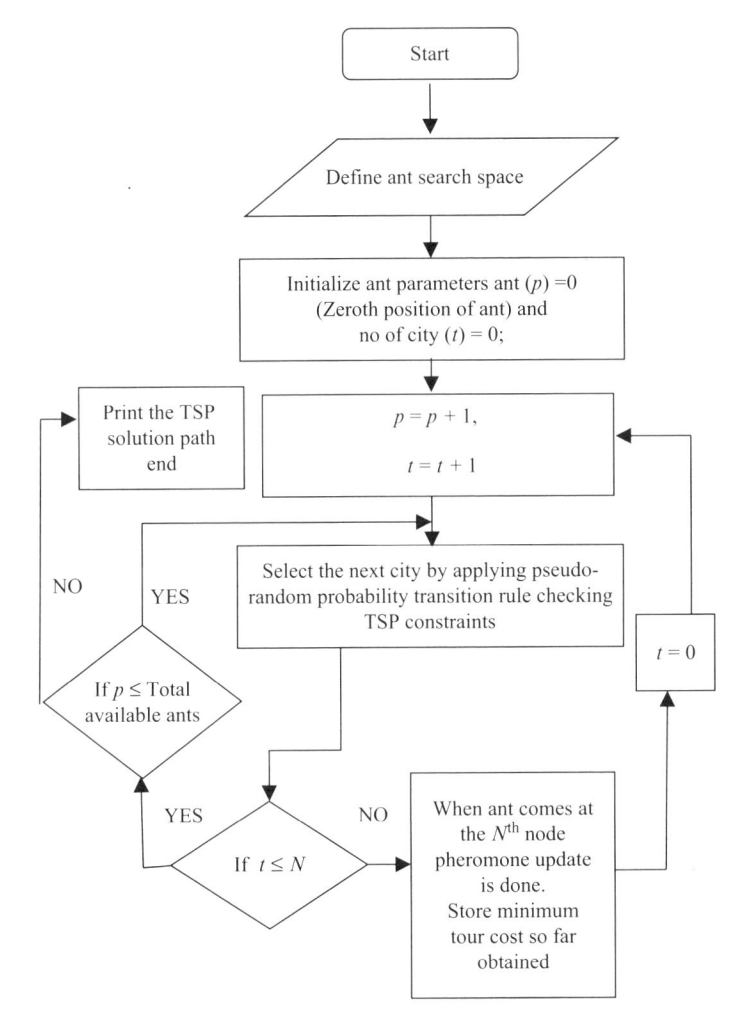

**Fig. 8.10** Flow chart for serial ant system model

heuristic function that depends on the Euclidean distance between the city nodes and the pheromone deposits. Here, elitist ants reinforces the edges belonging to $T$, the best tour found from the beginning of the trial, by a quantity $Q/L^+$, where $L^+$ is the length of $T^+$. At every cycle $e$ elitist ants are added to the usual ants so that the edges belonging to $T^+$ gets an extra reinforcement $e \times Q/L^+$. The idea is that the pheromone trail of $T^+$, so reinforced, will direct the search of all the other ants in probability towards a solution composed of some edges of the best tour itself.

The transition probability $P_{rs}^p(t)$ for the $p^{th}$ ant from one city node $r$ to next city node $s$ for AS models [22] are same and is given by:

$$P_{rs}^p(t) = \begin{cases} \dfrac{[\tau_{rs}(t)]^\alpha [\eta_{rs}]^\beta}{\sum_{p \in allowed_p}[\tau_{rs}(t)]^\alpha [\eta_{rs}]^\beta} & if\ s \in allowed_p \\ 0 & otherwise \end{cases} \qquad (8.9)$$

where

| | |
|---|---|
| $p$ | Index for an individual ant |
| $r, s$ | Index for states in the ASS |
| $\tau_{rs}$ | Trail intensity on edge $r, s$ |
| $\eta_{rs}$ | Heuristic function |
| $C_{rs}$ | Cost occurred during the passage of ants from $r$ to $s$ |
| $\alpha$ | Relative importance of the pheromone trail $\alpha \geq 0$ |
| $\beta$ | Relative importance of the visibility $\beta \geq 0$ |

'allowed$_p$' is the available states which the $p^{th}$ ant can choose from state $r$ to state $s$. Here, $p$ is the allowable states for the ants to move to Eq. (8.9).

In this model, pheromone deposition is updated globally by the following formula:

$$\tau_{rs}(t+N) = \rho\tau_{rs}(t) + \Delta\tau_{rs}^p(t, t+N) \quad (8.10)$$

where

$$\Delta\tau_{rs}^p = \begin{cases} Q/C_p & \text{if } p^{th} \text{ ant uses edge } (r, s) \text{ in its tour} \\ & \text{(between time } t \text{ and } t+N) \\ 0 & \text{otherwise} \end{cases} \quad (8.11)$$

where

$C_p$      Tour cost occurred by the $p^{th}$ ant

When an ant chooses any one of the city node present in the first column of the matrix, then $[\eta_{rs}]^\beta$ term present in the transition probability formulae is forced to be unity. Therefore the selection totally depends on the pseudo-random transition probability of the pheromone deposited.

### 8.5.2.4 Parameter Settings

Parameter settings for all the four models are set based on number of trial runs in which the best averages of TSP solution is obtained. The best selected parameters for all the four models are tabulated in Tables 8.2 and 8.3. As the length of the binary path increases the convergence of the solution is getting inferior in quality. When modified TACO is applied to TSP, the ants failed to find successful TSP solution and their major limitations are presented as follows:

(i) The length of the string. That is, when the number of city nodes increases, the sub-paths taken by the ants increases.
(ii) The ants are restricted to choose any of the two sub-paths, namely '1' or '0'. Therefore, the aforesaid restriction hinders the choice of having more number of sub-paths and hence, the ant exploration decreases.

The decision to select a specific bit by an ant is based only on the pheromone information obtained from the final evaluation of binary string. It does not include the pheromone information incorporating the transitional cost (TC) between two city nodes for local updating.

Table 8.2 Travelling salesman problem solutions for the test problems

| Test problem | TSP model | Average solution | Best solution | Average solution time (sec) |
|---|---|---|---|---|
| Burma 14 | AS(1000 iterations) | 31.20 | 30.88 | 70.68 |
| Oliver 30 | AS(1000 iterations) | 425.82 | 423.74 | 48.59 |
| Eilon 51 | AS(1000 iterations) | 434.66 | 430.34 | 223.23 |
| Burma 14 | TACO(1000 ants) | 35.45 | 33.41 | 17.41 |
| Oliver 30 | TACO(1000 ants) | 836.00 | 781.74 | 38.16 |
| Eilon 51 | TACO(1000 ants) | 1334.35 | 1291.16 | 64.55 |
| Burma 14 | Serial AS (1000 ants) | 31.72 | 31.48 | 3.71 |
| Oliver 30 | Serial AS (1000 ants) | 423.91 | 423.91 | 12.33 |
| Eilon 51 | Serial AS (1000 ants) | 456.08 | 449.81 | 32.36 |

The performance of AS with elitist concept is found to be good with more computations, and therefore solution time is found to be more as the TSP size increases. The parameters are chosen with the help of the literatures available for AS model for TSP and through trial runs for getting optimal solution. The serial movements of ants are simple in implementation and computationally fast when compared with TSP models considered in this chapter. It is very much competitive with AS model for TSP.

However, it requires more validation and performance evaluation with systematic approaches for setting the parameters. Since the convergence has been stopped for a fixed number of iterations for comparison purpose, the solution obtained may not be globally optimal for larger size problems. Therefore, the proposed model is found to be performing well and requires lot of enhancement. The computer hardware platform used for the implementation of UCP is Pentium IV processor, processor speed of 3.5 GHz, RAM of 1GB, and the software platform is MATLAB Version 7.4 (R14).

Table 8.3 Parameter settings

| S. No. | TSP model | Parameter settings |
|---|---|---|
| 1 | AS | $\alpha = 1$, $\beta = 5$, $Q = 10$, $\rho = 0.5$ |
| 2 | TACO | Pheromone evaporation factor = 0.5<br>Pheromone deposition factor = 0.001<br>Frequency Factor = 1 |
| 3 | Serial AS | $\alpha = 0.1$, $\beta = 0.9$, $Q = 1$, $\rho = 0.1$<br>Total number of Serial ants = 1000 |

## Example 8.2

Solve the TSP for the Oliver 30 city problem using an ant system model. Fix the control parameters for these models and check the difference in results. The data for the given problem is given in $X$–$Y$ coordinates of the graph with respect to their positions from the vertex.

| City node | 1 | 2 | 3 | 4 | 5 | 6 | 7 | 8 | 9 | 10 | 11 | 12 | 13 | 14 | 15 |
|---|---|---|---|---|---|---|---|---|---|---|---|---|---|---|---|
| X | 54 | 54 | 37 | 41 | 2 | 7 | 25 | 22 | 18 | 4 | 13 | 18 | 24 | 25 | 44 |
| Y | 67 | 62 | 84 | 94 | 99 | 64 | 62 | 60 | 54 | 50 | 40 | 40 | 42 | 38 | 35 |
| City node | 16 | 17 | 18 | 19 | 20 | 21 | 22 | 23 | 24 | 25 | 26 | 27 | 28 | 29 | 30 |
| X | 41 | 45 | 58 | 62 | 82 | 91 | 83 | 71 | 64 | 68 | 83 | 87 | 74 | 71 | 58 |
| Y | 26 | 21 | 35 | 32 | 7 | 38 | 46 | 44 | 60 | 58 | 69 | 76 | 78 | 71 | 69 |

## MATLAB Program 8.2

This program solves the TSP problem as discussed in section on serial ant system model with elitist ants.

```
%%%%%%%%%%%%%%%%%%%%%%%%%%%%%%%%%%%%%%%%%%%%%%
% TSP SOLUTION FOR OLIVER 30 CITY NODES USING AS
%%%%%%%%%%%%%%%%%%%%%%%%%%%%%%%%%%%%%%%%%%%%%%

Clear all                         % Clears  all previous variables
Ncity=30;                         % Number of cities on tour
Nants=Ncity;                      % Number of ants=Number of cities

% CITY LOCATIONS (X-Y CO-ORDINATES IN GRAPH)

xcor=[54 54 37 41 02 07 25 22 18 4 13 18 24 25 44 41 45 58 62 82 91 83 71 64 68 83 87 74
      71 58];
ycor=[67 62 84 94 99 64 62 60 54 50 40 40 42 38 35 26 21 35 32 07 38 46 44 60 58 69 76 78
      71 69];

% EUCLIDIAN DISTANCE BETWEEN CITIES

for i=1:Ncity
for j=1:Ncity
dij(i,j) = sqrt((xcor(i)-xcor(j))^2 + (ycor(i)-ycor(j))^2);
end
end

% INITIALISATION OF ANT PARAMETERS

hf=1./dij;                          % Heuristic function is 1/dij
phmone=0.1*ones(Ncity,Ncity);       % Initial pheromone deposited between cities
maxit=1000;                         % Max number of iterations
alpha=2;                            % Relative importance of the trail,alpha >=0
beta=10;                            % Relative importance of the visibility, beta>=0
rho=0.001;                          % rho - evoporation factor
Q=sum(1./(1:8));                    % Q - close to the lenght of the optimal tour
dbest=9999999;
```

```
% Max distance travelled assumed as reference to select the minimum distance
                                % so far obtained
e=5;                            % Elistic ants can be added if necessary (Optional)

% INITIALIZE TOURS

for k=1:Nants
tour(k,:)=randperm(Ncity);    % Intial random tours taken by ants
end
tour(:,Ncity+1)=tour(:,1);    % Tour ends on city it starts with

% FINDING THE CITY TOUR FOR EACH ANT

for it=1:maxit
for ii=1:Nants
for jj=2:Ncity-1
[jj tour(ii,:)];
cc=tour(ii,jj-1);             % Current city
nxt=tour(ii,jj:Ncity);        % Next cities to be visited

% CALCULATION OF PROBABILITY

num=((phmone(cc,nxt).^alpha).*(hf(cc,nxt).^beta));
deno=sum((phmone(cc,nxt).^alpha).*(hf(cc,nxt).^beta));
prob=num./deno;
rcity=rand;
for kk=1:length(prob)
if rcity<sum(prob(1:kk))
newcity=jj-1+kk;              % Next city to be visited
break
end
end
temp=tour(ii,newcity);        % Remaining cities that can be visited
tour(ii,newcity)=tour(ii,jj);
tour(ii,jj)=temp;
end
end

% CALCULATE THE LENGTH OF EACH TOUR AND PHEROMONE DISTRIBUTION

phtemp=zeros(Ncity,Ncity);
for i=1:Nants
dist(i,1) = 0;
for j=1:Ncity
dist(i,1)=dist(i)+dij(tour(i,j),tour(i,j+1));
phtemp(tour(i,j),tour(i,j+1))=Q/dist(i,1);
end
end

% SAVING THE BEST PATH SO FAR OBTAINED

[dmin,ind] = min(dist);
if dmin<dbest
dbest = dmin;
end

% EXTRA PHEROMONE DEPOSITED FOR ELITE PATH (BY ELITIST ANTS)

ph1=zeros(Ncity,Ncity);
for j=1:Ncity
ph1(tour(ind,j),tour(ind,j+1))=Q/dbest;
end
```

```
% PHEROMONE UPDATING

phmone=(1-rho)*phmone+phtemp+e*ph1;
dd(it,:)=[dbest dmin];
disp('Current Iteration');disp(it);
disp('Current Minimum Distance');disp(dmin);
disp('Minimum Distance Covered So Far');disp(dbest);
end

% SOLUTION AND DISPLAY

[tour,dist];
figure(1)
plot(xcor(tour(ind,:)),ycor(tour(ind,:)),xcor,ycor,'*')
xlabel('X-Co-ordinates of the cities')
ylabel('Y-Co-ordinates of the cities')
title('Tour Path- Solution for the TSP')
axis square
figure(2);plot([1:maxit],dd(:,1),[1:maxit],dd(:,2),':')
xlabel('Number of iterations')
ylabel('Total Distance')
title('Convergence plot for the TSP solution')
```

### Observation

Figure 8.11 shows the convergence plot for the TSP solution for 100 iterations for a typical trial. It also gives the tour completed in each iteration. The optimal tour got is shown in Fig. 8.12. Here again at every trial and for a fixed number of iterations, results may vary. However, it will stabilize to an optimal tour after some iteration. Ants not only try to get the best sub-path locally, but they always try to see that the global TSP solution emerges.

### Result (One-trial convergence plot)

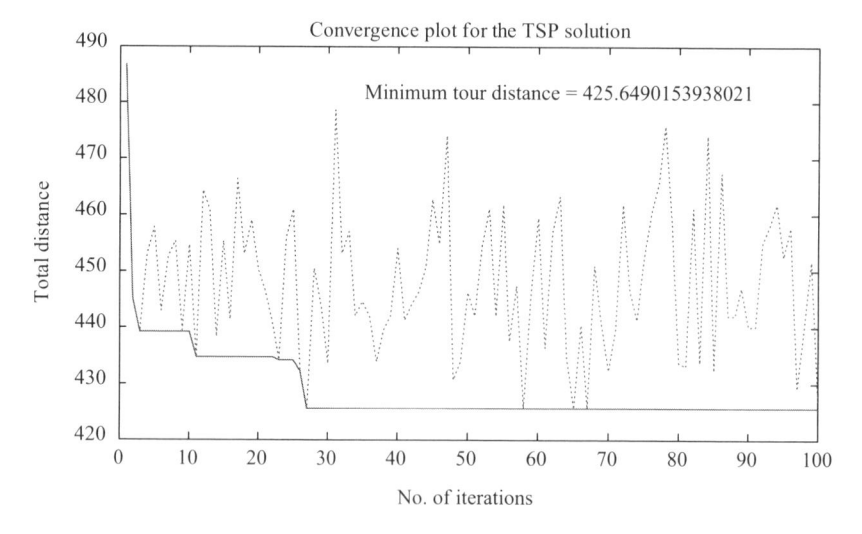

**Fig. 8.11** Convergence plot (A typical trial)

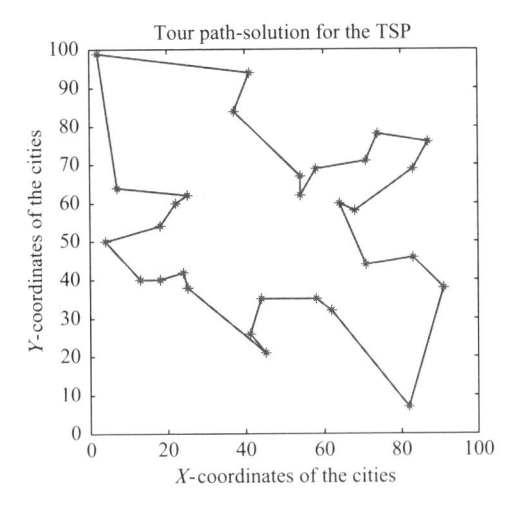

**Fig. 8.12** Convergence plot (A typical trial)

## 8.6 UNIT COMMITMENT PROBLEM

The need to obtain a globally optimum solution in the highly non-linear and computationally difficult power system environment has been a focus of research. The UCP is a hard combinatorial optimisation problem aimed at determining the optimum schedule of generating units (i.e., switching ON and OFF of $N$ generating units over a period of time for the demand forecasted to be served) by minimizing the overall cost of power generation while satisfying a set of system constraints. Finding a good solution to the UCP in reasonable amount of time is very critical since it could mean significant annual financial savings in power generating costs.

To 'commit' a generating unit is to 'turn it on', that is, to bring the unit up to speed, synchronize it to the system, and connect it so that it can deliver power to the network. The problem of 'committing enough units and leaving them online' is one of the economics. It is quite expensive to run too many generating units. A great deal of money can be saved by turning units off (de-committing them) when they are not needed. The generic UCP can be formulated as to minimize operational cost (OC) subject to minimum up time and down time constraints, crew constraints, ramp constraints, unit capability limits, deration of units, unit status, generation constraints, and reserve constraints.

The major limitations of the UCP lie in the problem's dimensions, large computational time, and complexity in programming and optimum results. Since optimum schedules for committing units can save millions of dollars per year in production costs, efforts are being made to solve the UCP using simulated annealing, expert systems, artificial neural networks, fuzzy systems, genetic algorithm (GA), evolutionary programming, and hybrid models. In this section, we solve the UCP with the help of the ant colony system model. The generic ACM-based unit commitment (UC) problem (UCP) can be formulated as discussed in the following section.

## 8.6.1 Minimize the Operational Cost

$$OC = \sum_{i=1}^{N}\sum_{t=1}^{T} FC_{it}(P_{it}) = ST_{it} + SD_{it} \quad (₹) \tag{8.12}$$

where $FC_{it}(P_{it})$ (fuel cost) is the input/output (I/O) curve that is modelled with a polynomial curve (normally a quadratic function):

$$FC_{it}(P_{it}) = a_i P_{it}^2 + b_i P_{it} + c_i \quad (₹/hr) \tag{8.13}$$

where, $a_i$, $b_i$ and $c_i$ are cost coefficients and $P_{it}$ is the power generated of unit $i$ during time period t in MW. The start-up cost is described by:

$$ST_{it} = TS_{it} F_{it} + (1 + e^{(D_{it} AS_{it})}) BS_{it} F_{it} + MS_{it} \quad (₹/hr) \tag{8.14}$$

where $TS_{it}$ is the turbine start–up cost, $BS_{it}$ is the boiler start-up, $MS_{it}$ is the start-up maintenance cost, $D_{it}$ is the down time in hours, and $AS_{it}$ is the boiler cool down coefficient. Similarly, the shutdown cost is described by:

$$SD_{it} = KP_{it} \quad (₹/hr) \tag{8.15}$$

where $K$ is the incremental shutdown cost.

**Subject to the following constraints:**
Minimum up time is as follows:

$$0 < T_{iu} \leq N_{G_i(online)} \tag{8.16}$$

where $T_{iu}$ is the minimum up time and $N_{G_i(online)}$ is the number of hour units for which $G_i$ has been online.
Minimum down time is given here:

$$0 < T_{id} \leq N_{G_i(offline)} \tag{8.17}$$

where $T_{iu}$ is the minimum down time and $N_{G_i(online)}$ is the number of hour units for which $G_i$ has been offline. The maximum and minimum output limits on the generators are as follows:

$$P_{it(min)} \leq P_{it} \leq P_{it(max)} \tag{8.18}$$

Those on the power rate are given here:

$$\nabla P_{it(min)} \leq \nabla P_{it} \leq \nabla P_{it(max)} \tag{8.19}$$

where, $\nabla P_{it}$ is the power rate of generator $i$ (in MW/hr). The power balance is represented as follows:

$$\sum_{i=1}^{N} P_{it} = load(H) \tag{8.20}$$

where $load(H)$ is the system load at hour $H$.

Let us take the numerical example of the four-unit system given in Table 8.4. The unit characteristics for the four-unit system are as follows:

Table 8.4  Numerical example of the four-unit system

|  | Unit 1 | Unit 2 | Unit 3 | Unit 4 |
|---|---|---|---|---|
| $P_{it}$(max) (MW) | 80 | 250 | 300 | 60 |
| $P_{it}$(min) (MW) | 25 | 60 | 75 | 20 |
| Ramp level (MW/hr) | 16 | 50 | 60 | 12 |
| Minimum up time (hr) | 4 | 5 | 5 | 1 |
| Maximum down time (hr) | 2 | 3 | 4 | 1 |
| Shutdown costs (₹) | 80 | 110 | 300 | 0 |
| Start-up costs (₹) |  |  |  |  |
| Hot | 150 | 170 | 500 | 0 |
| Cold | 350 | 400 | 1100 | 0.02 |
| Cold start time (hr) | 4 | 5 | 5 | 0 |
| Initial unit status | −5 | 8 | 8 | −6 |

*Initial unit status*: Hours offline (−) or online (+).

The following are the fuel cost equations:

$$C_1 = 25 + 1.5000 P_1 + 0.00396 P_1^2 \; ₹/hr \qquad (8.21)$$
$$C_2 = 72 + 1.3500 P_2 + 0.00261 P_2^2 \; ₹/hr$$
$$C_3 = 49 + 1.2643 P_3 + 0.00289 P_3^2 \; ₹/hr$$
$$C_4 = 15 + 1.4000 P_4 + 0.00510 P_4^2 \; ₹/hr$$

The ACS approach for solving the UCP [13] consists mainly of two phases. In the first phase, all the possible $S_t$ states of the $t^{th}$ hr that satisfy the load demand are determined; this is continued for the complete scheduling period of 24 hrs, which constitutes the ASS.

An ASS involving multi-decision states is seen in Fig. 8.13. Here, in the initialization part, the forecasted load demands and other relevant problem data from the system are taken for computation. Economic dispatch (ED) using the Lagrange multiplier method is used, which calculates the generator output and the production cost for each hour. The exhaustive enumeration technique is used to find all the possible combinations of the generating units available.

Once the search space is identified, the second phase involves the artificial ants that are allowed to pass continuously through the ASS. Each ant starts its journey from the initial condition, termed the starting node, reaches the end stage, and finally vanishes. Hence, it is a continuous flow of ants, and they never return. Once an ant reaches the end stage, a tour is completed and the overall generation cost path is generated. For each stage of the time period $t$, the ant selects an OC calculated for all $N$ generator units in order to minimize the overall OC. This is continued till the time period becomes $T$ and a tour is completed by that particular ant.

**Fig. 8.13** A multi-decision search phase

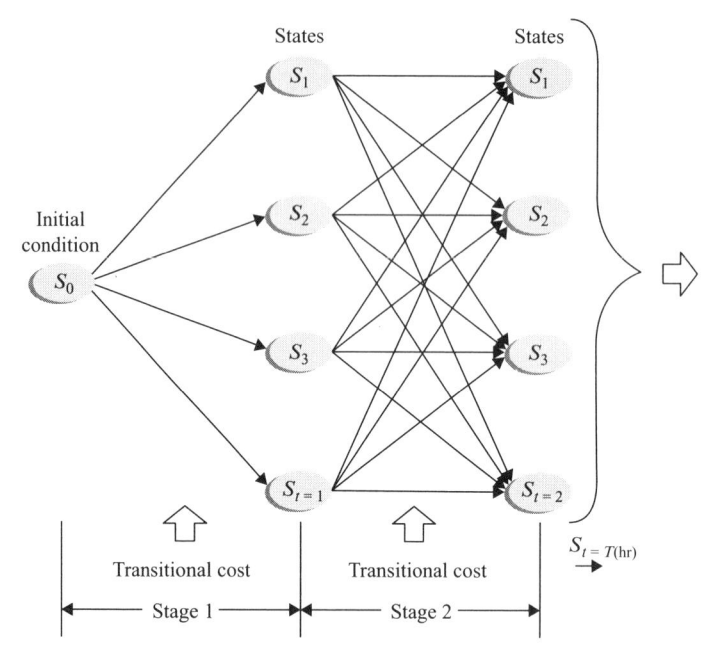

*$S_{t(hr)}$ is the eligible states satifying load demand for the $t$th hour.

Whenever a tour is completed by an individual ant and the total generation cost (TGC) is found to be less than the minimum cost paths taken by the previous ant, the present cost path is captured. This procedure is continued for all the remaining ants available at the starting node, which enables one to trace the optimal path.

The ACS mechanism can be divided into four parts: (a) initialization, (b) transition rule, (c) pheromone trail update rule, and (d) parameter settings (Fig. 8.13).

### 8.6.1.1 Initialization

During initialization, the parameters—requisite number of ants, relative importance of the pheromone trail, relative importance of the visibility, initial available pheromone trail, a constant related to the quantity of the trail laid by the ants, evaporation factor, tuning factor, number of elitist ants, etc.—have to be fixed and taken care of, which will be explained in detail in parameter settings.

### 8.6.1.2 Probability Transition Rule

The probability transition rule for the ACS (modified form of AS), as seen in (Eq. 8.9), is modified to allow explicitly for exploration. An ant $k$ in a state $i$ chooses the next state $j$ to move according to the following rule:

$$j = \begin{array}{l} \arg\max_{u \in J_i^k} \left\{ [\tau_{iu}(t)][\eta_{iu}]^\beta \right\} \quad \text{if} \quad q \leq q_0 \\ J \quad\quad\quad\quad\quad\quad\quad\quad\quad\quad \text{if} \quad q > q_0 \end{array} \quad (8.22)$$

where $\tau_{iJ(or)iu}$ is the trail intensity on edge $(i,j)$, $\eta_{ij} = 1/C_{ij}$ is the heuristic function and $C_{ij}$ is the transitional cost for that particular stage, $q$ is a random variable distributed over [0, 1], $q_0$ is a tuneable parameter $0 \leq q_0 \leq 1$, and $J \in J_j^k$ is a state that is randomly selected according to the probability given as follows:

$$P_{i,J}^k(t) = \frac{[\tau_{i,J}(t)][\eta_{i,J}]^\beta}{\sum_{l \in J_i^k} [\tau_{il}(t)][\eta_{il}]^\beta} \quad (8.23)$$

$q \leq q_0$ corresponds to the exploitation of the knowledge available about the problem, that is, the heuristic knowledge of the cost between states and the learned knowledge memorized in the form of pheromone trails, whereas $q > q_0$ favours more exploitation. Cutting exploration by tuning $q_0$ allows the system's activity to be concentrated on the best solutions instead of letting it explore constantly. Here $l$ denotes an allowable state [14].

### 8.6.1.3 Pheromone Trail Update Rule

Once the ants start choosing the minimum cost states, the pheromone trail update rule has to be implemented. In ACSs, the global trail-updating rule is given as follows:

$$\tau_{ij}(t) = (1-\rho)\tau_{ij}(t) + \rho \Delta \tau_{ij}(t) \quad (8.24)$$

where the $(i, j)$'s are the edges belonging to $T^+$, the minimum total operating cost path since the beginning of the trial, $\rho$ is the parameter governing pheromone decay, and the change in the pheromone concentration is given here:

$$\Delta \tau_{ij}(t) = 1/C^+ \quad (8.25)$$

where $C^+$ is the cost of $T^+$. This procedure allows only the best tour to be reinforced by a global update. Local updates are performed, so that other solutions can emerge. A local update is performed as follows: while performing a tour, ant $k$ is in state $i$ and selects a state $j \in J_j^k$, and the pheromone concentration of $(i, j)$ is updated using the following formula:

$$\tau_{ij}(t) = (1-\rho)\tau_{ij}(t) + \rho \tau_0 \quad (8.26)$$

where $\tau_0$ is the initial value of the pheromone trails.

The differences between an ACS and an AS are the following:

(a) An ACS uses a more aggressive action rule than an AS.
(b) Pheromone in an ACS is added only to arcs belonging to the globally best solution.
(c) Each time an ant uses a sub-path $(i, j)$ to move from stage t to stage $(t + 1)$ in ACS, it removes some pheromone from the sub-path.

It should be noted that in ACS, both local trail-updating and global trail-updating are used. In local trail-updating, the pheromone trail on the edges is modified; however in global trail-updating, an amount of pheromone is added after each of the ants has completed a tour. The amount of pheromone is inversely proportional to total operating cost path.

### 8.6.1.4 Parameter Settings

In the ACS model, the parameters $\beta$, $\rho$ and $q_0$ are those that affect the probability transition rule. The numerical example of a four-unit system for 24-hr scheduling period is tested for each parameter taking several values, all the others being constant (default settings; in each experiment only one of the values is changed), over 10 simulations in order to achieve some statistical information about the average evolution. The initial trail level $\tau_0$ is always set to 1. In the case of the ACS model, $\alpha = 1$; the number of ants allowed to pass through the ASS is 50. Table 8.5 shows the average TGCs for the various parameter settings.

Table 8.5  Parameter settings for the ACS model (Default settings $\beta = 1$, $\rho = 0.3$, $\tau_0 = 1$, $q_0 = 0.7$)

| $\beta$ | Av. TGC (₹/day) | $\rho$ | Av. TGC (₹/day) | $q_0$ | Av. TGC (₹/day) |
|---|---|---|---|---|---|
| 0 | 27,324.25 | 0 | 27,568.67 | 0.1 | 27,937 |
| 1 | 27,224.5 | **0.1** | **27,149.25** | 0.3 | 27,937 |
| 2 | 27,206 | 0.2 | 27,170.25 | 0.5 | 2.7478 |
| 5 | 27,115 | 0.3 | 27,328 | 0.7 | 27,328 |
| 7 | 27,107.5 | 0.5 | 27,373.5 | **0.9** | **27,135** |
| 10 | **27,030.25** | 0.7 | 27,442.67 | | |
| 15 | 27,151.5 | | | | |

The results of the experiment show that in this model, a high value of $\alpha$ means that the trail is very important, and therefore ants tend to choose edges chosen by other ants in the past. This is true until the value of $\beta$ becomes very high; in this case even if there is high amount of pheromone on a trail, there is always a high probability of an ant choosing another trail of lower cost. The ACS model performs well when the tuning factor is set to a high value, indicating that the model incorporates higher exploitation of the knowledge available about the problem. High values of $\beta$ and/or low values of $\alpha$ make the algorithm very similar to a stochastic *multi-greedy* algorithm (Fig. 8.14).

The evolution of the convergence of the minimum cost path can be seen in Fig. 8.15, where after the minimum number of ants have passed through the ASS and completed their tours, the convergence of the cost finally becomes stagnant. Even after the stagnant situation, ants still try to explore any of the minimum cost paths that are available, which indicates the strength of the ant colony system model. This can be understood from Fig. 8.16 by the oscillations for each individual ant taking its tour.

The test results indicate that an ant can absorb information from the experience gained from its fellow ants' behaviour to get the best results, which are almost globally optimum. Even though at one transition stage, the cost of the ACS

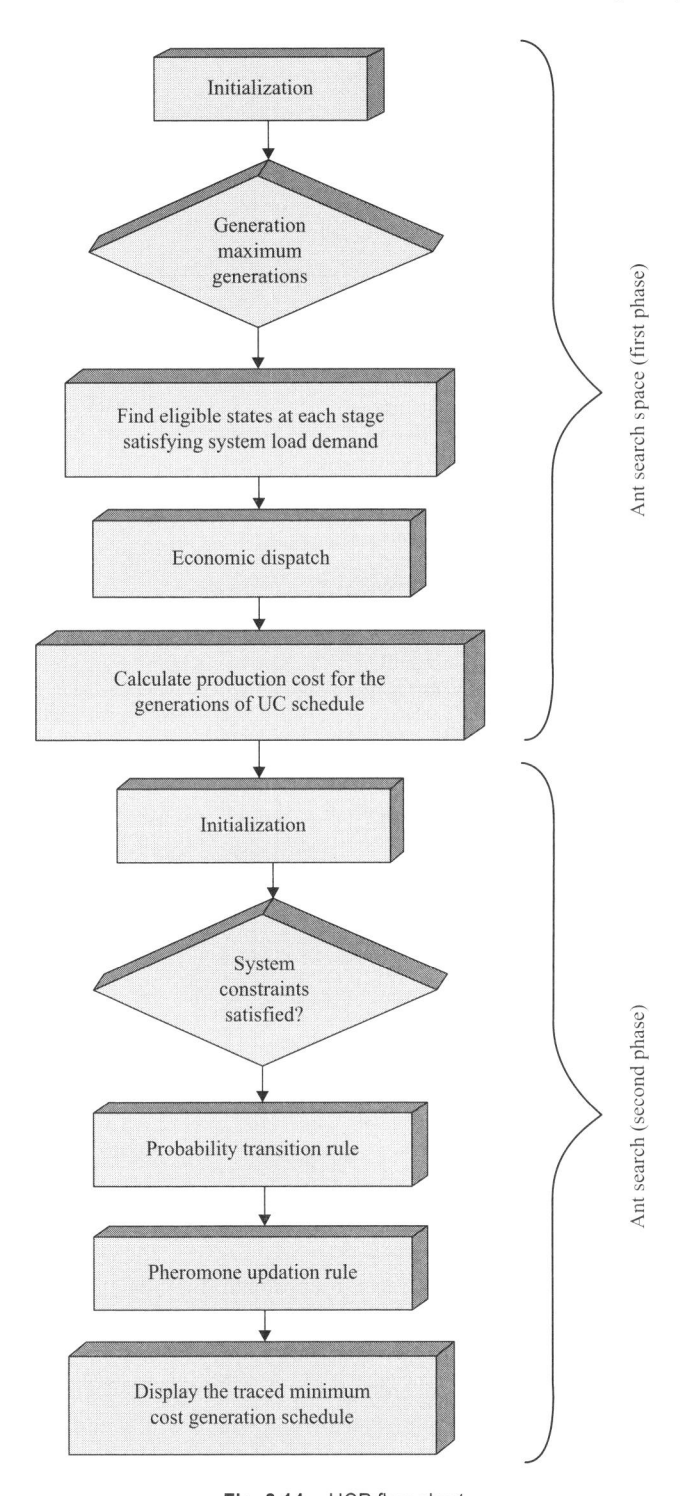

**Fig. 8.14** UCP flow chart

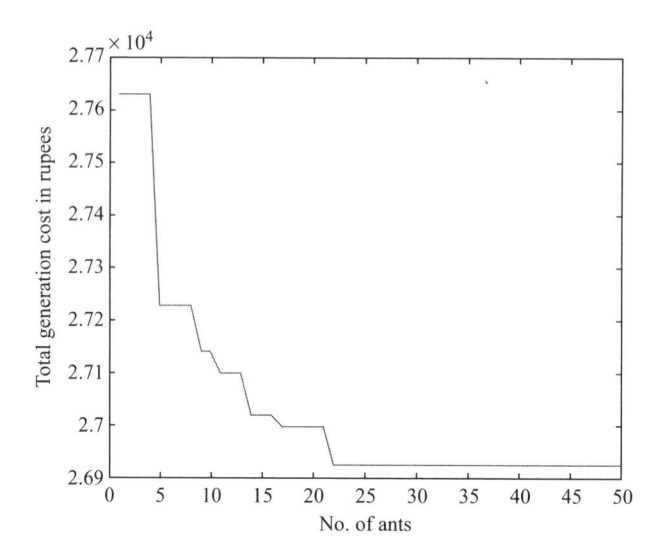

**Fig. 8.15** Convergence of TGC

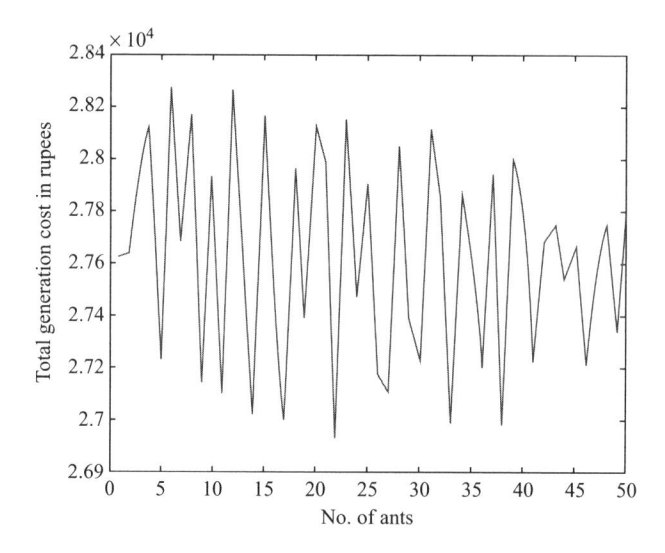

**Fig. 8.16** Total generation cost path taken by each ant

approach may be high as compared to DP approach, there is an overall reduction of generation cost because the ants can still foresee and pick out the stages coming afterwards which can belong to a low-cost path.

The DP approach is till date considered the best choice; however, the preceding results show that the ACS approach is performing successfully and helps to reduce the TGC more efficiently. The TGC for the four-unit system obtained using the DP approach is ₹27,541/day. Therefore, a saving of 2.2367 per cent is obtained using the ACS model. A comparison of the TC for the conventional DP and the ACS approach can be observed in Fig. 8.17 and Table 8.6.

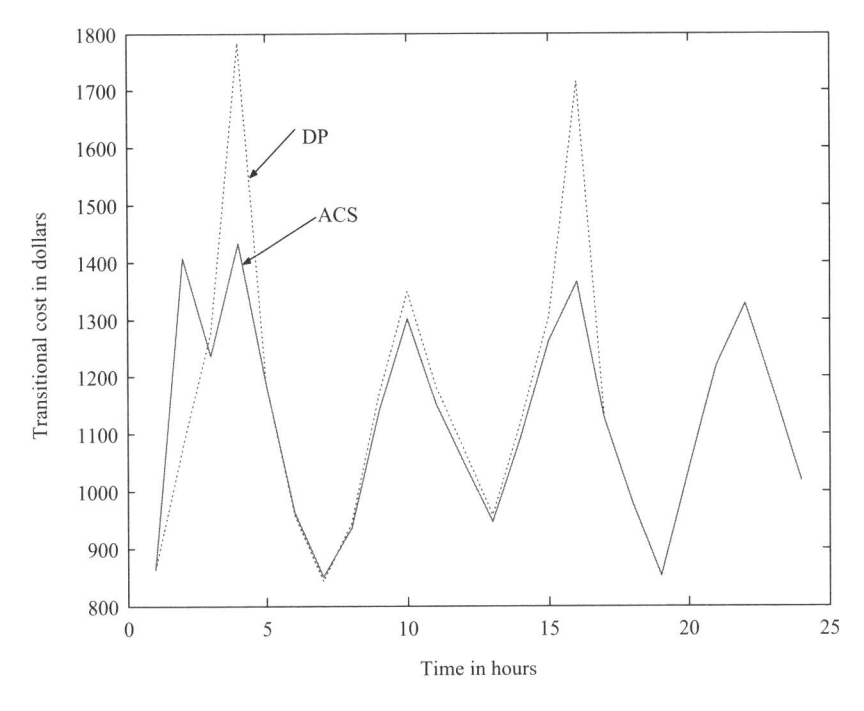

**Fig. 8.17** Comparison of generation cost

**Table 8.6** Transitional cost (TC)

| Period demand | | Dynamic programming | | Ant colony system | |
|---|---|---|---|---|---|
| (Hr) | (MW) | Unit status | TC (₹/hr) | Unit status | TC (₹/hr) |
| 1 | 410 | 0111 | 0864.30 | 0111 | 0864.30 |
| 2 | 500 | 0111 | 1,079.60 | 1111 | 1,407.50 |
| 3 | 575 | 0111 | 1,277.00 | 1111 | 1,237.40 |
| 4 | 650 | 1111 | 1,783.40 | 1111 | 1,433.40 |
| 5 | 555 | 1111 | 1,187.90 | 1111 | 1,187.90 |
| 6 | 450 | 0111 | 0957.30 | 1110 | 0963.20 |
| 7 | 400 | 0111 | 0841.70 | 1110 | 0850.40 |
| 8 | 445 | 0111 | 0945.40 | 1111 | 0935.30 |
| 9 | 535 | 0111 | 1,169.40 | 1111 | 1,139.50 |
| 10 | 600 | 0111 | 1,348.70 | 1111 | 1,300.90 |
| 11 | 540 | 0111 | 1,182.50 | 1111 | 1,151.50 |
| 12 | 495 | 0111 | 1,067.10 | 1111 | 1,046.00 |
| 13 | 450 | 0111 | 0957.30 | 1111 | 0946.10 |
| 14 | 516 | 0111 | 1,120.30 | 1111 | 1,094.60 |

*(Continued)*

**Table 8.6** (Continued)

| Period demand | | Dynamic programming | | Ant colony system | |
|---|---|---|---|---|---|
| (Hr) | (MW) | Unit status | TC (₹/hr) | Unit status | TC (₹/hr) |
| 15 | 585 | 0111 | 1,305.20 | 1111 | 1,262.60 |
| 16 | 625 | 1111 | 1,716.00 | 1111 | 1,366.00 |
| 17 | 530 | 1111 | 1,127.60 | 1111 | 1,127.60 |
| 18 | 465 | 1111 | 0978.80 | 1111 | 0978.80 |
| 19 | 405 | 1111 | 0851.20 | 1111 | 0851.20 |
| 20 | 492 | 1111 | 1,039.20 | 1111 | 1,039.20 |
| 21 | 568 | 1111 | 1,220.00 | 1111 | 1,220.00 |
| 22 | 610 | 1111 | 1,326.70 | 1111 | 1,326.70 |
| 23 | 550 | 1111 | 1,175.70 | 1111 | 1,175.70 |
| 24 | 483 | 1111 | 1,018.80 | 1111 | 1,018.80 |
| Total cost (₹/day) | | 27,541 | | 26,925 | |
| Time taken (sec) | | 5.875 | | 143.9840 | |

In this section, a new UC schedule has been presented using the ant algorithm approach. Since ant algorithms are more suitable for combinatorial optimisation problems and have the potential of finding nearly global optimum solutions, they are very well suited for solving the UCP. Along with determining the minimum cost path, other related features based on pheromone deposition, such as pheromone updating and optimal control parameters (e.g., the tuning factor and relative importance of the trail), have been discussed.

## 8.7 PARTICLE SWARM INTELLIGENT SYSTEMS

Particle swarm intelligent system (PSIS) was developed by Dr. Eberhart and Dr. Kennedy [15] as an optimisation technique known as particle swarm optimisation (PSO), inspired by the flocking of birds.

Let us try to understand the concept by means of an example. A villager used to offer food to crows in front of her house. It was really surprising to see that there used to be a loud cry of crows from different places. The cry calls seem to be the communication means for the crows, inviting the others to share the food. Immediately, many crows around respond with cry call, perhaps affirming their arrival at the food site as well.

We can try to decipher two responses from these crows positioned at different places. The first response may be that, 'I have already found a food nearby and I don't want to fly or travel much distance to your place and have it'. The second response may be that 'Another crow has called me to share the food and since the distance to fly in a particular speed or travel is less, I can reach there quickly and therefore, I won't be coming to have the food at your place'. The way the information is shared among them to find the food is amazing.

As stated before, PSO simulates the behaviour of bird flocking. Suppose the following scenario is observed: a group of birds are randomly searching food in an area. There is only one piece of food in the area being searched. All the birds do not know where the food is. However, they know how far the food happens to be in each iteration. Hence, what is the best strategy to find the food? The effective one is to follow the bird which is nearest to the food. PSO learned from the scenario can be used to solve the optimisation problems.

In PSO, each single solution is a 'bird' in the search space. We call it 'particle'. All of the particles have fitness values which are evaluated by the fitness function to be optimized, and have velocities which direct the flying of the particles. The particles fly through the problem space by following the current optimum particles.

The concept is simple, has few parameters, is easy to implement, and has found applications in many areas. This intelligent technique has been researched extensively, and scientists are exploring its potential as an optimizer applicable to many fields of engineering.

The PSIS originated as a simulation of a simplified social system. The main idea was to simulate the unpredictable choreography of a bird flock. These simulations were analysed to incorporate nearest-neighbour velocity matching, eliminate ancillary variables, and incorporate multi-dimensional search and acceleration by distance. Based on the observation of the evolution of the algorithm, it has been realized that the conceptual model is in fact an optimizer.

Particle swarm optimisation can be categorized into five parts: (i) algorithms, (ii) topology, (iii) parameters, (iv) merging or combining with other evolutionary techniques, and (v) applications. Initially, PSO was developed for real-valued problems; however, it can be extended to cover binary and discrete problems. Its most exciting industrial application has been ingredient mix optimisation by a major American corporation.

In this work, 'ingredient mix' refers to the mixture of ingredients that are used to grow production strains of microorganisms. The PSO provided an optimized ingredient mix that has over twice the fitness value found using traditional methods, at a very different location in ingredient space. The occurrence of an ingredient becoming contaminated hampered the search for a few iterations, but in the end did not give poor results; PSO is thus considered robust. Particle swarm optimisation by nature searches a much larger portion of the problem space than the traditional method. It was used for reactive power and voltage control by a Japanese electric utility; it was employed to find a control strategy with continuous and discrete control variables, resulting in a sort of hybrid binary and real-valued version of the algorithm. Voltage stability in the system was achieved using a continuous power flow technique.

Particle swarm optimisation has also proved its efficiency in evolving neural networks(i.e., training neural networks using particle swarms). Hence, like the other evolutionary computation (EC) algorithms, PSO can be applied to solve most optimisation problems as well as problems that can be converted into optimisation problems. It has been successfully applied for tracking dynamic systems and tackling multi-objective optimisation and constraint optimisation problems. The potential application areas also include classification, pattern recognition, biological system modelling, scheduling (planning), signal processing, games, robotic applications, decision-making, and simulation and identification. Examples include fuzzy controller design, job shop scheduling, real-time robot path planning, image segmentation, EEG signal simulation, speaker verification, time frequency analysis, modelling the spread of antibiotic resistance, burn diagnosing, gesture recognition, automatic target detection, etc. This natural phenomenon has thus proved successful and has paved the way for future research.

### 8.7.1 Basic PSO Method

Particle swarm optimisation is initialized by a population of random solutions and each potential solution is assigned a randomized velocity. The potential solutions, called particles, are then 'flown' through the problem space. Each particle keeps track of its coordinates in the problem space, which are associated with the best solution or fitness achieved so far. The fitness value is also stored. This value is called 'pbest'. Another 'best' value that is tracked by the global version of the PSO is the overall best value, and its location, obtained so far by any particle in the population. This value is termed 'gbest'.

Thus, at each time step, the particle changes its velocity (accelerates) and moves towards its pbest and gbest; this is the global version of PSO. When, in addition to pbest, each particle keeps track of the best solution, called nbest (neighbourhood best) or lbest (local best), attained within a local topological neighbourhood of the particles, the process is known as the local version of PSO. In addition, with respect to different applications, the discrete or binary version of PSO has come into existence. This is due to applications such as scheduling or routing problems, for which some changes have to be made in order to adapt to discrete spaces [16], [17].

### 8.7.2 Characteristic Features of PSO

The PSO method appears to adhere to the following five basic principles of swarm intelligence[17]:

(a) Proximity—the swarm must be able to perform simple space and time computations.
(b) Quality—the swarm should be able to respond to quality factors in the environment.
(c) Diverse response—the swarm should not commit its activities along excessively narrow channels.
(d) Stability—the swarm should not change its behaviour every time the environment alters.
(e) Adaptability—the swarm must be able to change its behaviour, when the computational cost is not prohibitive.

Indeed, the swarm in PSO performs space calculations for several time steps. It responds to the quality factors implied by each particle's best position and the best particle in the swarm, allocating the responses in a way that ensures diversity. Moreover, the swarm alters its behaviour (state) only when the best particle in the swarm (or in the neighbourhood, in the local variant of PSO) changes. Thus, it is both adaptive and stable [18].

### 8.7.3 Procedure of the Global Version

The procedure of the global version [19] is as follows:

(a) An array of population of particles with random positions and velocities on d dimensions in the problem space are initialized.
(b) Evaluate the fitness function in d variables for each particle.
(c) Compare particle's fitness evaluation with particle's 'pbest'. If the current value is better than 'pbest', then the current value is saved as the 'pbest' and the 'pbest' location corresponds to the current location in D–dimensional space.
(d) Compare fitness evaluation with the population's overall previous best. If the current value is better than the 'gbest', then current value is saved as 'gbest' to the current particle's array index and value.
(e) Modify the velocity and position of the particle according to the following equations:

$$v_{id}^{t+1} = v_{id}^t + c_1 rand()^t \times (p_{id}^t - x_{id}^t) + c_2 Rand()^n \times (p_{gd}^t - x_{id}^t), \quad (8.27)$$

$$x_{id}^{t+1} = x_{id}^t + v_{id}^{t+1} \quad (8.28)$$

(f) If the desired criterion is not met, go to step (b) otherwise stop the process. Usually the desired criterion may be a good fitness function or a maximum number of iterations.

Suppose that the search space is D-dimensional, then the $i$-th particle of the swarm can be represented by a D-dimensional vector, $X_{id} = (x_{i1}, x_{i2}, ..... x_{iD})^T$ The *velocity* (position change) of this particle, can be represented by another D-dimensional vector $V_{id} = (v_{i1}, v_{i2}, ..... v_{iD})^T$. The best previously visited position of the $i$-th particle is denoted as $P_{id} = (p_{i1}, p_{i2}, ......, p_{iD})^T$. Defining $g$ as the index of the best particle in the swarm (i.e., the $g^{th}$ particle is the best), and let the superscripts denote the iteration number, then the swarm is manipulated according to the two Eqs (Eqs 8.27 and 8.28), where $d = 1, 2, ..., D$; $i = 1, 2...N$, and $N$ is the size of the swarm; $c$ is a positive constant, called acceleration constant; $rand()$ and $Rand()$ are random numbers, uniformly distributed in [0, 1]; and $t$ determines the iteration number. The previous version with Eqs (8.27 and 8.28) is the basic version of PSO.

However, the basic version has no mechanism to control the velocity of the particle, which compelled to impose a maximum value $V_{max}$ in the positive direction and $-V_{max}$ in the negative direction. This can be explained in Eqs (8.29 and 8.30).

$$\text{if } v_{id} > V_{max}, \text{ then } v_{id} = V_{max} \tag{8.29}$$

$$\text{if } v_{id} < -V_{max}, \text{ then } v_{id} = -V_{max} \tag{8.30}$$

This parameter proved to be very critical because large values could result in particles moving away from good solutions, whereas small value results in inefficient exploration in the search space. This lack of control mechanism for the position velocity resulted in the lower performance of the PSO when compared to other EC.

In particular, PSO is able to locate the optimum area faster than the EC techniques, but fails in adjusting its velocity step size to continue the search for a finer grain. To overcome this limitation, the problem is addressed by incorporating a weight parameter for the previous velocity of the particle. Hence, the modified version of the equations is given as follows:

$$v_{id}^{t+1} = \varphi(wv_{id}^t + c_1 rand()^t \times (p_{id}^t - x_{id}^t) + c_2 Rand()^t \times (p_{gd}^t - x_{id}^t)), \tag{8.31}$$

$$x_{id}^{t+1} = x_{id}^t + v_{id}^{t+1}, \tag{8.32}$$

where $w$ is called inertia weight; $c_1$, $c_2$ are two positive constants, called cognitive and social parameter respectively; $rand()$, $Rand()$ are two random numbers independently generated; and $\varphi$ is a constriction factor, which is used alternatively to $w$ to limit velocity.

### 8.7.4 Parameters of PSO

It becomes necessary to choose the optimum value of setting the parameter for the best performance of PSO for different types of applications. Hence, the selection of the important parameters such as (1) pbest ($p_{id}$), (2) nbest ($p_{nd}$) and gbest ($p_{gd}$), (3) learning factors ($c_1$, $c_2$), (4) inertia weight ($w$), and (5) constriction factor ($\varphi$) have to be taken care of, which are discussed in this section.

#### 8.7.4.1 pbest ($p_{id}$)

'pbest' is the best position of the particle attained so far and can be considered as the particles memory and one memory slot is allotted to each particle. The best location does not necessarily always depend on the value of the fitness function. To adapt to different problems, many constraints can be applied to the definition of the best location. In certain non-linear constrained optimisation problems, the particles remember those positions in the feasible space and disregard unfeasible solutions. In some techniques, memory reset mechanism is adopted (i.e., in dynamic environments, particles 'pbest' will be reset to the current value if the environment changes).

#### 8.7.4.2 'nbest' ($p_{nd}$) and 'gbest' ($p_{gd}$)

The best position that neighbours of a particle achieved so far is the 'nbest', where 'gbest' is the extreme of 'nbest' and takes whole population as the neighbours of each particle. The neighbourhood of a particle is the social environment a particle encounters. The selection of the 'nbest' consists of two phases. In the first phase the determination of the neighbourhood come into picture and in the second phase the selection of the 'nbest' is done. Usually, certain predetermined conjunct particles are considered as neighbours.

Neighbours are defined as topological neighbours; neighbourhoods do not change during run. The number of neighbours or the size of the neighbourhood will affect the convergence speed of the algorithm. Larger the size of the neighbour more the convergence rate of the particles are observed. Premature or pre-convergence of the particles is prevented when the neighbourhood size is small. The selection of 'nbest' is usually determined by comparing fitness values among neighbours, that is, if the neighbourhood size is defined as two, for instance, particle (i) compares its fitness value with particle $(i-1)$ and particle $(i+1)$. The population size is problem-dependent and population sizes of 20–30 particles are probably most common. So far, smaller populations are optimal for PSO in terms of minimizing the total number of evaluations (i.e., population times the number of generations) to obtain a good solution. It will be difficult in the case of multi-objective optimisation environment, where multiple fitness values for each particle has to be taken care. In certain cases, the ratio of the fitness and the distance of other particles are used to determine the 'nbest'.

### 8.7.4.3 Learning Factors

The constants $c_1$ and $c_2$ are the learning factors, which represent the weighting of the stochastic acceleration terms that pull each particle towards 'pbest' and 'nbest' positions. Thus, adjustments of these constants change the amount of 'tension' in the system. Low values allow particles to roam far from target regions before being tugged back, whereas high values result in abrupt movement towards, or past, target regions. Generally $c_1$ and $c_2$ is set to 2.0, which will make the search cover all surrounding regions which is centred at the 'pbest' and 'nbest'.

### 8.7.4.4 Inertia Weight

Inertia weight $w$, has become very important for the convergence behaviour of the PSO. As already mentioned, maximum velocity $V_{max}$ has been a constraint to control the global exploration ability of a particle swarm. It has been understood larger $V_{max}$ facilitates global exploration, whereas a smaller $V_{max}$ encourages local exploitation. The concept of the inertia weight is developed to have a better-controlled exploration and exploitation. The inertia weight is initially set to a constant, but later experimental results suggested having a larger value initially, in order to promote global exploration of the search space, and gradually decrease it to get more refined solutions. Thus, an initial value of around 1.2 and a gradual decline towards 0 can be considered as a good choice for $w$. In addition randomized inertia weights are used in many reports, (i.e., the inertia weight can be set to $[0.5 + rand()/2.0]$.

### 8.7.4.5 Constriction Factor ($\phi$)

The constriction factor $\phi$ controls on the magnitude of the velocities, in a way similar to the parameter resulting in a variant of PSO, different from the one with the inertia weight [20]. Use of the constriction factor $\phi$ may be necessary to ensure convergence of PSO. The constriction factor is considered as function of the accelerating constants $c_1$ and $c_2$ as in the Eq. (8.33).

$$\varphi = \frac{2}{\left|2 - \psi - \sqrt{\psi^2 - 4\psi}\right|} \text{ where } \psi = c_1 + c_2, \ \psi > 4 \tag{8.33}$$

Here, the factor $\psi$ is set to 4.1 and thus the constant multiplier $\phi$ becomes 0.729. Even though initially it was thought that $V_{max}$ is not necessary, but from subsequent experimental results found from various research papers, $V_{max}$ can be limited and can be often set it at about 10–20 per cent of the dynamic range of the variable on each dimension and by also selecting an appropriate inertia $w$.

### 8.7.5 Comparison with Other EC Techniques

Particle swarm optimisation is an EC technique because it has the common evolutionary attributes as detailed in the following section [21], [22].

(a) During initialization, there is a population that is made up of a certain number of individuals, and each individual in the population is given a random solution initially.
(b) It has a mechanism for searching for a better solution in the problem space and producing a better new generation.
(c) The production of the new generation is based on the previous generation. Particle swarm optimisation can easily be implemented and is computationally inexpensive, since its memory and CPU speed requirements are low. Moreover, it does not require gradient information of the objective function under consideration, but only its values, and it uses only primitive mathematical operators. Particle swarm optimisation has been proved to be an efficient method for many global optimisation problems, and in some cases it does not suffer the difficulties encountered by other EC techniques.

In EC techniques, three main operators are involved: (a) recombination, (b) mutation, and (c) selection. Particle swarm optimisation does not have a direct recombination operator. However, the stochastic acceleration of a particle towards its previous best position as well as towards the best particle of the swarm (or towards the best particle in its neighbourhood in the local version) resembles the recombination procedure of EC. In PSO, information exchange takes place only between the particle's own experience and the experience of the best particle in the swarm, instead of being carried forward from 'parents' selected based on their fitness to descendants as in GAs.

Moreover, the PSOs directional position updating operation resembles the mutation of GAs, with a kind of in-built memory. This mutation-like procedure is multi-directional in PSO, like in GA, and includes control of the mutation's severity using factors such as $V_{max}$ and $\psi$.

Particle swarm optimisation is actually the only evolutionary algorithm that does not use the 'survival of the fittest' concept. It does not utilize a direct selection function. Thus, particles with lower fitness can survive during the optimisation and potentially visit any point of the search space.

## 8.7.6 Engineering Applications of PSIS and Future Research

Particle swarm optimisation is attractive due to easy implementation and very few parameters to adjust and, therefore, has been used in a wide variety of applications. Many PSO applications have already been pointed out in the previous sections. As mentioned before, it can be used in the place of the other EC techniques. Nowadays, it is also being used for training artificial neural networks; not only the network weights but also the network structure's evolution. As an example of evolving neural networks, PSO has been applied to the analysis of human tremor.

Particle swarm optimisation has become very popular and researchers are trying to apply it to various fields of engineering. However, it is necessary to know its scope in the near future. The still many unexplored areas of PSO are as follows [23]:

(a) Convergent analysis: It is still not clear how PSO converges, so thorough work has to be done in the theoretical research of swarm intelligence and chaos systems.
(b) The combination of various PSO techniques as well as other hybridized techniques with PSO dealing with complex problems has to be understood.
(c) Discrete/binary PSO: Available literature has shown the potential of EC techniques in dealing with discrete or binary variables. However, in the case of PSO, some difficulties have been encountered, which have yet to be solved.
(d) Particle swarm optimisation can be treated as an agent-based distributed computational technique; many of its computing characteristics still remain to be uncovered.

## 8.7.7 Working of PSO

The flow chart for the conventional PSO is given in Fig. 8.18.

Let us understand the working of PSO algorithm with the following example.

### Example 8.3

In this example, we discuss the basic features of PSO algorithm for optimizing a simple one-variable function. Let us consider the same function similar to the one discussed in Section 7.4.

$$\text{Min } f(x) = x \times \sin(10\pi \times x) + 1.0 \quad (8.34)$$

Subject to

$$-1 \leq x \leq 2$$

In a physical-dimensional search space, the position and velocity of individual $i$ are represented as the vectors $X_i = (x_{i1},\ldots,x_{iD})$ and $V_i = (v_{i1},\ldots,v_{iD})$, respectively, in the PSO algorithm. $D$ represents the number of variables in the function to be minimized.

Using the aforementioned particles, the velocity of individual is updated using Eqs (8.35) and (8.36).

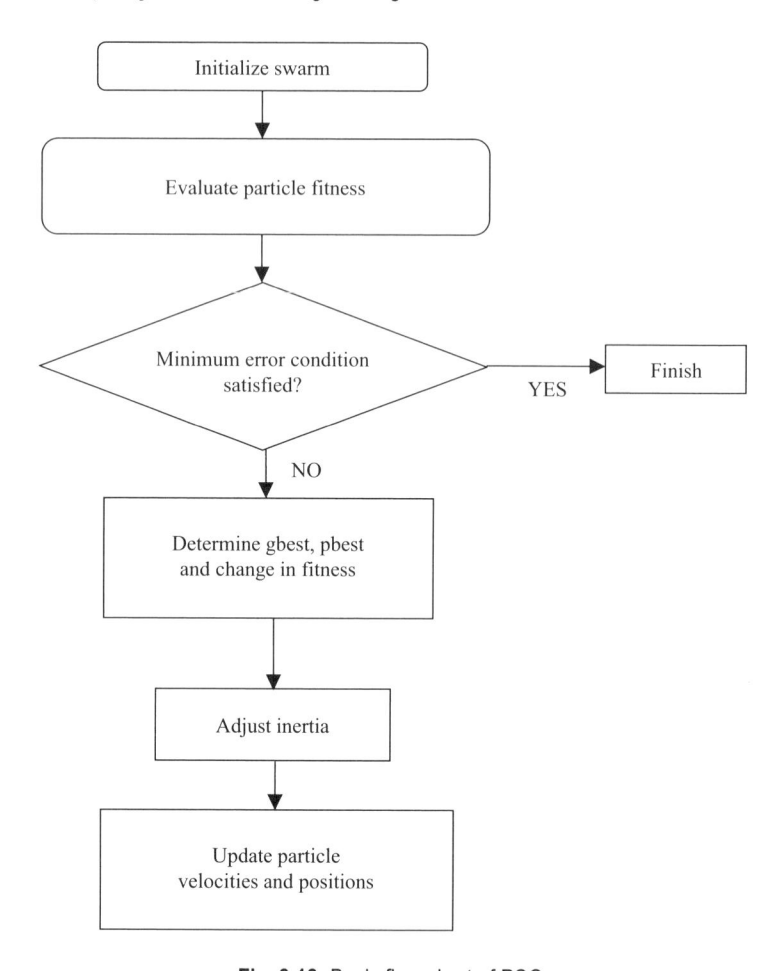

**Fig. 8.18** Basic flow chart of PSO

$$V_{ij}^{iter+1} = wV_{ij}^{iter} + c_1 rand_1 \times (Pbest_{ij}^{iter} - X_{ij}^{iter}) + c_2 rand_2 \times (Gbest_{ij}^{iter} - X_{ij}^{iter}) \tag{8.35}$$

and

$$w = ((w_{min} - w_{max})/(iter_{max} - 1)) \times (iter - 1) + w_{max} \tag{8.36}$$

Then, each individual moves from the current position to the next one by the modified velocity in using the following equation:

$$X_{ij}^{k+1} = X_{ij}^k + V_{ij}^{k+1} \tag{8.37}$$

where
$i \in \{1, 2, ...., Np\}$ and $j \in \{1, 2, ....., D\}$
$N_p$ is the number of particles.
$D$ is the number of parameters to optimize.
$V_{ij}^k$ is the velocity of individual at iteration.

$w$ is the weight parameter.
$c_1$ and $c_2$ are weight factors.
$rand_1$ and $rand_2$ are random numbers between 0 and 1.
$X_{ij}^k$ is the position of individual at iteration.
$Pbest_{ij}^k$ is the best position of individual until iteration.
$Gbest_{ij}^k$ is the best position of the group until iteration.
$iter_{max}$ is the maximum iteration number.
$iter$ is the current iteration number.

The computed output in a typical iteration is given in steps. The same can be verified with the MATLAB Program 8.3.

## Step 1: Initialization of PSO Control Parameters
*Assumption:*
Number of particles = 3
$c_1$ – acceleration const 1 (local best influence) = 2
$c_2$ – acceleration const 2 (global best influence) = 2
$w_{max}$ – Initial inertia weight = 0.9
$w_{min}$ – Final inertia weight = 0.2

*Given:*
Number of variables = 1
Upper limit of variable = [2]
Lower limit of variable = [−1]
Set Iteration, iter = 1
Set Iteration max = 100

## Step 2: Initial Generation of Population and Velocity
Generate random number for 1 variable $X_{ij}$ ($X_{i1}$) within the upper and lower limit, where '$i$' is number of particles ($N_p$) and $j$ is number of variables ($D$). (Here $i = 1\ldots5$ and $j = 1$.) Also the velocity $V_{ij}$ ($V_{i1}$) of the particles is generated randomly within the maximum and minimum limits.

Variables = $X_{i1}$
[−1.000000000000000
2.000000000000000
−0.267158235179544
1.284153871219337
0.188660719138083];

Velocity = $V_{i1}$
[3.946347013826481
4.000000000000000
1.678516053831895
−4.000000000000000
2.710274733465079];

## Step 3: Evaluation of Fitness of the Population
The formula to calculate the fitness value is given in Eq. (8.38).

$$\text{Fitness} = 1/(Obj + 1); \quad \text{when } Obj \leq 0 \quad (8.38)$$
$$= 1 + \text{abs}(Obj); \quad \text{when } Obj < 0$$

Corresponding objective and fitness value for the values $X_{i1}$ generated in step 2 is given as follows:

$Obj =$
[0.999999999999999
0.999999999999995
1.229269349800203
1.611585101150367
0.934201364304692]

$Fit =$
[1.000000000000001
1.000000000000005
0.813491363924866
0.62050710154008
1.070433033186887]

### Model Calculation for the 1st Particle (i.e., $i = 1$)
$X(1,1) = -1.0000$
$Obj = X \times \sin(10 \times pi \times X) + 1$ (using Eq. 8.34)
$\quad = -1.0000 \times \sin(10 \times pi \times -1.0000) + 1$
$\quad = 0.999999999999999$
$Fit = 1/(Obj + 1)$; (using Eq. 8.38)
$\quad = 1/(0.9999 + 1)$
$\quad = 1.0000$

## Step 4: Memorizes gbest Value
Memorize the particle which has maximum fitness value with corresponding fitness in gbest and gfit variables, respectively.
gbest = 0.188660719138083
gfit = 1.070433033186887
Pbest =
[−1.000000000000000
2.000000000000000
−0.267158235179544
1.284153871219337
0.188660719138083]

## Step 5: Set iteration, *iteration* = 1

## Step 6: Updating the Particle Velocity
The velocity of each particle is updated using Eqs (8.35) and (8.36).
Using Eq. (8.36), the weighting factor is calculated and given here:
Weighting factor for the 1st iteration $w = [0.9]$;

The velocities corresponding the weighting factor is calculated using Eq. (8.35).
$V =$

$$\begin{bmatrix} 3.896316461842095 \\ 1.346494210958751 \\ 1.978562185581112 \\ -3.535086449919751 \\ 2.814813406732314 \end{bmatrix}$$

*Note*: In case the velocities violate the maximum limit, set the velocity value to its maximum value. Similarly, if it violates the minimum limit, set the velocity value to its minimum value.

**Model Calculation**
The inertial weighting factor is calculated using Eq. (8.36).
$$w = ((0.2 - 0.9)/(100 - 1)) \times (1 - 1) + 0.9$$
$$= 0.9$$

Then, to calculate the velocity of each particle, we have to generate two random $rand_1$ and $rand_2$ values present in the equation to modify the position of one particle.

Generated first random value: $rand_1 = 0.549860201836332$, $rand_2 = 0.144954798223727$

For first particle $i = 1$ and first variable $j = 1$, using Eq. (8.35).
$$V'_{11} = (0.9 \times 3.9463) + (2 \times 0.5498) \times (-1 - (-1)) + (2 \times 0.1449)$$
$$\times (0.1887 - (-1))$$
$$= 3.8963$$

Similarly, for all the particles, the velocity is updated.

**Step 7: Modification of Particle Position**
Here the modification of position is carried out by the Eq. (8.37). The modified position is found as $X_{i1}$
Variables $= X_{i1}$

$$\begin{bmatrix} 2.000000000000000 \\ 2.000000000000000 \\ 1.711403950401569 \\ -1.000000000000000 \\ 2.000000000000000 \end{bmatrix}$$

*Note*: In case, if the variables violate the maximum limit, set that value to its maximu m value. Similarly, if it violates the minimum limit, set that value to its minimum value.

## Model Calculation:
For 1st particle and 1st variable (i.e., $i = 1$ and $j = 1$), we have

$X(1,1) = X(1,1) + V(1,1)'$
$= -1.0000 + 3.8963$
$= 2.8963$

It violates the upper limit value, hence $X(1,1)$ is set as 2.
Similarly, for all the particles, the position is modified.

## Step 8: Evaluation of Fitness of the modified particle position
Corresponding objective value and Fitness value for the values $X_{i1}$ and $X_{i2}$ are generated in step 2 and is given as follows:

$Obj =$
[0.999999999999995
0.999999999999995
0.399895266074140
0.999999999999999
0.999999999999995]

$Fit =$
[1.000000000000005
1.000000000000005
2.500654758475189
1.000000000000001
1.000000000000005]

*Note*: We can also keep both fitness function same as that of objective function.

## Step 9: Memorizes gbest and pbest value
Memorize the particle which has maximum fitness value with corresponding fitness in gbest and gfit variables, respectively.
gbest = 1.711403950401569
gfit = 2.500654758475189
pbest =
[2.000000000000000
2.000000000000000
1.711403950401569
−1.000000000000000
2.000000000000000]

**Step 10:** Memorize the best solution achieved so far. Increment the *iter* = *iter* + 1.

**Step 11:** Stop the process if the termination criterion is satisfied. Termination criteria used in this work is the specified maximum number of iteration. Otherwise, go to step 6.

## MATLAB Program 8.3

### Part A: Main program

```
%%%%%%%%%%%%%%%%%%%%%%%%%%%%%%%%%%%%%%%%%%%%%%%%%%%%%%%%%%%
% TO MINIMIZE OR MAXIMIZE A-SINGLE VARIABLE FUNCTION USING PSO
%%%%%%%%%%%%%%%%%%%%%%%%%%%%%%%%%%%%%%%%%%%%%%%%%%%%%%%%%%%

clear all;                    % Clear all previous variables

% INITIAL PSO PARAMETERS

minmax=0;                     % Minmax- (0- Minimize) (1- Maximize)
max_epoch=100;                % Maximum number of iterations (epochs) to train
ps_size=10;                   % Population size
max_vel=4;                    % Maximum particle velocity
ac1=2;                        % Acceleration const 1 (local best influence
ac2=2;                        % Acceleration const 2 (global best influence)
iw1=0.9;                      % Initial inertia weight
iw2=0.2;                      % Final inertia weight
iwe=100;     % Iteration (epoch) by which inertial weight should be at final value
D=1;                          % Number of variables in the objective function

% INITIALIZING THE DOMAIN RANGE FOR THE INPUT VARIABLE, -1 TO 2,

VRmin=ones(D,1)*-1;
VRmax=ones(D,1)*2;
VR=[VRmin,VRmax];

% INITIALIZE POPULATION OF PARTICLES AND THEIR VELOCITIES

for dimcnt=1:D
pos(1:ps_size,dimcnt)=normpos(randn([ps_size,1]),dimcnt,VR);
% Construct of random population
% positions bounded by VR

vel(1:ps_size,dimcnt)=normposv(randn([ps_size,1]),max_vel);
% Construct initial random velocities

end                           % between -max_vel,max_vel

% INITIAL PBEST POSITIONS VALUES

pbest=pos;
for j=1:ps_size               % Start particle loop
numin= '0';
for i=1:D
numin=strcat(numin,',',num2str(pos(j,i)));
end
evstrg=strcat('feval(''','obj' ,'''' ,numin(2:end),')' );
out(j)=eval(evstrg);          % Evaluate desired function with particle j
end
evstrg;
pbestval=out                  % Initially, pbest is same as pos

% ASSIGN INITIAL GBEST VALUES (GBEST AND GBESTVAL)

if minmax==1
[gbestval,idx1]=max(pbestval);   % This picks gbestval when we want to maximize the function
```

```
elseif minmax==0
[gbestval,idx1]=min(pbestval);    % This works for straight minimization
end

gbest=pbest(idx1,:)               % This is gbest position
tr(1)=gbestval                    % Save for output

% START PSO ITERATIVE PROCEDURES

cnt=0;    % Counter used for the stopping subroutine based on error convergence
for i=1:max_epoch                 % Start epoch loop (iterations)
for j=1:ps_size                   % Start particle loop
particle=j;
numin= '0' ;

% GETS NEW VELOCITIES, POSITIONS

if i<=iwe
iwt(i)=((iw2-iw1)/(iwe-1))*(i-1)+iw1;   % Get inertia weight, just a linear function
else                                     % w.r.t. Epoch parameter iwe
iwt(i)=iw2;
end
iwt;
for dimcnt=1:D
rannum1=rand(1);
rannum2=rand(1);
nc(j,1)=rannum1;
nc(j,2)=rannum2;
vel(j,dimcnt)=iwt(i)*vel(j,dimcnt) +ac1*rannum1*(pbest(j,dimcnt) -pos(j,dimcnt))...
+ac2*rannum2*(gbest(1,dimcnt) -pos(j,dimcnt));
end

% UPDATE NEW POSITION

pos(j,:)=pos(j,:)+vel(j,:);
postb=pos;
veltb(j,:)=vel(j,:);

% LIMIT VELOCITY/POSITION COMPONENTS TO MAXIMUM EXTREMES

for dimcnt=1:D
if vel(j,dimcnt)>max_vel
vel(j,dimcnt)=max_vel;
end
if vel(j,dimcnt)<-max_vel
vel(j,dimcnt)=-max_vel;
end

if pos(j,dimcnt)>=VR(dimcnt,2)
pos(j,dimcnt)=VR(dimcnt,2);
end

if pos(j,dimcnt)<=VR(dimcnt,1)
pos(j,dimcnt)=VR(dimcnt,1);
end
end

post=pos;
velt(j,:)=vel(j,:);
for dimcnt=1:D
```

```
numin=strcat(numin,',',num2str(pos(j,dimcnt)));
end
evstrg=strcat('feval(''','obj' ,'''',numin(2:end),')' );
out(j)=eval(evstrg);            % Evaluate desired function with particle j
e(j) = out(j);                  % Use to minimize or maximize function to unknown values

% UPDATE PBEST TO REFLECT SEARCHING FOR MAX OR MIN OF FUNCTION

if minmax==0
if pbestval(j)>=e(j);
pbestval(j)=e(j);
pbest(j,:)=pos(j,:);
end
elseif minmax==1
if pbestval(j)<=e(j);
pbestval(j)=e(j);
pbest(j,:)=pos(j,:);
end
end

% ASSIGN GBEST BY FINDING MINIMUM OF ALL PARTICLE PBESTS

if minmax==1
[iterbestval,idx1]=max(pbestval);
if gbestval<=iterbestval
gbestval=iterbestval;
gbest=pbest(idx1,:);
end
elseif minmax==0
[iterbestval,idx1]=min(pbestval);
% This picks gbestval when we want to minimize the
if gbestval>=iterbestval;      % function
gbestval=iterbestval;
gbest=pbest(idx1,:);
end
end
tr(i+1)=gbestval;               % Keep track of global best val
te=i;     % This will return the epoch number to calling program when done
end                             % End particle loop

disp('Best Variable (X)');
disp(gbest);
disp('Best Solution Obtained So Far');
disp(gbestval);
gbestfnplot(i,1)=gbestval;
disp('Number of Epochs');
disp(te);
end                             % Epoch loop

% DISPLAY OF RESULTS

figure(1)
plot(1:max_epoch,gbestfnplot);
xlabel('No of Iterations/Epoch');
ylabel('f(x)')
title('Convergence Plot using PSO')
```

## Part B: Sub programs (Subroutine functions)

<u>Objective Function</u>

```
function [out]=obj(x)
out=x*(sin(10*pi*x))+1;      % Function to minimised or maximised
```

<u>Mapping the initial random positions generated within variable's boundary limits</u>

```
function [out]=normpos(var1,dimcnt,var2)
X1=max(var1);
X2=min(var1);
Y1=var2(dimcnt,2);
Y2=var2(dimcnt,1);
out=((var1-X1)*(Y2-Y1)/(X2-X1))+Y1;   % Normalising using two line equation
```

<u>Mapping the initial random positions generated within velocity boundary limits</u>

```
function [out]=normposv(var1,max_vel)
X1=max(var1);
X2=min(var1);
Y2=-max_vel;
Y1=max_vel;
out=((var1-X1)*(Y2-Y1)/(X2-X1))+Y1;   % Normalising using a two line equation
```

### Observation

The program has been run for one trial and for 100 epochs. The minimum of the function is obtained and the convergence of the solution is shown in Fig. 8.19. The previous program can be modified and improved.

### Result (One-trial convergence plot)

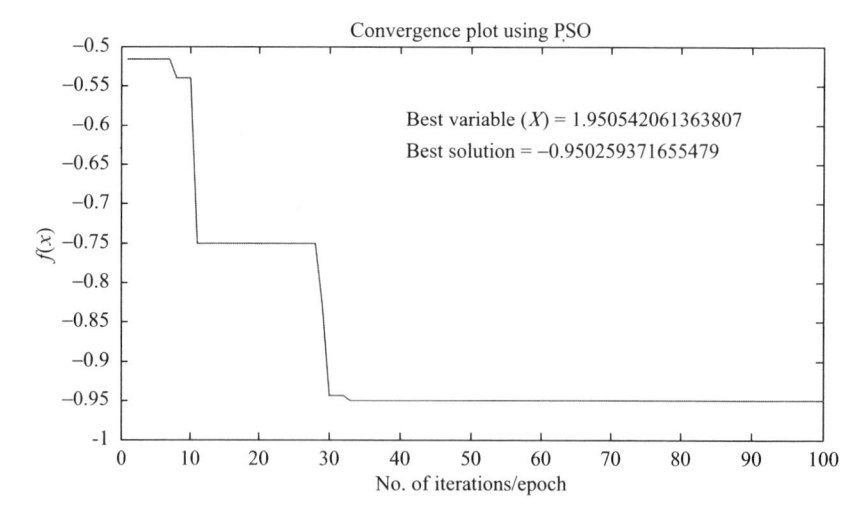

**Fig. 8.19** Convergence plot for minimization function

## 8.8 ARTIFICIAL BEE COLONY SYSTEM

The artificial bee colony (ABC) algorithm is a swarm-based meta-heuristic algorithm that was introduced for optimizing numerical problems. It has been developed by simulating the intelligent behaviour of honeybees. An important and interesting behaviour of bee colony is their foraging behaviour and, particularly how it flies around in a multi-dimensional search space and finding the food sources and back to the nest. Jonathan Swift [24] has quoted, 'We have chosen to fill our hives with honey and wax; thus furnishing mankind with the two noblest things, which are sweetness and light'.

In honey bee colonies, nectar foragers do not unload their nectar directly into cells. Instead, they transfer it to receiver (storer) bees, who then place it in cells. This is an example of *task partitioning* (Fig. 8.20). That is, the task of collecting and storing each load of nectar is divided into collecting and storing sub-tasks. For the system to function efficiently, there must be a balance in the numbers of foragers and receivers. Sometimes the functioning of foragers and receivers can be related to husband and wife managing things, at home. It can be related how efficiently they manage household activities effectively. The wife manages the things at the house and husband goes for work or vice versa or how both work and manage the activities of the home. The success in raising kids or managing the household activities depends upon how they equally balance and share things and live as one. This type of functioning in bee colony is achieved through self-organization, based on the reactions of foragers to the length of time they wait to be unloaded.

If a forager waits a long time it is more likely to make the *tremble dance*. A returning nectar forager is more likely to make the tremble dance, which recruits more nectar receivers, if she has had a long delay (search time) in being served by a receiver bee [25]. This recruits in-nest bees to act as receivers. If the delay is short a forager is more likely to make the *waggle dance*, which recruits additional workers to foraging and tells them where the flowers are. Waggle dances are mainly made in the dance floor area near the entrance. Tremble dances are made further into the nest, where there are younger bees. Foragers often transfer their nectar to several receivers. They probably do this to gain a better estimate of the average delay in being served. Each forager can only base its decision about whether to make a waggle dance, tremble dance, or no dance on its own 'local' experience and it can also be lucky or unlucky in how rapidly it is served. The communication or the interaction (information sharing) between these bees is done through their natural dancing ways.

**Fig. 8.20** Task partitioning—optimal balancing of work

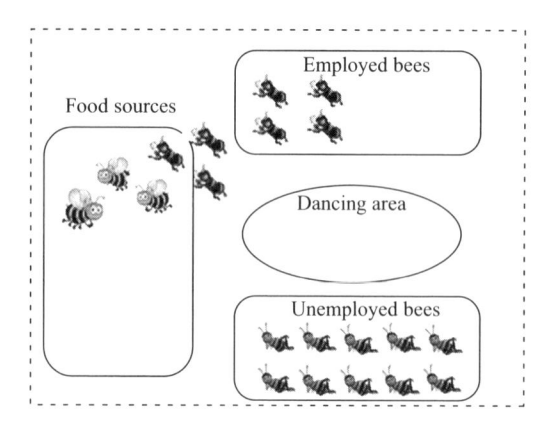

**Fig. 8.21** Behaviour of ABC

In ABC [26], the model consists of three essential components: employed bees (foragers), unemployed bees (receivers), and food sources (Fig. 8.21). It clearly shows the essential parts of the model, employed bees, unemployed bees, and food sources and dancing area. Employed bees fly around in a multi-dimensional search space and choose their food sources depending on their own experience. Once the employed bees complete their search process, it shares their food source information with unemployed bees or onlooker bees waiting in the hive by dancing in the dancing area.

Onlooker bees probabilistically choose their food sources depending on this information gained from the employed bees using Eq (8.38). If there is no improvement in the food source (fitness), then the scout bees fly and choose the food sources randomly without using experience.

$$Pro_p = \frac{fit_p}{\sum_{z=1}^{f} fit_z} \quad \text{or} \quad Pro_p = (0.9 \times fit_p / \max(fit)) + 0.1 \qquad (8.39)$$

where $fit_p$ is the fitness value of the solution $p$, which is proportional to the nectar amount of the food source in the position $p$, and $f$ is the number of food sources, which is equal to the number of employed bees, $n_e$. Now the onlookers produce a modification in the position selected by it using Eq. (8.39) and evaluate the nectar amount of the new source.

$$x'_{pq} = x_{pq} + \phi_{pq}(x_{pq} - x_{fq}) \qquad (8.40)$$

where $f \in \{1, 2\ldots n_e\}$ and $q \in \{1, 2\ldots D\}$ are randomly chosen indexes.

Although $f$ is determined randomly, it has to be different from $P$ and $D$ is the number of parameters to be optimized. $\varphi_{pq}$ is a random number generated between 0 and 1. It controls the production of neighbourhood food sources. If the nectar amount of the new source is higher than that of the previous one, the onlookers remember the new position; otherwise, it retains the old one. In other words, greedy selection method is employed as the selection operation between old and new food sources.

If a solution representing a food source is not improved by a predetermined number of trials, then that food source is abandoned and the employed bee associated with that food source becomes a scout. The number of trials for releasing a food source is equal to the value of 'limit', which is an important control parameter of ABC algorithm. The limit value usually varies from 0 to 100. If the abandoned source is $x_{pq}$, $q \in \{1, 2...D\}$, then the scout discovers a new food source $x_{pq}$ using Eq. (8.41).

$$x_{pq} = x_{q\min} + rand(0,1) \times (x_{q\max} - x_{q\min}) \qquad (8.41)$$

where $x_{q\min}$ and $x_{q\max}$ are the minimum and maximum limits of the parameter to be optimized. There are four control parameters used in ABC algorithm. They are the number of employed bees, number of unemployed or onlooker bees, the limit value, and the colony size. Thus, ABC system combines local search carried out by employed and onlooker bees, and global search managed by onlookers and scouts, attempting to balance exploration and exploitation process.

### 8.8.1 Working of ABC

Let us understand the working of ABC algorithm with the following example.

#### Example 8.4

In this example, we discuss the basic features of ABC algorithm for optimizing a simple one-variable function. Let us consider the same function similar to the one discussed in Section 7.4.

$$\text{Min } f(x) = x \cdot \sin(10\pi \cdot x) + 1.0 \qquad (8.42)$$

Subject to

$$-1 \leq x \leq 2$$

**Step 1: Initialization of ABC Control Parameters**

**Assumption:**
Number of colony = 10
Employed bees: Number of colony/2 = 5 (half the colony size selected)
Unemployed bees = Employed bees = Number of colony/2 = 5
Limit value LC = 2

**Given:**
Number of variables = 1 ($X$)
Upper limit of the variable: [2]
Lower limit of the variable: [−1]
Domain length = Upper limit−lower limit = [3]
Set Iteration = 1
Set iteration max = 100

**Step 2: Initial Generation of Population**
Generate random number for the variable $X_{pq}$ ($X_{p1}$) within the upper and lower limit. Where $p$ is number of employed bees and $q$ is number of variables. (Here $p = 1...5$ and $q = 1$.)

Variables = $X_{p1}$

[−1.000000000000000
2.000000000000000
−0.267158235179544
1.284153871219337
0.188660719138083]

## Step 3: Evaluation of Fitness of the Population
Formula to calculate Fitness value is given in Eq. (8.43)
$$\text{Fitness} = 1/(Obj + 1); \text{ when } Obj > 0 \quad (8.43)$$
$$1 + \text{abs}(Obj); \text{ when } Obj < 0$$

Corresponding objective value and fitness value for the values of $X_{p1}$ are generated in step 2 and are given here:

$Obj =$

[0.999999999999999
0.999999999999995
1.229275438930660
1.613198869656460
0.934205108171271]

$Fit =$

[0.500000000000000
0.500000000000001
0.448576242547974
0.382672750861653
0.517008250973687]

*Model calculation for the 1st value*
$X(1,1) = -1.000000000000000$
$Obj = X(1,1) \times \sin(X(1,1) \times pi \times 10) + 1$
  $= -1 \times \sin(-1 \times 10 \times pi) + 1$
  $= 0.9999$
$Fit = 1/(ObjVal + 1)$ (using Eq. 8.43)
  $= 1/(0.9999 + 1)$
  $= 0.5000$

**Step 4:** Set iteration = 1

## Employed Bee Phase

## Step 5: Modification of Position and Selection of Site by Employed Bees
Here modification of position is carried out by the Eq. (8.40).
$$x'_{p1} = x_{p1} + \phi_p (x_{p1} - x_{f1}) \quad (8.44)$$

where $f \in \{1, 2... n_e\}$ are randomly chosen indices. Although $f$ is determined randomly, it has to be different from $p$. $\Phi_p$ is a random number generated between −1 and 1.

Here, we have to generate two random values to modify the position of one employed bee.

- First a random value ($f$) is generated to choose a neighbour variable (i.e., current variable is modified with respect to neighbour variable).
- Second random value is $\Phi_p$. It controls the production of neighbourhood food sources.

**Employed bee 1:** It means $p = 1$
Generated first random = 3 (i.e., $f = 3$)

- It means, we are going to modify the variable (i.e., $X(1,1)$) with respect to the neighbour variable 3 (i.e., $X(3,1)$).

  Generated second random value: 0.081478674248819

- Nothing but $\Phi_p$ value.

  Hence using Eq. (8.41), we have the following:
  $X(1,1) = X(1,1) + 0.0815 \times (X(1,1) - X(3,1))$
  $= -1 + 0.0815 \times (-1 - (-0.2672))$
  $= -1.0597$

*Note*: Here $X(1,1)$ and $X(3,1)$ values are taken from step 2.

**Employed bee 2:** It means $p = 2$
Generated first random value: 5 (i.e., $f = 5$)

- It means, we are going to modify the variable (i.e., $X(2,1)$) with respect to the neighbour variable 5 (i.e., $X(5,1)$).

  Generated second random value: −0.470441947048740

- Nothing but $\Phi_p$ value.

  Hence using Eq. (8.44), we have the following result:
  $X(2,1) = X(2,1) + -0.4704 \times (X(2,1) - X(5,1))$
  $= 2 - 0.4704 \times (2 - (0.1887))$
  $= 1.1478$

*Note*: Here $X(2,1)$ and $X(5,1)$ values are taken from step 2.

**Employed bee 3:** It means $p = 3$
Generated first random value: 2 (i.e., $f = 2$)

- It means, we are going to modify the variable (i.e., $X(3,1)$) with respect to the neighbour variable 2 (i.e., $X(2,1)$).

  Generated second random value: −0.475290263581540

- Nothing but $\Phi_p$ value.

  Hence using Eq. (8.44), we have the following:
  $X(3,1) = X(3,1) - 0.7615 \times (X(3,1) - X(2,1))$
  $= -0.2671 - 0.4752 \times (-0.2671 - 2)$
  $= 0.8105$

*Note*: Here $X(3,1)$ and $X(2,1)$ values are taken from step 2.

**Employed bee 4:** It means $p = 4$
Generated first random value: 1 (i.e., $f = 5$)

- It means, we are going to modify the second variable (i.e., $X(4,1)$) with respect to the neighbour variable 5 (i.e., $X(5,1)$).

  Generated second random value: 0.291103749945047

- Nothing but $\Phi_p$ value.

  Hence using Eq. (8.44), we
  $X(4,1) = X(4,1) + 0.2911 \times (X(4,1) - X(5,1))$
  $= 1.2841 + 0.2911 \times (1.2841 - 0.1886)$
  $= 1.6030$

*Note*: Here $X(4,1)$ and $X(5,1)$ values are taken from step 2.

**Employed bee 5:** It means $p = 5$
Generated first random value: 3 (i.e., $f = 3$)

- It means, we are going to modify the second variable (i.e., $X(5,1)$) with respect to the neighbour variable 3 (i.e., $X(3,1)$).

  Generated second random value: 0.278633922080217

- Nothing but $\Phi_p$ value.

  Hence using Eq. (8.44) we have
  $X(5,1) = X(5,1) + 0.2786 \times (X(5,1) - X(3,1))$
  $= 0.1886 + 0.2786 \times (0.1886 - (-0.2671))$
  $= 0.3157$

*Note*: Here $X(5,1)$ and $X(3,1)$ values are taken from step 2.
Now modified Employed bee variables are given as follows:
  Variables = $X_{p1}$
  [−1.059710975431736 [Limits to be fixed to −1.000000000000000]
  1.147870021945455
  0.810486133441718
  1.603056035829310
  0.315667342138107]

*Note*: Here all modified values are within the upper and lower bound. In case, if it violates the maximum limit, set that value to its maximum value. Similarly, if it violates the minimum limit set that value to its minimum value.

Using Eqs (8.42) and (8.43), the objective and fitness values are calculated for the aforesaid values of $X_{p1}$. The final values are given later. The model calculation to calculate *Obj* and *Fit* is given in step 3 of this step-by-step illustration.

$Obj =$
  [0.999999999999999
  −0.145301101449190
  1.262196514014268
  1.153670188017295
  0.850825252529134]

$Fit =$
[0.500000000000000
1.145301101449190
0.442048245501669
0.464323648794441
0.540299522406835]

The fitness of the modified employed bee position is compared with the fitness of the old position computed in step 3. If the new variables have equal or better fitness than the old variables, it is replaced with the old one in the memory. Otherwise, the old one is retained in the memory. Hence the obtained new variables by employed bees are given as follows:

Variables $= X_{p1}$
[−1.000000000000000
1.147870021945455
−0.267158235179544 → Replaced with Old value
1.603056035829310
0.315667342138107]

*Note*: Here, the fitness of the 3rd employed bee is less than old variable (i.e., variable generated in step 2) fitness value. Hence a 3rd employed bee is replaced with old value from step 2. Corresponding fitness and objective values for the aforementioned value is as follows:

$Obj =$
[0.999999999999999
−0.145301101449190
1.229275438930660 → (New objective value for the replaced variable)
1.153670188017295
0.850825252529134]

$Fit =$
[0.500000000000000
1.145301101449190
0.448576242547974
0.464323648794441
0.540299522406835]

### Step 6: Update limit value

*Note*: Here the fitness of unemployed bee 3 has lesser value than the old fitness value calculated in step 3. Hence the 3rd unemployed bee position is replaced with old value calculated in step 3 and then increment the limit value by 1 for the corresponding unemployed bee 3.

Therefore limit value, LC = [0 0 0+1 0 0]

*Note*: When iteration grows, if the limit count (LC) is greater the 2, then new scout value is introduced using Eq. (8.41). This is nothing but generating new random variables similar to step 2 and introduce it with the already existing variables.

## Unemployed Bee Phase

### Step 7: Recruit Onlooker or unemployed bees for selected sites and evaluate fitness

An onlooker bee evaluates the nectar information taken from all employed bees and chooses a food source with a probability $Pro_p$ using Eq. (8.39) related to its fitness value. Onlookers are placed onto the food source sites by using a fitness-based selection technique (roulette-wheel selection).

$$Pro_p = (0.9 \times fit_p / \max(fit)) + 0.1 \qquad (8.45)$$

Using the previous equation, the probability for the fitness (step 5) is calculated and given here:

$Pro_p =$
[0.492909776678464
1.000000000000000
0.452499982565578
0.464874602308707
0.524577929376701

### Model Calculation

For the 1$^{st}$ value, $Fit(1) = 0.500000000000000$
Max(Fit) = 1.145301101449190
$Pro(1) = ((0.9 \times 0.5)/(1.1453)) + 0.1$
= 0.4929

### Step 8: Modification of Position by Onlookers and introduction of Scout bee

Here we are generating one random value between (0 and 1) for each of the bees. If the randomly generated value is less than the probability value calculated in the previous step, then the unemployed or onlooker bee modifies its position using the Eq. (8.40).

**Unemployed bee 1:** It means $p = 1$
Generated random value = 0.226187679752676
Here, the generated random value is less than the probability value (0.4929) calculated in step 7. Hence, the unemployed bee has to modify the position using Eq. (8.40). To modify the position again we need to generate two random values as discussed already in step 5.
Generate first random value = 3 (i.e., $f = 3$)

- It means, we are going to modify the variable $X(1,1)$ with respect to the neighbour variable 3 (i.e., $X(3,1)$).

  Generate second random value = −0.496387755055374

- Nothing but $\Phi_p$ value.

Hence, using Eq. (8.40) we get the following:
$X(1,1) = X(1,1) + (−0.4964) \times (X(1,1) − X(3,1))$
   $= −1.0597 + (−0.4964) \times (−1.0597 − 1.1478)$
   $= 0.0361$

*Note*: Here $X(1,1)$ and $X(3,1)$ are the variable values taken from step 5.

**Unemployed bee 2:** It means $p = 2$
Generated random value = 0.730248792267598
Here, the generated random value is less than the probability value (0.730248792267598) calculated in step 7. Hence, the unemployed bee has to modify the position using Eq. (8.40). To modify the position again we need to generate two random values that we discussed in step 5.
Generated first random value = 5 (i.e., $f = 5$)

- It means, we are going to modify the variable $X(2,1)$ with respect to the neighbour variable 5 (i.e., $X(5,1)$).

  Generate the second random value = −0.596387755055374

- Nothing but $\Phi_p$ value.

  Hence using Eq. (8.40) we have the following result:
  $X(2,1) = X(2,1) + (-0.5964) \times (X(2,1) - X(5,1))$
  $= 1.1478 + (-0.5964) \times (1.1479 - 0.3156)$
  $= 0.6515$

*Note*: Here $X(2,1)$ and $X(5,1)$ values are taken from step 5.

**Unemployed bee 3**
Generate random value = 0.730248792267598
 Generated random value is greater than the probability value (0.4525) calculated in step 7. Hence, the unemployed bee is same as the one calculated in step 5.

**Unemployed bee 4**
Generated random value = 0.837856765675564
 Generated random value is greater than the probability value (0.4649) calculated in step 7. Hence, the unemployed bee is same as the one calculated in step 5.

**Unemployed bee 5**
Generated random value = 0.230265467673456
 Generated random value is greater than the probability value (0.5246) calculated in step 7. Hence, the unemployed bee has to modify the position using Eq. (8.40). To modify the position again we need to generate two random values us we discussed in step 5.
 Generated first random value = 2 (i.e., $f = 2$)

- It means, we are going to modify the variable $X(5,1)$ with respect to the neighbour variable 5 (i.e., $X(2,1)$).

  Generate the second random value = −0.496387

- Nothing but $\Phi_p$ value.

  Hence using Eq. (8.40) we have the resultas follows:
  $X(5,1) = X(5,1) + (-0.4964) \times (X(5,1) - X(2,1))$
  $= 0.3157 + (-0.4964) \times (0.3157 - 1.1478)$
  $= 0.7287$

*Note*: Here $X(5,1)$ and $X(2,1)$ values are taken from step 5.

Variables = $X_{p1}$
[0.036074302500000
0.651444991510000
−0.267158235179544 → Fetch Old values
1.603056035829310 → Fetch Old values
0.728727175776198]

*Note*: Here, the generated random value is greater than the probability of 3$^{rd}$ and 4$^{th}$ employed bee's value calculated in step 7. Hence the unemployed bee fetches the old positions from step 5.

Using Eqs (8.42) and (8.43), the objective and fitness values are calculated for the aforementioned values of $X_{p1}$ and are given later. The model calculation to calculate *Obj* and *Fit* are given in step 3.

*Obj* =
[1.032676769688313
1.650773866371125
1.229275438930660
1.153670188017306
0.428448897428125]

*Fit* =
[0.491962133336791
0.377248324606801
0.448576242547974
0.464323648794439
0.700060045410422]

Now the fitness of the modified unemployed bee position is compared with the fitness of the old position computed in step 5 (Table 8.7). Now, the variables which correspond to the best fitness values of both the Employed and Unemployed Bee phase are the final bee position that proceeds for next generation.

Table 8.7 Comparing the employed bee and unemployed bee phase

| Calculated values | $X_{p1}$ | Fitness value |
|---|---|---|
| Employed bee phase | [−1.000000000000000<br>1.147870021945455<br>−0.267158235179544<br>1.603056035829310<br>0.315667342138107] | [**0.500000000000000**<br>**1.145301101449190**<br>0.448576242547974<br>0.464323648794441<br>0.540299522406835] |
| Unemployed bee phase | [0.036074302500000<br>0.651444991510000<br>−0.267158235179544<br>1.603056035829310<br>0.728727175776198] | [0.491962133336791<br>0.377248324606801<br>0.448576242547974<br>0.464323648794439<br>**0.700060045410422**] |

**Final bee variables (for next generation)** = $X_{p1}$
[−1.000000000000000 → Replaced with old values
 1.147870021945455 → Replaced with old values
 − 0.267158235179544
 1.603056035829310
 0.728727175776198]

Whenever the food sources of the bees are not improved in the unemployed bee phase, LC is incremented. Once the LC reaches a threshold value which is set initially, scout bee will be introduced as in Eq. (8.41), and the new food source (fitness) is determined. *Note*: Here the fitness of unemployed bee 1 and 2 has lesser value than the old fitness value calculated in step 5. Hence the 1$^{st}$ and 2$^{nd}$ unemployed bee position is replaced with the old values calculated in step 5. Now increment the limit value by 1 to the corresponding unemployed bee position 1 and 2.

Here the LC for this iteration is incremented as:
LC = [0 + 1 0 + 1 1 0 0]

**Step 9:** Memorize the best solution achieved so far. Increment the iteration = iteration + 1.

**Step 10:** Stop the process if the termination criterion is satisfied. Termination criteria used in this work is the specified maximum number of iteration. Otherwise, go to step 5.

## MATLAB Program 8.4

### Part A: Main program

```
%%%%%%%%%%%%%%%%%%%%%%%%%%%%%%%%%%%%%%%%%%%%%%%%%%%%%
% MINIMIZATION OF SINGLE VARIABLE FUNCTION USING ABC ALGORITHM
%%%%%%%%%%%%%%%%%%%%%%%%%%%%%%%%%%%%%%%%%%%%%%%%%%%%%

clear all              % The number of colony size (employed bees+onlooker bees)

% INITIALIZATION OF ABC CONTROL PARAMETERS

NP=50;                 % Colony size
FoodNumber=NP/2;       % The number of food sources equals the half of the colony size
limit=2;               % A food source which could not be improved through "limit" trials is
                       % abandoned by its employed bee
maxCycle=100;          % No of epochs

% PROBLEM SPECIFIC VARIABLES

objfun='obj';          % Cost function to be optimized
D=1;                   % The number of parameters of the problem to be optimized
ub=ones(1,D)*2;        % Lower bounds of the parameters.
lb=ones(1,D)*(-1);     % Upper bound of the parameters.

% CREATING THE SEARCH SPACE (FOOD SOURCES)
% GENERATION OF INITIAL POPULATION

Range = repmat((ub-lb),[FoodNumber 1]);    % Lower limit of food sources
Lower = repmat(lb, [FoodNumber 1]);        % Upper limit of food sources
```

```matlab
Foods = rand(FoodNumber,D) .* Range + Lower
% Generation of Food sources(variable populations)

ObjVal=feval(objfun,Foods);
% Objective value computed for all the food sources
Fitness=calculateFitness(ObjVal)            % Fitness computed for all the food sources

% RESET TRIAL COUNTERS

trial=zeros(1,FoodNumber);                  % Initialization of Limit Count

% THE BEST FOOD SOURCE IS MEMORIZED

BestInd=find(ObjVal==min(ObjVal));
BestInd=BestInd(end);
GlobalMin=ObjVal(BestInd);
GlobalParams=Foods(BestInd,:);
iter=1;                                     % Initialization of bee cycle
while ((iter <= maxCycle))

% EMPLOYED BEE PHASE

for  i=1:(FoodNumber)
neighbour=fix(rand*(FoodNumber))+1;
% Randomly chosen solution is used for modifying position of the ithemployed bee
while (neighbour==i)
neighbour=fix(rand*(FoodNumber))+1;
% Randomly selected position must be different from the previous position
end;
sol=Foods(i,:);
PR=(rand-0.5)*2;
sol=Foods(i)+(Foods(i)-Foods(neighbour))*PR;
% Modifying the position of the current employed bee

% GENERATED PARAMETER FIXED WITHIN LIMIT IF BOUNDARY LIMITS ARE VIOLATED

ind=find(sol<lb);
sol(ind)=lb(ind);
ind=find(sol>ub);
sol(ind)=ub(ind);
sol;

% EVALUATE NEW SOLUTION

ObjValSol=feval(objfun,sol);
FitnessSol=calculateFitness(ObjValSol);


% GREEDY SELECTION IS APPLIED BETWEEN THE CURRENT SOLUTION AND ITS MODIFIED SOLUTION

if (FitnessSol>Fitness(i))
% If the modified solution is better than the current solution
Foods(i,:)=sol;
% Replace the solution with the modified one and reset the trial counter
Fitness(i)=FitnessSol;
ObjVal(i)=ObjValSol;
trial(i)=0;
else
trial(i)=trial(i)+1;
% If the solution i(current employed bee) cannot be improved, increase its Limit Counter
end ;
end ;
```

```
prob =(0.9.*Fitness./max(Fitness))+0.1;        % Evaluating the probability of fitness

% UNEMPLOYED BEE PHASE

i=1;
t=0;
while (i<=FoodNumber)
DR=rand;
if(DR<prob(i))
t+1;
neighbour=fix(rand*(FoodNumber))+1;

% Randomly chosen solution is used for modifying position of the ith unemployed bee
while (neighbour==i)
neighbour=fix(rand*(FoodNumber))+1;
% Randomly selected position  must be different from the previous position
end ;
sol=Foods(i,:);
PR=(rand-0.5)*2;
sol= Foods(i)+(Foods(i)-Foods(neighbour))*PR;

% GENERATED PARAMETER FIXED WITHIN LIMIT IF BOUNDARY LIMITS ARE VIOLATED

ind=find(sol<lb);
sol(ind)=lb(ind);
ind=find(sol>ub);
sol(ind)=ub(ind);
sol;

% EVALUATE NEW SOLUTION

ObjValSol=feval(objfun,sol);
FitnessSol=calculateFitness(ObjValSo);

% GREEDY SELECTION IS APPLIED BETWEEN THE CURRENT SOLUTION AND ITS MODIFIED SOLUTION

if (FitnessSol>Fitness(i))

% If the modified solution is better than the current solution
Foods(i,:)=sol;

% Replace the solution with the modified one and reset the trial counter
Fitness(i)=FitnessSol;
ObjVal(i)=ObjValSol;
trial(i)=0;
else
trial(i)=trial(i)+1;

% If the solution i(current employed bee) cannot be improved, increase its Limit Counter
end ;
else
sol=Foods(i,:);
end ;
i=i+1;
end  ;
trial;
Foods;

% THE BEST FOOD SOURCE IS MEMORIZED

ind=find(ObjVal==min(ObjVal));
ind=ind(end);
```

```
if (ObjVal(ind)< GlobalMin)
GlobalMin=ObjVal(ind);
GlobalParams=Foods(ind,:);
end;

% SCOUT BEE PHASE

ind=find(trial==max(trial));
ind=ind(end);
if (trial(ind)>limit)
Bas(ind)=0;
sol=(ub-lb).*rand(1,D)+lb;
ObjValSol=feval(objfun,sol);
FitnessSol=calculateFitness(ObjValSol);
Foods(ind,:)=sol;
Fitness(ind)=FitnessSol;
ObjVal(ind)=ObjValSol;
end;
globsol(iter)=GlobalMin;
disp('Iteration Number');
disp(iter);
disp('Best Solution Obtained So Far')
disp(GlobalMin);
disp('Best Variable (X) Obtained So Far');
disp(GlobalParams);
iter=iter+1;
end                             % End of ABC

% DISPLAY OF RESULTS

figure(1)
plot(globsol);
xlabel('No of Iterations/Epoch');
ylabel('f(x)')
title('Convergence Plot using ABC')
```

## Part B: Sub programs (Subroutine functions)

Objective Function
```
function ObjVal = obj(Chrom,switc);
Dim=size(Chrom,2);              % Dimension of objective function
[Nind,Nvar] = size(Chrom);      % Compute population parameters
Chrom;
var1 = Chrom(:,1:Nvar);
for k=1:length(var1)
ObjVal(k) = var1(k)*(sin(var1(k)*pi*10))+1;
end
```

Fitness Function
```
function fFitness=calculateFitness(fObjV)
fFitness=zeros(size(fObjV));
ind=find(fObjV>=0);
fFitness(ind)=1./(fObjV(ind)+1);
ind=find(fObjV<0);
fFitness(ind)=1+abs(fObjV(ind));
```

**Result (One-trial convergence plot)**

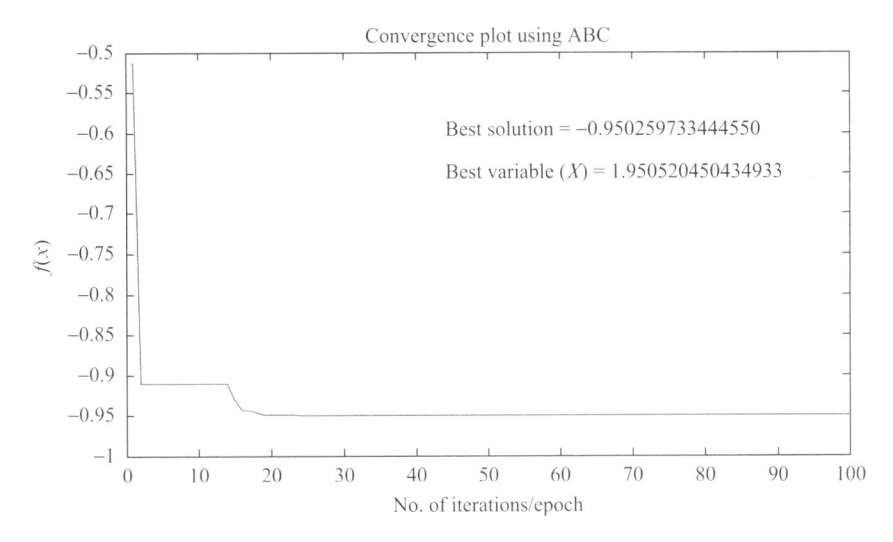

**Fig. 8.22** Convergence plot for minimization function

Best solution = −0.950259733444550
Best variable ($X$) = 1.950520450434933

**Observation**

The program has been run for one trial and for 100 epochs. The minimum of the function is obtained and the convergence of the solution is shown in Fig. 8.22. The earlier program can be modified and improved.

## 8.9 CUCKOO SEARCH ALGORITHM

In this section, the breeding behaviour of cuckoos and the characteristics of Levy flights in reaching best habitat societies are discussed. Cuckoo search algorithm (CSA) is one of the most recently defined algorithms by Xin-She Yang and Suash Deb in 2009[27]. It has been developed by simulating the intelligent breeding behaviour of cuckoos. It is a population-based search procedure that is used as an optimisation tool, in solving complex, non-linear, and non-convex optimisation problems.

The cuckoo species is a common migrative bird during summer in Europe and Asia; and during winters in Africa. They are called brood parasite, which means it lays eggs in the nests of other bird species, particularly of dunnocks, Meadow pipits, Eurasian reed warblers, Indian jungle crow, or house crow. In Indian scenario this is unending story between Indian koel (cuckoo) and the crow.

Figure 8.23 presents some of the sequence of cuckoo's habitat with crows. Cuckoo birds regularly infiltrate into the host nest of crow's nest. Then they lay eggs without the knowledge of host's, thereby the foster parents raise the cuckoo chicks. The cuckoo chicks are hatched earlier and usually throw or push away the crow's eggs, before the host's eggs get hatched, thereby robbing the host's chance for reproduction.

The bio-inspired cuckoo habitat shows the success of the parasitic behaviour of cuckoo in their continued existence. Cuckoo eggs mimic those of their most

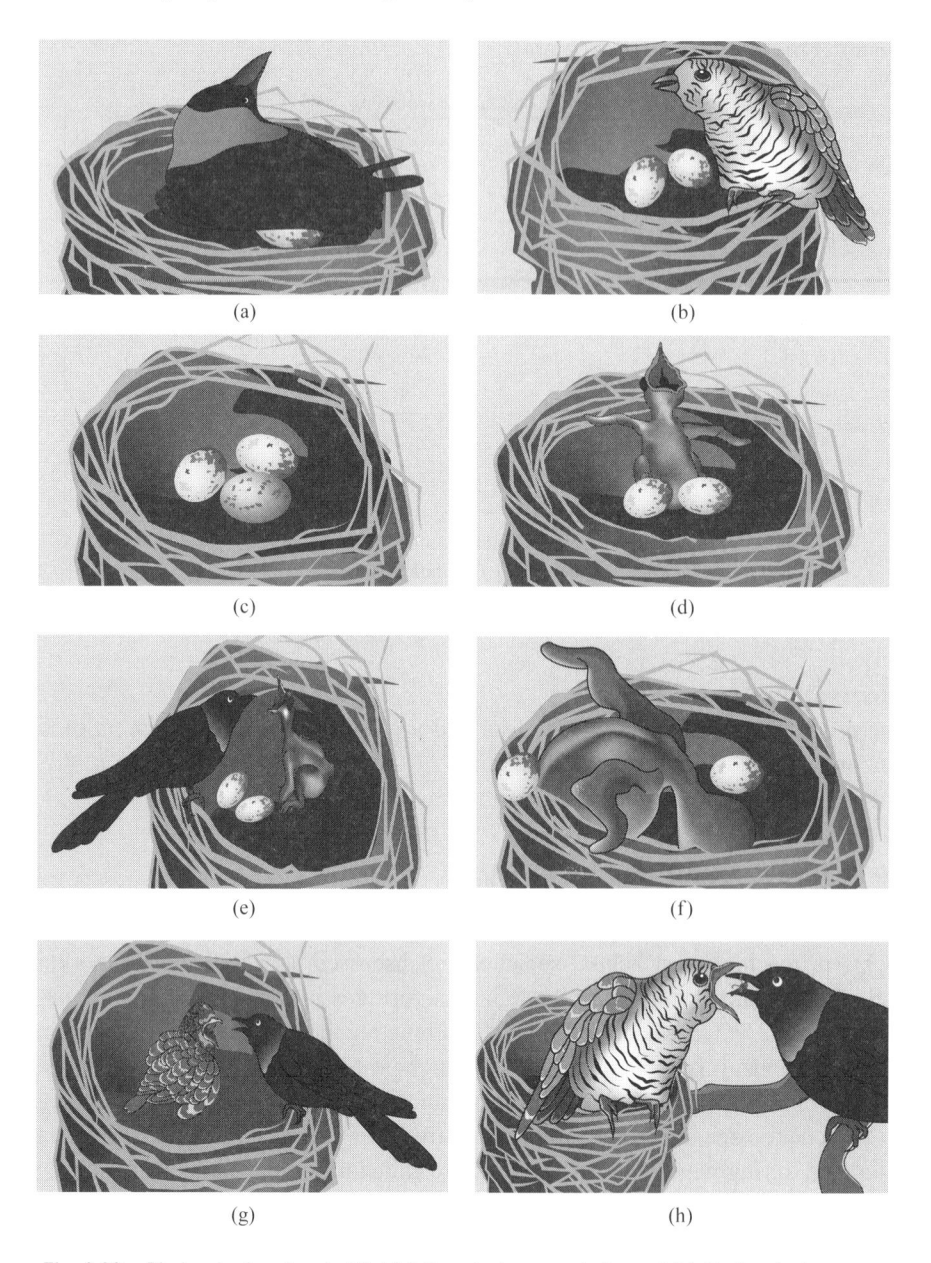

**Fig. 8.23** Bio-inspired cuckoo habitat (a) Crow laying eggs in its nest (b) Cuckoo laying egg in crow's nest (c) Cuckoo's egg mixed with crow's eggs (d) Cuckoo's egg hatches early (e) Crow feeding cuckoo's chick (f) Cuckoo's chick throws out crow's eggs (g) Cuckoo's chick fed by crow (foster parents) (h) Cuckoo's chick (larger size) fed by crow

common hosts. Female parasitic cuckoos specialize and lay eggs that closely resemble the eggs of their chosen host nest (i.e., nest is built by other species bird). Cuckoo chooses this host nest by natural selection. The shell of the cuckoo egg is usually thick. They have two distinct layers with an outer chalky layer that is believed to provide resistance to cracking when the eggs are dropped in the host nest. If the hosts notice the extra egg they will abandon the nest. The newly hatched cuckoo chick immediately ejects other eggs and chicks from the nest of its host.

A cuckoo chick will often grow to be much larger than its unsuspecting foster parent. The cuckoo egg hatches earlier than the host bird's egg, and the cuckoo chick grows faster. Alien eggs (i.e., remaining cuckoo's egg in the nest) are detected by host birds with a probability $P_a \varepsilon [0, 1]$ and these eggs are thrown away or the nest is abandoned, and a completely new nest is built, in a new location by host bird [28]. The mature cuckoo form societies and each society have its habitat region to live in. The best habitat from all of the societies will be the destination for the cuckoos in other societies. Then they immigrate towards this best habitat. Thus CSA mimics the breeding behaviour of cuckoos, where each individual searches the most suitable nest to lay an egg (compromise solution) in order to maximize the egg's survival rate and achieve the best habitat society [29].

A randomly distributed initial population of host nest is generated and then the population of solutions is subjected to repeated cycles of the search process of the cuckoo birds to lay an egg. The cuckoo randomly chooses the host nest position ($V_{pq}$) to lay an egg using Levy flights random-walk and is given in Eqs (8.46 and 8.47).

$$V_{pq}^{t+1} = V_{pq}^{t} + s_{pq} \times Levy(\lambda) \times \alpha \tag{8.46}$$

$$Levy(\lambda) = \left| \frac{\Gamma(1+\lambda) \times \sin(\frac{\pi \times \lambda}{2})}{\Gamma(\frac{(1+\lambda)}{2}) \times \lambda \times s^{\frac{(\lambda-1)}{2}}} \right|^{\frac{1}{\lambda}} \tag{8.47}$$

where $\lambda$ is a constant ($1 \leq \lambda \leq 3$) and $\alpha$ is a random number generated between $-1$ and $1$. In addition, $s > 0$ is the step size which should be related to the scales of the problem of interests. If $s$ is too large, then the new solution generated will be too far away from the old solution (or even jump out of the bounds). Then, such a move is unlikely to be accepted. If it is too small, the change is too small to be significant, and consequently such search is not efficient. Hence, a proper step size is important to maintain the search as efficiently as possible. Hence, the step size is calculated using Eq. (8.48).

$$s_{pq} = V_{pq}^{t} - V_{fq}^{t} \tag{8.48}$$

where $p, f \in \{1, 2,..., m\}$ and $q \in \{1, 2...D\}$ are randomly chosen indexes. Although $f$ is determined randomly, it has to be different from $p$. $D$ is the number of parameters to be optimized and $m$ is the total population of host nest positions.

Using Eq. (8.46) the cuckoo chooses the host nest or communal nest and an egg laid by a cuckoo is evaluated. The host bird identifies the alien egg with the probability value associated with that quality of an egg using Eq. (8.49).

$$Pro_p = (0.9 \times Fit_p/\max(Fit)) + 0.1 \qquad (8.49)$$

where $Fit_p$ is the fitness value of the solution $p$ which is proportional to the quality of an egg in the nest position $p$ and $Pro_p$ gives the survival probability rate of the cuckoo's egg. If the random generated probability $P_a \in [0, 1]$ is greater than the $Pro_p$, then the alien egg is identified by the host bird. Then the host bird, destroys the alien egg away or abandon the nest and, cuckoo find a new host's nest (in new position) using Eq. (8.50) for laying an egg. Otherwise, the egg grows up and be alive for the next generation based on the fitness function.

$$x_p = x_{p\min} + rand\,(0,1) \times (x_{p\max} - x_{p\min}) \qquad (8.50)$$

where $x_{p\min}$ and $x_{p\max}$ are the minimum and maximum limits of the parameter to be optimized.

### 8.9.1 Working of CSA

Let us understand the working of CSA algorithm [29] with the following example.

**Example 8.5**

In this example, we discuss the basic features of CSA algorithm for optimizing a simple one-variable function. Let us consider the same function similar to that one discussed in Section 7.4.

$$\text{Min } f(x) = x \times \sin(10\pi \times x) + 1.0 \qquad (8.51)$$

Subject to
$$-1 \leq x \leq 2$$

*Solution:*
**Step 1:** *Initialization of CSA parameter*
Initial population of host nest, $m = 5$
$\lambda$ (Constant value, $1 \leq \lambda \leq 3$) = 1
Maximum generation limit = 100
**Given:**
Number of variables to optimize, $D = 1$ (i.e., $X$)
Upper limit of the variable = 2
Lower limit of the variable = $-1$

**Step 2: Initial Generation of host nest population**
Generate random number for the single variables $X_{pq}$ ($X_{p1}$) within the upper and lower limit using Eq. (8.50) (i.e., $p = 1,\ldots, m$ and $q = 1,\ldots, D$). However, here $m = 5$ and $q = 1$.

Variables =  $X_{p1}$
[−1.000000000000000
2.000000000000000
−0.267158235179544
1.284153871219337
0.188660719138083]

## Step 3: Evaluation of fitness for generated nest position

Here fitness value of each host nest with an egg is calculated using Eq. (8.52).

$$Fit = 1/(F+1); \text{ when } F >= 0 \qquad (8.52)$$
$$= 1 + abs(F); \text{ when } F < 0$$

The objective value $F$ and fitness value $Fit$ for the values $X_{p1}$ are generated in step 2 is given here:

$Obj =$
[0.999999999999999
0.999999999999995
1.229275438930660
1.613198869656460
0.934205108171271]

$Fit =$
[0.500000000000000
0.500000000000001
0.448576242547974
0.382672750861653
0.517008250973687]

### Model calculation for the 1st nest position
$X(1,1) = -1.000000000000000$
$Obj = X(1,1) \times \sin(X(1,1) \times pi \times 10) + 1$
$= -1 \times \sin(-1 \times 10 \times pi) + 1$
$= 0.9999$

$Fit = 1/(ObjVal + 1) \longrightarrow$ (using Eq. 8.52)
$= 1/(0.9999 + 1)$
$= 0.5000$

## Step 4: Set generation = 1

## Step 5: Modification of nest position to lay an egg using Levy flights random-walk

Modification of nest position is carried out using the Eq. (8.46). Here, two random values are generated to modify the position of one host nest position. However, if there are more than one variable(i.e., $q > 1$), then more than one random values should be generated for which the extra one is for choosing the corresponding variable to be selected and modified. However, here in this case, always $q = 1$(one variable).

- First random value ($f$) is used to choose a neighbour's nest within the population. That is, the selected variable has to be modified with respect to the neighbour's nest.
- Second random value $\alpha$ controls the laying of an egg within available host nests through Levy flights equation.

## Model calculation for the modification 1st nest position
Host nest 1: It means $p = 1$

- Generated first random value is 5 (i.e., $f = 5$). It means the variable $X(1,1)$ is modified with respect to $X(5,1)$.
- Generated second random value $\alpha$ is 0.3383.

Also from Eqs (8.47) and (8.46), $X(1,1)$ is modified as follows:
$$X(1,1) = X(1,1) + 0.3383 \times (X(1,1) - X(5,1)) \times 0.8940$$
$$= (-1) + 0.3383 \times (-1 - (0.1887)) \times 0.8940$$
$$= -1.3595$$

*Note*: Here $X(1,1)$ and $X(5,2)$ values are taken from step 2. In addition, there will not be any change in the first value. First value ($X(1,1)$ will be same as that of step 2. Similarly, the remaining four nest positions are modified with corresponding random values generated for $q = 1$(in this case), $f$ and $\alpha$ and are given as follows:

$f = [3\ 5\ 1\ 1]$
$\alpha = [0.9632 - 0.2895 - 0.1434\ 0.1790]$

Therefore a new modified host nests using previously generated values are given here:

Variables = $X_{p1}$
[−1.3595
3.9523
−0.1492
0.9913
0.3789]

*Note*: Here the modified values, 1st and 2nd positions, are violating the limits. In this case, since it violates the maximum limit, set that value to its maximum value. Similarly, if it violates the minimum limit, set the value to its minimum value.

Hence the final modified values are as follows:

Variables = $X_{p1}$
[−1.0000 (Limits fixed)
2.0000 (Limits fixed)
−0.1492
0.9913
0.3789]

## Step 6: Evaluation of Fitness for modified nest position
Using Eqs (8.51) and (8.52), the objective function $F$ and corresponding fitness *Fit* are calculated for the aforesaid values ($X_{p1}$) and are given later. (Model calculation to calculate $F$ and *Fit* is given in step 3.)

$Obj =$
[1.0000
1.0000
0.8508
0.7324
0.7668]

$Fit =$
$\quad$ [0.5000
$\quad$ 0.5000
$\quad$ 0.5403
$\quad$ 0.5772
$\quad$ 0.5660]

### Step 7: Evaluation of Probability, $Pro_p$

Survival of the host nest in the population is determined using $Pro_p$ using Eq. (8.49). The probability for the Fitness (calculated in step 6) is calculated as follows:

$Pro_p =$
$\quad$ [0.8796
$\quad$ 0.8796
$\quad$ 0.9424
$\quad$ 1.0000
$\quad$ 0.9825]

**Model Calculation**
For the 1$^{st}$ value,
$Fit(1) = 0.5000$
$\text{Max}(Fit) = 0.5772$
$Pro(1) = ((0.9 \times 0.5000) / (0.5772)) + 0.1$
$\quad\quad\quad = 0.8796$

### Step 8: Generation of new host nest population

Here one random number $P_a$ is generated between 0 and 1 for each of the host nest. If the random generated number $P_a \in [0, 1]$ is greater than the $Pro_p$, then the alien egg is identified by the host bird. Then the host bird throws the alien egg away or abandon the nest and cuckoo finds a new host's nest (in new position), using Eq.(8.50), for laying an egg. Otherwise, the egg grows up and will be alive for the next generation based on the fitness function.

*Model calculation for 1st nest position*
**Host nest 1:** It means $p = 1$
Generated random number $P_a$ is 0.8961.
$\quad$ Here $P_a$ is greater than $Pro(1)$, since there is a chance that the host nest 1 may not survive and therefore cuckoo searches for new host nest using Eq. (8.50). To find a new nest position, generate a random number (i.e., rand (0, 1) value in the Eq. (8.50)).
$\quad$ rand $(0, 1) = [0.7309]$
$\quad$ Hence using Eq. (8.50), the $X(1,1)$ are calculated as follows:
$\quad X(1,1) = X_{min,1} + (0.7309) \times (X_{max,1} - X_{min,1})$
$\quad\quad\quad\quad = -1 + (0.7309) \times (3)$
$\quad\quad\quad\quad = 0.1926$

Here, the new nest position with an egg is added with the existing host nest positions which are not destroyed and hence the size of the host nest population is increased by one. (i.e., number of population of host nest = 5 + 1). Now a new added host nest with the available host nest population are given in the following steps with bold.

Variables = $X_{p1}$
[−1.0000
2.0000
−0.1492
0.9913
0.3789
**0.1926**]

Similarly, for the remaining host nests ($p$ = 2 to 5) random value, $P_a$ is generated which is given as

$P_a$ = [0.932359246225410   0.097540404999410
0.778498218867048   0.54688151920494]

When $p$ = 2, the generated random is greater than the probability calculated in step 7. Hence another one additional nest positions are added using Eq. 8.50 with the existing host nest positions. The generated rand (0,1) is 0.6215666. Thereby the size of the host nest is increased to 7 (i.e., number of population of host nest = 5 + 1 + 1). The new populations of the host nest with the newly added host nest variable which are represented as bold are given as follows:

Variables = $X_{p1}$
[−1.0000
2.0000
−0.1492
0.9913
0.3789
**0.1926**
**0.8647**]

*Note*: Here all modified values are within the upper and lower bound, and therefore no need for limit violation correction.

### Step 9: Evaluation of fitness for the new host nest population

Using Eqs (8.51) and (8.52), the objective function $F$ and fitness $Fit$ are calculated for the previously given values of $X_{p1}$ are given here. (Model calculation to calculate $F$ and $Fit$ is given in step 3.)

Obj =
[1.0000
1.0000
0.8508
0.7324

$$
\begin{aligned}
&\phantom{Fit=[}0.7668\\
&\phantom{Fit=[}0.9556\\
&\phantom{Fit=[}1.7741]
\end{aligned}
$$

$$
Fit = \begin{bmatrix}0.5000\\0.5000\\0.5403\\0.5772\\0.5660\\0.5113\\0.3605\end{bmatrix}
$$

## Step 10: Survival of the host nest with cuckoo's egg

Sort the fitness function *Fit* of the new population in descending order with the corresponding nest position.

$$
\begin{array}{cc}
Fit & X_{p1}\\
[0.5772 & 0.9913\\
0.5660 & 0.3789\\
0.5403 & -0.1492\\
0.5113 & 0.1926\\
0.5000 & -1.0000\\
0.5000 & 2.0000\\
0.3605 & 0.8647]
\end{array}
$$

The first highest fitness value of '*m*' number ($m = 5$) of nest positions is picked up for next generation.

$$
\begin{array}{cc}
Fit & X_{p1}\\
[0.5772 & 0.9913\\
0.5660 & 0.3789\\
0.5403 & -0.1492\\
0.5113 & 0.1926\\
0.5000 & -1.0000]
\end{array}
$$

Remaining nests with a cuckoo/alien egg (solution which is away from the optimal value) are identified by the host bird and abandoned. The first highest fitness values of *m* nest positions with cuckoo's egg are alive for next generation.

**Step 11:** Memorize the best solution achieved so far.
Increment the generation = generation + 1.

**Step 12:** Stop the process if the termination criterion is satisfied. A termination criterion is fixed as the specified maximum number of generation. Otherwise, go to step 5.

## MATLAB Program 8.5

### Part A: Main program

```
%%%%%%%%%%%%%%%%%%%%%%%%%%%%%%%%%%%%%%%%%%%%%%%%%%%%%%
% AN OPTIMISATION ALGORITHM (CSA) USING CUCKOO INTELLIGENCE
%%%%%%%%%%%%%%%%%%%%%%%%%%%%%%%%%%%%%%%%%%%%%%%%%%%%%%

clear all                          % All the previous variables are cleared

% INITIALIZATION OF CSA PARAMETER

n=150;                             % Number of nests (or different solutions)
nd=1;

% SIMPLE BOUNDS OF THE SEARCH DOMAIN

Lb=-1*ones(1,nd);                  % Lower bounds
Ub=2*ones(1,nd);                   % Upper bounds

% INITIAL GENERATION OF HOST NEST POPULATION

for i=1:n,
nest(i)=Lb+(Ub-Lb).*rand(size(Lb));   % Random initial solutions
end

% EVALUATION OF FITNESS FOR GENERATED NEST POSITION

for k=1:length(nest)
OBJ(k)=nest(k)*(sin(nest(k)*pi*10))+1;
end

fObjV=OBJ';
fFitness= zeros(size(fObjV));
ind=find(fObjV>=0);
fFitness(ind)=1./(fObjV(ind)+1);
ind=find(fObjV<0);
fFitness(ind)=1+abs(fObjV(ind));
fFitness;

% MEMORIZE THE BEST SOLUTION OBTAINED SO FAR

BestInd=find(OBJ==min(OBJ));
BestInd=BestInd(end);
GlobalMin=OBJ(BestInd)
GlobalParams=nest(BestInd)

% CUCKOO GENERATION COUNT START

for gen=1:100

% MODIFICATION OF NEST POSITION THROUGH LEVY FLIGHTS RANDOM WALK

lamda=2;
levy=(gamma(1+lamda)*sin(pi*lamda/2)/(gamma((1+lamda)/2)*lamda*2^((lamda-1)/2)))^(1/lamda);

for i=1:(n)
```

## Swarm Intelligent System

```
% RANDOMLY CHOSEN SOLUTION IS USED IN PRODUCING A MODIFIED SOLUTION

neighbour=fix(rand*(n))+1;
while(neighbour==i)
neighbour=fix(rand*(n))+1;
end;
neighbour;
sol=nest(i);
alpha=(rand-0.5)*2;
SPR(i)=alpha;
sol=nest(i)+(nest(i)-nest(neighbour))*alpha*levy;    % Modifying the position

% GENERATED PARAMETER VALUE FORCED WITHIN THE BOUNDARY LIMITS

ind=find(sol<Lb);
sol(ind)=Lb(ind);
ind=find(sol>Ub);
sol(ind)=Lb(ind);
sol;

% EVALUATION OF FITNESS FOR MODIFIED NEST POSITION

ObjValSol=sol*(sin(sol*pi*10))+1;
FitnessSol=calculateFitness(ObjValSol);
nest(i)=sol;
OBJ(i)=ObjValSol;
FIT(i)=FitnessSol;
End

% EVALUATION OF PROBABILITY

 prob=(0.9.*FIT./max(FIT))+0.1 ;

% ALIEN EGG IS IDENTIFIED BY THE HOST BIRD WITH CERTAIN PROBABILITY

for i=1:n
PRO(i)=rand;
if(PRO(i)>prob(i))

% RANDOMLY CHOSEN SOLUTION IS USED IN PRODUCING A MODIFIED SOLUTION

neighbour=fix(rand*(n))+1;
while(neighbour==i)
neighbour=fix(rand*(n))+1;
end;
sol=nest(i);
alpha=(rand-0.5)*5;
sol=nest(i)+(nest(i)-nest(neighbour))*alpha*levy;

% GENERATED PARAMETER VALUE FORCED WITHIN THE BOUNDARY LIMITS

ind=find(sol<Lb);
sol(ind)=Lb(ind);
ind=find(sol>Ub);
sol(ind)=Lb(ind);
sol;

% EVALUATION OF FITNESS FOR MODIFIED NEST POSITION

ObjValSol=sol*(sin(sol*pi*10))+1;
FitnessSol=calculateFitness(ObjValSol);
```

```
% Calling subroutine function for fitness calculation
ii=length(nest)+1;
nest(ii)=sol;
OBJ(ii)=ObjValSol;
FIT(ii)=FitnessSol;
end;
end

% THE NEST WITH BEST QUALITY OF EGG IS MEMORIZED

ind=find(OBJ==min(OBJ));
ind=ind(end);
if (OBJ(ind)<GlobalMin)
GlobalMin=OBJ(ind);
GlobalParams=nest(ind);
end;
globsol(gen)=GlobalMin;
[p q]=sort(OBJ);
x=1;
for k=1:length(FIT)
Nnest(x)=nest(q(k));
NOBJ(x)=OBJ(q(k));
NFIT(x)=FIT(q(k));
x=x+1;
end

% SURVIVAL OF THE HOST NEST WITH CUCKOO'S EGG
% I.E., REMAIN ING NEST ALIVE FOR NEXT GENERATION

nest=Nnest(1:n);
OBJ=NOBJ(1:n);
FIT=NFIT(1:n);
disp('Generation of Cuckoo Nest')
disp(gen);
disp('Best Variable(X) Obtained So Far');
disp(GlobalParams);
disp('Best solution Obtained So Far')
disp(globsol(gen));
clear Nnest OBJ FIT
end

% DISPLAY OF RESULTS

figure(1)
plot(globsol);
xlabel('Number of Cuckoo Generations'); ylabel('f(x)')
title('Convergence Plot of CSA')
```

## Part B: Sub programs (Subroutine functions)

### Fitness Function

```
function fFitness=calculateFitness(fObjV)
fFitness=zeros(size(fObjV));
ind=find(fObjV>=0);
fFitness(ind)=1./(fObjV(ind)+1);
ind=find(fObjV<0);
fFitness(ind)=1+abs(fObjV(ind));
```

## Result (One-trial convergence plot)

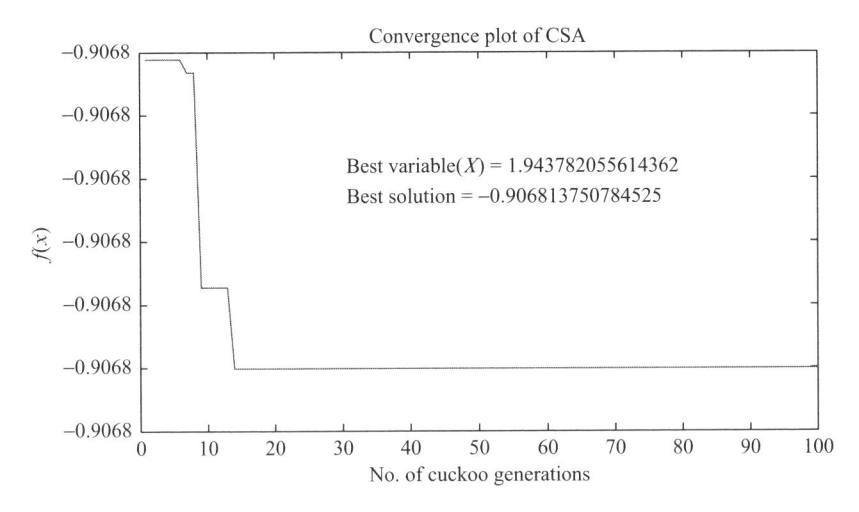

**Fig. 8.24** Convergence plot of CSA

## Observation

The program has been run for 1 trial and for 100 epochs. The minimum of the function is obtained and the convergence of the solution is shown in Fig. 8.24 The previous program can be modified and improved.

## 8.9.2 A Simple Economic Dispatch Problem

Power generators are to be operated in order to meet the load for any practical power systems. However, it is not economical to run all the generating units available at all the time. Therefore, it is vital to determine the units of a plant that should operate for a particular load in the problem of UC, which is already discussed and solved using ant algorithms.

The sub-problem of UCP is to get the load sharing among committed generators. Therefore, to determine the most efficient and economic operation of a power system, we go for economic load dispatch. The primary objective of ED problem (EDP) is to find the optimal combination of power outputs of generating units to *minimize the total fuel cost* while satisfying the load demand and other operational constraints.

### 8.9.2.1 Problem Formulation

The EDP is to find the optimal combination of power generation that minimizes the total fuel cost while at thermal power units satisfying the total demand subjected to the operating constraints of a power system with a defined interval (typically 1 h). The essential operation constraints are the power balance constraint, where the total generated power must be equals to the load demand [30]. Here, in this problem, the transmission losses and other constraints are not considered.

The mathematical formulation of the total fuel cost function is formulated as follows:

$$\text{Minimize } \sum_{i=1}^{n} F_i(P_i) \text{ (₹/hr)} \quad (8.53)$$

where, $F_i$ is the total fuel cost for the $i^{th}$ generator (in ₹/h), $P_i$ is the power of generator $i$ (in MW) and '$n$' is the number of generators in the system. Generally, the fuel cost of thermal generating unit is represented in polynomial function as shown here:

$$F_i(P_i) = a_i P_i^2 + b_i P_i + c_i \text{ (₹/hr)} \quad (8.54)$$

where $a_i$, $b_i$ and $c_i$ are cost coefficients of generator $i$.

**Subject to:**
**(a) Power Balance Constraints**
In this context, for power balance, an *equality constraint* should be attempted. The generated power should be the same as the total load demand.

$$\sum_{i=1}^{n} P_i - P_D = 0_i \quad (8.55)$$

Here, $P_D$ is the systems total demand (in MW)

**(b) Generation Operation Limits**
Inequality constraints for each generator must be also satisfied. Generation power of each generator should be laid between maximum and minimum limits. The inequality constraint for each generator is given as follows:

$$P_i^{min} \le P_i \le P_i^{max} \quad (8.56)$$

where $P_i^{min}$ and $P_i^{max}$ are the output of the minimum and maximum operation of the generating unit i.

The EDP has to be solved using CSA algorithm. Here CSA has to be implemented in finding this power variables $P_i$ where $i = 1\ldots n$, thereby minimizing the Eq. (8.53) and satisfying Eqs (8.55) and (8.56). Since there is a difficulty of randomness to satisfy Eq (8.55) by keeping all the $n$ power variables as unknown variables, one of the variable, say $P_n$ can be obtained in terms of total demand $P_D$ subtracted by the sum of the other $(n - 1)$ unknown variables. Let us try to solve a simple EDP for the aforementioned type.

**Example 8.6**

Solve a simple *ED* problem for three generating units ($n = 3$) using CSA. Minimize the fuel cost $F(P)$ such that the total power dispatch is $P_1 + P_2 + P_3 = 850$.

$$\text{Minimize } F(P) = \sum_{i=1}^{n} a_i P_i^2 + b_i P_i + c_i \quad (8.57)$$

*Generation limits*

$150 \le P_1 \le 600$

$100 \le P_2 \le 400$

$50 \le P_3 \le 200$

*Generator cost coefficient*
Unit 1: $a = 0.001562$, $b = 7.92$ and $c = 300$
Unit 2: $a = 0.00194$, $b = 7.85$ and $c = 320$
Unit 3: $a = 0.00482$, $b = 7.97$ and $c = 329$

The following MATLAB Program will solve the previous problem using CSA algorithm.

## MATLAB Program 8.6

### Part A: Main program

```
%%%%%%%%%%%%%%%%%%%%%%%%%%%%%%%%%%%%%%%%%%%%%%%%%%%%%%%%%%%%%%%
% A SIMPLE ECONOMIC DISPATCH PROBLEM USING CUCKOO INTELLIGENCE
%%%%%%%%%%%%%%%%%%%%%%%%%%%%%%%%%%%%%%%%%%%%%%%%%%%%%%%%%%%%%%%

clear all                 % All the previous variables are cleared

% GENERATION LIMITS

plims=[150 600;
       100 400;
        50 200];

% GENERATOR COST COEFFICIENTS

gencos=[0.001562  7.92  300;
        0.00194   7.85  320;
        0.00482   7.97  329];

% INITIALIZATION OF CSA PARAMETER

n=100;                    % Number of nests (or different solutions)
nd=3;                     % No of generating units (P1,P2 AND P3)

% INITIAL GENERATION OF HOST NEST POPULATION

for i=1:n,
for j=1:(nd-1)             % Random initial solutions within generation limits
nest(i,j)=plims(j,1)+(plims(j,2)-plims(j,1)).*rand;
end
nest(i,j+1)=850-sum(nest(i,:));   % Here P3=850-(P1+P2)
end

% EVALUATION OF FITNESS FOR GENERATED NEST POSITION

for k=1:length(nest)
OBJ(k)=fuelfitness(nest(k,:));    % Evaluation of fuel cost by calling subroutine function
end

% MEMORIZE THE BEST SOLUTION OBTAINED SO FAR

BestInd=find(OBJ==min(OBJ));
BestInd=BestInd(end);
```

```
GlobalMin=OBJ(BestInd);
disp(GlobalMin)
GlobalParams=nest(BestInd,:);

% CUCKOO GENERATION COUNT START

for gen=1:10000;

% MODIFICATION OF NEST POSITION THROUGH LEVY FLIGHTS RANDOM WALK

lamda=2;
levy=(gamma(1+lamda)*sin(pi*lamda/2)/(gamma((1+lamda)/2)*lamda*2^((lamda-1)/2)))^
(1/lamda);

for i=1:(n)

% RANDOMLY CHOSEN SOLUTION IS USED IN PRODUCING A MODIFIED NEST POSITION

neighbour=fix(rand*(n))+1;

% RANDOMLY SELECTED NEST POSITION MUST BE DIFFERENT FROM THE PREVIOUS POSITION

while (neighbour==i)
neighbour=fix(rand*(n))+1;       % Generating random value for selecting neighbour
end;
neighbour;
sol=nest(i,:);
alpha=(rand-0.5)*2;
SPR(i)=alpha;
sol=nest(i,:)+(nest(i,:)-nest(neighbour,:)).*alpha.*levy;    % Modifying the nest
position

% GENERATED PARAMETER VALUE IS MADE WITHIN THE GENERATOR UNIT LIMITS IF VIOLATED

for k=1:nd,

if (plims(k,1)>sol(1,k))
sol(1,k)=plims(k,1);
end
if (plims(k,2)<sol(1,k))
sol(1,k)=plims(k,2);
end
end
sol(1,3)=850-(sol(1,1)+sol(1,2));      % Here P3=850-(P1+P2)

% EVALUATION OF FITNESS FOR MODIFIED NEST POSITION

FitnessSol=fuelfitness(sol);           % Evaluating fule cost
nest(i,:)=sol;
FIT(i)=FitnessSol;
end

% EVALUATION OF PROBABILITY, PROP

prob=(0.9.*FIT./max(FIT))+0.1 ;

% ALIEN EGG IS IDENTIFIED BY THE HOST BIRD WITH THE PROBABILITY RAND

for i=1:n
PRO(i)=rand;
if(PRO(i)>prob(i))
```

```
% MODIFICATION OF NEST POSITION

% A RANDOMLY CHOSEN SOLUTION IS USED IN PRODUCING A MODIFIED NEST POSITION

neighbour=fix(rand*(n))+1;

% RANDOMLY SELECTED NEST POSITION MUST BE DIFFERENT FROM THE PREVIOUS POSITION

while (neighbour==i)
neighbour=fix(rand*(n))+1;
end;
sol=nest(i,:);
alpha=(rand-0.5)*5;
sol=nest(i,:)+(nest(i,:)-nest(neighbour,:))*alpha*levy;

% GENERATED PARAMETER VALUE IS MADE WITHIN THE GENERATOR UNIT LIMITS IF VIOLATED

for k=1:nd,
if (plims(k,1)>sol(1,k))
sol(1,k)=plims(k,1);
end
if (plims(k,2)<sol(1,k))
sol(1,k)=plims(k,2);
end
end
sol(1,3)=850-(sol(1,1)+sol(1,2));      % Here P3=850-(P1+P2)

% EVALUATION OF FITNESS FOR MODIFIED NEST POSITION

FitnessSol=fuelfitness(sol);
ii=length(nest)+1;
nest(ii,:)=sol;

FIT(ii)=FitnessSol;
OBJ(ii)=FitnessSol;
end;
end

% THE NEST WITH BEST QUALITY OF EGG IS MEMORIZED

ind=find(OBJ==min(OBJ));
ind=ind(end);
if (OBJ(ind)<GlobalMin)
GlobalMin=OBJ(ind);
GlobalParams=nest(ind,:);
end;
globsol(gen)=GlobalMin;
[p q]=sort(OBJ);
x=1;
for k=1:length(FIT)
Nnest(x,:)=nest(q(k),:);
NOBJ(x)=OBJ(q(k));
NFIT(x)=FIT(q(k));
x=x+1;
end

% SURVIVAL OF THE HOST NEST WITH CUCKOO'S EGG AND NEST ALIVE FOR NEXT GENERATION

nest=Nnest(1:n,:);
OBJ=NOBJ(1:n);
FIT=NFIT(1:n);
disp('Generation of Cuckoo Nest')
disp(gen);
disp('Best Power Dispatch Obtained So Far-P1-P2-P3- in MW');
```

```
disp(GlobalParams);
disp('Best Fuel Cost Solution Obtained So Far')
disp(globsol(gen));
end

% DISPLAY OF RESULTS

figure(1)
plot(globsol);
xlabel('Number of Cuckoo Generations'); ylabel('Fuel Cost Solution (₹)')
title('Convergence Plot of CSA')
```

### Part B: Sub programs (Subroutine functions)

Fitness Function

```
function fit=fuelfitness(dispatch)

gencos=[0.001562    7.92    300;
        0.00194     7.85    320;
        0.00482     7.97    329];

fit =(gencos(1,1).*dispatch(1,1).^2+gencos(1,2).*dispatch(1,1)+gencos(1,3))+...
     (gencos(2,1).*dispatch(1,2).^2+gencos(2,2).*dispatch(1,2)+gencos(2,3))+...
     (gencos(3,1).*dispatch(1,3).^2+gencos(3,2).*dispatch(1,3)+gencos(3,3));
```

### Result (One-trial convergence plot)

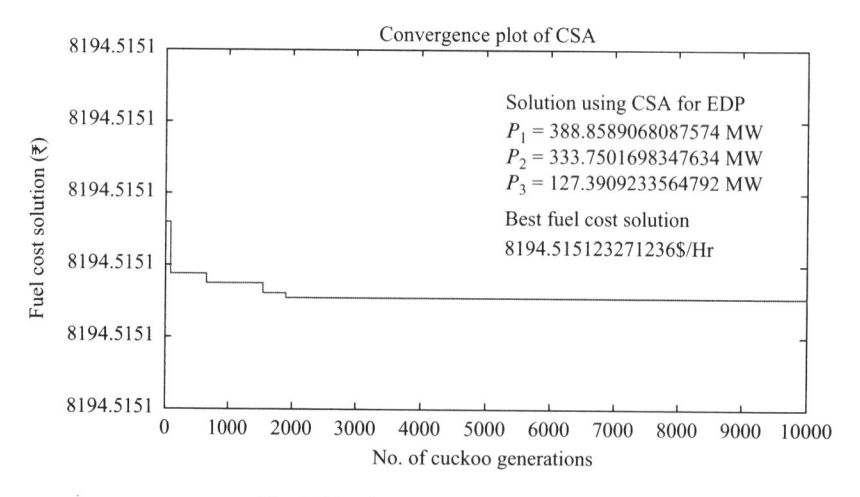

**Fig. 8.25** Convergence plot of CSA

Solution using CSA for EDP
$P_1 = 388.8589068087574$ MW
$P_2 = 333.7501698347634$ MW
$P_3 = 127.3909233564792$ MW

Best fuel cost solution
8194.515123271236$/Hr

### Observation

The program has been run for one trial and for 10,000 generations. The minimum of the cost function is obtained and the convergence of the solution is shown in Fig. 8.25. The aforecited ED program can be modified and improved.

# SUMMARY

- Swarm intelligence is the term used for the collective behaviour of a group (swarm) of animals as a single living creature, where via grouping and communication a *collective intelligence* emerges that actually results in more successful foraging for each individual in the group.
- Swarm intelligent searches the solution through exploration and exploitation.
- The two ways in which random numbers can be generated are: (i) through any physical phenomenon and (ii) through computational algorithms.
- The collective behaviour of the agents *natural* or *artificial* in a system should lead to the ultimate intelligence behaviour through proper convergence.
- An AACS is a population-based heuristic algorithm on agents that simulate the natural behaviour of ants developing mechanisms of cooperation and learning which enables the exploration of the positive feedback between agents as a search mechanism.
- Particle swarm optimisation incorporates nearest-neighbour velocity matching, eliminate ancillary variables, and incorporate multi-dimensional search and acceleration by distance.
- An important and interesting behaviour of bee colony is their foraging behaviour and, particularly how it flies around in a multi-dimensional search space and finding the food sources and back to the nest.
- Cuckoo search algorithm is developed by simulating the intelligent breeding behaviour of cuckoos through Levy flight equation.

# EXERCISES

## Part A Short-answer Questions

1. What is meant by 'swarm intelligence'? Name any two popular swarm intelligent systems.
2. What do you understand by 'optimal foraging policy'?
3. What is meant by 'exploitation and exploration in swarm intelligent systems'?
4. What is self-organization in social insects? Give a couple of day-to-day examples.
5. How are pseudo-random numbers generated?
6. What is meant by particle swarm optimisation?
7. Define an 'artificial ant colony system'.
8. List out the similarities and differences between the biological ant colony system and the artificial ant colony system.
9. What are the different modes of communication in ants?
10. What is 'pheromone trail-updating'? Why is it necessary?
11. List out the differences between the AS and ACS models.
12. What are 'elitist ants'?
13. Why is evaporation important in ant colony models?
14. Why are ant colony models more suitable in combinatorial optimisation problems?
15. What is the significance of TSP?
16. How do you regard other intelligent techniques with respect to ant colony intelligent systems?
17. Name some areas of applications (not the ones discussed in this chapter) in which the ant colony intelligent system can be successfully implemented.
18. What are the two main equations involved in PSO? Explain the variables used in these equations.
19. What do you understand by 'inertia weight'?
20. What is the local version of PSO?
21. How is PSO different from other evolutionary computational techniques?
22. What do you understand by task partitioning?
23. What are the two types of dances performed by honey bees?
24. What is an 'ABC algorithm'?
25. What is meant by 'employed and unemployed bees'?
26. What is 'brood-parasitism'?
27. What is the use of 'Levy-flight equation'?
28. Does a crow identify a cuckoo's egg? Explain what happens.

## Part B Long-answer Questions

1. Solve the TSP for the Oliver 30 city problem using both serial ant system models and compare their results. Fix the control parameters for these models and check the difference in results. The data for the given problem are given in X–Y coordinates of the graph with respect to their positions from the vertex.

| City node | 1 | 2 | 3 | 4 | 5 | 6 | 7 | 8 | 9 | 10 | 11 | 12 | 13 | 14 | 15 |
|---|---|---|---|---|---|---|---|---|---|---|---|---|---|---|---|
| X | 54 | 54 | 37 | 41 | 2 | 7 | 25 | 22 | 18 | 4 | 13 | 18 | 24 | 25 | 44 |
| Y | 67 | 62 | 84 | 94 | 99 | 64 | 62 | 60 | 54 | 50 | 40 | 40 | 42 | 38 | 35 |
| City node | 16 | 17 | 18 | 19 | 20 | 21 | 22 | 23 | 24 | 25 | 26 | 27 | 28 | 29 | 30 |
| X | 41 | 45 | 58 | 62 | 82 | 91 | 83 | 71 | 64 | 68 | 83 | 87 | 74 | 71 | 58 |
| Y | 26 | 21 | 35 | 32 | 7 | 38 | 46 | 44 | 60 | 58 | 69 | 76 | 78 | 71 | 69 |

2. A department head has four subordinates, and four tasks to be performed. The subordinates differ in efficiency and the tasks differ in their intrinsic difficulty. The estimate, of the time each man would take to perform each task, is given in the matrix here:

| Tasks | Men | | | |
|---|---|---|---|---|
|  | E | F | G | H |
| A | 18 | 26 | 17 | 11 |
| B | 13 | 28 | 14 | 26 |
| C | 38 | 19 | 18 | 15 |
| D | 19 | 26 | 24 | 10 |

How should the tasks be allocated with the help of ACS model, one to a man, so as to minimize the total man hours? (Assignment problem)

3. A marketing manager has five salesman and five districts. Considering the capabilities of the salesman and nature of districts, the marketing manager estimates that sales per month (rupees in hundreds) for each salesman in each district would be as follows:

| Job | Machine | | | | |
|---|---|---|---|---|---|
|  | A | B | C | D | E |
| 1 | 32 | 38 | 40 | 28 | 40 |
| 2 | 40 | 24 | 28 | 21 | 36 |
| 3 | 41 | 27 | 33 | 30 | 37 |
| 4 | 22 | 38 | 41 | 36 | 36 |
| 5 | 29 | 33 | 40 | 35 | 39 |

Find the assignment of salesman to districts using AS model that will result in maximum sales. (Assignment problem)

4. Determine the optimal sequence of jobs using ACS that minimizes the total elapsed time based on the following information. Processing time on machines is given in hours and passing is not allowed.(Job sequencing problem)

| Job | A | B | C | D | E | F | G |
|---|---|---|---|---|---|---|---|
| Machine M1 | 3 | 8 | 7 | 4 | 9 | 8 | 7 |
| Machine M1 | 4 | 3 | 2 | 5 | 1 | 4 | 3 |
| Machine M1 | 6 | 7 | 5 | 11 | 5 | 6 | 12 |

5. A project consists of a series of tasks labelled A, B, H, and I with the following relationships ($W < X$, $Y$ means $X$ and $Y$ cannot start until $W$ is completed; $X, Y < W$ means W cannot start until both X and Y are completed). With this notation construct the network diagram having the following constraints:

$$A < D, E; B, D < F; C < G; B, G < H; F G < I.$$

Find also the minimum time of completion of the project using ACS, when the time (in days) of completion of each task is as follows: (Critical path problem)

| Task | A | B | C | D | E | F | G | H | I |
|---|---|---|---|---|---|---|---|---|---|
| Time | 23 | 8 | 20 | 16 | 24 | 18 | 19 | 4 | 10 |

6. A computer centre has got four expert programmers. The centre needs four application programs to be developed. The head of the computer centre, after studying carefully the programs to be developed, estimates the computer time (in minutes) required by the respective experts to develop the application programs as follows: (Assignment problem)

| | | A | B | C | D |
|---|---|---|---|---|---|
| | 1 | 120 | 100 | 80 | 90 |
| Programmers | 2 | 80 | 90 | 110 | 70 |
| | 3 | 110 | 140 | 120 | 100 |
| | 4 | 90 | 90 | 80 | 90 |

Assign the programmers to the programs in such a way that the total computer time is minimum.

7. Six jobs go first on Machine A, then on Machine B, and lastly on Machine C. The order of the completion of jobs and three machines are as follows:

| Jobs | Processing time (in hours) | | |
|---|---|---|---|
| | Machine A | Machine B | Machine C |
| 1 | 8 | 3 | 8 |
| 2 | 3 | 4 | 7 |
| 3 | 7 | 5 | 6 |
| 4 | 2 | 2 | 9 |
| 5 | 5 | 1 | 10 |
| 6 | 1 | 6 | 9 |

Find the sequence of the jobs that minimizes elapsed time to complete the jobs using ant algorithm. (Job sequencing problem)

8. Solve the TSP for the Burma 14 city problem using the ant model. The data for the given problem is given in $X$-$Y$ coordinates of the graph with respect to their positions from the vertex.

| City No. | 1 | 2 | 3 | 4 | 5 | 6 | 7 | 8 | 9 | 10 | 11 | 12 | 13 | 14 |
|---|---|---|---|---|---|---|---|---|---|---|---|---|---|---|
| X | 16.47 | 16.47 | 20.09 | 22.39 | 25.23 | 22.00 | 20.47 | 17.20 | 16.30 | 14.05 | 16.53 | 21.52 | 19.41 | 20.09 |
| Y | 96.10 | 94.44 | 92.54 | 93.37 | 97.24 | 96.05 | 97.02 | 96.29 | 97.38 | 98.12 | 97.38 | 95.59 | 97.13 | 94.55 |

9. The following figure gives the mileage of the feasible links connecting nine offshore natural gas wellheads with an inshore delivery point. Because the location of well head 1 is the closest to shore, it is equipped with sufficient pumping and storage capacity to pump the output of the remaining eight wells to the delivery point. Determine the minimum pipeline network using PSO that links the well heads to the delivery point. (Shortest path problem)

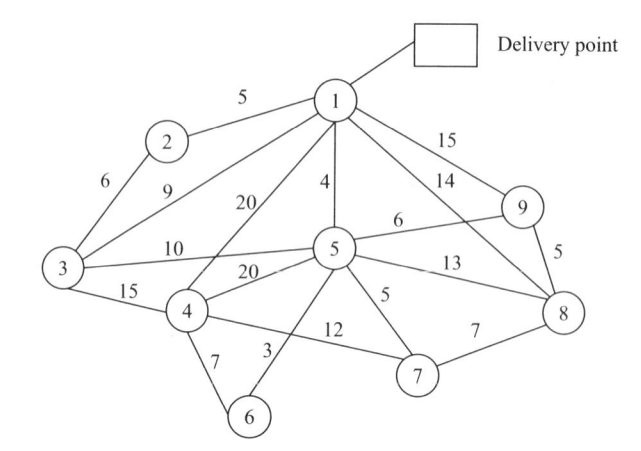

10. Find the shortest highway route using any ant model between two cities. The network in the figure given here provides the possible routes between the starting city at node 1 and the destination city at node 7. The routes pass through intermediate cities designated by nodes 2 to 6. (Shortest path problem)

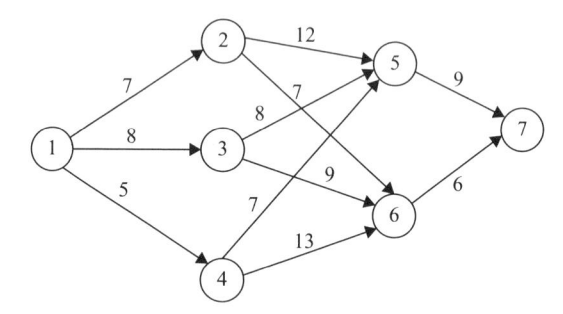

11. Solve the Oliver 30 city problem using PSO. Refer Q(1): Why is the constriction factor used in PSO?
12. Solve the unconstrained optimisation problems given here using PSO.
    (a) Maximize $F(X, Y) = X \sin(4\pi X) + Y \sin(20\pi X)$
        subject to
        $-3.0 \leq X \leq 12.1$
        $4.1 \leq Y \leq 5.8$
    (b) Minimize $F(X) = X \operatorname{Sin}^2(10\pi X) + 1$
        subject to
        $-1 \leq X \leq 2$
13. Solve a simple ED problem for three generating units ($n = 3$) using ABC. Minimize the fuel cost $F(P)$ such that the total power dispatch is $P_1 + P_2 + P_3 = 850$.

Minimize $F(P) = \sum_{i=1}^{n} a_i P_i^2 + b_i P_i + c_i$

Generation limits

$150 \leq P_1 \leq 600$
$100 \leq P_2 \leq 400$
$50 \leq P_3 \leq 200$

Generator cost coefficients
Unit 1: $a = 0.001562, b = 7.92$ and $c = 300$
Unit 2: $a = 0.00194, b = 7.85$ and $c = 320$
Unit 3: $a = 0.00482, b = 7.97$ and $c = 329$

## Part C Practical Exercises

1. To actually see ants finding their food source, go to a garden or any place where you can find an ant nest. Place a piece of sweet a little far away from the nest. Make a set-up in which the ants have room to take only any one of the two paths of different lengths to go near the sweet. Note the timings and watch these interesting creatures carefully and describe the events.

## REFERENCES

[1] Passino, Kevin M., *Biomimicry for Optimization, Control, and Automation*, Springer -verlag 2005 edition, London, UK
[2] Kroese, D. P., Taimre, T., and Botev, Z.I., *Handbook of Monte Carlo Methods*. John Wiley & Sons, New York,2011.
[3] Bonabeau, Eric, Marco Dorigo, and Guy Theraulaz, *Swarm Intelligence: From Natural to Artificial Systems*, Oxford University Press, USA, 23 September 1999.
[4] Dorigo, M. and G. Di Caro, The ant colony optimization meta-heuristic, in I.D. Corne, M. Dorigo, and F. Glover (eds.), *New Ideas in Optimization*, McGraw-Hill, London, pp. 11–32, 1999.
[5] Dorigo, M., V. Maniezzo, and A. Colorni, The ant system: Optimization by a colony of cooperating agents, *IEEE Transactions on Systems, Man, and Cybernetics,* Part B, Vol.26, Issue 2, pp. 29–41, 1996.
[6] Dorigo, M., G. Di Caro, and L.M. Gambardella, Ant algorithms for distributed discrete optimization, *Artificial Life*, Vol. 5, Issue. 3, pp. 137–72, 1999.
[7] Dorigo, M., V. Maniezzo, and A. Colorni, Positive feedback as a search strategy, *Technical Report/91-016/Politecnico di Milano/Italy*, 1991.
[8] Dorigo, Marco and Thomas Stützle, ACO algorithms for the travelling salesman problem, *Technical Problem Report/IRIDIA/1999*, Universite' Libre de Bruxelles, Belgium, 1999.
[9] Dorigo, Marco and Thomas Stützle, The ant colony optimization metaheuristic: Algorithms, applications, and advances, *Technical Report/IRIDIA/2000-36*, Universite' Libre de Bruxelles, Belgium, 2000.
[10] Hiroyasu, T., M. Miki., Y. Ono, and Y. Minami, Ant colony for continuous functions. *The Science and Engineering*, Doshisha University XX(Y), 2000.
[11] Simon, Sishaj P., N.P. Padhy, and R.S. Anand, Ant colony system: An application to the travelling salesman problem, *Proceedings of the NationalSystem Conference*, IIT Kharagpur, India, pp. 215–20, 2003.
[12] Karaboga, N., A. Kalinli, and D. Karaboga, Designing digital IIR filters using ant colony optimisation algorithm, *Engineering Applications of Artificial Intelligence*, Elsevier Publisher, Volume 17, Issue 3, pp. 301–309, 2004.
[13] Simon, S. P., N. P. Padhy, and R. S. Anand, An ant colony system approach for unit commitment problem, *International Journal of Electrical Power & Energy Systems* Elsevier Science Ltd., Vol. 28, Issue. 5, pp. 315–323, 2006.
[14] Dorigo, M. and L.M. Gambardella, Ant colony system: A cooperative learning approach to the traveling salesman, *IEEE Transactions on Evolutionary Computation*, Vol. 1, Issue 1, pp. 53–65, 1997.
[15] Eberhart, R.C. and J. Kennedy, A new optimizer using particle swarm theory, *Proceedings of the Sixth Symposium on Micro Machine and Human Science*, IEEE Service Center, Piscataway, NJ, pp. 39–43, 1995.
[16] Eberhart, R.C., P. Simpson, and R. Dobbins, *Computational Intelligence PCTools*, Academic Press, New York, 1996.
[17] Angeline, P.J., Evolutionary optimization versus particle swarm optimization:Philosophy and performance differences, in V.W. Porto, N. Saravanan, D. Waagen, and A.E. Eiben (eds.), *Evolutionary Programming*, Springer-Verlag, Berlin, Vol. VII, pp. 601–10, 1998.
[18] Parsopoulos, K.E. and M.N. Vrahatis, Recent approaches to globaloptimization problems through particle swarm optimization, *Natural Computing*, Vol. 1, Kluwer Academic Publishers, Dordrecht, pp. 235–306, 2002.
[19] Eberhart, Russell C. and Yuhui Shi, Guest editorial special issue on particleswarm optimization, *IEEE Transactions on Evolutionary Computation*, Vol.8, Issue 3, pp. 201–3, 2004.
[20] Clerc, M., The swarm and the queen: Towards a deterministic and adaptiveparticle swarm optimization, *Proceedings of the Congress on Evolutionary Computation*, Washington, DC, Piscataway, NJ, pp. 1951–7, 1999.
[21] Kennedy, J. and R.C. Eberhart, *Swarm Intelligence*. Morgan Kaufman Publishers, San Francisco, 2001. USA
[22] Padhy, N.P., *Artificial Intelligence & Intelligent Systems*, 1/e, Oxford University Press, 2005, India
[23] BijayaKetan Panigrahi, Ajith Abraham, and Swagatam Das,*Computational Intelligence in Power Engineering*, Springer Science & Business Media, 20 September 2010.
[24] Jonathan Swift, *The Battle of the Books and Other Short Pieces*, Echo Library, United Kingdom, 132 p, 1 February 2007.

[25] Karaboga, D., and B. Basturk, Artificial bee colony (ABC) optimization algorithm for solving constrained optimization problems, *Advances in Soft Computing: Foundations of Fuzzy Logic and Soft Computing*, Vol.4529/2007 of LNCS, pp. 789–798, Springer, Berlin, 2007.
[26] Karaboga, D, An idea based on honey bee swarm for numerical optimization. *Technical Report TR06*, Erciyes University, Engineering Faculty, Computer Engineering Department, 2005.
[27] Yang, X.-S., and S. Deb, Cuckoo search via Lévy flights,*World Congress on Nature & Biologically Inspired Computing (NaBIC 2009)*. IEEE Publications. pp.210–214, 2009.
[28] X.-S. Yang and S. Deb, Engineering optimisation by cuckoo search, *International Journal Mathematical Modelling and Numerical Optimisation*, Vol. 1, Issue 4, pp. 330–343, 2010.
[29] Chandrasekaran, K., and S. P. Simon Swarm, *Multi-objective scheduling problem: Hybrid approach using fuzzy assisted cuckoo search algorithm, and Evolutionary Computation 5*, pp. 1–16, Elsevier publisher, 2012.
[30] Basu, M., and A. Chowdhury, *Cuckoo search algorithm for economic dispatch, Energy*, Vol.60, pp. 99–108, Elsevier publisher, 1 October 2013.

## e-References

1. www.conservapedia.com/Henry_Ford (last accessed on 13/09/2014).

2. www.brainyquote.com/quotes/authors/g/george_halas.html (last accessed on 13/09/2014).

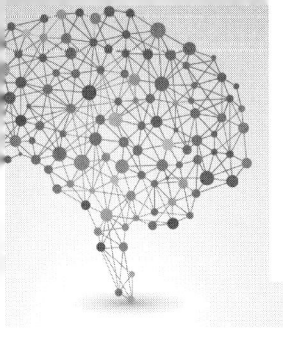

# Appendix A: Model Question Papers

## MODEL QUESTION PAPER I

Duration: 3 hours
Max. marks: 100

I. Answer the following questions: $(10 \times 2 = 20)$

1. List the strengths and weaknesses of artificial neural network.
2. How do you select the number of hidden-layer neurons according to Kolomogorov's theorem?
3. Name few fuzzy logic applications with examples.
4. Why fuzzy logic is misconceived as imprecise logic?
5. Arrange the following jumbled sequence of operations of a GA in order:
   encoding → solutions → crossover → offspring → new population → chromosomes → solutions → fitness computation → decoding → selection → evaluation → mutation
6. What do you understand by 'roulette-wheel selection'?
7. What do you understand by the term 'chunk' in rule-based expert system?
8. What is rule-based expert system? Give an example.
9. What do you understand by 'optimal foraging policy'?
10. Define 'brood parasitism'.

$(4 \times 20 = 80)$

II. a) Illustrate and explain biological neural network. [10]
   b) For the data given below, perform the learning using Hebbian rule for the input patterns. Use hardlimit as the activation function. Assume the desired response $D$ to have binary rather than bipolar values.

| $x_1$ | $x_2$ | $D$ |
|---|---|---|
| 1 | 1 | 0.3 |
| 1 | 0 | 0.3 |
| 0 | 1 | −0.3 |
| 0 | 0 | −0.3 |

Let threshold be 0.5, learning rate be 0.6, bias be −2, and weight values $w_1 = 0.3$ and $w_2 = 0.7$. [10]

**(OR)**

III. a) Explain the weight updation process in a BPNN network in both hidden layer and output layer using sigmoidal function. [10]

b) Discuss in detail the steps in solving an optimization problem with using Hopfield network. [10]

IV. a) Explain the spike propagation algorithm with relevant sketches. [10]
b) Write short notes on the following:
   i) Fuzzy-Genetic algorithm [5]
   ii) Neuro-Fuzzy system [5]

V. a) Let the term *true* of the linguistic variable 'Truth' be characterized by the membership function

$$T(v,\alpha,\beta,\gamma) \begin{cases} 0 & \text{if } v \leq \alpha \\ 2\left(\dfrac{v-\alpha}{\gamma-\alpha}\right)^2 & \text{if } \alpha \leq v \leq \beta \\ 1-2\left(\dfrac{v-\gamma}{\gamma-\alpha}\right)^2 & \text{if } \beta \leq v \leq \gamma \\ 1 & \text{if } v \geq \gamma \end{cases}$$

Draw the membership function of 'true'. Determine the membership functions of 'rather true' and 'very true'. What is the membership function of 'false' = not 'true' and what of 'very false'? [10]

b) The voltage drop across an element in a series circuit is equal to the series current multiplied by the elements impedance. The current $I$, impedance $R$, and voltage $V$ are presumed to be fuzzy variables. Membership functions for the current and the impedance are as follows:

$I = \{0/0 + 0.8/0.5 + 1/1 + 0.8/1.5 + 0/2\}$
$R = \{0.5/500 + 0.9/750 + 1/1000 + 0.9/1250 + 0.5/1500\}$

Find the arithmetic product for $V = I.\ R$ using the extension principle. [10]

VI. a) Write short notes on the following arithmetic crossover mechanisms:
   i) Linear crossover [4]
   ii) Directional crossover [4]
b) Discuss the various steps involved in a maximization problem using PSO with flow chart. [12]

**(OR)**

VII. a) Illustrate the steps involved in GA to minimize $f(x) = x \times \sin(x) + 1$ such that $x$ takes the value between $[-1\ 2]$ for one generation. The value of crossover probability and mutation probability are 0.4 and 0.02, respectively and the population size is 6. [12]

b) Two parent strings $A$ and $B$ are given as follows. Generate offspring using
   i) Order crossover
   ii) Position crossover
   
   A ⟶ 1 2 4 9 8 6 7 3 5
   B ⟶ 2 3 6 8 5 1 4 7 9 [6]

# MODEL QUESTION PAPER II

Duration: 3 hours
Max. marks: 100

I. Answer the following questions: (10 × 2 = 20)

1. How are third-generation neural networks different from second-generation neural networks?
2. What are 'synaptic vesicles'?
3. 'Behaviour of fuzzy logic is deterministic.' Justify.
4. How is fuzzy logic system different from crisp systems?
5. What do you understand by a 'schema'?
6. What do you understand by inversion, deletion, duplication, and segregation?
7. What is backward chaining and forward chaining in rule-based expert system?
8. Name some programming language used for building an expert system.
9. What is 'pheromone trail updating'? Why is it necessary?
10. What are the two types of dances performed by honey bees?

(4 × 20 = 80)

II. a) Give the algorithm of Madaline network. Discuss its potential in solving an XOR problem, which is linearly inseparable. [10]

b) A 3-input 2-output neural network has the weight values $w_{11} = 0.6$, $w_{12} = 1.1$, $w_{21} = 0.7$, $w_{22} = 0.5$, $w_{31} = 0.8$, $w_{32} = 0.2$. It is given an input of $[0.3\ 0.7\ 1.6]^T$. Find the value of the output if a binary sigmoid is used as a transfer function. Also, find the new weights if the delta learning rule is used. Assume the desired output to be $[1.5\ 1.2]^T$, $\eta = 0.6$ and $s = 0.5$. Assume a threshold of 1.5. [10]

**(OR)**

III. a) Explain the architecture and algorithm of the Hopfield neural network. [10]

b) What is a Boltzmann machine neural network? Explain its architecture with a neat sketch. Also discuss the procedure involved in updating of weights. [10]

IV. a) Explain the process of information between neurons in terms of spikes with relevant sketches. [10]

b) Write short notes on the following:
  (i) Conductance-based response model [4]
  (ii) Compartment models [3]
  (iii) Rate models [3]

V. a) Given a fuzzy set $A$ describing pressure $P$ is higher than 15 units, through the membership function, and fuzzy set $B$ describing pressure $P$ is approximately equal to 17 units. Find the membership function of the fuzzy set $C$ describing pressure $P$ is higher than 15 units and approximately equal to 17 units and also plot it.

$\mu_A(x) = 1/1 + (x - 15)^{-2}$ for $x > 15$ and $0$ for $x \leq 15$
$\mu_B(x) = 1/1 + (x - 17)^4$ [10]

b) Show that the average squared reconstruction error of the real-valued sequencer $x(0)\ldots x(M-1)$ equals the average squared reconstruction error of the transformed values:

$$\frac{1}{M}\sum_{m=0}^{M-1}[x(m)-x(m)]^2 = \frac{1}{M}\sum_{u=0}^{M-1}|X(u)-X(u)|^2$$

If $[X(0)\ldots X(M-1)] = [x(0)\ldots x(M-1)]\,U$; $U$ denotes a unitary matrix and $U^*$ denotes its complex conjugate transpose. So $U^*U = I$, where $I$ denotes the $M$-by-$M$ identity matrix. [10]

VI. a) If $4x + 2y = 8$ and $3x + 4y = 12$, find the value of $x$ and $y$ at the end of first iteration using GA when $x$ lies between $-2$ and $2$ and $y$ lies between $-1$ and $3$. [12]

b) Explain the following operator:
   i) Single-point crossover [2]
   ii) Double-point crossover [2]
   iii) Multiple-point crossover [2]
   iv) Uniform crossover [2]

**(OR)**

VII. a) Discuss the various steps involved in a minimization problem using genetic algorithm. [14]

b) For a minimization problem, find the normalised fitness values of the given chromosomes. [6]

| Chromosome, k | 1 | 2 | 3 | 4 | 5 | 6 | 7 | 8 | 9 | 10 |
|---|---|---|---|---|---|---|---|---|---|---|
| Raw fitness, $F_k$ | 12 | 45 | 33 | 27 | 50 | 24 | 42 | 36 | 15 | 30 |

## MODEL PAPER III

Duration: 3 hours
Max. marks: 100

I. Answer the following questions: $(10 \times 2 = 20)$

1. Why artificial neural network is called an intelligent network?
2. Why do we need a MAXNET in Hamming neural network?
3. What is intuitionist fuzzy logic? How is it different from fuzzy logic?
4. "Fuzzy logic is no better alternative to linear control" Justify.
5. Define 'crossover rate' and 'mutation rate'.
6. How is GA different from evolutionary programming?
7. List out the various categories of expert system application.
8. List out the major errors that occur while developing expert system.
9. Why is evaporation important in ant colony models?
10. What is meant by 'employed and unemployed bees'?

$(4 \times 20 = 80)$

II. a) Discuss on the neuronal communication that takes place at synapse with necessary diagrams. [10]

b) Solve the following AND function having binary input and binary targets using learning rule. Given training data are as follows:

| Input | | Target |
|---|---|---|
| $X_1$ | $X_2$ | 1 |
| 1 | 1 | 1 | 1 |
| 1 | 0 | 1 | 0 |
| 0 | 1 | 1 | 0 |
| 0 | 0 | 1 | 0 |

Use Learning rate (0.8), Threshold value ($\theta = 0.5$); Initial weights and Bias ($w_1 = 2$, $w_2 = 1$, $b = -3$). The output of the neuron is 1 when the sum potential is greater than $\theta$ and is $-1$ when lesser than $-\theta$, otherwise it is zero. [10]

**(OR)**

III. a) Derive the generalized expression for the feed forward back propagation neural network with a neat sketch for its weight upgrade with linear function $\varphi(I) = I$ in both hidden layer and sigmoidal function output layer. [10]
b) Discuss the architecture and algorithm of KNN network with a neat sketch. [10]

IV. a) Explain the different threshold-fire models in detail. [10]
b) Explain the spike propagation algorithm with relevant sketches. [10]

V. a) Consider a fuzzy inference system given by the following rules:
i) IF colour is Dark AND Texture is soft THEN Fruit quality is rotten.
ii) IF colour is Light OR Texture is Hard THEN fruit quality is ripe.
The membership functions for Dark, Light, Soft, Hard, Rotten, and ripe are expressed by the following fuzzy sets.

$A_{dark}(x) = 0/1 + 0.25/2 + 0.5/3 + 0.75/4 + 1/5 + 0.75/6 + 0.5/7 + 0.25/8 + 0/9$.

$A_{light}(x) = 0/6 + 0.25/7 + 0.5/8 + 0.75/9 + 1/10 + 0.75/11 + 0.5/12 + 0.25/13 + 0/14$.

$A_{soft}(x) = 0/1 + 0.25/2 + 0.5/3 + 0.75/4 + 1/5 + 0.75/6 + 0.5/7 + 0.25/8 + 0/9$

$A_{hard}(x) = 0/6 + 0.25/7 + 0.5/8 + 0.75/9 + 1/10 + 0.75/11 + 0.5/12 + 0.25/13 + 0/14$.

$A_{rotten}(x) = 0/0 + 0.25/0.25 + 0.5/1 + 0.75/1.5 + 1/2 + 0.75/2.5 + 0.5/3 + 0.25/3.5 + 0/4$

$A_{ripe}(x) = 0/3 + 0.25/3.5 + 0.5/4 + 0.75/4.5 + 1/5 + 0.75/5.5 + 0.5/6 + 0.25/6.5 + 0/7$

iii) Evaluate the antecedent membership functions for the input colour = 3 and Texture = 6 using the max–min composition operator. [10]

b) Three variables of interest in power transistors are the amount of current that can be switched, the voltage that can be switched, and the cost. The following membership functions for power transistors were developed from a hypothetical components catalogue:

Average current (in amps) = $I = \{0.4/0.8 + 0.7/0.9 + 1/1 + 0.8/1.1 + 0.6/1.2\}$
Average voltage (in volts) = $V = \{0.2/30 + 0.8/45 + 1/60 + 0.9/75 + 0.7/90\}$

Keep in mind that the Cartesian product is different from the arithmetic product. The Cartesian product expresses the relationship between $Vi$ and $Ij$, where $Vi$ and $Ij$ are individual elements in fuzzy sets $V$ and $I$.

    i) Find the fuzzy Cartesian product $P = V \times I$. Now let us define a fuzzy set for the cost $C$ in dollars of a transistor, for example, $C = \{0.4/0.5 + 1/0.6 + 0.5/0.7\}$

    ii) Using a fuzzy Cartesian product, find $T = I \times C$. what would this relation, $T$, represent physically?

    iii) Using max–min composition, find $E = P$ o $T$. What would this relation, $E$, represent physically?

    iv) Using max-product composition, find $E = P$ o $T$. What would this relation, $E$, represent physically? [10]

VI. a) Write short notes on the following mutation operator: [10]
    i) Shift left and Shift right mutation
    ii) Inversion mutation
    iii) Insertion mutation
    iv) Displacement mutation

  b) Apply both order crossover and position crossover on the two strings given as follows to generate two offsprings?
A ⟶ 1 2 4 9 8 6 7 3 5
B ⟶ 2 3 6 8 5 1 4 7 9 [10]

**(OR)**

VII. a) Illustrate the steps involves in PSO to minimize $F(b) = 4 \times b \sin^2(10\pi b) + 1$ subject to $-1 \leq X \leq 2$ for one iteration. Let the population size be 6. [10]

  b) Describe various steps in implementation of GA to any of the optimization problem. [10]

## MODEL PAPER IV

Duration: 3 hours
Max. marks: 100

I. Answer the following questions: $(10 \times 2 = 20)$

1. How is neurocomputing different from conventional computing?
2. What do you understand by 'self-training' in expert system?
3. What do understand by 'tournament selection'?
4. What do you understand by resonance in ART networks?
5. What is the local version of PSO?
6. What do you understand by a 'schema'?
7. List out the differences between the AS and ACS models.
8. What are the different modes of communication in ants?
9. What is a confidence factor in an expert system?
10. What do you understand by knowledge base editor in expert system?

$(4 \times 20 = 80)$

II. a) Give a detailed account of Adaline and Madaline networks. [8]
  b) Apply the perceptron learning algorithm to classify the following three-dimensional unipolar binary patterns before augmentation:

Class A: $\{x\} = \{(0, 0, 0), (1, 1, 1)\}$
Class B: $\{x\} = \{(0, 0, 1), (0, 1, 1)\}$

Also, draw a figure of the perceptron obtained, with its connections, weights, threshold, and transfer characteristic specified. [12]

**(OR)**

III. a) A two-input, single-output, two-layer feed forward neural network has the hidden-layer weights $w_{hp,j} = [0.3\ 0.4;\ 0.2\ 0.8;\ 0.1\ 0.6]$ and output-layer weights $w_{pq,k} = [0.22\ 0.47\ 0.36]$. The bias values are $b_j = 0.5$ and $b_k = 0.45$. Consider a sigmoidal function with $s = 0.2$ as activation function. What is the output of the neural network if the input is $I = [0.5\ 0.2]^T$? Find the change in weights using gradient descent method given target is 0.7 and $\eta = 0.6$. [12]

b) Explain the architecture and algorithm of a Hamming neural network (HNN). [8]

IV. a) Discuss in detail the real cortical neuronal spiking responses during the injection of simple DC pulses. [10]

b) Explain the significance of Intuitionistic fuzzy sets. [10]

V. a) Apply the fuzzy Modus Ponens rule to deduce rotation is quite slow given that, if the temperature is high then the rotation is slow. The temperature is very high. Let $H$ (high), $VH$ (very high), $S$ (slow), and $QS$ (quite slow) indicate the associated fuzzy sets as follows:

For $X = \{30, 40, 50, 60, 70, 80, 90, 100\}$, the set of temperature and $Y = \{10, 20, 30, 40, 50, 60\}$ the set of rotations per minute.
$H = \{(70, 1)\ (80, 1)\ (90, 0.3)\}$, $VH = \{(90, 0.9)\ (100, 1)\}$, $QS = \{(10, 1)\ (20, 0.8)\}$, and $S = \{(30, 0.8)\ (40, 1)\ (50, 0.6)\}$ [10]

b) In the field of computer networking, there is an imprecise relationship between the level of use of a network communication bandwidth and the latency experienced in peer-to-peer communications. Let $X$ be a fuzzy set of use levels (in terms of the percentage of full bandwidth used) and $Y$ be a fuzzy set of latencies with the following membership functions:

$X = \{0.2/10 + 0.5/20 + 0.8/40 + 1.0/60 + 0.6/80 + 0.1/100\}$
$Y = \{0.3/0.5 + 0.6/1 + 0.9/1.5 + 1.0/4 + 0.6/8 + 0.3/20\}$

Find the Cartesian product represented by the relation $R = X \times Y$. And, we have a second fuzzy set of bandwidth usage given by,

$Z = \{0.3/10 + 0.6/20 + 0.7/40 + 0.9/60 + 1/80 + 0.5/100\}$

Find the $S = Z_{1\times6}\ \text{o}\ R_{6\times6}$ [10]

VI. a) Apply arithmetic crossover on the four variable vectors $X_1, X_2$ given below, with different weightage combinations.

$X_1 = [\ 1.5\quad 2\quad 3\quad 5.6\ ]$
$X_2 = [\ 2\quad 1.8\quad 2.5\quad 6\ ]$ [10]

b) Explain in detail about roulette wheel selection mechanism in GA. [10]

**(OR)**

VII. a) For the following binary strings, apply 1's compliment mutation operator with a probability of 40%, $A = (10001011)$, $B = (01001101)$, $C = (10101010)$, $D = (10101100)$, $E = (01100100)$. [8]

b) Explain in detail about the cuckoo search algorithm used to solve optimization problem. [12]

# MODEL PAPER V

Duration: 3 hours
Max. marks: 100

I. Answer the following questions: $(10 \times 2 = 20)$

1. What are 'neurotransmitters'? Give examples.
2. List the jobs performed by a knowledge engineer.
3. Why is it said that genetic algorithms + data structures = evolution programs?
4. What are support vectors?
5. What is an 'ABC algorithm'?
6. How are the top-down weights and bottom-up weights set in an ART-1 network?
7. What is self-organization in social insects? Give a couple of day-to-day examples.
8. Define 'crossover rate' and 'mutation rate'.
9. What is a classifier system? Give an example.
10. What are redundant rules? Give an example.

$(4 \times 20 = 80)$

II. a) Design a feed forward network for the example training set containing linearly non-separable patterns of three classes as shown in the following figure. [12]

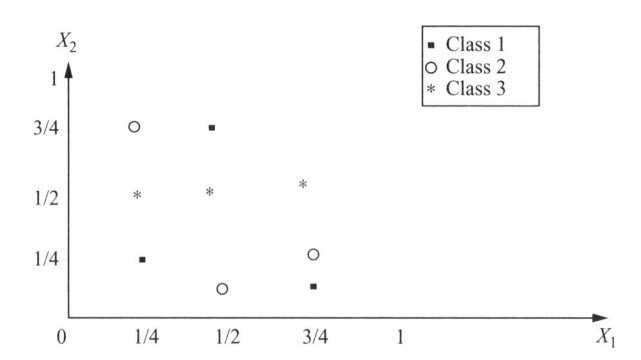

b) How BPNN can be used for character-recognition problems? Explain with necessary illustations. [8]

**(OR)**

III. a) Consider a four-input two-cluster Kohonen neural network with the weight values $w = [0.1\ 0.5;\ 0.7\ 0.3;\ 0.4\ 0.7;\ 0.2\ 0.9]$. Two input patterns $I = [1\ -1\ 1\ 1;\ 1\ -1\ -1\ -1]$ are given to the neural network. Calculate the Euclidean distance to each cluster for each input pattern. Update the weights after the first input pattern is presented and then find and check the Euclidean distances of the second input pattern. Use a learning rate of 0.6. [14]

b) Write short notes on the following: [6]
   i) Conductance-based response model
   ii) Compartment models
   iii) Rate models

IV. a) Explain the procedures involved in the weight update in SVM. [10]
b) Write short notes on *Intuitionistic Fuzzy Sets* operation. [10]

V. a) Let $R$ and $S$ be two fuzzy relations defined as follows: [10]

$$R = \begin{array}{c} \\ x_1 \\ x_2 \end{array} \begin{array}{c} y_1 \quad y_2 \quad y_3 \\ \begin{bmatrix} 0.0 & 0.2 & 0.8 \\ 0.3 & 0.6 & 1.0 \end{bmatrix} \end{array}$$

$$S = \begin{array}{c} \\ y_1 \\ y_2 \\ y_3 \end{array} \begin{array}{c} z_1 \quad z_2 \quad z_3 \\ \begin{bmatrix} 0.3 & 0.7 & 1.0 \\ 0.5 & 1.0 & 0.6 \\ 1.0 & 0.2 & 0.0 \end{bmatrix} \end{array}$$

Compute the result of $R \circ S$ using max–min composition.

b) Amplifier capacity on a normalized universe, say [0, 100] can be described linguistically by fuzzy variables like these: [10]
'Powerful' = $\{0/1 + 0.4/10 + 0.8/50 + 1/100\}$
'Weak' = $\{1/1 + 0.9/10 + 0.3/50 + 0/100\}$
Find the membership functions for the following linguistic phrases used to describe the capacity of various amplifiers:
i) Powerful and not weak
ii) Very powerful or very weak
iii) Very, very powerful and not weak

VI. a) Explain the process of pheromone update in ant colony optimization algorithm and describe the various types of pheromone update. [12]
b) Find the value of four-bitstring '$X$' = 19A5 represented in hexadecimal system, where $100 \leq X \leq 150$. [8]

**(OR)**

VII. a) Apply arithmetic crossover on the four variable vectors $X_1$, $X_2$ given as follows, with
i) Convex operator; ii) Affine operator; and iii) Linear operator weightage combinations.
$X_1 = [1.5 \quad 2 \quad 3 \quad 5.6]$
$X_2 = [2 \quad 1.8 \quad 2.5 \quad 6]$ [10]
b) Explain the impact of population size on exploration and exploitation capability in a population-based heuristic algorithm. [10]

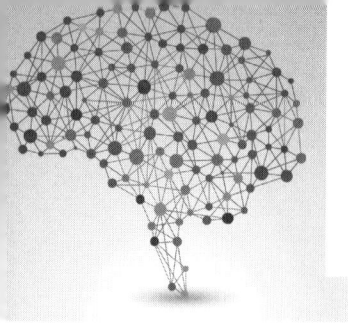

# Appendix B: MATLAB Tutorial

## Introduction

MATLAB (Matrix Laboratory) software, a numerical computing environment, is developed by Mathworks an American privately held corporation. It is a fourth-generation programming language that allows matrix manipulations, plotting of functions and data, implementation of algorithms, creation of user interfaces, and interfacing with programs written in other languages, including C, C++, Java, and Fortran.

Although MATLAB is intended primarily for numerical computing, many toolboxes cater different fields of science and engineering in direct implementation and applications. Also additional packages like Simulink adds graphical multi-domain simulation and model-based design for dynamic and embedded systems.

The MATLAB consist of the following main components:

- **Development Environment** This is the set of tools and facilities that help you use MATLAB functions and files. Many of these tools are graphical user interfaces. It includes the MATLAB desktop and Command Window, a command history, an editor and debugger, and browsers for viewing help, the workspace, files, and the search path.
- **The MATLAB Mathematical Function Library** This is a vast collection of computational algorithms ranging from elementary functions, such as sum, sine, cosine, and complex arithmetic, to more sophisticated functions like matrix inverse, matrix eigen values, Bessel functions, and fast Fourier transforms.
- **The MATLAB Language** This is a high-level matrix/array language with control flow statements, functions, data structures, input/output, and object-oriented programming features. It allows both 'programming in the small' to rapidly create quick and dirty throw-away programs, and 'programming in the large' to create large and complex application programs.
- **Graphics** MATLAB has extensive facilities for displaying vectors and matrices as graphs, as well as annotating and printing these graphs. It includes high-level functions for two-dimensional and three-dimensional data visualization, image processing, animation, and presentation graphics. It also includes low-level functions that allow you to fully customize the appearance of graphics as well as to build complete graphical user interfaces on your MATLAB applications.
- **The MATLAB Application Program Interface** This is a library that allows you to write C and Fortran programs that interact with MATLAB. It includes facilities for calling routines from MATLAB (dynamic linking), calling MATLAB as a computational engine, and for reading and writing MAT-files.

Figure.1 shows the desktop environment with the command window when the MATLAB software icon is clicked and opened.

Appendix B: MATLAB Tutorial 647

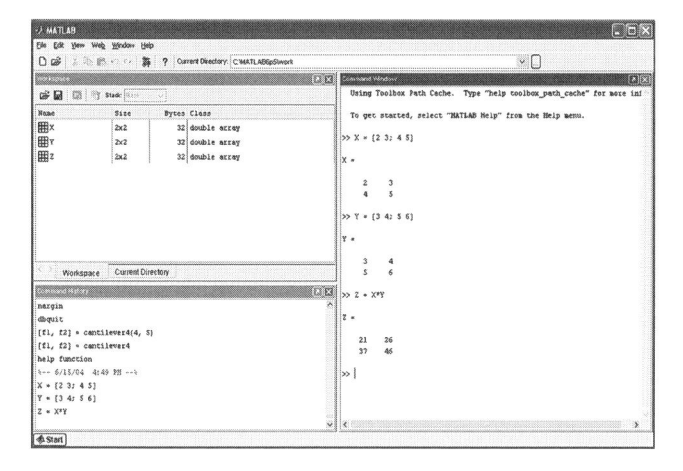

**Fig. 1** MATLAB desktop environment

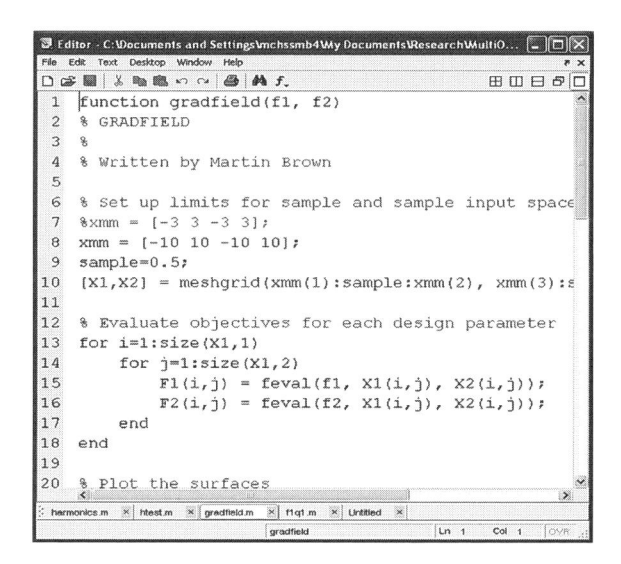

**Fig. 2** MATLAB editor

Commands can be typed directly into the command window (like a calculator), or they can be grouped together into a script file (or function). A script is a text file with a ".*m*" extension. A script file can be created using the MATLAB editor as shown in Fig. 2.

## Simple Calculations and Built-in Functions

### Entering Vectors and Matrices

The following commands show how to enter numbers, vectors, and matrices, and assign them to variables (>> is the MATLAB prompt on computer; it may be different with different computers or different versions of MATLAB):

```
>> a = 2
a =
    2
>> x = [1;2;3]
x =
    1
    2
    3
>> A = [1 2 3;4 5 6;7 8 0]
A =
    1   2   3
    4   5   6
    7   8   0
```

*Notice that the rows of a matrix are separated by semicolons, while the entries on a row are separated by spaces (or commas).*

## Certain Useful Built-in Variables and Functions:

### whos:

A useful command is "**whos**", which displays the names of all defined variables and their types:

```
>> whos
   Name      Size       Bytes  Class
   A         3x3           72  double array
   a         1x1            8  double array
   x         3x1           24  double array
```

*Note that each of these three variables is an array; the "shape" of the array determines its exact type. The scalar a is a $1 \times 1$ array, the vector x is a $3 \times 1$ array, and A is a $3 \times 3$ array (see the "size" entry for each variable).*

### help:

At this point, rather than providing a comprehensive list of functions available in MATLAB, An extensive online help system can be accessed by commands of the form help <command-name>.

For example,

```
>> help ans

   ANS    The most recent answer.
          ANS is the variable created automatically when expressions
          are not assigned to anything else. ANSwer.

>> help pi

   PI     3.1415926535897....
          PI = 4*atan(1) = imag(log(-1)) = 3.1415926535897....
```

A good place to start is with the command 'help', which explains how the help system works as well as some related commands. Typing 'help' by itself produces a list of topics for which help is available; looking at this list we find the entry 'elfun--elementary math functions'. Typing help elfun produces a list of the mathemathcal functions available. We see, for example, that the inverse tangent function (or arctangent) is called atan:

## Arithmetic Operations on Matrices

MATLAB can perform the standard arithmetic operations on matrices, vectors, and scalars (that is, on 2-, 1-, and 0-dimensional arrays): addition, subtraction, and multiplication. In addition, MATLAB defines a notion of matrix division as well as 'vectorized' operations. All vectorized operations (these include addition, subtraction, and scalar multiplication, as explained later) can be applied to $n$-dimensional arrays for any value of $n$, but multiplication and division are restricted to matrices and vectors ($n \leq 2$).

### Standard Operations

If $A$ and $B$ are arrays, then MATLAB can compute $A + B$ and $A - B$ when these operations are defined. For example, consider the following commands:

```
>> A = [1 2 3;4 5 6;7 8 9];
>> B = [1 1 1;2 2 2;3 3 3];
>> C = [1 2;3 4;5 6];
>> whos
  Name      Size         Bytes  Class
  A         3x3             72  double array
  B         3x3             72  double array
  C         3x2             48  double array
Grand total is 24 elements using 192 bytes.
```

### Matrix addition

```
>> A+B
ans =
    2     3     4
    6     7     8
   10    11    12
>> A+C
??? Error using ==> +
Matrix dimensions must agree.
```

### Matrix multiplication

```
>> A*C
ans =
   22    28
   49    64
   76   100
>> C*A
??? Error using ==> *
Inner matrix dimensions must agree.
```

If $A$ is a square matrix and m is a positive integer, then $A\wedge m$ is the product of $m$ factors of $A$.

However, no notion of multiplication is defined for multi-dimensional arrays with more than 2 dimensions.

### Solving Matrix Equations using Matrix Division

If $A$ is a square, non-singular matrix, then the solution of the equation $Ax = b$ is $x = A^{-1}b$. MATLAB implements this operation with the backslash operator:

```
>> A = rand(3,3)
A =
    0.2190    0.6793    0.5194
    0.0470    0.9347    0.8310
    0.6789    0.3835    0.0346
>> b = rand(3,1)
b =
    0.0535
    0.5297
    0.6711
>> x = A\b
x =
 -159.3380
  314.8625
 -344.5078
```

```
>> A*x-b
ans =
   1.0e-13 *
   -0.2602
   -0.1732
   -0.0322
```

It should be noted that the use of the built-in function rand, which creates a matrix with entries from a uniform distribution on the interval (0,1). (See help rand for more details.) Thus $A \backslash b$ is (mathematically) equivalent to multiplying $b$ on the left by $A^{-1}$ (however, MATLAB does *not* compute the inverse matrix; instead it solves the linear system directly). When used with a non-square matrix, the backslash operator solves the appropriate system in the least-squares sense; see help slash for details. Of course, as with the other arithmetic operators, the matrices must be compatible in size. The division operator is not defined for $n$-dimensional arrays with $n > 2$.

## Vectorized Functions and Operators; More on Graphs

### Creating the Special Matrices

MATLAB has many commands to create special matrices; the following command creates a row vector whose components increase arithmetically:

*Example 1*
```
>> t = 1:5
t =
   1   2   3   4   5
```

*Example 2*
The components can change by non-unit steps:
```
>> x = 0:.1:1
x =
  Columns 1 through 7
        0    0.1000    0.2000    0.3000    0.4000    0.5000    0.6000
  Columns 8 through 11
   0.7000    0.8000    0.9000    1.0000
```

*Example 3*
A negative step is also allowed. The command linspace has similar results; it creates a vector with linearly spaced entries. Specifically, linspace $(a,b,n)$ creates a vector of length $n$ with entries

$$a, a + (b-a)/(n-1), a + 2(b-a)/(n-1), \ldots, b$$

```
>> linspace(0,1,11)
ans =
  Columns 1 through 7
        0    0.1000    0.2000    0.3000    0.4000    0.5000    0.6000
  Columns 8 through 11
   0.7000    0.8000    0.9000    1.0000
```

*Example 4*
There is a similar command logspace for creating vectors with logarithmically spaced entries:
```
>> logspace(0,1,11)
ans =
  Columns 1 through 7
   1.0000    1.2589    1.5849    1.9953    2.5119    3.1623    3.9811
  Columns 8 through 11
   5.0119    6.3096    7.9433   10.0000
```

## Vectorized Operation

A vector with linearly spaced entries can be regarded as defining a one-dimensional grid, which is useful for graphing functions. To create a graph of $y = f(x)$ (or, to be precise, to graph points of the form $(x, f(x))$ and connect them with line segments), one can create a grid in the vector $x$ and then create a vector $y$ with the corresponding function values.

It is easy to create the needed vectors to graph a built-in function, since MATLAB functions are *vectorized*. This means that if a built-in function such as sine is applied to an array, the effect is to create a new array of the same size whose entries are the function values of the entries of the original array. For example,

```
>> x = (0:.1:2*pi);
>> y = sin(x);
>> plot(x,y)
```

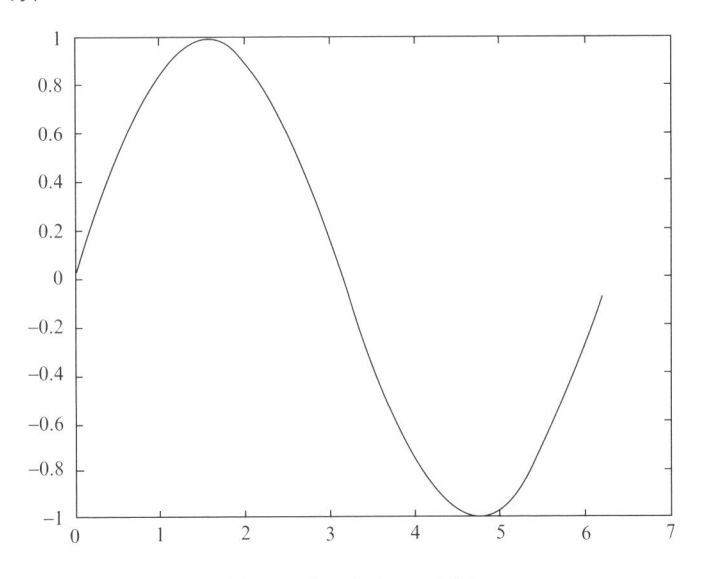

**Fig. 3** Graph of $y = \sin(x)$

MATLAB also provides vectorized arithmetic operators, which are the same as the ordinary $y = x/(1 + x^2)$ operators, preceded by ".". For example, to graph:

```
>> x = (-5:.1:5);
>> y = x./(1+x.^2);
>> plot(x,y)
```

Thus $x.\wedge 2$ squares each component of $x$, and $x./z$ divides each component of $x$ by the corresponding component of $z$. Addition and subtraction are performed component-wise by definition, so there are no ".+" or ".–" operators. Note the difference between $A\wedge 2$ and $A.\wedge 2$. The first is only defined if $A$ is a square matrix, while the second is defined for any $n$-dimensional array $A$.

## Programming in MATLAB

The capabilities of MATLAB can be extended through programs written in its own programming language. It provides the standard constructs, such as loops and conditionals; these constructs can be used interactively to reduce the tedium of repetitive tasks, or collected in programs stored in "m-files" (nothing more than a text file with extension ".m").

## Conditionals and Loops
### if-else:
The general form of the If statement is,

```
if expr1
    statements
elseif expr2
    statements
   .
   .
   .
else
    statements
end
```

The first block of statements following a non-zero *expr* executes.

MATLAB has a standard if-else conditional Structure. For illustration lets look at an example given below.

### Example 5

```
weight= input('Enter your weight in kg unit:');
height= input('Enter your height in cm unit:');
bmi=weight/(height*0.01)^2;
disp( 'Your Body Mass Index is:'   );
bmi
if bmi <= 18.5
disp('You are under weight. Have a healthy food');
elseif  bmi > 18.5 && bmi <= 25
disp('You are maintaining normal weight. Keep it up');
elseif  bmi > 25 && bmi < 30
disp('You are overweight. Avoid junk food');
elseif bmi >= 30
disp('You are obesity. Do exercise and avoid junk food');
end

Enter your weight in kg unit:41
Enter your height in cm unit:161
Your Body Mass Index is:

bmi =

   15.8173

You are under weight. Have a healthy food
```

## Logical Operations

The logical operators in MATLAB are $<, >, <=, >=, ==$ (logical equals), and $\sim=$ (not equal). These are binary operators which return the values 0 and 1 (for scalar arguments):

```
>> 5>3
ans =
     1
>> 5<3
ans =
     0
>> 5==3
ans =
     0
```

## Loops

MATLAB provides two types of loops, a for-loop (comparable to a Fortran do-loop or a C for-loop) and a while-loop.

## for-loop:

A for-loop repeats the statements in the loop as the loop index takes on the values in a given row vector:

```
>> for i=[1,2,3,4]
       disp(i^2)
   end
     1
     4
     9
    16
```

It should be noted that the use of the built-in function disp, which simply displays its argument. The loop, like an if-block, must be terminated by end. This loop would more commonly be written as,

```
>> for i=1:4
       disp(i^2)
   end
     1
     4
     9
    16
```
(recall that 1:4 is the same as [1,2,3,4]).

## while-loop:

The while-loop repeats as long as the given expression is true (non-zero):

```
>> x=1;
>> while 1+x > 1
       x = x/2;
   end
>> x
x =
   1.1102e-16
```

## SWITCH/CASE/OTHERWISE

Switch among several cases based on expression.

Syntax:

```
switch switch_expression
   case case_expression
       statements
   case case_expression
       statements
   ...
   otherwise
       statements
end
```

The switch/case/otherwise can be understood by the example given below

### Example 6

```
prob=input('Whether you have pain? :',' s');
switch prob
    case 'head'
        disp('You are forwarded to Neurologists');
    case 'stomach'
        disp('You are forwarded to Gastroenterology');
    case 'eye'
        disp('You are forwarded to Ophthalmologists');
```

```
        case 'chest'
            disp('You are forwarded to Cardiology');
        case 'teeth'
            disp('You are forwarded to Dentist');
        case 'skin'
            disp('You are forwarded to Dermatologists');
        otherwise
            disp('Please enter your problem');
    end
Whether you have pain?: chest
You are forwarded to Cardiology
```

## Functions

Much more powerful than scripts are functions, which allow the user to create new MATLAB commands. A function is defined in an m-file that begins with a line of the following form:

```
function [output1,output2,...] = cmd_name(input1,input2,...)
```

The rest of the m-file consists of ordinary MATLAB commands computing the values of the outputs and performing other desired actions. It is important to note that when a function is invoked, MATLAB creates a local workspace. The commands in the function cannot refer to variables from the global (interactive) workspace unless they are passed as inputs. By the same token, variables created as the function executes are erased when the execution of the function ends, unless they are passed back as outputs.

Here is a simple example of a function; it computes the function $f(x) = \sin(x^2)$. The following commands should be stored in the file fcn.m (the name of the function within MATLAB is the name of the m-file, without the extension):

```
function y = fn(x)

y = sin(x.^2);
```

It should be noted that a vectorized operator .^ is used so that the function fn is also vectorized. With this function defined, we can now use *fn* just as the built-in function sin:

```
>> x = (-pi:2*pi/100:pi)';
>> y = sin(x);
>> z = fn(x);
>> plot(x,y,x,z)
>> grid
```

Although there are more things to be learnt in MATLAB, this appendix section only introduces MATLAB and a little bit of programming.

Other than programming, MATLAB software package provides software tools for particular subjects. Fuzzy Logic MATLAB Tool Box is well explained in Chapter 6 even with the graphical user interface called the FIS (Fuzzy Inference System). Artificial neural network MATLAB Tool Box is explained with electrical load forecasting example in the end of the Chapter 3. The only limitation with these tool boxes is that the clarity in the execution of the soft computing programs and the steps involved or coded in a program may not be visible or understood directly unless the subject is thoroughly understood. The reader can go to www.mathworks.in for further learning.

# Glossary

*Accuracy*   It explains how close the instrument reading is to the true value.

*Activation function*   A function that defines the output of the neuron by comparing with a threshold value.

*Artificial intelligence*   A field of study that encompasses computational techniques for performing tasks that apparently require intelligence when performed by humans.

*Batch training mode*   Update of weights is performed as a sum over the entire training set.

*Bias*   It is another weight whose weight value is always equal to unity, and which helps in the process of initial learning.

*Biomimetics*   Inventions that mimic nature.

*Break package*   A de-bugging procedure that guides the user when to stop the program execution before some recurring error, thereby examining the current values in the database.

*Chunk*   A rule that corresponds to a small modular collection of knowledge.

*Content-addresable memory*   A special type of computer memory used in certain very high speed searching applications with binary threshold units that allows the recall of data on the degree of similarity between the input patterns and the patterns stored in memory.

*Crisp set*   A collection of distinct (precisely defined) elements.

*Crossover*   A core genetic operator, which is considered as an axle for the generation of new offspring with strong characteristic features of new genetic information obtained as a result of the exchange of genetic material among the individuals of the chromosomal population.

*Degree of membership*   The numerical value of the membership function.

*De-polarizing*   A biological phenomenon in a neuron where an input at an excitatory synapse reduces the negative polarization of the membrane.

*Domain of fuzzy set*   The range of values covered by a particular fuzzy set with its elements' degree of membership greater than zero.

*Empty fuzzy set*   A fuzzy set A is said to be an empty set if it has no members and its membership function is zero everywhere in its universe of discourse.

*Equal fuzzy sets*   If the membership functions of any two fuzzy sets A and B are equal everywhere in the universe of discourse, then the two fuzzy sets are said to be equal.

*Expert system*   Intelligent computer programs that use expertise knowledge and inference schemes for solving problems, thereby emulating the decision making like a human expert.

*Explanation sub-system*   A mechanism that provides to trace the rules used and, thereby, justifies its conclusions.

*Explicit solution evaluation*   A measure of the quality of the solution generated that is used to decide how much pheromone should be deposited by an ant.

*Foraging theory*   A theory based on the assumption that animals search for and obtain nutrients in a way that maximizes their energy intake $E$ per unit time $T$ spent foraging.

*Fuzzification*   A process of converting the crisp values to fuzzy variable.

*Fuzzy concentration*   A process that tends to concentrate or reduce the fuzziness of the elements in a fuzzy set by reducing the degree of membership of all elements that are only 'partly' in the set.

*Fuzzy dilation*   A process that tends to dilate or increase the fuzziness of the elements in a fuzzy set by increasing the degree of membership of all elements that are only 'partly' in the set.

*Fuzzy intensification*   A process that tends to dilate and concentrate the fuzziness of the elements in a fuzzy set by increasing and decreasing the degree of membership of all elements that are only 'partly' in the set.

*Fuzzy logic*   A form of reasoning, derived from fuzzy set theory, whereby a truth value need not be exactly zero (false) or 1(true), but rather can be zero, 1, or any value in between.

*Fuzzy set*   A collection of distinct elements with a varying degree of relevance or inclusion.

*Gbest*   The 'best' value that is tracked by the global version of the particle swarm optimizer, which is the overall best value, and its location, obtained so far by any particle in the population.

*Genetic algorithm*   (1) An iterative procedure maintaining a population of structures that are candidate solutions to specific domain challenges. (2) The genetic algorithm is a randomized search and optimization technique guided by the principle of natural genetic systems.

*Genetic programming*   An extension of the genetic model of evolutionary programs where bits or objects that constitute the population are not fixed-length character strings that encode possible solutions to the problem at hand. Nevertheless, they are programs expressed as parse trees rather than lines of code or using a suitable data structure when executed and are the candidate solutions to the problem.

*Hamming distance*   The number of components between any two vectors by which they differ.

*Hyperpolarizing*   A biological phenomenon in a neuron where an inhibitory synapse increases the negative polarization of the membrane even further.

*Implicit solution evaluation*   A measure of the quality of the solution that ants exploit through differential path length effect of real ants foraging behaviour, i.e., the fact that if the ant chooses a shorter path then it is the first to deposit pheromone and to bias the search of forthcoming ants.

*Incremental training mode*   Updating of weights, which is performed after the presentation of each pattern.

*Inexactness*   It represents the inability to measure variables very close to its true value.

*Inference engine*   A platform where new facts are inferred by using the information from the knowledge base and the user.

*Knowledge acquisition facility*   Dedicated modules only for updating the knowledge base where the knowledge engineer transfers the knowledge from the human expert to the computer-based expert system.

*Knowledge base editor*   A platform that helps the expert or knowledge engineer to continuously update information with ease and verify the knowledge base.

*Knowledge base*   A domain in which the knowledge of a human expert on a particular subject is contained in a structured format that is easy to read and interpret.

*Knowledge engineering*  A process of building an expert system through acquisition of knowledge from a human expertise or from any other source.

*Knowledge-engineering language*  A kind of programming language that is used to build, construct, and debug expert systems.

*Linear separability*  A property in a two-dimensional space where two sets of points can be separated by a single line.

*MAXNET*  The second layer of the Hamming neural network that finds the unit with the largest net input.

*Membership function*  Representation of a physical variable as a continuous curve.

*Membrane potential*  The potential difference that exists between the interior of the neuron cell and its surrounding.

*Meta-heuristic*  Higher-level search.

*Momentum term*  A term that directs the weight change as a combination of the current gradient and the previous gradient.

*Multi-layer network*  A multi-layer net is a net with one or more layers (or levels) of nodes (the so-called hidden units) between the input units and the output units.

*Mutation*  A core genetic operator that maintains the genetic diversity from one generation of a population of chromosomes to the next.

*Nbest*  Each particle that keeps track of the best solution within a local topological neighbourhood of the particles is called nbest (neighbourhood best) or lbest (local best).

*Neural network*  (1) A computer architecture in which a number of processors are interconnected in a manner suggestive of the connections between neurons in a human brain and which is able to learn by a process of trial and error. (Merriam-Webster dictionary) (2) An information processing system that mimics certain performance characteristics of the biological neural systems of the brain.

*Neurotransmitter*  Chemical substances that help in synaptic transmission.

*Normal fuzzy set*  A fuzzy set A is said to be normal if it has a membership function that includes at least one singleton equal to unity in its universe of discourse.

*Pbest*  Each particle that keeps track of its coordinates in the problem space, which are associated with the best solution or fitness achieved so far, is called pbest.

*Perceptron*  A linear classifier that can classify an input into one of the two possible outputs.

*Pheromone*  A chemical substance laid by ants during traverse.

*Plasticity*  A property in which learning instability occurs because of the network's adaptability, which causes prior learning to be eroded by more recent learning.

*Possibility theory*  A theory that handles imprecision.

*Precision*  It refers to the number of numerical digits used to represent the measured output.

*Probability theory*  A theory that attempts to explain events occurring in a random space. It handles the likelihood of occurrence.

*Programming language*  An artificial language developed to control and direct the operation of a computer.

*Radial basis functions*  Functions that produce localized, bounded, and radially symmetric activations that decreases the distance from the function's centres.

***Reinforced learning*** An intermediate form of the earlier two types of learning (Supervised and Unsupervised) that reinforces the weights by grading the updating of weights as good (rewarding) or bad (punishable) based on the environmental response and accordingly adjusts its network parameters.

***Rule-based expert systems*** Expert systems that represent knowledge in a rule format.

***Sigmoidal function*** A logistic function that monotonically increases from a lower limit (0 or −1) to an upper limit (+1) as sum increases.

***Soft computing*** A domain of methodologies that exploits the tolerance for imprecision, uncertainty, and partial truth in solving a problem that involves information processing.

***Spike train*** A chain of pulses emitted by a single neuron, which is a sequence of stereotyped events that occur at regular or irregular intervals.

***Stigmergy*** Indirect communication mediated by pheromone deposition observed in ants.

***Supervised learning*** A learning method by an algorithm that minimizes the error difference (error vector) between the actual output (output feature) and target output.

***Swarm intelligence*** A term that is used for the collective behaviour of a group (swarm) of animals as a single living creature, where via grouping and communication, a collective intelligence emerges, which actually results in more successful foraging for each individual in the group. In other words, collective behaviour of a group of animals, especially social insects such as ants, bees, and termites, that are each following very basic rules.

***Synapse*** An interface between neurons where transfer of information takes place.

***Tracing*** A de-bugging procedure that provides the user with a trace or display of system operation where a list of names are fired by the rules or the names of all the sub-routines.

***Undecidability*** It refers to the inability to distinguish between various states of an event.

***Universe of discourse*** The complete range of the model variable.

***Unsupervised learning*** A learning method by an algorithm that updates the weights based on the (output) unit that is trained to respond to clusters of pattern within the input.

***User interface*** A platform that allows the system user to enter rules and facts about a particular situation, ask questions to the system, and provide responses to user requests.

***Validation*** A procedure in expert system that demonstrates the exactness of the final product satisfying the needs of a user in solving the problem.

***Verification*** A procedure in expert system that ensures that an expert system is developed correctly and which does not contain technical errors.

***Vigilance parameter*** User-specified value to decide the degree of similarity essential for the input patterns to be assigned to a cluster unit in the ART network.

***Weights*** They represent the strength of the connection between an input and a neuron by a value.

# Index

Accommodation, 258
 flat ramp, 258
 inhibition-induced spiking, 258
 step ramp, 258
Accuracy, 286
Action potential, 70
 excitory, 71
 inhibitory, 71
 neuronal spike, 70
Activation/transfer function, 80
 arbitrary-order polynomial, 82
 binary sigmoid (logsig), 81
 binary step function, 81
 bipolar sigmoid function (tansig), 81
 conditional stimulus, 86
 Gaussian, 82
 hard limit (hardlim), 81
 identity function (purelin), 81
 inner product kernel, 82
 inverse multiquadratics, 82
 logistic function, 80
 multiquadratics, 82
 saturating linear (satlin), 82
 sigmoid function, 80
 support vectors, 82
 symmetrical hard limit (hardlims), 82
 symmetric saturating linear (satlins), 82
 unconditional stimulus, 86
Adaline network, 101
 adaptive linear neuron, 101
 least mean squares (LMS), 101
 Widrow-hoff rule, 101
Adaptive resonance theory (ART), 208
 ART-1, 209
 ART-2, 209
 ART-3, 209
 degree of expectations, 209, 210
 encoder problem, 212
 energy, 214
 energy gap, 214
 global state, 214
 input interface layer, 209
 input processing layer, 209
 output layer, 209
 plasticity, 208
 random asynchronous updation, 211
 reset layer, 209
 reset mechanism, 209
 resonance, 209
 simulated annealing technique, 212
 thermodynamic systems, 214
 vigilance parameter, 209
Ant search phase, 558
 evaluation function, 557

 evaporation parameter, 560
 pheromone evaporation, 560
 pheromone updating, 559
 pseudo-random probability function, 559
Artificial ant colony system, 554
 backtracking, 554
 elitist approach, 554
 local stigmergetic communication, 554
 population-based heuristic algorithm, 554
 ranking-based, 554
 trail, 554
Artificial bee colony system, 599
 employed bees, 600
 foragers, 599
 meta-heuristic algorithm, 599
 receivers, 599
 scout bees, 600
 task partitioning, 599
 tremble dance, 599
 unemployed bees, 600
 waggle dance, 599
Artificial neural networks, 7

Backward chaining, 32
Bias term, 71
 Adaline, 73
 auxiliary hybrid models, 74
 content-addressable memory, 73
 delta rule, 73
 embedded, 74
 exclusive-OR (XOR), 73
 generalization, 73
 hybrid ANN models, 74
 logic functions, 73
 Madaline, 73
 network architecture, 74
 non-probabilistic binary linear classifier, 73
 self-organizing maps, 73
 sequential, 74
 spiking NNs (SNNs), 74
 supervised learning, 73
 training/learning, 74
Bi-directional associative memeory, 186
 associative memory neural networks, 186
 asynchronous updating, 187
 auto-AMNN, 186
 hetero-AMNN, 186
 lyapunov function, 187
Bi-directional associative memories, 197
 two-way associative search, 197
Binary representation, 453
 binary coding, 453
 gray coding, 453
 octal representation, 454

## 660  Index

Biological neural networks, 67
  axon tracts, 67
  cell bodies, 67
  dendrites, 67
  grey matter, 67
  ionic channels, 69
  lock-and-key, 70
  membrane potential, 70
  mitochondria, 67
  myelin, 67
  neurotransmitters, 68
  Organelles, 67
  permeability, 70
  post-synaptic, 70
  presynaptic vesicle, 70
  receptor sites, 70
  synaptic transmission, 68
  synaptic vesicles, 68
  unidirectional, 68
  white matter, 67
Biomimetics, 2
  expert systems, 2
  fuzzy logic systems, 2
  neural networks, 2
  swarm intelligence, 2
Bi-stability of resting and
    spiking states, 258
  resting and tonic spiking, 258
Boundary mutation, 480
  plain mutation, 480

Class 1 excitability, 258
Class 2 excitability, 258
Compartmental models, 259
Conditional and qualified
    propositions, 338
  fuzzy truth qualifier, 338
Conditional and unqualified
    propositions, 338
Conductance-based, 259
Confabulation theory, 7
Continous BAM, 200
Convex Fuzzy Sets, 295
  Gaussian membership function, 297
  linearly expressed gamma membership
    function, 297
  L membership function, 297
  sigmoidal membership function, 297
  trapezoidal membership function, 297
  triangle membership function, 297
Cuckoo search algorithm, 613
  alien eggs, 615
  brood parasite, 613
  dunnocks, 613
  eurasian reed warblers, 613
  indian jungle crow, 613
  indian koel, 613
  levy flights, 615
  meadow pipits, 613
  natural selection, 614
  reed warbler, 613

De-fuzzification, 350
  assessment of de-fuzzification
    methods, 358
  centre of area (COA) de-fuzzification, 352
  centre of largest area (COLA), 356
  centre of sums (COS), 354
  computational complexity, 359
  continuity, 358
  disambiguity, 358
  first of maxima, 356
  last of maxima, 357
  max-membership (height method), 351
  mean of maxima (MOM), 354
  plausibility, 359
  weighted average method, 353
  weighting methods, 359
Degree of fulfilment, 344
Degree of membership, 291
Depolarizing, 254
Depolarizing after-potentials, 258
  after-hyperpolarization (AHP), 258
  depolarized after potential (DAP), 258

Economic dispatch (ED), 575
  global trail-updating, 577
  lagrange multiplier method, 575
  local trail-updating, 577
  multi-greedy algorithm, 578
Economic dispatch problem, 625
  equality constraint, 626
Electrical load forecasting, 227
  auto regressive integrated moving
    average, 228
  auto regressive moving average, 228
  commercial, 228
  demographic, 227
  humidity, 228
  industrial, 228
  load profile, 228
  long-term load forecasting, 227
  medium-term, 227
  regression models, 228
  residential, 228
  seasonal variation, 227
  short-term, 227
  similar-day approach, 228
  temperature, 228
  time series, 228
Electrical load forecasting, 267
  classical, 267
  cross-correlation function, 274
  day-ahead correlation, 271
  error variance, 275
  mean absolute percentage error, 275
  non-conventional, 267
  normalized mean square error, 275
  population coding, 267
  similar-day correlation, 271
  spike propagation algorithm, 268
  synaptic efficacy, 268
  temporal encoding, 267

Index    661

Evolutionary programming, 19, 531
  bucket brigade algorithm, 535
  classifiers, 534
  classifier store, 535
  competition, 531
  constant scaling factor, 533
  effectors, 535
  finite-length message list, 535
  Initialization, 531
  machine learning classifier system, 533
  mutation, 531
  penalty factor, 533
  probabilistic search technique, 532
  selection, 531
Evolutionary strategy (ES), 21
  bioinformatics, 22
  crossover mechanism, 21
  finite state machines, 22
  genesis, 23
  genitor, 23
  hypergen, 23
  LibGA, 23
  natural adaptation, 22
  pharmacometrics, 22
  phylogenetics, 22
  recombination, 21
  stochastic tournament selection, 21
Excitatory post-synaptic potential (EPSP), 254
Expert system-building tools, 54
  1st class, 56
  ART, 56
  custom CMOS chip, 57
  domain-specific tools, 54
  EXSYS, 56
  GURU, 56
  hybrid tools, 54
  *HYCONES II*, 55
  inductive tools, 54
  information management systems (IMS), 56
  KES, 56
  knowbel, 55
  oracle RDBMS, 56
  PC PLUS, 56
  simple-rule-based tools, 54
  structured-rule-based tools, 54
Expert systems, 27
  autopilot, 27
  case specific data, 28
  chunk, 31
  explanation sub-system, 29
  inference engine, 29
  knowledge acquisition facility, 29
  knowledge base editor, 28
  knowledge base (KB), 28
  rule-based expert systems, 28
  self-training, 29
  user interface, 28
Expert system tools, 51
  advanced engineering language, 52
  cobol, 52
  core engineering language, 52
  fortran, 52
  GPSS, 52
  knowledge-engineering language, 51
  knowledge ware solution, 52
  Lisp, 52
  mathematical engineering language, 52
  programming language, 51
Exploitation, 548
Exploration, 548
  artificial immune systems, 549
  bird flocking, 549
  cuckoo's habitat, 549
  fish schooling, 549
  initial key, 548
  pheromone, 549
  probabilistic behaviour, 548
  pseudo-random numbers, 548
  random perturbation, 549
  seed/fixed number, 548
  self-organized, 549
  social life forms, 549
  stochastic behaviour, 548

First-generation neurons, 253
  integrate-and-fire units, 253
First-generation NNs, 9
  adaptive resonance theory, 9
  back propagation NN, 9
  hopfield NN, 9
  kohonnen NN, 9
  McCulloch-pitts threshold neurons (1943), 9
  perceptron NN, 9
  radial basis NN, 9
  spiking or Pulsed NN, 9
  support vector machines, 9
Floating-point representation, 456
  Caley's theorem, 457
  edge encoding, 457
  leaf vertex, 458
  link, 458
  minimum spanning tree, 456
  node-biased encoding, 458
  prim's algorithm, 458
  prüfer number, 457
  tree representation, 456
  vertex encoding, 457
Forward chaining, 32
  circular rule chains, 47
  confidence factors, 48
  conflicting rules, 41
  consequence-driven reasoning, 33
  control, 39
  dead end goals, 48, 50
  dead end IF conditions, 48
  debugging, 39
  designing, 38
  diagnosis, 38
  goal-directed, 33
  illegal attribute values, 48

## Index

instruction, 39
interpretation, 38
knowledge engineer, 37
knowledge engineering, 37
monitoring, 39
planning, 38
prediction, 38
redundant rules, 39
subsumed rules, 42
unnecessary IF conditions, 43
unreachable conclusions, 48
unreachable IF conditions, 45
unreferenced attribute values, 48
validation, 39
verification, 39
Frequency preference and resonance, 258
   resonators, 258
   sub-threshold oscillations, 258
Fuzzification, 310, 335
   fuzzy propositions, 337
   logic variable, 337
   proposition variable, 337
   sentence, 337
Fuzzy arithmetics, 308
   alpha-cut method, 313, 314
   alpha-cuts, 312, 313
   continuous fuzzy Set, 314
   discrete fuzzy set, 308, 313
   extension principle, 308
   fattening, 318
   fuzzy numbers, 308
   higher order arithmetic operations, 319
   many-to-one mapping, 309
   resolution principle, 313
Fuzzy composition, 323
   composition of fuzzy relation, 323
Fuzzy connectives, 338
   antecedent, 338
   conjunction, 338
   consequent, 338
   disjunction, 338
   implication, 338
   implication operator, 338
   negation, 338
Fuzzy controllers, 385
   centre of area, 393
   de-fuzzification module, 387
   de-fuzzifier, 387
   degree of fulfilment, 392
   derivative gain constant, 386
   first-order Sugeno controller, 395
   fuzzification module, 387
   fuzzifier, 387
   fuzzy associative memory (FAM), 391
   fuzzy logic (FL) tools, 389
   fuzzy opinion matrix, 396
   generalized modus ponens, 391
   inference engine, 387
   integral gain constant, 386
   integral term, 386
   integration variable, 386
   knowledge base, 387
   Larsen product, 394
   max-membership, 395
   normalization, 388
   overshooting, 387
   proportional gain constant, 386
   proportional integral derivative, 387
   proportional term, 386
   quantization, 388
   reset constant, 387
   rule base, 387
   scaling, 388
   smoothing, 388
   Sugeno, 395
   TSK form, 395
   zero-order Sugeno controller, 395
Fuzzy distance approach, 398
   FIS editor, 402
   fuzzy associative memory, 421
   fuzzy hamming distance, 398
   fuzzy inference system, 400
   hydel power plant, 419
   implication method, 422
   kinetic energy, 419
   surface viewer, 403
Fuzzy genetic, 435
   genetic fuzzy, 435
Fuzzy implication relations, 339
   arithmetic, 340
   boolean, 340
   bounded product, 340
   drastic product, 340
   godelian, 340
   gougen, 340
   Larsen product, 340
   mamdani min, 340
   method of implication, 339
   Standard sequence, 340
   zadeh max-min, 340
Fuzzy inference algorithms, 349
Fuzzy inference procedures, 341
   generalized modus ponens (GMP), 341
   generalized modus tollens (GMT), 342
   rule of definition, 341
   rule of detachment, 341
   rule of substitution, 341
Fuzzy logic, 283
   human thinking, 283
   interpretation, 283
   machine, 283
Fuzzy logic applications, 385
   closed loop, 385
   fuzzy decision-making, 385
   fuzzy logic-based control, 385
   proportional integral derivative, 385
Fuzzy relations, 321, 322
   cartesian products, 322
   cartesian product space, 322

completely related, 321
continuous cartesian product, 322
discrete cartesian product, 322
non-related, 321
Fuzzy set operations, 305
  adsorption, 307
  associative Property, 307
  commutativity, 307
  De Morgan's laws, 307
  distributive Property, 307
  double negation law, 306
  empty fuzzy set, 305
  equal fuzzy sets, 305
  fuzzy set multiplication by a crisp
      number, 306
  fuzzy set support, 306
  idempotency, 306
  law of contradiction, 307
  law of excluded middle, 307
  normal fuzzy set, 305
  power of a fuzzy set, 306
  product of fuzzy sets, 306
  subnormal, 305
Fuzzy set operations, 297
  analytical solutions, 297
  complement, 298
  crisp decision-making, 303
  curved function, 301
  fuzzy union, 302
  intersection, 298
  logical NOT operation, 303
  ramping membership function, 300
  union, 298
Fuzzy systems, 13
  blue circle cement, 16
  boolean logic, 13
  deductive reasoning, 14
  degrees of truth, 13
  fuzzification, 15
  fuzzy set theory, 13
  laboratory for international fuzzy engineering
      research (LIFE), 16
  ministry of international trade and industry
      (MITI), 16
  possibility theory, 14
  probability theory, 14
  real-world vagueness, 13
  sendai subway system, 16

Genetic algorithm, 445
  chromosomes, 445
  DNA strands, 446
  genetics, 445
  inheritance, 445
  simple living cell, 446

Hamming neural network, 175
Hard computing, 2
  analytical model, 3
  data mining, 3

decision support, process, 3
deterministic, 3
fault diagnosis, 3
forecasting applications, 3
human machine interface, 3
machine intelligence quotient
    (MIQ), 3
pattern recognition, 3
process optimisation, 3
robotics, 3
signal and image processing, 3
stochastic, 3
system control, 3
system integration, 3
virtual reality, 3
Hebbian rule, 88
  decay factor, 88
  extended delta rule, 90
  linearly independent, 89
  orthogonal, 89
  squared error (SE), 89
  weighted sum, 89
Hopfield neural network, 186
Human learning ability, 285
Hybrid techniques, 434
Hybrid technologies, 18
  genetic-neuro-fuzzy, 18
  neuro-fuzzy systems, 18
Hyperpolarizing, 254
  absolute refractoriness effect, 255
  absolute refractory period, 255
  firing time, 255
  generic PSP, 255
  real cortical neuronal, 256
  relative refractory period, 255
  spike after potential (SAP), 255

Icosytems, 23
  bird flocking, 24
  emergent behaviour, 26
  firefly systems, 24
  fish schooling, 24
  foraging scheme, 26
  non-controllable, 26
  non-optimal, 26
  non-predictable, 26
  self-organization, 24
Imprecise logic, 17
  bivalence states, 17
  defuzzification, 17
  inference mechanism, 17
  possibility distribution, 18
Imprecision, 285
Inexactness, 286
Information processing system, 7
Inhibition-induced bursting, 258
Inhibition-induced spiking, 258
Inhibitory post-synaptic potential, 254
  axonal delay, 254
  negative polarization, 254

# Index

Integrate-and-fire models, 259
  absolute refractoriness, 261
Integration and coincidence detection, 258
  integrator, 258
Intelligence, 4
  expert system, 4
  natural language, 4
  panasonic microcomputer-controlled fuzzy logic® rice cooker, 4
  planning, 4
Intelligent systems, 4
Intuitionist fuzzy logic, 18
Intuitionistic fuzzy sets, 435
  degree of membership, 436
  degree of non-determinacy, 436
  hesitation, 435
  membership function, 435
  non-membership function, 435

Kohonen neural network, 153
  euclidean distance (ED), 153
  map, 153
  self-organizing map, 153
  topological parameter, 159

Learning vector quantization, 164
Linear seperability, 99
Linguistic modifiers, 329
  concentration, 330
  dilation, 332
  intensification, 333

Madaline network, 104
MATLAB NN toolbox, 231
  command prompt, 231
  gradient descent algorithm, 232
  mean absolute percentage error, 235
  network/data manager, 235
  nntool, 231
  performance, 234
  regression, 235
  simulate network, 235
  training state, 234
  train network, 234
  validation, 232
  workspace, 231
Max-average composition, 325
Max-min composition, 324
MAXNET, 175
  Hamming distance (HD), 175
Max-product composition, 325
Max-star composition, 324
Membership function, 291
Metaheuristic, 19
  black-box, 19
  chromosomes, 20
  derivative-free, 19
  direct search, 19
  generation, 20
  heuristics, 19

Lisp (Locator/Identifier Separation Protocol), 20
  meta, 19
  offspring, 19
  random mutation, 19
  simulated evolution, 20
Mixed model, 257
  mammalian neocortex, 257
Mutation, 480
  uniform mutation, 480

Natural evolution, 446
Natural inheritance operators, 485
  any-pattern mating, 490
  benchmark problem, 506
  best-pattern mating, 490
  complement, 489
  crossover operation, 501
  cumulative probability, 501
  deletion, 487
  diploidy, 485
  dominance, 485
  economic load dispatch, 513
  gradient descent learning, 527
  haploid chromosome, 486
  heterozygous, 486
  homologous chromosomes, 485
  homologous mating, 487
  homozygous, 486
  immigrants, 489
  intrachromosomal duplication, 488
  lagrangian multiplier method, 512
  linear + end inversion, 486
  linear inversion, 486
  massively parallel GAs, 530
  mating, 490
  migration, 489
  mutation operation, 501
  niche, 489
  parallel GA, 530
  parallel hybrid GAs, 530
  parallel island models, 530
  piece-wise linear, 513
  position-based crossover, 506
  prime ordering, 490
  probability distribution function, 501
  reciprocal exchange mutation, 506
  re-generation, 488
  root mean square, 529
  roulette-wheel selection, 500
  segregation, 488
  sharing, 489
  speciation, 489
  strict homology mating, 490
  termination criterion, 502
  translocation, 488
  valve-point effect, 513
  viability mating, 490
Natural language, 328
  atomic terms, 328
  compound terms, 328

Index  665

fuzzy interpretations, 328
phrases, 328
primary terms, 328
Natural selection, 446
  alleles, 449
  biological evolution, 448
  crossover, 449
  encoding, 452
  evolutionary programming, 447
  evolution strategies, 448
  fitness, 448
  generations, 450
  genetic algorithms, 447
  genotypes, 449
  loci, 449
  mutation, 449
  objective, 448
  offspring, 446
  phenotype, 449
  probabilistic transition rules, 451
  randomized search, 448
  re-combination, 449
  roulette-wheel selection, 450
  simulated evolution, 449
Neural computing, 11
  von neumann machine, 11
Neural network architecture, 74
  actual output (output feature), 78
  competitive neural network, 76
  error difference (error vector), 78
  feed-back NNs, 76
  feed-forward NNs, 76
  hopfield net architecture, 75
  MAXNET, 76
  multi-layer neural network, 76
  recurrent NNs, 76
  single-layer neural network, 75
  source (input feature), 78
  target data (desired), 78
  target output, 78
  unsupervised hebb learning, 79
Neural networks, 63
  association, 63
  cerebral cortex, 64
  deep blue, 67
  deep thought, 67
  memory, 63
  neocortical neurons, 63
  neuro-anatomy, 64
  outcome, 63
  synapses, 64
  training, 63
Neuro-fuzzy, 434
Non-convex, 295
Non-uniform mutation, 480
  displacement, 483
  displacement, 484
  heuristic mutation, 484
  insertion, 483, 484
  inversion, 483

logical bit-wise operator, 480
mask, 483
masking operator, 480, 483
one's complement operator, 480
reciprocal exchange, 483, 484
shift left operator, 482
shift operator, 480, 482
shift right operator, 483
unary operator, 481

Operations on fuzzy relations, 323
  complement, 323
  containment, 323
  intersection, 323
  union, 323
Optimal foraging policy, 547
  Foraging theory, 547
  information sharing, 548
  mate-finding, 548
  shelter-building, 548

Parameter settings, 568
  modified TACO, 568
  transitional cost, 568
Particle swarm intelligent
    system, 582
  acceleration constant, 585
  cognitive, 586
  constriction factor, 586
  gbest, 584
  inertia weight, 586
  lbest, 584
  mutation, 588
  nbest, 584
  particle, 583
  pbest, 584
  recombination, 588
  selection, 588
  social parameter, 586
  velocity, 585
Perceptron, 91
  linear classifier, 91
  perceptron learning rule, 92
  undecided region, 92
Permutation representation, 459
  completion-time-based, 460
  cumulative probability, 461
  disjunctive-graph-based, 460
  grammatical encoding, 460
  job-based, 460
  job-pair-relation-based, 460
  machine-based, 460
  operation-based, 460
  order representation, 459
  path, 459
  preference-list-based, 460
  priority-rule-based, 460
  random keys representation, 459
  random keys representations, 460
  roulette wheel, 460

travelling salesman, 459
Phasic bursting, 256
Phasic spiking, 256
Pheromone updating, 555
   off-line pheromone updates, 556
Possibility theory, 287
   characteristic function, 288, 289
   classical sets, 288
   fuzziness, 289
   fuzzy conjunction, 288
   fuzzy set, 289
   imprecise constraint, 287
   linguistic variables, 288
   list method, 289
   possibility distribution, 287, 288
   probability distribution, 288
   rule method, 289
   solution space, 287
   superset, 288
   universe of discourse, 288
   word function, 289
Precision, 286
Principle of incompatibility, 284
   fuzzy sets, 284
   human interpretation, 285
   human reasoning, 285
   imprecision, 284
   two-valued logic, 284
   uncertainty, 284
   vagueness, 284
Probabilistic transition rule, 554
   artificial pheromone trail, 555
Probability theory, 287

Radial basis function neural networks, 218
   bell-shaped RBF, 218
   Gaussian function, 219
   k-means clustering, 221
   orthogonal least sqares, 221
Rate models, 259
Rebound burst, 258
   sleep oscillations, 258
   thalamo-cortical system, 258
Rebound spike, 258
   post-inhibitory (rebound) spike, 258
Reinforced learning, 79
   batch training mode, 80
   incremental training mode, 80
   offline mode, 80
   online mode, 80
   testing mode, 80
   training mode, 80
   using mode, 80

Second-generation neural networks, 118
   arctangent, 121
   asymptotically, 120
   automatic gain control, 122
   bias, 129
   character recognition, 142
   hyperbolic tangent, 121
   Kolomogorov's theorem, 124
   learning rate, 125
   logistic function, 120
   momentum, 129
   momentum coefficient, 130
   monotonically, 120
   multi-layer perceptrons, 119
   weight assignment problem, 119
Second-generation neurons, 253
   rate encoding, 253
Second-generation NNs, 10
   back propagation of errors, 10
   cognition, 11
   consciousness, 11
   perception, 11
   pseudo-random numbers, 11
   simulated annealing, 11
   third-generation networks, 10
Selection, 461
   block selection, 463
   crowding strategy, 461
   deterministic sampling, 463
   elitist selection, 464
   enlarged sampling space, 462
   generational replacement, 461
   mixed sampling, 463
   proportionate selection, 463
   random perturbation, 462
   regular sampling space, 461
   reproductive plan, 462
   sampling mechanism, 461, 463
   sampling space, 461
   selection probability, 461
   steady-state reproduction, 464
   steady-state selection, 464
   stochastic sampling, 463
   stochastic tournament selection, 464
   stochastic universal sampling, 463
   super-chromosomes, 463
   survival probability, 463
   tournament selection, 464
   tournament size, 464
   truncation selection, 463
Selection probability, 464
   affine combination, 478
   affine crossover, 479
   arithmetical operators, 470
   arithmetic crossover, 478
   average, 479
   blend crossover, 474
   Boltzman selection, 467
   canonical, 474
   conventional operators, 470
   convex crossover, 479
   convex set theory, 478
   cycle crossover (CX), 476
   directional crossover, 479
   directional selection, 468
   direction-based operators, 470

disruptive selection, 468
double-point crossover, 470
dynamic scaling, 465
exponential ranking, 468
extended intermediate crossover, 479
fitness scaling, 465
flat crossover, 474
heuristic, 474
heuristic crossover, 478
hyper-rectangle, 474
intermediate crossover, 479
linear combination, 478
linear crossover, 479
linear scaling, 465
logarithmic scaling, 465
multiple-point crossover, 471
neo-darwinism, 468
non-monotonic function, 469
normalizing, 467
normalizing selection, 468
order-based crossover, 476
order crossover, 475
partial-mapped crossover, 474
permutation-based crossover operations, 474
position-based crossover (OX), 475
power law scaling, 465
random crossover, 474
ranking method, 464
relationship mapping, 474
sigma truncation, 465
single-point crossover, 470
stabilizing selection, 468
static scaling, 465
sub-tour exchange crossover, 478
uniform crossover, 471
windowing, 466
Self-organizing systems, 549
altruism algorithm, 551
ant colony optimisation, 551
artificial bee colony algorithm, 551
artificial immune systems, 551
autocatalysis, 553
bacterial foraging techniques, 551
brood-parasitism, 551
charged system search, 551
cuckoo search, 551
differential path length, 553
firefly algorithm, 551
flashing behaviour, 551
gravitational search algorithm, 551
intelligent water drops, 551
particle swarm optimisation, 551
pheromone, 551
river formation dynamics, 551
self-propelled particles, 552
stochastic diffusion search, 552
travelling salesman problem, 563
Serial ant system model, 566
  ant search space, 566
  euclidean distance, 566
  heuristic function, 567
  matrix space, 566
  transition probability, 567
Simulated annealing, 214
  annealing schedule, 215
  environmental vectors, 216
  unclamped units, 216
Soft computing, 1
  bionic car, 2
  gecko tape, 2
  genetic algorithm, 2
  imprecision, 2
  mirasol displays, 2
  partial truth, 2
  particle swarm optimisation, 2
  uncertainty, 2
Solution evaluation, 556
  explicit solution evaluation, 556
  implicit, 556
  pseudo-random probability, 557
Spike frequency adaptation, 257
Spike latency, 258
Spike neuron models, 259
  Hodgkin–Huxley, 259
Spike response model (SRM), 261
  dynamic threshold, 262
  ionic channels, 263
  leakage conductance, 266
  leak current, 264
  naka-rushton function, 267
  nernst potential, 264
  sigmoidal units, 266
Spiking neuron models, 259
Spiking neurons, 253
Stigmergy, 553
  mass recruitment, 553
  recruitment, 553
Structure of fuzzy inference system, 335
  de-fuzzification, 335
  fuzzy singleton, 335
Sub-threshold oscillations, 258
Support vector machine (SVM), 222
  constrained optimisation problem, 223
  feature space, 222
  hyper plane classifiers, 222
  input space, 222
  kernel mapping, 226
  kernels, 226
  kernel trick, 226
  linear classifier, 222
  mercer theorem, 227
  optimal separating hyperplane, 222
  polynomial kernel, 227
  quadratic programming (QP) problem, 224
  radial basis function kernel, 227
  slack variables, 225
  soft margin hyperplane, 225
  sparse solution, 227
  support vectors, 222

Swarm intelligence, 547
  artificial or natural agents, 547
  collective intelligence, 547
  foraging, 547
  synergizing behaviour, 547
System-building aids, 53
  AGE, 53
  break package, 53
  respective reasoning, 53
  TEIRESIAS, 53
  tracing, 53

Training rule, 8
Third-generation neural networks, 253
Third-generation neurons, 253
  membrane potential, 254
  post-synaptic neuron, 254
  post-synaptic potentials, 254
  presynaptic neuron, 254
  spikes, 254
  spike train, 254
Threshold-fire, 259
Threshold-fire models, 259
  integrate-and-fire, 259
  spike response model, 259
Threshold variability, 258
Tonic bursting, 256
  cat neocortex, 256
  chattering neurons, 256
  gamma-frequency oscillations, 256
Tonic spiking, 256
  fast spiking inhibitory neurons (FS), 256
  low-threshold spiking neurons (LTS), 256
  regular spiking excitatory neurons (RS), 256
Travelling salesman problem, 563
  asymmetric TSP, 564
  elitist ants, 564
  Euclidean norm, 564
  Euclidean TSP, 564
  Hamiltonian circuit, 564
  hard combinatorial optimisation problem, 563
  initialization phase, 563
  search-and-update phase, 563
  serial AS model, 563
  state transition rule, 564
  symmetric TSPs, 564
  tabu list, 564
  touring ant colony model, 565
Truth function, 291
  continuous membership function, 293
  continuous universe of discourse, 293
  crisp sets, 293
  domain of fuzzy set, 295
  non-negative real numbers, 293
  ordered pairs, 291
  singleton, 292
  small integers, 293
  system variable, 294
  universe of discourse, 294
  valuation set, 291
Type-II fuzzy sets, 18

Uncertainty, 285
  association, 285
  distorted, 285
  generalization, 285
  human intelligence, 286
  imprecise, 285
  incomplete, 285
  information loss, 285
  partial truth, 285
  vague, 285
Unconditional and qualified propositions, 338
Unconditional and unqualified propositions, 337
Undecidability, 286
Unit commitment problem, 573
  input/output (I/O) curve, 574
  polynomial curve, 574
  start-up cost, 574

Weights, 71

# About the Authors

**N.P. Padhy** is currently Professor and Chair Professor of NEEPCO (North East Electric Power Company) in the Department of Electrical Engineering, IIT Roorkee. He has been involved in developing the course content for several courses related to soft computing. His professional interests include the application of expert systems, fuzzy logic, neural networks, genetic algorithms, evolutionary programming, and swarm intelligence to solve engineering problems. Professor Padhy's primary research interest is in the area of soft computing applications to power engineering. He has published over 200 research papers in various national and international conferences and journals.

Dr Padhy has been awarded the BOYSCAST post-doctoral fellowship (2004) and Alexander Von Humboldt experienced researcher fellowship (2009) and has been Fellow of Indian National Academy of Engineers (2014) and Fellow of The Institution of Engineering and Technology, UK (2014), for his research contribution mainly in the area of soft computing and its application in electrical engineering. He is the author of *Artificial Intelligence and Intelligent Systems* (OUP, 2005) and prepared the SI edition for *Power System Analysis Design* (2010).

**S.P. Simon** is currently Assistant Professor, Department of Electrical and Electronics Engineering, National Institute of Technology, Tiruchirappalli. He has published nearly 50 research papers in various national and international conferences and journals. He has been organizing various workshops and staff development programmes on soft computing to engineering applications. His research focuses on developing intelligent models using soft computing tools in the field of engineering.

# Related Titles

## Mobile Computing, 2e
[9780198068914]

**Raj Kamal**, *Devi Ahilya University, Indore*

The second edition of this book is a comprehensive text with updated coverage of recent trends and advancements in the fast moving field of computing in mobile environment. Designed to serve as a textbook for the students of CSE, IT, ECE, and those pursuing MCA, it offers an insight into the fundamental principles behind different access technologies as well as their service and application aspects.

*Key Features*
- New sections on emerging technologies such as IPsec, i-mode, WAP, Ultra-wide-band, Near-field Communication, VoIP, and ZigBee
- Detailed discussion on application development platforms, and the latest mobile operating systems such as Phone 7, Symbian, and Android
- Numerous examples on modulation techniques, CDMA, spread spectrum, OFDM, and other communication protocols
- Provides an up-to-date coverage of Wireless LAN, DECT, HSPA, WCDMA, WiMax, LTE, mobile ad-hoc, and wireless sensor networks
- Contains programs and sample codes for building successful mobile applications

## Software Testing: Principles and Practices, 1e
[9780198061847]

**Naresh Chauhan**, *YMCA University of Science and Technology, Faridabad*

*Software Testing* focuses on software testing as not just being a phase of software development life cycle (SDLC) but a complete process to fulfil the demands of quality software.

*Key Features*
- Advocates the notion of effective and systematic software testing in place of exhaustive testing
- Provides a comprehensive coverage of software testing techniques through a large number of test cases and diagrams
- Comprises separate chapters on regression testing, software quality assurance, test maturity model, and debugging for better understanding of software testing process

- Covers testing techniques for two specialized environments: object-oriented software and Web-based software

## Artificial Intelligence and Intelligent Systems
[9780195671544]

**N.P. Padhy**, *IIT Roorkee*

It provides a comprehensive coverage of the fundamental concepts and techniques in artificial intelligence (AI). The book discusses current trends in AI and its application in various fields. Intelligent systems such as expert systems, fuzzy systems, artificial neural networks, genetic algorithms, and swarm intelligent systems are discussed in detail with examples to facilitate in-depth understanding of AI.

*Key Features*
- Includes real-world examples to illustrate concepts
- Contains a separate chapter on programming languages in AI
- Includes new topics such as swarm intelligent systems
- Explains genetic algorithms and swarm intelligence using examples

## Data Warehousing
[9780195699616]

**Reema Thareja**, *University of Delhi*

This book provides a thorough understanding of the fundamentals of data warehousing and imparts a sound knowledge base to users for the creation and management of a data warehouse.

*Key Features*
- Incorporates a step-by-step approach to designing and building a data warehouse
- Contains a running case study to bring out the practical aspects of building and maintaining a data warehouse
- Illustrates difficult concepts through several examples

## Other Related Titles

9780195686289    Vikram Pudi & P. Radha Krishna: *Data Mining*
9780198070788    S. Sridhar: *Digital Image Processing*